YORK ON OLD POSTCARDS

Compiled by

Joe Dickinson

ii A corner of old York (Little Shambles). Raphael Tuck
'Oilette' – York series III.

£6.95

**Designed and Published by
Reflections of a Bygone Age,
Keyworth, Nottingham**
First published 1989. Reprinted 1997.

ISBN 0 946245 20 7

iii A quaint corner of the Great Shambles, on a card published by Raphael Tuck & Sons ('Oilette' 7088).

Cover pictures:

Front: Henry B. Wimbush painted this scene of Micklegate Bar for Raphael Tuck & Sons in their 'Oilette' series V.

Back: (top) The Black Bull, by Tuck — York series III.
(bottom) 1907 Advert card for Joseph Terry & Sons Ltd. — view from the river of Clementhorpe factory, near Skeldergate Bridge. Today the whole of the old Terry's factory has been demolished to make way for new houses and flats.

**Printed by
Adlard Print and Typesetting Services,
Ruddington, Notts.**

iv Raphael Tuck 'Heraldic' Postcard no. 943. This card was published in 1901, and as only the address could be written on the reverse, according to Post Office regulations, any message had to be written on the front.

CONTENTS

To my beloved wife Hilary

ACKNOWLEDGEMENTS

For help in supplying historical information, and for much encouragement and kindness while I was compiling this book, I'm indebted to the following: the staff of York reference library; my wife Hilary and her father Mr. E. Woodward; Mr. & Mrs. Jack Stasiak; Mrs. Patricia Hawe and her mother Mrs. Frances Moore.

Introduction

To have been born and brought up among the great heritage of the City of York is in itself a lucky and unique honour. I've often heard people ask *"do the citizens of York appreciate their city and its great history?"* I'm sure many of them do. It gives a feeling of gratitude having lived in a background which encouraged a pride and appreciation of the City of York, to enjoy the history and learn the importance of its heritage, architectural treasures preserved to us through the ages: a most enlightening experience.

The old postcard photograph is an historic document from the turn of the century onwards, though some cards show much earlier events from old engravings and paintings which predate the camera. All these items are valuable in that they give a detailed illustration of past life in our city, and an opportunity to study life in the days of our grandparents and great-grandparents. Their struggle through war and peace, in times of social poverty, their life-long fight to strive for a better life for working men and their wives and children, and men who gave their lives in the battle for freedom for their families to dismiss fears of the future, have all made their own major contribution to what has become our present.

I hope this postcard pictorial will help to promote a new and greater interest among many people, who can identify with, be a part of, and reminisce over bygone days in this city, their home and work place: an ancient walled city of two thousand years history, which should not be spoiled but preserved and passed on to the unborn future generations as it was for us all.

Many important buildings and historic sites in York have already been destroyed over the years, some to make way for the traffic of the day: in widening streets, taking corners off and constructing new streets, names of streets were changed for varying reasons. York suffered great losses of antiquity: churches, windmills, buildings, houses, hotels and inns were all demolished.

Even today, York still loses old buildings that are replaced with modern concrete structures as offices, hotels, flats and shops with twenty-foot plate glass windows. This puts York in danger of becoming a concrete jungle and fast losing its old respected character. The city will be in danger of having little to offer future generations if the old landscape continues to be demolished. Let us hope that recognition of the need to preserve our heritage prevails.

I'm now in my 29th year as a Rowntree employee, and in that time I've seen at first hand tremendous continuous changes. The recent Nestlé takeover was the biggest and most surprising of these. Ironically, at the same time the takeover battle was on, the former Tanner's Moat factory used by Rowntrees up to the turn of the century — and where the very foundation of the business was built — was being demolished. The takeover by Nestlé was seen by many as being a sad day for the city, but as Rowntree chairman Kenneth Dixon said: *"What we have here is a good deal for employees, for shareholders, and for the City of York. I believe York has nothing to fear. What we now have to do is to look forward and build on the new future."*

Joe Dickinson
York, February 1989

The role of the Picture Postcard

Picture Postcards were not introduced in Britain until 1894, though they had been popular on the Continent for over 20 years. The early British cards were known as Court Cards (size 115 x 89 mm), smaller than the Continental size of 140 x 89 mm, and the message had to be written on the same side as the picture, leaving the back for the stamp and address. This obviously inhibited the possibilities for illustrations, so when the Post Office permitted the use of the larger-size card (1899) and the 'divided back' (1902) where message and address occupied the same side, the publishers were able to exploit the postcard much more effectively, and a flood of cards on every imaginable subject was produced.

The postcard fulfilled several functions: it was a medium for communicating simple messages and greetings (mail was reliably delivered within 24 hours, and over short distances, on the same day). Firms used them as advertising material and correspondence cards. Photographs of special events and disasters provided a unique pictorial record of local happenings. Comic postcards gave people the opportunity to send risqué messages to their friends. Soon, the collecting of all these cards became a major hobby, and the reign of Edward VII paralleled the 'golden age' of Picture Postcards, with many thousands of families amassing vast numbers sent from all over Britain (and, for those with wealthy connections, the Continent). Specialist magazines catered for the craze, and publishers produced cards on all kinds of themes: railways, actresses, military, shipping, glamour, children, heraldic, royalty, political — as well as greetings, comic cards and street scenes. The Great War saw new themes developed — patriotic, political satire, and beautiful silk cards, embroidered in France, and sent home by British tommies to be lovingly treasured. Postcard collecting ceased to have the same meaning and appeal after the war, though. The quality of production deteriorated (some of the best pre-1914 cards had been printed in Germany), the postage rate doubled, and the national mood and social conditions had changed out of all recognition: it was a new era, with changed values and priorities. 'Golden Age' postcards lay neglected in their albums in attics for years, until a few enthusiasts in the 1950's ushered a new-found appreciation for the beautiful old cards to a whole new generation. Their availability, though, remained confined to the shelves of occasional book and antique shops, and new-wave collectors didn't find it easy to build up collections. All that changed in the 1970's. A travelling exhibition organised by the Victoria and Albert Museum, the emergence of specialist dealers, magazines, catalogues and fairs, had the effect of encouraging a host of new collectors and a consequent upsurge in prices. By then, Edwardian albums were emerging from the attics, as their original owners or their sons and daughters died. Now, the hobby is thriving, and the beautiful postcard issues of the Edwardian era are once again lovingly collected.

1. Ousegate, mentioned as early as 1120, means the road to the Ouse. It is thought that not far from here lay the original track across the glacial moraine by which, through countless centuries, the first dwellers approached the ford over the river. These would have been tribes of the Brigantes who, from about the Bronze Age, inhabited the lowlands of Yorkshire until the Roman invasion. The postcard is 'City Series no. 4' by T.D.Y., and was posted from York in August 1923. *"I am having a glorious time"* wrote the sender.

OUSEGATE, YORK.

OLD HOUSE, NORTH STREET, YORK

2. North Street dates back to the tenth century, when York was a great trading centre. In mediaeval times, York merchants lived in large fine houses here because of its convenient access to the only bridge over the river, Ousebridge, and the then busy docks at Kings Staith. This fine real photographic card by William Hayes, a noted York postcard publisher, features the premises of Sutton & Co., general carriers, to the right, and dates from around 1910.

3. First mention of this street is also 1120. By 1245 it had become Ousegate, but the street is many centuries older still. Between the church of St. Michael, visible on the left, and the river, was the old churchyard, later built over by housing. Many city centre churches lost their churchyards as the city was built up. The Ouse Bridge restaurant is prominent on the right. Card published by Soloman Brothers of London in their series 48.

LOW OUSEGATE, YORK.

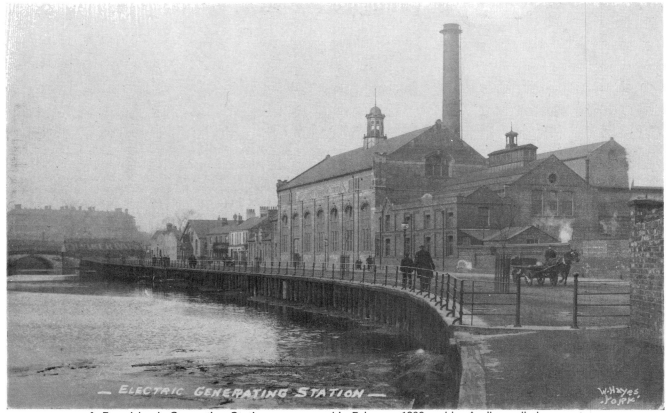

4. Foss Islands Generating Station was opened in February 1900 and by April supplied power to 16,470 consumers, as well as lighting the streets and public buildings. In 1901 the figures, in millions for the units sold were: Domestic 180; public lighting 38; industrial 1, totalling 219. In 1951 those figures read: domestic 68,083; public lighting 2,592; industrial 76,533, totalling 147,208 million units. Another William Hayes card.

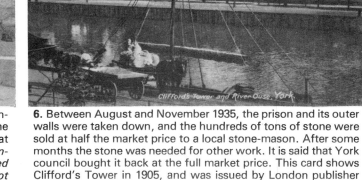

5. Tower Gardens on a postcard by Photocrom Co. Ltd. of London. This card was sent from the city in December 1908. The sender writes *"Another view to your collection"* and tells us that *"you can see the white tower where Daniel Defoe wrote 'Robinson Crusoe' while imprisoned; also hundreds of Jews killed themselves by jumping into a well there. I have been inside (not doing time) and seen the well"*. The first stone of the exterior wall visible here was laid on March 20 1826; gritstone was used for strength. The lofty walls, 35 feet high, have numerous buttresses at regular intervals. The cost of the operation — £175,874-3s-10d — seems a large sum for that sort of job when people were very poor.

6. Between August and November 1935, the prison and its outer walls were taken down, and the hundreds of tons of stone were sold at half the market price to a local stone-mason. After some months the stone was needed for other work. It is said that York council bought it back at the full market price. This card shows Clifford's Tower in 1905, and was issued by London publisher Hartmann.

7. Pavement. These jetted buildings in a derelict state were pulled down in 1910 to make way for Piccadilly. This row of characteristic beautiful timbered buildings overlooked the old corn market where the large Corn Bell was rung at market opening time, 10 a.m. Here also was built in 1579 a capon call, a structure for the sale of fowls. Postcard by William Hayes.

8. All Saints, Pavement, is mentioned in the Domesday book and on a document dated 1160. The list of rectors dates back to 1238. In 1579 at this market place were sold corn, butter, cheese, eggs and poultry. Near St. Crux church was a bull ring for baiting bulls, and a town crier stood here. In Edwardian times, Melias Tea Stores, "Largest Retailers in the Kingdom", occupied the premises on the left. No publisher is indicated on the card, though it could be another Hayes effort.

9. Pavement looking to High Ousegate, a very busy thoroughfare for centuries. After twenty years of talks and an act of Parliament, Parliament Street was built in 1836, thus uniting the old Pavement market with the old Thursday market of St. Sampsons Square, at the same time causing the destruction of a large part of Little Shambles. W. Dove & Son (ironmongers) are on the right. This, like the other two horizontal cards on this page, was another example of Hayes' postcard work.

Sir Thomas Herbert's House - The Pavement. York.

11. Monkgate is first mentioned in 1070 as Munecagate, which could mean 'monks' street'. Heavy wagons could not pass through the bars here except on payment of high tolls. Though the land here was within the boundaries of the Forest of Galtres the city was empowered, by a statute of 1569, to hold a horse fair here, and to keep the tolls and customs. Card postally used from York in May 1905.

12. Monkgate extended from the bar to Monk Bridge, and was the main approach to the city from the North-East. None of the surviving domestic buildings antedate the civil war. To the right of this scene is the old business of Bowmans, the removal contractors and storers. Part of this building collapsed in the early 1960s avoiding the need for demolition! William Hayes postcard. *(see also illus. 114)*

10. Pavement was the oldest open space in York, used in pre-Norman days for people to assemble. Through mediaeval times it was a place of punishment, even of executions, and proclamations. It may have received its name from being the earliest paved area. The buildings to the left were demolished in the early 1950s to make way for a new street called The Stonebow, which is from that point to Peasholme Green. The postcard is by Arthur & Co. of York.

MONK BAR. YORK.

13. Monk Bar. When the stone defences were built the old gate was replaced by the one on the present site. In 1435 the house above the bar was rented for four shillings a year to Thomas Pak, the Minster's master stonemason. Monk Bar is the highest of the bars, and still has its portcullis, part of the hoisting apparatus, and the two rooms above. This is a 1920's view on a card in 'City Series no. 2' by T.D.Y., and was posted in July 1925.

14. A privately-produced card of York market, postally used in October 1905. An act of 1833 re-affirmed the corporation's power to regulate all markets and fairs in the city. By law, rates for tolls were established in 1873, and full control was confirmed by the York Extension and Improvement Act of 1884.

CLARENCE STREET - YORK -

15. The houses in Clarence Street were not built until about 1835. The full length of this street to the left was for centuries an open space of several acres which bore the name of 'The Horsefair'. From 1218 three big fairs were held there every year. Tolls from two of them were paid to the mayor and people of York while tolls from the third went to the Archbishop of York. This scene is dated about 1905, and features W. Hardgrave's ironmongery on the right. Another marvellous William Hayes photographic card.

York. Exhibition Square.

16. Exhibition Square was created in 1876 from a corner of St. Mary's Abbey grounds called Bears Park Garden. An old house and a public house, 'Bird-in-Hand', were demolished. In 1879 the city art gallery was built. A central point of importance missing from this scene is the William Etty statue, thus dating the card, by Arthur & Co., before 1911.

17. An old curiosity shop at the end of the Shambles, a fitting scene for an ancient corner of the city. The Domesday Book of 1087 mentions the Shambles and the King's Court. A privately-produced card of April 1938.

18. Gillygate. The street, called 'Invico Sancti Egidii' in 1161, bore by 1373 the name of Giligate after the church of St. Giles which was declared redundant and demolished in 1547. It stood in the area of the present Salvation Army hall and Claremont Terrace. In 1644 the moats of the walls were cleared of all buildings. This picture postcard shows the High Petergate end of Gillygate before it lost its corner building. Shops featured include F.W. Rose (baker), W.R. Fletcher, and Dickenson, while the cart on the right belongs to Forster and Coverdale, aerated water manufacturers, of Hull Road. This W. Hayes card was actually posted to Brussels, where it arrived in September 1909.

York. Davygate.

19. Davygate is named after David Le Lardiner, whose family was given land in the area by King Stephen in 1135. The Lardiner family were the King's custodians for the forest of Galtres, and collected taxes from butchers, bakers, fishmongers and corn dealers. Their mansion, called Lardiner Hall, and later Davy Hall, is visible to the left of this picture, today the site of the Davygate arcade. Postcard published by Arthur & Co., and posted to Bridlington in July 1908.

20. Children playing at the end of Nunmill Street in 1905 seem to be happy with their hoops and sticks. They would also have whips and tops. In mediaeval days there were windmills in this area, and up to 1885 many corporation-owned mills. Each working mill had to pay rent to the Crown. This photographic card is crudely inscribed 'P. Preston', and even the caption is handwritten. It was sent from York in July 1905.

NUNMILL ST YORK   P P Preston

BISHOPTHORPE. RD.

21. Bishopthorpe Road is an ancient place: in 1405 the 42nd Archbishop of York, Richard Scrope, and the Earl of Nottingham were tried for high treason by King Henry IV. He personally took part in the tribunal and condemned them both to death. They were taken to a field on the side of Bishopthorpe Road and beheaded, the punishment for this offence. On this scene, in happier times about 1905, there seems to be an air of contentment, with many street residents having turned out for the photographer, whose name appears to be Rowles.

22. Galman was the ancient name of the street which has been known as Bootham since mediaeval times. Galman extended from Bootham Bar to a wooden gate at the end of Marygate which was called "Galmhowlith" meaning the gate. In this interesting 1930's view can be seen the busy street of those days; note the barrow boy. No publisher indicated on the card, though from its number, 10732, it must have been by a prolific issuer.

23. This card shows a pleasant Edwardian scene with typical transport, horse and trap, under the Bar. When the Romans built York, High to Low Petergate followed the line of the central thoroughfare or, "Via Principalis". Bootham Bar stands where the Roman gate stood at one end of the street. The other gate stood at the end of Goodramgate near Kings Square. Bootham Bar to Monk Bar and the Bar Walls stand on the original site of the Roman wall of York. Postcard in the 'Queen' series by Scarborough publishers E.T.W. Dennis, and posted in August 1908.

24. There were some powers in York who would have robbed the city's future generations of their heritage of the Bars, Posterns and Walls. In 1832 Bootham Bar's Barbican was removed and only by strong public protest was the Bar preserved from destruction. This scene about 1904 shows the Bar much the same as it is today. Hunt of Manchester was responsible for publishing the photograph.

25. A William Hayes postcard of Haxby Road, known up to 1851 as Peppermill Lane after the Randerson family's working peppercorn windmill, which stood opposite Fountayne Street. After this closed and was later demolished, the name of Haxby Road became used. Card postally used in May 1906.

26. On the horizon of this card is Rowntrees Cocoa Works. Just below is the York Rugby Ground and to the right of the scene Clarence Gardens. The crowd seen here on this 1906 view by Hayes were probably on their way to a rugby match. In 1379 the Dean and Chapter had a gallows which stood in the Horse Fair by a stone wayside cross near the present junction of Haxby Road and Wigginton Road. Also at the junction in 1893 the city boundary was extended and brought into the city area.

27. G. Dickenson & Son, Tea Dealers. In 1795 Mr John Tesseyman began this grocery business. By 1869 Mr George Dickenson acquired the business and in 1886 it became Mr George Dickenson & Son. The rapid expansion led to the opening of the Fishergate and Gillygate branches. They were grocers, provision merchants, and warehousemen. Their roasted coffee was a speciality, English jams were made and 3lb parcels of orders were posted. The shops were at 1 Bootham and 1 Gillygate. *(See illus. 18)*. Note the firm's delivery horse and cart on this postcard, which was used by the firm as a publicity handout. This example was posted in August 1906.

G. DICKENSON & SON. Tea Dealers, York.

28. The construction of Oxford Street which is off Holgate Road to Rosary Terrace in 1851, may well have been for railway workers who originally settled there. It was for this section of the working classes that York Equitable Industrial Society (better known as the Co-op) opened its first suburban branch in Holgate Road. This photographic postcard was taken before 1907, showing an interesting view of the street and its residents, all of whom were pleased to pose for the photographer — who remained anonymous.

29. Gordon Street, off Heslington Road, has 35 houses. The corner shop seen here and known as 26 Heslington Road was J. Kirby, tailor and draper, at least as early as 1893. By 1927 they had become general dealers and were still there in 1950. In 1974 the shop was used by T.E. & A. Downs, newsagents. Today it is simply known as Heslington Road Newsagents. This postcard, again by unidentified publisher, is of c.1905 vintage.

York. — Théâtre Royal.

30. The first building designed as a cinema was the "Electric Theatre" on Fossgate which opened in 1911. It was better known in the 40s and since as the *Scala.* By 1951 it had closed as a cinema and was sold for use as a furniture shop. In the early part of the century films were shown in a variety of public and music halls. Goodramgate's Victoria Hall was a classic example, but any makeshift accommodation possible was used. This postcard was published by Bramley (The Electric Printing Works), Cross Gates, Leeds, and postally used in 1917.

31. On October 1st, 1734 Thomas Keregan founded and built York's first theatre in the Minster Yard, but this soon proved to be inadequate. By 1744 Keregan's widow leased the St. Leonards Cloisters Hospital from the corporation, and built York's first permanent theatre. In 1761 Joseph Baker got the lease in order; he spent £500 on improvements by 1765: the York Company became a circuit company and toured locally. The front face of the theatre building has been changed over the years. In 1967 cleaning of stonework and removal of an old glass canopy, also the construction of a glass and concrete foyer wing to the north wall, caused a major change. Card by Arthur and Co. Ltd., around 1907.

32. An early – around 1904 – view of Museum Street on a *Silverette* card by Raphael Tuck & Sons, probably the top publishers of postcards ever. Over the centuries, this street had a variety of names such as St. Leonards Hill, Ficteles Lane, Finkle Street, Back Lendal. It was reconstructed and widened when Lendal Bridge was constructed in 1859-62. Before this date a ferry operated for many years. Buildings on the right are now replaced with modern ones. To the left under the trees is the entrance to the Museum Gardens.

33. Walmgate is another very ancient street; just off it were alleys, courts and yards, usually situated behind the public houses and inns such as the Old Malt Shovel, Bay Horse, The Barley Corn and The Duke Of York. Most of the buildings on this scene on each side of the road have been demolished and replaced with modern housing and flats. Card published by W.A.R. Co. and numbered 22-1; it dates from the 1920's.

34. Poverty in Walmgate. Many of the slum dwellers were poor working-class Irish citizens, who in the 1840s came to York at the time of the famine in Ireland. Through the century, the inhabitants of this locality had a higher death rate than in other parts of the city. Unhealthy living conditions contributed to this problem: families lived in cold, damp and badly-lit hovels. This excellent photograph was by an anonymous publisher.

35. This early Edwardian postcard by the Photocrom Co. Ltd. shows a classic view of the 16th century Walmgate Bar and its barbican, the only bar to retain this unique feature. The inner face of the bar is 16th century, a two-storey wooden structure. The barbican and bar was badly damaged in the 1644 siege of York, but restored in 1648. The bar today stands among some of York's busiest traffic. The card was postally used — at Epping! — in June 1908.

36. Judges of Hastings were famous for their sepia photographic scenes encompassing the whole of the British Isles. This card of Walmgate Bar is numbered 12815, an indication of their tremendous output. Walmgate bore the name of Walbegate from 1070 until 1186. An almshouse at the foot of Foss Bridge was founded and endowed in 1717 by Mrs Dorothy Wilson, a maiden gentlewoman who lived in the parish of St. Denys. She left, in her will, land for the maintenance of ten women who had a room each in the hospital and the sum of £6 10s 0d per annum. By order of the trustees in 1765 the Dorothy Wilson's Hospital was taken down and rebuilt. Shown here is quite a tranquil scene from the 1920's.

37. William Hayes again – a postcard showing the Crescent, off Blossom Street, which was constructed in a wide and spacious area between 1851 and 1867. On the left is the corner shop of Henry Coning (19 Blossom Street), family grocers and provision merchants. This was the same family business that took over the old Joseph Rowntree shop in Pavement.

38. William Hayes captured a marvellous scene here: Blossom Street in coaching days. It seems really unrecognisable until you see Micklegate Bar in the background: most of the buildings to the left are now demolished. This early Edwardian scene shows the street before the building of the Odeon cinema – now the only one left in the city. Modern offices have also replaced old buildings on the left of the street. This card, like several others in the book, carries on the reverse the handstamp of the retailer: W.H. Campbell, 38 Micklegate.

39. Micklegate Bar and Blossom Street. The white building behind the black car on this view is the Windmill Hotel, built in 1770. In those days its large windows offered a panoramic view of the Nunmill on Bishopthorpe Road. Two windmills on the Mount could also be seen and enjoyed by the hotel guests. Only one windmill survives today on Acomb Road and its future is very uncertain. 'City Series no. 3' card by T.D.Y., postally used in September 1925.

40. William Hayes postcard of Micklegate Bar, showing a view leaving Blossom Street. Thomas Percy, Earl of Northumberland, a leader of the rebellion against Queen Elizabeth in 1569, was beheaded in York on 22nd August 1572. His head was set on a high pole on Micklegate Bar, where it remained for two years, as a lesson to anybody trying a similar action. If anybody removed heads from the bar illegally they could lose theirs too.

41. Like many other city streets, Micklegate acquired its current name gradually: in 1161 it was Myglagate, and by 1180 had become Myklegate. It dates back to Roman times, and many remains have been discovered. In the area, too, were a Benedictine priory with three parish churches, and large houses belonging to merchants – the docks were close by. On each side, going down to the river, were open drains called the King's Ditches – the only form of sanitation for many centuries. On this uncredited card W. Merry's Priory Bakery features prominently on the right, while next door is W.H. Campbell *(see caption 38).*

42. Micklegate House, in the centre of this postcard, was built in 1752 as the town house of the Bourchiers of Beningbrough. Mr William Peckitt (York painter) painted two panels portraying dogs, signed and dated 1755-6. John Bouchier paid £2 12s 6d for the glass paintings. Today, Micklegate House is in the hands of York University who used it in 1960 for the storage of books. Another W. Hayes postcard.

43. Jubbergate goes back in name to its predecessors of Jubretgate (1356), and Jubergate (1443). It was originally much longer than it is today, for it was cut in two when Parliament Street was constructed in 1836. To the left was once York's first, very small, police station, and the buildings to the right are now demolished. In the street leading off in the distance can be seen Dalby's Boot Stores; in the centre is F. Orrington, furniture dealer and repairer, who advertises 'Perambulators for Hire'. W. Robinson, butcher, has a shop on the right. No publisher identified on the card.

44. Leading away from F. Orrington's shop is Little Shambles, quite a long, narrow street in its day, and built in the image of the greater Shambles. Little Shambles was pulled down to make way for York Market, which was considered an obstruction in Parliament Street. Could such an example of vandalism happen today?

45. Little Shambles, also known as Haymonger Lane in times of old, used to go right through to Peter Lane. After twenty years of argument about change, part of Little Shambles was demolished by an act of parliament in order to construct Parliament Street. The other part from The Shambles to Jubbergate was pulled down later. It's a shame for York to have lost such a wonderful heritage of this street, full of old timbered buildings. Raphael Tuck *Oilette* card: York series III, no. 7088, postally used in October 1906.

46. Fossgate, mentioned as early as 1120, formed part of the Roman road out of Eboracum. Fossbridge, at the foot of Fossgate, is very ancient: workmen employed in making a drain near the bridge in 1825 found very old pavements below the surface, the lowest as deep as twelve feet. These appeared to have been laid on swampy ground. Also found were slips of untanned leather. Mediaeval documents tell of Fossbridge, "over the fishpond" rather than the Foss. This photograph, showing a cobbled Fossgate and a busy thoroughfare, features Calpine's Printing Office (and frame maker) on the right.

47. The Shambles is mentioned in the Domesday Book. In 1087 the Latin name for the street was "In Macello". York's mediaeval street was also called Haymongergate, and Needlergate because needles were made there from animal bones. Hanging meat and open sewers were an invitation to the spread of disease. This photographic card was posted from York in May 1906.

48. This is Petergate, the ancient street to which the Via Principalis of the Roman fort ran at right angles. Massive column bases were found near the west end of St. Michael-Le-Belfrey church, which, with another found in the Minster are all that remain of the old fort. Off Petergate in 1570 on 16th April was born Guy Fawkes, baptized at St. Michael-Le-Belfrey and educated at St. Peters School Clifton York, before his unsuccessful attempt to destroy the establishment. The postcard was published by Valentine of Dundee about 1906. Shops visible on the left are H.J. Lloyd's cycle works, L. Wright (beef and pork butchers), and the Petergate Cafe. The establishment on the right at no. 63 is a pawnbroker's.

49. This view of Goodramgate shows a changed area: most of the buildings on the left are now demolished and have been replaced with modern ones. In 867, the Danes took the city and the chieftains established themselves here. It is possible that the name of the street came from the Danish name of Guthrum, as the ancient name was Gutherungate. The 'Cross Keys' public house shown on the left (in the distance) was built in 1904 and is still open for business today. No indication of who published the card, of c.1906 vintage. Shops on the left are Britton, tobacconist, at no. 24, with G. Benson, bootmaker, next door at no. 26.

50. These quaint old houses in Trinity Lane off Micklegate were pulled down this century. The woman standing in the first doorway wearing an apron is Mrs Frances Proctor, who lived in the street for many years. Note the cobbled roadway. A William Hayes postcard.

51. Jacob's Well was an old house in Trinity Lane which was originally built in 1472 as the residence of the chancery priests of Holy Trinity Priory. In 1820 it became a public house with the name shown on this 1903 postcard by Hayes, though two years later was turned into a church hall for the parish of Holy Trinity. It is still here today.

52. A glimpse of Fishergate from the city walls in 1908 – the old walls of York Castle can be seen in the distance. The houses on the right (one displaying an advert for Veno's Cough Cure on the wall) have long since been pulled down. On the left a delivery cart belonging to the bakers Whittaker & Son, and advertising Hovis, stands outside the 'Mason's Arms'.

As long ago as 1070, a street called Fiscergate, part of which was known as Nowtgate, existed. There was also once a church called All Saints Fishergate, built in the reign of William II, which was pulled down about 1585.

53. A well-known site in Coney Street for nearly three centuries before the air raid of 29th April 1942 was the large street clock in the centre of this scene. It was a casualty of that night, but is now reinstated in its rightful place, on the site of the present Leak and Thorp store. The building on the left was originally the 'Old George Inn', dating from the fourteenth century but demolished in 1869. This postcard was actually given away free – as part of a large series – with a magazine called *Dainty Novels.*

54. St. Helens Square before it was widened. It was originally created in 1733 from the graveyard of St. Helens Church. Here it can be seen as a narrow cobbled area. The shops on the right were removed with the 'Harkers Hotel'. This postcard by Arthur & Co. was postally used in December 1910.

55. Many people will remember the County Hospital, seen here on this postcard in the days of gaslight. Philanthropist Lady Elizabeth Hastings left £500 in her will in 1730 to go towards an infirmary, which started in a house in Monkgate in 1740. The County Hospital soon replaced this.

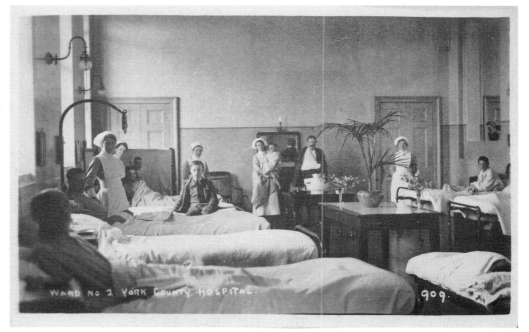

56. In November 1858, at a meeting at the old 'George Hotel', it was decided to hold a floral and musical exhibition on or about June 1859. From that date, for about sixty-five years, Bootham Park Hospital grounds were the scene of York's greatest public holiday, the Grand Yorkshire Gala. This soon became a central attraction to thousands of visitors who travelled miles to enjoy the event. On this 1908 postcard by Hanstock of York, the balloon ascent is the principal feature. More fixed attractions seen here are the helter-skelter (Holdsworth's Alpine Glassade), a bandstand, and various roundabouts. The card was sent from York on June 18th, 1908 with the message *"we are spending the day in York, it being the Gala. Am having a lovely time."*

YORK GALA

57. Bramley of Leeds published this view of the 1912 event. Balloon ascents and nightly firework displays were regular attractions of the Gala, which rapidly developed into a three-day festival. Tens of thousands of people — both locals and visitors — passed through the turnstiles annually.

58. The 1905 Gala on an anonymously-published card, which was strangely not sent through the post until 1962. Bootham Park grounds were always spoken of as 'the Gala fields'. The Gala was so popular an event that for a few years York races suffered and were miserably attended. Could anyone imagine this happening today!

Showing the Captive Balloon which escaped with eight passengers.

Balloon Ascent Grand Yorkshire Gala.

59. *'The Captive Balloon which escaped with eight passengers'* proclaims this card by Arthur & Co. — no year indicated, but possibly 1912. Other regular attractions at the Gala included acrobatic and juggling shows, regimental bands, swings, roundabouts, shooting galleries and refreshments.

60. Another Bramley of Leeds card of 1906. All the profits from the Gala were distributed annually among York charities. Older citizens may well view the Grand Yorkshire Gala as the best of Victorian prosperity, spirit and merriment, reviving memories of their youth and the good old days. Or perhaps just the pleasanter days away from the long hours of a hard working week.

YORK GALA JUNE 21ST '06

YORK GALA

61. Superb fashion parade at one of the Edwardian Galas on another Bramley postcard. The event ran until 1923 at the Bootham site, moved to Fulford in 1924, before transferring to the Knavesmire. It had lasted 65 years at Bootham.

AVIATION

62. The Royal Flying Corps' first visit to York on 21st February 1913. Photographic postcard by Hanstock, retailed by Bilton (The York Picture Postcard Emporium). To the left of the picture is another photographer with his large box camera on tripod.

63. Another card in the same series. After German battleships attacked the East Coast in 1914 Royal Flying Corps home defence units were stationed in Yorkshire, where they particularly used the racecourses among other flat areas. Long before the Royal Air Force was formed, army airmen were flying planes.

64. Henri Salmet was one of the pioneer aviators who became a celebrity as he toured Britain appearing at the aviation meetings which became extremely popular attractions. Hanstock recorded his visit to York Racecourse on 18th September 1913.

65. Army airmen on the Knavesmire in 1913. The Royal Flying Corps was composed of ex-cavalrymen and partially took over the aerial defence of the country when the Great War began in August 1914. In York the Knavesmire was put to use, but on May 2nd and 3rd, 1916 Zeppelin L-21 dropped bombs on York, with the result that the citizens demanded that 33 squadron be moved from the Knavesmire in case further night raids were attracted by their presence. York was actually attacked three times during the war, with 9 deaths and 28 serious injuries.

EVENTS AND DISASTERS

YORK FAT STOCK SHOW

66. Instituted in 1857, the York Fat Stock Show was held up to the second world war. In its heyday the show was a big event attracting many visitors from near and far, who travelled to York by early rail transport, horse-drawn coaches and on foot. It has now been replaced by the younger Yorkshire Show. This advertising postcard, used by Mawson's to publicise their appearance at the show was posted from York in February 1916.

67. For many years, numerous small markets and fairs were held in the city streets, causing great inconvenience. In 1826 a permanent six-acre site was found in Paragon Street near the 'City Arms' inn, and became York Cattle Market. This closed in the sixties and moved to Murton, which held its first sale on 1st March 1971, at the York Livestock Centre. Postcard published by the Yorkshire Herald Co., Coney Street, York, but undated — probably 1909-12 period.

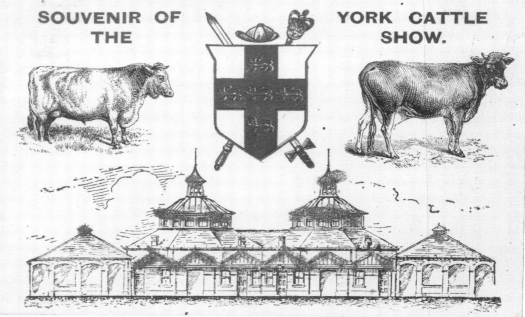

SOUVENIR OF THE — YORK CATTLE SHOW.

68. The Hospital Saturday procession route started on St. Georges Field, then to Fishergate, Cemetery Road, Barbican Road, Walmgate, Fossgate, Pavement, Skeldergate Bridge, Bishopsgate Street, Bishopthorpe Road, Nunthorpe Road, Moss Street, Blossom Street, Micklegate, Bridge Street, Low Ousegate, Spurriergate, Coney Street, St. Helens Square, Blake Street, Duncombe Place, Petergate, Goodramgate, Monkgate, Penleys Grove Street, Townend Street, and Haxby Road to Rowntrees Pleasure Grounds, where prize distribution took place. Total sum collected on July 13th, 1907 was £66. This W. Hayes postcard was sent to Hessle from York five days later.

69. The Hospital Saturday movement existed from 1900 to 1939, and was intended to replenish the funds of the County Hospital. This postcard was published by Wheatley of Regent Street — notice the amateurish handwritten caption.

70. Collections began at 10 a.m. Ladies, boys and girls walked the streets with collecting boxes, and policemen were even known to use their helmets, such was the community atmosphere. Featured in this postcard from Outhwaite's Premier York Postcard Den are the Hungate Mission Band of Hope with their 1907 May Queen, Miss Edwards, in an open carriage.

OPENING OF SKELDERGATE BRIDGE APRIL 1st 1914

71. From about 1541 there was a ferry in the area of Skeldergate Bridge. In 1873 a proposal for a bridge was passed and in 1878 the foundation stone laid. Three years later the bridge was opened, having cost £56,000. Although a toll of ½d per person was imposed, it was ignored in favour of a rate of three-farthings in the pound for twenty years, as an easier and more convenient way of paying. However, the cost turned out to be 40% more than had been anticipated, so a traffic toll was imposed. This ended in 1914 and the bridge was 'freed', as commemorated in this ceremony on April 1st. Broars of York was responsible for the postcard.

72. A similar card by Edwin F. Fox of Micklegate. The tower visible behind the dignitaries contains the lifting gear for raising the bridge, although it has now been immobilised for safety. In 1938-9 the bridge was reconstructed to a solid design and the four spans were strengthened, at a cost of £15,000.

THE LORD MAYOR CUTTING THE RIBBON TO FREE THE BRIDGE.

73. Special day at the Groves Wesleyan Chapel on 25th September 1907 for Mr H.E. Hawking and Miss Lily Agar, who were married there. Published by T.J. Hanstock, the card was soon on sale, for this example was posted from York on 30th September.

The Groves Chapel was built in 1888 at a cost of £5,721, to accommodate 800 people. The organ was installed for £450.

Wigginton Road, seen stretching away in the distance, was much narrower then. On its left is an area where today the York District Hospital stands.

Marriage of Mr H.E. Hawking & Miss Lily Agar
Sept 25-07

THE GROVES WESLEYAN CHAPEL AND WIGGINTON ROAD YORK

74. The 1909 pageant, held in Museum Gardens, was a dramatic representation of the city's history in seven episodes from 800 B.C. to 1644, that being the date of the great siege of York in the civil war. Pageantry is a way of keeping our interest alive and reminding us that the history of York is the very foundation of our birth place, our home, and our work place. This sepia photographic card was by 'H.J.S.'.

75. William Etty, a native of York whose statue stands in the centre of Exhibition Square, is well-represented in the York Gallery collection. Today we have more than his paintings to thank him for; he and his friends successfully fought to preserve the city's bars and walls from the threat of demolition. This 1911 card shows the unveiling of the statue.

76. S.H. Smith published this card of a fire engine on its way to Wales & Son's premises on 30th July 1906. The firm, situated off Goodramgate, were established in 1825, as contructors of carriages and motor cars, and as engineers and cycle agents. Their garage is represented at York Castle Museum today.

This postcard view is looking up the narrow street of Ogleforth where the fire took place.

77. The entrance to Ogleforth, showing the arrival of Rowntree's fire brigade at the Wales fire. They often attended conflagrations in York by agreement with the city fire authority. This card — and the previous one — are fascinating mementoes of the chocolate factory brigade in action. The engine can today be seen in all its splendour at the entrance of York Castle Museum.

78. The great fire of November 8th 1910 badly gutted Boyes & Co. Ltd. Insurance payout was £11,421. The store first opened in 1906 at Bridge Street, York, and by July 1912 the new store was opened. In the 1960s it was expanded at the cost of £132,933. Then in February 26 1983, Boyes closed down in York, much to the dismay of the regular shoppers, and was sold for £500,000. In May 1987 Boyes re-opened in Goodramgate. Postcard by Hanstock, and posted in December 1910. *(see illus. 107)*

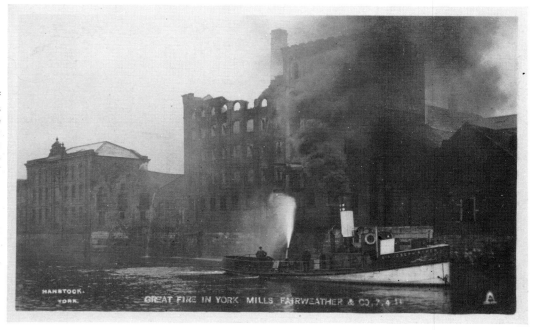

79. Another Hanstock card, of a fire at Fairweather & Co's mills on 7th April 1911. It broke out at 2 a.m., and spread with surprising rapidity, involving the services of six fire engines and a river float in a 12-hour battle against the intense heat, smoke and massive flames. Huge stocks of grain and machinery were destroyed: total damage was put at £50,000. The cause of the great fire remained a mystery.

80. The regular judge's visit to the Minster before the assize courts. This card depicts the scene in July 1911, and was another Hanstock publication.

81. A Brooks postcard of the York Hospital Saturday Sports, sometime pre-1914. Ambulance work is the activity going on here.

82. Alderman William Bentley, Lord Mayor of York, who died on 30th January 1907, aged 53, had won great respect in the city as a kind-hearted gentleman who had the art of communication with the citizens. At the funeral on February 4th, the whole city joined in an expression of common grief, a remarkable tribute to the Mayor. This postcard shows the procession in Fishergate.

83. The funeral procession passes the 'Mason's Arms' on Fishergate, captured on a William Hayes postcard. Lining the route of the funeral were troops from the 18th Hussars, York and Lancaster Regiment, and West Yorkshire Regiment. A double line of military personnel stretched from Coney Street past the Mansion House to the west door of York Minster for the service.

84. The coronation day of George V on 22nd June 1911 showed York to be a blaze of colour, flags, streamers, lamps and flowers. On this day 2,000 children gathered on Bootham Park field at a fete, where the philanthropist Mr Joseph Rowntree gave boxes of chocolates, specially designed as a souvenir of the occasion. York's electric trams were also decorated. Postcard by Hanstock.

85. Some of the Moss Street children in fancy dress during the 1918 peace celebrations. The street parties were organised by residents who contributed tables, seating and food for families to remember the sacrifice of the soldiers who had fought and died.

86. William Hayes was on hand (about 1906?) to record the Layerthorpe Junior Section Minstrel Troupe at Bilton Street school or St. Cuthbert's, built in 1831 for 150 boys. The school closed in 1956. Layerthorpe was a poor area of York, with inferior housing and fewer job opportunities. Few postcards exist to record this part of the city.

87. York citizens made a solemn protest over the Welsh church disestablishment bill, and demonstrations in the city on June 25th, 1913 were organised by four Welsh bishops. An intercession service was held at York Minster, where eight thousand attended. This Hanstock postcard shows the Archbishop of York speaking outside Shepherd's City Baths.

88. York Band of Hope Gala 1906, an annual gathering where collections were made to help those most desperately in need. The Band of Hope's motto was *"Save the children: are they not the hope of the nation?"* It was connected to Methodist Churches – in York Wesleyan Methodists were founded in 1744, and Primitive Methodists in 1819.

89. The Band of Hope's annual event involved a great long procession through the streets of York, with splendid tableaux and fancy costumes. This card shows part of a huge crowd in Skeldergate, outside J.W. Todd's grocery and provision stores.

90. Another - presumably - Edwardian postcard showing some of the 1,300 poor children lined up for a Christmas tea by the York Salvation Army, outside the Gillygate Citadel. This was built very near to the 12th century St. Giles church, long since pulled down.

TRAMS

91. A trace-horse was stationed at the bottom of Micklegate Hill, where a massive leather nose-bag was tied to a lamp-post. His job was to provide extra horse-power up the hill. The horse refused to go a yard further than he needed, but trotted back at speed to his nose-bag. Here they are starting off up the hill, outside the Family and Commercial Hotel, probably in 1909.

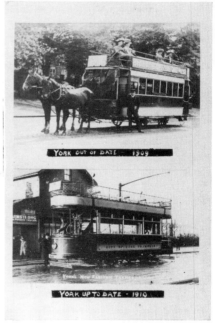

92. The change-over from horse trams in 1909 saw the end of an era for the city of York. By 1910 the lines had been electrified and the new electric cars were running. In 1911 the corporation's electricity and tramways committees were amalgamated, and the tram cars were not challenged by buses until 1914. Previously the city had rejected an offer to run a petrol-electric bus service, but in 1914 it authorised private enterprise to run motor and trolley buses. Message on the reverse of this card says *"just a line to send you one of our new trams, but we have not got them into Blossom St. yet, though we shall not be long"*. It was posted from the city in February 1910.

93. A line from Castle Mills Bridge to Fulford was opened on 27 October 1880, when an experimental steam tram was tried for a few months. People living on the line of the route complained about the noise of the engine, with the result that horses remained the sole source of power for York trams until 1910 when electric trams were introduced. Note the advert for Wood Milne shoe polish on the front of the tram as it stands in Fulford Road.

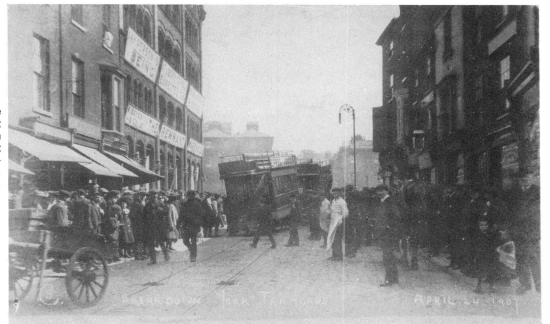

94. A dramatic scene outside Boyes' store in Bridge Street on 24th April 1907, with a horse-drawn tram having left the rails, snapping the front axle in two. After a long delay, the passengers had to walk. Postally used on 29th April, five days after the incident.

YORK'S FIRST ELECTRIC CAR

95. In 1909 the tramways were bought by the City Council from the private York Tramways Company for £8,856, and in the same year were electrified at a cost of £89,741. This view shows the first run of the electric car (20 January 1910) in Clifford Street on its way to Fulford, with the Lord Mayor and other officials on board.

96. The first day run of York's electric cars brought crowds thronging into the streets, lining the route to witness the historic event. This scene is in Fishergate, and the tram is proceeding from Fulford to Dringhouses. The very first car was driven by the Lord Mayor (with assistance from driver J.A. Stewart).

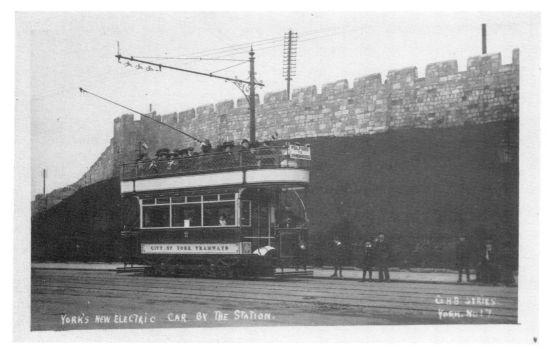

YORK'S NEW ELECTRIC CAR BY THE STATION.

G.H.B. SERIES
YORK. No.17

97. G.H.B. series postcard showing one of the new trams at the corner of Queen Street.

98. A much later scene near the Minster in July 1925. Postcard by W. Bramley of Cross Gates, Leeds.

MUSEUM ST. CAR YORK.

99. The Doncaster Rotophoto Co. Ltd. travelled far afield in the 1920's to produce picture postcards, and their York series was prefixed 562 – this is no. 63. The scene is Clarence Street, and the tramcar in the distance ran from Duncombe Place to Haxby Road, with its terminus in Rowntrees factory. In 1927, the approximate date of this card, there was a regular service every thirty minutes.

100. The tramway was purposely routed by way of the new railway station to avoid Micklegate Hill, and went to Holgate Bridge. The Haxby Road to Acomb routes were constructed at the same time, though Lendal Bridge had to be strengthened to take the extra traffic. Many tram shelters were built, like the one on the right of this scene.

101. W. Bramley postcard of a tramcar proceeding down Gillygate in June 1910, on its way from the railway station to Haxby Road. C.E. Britton's shop is to the right.

102. The same publisher, and another scene on Gillygate, with the two drivers having a chat, and two young lads looking on with interest. The only other visible traffic is a lone cyclist. Precious & Co's outfitters is to the left.

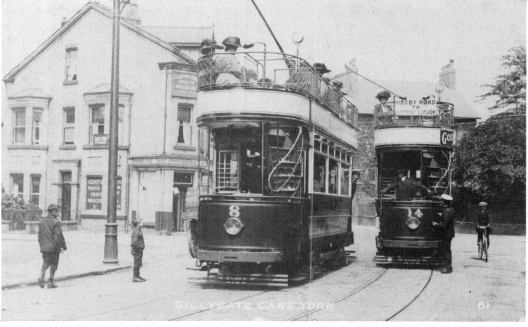

103. Every weekday morning before 8 a.m., and at noon there were special trams to carry people to and from work. Fares on trams and buses were the same at 2d a journey. By 1921 the Fulford tram depot was supplemented by a bus depot in Piccadilly, and in 1931 a bus garage was built at the Fulford depot. This is a scene in Spring 1911.

104. The Fulford, Haxby Road, Acomb and South Bank routes all ran at 7½ minute intervals between 8 a.m. and 9 a.m., and thereafter every ten minutes until 12 a.m., reverting then to every 7½ minutes until 11 p.m. The Saturday service ran every ten minutes. The fare was 2d per trip. When in 1916 the Haxby Road line was extended, the tram-line system was at its largest with 8½ miles, compared with only 3 miles in the days of the horse trams. Superb photographic postcard by Fox of the Dringhouses to Fulford tram.

105. Even in 1927 tramcar fares were still at the same level. Passengers could travel any distance on any route for a universal fare of 2d and could obtain a 2d ticket for transferring at Queen Street corner. Here we see Lendal Bridge in the 1920s.

106. This is the Haxby Road terminus. In 1916 the line was extended over the hump-back railway bridge in the distance, and beyond Rowntree's chocolate factory. Postcard by Bramley, posted in October 1914.

107. Boyes store, so well-liked by shoppers and seen here rebuilt after the 1910 fire, no longer stands on Ouse Bridge, over which tramcar no. 36 is on its way out of the city. This 1915 card was printed and published as an advertising item for Boyes by Delittle, Fenwick & Co. *(see illus. 78)*

108. Tramcar coming out of Queen Street (formerly Thief Lane), which at one time stretched to North Street Postern on the outside of the city walls. The corner of Queen Street was widened in 1877, when Brown Brothers and Taylors shop was demolished. Postcard by the London firm Soloman Brothers.

109. Posted in April 1916, this superb photographic card shows Micklegate Bar and Blossom Street, originally called Ploxamgate, and dating back to Roman times, when it formed part of the road to London – in fact it continued to be the high road to the capital until 1792. Note the beautifully-made lamp-post on the left.

110. The Mount, York, with a no. 14 tram, about 1912 on a postcard by Fox. Trams ran in York until 1935.

111. In a corner of St. George's Field – about 1910 – this W.D. and H.O. Wills advertisement stand, perched somewhat precariously on a bicycle, was part of the great procession of the Hospital Saturday annual event. Such promotion of smoking would certainly be frowned on today – in this photograph the majority of onlookers are young children.

112. Plain Mr York, a larger-than-life working model, would hand you a postcard of himself when confronted. This worked on a clockwork suction system. The advertising gimmick from the 1920s was a children's favourite. Plain Mr York was still working at an exhibition called "Sweet Memories" at Rowntrees' factory in May 1984. According to the information on the reverse of this postcard, Rowntree's cocoa and chocolate works estate covered 200 acres and employed over 6,000 people.

113. A typical poster advertising postcard for the largest and most famous of York's pageants – that of 1909, in which many of York's citizens and their children took part on a massive scale. The drawing was by Archie Ward, the postcard published by Delittle, Fenwick & Co., and posted from York in June 1908, thirteen months before the advertised pageant.

114. Thomas Bowman, furniture dealer and remover, bought in 1908 the New Street Methodist chapel for £5,900. At a later date Bowman and Sons moved to Monkgate and were still there in the 1960s. This postcard shows just one of their steam-powered removal vehicles. *(see illus. 12)*

115. W.T. Forsselius sold cars at the Blossom Street garage from 1908 until 1982, when they left York for Poppleton. Trade fell dramatically then, however, causing losses, and the old firm have since gone into liquidation. This photographic card by Edwin Fox features a marvellous range of early motors for sale, and Forsselius advertise themselves as agents for Flanders and E.M.F. Cars.

116. Advertising postcard for Isaac Walton & Co. Tailors and Outfitters, of 39/40 Parliament Street. The reverse was used for appointments/confirmation of orders. Parliament Street did not exist until 1836, so there was no connecting road between St. Sampson's Square and Pavement. Because the Thursday market and the Pavement market were too small for the city, an act of Parliament was passed after twenty years of talks whereby the old market places were connected by Parliament Street. Even today there are controversial arguments about the proposed future of the street. The buildings on the right of this scene have been demolished.

117. Another Tailor, A.W. Wansbrough of Coney Street; the firm went out of business in 1909. Miss E. Ward, costumier, was at this address in 1927. A year later, no. 56 disappeared when buildings were taken down to make the Square bigger — the site is now part of a bank. F. Burgin, chemist, also featured on this card, is still in business today.

118. One of a fine series of poster reproductions by Raphael Tuck of London. "Celebrated Posters" were described on the card as a 'Collector's Postcard Series' — this one is numbered 1501. The whole of the reverse was designated for the address (the card was posted in July 1903) so that the message had to be squeezed beneath the picture on the front. The design, by Beggarstaffs, advertised Rowntree's Elect Cocoa.

In the 1920's, Arnold Rowntree, the director of advertising and sales, had a car specially designed in the shape of a large tin of Elect Cocoa.

119. This is an early view of the old Rowntree shop in Pavement. It may well have looked like this when Joseph Rowntree as a boy of 15 joined the shop, though the face of the shop building has changed often over the years. The two lamps in front of the shop look quite impressive with advertising on their sides. The picture was taken after T. Coning & Sons had taken over the shop. They sold cocoa which was specially packed in their name, in a cylindrical tin with a white paper label printed in gold. Palethorpe's Royal Cambridge sausages are prominently advertised. The postcard, published by Burrow of Cheltenham, carries on the reverse the name and address of Coning & Sons.

120. St. Sampsons Square, the site of the ancient Thursday Market. Excavations in 1936 showed that this market went as far back as the fourth century, when the 'square' was a real square. It lost its original look when Parliament Street was constructed, uniting it with the old Pavement market. The name 'Thursday Market' was not recorded until the time of King John. Photographic card by Hayes, with reverse message, though not postally used.

121. The old Rowntree shop in the Pavement, run by Joseph Rowntree's father, was taken over early this century by Coning & Sons, provision merchants *(see also illus. 119),* and is seen here as 'The Cremery Restaurant'. It was also, from the 1920's to the 1960's, York Coffee House Ltd., until it became Rowntree's grocers of Scarborough.

Pavement, York.

122. Leopard Yard, so named after the closure of the 'Leopard Inn' in 1906, separated no. 45 and 47 Coney Street. The Leopard Yard housed three residents from 1906 to 1925. In 1926 building took place to construct York's first arcade which became the Leopard Arcade. Some of its shops were Saxon Co. Ltd., S.M. Gawthorne Co. Ltd. and the Northern Motor Utilities Co. Ltd. This is Gawthorne's advertising card.

123. Frances, Muriel, Jessy and Olive standing outside the shop of W. Hardy, tobacconist, of 30, Walmgate, one day in 1922, when Woodbines, Robins and Park Drive were 2d for five and 4d for ten, Players and Gold Flake were 6d for ten and 1/- for twenty, and Robin and Twist tobacco were 8d an ounce, and St Bruno 10d.

124. W.J. Scott of 36, Fossgate, provision stores, was set up in 1895. By 1909 William Joe had moved to 41 Fossgate, and had premises on Skeldergate. By 1927 the business had ceased. This postcard was published in 1905, and posted from the city on 31st July that year.

COLLECTING POSTCARDS

Anyone wanting to put together a collection of old postcards of York will find local collectors' fairs a helpful source. Many national dealers provide approvals (list in *Picture Postcard Annual,* obtainable from the publishers of this book) and most towns and cities have collectors' shops where old postcards are sold. A useful source locally is the Collectors Centre at 63 Micklegate. A specialist magazine, *Picture Postcard Monthly,* is the hobby's premier guide.

THE RIVER

125. Superb photographic postcard of the Ouse at Skeldergate Bridge by Bramley of Leeds. The barges are James Mary of Clifton (left) and Industry of York.

126. For hundreds of years the River Ouse was the chief means of transporting cargo to York. In its heyday the docks became quite large for the size of the city. By 1892 there were shipments of wheat, sugar, timber, cement, oil cake, barley, coal, flour, builders' sand and gravel, all of which have now declined. This photographic card by Hayes shows a scene looking towards York with Skeldergate Bridge in the distance.

127. The Ouse at Lendal Bridge frozen over in 1948 on a photographic postcard from the *Yorkshire Herald*. This event has by no means been uncommon in the river's history. The severe winter of 1784 caused the Ouse to be frozen for eight successive weeks. Events on the ice have included the roasting of chestnuts and skating. In 1740, booths were erected and football and other games played. In 1607, there was even horse-racing from the Tower to Marygate.

128. A mysteriously low tide in 1910 pictured on this Ryder's Series postcard, despite the existence of the Naburn Locks, built in 1757 at a cost of £10,000. Prior to this, when the Ouse was still a tidal river, there were often very low water levels, the worst perhaps 1723, when there was an extreme drought. Compare this scene, looking from Ouse Bridge towards Skeldergate Bridge, with illus. 131.

129. Conversely, the Ouse has for hundreds of years been subject to rapid rises in the water level, creating fast-flowing currents and causing severe flooding in the city. Only recently has anything been done to counteract this devastation and damage to homes and businesses. Date of this photographic postcard from Outhwaite's Premier York Postcard Depot uncertain, but probably around 1907. Scene looking from Skeldergate Bridge across St. Georges Park to Cliffords Tower.

130. 'Dent' series postcard, postally used in September 1905, featuring Ouse Bridge, the foundation stone of which was laid in 1810, and the structure completed in 1820. Until June 1829 a toll was charged to help pay the enormous cost of the bridge, £30,000. An act was passed to obtain money out of the county rates by five yearly instalments of £6,000. Until 1863 it was the only major bridge to span the river – then Lendal Bridge was opened.

131. The Riverside adjacent to Friars Temple and South Esplanade *(cf. illus. 128).* On the left of this scene are the remains of the Franciscan friars wall, all that remains of what was a large site until the dissolution in 1539. Despite the height of the houses on this bank, built in the 1850s, they are badly affected by floods. As I lived in the nearest one for sixteen years I have first-hand experience of this annual event. 1920s card by Doncaster Rotophoto Co. Ltd. (no. 562-38).

THE FERRY, WATER END, CLIFTON, YORK.

132. 'City Series' no. 89 by T.D.Y., posted in October 1923, and featuring Clifton Scope, the ancient lane from the green to the river, where a thirty-foot cliff is still in evidence, and where stands Clifton Bridge, replacing the old ferry which went back hundreds of years. The cliff overlooks the flood plain and flat common land of the Ings. A map of 1836 shows a pub called the 'Marquee Inn' nearby. Today a number of new houses stand on the cliff.

133. Interesting scene on Ouse Bridge on a postcard by J. Hodgson of Cleckheaton, postally used from the city on 26 June 1904. B. and L. Bushell, Ironmongers, are prominent on the right.

134. In 1901 master mariner Captain Edward Grace brought the first *River King* to York and moored the 69-foot steamer at Kings Staith. Without casualties it sank in 1932 and was immediately replaced by the second *River King*. This was a 72-foot long steel-hulled vessel, diesel-powered and capable of carrying 291 passengers in summer. Out of season it could work carrying 50 tons of cocoa beans or 110 tons of silver sand, thereby working all year round. It left York in 1938 and today still works in Stourport. This postcard features a 1907 scene with the original steamer. *(see illus. 166)*

RIVER. KING. YORK.

ROYAL VISITS

135. H.R.H. Princess Henry of Battenberg arrived at York station on 24th October 1905, visiting the city to unveil the Queen Victoria memorial, sculpted by George Milburn, in the Guild Hall. The fullsize marble figure had been paid for by public subscription to commemorate the Queen's reign. Chadwick & Allen of Hull published the card, which was posted from York on November 12th, 1905.

136. Another card from the same publisher, showing the Princess leaving the Mansion House after lunch. A guard of honour from the 2nd York and Lancaster Regiment was on parade. Before she left York on the 4.53 train north, Princess Henry also opened a lifeboat bazaar.

137. The Duke and Duchess of York (George VI and current Queen Mother) arriving at the Mansion House in 1925 en route to unveil the Cenotaph in Leeman Road Gardens. The shield on the wall was to commemorate this royal visit. Postcard by T.J. Hanstock of Clarence Street.

138. The royal visit of the Prince of Wales (later Edward VIII) to York on 31st May 1923 was arranged so he could become a freeman of the city. His day included a call at Rowntree's Cocoa Works, where 7,500 employees gave him a great reception. A casket of chocolate was presented to him on a very happy day for the city of York. Pathé Fréres Cinéma Ltd. published this souvenir card, showing a view looking down Station Rise.

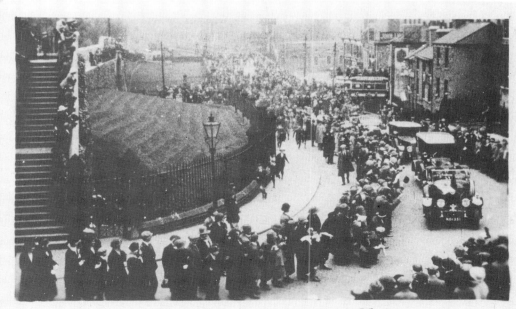

139. York's first Minster was built of wood in 633 by Edwin under the guidance of Paulinus, though the Minster as we know it was built between 1227 and 1472. Over 500 feet long, 100 feet wide and 200 feet high at the central tower, it is one of the largest of English cathedrals, with some of the finest stained glass in Europe. Postcard by Valentine of Dundee.

140. All Saints, Pavement has, as its most notable feature, an octagonal lantern tower, in which a large lamp used to hang. This was lit at night as a mark for travellers passing through the Forest of Galtres to the city. Coppergate to the left is a scene much changed today. Gray & Co. Ltd., Eboracum Series, York.

141. Here we see the church of Holy Trinity in The King's Court. Commonly called Christ Church, it was a mediaeval structure rebuilt in 1860 and demolished in 1937. It was the butchers' church, serving Shambles, which was earlier known as Ketmongergate, the street of fleshmongers. After 1836 it ceased to be used as a church, and in 1896 sheep awaiting slaughter were housed there by some parishioners for easy access to Shambles. This photographic card was posted from York in May 1911 with the message *"This is the old church we scholars went to on Sundays. This is the one they want to turn into a covered market."*

142. St. Sampson's is an old church rebuilt with new stone in 1844. It has for some years had a new lease of life as the meeting place for many of York's senior citizens who rest, drink tea and reminisce there. On this card (by Bramley of Leeds, whose York agent was W.A. Bilton, King's Square) Gilbertson's Wholesale & Retail Newsagents and Stationers is on the right.

143. E.T.W. Dennis 'Dainty' series postcard, postally used in March 1910, showing St. Maurice's Church. A new church was erected in 1877-8 on the corner of Monkgate and Lord Mayors walk, after the old church was pulled down. In later years it fell into decline and was demolished in the 1970s.

MILITARY EVENTS

144. Military Sunday was an extraordinarily popular event. The city was crowded on every occasion, with thousands coming by road and rail. Here we see two officers at the 1906 event, which, like the others, was colourful, smart and uplifting, with military brass bands. The nearest comparison today is Remembrance Day in November. Chadwick and Allen of Hull published this photographic postcard.

145. Duncombe Place: marching to the Minster. Here an unfortunate adjustment to a busby helmet by a member of the Hussars caught the cameraman's eye.

146. The first Military Sunday was held at the Minster on 19 April 1885 as a memorial service for General Gordon who had been killed in Khartoum the previous January. The special military service was repeated annually. This interesting view of Clifford Street shows the parade returning from the Minster and the crowds looking on. The actual year is not specified.

147. From 1885 to the outbreak of the second world war in 1939 the annual Military Sunday was held in mid-summer, with the territorial troops in the city taking part. In this unusual scene, taken in 1913 in Clifford Street, they are marching to the Minster with the City Castle prison walls dominant. Also to be seen are two sets of tramlines in the roadway. Postcard by Valentine of Dundee.

ST. JOHN'S AMBULANCE, YORK.

148. St. John's Ambulance on standby during the First World War. The York centre of the Association was formed in 1890 and has been active in the city and neighbourhood since then. For many years its centre was in High Ousegate. Always at public gatherings and ready to help, they still serve York in an admirable way.

YORK MILITARY HOSPITAL DURING THE EUROPEAN WAR 1914.

149. Postcard by George Brooks, 11 Leake Street, of temporary tents erected on the lawns of the York military hospital in 1914. The hospital, built on Fulford Road in 1854, was enlarged in 1878, 1893 (when it had room for 120 patients), and in 1906.

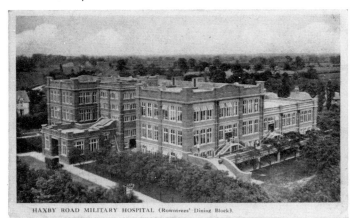

HAXBY ROAD MILITARY HOSPITAL (Rowntrees' Dining Block).

150. Rowntree's dining block was used as a military hospital in the 1914-18 war, for there was such a lot of war wounded coming home that the hospitals could not cope. Public halls, buildings and anywhere that could be used became temporary hospitals.

SIGNALLING FROM THE MINSTER to the BARRACKS

151. Military officials stand on the roof of York Minster in this exercise of signalling messages to Fulford barracks. Apart from Military Sunday, and other services, the use of a religious building for military purposes must be an unusual event, and certainly attracts the attention of the visitors on the right. W. Hayes published the card.

152. The arrival on 3rd August 1905 of Lord Roberts to the opening ceremony of the South African war memorial, an octagonal column set on steps with a lantern top. 1,320 Yorkshire lives were lost in the Boer War. The unveiling took place on a wet day amid hundreds of citizens. Photographic card by Chadwick & Allen of Hull.

153. Fishergate church parade in 1911, with the Scots Greys on the march. The buildings in the background have been demolished and replaced by flats. This card was posted from York in May 1911.

154. Anonymously-published card of one of the invaluable A.R.P. groups during the second world war. Wardens like this would have had to face the Beadeker raid on 29th April 1942, when twenty enemy bombers unloaded their deadly cargo on the city — York's blackest day since the siege of 1644. The Minster, however, was undamaged.

155. Outhwaite published this postcard commemorating York soldiers who died in the Great War. Gunner A. Brown (second row, second from right), 48853 65th Battery Royal Field Artillery, was killed in action on 7th December 1914, aged 24, at Ypres. He was buried in Dranoutre Military Cemetery in Belgium. Gunner Brown hailed from Leeman Road, and is featured with other local casualties here.

RAILWAYS

156. Few among the railway pioneers – except probably George Hudson – could have foreseen the massive growth in railway traffic that took place during the nineteenth century: but York certainly played a crucial part in the network. This 1930s view shows no. 1405 leaving on a York-Manchester express.

157. The 1911 York railway strike seems to have been quite an attraction: industrial harmony clearly did not exist in these days either. Queen Street bridge, where the crowd is standing, was built in 1880. In the days of the old station of 1840 there was a level crossing here. Queen Street was formerly known as Thief Lane, a very narrow thoroughfare. This card was probably published by Hayes. It was posted to Durham in September 1911.

② — YORK STATION — W·HAYES

158. The first station at York was built outside the city walls and made of wood. The next, inside the walls and opened in 1840, is now offices. The current station was opened in 1877, after six years of construction: the architect was Thomas Prosser. This rare photographic card by Hayes dates from around 1908.

159. Francis Frith of Reigate was one of the country's most famous publishing firms, and covered locations far away from their Surrey base. In this c.1905 view, the photographer has assembled a cross-section of the station staff for his postcard view, which shows the magnificent curved roof – 800 feet long and 234 feet wide – to good effect. The largest of the wrought-iron roof ribs rises to 42 feet above platform level. When it first opened, it was the world's biggest station.

York Station.

160. Another Frith view, taken at almost exactly the same spot on, presumably, the same day.

● York station cost £400,000 to build
● The massive side walls are built of yellow Scarborough bricks with stone dressings
● Its roof was erected by John Butler of Stanningley
● The main platform is 500 feet long
● Locomotives from many companies worked into York, though its joint operators were the Great Northern and North Eastern

161. A schoolboy leaving school in York for the last time sent this postcard to Jackley, Oxfordshire on 16 May 1906.

4354. YORK

162. One of F. Moore's (Locomotive Publishing Co.) postcards of the 1920s, featuring the array of signals for which York is famous. Photograph looking southbound.

N. E. R. York Station.

163. Locomotive Publishing Co. card from c.1906. York at this time must have been a paradise for the railway enthusiast, with a tremendous variety of locomotives and rolling stock to be seen. View taken from the south of York station.

D.V.L.R.

164. This was the scene at Layerthorpe station when Lady Deramore, the wife of the chairman, opened the Derwent Valley Light Railway on 19 July 1913. The first class fare was 3d per mile, second class 2d, and third 1d. All trains stopped at Osbaldwick, Aurton Lane, Dunnington, Elvington, Wheldrake, Cottingwith, Thorganby, Skipwith and North Duffield. Passenger excursions ceased on 31 August 1979, and special party bookings on November 1979. This postcard by Hanstock was posted a week after the opening.

LOADING UP COCOA   ROWNTREE'S PRIVATE RAILWAY STATION, YORK

165. Rowntree's private railway station, on a postcard published by the firm and used as a correspondence card. It was sent from South-East London on 11 December 1922; Rowntree's had a representative in Catford. The picture shows cocoa being loaded onto trains. This private station was closed in 1987; road transport has taken over.

PERSONALITIES

167. An Edwardian postcard reproducing a picture of Richard Naylor, York's last bellman, who died in 1873.

166. Captain Grace of the 'River King' steamer *(see illus. 134).*

168. Mrs. Cattle was born in 1803, and featured on this postcard in her 104th year, on 24 November 1906.

ROWNTREES

YORK.

ROWNTREE & CO., Ltd.—PACKING DEPARTMENT.

169. In this scene showing the packing department, wooden casing goes back to the earliest factories and was still in use (called the export roller department) in the 1960s. Today Rowntree Mackintosh P.L.C. has become a giant worldwide organisation, with the power of mass production and modern plant. It has, however, lost many of its old values with expense cuts to please its shareholders, to whom money is all-important: a far cry from the days when philanthropy was seen as important while the foundations of the business was being built up.

This undivided back postcard (the address had to occupy the reverse, and there was a space on the front for the message, as evidenced on the picture) was published by Tillotson & Son Ltd., and postally used in November 1903.

170. In 1890, 23 acres of land at the Haxby Road site were bought. By 1897 a limited liability company, Rowntrees & Co. Ltd., with Joseph as the chairman, issued capital of £226,000 and employed about 1200 workers. By this time work in the Haxby Road factory was in the early stages. Though Rowntrees was expanding rapidly, Joseph felt the new factory was too large and impersonal, so evening classes and social events were introduced.

By the time this postcard was published by Rowntrees themselves about 1907, the estate covered 222 acres and the number of employees had grown to almost 7,000. The multi-view here features a view through the entrance arch, office avenue, the company's private railway station (see illus. 165) and a panoramic view of the works.

YORK.

Rowntree & Co., Ltd.—Where Employees' Meals are Cooked.

171. Another card in Tillotson's series (and used in October 1903). The Rowntree family were great social reformers: the board of directors and the factory workers were then a close community with a united aim of producing a large variety of high-quality products. People and their jobs were of unique importance apart from growth and profits. A working relationship was built up with union, management and employees, and a working democracy was encouraged in the factory departments.

172. In 1899 these girls were working on the royal order from Queen Victoria, of 40,000 tin boxes in red, blue and gold specially packed for the troops in South Africa on the Boer War battlefield. This was a 1900 new year gift which carried the message "A HAPPY NEW YEAR" and was signed by the Queen. These girls stood all day as seen here – they did not wear head cover such as turbans or hats as they do today.

173. Chocolate packing in the early days was a work of art by the packers, who had to work rapidly to a set pattern, placing each chocolate into an individual paper cup. The packed box then had to be lightly brushed, finished and hand-wrapped in cellophane. The girls would be on a high piecework rate.

174. The old Rowntree fire brigade station was built in 1908; Captain Lawrence had a staff of 6 firemen and 15 auxiliaries. An old horse-drawn steam fire engine was superseded by a motor fire engine, and a motor ambulance. The brigade protected New Earswick, and gave assistance to the city brigade when called upon, sometimes attending large York fires *(see illus. 77)*. They now have a new station with modern engines and equipment. This is another postcard in the Tillotson series.

OTHER LOCAL INDUSTRY

175. Joseph Terry & Sons had, by the 1920s, outgrown their factory and were unable to expand on that site. So between 1925 and 28, their new factory on Bishopthorpe Road was built, and opened. They have been there ever since. Some of the early products made were chocolate, boiled sugars, sugared almonds, peppermints, marzipan and calves jelly. Terry's are well represented in York Castle Museum. This postcard (by Aero Pictorial of London) was overprinted as a correspondence card on the reverse.

176. A postcard by W. & T. Gaines of Leeds, featuring J.B. Inglis of 4 Coney Street, a watchmaker, jeweller and engraver who started up in business in 1885. His stock of silver and watches, he claimed, was the largest with the lowest prices. His services were repairing and engraving, and the work was done in Castlegate as seen here. They also crown-plated, nickle-plated, guilded, enamelled and lacquered.

177. In 1915, land was purchased at Tanghall for urgent erection of working-class houses. York's housing shortage was then very serious: 1250 homes were needed at once. A sum of £200,000 was borrowed by the corporation, and the 1919 housing act provided some subsidies. 367 houses were built in Tanghall by 1925, and by 1928 1,272 were completed with another 210 in progress. These days this sort of housing does not get built.

SPORT AND ENTERTAINMENT

178. Fun fairs were moved, in 1924, from Parliament Street to St Georges Field, where the August Bank Holiday fair was established during the second world war. City pleasure fairs are still held there, although they are now much smaller affairs, less crowded and less of a family outing than in the old days. This postcard of Corrigan's speedway comes from a famous series published by Jack Mellor of Halifax: he specialised in fairground subjects.

180. Chadwick & Allen published a long series featuring Ebor Day at York Racecourse; this is no. 24. Prior to 1731, York races were held on Clifton Ings, and since then on the Knavesmire. The first Ebor Day was in August 1843, the first Ebor Handicap winner was *Pagan* ridden by Colonel Templeman over a 2-mile course. From then on Ebor Day was usually held on the Wednesday of August holiday week.

179. Some of the staff of the *City Picture Palace* before it was renamed *The Rialto* in the early 1930s. By 1935 it had burnt down and was quickly replaced by a new cinema. The new *Rialto* did not, however, offer roller skating, but dancing did continue. In the late 1960s it became a bingo hall and was renamed *'The Cat's Whiskers'*. Recently it has returned to being the *Rialto*. Card by Avison & Co., Daylight & Electric Studios, 9 Fishergate.

181. No. 23 in the same series, a superb photographic card. The Ebor race was eventually cut down to one and three-quarter miles, and Ebor day became a centre for all classes of people from many parts of the country. One meeting in 1954 was hit by a monsoon which virtually reduced the course to a lake.

HOTELS

182. The Bay Horse Hotel just outside Monkgate Bar on a photographic card by unidentified publisher, taken about 1909, when J. Dobson was the landlord. It offered "good accomodation for cyclists, visitors and commercial gentleman".

183. Coppergate has undergone much change over the centuries. The public house on this postcard scene was originally called 'The Leopard' but renamed the Market Tavern in 1770. The newly developed Coppergate site and the latest of York's squares, St. Mary's Square, has become world-famous with the very popular Viking Centre its main attraction to many thousands of visitors.

184. Fine advertising card for the Old George Hotel, published by Delittle, Fenwick & Co. of York. The hotel was built in 1770, and was a family and commercial hotel for 180 years, until it was demolished in the early 1950s to construct the Stonebow. The modern building that stands close to this site is Stonebow House, a most unsightly structure of shops and offices.

185. In 1770 cottages were removed on this site, and the York Tavern was erected. The Inn took its name from Christopher Harker, a former butler. This high-quality Georgian building with an equally handsome interior was a well-known coaching Inn. Unfortunately, on 31st October 1928, it was shamefully demolished to widen St. Helens Square. This advertising postcard was actually sent from Hove in August 1910.

186. This is an example of one of the rooms in the much loved Georgian building The Queens Hotel, that stood in Micklegate for over 260 years and should still be there in its original state today, instead of the empty space that remains of it. Another Delittle, Fenwick & Co. postcard.

187. The Old Black Swan in Peaseholme Green dates back to the 14th century, and boasts fine panelled rooms, a massive oak staircase and wonderful old fireplace. It was the birthplace of General Wolfe in 1727; today, apart from being a public house, it offers hot and cold meals. *Silverette* type card published by Raphael Tuck in series 1882, 'Quaint Corners, York', and posted from the city in August 1905.

188. W. Bramley of Leeds published this photographic card of The White Swan in Pavement, a coaching inn built in 1733. The ground floor exterior has been changed since the postcard was issued, and is now taken up by shops. The hotel became a corner building, making it more prominent, when in 1910 old timbered buildings were demolished to make way for the construction of Piccadilly. The hotel was renovated after an internal fire a few years ago.

LOCAL POSTCARD PUBLISHERS

Many cards of York were published by small firms or individuals, with William Hayes the most prolific. Often these postcards were produced by a photographic process in very small quantities, and consequently are today difficult to find. Much research needs to be done to determine the scope of their output, and the publishers would be pleased to receive any further information about them, or indeed about any hitherto undiscovered postcard publishers. The following is a list of those whose work features in this book.

York publishers

Arthur & Co.
Avison & Co., Daylight and Electric Studios, 9 Fishergate
Broars
George Brooks, 11 Leake Street
Delittle, Fenwick & Co.
'Dent' series
E.F. Fox, Micklegate
G.H.S.
Gray & Co., 'Eboracum' series
H.J.S.
T.J. Hanstock, Clarence Street
William Hayes
Outhwaite's Premier York Postcard Den
P. Preston
Rowles
Rowntrees
Ryder's series
T.D.Y.
Wheatley, Regent Street
Yorkshire Herald Co.

Local publishers outside York

W. Bramley (Leeds)
E. Burrow (Cheltenham)
Chadwick & Allen (Hull)
Debenham & Co.
Doncaster Rotophoto Co.
W. & T. Gaines (Leeds)
J. Hodgson (Cleckheaton)
Hunt (Manchester)
Jack Mellor (Halifax)
Tillotson & Sons Ltd.
W.A.R. Co.

In addition, many local firms published their own advertising postcards.

NATIONAL POSTCARD PUBLISHERS

Because York was a popular Tourist centre, most of the top British publishers issued cards, often in sets of six. These had high print runs, were frequently in colour, and are normally easy to collect now.

Aerofilms
Aero Pictorial
Cynicus Publishing Co. (Tayport)
E.T.W. Dennis (Scarborough)
F. Frith (Reigate)
F. Hartmann (London)
Judges (Hastings)

Locomotive Publishing Co./F. Moore (London)
Pathé Freres Cinema
Photocrom (Tunbridge Wells)
Solomon brothers (London)
Raphael Tuck & Sons (London)
J. Valentine (Dundee)

189. Photographic card of York Gala viewed from one of the balloons that made an ascent from the gala field. The card was posted at York in August 1910.

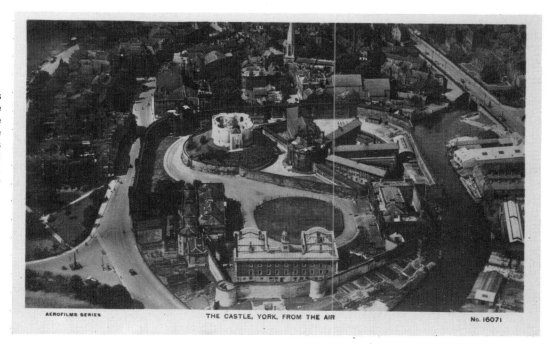

190. Aerofilms published this postcard of York castle in the 1920s. Cliffords Tower is in the centre of the picture with the old prison (built in 1705) to its right. Included were two small cells for solitary prisoners and three special cells for those condemned to death.

AEROFILMS SERIES   THE CASTLE, YORK, FROM THE AIR   No. 16071

AEROFILMS SERIES   AIR VIEW OF THE RIVER OUSE, YORK   No. 6632

191. Another Aerofilms card showing a view of the River Ouse with the steeple of All Saints, North Street, dominant, as it had been for centuries before it was overpowered by the Viking Hotel. This is an area of much change, where many properties have for years been affected by the floods of the Ouse.

SKELDERGATE BRIDGE WORKS, YORK.

192. Also by Aerofilms, this card features Skeldergate Bridge. Isaac Richardson, a quaker, bought a plot of land at Skeldergate Postern in 1780, including a cherry orchard known as Cherry Hill. He built up a tanning business which his son William eventually converted to agriculture. The firm underwent ownership transitions, too, through Anderton Richardson and Hargreaves to Britag. Now the old works on this site have given way to new houses and flats.

COMIC CARDS

193. The end of horse-drawn trams in York portrayed on a comic card published by Delittle, Fenwick & Co.

194. Similar tram caricature by the same firm in their *Defco* series.

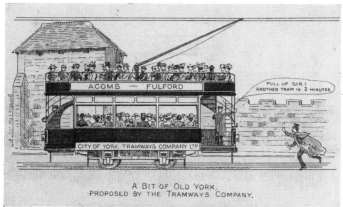

195. More satirical tram humour.

196. Delittle, Fenwick & Co's view of York's uncovered market, postally used in November 1906.

197. This card by the Cynicus Publishing Co. of Tayport, Fife, was a standard design, overprinted for use in hundreds of different places. This York version was posted from the city in August 1907.

198. The virtue of patience at York's public library, by D.F. & Co. in their *Defco* series.

199. Another nationally sold card, captioned according to where it was to be marketed, and reflecting the popularity of roller skating at special rinks in the Edwardian era. Published by Valentine of Dundee, it was posted in September 1909.

League Express

LEAGUE
Publications Ltd

RUGBY LEAGUE
2018-2019
End of jeopardy

For Malcolm Andrews

First published in Great Britain in 2018 by
League Publications Ltd, Wellington House, Briggate, Brighouse, West Yorkshire HD6 1DN

Copyright © League Publications Ltd

A CIP catalogue record for this book is available from the British Library
ISBN 978-1-901347-37-1

Designed and Typeset by League Publications Limited
Printed by H Charlesworth & Co Ltd, Wakefield

Contributing Editor
Tim Butcher

Statistics, production and design
Daniel Spencer

Contributors
Thomas Alderson
Malcolm Andrews
Robbie Andrews
Peter Bird
Aaron Bower
Steve Brady
Martin Butcher
Michael Butcher
Phil Caplan
Josh Chapman
Tom Coates
John Cox
Joseph Crabtree
Drew Darbyshire
Alex Davis
John Drake
Daniel Fowler
Ian Golden
Sian Golden
Ryan Gould
Michael Hale
Sean Hayes
Ian Henshaw
Phil Hodgson
Ash Hope
Mike Hyde
Andrew Jackson
Chris Jackson
Steve Kilmartin
David Kuzio

Melvin Levongo
Lorraine Marsden
Steve Mascord
Bryn May
Keith McGhie
Charlie O'Connor-Clarke
Michael Park
Dave Parkinson
Josh Pay
Huw Richards
Ian Rigg
Chris Roberts
Andrew Robson
Martyn Sadler
David Saffer
Matthew Shaw
Steve Slater
James Stott
Mitchell Tierney
Jeff Tyldesley
Callum Walker
Gareth Walker
John Walsh
Jordan Weir
Ricky Wilby
Gavin Willacy
Gavin Wilson
Ian Wilson
Peter Wilson
Jack Wynne

Pictures
NRL Imagery
Steve Gaunt
Matthew Merrick
Craig Milner
Steve Jones/RLPix
Dean Williams
Magi Haroun
SWpix
Paul Clayton
Bernard Platt
Mark Cosgrove
Craig Cresswell
Craig Hawkhead
Steve Miller
Prime Images
Richard Long
Melanie Allatt
Simon Davies
Sean Gosling
Neko Grouch
Richard Land
Steve McCormick
Bob Brough
Paul Butterfield
Graeme Crowther
Terry Donnelly
Paul McCarthy
Gary McKeating
Dave Murgatroyd
Bernard Rieu
John Rushworth
Paul Smith
Troy Taule
Craig Thomas
Mal Walker

Main cover picture
Craig Milner

CONTENTS

ACKNOWLEDGEMENTS

The *League Express Yearbook 2018-2019* is the 23rd of League Publications Ltd's annual series of Rugby League Yearbooks, which began in the first year of Super League in 1996.

This is the first year we have produced the book without the involvement of Malcolm Andrews, who compiled the Australian section of the book since its inception. We had to say goodbye to our good mate when he sadly passed away late in the year.

We have always believed that a historical record of the Rugby League year is a vital source for Rugby League supporters and for future generations. And as always we rely on the hard work and dedication of all the contributors to *Rugby Leaguer & Rugby League Express*, *Rugby League World* magazine and totalrl.com website to make this publication possible.

We are able to include some wonderful action photography provided by, in particular NRL Imagery, Steve Gaunt, Matthew Merrick, Craig Milner, Steve Jones at RLPix, Dean Williams and Magi Haroun.

Thanks to the Rugby Football League for their help during the year and to the historians and statisticians at clubs who help us resolve any anomalies.

Acknowledgement also to the Rothmans Yearbook 1999, compiled by our late friend Ray Fletcher, the British Rugby Records Book from London Publications and to the club officials, and some supporters, who helped us verify records.

Thanks also to Opta Sportdata, who compile the Opta Index Analysis in our statistical section.

Special thanks to Matthew Shaw, Lorraine Marsden and Alex Davis, who respectively wrote the Championship, League 1 and NRL sections.

The comprehensive statistical review is once again a work of wonder, put together, as always, by Daniel Spencer, who also designed the book.

TIM BUTCHER
Contributing Editor

INTRODUCTION

The Rugby League year is never dull and 2018 has provided more wonderful moments that will be remembered for many years to come.

Freshest in the memory is England's series win over New Zealand, who came to the UK for their Autumn tour on the back of a convincing win over World Champions Australia only two weeks before.

The series win was a great fillip for British Rugby League but it was the manner of the success and the emergence of a new breed of England international player that proved the most satisfying. The Kiwis were far from pushovers - they certainly proved that in the third game of the series - but were beaten after two high-standard Test matches which whetted the appetite for more international football.

The man responsible for providing an expanded international fixture list is Nigel Wood, who took over as chief executive of the Rugby League International Federation in mid-season after his ten-year tenure as chief executive of the Rugby Football League came to an end at the start of the year.

It was certainly a season of change, as the Super League appointed its own chief executive in Rob Elstone and engineered the scrapping of the three-eights fixture system which was the brainchild of Wood. 2018 was the fourth and last season of the Super 8s system.

The next season was to see the re-introduction of one-up, one-down and the top-five play-offs that had been in place from 1998 to 2001. The unilateral announcement was made by a group of Super League chairmen at the media unveiling of former Everton FC CEO Elstone in early June. Not even all Super League club officials were behind it, with Leeds chief executive Gary Hetherington accusing the group involved of a 'power grab' and there was furore from representatives of Championship and League 1 clubs. No decision had indeed been made but a special general meeting of the RFL at the end of the season waved the changes through.

Whatever the fixture format and squabbles off the field, on the field there will always be some special moments and the celestial scriptwriters could be well satisfied with their work by the end of the season. It must have been written in the stars that Shaun Wane should finish off a 35-year association with Wigan Rugby League by leading the Warriors to Grand Final glory. The 12-4 win over Warrington at Old Trafford couldn't have summed up better the will to win that Wane had instilled in his group of players, with three of them playing their last games for the club.

Sam Tomkins was bound for the Catalans, while John Bateman and Ryan Sutton were to join the player drain to the NRL and join Canberra Raiders. Leeds and England winger Ryan Hall would head that way too to play for NRL Premiers Sydney Roosters.

The Rhinos' dream finish of 2017 turned into another nightmare as they failed to reach the top-eight for a second time in three years. They secured their place via the Qualifiers in reasonably comfortable fashion but parted company with four-times Championship coach Brian McDermott, as well as recording a record home crowd for Super League when 23,246 people turned out to see them play Castleford at Elland Road,

Catalans Dragons show off the Challenge Cup to their supporters after a stunning Wembley win

the switch of venues enforced because of the on-going refurbishment of the stadium at Headingley.

It was the year that saw the first time a Super League fixture had been played outside Europe as Wigan beat Hull FC in Wollongong, New South Wales by 24-10, 12,416 turning out for the round-two game on the Saturday night, a higher attendance than any of the three league fixtures between the two teams in 2017.

Super League champions Leeds fell to a 38-4 World Club Challenge defeat to the Storm at AAMI Park in Melbourne, the first time the game had been played in Australia since 1994.

The so-labelled 'Beast from the East' arrived in March and caused postponements and disruption in round four and round six. We had the first abandonment of a game because of blizzards when the players of Wakefield and Widnes had to walk off the pitch 26 minutes into their round six game. The cold and wet weather continued through April before an inordinately dry and hot summer set in and fans at last got the warm-weather football they had dreamed of.

One club that got better along with the weather was Catalans Dragons, who created history by winning the Challenge Cup, Lance Todd Trophy winner Tony Gigot completing a rollercoaster two years by leading his team to a 20-14 victory over Warrington. In the early part of the season, the Dragons had looked like bottom-four certainties.

The Wolves enjoyed a renaissance under new coach Steve Price and reached the two major finals but found Wigan and Catalans too good for them on the big days. St Helens won the third trophy with room to spare by lifting the League Leaders Shield by finishing top of the table by some distance. But they fell at the semi-finals stage in both major competitions, despite thrilling the crowds with what looked for the bulk of the season as unstoppable football. On the back of that they had seven players in the end-of-season Super League Dream team as well as their mercurial fullback Ben Barba being named Steve Prescott Man of Steel.

Introduction

Of the rest, Castleford couldn't repeat their top-of-the-table feat of 12 months before, with reigning Man of Steel Luke Gale absent injured for most of the season but still in with a shout come the semi-finals; Wakefield finished in fifth spot for the second year running, having three players in the Dream Team while Huddersfield got a new coach mid-season and almost made the top-four from an unpromising position. Hull FC made a mesmeric descent towards the end of the season on the back of an injury run, losing their last eleven matches when they had not long before looked a fair bet for the top four.

The anxiety of finishing in the bottom four ended in 2018 and bottom club Widnes didn't even make the fourth v fifth Million Pound Game after the Qualifiers, as Denis Betts was sacked as coach in the middle of an eight-match losing run in Super League.

Instead, two Championship teams contested the play-off, with London Broncos stunning Toronto Wolfpack in a try-less game in Canada. That stymied plans for a North American team in Super League and applications for entry into the RFL from other cities in Canada and the USA didn't make any obvious progress. England and New Zealand did play a Test match in Denver, Colorado in June as part of the build-up to a possible World Cup in the USA.

It's all in this book. We hope you will enjoy re-living your Rugby League season.

TIM BUTCHER
Contributing Editor

The 23rd League Express Yearbook contains the full story of the domestic year, the Australian season and match facts for all Super League, Challenge Cup games involving professional teams, Championship and Championship One games. Every player who has played Super League is also listed along with those players to have made their debuts this year. We have also selected five individuals who we judge to have made the biggest impact on Rugby League in 2018. There are scoring and attendance records for every club as well as League wide records. A full record of the 2017 World Cup is also included and the 2018 Test series between England and New Zealand is also detailed.

* League Publications publishes the weekly newspaper Rugby Leaguer & Rugby League Express, as well as the monthly glossy magazine Rugby League World and the UK's most popular League website 'totalrl.com'.

1
THE 2018 SEASON

DECEMBER 2017
So near, yet...

December started in heart-stopping fashion as England came within an ankle-tap of denying Australia their 11th World Cup at the Suncorp Stadium on the first Saturday of the month. Only a desperate lunge by Australian centre Josh Dugan prevented Kallum Watkins from keeping his feet and finding inside support for what would have been an equalising score.

In the end a 6-nil defeat to the reigning world champions reflected well on Wayne Bennett-coached England and on international Rugby League, which was already riding high on the performance of Pacific Island nations, especially Tonga, who themselves came within a whisker of toppling England in the semi-final.

Not surprisingly, the performance of Super League players caught the eye of NRL clubs.

Huddersfield winger Jermaine McGillvary was a target, even though he was contracted to his hometown club until 2020. The 29-year-old produced an impressive World Cup campaign for England, scoring six tries in four games and was named on a four-man shortlist for the Golden Boot award. McGillvary's clubmate Oliver Roberts was also highly fancied in Australia after standing out for Ireland, who registered two wins out of three games but still didn't qualify for the quarter-finals because of the contrived 14-team draw.

St Helens prop Alex Walmsley also took the eye after making his Test debut for England in a 29-10 victory over Lebanon, just five years on from playing open-age amateur rugby with Dewsbury Celtic.

It wouldn't be one-way traffic, as former England centre Dan Sarginson rejoined Wigan on a two-year deal after having secured a release from Gold Coast Titans, just twelve months on from joining the NRL club, where his season was dogged by injury.

Wakefield Trinity's long-running uncertainty over a new stadium dragged on and on and by the end of the year there was still a question mark over whether they would be granted permission to play at Belle Vue in 2018, their home since 1879. Developers Yorkcourt Properties, tasked with delivering a community stadium for the city of Wakefield, had not followed through on assurances made at the out-of-town Newmarket site. Trinity were considering a potential court case against Wakefield Council after several years of high-profile disputes.

On the field, Trinity were keen to build on their fifth-placed finish of 2017 and completed their squad for 2018 with the signing of former Leigh and Wigan utility player Ryan Hampshire.

Catalans Dragons, who had secured their place in Super League via the Million Pound Game, continued their recruitment for 2018 with the signing of Samisoni Langi, who had finished the previous season at Leigh. The versatile Tongan international signed a two-year contract. New Zealand international Krisnan Inu was released after two-and-a-half years in the south of France and secured a move to Widnes Vikings.

Vikings CEO James Rule revealed that the club had 'genuine interest' earlier in the year from parties interested in buying their Super League licence and relocating them. At the time Vikings officials had declined to comment on any such activity but, following the announcement the Vikings had agreed a new five-year deal to remain at Halton Stadium, Rule said the board eventually rejected offers of relocation and significant financial investment.

Salford Red Devils delved into the international market with the addition of Fiji prop Ben Nakubuwai, who had played a prominent role on his nation's progress to the World Cup semi-finals.

There was controversy off the field as some Championship clubs voiced their anger after it emerged Leigh Centurions had received a £500,000 parachute payment following relegation from Super League. The sum came from Super League Europe after clubs in the top flight agreed to make the payment. Championship clubs predicted Leigh would have an unfair advantage due to the additional distribution.

Boxing Day saw the traditional Leeds-Wakefield challenge switched to Belle Vue because of ongoing re-building work at Headingley and the Rhinos came away with a 17-10 victory. With Danny McGuire's replacement as captain not yet announced publicly, prop Brad Singleton had the honour of wearing the armband in the win over Trinity, which augured well for 2018.

In the other Boxing Day games, Batley won at Dewsbury 28-16, Featherstone won at Castleford 32-16 and Bradford, in League 1 in 2018 and with John Kear as new head coach, beat Halifax 22-6.

Denis Betts hailed the performance of young fullback Olly Ashall-Bott after he starred in Widnes's pre-season home victory over Warrington later in the week. The 20-year-old was making his first appearance for over a year following a serious knee injury and scored two tries to cap a superb return as the Vikings defeated the Wolves 26-22.

At the end of year, Castleford Tigers halfback Luke Gale was named Player of the Year in League Express's annual readers poll, taking 46 per cent of the votes, with nearest rival Alex Walmsley, his England team-mate and St Helens prop, on 18 per cent.

Gale, who shone as his side won the League Leaders' Shield only to lose out to Leeds Rhinos in the Grand Final, was the 2017 Man of Steel and also won the Albert Goldthorpe Medal as the player gaining the most points from League Express reporters throughout the season. It was his third successive Albert Goldthorpe Medal success. St Helens' Regan Grace was voted the Young Player of the Year and the best domestic newcomer in 2017.

JANUARY
Room at the top

The Rugby Football League was starting the search for a new chief executive at the start of 2018 when it was announced that Nigel Wood was to stand down after ten years in the role.

Wood, who was also chairman of the Rugby League International Federation (RLIF), had served on the RFL board since 2001. He was credited with putting the governing body on a more stable financial footing after the financial fall-out of the 2000 World Cup. He was also the brains behind the two twelves/three eights system that had gathered many critics since its introduction in 2015.

Chief operating officer Ralph Rimmer was to act as interim chief executive while the RFL searched for Wood's successor.

In the meantime Wood was tasked with making a fact-finding mission to North America to assess the validity of a bid from a consortium in New York to join the competition. On the back of the meteoric success of Toronto Wolfpack since their introduction in 2017, proposed Rugby League franchises in Boston and Hamilton (Canada) had also expressed interest in joining the RFL as early as the 2019 season.

The man behind a proposed new club in the American city of Boston was thought to be Mark Evans, the former CEO of NRL club Melbourne Storm. Evans was at the Storm for over two years, taking the role in May 2013 before leaving in July of 2015.

According to reports in Australia, the RLIF was in the process of suing IMG, the tournament promoters of the World Cup, for over half a million Australian dollars, alleging they had withheld a significant sum of money from the tournament in relation to the three games that were played in Papua New Guinea. IMG were arguing the initial contract for the tournament didn't involve a venue outside Australia and New Zealand, with a heavy additional cost coming as a result of the three games in Port Moresby.

The three matches in question proved to be a success, with all of them being sell-outs. But the dispute was about whether the games should have been played there at all and whether the RLIF could enforce payment for them. If the matter was ever resolved, it was kept secret.

Meanwhile the RLIF at last gained recognition from the Global Association of International Sports Federations (GAISF), previously known as Sport Accord, by being given observer status. The recognition would give the RLIF status when approaching national governments to help establish Rugby League teams and competitions.

The Rugby League world was stunned by the sudden death of Papua New Guinea centre Kato Ottio, a star of the Kumuls' World Cup campaign who, along with prop Wellington Albert, had been signed by Widnes Vikings.

The 23-year-old Ottio collapsed just days before he and Albert were due to fly to the UK. His sudden death happened after he collapsed while on a second five-mile run in temperatures reaching 33 degrees in a bid to show youngsters in his homeland what it took to be a professional. He died at the Pacific International Hospital in Port Moresby, just two days before he was due to fly to England.

The Vikings subsequently launched a crowdfunding page and raised over £4,000 for

Ottio's family at their pre-season game against Whitehaven.

Michael McIlorum said he was ready for a new challenge after joining Catalans Dragons on a two-year contract from Wigan Warriors.

The 29-year-old Ireland hooker, who still had two years to go on his Wigan contract, became the sixth player involved in the 2017 World Cup to put pen to paper with the Perpignan club. Steve McNamara had also signed Scotland back Lewis Tierney permanently from Wigan, France prop Antoni Maria from Leigh Centurions, France centre or back row Benjamin Jullien from Warrington Wolves and Papua New Guinea captain David Mead from Brisbane Broncos.

A new, not-for-profit holding company, Salford RD Holdings, took control of the Salford Red Devils club from Dr Marwan Koukash, who had owned the club since 2013. A four-strong board of directors, intended to represent fans and the Salford community, was to take over.

Red Devils head coach Ian Watson launched an attack on Hull Kingston Rovers following the Robins' official bid for Robert Lui. Watson was angered by Rovers' attempt to sign his leading halfback on the eve of the season.

Another Australian, Huddersfield forward Tom Symonds suffered another injury setback. The backrower aggravated the knee injury that saw him manage just two appearances throughout the 2017 season. He subsequently managed just one game in 2018 and was released from his contract shortly after

The Giants were also hit with the news that captain Leroy Cudjoe was to miss the first month of the season as he continued to recover from a knee injury. The 29-year-old missed the final month of the 2017 campaign to undergo an operation.

Wakefield winger Tom Johnstone admitted he had doubts whether he would be the same player after a serious knee injury before marking his return to action with a hat-trick in Trinity's comfortable 62-0 home pre-season win over Halifax.

Hull Kingston Rovers triumphed in the battle for the Clive Sullivan Memorial Trophy, defeating their rivals Hull FC 34-26 at the KCOM Stadium. But it came at a cost as Danny Addy was ruled out for the season with a knee injury.

Micky Higham said he had mixed emotions on having played his last game of professional Rugby League. The 37-year-old captained his hometown club Leigh Centurions in a pre-season testimonial game against his former side Wigan Warriors, with Wigan claiming a 22-14 victory. But the following month Higham came out of retirement to help Leigh's cause after a poor start to the season and the resignation of coach Neil Jukes.

LADBROKES CHALLENGE CUP - ROUND 1

Saturday 27th January 2018
British Army 48 Milford Marlins 10
Distington 32 Queens 24
East Leeds 10 Thornhill Trojans 28
Featherstone Lions 34 Skirlaugh 14
Hunslet Warriors 0 Wath Brow Hornets 30
Kells 40 British Police 8
Leigh Miners Rangers 18 Myton Warriors 22
Lock Lane 48 Hindley 0
London Chargers 18 Hammersmith Hills Hoists 0
Loughborough University 4 Bradford Dudley Hill 38
Millom 36 Strathmore Silverbacks 18
Orrell St James 34 Northampton Demons 0
Oulton Raiders 28 Siddal 26
Rochdale Mayfield 28 Crosfields 0
Royal Air Force 12 Drighlington 4
Royal Navy 11 Normanton Knights 12 (aet)
Saddleworth Rangers 12 Thatto Heath Crusaders 22
Underbank Rangers 16 Batley Boys 17 (aet)
University of Hull 24 Hensingham 10
Wallsend Eagles 6 Pilkington Recs 42
York Acorn 16 Askam 32
Sunday 28th January 2018
West Hull 58 Longhorns 10
Saturday 3rd February 2018
Shaw Cross Sharks 18 Beverley 0

Hunslet Club Parkside v Valley Cougars - *Tie awarded to Hunslet*

LADBROKES CHALLENGE CUP - ROUND 2

Saturday 10th February 2018
Askam 16 West Hull 4
Batley Boys 13 Royal Air Force 12 (aet)
British Army 26 London Chargers 14
Distington 12 Lock Lane 4
Featherstone Lions 18 Thatto Heath Crusaders 6
Hunslet Club Parkside 24 Wath Brow Hornets 6
Kells 8 Orrell St James 6
Millom 24 Bradford Dudley Hill 12
Oulton Raiders 24 Shaw Cross Sharks 10
Pilkington Recs 16 Thornhill Trojans 0
Rochdale Mayfield 4 Normanton Knights 8
University of Hull 18 Myton Warriors 22

FEBRUARY
Saints on fire

Round 1

Champions Leeds kicked off Super League XXIII on the first Thursday night of February and were good value for their 16-12 televised win at Warrington, with 18-year-old fullback Jack Walker producing a number of try-saving tackles.

New halfback Richie Myler had a steadying effect on the Rhinos, who dominated the first half and should have been further in front than 12-6 at the break. Jamie Jones-Buchanan scored the first try of the game on 15 minutes as Leeds kept the ball alive and Joel Moon had all the time in the world to kick over the defence to set up the veteran back-rower, who caught the ball superbly and forced his way over.

Three minutes later Myler picked out Ryan Hall with a kick over the defence to the left corner to give the visitors a 10-0 lead with 18 minutes gone, extended by two points on 26 minutes as new Leeds skipper Kallum Watkins, on his 250th career appearance, potted a penalty. At that point the Rhinos looked well in control.

The Wolves had marquee player Tyrone Roberts, Ben Murdoch-Masila and Bryson Goodwin on debut and it was former Kiwi international Goodwin, after having left the field moments earlier with a head injury, who gave them a lifeline, powering through a sea of Leeds players with ten minutes remaining until half-time.

Warrington were firing after the break, with Ryan Atkins held on the line in a great tackle by Walker, who not much later held up Murdoch-Masila.

But Hall's second try, as he broke 80 metres downfield before rounding Stefan Ratchford and dotting down in Jack Hughes' heroic tackle-effort, gave Leeds the mental edge with 55 minutes gone.

Atkins looked certain to have brought the Wolves back to within two points after Roberts and Murdoch-Masila created space down the right but Walker's brilliant try-saving tackle as the Wolves centre tried to fly through the air maintained a six-point cushion for the Rhinos.

With two minutes of the match to go, Tom Lineham gave Warrington a slender chance of snatching victory when he capitalised on Walker dropping Roberts' high kick before diving over, with Goodwin converting to reduce the gap to four points. But it was too little, too late, as Leeds held on to claim their first two points of the new campaign.

Wolves captain Chris Hill left midway through the second half to be with his wife, who had gone into labour while attending the game herself. Hill's wife Kathryn later gave birth to their fourth child, Iris-Kay.

On the same night, Hull FC got off to a flyer with a 38-12 home win over Huddersfield.

The Giants got themselves 12-4 up after 35 minutes but then self-imploded, conceding 34-unanswered points. All eyes were on new Hull signing Bureta Faraimo's right wing but Fetuli Talanoa stole the show from the left with a second-half hat-trick.

Hull started with two debutants, USA international Faraimo and Mickey Paea, the latter returned from Newcastle Knights and making his first Hull FC appearance since

2015. The Giants welcomed back Jake Mamo for his first game since the previous June because of a serious foot injury and gave new signing Adam Walne a debut. He impressed with his strong running but they missed Jermaine McGillvary, included in the 19-man squad but not recovered from a knee injury sustained in the World Cup.

Hull's last try summed up the Giants' second half. A high Albert Kelly kick was dropped by Mamo, allowing Jamie Shaul to stroll in unchallenged.

Super League sponsors Betfred received a flood of money over the weekend for St Helens to win the Super League Grand Final after Saints demolished Castleford Tigers 46-6 at the Totally Wicked Stadium on the Friday night. Saints were now 3/1 favourites, in from 5/1.

Ben Barba won the man of the match award and his odds to win the Steve Prescott Man of Steel award shortened from 8/1 to 4/1. Second favourite was Saints captain James Roby, whose odds also fell.

It was a thumping win over the Tigers that rounded off a strong week for St Helens, after Alex Walmsley committed his long-term future with a new four-year deal. Barba produced the kind of performance that led to him being voted the best in the NRL in 2012 by touching down twice and creating four other tries, including a hat-trick for England centre Mark Percival. With Roby at his industrious best in the middle, Saints overwhelmed a Tigers side that was labelled 'embarrassing' by coach Daryl Powell.

Castleford still hadn't won at St Helens since a 12-8 Regal Trophy victory on 19th December 1992 and the glaring hole in their 2017 attack was Zak Hardaker, suspended two days before the previous year's Grand Final for failing a drugs test. Ben Roberts played fullback and looked less than comfortable, although the game was lost in the forwards where Saints got on an unstoppable roll.

Wigan, with stand-off George Williams irrepressible, got off to a lightning start too with a 40-12 win at Salford, a promised new attacking approach reaping immediate dividends. Sam Tomkins started at fullback then moved to halfback as Morgan Escare came off the bench. But Wigan never lost the groove that saw them cut the Red Devils up out wide, with Liam Marshall and Oliver Gildart scoring two tries apiece.

After Salford's Kris Welham and Wigan's Tom Davies exchanged tries, Gildart edged the visitors in front and secured a 10-6 half-time lead. Escare added to it after the break as Marshall scored two quick tries to extend the lead to 28-6. Gildart and Tony Clubb also went over for the visitors in the second half, while Niall Evalds scored a late consolation for Salford.

In the week Salford had been hit by the news that winger Manu Vatuvei had been ruled out for the year with a serious Achilles tendon injury suffered in training on the eve of the season.

Winger Tom Johnstone's acrobatic hat-trick ensured Wakefield spoiled Hull KR's return to Super League, Trinity coming away from east Hull with a 28-6 win. The 22-year-old winger had been out of competitive action for nine months after suffering a season-ending knee injury in April the previous year but the youngster showed no ill-effects

Johnstone grabbed his first three tackles after Rovers halfback Matty Marsh had been sin-binned for a tackle off the ball and further tries to Bill Tupou, Liam Finn, and Johnstone's second on the stroke of half-time sent Trinity into the break deservedly 18 points to the good.

After an error-strewn first half, the Robins battled back after the break, with Marsh denied a try for obstruction and Justin Carney held up over the line by new forward Pauli Pauli and Scott Grix before Chris Clarkson finally cracked Wakefield's resistance from Danny McGuire's pass. However, Johnstone's spectacular third try twelve minutes from time and a late score from debutant Ryan Hampshire gave Wakefield a deserved win.

Hull KR that week made two squad additions in USA international centre Junior Vaivai and experienced former England forward Danny Tickle.

Widnes sat second on the early Super League table after a thumping Sunday-afternoon 40-12 win over Catalans. It had taken them until April to win their first game of the season a year before.

The Catalans' discipline was poor as they conceded 15 penalties to the Vikings' four. Five of those were in the first eleven minutes that saw Sam Moa sin-binned for a late tackle on Joe Mellor and coach Steve McNamara said his side's second-half collapse, after being level at 12-12 at half-time, was unacceptable. Moa got a two-match ban.

Prop Chris Houston, co-captain Mellor and Rhys Hanbury all impressed for Widnes along with two-try Chris Dean, his second on 55 minutes opening up an unassailable 24-12 lead. Debutants David Mead and Benjamin Jullien scored the two first-half tries for the Dragons.

The only downside for the impressive Vikings was that winger Patrick Ah Van broke his arm scoring a try in the 71st minute.

The following day, League Express revealed that contact had been made between the Rugby Football League and Matchroom Sports, the Essex firm founded by Barry Hearn, which had revived the sports of snooker, boxing and darts, to sound out whether the organisation could use its skills

Eddie Hearn, son of Barry, told Talksport radio he would be open to the challenge of reviving Rugby League, although he warned that his methods might not go down well with some key figures in the game.

* Wayne Bennett signed a new two-year deal to stay on as coach of the England team. Castleford coach Daryl Powell turned down the chance become his assistant with a view to succeeding to the head coaching job in 2020.

Round 2

The second round of games in Super League XXIII provided a first for the sport when Wigan beat Hull FC 24-10 at WIN Stadium in Wollongong in the first ever game to be played outside Europe.

A crowd of 12,416 turned up on the Saturday night, a higher attendance than any of the three league fixtures between the two teams in 2017. It was estimated that Wigan, who forfeited home advantage in the round-two match, and Hull split £1 million generated by sponsorship of the trip, which was backed by the New South Wales Government via its tourism and major events agency. Around 5,000 Wigan and Hull fans headed to New South Wales for the historic fixture. Most stayed on for the following Saturday's friendly double header, with Wigan facing South Sydney and Hull taking on St George Illawarra at the ANZ Stadium.

Wigan got the win against a Hull side left desperately depleted by early injuries to key players Bureta Faraimo, with a head knock in the third minute, and Danny Houghton, who tore a calf after 25 minutes.

The Warriors were always in control despite both teams struggling with the warm conditions. They were 10-0 up after two scintillating tries from winger Liam Marshall down Hull's makeshift right edge. It was a scrap from then on, with Fetuli Talanoa and Jordan Abdull tries levelling, although a Sam Tomkins penalty just before half-time gave Wigan a 12-10 lead at the break.

On 45 minutes, George Williams threw an offload to Sam Powell and he gave a flat pass to Ryan Sutton, who crashed over the line from short-distance. Sam Tomkins' conversion extended the lead to eight points. And Wigan finally wrapped the match up in the 70th minute. With 15-man Hull tiring, Powell gave a short pass to Ben Flower and the Wales international had too much power for Hull's defenders as he stayed low and grounded the ball.

The main event in Australia the following week was the World Club Challenge between Melbourne and Leeds Rhinos and on the Thursday night of round two the

Rhinos came back to win 20-11 over Hull KR at Elland Road.

Not in the original 19 for the round-two game, drafted-in Jimmy Keinhorst secured a place on the plane to Melbourne with a hat-trick of tries for the Rhinos, to see off the much-improved Robins. Keinhorst's performance included two tries in five minutes late on to erode Hull KR's narrow lead after a game dogged by greasy, spilt ball in constant, teeming rain.

Rovers were 10-0 up after 22 minutes with two finely crafted tries, first when Chris Clarkson and Maurice Blair sent Andrew Heffernan into space from deep and Ryan Shaw stepped and slid his way over the line before landing a superb touchline conversion. Then, on the last tackle of their next attacking set, which included a couple of excellent offloads, Chris Atkin's clever short ball saw Adam Quinlan cross, with Shaw's shot at the conversion hitting the post.

But two tries in a similar spell just after the half-hour found the Rhinos level. For the first, Stevie Ward's peach of a pass sent Adam Cuthbertson scampering untouched to the posts. For the second, Cuthbertson's lobbed ball on the back of a Carl Ablett charge allowed Keinhorst to get around Blair - out in the centre after Heffernan left the field with a head knock from an unspotted high Keinhorst tackle - and away from Danny McGuire. Richie Myler goaled the first but missed the second conversion attempt.

Level at the break, Atkin nudged Rovers ahead with a field goal at the start of the second half and it remained that way until the 67th minute when Ablett's disguised pass sent Keinhorst angling to the posts, with Myler goaling for a five-point Rhinos lead.

Five minutes later Ryan Hall caught Myler's bomb to the corner and fed Keinhorst on his outside for his treble.

With the extensive refurbishment at Headingley not completed all season, over 16,000 fans flocked to Elland Road to see the return to Leeds of new Robins skipper McGuire, although it was his halfback partner Atkin, on Super League debut, who took the eye and was the principal reason behind their 7-0 dominance in goal-line drop-outs.

Leeds forward Anthony Mullally suffered a broken finger that ruled him out of the trip to Australia, with Josh Walters being called up to the squad to replace him. Meanwhile the Robins began efforts to bring Todd Carney back to Super League.

Also on the Thursday night, the Giants picked up their first victory of the season, beating Warrington, missing injured marquee signing Tyrone Roberts, at home by 20-6.

The Giants went into the match without Jermaine McGillvary for a second game running and Michael Lawrence, captain in round one, was unavailable, leaving Ryan Hinchcliffe to skipper the side.

Huddersfield mastered the wet and slippery conditions to consign the Wolves, under new coach Steve Price, to two defeats out of two.

The Wolves were first on the scoreboard after five minutes. A Jordan Rankin grubber on the Warrington line was stopped and pounced on by Kevin Brown who set Ben Currie away. With the England star stopped 20 metres short, on the next play, Stefan Ratchford chipped to the corner for Tom Lineham to slide, catch and score brilliantly.

But Huddersfield took control as converted tries from Dale Ferguson and Darnell Mackintosh made it 12-4. Danny Brough's goal extended their lead before Bryson Goodwin hit back with a penalty on the stroke of half-time. Jordan Turner's 63rd minute score in the corner settled it, with the visitors unable to find a way back into the game.

Wakefield coach Chris Chester admitted his side 'got out of jail' after they edged a tight home clash with Salford 14-12 after a dramatic finish. Trinity should have made sure of their win when on the attack and six points ahead in the closing stages but instead had to watch anxiously on as Gareth O'Brien lined up a touchline conversion to Kris Welham's last minute try. It just drifted to the right of the posts.

Trinity led 8-0 at the break after a first half that had more penalties than points but the Red Devils, who gave a debut to Fijian Ben Nakubuwai, who with fellow prop Craig

Kopzcak and hooker Logan Tomkins came off the bench to gain ascendancy, were level by the 53rd minute.

But with the teams locked at 8-8, Ryan Hampshire emerged from the bench for Wakefield to turn the tide. The well-travelled utility back, who was on his home debut, produced a superb kick under pressure for Jacob Miller to collect and dive under the posts. Lim Finn's third goal made it 14-8.

And Wakefield looked set to make sure of victory when a Scott Grix break laid the position for a decisive field goal, only for David Fifita to be penalised for an improper play the ball to give Salford one last shot.

They took it when Weller Hauraki attacked the blindside and Kris Welham sneaked over in the right corner. But O'Brien's conversion attempt after the hooter just drifted wide to leave the Red Devils still looking for their first point and Wakefield continuing their 100 per cent start to the campaign.

On the Saturday, St Helens also kept up a 100 per cent record with a 21-12 win at Catalans. A masterful kicking display from young halfback Danny Richardson and the elusive brilliance of Ben Barba, combined with Alex Walmsley's brute force, was enough to see Saints through, despite the dismissal of Morgan Knowles on 52 minutes for a spear tackle on Thibaut Margalet, although Benjamin Jullien was sin-binned just after for a suspected crusher on Jonny Lomax.

Saints established a first-half lead with tries by Lomax and Regan Grace, as Catalans went in scoreless. David Mead's score reduced the deficit before Knowles was sent off and Adam Swift scored from an unpromising position in the right corner for Richardson's conversion to make it 18-6. Alrix Da Costa's short-range reply five minutes later closed the gap but Richardson, keeping Matty Smith out of the Saints side, steadied the ship with a field goal before sealing the win with a late penalty.

Knowles was subsequently banned for four games while Jullien got one game.

A patched-up Dragons, missing halves Luke Walsh and Samisoni Langi, both injured the previous week, had 19-year-old Lucas Albert teamed up with 34-year-old Greg Bird at halfback but were much improved from their defeat at Widnes.

Meanwhile the Dragons received a major boost after Tony Gigot successfully appealed his two-year anti-doping suspension. The fullback had been fighting the case for over a year after initially being banned in 2016, despite never actually failing a test. He was deemed to have acted inappropriately towards a tester and subsequently handed a two-year ban.

The ban was overturned in 2017, which allowed for a return mid-season, only for the decision to be changed again. However Gigot was now free to resume his playing career once again with the Dragons.

After the shock of their first-round hammering at St Helens, Castleford got off the mark with a scratchy 13-12 home win over Widnes.

The Vikings battled back from falling two scores behind in the final few minutes to set up a grandstand finale when young forward Jay Chapelhow scored with seven minutes remaining - and had Tom Gilmore not hooked two late field-goal attempts wide, may have had something to show for their efforts.

England back row Mike McMeeken had a try disallowed for obstruction. And Jy Hitchcox dropped a potential try-scoring pass from Michael Shenton before winger Greg Minikin touched down in the final minute of the first half. Luke Gale missed his touchline conversion attempt. But nine minutes after the break, Matt Whitley reacted quicker than fullback Ben Roberts to reach Gilmore's reverse grubber kick. Gilmore goaled for a shock lead.

However, with 13 minutes left Jamie Ellis's high kick was re-cycled to the left wing where skipper Shenton sent in Hitchcox. Gale goaled and added a 68th minute penalty before landing a field goal from in front of the posts on 72 minutes to nudge the Tigers 13-6 in front, which proved just enough.

World Club Challenge

Super League champions Leeds Rhinos fell to a 38-4 World Club Challenge defeat to the Storm at AAMI Park in Melbourne, the first time the game had been played in Australia since 1994.

With four injured prop forwards unavailable for selection - Keith Galloway, Mitch Garbutt, Anthony Mullally and Mikolaj Oledzki all missing - the first-half losses of Jack Walker and Stevie Ward to knee and calf injuries respectively left the Rhinos unable to resist a brilliant team performance from the Storm.

The first 15 minutes went well for Leeds. They picked up two early penalties before Ward engineered a superb try for Ryan Hall with a brilliant cutout pass.

But they were unable to score again and the Storm, guided around the field by Cameron Smith and 20-year-old Brodie Croft, stepping into the shoes vacated by Cooper Cronk who had moved onto Sydney Roosters, scored seven tries, with Croft grabbing one himself and having a hand in most of the others.

Jesse Bromwich, Croft and Suliasi Vunivalu tries had the Storm in front by 18-4 at half-time. After the break it was virtually one-way traffic as tries from Nelson Asofa-Solomona, Felise Kaufusi, Will Chambers and Dale Finucane sealed a convincing Melbourne victory.

* There was no World Club Series in 2018, though Hull FC and Wigan Warriors played double header friendlies on the Saturday at ANZ Stadium. Almost 19,000 fans turned up to see Hull edged 24-18 by St George Illawarra Dragons in a highly competitive game before South Sydney beat Wigan 18-8.

DOWNER WORLD CLUB CHALLENGE

Friday 16th February 2018

MELBOURNE STORM 38 LEEDS RHINOS 4

STORM: 1 Billy Slater; 2 Suliasi Vunivalu; 3 Will Chambers; 4 Curtis Scott; 5 Josh Addo-Carr; 6 Cameron Munster; 7 Brodie Croft; 8 Jesse Bromwich; 9 Cameron Smith (C); 10 Tim Glasby; 11 Felise Kaufusi; 12 Ryan Hoffman; 13 Dale Finucane. Subs (all used): 14 Brandon Smith; 15 Nelson Asofa-Solomona; 16 Kenny Bromwich; 17 Christian Welch.
Tries: J Bromwich (17), Croft (24), Vunivalu (40), Asofa-Solomona (49), Kaufusi (57), Chambers (71), Finucane (80); **Goals:** C Smith 4/7, Munster 1/1.
RHINOS: 24 Jack Walker; 2 Tom Briscoe; 3 Kallum Watkins (C); 4 Liam Sutcliffe; 5 Ryan Hall; 6 Joel Moon; 7 Richie Myler; 8 Adam Cuthbertson; 9 Matt Parcell; 10 Brad Singleton; 11 Jamie Jones-Buchanan; 12 Carl Ablett; 13 Stevie Ward. Subs (all used): 14 Brad Dwyer; 15 Brett Delaney; 18 Jimmy Keinhorst; 23 Jack Ormondroyd.
Try: Hall (9); **Goals:** Watkins 0/1.
Rugby Leaguer & League Express Men of the Match: *Storm:* Nelson Asofa-Solomona; *Rhinos:* Kallum Watkins.
Penalty count: 9-4; **Half-time:** 18-4;
Referees: Ben Cummins & Gerard Sutton;
Attendance: 19,062 *(at AAMI Park).*

Round 11

Hull KR got off the mark in the first of the two games brought forward to accommodate the previous year's bottom four clubs' entry into the Challenge Cup in the fifth round with a Thursday night 23-4 home win over Catalans.

An early Ryan Shaw try was the only score separating the teams for much of a disjointed first half but the introduction off the bench of Mose Masoe and Rovers skipper Shaun Lunt signalled a step-up in tempo from the Robins.

Celebrating his 300th career appearance, Lunt first created a try for Masoe, then helped himself to one just before the break. And when on-debut Danny Tickle went over ten minutes into the second half to make it 22-0, there was no way back for a Catalans team who were their own worst enemies for much of the game. They did score through David Mead but seemed to go backwards from the previous week's display against St Helens.

Chris Atkin finished off an uninspiring 80 minutes for the TV viewers with a late field goal.

The night after, Stefan Ratchford produced a man-of-the-match display at the Halton Stadium, touching down in the first half and creating a second-half effort for Ryan

February

Atkins in Warrington's 18-10 win over the Vikings.

The Wolves had lost their first two fixtures against Leeds and Huddersfield Giants but they fought hard for their first win of the season.

It was a chaotic derby that saw referee Phil Bentham injured, helped from the field in the 54th minute after Widnes forward Chris Houston ran into the back of him while chasing a kick, an incident that was placed on report.

Bentham, who was replaced by Scott Mikalauskas, missed a frantic final half-hour that included a number of skirmishes and a decisive tackle by Ratchford on Widnes prop Jay Chapelhow.

The Wolves were 10-0 up inside 14 minutes. Declan Patton's delicate chip saw Ryan Atkins jump the highest to touch down before Ben Currie's flat pass put Ratchford over from close range.

Krisnan Inu touched down a Joe Mellor kick before half-time but the Vikings fell further behind five minutes after the restart. Again Atkins was the scorer and again it came from a cross-field kick, this time Ratchford putting boot to ball to make it 16-4 with Bryson Goodwin's conversion.

Tom Lineham had a try chalked off for a Currie forward pass before Bentham's exit sparked a manic last half-hour. Goodwin edged the Wolves further ahead with a penalty, before Jack Hughes raced away to score, only to be eventually brought back for a skirmish started by Currie and Inu that saw the otherwise impressive Daryl Clark penalised for his involvement.

Widnes threatened a late rally when Inu replicated Atkins' efforts to touch down a Tom Gilmore kick for a try that was converted. But the Vikings' best chance slipped away when a desperate Ratchford tackle dislodged the ball from Chalpelhow's grasp as he reached for the line.

There was another minor set-to under the Warrington posts between Houston and Dom Crosby and the Wolves finished the match with twelve men when Mike Cooper was sin-binned for a professional foul on Olly Ashall-Bolt.

Widnes coach Denis Betts, like most observers, reckoned Houston's collision with Bentham was accidental. Nevertheless he accepted the two-match ban that was handed to Houston early the next week.

Round 3

Wigan coach Shaun Wane refused to use the Warriors' travels down under as an excuse after his side were dominated by Warrington on the last Friday of February, the final score of 16-10 at Halliwell Jones Stadium not truly reflecting the Wolves' superiority on the night.

Only six days after playing their last game against Souths in Sydney the Warriors looked anything but exhausted, as they threatened to come back into the game in the final quarter. By that stage Warrington were leading 16-0 and although Liam Marshall pulled a try back for Wigan on 62 minutes, the Warriors could only breach an impressive Wolves defence one more time, when Tony Clubb forced his way over in the final minute of the game, with no time left for a restart.

It was a feisty affair at times, with several clashes including George Williams and Ben Murdoch-Masila, Tony Clubb and Ben Westwood and Bryson Goodwin and Sam Tomkins. But the Wolves kept their cool for the most part and, had Ryan Atkins not knocked on with the line wide open in the 40th minute and then seen a try ruled out for Murdoch-Masila's fumble straight after the restart, their victory would have been much more comprehensive.

There were two Warrington debutants, with Mitch Brown replacing Matty Russell on the right wing, while Sitaleki Akauola came in for Joe Philbin as a substitute.

High-flying St Helens came home from Huddersfield on the same night with a hard-fought 26-12 win. Jon Wilkin and Danny Brough swapped converted tries and Danny Richardson and Brough swapped penalty goals to make it 8-all three minutes from the half-time hooter. The parity lasted just a minute, however, as Jake Mamo fumbled the kick-off before James Roby stretched over from dummy-half.

Jonny Lomax put Zeb Taia through a surprisingly big gap in the Giants' defence as St Helens extended their advantage nine minutes into the second half. Mark Percival then impressively beat Mamo to Jonny Lomax's high kick before placing the ball down under the posts as Saints made it two tries in three minutes.

The Giants hit back four minutes later as Oliver Roberts spun a would-be tackler and fell across the line, but the Saints defence stood firm to secure the points.

Salford were far too strong for Hull KR, without Danny McGuire, out with a minor injury, down the road at the AJ Bell Stadium, emerging 36-12 winners. After going behind to a converted third minute Thomas Minns try, tries from Gareth O'Brien, Junior Sa'u and Jake Bibby gave Salford an 18-6 half-time lead and the Red Devils were well on their way to their first win of the season.

Junior Sa'u was in rampaging form and hooker Josh Wood secured the win when he broke downfield just after the break and sent Robert Lui in. Adam Quinlan's try gave the visitors hope but two tries from Niall Evalds ended that.

On the Saturday afternoon, halfbacks Jamie Ellis and Luke Gale turned on the style and captain Michael Shenton, switched from the centre to the wing following an injury to Greg Eden, grabbed two tries as Castleford, looking much more like the side that lit up Super League in 2017, registered a 28-18 home win over Hull FC.

The Tigers overturned an 8-0 deficit to finish as comfortable winners against the Challenge Cup holders, who like Wigan had returned that week from Australia. Ellis, back at the Mend-A-Hose Jungle after four years at Huddersfield and Hull KR, was central to the Tigers' recovery and had a hand or a boot in the first three of the hosts' five tries.

Later that day in cold Perpignan, Wakefield maintained their 100 per cent start, but only just, as they edged the Dragons 16-14.

Tom Johnstone's 80-yard burst to score on the left on 30 minutes was the highlight of a game that simmered throughout but never really caught fire, with injury-hit Catalans providing a fierce physical challenge. Michael McIlorum, Paul Aiton, Luke Walsh and Samisoni Langi were all missing injured.

Ben Garcia's try and three kicks from Lucas Albert put Dragons 10-8 up at the break, with Trinity's scores coming from Reece Lyne and Johnstone. The latter was a beauty. A charged down field-goal attempt by Albert was taken by Pauli Pauli, who fed Bill Tupou for the centre to release the flying winger wide on the left. David Mead set off in pursuit but could only paw at him after 80 metres as Johnstone gracefully avoided touch to score the try of the match.

A third Wakefield try on 51 minutes from David Fifita - the home crowd were convinced he had been tackled but video evidence proved otherwise - restored the visitors' lead before Liam Finn converted and then landed the crucial penalty.

Crucial because Albert couldn't land the touchline conversion to Lewis Tierney's finely worked try on 64 minutes and that proved to be the final margin.

Leeds coach Brian McDermott refused to blame the club's WCC trip to Australia or their growing injury list as the reason for their first Super League defeat of the season on the Sunday. The Rhinos lost 23-6 to in-form Widnes at the Select Security Stadium to end their unbeaten start to the defence of their Super League title, with McDermott unable to call on a number of frontline players.

Widnes were far too good, with Krisnan Inu the gamestar, ending with two tries as young hooker Danny Walker's try with eight minutes remaining secured victory.

BETFRED SUPER LEAGUE
Sunday 25th February

	P	W	D	L	F	A	D	Pts
St Helens	3	3	0	0	93	30	63	6
Wakefield Trinity	3	3	0	0	58	32	26	6
Widnes Vikings	4	2	0	2	85	49	36	4
Wigan Warriors	3	2	0	1	74	38	36	4
Warrington Wolves	4	2	0	2	52	56	-4	4
Leeds Rhinos	3	2	0	1	42	46	-4	4
Castleford Tigers	3	2	0	1	47	76	-29	4
Hull FC	3	1	0	2	66	64	2	2
Salford Red Devils	3	1	0	2	60	66	-6	2
Huddersfield Giants	3	1	0	2	44	70	-26	2
Hull Kingston Rovers	4	1	0	3	52	88	-36	2
Catalans Dragons	4	0	0	4	42	100	-58	0

MARCH
The big freeze

Round 4

The start of March 2018 saw the arrival of an icy cold airstream from the east, combined with high winds that almost paralysed parts of Britain for days on end. It was quite a feat that only two of the Super League games were postponed, although two were delayed from the Friday night to the Sunday afternoon.

The much anticipated Thursday-night visit of Castleford to Hull KR, where the clubs were due to play for the Roger Millward Trophy, was the first fixture to fall victim to the snow and ice, with Leeds-Catalans the following night an understandable early cancellation as airports around the country were closed.

Two Friday-night games did go ahead, with attendances well down on what would have been expected. The Sky TV cameras were switched from Wakefield to Hull for the feisty clash between Hull FC and Warrington, in which the Airlie Birds claimed their second win of the campaign at the expense of a committed Wolves side, who almost battled back to grab victory, despite plenty of adversity in sub-zero temperatures.

The Wolves, who had to travel to Hull by train because of a day-long closure of the M62 motorway, lost 21-12. However, they set up a thrilling finale following the 49th-minute dismissal of Declan Patton after a high tackle on Bureta Faraimo, coming from 18-0 down to within six points before Hull, who had Liam Watts sent off late in the game themselves for a head-butt, regained enough composure to close out the win in the final stages.

Hull were still without captain Danny Houghton, meaning Danny Washbrook made his 200th appearance for the club at hooker, but they welcomed back England international Scott Taylor after two weeks out with appendicitis that had struck him in Australia.

Hull led 10-0 after 50 minutes when Patton saw red and a further score from Carlos Tuimavave off a superb drop-off move involving Fetuli Talanoa, helped Hull go 18-0 up. But Jack Hughes and Ryan Atkins crossed as the Wire got to within six points of the hosts. Marc Sneyd calmed home nerves with a penalty goal and a last-second field goal.

Hull coach Lee Radford insisted he had no sympathy for prop Watts following the 'pathetic' incident that saw him receive a fourth red card in less than a year. Watts was frustrated by Dom Crosby carrying on an upright wrestle well after referee Ben Thaler called held and marched towards the Wolves prop and head-butted him before playing the ball. It was more of a gesture than an attempt to wound but his coach admitted he deserved any ban coming his way.

Watts got three matches and it proved to be the end of his Hull FC career. Patton was hit with a five-match ban.

Wigan got back on the winning trail on the same night, as they recovered from a 16-4 half-time deficit to beat Widnes 32-16 at a bitterly cold DW Stadium.

Widnes played a near-perfect opening 40 minutes as they deservedly led thanks to tries from Matt Whitley and Stefan Marsh and four goals from Tom Gilmore. But a late score from Joe Burgess on the hooter gave the Warriors a glimmer of hope.

The Warriors looked a completely different side after the break to run in five unanswered second-half tries - from Ryan Sutton, Thomas Leuluai, Liam Farrell, Sam

Tomkins, a 70-metre beauty after collecting a Joe Mellor kick, and Tom Davies - to make it three wins from four for Shaun Wane's men.

In the first of the games postponed to the Sunday, Wakefield made it four wins from four - their best ever start to a season since 1945 - with an eventually convincing 22-4 win over Huddersfield.

For large periods of the opening 40 minutes in particular, it was all Huddersfield. But they couldn't find a way through, despite forcing three GLDOs on the first ten minutes. And they could only score one try all game when a Jake Mamo drive to the line and a quick play the ball allowed Lee Gaskell to go over untouched from short range in the right centre. That was in response to a Ben Jones-Bishop try which Liam Finn converted from wide out but with Danny Brough missing the conversion it was 6-4 at half-time.

Finn kicked two easy penalties after the break as Trinity got on top and produced a superb dink to the right corner, following Kruise Leeming's yellow card as the unlucky man to be penalised following a team warning, for Jones-Bishop to take on the full and touch down. Mason Caton-Brown's last-minute chase and touch down of a Bill Tupou kick on a free play ended the contest.

St Helens stayed above Wakefield on points difference after they too kept up their 100 per cent start with a 34-2 home win over Salford, Ben Barba once again instrumental with a hand in all but two of Saints' tries.

The visitors had the better of the opening 20 minutes and took a deserved two-point lead when, after receiving a penalty for offside, they opted to kick for goal and Gareth O'Brien slotted the ball between the posts. But Saints led 8-2 at the break with tries from Tommy Makinson and Barba.

Barba stepped his way to the line again straight after the break, to which Danny Richardson this time applied the extras, adding a penalty when Salford were penalised in front of the sticks when O'Brien's drop-out went straight into touch. And although the hosts failed to capitalise when former Saints prop Lama Tasi was sin-binned for three consecutive late shots, they ran in three late tries.

Louie McCarthy-Scarsbrook bundled over after an initial break from Jonny Lomax, who got in on the act himself before form prop Luke Thompson completed the scoring when Barba and Richardson kept the ball alive.

* That week confirmation was released that England and New Zealand would play a Test match in Denver, Colorado on 23rd June.

Round 5

Leeds played at Headingley for the first time in 2018, with a temporary stand in place of the demolished main stand and only a tiny part of the newly built South Stand open. And despite more overnight snow causing problems for the groundstaff, the Rhinos were rewarded with a 20-16 win over Hull FC.

Kallum Watkins and Tom Briscoe scored first-half tries for the Rhinos, who had not lost a home match against the Black and Whites since September 2007. But Hull were back in it at 10-6 at half-time thanks to a Dean Hadley try and could have been in the lead when the video referee spotted an irrelevant obstruction in the build up to Josh Griffin's try. Jack Logan, back after almost two years plagued with various injuries, had already had a try denied when he picked up Jake Connor's improvised kick in an offside position. It was close.

Second tries to Watkins and Briscoe looked to have the Rhinos safe by the hour mark but Hull finished the stronger, the outstanding Jordan Abdull and Fetuli Talanoa scoring tries, with young forward Jordan Lane prominent on debut.

Widnes's bright start was beginning to dim as they lost their second match in succession on a rain-soaked Friday night when they lost 28-16 at home to workmanlike Huddersfield.

The Giants were 14-0 up at half-time after Jake Mamo and Ryan Hinchliffe crossed and further tries from Oliver Roberts and then Jermaine McGillvary, soon after the

March

Vikings' PNG prop Wellington Albert had been sent off for a dangerous tackle, appeared to put them out of sight at 24-0.

The 12-man Vikings rallied with scores from Joe Mellor, Matt Whitley and Stefan Marsh but Danny Brough's two late penalties ended their hopes.

Albert got a two-match ban for the cannonball on McGillvary.

Just down the road, Warrington also fell to their second straight defeat as St Helens' perfect run continued when they beat the Wolves 30-16 at the Halliwell Jones Stadium.

Centre Mark Percival grabbed a hat-trick, while halfback Danny Richardson showed great maturity for a 21-year-old. James Roby was at his best and Luke Thompson and Dominique Peyroux were outstanding in the pack.

Saints led by two points at half-time after Percival and Toby King swapped tries and Richardson slotted a penalty.

After the break, Roby scooted over next to the posts from dummy-half. The hosts were soon back within two points though. Toby King collected Tyrone Roberts' kick and, despite being wrapped in the tackle near the line, he managed to free the ball to sub Harvey Livett, who dived over in the left corner.

Shortly afterwards, Alex Walmsley took a knock in the tackle, left the field groggily and had to sit out the remainder of the game because of concussion. It turned out to be a neck injury that required surgery and kept the England prop out for the season.

Percival got his second and with 13 minutes left on the clock Saints established a two-try advantage when Richardson spotted a gap and broke through on the last play. He had options on both sides and put in a perfectly-timed grubber towards the left corner, where Percival gathered to complete his hat-trick.

The try that finally settled it saw a role reversal as Percival put in a neat grubber towards the posts and Richardson collected to dive over in front of the jubilant Saints fans.

Catalans got off the mark at the fifth attempt the night after with an 18-16 home win over Hull KR.

It wasn't pretty. All four tries were scored from kicks and there were a series of contentious decisions that had both sets of fans grumbling. It was tit for tat throughout, with Justin Carney's converted try on 66 minutes levelling at 16-all before Lucas Albert effectively won the match with a 70th-minute penalty.

Robins coach Tim Sheens was furious at the penalty decision. Catalans hooker Michael McIlorum picked up at dummy-half, passed the ball into the kneeling Maurice Blair and referee Scott Mikalauskas went for the whistle, providing the Dragons with the two points that became the ultimate winning margin.

On the Sunday, Wigan moved above Wakefield into second place on the Super League table after ending Trinity's unbeaten start to the new campaign, Sam Tomkins starring and Joe Burgess finishing with a hat-trick in a 30-18 home win.

Ben Jones-Bishop's two tries helped Trinity lead 12-10 at the break, with Burgess and Taulima Tautai - making his 100th Wigan appearance – replying.

It took only six minutes of the second half for the Warriors to go back in front when Burgess claimed his second - before a crucial moment in the contest soon after. It looked like Jones-Bishop had scored his hat-trick following a cut-out pass from Finn, before referee Chris Kendall pulled the play back for a forward pass.

Two tries in five minutes soon after - one to Tom Davies and Burgess' hat-trick try - opened up a three-score lead which, given how well Wigan were defending, was game-deciding.

Wakefield kept fighting and they scored the game's final try to potentially set up a grandstand finish when Tinirau Arona capitalised on a Craig Huby offload to barge his way over. But any Wigan nerves were calmed in the final moments when Sam Tomkins kicked a late penalty to ensure Wigan moved up to second spot.

Tara Jones, one of two in-goal judges for the game, became the first ever on-field female official for a Super League match.

Castleford, helped by an error-strewn display by the Red Devils, particularly in the first half, posted a third successive victory with a 22-8 home win over Salford.

The Tigers went in at the break 20-0 ahead - through Michael Shenton, James Clare and Luke Gale - but two of their three tries arose directly from errors by the Red Devils, while the other was scored a couple of plays after a Salford error.

After half-time, Junior Sa'u crossed in the corner for Salford, before both sides were briefly reduced to 12 men, with Grant Millington and Logan Tomkins sin-binned for fighting. Jake Bibby added a late consolation for the visitors but neither of Salford's second-half scores were converted.

Gale's five successful kicks for the hosts - including two tough conversions from out wide on the touchline early in the first half - proved key.

Tigers second rower Oliver Holmes was also sin-binned midway through the first half for dumping Salford loose forward Tyrone McCarthy. Holmes got one match.

Gareth O'Brien was missing for Salford and it emerged he had signed for Toronto Wolfpack in a big-money deal, prompting rumours that the Red Devils were about to offload more players.

And in the days following, Hull FC prop Liam Watts completed a move to his original Academy club, Castleford, with the Tigers paying a significant fee. Hull coach Lee Radford had reportedly run out of patience with Watts' poor discipline.

Round 6

The snow and ice was back two weeks after it had disrupted round four but its arrival on the Saturday allowed four Super League matches to go ahead.

In the exciting Friday-night TV game, Leeds produced a fine second-half display to become the first team to beat St Helens in 2018, with a 28-20 victory at the Totally Wicked Stadium.

The Rhinos played 74 minutes with only three subs after fullback Ashton Golding failed a concussion assessment in the opening stages of the match. And they were without first-team forwards Adam Cuthbertson, Brett Ferres, Mitch Garbutt and Nathaniel Peteru. Youngsters Cameron Smith, Mikolaj Oledzki, Josh Walters and Jack Walker all played well after their introduction off the bench. And Ash Handley, who was named at left centre, touched down two kicks in the space of five second-half minutes to make it a remarkable ten tries in six games against Saints.

It was 12-12 at the break after Ben Barba and Adam Swift scored for Saints in between converted Leeds tries from Anthony Mullally and Richie Myler. Danny Richardson and Kallum Watkins swapped penalty goals and although Barba got a second try after Handley's double, Rhinos hooker Matt Parcell's late try sealed it.

Saints sorely missed prop Alex Walmsley, set to miss England's mid-season international against New Zealand with a neck injury.

The night before, Huddersfield suffered a fifth defeat in seven games, going down 38-6 at home to Hull KR, despite dominating both territory and possession.

The Giants opened the scoring through in-form second-rower Oliver Roberts off a superb flat Danny Brough pass. Brough added the conversion to give the Giants a 6-0 lead.

But Hull KR were level after scoring off a clever set play. From a tap penalty, Chris Atkin came back against the grain, before Adam Quinlan's quick pass found Andrew Heffernan, who stepped gracefully through three Giants defenders before diving over. Ryan Shaw, who was faultless with the boot throughout, nailed the conversion to level the scores.

Heffernan then turned provider when he found space off a Chris Clarkson pass. The centre fed Quinlan on his inside, and the fullback rounded under the posts. With half-time approaching, Rovers stretched their lead to eight through Shaw after Huddersfield were penalised for holding down Mose Masoe.

But Hull KR weren't finished yet in the first half as a clever cut-out pass from Atkin found Quinlan, who quickly grubbered for the unmarked Shaw. The winger's conversion gave the Robins a 20-6 lead at the break.

The killer try came 14 minutes after the break as the Giants desperately tried to get back into the game. Jordan Rankin attempted to grubber into the in-goal but the ball ended up with prop Robbie Mulhern, who showed immense pace to streak away. Brough and Jermaine McGillvary were closing. However, Mulhern handed off the halfback and managed to evade McGillvary long enough, despite being knocked to the ground, to pass the ball onto James Greenwood, who charged over.

Hull KR were beginning to enjoy themselves and extended their lead further with another highlight reel-worthy try. Danny McGuire and Quinlan combined in centre-field to send Heffernan haring through a hole. The centre only had to draw and pass to send Shaw in at the corner for his second of the evening.

Rovers rubbed salt into the wounds of the Giants with another long-ranger down the right. This time, Atkin and McGuire teamed up to send Shaw away. The winger found McGuire back on the inside, via Quinlan, allowing the halfback to score his first in Hull KR colours and seal a well-deserved Rovers victory.

There was a return for Rovers' James Donaldson, after a ten-month injury lay-off due to a damaged anterior cruciate ligament.

On the Friday, Salford suggested that social media talk of a player sell-off might be wide of the mark with a 24-8 home win over Hull FC.

After back-to-back defeats, Ian Watson's men put in a much-improved performance and played with too much physicality and energy for Hull, who never looked like scoring for large parts of the game.

On the back of a strong and effective forward pack, Robert Lui ran the show, running the Airlie Birds' defence ragged. The ex-NRL star scored a try and adding four goals to really offset the departure of Gareth O'Brien in a performance that brought confidence back to the AJ Bell Stadium.

Ben Nakubuwai, Jack Littlejohn, Lui and Greg Johnson scored their four tries. Hull's points, all scored in the first half, came from a Dean Hadley try and two Marc Sneyd goals.

Off the field, Salford head of rugby Ian Blease confirmed that the Red Devils were working with the people behind a New York Rugby League bid to take one of their Super League fixtures to the USA.

Dark clouds gathered in cold and wet Perpignan on the Saturday night as Catalans Dragons crashed to their fifth defeat of the season, by 26-0 to Warrington, their first ever nilling at home. Catalans president Bernard Guasch insisted the club would continue to support coach Steve McNamara's plans for the team.

Bryson Goodwin's return from injury gave the Wolves a fillip, but it was the forwards who got a grip of the game. Chris Hill, Mike Cooper and the irrepressible Ben Westwood lapped up the atrocious conditions to keep the Catalans on the back foot in a one-sided contest.

Kevin Brown and Tyrone Roberts kicked the Catalans to death, pinning them back with deft precision, despite the elements. The Wolves were 14-0 up at the break, with Mitch Brown crossing out wide, Daryl Clark sneaking in and Ben Murdoch-Masila going in on the right. Murdoch-Masila rumbled in again to add to the lead after half-time. And Harvey Livett crossed late on for the Wolves to give their hardy travelling fans extra cheer.

Catalans - still missing injured halfbacks Luke Walsh and Samisoni Langi - were devoid of ideas, with Greg Bird's second-half touchdown ruled out for obstruction.

Around the same time, a group of volunteers at Wakefield's Mobile Rocket Stadium, that included chairman Michael Carter, worked hard to clear lines after snow began to fall. The game against Widnes kicked off at 6.30pm but after 26 minutes and with Wakefield leading 2-nil, referee Liam Moore led the players off the pitch and the game was abandoned.

It was the first time in the history of Super League that a game had been abandoned because of heavy snow falling after the kick-off.

Unsurprisingly, Castleford's home game with Wigan the following day was postponed, meaning the Tigers had two games to re-arrange later in the season.

Round 7

The reconstruction of the two side stands at Headingley was continuing apace but Leeds' decision to move their game with Castleford to Elland Road paid dividends, the Grand Final rematch drawing an attendance of 23,246, the Rhinos' biggest home crowd in the Super League era, beating their attendance against Bradford Bulls in 2003.

They and the live Friday-night TV audience were rewarded with a cracking game, with both coaches saying that the other side deserved to win.

Trailing 24-0 and then 25-10, Leeds got to within a point of the Tigers before Kallum Watkins' late conversion was pushed wide, meaning the Rhinos lost 25-24. In the end, a near-nonchalant, 40-metre field goal to end the first half by Luke Gale was all that split the sides.

The Tigers were irresistible early on, posting 18 points in eleven opening minutes and 24 in even time. But the Rhinos scored five tries to four and nilled the Tigers in the second half, despite being down to twelve men following Brad Singleton's sin-binning for a high challenge on Junior Moors.

Jamie Ellis, James Clare, Alex Foster and Junior Moors all went over for the Tigers in an excellent first-half display, putting the Tigers 24-0 up. But Kallum Watkins and Ash Handley replied for the hosts, before Gale's one-pointer gave Tigers a 25-10 half-time lead.

After the break, Watkins and Handley both got their second tries before Ryan Hall's acrobatic late score presented Watkins with the chance to put Leeds ahead for the first time but the touchline kick drifted wide as the Tigers made it four wins a row.

On the same night - with Easter a week away round seven was over by Friday night - Warrington showed signs they were turning a corner after a clunky start under new coach Steve Price. with a 34-24 home win over Wakefield.

The Wolves were unchanged from the 26-0 win over Catalans, the match coming too early for Josh Charnley, who completed his switch back to Rugby League from union earlier in the week and there was a blow for Wakefield when David Fifita pulled up injured in the warm-up.

The game was finely poised at half-time with Trinity 14-12 up but in the second period, Warrington's clinical attack proved to be the difference between the two sides, winger Tom Lineham finishing with a hat-trick. Lineham killed off any chance of a Trinity comeback on 77 minutes when he broke the line directly from a scrum and raced 90 metres upfield for his third.

Ben Murdoch-Masila also scored a barnstorming try with 18 minutes left, with gamestar Stefan Ratchford's subsequent conversion extending Warrington's lead to 16 points.

Wigan Warriors thrashed Huddersfield Giants 48-10 at the DW Stadium with their best performance of the season.

The Warriors were unstoppable in the opening 40 minutes as a brace from Tom Davies and further tries from Oliver Gildart, Joe Burgess and John Bateman saw them outclass the Giants, with the visitors' only score of the half, from Jermaine McGillvary, coming from a Warriors error.

Sam Tomkins, Sam Powell, George Williams and Liam Farrell caused the Giants untold problems in the first half and the likes of Davies, Burgess, Gildart and Bateman were on hand to pick up the scraps.

Wigan didn't need to be at their best in the second half as the damage had already been done, but a fine solo try from George Williams and further scores from Ryan Sutton, Willie Isa and another from Burgess saw them cruise to victory to leave Huddersfield with just two wins so far, Ryan Hinchcliffe scoring a consolation seven minutes from the end.

The game turned out to be Rick Stone's last game in charge at the Giants as he was sacked the following Monday. The 51-year-old Australian was appointed at the John Smith's Stadium in July 2016 and helped the Giants to a top-eight finish in 2017.

March

Huddersfield were currently 11th in Super League and had the worst defensive record.

Assistant Chris Thorman was placed in temporary charge for the two Easter games against Leeds and Catalans.

Leaders St Helens returned to winning ways with a clinical five-try 30-6 win at Hull KR. Sparked by another Ben Barba masterclass, they produced an assured and composed performance to get the better of a dogged Rovers side.

The scoreline didn't do justice to the home side's application and effort but they struggled to find the cutting edge to get past a stubborn Saints defence, especially after losing hooker George Lawler to a fractured ankle, and three others, including Danny McGuire, to head knocks.

Barba's second try midway through the second half sealed victory for Saints, for whom Luke Thompson was a standout in the continued absence of Alex Walmsley.

Meanwhile, the Robins' pursuit of a new halfback remained up in the air after the club had two approaches for two different players rejected. They made a six-figure offer to Salford for long-time target Robert Lui, but the Red Devils rejected it. And a fresh approach for Leigh Centurions scrum-half Drew Hutchinson was knocked back by the Championship club.

On the other side of the city, Catalans' nightmare start to the season showed no sign of ending as they were put to the sword by Hull FC, who picked up a first win in three with a 42-16 success.

Languishing at the bottom of the table with only one win in seven matches, the Dragons looked desperately low on confidence and were punished by the Airlie Birds, who welcomed back talismanic halfback Albert Kelly after injury. They looked far more accomplished with the ball as they ripped the Catalans defence to pieces in the second half after a tight opening 40 minutes.

The Dragons, dealt a blow before kick-off when they lost key dummy half Michael McIlorum in the warm-up, were in the contest at only 12-4 behind at half-time. But Steve McNamara's men collapsed in the third quarter of the game, conceding four quick tries as Hull ran riot.

Stand-in skipper Scott Taylor had spoken about Hull mounting a response after the defeat at Salford and he led the way.

The round had opened the night before as Widnes made a significant gain in what, at this stage, looked to be a five-team battle to avoid the Middle Eights, with a vital 24-16 home victory over the Red Devils, coming back from 10-6 down at the break.

Aaron Heremaia was the game's undisputed star, producing an 80-minute display in the middle of the field which ultimately proved pivotal, scoring the try with four minutes left which secured victory.

Salford twice had the lead, including going into the final ten minutes, when they overcame the loss of prop Lama Tasi due to a yellow card for a dangerous tackle on Heremaia.

Tasi's return from the bin on 54 minutes helped the Red Devils get back on the front foot, laying the platform for them to go back ahead when Robert Lui's clever kick was pounced on by Jake Bibby, who put Weller Hauraki over.

Lui couldn't convert but did take another two points with a penalty goal to make it 16-12 - however, as the final 15 minutes approached, Salford began to unravel.

They conceded a needless penalty when debutant winger Derrell Olpherts blocked a chasing Widnes attacker as Niall Evalds claimed a high ball, and it was crucial. Three tackles later, Widnes were back in front when Greg Burke crashed over, with Krisnan Inu converting.

They would not fall behind again, eventually rubber-stamping victory when Heremaia fittingly scored the match-winning try after Evalds spilled a Danny Craven kick following back-to-back drop-outs.

Round 8

The Good Friday programme opened on the Thursday night as heavy rain tried to ruin the clash between Wakefield and Castleford, which ended with the Tigers leapfrogging their neighbours in the table after a mud-bound 11-6 win.

Wakefield, while missing their captain Danny Kirmond, were able to welcome back David Fifita after the big prop wasn't named in the initial 19-man squad because of a groin injury but insisted on playing. Wakefield also fielded the returning Kyle Wood, who was the shining light for Trinity and the source of most of their good play with his quick and penetrative runs from dummy-half.

The Tigers chose to play young halfback Jake Trueman from the start at fullback in place of Ben Roberts, who moved to the halves, with Jamie Ellis playing the part of an unused sub on the bench.

Castleford started the game on the front foot and forced a couple of dropouts early on. But Wakefield were enthused by keeping the Tigers at bay and they went close to opening the scoring when Anthony England rumbled towards the try line from a quick play-the-ball, before Oliver Holmes' heroics held up the former Tigers junior.

The scoring was opened only four minutes later in the 17th minute as Roberts provided a slick pass to Mike McMeeken for the England international to glide over. Luke Gale's conversion was never in doubt.

The first half belonged to the Tigers but Wakefield went close again when Fifita ran towards the line but McMeeken's try-saver managed to dislodge the ball and send it over the dead ball line. Trinity fans were convinced the ball was stolen but the video referee ruled a knock on.

Luke Gale's field goal with three minutes of the first half remaining gave Castleford a two-score lead which proved psychologically significant as Wakefield upped the ante after the turnaround and deservedly got back into the game on the hour mark. In their own half, Kyle Wood ran from dummy half and fed Liam Finn, whose planned long kick into the right corner produced a foot race as Ben Jones-Bishop outpaced his opposite number James Clare to the ball. Finn's conversion made it a one-point ball game.

Castleford's lead extended out to five points, though, through two Gale penalties when Grix fumbled the ball into his own player who was stood in front of him and Tinirau Arona was judged to be offside when making a tackle on dummy-half Paul McShane.

Wakefield knocked on the door in the closing minutes but couldn't penetrate the Tigers' defence. Pauli Pauli came close when he threw the ball into touch attempting to find Jones-Bishop and Tom Johnstone lost the ball close to the line with three minutes to play.

It was a grafting win for the Tigers, with forward Holmes outstanding, having signed a new two-year deal with the club.

Good Friday produced drier weather and some cracking derbies.

Hull KR attracted a record crowd to KCOM Craven Park as Hull FC overcame the early sending-off of winger Bureta Faraimo to win a controversial game by 30-22. The USA international was shown a straight red card for late contact on Hull KR halfback Chris Atkin. It was an afternoon packed with talking points, with both coaches fuming at calls made by referee Chris Kendall and video referee Phil Bentham, in a contest that took over two hours to complete.

Hull coach Lee Radford was full of praise for his side, and in particular Carlos Tuimavave, who created three tries for his team-mates and was a stand-out performer for the Black and Whites. He criticised the red card, while Hull KR coach Tim Sheens blasted Bentham for chalking off an Adam Quinlan try for obstruction.

Jake Connor's touchdown on the hour mark proved decisive as Rovers looked to be brewing a comeback heading into the final quarter. Faraimo received a one-match penalty notice.

St Helens extended their lead at the top of the table to four points, ending their nine-year wait for a victory against Wigan on Good Friday with a 21-18 success.

Saints led 12-2 at the break after Morgan Escare opened the scoring with a penalty goal. Jon Wilkin, making his 400th appearance for Saints, combined sweetly with prop Luke Thompson to put Ben Barba clear and, from just inside his own half, the Australian rounded Escare with ease.

Danny Richardson added the conversion and Saints increased their lead five minutes before half-time when second-rower Zeb Taia took a short pass from impressive captain James Roby.

But, six minutes after the break, Wigan got back to within four points when Joel Tomkins took George Williams' inside pass to touch down for a try that Escare converted.

The Warriors then went ahead on 65 minutes when second-rower Willie Isa scooped up a loose ball to score and Williams added the extras.

But, in a frenetic finale, once Richardson's penalty had tied up the scores once more and Wigan halfback Sam Powell had missed with a field-goal attempt, Ryan Morgan's break created the opening for Jonny Lomax's pass to winger Regan Grace's winning try in the left corner.

Richardson converted, then also crucially added a killer field goal before Joel Tomkins' brave second try. With less than a minute to go, Wigan surprisingly took the touchline kick, Williams slicing wide - and that ran down the clock.

It was even closer at the John Smith's Stadium as the Giants and Leeds ended all square at 22-all, the first Super League draw of the season. Despite being denied victory through Ash Handley's late score, the Giants, with interim coach Chris Thorman in charge, were arguably the better team against the reigning champions.

Thorman made seven changes to the squad that had lost heavily at Wigan in the previous round. The incoming players included first-team debutants winger Louis Senior and back-rower Sam Hewitt.

The Giants led 14-6 at half-time thanks to winger Jared Simpson's double, with Kallum Watkins scoring in reply. Ryan Hall and Handley tries put Leeds ahead but Adam O'Brien crossed to swing the game back Huddersfield's way until Watkins converted Handley's try to level with three minutes to go.

Winger Josh Charnley scored a brace on his Warrington debut as the Wolves produced a much-improved second-half display to see off Widnes Vikings at home by 32-16 and make it three wins on the trot in Super League. And as in their victory over Wakefield Trinity a week earlier, Warrington had to turn around a half-time deficit, trailing 12-10 at the break.

Toby King also scored two tries and Sitaleki Akauola and Ben Westwood both crossed too as Wire ran in six in total. For Widnes, winger Ed Chamberlain scored two tries and Rhys Hanbury one.

Salford moved level on points with the Vikings after a 32-16 home win over Catalans, a third straight league victory on home soil. Back-to-back tries from Jake Bibby and Niall Evalds gave Salford early control but Fouad Yaha replied to reduce Catalans' deficit to 12-4 at the break. Greg Johnson extended the Red Devils' lead before Yaha went 90 metres to keep the Dragons in the contest. Further tries from Josh Jones and Kris Welham eased Salford clear before Greg Bird's last-minute consolation score.

After losing seven of their opening eight games, with Luke Walsh looking increasingly unlikely to play again due to ongoing injury problems, the Dragons were considering re-registering legendary halfback and current assistant coach Thomas Bosc to solve their problems in the pivots.

BETFRED SUPER LEAGUE
Friday 30th March

	P	W	D	L	F	A	D	Pts
St Helens	8	7	0	1	228	96	132	14
Wigan Warriors	7	5	0	2	202	103	99	10
Warrington Wolves	9	5	0	4	168	149	19	10
Castleford Tigers	6	5	0	1	105	114	-9	10
Leeds Rhinos	7	4	1	2	136	129	7	9
Hull FC	8	4	0	4	183	158	25	8
Wakefield Trinity	7	4	0	3	128	111	17	8
Widnes Vikings	8	3	0	5	159	157	2	6
Salford Red Devils	8	3	0	5	142	170	-28	6
Huddersfield Giants	8	2	1	5	114	216	-102	5
Hull Kingston Rovers	8	2	0	6	134	172	-38	4
Catalans Dragons	8	1	0	7	92	216	-124	2

APRIL
Beware the demon Barba

Round 9

On a wet and cold Easter Monday, St Helens remained four points clear at the top of the table after they backed up their last-minute win over Wigan Warriors on Good Friday with a 28-6 victory over Widnes at the Select Security Stadium.

Widnes started the better side. But St Helens, who had Matty Smith making his first appearance of 2018, on the bench, hit back and went 10-0 up as Ryan Morgan went in before Mark Percival notched the second, with both assists by Ben Barba.

Wellington Albert scored his first try for Widnes when he stormed on to an Aaron Heremaia pass but Percival got his second five minutes later, this time on the end of a Danny Richardson grubber.

After half-time, Luke Douglas was sin-binned for a crusher tackle on Danny Craven. But after Widnes had a Ryan Ince try disallowed as the ball went dead, Saints went up to the other end of the field and Barba struck, although TV replays suggested he had dropped the ball in the act of scoring.

St Helens put some gloss on the result when Tommy Makinson acrobatically finished off two flowing moves in the right-hand corner. Douglas escaped a ban on a penalty notice.

Winger Liam Marshall scored four of Wigan's eight tries as they comfortably saw off Hull Kingston Rovers at home by 44-6.

Sam Tomkins, back after missing the Good Friday trip to St Helens through illness, grabbed the first of Wigan's five first-half tries in the 24th minute, with Liam Farrell's double coming either side of four-pointers from George Williams and Marshall.

Chris Atkin scored after the break before Marshall went over again. With Rovers' Josh Johnson in the sin bin, Marshall added a further two tries to complete the victory. Pre-season recruit from South Sydney, prop Gabe Hamlin, made an impressive debut for the Warriors.

Warrington made it four successive victories after emerging through horrendous conditions at the Jungle to inflict a second defeat of the season on Castleford, by 18-6.

Driving rain throughout the early hours of Easter Monday left large parts of the Tigers' pitch covered in standing water but referee Robert Hicks' pitch inspection deemed the surface playable.

Tries from Toby King and the outstanding Daryl Clark helped the Wolves back up their Good Friday victory against Widnes. Clark, in particular, was a menace for his former club all afternoon, with the boot of Stefan Ratchford also pivotal as he kicked five goals that, in testing conditions, were always likely to be vital.

Two penalties from Ratchford inside the opening quarter put Warrington 4-0 ahead and, with half-time just seconds away, the Wolves scored a try that was impressive given the conditions, as Jack Hughes and Josh Charnley combined to send King splashing over the line. Ratchford converted to open up a 10-0 lead.

Castleford continued to apply pressure on the Wolves' line after the break and they eventually earned reward when Luke Gale's kick deflected into the path of Oliver Holmes, with the halfback converting to reduce the deficit to just four points.

Another penalty from Ratchford steadied the Wolves' nerves but not before the Tigers thought they had levelled the scores via Jake Webster. However, his try was ruled out after he was adjudged to have kicked the ball out of Ratchford's hands. And, having survived that scare, Clark sealed a brilliant individual display by wrapping up victory with seconds remaining.

Marc Sneyd dropped a field goal from inside his own half with just moments remaining to move Hull FC into fifth in the table with a nail-biting 27-26 win over Wakefield at the KCOM Stadium.

Two tries from Bill Tupou and one from Mason Caton-Brown put Trinity 18-8 up at the break, with Hull's only first-half try coming from Jordan Abdull. But tries from Albert Kelly and Fetuli Talanoa edged the hosts ahead 20-18 in the 54th minute. Talanoa and Caton-Brown then traded tries and, with scores level late on, Sneyd landed the match-winning kick.

Despite sleeting and snowy conditions at Headingley, Leeds Rhinos held firm to take a 20-0 win against Salford.

Tom Briscoe registered Leeds' opening try and Ash Handley capitalised on Niall Evalds' error to extend the lead. Kallum Watkins converted in-form Handley's score - the centre's seventh try in his past four matches - and later kicked a penalty to give reigning champions Leeds a 12-0 half-time advantage.

Another Watkins penalty and Josh Walters' try completed the scoring.

Catalans remained bottom but earned their second win of the season, by 27-6 in Perpignan against depleted Huddersfield Giants.

Huddersfield fielded a patched-up squad under interim head-coach Chris Thorman, with Louis Senior replaced by his twin brother Innes for his debut, while Danny Brough and Oliver Roberts missed out.

The Giants got the scoreboard ticking when Ukuma Ta'ai's barnstorming run set up Jordan Turner to find Aaron Murphy out wide. But they dropped the kick-off, allowing Catalans to get straight back into the game through Jodie Broughton.

After the break, Catalans took a lead they never relinquished. Tony Gigot kicked to the corner for Fouad Yaha to bat the ball back to Benjamin Jullien before Greg Bird broke free and found PNG star David Mead on his outside.

Mead added a second when Samisoni Langi and Gigot combined to set the fullback away. Broughton rounded off the try-scoring after he was again found by Michael Mcllorum.

A late penalty and field goal from Gigot rubbed further salt into the gaping wounds of the Giants.

Round 10

The standard of play the week after the gruelling Easter period wasn't at its highest but that did not mean there was no excitement in round ten.

St Helens and Hull FC drew the short straw and had to back up for the TV game on the Friday night as runaway league leaders Saints proved they were far from a one-man team, winning 26-12 at home.

Saints were in control for large parts of the match to claim their third win in as many games over the Easter period, despite Steve Prescott Man of Steel favourite Ben Barba being ruled out due to illness. And James Roby sustained a rib injury early in the second half.

Solid up front and with a superior cutting edge out wide, where Tommy Makinson was excellent, they were clearly the better side against a gallant Hull FC team that had its own injury issues. The first-half loss of Fetuli Talanoa and Brad Fash with a broken jaw significantly hindered coach Lee Radford's options.

Jonny Lomax had a fine game filling in at fullback for St Helens and Theo Fages retained his place at stand-off as Zeb Taia finished with a try double.

A brilliant try from Albert Kelly after a superb flick to Jack Logan on the right wing from Jake Connor made it 14-6 at the hour mark but Taia's second try on 67 minutes settled it before the powerful Luke Thompson and Chris Green traded tries.

After the game Lee Radford bemoaned the trend for players 'advertising staying down', seemingly leading to harsher punishments for marginal tackles. Jordan Abdull was placed on report for an apparent crusher tackle on halfback Danny Richardson. Richardson stayed down after the incident and, after a break in play, Abdull was put on report by Robert Hicks. No charge followed.

There was real excitement the following evening in the south of France where Wigan produced a the mother of all comebacks, coming from 21-0 down after 45 minutes to beat Catalans 32-23.

Wigan skipper Sean O'Loughlin's leadership and passing skills were immense in an epic fightback which saw his team take the points home against the odds.

Steve McNamara said his players were 'distraught' at losing a game after leading for so long. Injuries to loose forward Greg Bird and the late sin-binning of Mickael Simon didn't help, but McNamara reckoned the penalty count was a significant factor in the defeat.

A disallowed try for the home team, an apparent ball-steal and possible forward pass leading to a Wigan try left fiery Dragons President Bernard Guasch in a furious mood as he launched a furious attack on 'scandalous' refereeing decisions.

Catalans led 15-nil at the break, with Tony Gigot kicking a penalty and a field goal to add to tries from Benjamin Jullien and David Mead, who lit up the game with an 85-metre romp up the middle of the pitch to score on 38 minutes.

Ben Garcia went over to stretch the lead two minutes into the second half but Dan Sarginson's try sparked the Warriors comeback soon after. Wigan added five more as Oliver Gildart, Joe Burgess, Liam Farrell, Sam Tomkins and Tony Clubb sealed the win.

The big buzz around the game was the news that Wigan's Sam Tomkins was likely to become a Catalans Dragons player in 2019.

Warrington made it five wins in a row and three victories in eight days over the Easter period with a 22-6 Saturday-afternoon win at Salford.

The Wolves raced into a 14-point lead early on and were having particular joy down their right, where Salford found high bombs from Tyrone Roberts and Kevin Brown and the threat of Toby King and Josh Charnley difficult to handle.

Brown, along with halfback partner Roberts, was excellent and his try with seven minutes left took Warrington's lead to 14 points and secured the victory.

Justin Carney grabbed a brace of tries as Hull KR ground out a much-needed Saturday evening 31-12 home win over fellow strugglers Widnes.

For the most part, it was a tight contest, with little to separate two sides that were lacking confidence and already feeling the pressure of being at the wrong end of the table. The Robins came out on top through a mixture of resilience and the misfortune of their opponents, who were left playing the final half-hour with no fit replacements after suffering a raft of injuries at the end of an exhausting Easter programme.

Widnes coach Denis Betts was left to count the cost of his side's defeat, with 19-year-old Keanan Brand suffering a broken leg just seven minutes into his Super League debut, while Danny Craven, Wellington Albert and Gil Dudson were also left watching from the sidelines as their team ran out of steam.

Rovers didn't have everything their own way though, losing centre Andrew Heffernan to concussion and having to overcome the sin-binning of Chris Clarkson early in the second half. But coach Tim Sheens was pleased with his team's determination to grind out the win.

It was 12-all until the hour mark but Danny Tickle's try and Danny McGuire's field goal opened up a seven-point gap before James Greenwood and Carney tries gave the scoreline a lopsided look.

It added to a terrible week for the Vikings on the injury front, with star centre Krisnan Inu facing several months on the sidelines after breaking his leg in the Good Friday defeat to Warrington. Patrick Ah Van was still out with a broken arm, Hep Cahill with ligament damage, Lloyd White a calf injury and Jay Chapelhow a broken thumb.

Castleford got a 40-28 win at Huddersfield on the Sunday. The scoreline was comfortable in the end but it was anything but after what was truly a game of two halves.

April

The Tigers looked to be easing to victory at half-time, leading 28-6 and looking dangerous every time they had the ball in hand. However, the Giants had different ideas, fighting back to move within eight points on two occasions with the Tigers just about holding on for the victory.

Alex Foster was the star of the show for Castleford with a brace, while 17-year-old Innes Senior also took home plenty of plaudits for his double for the hosts. Foster's 73rd minute try sealed the win after a nervy second half from the Tigers.

Wakefield and Leeds produced a thrilling match at the Mobile Rocket Stadium (the name for Belle Vue in 2018), with the Rhinos fighting hard for their 28-26 victory.

Both sides were without experienced players, with Wakefield resting Liam Finn and Scott Grix, with David Fifita having gone back to Australia to recuperate from a groin injury. Joel Moon was missing for Leeds, with Liam Sutcliffe coming in at stand-off, with props Adam Cuthbertson and Mitch Garbutt also absent. Kallum Watkins' leadership qualities helped inspire the Rhinos to victory as he finished with 16 of Leeds' 28 points as they moved into the top four.

Leeds led early on as Watkins touched down from Richie Myler's kick but the Rhinos trailed 12-6 at half-time after tries from Jacob Miller and Kyle Wood. Ash Handley's try on 47 minutes tied the game but a Ryan Hampshire penalty goal restored Trinity's lead before Matty Ashurst's try under the sticks made it eight points difference.

But Leeds looked the most likely, with Handley and fullback Ash Golding running strongly before Watkins and Brad Singleton went over for Leeds.

Josh Walters put Leeds eight points ahead when he touched down Watkins' dab into the right corner, before Max Jowitt's late try set up a thrilling last minute as a Reece Lyne break gave Trinity one last attack that the Rhinos bravely repelled.

The result meant Wakefield were on the back of five straight defeats, the last three by margins of five, one and two points. That week they had tied up stand-off Jacob Miller on a new four-and-a-half year contract but rumours that loose forward Joe Westerman was on his way to Belle Vue from Toronto Wolfpack were denied.

That week Watkins committed his long term future to the Rhinos by signing a contract extension until the end of 2021.

Round 11

St Helens' lead at the top of the table was cut to two points as Wakefield inflicted a defeat on the league leaders to reinvigorate their own flagging top-four hopes, winning a thrilling Sunday-afternoon contest at Mobile Rocket Stadium by 24-20.

Trinity, with Liam Finn and Scott Grix back, but star winger Tom Johnstone not selected, were impressive for large periods. They led 22-6 after just 22 minutes, with four tries - from Ben Jones-Bishop, Reece Lyne, Justin Horo and Bill Tupou - in a blistering 17-minute passage of play.

It had looked an unlikely scenario after Mark Percival scored a try in the second minute after a long-range break from Jon Wilkin that Danny Richardson was an inch away from finishing off.

By half-time, that 16-point cushion had been hauled back to just eight with tries to Tommy Makinson and another to Percival. Makinson's try was a spectacular effort he replicated on several occasions in 2018, touching down as his body hovered in touch. Seven minutes after the break, Luke Douglas reduced the deficit to just two points, crashing onto a brilliant disguised pass from Theo Fages.

After Liam Finn kicked a 73rd-minute penalty the excitement went up a notch as Saints, without James Roby, threw the kitchen sink at Wakefield and looked favourites to impose a sixth straight narrow defeat on Trinity.

Ben Barba, closely policed up to that point, broke and sent Jonny Lomax to the line, only for Tyler Randell to stop him with a high tackle, for which he was sin-binned.

Then Percival kicked through to the line, only to be sin-binned himself when he insisted too strongly that he had been brought down by Finn. One desperate last-second attack saw Lomax's long ball to the right spilled by Makinson.

Wigan had already moved to within two league points of Saints with another comeback, this time winning by 9-8 at Leeds on the Friday night.

Trailing 8-0 with nine minutes left - Tom Briscoe getting the only try before that on 21 minutes from a superb floated ball from Richie Myler - and having survived the ten-minute absence of Sam Powell, the Warriors seemed destined to end empty-handed in a rain-affected game. But twice Sam Tomkins was involved in getting the ball down to the Western terrace end as time ebbed away, with broken-nosed Ash Handley superbly keeping out Dan Sarginson on the Wigan right. The ball was swung left, where John Bateman found Liam Farrell with a glorious flicked pass and his lobbed ball put Oliver Gildart over in the corner, with Tomkins goaling from touch.

Five minutes later, after Leeds had hit ultra-conservative mode, Sam Tomkins landed a penalty to level after Brett Delaney had gone high on Powell. And then came his coup de grace, after Leeds had surprisingly gone short from the re-start.

Bateman and Sean O'Loughlin made midfield metres but Wigan seemed to have gone up a blind alley out wide on the fifth. Unexpectedly, from ten in and forty metres out, Sam swung his right foot and landed a peach of a field goal.

An error-strewn game had once again raised complaints about the performance of the Rhino balls used in Super League.

Warrington were also on 16 league points, though they had played two more games than Wigan, after a 40-26 home win over Hull KR on the Saturday afternoon.

With the hosts leading 22-2 at the break, with tries from Mike Cooper and Ben Currie, and two from Jack Hughes, it looked as though they would be heading for a routine victory. But Rovers staged a rapid comeback and trailed by just two points on 49 minutes. Maurice Blair, James Donaldson and Chris Atkin scored three tries in quick succession to give Rovers hope.

Ultimately, though, Warrington's class showed in the final 20 minutes as they ran away from an injury-hit Robins side. Tom Lineham, Stefan Ratchford and Ryan Atkins crossed to ensure Wire's win before Danny McGuire went over for a consolation.

Rovers were expected to head into the transfer market for a replacement for captain Shaun Lunt, taken off just two minutes into the game with a knee ligament problem.

Injuries were proving a particular problem for Widnes. Their coach Denis Betts said he felt like he was in 'some kind of vortex' after Chris Dean and Chris Houston were added to his lengthy casualty list during the Thursday-night 39-20 defeat to Hull FC at the Select Security Stadium.

Dean was helped off in the early stages of the game with a torn bicep and was followed in the 46th minute by Houston with a knee injury.

Hull, who themselves played with 16 men after a pre-match pain-killing injection that reacted badly ruled out Carlos Tuimavave, offered no sympathy, with an accomplished spell of three tries in six second-half minutes proving decisive in what was a highly competitive game.

Centre Josh Griffin got one of those tries in a man of the match display, adding a second four minutes from the end.

The down-at-heel Vikings led 14-12 until Masi Matongo's first try for Hull FC in the 54th minute before Hull pulled away, with two-try Tom Olbison a stand-out.

The Vikings took Leeds utility Jimmy Keinhorst on a month's loan.

Salford climbed out of the bottom four with a 30-12 victory at Huddersfield on the Sunday - their first away win in 11 months - with Robert Lui in sparkling form.

A day of frustration for the Giants was summed up when acting captain Danny Brough was dismissed for dissent in the 75th minute, with the Red Devils already leading 22-12 and two brilliantly worked tries from right wing Jake Bibby followed.

Only Catalans Dragons sat below Huddersfield on the league ladder and they showed no sign of moving off the bottom on the Sunday with a sub-standard 41-0 defeat at Castleford, who were now two points behind leaders St Helens with two games in hand.

It took 15 minutes for the Tigers to score their first try but it was a procession thereafter. The hosts took complete control by half-time through converted tries from Paul McShane, Michael Shenton and Oliver Holmes and a late Luke Gale field goal.

McShane went over for his second after the restart before James Clare touched down in a dominant Tigers display. Joe Wardle scored his first try for the club and Holmes finished the scoring with his second of the day as Catalans failed to get on the scoresheet.

To compound the Dragons' misery, star player David Mead limped off just before half-time with a hamstring injury.

No Catalans directors were at the game. 'No directors will head to Castleford and perhaps York (for a Challenge Cup tie the following week),' explained Bernard Guasch. 'I want to show the English that I am not happy with the way we are treated by the referees.'

Round 12

For the second time in as many weeks, Leeds suffered the heartbreak of defeat by a single point after Marc Sneyd kicked a 76th-minute field goal at the KCOM Stadium to seal a 19-18 Hull FC victory.

The reigning champions rallied from 14-0 down to lead by four points thanks to three quick tries in the second half. However, Hull produced their best performance of the season, showing the belief to secure a victory at the death, earning their first win over Leeds in the league since 2014.

Rhinos veteran Jamie Jones-Buchanan made his 400th appearance for the club but the Airlie Birds made it an unhappy night for one of the Leeds greats as Hull leapfrogged their opponents into the top four.

Jake Connor and Bureta Faraimo's tries on the right gave the Airlie Birds an 8-0 lead at half-time. Hull opened the second half with three consecutive sets on the Rhinos' line and it brought a third try of the evening. A brilliant cut-out pass from Albert Kelly put Connor on the outside of Ash Handley to score his second down the right and this time Sneyd added the conversion to take the Airlie Birds out to a three-score lead.

Leeds needed a response and they got it from England international Ryan Hall. After camping down the Hull end for two sets in succession, the Rhinos spread the ball well to the left and gave the big winger just enough space to squeeze the ball to the line for a try only he could have scored, bringing his side back into the contest.

And they cut the gap to two on the hour mark. A brilliant run around play involving Brett Ferres gave Joel Moon the space to race over on the left. Referee Ben Thaler had gone to the video-referee without approving the try, suggesting there may have been an obstruction, but he was overruled by Phil Bentham.

And two minutes later Bentham awarded Matt Parcell a penalty try when a teasing kick ricocheted off the uprights into the arms of the hooker but Josh Bowden dislodged the ball with a lunging leg. The try was awarded under the posts and Watkins converted to give the Rhinos a four-point buffer.

Hull found some energy to snatch a game-levelling score inside the final ten minutes. A floating Kelly kick was taken by Fetuli Talanoa, who did well to offload to his centre Carlos Tuimavave for the score. But Sneyd dragged the conversion wide to leave the scores level. Sneyd made amends shortly after as he stepped up to slot the field goal that brought the house down.

In the wake of the game, Leeds coach Brian McDermott criticised referees for officiating the game 'with a microscope,' claiming the game was refereed differently in the opening two-thirds of the season and that officials were influenced too heavily by the crowd. 'Too many possessions are decided by whether an opposition's defence concedes a penalty,' said McDermott.

Referees boss Steve Ganson countered by insisting that an increase in gamesmanship from players was at the root of the problem.' When there's a milking of penalties, occasionally referees will fall for it,' he said. 'But coaches have a high-level input and when you look at moving off the mark, pushing forward and all those sort of things, they're coached. It needs some joined-up thinking.'

Castleford coach Daryl Powell heaped praise on winger Garry Lo after he impressed in their 28-12 defeat at Wigan on the Friday.

Lo, who starred for Papua New Guinea in the 2017 World Cup, was recalled from a loan spell with Sheffield Eagles to line up against the Warriors in place of James Clare and he marked his Super League debut with a try.

An enthralling opening 40 minutes saw just two points separate the sides at the break. Wigan, with Sam Tomkins in brilliant form, had raced into a 14-2 lead thanks to tries from Oliver Gildart and Liam Farrell and they were looking good for a comfortable win. A try from Oliver Holmes gave the Tigers a lifeline but the game should have been over when Willie Isa spilled the ball with the line at his mercy following a neat kick from George Williams. Castleford took full advantage of that mistake and went up the other end, with Lo going over to reduce the gap to two at half-time.

A try from nothing for Gildart after the break, following another strong run from Joe Burgess, saw Wigan extend their lead to six points, while further scores from Williams and Tony Clubb saw them clinch victory

On the same night, Salford leapfrogged Wakefield into seventh place after their stunning 38-4 home victory over a Trinity side that had taken the scalp of runaway leaders St Helens five days before.

Junior Sa'u's second-minute try out wide was the only try of a low-key first half, which saw home halfback Robert Lui forced off with a calf injury.

Wakefield had Reece Lyne sin-binned for a professional foul five minutes into the second half and Tyrone McCarthy and Ryan Lannon crossed before Joe Arundel pulled a try back.

But Jake Bibby went over twice, with gamestar George Griffin and Greg Johnson also scoring as Salford ran riot late on.

Jonny Lomax scored a hat-trick to inspire an emphatic St Helens response against injury-ravaged Huddersfield Giants following the defeat at Wakefield. The 66-4 home win kept them two points clear of second-placed Wigan as Ben Barba, Louie McCarthy-Scarsbrook and Ryan Morgan also collected braces in a twelve-try haul.

Challenge Cup Round 5

Last year's bottom four teams were involved in the fifth round of the Challenge Cup and all four progressed.

Catalans Dragons were given an almighty scare by League 1 side York in front of a bumper crowd at Bootham Crescent of 3,081, eventually winning 34-22. Warrington breezed into the last 16 with a 54-6 win over now in League 1 Bradford Bulls in a game which proved to be England international Ben Currie's last of the season after he injured the same knee that saw him miss almost a year of action earlier in his career.

Widnes scored 17 tries through ten different players as they romped into round six with a club-record win, beating League 1 Coventry Bears at home by 90-0. Danny Craven claimed four tries and Rhys Hanbury and Patrick Ah Van, back after a broken arm, three apiece as Widnes bettered their 90-4 second-tier win at Doncaster in 2007.

Hull KR made sure there was no repeat of their shock elimination in 2016 by Oldham as USA international Junior Vaivai was outstanding in a 40-minute spell and Adam Quinlan scored a hat trick in a 32-0 away win.

Rovers had been rocked by Thomas Minns's failed drugs test and went into the tie without Danny McGuire, Justin Carney, Chris Clarkson and Shaun Lunt. Minns tested positive for a banned, non-performance-enhancing substance following a game with Huddersfield in March. He admitted his guilt, claiming he took the unspecified substance on Mother's Day as he struggled to come to terms with his mother's death.

Round 13

Frontrunners St Helens ran in eleven tries, including a hat-trick from Ben Barba, to seal an impressive 60-10 win over Salford Red Devils at the AJ Bell Stadium on the Thursday evening.

Backing up their big home win over Huddersfield it meant Saints had racked up 126 points in two games and they had to play 42 minutes of the game with twelve men after seeing substitute Matty Lees sent off for a swinging arm on Niall Evalds just before half-time.

That incident with Lees was one of two drawbacks on an otherwise fine night's work for the Red Vee. Man of the match Barba was stretchered off in a neck brace close to the end of the game after falling awkwardly. The injury transpired to be none too serious. Lees received a two-match penalty notice.

Injuries were also hitting the Red Devils hard and the news they had been beaten to the signature of Warrington winger Matty Russell by Toronto Wolfpack, after the Canadian club made an eleventh hour swoop for the Scotland star, was a blow.

Wigan stayed two points behind Saints after they came from 18-4 down at half-time to win 32-24 against the Vikings at the Halton Stadium on the Friday night. The Warriors were firm outsiders at the break with Thomas Leuluai still in the sin bin and Widnes having controlled the second quarter with an impressive performance.

But a blitz of three tries in consecutive sets ten minutes after the restart swung the game dramatically and the Warriors - who had a stand-out performance from forward Ryan Sutton and a couple of moments of magic from fullback Morgan Escare - then edged the closing stages of a thoroughly entertaining contest.

In the absence of Joe Mellor, Tom Gilmore led the Vikings, who gave a debut to Leeds loanee Jimmy Keinhorst, well and produced an excellent attacking kicking game, while Ryan Ince finished with two tries and Tom Olbison was typically unrelenting at loose forward.

The game flipped around in six dramatic minutes at the start of the second half. Oliver Gildart sent Joe Burgess over directly from a scrum before Escare took a Taulima Tautai offload and showed outstanding feet to dance over under the posts. The Warriors then touched down in a third consecutive set when Isa charged over and Sam Powell's conversion had the visitors two points ahead.

A Gilmore penalty, which was awarded for a Dan Sarginson high tackle on Rhys Hanbury, drew the sides level, before Sutton powered over for a six-point cushion.

A smart Rhys Hanbury cut-out pass put Ince over for his second and gave Gilmore the chance to level again from the right touchline. But his difficult attempt drifted wide and in the dying stages Tautai stormed over to formally seal matters.

Warrington remained two points behind Wigan after their 38-4 home win over threadbare Huddersfield on the same night.

The Giants' season had been hindered by injuries. Jake Mamo, Michael Lawrence, Sebastine Ikahihifo and Tyler Dickinson all returned but this match proved no different. Lee Gaskell was injured in the warm-up while Aaron Murphy and Jared Simpson were pulled from the field with a torn adductor and concussion respectively.

Warrington punished them without hitting top gear. Josh Charnley completed his second-half hat-trick down the wing and Steve Price's men never looked in danger as fullback Stefan Ratchford scored two tries and set up several others.

That week the Giants handed a two-and-a-half-year contract to former Canberra Raiders captain Simon Woolford to become their new head coach. Woolford was currently working as an assistant to former Giants and St Helens coach Nathan Brown at the Newcastle Knights in the NRL.

Leeds moved to within a point of fourth-placed Castleford following a nerve-jangling 20-18 victory at Hull KR on the Sunday, after back-to-back one-point defeats in their previous outings.

It could have been the same outcome at KCOM Craven Park. Having twice led in the first half, the Robins put an enormous amount of pressure on the Rhinos' line in the final quarter after Kallum Watkins' 55th minute penalty goal marked the final score of the match. Rovers also had two tries - to Robbie Mulhern and Chris Atkin - disallowed. Junior Vaivai and Justin Carney also came desperately close to scoring. Ryan Hall scored the try that brought Leeds level at 18-all while Mose Masoe was in the sin bin for a high tackle.

The Tigers beat Wakefield at home in the Friday-night game by 24-4. The derby, which was played for the Adam Watene Trophy on the tenth anniversary of the death of the former Castleford and Trinity player, was much more closely contested than the result would suggest and the game was in the balance until midway through the second half with Castleford, who were only 16-4 ahead as the match drew to a conclusion, only sealing victory in the last seven minutes with a breakaway Paul McShane try.

Worrying for home fans was the knee injury to halfback Luke Gale in the 27th minute, which was expected to rule out the reigning Man of Steel and Albert Goldthorpe medal holder for up to three months.

Kumul winger Garry Lo was missing, having been stood down by the Castleford club after he had volunteered to assist police with an unspecified inquiry.

Catalans climbed off the foot of the table for the first time in 2018 with a nailbiting 25-24 win over Hull in Perpignan on the Saturday night.

A dream debut for Josh Drinkwater helped to give the Dragons their most significant victory of the season in a bitter nip-and-tuck tussle. The former London and Leigh halfback was signed from Western Suburbs Magpies after the decision of injured halfback Luke Walsh to retire and was only cleared to play hours before kick-off as the Dragons awaited his RFL registration. But he slotted seamlessly into the side, scored a try and landed six goals from six.

The game was marred by an injury to Hull's Jordan Abdull who was taken to hospital with a broken leg. Team-mate Albert Kelly and Catalans' David Mead also picked up injuries during the match.

Scott Taylor and Hakim Miloudi tries put Hull FC up at the break, with Brayden Wiliame grabbing Dragons' four-pointer in response.

Drinkwater and Tony Gigot tries then edged Catalans ahead, only for Taylor and two Jake Connor goals to regain the lead for Hull, though Drinkwater then kicked a penalty goal to level.

After Connor and Michael McIlorum went to the bin after an altercation and with Abdull on his way to hospital, Drinkwater and Connor exchanged penalties which set the scene for Gigot to kick the winning field goal in the last minute, the ball only just clearing the crossbar from close range.

BETFRED SUPER LEAGUE
Sunday 29th April

	P	W	D	L	F	A	D	Pts
St Helens	13	11	0	2	428	152	276	22
Wigan Warriors	12	10	0	2	347	176	171	20
Warrington Wolves	13	9	0	4	286	191	95	18
Castleford Tigers	11	8	0	3	228	192	36	16
Leeds Rhinos	12	7	1	4	230	201	29	15
Hull FC	13	7	0	6	304	273	31	14
Wakefield Trinity	12	5	0	7	212	248	-36	10
Salford Red Devils	13	5	0	8	226	288	-62	10
Widnes Vikings	12	3	0	9	221	287	-66	6
Hull Kingston Rovers	12	3	0	9	215	288	-73	6
Catalans Dragons	12	3	0	9	167	319	-152	6
Huddersfield Giants	13	2	1	10	168	417	-249	5

* That weekend York City Knights recorded a 144-0 victory over West Wales Raiders. Their 144-point haul was the most scored in one game, surpassing Huddersfield's 142 points scored against Blackpool Gladiators, while the margin of victory was six points better than the previous 138-point margin registered by Huddersfield and by Barrow, who beat Nottingham City 138-0. Both records had been in place since 1994, coincidentally both being set on the same day in the Regal Trophy.

MAY
Magic May

Round 14

The top three were four points clear of the chasing pack after the first week in May, with Warrington's Friday-night TV victory at Headingley the most significant result.

Summer conditions arrived at last as the Wolves emerged 33-22 winners after establishing first-half dominance at 10-0 before finding themselves 22-11 down at the start of the last quarter.

There was a top performance from youngster, flame-haired backrower Harvey Livett, out of contract at the end of the season and covering for out-for-the season Ben Currie. Moving to centre to cover a head injury to Bryson Goodwin, he posted his first senior hat-trick.

Livett's first try on 18 minutes saw him roll through Rhinos skipper Kallum Watkins on a last-tackle power play. His others in the 69th and 72nd minute showed great speed, confidence and footwork to capitalise principally on dynamic work in the middle from the outstanding Daryl Clark, linking from the back via Stefan Ratchford featuring a glorious, instinctive flicked pass and the precision engineering of Tyrone Roberts, who was starting to hit his straps.

On the other side, it was a torrid night initially for Ashton Golding, who started the game at hooker, despite Brett Ferres being named in the role and was withdrawn after twelve minutes for usual rake Matt Parcell.

Golding uncharacteristically spilled two high kicks as Leeds were bent to almost breaking point in the opening half-hour. But the young custodian then showed great resolve to escape Livett to score the Rhinos' first points. He went on to make six tackle busts, which was a joint game high with Clark's figures.

Ben Murdoch-Masila's contribution off the bench seemed to consist predominantly of errors and concession of penalties but, when it mattered at the end, with Warrington not quite in the comfort zone at 27-22, he called for the ball and with a close-in unstoppable charge managed to seal the points and the Wolves' eighth successive Super League win.

St Helens had recorded a comfortable 26-12 home win over Catalans the night before, despite the absence of Ben Barba. Skipper James Roby returned from injury and had a big impact in the 60 minutes he was on the field.

Jonny Lomax was at the heart of everything St Helens did well with the ball, involved in a number of try-scoring plays as well as scoring one himself. And Tommy Makinson continued his great form as Regan Grace's eye-catching second try put the result beyond doubt, giving the improving but unimaginative Catalans nothing to play for but pride in the final ten minutes.

Wigan, two points ahead of Warrington and two behind St Helens, had little trouble beating Salford at home on the Friday night by 30-0.

Captain Sean O'Loughlin was absent as Wigan dominated from start to finish. After wasting a couple of early chances they took the lead through Oliver Gildart, while further tries from Tony Clubb and George Williams saw them in full control at the break. The Red Devils looked a tired outfit, mainly because of all the tackling they were made to do. That pattern didn't really change in the second half as Wigan spent the majority of it camped in Salford's half. Sam Tomkins helped himself to a brace of tries in the second half, while John Bateman had the final say with a try.

Sam Tomkins was to move to the Catalans at the end of the season, with Wigan already thought to have signed former Castleford fullback Zak Hardaker. Hardaker was handed a 14-month suspension by UK Anti-Doping the previous week, due to expire on 7th November that year. His legal team was able to successfully argue that his ban should be reduced due to 'exceptional circumstances.'

Despite having sacked him, the Tigers could in theory seek compensation from the Warriors for Hardaker's signature, having paid £150,000 to Leeds Rhinos to sign Hardaker on a permanent basis in June 2017, just four months before he was suspended by UKAD.

On the Saturday afternoon, Sika Manu and Bureta Faraimo both scored twice as a ruthless Hull FC put an injury-ravaged Castleford to the sword by 36-12.

Jake Connor, who was playing in the halves following an injury to new two-year deal Hull hero Albert Kelly, played a blinder and set the ball rolling when he sent in Manu for his first on 12 minutes.

Paul McShane got a try back but it was 20-6 at the break after Jamie Shaul, Manu and Faraimo tries.

Already without Luke Gale, Greg Eden, Ben Roberts and Nathan Massey, Castleford were dealt another blow before kick-off as Jake Webster withdrew from the squad. Alex Foster came into the centres with youngster Calum Turner taking Foster's place on the bench. Debutant Turner got the only Cas try in the second half.

Joe Westerman made his second debut for Hull off the bench after signing from Toronto Wolfpack.

Hull confirmed just prior to the game that Kelly had agreed a new two-year deal, contracting him to the club until the end of the 2020 season. However, Kelly's halfback partner Marc Sneyd was helped from the field shortly after half-time with a knee injury.

Huddersfield, awaiting the arrival of new coach Simon Woolford, climbed off the foot of the table, leapfrogging Widnes with a 28-12 Friday-night home win over the Vikings.

Centre Jake Wardle, brother of Castleford's Joe, made an unbelievable debut, scoring two tries, both by collecting high kicks cleanly. But then he was sin-binned on the 68th minute for a spear tackle on Rhys Hanbury. He was banned for three games.

Oliver Russell also made a promising debut at scrum-half, playing alongside fellow young stars Darnell McIntosh, Sam Wood and Matty English.

Vikings coach Denis Betts couldn't hide his frustration after the game. 'They are rubbish, we are rubbish,' he said.

By the Sunday afternoon of a bank holiday weekend it was getting really hot as Hull KR's injury list got the better of them at Wakefield, Trinity putting on a second-half masterclass to finish 54-18 winners.

Winger Tom Johnstone, dropped after the defeat to Leeds despite his call-up to the England Elite training squad, responded in style and scored a hat-trick for the second time in 2018 against Hull KR. Fullback Scott Grix got another two tries as Jacob Miller was at the centre of some thrilling dry-weather football.

The one-sided scoreline looked unlikely ten minutes before half-time after the Robins had fought back from 12-0 down to 12-all and could well have been in the lead had the touch-judge not disallowed what looked a fair try by Liam Salter in the left corner.

Missing Shaun Lunt, Andrew Heffernan and Justin Carney, with young, on-loan Saints hooker Aaron Smith on debut, the Robins couldn't cope with a lack of possession after half-time, despite the best efforts of fullback Adam Quinlan.

May
Challenge Cup Round 6

Leigh Centurions, intent on making a return to Super League after their Million Pound Game relegation in 2017, repeated their 2015 Cup heroics to knock out Salford with a 22-10 home win over the Red Devils.

Leigh had stand-out performers in skipper Harrison Hansen and fullback Peter Matautia, as they came back from a 10-0 deficit after only 12 minutes. The Red Devils badly missed the mercurial talents of knee-injury victim Robert Lui but looked destined to progress as Niall Evalds eased his way over on the right. On-loan from Wigan halfback Jake Shorrocks put his conversion attempt wide but kicked the extras when George Griffin crashed through from close range.

But Leigh's comeback started four minutes later when Ben Reynolds shot through before former Salford man Hansen twisted through four tacklers to cross following a pass from Aussie halfback Drew Hutchison. Reynolds converted both tries to make it 12-10 to the Centurions after 20 minutes. That's how it remained after a nip-and-tuck first half.

Nine minutes after half-time, Hutchison reached the line to be denied by the video referee. Two tackles after that, there was no denying Daniel Mortimer, who was playing his first game since February. The pivot burrowed over from a quick play-the-ball by Bodene Thompson and Reynolds nudged over his third goal.

Super League Salford looked nervous as they regularly spilled possession and Leigh cemented their win after 77 minutes as Hutchison stepped and twisted and found his way to four points.

Another top Championship side, Toronto Wolfpack, looked like causing another major shock on the Sunday afternoon as they led 10-0 at in-form Warrington after stunning the Wolves with some high-speed and expansive football. But after Mike Cooper had got Warrington on the board on 23 minutes, the Wolfpack imploded as their discipline fell apart.

Liam Kay was shown a yellow card for a dangerous tackle on Josh Charnley. Then Andrew Dixon's moment of madness three minutes before half-time, when he punched Harvey Livett after a dispute at a play-the-ball, was inexplicable. Toronto had earlier rode out the 10-minute period without Kay successfully and it looked as they would lead 10-6 heading into the break.

But when Josh Charnley crossed on the stroke of half-time, it put Warrington ahead and that try was the start of a 60-point run of unanswered scores as the Wolves finished 66-10 winners.

At one stage, Toronto had just ten men on the field after Darcy Lussick and their captain Josh McCrone were both sin-binned for two separate incidents of dissent.

Thursday's TV game at Featherstone, which Hull FC won 38-20, was also an indisciplined affair. Lee Radford compared a chaotic conclusion to a game in the local park after Jake Connor guided his team through despite Hull finishing the game with nine men.

Hull had three men in the sin bin when winger Bureta Faraimo was shown a red card after the final hooter for a late, high hit on opposite winger Shaun Robinson, leaving the Black and Whites to defend one tackle four men short. Featherstone also had three players yellow-carded during the second half.

In the end Connor's two early tries helped the current holders into a commanding 18-0 lead inside the first 13 minutes and, despite plenty of effort and no little skill, that was always likely to prove too much for Championship side Featherstone.

The marquee game on the Saturday afternoon saw St Helens emerge 36-18 winners at Castleford. Ben Barba – and St Helens' strong defence – were the differences between the sides. Barba not only helped himself to a hat-trick but had a hand in two of the Saints' other three touchdowns. His hat-trick score was a stupendous solo effort in which the fullback beat four men in a memorable 70-metre run.

Danny Richardson's try on 63 minutes opened up an 18-point gap and finally put paid to the Tigers' hopes, with Luke Gale's lengthy injury absence seemingly hitting them hard.

With new head coach Simon Woolford due to arrive the next week, Huddersfield Giants started to hit form under interim Chris Thorman and on the Friday night they knocked out Wakefield with a 24-14 home win.

Huddersfield were 8-6 behind at the break but gained complete control during the second half and racked up a 16-point lead with only 15 minutes left, with Lee Gaskell's score the coup de grace.

The 20-year-old prop Matty English came off the bench and constantly got the Giants supporters off their feet, scoring his first-ever Huddersfield try. The next week he signed a new four-year contract with the Giants.

Also on the Friday evening, Leeds survived a late onslaught to book their place in the quarter-finals with a 23-20 win at Widnes.

Trailing 23-4 after Ash Golding and Stevie Ward tries early in the second half, the game appeared up for the Vikings. But, as was the case more than once in 2018, they sparked into life when the game looked lost. Three tries in twelve second-half minutes, from Matt Whitley, Alex Gerrard and Charly Runciman, put them right back in the contest. But Leeds, under enormous pressure, managed to hold on for the final 20 minutes to book their place in the last eight. Dramatically, Aaron Heremaia had a try ruled out with minutes remaining after referee Greg Dolan adjudged he had lost the ball in the process of scoring.

Catalans progressed with a 56-10 home win over Whitehaven on the Saturday, Jodie Broughton finishing with a try hat-trick and debutant forward Mickael Goudemand scoring twice, while Wigan, the day after, struggled past twelve-man Hull KR by 28-10 at KCOM Craven Park.

There was little to separate the sides for much of a tight tie but, after already having had Adam Quinlan sin-binned, Rovers were hampered when Danny Tickle was given his marching orders on half-time for punching John Bateman, who was yellow carded.

Sam Tomkins was at the heart of every positive thing Wigan produced and his precision with the boot kept his side ahead, with his 62nd-minute try tipping the scales decisively in Wigan's favour.

That week it was confirmed that Tomkins had signed a three-year deal from 2019 with Catalans Dragons and that Zak Hardaker, free to return to action on November 8th at the end of his drugs ban, had signed for the Warriors.

Round 15

Magic Weekend was staged in Newcastle for the fourth successive year and 64,319 fans attended St James' Park, with 38,881 on the Saturday and 25,438 attending on Sunday in soaring temperatures.

The figures were down on the most popular Magic Weekend, which was in 2016, when 68,276 attended, while the attendances on both days failed to beat the records set for Saturday of 40,871 in 2015 and 32,953 for Sunday in 2012, when the event was held at Manchester's Etihad Stadium.

On the Friday night, Newcastle Thunder attracted a record crowd of 4,137 to their League 1 clash against Bradford Bulls.

The weekend opened with a Championship clash. Winger Liam Kay scored a hat-trick as Toronto Wolfpack put their Warrington nightmare behind them with an accomplished 43-30 win over Toulouse that moved them five points clear at the top of the table.

In the opening Super League game, St Helens marched on with a 38-18 win over

Widnes Vikings, who were well in touch at half-time when they trailed only 22-18. But Saints controlled the contest far more effectively in the second half and, as time wore on, it looked increasingly unlikely that Widnes, who ran out of steam after an hour, were going to pull off a shock.

Although Ben Barba was highly influential in the first half, it was 21-year-old halfback Danny Richardson who pulled the strings in the second and fuelled calls for him to gain England selection.

Ryan Morgan's second try on 63 minutes, taking Saints' lead to 14 points ended Widnes's challenge.

Wigan ominously produced their best performance of the season as they emphatically ended Warrington's run of ten straight wins with a 38-10 victory, extending their own run to eight games. Without captain Sean O'Loughlin, Sam Tomkins played superbly, as did centre John Bateman.

The Wolves played a big part in the first-half arm-wrestle, scoring twice through Harvey Livett and Stefan Ratchford. But Wigan also scored two tries through Sam Powell and Sam Tomkins, who kicked four goals, to lead 16-10 at half-time.

It was one-way traffic after the break as Wigan kept Warrington scoreless to rack up 22-unanswered points, tries for Bateman, George Williams, Liam Marshall and Tom Davies capping a convincing win.

In the final game of the Saturday, Castleford put Leeds to the sword by the same scoreline, 38-10, Jesse Sene-Lefao a standout in a dominant Tigers pack, with young halfback Jake Trueman playing a starring role. Backrower Alex Foster was also a revelation in the centre. Almost unstoppable with his mazy charges out wide, his run to set up Michael Shenton's score at the start of the second half was one of the highlights of Magic day one.

The Tigers scored three tries without reply in the first half through Jy Hitchcox, Foster and Junior Moors. Jamie Ellis converted all three and kicked two penalty goals for a 22-0 lead. And he converted Shenton's try before prop Mikolaj Oledzki's first Super League try got the Rhinos on the board. But there was little hope for Leeds as Adam Milner and Oliver Holmes scored tries before a late Brett Ferres consolation.

The Rhinos suffered a major blow when captain Kallum Watkins limped off with what turned out to be a season-ending knee injury.

In the day-two opener Jodie Broughton claimed a second-half hat-trick against his old club Salford to help Catalans Dragons climb off the foot of the table for only the second time in 2018 with a 26-12 win.

Broughton, who made nearly 100 appearances across four seasons for the Red Devils, ran in his treble during a 14-minute purple patch which sealed the two much-needed league points. Had either Josh Drinkwater or Tony Gigot had their kicking boots on, the final margin would have been greater.

The Red Devils, wearing yellow shirts specially designed to commemorate the Manchester Arena bomb attack of the previous year, made a strong start and appeared to have struck first.

A Robert Lui kick was patted back by Kris Welham for Derrell Olpherts to scoot over but, after a couple of video replays, the try was ruled out by the video referee. Salford were not to be denied though and Weller Hauraki crossed shortly afterwards after latching onto a Mark Flanagan offload and swatting away a couple of attempted tackles.

But Ben Garcia and Julian Bousquet replied for the Dragons, who also had a try ruled out, establishing a 10-6 half-time lead. Broughton's ruthless finishing in the second half, regardless of George Griffin's try four minutes from time, killed off the Red Devils.

Resurgent Huddersfield Giants completed a quick-fire double over Wakefield ahead of the delayed arrival of new head coach Simon Woolford, hanging on grimly to win 25-22, nine days after beating them 24-14 to reach the quarter-finals of the Challenge Cup. It made it three wins on the trot for interim boss Chris Thorman as the Giants waited for

Woolford to receive his work permit. Thorman revealed that he was already having a major input into the team via the internet.

Aaron Murphy, playing in the back row, Adam O'Brien and Jake Mamo tries had the Giants 18-0 up at the half hour mark on the back of some exciting ball movement. Wakefield looked unable to cope before Matty Ashurst crossed, grounding his own ricocheted grubber to the in-goal. A Danny Brough field goal put Giants 19-6 up at the break, capitalising on his own 40/20.

Wakefield started the second half the stronger and, after referee James Child had just put the Giants on a team warning for conceding a string of penalties, Kruise Leeming was sent to the sin bin for holding down in the 44th minute. Two minutes later, Jacob Miller kicked through for Ben Jones-Bishop to touch down, with Liam Finn landing the goal. But the twelve-man Giants went back downfield and sent the ball out to the left for Darnell McIntosh to finish smartly in the corner. Brough landed the touchline conversion and the lead was back up to 13 points.

Jones-Bishop added his second in the 57th minute and Finn kicked goal number three. And with seven minutes remaining, a nerve-tingling finale was guaranteed as Reece Lyne handed off Jake Mamo to grab his side's fourth try. Finn was off target with his goal attempt but there were now just three points between the sides and a nail-biting finish as Huddersfield hung on.

The Hull derby provided the finale to the Magic Weekend, with the Airlie Birds winning 34-22 after a battle of two injury-hit sides, keeping them level on points with fourth-placed Castleford.

All eyes were on Kirk Yeaman, the club's 15-year stalwart who came out of retirement to help make up the numbers. And the performance of a young halfback who'd never donned the club's colours grasped the spotlight. Many Hull FC fans will have had to do a google search to find out who Liam Harris was when the club announced his signing from Doncaster the previous week. Not only did he score, his overall display of fearlessness with the ball caught the eye. Centre Cameron Scott was also a debutant.

The Black and Whites led 24-10 at half-time as Jamie Shaul scored two of their four tries, the others coming from Scott Taylor and Harris, to two from Kieren Moss, helped them pull away after a tit-for-tat start.

Moss's hat-trick try on 56 minutes, converted by Ryan Shaw, gave Rovers' supporters hope of a comeback. But, with the game still in the balance, Jake Connor, thriving in the absence of Marc Sneyd and Albert Kelly, created a score for Jack Logan out wide and then danced through himself to confirm the Black and Whites' seventh successive derby win before Tommy Lee's effort provided consolation six minutes from time.

Round 16

New Huddersfield coach Simon Woolford watched on as the Giants moved into the top eight with a 24-16 Friday-night win at Salford, the Red Devils slipping into the bottom four.

It had all started so well for the Red Devils, Junior Sa'u crossing from Niall Evalds' short ball. However, the Giants hit back in the 19th minute as Jake Mamo's cut-out pass caught Salford cold, allowing Darnell McIntosh to go in at the corner. Danny Brough's missed conversion, coupled with Robert Lui's penalty goal, meant Salford still held the lead, although a Brough penalty did bring parity. But Salford retained their advantage through the opportunistic Evalds as Jordan Rankin tried to shepherd the ball dead.

The introduction of Kruise Leeming in the second half changed the pace of the game, with the hooker playing a key role in all of Huddersfield's second-half tries. They hit the front in the 51st minute when Leeming ran laterally and popped a pass to the excellent Daniel Smith, who barged over from close range. Jordan Turner scored what would prove to be a crucial try, as he freed his arm to score. And Huddersfield wrapped it up in the 74th minute as Leeming came out of dummy-half and planted the ball down, despite the efforts of two Salford defenders.

Junior Sa'u scored a fine individual try at the end, skittling several defenders on his way to his brace but the points were in the Giants' bag.

Off the field, former Salford owner Marwan Koukash had agreed to write off debt in excess of £5 million. And the Red Devils announced they would not be offering Manu Vatuvei a new contract in 2019. A serious Achilles tendon injury on the eve of the season had ruled him out for the year.

On the same night, USA international Junior Vaivai's brace of tries saw Hull KR bag a shock 24-8 home win over second-placed Wigan.

A try from Joel Tomkins and a pair of goals from brother Sam had given the Warriors an early lead but two quick-fire tries from Vaivai and Adam Quinlan fired Rovers into a slender half-time advantage before Chris Atkin went over early in the second half to swing the contest firmly in the Robins' favour.

Vaivai denied John Bateman a certain try midway through the second half and, as Wigan's frustration built, Joel Tomkins was sin-binned before Vaivai helped himself to his second try to seal Rovers' first Super League win since 7th April.

On the downside, Robins winger Justin Carney was facing a spell on the sidelines after breaking his hand in the first half.

Meanwhile, former Wigan great Shaun Edwards had emerged as favourite to take over from Shaun Wane as the Warriors' new head coach at the conclusion of the 2018 campaign. Former Wigan forward Wane announced he would be leaving the club. He was initially Michael Maguire's assistant before he succeeded him as head coach at the start of the 2012 campaign.

Wakefield registered a crucial 19-6 win at Widnes, thanks to a three-try first half. Stefan Marsh's penalty gave the hosts the lead but tries from Pauli Pauli, Tom Johnstone - with a superb dive into the corner from an excellent looped ball from Jacob Miller - and David Fifita put Trinity 16-2 up at half-time.

Patrick Ah Van touched down for Widnes to cut the deficit to 10 points but in a second half of few chances for either side gamestar Miller kicked a late field goal to seal Trinity's win.

The defeat left Widnes rooted to the bottom of the Super League table after Hull KR's shock win against Wigan.

In the following week the Vikings sacked long-serving head coach Denis Betts after seven-and-a-half years at the helm.

The Vikings were four points behind tenth placed Catalans after the Dragons beat understrength Leeds 33-20 in Perpignan on the Saturday night. The early season strugglers produced a power-packed performance, led by a rampant Remi Casty, which had the Rhinos rattled throughout.

Rhinos call-ups Jimmy Keinhorst and Jordan Lilley worked tirelessly to plug the gaps left by injuries to Kallum Watkins and Jamie-Jones Buchanan but for long periods the Dragons were utterly dominant. They led 16-0 after half an hour and 17-4 at the break after Ash Handley got the Rhinos on the board. The Rhinos had a mini-revival in the third quarter with Brett Ferres and Ryan Hall tries and scored a late consolation try through Brad Dwyer but couldn't match the Catalans for pace and power when it mattered. Tony Gigot, Josh Drinkwater and Jodie Broughton scored further tries before Dwyer's consolation.

Warrington provided a great fightback, recovering from a 12-0 half-time deficit to finish as relatively comfortable 30-12 home winners, although patched-up Hull FC played their full part in an entertaining TV clash.

In the end the cutting edge of backrowers Harvey Livett, who had signed a new contract that week, and Ben Murdoch-Masila, feeding off the creativity of Kevin Brown, Stefan Ratchford and Tyrone Roberts, proved too much for a injury-hit Black and Whites side that had threatened an upset at the break.

For Hull, there was a typical non-stop effort from Danny Houghton to go alongside several encouraging performances from youngsters, in a gutsy team display that earned a deserved ovation from the travelling support at the end of the game.

Hull opened the scoring in the sixth minute when Liam Harris's pin-point kick was fumbled by Tom Lineham and Sika Manu patted the ball back to makeshift centre Dean Hadley to score. Seven minutes later the visitors were over again, this time with Mickey Paea crashing over under the posts. Two conversions from Jake Connor gave them a two-score cushion that they would preserve until the break.

A thrilling first half finished in controversy when Chris Hill made a biting allegation against Hakim Miloudi. The Frenchman was later found to have no charge to answer.

Trailing 12-0, Warrington were level by the 53rd minute. After Miloudi conceded a goal-line drop-out from a shrewd Roberts kick, Kevin Brown's smart pass put Livett over. Soon after it was Brown himself twisting out of a tackle to score, with two Livett conversions making it 12-12. The impetus was now all with the home side and Murdoch-Masila - who made a number of stirring charges - stole over from dummy-half before smart hands to the right saw Ratchford and Ryan Atkins combine to put Josh Charnley over. Ryan Atkins completed the scoring by stepping through from close range and not even a late disallowed try to Livett for a push in the back of Danny Washbrook could dampen the Wolves' mood.

Wigan's defeat at Hull KR gave St Helens the chance to go four points clear at the top and they took it with both hands, winning 40-18 at Castleford.

For once, Jonny Lomax, thriving at stand-off in 2018, took the limelight from Ben Barba, shining amongst an eight-try masterclass.

Kyle Amor touched down inside three minutes for Saints but Cas responded immediately through Mike McMeeken. Barba ran 90 metres for a try after Adam Swift had knocked back a high kick before Lomax and Dominique Peyroux extended their lead.

Ryan Morgan and Theo Fages crossed twice for Saints in the second half before Jy Hitchcox, Jake Trueman and Oliver Holmes helped the Tigers, with a makeshift backline, finish the match with a flourish.

BETFRED SUPER LEAGUE
Sunday 27th May

	P	W	D	L	F	A	D	Pts
St Helens	16	14	0	2	532	200	332	28
Wigan Warriors	15	12	0	3	423	210	213	24
Warrington Wolves	16	11	0	5	359	263	96	22
Hull FC	16	9	0	7	386	337	49	18
Castleford Tigers	14	9	0	5	296	278	18	18
Leeds Rhinos	15	7	1	7	282	305	-23	15
Wakefield Trinity	15	7	0	8	307	297	10	14
Huddersfield Giants	16	5	1	10	245	473	-228	11
Salford Red Devils	16	5	0	11	254	368	-114	10
Catalans Dragons	15	5	0	10	238	377	-139	10
Hull Kingston Rovers	15	4	0	11	279	384	-105	8
Widnes Vikings	15	3	0	12	263	372	-109	6

JUNE
Champions stumble

Challenge Cup Quarter-finals

Catalans became the first side to book their place in the semi-finals with a 20-6 win at Huddersfield on the Thursday night. Tries from David Mead and Greg Bird, plus six goals from Josh Drinkwater, separated the sides on a perfect summer's evening, in a scrappy, stop-start game.

Dragons coach Steve McNamara had special praise for centre Brayden Wiliame, whose grandmother had passed away the previous week. He had made a return trip to Australia after the Dragons' victory over Leeds and only arrived back in Manchester on the day of the Cup match.

Catalans also obtained clearance on the day of the game to include new signing Kenny Edwards, who had been released by Parramatta after an off-field incident and faced a Sydney court hearing for a charge of driving on a suspended licence. He made a big impression. The second-rower came off of the bench to make his debut after only 15 minutes when Greg Bird was forced off while clutching a towel to a head wound.

The Dragons also lost prolific scoring winger Jodie Broughton during a try-less first half, at the end of which just two Drinkwater penalties separated the sides.

The Giants welcomed back skipper Leroy Cudjoe after nine months out with a knee injury as new coach Simon Woolford took the reins fully for the first time since his arrival in Britain seven days before. Cudjoe got Huddersfield's only try, on 42 minutes, after mesmeric work in centre field from Kruise Leeming and Danny Brough's towering conversion gave the Giants a 6-4 lead.

But the Dragons hit back swiftly as Tony Gigot's kick to the corner wasn't dealt with and David Mead pounced to score. Drinkwater landed his third goal and after that the Dragons strangled the life out of the home side.

Brough was sin-binned on 22 minutes for a crusher tackle on Edwards. He was handed a two-match penalty notice and then copped a further game for an 'unreasonable' appeal.

Leeds were forced to play their Friday-night home tie with Championship Leigh at Featherstone because of a cricket test match at Headingley and went through by 52-22.

Leigh went into the game with real hope of a second Cup upset against an injury-plagued Rhinos side, after beating Salford in the previous round. But Peter Matautia's spear tackle on Matt Parcell, which saw him red-carded in the ninth minute after the Centurions had got off to a rousing start, completely altered that dynamic. Down a man, playing up the hill, the toll was immediate, as the Rhinos posted six tries in 17 mesmerising minutes, four of them in an electrifying back-to-back spell where the Centurions were reduced to kicking off and standing behind their posts.

For Leeds, Ashton Golding was superb, offering speed and decisiveness out of dummy-half as a makeshift hooker, following Parcell's departure with the concussion suffered as a direct result of the red-card offence. But the gamestar was again Jack Walker.

His searing breaks from the back, beautifully timed incursions into the line and confident takes of the high ball, allied to a wonderfully balanced, stepping run for his side's third try, were the catalyst for the ensuing try-fest.

Matautia got a four-match ban and Matt Dawson-Jones five matches after being sent off near the end of the game for 'questioning the integrity of the referee'.

On the Sunday, St Helens ended Hull's three-year unbeaten run in the Cup with a nerve-jangling 25-22 victory at the Totally Wicked Stadium.

Favourites Saints were pushed every single step of the way by a Hull side who, given the circumstances and the events which played out during the game, probably had no right to be anywhere near the final losing margin of three points. They had three players sin-binned on separate occasions and more injury problems. Dean Hadley went down in the first minute and limped off. Danny Houghton left the field with a head knock and didn't return. Sika Manu also departed with around half an hour left.

Mark Percival and Regan Grace opened the scoring before Hull replied through Albert Kelly and Chris Green. Hull had Houghton (crusher) and Danny Washbrook (use of knees) sin-binned within two minutes, then Percival and Grace both crossed again as Saints made their advantage count. A Danny Richardson field goal on the half-time hooter made it 23-12.

Scott Taylor scored for Hull on 53 minutes and Jake Connor converted for 23-18 before Masi Matongo was sent to the bin for a late challenge on Jonny Lomax. Richardson's penalty goal made it 25-18 but with ten minutes left and the Saints unable to completely kill Hull off, Hakim Miloudi leaped highest to claim a brilliant Albert Kelly kick. It set up a thrilling closing stage that was ended when Jamie Shaul's exhausted dummy-half pass to an equally exhausted Kelly went forward.

The day before, Warrington put the cleaners through Wigan, who had beaten them resoundingly two weeks before at the Magic Weekend, winning 23-0 at the Halliwell Jones Stadium.

Kevin Brown wrong-footed the Wigan defence to open the scoring after a frenetic first 10 minutes. And the Wolves led 16-0 at half-time as Ben Murdoch-Masila crashed over and Josh Charnley ran in against his old club.

Wigan had Tommy Leuluai sin-binned after the interval and Declan Patton's late try, after the outstanding Tyrone Roberts potted a field goal, produced a scoreline that reflected Warrington's dominance.

It was a second straight defeat for Wigan since Shaun Wane revealed he was to depart the club at the end of the season and by the end of the match the Warriors had not scored a try in over two hours of action.

And there was further trouble for the Warriors after a video of Joel Tomkins man-handling and abusing bar staff at a pub in Standish went viral on the Saturday evening. Wigan suspended Joel Tomkins for four weeks and fined him £10,000. The dual-code international was in the company of his brother, Sam, who said little in the five-minute video. The fullback was fined £5,000 but not banned.

Round 4

On the Friday night of the Cup round, Castleford turned on the style as they claimed the inaugural Roger Millward Trophy with a 42-14 win over Hull KR. The game had been postponed at the start of March because of the so-labelled 'Beast from the East'.

The Tigers flew out of the blocks and had the game sewn up by half-time with a whirlwind opening quarter that saw them run in 22-unanswered points.

Rovers stemmed the tide in the second half but the damage was done as wingers Kieran Gill and Jy Hitchcox grabbed two tries apiece in an eight-try showing.

June
Round 17

The Friday-night TV game between Warrington and Castleford was rated by many as the game of the season, the injury-denuded Tigers emerging with a 34-30 victory.

The Tigers were already without key men in reigning Man of Steel Luke Gale, Ben Roberts, Liam Watts, Junior Moors, Jamie Ellis and Jake Webster. When Greg Eden and Paul McShane pulled out late due to injuries a win for the Wolves, with home advantage and a week after their Cup hammering of Wigan, looked a formality.

The Tigers had signed former Sheffield Eagles stalwart Quentin Laulu-Togagae, who had been released by Toronto, and he made his debut in Super League at the age of 33, though he was playing in the unfamiliar position of halfback when he had spent the previous ten years playing at fullback. He was partnering 19-year-old Jake Trueman in the halves, while 19-year-old fullback Calum Turner was in for Greg Eden at fullback after being called up from the Tigers' Academy side that morning, without having trained with the first team.

Castleford raced out to an early 12-point lead with two pieces of good fortune. First, Mike McMeeken grubbered a kick that went through Stefan Ratchford's legs for the Tigers forward to touch down. And their second try came when a grubber kick from Trueman freakishly bounced up to hit the crossbar and fall into Turner's hands for a second try.

But after 31 minutes the Wolves had cruised into a 20-12 lead through tries to Tyrone Roberts, Ratchford, Daryl Clark and Sitaleki Akauola.

But instead of Warrington running away with it, the Tigers levelled the scores at half-time with a peach of a try from Jy Hitchcox, which came with a brilliant final pass from Tigers skipper Michael Shenton, converted from the touchline by Turner, who then kicked a penalty after Josh Charnley tackled him high.

Charnley made amends 13 minutes into the second half with a try in the right corner to regain a four-point lead. But that wasn't enough to disrupt the QLT show, as the Tigers' new recruit scored a fine try from a Jesse Sene-Lefao offload before making the sort of break that supporters of Championship clubs were used to watching to put Oliver Holmes in for the decisive try.

With the score at 32-24, Castleford had a lead to hold on to, but Turner dropped a high kick and from the free play Charnley bagged his second with a fine diving effort. Turner went off soon after with a hamstring problem, leaving Castleford further depleted with just a two-point advantage. They extended that to four when Adam Milner kicked a penalty goal and, with six minutes left, they held on for a memorable victory.

Wakefield extended Wigan's losing run in the Thursday TV game, emerging with a deserved 32-16 win at the Mobile Rocket Stadium.

The Warriors, who remained without a win since Shaun Wane announced he would be leaving at the end of the season, travelled across the Pennines without four frontline forwards and it was the home side's pack that did much of the damage. The outstanding David Fifita was hard to handle in his two long spells and he got commendable support from the likes of Matty Ashurst and Pauli Pauli.

Wane handed a debut to young winger Craig Mullen after Liam Marshall withdrew due to illness, while Romain Navarrete and Callum Field were drafted in to plug the shortfall in their pack.

Two tries from Ben Jones-Bishop, one in each half, and four-pointers from Bill Tupou, Tom Johnstone and Pauli Pauli were reward for Trinity's dominance. Gabe Hamlin scored his first Warriors try just before half-time that made it 14-6 at the break, while Tom Davies and Morgan Escare scores came too late in the last ten minutes.

Wigan's defeat meant St Helens were now six points clear at the top of the table after a 26-4 home win over Hull KR the following night.

Despite Saints not being at their best, they never had to be and they didn't move out of first gear from the moment they took a 12-0 lead within the opening ten minutes.

Rovers had to do it tough as Matty Marsh left the field early on with a broken nose and concussion but they were their own worst enemy at times. Saints led 18-0 at the break after converted tries from Ryan Morgan, the in-form James Roby and Ben Barba. After Junior Vaivai pulled one back for Rovers, Mark Percival got on the end of a kick to score before top scorer Barba's second try with a late breakaway.

On a busy Friday night, a first-half massacre paved the way for Hull FC to bounce back to winning ways, by 45-14, over a struggling Salford Red Devils side that was now firmly positioned in Super League's bottom four. A field goal and six conversions from Jake Connor to six tries gave Hull a whopping 37-0 half-time lead. A Bureta Faraimo hat-trick was the highlight as Connor made another case for an England call-up.

There was a first victory for new coach Simon Woolford as Huddersfield recorded a 25-18 win at Leeds.

The Rhinos were still understrength but so were the Giants, who stayed in eighth spot after a fourth straight league win. Benchman Sebastine Ikahihifo provided Huddersfield with great go-forward and he was backed up by youngster Matty English and fellow replacement Daniel Smith, who was everywhere. The way the Giants went about their work was perfectly summed up by the outstanding display of Alex Mellor, who made the most metres, tackles and tackle busts for his side, together with a try and an assist.

The contest was summed up in a five-minute spell leading up to the 70th minute, with the Giants leading by a converted try. Three times they lost the ball in their own half, twice at the play-the-ball and once spilling a Brett Ferres grubber. But Leeds never had the right man in position to execute an effective last-tackle play. The in-tune Huddersfield defence pleased Woolford the most, along with the performance of young pivot Oliver Russell, who kicked the conclusive field goal minutes from time with his second attempt.

On the Saturday, Catalans kept within a point of the Giants with a 32-12 home win over bottom-of-the-table Widnes.

With interim coach Francis Cummins in charge for the first time, the Vikings looked well capable of causing a shock, racing into a 10-0 lead through Ted Chapelhow and Rhys Hanbury tries and having two more disallowed by the video referee. But by half-time Tony Gigot and Brayden Wiliame tries and three Josh Drinkwater goals had the Dragons in a 12-10 lead.

Referee Chris Kendall was forced to reach for a yellow card six minutes after the break when Julian Bousquet tackled Jay Chapelhow off the ball. Antoni Maria stumbled awkwardly over the prone Vikings player and damaged an ankle, so he had to follow his teammate from the pitch. Patrick Ah Van took over kicking duties for Widnes and landed the penalty goal to level the scores.

With 20 minutes to go, Remi Casty returned from the bench and Louis Anderson began to terrorise the visitors. With Kenny Edwards, Sam Moa and Greg Bird adding extra poundage, the strength of the Catalans pack took its toll.

But it was more brain than brawn that led to the next score for the Dragons. Gigot was forced to drop-out from under the posts and shaped to launch a lengthy clearance but dummied the Vikings defence with a deft low shot which he regathered before racing 60 metres. He was held down when tackled and Drinkwater converted the penalty to put his side ahead once more.

Casty made sure with his second effort over the line, crossing on his back in the 60th minute to the left of the posts. Drinkwater added the conversion and it was 20-12. And Edwards then managed to score on his home debut, taking a short ball from a busy Michael McIlorum to barge over on the left, with Drinkwater's kick making it 26-12.

To their credit, Widnes fought to the end but an impressive performance from Fouad Yaha on the wing was crowned by a try with three minutes left and another conversion completed the scoring.

The Dragons had won five in a row and were just one point from reaching the top eight with a game in hand on nearest rivals Huddersfield Giants, who they were due to play on the following Friday.

June
Round 18

The media unveiling of former Everton FC CEO Rob Elstone as chief executive of Super League Europe went far from smoothly.

At a Tuesday morning media conference at the Halliwell Jones Stadium in Warrington, representatives of some Super League clubs, led by Wigan Chairman Ian Lenagan, announced that the structure of the game would change the next year from the current model of two-twelves, three-eights that had been in operation since the start of the 2015 season, to one-up one down. The announcement gave rise to a strong riposte from Leeds Rhinos chief executive Gary Hetherington, who accused the chairmen involved of a 'power grab' and furore from representatives of Championship and League 1 clubs who insisted that no such decision had been made.

The next day a Rugby Football League statement made clear that no decision had been made but the episode hung over the following weekend's games.

Fortunately it was one of the season's most exciting rounds with a total winning margin of 22 points over six games, giving an average winning margin of less than four points. There was a drawn game at Castleford on the Sunday, two games with winning margins of one point on the Friday night at Leeds and Huddersfield, a game with a winning margin of two points at Wakefield on the Sunday, a winning margin of four points for Wigan at Hull FC on the Saturday and a winning margin of 14 points for Salford over Widnes on the Thursday night at the A J Bell Stadium.

Stand-off Robert Lui steered the Red Devils to a much-needed first win in seven games, by 26-12, as the 69th minute dismissal of captain Chris Houston for sarcastically applauding referee James Child after he was sin-binned for a late hit on former team-mate Greg Burke compounded a miserable night for the Vikings.

It was a tenth straight league defeat that left Widnes rooted at the bottom of the table but they hit a new landmark since the introduction of their Academy ten years before. Of the 17 players included in their squad for the defeat, nine were Academy graduates at the club. Dan Norman joined the growing contingent of home-grown players to represent the club in Super League as he made his debut from the bench.

Burke and Ed Chamberlain had joined Salford on loan, with Weller Hauraki going the other way and 25-year-old prop Burke scored a try on debut that put Salford back in front on the hour mark. Lui converted that, kicked a penalty goal and converted his own long-range charge-down try three minutes from time.

Houston was subsequently banned for two matches.

Huddersfield opened a three-point gap between them and the bottom four with a 26-25 home win over Catalans. New coach Simon Woolford had to admit his side 'got lucky' after a dramatic end to a game in which Huddersfield were twice 18 points in arrears. Three refereeing decisions in the closing minutes went the way of the Giants, the most crucial the penalty for a ruck infringement that gave Oliver Russell an easy goal kick to win the game.

Another bonus for the Giants was a crowd of 9,121 that turned out after the Giants offered free admission in an attempt to improve attendances long term. Sam Moa would miss the next two Catalans games after being charged with a high tackle.

Leeds and St Helens put on a brilliant game at Headingley for the TV cameras, a rip-roaring spectacle that was settled at 23-22 by a last-gasp field goal from Saints' boom scrum-half Danny Richardson.

Injury-hit Leeds were stretched to the point of naming unused teenage prop Tom Holroyd on the bench after Stevie Ward's late withdrawal. But with hooker Matt Parcell setting a sensational lead out of dummy-half, this was a game they could well have edged.

Tom Briscoe gave the Rhinos an early lead but Saints hit back with tries from Ben Barba and Jonny Lomax. Briscoe's second score levelled and, after Mark Percival put the visitors back ahead, Mitch Garbutt and Brett Ferres crossed to put Leeds 22-16 up.

Liam Sutcliffe couldn't add the conversion, which would have given Leeds a two-score cushion with nine minutes to go and Saints admirably found a way to win. Lomax regathered the short kick-off and Percival brilliantly crabbed across the Leeds line, finding a gap to release Ryan Morgan, who stepped and scrambled over. Richardson converted from far out on the right this time, to make it 22-all.

Luke Thompson and the unquenchable James Roby made significant metres and Richardson, Luke Douglas and Dom Peyroux put Morgan clear but his flick pass with Makinson free went into touch behind the winger. But again Roby shot clear up the middle and Richardson's boot did the rest, with a joyous field goal towards the Saints fans massed on the Western terrace.

St Helens Chairman Eamonn McManus had lambasted the 'incredibly unprofessional' reports claiming that Ben Barba was to return to the NRL in 2019, insisting that the Saints fullback was 'very happy' at the Super League leaders. Barba was the outright favourite for the Man of Steel award and leading the Albert Goldthorpe Medal table after 18 rounds of the competition. His form had inevitably attracted the attention of a number of NRL clubs, but he remained under contract for 2019.

Lee Radford lamented a missed opportunity for Hull to climb into Super League's play-off places after their 14-10 home loss to Wigan, their first home defeat of the season as the Warriors ended their three-match losing run to stay second in the Super League table. Hull led 10-8 for much of the second half before Liam Marshall's try five minutes from time.

The Cherry and Whites led 8-6 at half-time, with Bureta Faraimo crossing for Hull after Dan Sarginson's opener. Faraimo scored his second try after the break to complete the turnaround but a Sam Tomkins penalty made it 10-10.

Marshall's winner came in fortuitous fashion when Sam Tomkins' field-goal attempt hit the bar and Sean O'Loughlin teed up the left winger to go over in the corner.

Jamie Shaul did not return for the second half of the Saturday afternoon clash, with coach Lee Radford later revealing he was suffering from plantar fasciitis (a heel injury).

Warrington remained within two league points of Wigan after they hung on for dear life at Wakefield before finishing 32-30 winners.

After 23 minutes, the Wolves led 20-0 courtesy of two tries to stand-out Stefan Ratchford and another for Tom Lineham, coupled with four goals from the boot of Harvey Livett. Trinity looked at that stage to be on for a real hammering but incredibly they battled back. Indeed, for a few frenetic seconds at the end, after the sin-binning of Sitaleki Akauola for a high tackle, there was a sniff of an unlikely victory for Wakefield, who scored twice, through Tom Johnstone and Pauli Pauli, in three minutes to give themselves 20 seconds to snatch a win from the jaws of defeat.

It was even closer down the road at Castleford as winger Jy Hitchcox crossed for four tries but was still unable to celebrate a Tigers triumph as Hull KR battled back for a thrilling 24-all draw, with Rovers halfback Chris Atkin twice having field-goal attempts to win the game.

Opposite number Jake Trueman also had a late tilt at a one-pointer in the final nerve-wracking exchanges, although it would have been harsh on the visitors had they been denied after they had been behind for almost all of the contest, including finding themselves 14-0 down by the 24th minute.

The Tigers led 14-0 through Mike McMeeken's try and two from Hitchcox. Junior Vaivai went over before the break for Rovers and Adam Quinlan went over straight after half-time. Hitchcox added two more to put the Tigers 24-12 up but Mose Masoe and then Vaivai replied for the Robins, Ryan Shaw holding his nerve to land the 77th-minute conversion which levelled the scores and set up a thrilling finale.

Hull KR had Joel Tomkins on debut after his resignation at Wigan following the high-profile incident in a bar in the town, which resulted in the Warriors suspending him for four weeks.

June

With a weekend kept free to make room for England's mid-season international against New Zealand in Denver, three catch-up games left over from two snow-affected weekends in March were played as hot summer conditions arrived.

Round 4

Catalans' reviving fortunes continued with a 28-25 win at Leeds, a despairing Fouad Yaha tackle late in the game on Tom Briscoe extending the Champions' losing run to six games.

With only a 72nd-minute field goal from Liam Sutcliffe to show after the break - having dominated the first half to lead 24-10 but then being overpowered by the huge Dragons bench - Leeds offered their first real threat of the second half with less than two minutes left. Sutcliffe grubbered through and the elder Briscoe, Tom - the brothers were reunited for a third time at Headingley with Luke's re-acquisition from Featherstone - hared for the ball, hacked it on, regathered and set sail for the clinching score. Catalans winger Yaha hauled him down, deliberately holding on for too long and being sin-binned but with the job done.

Sutcliffe's field goal had put Leeds back in the lead at 25-24 but recent Dragons arrival Kenny Edwards charged over two minutes later to set up the exciting finish.

Round 6

Jamie Ellis kicked a last-minute field goal to give Castleford a 19-18 Friday night home win over Wigan.

Tigers coach Daryl Powell was forced to field no fewer than eight front-rowers in his 17 - five in the starting pack and three on the bench. But despite that and Matt Cook's 69th minute sin-binning, the Tigers found a way to win when Ellis made it third time lucky in a late one-point shoot-out.

Wigan had their own absentees - not least England trio Sean O'Loughlin, John Bateman and George Williams - and had back-rower Liam Paisley on debut.

After Sam Tomkins' opening try was cancelled out by Quentin Laulu-Togagae, Wigan led 12-4 at half-time thanks to Liam Marshall's 75-metre breakaway try, converted by Tomkins, who also kicked a penalty goal. But Cas hit back with tries from Michael Shenton and Cook, either side of an Ellis penalty.

Wigan crossed again through Tom Davies, a try goaled by Tomkins, after Cook's late yellow card but Ellis finally won it with his one-pointer.

Williams didn't play in the Denver Test. A scan on a knee injury he had picked up in the win at Hull ruled him out.

On the Sunday, Wakefield were worthy 44-22 winners over bottom side Widnes, extending their cushion over ninth-placed Catalans to four points with five games left. A superior points difference effectively made the gap five points.

Trinity were 22-0 ahead at half-time and then 28-0 in front on 44 minutes when gamestar Bill Tupou shrugged off several tacklers on a determined run for his second try. But fired by substitute hooker Danny Walker the Vikings hit back to score four tries, though further tries to James Batchelor and Reece Lyne meant there would be no miracle comeback win.

Tom Johnstone's mazy solo effort that opened the scoring was the pick of the tries after he was put away in his own half by Tupou's flick and turned several cover defenders inside out to reach the line.

* A Saturday afternoon crowd of 19,320 at Mile High Stadium, Denver, Colorado, saw England beat New Zealand 36-18.

Round 19

St Helens kept their six-point lead at the top of the table after a nip-and-tuck Friday-night TV home game with Wakefield, which they eventually won by 34-30.

Three team tries and four goals from the boot of Danny Richardson had St Helens in a 20-6 half-time lead on a searing hot night. But Trinity not only made a fightback, they led heading into the final quarter and looked well capable of finishing the job.

But with substitute hooker Kyle Wood dabbing a grubber into the in-goal on 65 minutes, with Trinity leading 26-20, the game turned back Saints' way. Jony Lomax shot back into play and played the ball lightning fast. Within the blink of an eye the ball was moved left and Regan Grace was racing away down the wing. Wakefield got across in numbers but somehow Grace manage to turn them inside out before shooting over for the try. Gamestar James Roby was soon crashing over and Zeb Taia got a try from close range, even though video replay suggested he hadn't grounded the ball.

Reece Lyne pulled back another try, the conversion attempt was declined but Wakefield couldn't get out of their half in the seconds remaining.

On the same night, Adam Quinlan and Ryan Shaw both crossed twice as a strong Hull KR side brushed aside an error-strewn Huddersfield by 37-10 to keep their faint top-eight hopes alive.

The Giants had won their previous five Super League games but despite going ahead early through a Darnell McIntosh score, the Robins responded with 36-unanswered points, Aaron Murphy getting the last try of the game, to seal a comfortable home win. Chris Atkin capped it off with a last-second field goal, with Joel Tomkins getting his first try for the Robins on his home debut.

Hull KR were still four points adrift of the Giants in joint-eighth spot but only a point now behind Salford after the Red Devils fought hard but eventually lost 30-14 at Warrington.

After their international excursions in Denver, England stars Chris Hill and Stefan Ratchford were rested by Steve Price, with Harvey Livett and Ryan Atkins both sidelined through injury.

Sitaleki Akauola, Tom Lineham and Toby King scored before the break to earn a narrow 14-10 lead as Jack Littlejohn scored twice for the Reds. After being pegged back to 14-14 by Jake Bibby's try, Wire then eased clear with three unanswered tries. Josh Charnley, Daryl Clark and Mike Cooper crossed to wrap up victory.

Mitch Brown was excellent as he stepped in for Ratchford, looking assured under the high ball, making plenty of eye-catching breaks and returns.

On the following Monday, League Express revealed the Wolves' attempt to lure former St Helens halfback Kyle Eastmond back to Super League had stalled. Tyrone Roberts had confirmed he was returning to the NRL at the end of this season, a clause in his three-year deal with the Wolves allowing him to leave after one season if he wished.

Widnes Vikings, after 12 straight defeats, were mathematically certain to be in the Qualifiers but they played strongly in a 31-24 defeat at Hull FC.

With the game in the balance deep in the final quarter and having seen their 16-0 lead evolve into a 24-22 deficit, thanks to four well-worked tries by the Vikings, Hull showed superior game management to close out the contest and keep pace with the top four.

Barely six days after making a big impression on his England debut in the USA against New Zealand and on the day of announcing a fresh three-year deal at the club, in-form utility back Jake Connor produced several hugely important plays in the second half to steer Hull to victory.

In the second half, Connor made the switch from the centres to the halves, where he had been so dangerous in recent weeks. It turned out to be a stroke of genius as he set up a try, kicked a long-range penalty and a field goal to edge Hull in front before adding a high-pressure touchline conversion to seal the win for the Black and Whites.

After Connor had established a 25-24 lead, Bureta Faraimo's late try spelt the end of the Widnes resistance.

Owen Buckley became the latest Vikings Academy product to play first-grade level for the club, with the occasion made even more memorable as he scored a try on debut.

On the Saturday it was just like old times for Catalans as over 10,000 fans turned out in the sun to witness the Dragons' 44-16 hammering of Castleford, a win that lifted them out of the bottom four.

A heavyweight performance by the Catalans pack allowed Aussie scrum-half Josh Drinkwater to run riot, scoring a hat-trick of tries and six goals. His acquisition at the end of April was turning out to be one of the signings of the season.

Castleford had no answer to the pace and power of the home team and wilted in the 33-degree heat and 90 per cent humidity, despite their decision to travel early to train and acclimatise to the conditions.

The first game of the round had seen Wigan demolish Leeds at home by 46-8 in the Thursday-night TV game.

Wigan looked slick and well organised, with Liam Marshall scoring a hat-trick of tries. Leeds scored first after starting the stronger but from then on the Warriors dominated the rest of the first half. Brett Ferres capitalised on a mix up in the Wigan defence to score the opening try, before a quickfire brace from Marshall, one from Josh Woods, the young halfback having a wow of a game, and five goals from Sam Tomkins saw the Warriors lead 22-4 at the break.

Liam Farrell and Thomas Leuluai ensured there would be no miracle comeback from the Rhinos and, despite Joel Moon going over, the Warriors finished strongest with Tom Davies going over and Marshall completing his hat-trick in the dying minutes.

John Bateman and Sean O'Loughlin both returned following the Test match in Denver, while former St Helens second row forward Joe Greenwood, signed from Gold Coast Titans made a solid debut off the bench.

It was a seventh successive league defeat for reigning Champions Leeds Rhinos who were now in eighth spot courtesy only of a superior points difference than Huddersfield.

The following Monday they announced they had sacked four-time Grand Final winner Brian McDermott as head coach.

BETFRED SUPER LEAGUE
Sunday 1st July

	P	W	D	L	F	A	D	Pts
St Helens	19	17	0	2	615	256	359	34
Wigan Warriors	19	14	0	5	517	279	238	28
Warrington Wolves	19	13	0	6	451	341	110	26
Castleford Tigers	19	12	1	6	431	408	23	25
Hull FC	19	11	0	8	472	389	83	22
Wakefield Trinity	19	9	0	10	443	401	42	18
Catalans Dragons	19	8	0	11	367	456	-89	16
Leeds Rhinos	19	7	1	11	355	427	-72	15
Huddersfield Giants	19	7	1	11	306	553	-247	15
Salford Red Devils	19	6	0	13	308	455	-147	12
Hull Kingston Rovers	19	5	1	13	358	486	-128	11
Widnes Vikings	19	3	0	16	333	505	-172	6

JULY
Giants awake

Round 20

Leeds moved quickly to replace Brian McDermott as the following Thursday they announced that Rhinos legend Kevin Sinfield had been appointed the club's first-ever director of rugby.

Sinfield was to head up a new-look coaching team at the Rhinos alongside former hooker James Lowes, who would be first-team coach until at least the end of the season. Sinfield was to scale back his commitments with the Rugby Football League, where he was Director of Rugby with a key role for the England team, to one day a week

Sinfield's chances of guiding Leeds into the top eight took a blow on the Sunday afternoon at the Mend-a-Hose Jungle, as Castleford Tigers were far too strong for the Rhinos, winning 42-10, leaving Leeds in ninth place on 15 points. They were two points behind eighth placed Huddersfield and with a crucial game to come against Wakefield Trinity, three points above them, at Headingley the following Friday.

A second-half scoreline of 26-0 against underlined the size of the task for Sinfield, as the Tigers started to show the form that had taken them to the Grand Final in 2017. Star of the show was teenage halfback Jake Trueman, revelling after being thrust in at the deep end with the long-term injury to Luke Gale. With the game finely poised at half-time, Trueman scored twice and created two more tries for Jesse Sene-Lefao.

The win took Castleford into third spot with Warrington having been edged out by 13-12 at Wigan on the Friday night. Reserve halfback Josh Woods was the toast of the town as his last-gasp field goal sealed a dramatic win. The victory for the Warriors still had them six points behind leaders St Helens but they had opened up a four-point gap between themselves and the Wolves.

It was always going to be a blood and thunder affair and defences played their part in the opening 40 minutes, with just three tries being conceded as both teams scrambled to keep their line intact.

It was Wigan, still smarting from that 23-0 Cup loss at the Halliwell Jones the previous month, who struck first, with Tom Davies getting on the end of a neatly worked move orchestrated by Sam Tomkins, only for Toby King to quickly reply for the Wolves. Liam Paisley grabbed his first try for the club in only his second appearance to put the Warriors into a deserved 12-4 half-time lead.

The second half was an even tighter affair with Warrington dominating with ball in hand. They scored the only points of the half through tries from Tom Lineham and Josh Charnley to level matters heading into the dying seconds, only for Woods to pinch it at the death for Wigan with a dramatic field goal.

That week it was announced that England utility John Bateman would be joining the player-drain to the NRL alongside teammate Ryan Sutton, with the pair set to join Canberra Raiders at the end of the season. Wigan received a significant transfer fee for 24-year-old Bateman and reached an agreement for him to return to the Super League club as their marquee player should he return to the UK.

There was some other bad news for Wigan fans when Liam Farrell was forced off during the first half of the game with a shoulder injury, with some doubt as to when he would be able to return.

Leaders St Helens had little trouble getting past Widnes at home, with Adam Swift getting a hat-trick in a 36-6 win. It was only Swift's seventh game of the season as he came in to replace Tommy Makinson, with Ben Barba, increasingly linked with a move back to the NRL, absent, Jonny Lomax slotting back into fullback and playing a blinder.

After establishing a 20-point lead by the break, it was always comfortable for Saints and the game fizzled out, despite Widnes, three points adrift at the bottom of the table, at least asking more questions in the second half.

Huddersfield, rejuvenated since the arrival of Simon Woolford as head coach, were in the top eight after their Thursday night 29-18 home win over fading Hull FC.

Hull were missing the injured Jamie Shaul, Marc Sneyd and Fetuli Talanoa, with Sika Manu suspended for three games for dangerous contact in the win over Widnes, but coach Lee Radford admitted they were beaten in every position. Hull had won two of their last five games and were well off the pace for fourth, four points separating them from Warrington.

Giants centre Jordan Turner was at the top of his game as Darnell McIntosh finished with a try-brace, Danny Brough's return from suspension also pivotal.

Huddersfield were now only one point behind sixth placed Wakefield as the Catalans moved level on points with Wakefield with a 35-18 Saturday evening win at Belle Vue.

After a season when they had been tipped for the top four, Trinity were now in danger of entering the dogfight to avoid the Qualifiers after the Dragons, who themselves had looked doomed to another battle for survival in the Qualifiers in the first half of the season. But seven wins from their last nine Super League outings had them on an upward curve, the form they showed at Wakefield good enough to make a late challenge for the top four.

After going behind to an early try from old boy Justin Horo they looked in total control at 22-6 by the half-time hooter when they were awarded a penalty on halfway. Josh Drinkwater decided to kick for goal. The kick missed, Ryan Hampshire collected and fed Liam Finn, who kicked long for Tom Johnstone to collect and race away.

The Dragons could have been rattled, especially after Horo got a second six-pointer to make it 22-18. But from then on the Dragons bossed the middle, Brayden Wiliame getting his second try and Fouad Yaha settling it late on.

Danny McGuire's hat-trick inspired an emphatic 52-22 home Hull KR win over a disappointing Salford side on the Friday night.

The Red Devils had started well and edged ahead thanks to an early Greg Johnson try but Rovers hit back with a flurry of points, running in five tries in 20 minutes to effectively seal the win by half-time.

Junior Sa'u went over just after the restart, but another blitz of three tries in seven minutes saw McGuire complete his hat-trick while young winger Will Oakes grabbed a brace as the Red and Whites leapfrogged Salford in the battle for positions in the bottom four.

* Toronto Wolfpack secured back-to-back league titles, just one defeat to their name, with a 68-4 home Championship win over Sheffield Eagles,

Round 21

While public bickering over the re-formatting of the leagues between some Super League chairmen and their counterparts from the lower divisions continued, the battle to escape from the bottom four and the consequent jeopardy of the Qualifiers was far from over.

Salford's defeat against Castleford on the Friday night had consigned them to the Qualifiers, along with Widnes. But after round 21, with two games to go, any two from Wakefield, Catalans, Huddersfield, Leeds and Hull Kingston Rovers would be joining them.

All five of those sides picked up at least a point in a thrilling weekend of football. Thursday night saw the Giants and the Dragons climb above Trinity with a win and draw respectively, before Wakefield regained sixth place, but only on points difference, following a 20-all draw at Leeds. That point saw the Rhinos remain three points adrift of safety.

The depleted Red Devils went down to a 24-6 defeat to the Tigers at the AJ Bell Stadium, at the end of a week in which they announced the signing of NRL halfback Jackson Hastings, who had been dropped from Manly's first-grade roster before being released.

With the pitch greasy following torrential downpours across the north west, it was far from a classic. Jake Webster touched down early on to send the Tigers ahead but Jake Bibby crossed before the break to level. Michael Shenton and Webster both scored tries early in the second half as the visitors moved clear. With Paul McShane kicking all the conversions, Kieran Gill's late try to extend the lead to 18 points sealed the result.

The Vikings narrowly lost at home by 26-24 to Hull KR, which meant they would finish bottom of the table heading into the Qualifiers.

Francis Cummins' youthful Widnes side had given themselves an outside chance of victory with a little over 60 seconds remaining, after Owen Buckley's second try, coupled with Krisnan Inu's goal, reduced Hull KR's lead to just two points.

Widnes, with young fullback Olly Ashall-Bott a standout, had one set to try and snatch a victory which, although it wouldn't have saved them from the Qualifiers, would have ended a run of 13 straight league defeats and begun to rebuild confidence ahead of the split.

However, Charly Runciman spilled the kick-off. Hull KR survived the final seconds in possession and, in the process, kept alive their own hopes of escaping the bottom four in the final fortnight.

Shaun Lunt, thrust into the starting line-up at the last minute after Tommy Lee pulled out, was magnificent, delivering an 80-minute performance in energy-sapping conditions in the middle of the park to lead Rovers to victory.

Leeds stood on the precipice of the Qualifiers after, for the fourth time in their previous six home games, failing to hold on to a lead in the closing stages. And they only managed the draw thanks to a post, as Jacob Miller's field-goal attempt with four minutes remaining bounced back into play. It meant that the Rhinos held on to salvage a point at 20-all, averting an eight-match losing run, but not giving director of rugby Kevin Sinfield victory on an adulated return to Headingley.

The change in Trinity's fortunes came with the introduction of Kyle Wood as one of three simultaneous substitutes put on by coach Chris Chester after the Rhinos had gone 18-6 up. Wood's sharpness up the middle, with his support and distribution, brought a different dimension to an attack that had generally been handled by Leeds. His try in the 71st minute, when he latched on to a Miller grubber to the post, was due reward for a tremendous stint that also included 40 tackles.

Catalans recovered from being 18-8 down midway through the first half to earn a share of the spoils at Warrington, the Thursday-night game ending all square at 22-all, both teams missing field-goal attempts in the rain-soaked closing stages.

The Dragons led 20-18 after an open first half that was high on points and entertainment and there was no letting up on the excitement after the break, even if only three penalty goals followed. Wolves winger Josh Charnley, who otherwise had another excellent game, missed a late chance to win it when the ball squirted from his grasp as he dived for the line and Tyrone Roberts saw his field-goal attempt drift wide.

Under the guidance of new head coach Simon Woolford, initially from afar before a closer presence, Huddersfield had gone from top eight no-hopers to near Super 8 certainties. And they confirmed they were a team to be avoided with a 20-12 Thursday-night home win over Wigan.

The Warriors were hindered by the early withdrawal of Sean O'Loughlin, who went off due to a recurrence of a calf injury. The skipper had returned to the side after missing the previous week's win over Warrington and they were without John Bateman and Liam Farrell through injury too. The young, giant prop Samy Kibula was brought in for his debut as a result.

July

Sam Tomkins opened the scoring for Wigan but Darnell McIntosh and Alex Mellor hit back for the Giants. McIntosh crossed over for his second try soon after the break before Leroy Cudjoe further extended the lead. Tom Davies ran in a late try for the visitors but they could not overturn the Giants' advantage.

St Helens extended their lead at the top of the table to eight points the following night after battling back to beat Hull FC at the KCOM Stadium by 34-18. The first 55 minutes was an almighty battle but Saints were able to click into gear and lift to another level of intensity.

Hull came into the game desperate for a win after falling four points adrift of the top four. They produced a sterling effort, knocking Saints off their stride to lead by two scores deep into the second half. But five unanswered tries in a devastating last 25 minutes showed why Saints had dominated the competition.

The change in momentum late in the game was thanks largely to the input of their skipper James Roby and the outstanding Jonny Lomax, who finished with two tries alongside Ben Barba.

Hull's disappointment was compounded by the loss of Jake Connor and Albert Kelly to injury. Connor's hamstring was thought to have ended his season.

Round 22

The top-eight/bottom four split was decided with a week to go as Huddersfield and Catalans confirmed their resurgence and Wakefield produced one of the most stunning scorelines of the season.

It meant that champions Leeds Rhinos would be in the Qualifiers for the second time in three seasons, despite their 34-0 victory over Widnes Vikings on the Friday. And they would be joined by Hull KR who only had the slightest mathematical chance of avoiding the Qualifiers before round 22.

The Giants produced a commanding 32-18 victory at Castleford on the Friday night, as Danny Brough produced a halfback master-class and Jermaine McGillvary finished with a hat-trick of tries.

Castleford looked very much on course to move above Wigan into second spot when, in a whirlwind opening, two tries were registered against a nervy Giants' defence. But by half-time it was 18-all after the teams shared six tries, with Jamie Ellis, Jake Trueman and Junior Moors going over for the hosts and Jermaine McGillvary, twice, and Lee Gaskell crossing for the Giants.

Inside the first four minutes of the second half the Giants went in front for the first time as Greg Eden allowed a last-tackle kick to by-pass him, only for Leroy Cudjoe to dive majestically, somehow avoiding contact with the dead-ball line, for a try, his 100th for Huddersfield, which was given the thumbs up on referral.

Just three minutes later a penalty awarded against Paul McShane for a high tackle on Brough led to Lee Gaskell sending Darnell McIntosh over, meaning he had now scored in each of his side's last five outings.

And, after Giants packman Dale Ferguson had clattered Quentin Laulu-Togagae with a fearsome hit, Adam O'Brien burst through from halfway, with Jordan Rankin's floated pass sending McGillvary in for his hat-trick effort on 52 minutes.

Eden, who had scored in each of the Tigers' previous three meetings with Huddersfield, had an effort ruled out on referral, the ball having scraped the in-goal touchline. And when Mitch Clark was penalised for a high tackle on the hour, Brough landed what turned out to be the last score of the game with his penalty, Gaskell and Eden, again, having subsequent touchdowns declined on referral.

The Tigers dropped to fourth position but their fans were boosted when it was announced that forward Adam Milner had agreed a three-year contract extension to end speculation over a move to Australia.

The Dragons secured their top-eight slot on the Saturday with a 44-10 home victory over fading Salford, completing a sensational transformation in the club's fortunes. After the worst start to a season in the club's eleven-year top-flight history, Catalans were still bottom of the table until the end of April, when a last-minute 25-24 win against Hull at home seemed to be the turning point. Four tries from rugby-union bound Fouad Yaha were enough to see off the Red Devils in a one-sided romp.

There were many pre-match jitters at Wakefield's Mobile Rocket Stadium on the Sunday as defeat to Hull FC would make Trinity favourites for the Qualifiers with a daunting trip to in-form Huddersfield to come on the Friday while Leeds headed to off-form Salford. But when the pressure was at its most extreme, Trinity produced a performance that beggared belief, running out 72-10 winners in the sun.

It was 38-0 by half-time through tries from Tom Johnstone, David Fifita - a 50-metre effort - Jacob Miller, Pauli Pauli, Reece Lyne and James Batchelor. Ben Jones-Bishop scored two second-half tries, while Miller, Lyne and Pauli ran in for their doubles.

Max Jowitt went over for Trinity's 12th try, while Ryan Hampshire kicked 24 points before Liam Harris and Bureta Faraimo scored late consolations.

Hull played terribly, despite being boosted by the return of several of their key stars. Jamie Shaul, Fetuli Talanoa, Marc Sneyd and Joe Westerman all returned from injuries to feature in the starting line-up. Coach Lee Radford apologised to their fans. With two of the top four losing earlier in the weekend, the game was a chance to resurrect their play-off hopes. Instead they were seven points adrift, with an inferior points difference

Leeds' previous win at home was on Easter Monday when they nilled their opponents, who on that day were Salford Red Devils. And they did the same to wooden-spooners Widnes on the Friday night, on-loan from Warrington debutant prop Dom Crosby impressive on his first appearance in a 34-0 win. Hookers Brad Dwyer and Matt Parcell also excelled alongside fullback Jack Walker.

It was revealed in the week that winger Ryan Hall was to head to the NRL at the end of the season. Hall, 30, signed a two-year contract with the Sydney Roosters after spending twelve seasons at Headingley, making his Leeds debut in the 2007 Magic Weekend in Cardiff.

St Helens hooker James Roby insisted he had no potential retirement date in his plans following another masterful performance in his side's 14-6 win at local rivals Wigan on the Thursday night.

The 32-year-old spoke after leading the Super League pacemakers to become the first team to win at Wigan in 2018, extending their lead at the summit to ten points.

It was a blood and thunder affair, with more big hits than try scoring opportunities. But it was Saints who held a slender 8-0 lead at the break thanks to a try from Dominique Peyroux and four points from the boot of Danny Richardson. The Warriors - without Oliver Gildart, Joe Burgess, George Williams, Liam Farrell, Dom Manfredi, Sean O'Loughlin and Ryan Sutton - fronted up well in defence and could have easily conceded a few more tries but it was in attack where they were severely lacking as they looked completely out of sorts with the ball in hand.

St Helens were not at their fluent best but they didn't need to be as their defence made Wigan look ordinary at times. They extended their lead shortly after the break, with Morgan Knowles going over. A late try from Sam Tomkins set up a tense finish but Saints deserved their win in the end.

The following night, Tyrone Roberts' 14-point haul saw Warrington climb up to third spot and consign Hull KR, themselves on a three-match winning run, to the Qualifiers with a 34-20 win at KCOM Craven Park.

Rovers had led briefly through Elliot Wallis's first-half double after Mike Cooper gave the Wolves an early lead. But a converted Stefan Ratchford try gave Warrington a 12-8 half-time advantage. A Robbie Mulhern try three minutes after the break converted by Danny Tickle put the Robins in front. But Warrington never trailed again after Roberts' try regained the lead, Toby King scoring four minutes after. Kevin Brown and Declan Patton both crossed, after Chris Atkin's try brought Rovers within two points on the hour mark.

Round 23

St Helens finished the regular season a convincing ten points clear at the top of the table and their place in the end-of-season play-off already secure after a nail-biting 14-12 home win over Warrington in the Thursday TV game.

With the scores locked at 12-all, Ben Murdoch-Masila was penalised in the last tackle of the game. And the hooter had long sounded when halfback Danny Richardson showed nerves of steel to step forward and boot a 54-metre penalty.

Saints were 8-0 down at half-time - Daryl Clark's 11th minute score the only try of the first half, Tyrone Roberts adding a conversion and a penalty. A minute after the break, gamestar Jonny Lomax half broke and sent Mark Percival away down the left wing and Ben Barba was on his inside for the try.

Roberts kicked two more penalty goals before Lomax crashed over off Zeb Taia's inside dink and Richardson converted for 12-all with 15 minutes to go.

Saints looked likely to suffer a first defeat in 14 matches as the Wolves camped inside their 20-metre area for the last ten minutes. Roberts, twice, Richardson and Stefan Ratchford all failed with one-point efforts before Richardson stepped forward with his nerves of steel.

Sam Tomkins gave his future employers a glimpse of what they could expect the following season as he guided Wigan to a hard-fought 25-20 win over 12-man Catalans to ensure they headed into the Super 8s in second place.

Wigan led 8-6 at the break after falling behind early on but the main talking point came in the dying seconds of the half as Kenny Edwards was sent from the field for a late and high tackle on John Bateman after the Wigan man had kicked ahead.

The Warriors looked to be cruising at the start of the second half as quick tries from Morgan Escare and Tomkins put them 20-6 ahead and seemingly on course for a comfortable win. But the French side refused to play the part of the whipping boys and they hit back with Alrix Da Costa and Fouad Yaha going over to reduce the gap to two points before Lucas Albert kicked a penalty to level the game with 13 minutes remaining. Neither team was interested in the draw and that was evident when Tomkins dropped a field goal with seven minutes left. The Dragons couldn't conjure up that final magic moment and it was the Warriors who sealed it late on with Joe Greenwood going over for his first Wigan try since joining from Gold Coast Titans.

Edwards got sending off sufficient when the RFL match review panel found initial contact had been on the chest. But Catalans forward Greg Bird was banned for four games for a dangerous tackle on Wigan prop Gabe Hamlin which had gone unpenalised in the 22nd minute of the game, potentially significant with the Dragons set for a Challenge Cup semi-final the following week.

Castleford went above Warrington into third spot with a 52-24 win at Widnes on the Sunday, a 16th straight loss for the Vikings. The Tigers' devastating four-try, seven-minute first-half spell turned the game and established a 28-18 half-time lead after Widnes had led early on. And they scored four tries after the break to bring up the 50-point mark and secure a third win in four games.

Greg Eden finished with a hat-trick and Quentin Laulu-Togagae scored a double, with Peter Matautia, signed from a player exodus from Leigh, making a steady debut.

Widnes also had new signings Liam Finn, on loan from Wakefield, and Harrison Hansen on debut and had also signed prop Charlie Gubb from Canberra as they geared up for another Qualifiers campaign.

Huddersfield coach Woolford refused to rule out a top-four finish after Huddersfield's stunning run of form hit new heights on the Friday night. A 40-28 home victory over Wakefield saw them finish the regular season in fifth place, just six points behind the top four.

The Giants had no interchanges left on their bench after Michael Lawrence limped off. But their free-flowing and almost error-free Rugby League of the first half had all but won the game by half-time.

Jermaine McGillvary got his second consecutive hat-trick playing outside Leroy Cudjoe, back to the form that made him an England centre earlier in the decade.

Lawrence's hamstring injury blow was softened by the news that Suaia Matagi was to join the Giants earlier than expected from Parramatta. The Samoan prop forward was due to join the club in 2019 but had been granted an early release to join them for the remainder of the year.

Salford comfortably beat Leeds Rhinos at home by 38-22 to pick up only their second win in twelve matches, gaining some momentum ahead of the Super 8s Qualifiers, despite having to play for more than an hour with twelve men. Even though the Red Devils were 16 points ahead at the time, it was a big ask for them to record the victory when Lee Mossop was given a red card for a headbutt on Brad Singleton on 19 minutes.

Although Jackson Hastings, who flew into the UK earlier in the week, was taken off as a precaution after 23 minutes, he was outstanding during his cameo appearance and showed precisely what he was going to offer Salford in the Qualifiers. He certainly brought the best out of Robert Lui, who was outstanding and pulled the majority of the strings for Salford, while Niall Evalds finished with a try double.

Leeds handed a debut to Jordan Thompson, who joined from Leigh Centurions ahead of the transfer deadline, but they looked unsure despite Brad Dwyer giving them an early lead. Mossop escaped any further punishment after the MRP found he'd made only light contact with his head.

Dramatic thunderstorms struck the city of Hull just before the kick-off on the Friday night. But the torrential rain did little to dampen the excitement of the 232nd Hull derby, with Hull Kingston Rovers holding off a second-half fight back from Hull FC to claim their first derby win, by 20-16, from their last eight meetings.

A first half full of patience had the Robins in total control but three tries without reply from the Black and Whites saw them claw themselves back level going into the final quarter.

However, Rovers landed two late penalties from the boot of former FC man Danny Tickle and showed some unwavering desperation and spirit in defence to take home the bragging rights ahead of the Super 8s competitions.

Both sides fielded largely different teams to the previous week, as the injury toll continued to plague both sides of the city. Rovers in particular were missing no fewer than eleven first-teamers through either injury or suspension, Danny McGuire, Mose Masoe and James Greenwood all picking up bans after the defeat by Warrington, meaning Tim Sheens gave debuts to Ben Crooks, Todd Carney and a second club debut to Craig Hall, after they all joined the club just days before.

It turned out to be a masterstroke from the former Australia national coach as Hall bagged two tries to haunt his old side, whilst his centre partner Crooks never missed a beat in defence.

BETFRED SUPER LEAGUE
Sunday 29th July

	P	W	D	L	F	A	D	Pts
St Helens	23	21	0	2	713	298	415	42
Wigan Warriors	23	16	0	7	573	345	228	32
Castleford Tigers	23	15	1	7	567	480	87	31
Warrington Wolves	23	14	1	8	531	410	121	29
Huddersfield Giants	23	11	1	11	427	629	-202	23
Hull FC	23	11	0	12	534	544	-10	22
Wakefield Trinity	23	10	1	12	581	506	75	21
Catalans Dragons	23	10	1	12	488	531	-43	21
Leeds Rhinos	23	8	2	13	441	527	-86	18
Hull Kingston Rovers	23	8	1	14	476	582	-106	17
Salford Red Devils	23	7	0	16	384	597	-213	14
Widnes Vikings	23	3	0	20	387	653	-266	6

BETFRED CHAMPIONSHIP
Sunday 29th July

	P	W	D	L	F	A	D	Pts
Toronto Wolfpack	23	20	1	2	866	374	492	41
London Broncos	23	16	1	6	907	423	484	33
Toulouse Olympique	23	16	1	6	900	438	462	33
Halifax	23	16	1	6	643	416	227	33
Featherstone Rovers	23	16	0	7	819	420	399	32
Leigh Centurions	23	16	0	7	849	508	341	32
Batley Bulldogs	23	8	0	15	523	703	-180	16
Sheffield Eagles	23	7	0	16	437	843	-406	14
Dewsbury Rams	23	6	1	16	424	746	-322	13
Barrow Raiders	23	5	3	15	382	816	-434	13
Swinton Lions	23	3	2	18	402	866	-464	8
Rochdale Hornets	23	4	0	19	327	926	-599	8

AUGUST
History-making Dragons

Challenge Cup Semi-finals

The 2018 Challenge Cup semi-finals were played as part of a double-header at Bolton, with Catalans Dragons and Warrington Wolves winning the right to meet at Wembley in front of a sell-out crowd of 26,086 on the first Sunday of August.

The Dragons stunned Super League leaders St Helens, winning 35-16 in the first game, their power in the middle of the park, despite missing the suspended Greg Bird, totally overwhelming the runaway league leaders.

First-half tries to Lewis Tierney, Benjamin Garcia, two, and Tony Gigot, combine with five Josh Drinkwater goals and a Gigot field goal helped the French side build a formidable 27-0 half-time lead, with St Helens having backrower Morgan Knowles sin-binned for a high tackle on Kenny Edwards in the 34th minute.

The lead was extended by two points following a third Drinkwater penalty goal soon after the restart, before Saints finally found a response.

Mark Percival, who had just clattered Tierney with a huge tackle on a kick-chase, was the scorer, finishing off a smart pass from Ben Barba to score in the left corner. Five minutes later Saints were over again, with Louie McCarthy-Scarsbrook just making it to the line and Danny Richardson's conversion closing the gap to 19 points with 25 minutes still to play.

But any hope of an unlikely comeback were extinguished by the Dragons, by then being cheered on by Warrington and Leeds fans awaiting their clash, just after the hour mark, as Sam Moa capped a power-packed performance by barging over Lomax to ensure the win. Percival did grab a second try in the same left-hand corner but Saints' frustrating afternoon was summed up in the closing stages when McCarthy-Scarsbrook burst through the middle, only to see his attempted offload hit the ground.

The second game went to form with Warrington overwhelming Leeds by 48-12, even though the Rhinos started the better of the two sides. They took the lead when, after Tyrone Roberts kicked the Wolves into a 2-0 lead, Ryan Hall exploited some fine short-side play to muscle his way over the line from close-range. But thereafter, Leeds fell apart.

From a scrum, Tom Lineham stormed through some timid Leeds defending - not for the first time - before racing the length of the field, with Roberts' goal from in front putting Warrington ahead. Josh Charnley ran in soon after and Kevin Brown and Ben Murdoch-Masila extended their lead to 26-6 by half-time.

After the break, Adam Cuthbertson reduced Leeds' deficit but Charnley scored once more before Toby King, Bryson Goodwin and Lineham touched down to send Warrington to their second final in three seasons.

After the game, newly appointed CEO Ralph Rimmer admitted the Rugby Football League would have to implement its 'plan B'. With less than three weeks to the final there was some concern at being able to promote the game, with late travel arrangements from France in the middle of the holiday period an obvious problem. Rimmer insisted the RFL would adjust its marketing campaigns accordingly to generate a big crowd.

Super League Super 8s - Round 1

Just like Castleford 12 months before, St Helens went into the seven-round play-off with a ten point lead at the top of the table and were already a sure bet for the League Leaders Shield.

But their lead was chopped to eight after the opening round of the Super 8s as they fell to a 16-12 home defeat to Huddersfield. The Giants established a 16-0 lead as Saints failed to fire, marquee player Ben Barba, who had been a shoo-in for the Man of Steel award for most of the season, looking particularly off colour amid reports that he was to be released by Saints at the end of the season to go back to the NRL.

Darnell McIntosh grabbed a double and Alex Mellor went over to put Huddersfield 16-0 up before Super League's leading try-scorer Barba replied just before the break. Form prop Luke Thompson crashed over for Saints' second try with 21 minutes remaining. But the Giants soaked up everything St Helens could throw at them.

Victory for Huddersfield moved them to within six points of Castleford in fourth after the Tigers fell just short at Wigan on the same Friday night by 24-22.

The Warriors welcomed back George Williams and Ryan Sutton following long lay-offs with knee injuries, with Oliver Partington coming onto the bench for his debut.

Liam Marshall, Gabe Hamlin, Dan Sarginson and Sutton tries helped establish a 20-0 half-time Wigan lead. The Tigers came back out fired up and scored through Jake Trueman, James Clare and Paul McShane to put the pressure on. Morgan Escare added a penalty goal early in the second half and Sam Tomkins' penalty five minutes from time proved to be decisive as it put the Warriors eight in front, meaning the Tigers needed to score twice in the last ten minutes. Mitch Clark's last-minute score proved a consolation.

The win came at the end of a week in which Wigan announced that former halfback Adrian Lam would return for 2019 as head coach until club legend Shaun Edwards took up the job in 2020.

Down the road, Warrington's 56-6 win over Catalans moved them back into third, three points behind Wigan.

Catalans made twelve changes to the team that stunned St Helens in the Cup five days earlier, handing debuts to young trio Ugo Martin, Robin Brochon and Arthur Mourgue, the latter two who were in Serbia the day before the game with France under-19s.

The Wolves left three of their own semi-final winning side out, but still had far too much for the Dragons, with Kevin Brown and Tyrone Roberts excellent in midfield and Josh Charnley and hat-trick scorer Tom Lineham causing havoc on the wings.

Back-rower Bodene Thompson, who joined from Leigh just before the signing deadline, made a solid debut.

The Dragons were still without veteran forward Greg Bird whose appeal against the severity of his four-match suspension had failed, meaning he would also miss the Challenge Cup final.

Wakefield produced a dominant and controlled second-half performance to overhaul Hull FC at KCOM Stadium by 31-13, their second impressive win over the East Yorkshire side in three weeks to keep themselves mathematically in the hunt for a semi-final berth.

Trinity found themselves 13-7 behind with just half-an-hour remaining, after a disjointed but close-run second half, but they clicked into gear, particularly in the final quarter, to run in three unanswered tries, from Bill Tupou, Pauli Pauli and Tom Johnstone. It was Hull's fifth straight defeat, effectively ending their campaign.

Super 8s, The Qualifiers - Round 1

The first game of the Qualifiers on the Thursday night indicated this year would provide the most fiercely-fought competition to date as London Broncos stunned Super League Widnes on their own patch, with Jarrod Sammut landing a field goal with just 48 seconds remaining to seal a 21-20 win.

The Broncos finished second in the Championship table after the regular campaign on points difference over Toulouse and were unbeaten in their previous eight games. But at 14-4 behind on 55 minutes, superior Super League fitness looked destined to carry the Vikings home.

Widnes led 6-0 at half-time through an Olly Ashall-Bott try on the half-hour and then extended their lead to 14-4 after London hit back with a Mark Ioane try, two Krisnan Inu goals and a Chris Dean try stretching their lead.

But three tries in eight minutes, one from Daniel Harrison and two from Kieran Dixon, without reply put the Broncos in front, before Inu's try levelled at 20-all and set up the finale.

There was further disappointment for Widnes late on as new signing Charlie Gubb picked up a knee injury and had to crawl off the field.

The night after, Salford struck a telling blow with a 28-10 win at Hull KR.

There had been little between the sides in the first 50 minutes, with Niall Evalds' opening score cancelled out by a Craig Hall touchdown and two Salford penalty goals giving them a slender lead. However a 90-metre Robert Lui interception broke the game wide open in the 56th minute. From there the physically dominant Salford side managed the game in textbook fashion through the kicking game of the impressive Jackson Hastings, with debutant Joey Lussick and Josh Wood going over late on to seal the win for a Red Devils side that had looked dead in the water until their round 23 win over Leeds.

The Rhinos got off to a flying start too, albeit against Championship opposition, as they beat Toulouse at home by 48-22. But it was far from plain sailing as Olympique played a thrilling brand of football and had Stanislas Robin not bombed a try that would have given them a 22-20 lead there could have been a different outcome.

But the Rhinos regrouped and physically drained their opponents, with Richie Myler the chief in turning the screw and Brad Dwyer best exploiting the resulting space created. With three tries in seven minutes after the hour mark the Rhinos pulled away.

Another negative for Toulouse coach Sylvain Houles was a broken foot to experienced forward Eddy Pettybourne.

Toronto had run away with the Championship and the Canadian High Commission had agreed to take special measures to ensure the Qualifiers, in which the Wolfpack would play four home games, were not disrupted by the Canadian immigration authorities refusing to grant visas to players who had minor criminal convictions. Several Championship clubs had to leave players at home earlier in the season after visas were refused.

In week one Toronto travelled to Halifax, the only part-time team in the competition, and recorded a hard-fought 14-0 win. Tries to Andy Ackers and Andrew Dixon either side of the break proved the difference. But prolific winger Liam Kay was out for the rest of the season with a broken ankle.

Super League Super 8s - Round 2

St Helens recovered their composure after two straight defeats with a 36-16 win at Wakefield in the Thursday TV game.

The runaway league leaders spent a prolonged spell in the first half on the back foot as Trinity started well and restricted them to long spells in their own half. But the minute Wakefield's standards dipped, Saints ruthlessly cut them to ribbons. Three tries in ten minutes before the break, two from Tommy Makinson and one from Jonny Lomax, to make it 16-0, ultimately won them the game, though they had to come up with two key second-half scores - one while Trinity prop Craig Huby was in the sin bin - to snuff out potential comebacks.

Wakefield's chances of the semi-finals were just about gone but Huddersfield found themselves within four points of the top four after a sixth consecutive win, this one a 26-6 home success over Hull FC.

On a drizzly Friday night, the sides were locked at 0-0 at half-time after a 40-minute battle where neither team was able to create a clear-cut opening. The deadlock was finally broken three minutes after the break when Josh Griffin lost the ball trying to run away from his own line and Danny Brough sent Alex Mellor scampering across the line.

Within two minutes Lee Gaskell was in again for the Giants, after supporting an Adam O'Brien break, and Brough added the 1,000th two-pointer of his career to simultaneously move into seventh place in the all-time scorers list - a point ahead of former Hull KR and Featherstone favourite Cyril Kellett.

Bureta Faraimo got a try and goal back but further scores to Ryan Hinchcliffe and Ukuma Ta'ai saw the Giants home.

It was a sixth straight defeat for Hull, missing their three main creators, Marc Sneyd, Jake Connor and Albert Kelly.

Castleford's 28-18 win over Warrington meant the Wolves were the team in the Giants' sights.

Wembley-bound Warrington, barely in the contest in the first half, during which Castleford established a 16-0 lead through tries from James Clare, Junior Moors and Greg Eden, responded by clawing their way back to 16-12 within seven minutes of the resumption. Kevin Brown set up Stefan Ratchford and Bryson Goodwin as the visitors made a great start to the second half.

The reintroduction of props Liam Watts and Grant Millington around the hour mark helped steady the Tigers, who were rocking. The duo immediately gained the territory from which Eden scored his second try. Four minutes later Mike McMeeken powered over before Ratchford went over for a late consolation for the Wire.

Warrington's Wembley opponents, Catalans Dragons, found Wigan too hot to handle in Perpignan, losing 35-6.

A one-sided affair was marred by an early blow for Wigan winger Liam Marshall, who had to be helped from the pitch with a season-ending ACL injury.

Sam Tomkins had his future fans in Perpignan standing to applaud a fullback masterclass. An 80th-minute field goal provided a fitting finish to a composed and controlled performance by the Dragons' star signing for 2019.

Super 8s, The Qualifiers - Round 2

Hull KR became the first Super League side to play in Toronto, and they avoided a 0-2 start to the Qualifiers with a dramatic 28-22 victory over the Wolfpack, becoming just the second team to beat Toronto on Canadian soil.

Andrew Dixon scored a pair of tries for the Wolfpack but it was Hull KR's defence that won the day as they consistently foiled the home side throughout the match. Former Wolfpack captain Craig Hall was also a thorn in his former club's side as he converted a pair of penalties and scored a first-half try. Another first-half intercept try, from Junior Vaivai - on the back of Rovers fullback Adam Quinlan's pace and awareness - gave Hull KR a 14-6 half-time lead after Wolfpack winger Nick Rawsthorne opened the try-scoring.

Dixon's first try and three Gareth O'Brien goals gave Toronto a 16-14 lead but Chris Atkin and Chris Clarkson completed the Robins' scoring before Dixon's second set up a pulsating last few minutes, capped off by Hall's late penalty goal.

Salford Red Devils came from behind to win 32-6 and ruthlessly condemn struggling Widnes to back-to-back losses in the second stage of the campaign.

Charly Runciman's early try put the visitors ahead but Salford, with Jackson Hastings once again a standout, exploited Widnes' right edge to score twice through

Junior Sa'u and move ahead. Further tries by Rob Lui, Niall Evalds and Mark Flanagan secured the win

The Vikings had now lost 15 consecutive games dating all the way back to April. A season-ending knee injury to fullback Olly Ashall-Bott was another blow for the Vikings.

Toulouse Olympique picked up their first points of the Qualifiers with a comprehensive 28-6 home victory against Halifax. Late recruit, Italy international Chris Centrone continued his impressive form with two tries, while Paul Marcon, Stanislas Robin and Anthony Marion also crossed.

Centrone's solo effort on 33 minutes saw him beat just about every opponent from 60 metres out. Dan Fleming got a late consolation try that Shane Grady goaled.

Leeds had little trouble getting their second win as they outclassed London Broncos 48-32 in sunny Ealing, a late burst of four tries from the Broncos making the final score more respectable.

Leading 28-6 at the break - Joel Moon scoring a genuine hat-trick with the first three tries of the game - thanks to an extremely accomplished display, the chance of the Rhinos surrendering a lead of that scale, which was extended to 48-10 at one stage, always seemed remote.

Challenge Cup Final

Catalans Dragons created Wembley history on the last Saturday of August, becoming the first non-English club to win the Challenge Cup with a 20-14 win over Warrington.

With the Marseillaise being sung before the game and the Dragons having received a message of support from the French President Emmanuel Macron, it was always going to be a different final.

As well as Catalans becoming the first French club to win the Challenge Cup, their fullback Tony Gigot became the first French player to win the Lance Todd Trophy.

Gigot played a vital role in the Catalans' victory, as he had done in the semi-final hammering of St Helens. And it wasn't until February that the Avignon-born fullback, who rejoined Catalans in 2015, was able to resume his career after winning an appeal against the suspension, previously reduced to three months before it was restored in full, for an 'inappropriate exchange' with an anti-doping official in 2016.

Michael McIlorum, Lewis Tierney and Remi Casty also caught the eye for the

BETFRED SUPER LEAGUE - SUPER 8s
Sunday 19th August

	P	W	D	L	F	A	D	Pts
St Helens	25	22	0	3	761	330	431	44
Wigan Warriors	25	18	0	7	632	373	259	36
Castleford Tigers	25	16	1	8	617	522	95	33
Warrington Wolves	25	15	1	9	605	444	161	31
Huddersfield Giants	25	13	1	11	469	647	-178	27
Wakefield Trinity	25	11	1	13	628	555	73	23
Hull FC	25	11	0	14	553	601	-48	22
Catalans Dragons	25	10	1	14	500	622	-122	21

SUPER 8s - THE QUALIFIERS
Sunday 19th August

	P	W	D	L	F	A	D	Pts
Salford Red Devils	2	2	0	0	60	16	44	4
Leeds Rhinos	2	2	0	0	96	54	42	4
Toronto Wolfpack	2	1	0	1	36	28	8	2
Toulouse Olympique	2	1	0	1	50	54	-4	2
Hull Kingston Rovers	2	1	0	1	38	50	-12	2
London Broncos	2	1	0	1	53	68	-15	2
Widnes Vikings	2	0	0	2	26	53	-27	0
Halifax	2	0	0	2	6	42	-36	0

LADBROKES CHALLENGE CUP FINAL

Saturday 25th August 2018

CATALANS DRAGONS 20 WARRINGTON WOLVES 14

DRAGONS: 31 Tony Gigot; 20 Lewis Tierney; 1 David Mead; 4 Brayden Wiliame; 5 Fouad Yaha; 6 Samisoni Langi; 33 Josh Drinkwater; 15 Mickael Simon; 19 Michael McIlorum; 10 Sam Moa; 21 Benjamin Jullien; 12 Benjamin Garcia; 8 Remi Casty (C). Subs (all used): 14 Julian Bousquet; 17 Jason Baitieri; 34 Kenny Edwards; 32 Mickael Goudemand.
Tries: Tierney (2), Garcia (34), Wiliame (46);
Goals: Drinkwater 4/4.
WOLVES: 1 Stefan Ratchford; 2 Tom Lineham; 3 Bryson Goodwin; 18 Toby King; 27 Josh Charnley; 6 Kevin Brown; 7 Tyrone Roberts; 8 Chris Hill (C); 9 Daryl Clark; 10 Mike Cooper; 20 Harvey Livett; 12 Jack Hughes; 34 Ben Westwood. Subs (all used): 13 Ben Murdoch-Masila; 19 George King; 15 Declan Patton; 17 Joe Philbin.
Tries: Murdoch-Masila (28), G King (56); **Goals:** Roberts 3/3.
Rugby Leaguer & League Express Men of the Match:
Dragons: Tony Gigot; *Wolves:* Toby King.
Penalty count: 6-10; **Half-time:** 14-6; **Referee:** Robert Hicks;
Attendance: 50,672 *(at Wembley Stadium).*

winners as a 100 per cent completion rate in the first half laid the foundation for the Catalans' win.

The Dragons couldn't have wished for a better start. Hardly 100 seconds had elapsed when Stefan Ratchford dropped Samisoni Langi's towering kick. The Catalans pounced on the ball for a repeat set and, before the Wolves had restored order in their defensive line, David Mead and Benjamin Jullien combined brilliantly to put Tierney over in the right corner.

The opening stages were a sign of what was to come for the Wolves. Their first-half display was clumsy and tentative. They looked, for large parts, spooked by the occasion.

Catalans did not. They were dominant, pugnacious and played with fiery intent. It soon forced Ben Westwood to surrender a penalty in front of his own posts for holding down Sam Moa which saw Josh Drinkwater extend the lead to eight points with his second goal.

Eventually, Warrington worked their way into the game. But while their nerves perhaps faded, their lack of composure did not, as evidenced by Kevin Brown's woefully flung out pass to Tom Lineham when they'd got the ball back from an unclaimed kick. And they had a try ruled out when Lineham's score in the corner was ruled out by the video referee due to an obstruction by decoy runner Joe Philbin on Langi.

The Wolves did score next, however. A high kick from Ratchford saw the ball drop loose after Fouad Yaha and Toby King contested the aerial duel and that allowed Ben Murdoch-Masila to pick up and score with his first touch, with video referee Ben Thaler approving the try when he confirmed that King hadn't knocked it forward.

That was the foothold Warrington needed in the game. Six minutes later they relinquished it. Ben Garcia's forceful scoot from close range saw him roll the ball down the boot of Ratchford and over the try line, video referral again needed. Drinkwater's conversion made in 14-6 at the break.

Gigot set up the try that effectively won Catalans the Cup six minutes into the second half. A majestic 40/20, followed by a sweet delayed short pass, saw Brayden Wiliame claw his way over the line. A 14-point lead was established, and the trophy was heading across the Channel.

Warrington had other ideas though. They were handed a lifeline ten minutes later. Brown's reverse kick was spilt by Drinkwater, allowing Tyrone Roberts to pick the ball up and offload to George King to score.

Catalans became nervy. Their 100 per cent completion rate took a nosedive. They started dropping the ball and conceding penalties. Warrington's following began to roar in anticipation.

But by the fortune of luck and sheer will the French side clung on. Warrington did themselves no favours with their toothless attack, which was evident by their decision to opt for two when trailing by eight points. While the Dragons were desperate, they remained resolute. To a man, they defended like their lives, like history, depended on it. The one time they were breached, Ben Westwood failed to cling on to Roberts' hard pass.

When Gigot, with blood smeared on his face, claimed a low grubber kick with a minute to go, the Catalans fans celebrated frantically.

SEPTEMBER
Saints march in

Super League Super 8s - Round 3

St Helens would have lifted the League Leaders' Shield on the first Friday of September had they beaten Wigan at home but, instead, the Warriors reduced the gap between the pair to six points with a stunning 30-10 victory over their old enemy.

Former Saint Joe Greenwood was the gamestar after some destructive contributions out wide, his back row partner John Bateman his usual bustling presence, George Williams back to his best at stand-off and hooker Sam Powell non-stop in the middle. And Morgan Escare produced some vital plays after being a late call-up for Sam Tomkins, who injured a knee in the warm-up.

Dan Sarginson's double and Bateman's try before Tommy Makinson's reply put Wigan 14-4 ahead at the break. Makinson's stunning finish for his spectacular 40th minute try was spectacular as he took Danny Richardson's kick over the head of Oliver Gildart, spun and managed to plant the ball in the corner.

But any chance of a Saints comeback was snuffed out moments after the restart as Tom Davies nudged over for Wigan's fourth.

Makinson clawed a second try back for Saints after a brilliant one-handed offload from Louie McCarthy-Scarsbrook and, with 30 minutes to play, there were only eight points in it.

But Wigan turned on the class in the closing quarter, Gildart stunning the home crowd with a try from inside own half as he sprinted and outfoxed Ben Barba to cross the try line.

Sean O'Loughlin then made it a night to remember for the Warriors as he crashed over from close range for his first try of the season.

Bryson Goodwin scored five of Warrington's 14 tries on the Thursday as they demolished Hull 80-10 at the Halliwell Jones Stadium, just five days after their Challenge Cup Final defeat to Catalans Dragons.

Warrington played at a tempo and pace that Hull couldn't respond to and they cut the Black and Whites to shreds with six well-worked tries in the first half to effectively wrap the game up.

It was Hull's heaviest defeat of the Super League era and their seventh in succession. In the days after, Hull FC owner Adam Pearson insisted he would stick by under-fire coach Lee Radford, but pledged a squad shake-up.

The Wolves' semi-final spot looked secure after Huddersfield's faint top-four hopes were ruined by Wakefield on the same night, with a 42-16 defeat ending their six-match winning run and leaving them six points behind Warrington with four games to play.

Trinity wore down their hosts by throwing the ball around and tiring out the Giants' big pack, overturning 12-0 and then 16-6 deficits with 36 unanswered points in the second half, with a Tom Johnstone interception try six minutes into the second half reversing the game's momentum.

Wakefield's win overshadowed Danny Brough's latest incursion into the record books. Brough's 13th minute conversion of the Giants' opening try made the Scottish international Super League's fourth highest all-time points scorer, overhauling Pat Richards' tally of 2,284

Catalans' post-Wembley celebrations meant they weren't at their best when they travelled to Castleford on the following Friday, the Tigers winning 36-4.

Greg Eden led the way with a hat-trick. Michael Shenton, Jake Trueman and Oliver Holmes, after a classic defence-to-attack move, also crossed. Luke Gale also kicked six goals on his return after four months out. Gale, making his 100th appearance for Castleford, was playing his first game since the match with Wakefield on 27th April. And Ben Roberts was on the bench for his first outing since the fixture with Wigan in the same month.

Castleford, chasing a top-two finish and subsequent home semi-final, were now back to within three points of second-placed Wigan.

Super 8s, The Qualifiers - Round 3

The prospect of Widnes being relegated after a seven-year spell in Super League loomed large after a 44-22 defeat at Championship Toulouse.

The Vikings fell behind early when playmaker Johnathon Ford created the first of two tries for fullback Mark Kheirallah, who added the goal. Centre Krisnan Inu pulled a try back for the visitors shortly afterwards after being put through a gap by stand-off Joe Mellor and they took the lead on 25 minutes when back rower Harrison Hansen forced his way over.

Inu added the conversion to make it 10-6 but Toulouse hit back through Kheirallah, who collected Ford's kick over the defence for his second score. Then Chris Centrone picked up a loose ball to race the full length of the field and Kheirallah converted both tries to stretch the French club's lead to 18-10 at the break.

Widnes got back to within two points early in the second half when halfback Tom Gilmore put second-rower Weller Hauraki through a gap for their third try, with Inu adding the goal. Gil Dudson, who was Vikings captain for the day on his 200th professional appearance limped off on 53 minutes as Toulouse looked to break free from the Vikings' period of dominance.

An exquisite kick over the top from Stanislas Robin towards the posts was met by the rangy Ford on 58 minutes. He plucked the ball out of the air with three defenders looking on and touched down under the posts. Kheirallah converted with ease to stretch the lead back to eight points.

A couple of minutes later Widnes suffered a blow as the inspirational Aaron Heremaia limped off. Further tries from Centrone and Robin sealed it. Lloyd White pulled a try back for the Vikings eight minutes from time but Toulouse had the last word when halfback William Barthau went over for their seventh try and Kheirallah took his goal tally to seven as he finished with a 22-point haul.

The long, hot summer continued as Leeds and Hull KR fought out an end-to-end encounter, with the Robins ending 38-36 winners at Headingley, with Craig Hall finishing with a try hat-trick, fullback Adam Quinlan outstanding.

Jackson Hastings was in majestic form once again on the Sunday as the Red Devils notched up their third straight win in the Qualifiers with a 62-4 hammering of Halifax at the Shay. Hastings scored twice and created many others in a masterful performance that further emphasised his value to the Red Devils. Winger Derrell Olpherts finished with a hat-trick.

And over in Toronto, the Wolfpack made it two wins from three with a 34-22 win over London Broncos, after leading 20-0 at half-time. Four tries in ten minutes in the second half from London made for a nervy end to the match for the home supporters.

September

Super League Super 8s - Round 4

The top-four teams were decided after Warrington edged a 26-24 Friday-night, home win over Huddersfield.

The lead changed hands several times throughout the match though neither side looked comfortable whenever they had established an advantage. Ultimately, the difference between the two teams was their goal-kicking. While the vast majority of Danny Brough's conversion attempts for Huddersfield were out wide and difficult to land, Warrington managed to score more of their tries centrally, making it easier to add the points.

Jake Mamo, playing on the right wing, scored a first-half hat-trick but Ryan Atkins, playing his first game since June, and Bryson Goodwin tries kept Warrington in touch.

Stefan Ratchford and Tom Lineham crossed for Wire after the break, and Goodwin restored their eight-point lead after Lee Gaskell's try for Giants. Jake Wardle went over to reduce the gap to two points with three minutes to go but Brough couldn't level with the conversion.

On the full-time hooter, Warrington were penalised for holding down in the ruck and Brough had another opportunity to level the scores but his attempt from out wide on the halfway line fell agonisingly short.

Wigan remained favourites to finish second after a 25-10 Thursday-night home win over Wakefield.

Oliver Gildart went over after just 82 seconds and Wigan led 10-0 at one stage thanks to a short-range Sam Powell try. But Trinity deservedly got back in the game before half-time thanks to a breakaway try from Tom Johnstone just seconds after Trinity were reduced to twelve men when Matty Ashurst was sin-binned for a crusher tackle.

Until that point the Warriors were unbreakable in defence, with Joe Greenwood, Romain Navarrete, Dan Sarginson and John Bateman all making telling contributions.

In the second half, Wakefield continued to ask questions of the Wigan defence, despite a final 13-4 penalty count against them, with Tyler Randell impressing. They trailed by just three points heading into the final 20 minutes, but late tries from Morgan Escare and Joe Greenwood saw the Warriors home.

Before the game there was a minute's silence for the younger brother of Wigan centre Dan Sarginson, who made the decision to play just days after his sibling's death.

Wakefield also had Scott Grix yellow carded in the second half but both he and Ashurst escaped censure. Joe Greenwood however was subsequently banned for one game for dangerous contact.

That week Zak Hardaker began pre-season training with the Warriors. The former Castleford and England fullback had been suspended for 14 months, having tested positive for cocaine towards the end of the previous season. He would be available from the start of the 2019 season for his new club.

Wigan could still theoretically catch leaders Saints, who sneaked a late 26-22 win at Catalans on the Saturday.

Catalans were ahead for long periods of the game but a decision to award a scrum to the visitors two minutes from time, which led to the match-winning try by Morgan Knowles, resulted in an explosion of anger from Dragons supporters. Coach Steve McNamara blamed the referee too.

 Saints, with James Roby and Ben Barba rested, trailed 22-14 with ten minutes to go. But gamestar Jonny Lomax, playing at fullback, was on hand to support a Mark Percival break down the left and then, after that crucial scrum call, Knowles took a short ball from Theo Fages and spun through the Dragons' defence on 78 minutes to strike the killer blow, with Danny Richardson converting both tries.

Castleford secured their top-four spot with a 28-8 win at Hull FC, who, still missing nine members of their first team, were much improved from their humiliation at Warrington the week before.

Mike McMeeken went over to put Tigers ahead, before Junior Moors powered over for the visitors' second try. Greg Eden ran in their third from 90 metres out after intercepting a pass off team-mate Michael Shenton's head. Tries from Eden and James Clare further extended the lead, before Carlos Tuimavave and Hakim Miloudi crossed to restore some pride for the hosts.

Super 8s, The Qualifiers - Round 4

Salford needed just one more win to confirm Super League safety after making it four from four despite two reds cards in a 28-16 televised victory over Toronto.

Luke Burgess was dismissed for a high tackle on Jake Emmitt in the 53rd minute and Jackson Hastings followed him with 13 seconds left after his swinging arm connected directly with Gareth O'Brien's head. The Red Devils also had Lama Tasi sin-binned in the first half for another hit on O'Brien but did enough in the first 40 minutes to clinch another vital win.

With Hastings and Robert Lui to the fore, they established a 20-0 interval lead and held firm amid the Wolfpack fightback, aided by Chase Stanley's 60th minute yellow card. Red Devils winger Ed Chamberlain finished with a try, six goals from six and made several decisive defensive interventions in that second half.

Hastings, strongly linked with a move to Wigan, got a two-match penalty notice and Burgess one-match.

Leeds, who had announced David Furner as their new head coach for 2019, took a significant step towards Super League survival on the Sunday, emerging through a tense and low-quality affair at Widnes by 16-6.

It was dramatic and nerve-jangling to the end. Only when Richie Myler scored with three minutes remaining was this contest ever truly decided.

The game was tense and it wasn't until seven minutes before half-time when the deadlock was broken. Both teams had spurned glorious opportunities to go ahead, and after a loose pass was collected by Myler on the Leeds line, he passed to Luke Briscoe, who raced away from Joe Mellor to touch down.

However, Widnes came roaring back before the break. After earning a penalty, it was Tom Olbison who crashed over the top of Nathaniel Peteru, with Krisnan Inu converting to make it 6-4 at half-time.

Widnes had their chances but couldn't take them and, eventually, Leeds made them pay when, after a great piece of play from Jack Walker on the back of a Liam Sutcliffe 40/20 put Leeds in position, Matt Parcell took advantage from the quick play-the-ball to dart over.

With time ticking away, there were still huge chances for Widnes. A great kick from debutant youngster Joe Lyons found Inu and he turned the ball inside for Patrick Ah Van. All the winger had to do was collect and race away - but he dropped the ball.

It was pivotal. Within seconds, Sutcliffe had broke away down the right and turned the ball inside for Myler and Leeds were home and dry.

Coach Francis Cummins was adamant afterwards that the Vikings could win their final three games and at least shoehorn their way into a Million Pound Game place, despite a run of 17 consecutive losses.

There was a major shock in west London as the Broncos took Toulouse to the cleaners with a 34-8 win. Jarrod Sammut ran the game with his tactical kicking and landed seven goals with unerring accuracy. At 26-4 at the break the outcome was already decided.

Craig Hall helped himself to four tries at KCOM Craven Park as Hull KR survived a Halifax comeback to seal their third Qualifiers victory.

The Robins raced into a 24-0 lead inside 27 minutes but almost paid the penalty for a scrappy second half as Halifax grew in confidence after the break with some eye-catching rugby of their own.

The result came at a cost for Tim Sheens' side though as the in-form Adam Quinlan and Justin Carney picked up season-ending injuries.

September
Super League Super 8s - Round 5

St Helens secured the League Leaders Shield with two games to spare by beating Hull FC 38-12 at the Totally Wicked Stadium, the club's seventh table-topping finish of the Super League era.

Hull, for whom Jake Connor made a shock return from a hamstring injury, had threatened an upset when they fought back from 12-0 down to level the game four minutes before half-time. But Luke Thompson scored their third try moments from the break and Saints never looked back.

Saints, needing only a point to ensure they would finish top, took an early lead with tries from Mark Percival and Morgan Knowles. Jordan Lane and Brad Fash crossed for Hull, but Thompson's try steadied the Saints ship.

The hosts pulled away after half-time as two tries from Regan Grace and Percival's second, with Danny Richardson kicking seven goals, sealed the result.

Wigan remained three points clear in second with two games to go as a late trio of tries, while Tom Lineham was in the sin bin for a high tackle, produced a 26-6 home win over Warrington to make it five wins in a row.

It was a dream comeback after two years out with injury for Dom Manfredi, who crossed twice in the final nine minutes, while Ryan Sutton also scored after George Williams' goal had given them a two-point lead.

Thomas Leuluai's try on 38 minutes from John Bateman's kick through, which resulted in a dislocated finger, was the only score of a bruising first half. Stefan Ratchford's score 14 minutes after the break when he chased down Tyrone Roberts' disguised short grubber, with Sam Tomkins in the sin bin for dissent, put the Wire in the contest, before the late flurry.

For the Wolves, forward Luis Johnson made an impressive debut from the bench.

Castleford finished with a flourish to end up 44-12 winners at home to Huddersfield, missing the potent right-wing pairing of Leroy Cudjoe and Jermaine McGillvary.

Prop Junior Moors was the star of the show with two tries as the Tigers came from 12-4 down to win 44-12 and give them a faint hope of catching second-placed Wigan.

Luke Gale was a late withdrawal with a minor leg strain but not for the first time 19-year-old Jake Trueman excelled. At times, the game-management of the teenager was inch-perfect, as was his kicking game. He played a major role in taking the game away from Huddersfield, with a hand in a number of the five second-half tries which put a hint of gloss on the scoreline.

Wakefield moved into fifth and ensured a top-six finish at least with a 34-22 home win over Catalans.

Winger Tom Johnstone led the charge with a hat-trick as Trinity scored three vital, quick-fire tries in the ten minutes before half-time to lay a platform for victory.

The Cup winners, who'd been so cruelly undone by St Helens a week earlier, played their part in a tight contest for the first half-hour but an acrobatic score from Johnstone, followed by tries from Tyler Randall and Reece Lyne quickly afterwards, handed Trinity a cushion they wouldn't relinquish.

When Johnstone scored his third try after 49 minutes it looked all over at 34-12. But David Mead got a try back chasing a Lucas Albert grubber and with Ryan Hampshire having kicked only three of his conversion attempts, the Dragons were a chance.

In a chaotic last fifteen minutes they got closer after Craig Huby was sin-binned for a high tackle on Mickael Simon, as Brayden Wiliame scythed through for a try.

Almost as soon as Huby returned he was met with a high tackle from Simon and after the ensuing melee Simon and Jacob Miller were red-carded. There was still time for the Dragons to go close during another set-to involving Huby, this time with Jason Baitieri and in the scramble Johnstone ended up prone with a knee injury. After ten minutes of treatment, the winger was on his feet and managed to walk off.

Super 8s, The Qualifiers - Round 5

A last-minute Liam Sutcliffe penalty from 25 metres out gave Leeds an 18-16 home win over Salford to draw the sides level at the top of the Qualifiers.

Salford coach Ian Watson felt aggrieved that the late indiscretion, a challenge on Richie Myler, was pulled up and insisted his side should have had a cast-iron shot at goal of their own in a dramatic finale after Jack Walker lost Robert Lui's high kick and Nathaniel Peteru then held out debutant Jansin Turgut.

'I think we were robbed in the end, if I'm honest,' said Watson. But victory was as much down to the intervening set between those decisions at either end of the field and Matt Parcell's heroic charge-down to thwart Lui's shot at a field goal, after Craig Kopczak had been held up.

In another tense encounter, Tom Briscoe and Jimmy Keinhorst tries, with Niall Evalds in reply, gave the Rhinos an 8-4 first-half lead. Tries were then traded again, as Briscoe's second was cancelled out by Greg Burke and Derrell Olpherts scores. The draw seemed likely before Sutcliffe slotted home the decider.

That seemed a likely outcome too across the Atlantic as the Wolfpack attracted a crowd of 7,923 to the Lamport Stadium, clinching a 13-12 victory over Toulouse with a field goal from Gareth O'Brien in the 77th minute of the game.

A missed, highly kickable conversion from William Barthau after Toulouse tied the match in the 72nd minute opened the door for O'Brien.

Level 8-8 at the break, Toronto went ahead early in the second half with a Chase Stanley try and then absorbed Toulouse pressure until a Stanislas Robin try in the 71st minute made it 12-12.

The game wasn't without controversy, with the Wolfpack's opening try by winger Mason Caton-Brown being incorrectly awarded, when slow-motion replays clearly indicated he lost control of the ball over the line.

And Wolfpack forward Jack Bussey was in hot water after being caught biting the ear of Toulouse's Bastien Ader. Bussey was suspended for eight games after pleading guilty to the offence. He also got an extra two matches for a high tackle on Barthau.

Hull KR were one step away from safety as James Greenwood's double edged them closer to Super League survival with a hard-fought 30-18 home, Saturday evening win over London Broncos.

A week after holding off a Halifax comeback, Rovers again kept their nerve as a spirited Broncos side battled back from 20-6 down at half-time to trail by just two points heading into the final ten minutes, when Greenwood's second and a late Junior Vaivai score saw the Robins home.

A fine performance from Krisnan Inu kept Widnes Vikings' slim Super League hopes alive for another week and ended the club's 17-match losing run with a 26-12 home win over Halifax.

Not since breezing past League 1 Coventry Bears in the Challenge Cup in April had the Vikings had chance to sing their post-match winning song. They were significantly tested at times by a committed and well-organised Halifax side that was led around the park by wily veteran Scott Murrell. But Inu's two tries and an assist were ultimately the difference between the teams, and it meant the Vikings are not yet officially condemned to relegation.

* On the 14th September, an extraordinary general meeting of the RFL Council in Salford voted to scrap the Super 8s system after four seasons and revert to one up-one down promotion to Super League, with the season ending in top-five play-off to decide the champions.

Super League Super 8s - Round 6

With the top four spots already decided the Super 8s took on a dead rubber sheen and made most people think that a reversion to the top-five play-off system from 2019 might be a good thing.

September

That's not to say there was no entertainment, particularly on the Saturday afternoon when St Helens went to Warrington for an enticing semi-final dress rehearsal, which the League Leaders won 34-14.

A 13th-minute bust up after Matty Lees accidentally made contact with his knee on a stumbling Tyrone Roberts set the tone for a feisty first half. Lees was sin-binned and was joined by teammate Mark Percival and Warrington's Ryan Atkins, who had both run to join the melee. All had no charge to face the following week.

Roberts left the field for good with a concussion and Kevin Brown suffered a hamstring problem and missed the second half. Brown's try had opened the scoring on 23 minutes but two tries in the final ten minutes of the first half, from Luke Douglas and Regan Grace, gave Saints the lead and, after the break, they were red hot. Three quick-fire tries between the 51st and 58th minutes put St Helens in the ascendency and they saw the game out comfortably from there.

After the game, Saints coach Justin Holbrook insisted Ben Barba was over the niggling injuries that had contributed to a downturn in form. Barba scored twice and appeared back to his best.

St Helens would have home advantage two weeks later and Wigan guaranteed they would be the other home semi-finalist after a hard-fought 13-6 win at Huddersfield on a rainy Thursday night.

Both sides were plagued by handling errors in a near constant deluge, keeping scoring chances at a premium. Morgan Escare, who came into the starting line-up after Tommy Leuluai was a late withdrawal through injury, took one of those by evading Lee Gaskell to score in the first half. And when he slotted over a field goal just after the hour mark it created a two-score lead that was always likely to be enough in the wet conditions.

Kruise Leeming forced his way over from dummy-half to close the gap to one point with Danny Brough's conversion on 71 minutes. But any hopes the Giants had of mounting a stirring late comeback evaporated when Brough was sin-binned for a high tackle on Escare. In the ensuing set, Oliver Gildart touched down George Williams' kick to confirm Wigan's win.

The following night, Greg Eden raced over for four tries and Luke Gale landed seven goals from as many attempts as Castleford clinched third place and a play-off semi-final at Wigan with a 42-10 home win over weakened Wakefield.

Trinity lacked stand-off Jacob Miller, a flu victim, and also badly missed the likes of props David Fifita and Anthony England, together with free-scoring winger Tom Johnstone (knee), although Ben Jones-Bishop, who missed the previous week's game at Wigan because of the birth of his child, was back in the side.

And their prospects were further hit by the departure of fullback Scott Grix in the early stages with a suspected fractured cheekbone after he tackled Michael Shenton close to the line.

The Tigers were 18-0 up before the opening quarter was out and although Trinity subsequently offered more resistance, the damage was done in a game which only went ahead through tremendous work by the Castleford ground staff after heavy rain in the previous 24 hours.

Tigers centre Jake Webster was seen off in style following his last match at the Mend-A-Hose Jungle. The 34-year-old former New Zealand international, who was moving to Bradford, was given a grand finale when his teammates performed a haka in tribute.

On the Saturday evening two tries in the last six minutes, after Hull had gone in front for the first time with nine minutes left, helped Catalans snatch a dramatic 26-20 victory, their first since beating Warrington in the Ladbrokes Challenge Cup Final, ending a six-match losing run in Super League.

Hull FC looked likely winners when, on 70 minutes, winger Bureta Faraimo burst through from inside his own half and, on reaching the Dragons' 20, fed hooker Danny

Houghton, who sent fullback Jamie Shaul over the line,. Scrum-half Jake Connor landed his second goal to help the home side go 20-16 up.

But just three minutes later Catalans regained the lead, with Kenny Edwards and loose forward Greg Bird linking to send Iain Thornley down the touchline, the winger putting centre Brayden Wiliame over with his inside pass. Josh Drinkwater was unable to add the conversion and a draw, which would possibly have been the fairest result in an error-strewn game, looked the most likely outcome. However, Catalans hooker Michael McIlorum and Bird combined in midfield to work space for substitute Edwards to tear onto Bird's neat pass, his well-chosen angle completely wrong-footing the home side. Edwards, approaching Shaul at pace, easily rounded the fullback to dive under the posts for a score that effectively ended Hull's hopes.

Super 8s, The Qualifiers - Round 6

The real excitement of the weekend came in the Qualifiers, when the table was put into turmoil by three games played in different countries.

Widnes's seven-year stay in Super League was ended on the Saturday after they suffered a 20-12 defeat to the Wolfpack in front of a crowd of over eight thousand people at Lamport Stadium in Toronto.

The match was back and forth throughout, finely poised at 10-8 to the home side at half-time, but a try scored by Blake Wallace in the 57th minute and a pair of penalties converted by Gareth O'Brien allowed Toronto to pull away.

On the same Saturday afternoon there was a massive shock in wet west London as the Broncos shocked Salford with an 11-8 win.

Two early scores gave London an edge they never lost. The first, an eleventh minute penalty followed a fumble from Luke Burgess in London territory. An improvised mixture of handling, scramble and calculated footwork drove the Broncos forward 60 metres to where Salford offended and Jarrod Sammut landed the goal.

Two minutes later Jay Pitts, apparently held above the Salford line, corkscrewed downwards through two defenders for the try and Sammut kicked the goal to make it 8-0. London conceded a plethora of penalties, culminating with the sin-binning of Eddie Battye as they offended once too often. But Salford made nothing of their advantage, instead falling further behind in the final seconds of Battye's ten-minute absence. Sammut's cool 20-metre field goal was a single point worth far more in terms of what it said of London's control, making it 9-0 at the interval.

Greg Johnson got a try back but Eloi Pelissier's quick thinking earned a penalty chance, which Sammut converted unerringly from 20 metres, taking their lead back to seven points.

Johnson, again given space by Kris Welham, dived over with three minutes to go, making for a tense finale. But Ed Chamberlain sliced the conversion from the far left, which might have taken them to within a point, and the chance of guaranteeing Super League survival with a last-gasp field goal.

Later in the day Hull KR were 19-0 ahead in Toulouse but then conceded 34 consecutive points to throw the Qualifiers wide open going into the final round.

The Robins were comfortably placed when Chris Atkin went over for their third try on 24 minutes, with Danny Tickle's goal taking their lead out to 19-0. But the game was turned on its head after Toulouse scored three tries in six minutes just before half-time.

Second-rower Rhys Curran, centre Chris Centrone and halfback Stanislas Robin all went over for tries which were converted by Mark Kheirallah to bring his side to within a point at 19-18. And with stand-off Johnathon Ford continuing to run the show Olympique came home under a wet sail to the delight of the 4,127 crowd at Stade Ernest Argeles.

The shock defeat meant Hull KR were now fourth in the Qualifiers, behind Toronto and needed to put plenty of points on Widnes the next weekend to avoid the dreaded Million Pound Game.

September

Only Leeds had secured a Super League spot for 2019 as they registered a 34-6 win at Halifax. They were held 6-6 at half-time after Richie Myler's opening try had been cancelled out by Steve Tyrer converting his own try. But Leeds surged clear in the second half with five more, two from Brad Dwyer and the rest from Liam Sutcliffe, Cameron Smith and Luke Briscoe.

That week the Rhinos announced that David Furner was to be their head coach from 2019, 15 years on from playing in the club's 2004 Grand Final-winning side.

Super League Super 8s - Round 7

Liam Farrell made his return from a shoulder injury after ten weeks out as Wigan became the first (and with the ditching of the system, last) ever team to win all seven Super 8s fixtures as they beat Hull FC 14-12 at the DW Stadium.

It wasn't a classic. The first half was a slow burner that only got going when Hull went 12-0 in front after 29 minutes thanks to tries from Carlos Tuimavave and Jamie Shaul, both converted by Jake Connor, before Gabe Hamlin reduced the deficit to six before the break. The Warriors were the superior side after the break with tries from Dan Sarginson and Oliver Gildart sealing the win.

The end of the season couldn't have come soon enough for Hull FC. They had lost their last eleven games.

Off the field, Wigan were rocked by the news that Zak Hardaker, who had started training with the Warriors, was to appear in court after being arrested for drink driving. Hardaker, who was suspended by Castleford two days before last year's Grand Final, was due to appear in court two days before this year's event.

St Helens headed into the semi-finals on the back of a four-game winning streak after shutting out an underperforming Castleford Tigers on the same Friday night, finishing 26-0 winners, with Ben Barba getting another two tries to finish Super League's top try-scorer with 28.

That week Saints announced they had signed former Penrith and North Queensland fullback Lachlan Coote on a three-year deal following the confirmed departure of Ben Barba to the Cowboys.

Four second-half tries by David Mead sealed a rollercoaster season for the Catalans Dragons with a 22-12 home win over Huddersfield after being behind 12-0 at half-time.

In unusually cool and damp conditions in Perpignan, the Catalans once again blew hot and cold but Mead's incredible try-surge after the break ensured a convincing victory.

That week Jermaine McGillvary signed a new contract extension with the Giants until the end of the 2022 campaign.

Huddersfield's defeat meant that Wakefield finished in fifth position for the second year running, even though they had lost 36-23 at home to Warrington the night before.

The Wolves were without halfbacks Tyrone Roberts and Kevin Brown but managed to come back from a 13-12 half-time deficit to pull away in the second half.

They took the lead in controversial circumstances. Wakefield attempted a free play after they thought the Wolves had knocked on but dropped the ball themselves inside their own '20'. Stefan Ratchford kicked forward and scored.

It left Wakefield reeling and minutes later they were hit with another sucker-punch as a Declan Patton grubber took a few ricochets and presented itself for Jack Hughes to score under the sticks. Suddenly, Warrington were eleven points ahead and that was enough to carry them home.

* That week League Express confirmed Castleford halfback Jake Trueman as Albert Goldthorpe Rookie of the Year in the week that the Albert Goldthorpe Medal itself was won by Warrington Wolves fullback Stefan Ratchford.

Super 8s, The Qualifiers - Round 7

Jackson Hastings' cult hero status at Salford reached new levels as he guided the Red Devils to Super League safety with a memorable 44-10 Thursday-night home win over Toulouse.

The Australian halfback was returning from a two-match ban, with Ian Watson's side having stumbled in his absence in narrow defeats to Leeds and London. But he made it six wins from his six appearances for the club so far, scoring a first-half try and kicking seven goals. The end of the game saw him mobbed by Salford supporters and chair-lifted around, having already given away most of his playing kit.

Toulouse recovered from 14-0 down - Hastings opening the scoring with a rare eight-point try when Olympique fullback Mark Kheirallah needlessly carried on with the tackle after the halfback had touched down - to trail by just four early in the second half. But they failed to make the most of their attacking opportunities at that point, mainly because of Salford's defensive line speed. The big defeat meant that London would have to lose at home to Halifax by 25 points on the Saturday night for Toulouse to make the Million Pound Game.

The Broncos didn't, winning 23-16, despite win-less Halifax racing into an early 12-0 lead. First an attack marked by the probing of Ben Johnston ended with Ben Kaye crossing deftly from dummy-half. Then the airborne Steve Tyrer took Scott Murrell's superb reverse chip to splash down for the try. Tyrer converted both and at 12-0, there were hints of a remarkable reprieve for Toulouse.

But Jarrod Sammut ran from a scrum to angle his way across from 15 metres in the 20th minute before Eloi Pelissier's score from dummy-half. Sammut's conversions made it 12-12 after 23 minutes, but Halifax struck back again to lead deservedly 16-12 at the break as Adam Tangata broke a tackle close to the line.

The Broncos improved after half-time, gradually gaining a territorial edge. The breakthrough came just before the hour. This time Kieran Dixon was first both to the high ball, then to Sammut's deft response, and he crossed in the corner. Sammut converted via a post, and the home side finally led.

Elliot Kear crossed to make it 22-16 to London with 14 minutes left. But even after having Brandon Moore sin binned for dissent, Halifax battled on to the end, their defeat only sealed by Sammut's field goal in the final seconds.

The Wolfpack had ended Friday night inside the automatic promotion places after Gareth O'Brien's field goal handed them a historic 17-16 victory at Leeds, before Hull KR overhauled them on the Sunday after beating Widnes by at least the 14-point margin required.

The Robins sauntered to a 30-0 home victory over the Vikings. Danny McGuire was absolutely imperious in the first 40 minutes, by which time the Robins had already eclipsed the 14-point winning margin required to rubber-stamp safety. There were three Hull KR tries in that opening half and McGuire had a hand in each of them. And Junior Vaivai's try around the hour mark settled the all-too obvious Hull KR nerves once and for all.

BETFRED SUPER LEAGUE - SUPER 8s
Final table - Sunday 30th September

	P	W	D	L	F	A	D	Pts
St Helens	30	26	0	4	895	408	487	52
Wigan Warriors	30	23	0	7	740	417	323	46
Castleford Tigers	30	20	1	9	767	582	185	41
Warrington Wolves	30	18	1	11	767	561	206	37
Wakefield Trinity	30	13	1	16	747	696	51	27
Huddersfield Giants	30	13	1	16	539	794	-255	27
Catalans Dragons	30	12	1	17	596	750	-154	25
Hull FC	30	11	0	19	615	787	-172	22

SUPER 8s - THE QUALIFIERS
Final table - Sunday 30th September

	P	W	D	L	F	A	D	Pts
Salford Red Devils	7	5	0	2	218	75	143	10
Leeds Rhinos	7	5	0	2	216	137	79	10
Hull Kingston Rovers	7	5	0	2	197	162	35	10
Toronto Wolfpack	7	5	0	2	136	118	18	10
London Broncos	7	4	0	3	161	164	-3	8
Toulouse Olympique	7	3	0	4	156	190	-34	6
Widnes Vikings	7	1	0	6	92	173	-81	2
Halifax	7	0	0	7	68	225	-157	0

OCTOBER
High five for Warriors

Super League Semi-finals

Warrington Wolves won through to their fourth Grand Final in seven seasons with a surprise 18-13 win at runaway League Leaders St Helens in the first semi-final on the Thursday night.

After a try-less first half, with a Danny Richardson field goal giving Saints a 3-2 advantage at the break, the Wolves outscored the pre-match favourites three-to-one, with winger Tom Lineham showing terrific determination for two of them and Jack Hughes the other.

Prop Luke Thompson provided another mighty contribution up front for St Helens. But the fluent attack that had hurt so many teams in 2018 didn't fire when it mattered most.

The game exploded into life in the second half after prop Luke Douglas broke the try-scoring deadlock. But Warrington hit back immediately as Hughes, who had been named England Knights skipper during the week, stepped past Mark Percival and Jonny Lomax and beat Ben Barba to the corner.

Soon after, Hughes conceded a penalty that saw Richardson make it 11-6. And the home side continued to create attacking opportunities, with a spiralling kick seeing Ratchford forced into touch near his own line. But the Wolves were the next to cross. Smart hands from Kevin Brown and Bryson Goodwin gave Lineham enough space to dive low and early and scramble over the line. This time Roberts converted from the touchline and the Wolves were back ahead by 12-11.

Richardson missed a penalty attempt from out wide after Joe Philbin hit him late following a kick but he levelled the scores with a field goal immediately afterwards and then edged his side a point in front with another one-pointer.

The drama wasn't over though, with Lineham beating Richardson, stepping inside Barba and proving too strong for Dominique Peyroux to stop him from going over the line with six minutes remaining. Roberts' conversion made it a five-point gap, with the Wolves seeing out the final stages to book their ticket to Old Trafford.

After the following night's 14-0 home win by Wigan over Castleford, the size of the Wolves' task in the Grand Final became crystal clear.

The Warriors' defence was absolutely stifling and the Tigers rarely looked like scoring, other than on one occasion when Paul McShane dropped the ball when he was trying to touch down. Sam Tomkins pulled all the strings for Wigan as he extended his Warriors career by 80 minutes. His kicking game was spot on and he came away with a personal haul of ten points.

Wigan established their dominance in the first half. They led 7-0 at the interval with Thomas Leuluai celebrating his 250th appearance for the club with a try, while three points came from the boot of Tomkins. Tomkins extended Wigan's lead with a try and a penalty to put them 13-0 in front, before sealing victory with a field goal on the final hooter.

It was another disappointing end to the season for the Tigers.

Million Pound Game

There was a major blowout in the promotion play-off as London Broncos stunned runaway Championship winners Toronto on their own patch with a 4-2 victory. Two Jarrod Sammut conversions ultimately secured the return of the Broncos to Super League.

The Wolfpack's best moment of a cagey opening quarter came in the opening 60 seconds. Josh McCrone's high kick was spilt by Alex Walker under pressure from Gareth O'Brien. McCrone picked up and scored under the sticks. Thankfully for London, the try was, eventually, disallowed as O'Brien was deemed offside.

The subsequent penalty saw London gain territory and they kept it. They carried hard, ended sets well and made life difficult for Toronto. It wasn't the free-flowing rugby associated with the 2018 Broncos. But it was effective. Ultimately it gave them a two-point lead, with a penalty allowing Jarrod Sammut to slot a goal in the ninth minute.

Frustration and anxiety started to creep into the Wolfpack's game, the most notable example coming through Andy Ackers who, just moments after coming on, needlessly hit Eloi Pelissier late and was sin-binned.

After the break, Toronto came out stronger. They started to dominate down the middle and exerted strong pressure on the Broncos. Ashton Sims went close as he barged towards the posts but was held up by sheer will and several London limbs.

Eventually, Toronto drew level. London agonisingly kicked out on the full and made things worse when they conceded a penalty that allowed O'Brien to convert.

But then Toronto had a disaster of their own. Blake Wallace dropped the restart, Jack Buchanan conceded a penalty and a second Sammut penalty put London back ahead within a few seconds of being pegged back.

The Wolfpack came agonisingly close as O'Brien pulled a long-range conversion wide and then, the big chance, the big moment, came.

Blake Wallace took off from his deceptive left foot. Dan Hindmarsh looked on helplessly as Wallace darted to the line. A try beckoned. But then, young fullback Walker grabbed Wallace, got his legs underneath the ball and wrapped up the halfback. It was, ultimately, the million-pound tackle.

Super League Grand Final

Wigan coach Shaun Wane's 35-year association with his hometown club ended with a fifth Super League title, as the Warriors defeated Warrington 12-4 to become champions again.

Wane was filled with emotion surrounding his exit as he prepared to begin a role as defensive coach in Scottish rugby union. It was also a perfect way to say farewell for the departing trio of Catalans-bound Sam Tomkins and John Bateman and Ryan Sutton, both heading for Canberra Raiders.

Right winger Dom Manfredi scored twice in only his fifth game since returning from two serious knee injuries which had robbed him of the last two years of his career. Manfredi was excellent, not only in attack but in defence, providing a try-saving tackle on Tom Lineham that left him with a gruesome cut on his eyelid that forced him to require treatment. But he shrugged it off, got it bandaged up and returned to score the winning try with three minutes left on the clock.

The win was typical of the Wane-coached Warriors, with a total commitment to defence strangling the life out of the Wolves. Warrington could have no real complaints. While they were left aggrieved that no further punishment was inflicted on Sam Tomkins for two dubious challenges in the first half, they had lacked the quality to win the game. In 2018's two finals, despite a weight of possession and numerous good sets, they didn't provide the flair or the magic to win the big prize.

They had the consolation of seeing fullback Stefan Ratchford becoming the fourth player from a losing team to win the Harry Sunderland Trophy as man of the match.

Both teams were, unsurprisingly, unchanged from their semi-final victories. From the off it was gritty and fiery. Neither side budged defensively. Thomas Leuluai ripped in without a moment's thought, while Mike Cooper bludgeoned and barrelled into tackles. There were four mistakes in the opening eight minutes.

But in the twelfth minute came the first breakthrough. Wigan conceded a penalty to put Warrington in striking position for the first time. The ball was shifted right. Ratchford grasped the ball, crafted a pass of the finest to Josh Charnley, who dived in for his first try at Old Trafford since scoring for Wigan against Warrington two years earlier.

Wigan weren't fazed by the early setback. They rode their luck, though. Tomkins found himself in hot water after a trip on Bryson Goodwin. Referee Robert Hicks gave him a good telling off but no further punishment.

BETFRED SUPER LEAGUE GRAND FINAL

Saturday 13th October 2018

WARRINGTON WOLVES 4 WIGAN WARRIORS 12

WOLVES: 1 Stefan Ratchford; 2 Tom Lineham; 3 Bryson Goodwin; 18 Toby King; 27 Josh Charnley; 6 Kevin Brown; 7 Tyrone Roberts; 8 Chris Hill (C); 9 Daryl Clark; 10 Mike Cooper; 30 Bodene Thompson; 12 Jack Hughes; 34 Ben Westwood. Subs (all used): 17 Joe Philbin; 13 Ben Murdoch-Masila; 19 George King; 15 Declan Patton.
Try: Charnley (12); **Goals:** Roberts 0/1.
WARRIORS: 1 Sam Tomkins; 21 Dom Manfredi; 4 Oliver Gildart; 3 Dan Sarginson; 2 Tom Davies; 6 George Williams; 9 Thomas Leuluai; 25 Romain Navarrete; 7 Sam Powell; 10 Ben Flower; 40 Joe Greenwood; 14 John Bateman; 13 Sean O'Loughlin (C). Subs (all used): 20 Morgan Escare; 15 Ryan Sutton; 12 Liam Farrell; 8 Tony Clubb.
Tries: Manfredi (25, 77), Davies (31); **Goals:** S Tomkins 0/4.
Rugby Leaguer & League Express Men of the Match:
Wolves: Stefan Ratchford; *Warriors:* Dom Manfredi.
Penalty count: 7-4; **Half-time:** 4-8; **Referee:** Robert Hicks; **Attendance:** 64,892 *(at Old Trafford, Manchester).*

Warrington fans were left incensed and their anger was multiplied a few minutes later when Wigan dew level. Wigan raided down the right edge and came up trumps, with Oliver Gildart stepping Kevin Brown and Goodwin inside and out before delivering a fine pass to Manfredi to stagger in at the corner.

There was no luck involved with Wigan's next and, ultimately, crucial try four minutes later. George Williams handled the occasion excellently, his kicking game, in particular, of significant importance. It was his vision that saw Wigan go ahead. After coming away from broken play with the ball in hand, he picked out Tom Davies's signal to kick the ball through and Davies hurtled past Charnley and planted the ball down in the in-goal, with the video-referee confirming he hadn't been offside when Williams kicked the ball. All three conversions were missed, leaving the scoreline at 8-4.

If Warrington fans weren't already frustrated, they most certainly were as the first half ended. Tomkins again found himself in trouble after a clumsy 'tackle' on Daryl Clark. Tomkins led with the knees as Clark grasped a loose ball, with the fullback catching him hard in the back of the head. Tomkins, somehow, once again got away with nothing more than a telling-off. At the following week's Match Review Panel he was banned for one game on a penalty notice. And Leuluai got the same for dangerous contact on Ratchford in the 23rd minute.

With tempers rising, unsavoury scenes ensued at the break. As the teams trudged off the field, Wigan players were showered by drinks directed at them from the Warrington end. Then Goodwin and Morgan Escare argued and a minor scuffle commenced in the tunnel.

After the break, Warrington failed to spark when it mattered as Wigan suffocated them with their meticulous kicking and fervid defence creating a choke hold from which they never managed to break free.

The only player who appeared capable of doing so was Ratchford, who went on a one-man pursuit of a Grand Final winner's ring with two marauding runs down the middle of the pitch in the space of four minutes. But he was hounded down by a pack of cherry and white dogs, with none in primrose and blue anywhere in sight.

Ultimately, it was Manfredi's night, along with Wane, Bateman, Tomkins and Sutton. He capped off a wonderful performance and a wonderful evening for Wigan with the winning try, diving in at the corner after a fluid move down the right. Wigan's bench erupted, Wane, with tears in his eyes, pumped the air triumphantly. The dream was complete.

WOMEN'S LEAGUE
Warrior Spirit

WIGAN WARRIORS and **LEEDS RHINOS** capped their debut season's in Women's Rugby League by playing out an enthralling Super League Grand Final at the Manchester Regional Arena.

A Charlotte Foley penalty in the final moments was all that separated the sides as Wigan, who won 18-16, were crowned Champions, while Leeds had to settle for the Challenge Cup and League Leaders Shield they had previously secured.

Despite Rhiannon Marshall opening the scoring for Leeds, with Courtney Hill converting, Wigan were soon to open up a commanding lead. A Rachel Thompson hat-trick and a score from Georgia Wilson gave Wigan a 16-6 lead midway through the second half and it could have been more had Michelle Davis added her three conversion attempts and Foley her one.

But Leeds hit back with tries from Suze Hill and teenage sensation Caitlin Beevers. Courtney Hill's second goal of the afternoon levelled matters and gave Leeds hope, before they were penalised for offside, allowing Foley to step up to be the hero.

Leeds did finish the season with some silverware though after finishing top of the table, as well as lifting the Challenge Cup at Warrington's Halliwell Jones Stadium in August, after a late Lois Forsell try secured a 20-14 win over Castleford Tigers.

As a curtain raiser to Leeds' victory, last year's Challenge Cup winners **BRADFORD BULLS** beat Championship side Stanningley to claim the Challenge Shield. Fullback Leah Jones contributed 16 points as the Bulls ran out 44-16 winners - but it wasn't as easy for them as the scoreline suggested, with Stanningley pushing them all the way.

On the league front, Leeds Rhinos showed their title credentials from the off with a 32-16 win over 2017 champions Bradford. The Rhinos, coached by first team prop Adam Cuthbertson, lost just twice all season - away at St Helens and by a single-point against Wigan, but a season-ending injury to Forsell weeks before the Grand Final proved crucial to the end of their campaign.

Champions Wigan finished second behind the Rhinos after an impressive year under Amanda Wilkinson. What made their achievements all the more impressive was that around half of the squad had no prior experience. Former England international Gemma Walsh however added crucial experience and was a guiding light on the field.

ST HELENS may have been a new team in name but having joined forces with local club Thatto Heath St Helens, who had enjoyed much success in Women's Rugby League in recent years, they were far from being a new kid on the block. With many of the players knowing each other prior to this season, Saints were able to hit the ground running and racked up the points in each of their opening three games. Consecutive defeats to Wigan and Leeds in the final months of the campaign ultimately proved crucial to their hopes of the title.

CASTLEFORD TIGERS made up the top four and set-up a semi-final tie against the Rhinos - a team they failed to beat in four attempts in 2018 (twice in the league, once in the play-off and in the Challenge Cup Final). Their young squad continued to make progress in their second year in the top flight, with Georgia Roche shining to become the first ever Woman of Steel. She also claimed national recognition by being nominated for the BBC Young Sports Personality of the Year.

Women's League

Bradford, who won last year's smaller Super League competition will have been disappointed to miss out on the play-offs but having seen many players retire or move to other clubs, with many joining rivals Leeds Rhinos, it was always going to be difficult for the Bulls to be as dominant as they were in 2017.

FEATHERSTONE ROVERS, another team to have experienced the highs in recent years, struggled to live up to past reputation. The arrival of England international Katie Hepworth in the closing weeks of the season did add an extra spark that they will be hoping to utilise in 2019 as they aim to win more than a solitary game.

YORK CITY KNIGHTS made the biggest step up in 2018, coming into Super League from the Merit League. And they will have been buoyed by a season of continued development on the field, which resulted in their opening league win of the season coming against Featherstone at the start of September. Big wins against two Championship sides in the cup competition re-enforced their belief they were right to have joined the Super League.

In the Championship, **WAKEFIELD TRINITY**, who are thought to be entering Super League in 2019, finished as Minor Premiers, level on points with second placed **STANNINGLEY**, who went on to beat Leigh Miners Rangers in the Grand Final.

WOMEN'S ROUND-UP

SUPER LEAGUE - FINAL TABLE

	P	W	D	L	F	A	D	Pts
Leeds Rhinos	12	10	0	2	438	139	299	20
Wigan Warriors	12	9	1	2	324	128	196	19
St Helens	12	8	1	3	316	130	186	17
Castleford Tigers	12	6	2	4	318	228	90	14
Bradford Bulls	12	5	0	7	292	312	-20	10
Featherstone Rovers	12	1	0	11	180	461	-281	2
York City Knights	12	1	0	11	78	548	-470	2

SUPER LEAGUE GRAND FINAL

Saturday 13th October 2018

LEEDS RHINOS 16 WIGAN WARRIORS 18

RHINOS: 1 Caitlin Beevers; 2 Suze Hill; 3 Charlotte Booth; 4 Sophie Robinson; 5 Madison Laverick; 6 Hanna Butcher; 7 Courtney Hill; 8 Amy Johnson; 9 Rhiannon Marshall; 10 Danielle Anderson; 11 Aimee Staveley; 12 Manina Spurr; 13 Shannon Lacey. Subs (all used): 14 Frankie Townend; 15 Sophie Nuttall; 16 Chloe Kerrigan; 17 Ellie Oldroyd.
Tries: Marshall (7), Beevers (63), S Hill (77); **Goals:** C Hill 2/4.
WARRIORS: 1 Rebecca Greenfield; 2 Alison Burrows; 3 Rachel Thompson; 4 Georgia Wilson; 5 Michelle Davis; 6 Gemma Walsh; 7 Sarah Harrison; 19 Hannah Goodburn; 26 Claire Hall; 8 Chloe Hammond; 25 Amanda Sibbald; 24 Vanessa Temple; 10 Joanie Alpin. Subs (all used): 14 Holly Speakman; 9 Charlotte Foley; 23 Lucy Baggaley; 15 Gemma Hennessey.
Tries: Thompson (10, 39, 57), Wilson (46); **Goals:** Davis 0/3, Foley 1/2.
Rugby Leaguer & League Express Women of the Match:
Rhinos: Charlotte Booth; *Warriors:* Rachel Thompson.
Penalty count: 4-7; **Half time:** 6-8; **Referee:** Alan Billington;
Attendance: 1,189 (at Manchester Regional Arena).

SUPER LEAGUE SEMI-FINALS
Sunday 7th October 2018
Leeds Rhinos 24 ....Castleford Tigers 10
Wigan Warriors 10 .... St Helens 6

CHALLENGE CUP FINAL

Saturday 4th August 2018

CASTLEFORD TIGERS 14 LEEDS RHINOS 20

TIGERS: 1 Tara Stanley; 2 Maisie Burton; 32 Courtney Pointon; 4 Lacey Owen; 5 Kelsey Gentles; 6 Georgie Hetherington; 7 Olivia Grace; 27 Lucy Eastwood; 9 Sinead Peach; 10 Jasmine Rowley; 11 Katie Hepworth; 24 Beth Weir; 13 Georgia Roche. Subs (all used): 14 Jasmine Cudjoe; 15 Tamzin Renouf; 25 Grace Field; 17 Emma Lumley; 33 Marie Colley; 19 Katie Tordoff; 20 Shannelle Mannion.
Tries: Hepworth (18), Stanley (29), Roche (39); **Goals:** Hepworth 1/3.

RHINOS: 1 Charlotte Booth; 2 Suze Hill; 3 Sophie Nuttall; 4 Sophie Robinson; 5 Caitlin Beevers; 6 Hanna Butcher; 7 Courtney Hill; 8 Amy Johnson; 9 Lois Forsell; 10 Danielle Anderson; 11 Aimee Staveley; 12 Manina Spurr; 17 Shannon Lacey. Subs (all used): 14 Frankie Townend, 15 Madison Laverick; 16 Chloe Kerrigan; 13 Rhiannon Marshall; 18 Megan Price; 19 Ellie Oldroyd.
Tries: S Hill (33), Beevers (41), Staveley (64), Forsell (78); **Goals:** C Hill 2/4.
Rugby Leaguer & League Express Women of the Match:
Tigers: Katie Hepworth; *Rhinos:* Lois Forsell.
Penalty count: 6-6; **Half-time:** 14-6; **Referee:** Alan Billington;
Attendance: 1,022 (at Halliwell Jones Stadium, Warrington).

CHALLENGE CUP SEMI-FINALS
Sunday 15th July 2018
Castleford Tigers 48 .... York City Knights 12
Wigan Warriors 8 ....Leeds Rhinos 26

CHALLENGE SHIELD FINAL

Saturday 4th August 2018

BRADFORD BULLS 44 STANNINGLEY 16

BULLS: 20 Leah Jones; 16 Adara Telemacque; 1 Savannah Andrade; 3 Jess Courtman; 2 Becky Conlon; 31 Danielle Bose; 12 Amy Boardman; 8 Lauren Hickey; 17 Chrissi Nettleton; 21 Vicky Rhodes; 11 Shona Hoyle; 23 Heather McDonald; 28 Reagan Walker. Subs (all used): 5 Haylie Hields; 19 Memphis Jubb; 7 Stacey Greenwood; 30 Stacey Wilson; 4 Amy Hardcastle; 9 Kirsty Maroney; 32 Beth Sutcliffe.
Tries: Jones (8), Hoyle (18), Walker (21, 76), Conlon (35), Hardcastle (46, 79), Courtman (69); **Goals:** Jones 6/8.
STANNINGLEY: 1 Hayley Fielding; 2 Allana Waller; 3 Sophie Bickerdyke; 4 Elychia Watson; 5 Lauren Waller; 6 Chloe Wainwright-Morley; 7 Laura Dyson; 8 Rachael Barker; 9 Grace Ramsden; 10 Lyndsey Cunnett; 11 Jodie Davies; 12 Olivia Wood; 13 Demi Fisher. Subs (all used): 14 Markella Morgan; 15 Louise Travers; 16 Loren Gregory; 17 Leanne May.
Tries: Fielding (14), Watson (39); **Goals:** Wainwright-Morley 4/4.
Rugby Leaguer & League Express Women of the Match:
Bulls: Leah Jones; *Stanningley:* Rachael Barker.
Penalty count: 5-8; **Half-time:** 20-14; **Referee:** Neil Pascall.
(at Halliwell Jones Stadium, Warrington).

CHALLENGE SHIELD SEMI-FINALS
Sunday 15th July 2018
Stanningley 66 .... Brighouse Rangers 4
Wakefield Trinity 0 ....Bradford Bulls 58

2
CHAMPIONSHIP
& LEAGUE 1 2018

CHAMPIONSHIP SEASON
Capital gains

LONDON BRONCOS headed into 2018 with modest expectations. Coach Andrew Henderson had departed for Warrington Wolves, as assistant, after two excellent seasons with the Broncos when they secured back-to-back second-placed finishes.

Assistant Danny Ward was tasked with replacing him. He would have to do so without Andy Ackers and William Barthau, two key players who departed for Toronto Wolfpack and Toulouse Olympique respectively. The pair weren't replaced as the Broncos slashed their budget for the campaign.

Some pundits predicted they could finish as low as tenth.

However, London proved straight away that that wouldn't be the case as they topped the division early on, highlighted by a hammering of the Toronto Wolfpack in round four.

While there was a slight blip thereafter, with defeats to Toulouse Olympique, Leigh Centurions and Halifax, the Broncos ultimately recovered and picked up their place in the Qualifiers in stunning style, earning a draw in France against Toulouse, while defeating Halifax and Featherstone in three consecutive weeks that ultimately secured their place in the top four.

The Broncos weren't seriously expected to compete for a spot in Super League. But having secured second place in the Championship due to their superior points difference over Toulouse, they set their stall out when defeating Widnes Vikings 21-20.

The heroics continued. They defeated Toulouse at home, followed by an outstanding home victory over Salford and a win over Halifax secured a place in the Million Pound Game.

Despite overcoming the odds already, they were again written off heading into the game - a daunting trip to Toronto for the third time in the season. The Broncos had lost heavily in their two trips before but stunned the world when it mattered the most, winning 4-2 and sparking memorable scenes and the return of the capital club to Super League.

The name **TORONTO WOLFPACK** remains on the lips of everyone after their second year in the European competition. Despite that, and a number of memorable moments, they ultimately didn't secure a place in Super League following an agonising 4-2 defeat at the hands of London Broncos in the Million Pound Game.

They won the Championship at a canter, dropping just five points on their way to securing the League Leaders' Shield.

Playing in blocks of home and away games, the Wolfpack ended their European tour top of the league with notable wins over Leigh Centurions, Toulouse Olympique and Halifax. The only blemishes on their record came with a draw at Barrow Raiders, a heavy defeat in London and their first ever home defeat to Featherstone Rovers on the final day of the regular season.

London's Matt Davis flies in for a try during the Broncos' big early-season victory against Toronto Wolfpack

They continued to make headlines, having played a part in the first Magic Weekend all-Championship clash against Toulouse Olympique and making high-profile signings such as Gareth O'Brien, Chase Stanley and Darcy Lussick.

Despite all that, they never truly convinced anyone they were ready for Super League during the Qualifiers, although they did pick up a famous victory over Leeds Rhinos at Headingley in the penultimate round of the Qualifiers competition, while also triumphing against Widnes.

It wasn't enough for them to gain an automatic promotion spot and their season ended in disappointment, going down to Danny Ward's Broncos.

TOULOUSE OLYMPIQUE overcame the heartbreak of 2017 by securing an impressive third-place finish in the Championship in just their second year in the competition.

Aided by the excellence of Mark Kheirallah and Johnathon Ford, Sylvain Houles' side never dropped out of the top four, despite the mad scramble for the positions in the Championship.

The club's home form was impressive, falling to defeat only to Leigh Centurions and Toronto Wolfpack in the regular rounds, while in the Qualifiers they defeated Widnes Vikings, Halifax and Hull KR.

Winning all three of their home games in the Qualifiers could only provide them with a sixth-placed finish.

Nevertheless, that was still an excellent return for the French club, who continue to show great strides of improvement as they set their sights on Super League.

They even made an appearance at the Magic Weekend. The Championship kicked off the event on the Saturday, with Toronto Wolfpack prevailing 43-30 in a highly entertaining game.

Championship Season

One of the great achievers of the year were **HALIFAX**, who once again defied the odds to reach the Qualifiers for the third time in four years.

With the likes of Toronto and Leigh spending eye-watering amounts and London, Toulouse and Featherstone all spending comfortably more, it seemed unrealistic for Fax to make the four again.

But Fax stuck around those positions from the get-go. Early wins over Leigh and London put them within touching distance and, crucially, they dropped just one point all season against teams in the bottom half of the league.

A superb win over Featherstone at the Summer Bash, largely down to the stunning display of talismanic halfback Scott Murrell, proved to be one of their key moments in a top-four race that saw teams between second and sixth jockey for position all season.

Ultimately, Fax went into the run-in with successive games against Featherstone, London and Toulouse knowing two wins would all but secure their place in the four.

A 34-20 triumph over Featherstone was followed by a narrow 20-18 defeat to London.

That left them needing victory over Toulouse, and they delivered, with Shane Grady's late try securing a 19-14 win.

While they failed to win a game in the Qualifiers once again, Fax did retain their spot as the country's best part-time team and notably put in an excellent effort against the defending Super League champions Leeds, going into half-time level with the Rhinos before falling to defeat.

A year, ultimately, of frustration for Jon Duffy's side, as **FEATHERSTONE ROVERS** narrowly missed out on a place in the top four for a third consecutive year.

An eye-catching recruitment drive had seen the likes of Gareth Hock, Martyn Ridyard and Tom Holmes all join the club in the off-season and when they beat Halifax and Toulouse in the opening two weeks of the season, it appeared Rovers were ready to make a push towards Super League in 2019.

But sadly, Featherstone became renowned for coming up short in the big games. In round three they lost to London, with top spot in the table up for grabs, and when the opportunity presented itself again on Good Friday, they went down 24-16 to Toronto.

They were, however, scorching past the rest of the competition, frequently handing out beatings. By the end of the year, they had scored over 1,000 points in their 30 league games.

But perhaps the crucial moment of their season was when Martyn Ridyard suffered a shoulder injury in May that would see him miss the top four run-in. Without him, Rovers lost twice to Halifax, thus extending their winless run at the Summer Bash in the process, while also losing out to Leigh, Toulouse and London.

As a result, their top-four hopes were squashed. Holmes was cruelly also ruled out for the year after an injury picked up in their Blackpool defeat to Fax. While Featherstone still had no problem defeating the bottom-half sides without those key players, the absence of their first-choice partnership in the big games was telling.

Despite that, they ended the year making two pieces of history, becoming the first side to defeat Toronto Wolfpack in Canada after an excellent 30-12 victory in the final game of the regular season, before being named the final winners of the Championship Shield after defeating Leigh in the final.

2018 proved to be a disastrous campaign for **LEIGH CENTURIONS**, who failed to make the top four after their relegation from Super League.

The Centurions had received a £500,000 parachute payment which facilitated the recruitment of 19 players from Super League and the NRL but they found the going tough in the second tier with an awful start to the year seeing the club lose five of their opening six games.

Shaun Robinson dives past Ben Heaton to score during Featherstone's opening round win against Halifax

Coach Neil Jukes subsequently resigned and was replaced by Kieron Purtill and that resulted in a huge upturn in form that saw Leigh move to within touching distance of the top four.

Sadly for them, however, two defeats, first at the Summer Bash to Toronto and then defeat in Canada to the Wolfpack, meant they just ran out of time and ultimately failed to make the top four.

As a result, the club tried to strip their assets, with financial troubles set to damage the club significantly, given the reduction in central funding they would receive.

This had an effect on their Championship Shield campaign with the club failing to raise enough players for several games before only having a handful of players to play in the final against Featherstone Rovers.

The Centurions were granted special dispensation to sign emergency players in order to fulfil the fixture and they lost 42-10 to the Rovers after putting in a valiant effort in troubled circumstances.

It was very much a case of same old, same old for **BATLEY BULLDOGS**, as coach Matt Diskin oversaw another season with the club firmly in mid-table.

Batley ultimately finished seventh, one place and two wins worse off than his maiden season in charge.

But with the arrival of Toronto and Leigh in the division, it marked a steady return for the Bulldogs, who were very much the best of the rest in a competition that was split in half.

Batley's attack saw steady improvement on their previous season.

The main example came in round 11 when Batley stunned French counterparts Toulouse, who left West Yorkshire humbled after being on the receiving end of a 46-22 hammering.

Championship Season

Sadly, that victory was their only one against top-half opposition in the regular rounds and while they did beat a much-changed Leigh side in the Championship Shield, there remains a bridge for the Bulldogs to cross before pushing higher up the league.

However, the Bulldogs ended the year very much with an eye on the future. A strong recruitment drive saw them strengthen ahead of 2019, with livewire halfback Louis Jouffret agreeing to stay at the club after impressing during an initial short-term deal with the club.

For **DEWSBURY RAMS**, 2018 was a continuation of their mid-table status in the Championship, finishing eighth in the league, comfortably clear of relegation but nowhere near the top four.

A strong start to the season saw Neil Kelly's side win three of their opening four games before a ten-game losing streak saw them plummet down the table and get knocked out of the Challenge Cup by League 1 side Whitehaven.

However, a credible draw with Halifax in round 14, followed by a dramatic 20-18 victory over bitter rivals Batley at the Summer Bash eased fears and, eventually, they saw the season out steadily, winning four of their seven Championship Shield games, including a 52-6 demolition of Leigh.

That proved to be Kelly's final game in charge, as the stalwart's second spell with the club ended with just one full season under his belt.

Kelly resigned from the post, citing a drop in budget as one of the factors behind his decision to leave.

The club ended the year by appointing former Gloucestershire All Golds coach Lee Greenwood as Kelly's replacement.

2018 was a year to remember for promoted **BARROW RAIDERS** as they enjoyed and endured many highs and lows.

But ultimately, they ended the season having fulfilled their initial goal of consolidating their place in the second tier.

Barrow's return to Championship rugby saw them host the league's two favourites in rounds two and three. Toronto and Leigh went to Cumbria and were widely expected to leave with two league points.

Between them, they left with one. Paul Crarey's side battled out in the rain, sleet and hail to earn a fantastic point against the Wolfpack thanks to a Dan Toal try that secured an 8-8 stalemate.

It meant Leigh were well aware of the challenge ahead when they made the trip a week later and, initially, it looked like they had things sorted as they raced into a lead.

However, Dan Toal scored a hat-trick to secure a stunning 24-20 win and leave the Championship well aware of the danger presented by the Raiders.

Unfortunately, the going got tough both on and off the field as the season progressed. The Raiders revealed the severity of financial troubles that threatened the club's existence and that coincided with a downturn in form.

However, the club ended the year making strong strides towards securing its future, while they were never truly threatened by relegation, ending the year in ninth spot.

2018 was another bitterly disappointing one for **SHEFFIELD EAGLES**, who registered one of their worst league finishes in recent history.

With the club still coming to terms with returning to part-time status after one year as a full-time club in 2016, the Eagles found the going tough and ultimately ended the year with only eight wins to their name.

However, the overriding positive was a move back to the city with the club making the move to the Olympic Legacy Park, having played in Wakefield the year before. The club had been on the road for many years after the demolition of the Don Valley Stadium at the end of 2013.

Their first game at the Olympic Legacy Park saw them defeated by Toronto Wolfpack. However, the return to the stadium is expected to have huge ramifications for the club in the future.

The Eagles ended the year recruiting impressively for 2019 with the likes of Joel Farrell, Pat Walker (Batley Bulldogs), Josh Guzdek, Aaron Brown (Dewsbury Rams) and Bradley Knowles (Featherstone Rovers) all arriving at the club as Mark Aston looks to end three years of struggle.

ROCHDALE HORNETS once again punched above their weight. Having consolidated their position in the Championship the year before, Alan Kilshaw looked to have a formidable task ahead of him after financial troubles saw the club releasing some of their top performers to rival clubs on the eve of the season.

It was evident early on that it would be a tough year, as Hornets won only one of their opening ten games - a 24-12 victory at home to Barrow Raiders.

However, a 32-27 victory over Dewsbury got them up and running. And while the victories were few and far between they did just about enough to keep themselves within touching distance of the sides above them in the table.

The league restructuring late in the season provided them with a lifeline, with only the bottom-placed side, instead of the bottom two, under threat of relegation. Even then, the bottom side would play off against a team from League 1 for the right to play in the Championship in 2019.

The Hornets won their final two games of the season, against Dewsbury and Sheffield. As a result, they leapfrogged Swinton on the final weekend of the season.

Coach Alan Kilshaw left the club at the end of the year after three successful seasons, having guided Hornets to promotion from League 1, and then secured the club's second-tier status despite the odds against them.

SWINTON LIONS ensured they would be playing Championship rugby once again in 2019 despite finishing bottom of the table at the end of the year.

The league restructuring decided on in mid-September, which would see the Championship expanded from 12 to 14 teams in 2019, proved invaluable for the Lions as it provided them with one last chance to protect their status in a promotion play-off final against Workington Town. The Cumbrians had been beaten 27-8 at Bradford on the previous Sunday, meaning they finished third in League 1, before then losing the coin toss to determine who got home advantage in the match to decide the 14th and final team in the Championship.

Swinton won the game 33-20 in front of a joyous crowd at Heywood Road.

Stuart Littler's first full year as head coach proved to be a difficult one, with the Lions managing just four wins all season and conceding 1,112 points in 30 league games.

However, they ultimately survived and new owner Andy Mazey has begun to get his business plan for the club underway as they look to a brighter future.

CHAMPIONSHIP AWARDS

PLAYER OF THE YEAR
Mark Kheirallah
(Toulouse Olympique)

YOUNG PLAYER OF THE YEAR
Matthew Costello
(Sheffield Eagles)

COACH OF THE YEAR
Danny Ward (London Broncos)

CLUB OF THE YEAR
Toronto Wolfpack

LEAGUE 1 SEASON
Arise the Knights

YORK CITY KNIGHTS had enjoyed a huge turn around in fortunes since they went bust two seasons before.

After missing out on promotion through the play-offs in the previous four seasons, coach James Ford was determined to get an automatic spot into the Championship for 2019 to continue the development the club had made under the stewardship of new owner Jon Flatman.

The signing of former Super League star Ben Cockayne proved a masterstroke by Ford and his re-signing for 2019 will boost the Knights' hopes of remaining in the Championship. The 35 year-old, with 10 years of Super League experience behind him, initially featured at fullback before injuries saw him step into the halves and create the league's deadliest halfback partnership with eventual League 1 Player of the Year Connor Robinson.

Cockayne's experience, plus that of the dual registered players from Hull Kingston Rovers who Ford utilised at strategic points throughout the year, proved vital. Especially when they travelled to Odsal to take on promotion favourites Bradford Bulls in July. A late touchline conversion miss from Bradford's Dane Chisholm ensured a victory for York that saw them draw level on points with Bradford at the top of the league.

And they didn't drop another point all season, so when the final hooter sounded in the last match of the season against Whitehaven there were jubilant scenes at Bootham Crescent. There would be no more play-off heartache.

Four-time Super League champions **BRADFORD BULLS** were tipped to bounce straight back up to the Championship at the first attempt. But they certainly didn't have it all their own way as one of their former favourites came back to haunt them, not once, but twice in 2018.

Leon Pryce, who had hung up his boots midway through the previous season, held the reins at a Workington Town side that proved John Kear's league nemesis.

Two defeats to Town, plus another to York City Knights at Odsal, meant the Bulls had to rely on the play-offs to make it back to the Championship at the first attempt.

But Kear did what Kear does best in knock-out rugby and inspired the team to produce their best two performances of the season in the play-offs.

A 47-0 win over Oldham set up a third meeting of the year with their Cumbrian adversaries and Kear proved why he had been top of Bradford's wish list when it came to getting a new coach following Geoff Toovey's decision not to return to the club following their relegation in 2017.

Aside from the three defeats, the Bulls were a dominant force throughout the year, finishing the campaign with both the best offensive and defensive records.

With the club's Academy producing a number of the year's standout stars, plus the addition of players like Jake Webster, the former Super League champions were back on an upward curve.

Ben Cockayne leads the York celebrations following the City Knights' vital win at Bradford

DONCASTER went into the year looking to give Bradford and York a run for their money and an unbeaten three-match run at the start of the season filled them with the confidence that it could be done.

Ultimately though, four defeats to the Bulls and the City Knights proved their undoing and they were unable to keep up with the League's pacesetters.

Coach Richard Horne definitely benefitted from having a full pre-season in charge and used his contacts at Super League Hull FC to bring in the added numbers and experience when needed.

One of Horne's greatest achievements was the self-belief he managed to instil across a relatively small squad.

That culminated in a nine-match winning run at the end of the season, a streak that was only ended by Workington in the play-offs.

With the vast majority of the squad staying in 2019 and the domestic restructure, promotion to the Championship will be a more viable opportunity for the South Yorkshire club.

WORKINGTON TOWN were a revelation under the stewardship of former Great Britain international and Grand Final winner Leon Pryce.

If League 1 was meant to all be about York City Knight and Bradford Bulls in 2018, Pryce and Town didn't get the memo and they had a big say in the eventual outcome of the league.

Town only lost narrowly when York visited Derwent Park in September but Pryce proved the thorn in Bradford's side, beating his boyhood club, who he'd only left as a player the previous year, both home and away. These results ultimately saw Bradford miss out on automatic promotion and set up a third game between the two sides in the play-off final. Bradford may have got their revenge but Town never gave up and that never-say-die attitude carried through to a second-chance game against Swinton Lions.

League 1 Season

With the game only being announced within a month of the end of the season to tie in with the new league structure for 2019, Town were down on numbers due to injuries but again they battled to the end only, narrowly missing out on promotion.

Whilst largely having a Cumbrian-based side, Pryce was able to call upon his many connections in the game to bring players like the experienced Sean Penkywicz and Fuifui Moimoi to Derwent Park. When games were tight against their play-off rivals, the experience of these players, along with the likes of Oliver Wilkes, proved invaluable for the rookie coach.

OLDHAM went into the season with one of the smallest squads but managed to prove that bigger doesn't always mean better.

Even when injuries hit and coach Scott Naylor was unable to call on any dual-registered players - as they hadn't played enough games for the club before the cut off point in September - Oldham kept fighting and a win over London Skolars on the final weekend ultimately secured their spot in the top five.

One area that will have frustrated Naylor though is that, with the exception of two of their three defeats to Bradford (30-12 in the league and 47-0 in the play-offs), they only lost their games by a maximum of eight points.

Unfortunately for Oldham, they seemed to save their worst performance of the season until the end, bowing out of the play-offs in forgettable style. That game though mirrored most of the ten defeats they'd suffered throughout the season. They started well for the opening quarter before mistakes started to creep in and proved their undoing.

All in all it was a season of missed opportunities and 'what if' moments.

WHITEHAVEN will have a very different feel about them in 2019 after a tumultuous season took its toll across the board.

Serious financial problems severely threatened the club's existence, meaning big cuts had to happen and the biggest of those was the departure of player-coach Carl Forster, who stood down at the end of the year.

Forster had rejuvenated the club over two seasons and seen them in with a realistic chance of getting back to the Championship.

With already limited options due to injuries constantly limiting Whitehaven to around 19 players, talks of financial problems could have made things worse with players seeking opportunities elsewhere. But such is the spirit Forster built at the club, not one player asked to leave and they all stuck it out until the end.

Special measures imposed by the RFL because of the financial situation meant Haven were unable to sign any players as the season progressed. So missing out on the play-offs on points difference was achievement in itself.

It wasn't just in the League though that 'Haven impressed, making it all the way to the sixth-round and losing out to eventual winners Catalans Dragons. Along the way they beat Championship sides Rochdale Hornets and Dewsbury Rams.

HUNSLET continued their impressive form under head coach Gary Thornton, who had come in and worked wonders half way through the 2017 season.

Many of 2018's squad have already agreed to stay and the injection of Championship experience with the likes of Ben Heaton and Gareth Potts could see Hunslet really take League 1 by storm.

Even the disruption of losing captain George Flanagan to Bradford Bulls just weeks before the new season was due to kick-off couldn't derail the South Leeds club. While there was no direct replacement incoming for Flanagan straight away, players elsewhere stepped up and Hunslet went on to win four of their opening six games to get themselves into the play-off race from the start.

Flanagan's departure saw Duane Straugheir step into the captain's role and he was at the heart of everything good the club produced throughout a generally satisfactory season for them.

continued on page 113

Tommy Makinson

St Helens & England

Tommy Makinson finished 2018 on top of the world.

The St Helens winger's Golden Boot award came at the end of an unbelievable year as he starred for the eventual League Leaders at club level, before producing three outstanding performances for England.

Makinson came off the bench for his international debut in the 36-18 win over New Zealand in Denver in June, coming up with a superb piece of skill to set up Elliott Whitehead's pivotal try, before scoring a beauty of his own ten minutes later.

There were no spectacular tries from him in the first game of the three-match Test series on home soil against the Kiwis but Makinson epitomised the modern-day winger with his explosive returns from his own territory.

He defended for his life in game two, as well as scoring a magical hat-trick of tries.

In game three he scored twice, although both 'tries' were ruled out by the video referee.

Makinson could easily have been a forgotten man. A broken ankle in the middle of the 2015 season, followed by a ruptured anterior cruciate ligament on his comeback at the start of 2016, effectively put him out of the game for nearly two years.

According to England coach Wayne Bennett, his international performances had put him 'in a league of his own'. Few would argue with that.

ENGLAND V NEW ZEALAND
4 NOVEMBER 2018

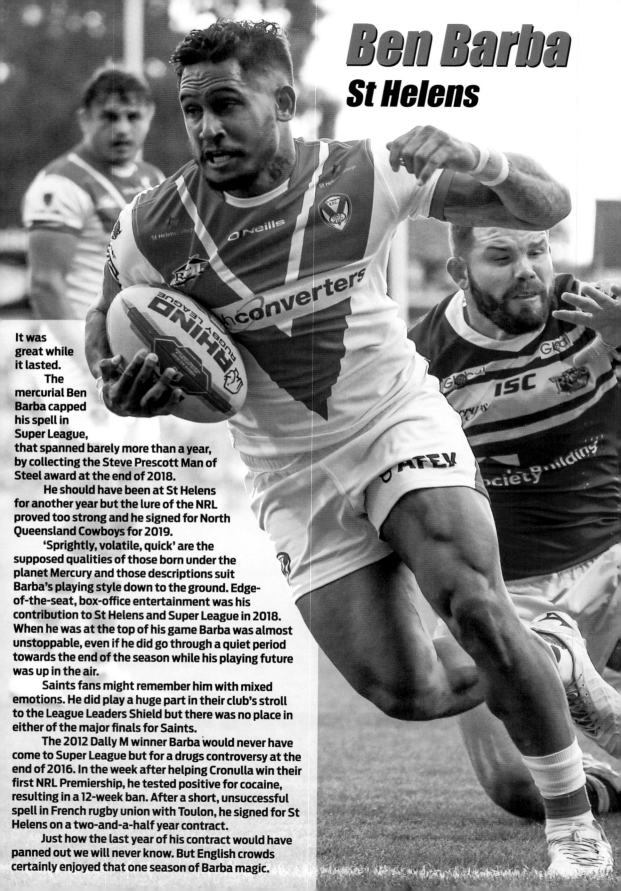

Ben Barba
St Helens

It was great while it lasted.

The mercurial Ben Barba capped his spell in Super League, that spanned barely more than a year, by collecting the Steve Prescott Man of Steel award at the end of 2018.

He should have been at St Helens for another year but the lure of the NRL proved too strong and he signed for North Queensland Cowboys for 2019.

'Sprightly, volatile, quick' are the supposed qualities of those born under the planet Mercury and those descriptions suit Barba's playing style down to the ground. Edge-of-the-seat, box-office entertainment was his contribution to St Helens and Super League in 2018. When he was at the top of his game Barba was almost unstoppable, even if he did go through a quiet period towards the end of the season while his playing future was up in the air.

Saints fans might remember him with mixed emotions. He did play a huge part in their club's stroll to the League Leaders Shield but there was no place in either of the major finals for Saints.

The 2012 Dally M winner Barba would never have come to Super League but for a drugs controversy at the end of 2016. In the week after helping Cronulla win their first NRL Premiership, he tested positive for cocaine, resulting in a 12-week ban. After a short, unsuccessful spell in French rugby union with Toulon, he signed for St Helens on a two-and-a-half year contract.

Just how the last year of his contract would have panned out we will never know. But English crowds certainly enjoyed that one season of Barba magic.

Danny Ward
London Broncos

What have we done?' Danny Ward's post-match reaction to his side London Broncos' astonishing 4-2 win over highly fancied Toronto Wolfpack in the Million Pound Game was echoed across the world.

But it finally sank in. The Broncos had overturned the odds and won back their place in Super League by winning the play-off between fourth and fifth in the Super 8s qualifiers.

Less than two weeks before, Ward had been named Championship coach of the year, mainly on the back of getting his side into the Middle Eights and making a fist of it in the play-offs, beating two Super League sides along the way. But not many people outside the Broncos camp seriously thought London would be back in Super League two weeks later.

Danny Ward's association with London Rugby League's senior club goes back to 2008 when he joined then-named Harlequins, playing for four seasons before moving into coaching, first with the Academy and then as Andrew Henderson's assistant.

At the start of 2018, with Henderson left for Warrington as assistant and star man Andy Ackers joining Toronto, former Leeds prop Ward stepped into the head coaching role. The Broncos weren't expected to make the top four for the third year running. And even when they did, they were predicted to merely make up the numbers. How wrong could you be?

Because the Broncos, one of the founding members of Super League in 1996, were back

Tony Gigot would be an automatic choice as one of 2018's personalities simply for being the first Frenchman to win the Lance Todd Trophy in its 73-year history. But Gigot's backstory is like no other.

Gigot played a huge part in the Dragons getting to Wembley with a man-of-the-match performance in Catalans' 35-16 win over St Helens in the semi-final but at the start of the year his career was in tatters.

It wasn't until February that the Avignon-born fullback was able to resume his career after winning an appeal against a two-year suspension imposed by the French anti-doping authorities.

The ban had first been imposed a year before, was reduced on appeal to three months, allowing Gigot to play again from April 2017, then re-imposed in August that year for an 'inappropriate exchange' with an anti-doping official at an international camp in 2016. He never failed a drugs test.

Gigot's re-signing was significant for the Dragons and their mid-season revival owed a lot to switching Gigot to fullback, with David Mead moving into the centres.

The years leading up to Catalans' 20-14 win over Warrington at Wembley hadn't been plain sailing either for Gigot - on loan at Toulouse, released by the Dragons and playing for Avignon in the French Elite, attempting in vain to get an NRL start at Cronulla Sharks, lasting two games at London Broncos, back to Avignon and, finally, re-signed by Catalans in May 2015.

And now he could add the Lance Todd Trophy to that colourful CV.

Tony Gigot
Catalans Dragons & France

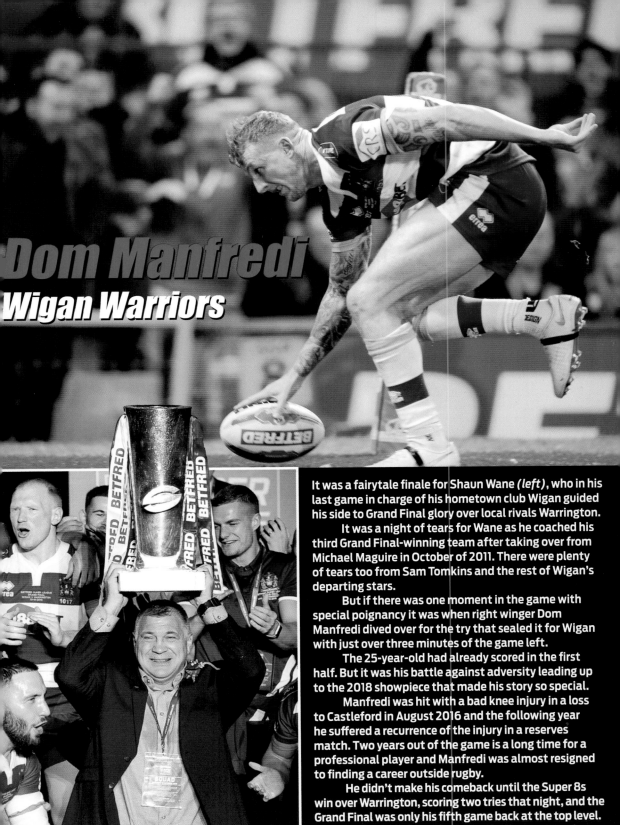

Dom Manfredi
Wigan Warriors

It was a fairytale finale for Shaun Wane (*left*), who in his last game in charge of his hometown club Wigan guided his side to Grand Final glory over local rivals Warrington.

It was a night of tears for Wane as he coached his third Grand Final-winning team after taking over from Michael Maguire in October of 2011. There were plenty of tears too from Sam Tomkins and the rest of Wigan's departing stars.

But if there was one moment in the game with special poignancy it was when right winger Dom Manfredi dived over for the try that sealed it for Wigan with just over three minutes of the game left.

The 25-year-old had already scored in the first half. But it was his battle against adversity leading up to the 2018 showpiece that made his story so special.

Manfredi was hit with a bad knee injury in a loss to Castleford in August 2016 and the following year he suffered a recurrence of the injury in a reserves match. Two years out of the game is a long time for a professional player and Manfredi was almost resigned to finding a career outside rugby.

He didn't make his comeback until the Super 8s win over Warrington, scoring two tries that night, and the Grand Final was only his fifth game back at the top level.

At the end of the Final, Manfredi was a blood-spattered hero after re-taking the field for treatment on a nasty cut on his eyelid. It summed up the courage

2018 SEASON REVIEW

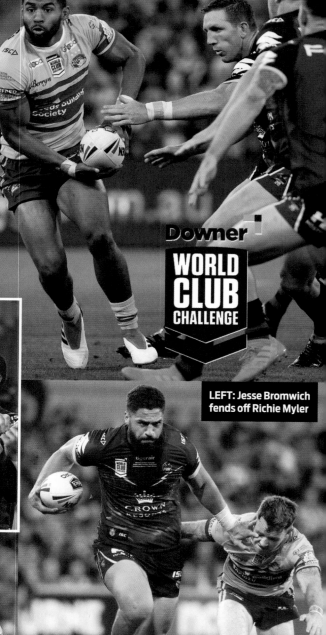

MELBOURNE STORM...........................38
LEEDS RHINOS....................................4

RIGHT: Kallum Watkins looks for support from Jamie Jones-Buchanan as the Melbourne defence closes in

BELOW: The victorious Melbourne Storm side celebrate winning the World Club Challenge

Downer

WORLD CLUB CHALLENGE

LEFT: Jesse Bromwich fends off Richie Myler

RIGHT: Wigan's Morgan Escare gets a pass away under pressure from Hull FC's Albert Kelly as Super League heads Down Under

DACIA MAGIC WEEKEND

RIGHT: Hull FC's Scott Taylor crosses for a try against Hull KR

BELOW: St Helens' Ryan Morgan stretches towards the Widnes tryline

BELOW: Castleford's Alex Foster dives over against Leeds

RIGHT: Catalans' Greg Bird takes on Salford duo Logan Tomkins and Lee Mossop

BELOW: Wigan's Sam Tomkins kicks for goal against Warrington

RIGHT: Huddersfield's Adam O'Brien shows his delight at scoring against Wakefield

SUPER LEAGUE AWARDS

STEVE PRESCOTT MBE MAN OF STEEL
Ben Barba (St Helens)

YOUNG PLAYER OF THE YEAR
Jake Trueman (Castleford Tigers)

COACH OF THE YEAR
Shaun Wane (Wigan Warriors)

CLUB OF THE YEAR
Warrington Wolves

TOP TRY SCORER
Ben Barba (St Helens) (28)

TOP METRE MAKER
Bill Tupou (Wakefield Trinity) (4,114)

TOP TACKLER
Paul McShane (Castleford Tigers) (1160)

(totals include regular season & Super 8s only)

SUPER LEAGUE DREAM TEAM
(previous selections in italics)

1. Ben Barba (St Helens) *Debut*
2. Tommy Makinson (St Helens) *2014*
3. Mark Percival (St Helens) *2017*
4. Bill Tupou (Wakefield) *Debut*
5. Tom Johnstone (Wakefield) *Debut*
6. Jonny Lomax (St Helens) *Debut*
7. Danny Richardson (St Helens) *Debut*
8. Luke Thompson (St Helens) *Debut*
9. James Roby (St Helens)
   2007, 2010, 2011, 2012, 2015
10. Remi Casty (Catalans Dragons) *2012*
11. John Bateman (Wigan) *Debut*
12. Matty Ashurst (Wakefield) *Debut*
13. Sean O'Loughlin (Wigan)
   2010, 2011, 2012, 2013, 2014, 2017

ALBERT GOLDTHORPE MEDAL
Stefan Ratchford (Warrington Wolves)

ALBERT GOLDTHORPE ROOKIE OF THE YEAR
Jake Trueman (Castleford Tigers)

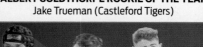

ABOVE: Jake Trueman - 2018 Young Player of the Year

RIGHT: Ben Barba and Georgia Roche show off their awards

BELOW: The 2018 Super League Dream Team

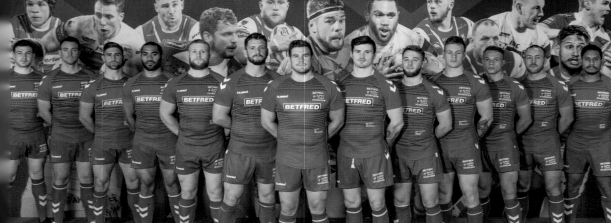

RIGHT: St Helens are presented with the League Leaders' Shield

BELOW: The Wakefield defence puts a stop to the progress of Castleford's junior Moors

LEFT: Huddersfield's Suaia Matagi brought down by St Helens' Jonny Lomax

LEFT: Catalans' Antoni Maria offloads under pressure from Hull FC's Scott Taylor

BETFRED SUPER LEAGUE SUPER 8s

RIGHT: Warrington matchwinner Tom Lineham celebrates reaching the Grand Final with the Wolves' fans, after victory against St Helens

RIGHT: Wigan's Dom Manfredi races past Adam Milner as the Warriors nil Castleford to reach Old Trafford

The ecstatic Catalans Dragons team show off the Challenge Cup

Ladbrokes
CHALLENGE CUP

**RIGHT: A dejected
Stefan Ratchford
reflects on defeat as
Catalans celebrate**

**FAR RIGHT: Brayden
Wiliame holds off
Josh Charnley to score**

Departing coach Shaun Wane lifts the Super League Trophy, flanked by his victorious Wigan squad

BELOW: Sam Tomkins races to congratulate Dom Manfredi on scoring the winning try

BELOW: Morgan Escare breaks away from Joe Philbin and Bodene Thompson

BETFRED SUPER LEAGUE
GRAND FINAL

MELBOURNE STORM............................ 6
SYDNEY ROOSTERS 21

TOP: Sydney Roosters celebrate their Grand Final success

ABOVE: Billy Slater can't stop Latrell Mitchell from scoring

LEFT: Jared Waerea-Hargreaves gives coach Trent Robinson a Gatorade shower

GRAND FINAL
SYDNEY 2018

LEFT: Toronto Wolfpack's Gareth O'Brien shows his delight at landing the winning field goal against Leeds

ABOVE: Jackson Hastings throws his boots to fans as Salford survive

SUPER 8s
THE QUALIFIERS

LEFT: Hull KR's Craig Hall on the charge against relegated Widnes

FAR LEFT: Halifax's Kieren Moss meets Leeds duo Liam Sutcliffe and Adam Cuthbertson head on

BELOW: The champagne flows as London Broncos celebrate promotion to Super League

£1M GAME

RIGHT: Barrow's Shane Toal celebrates a try against Sheffield

BETFRED CHAMPIONSHIP

BELOW: Toulouse Olympique's Chris Centrone charges away from London Broncos' James Cunningham and Rhys Williams

RIGHT: Dewsbury's Josh Guzdek and Batley's Joel Farrell contest a high ball at The Summer Bash

BELOW: Toronto's Ashton Sims lifts the League Leaders' Shield as the Wolfpack celebrate

RIGHT: Leigh's Rhys Evans leaves Rochdale's Declan Kay trailing

York coach James Ford leads the celebrations as the City Knights are crowned League 1 champions

BELOW: Joel Edwards is mobbed by teammates after scoring during York's last-day win against Whitehaven

BETFRED LEAGUE 1

ABOVE: Bradford coach John Kear is chaired from the field as the Bulls earn a return to the Championship

RIGHT: Bradford's Jy Hitchcox beats Workington's Jamie Doran to score in the corner

ABOVE: Swinton's Rob Fairclough makes a break as the Lions survive, and deny Workington promotion

RIGHT: Matty Wildie gets the ball away during Featherstone's Championship Shield Final win against Leigh

BETFRED CHAMPIONSHIP SHIELD SUPER 8s

WOMEN'S SUPER LEAGUE
GRAND FINAL
MANCHESTER 2018

WOMEN'S SUPER LEAGUE

ABOVE: Wigan Warriors celebrate their Super League Grand Final win

LEFT: The Wigan defence wraps up Leeds' Manina Spurr during the Grand Final

RIGHT: Woman of Steel Georgia Roche in action against Leeds

LEFT: Leeds' Lois Forsell scores the winning try in the Challenge Cup Final

ABOVE: Bradford captain Kirsty Moroney on the attack as the Bulls defeat Stanningley to win the Challenge Shield

WINNERS

RUGBY FOOTBALL LEAGUE

ABOVE: Leeds Rhinos show their delight as they lift the Challenge Cup, following victory against Castleford

continued from page 96

NEWCASTLE THUNDER continue to be one of the shining lights in Rugby League.

With a young British coach in charge in Jason Payne, an excellent youth system at the club that has provided many an up-coming first team player, and great facilities at Kingston Park, Thunder will be the envy of even some Super League clubs. So it is no wonder they one day aspire to be in the top tier.

After ending 2017 as somewhat of a surprise packet under Payne, many expected Thunder to be challenging again and they weren't far off in what mainly proved to be a tight and competitive season. With York and Bradford expected to go up from the start, it realistically meant there was three play-off spots available and about seven teams with realistic chances of making them, so it was always going to be hard for Newcastle to repeat the feats of the previous year.

That said they still put in some impressive performances and finished the year in style, beating West Wales Raiders 98-6 - their biggest ever margin of victory - with a team that contained ten players that had come through their own youth system.

Payne admitted a lack of experience was their undoing at certain points of the year and he has addressed that with the signings of former Super League stars Liam Finn and Keal Carlile for 2019.

KEIGHLEY COUGARS once again went into the season full of hope and expectations of making the play-offs after narrowly missing out the previous season.

A 44-34 win over Workington Town on the opening day filled the club with optimism and they were still well within a shout of making the top five when the news broke at the end of June that they had come within hours of going out of business.

The setback prompted several players to move on, leaving coach Craig Lingard with far fewer options at his disposal for the second half of the year.

New investors were found and former Castleford Tigers chief Steve Gill came in to steady the ship and offer his expertise but by then a lot of the damage had already been done. So when injuries further hit the squad as the season progressed, it was very much a case of the Cougars limping to the finish line with whatever resources they still had available.

Lingard, whose position was unsure at the end of the season, will be working on a much tighter budget in 2019 to avoid a recurrence of those problems.

NORTH WALES CRUSADERS were the first team to make a coaching change in 2018 when Mike Grady moved on after just three league games.

Two defeats and a draw in those games, plus a heavy loss to Featherstone Rovers in the Challenge Cup, saw the Crusaders make a slower start to the campaign than they would have envisaged after only just missing out on a place in the 2017 League 1 Shield final by two points.

They were sitting 11th when Grady left and was replaced by former coach Anthony Murray, who oversaw a victory in his first match against West Wales Raiders. Although the Crusaders then went on to lose the next three games, performances were improving and it soon started paying off with wins - particularly impressive were those at Whitehaven and Newcastle as the season progressed.

COVENTRY BEARS may have had to settle for another lower mid-table finish in League 1 but they continued to lead the way where other expansionist clubs floundered.

Another year of steady improvement on the field and the continuation of work being done off it, was rewarded with seven wins across the season, making it the Bears' most successful season since 2016, when they picked up a total of eight wins and a draw.

But it was the nature of two of those wins that will have pleased coach Tom Tsang the most.

League 1 Season

In July, when a number of the Bears players were away playing in the Student Four Nations, the Bears put in a strong and determined performance from the start against Keighley Cougars to claim their first-ever win over a traditional northern club. It wasn't to be a one-off occurrence either as the Bears then beat a second heartland team in Hunslet in the final match of the season, proving to Tsang and the team that their decision to put their faith in locally based players was finally starting to pay off.

LONDON SKOLARS' season never really got started as long-term injuries to key players throughout the season took their toll and it became difficult for the club to ever find any real consistency.

Halfbacks Mike Bishay and Jy-mel Coleman were on the sidelines for large chunks of the season and their experience was missed on the field.

With more points scored than any of the bottom five teams, finding their way to the line was never really the issue for Skolars, so coach Jermaine Coleman will now doubt be looking to work to tighten up what they do without ball in hand.

On numerous occasions the Skolars showed they could compete with the sides battling for the play-offs for long periods, but lapses in concentration at key points of the game proved their undoing more than once.

In 2019 Skolars will find themselves the only non-Super League team based in the south of England, meaning they could have a larger playing pool available to them. If they strengthen wisely they could find themselves in a good position to challenge for a higher league finish.

HEMEL STAGS endured another season of struggle in League 1.

A move to a Sheffield base saw the Stags stick to their original plan of gradually moving back to the Hertfordshire town but it still didn't improve their fortunes as the only games they won were against West Wales Raiders.

They were able to compete for small periods of games but a lack of experience meant they were unable to sustain it for prolonged spells.

With long-standing coach Troy Perkins gone before the season started, director of rugby Dean Thomas took charge for most of the season, before assistant coach, former Sheffield Eagles star Jack Howieson, stepped up to the head coach role, coming out of retirement to add some knowledge on the field too.

The season ended with much uncertainty over their future in the league and it was confirmed in late October they were to move back to Hemel Hampstead and withdraw from the league to concentrate on developing their community programme. They plan to return to League 1 in 2020.

WEST WALES RAIDERS' first season in the league was one to forget as they became the first team since Nottingham City in 1991-92 to lose every game in a season.

It had been hoped that the new club in Llanelli would develop local talent and bring a strong Rugby League presence to the area. But inexperienced showed and they conceded an average of 81 points in their 26 league games. Add to that an 82-6 defeat at Bradford Bulls in the Challenge Cup and new coach Kim Williams certainly had his work cut out to shore up the defence.

The record 144-0 defeat to York signalled the end of Jon Ellis's short stint as coach, with assistant and former South Wales Ironman coach Phil Carleton taking the reins. But he too left before the end of the season when an offer from rugby union proved too good to turn down.

Welsh internationals Steve Parry and Morgan Evans worked alongside owner and chairman Andrew Thorne to steer the ship for the rest of the season. Williams, a former performance manager at Melbourne Storm, will be looking for improvement.

LEAGUE 1 PLAY-OFFS
Bulls revival

Promotion from League 1 into the Championship went to the side topping the table after 26 rounds, with a second promotion place going to the winner of a four-team play-off. York went up automatically, pipping Bradford Bulls by two league points, leaving the Bulls, Doncaster, Workington and Oldham to play off.

However, after an extraordinary meeting of the Rugby Football League on September 14th 2018 decided to re-structure the competitions for 2019, the loser of the final of the top-four play-off would enter a promotion play-off against the bottom side in the Championship.

Favourites Bradford had little difficulty in progressing to the final with a highly efficient 47-0 home demolition of Oldham, the team they were relegated alongside in 2017.

League 1 Young Player of the Year Ethan Ryan took his season's try tally in the league to 34 with a brace, while Elliot Minchella also claimed two as the Bulls ran in a total of eight touchdowns. Joe Keyes added seven goals, two of them from penalties. And Dane Chisholm comprehensively out-thought Oldham throughout with some astute and pinpoint kicking.

The previous week the Bulls rested a host of first-choice players, so had the significant additions of Ryan, Minchella, Keyes, Gregg McNally, Steve Crossley and George Flanagan, while Oldham were without four suspended players in Danny Bridge, Luke Hooley, Ben Davies and Luke Nelmes.

Workington would be the Bulls' opponents the following week after a 30-18 win at third-placed Doncaster.

Doncaster had a psychological edge going into the game after beating Town 44-32 - their ninth straight victory - in the final game of the regular season. But Workington coach Leon Pryce brought back a number of his frontline players, including Jamie Doran, Sean Penkywicz and Oliver Wilkes and the experience told.

Joe Hambley's try with a quarter of the game remaining clinched Workington's place in the play-off final as Doran controlled things for Town.

League 1 Promotion Final

Jy Hitchcox, on loan from Castleford, scored a memorable hat-trick to help Bradford Bulls complete the first part of coach John Kear's 'masterplan' to restore them to former glories with a hard-fought 27-8 League 1 play-off final victory over Workington.

Kear, in his first year at Odsal, has steered his charges back into the Championship at the first attempt, albeit not as most expected, automatically through topping the table.

But Hitchcox's spectacular treble - all diving horizontally in by the corner flag - plus tries from George Flanagan, Joe Keyes and Dane Chisholm were enough to see the Bulls home - and it would surely have been by more had three different goal-kickers managed more than one success out of seven attempts.

Workington were largely responsible for the Bulls' failure to finish above York after inflicting two of the three losses incurred by the former Super League champions during the season. But completing an unlikely treble proved a bridge too far for the plucky part-timers.

Leon Pryce, like Kear in his first year at the helm but also in his maiden coaching role, could be proud of his and his players' achievements.

And the Cumbrians still had one more opportunity to end their two-year stint in the sport's third-tier when they faced Championship basement-dwellers Swinton the next weekend, losing a coin toss to determine who got home advantage. Pryce admitted it would be 'touch and go' over whether his side could even field a full 17, with players on pre-booked holidays due to the late nature of the fixture's arrangement.

Championship Promotion/Relegation Play-off

Swinton secured their place in the second tier after overcoming gutsy Workington.

Workington had unsuccessfully attempted to gain special dispensation to sign players for the match and were just about able to field 17 players despite several carrying injuries.

Even though they all took to the field, most of the substitutes only played a handful of minutes before retreating.

It was a very close encounter, with man of the match Kyle Shelford edging the Lions 26-20 in front on the hour mark, for the first time since the eighth minute. But Town pushed hard, with Jamie Doran leading his troops well. When they won a penalty which put them within striking distance, they looked capable of levelling again.

But a try never materialised and Swinton secured the win late on. Josh Woods nailed a field goal in the 77th minute to finally put breathing space between the two teams for the first time, then Rhodri Lloyd crashed over for his second try.

BETFRED LEAGUE 1 - PROMOTION FINAL

Sunday 7th October 2018

BRADFORD BULLS 27 WORKINGTON TOWN 8

BULLS: 14 Gregg McNally; 35 Jy Hitchcox; 3 Ashley Gibson; 4 Ross Oakes; 2 Ethan Ryan; 6 Joe Keyes; 7 Dane Chisholm; 8 Liam Kirk; 38 Jordan Lilley; 10 Steve Crossley; 12 Elliot Minchella; 11 Matt Garside; 19 Mikey Wood. Subs (all used): 37 James Green; 21 George Flanagan; 17 Ross Peltier; 32 Matthew Storton.
Tries: Hitchcox (4, 63, 74), Flanagan (35), Keyes (38), Chisholm (79);
Goals: Keyes 0/2, Chisholm 1/4, Crossley 0/1; **Field goal:** Chisholm (67).
Sin bin: Garside (14) - dissent.
TOWN: 24 Tyllar Mellor; 2 Joe Hambley; 22 Elliot Miller; 16 Ben Morris; - Scott Rooke; 6 Jamie Doran; 7 Carl Forber; 8 Oliver Wilkes; 20 Sean Penkywicz; 28 Tyler Dickinson; 21 Jake Moore; 18 Karl Olstrom; 10 Stevie Scholey. Subs (all used): 9 James Newton; 15 Tom Curwen; 11 Andrew Dawson; 17 Fuifui Moimoi.
Try: Miller (51); **Goals:** Forber 2/2.
Dismissal: Moimoi (68) - high tackle on Kirk.
Rugby Leaguer & League Express Men of the Match:
Bulls: Jy Hitchcox; *Town:* Tyllar Mellor.
Penalty count: 11-9; **Half-time:** 12-2; **Referee:** Marcus Griffiths;
Attendance: 6,011.

BETFRED CHAMPIONSHIP - PROMOTION/RELEGATION PLAY-OFF

Sunday 14th October 2018

SWINTON LIONS 33 WORKINGTON TOWN 20

LIONS: 7 Jack Hansen; 16 Ryan Gray; 11 Rhodri Lloyd; 4 George Tyson; 32 Craig Mullen; 30 Rob Fairclough; 31 Josh Woods; 8 Andy Bracek; 9 Luke Waterworth; 10 Andy Thornley; 17 Kyle Shelford; 33 Liam Paisley; 25 Will Hope. Subs (all used): 15 Ben Austin; 34 Josh Ganson; 24 Aaron Hall; 35 Paddy Jones.
Tries: Waterworth (6, 20), Lloyd (40, 79), Woods (55), Shelford (59);
Goals: J Hansen 4/6; **Field goal:** Woods (77).
TOWN: 24 Tyllar Mellor; 2 Joe Hambley; 12 Kurt Maudling; 16 Ben Morris; - Scott Rooke; 6 Jamie Doran; 7 Carl Forber; 28 Tyler Dickinson; 9 James Newton; 15 Tom Curwen; 4 Gordon Maudling; 21 Jake Moore; 18 Karl Olstrom. Subs (all used): 8 Oliver Wilkes; 20 Sean Penkywicz; 5 Perry Singleton; 11 Andrew Dawson.
Tries: Hambley (8), Rooke (37), Mellor (53); **Goals:** Forber 4/4.
Rugby Leaguer & League Express Men of the Match:
Lions: Kyle Shelford; *Town:* Carl Forber.
Penalty count: 7-6; **Half-time:** 16-14; **Referee:** Greg Dolan;
Attendance: 703.

LEAGUE 1 AWARDS

PLAYER OF THE YEAR
Connor Robinson
(York City Knights)

YOUNG PLAYER OF THE YEAR
Ethan Ryan (Bradford Bulls)

COACH OF THE YEAR
James Ford (York City Knights)

CLUB OF THE YEAR
York City Knights

4
SEASON DOWN UNDER

NRL
Roosters crowing

In front of over 80,000 fans at Sydney's ANZ Stadium, Sydney Roosters produced a brilliant all-round performance to take Melbourne's crown with a 21-6 victory over the Storm.

The build-up to the game had been completely dominated by talk of the two old teammates that would, or wouldn't, face off for the final time in their careers.

Whilst it wasn't the end for Cooper Cronk, who would be playing on with the Roosters the next year, it was the final curtain for perhaps the greatest fullback of all time. Billy Slater was credited for changing what it meant to be a fullback, just as Clive Churchill had done decades before. His ball skills matched his pace and evasion while his work through the middle of the ruck, often in conjunction with Cameron Smith and Cronk, was legendary.

In the week before the game, Slater's swan song was in huge doubt. 'Billy Whiz' had been charged with a shoulder charge against Sosaia Feki in Melbourne's semi-final win over Cronulla and was sent before a judicial panel with a ban looming. The verdict, however, went in his favour and he was allowed to play, although he was booed by a majority of the Grand Final crowd.

Melbourne were attempting to earn back-to-back titles, a feat not accomplished since Brisbane managed two successive victories over St George in 1992 and 1993.

But as they did in the race for the Minor Premiership the Roosters ran out victors and there was very little Melbourne could do about it on the day.

They had found themselves 18-0 up a year before in 2017's Grand Final but were left stranded 18-0 down at the break in this year's showpiece, as the Roosters scored three first-half tries to all but end the contest before the teams returned to the sheds at half-time.

Storm had no answer as the Roosters' left edge did most of the damage in the opening twenty minutes. First a sweeping move ended with Daniel Tupou diving in at the corner. Then Latrell Mitchell stepped between defenders on the same side to make the lead twelve.

Young Kiwi Joseph Manu had often been left in Mitchell's shadow as Sydney's other centre but he joined the party when he went over on the right-hand side.

While the only try of the second half went to Melbourne flyer Josh Addo-Carr, the game was seen out imperiously by the Roosters.

Cameron Munster, despite an excellent season at stand-off for Melbourne, gained an unwanted record being the first player in Grand Final history to be sin-binned twice. He was first sent for ten minutes for a professional foul and then for kicking out in the final moments of the game.

Here's how all sixteen teams fared in 2018.

SYDNEY ROOSTERS (Premiers/Minor Premiers)
Top pointscorer: Latrell Mitchell (248); *Top tryscorer:* Blake Ferguson (18)

Sydney Roosters won both trophies in 2018. They secured the Minor Premiership in dramatic style with a 44-10 win over wooden spooners Parramatta Eels. Then the Roosters won all three of their Finals games, conceding just 22 points in the process as they defended their way to a Premiership.

Daniel Tupou skips past the despairing dive of Suliasi Vunivalu to score the opening try in the NRL Grand Final

Headed up by their 26-year-old captain Boyd Cordner, who also captained New South Wales to victory in Origin, the Roosters were widely expected to be challenging at the top in 2018 after a poor season in 2017 by their high standards.

The acquisitions of both James Tedesco and Cooper Cronk had the hallmarks of signings that would be crucial come the big games at the end of the year.

And so it proved.

Even with Cronk going into the Grand Final against Melbourne Storm with the full use of only one of his arms, he coached his side to victory from the field. Tedesco proved a solid fullback, in both attack and defence, throughout an incredibly successful season for the Bondi boys.

Their home, Allianz Stadium, the former Sydney Football Stadium, was closed at the end of the season for redevelopment. A new stadium is expected to reopen in 2022 and they will play their home games until then at the Sydney Cricket ground.

MELBOURNE STORM (Runners-up)
Top pointscorer: Cameron Smith (201); *Top tryscorer:* Josh Addo-Carr (18)

After a hugely successful season in 2017, Melbourne Storm became the nearly men of 2018.

After saying goodbye to Cooper Cronk at the end of 2017, they then farewelled a second of their infamous 'Three Musketeers' as Billy Slater announced his retirement at the end of the season.

Slater wouldn't go out with a Premiership as the Storm were beaten in the Grand Final by his old friend Cooper Cronk and the Sydney Roosters.

Melbourne also lost out on the Minor Premiership thanks to a final round defeat to Penrith and the Roosters' big victory over Parramatta.

Despite coming away, in the end, empty handed, the Storm provided some real highlights in the NRL. Their flying winger Josh Addo-Carr soared to new heights while Nelson Asofa-Solomona really came of age as he rumbled through the middle of many an NRL team.

The Storm were also boosted when Craig Bellamy signed a new deal mid-way through the season keeping the coach at the club for the foreseeable future, ending speculation he would move to Brisbane Broncos.

SOUTH SYDNEY RABBITOHS (3rd)

Top pointscorer: Adam Reynolds (211); *Top tryscorer:* Robert Jennings (19)

After winning the Grand Final in 2014, South Sydney Rabbitohs have been in indifferent form. Many didn't expect this to change either with relative rookie, former South Wales Scorpions boss, Anthony Seibold appointed as head coach at the end of the previous season.

But Seibold proved to be an inspired choice as the Rabbitohs became the most exciting team to watch in the NRL.

Led by the back-in-form Burgess twins Tom and George, Souths were able to play fast and explosive Rugby League on the back of their lightning quick hooker Damien Cook.

After the international retirement of Cameron Smith during the season, the Australian hooking spot was up for grabs and Cook snatched it with both hands. His immense speed out of dummy half, coupled with the Burgess twins' quick play-the-balls made Souths a real handful.

Ultimately, their season ended in disappointment. They were beaten by arch-rivals the Roosters in the Preliminary Final. But 2018 was still a season of great promise for the Bunnies.

It ended with the announcement that Wayne Bennett would be coaching the side from 2020 with Seibold tipped to move to the Broncos.

CRONULLA SHARKS (4th)

Top pointscorer: Chad Townsend (148); *Top tryscorer:* Valentine Holmes (22)

Cronulla Sharks made the NRL Finals once again under coach Shane Flanagan in 2018. After falling at the first hurdle the year before, the Sharks made it all the way to the Preliminary Final, losing to Melbourne after finishing the regular season in fourth position.

The real highlight for the Sharks this season was the further emergence of Valentine Holmes as a genuine contender for individual honours at the end of the year.

Holmes, while playing much of his early and international career on the wing, secured himself a spot in his preferred position at fullback, with Josh Dugan suffering an injury-ravaged campaign. Holmes notched 22 tries in all as he proved a constant menace for defending teams.

Meanwhile, old-timers such as Luke Lewis, who retired at the end of the season, and Paul Gallen continued to inspire their team with sensational performances. Matt Prior became the seventh oldest State of Origin debutant in Game II as he produced his career best form with the Sharks in 2018 at the age of 31.

PENRITH PANTHERS (5th)

Top pointscorer: James Maloney (126); *Top tryscorer:* Waqa Blake (13)

Penrith Panthers had a turbulent 2018.

While performances on the pitch were generally good as they comfortably secured a spot in the Finals, they were heavily involved in the general coaching merry-go-round towards the end of the season.

With the Finals looming, General Manager Phil Gould thought it necessary to sack head coach Anthony Griffin, with Cameron Ciraldo stepping up to take charge for the rest of the season.

The Panthers' season faltered towards the end but they were within a whisker of the Preliminary Final before losing to Cronulla Sharks in their second Finals game.

Both James Maloney and Nathan Cleary, the club's halfback pairing, were called up to the New South Wales squad as the Panthers gained a reputation as the side that would always come back to win: In both their opening two games, they came from 14-0 down to take the points.

New head coach Ivan Cleary is heading back to the club that sacked him at the end of 2015. The Panthers are expected to go from strength to strength with a young squad, despite losing Tyrone Peachey and Corey Harawira-Naera to Gold Coast Titans and Canterbury Bulldogs respectively.

ST GEORGE ILLAWARRA DRAGONS (6th)

Top pointscorer: Gareth Widdop (205); *Top tryscorer:* Matt Dufty (13)

It seems to have become the norm in recent years. St George Illawarra Dragons' season starts off incredibly well as they lead the competition through the opening rounds. But come the mid-point of the season, their tail-off begins.

Last year, they dropped out of the Finals positions altogether. Thankfully for the Dragons, they didn't go that far this year and were able to book their position in the play-offs.

A huge victory over Brisbane at Suncorp followed but their run in the Finals was ended by South Sydney Rabbitohs.

English duo Gareth Widdop and James Graham were pivotal for the Dragons, who played a pre-season game against Hull FC in Wollongong as part of the Black and Whites' tour down under.

Young gun Matt Dufty proved to be an inspiration at fullback, while Jason Nightingale played his final season with the Red Vee after joining the club in 2007.

BRISBANE BRONCOS (7th)

Top pointscorer: Jamayne Isaako (239); *Top tryscorer:* Corey Oates (18)

Without Ben Hunt, who had joined St George Illawarra Dragons, many pundits questioned the Broncos' halfback pairing of Kodi Nikorima and Anthony Milford. But Nikorima stepped up well into the number seven role as the Broncos secured a top-eight finish under head coach Wayne Bennett.

But the Broncos' season ended in emphatically poor style with a hefty home defeat to the Dragons in the first round of the Finals.

Speculation surrounding the Broncos and their coaching position was rife throughout the campaign. The press had a field day after Bennett didn't turn up for a club barbecue at the house of CEO Paul White, speculating the pair had fallen out over an extension of Bennett's contract, which ran out at the end of 2019.

At the end of the season, Bennett signed with South Sydney Rabbitohs from 2020 onwards.

The Broncos also said farewell to one of their greats in Sam Thaiday, who announced his retirement in typical style, dressing up as old man during his press conference. He also paid tribute to all the NRL's retiring players at the Dally M Awards evening in Sydney.

NEW ZEALAND WARRIORS (8th)

Top pointscorer: Shaun Johnson (142); *Top tryscorer:* David Fusitu'a (23)

New Zealand Warriors enjoyed a good campaign in 2018.

Having not made it into the Finals since they played in the Grand Final in 2011, a season like 2018 was long overdue for the Warriors.

With Shaun Johnson playing more games than in recent seasons and the excellent form of fullback Roger Tuivasa-Sheck, the Warriors produced a well-timed late surge to beat West Tigers to the last play-off place.

Tuivasa-Sheck was to go on and make history. The Kiwi International became the first Warrior to win the Dally M Medal as the NRL's best player. Tuivasa-Sheck was instrumental to the Warriors throughout the season as he ran for almost 4,000 metres.

Meanwhile David Fusitu'a was the NRL's top tryscorer as the winger crossed the whitewash 23 times in all, including some brilliant finishes on the right wing.

WESTS TIGERS (9th)

Top pointscorer: Esan Marsters (124); *Top tryscorer:* Corey Thompson (9)

Wests Tigers were so close to achieving what most thought almost impossible at the start of the season, making the top eight.

The Tigers weren't fancied heading into 2018, with the club losing some key players.

Origin stars James Tedesco and Aaron Woods both left for pastures new, with Super League duo Mahe Fonua and Corey Thompson heading to Leichhardt.

Thompson, the Tigers' leading tryscorer, proved to be a brilliant signing as he played a key part in the Tigers' season.

Renowned for their stern defence, the Tigers were led around the park by the impressive Luke Brooks and some flair was added by the mid-season signing of Moses Mbye from Canterbury Bulldogs.

Michael Maguire will take the coaching reins in 2019 as Ivan Cleary was released early to move to Penrith.

CANBERRA RAIDERS (10th)

Top pointscorer: Jarrod Croker (154); *Top tryscorer:* Joey Leilua (14)

The Raiders, as has been the case for the past few seasons, were one of the best sides to watch in the NRL, although the results didn't always come with the performances.

While Jordan Rapana and Joey Leilua continued their potent combination on the right edge, Josh Hodgson endured an injury-hit campaign after his incredible 2017. The Raiders' ever-dependable captain Jarrod Croker was also struck by injury towards the end of the season.

In the end, too many defeats by small margins led to them comfortably missing out on the Finals. But with more English talent flooding to the Australian capital in 2019 in John Bateman and Ryan Sutton, the Raiders' tale could be different next year.

Towards the end of the season, Blake Austin showed Warrington Wolves fans what was in store for them in the next few years with some excellent performances.

Their star fullback Jack Wighton was suspended by the NRL in July for ten games - the Raiders banned him for six weeks but were over-ruled by the governing body - after he pleaded guilty in court to five counts of assault and one of public urination. Wighton's season was over and that was probably the moment the Raiders' Finals push ended.

NEWCASTLE KNIGHTS (11th)

Top pointscorer: Ken Sio (98); *Top tryscorer:* Ken Sio (12)

After two successive wooden spoons, the only way was up for the Knights. They certainly could be satisfied with their efforts in 2018.

For most of the opening half of the season, it looked as if Newcastle were set to compete well into September but an injury to star halfback Mitchell Pearce put pay to any play-off hopes harboured by the Knights.

Kalyn Ponga, the teenage signing from North Queensland Cowboys, was one of the signings of the season.

His footwork and ball skills out the back made the Knights a very difficult football team to handle. Their defence did, however, let them down. Only Manly Sea Eagles had a worse defensive record than the Knights.

More good signings like Tim Glasby from Melbourne Storm could see the Knights improve further in 2019.

CANTERBURY BULLDOGS (12th)

Top pointscorer: Rhyse Martin (88); *Top tryscorers:* Brett Morris/Josh Morris (9)

The Bulldogs were in transition during 2018. After Des Hasler left the club at the end of 2017, Dean Pay came in to replace him and the Bulldogs found it tough going. They had also lost their captain James Graham to St George Illawarra Dragons.

But it wasn't all doom and gloom for the Bulldogs. They unearthed some potential stars of tomorrow during the season.

Lachlan Lewis, nephew of namesake Wally Lewis, proved to be an inspired addition from the club's youth system as he slotted seamlessly into their halfback partnership. Rhyse Martin, the sharp-shooting second-row forward scored a hat-trick against Canberra Raiders and kicked conversions with unbelievable accuracy. He kicked 36 goals and missed only two to give him a final percentage of 94.7.

The Bulldogs are losing both Morris twins to different Sydney sides in 2019. As the pair were the club's joint leading scorers this year, they could prove to be a big loss for the club. The emergence of Reimis Smith towards the end of the season could prove useful in replacing the Morris twins.

NORTH QUEENSLAND COWBOYS (13th)

Top pointscorer: Johnathan Thurston (166); *Top tryscorer:* Kyle Feldt (14)

2018 was generally a disaster for North Queensland Cowboys. After losing in the Grand Final in 2017 despite the lack of Johnathan Thurston, many expected them to improve with their star player back in the side.

With the likes of Jason Taumalolo and Michael Morgan aiding Thurston, it was a shock to see the Cowboys struggle so much.

An almost season-ending injury to key off-season signing Jordan McLean within the first month of the season didn't help.

The Cowboys then had to bid farewell to Thurston as he retired at the end of the season.

Thurston will go down as one of the best players of all time. He will always have a special place in Townsville as the man that led them to their Premiership in 2015 with that famous field goal.

GOLD COAST TITANS (14th)
Top pointscorer: Michael Gordon (132); *Top tryscorer:* Anthony Don (15)

Gold Coast Titans, under a new coach in Garth Brennan, just didn't have the strike within their team to threaten the finals positions. While they had some excellent young talent in Ash Taylor, Jai Arrow and Jarrod Wallace, 2018 was perhaps a year too early for them for them to make an impact.

Taylor is without doubt the key for them to have future success. His acquisition from the Broncos was an inspired one and even at the tender age of just 23, he leads his side around with great aplomb.

Late bloomer Anthony Don is Mr Reliable for the Titans and he weighed in with an impressive 15 tries while youngster Phillip Sami also impressed, scoring 14 tries in his 23 appearances in the threequarters.

MANLY SEA EAGLES (15th)
Top pointscorer: Daly Cherry-Evans (166); *Top tryscorers:* Shaun Lane/Tom Trbojevic (9)

Manly Sea Eagles had a very troubled campaign in 2018.

They were charged with salary cap violations by the NRL and fined, while their decent start to the season soon went south when rumours of bust ups within the camp surfaced.

Salford Red Devils didn't mind. They were able to acquire Jackson Hastings in the aftermath while Daly Cherry-Evans, the other rumoured party, went on to captain Australia's Prime Minister's XIII against Papua New Guinea.

Head coach Trent Barrett fell out with the club over infrastructure and support issues and gave 12-months notice in July. He was replaced by Des Hasler at the end of the season.

While the Sea Eagles generally struggled, the Trbojevic brothers, Jake and Tom had impressive seasons while lanky second-row forward Shaun Lane top scored for the club alongside alongside Tom Trobjevic in an excellent rookie campaign.

PARRAMATTA EELS (16th)
Top pointscorer: Mitchell Moses (106); *Top tryscorer:* Jarryd Hayne (10)

It was a miserable campaign for the Parramatta Eels who showed such promise in 2017. But 2018 was one to forget for the NRL's bottom side.

One of the few positives for the club was the return of Eels legend Jarryd Hayne to Parramatta. He top scored with ten tries and looked as close to his old form as he had done for many a year.

The club won just six games all season and didn't win any of their 12 away games.

The signings of Blake Ferguson and Shaun Lane for 2019 could prove crucial for the Eels, although they will miss Beau Scott, who retired at the end of the season.

NRL PREMIERSHIP FINALS SERIES

QUALIFYING FINALS
Friday 7th September 2018
Melbourne Storm 29 .... South Sydney Rabbitohs 28
Saturday 8th September 2018
Sydney Roosters 21 .... Cronulla Sharks 12

ELIMINATION FINALS
Saturday 8th September 2018
Penrith Panthers 27 ....New Zealand Warriors 12
(at ANZ Stadium, Sydney)
Sunday 9th September 2018
Brisbane Broncos 18..St George Illawarra Dragons 48

SEMI-FINALS
Friday 14th September 2018
Cronulla Sharks 21 ....Penrith Panthers 20
(at Allianz Stadium, Sydney)
Saturday 15th September 2018
South Sydney Rabbitohs 13 .... St George Illawarra Dragons 12

PRELIMINARY FINALS
Friday 21st September 2018
Melbourne Storm 22.. Cronulla Sharks 6
Saturday 22nd September 2018
Sydney Roosters 12 ....South Sydney Rabbitohs 4

NRL GRAND FINAL

Sunday 30th September 2018

MELBOURNE STORM 6 SYDNEY ROOSTERS 21

STORM: 1 Billy Slater; 2 Suliasi Vunivalu; 3 Will Chambers; 4 Curtis Scott; 5 Josh Addo-Carr; 6 Cameron Munster; 7 Brodie Croft; 8 Jesse Bromwich; 9 Cameron Smith (C); 10 Tim Glasby; 11 Felise Kaufusi; 12 Joe Stimson; 13 Dale Finucane. Subs (all used): 14 Kenny Bromwich; 15 Christian Welch; 16 Brandon Smith; 17 Nelson Asofa-Solomona.
Try: Addo-Carr (63); **Goals:** C Smith 1/1.
Sin bin: Munster (30) - professional foul, (78) - kicking out at Manu.
ROOSTERS: 1 James Tedesco; 2 Daniel Tupou; 3 Latrell Mitchell; 4 Joseph Manu; 5 Blake Ferguson; 6 Luke Keary; 23 Cooper Cronk; 8 Jared Waerea-Hargreaves; 9 Jake Friend; 10 Sio Siua Taukeiaho; 11 Boyd Cordner (C); 7 Mitchell Aubusson; 13 Victor Radley. Subs (all used): 12 Isaac Liu; 14 Dylan Napa; 15 Zane Tetevano; 17 Ryan Matterson.
Tries: Tupou (8), Mitchell (15), Manu (37); **Goals:** Mitchell 4/6;
Field goal: Keary (69).
Clive Churchill Medal: Luke Keary (Sydney Roosters).
Rugby Leaguer & League Express Men of the Match:
Storm: Josh Addo-Carr; *Roosters:* Luke Keary.
Half-time: 0-18; **Referees:** Ashley Klein & Gerard Sutton;
Attendance: 82,688 *(at ANZ Stadium, Sydney)*.

NRL PREMIERSHIP - FINAL TABLE

	P	W	D	L	B	F	A	D	Pts
Sydney Roosters	24	16	0	8	1	542	361	181	34
Melbourne Storm	24	16	0	8	1	536	363	173	34
South Sydney Rabbitohs	24	16	0	8	1	582	437	145	34
Cronulla Sharks	24	16	0	8	1	519	423	96	34
Penrith Panthers	24	15	0	9	1	417	461	56	32
Brisbane Broncos	24	15	0	9	1	556	500	56	32
St George Illawarra Dragons	24	15	0	9	1	519	472	47	32
New Zealand Warriors	24	15	0	9	1	472	447	25	32
Wests Tigers	24	12	0	12	1	377	460	-83	26
Canberra Raiders	24	10	0	14	1	563	540	23	22
Newcastle Knights	24	9	0	15	1	414	607	-193	20
Canterbury Bulldogs	24	8	0	16	1	428	474	-46	18
North Queensland Cowboys	24	8	0	16	1	449	521	-72	18
Gold Coast Titans	24	8	0	16	1	472	582	-110	18
Manly Sea Eagles	24	7	0	17	1	500	622	-122	16
Parramatta Eels	24	6	0	18	1	374	550	-176	14

LEADING POINTSCORERS

Latrell Mitchell	Sydney Roosters	248
Jamayne Isaako	Brisbane Broncos	239
Adam Reynolds	South Sydney Rabbitohs	211
Gareth Widdop	St George Illawarra Dragons	205
Cameron Smith	Melbourne Storm	201

TOP TRYSCORERS

David Fusitu'a	New Zealand Warriors	23
Valentine Holmes	Cronulla Sharks	22
Robert Jennings	South Sydney Rabbitohs	19
Josh Addo-Carr	Melbourne Storm	18
Blake Ferguson	Sydney Roosters	18
Corey Oates	Brisbane Broncos	18

STATE CHAMPIONSHIP *(Winners of Queensland and NSW Cups)*
Sunday 30th September 2018
Canterbury Bulldogs 42 .... Redcliffe Dolphins 18
(at ANZ Stadium, Sydney)

NRLW GRAND FINAL *(Women's Premiership)*
Sunday 30th September 2018
Brisbane Broncos 34 ....Sydney Roosters 12
(at ANZ Stadium, Sydney)

DALLY M AWARDS

Dally M Medal (Player of the Year):
Roger Tuivasa-Sheck (New Zealand Warriors)
Provan Summons Medal (People's Choice):
Damien Cook (South Sydney Rabbitohs)
Coach of the Year: Anthony Seibold (South Sydney Rabbitohs)
Captain of the Year: Cameron Smith (Melbourne Storm)
Rookie of the Year: Jamayne Isaako (Brisbane Broncos)
Female Player of the Year: Brittany Breayley (Brisbane Broncos)

STATE OF ORIGIN
Bluesbreakers

The Queensland dominance was finally broken in 2018.

New South Wales had lost eleven out of the last 12 State of Origin series going into 2018, but the Blues managed a 2-1 victory over Queensland.

Every series since 2010 has finished 2-1, now twice to New South Wales and six times to Queensland.

The Blues won the opening two games to secure the series without needing a decider which, in the end, Queensland won in Brisbane.

It's perhaps no surprise that the Blues were triumphant in this series with the bulging list of recent retirements in the Queensland side. While this was Billy Slater's last series before his retirement, there was no Cameron Smith, Johnathan Thurston, Cooper Cronk, Nate Myles or Matt Scott, all of whom had played key parts in Queensland's recent domination of the competition.

Not that New South Wales were experienced as new Blues coach Brad Fittler went for raw and unexperienced Origin players. And it worked a treat.

Fittler fielded 11 debutants in the opening game, which was played in Melbourne at the MCG in front of 87,122 fans. It was the most inexperienced Blues side fielded since the 1980s but they won through 22-12.

Queensland were led by new captain Greg Inglis who, despite ending up on the losing side in the Victorian capital, was in inspired form. He constantly shot out of the line to rally his troops with a big shot on a Blues attacker.

The Blues' speed up the middle, provided from dummy half by Damien Cook, who combined with James Maloney, saw the supporting James Tedesco break the deadlock. But Maloney then turned villain and threw an intercept pass to Valentine Holmes, who raced away to bring Queensland back into the game.

Queensland took the lead when Dane Gagai crossed after three minutes of the second half but Latrell Mitchell replied to even the game up.

But two more debutants on the New South Wales team sealed the game for the Blues. Tom Trbojevic, playing on the wing rather than his usual position of fullback, and Josh Addo-Carr both scored to hand the Blues a ten-point win.

STATE OF ORIGIN - GAME I

Wednesday 6th June 2018

NEW SOUTH WALES 22 QUEENSLAND 12

NEW SOUTH WALES: 1 James Tedesco (Sydney Roosters); 2 Tom Trbojevic (Manly Sea Eagles); 3 Latrell Mitchell (Sydney Roosters); 4 James Roberts (Brisbane Broncos); 5 Josh Addo-Carr (Melbourne Storm); 6 James Maloney (Penrith Panthers); 7 Nathan Cleary (Penrith Panthers); 8 David Klemmer (Canterbury Bulldogs); 9 Damien Cook (South Sydney Rabbitohs); 10 Reagan Campbell-Gillard (Penrith Panthers); 11 Boyd Cordner (Sydney Roosters) (C); 12 Tyson Frizell (St George Illawarra Dragons); 13 Jack de Belin (St George Illawarra Dragons). Subs (all used): 14 Paul Vaughan (St George Illawarra Dragons); 15 Jake Trbojevic (Manly Sea Eagles); 16 Angus Crichton (South Sydney Rabbitohs); 17 Tyrone Peachey (Penrith Panthers).
Tries: Tedesco (22), Mitchell (48), T Trbojevic (51), Addo-Carr (69);
Goals: Maloney 3/5.
QUEENSLAND: 14 Michael Morgan (North Queensland Cowboys); 2 Valentine Holmes (Cronulla Sharks); 3 Greg Inglis (South Sydney Rabbitohs) (C); 4 Will Chambers (Melbourne Storm); 5 Dane Gagai (South Sydney Rabbitohs); 6 Cameron Munster (Melbourne Storm); 7 Ben Hunt (St George Illawarra Dragons); 8 Dylan Napa (Sydney Roosters); 9 Andrew McCullough (Brisbane Broncos); 10 Jarrod Wallace (Gold Coast Titans); 11 Gavin Cooper (North Queensland Cowboys); 12 Felise Kaufusi (Melbourne Storm); 13 Josh McGuire (Brisbane Broncos). Subs (all used): 15 Josh Papalii (Canberra Raiders); 16 Coen Hess (North Queensland Cowboys); 17 Jai Arrow (Gold Coast Titans); 19 Anthony Milford (Brisbane Broncos).
Tries: Holmes (28), Gagai (43); **Goals:** Holmes 2/2.
Rugby Leaguer & League Express Men of the Match:
New South Wales: James Tedesco; *Queensland:* Greg Inglis.
Half-time: 8-6; **Referees:** Ashley Klein & Gerard Sutton;
Attendance: 87,122 (at Melbourne Cricket Ground).

The jubilant New South Wales players celebrate their State of Origin series win

They had to win their next match in Sydney to seal the series.

Led by captain Boyd Cordner, they did just that.

In front of a packed house - 82,223 fans - at ANZ Stadium, the Blues once again ran out on top, though only just, with an 18-14 comeback win.

It would have been easy for the Blues to panic early on when they found themselves down by ten points after only a quarter of the game. Queensland were inspired by the inclusion of Billy Slater, the eventual Wally Lewis Medal winner, awarded to the player of the series.

Holmes scored his second try of the series before Gagai repeated the feat with his second.

But the Blues were in front at the break thanks to two tries in six minutes. Maloney was at the heart of both tries. He

STATE OF ORIGIN - GAME II

Sunday 24th June 2018

NEW SOUTH WALES 18 QUEENSLAND 14

NEW SOUTH WALES: 1 James Tedesco (Sydney Roosters); 2 Tom Trbojevic (Manly Sea Eagles); 3 Latrell Mitchell (Sydney Roosters); 4 James Roberts (Brisbane Broncos); 5 Josh Addo-Carr (Melbourne Storm); 6 James Maloney (Penrith Panthers); 7 Nathan Cleary (Penrith Panthers); 8 David Klemmer (Canterbury Bulldogs); 9 Damien Cook (South Sydney Rabbitohs); 10 Matt Prior (Cronulla Sharks); 11 Boyd Cordner (Sydney Roosters) (C); 12 Tyson Frizell (St George Illawarra Dragons); 13 Jack de Belin (St George Illawarra Dragons). Subs (all used): 14 Paul Vaughan (St George Illawarra Dragons); 15 Jake Trbojevic (Manly Sea Eagles); 16 Angus Crichton (South Sydney Rabbitohs); 17 Tyrone Peachey (Penrith Panthers). **Tries:** Addo-Carr (25), Cordner (31, pen), Mitchell (50); **Goals:** Maloney 3/3. **Sin bin:** Roberts (69) - professional foul.
QUEENSLAND: 1 Billy Slater (Melbourne Storm); 2 Valentine Holmes (Cronulla Sharks); 3 Greg Inglis (South Sydney Rabbitohs) (C); 4 Will Chambers (Melbourne Storm); 5 Dane Gagai (South Sydney Rabbitohs); 6 Cameron Munster (Melbourne Storm); 7 Ben Hunt (St George Illawarra Dragons); 8 Dylan Napa (Sydney Roosters); 9 Andrew McCullough (Brisbane Broncos); 10 Jarrod Wallace (Gold Coast Titans); 11 Gavin Cooper (North Queensland Cowboys); 12 Felise Kaufusi (Melbourne Storm); 13 Josh McGuire (Brisbane Broncos). Subs (all used): 14 Kalyn Ponga (Newcastle Knights); 15 Josh Papalii (Canberra Raiders); 16 Coen Hess (North Queensland Cowboys); 17 Jai Arrow (Gold Coast Titans). **Tries:** Holmes (13), Gagai (20), Chambers (62); **Goals:** Holmes 1/3.
Rugby Leaguer & League Express Men of the Match:
New South Wales: James Maloney; *Queensland:* Billy Slater.
Half-time: 12-10; **Referees:** Ashley Klein & Gerard Sutton; **Attendance:** 82,223 (at ANZ Stadium, Sydney).

sent a cut-out pass to Addo-Carr for the first before kicking through the line for Cordner. Cordner was impeded on his way to the ball but was awarded a penalty try by the video referee.

Mitchell continued his excellent debut series with his second Origin try just ten minutes after the break.

That gave the Blues a two-try lead which they didn't give up. Will Chambers' try with 18 minutes to go ensured it wasn't a comfortable finish but the Blues held on to claim the series in front of their delirious supporters.

Anyone that says that the third game in an already decided Origin series is a dead rubber has obviously never seen any Origin games.

Despite their being, on the face of it, nothing to play for, the third game in the series didn't disappoint as the Maroons avoided the embarrassing whitewash in front of their home supporters at Suncorp Stadium with an 18-12 win.

The game was Billy Slater's last in the Maroon of Queensland while it also saw the return of Daly Cherry-Evans to the Origin scene. And he made it count.

Ben Hunt had taken a fair bit of criticism for Queensland's defeat in Game II and was dropped to the bench by Kevin Walters in favour of Cherry-Evans. His decision was justified with Cherry-Evans' man-of-the-match performance. Slater captained the Maroons in the absence of Inglis and it was a dream farewell.

Holmes kickstarted Queensland's performance. He snapped up Tedesco's loose pass to score his second intercept try of the series.

But the Blues replied in kind when Tom Trbojevic intercepted Cameron Munster's pass.

Then, with the home side reeling, New South Wales took the lead with a simple try for Tedesco made by Cook.

But a second try for Holmes and a well-deserved score for Cherry-Evans won the game for the home side.

The Blues didn't mind too much. They still lifted the shield at the end of the game in the heart of Queensland.

Slater's awarding of the Wally Lewis Medal provoked much discussion after only playing two games and featuring on the losing side. The Sydney press believed a New South Wales player deserved the award.

STATE OF ORIGIN - GAME III

Wednesday 11th July 2018

QUEENSLAND 18 NEW SOUTH WALES 12

QUEENSLAND: 1 Billy Slater (Melbourne Storm) (C); 2 Valentine Holmes (Cronulla Sharks); 3 Dane Gagai (South Sydney Rabbitohs); 4 Will Chambers (Melbourne Storm); 5 Corey Oates (Brisbane Broncos); 6 Cameron Munster (Melbourne Storm); 7 Daly Cherry-Evans (Manly Sea Eagles); 8 Jai Arrow (Gold Coast Titans); 9 Andrew McCullough (Brisbane Broncos); 10 Josh Papalii (Canberra Raiders); 11 Gavin Cooper (North Queensland Cowboys); 12 Felise Kaufusi (Melbourne Storm); 13 Josh McGuire (Brisbane Broncos). Subs (all used): 14 Ben Hunt (St George Illawarra Dragons); 15 Jarrod Wallace (Gold Coast Titans); 16 Coen Hess (North Queensland Cowboys); 17 Tim Glasby (Melbourne Storm). **Tries:** Holmes (11, 51), Cherry-Evans (58); **Goals:** Holmes 3/4.
NEW SOUTH WALES: 1 James Tedesco (Sydney Roosters); 2 Tom Trbojevic (Manly Sea Eagles); 3 Latrell Mitchell (Sydney Roosters); 4 James Roberts (Brisbane Broncos); 5 Josh Addo-Carr (Melbourne Storm); 6 James Maloney (Penrith Panthers); 7 Nathan Cleary (Penrith Panthers); 8 David Klemmer (Canterbury Bulldogs); 9 Damien Cook (South Sydney Rabbitohs); 10 Paul Vaughan (St George Illawarra Dragons); 11 Boyd Cordner (Sydney Roosters) (C); 12 Tyson Frizell (St George Illawarra Dragons); 15 Jake Trbojevic (Manly Sea Eagles). Subs (all used): 13 Jack de Belin (St George Illawarra Dragons); 14 Tariq Sims (St George Illawarra Dragons); 16 Angus Crichton (South Sydney Rabbitohs); 17 Tyrone Peachey (Penrith Panthers).
Tries: T Trbojevic (37), Tedesco (40); **Goals:** Cleary 2/2.
Sin bin: Maloney (31) - professional foul.
Rugby Leaguer & League Express Men of the Match:
Queensland: Daly Cherry-Evans; *New South Wales:* Tom Trbojevic.
Half-time: 8-12; **Referees:** Ashley Klein & Gerard Sutton;
Attendance: 51,214 (at Suncorp Stadium, Brisbane).

Wally Lewis Medal (Man of the Series): Billy Slater (Queensland)

RUGBY LEAGUE
W☮RLD CUP
2017

The 2017 Rugby League World Cup produced the most exciting and diverse global competition in history as Pacific Island teams competed for the first time on the same terms as Tier One nations Australia, New Zealand and England.

Fourteen nations were involved in the 15th global tournament in four groups, with unbeaten Australia eventually winning their 11th World Cup with a narrow win against England in the final in Brisbane.

Australia won the opening game of the 2017 World Cup on the last Friday in October in Melbourne, defeating England 18-4. But the win flattered the Kangaroos thanks to eight points in the final five minutes, that after star England forward Sam Burgess had limped off in the 36th minute.

It was a close encounter that England had led after five minutes. Given field position by their only penalty of the game, a sharp pass from Sean O'Loughlin and a long ball from Gareth Widdop gave Jermaine McGillvary enough space to touch down in the right corner. Widdop pulled the conversion wide.

McGillvary also made several key defensive contributions, particularly in the first half, and with the ball racked up almost 200 metres, five tackle busts and three clean breaks. Man of the match was Billy Slater, one of three Australian try scorers alongside Matt Gillett and Josh Dugan, while Cameron Smith was imperial around the ruck.

England coach Wayne Bennett was forced into a change in his line-up on the day of the game, with St Helens prop Alex Walmsley succumbing to a virus as Warrington utility Ben Currie got his first cap off the bench.

Australia established a grip on the game with a period of sustained pressure after McGillvary's try, Cooper Conk's kicking game keeping England on the back foot. Gillett and Slater tries, both through the right centre, and a Smith conversion saw them lead 10-4. That was how it stayed until a late Smith penalty for a dubious ball steal and Dugan's 80-metre try from a Widdop kick finished the game off.

The third team to qualify from Group A was also effectively settled on the first Sunday in Canberra when Lebanon beat France 29-18, their first win in a World Cup. It was a lot closer then the final score suggested, the sides level at 18-all until the 74th minute when star Parramatta stand-off Mitchell Moses potted a field goal and two minutes later broke, chipped French fullback Mark Kheirallah, collected his own kick and touched down to seal the win. Winger Travis Robinson got another try at the final whistle.

England won their remaining two games, beating Lebanon at the Sydney Football Stadium by 29-10 and France 36-6 in Perth. McGillvary scored a try in the win over Lebanon but faced a charge in the week after Cedars halfback Robbie Farah alleged he had been bitten by the Huddersfield winger. A three-man disciplinary panel took just three minutes to deliver their not-guilty verdict. McGillvary took his place against France and scored another two tries.

Wade Graham scored a first half hat-trick and added another try in the second half as Australia sealed their place in the quarter-finals with a comfortable ten-try, 52-6 win over the French in Canberra. Cameron Munster also scored two tries on debut. And a week later at Sydney Football Stadium, they breezed into the quarter-finals with a comfortable 34-0 win over Lebanon, Munster collecting two more tries.

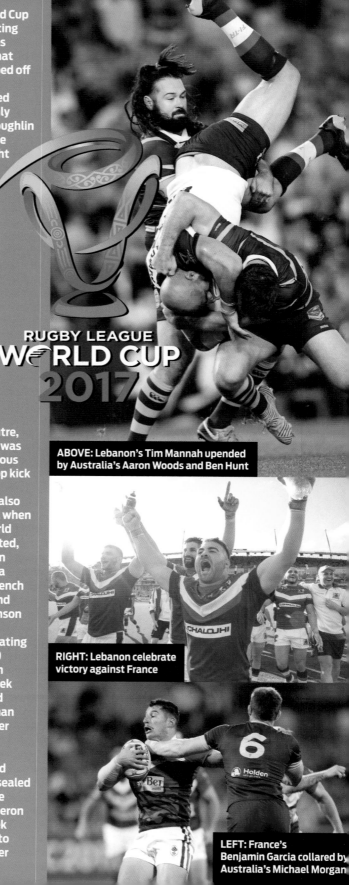

RUGBY LEAGUE
WORLD CUP
2017

ABOVE: Lebanon's Tim Mannah upended by Australia's Aaron Woods and Ben Hunt

RIGHT: Lebanon celebrate victory against France

LEFT: France's Benjamin Garcia collared by Australia's Michael Morgan

BELOW: England's Gareth Widdop acrobatically claims possession against Australia

BOTTOM LEFT: England's James Roby takes on France's Benjamin Jullien

BOTTOM RIGHT: England's Alex Walmsley looks for support against Lebanon

GROUP A

BELOW: New Zealand's Adam Blair displays intensity during the Haka before the Kiwis' clash with Scotland

GROUP B

LEFT: Tonga's Mahe Fonua looks to offload against New Zealand

RUGBY LEAGUE
W RLD CUP
2017

ABOVE: Scotland's Danny Addy takes on Samoa's Bunty Afoa

DIE FOR TONG

ABOVE: Tonga fans celebrate victory against Samoa

BELOW: New Zealand's Kodi Nikorima dives past Samoa's Young Tonumaipea to score

LEFT: Tonga's Michael Jennings leaves Scotland's Luke Douglas grounded

Tonga turned world Rugby League upside down by winning four-team group B, which featured games in Australia and New Zealand.

The decisions by Jason Taumalolo, Manu Ma'u, David Fusitu'a and Sio Siua Taukeiaho to turn their backs on New Zealand and Andrew Fifita to do the same with Australia, at great financial personal loss, and play for their home nation gave Tonga a strong spine. But their 28-22 win over the Kiwis in Hamilton on the last Saturday of the qualifiers still came as a major shock.

A sell-out crowd was made up mostly of Tongans. The excitement started before kick-off, with a stirring Haka by the Kiwis followed by a fearsome Sipa Tau as players ended up nose to nose.

Tonga trailed 16-2 at half-time, only to storm back, scoring four tries in 17 spellbinding minutes to take the lead, amid rapturous scenes.

The Kiwis threatened a comeback, with a Roger Tuivasa-Sheck special closing the gap to two points with eight minutes left. But Fusitu'a iced the result with his third try of the match and post-match celebrations filled the streets for days to come.

Tonga had given warning two weeks earlier with a 50-4 win over Scotland in the heat of Cairns, on the north Queensland coast. Parramatta centre Michael Jennings tore the Bravehearts to shreds, finishing with three tries, striking before Scotland had handled the ball, at the end of an adventurous first set. It would have been a point a minute in the first half had NZ Warriors half Ata Hingano not hit a post with his second kick at goal.

Danny Addy got Scotland's only try, dummying from a play-the-ball a metre out and diving over.

The week after, Tonga beat Samoa 32-18 in front of almost 20,000 Pacific Islanders, who cheered every try by both sides at the Waikato Stadium in Hamilton.

New Zealand were also unbeaten leading up to the Tonga game, having little difficulty in beating Samoa, by 38-8, at Mount Smart Stadium in Auckland. It was a decisive victory but the Kiwis were hardly impressive, turning in an error-ridden display. They clung to a narrow 10-4 lead at the interval, but ran riot in the second half, scoring five unanswered tries, before allowing the Samoans in for a consolation try in the closing seconds.

A week later in Christchurch, the Kiwis looked much more impressive in a 74-6 win over Scotland, Melbourne giant Nelson Asofa-Solomona again impressing off the bench. Te Maire Martin and Peta Hiku both got hat-tricks.

Scotland, surprisingly, could still make the quarter-finals if they beat Samoa in their last game, back in Cairns. But their chances looked remote when captain Danny Brough and forwards Jonny Walker and Sam Brooks were sent home in disgrace after the airline taking the Scots to Australia refused to let the drunken trio on-board.

But Scotland went home with their heads held high after a battling 14-all draw with Samoa, gamestar Danny Addy pulling a 42-metre penalty just left on 72 minutes, and then, with a minute remaining, putting a field-goal attempt wide from 40 metres.

Papua New Guinea thoroughly enjoyed hosting their three home group games in front of sell-out crowds in Port Moresby, as they qualified unbeaten for the quarter-finals.

The crucial game came on the second weekend of the qualifiers when the Kumuls drove the locals wild with a 14-6 win over Ireland. But, backed by their vociferous, flamboyant and partisan army of followers, PNG were given an almighty scare, with scrum-half Watson Boas's try two minutes from time allowing Michael Marum's side to finally rest easy.

In a wonderful, physical encounter in searing heat, Michael McIlorum opened the scoring for Ireland but Sheffield winger Garry Lo pulled a beauty back and St George's Nene Macdonald's try in the right centre gave PNG that 8-6 lead. It was tense from then on. With ten minutes remaining, Ireland's Louie McCarthy-Scarsbrook knocked on over the line trying to touch down a Liam Finn grubber and, seconds later PNG winger Justin Olam had a try disallowed for a forward pass. But when Ireland lost possession, Watson Boas was on hand to kick on and score the winner.

The Kumuls had beaten Wales the week before, running riot in a 50-6 victory, their aggressive style of play too much for a side containing only three Super League players. Wales missed 76 tackles compared to PNG's 19 and St Helens winger Regan Grace's last-second try was all they could muster.

With only three teams in the group, each side played a cross-group game with Group D and Ireland had won their's in week one, a nigh-on perfect team performance upsetting strongly fancied Italy by 36-12 in scorching Cairns.

Liam Finn was the game's star, setting the tempo perfectly for the Irish, and linking with Wakefield clubmate Scott Grix to create Liam Kay's opening try in the third minute. Finn wisely kicked a penalty for 14-0 at the much-needed drinks break. Kay's second try off Finn's long pass, superbly converted by Finn, made it 20-0 and despite a comeback, with James Tedesco a danger throughout, that was too much for Italy.

Though defeat in Port Moresby meant that Ireland's hope of qualification had gone, they finished with two wins from three after a 34-6 win over Wales in Perth, in the first of a double header with the England-France game.

Api Pewhairangi, Oliver Roberts twice, Joe Philbin, Liam Finn and Liam Kay all scored tries for Ireland. Ben Morris's try just after half-time gave Wales some consolation but Finn's try just before the interval ensured Wales didn't look like getting back into it.

But by the time that game wrapped up, PNG were already guaranteed to top the group table after a 64-0 win over USA, giving the Kumuls a quarter-final crack at England in Melbourne. The Kumuls gave a bow to Lachlan Lam, son of their former great Adrian Lam, and he scored two tries in the rout.

GROUP C

ABOVE: Ireland's Michael McIlorum drives forward against Papua New Guinea

RUGBY LEAGUE
WORLD CUP
2017

ABOVE: Ireland's Scott Grix bursts through the Wales defensive line

ABOVE: Wales' Elliot Kear brings down Papua New Guinea's Watson Boas

BELOW: Fiji's Jarryd Hayne tries to escape the clutches of Italy's Josh Mantellato

RUGBY LEAGUE
WORLD CUP
2017

GROUP D

RIGHT: Italy's Chris Centrone spots a gap against USA

ABOVE: Ireland's Kyle Amor celebrates scoring against Italy with Brad Singleton and Michael McIlorum

BELOW: Papua New Guinea's Lachlan Lam brought to ground against USA

ABOVE: Fiji celebrate a try against Wales

RIGHT: USA's Matthew Shipway looks for a way through against Fiji

Fiji, coached by former Catalans and St Helens coach Mick Potter, looked a good bet to make the semi-finals for the third successive tournament as they swept through their qualifiers.

They opened with a 58-12 hammering of an under-powered USA in Townsville. Within 12 minutes of the start, Fiji scored three quick tries down the right, despite USA moving Hull-bound Bureta Faraimo to left centre in a bid to combat the threat of winger Suliasi Vunivalu. Centre Taane Milne caused the initial damage, first taking Vunivalu's offload to score after three minutes, then setting up fullback Kevin Naiqama with a neat inside kick soon after.

On twelve minutes, Milne shoved off two attempted tacklers to cross, and when Jarryd Hayne threw a long pass out to the left, Akuila Uate danced in with the delight of a man finally getting some possession.

Half the USA team had yet to touch the ball as they struggled to get near to completing a set, and Leeds boss Brian McDermott's side trailed 26-0 after 17 painful minutes as prop Kane Evans ploughed over, breaking his wrist in the process.

There were cheers all round the sparsely-occupied stadium after 20 minutes when USA second rower Matt Shipway stepped his way to the line but Naiqama strolled in for his second try (Fiji also had two ruled out) and Vunivalu finally got over after 35 minutes.

There were boos when USA centre Junior Vaivai had his opportunistic effort disallowed by the video referee for having put his foot in touch before grasping a bouncing ball seconds before the hooter, although he went on to score the last try of the game.

A week later at the same venue, the Batis were even more impressive in beating Wales, in a first ever meeting between the two nations, in a cross-group game. The 72-6 scoreline was a record World Cup defeat for Wales, beating their defeat in Port Moresby the previous week.

Jarryd Hayne was outstanding in his creation of tries and made it look simple as Melbourne's Vunivalu scored a try hat-trick.

Coming into the last qualifier in Canberra, Italy needed a 48-point victory over Fiji to make the knockout stages, and while that never looked possible, it was a remarkable nine-minute hat-trick by Vunivalu late on that sealed the game for Fiji, who faced a mouth-watering clash with New Zealand in Wellington the following Saturday after their 38-10 win over the Azzurri.

Italy's 36-12 cross-group defeat to surprise packet Ireland in scorching Cairns in week one had scuppered their chances, a 20-0 deficit after half an hour too much to make up. But they kept their slim hopes alive the week after, running in eight tries to swamp USA 46-0, despite the game's build-up being overshadowed by a reported bar brawl between teammates Shannon Wakeman and James Tedesco. Sydney Roosters-bound Tedesco started at stand-off and scored two tries while Huddersfield front row Wakeman was on the bench.

USA's trip to Port Moresby for the third game looked a lost cause before kick-off and so it proved for a side containing six players from north American clubs.

AUSTRALIA 46 ....SAMOA 0

Cronulla Sharks winger Valentine Holmes set an all-time World Cup record haul of five tries as Australia shrugged off the steamy, tropical conditions in Darwin to book a spot in the semi-finals with a whitewash of Samoa.

The Samoans - who hadn't won a game in the competition despite fielding some top NRL players - were outclassed in every facet of the game in the first Test match ever staged in the capital of the Northern Territory. They conceded eight tries to the defending world champions, including a brace to stand-off Michael Morgan and one to fullback Billy Slater, who was at his dazzling best.

Slater equalled Jarryd Hayne's record for scoring the most tries in World Cup history while his captain Cameron Smith equalled Bob Fulton's record of 15 World Cup appearances in the green and gold jersey.

Cooper Cronk and Smith steered the Aussies around the pitch while props David Klemmer and Jordan McLean stood out. Brisbane's Josh McGuire was also outstanding against his former Test teammates.

NEW ZEALAND 2 ....FIJI 4

Fiji qualified for the semi-finals for the third tournament running in one of the greatest upsets in the history of Rugby League, thoroughly deserving their win in Wellington, in the first try-less game in a World Cup since 1970, when Great Britain defeated France 6-0.

It wasn't a lucky win or unexciting. The Batis had more desire, more discipline and more dynamism and were on top for most of the match, with the Kiwis not making a line break until the 70th minute.

It was a remarkable effort fuelled by a strong sense of national pride. Fiji had some top NRL talent, like Jarryd Hayne, Akuila Uate, Kevin Naiqama, Api Koroisau and Suliasi Vunivalu, but coach Mick Potter also had players drawn from the second-tier New South Wales and Queensland Cup competitions and others from various NRL Under-20's teams.

The winning penalty was kicked by centre Taane Milne in the 61st minute after Roger Tuivasa-Sheck saved two tries with last-ditch tackles and Brayden Wiliame crossed the line in the second half but was called back for a double movement.

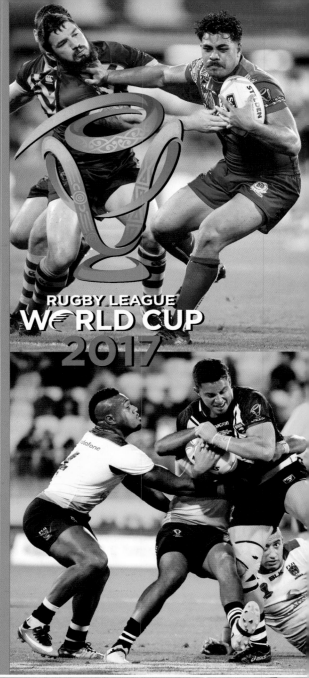

RUGBY LEAGUE
WORLD CUP
2017

ABOVE: Tonga's David Fusitu'a dives for the corner against Lebanon

LEFT: Samoa's Young Tonumaipea fends off Australia's Matt Gillett

LEFT: New Zealand's Joseph Tapine in the thick of the action against Fiji

BELOW LEFT: The Fiji and New Zealand teams take part in a group prayer following an intense Quarter Final

BELOW: England's Sam Burgess feels the effect of a high shot against Papua New Guinea

LEBANON 22 .... TONGA 24

Tonga secured a spot in their first ever World Cup semi-final but it was far from comfortable against a Cedars side coached by Brad Fittler that had in most people's eyes had already exceeded expectations.

Lebanon, marshalled superbly by NRL halves Robbie Farah and Mitchell Moses, trailed by only six points at the break and had a try after the restart ruled out by the video referee. Centre Adam Doueihi, a South Sydney youth player who had a great competition, was pulled back for a debatable obstruction, and soon after, a penalty goal from Ata Hingano extended Tonga's lead to eight points.

The Cedars eventually scored again through Abbas Miski, closing the gap to two points with ten minutes remaining, but Tonga held on to edge a thriller.

NZ Warriors winger David Fusitu'a, one of the players to turn his back on Kiwi selection, was the match-winner with two tries, a week after scoring a hat-trick in the win against New Zealand.

ENGLAND 36 .... PAPUA NEW GUINEA 6

England made the semi-finals, though coach Wayne Bennett said it was his side's worst performance so far in this year's tournament.

The Papuans headed into the clash in confident mood after having won all three of their group games but the loss of captain David Mead to a head injury in the opening minutes deprived them of one of their major strike forces.

England were never fully in control of the game, they finished with a completion rate of 56 per cent, but Ben Currie's try on 56 minutes gave them a twenty-point lead, comfortable enough to see them home. Huddersfield winger Jermaine McGillvary was again the star player, scoring another two tries to make it six from four games.

There was some disruption for England. Stand-off Kevin Brown was injured just before half-time after a Watson Boas tackle left him prone on the Melbourne Rectangular Stadium turf. Brown continued to play on for another 15 minutes before being replaced at half-time.

QUARTER FINALS

AUSTRALIA 54 .... FIJI 6

For the third World Cup semi-final running, Fiji found Australia too hot to handle. Valentine Holmes broke his own World Cup try-scoring record, set the week before against Samoa, netting six of the Kangaroos' ten tries. Billy Slater and Dane Gagai also crossed twice in a less than half-full Suncorp Stadium in Brisbane.

Holmes also passed Wendell Sailor's record for tries at one World Cup of 10, set in 2000, having scored 12 with one match left to play. And Slater took his tally at World Cups to 16 - taking him out on his own as the competition's all-time leading try scorer.

At least the Batis scored a try, through Melbourne winger Suliasi Vunivalu on 60 minutes, having lost to Australia by 52-0 in 2008 and 64-0 in 2013.

A Holmes knock-on gifted Fiji field position to attack the Australian line early on and from a penalty twenty metres out in front of the posts. Apisai Koroisau kicked the goal to give Fiji a 2-0 lead.

But from then on Australia, with Cooper Cronk's kicking game to the fore, were in control, Holmes' hat-trick try shortly after half-time giving the Kangaroos an unassailable 26-point lead.

ENGLAND 20 .... TONGA 18

England qualified for their first World Cup final since 1995 after one of the greatest matches - and occasions - in World Cup history in Auckland.

In front of a remarkable sea of red in the packed Mount Smart stands, they somehow stood firm amid a stirring late Tongan onslaught, having looked in control for much of an absorbing clash.

Leading 20-0 with little over seven minutes remaining, through tries from Jermaine McGillvary, Gareth Widdop and John Bateman, England had more than one foot in the Brisbane final, having defended superbly and taken three chances in accomplished style, with Widdop, at fullback, outstanding.

Tevita Pangai Junior's 73rd minute scrambled try looked little more than consolation. But back-to-back tries from Siliva Havili and Tuimoala Lolohea against a tiring England defence suddenly left Tonga within two points with two minutes on the clock, and they poured forward again.

England looked to have repelled the danger when Jermaine McGillvary intercepted a pass and ran out of defence. But he spilled the ball in a tackle and Tonga moved the ball left, where Cronulla prop Andrew Fifita burst past one tackle, only to be hauled in by a desperate effort from Elliott Whitehead that forced the ball free.

Referee Matt Cecchin ruled a knock-on even before Fifita had regathered and touched down, claiming a ball strip, and England had somehow held on. The official was quickly surrounded by Tongan players pleading to go to the video referee, but to no avail.

The next day two thousand Tongans marched through the streets of Auckland demanding the game be replayed because of the referee's decision.

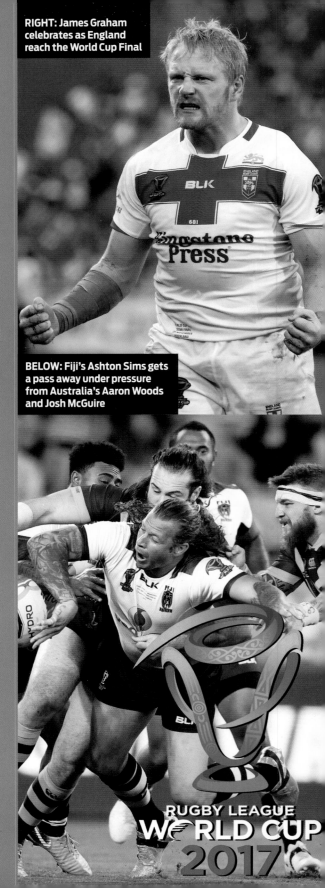

RIGHT: James Graham celebrates as England reach the World Cup Final

BELOW: Fiji's Ashton Sims gets a pass away under pressure from Australia's Aaron Woods and Josh McGuire

RUGBY LEAGUE
WORLD CUP
2017

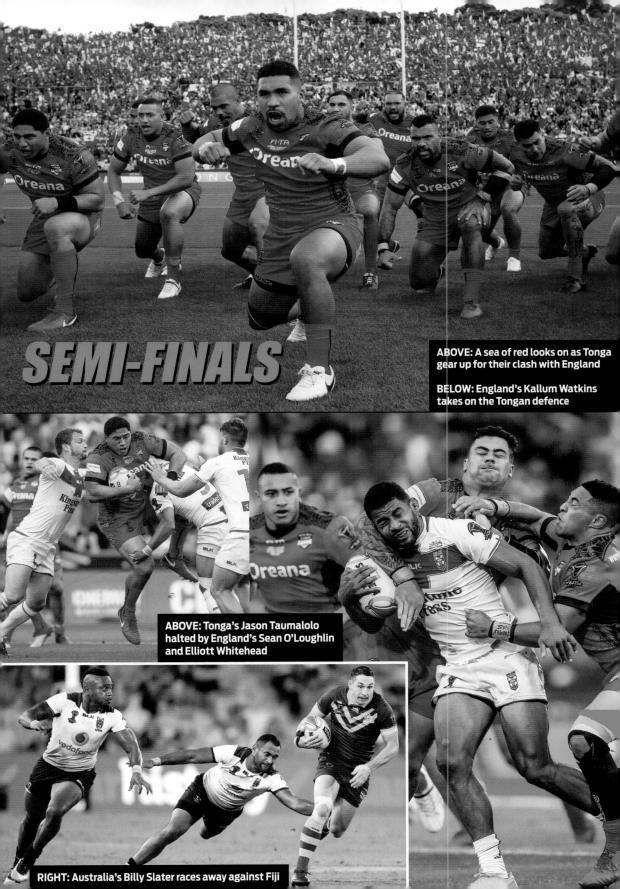

SEMI-FINALS

ABOVE: A sea of red looks on as Tonga gear up for their clash with England

BELOW: England's Kallum Watkins takes on the Tongan defence

ABOVE: Tonga's Jason Taumalolo halted by England's Sean O'Loughlin and Elliott Whitehead

RIGHT: Australia's Billy Slater races away against Fiji

BELOW: Michael Morgan tries to shake off the attentions of Elliott Whitehead

ABOVE: Cooper Cronk offers his commiserations to a dejected James Graham

RUGBY LEAGUE
W⊙RLD CUP
2017
FINAL

RIGHT: Tom Burgess takes on Tyson Frizell and Wade Graham

ABOVE: Josh Dugan manages to ankle-tap Kallum Watkins in the game's key moment

AUSTRALIA 6......................................ENGLAND 0

England came up just short as they attempted to win the Rugby League World Cup for the first time since 1972, in what was the closest contest between the old foes for many a year.

The only score of the game came on the 15-minute mark when, after a goal-line drop-out, Aussie skipper Cameron Smith picked up from dummy-half and fed Boyd Cordner down the left edge. The Sydney Roosters' back-rower stepped out of Kevin Brown's tackle and planted the ball down despite the effort of Gareth Widdop. Smith added the conversion.

Apart from that there was nothing in it, despite England missing Josh Hodgson, who had limped off against Tonga with a knee injury, his starting spot going to James Roby, as well as captain Sean O'Loughlin, ruled out late in the week with a quad injury. Jonny Lomax and Chris Heighington both came onto the bench in their absence.

By the closing stages, Australia were clinging on, content to make yardage and kick deep. But England didn't have the composure to get over the line. Their best chance came when Kallum Watkins broke through the right centre with 16 minutes to go, with support inside him. But a miraculous ankle-tap from Josh Dugan tripped him up and the chance was gone.

In the game's last play, England kept the ball alive brilliantly. But Jermaine McGillvary tried a desperate grubber kick around last man Billy Slater when he had teammates inside him.

Cooper Cronk, in his last international match, produced a performance of sheer quality, with a near faultless kicking game and superb execution, which saw him edge the man of the match award from his captain Smith, who described the game as one of the toughest of his career.

It was the lowest scoring World Cup Final of all time, beating the result from 1992 when Australia defeated Great Britain 10-6 at Wembley. It was also the first time a team has been nilled in a World Cup Final and the first time a team had won a World Cup Final on its own soil since Australia defeated Great Britain 13-12 at the Sydney Cricket Ground in 1977.

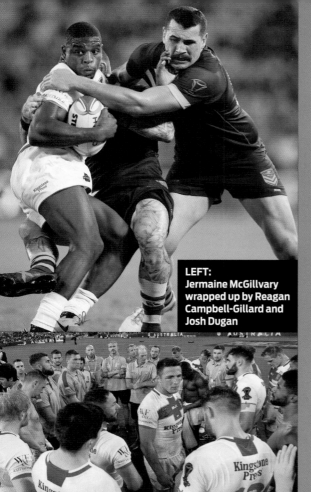

LEFT:
Jermaine McGillvary wrapped up by Reagan Campbell-Gillard and Josh Dugan

ABOVE: The England team reflect on defeat

BELOW: Cameron Smith leaves the Brisbane Stadium with the World Cup

LEFT: Oliver Gildart shows his delight at scoring England's winning try against New Zealand during the First Test in Hull

BELOW LEFT: Tommy Makinson dives in for the first of his hat-trick of tries in the Second Test at Anfield, and James Graham is halted by the New Zealand defence (**BELOW RIGHT**)

2018 TEST SERIES

BELOW: England show off the Baskerville Shield, despite defeat in the Third Test at Elland Road

6
INTERNATIONAL YEAR

WORLD CUP 2017
Statistical review

GROUP A

Friday 27th October 2017

AUSTRALIA 18 ENGLAND 4

AUSTRALIA: 1 Billy Slater (Melbourne Storm); 2 Dane Gagai (Newcastle Knights); 3 Will Chambers (Melbourne Storm); 4 Josh Dugan (St George Illawarra Dragons); 5 Valentine Holmes (Cronulla Sharks); 6 Michael Morgan (North Queensland Cowboys); 7 Cooper Cronk (Melbourne Storm); 8 Aaron Woods (Wests Tigers); 9 Cameron Smith (Melbourne Storm) (C); 10 David Klemmer (Canterbury Bulldogs); 11 Boyd Cordner (Sydney Roosters); 12 Matt Gillett (Brisbane Broncos); 13 Jake Trbojevic (Manly Sea Eagles). Subs (all used): 14 Wade Graham (Cronulla Sharks); 15 Jordan McLean (Melbourne Storm); 16 Josh McGuire (Brisbane Broncos); 17 Tyson Frizell (St George Illawarra Dragons).
Tries: Gillett (23), Slater (29), Dugan (79); **Goals:** Smith 3/4.
ENGLAND: 1 Jonny Lomax (St Helens); 2 Jermaine McGillvary (Huddersfield Giants); 3 Kallum Watkins (Leeds Rhinos); 4 John Bateman (Wigan Warriors); 5 Ryan Hall (Leeds Rhinos); 6 Gareth Widdop (St George Illawarra Dragons); 7 Luke Gale (Castleford Tigers); 8 Chris Hill (Warrington Wolves); 9 Josh Hodgson (Canberra Raiders); 10 James Graham (Canterbury Bulldogs); 11 Sam Burgess (South Sydney Rabbitohs); 12 Elliott Whitehead (Canberra Raiders); 13 Sean O'Loughlin (Wigan Warriors) (C). Subs (all used): 15 Chris Heighington (Cronulla Sharks); 16 Tom Burgess (South Sydney Rabbitohs); 17 James Roby (St Helens); 18 Ben Currie (Warrington Wolves).
Try: McGillvary (5); **Goals:** Widdop 0/1.
Rugby Leaguer & League Express Men of the Match:
Australia: Billy Slater; *England:* Jermaine McGillvary.
Penalty count: 3-1; **Half-time:** 10-4; **Referee:** Matt Cecchin (Australia); **Attendance:** 22,724 *(at Melbourne Rectangular Stadium)*.

Sunday 29th October 2017

FRANCE 18 LEBANON 29

FRANCE: 1 Mark Kheirallah (Toulouse Olympique); 5 Ilias Bergal (Swinton Lions); 4 Damien Cardace (Lezignan); 3 Bastien Ader (Toulouse Olympique); 2 Fouad Yaha (Catalans Dragons); 6 Theo Fages (St Helens) (C); 7 William Barthau (London Broncos); 8 Antoni Maria (Leigh Centurions); 9 Eloi Pelissier (Leigh Centurions); 10 Julian Bousquet (Catalans Dragons); 11 Benjamin Garcia (Catalans Dragons); 12 Benjamin Jullien (Warrington Wolves); 13 Jason Baitieri (Catalans Dragons). Subs (all used): 14 Clement Boyer (Toulouse Olympique); 15 Nabil Djalout (Catalans Dragons); 16 Thibaut Margalet (Catalans Dragons); 17 Lucas Albert (Catalans Dragons).
Tries: Ader (16, 52), Cardace (68); **Goals:** Barthau 3/4.
LEBANON: 1 Anthony Layoun (Parramatta Eels); 2 Travis Robinson (Newtown Jets); 3 James Elias (Wests Newcastle); 4 Jason Wehbe (Unattached); 5 Abbas Miski (North Sydney Bears); 6 Mitchell Moses (Parramatta Eels); 7 Robbie Farah (South Sydney Rabbitohs) (C); 8 Tim Mannah (Parramatta Eels); 17 Andrew Kazzi (Wests Tigers); 14 Mitchell Mamary (Wentworthville Magpies); 16 Jaleel Seve-Derbas (Wests Tigers); 12 Ahmad Ellaz (Auburn Warriors); 13 Nick Kassis (Blacktown Workers). Subs (all used): 9 Michael Lichaa (Canterbury Bulldogs); 10 Alex Twal (Wests Tigers); 15 Elias Sukkar (Wentworthville Magpies); 18 Adam Doueihi (South Sydney Rabbitohs).
Tries: Layoun (9), Robinson (40, 80), Doueihi (64), Moses (76); **Goals:** Moses 4/5; **Field goal:** Moses (74).
Rugby Leaguer & League Express Men of the Match:
France: Bastien Ader; *Lebanon:* Mitchell Moses.
Penalty count: 4-5; **Half-time:** 6-12; **Referee:** Gerard Sutton (Australia); **Attendance:** 5,429 *(at Canberra Stadium)*.

Friday 3rd November 2017

AUSTRALIA 52 FRANCE 6

AUSTRALIA: 1 Billy Slater (Melbourne Storm); 2 Tom Trbojevic (Manly Sea Eagles); 3 Will Chambers (Melbourne Storm); 4 Josh Dugan (St George Illawarra Dragons); 5 Josh Mansour (Penrith Panthers); 6 Michael Morgan (North Queensland Cowboys); 14 Cameron Munster (Melbourne Storm); 8 Jordan McLean (Melbourne Storm); 9 Cameron Smith (Melbourne Storm) (C); 10 Reagan Campbell-Gillard (Penrith Panthers); 11 Wade Graham (Cronulla Sharks); 12 Tyson Frizell (St George Illawarra Dragons); 13 Josh McGuire (Brisbane Broncos). Subs (all used): 15 Felise Kaufusi (Melbourne Storm); 16 Aaron Woods (Wests Tigers); 17 David Klemmer (Canterbury Bulldogs); 18 Valentine Holmes (Cronulla Sharks).
Tries: Graham (11, 13, 31, 66), Dugan (33), Munster (40, 74), Frizell (49), Slater (52), Holmes (78); **Goals:** Smith 6/8, Munster 0/2.
FRANCE: 1 Mark Kheirallah (Toulouse Olympique); 5 Ilias Bergal (Swinton Lions); 4 Olivier Arnaud (Avignon); 3 Bastien Ader (Toulouse Olympique); 2 Fouad Yaha (Catalans Dragons); 6 Remy Marginet (Sheffield Eagles); 7 Theo Fages (St Helens) (C); 13 Jason Baitieri (Catalans Dragons); 17 John Boudebza (London Broncos); 15 Mickael Rouch (Limoux Grizzlies); 10 Julian Bousquet (Catalans Dragons); 11 Benjamin Garcia (Catalans Dragons); 12 Benjamin Jullien (Warrington Wolves). Subs (all used): 8 Maxime Herold (Limoux Grizzlies); 9 Eloi Pelissier (Leigh Centurions); 14 Thibaut Margalet (Catalans Dragons); 16 Romain Navarrete (Wigan Warriors).
Try: Kheirallah (24); **Goals:** Marginet 1/1.
Rugby Leaguer & League Express Men of the Match:
Australia: Wade Graham; *France:* Mark Kheirallah.
Penalty count: 7-6; **Half-time:** 20-6; **Referee:** Robert Hicks (England); **Attendance:** 12,393 *(at Canberra Stadium)*.

Saturday 4th November 2017

ENGLAND 29 LEBANON 10

ENGLAND: 21 Stefan Ratchford (Warrington Wolves); 2 Jermaine McGillvary (Huddersfield Giants); 3 Kallum Watkins (Leeds Rhinos); 4 John Bateman (Wigan Warriors); 5 Ryan Hall (Leeds Rhinos); 6 Gareth Widdop (St George Illawarra Dragons); 7 Luke Gale (Castleford Tigers); 8 Chris Hill (Warrington Wolves); 9 Josh Hodgson (Canberra Raiders); 10 James Graham (Canterbury Bulldogs); 11 Ben Currie (Warrington Wolves); 12 Elliott Whitehead (Canberra Raiders); 13 Sean O'Loughlin (Wigan Warriors) (C). Subs (all used): 14 Alex Walmsley (St Helens); 15 Chris Heighington (Cronulla Sharks); 16 Tom Burgess (South Sydney Rabbitohs); 18 George Williams (Wigan Warriors).
Tries: Watkins (9), McGillvary (25), Hall (28), Currie (32), T Burgess (56); **Goals:** Widdop 4/5; **Field goal:** Widdop (80).
LEBANON: 1 Daniel Abou-Sleiman (Unattached); 2 Travis Robinson (Newtown Jets); 3 Bilal Maarbani (Manly Sea Eagles); 4 Adam Doueihi (South Sydney Rabbitohs); 5 Abbas Miski (North Sydney Bears); 6 Mitchell Moses (Parramatta Eels); 7 Robbie Farah (South Sydney Rabbitohs) (C); 8 Tim Mannah (Parramatta Eels); 16 Jamie Clark (Auburn Warriors); 14 Mitchell Mamary (Wentworthville Magpies); 10 Alex Twal (Wests Tigers); 12 Ahmad Ellaz (Auburn Warriors); 13 Nick Kassis (Blacktown Workers). Subs (all used): 9 Michael Lichaa (Canterbury Bulldogs); 15 Ray Moujalli (Canterbury Bulldogs); 17 Jason Wehbe (Unattached); 18 Elias Sukkar (Wentworthville Magpies).
Tries: Kassis (18), Wehbe (75); **Goals:** Moses 1/2.
Rugby Leaguer & League Express Men of the Match:
England: Jermaine McGillvary; *Lebanon:* Mitchell Moses.
Penalty count: 8-5; **Half-time:** 22-6; **Referee:** Ben Thaler (England); **Attendance:** 10,237 *(at Sydney Football Stadium)*.

Saturday 11th November 2017

AUSTRALIA 34 LEBANON 0

AUSTRALIA: 1 Valentine Holmes (Cronulla Sharks); 2 Dane Gagai (Newcastle Knights); 3 Tom Trbojevic (Manly Sea Eagles); 4 Cameron Munster (Melbourne Storm); 5 Josh Mansour (Penrith Panthers); 6 James Maloney (Cronulla Sharks); 7 Cooper Cronk (Melbourne Storm); 8 Aaron Woods (Wests Tigers); 9 Cameron Smith (Melbourne Storm) (C); 10 David Klemmer (Canterbury Bulldogs); 11 Boyd Cordner (Sydney Roosters); 12 Matt Gillett (Brisbane Broncos); 13 Felise Kaufusi (Melbourne Storm). Subs (all used): 14 Ben Hunt (Brisbane Broncos); 15 Jordan McLean (Melbourne Storm); 16 Reagan Campbell-Gillard (Penrith Panthers); 17 Wade Graham (Cronulla Sharks).
Tries: Munster (8, 50), Maloney (25), Cordner (54), Gagai (76), T Trbojevic (79); **Goals:** Smith 1/2, Maloney 4/4.
On report: Klemmer (21) - alleged high tackle; Woods (66) - alleged dangerous challenge on Mannah.
LEBANON: 1 Anthony Layoun (Parramatta Eels); 5 Abbas Miski (North Sydney Bears); 3 James Elias (Wests Newcastle); 4 Adam Doueihi (South Sydney Rabbitohs); 19 Danny Barakat (Wentworthville Magpies); 6 Mitchell Moses (Parramatta Eels); 7 Robbie Farah (South Sydney Rabbitohs) (C); 8 Tim Mannah (Parramatta Eels); 9 Michael Lichaa (Canterbury Bulldogs); 15 Ray Moujalli (Canterbury Bulldogs); 11 Chris Saab (Blacktown Workers); 12 Ahmad Ellaz (Auburn Warriors); 16 Jamie Clark (Auburn Warriors). Subs (all used): 10 Alex Twal (Wests Tigers); 14 Mitchell Mamary (Wentworthville Magpies); 17 Andrew Kazzi (Wests Tigers); 18 Jason Wehbe (Unattached).
Rugby Leaguer & League Express Men of the Match:
Australia: Cameron Munster; *Lebanon:* Mitchell Moses.
Penalty count: 9-12; **Half-time:** 10-0; **Referee:** James Child (England); **Attendance:** 21,127 *(at Sydney Football Stadium)*.

Sunday 12th November 2017

ENGLAND 36 FRANCE 6

ENGLAND: 1 Gareth Widdop (St George Illawarra Dragons); 5 Jermaine McGillvary (Huddersfield Giants); 3 Mark Percival (St Helens); 4 John Bateman (Wigan Warriors); 2 Stefan Ratchford (Warrington Wolves); 6 Kevin Brown (Warrington Wolves); 7 Luke Gale (Castleford Tigers); 8 Chris Hill (Warrington Wolves); 9 James Roby (St Helens); 10 James Graham (Canterbury Bulldogs); 11 Ben Currie (Warrington Wolves); 12 Mike McMeeken (Castleford Tigers); 13 Sean O'Loughlin (Wigan Warriors) (C). Subs (all used): 14 Alex Walmsley (St Helens); 15 Tom Burgess (South Sydney Rabbitohs); 16 Scott Taylor (Hull FC); 17 George Williams (Wigan Warriors).
Tries: Widdop (2), Ratchford (6), Graham (9), Percival (23), Bateman (29), McGillvary (42, 64); **Goals:** Widdop 4/7.
FRANCE: 1 Mark Kheirallah (Toulouse Olympique); 5 Ilias Bergal (Swinton Lions); 12 Benjamin Jullien (Warrington Wolves); 3 Bastien Ader (Toulouse Olympique); 2 Fouad Yaha (Catalans Dragons); 6 Theo Fages (St Helens) (C); 7 Lucas Albert (Catalans Dragons); 16 Maxime Herold (Limoux Grizzlies); 9 John Boudebza (London Broncos); 8 Antoni Maria (Leigh Centurions); 10 Julian Bousquet (Catalans Dragons); 11 Benjamin Garcia (Catalans Dragons); 13 Jason Baitieri (Catalans Dragons). Subs (all used): 14 Romain Navarrete (Wigan Warriors); 15 Thibaut Margalet (Catalans Dragons); 19 Mickael Rouch (Limoux Grizzlies); 20 Nabil Djalout (Catalans Dragons).
Try: Garcia (34); **Goals:** Albert 1/1.
Rugby Leaguer & League Express Men of the Match:
England: Gareth Widdop; *France:* Lucas Albert.
Penalty count: 4-4; **Half-time:** 26-6; **Referee:** Phil Bentham (England); **Attendance:** 14,744 *(at Perth Rectangular Stadium)*.

AUSTRALIA

	CLUB	APP(S)	T	G	FG	PTS
Reagan Campbell-Gillard	Penrith Panthers	1(4)	0	0	0	0
Will Chambers	Melbourne Storm	5	0	0	0	0
Boyd Cordner	Sydney Roosters	5	2	0	0	8
Cooper Cronk	Melbourne Storm	5	0	0	0	0
Josh Dugan	St George Illawarra Dragons	5	2	0	0	8
Tyson Frizell	St George Illawarra Dragons	1(4)	1	0	0	4
Dane Gagai	Newcastle Knights	5	3	0	0	12
Matt Gillett	Brisbane Broncos	5	1	0	0	4
Wade Graham	Cronulla Sharks	1(5)	4	0	0	16
Valentine Holmes	Cronulla Sharks	5(1)	12	0	0	48
Ben Hunt	Brisbane Broncos	(1)	0	0	0	0
Felise Kaufusi	Melbourne Storm	1(1)	0	0	0	0
David Klemmer	Canterbury Bulldogs	5(1)	0	0	0	0
James Maloney	Cronulla Sharks	1	1	4	0	12
Josh Mansour	Penrith Panthers	2	0	0	0	0
Josh McGuire	Brisbane Broncos	4(1)	0	0	0	0
Jordan McLean	Melbourne Storm	1(5)	0	0	0	0
Michael Morgan	North Queensland Cowboys	5	2	0	0	8
Cameron Munster	Melbourne Storm	2	4	0	0	16
Billy Slater	Melbourne Storm	5	5	0	0	20
Cameron Smith	Melbourne Storm	6	0	25	0	50
Jake Trbojevic	Manly Sea Eagles	1	0	0	0	0
Tom Trbojevic	Manly Sea Eagles	2	1	0	0	4
Aaron Woods	Wests Tigers	5(1)	0	0	0	0

ENGLAND

	CLUB	APP(S)	T	G	FG	PTS
John Bateman	Wigan Warriors	6	2	0	0	8
Kevin Brown	Warrington Wolves	4	0	0	0	0
Sam Burgess	South Sydney Rabbitohs	4	0	0	0	0
Tom Burgess	South Sydney Rabbitohs	(6)	1	0	0	4
Ben Currie	Warrington Wolves	3(3)	2	0	0	8
Luke Gale	Castleford Tigers	6	0	0	0	0
James Graham	Canterbury Bulldogs	6	1	0	0	4
Ryan Hall	Leeds Rhinos	5	2	0	0	8
Chris Heighington	Cronulla Sharks	(3)	0	0	0	0
Chris Hill	Warrington Wolves	6	0	0	0	0
Josh Hodgson	Canberra Raiders	4	0	0	0	0
Jonny Lomax	St Helens	1(1)	0	0	0	0
Jermaine McGillvary	Huddersfield Giants	6	7	0	0	28
Mike McMeeken	Castleford Tigers	1	0	0	0	0
Sean O'Loughlin	Wigan Warriors	5	0	0	0	0
Mark Percival	St Helens	1	1	0	0	4
Stefan Ratchford	Warrington Wolves	2	1	0	0	4
James Roby	St Helens	2(3)	0	0	0	0
Scott Taylor	Hull FC	(1)	0	0	0	0
Alex Walmsley	St Helens	(5)	1	0	0	4
Kallum Watkins	Leeds Rhinos	5	3	0	0	12
Elliott Whitehead	Canberra Raiders	5	0	0	0	0
Gareth Widdop	St George Illawarra Dragons	6	2	16	1	41
George Williams	Wigan Warriors	(2)	0	0	0	0

FRANCE

	CLUB	APP(S)	T	G	FG	PTS
Bastien Ader	Toulouse Olympique	3	2	0	0	8
Lucas Albert	Catalans Dragons	1(1)	0	1	0	2
Olivier Arnaud	Avignon	1	0	0	0	0
Jason Baitieri	Catalans Dragons	3	0	0	0	0
William Barthau	London Broncos	1	0	3	0	6
Ilias Bergal	Swinton Lions	3	0	0	0	0
Guillaume Bonnet	Lezignan	0	0	0	0	0
John Boudebza	London Broncos	2	0	0	0	0
Julian Bousquet	Catalans Dragons	3	0	0	0	0
Clement Boyer	Toulouse Olympique	(1)	0	0	0	0
Damien Cardace	Lezignan	1	1	0	0	4
Nabil Djalout	Catalans Dragons	(2)	0	0	0	0
Theo Fages	St Helens	3	0	0	0	0
Benjamin Garcia	Catalans Dragons	3	1	0	0	4
Maxime Herold	Limoux Grizzlies	1(1)	0	0	0	0
Benjamin Jullien	Warrington Wolves	3	0	0	0	0
Mark Kheirallah	Toulouse Olympique	3	1	0	0	4
Thibaut Margalet	Catalans Dragons	(3)	0	0	0	0
Remy Marginet	Sheffield Eagles	1	0	1	0	2
Antoni Maria	Leigh Centurions	2	0	0	0	0
Romain Navarrete	Wigan Warriors	(2)	0	0	0	0
Eloi Pelissier	Leigh Centurions	1(1)	0	0	0	0
Mickael Rouch	Limoux Grizzlies	1(1)	0	0	0	0
Fouad Yaha	Catalans Dragons	3	0	0	0	0

LEBANON

	CLUB	APP(S)	T	G	FG	PTS
Daniel Abou-Sleiman	Unattached	1	0	0	0	0
Danny Barakat	Wentworthville Magpies	1	0	0	0	0
Jamie Clark	Auburn Warriors	2(1)	0	0	0	0
Adam Doueihi	South Sydney Rabbitohs	3(1)	2	0	0	8
James Elias	Wests Newcastle	3	1	0	0	4
Ahmad Ellaz	Auburn Warriors	4	0	0	0	0
Robbie Farah	South Sydney Rabbitohs	4	0	0	0	0
Nick Kassis	Blacktown Workers	3	1	0	0	4
Andrew Kazzi	Wests Tigers	1(1)	0	0	0	0
Anthony Layoun	Parramatta Eels	3	1	0	0	4
Michael Lichaa	Canterbury Bulldogs	2(2)	0	0	0	0
Bilal Maarbani	Manly Sea Eagles	1	0	0	0	0
Mitchell Mamary	Wentworthville Magpies	3(1)	0	0	0	0
Tim Mannah	Parramatta Eels	4	0	0	0	0
Abbas Miski	North Sydney Bears	4	2	0	0	8
Mitchell Moses	Parramatta Eels	4	1	8	1	21
Ray Moujalli	Canterbury Bulldogs	1(2)	0	0	0	0
Travis Robinson	Newtown Jets	3	2	0	0	8
Chris Saab	Blacktown Workers	1	0	0	0	0
Raymond Sabat	Lycans FC	0	0	0	0	0
Jaleel Seve-Derbas	Wests Tigers	1	0	0	0	0
Elias Sukkar	Wentworthville Magpies	(3)	0	0	0	0
Alex Twal	Wests Tigers	2(2)	0	0	0	0
Jason Wehbe	Unattached	1(3)	1	0	0	4

GROUP A - FINAL STANDINGS

	P	W	D	L	F	A	D	Pts
Australia	3	3	0	0	104	10	94	6
England	3	2	0	1	69	34	35	4
Lebanon	3	1	0	2	39	81	-42	2
France	3	0	0	3	30	117	-87	0

World Cup 2017 - Statistical review

GROUP B

NEW ZEALAND 38 SAMOA 8

NEW ZEALAND: 1 Roger Tuivasa-Sheck (New Zealand Warriors); 5 Jordan Rapana (Canberra Raiders); 4 Brad Takairangi (Parramatta Eels); 3 Gerard Beale (Cronulla Sharks); 2 Dallin Watene-Zelezniak (Penrith Panthers); 6 Kodi Nikorima (Brisbane Broncos); 7 Shaun Johnson (New Zealand Warriors); 8 Martin Taupau (Manly Sea Eagles); 9 Thomas Leuluai (Wigan Warriors); 18 Jared Waerea-Hargreaves (Sydney Roosters); 12 Joseph Tapine (Canberra Raiders); 13 Simon Mannering (New Zealand Warriors); 10 Adam Blair (Brisbane Broncos) (C). Subs (all used): 14 Nelson Asofa-Solomona (Melbourne Storm); 15 Russell Packer (St George Illawarra Dragons); 16 Isaac Liu (Sydney Roosters); 17 Danny Levi (Newcastle Knights). **Tries:** Rapana (4), Johnson (19), Takairangi (46), Nikorima (53), Liu (55), Tuivasa-Sheck (69), Asofa-Solomona (72); **Goals:** Johnson 5/7.
SAMOA: 1 Young Tonumaipea (Melbourne Storm); 2 Peter Mata'utia (Newcastle Knights); 4 Joseph Leilua (Canberra Raiders); 3 Tim Lafai (St George Illawarra Dragons); 5 Ken Maumalo (New Zealand Warriors); 6 Joseph Paulo (Cronulla Sharks); 7 Ben Roberts (Castleford Tigers); 8 Junior Paulo (Canberra Raiders); 9 Jazz Tevaga (New Zealand Warriors); 10 Sam Lisone (New Zealand Warriors); 11 Josh Papalii (Canberra Raiders); 12 Frank Pritchard (Parramatta Eels) (C); 13 Leeson Ah Mau (St George Illawarra Dragons). Subs (all used): 14 Pita Godinet (Manly Sea Eagles); 16 Suaia Matagi (Parramatta Eels); 17 Bunty Afoa (New Zealand Warriors). **Tries:** Maumalo (36), Joseph Paulo (80); **Goals:** Mata'utia 0/1, Lafai 0/1.
Rugby Leaguer & League Express Men of the Match:
New Zealand: Kodi Nikorima; *Samoa:* Joseph Leilua.
Penalty count: 10-7; **Half-time:** 10-4; **Referee:** James Child (England); **Attendance:** 18,200 *(at Mount Smart Stadium, Auckland).*

SCOTLAND 4 TONGA 50

SCOTLAND: 1 Lewis Tierney (Wigan Warriors); 5 Will Oakes (Hull Kingston Rovers); 3 Ben Hellewell (London Broncos); 4 Lachlan Stein (Penrith Panthers); 2 Matthew Russell (Warrington Wolves); 6 Danny Brough (Huddersfield Giants) (C); 7 Danny Addy (Hull Kingston Rovers); 8 Luke Douglas (St Helens); 9 Kane Bentley (Toulouse Olympique); 10 Ben Kavanagh (Hull Kingston Rovers); 11 Frankie Mariano (Featherstone Rovers); 12 Dale Ferguson (Huddersfield Giants); 13 James Bell (New Zealand Warriors). Subs (all used): 14 Callum Phillips (Workington Town); 15 Andrew Bentley (Toulouse Olympique); 16 Sam Brooks (Featherstone Rovers); 17 Jonathan Walker (Darlington Point Roosters). **Try:** Addy (67); **Goals:** Brough 0/1.
TONGA: 1 Will Hopoate (Canterbury Bulldogs); 5 Manu Vatuvei (Salford Red Devils); 20 Konrad Hurrell (Gold Coast Titans); 3 Michael Jennings (Parramatta Eels); 2 Daniel Tupou (Sydney Roosters); 6 Tuimoala Lolohea (Wests Tigers); 7 Ata Hingano (New Zealand Warriors); 8 Andrew Fifita (Cronulla Sharks); 9 Siliva Havili (St George Illawarra Dragons); 10 Sio Siua Taukeiaho (Sydney Roosters); 11 Manu Ma'u (Parramatta Eels); 12 Sika Manu (Hull FC) (C); 13 Jason Taumalolo (North Queensland Cowboys). Subs (all used): 14 Sione Katoa (Penrith Panthers); 15 Sam Moa (Catalans Dragons); 16 Peni Terepo (Parramatta Eels); 17 Ben Murdoch-Masila (Salford Red Devils). **Tries:** Jennings (3, 20, 40), Taumalolo (17), Manu (23), Tupou (26, 73), Terepo (70), Hingano (76); **Goals:** Taukeiaho 6/7, Lolohea 1/2.
Rugby Leaguer & League Express Men of the Match:
Scotland: Lewis Tierney; *Tonga:* Michael Jennings.
Penalty count: 6-10; **Half-time:** 0-38; **Referee:** Phil Bentham (England); **Attendance:** 9,216 *(at Barlow Park, Cairns).*

NEW ZEALAND 74 SCOTLAND 6

NEW ZEALAND: 1 Roger Tuivasa-Sheck (New Zealand Warriors); 5 Peta Hiku (Warrington Wolves); 4 Brad Takairangi (Parramatta Eels); 3 Dean Whare (Penrith Panthers); 2 Jason Nightingale (St George Illawarra Dragons); 6 Te Maire Martin (North Queensland Cowboys); 7 Shaun Johnson (New Zealand Warriors); 8 Martin Taupau (Manly Sea Eagles); 9 Elijah Taylor (Wests Tigers); 10 Jared Waerea-Hargreaves (Sydney Roosters); 11 Kenny Bromwich (Melbourne Storm); 12 Joseph Tapine (Canberra Raiders); 13 Adam Blair (Brisbane Broncos) (C). Subs (all used): 14 Nelson Asofa-Solomona (Melbourne Storm); 15 Russell Packer (St George Illawarra Dragons); 16 Addin Fonua-Blake (Manly Sea Eagles); 17 Danny Levi (Newcastle Knights). **Tries:** Bromwich (9), Nightingale (13, 23), Tapine (15), Martin (32, 52, 76), Hiku (39, 59, 69), Packer (43), Whare (55), Johnson (61), Taylor (78). **Goals:** Johnson 9/14.
SCOTLAND: 1 Alex Walker (London Broncos); 2 Lewis Tierney (Wigan Warriors); 3 Ben Hellewell (London Broncos); 4 Lachlan Stein (Penrith Panthers); 5 Matthew Russell (Warrington Wolves); 6 Danny Brough (Huddersfield Giants) (C); 7 Oscar Thomas (Bradford Bulls); 8 Luke Douglas (St Helens); 9 Danny Addy (Hull Kingston Rovers); 10 Ben Kavanagh (Hull Kingston Rovers); 11 Jarred Anderson (Sydney Roosters); 12 Dale Ferguson (Huddersfield Giants); 13 James Bell (New Zealand Warriors). Subs (all used): 14 Kane Bentley (Toulouse Olympique); 15 Sam Brooks (Featherstone Rovers); 16 Brandan Wilkinson (Bradford Bulls); 17 Jonathan Walker (Darlington Point Roosters). **Try:** Thomas (72); **Goals:** Addy 1/1.
Rugby Leaguer & League Express Men of the Match:
New Zealand: Roger Tuivasa-Sheck; *Scotland:* Luke Douglas.
Penalty count: 2-5; **Half-time:** 28-0; **Referee:** Henry Perenara (New Zealand); **Attendance:** 12,130 *(at Christchurch Stadium).*

SAMOA 18 TONGA 32

SAMOA: 1 Young Tonumaipea (Melbourne Storm); 5 Ken Maumalo (New Zealand Warriors); 4 Joseph Leilua (Canberra Raiders); 3 Tim Lafai (St George Illawarra Dragons); 2 Ricky Leutele (Cronulla Sharks); 20 Jarome Luai (Penrith Panthers); 7 Ben Roberts (Castleford Tigers); 8 Junior Paulo (Canberra Raiders); 9 Jazz Tevaga (New Zealand Warriors); 10 Herman Ese'ese (Brisbane Broncos); 11 Josh Papalii (Canberra Raiders); 12 Frank Pritchard (Parramatta Eels) (C); 13 Leeson Ah Mau (St George Illawarra Dragons). Subs (all used): 14 Fa'amanu Brown (Cronulla Sharks); 15 Zane Musgrove (South Sydney Rabbitohs); 16 Sam Lisone (New Zealand Warriors); 17 Bunty Afoa (New Zealand Warriors). **Tries:** Tevaga (17), Roberts (65), Lafai (73); **Goals:** Lafai 3/3.
TONGA: 1 Will Hopoate (Canterbury Bulldogs); 5 David Fusitu'a (New Zealand Warriors); 4 Solomone Kata (New Zealand Warriors); 3 Michael Jennings (Parramatta Eels); 2 Daniel Tupou (Sydney Roosters); 6 Tuimoala Lolohea (Wests Tigers); 7 Ata Hingano (New Zealand Warriors); 8 Andrew Fifita (Cronulla Sharks); 14 Sione Katoa (Penrith Panthers); 10 Sio Siua Taukeiaho (Sydney Roosters); 11 Manu Ma'u (Parramatta Eels); 12 Sika Manu (Hull FC) (C); 13 Jason Taumalolo (North Queensland Cowboys). Subs (all used): 9 Siliva Havili (St George Illawarra Dragons); 15 Sam Moa (Catalans Dragons); 16 Peni Terepo (Parramatta Eels); 17 Ben Murdoch-Masila (Salford Red Devils). **Tries:** Jennings (10, 29), Terepo (52), Murdoch-Masila (59), Ma'u (77); **Goals:** Taukeiaho 4/4, Hingano 2/2.
Rugby Leaguer & League Express Men of the Match:
Samoa: Junior Paulo; *Tonga:* Ata Hingano.
Penalty count: 4-6; **Half-time:** 6-14; **Referee:** Ben Cummins (Australia); **Attendance:** 18,156 *(at Waikato Stadium, Hamilton).*

NEW ZEALAND 22 TONGA 28

NEW ZEALAND: 1 Roger Tuivasa-Sheck (New Zealand Warriors); 5 Jordan Rapana (Canberra Raiders); 4 Brad Takairangi (Parramatta Eels); 3 Dean Whare (Penrith Panthers); 2 Dallin Watene-Zelezniak (Penrith Panthers); 6 Kodi Nikorima (Brisbane Broncos); 7 Shaun Johnson (New Zealand Warriors); 8 Martin Taupau (Manly Sea Eagles); 9 Thomas Leuluai (Wigan Warriors); 10 Jared Waerea-Hargreaves (Sydney Roosters); 11 Simon Mannering (New Zealand Warriors); 12 Joseph Tapine (Canberra Raiders); 13 Adam Blair (Brisbane Broncos) (C). Subs (all used): 14 Nelson Asofa-Solomona (Melbourne Storm); 15 Russell Packer (St George Illawarra Dragons); 16 Isaac Liu (Sydney Roosters); 17 Danny Levi (Newcastle Knights). **Tries:** Watene-Zelezniak (20), Rapana (28), Tuivasa-Sheck (39, 72); **Goals:** Johnson 3/4.
TONGA: 1 Will Hopoate (Canterbury Bulldogs); 5 David Fusitu'a (New Zealand Warriors); 4 Konrad Hurrell (Gold Coast Titans); 18 Mahe Fonua (Hull FC); 2 Daniel Tupou (Sydney Roosters); 6 Tuimoala Lolohea (Wests Tigers); 7 Ata Hingano (New Zealand Warriors); 8 Andrew Fifita (Cronulla Sharks); 9 Sione Katoa (Penrith Panthers); 10 Sio Siua Taukeiaho (Sydney Roosters); 11 Manu Ma'u (Parramatta Eels); 12 Sika Manu (Hull FC) (C); 13 Jason Taumalolo (North Queensland Cowboys). Subs (all used): 14 Siliva Havili (St George Illawarra Dragons); 16 Peni Terepo (Parramatta Eels); 17 Ben Murdoch-Masila (Salford Red Devils); 21 Tevita Pangai Jnr (Brisbane Broncos). **Tries:** Fusitu'a (48, 59, 77), Lolohea (62), Hopoate (65); **Goals:** Taukeiaho 3/4, Lolohea 1/2.
Rugby Leaguer & League Express Men of the Match:
New Zealand: Roger Tuivasa-Sheck; *Tonga:* Jason Taumalolo.
Penalty count: 6-8; **Half-time:** 16-2; **Referee:** Gerard Sutton (Australia); **Attendance:** 24,041 *(at Waikato Stadium, Hamilton).*

SAMOA 14 SCOTLAND 14

SAMOA: 1 Young Tonumaipea (Melbourne Storm); 5 Matthew Wright (Manly Sea Eagles); 4 Joseph Leilua (Canberra Raiders); 3 Tim Lafai (St George Illawarra Dragons); 2 Ricky Leutele (Cronulla Sharks); 6 Jarome Luai (Penrith Panthers); 7 Fa'amanu Brown (Cronulla Sharks); 8 Junior Paulo (Canberra Raiders); 9 Jazz Tevaga (New Zealand Warriors); 10 Herman Ese'ese (Brisbane Broncos); 11 Josh Papalii (Canberra Raiders); 12 Frank Winterstein (Manly Sea Eagles); 13 Bunty Afoa (New Zealand Warriors). Subs (all used): 14 Pita Godinet (Manly Sea Eagles); 15 Joseph Paulo (Cronulla Sharks); 16 Leeson Ah Mau (St George Illawarra Dragons); 17 Sam Tagataese (Cronulla Sharks) (C). **Tries:** Junior Paulo (12), Wright (49), Tonumaipea (66); **Goals:** Wright 1/3.
SCOTLAND: 1 Lewis Tierney (Wigan Warriors); 2 Shane Toal (Barrow Raiders); 3 Ben Hellewell (London Broncos); 4 Lachlan Stein (Penrith Panthers); 5 Matthew Russell (Warrington Wolves); 6 Danny Addy (Hull Kingston Rovers); 7 Oscar Thomas (Bradford Bulls); 8 Luke Douglas (St Helens) (C); 9 Callum Phillips (Workington Town); 10 Ben Kavanagh (Hull Kingston Rovers); 11 Frankie Mariano (Featherstone Rovers); 12 Dale Ferguson (Huddersfield Giants); 13 James Bell (New Zealand Warriors). Subs (all used): 14 Kane Bentley (Toulouse Olympique); 15 Brandan Wilkinson (Bradford Bulls); 16 Andrew Bentley (Toulouse Olympique); 17 Jarred Anderson (Sydney Roosters). **Tries:** Tierney (5), Mariano (29); **Goals:** Addy 3/4.
Rugby Leaguer & League Express Men of the Match:
Samoa: Josh Papalii; *Scotland:* Dale Ferguson.
Penalty count: 7-7; **Half-time:** 6-14; **Referee:** Ashley Klein (Australia); **Attendance:** 4,309 *(at Barlow Park, Cairns).*

NEW ZEALAND

	CLUB	APP(S)	T	G	FG	PTS
Nelson Asofa-Solomona	Melbourne Storm	(4)	1	0	0	4
Gerard Beale	Cronulla Sharks	1	0	0	0	0
Adam Blair	Brisbane Broncos	4	0	0	0	0
Kenny Bromwich	Melbourne Storm	1	1	0	0	4
Addin Fonua-Blake	Manly Sea Eagles	(1)	0	0	0	0
Peta Hiku	Warrington Wolves	1	3	0	0	12
Shaun Johnson	New Zealand Warriors	4	2	18	0	44
Thomas Leuluai	Wigan Warriors	2	0	0	0	0
Danny Levi	Newcastle Knights	1(3)	0	0	0	0
Isaac Liu	Sydney Roosters	(3)	1	0	0	4
Simon Mannering	New Zealand Warriors	3	0	0	0	0
Te Maire Martin	North Queensland Cowboys	2	3	0	0	12
Jason Nightingale	St George Illawarra Dragons	1	2	0	0	8
Kodi Nikorima	Brisbane Broncos	2(1)	1	0	0	4
Russell Packer	St George Illawarra Dragons	(4)	1	0	0	4
Jordan Rapana	Canberra Raiders	3	2	0	0	8
Brad Takairangi	Parramatta Eels	4	1	0	0	4
Joseph Tapine	Canberra Raiders	4	1	0	0	4
Martin Taupau	Manly Sea Eagles	4	0	0	0	0
Elijah Taylor	Wests Tigers	1	1	0	0	4
Roger Tuivasa-Sheck	New Zealand Warriors	4	3	0	0	12
Jared Waerea-Hargreaves	Sydney Roosters	4	0	0	0	0
Dallin Watene-Zelezniak	Penrith Panthers	3	1	0	0	4
Dean Whare	Penrith Panthers	3	1	0	0	4

SAMOA

	CLUB	APP(S)	T	G	FG	PTS
Bunty Afoa	New Zealand Warriors	2(2)	0	0	0	0
Leeson Ah Mau	St George Illawarra Dragons	3(1)	0	0	0	0
Fa'amanu Brown	Cronulla Sharks	1(2)	0	0	0	0
Herman Ese'ese	Brisbane Broncos	2(2)	0	0	0	0
Pita Godinet	Manly Sea Eagles	(2)	0	0	0	0
Tim Lafai	St George Illawarra Dragons	4	1	3	0	10
Joseph Leilua	Canberra Raiders	4	0	0	0	0
Ricky Leutele	Cronulla Sharks	3	0	0	0	0
Sam Lisone	New Zealand Warriors	1(1)	0	0	0	0
Jarome Luai	Penrith Panthers	3	0	0	0	0
Suaia Matagi	Parramatta Eels	(2)	0	0	0	0
Peter Mata'utia	Newcastle Knights	1	0	0	0	0
Ken Maumalo	New Zealand Warriors	2	1	0	0	4
Zane Musgrove	South Sydney Rabbitohs	(1)	0	0	0	0
Josh Papalii	Canberra Raiders	4	0	0	0	0
Joseph Paulo	Cronulla Sharks	1(2)	1	0	0	4
Junior Paulo	Canberra Raiders	4	1	0	0	4
Frank Pritchard	Parramatta Eels	3	0	0	0	0
Ben Roberts	Castleford Tigers	3	1	0	0	4
Sam Tagataese	Cronulla Sharks	(1)	0	0	0	0
Jazz Tevaga	New Zealand Warriors	4	1	0	0	4
Young Tonumaipea	Melbourne Storm	4	1	0	0	4
Frank Winterstein	Manly Sea Eagles	1	0	0	0	0
Matthew Wright	Manly Sea Eagles	2	1	1	0	6

SCOTLAND

	CLUB	APP(S)	T	G	FG	PTS
Danny Addy	Hull Kingston Rovers	3	1	4	0	12
Jarred Anderson	Sydney Roosters	1(1)	0	0	0	0
James Bell	New Zealand Warriors	3	0	0	0	0
Andrew Bentley	Toulouse Olympique	(2)	0	0	0	0
Kane Bentley	Toulouse Olympique	1(2)	0	0	0	0
Sam Brooks	Featherstone Rovers	(2)	0	0	0	0
Danny Brough	Huddersfield Giants	2	0	0	0	0
Luke Douglas	St Helens	3	0	0	0	0
Dale Ferguson	Huddersfield Giants	3	0	0	0	0
Ben Hellewell	London Broncos	3	0	0	0	0
Ben Kavanagh	Hull Kingston Rovers	3	0	0	0	0
Frankie Mariano	Featherstone Rovers	2	1	0	0	4
Kieran Moran	Hull Kingston Rovers	0	0	0	0	0
Will Oakes	Hull Kingston Rovers	1	0	0	0	0
Callum Phillips	Workington Town	1(1)	0	0	0	0
Matthew Russell	Warrington Wolves	3	0	0	0	0
Dave Scott	Batley Bulldogs	0	0	0	0	0
Lachlan Stein	Penrith Panthers	3	0	0	0	0
Oscar Thomas	Bradford Bulls	2	1	0	0	4
Lewis Tierney	Wigan Warriors	3	1	0	0	4
Shane Toal	Barrow Raiders	1	0	0	0	0
Alex Walker	London Broncos	1	0	0	0	0
Jonathan Walker	Darlington Point Roosters	(2)	0	0	0	0
Brandan Wilkinson	Bradford Bulls	(2)	0	0	0	0

TONGA

	CLUB	APP(S)	T	G	FG	PTS
Andrew Fifita	Cronulla Sharks	5	0	0	0	0
Mahe Fonua	Hull FC	1	0	0	0	0
David Fusitu'a	New Zealand Warriors	4	5	0	0	20
Siliva Havili	St George Illawarra Dragons	3(2)	1	0	0	4
Ata Hingano	New Zealand Warriors	5	1	7	0	18
Will Hopoate	Canterbury Bulldogs	5	2	0	0	8
Konrad Hurrell	Gold Coast Titans	4	0	0	0	0
Michael Jennings	Parramatta Eels	4	5	0	0	20
Solomone Kata	New Zealand Warriors	1	0	0	0	0
Sione Katoa	Penrith Panthers	2(3)	0	0	0	0
Samisoni Langi	Leigh Centurions	0	0	0	0	0
Tuimoala Lolohea	Wests Tigers	5	3	1	0	14
Sika Manu	Hull FC	5	1	0	0	4
Manu Ma'u	Parramatta Eels	5	1	0	0	4
Sam Moa	Catalans Dragons	(2)	0	0	0	0
Ben Murdoch-Masila	Salford Red Devils	(5)	1	0	0	4
Joe Ofahengaue	Brisbane Broncos	1	0	0	0	0
Tevita Pangai Jnr	Brisbane Broncos	(3)	1	0	0	4
Ukuma Ta'ai	Huddersfield Giants	(1)	0	0	0	0
Sio Siua Taukeiaho	Sydney Roosters	4	0	16	0	32
Jason Taumalolo	North Queensland Cowboys	5	1	0	0	4
Peni Terepo	Parramatta Eels	(4)	2	0	0	8
Daniel Tupou	Sydney Roosters	5	2	0	0	8
Manu Vatuvei	Salford Red Devils	1	0	0	0	0

GROUP B - FINAL STANDINGS

	P	W	D	L	F	A	D	Pts
Tonga	3	3	0	0	110	44	66	6
New Zealand	3	2	0	1	134	42	92	4
Samoa	3	0	1	2	40	84	-44	1
Scotland	3	0	1	2	24	138	-114	1

151

World Cup 2017 - Statistical review

GROUP C

Saturday 28th October 2017

PAPUA NEW GUINEA 50 WALES 6

PAPUA NEW GUINEA: 1 David Mead (Brisbane Broncos) (C); 2 Justin Olam (Melbourne Storm); 4 Nene Macdonald (St George Illawarra Dragons); 3 Kato Ottio (Canberra Raiders); 5 Garry Lo (Sheffield Eagles); 6 Ase Boas (PNG Hunters); 7 Watson Boas (PNG Hunters); 8 Stanton Albert (PNG Hunters); 9 Wartovo Puara (PNG Hunters); 10 Luke Page (Burleigh Bears); 11 Rhyse Martin (Canterbury Bulldogs); 12 Willie Minoga (PNG Hunters); 13 Paul Aiton (Catalans Dragons). Subs (all used): 14 Kurt Baptiste (Canberra Raiders); 15 Wellington Albert (PNG Hunters); 16 James Segeyaro (Cronulla Sharks); 17 Enock Maki (PNG Hunters). **Tries:** Mead (5, 10, 60), Macdonald (22), Ottio (34), W Boas (37), Martin (43, 53), Olam (56), Aiton (70); **Goals:** A Boas 0/2, Martin 5/8.
WALES: 1 Elliot Kear (London Broncos); 5 Regan Grace (St Helens); 3 Michael Channing (London Broncos); 4 Andrew Gay (South Wales Ironmen); 2 Rhys Williams (London Broncos); 6 Courtney Davies (Gloucestershire All Golds); 7 Matt Seamark (Wynnum Manly Seagulls); 8 Craig Kopczak (Salford Red Devils) (C); 9 Steve Parry (Gloucestershire All Golds); 10 Phil Joseph (Workington Town); 11 Rhodri Lloyd (Swinton Lions); 17 Chester Butler (Halifax); 13 Morgan Knowles (St Helens). Subs (all used): 12 Ben Morris (St Helens); 14 Matty Fozard (Sheffield Eagles); 15 Sam Hopkins (Leigh Centurions); 16 Ben Evans (London Broncos). **Try:** Grace (80); **Goals:** Davies 1/1.
Rugby Leaguer & League Express Men of the Match:
Papua New Guinea: Rhyse Martin; *Wales:* Elliot Kear.
Penalty count: 9-6; **Half-time:** 26-0; **Referee:** Ben Cummins (Australia); **Attendance:** 14,800 *(at National Football Stadium, Port Moresby)*.

Sunday 5th November 2017

PAPUA NEW GUINEA 14 IRELAND 6

PAPUA NEW GUINEA: 1 David Mead (Brisbane Broncos) (C); 2 Justin Olam (Melbourne Storm); 3 Kato Ottio (Canberra Raiders); 4 Nene Macdonald (St George Illawarra Dragons); 5 Garry Lo (Sheffield Eagles); 6 Ase Boas (PNG Hunters); 7 Watson Boas (PNG Hunters); 8 Stanton Albert (PNG Hunters); 9 Kurt Baptiste (Canberra Raiders); 10 Luke Page (Burleigh Bears); 11 Rhyse Martin (Canterbury Bulldogs); 12 Willie Minoga (PNG Hunters); 13 Paul Aiton (Catalans Dragons). Subs (all used): 14 James Segeyaro (Cronulla Sharks); 15 Wellington Albert (PNG Hunters); 16 Stargroth Amean (PNG Hunters); 17 Enock Maki (PNG Hunters). **Tries:** Lo (16), Macdonald (26), W Boas (78); **Goals:** Martin 0/2, A Boas 1/1.
IRELAND: 1 Scott Grix (Wakefield Trinity); 2 Shannon McDonnell (Camden Rams); 3 Ed Chamberlain (Widnes Vikings); 4 Michael Morgan (Canterbury Bulldogs); 5 Liam Kay (Toronto Wolfpack); 6 Api Pewhairangi (London Broncos); 7 Liam Finn (Wakefield Trinity) (C); 8 Brad Singleton (Leeds Rhinos); 9 Michael McIlorum (Wigan Warriors); 10 Kyle Amor (St Helens); 11 Louie McCarthy-Scarsbrook (St Helens); 12 Oliver Roberts (Huddersfield Giants); 13 George King (Warrington Wolves). Subs (all used): 14 Tyrone McCarthy (Salford Red Devils); 15 James Hasson (Wakefield Trinity); 16 Joe Philbin (Warrington Wolves); 17 Anthony Mullally (Leeds Rhinos). **Try:** McIlorum (5); **Goals:** Finn 1/1.
Rugby Leaguer & League Express Men of the Match:
Papua New Guinea: Garry Lo; *Ireland:* Liam Finn.
Penalty count: 5-5; **Half-time:** 8-6; **Referee:** Matt Cecchin (Australia); **Attendance:** 14,800 *(at National Football Stadium, Port Moresby)*.

Sunday 12th November 2017

IRELAND 34 WALES 6

IRELAND: 1 Scott Grix (Wakefield Trinity); 2 Shannon McDonnell (Camden Rams); 3 Ed Chamberlain (Widnes Vikings); 4 Api Pewhairangi (London Broncos); 5 Liam Kay (Toronto Wolfpack); 6 Joe Keyes (Bradford Bulls); 7 Liam Finn (Wakefield Trinity) (C); 8 Anthony Mullally (Leeds Rhinos); 9 Michael McIlorum (Wigan Warriors); 10 Kyle Amor (St Helens); 11 Louie McCarthy-Scarsbrook (St Helens); 15 Will Hope (Sheffield Eagles); 13 Brad Singleton (Leeds Rhinos). Subs (all used): 12 Oliver Roberts (Huddersfield Giants); 14 George King (Warrington Wolves); 16 Joe Philbin (Warrington Wolves); 17 Matty Hadden (Rochdale Hornets). **Tries:** Pewhairangi (8), Roberts (31, 66), Philbin (34), Finn (39), Kay (74); **Goals:** Finn 5/6.
WALES: 1 Elliot Kear (London Broncos); 5 Regan Grace (St Helens); 3 Michael Channing (London Broncos); 17 Ben Morris (St Helens); 2 Rhys Williams (London Broncos); 6 Courtney Davies (Gloucestershire All Golds); 23 Josh Ralph (Tweed Heads Seagulls); 8 Craig Kopczak (Salford Red Devils) (C); 14 Steve Parry (Gloucestershire All Golds); 16 Ben Evans (London Broncos); 13 Morgan Knowles (St Helens); 9 Matty Fozard (Sheffield Eagles); 10 Phil Joseph (Workington Town). Subs (all used): 11 Rhodri Lloyd (Swinton Lions); 12 Joe Burke (Oldham); 15 Gavin Bennion (Rochdale Hornets); 18 Andrew Gay (South Wales Ironmen). **Try:** Morris (58); **Goals:** Davies 1/1.
Rugby Leaguer & League Express Men of the Match:
Ireland: Liam Finn; *Wales:* Rhodri Lloyd.
Penalty count: 5-8; **Half-time:** 22-0; **Referee:** Ben Thaler (England); **Attendance:** 14,744 *(at Perth Rectangular Stadium)*.

IRELAND

	CLUB	APP(S)	T	G	FG	PTS
Kyle Amor	St Helens	3	1	0	0	4
Ed Chamberlain	Widnes Vikings	3	0	0	0	0
Casey Dunne	Longhorns	0	0	0	0	0
Liam Finn	Wakefield Trinity	3	1	12	0	28
Scott Grix	Wakefield Trinity	3	0	0	0	0
Matty Hadden	Rochdale Hornets	(1)	0	0	0	0
James Hasson	Wakefield Trinity	(2)	0	0	0	0
Jack Higginson	Wigan Warriors	0	0	0	0	0
Will Hope	Sheffield Eagles	1	0	0	0	0
Liam Kay	Toronto Wolfpack	3	3	0	0	12
James Kelly	Sheffield Eagles	0	0	0	0	0
Joe Keyes	Bradford Bulls	1	0	0	0	0
George King	Warrington Wolves	2(1)	1	0	0	4
Tyrone McCarthy	Salford Red Devils	(2)	0	0	0	0
Louie McCarthy-Scarsbrook	St Helens	3	1	0	0	4
Shannon McDonnell	Camden Rams	3	0	0	0	0
Michael McIlorum	Wigan Warriors	3	1	0	0	4
Alan McMahon	Waterford Vikings	0	0	0	0	0
Michael Morgan	Canterbury Bulldogs	2	1	0	0	4
Anthony Mullally	Leeds Rhinos	1(2)	0	0	0	0
Api Pewhairangi	London Broncos	3	1	0	0	4
Joe Philbin	Warrington Wolves	(3)	1	0	0	4
Oliver Roberts	Huddersfield Giants	2(1)	2	0	0	8
Brad Singleton	Leeds Rhinos	3	0	0	0	0

PAPUA NEW GUINEA

	CLUB	APP(S)	T	G	FG	PTS
Paul Aiton	Catalans Dragons	4	1	0	0	4
Stanton Albert	PNG Hunters	2(1)	1	0	0	4
Wellington Albert	PNG Hunters	(2)	1	0	0	4
Stargroth Amean	PNG Hunters	(3)	1	0	0	4
Kurt Baptiste	Canberra Raiders	1(3)	0	0	0	0
Ase Boas	PNG Hunters	3	0	1	0	2
Watson Boas	PNG Hunters	4	2	0	0	8
Rod Griffin	Canterbury Bulldogs	1(1)	1	0	0	4
Lachlan Lam	Sydney Roosters	1	2	0	0	8
Garry Lo	Sheffield Eagles	4	2	0	0	8
Nene Macdonald	St George Illawarra Dragons	4	3	0	0	12
Enock Maki	PNG Hunters	(2)	0	0	0	0
Rhyse Martin	Canterbury Bulldogs	4	2	16	0	40
David Mead	Brisbane Broncos	4	4	0	0	16
Moses Meninga	PNG Hunters	2	0	0	0	0
Willie Minoga	PNG Hunters	3	0	0	0	0
Justin Olam	Melbourne Storm	4	4	0	0	16
Kato Ottio	Canberra Raiders	4	1	0	0	4
Luke Page	Burleigh Bears	4	0	0	0	0
Wartovo Puara	PNG Hunters	1	0	0	0	0
Nixon Putt	PNG Hunters	(1)	0	0	0	0
James Segeyaro	Cronulla Sharks	2(2)	1	0	0	4
Thompson Teteh	Redcliffe Dolphins	(1)	0	0	0	0

* Only 23 players named in squad

WALES

	CLUB	APP(S)	T	G	FG	PTS
Danny Ansell	Hunslet	(1)	0	0	0	0
Matt Barron	Newcastle Thunder	(1)	0	0	0	0
Gavin Bennion	Rochdale Hornets	(1)	0	0	0	0
Joe Burke	Oldham	1(1)	0	0	0	0
Chester Butler	Halifax	1	0	0	0	0
Michael Channing	London Broncos	3	0	0	0	0
Courtney Davies	Gloucestershire All Golds	3	0	3	0	6
Ben Evans	London Broncos	1(2)	0	0	0	0
Matty Fozard	Sheffield Eagles	1(2)	0	0	0	0
Andrew Gay	South Wales Ironmen	1(1)	0	0	0	0
Regan Grace	St Helens	3	1	0	0	4
Dalton Grant	London Broncos	1	0	0	0	0
Sam Hopkins	Leigh Centurions	(1)	0	0	0	0
Phil Joseph	Workington Town	3	0	0	0	0
Elliot Kear	London Broncos	3	0	0	0	0
Morgan Knowles	St Helens	3	1	0	0	4
Craig Kopczak	Salford Red Devils	3	0	0	0	0
Rhodri Lloyd	Swinton Lions	2(1)	0	0	0	0
Ben Morris	St Helens	1(1)	1	0	0	4
Steve Parry	Gloucestershire All Golds	3	0	0	0	0
Josh Ralph	Tweed Heads Seagulls	1	0	0	0	0
Christiaan Roets	South Wales Ironmen	1	0	0	0	0
Matt Seamark	Wynnum Manly Seagulls	1	0	0	0	0
Rhys Williams	London Broncos	3	0	0	0	0

GROUP D

Saturday 28th October 2017

FIJI 58 USA 12

FIJI: 1 Kevin Naiqama (Wests Tigers) (C); 2 Suliasi Vunivalu (Melbourne Storm); 3 Taane Milne (St George Illawarra Dragons); 4 Akuila Uate (Manly Sea Eagles); 5 Marcelo Montoya (Canterbury Bulldogs); 6 Jarryd Hayne (Gold Coast Titans); 7 Henry Raiwalui (Blacktown Workers); 8 Ashton Sims (Warrington Wolves); 9 Apisai Koroisau (Manly Sea Eagles); 10 Kane Evans (Sydney Roosters); 11 Viliame Kikau (Penrith Panthers); 18 Brayden Wiliame (Catalans Dragons); 13 Tui Kamikamica (Melbourne Storm). Subs (all used): 14 Joe Lovadua (St George Illawarra Dragons); 15 Jacob Saifiti (Newcastle Knights); 16 Eloni Vunakece (Sydney Roosters); 17 Ben Nakubuwai (Gold Coast Titans).
Tries: Milne (3, 12), Naiqama (7, 30), Uate (14), Evans (17), Vunivalu (35, 64), Hayne (46), Kikau (59), Raiwalui (66); **Goals:** Koroisau 5/8, Milne 2/3.
USA: 1 Corey Makelim (Mounties); 2 Ryan Burroughs (Toronto Wolfpack); 4 Jonathan Alley (Central Florida Warriors); 3 Junior Vaivai (Illawarra Wests Devils); 5 Bureta Faraimo (New Zealand Warriors); 6 Kristian Freed (White Plains Wombats); 11 Daniel Howard (Wentworthville Magpies); 8 Eddy Pettybourne (Tweed Heads Seagulls); 9 David Marando (Belrose Eagles); 10 Mark Offerdahl (London Broncos) (C); 16 Stephen Howard (Mounties); 12 Matthew Shipway (South Newcastle); 13 Nicholas Newlin (Atlanta Rhinos). Subs (all used): 7 Tui Samoa (Unattached); 15 Andrew Kneisly (Philadelphia Flight); 19 Joe Eichner (Toronto Wolfpack); 21 Joshua Rice (New York Knights).
Tries: Shipway (20), Vaivai (72); **Goals:** Faraimo 2/2.
Rugby Leaguer & League Express Men of the Match:
Fiji: Taane Milne; *USA:* Junior Vaivai.
Penalty count: 5-4; **Half-time:** 36-6; **Referee:** Henry Perenara (New Zealand); **Attendance:** 5,103 *(at Townsville Stadium).*

Sunday 5th November 2017

ITALY 46 USA 0

ITALY: 2 Mason Cerruto (Penrith Panthers); 14 Chris Centrone (Wyong Roos); 3 Justin Castellaro (Northern Pride); 4 Nathan Milone (Wests Tigers); 5 Josh Mantellato (Wong Roos); 1 James Tedesco (Wests Tigers); 7 Ryan Ghietti (Northern Pride); 8 Paul Vaughan (St George Illawarra Dragons); 9 Joe Tramontana (Canterbury Bulldogs); 10 Daniel Alvaro (Parramatta Eels); 17 Jayden Walker (Cronulla Sharks); 12 Mark Minichiello (Hull FC) (C); 13 Nathan Brown (Parramatta Eels). Subs (all used): 11 Joel Riethmuller (Northern Pride); 15 Brendan Santi (Sydney Roosters); 16 Shannon Wakeman (Huddersfield Giants); 21 Christophe Calegari (Palau Broncos).
Tries: Tramontana (8, 36), Tedesco (14, 44), Mantellato (20), Ghietti (26), Vaughan (59), Cerruto (72); **Goals:** Mantellato 7/8.
USA: 1 Corey Makelim (Mounties); 2 Ryan Burroughs (Toronto Wolfpack); 3 Junior Vaivai (Illawarra Wests Devils); 21 Joshua Rice (New York Knights); 5 Bureta Faraimo (New Zealand Warriors); 6 Kristian Freed (White Plains Wombats); 7 Tui Samoa (Unattached); 8 Eddy Pettybourne (Tweed Heads Seagulls); 9 David Marando (Belrose Eagles); 10 Mark Offerdahl (London Broncos) (C); 11 Daniel Howard (Wentworthville Magpies); 12 Matthew Shipway (South Newcastle); 17 Gabriel Farley (Philadelphia Fight). Subs (all used): 14 Sam Tochterman-Talbott (Tweed Heads Seagulls); 15 Fotukava Malu (Atlanta Rhinos); 18 Charles Cortalano (White Plains Wombats); 20 David Ulch (Tampa Mayhem).
Rugby Leaguer & League Express Men of the Match:
Italy: James Tedesco; *USA:* Corey Makelim.
Penalty count: 8-6; **Half-time:** 28-0; **Referee:** Ashley Klein (Australia); **Attendance:** 7,732 *(at Townsville Stadium).*

Friday 10th November 2017

FIJI 38 ITALY 10

FIJI: 1 Kevin Naiqama (Wests Tigers) (C); 2 Suliasi Vunivalu (Melbourne Storm); 3 Taane Milne (St George Illawarra Dragons); 4 Akuila Uate (Manly Sea Eagles); 5 Marcelo Montoya (Canterbury Bulldogs); 6 Jarryd Hayne (Gold Coast Titans); 7 Henry Raiwalui (Blacktown Workers); 8 Ashton Sims (Warrington Wolves); 9 Apisai Koroisau (Manly Sea Eagles); 10 Eloni Vunakece (Sydney Roosters); 11 Viliame Kikau (Penrith Panthers); 12 Brayden Wiliame (Catalans Dragons); 13 Tui Kamikamica (Melbourne Storm). Subs (all used): 15 Jacob Saifiti (Newcastle Knights); 16 Junior Roqica (London Broncos); 17 Ben Nakubuwai (Gold Coast Titans); 18 James Storer (Port Kembla Blacks).
Tries: Naiqama (28), Raiwalui (40), Wiliame (54), Vunivalu (60, 63, 68), Montoya (75); **Goals:** Koroisau 3/4, Milne 2/3.
Sin bin: Hayne (34) - fighting.
ITALY: 2 Mason Cerruto (Penrith Panthers); 20 Richard Lepori (Oldham); 18 Christophe Calegari (Palau Broncos); 4 Nathan Milone (Wests Tigers); 5 Josh Mantellato (Wyong Roos); 1 James Tedesco (Wests Tigers); 6 Terry Campese (Queanbeyan Blues); 8 Paul Vaughan (St George Illawarra Dragons); 9 Joe Tramontana (Canterbury Bulldogs); 10 Daniel Alvaro (Parramatta Eels); 17 Jayden Walker (Cronulla Sharks); 12 Mark Minichiello (Hull FC) (C); 13 Nathan Brown (Parramatta Eels). Subs (all used): 7 Ryan Ghietti (Northern Pride); 11 Joel Riethmuller (Northern Pride); 15 Brendan Santi (Sydney Roosters); 16 Shannon Wakeman (Huddersfield Giants).
Tries: Mantellato (19), Milone (43); **Goals:** Mantellato 1/2.
Sin bin: Walker (12) - professional foul; Tramontana (34) - fighting.
Rugby Leaguer & League Express Men of the Match:
Fiji: Suliasi Vunivalu; *Italy:* Josh Mantellato.
Penalty count: 10-11; **Half-time:** 12-4; **Referee:** Robert Hicks (England); **Attendance:** 6,733 *(at Canberra Stadium).*

FIJI

	CLUB	APP(S)	T	G	FG	PTS
Kane Evans	Sydney Roosters	1	1	0	0	4
Salesi Faingaa	Parramatta Eels	1	1	0	0	4
Jarryd Hayne	Gold Coast Titans	5	2	0	0	8
Tui Kamikamica	Melbourne Storm	5	0	0	0	0
Viliame Kikau	Penrith Panthers	5	3	0	0	12
Apisai Koroisau	Manly Sea Eagles	5	0	14	0	28
Joe Lovadua	St George Illawarra Dragons	(4)	1	0	0	4
Taane Milne	St George Illawarra Dragons	5	4	8	0	32
Sitiveni Moceidreke	South Sydney Rabbitohs	0	0	0	0	0
Marcelo Montoya	Canterbury Bulldogs	5	2	0	0	8
Kevin Naiqama	Wests Tigers	5	3	0	0	12
Ben Nakubuwai	Gold Coast Titans	(5)	1	0	0	4
Henry Raiwalui	Blacktown Workers	5	3	0	0	12
Mikaele Ravalava	Canberra Raiders	0	0	0	0	0
Junior Roqica	London Broncos	(4)	0	0	0	0
Jacob Saifiti	Newcastle Knights	(5)	0	0	0	0
Pio Seci	Nabua Broncos	0	0	0	0	0
Ashton Sims	Warrington Wolves	5	0	0	0	0
Korbin Sims	Brisbane Broncos	0	0	0	0	0
James Storer	Port Kembla Blacks	(1)	0	0	0	0
Akuila Uate	Manly Sea Eagles	5	1	0	0	4
Eloni Vunakece	Sydney Roosters	4(1)	1	0	0	4
Suliasi Vunivalu	Melbourne Storm	5	9	1	0	38
Brayden Wiliame	Catalans Dragons	4	1	0	0	4

ITALY

	CLUB	APP(S)	T	G	FG	PTS
Daniel Alvaro	Parramatta Eels	3	0	0	0	0
Mirco Bergamasco	Saluzzo Roosters	0	0	0	0	0
Nathan Brown	Parramatta Eels	3	0	0	0	0
Christophe Calegari	Palau Broncos	1(1)	0	0	0	0
Terry Campese	Queanbeyan Blues	1	0	0	0	0
Justin Castellaro	Northern Pride	2	1	0	0	4
Gioele Celerino	Saluzzo Roosters	0	0	0	0	0
Chris Centrone	Wyong Roos	1	0	0	0	0
Mason Cerruto	Penrith Panthers	3	1	0	0	4
Ryan Ghietti	Northern Pride	2(1)	1	0	0	4
Gavin Hiscox	Central Queensland Capras	0	0	0	0	0
Jack Johns	Newcastle Knights	1	0	0	0	0
Richard Lepori	Oldham	1	0	0	0	0
Josh Mantellato	Wyong Roos	3	2	10	0	28
Nathan Milone	Wests Tigers	3	2	0	0	8
Mark Minichiello	Hull FC	3	0	0	0	0
Joel Riethmuller	Northern Pride	1(2)	0	0	0	0
Brendan Santi	Sydney Roosters	(3)	0	0	0	0
James Tedesco	Wests Tigers	3	2	0	0	8
Joe Tramontana	Canterbury Bulldogs	2(1)	2	0	0	8
Paul Vaughan	St George Illawarra Dragons	3	1	0	0	4
Shannon Wakeman	Huddersfield Giants	(3)	0	0	0	0
Jayden Walker	Cronulla Sharks	2(1)	0	0	0	0
Colin Wilkie	Northern Pride	1	0	0	0	0

USA

	CLUB	APP(S)	T	G	FG	PTS
Jonathan Alley	Central Florida Warriors	1	0	0	0	0
Ryan Burroughs	Toronto Wolfpack	3	0	0	0	0
Charles Cortalano	White Plains Wombats	(1)	0	0	0	0
Joe Eichner	Toronto Wolfpack	1(1)	0	0	0	0
Bureta Faraimo	New Zealand Warriors	3	0	2	0	4
Gabriel Farley	Philadelphia Fight	2	0	0	0	0
Kristian Freed	White Plains Wombats	3	0	0	0	0
Daniel Howard	Wentworthville Magpies	3	0	0	0	0
Stephen Howard	Mounties	2	0	0	0	0
Martwain Johnston	Delaware Black Foxes	(1)	0	0	0	0
Andrew Kneisly	Philadelphia Fight	(1)	0	0	0	0
Corey Makelim	Mounties	3	0	0	0	0
Fotukava Malu	Atlanta Rhinos	(1)	0	0	0	0
David Marando	Belrose Eagles	3	0	0	0	0
Nicholas Newlin	Atlanta Rhinos	1	0	0	0	0
Mark Offerdahl	London Broncos	3	0	0	0	0
Eddy Pettybourne	Tweed Heads Seagulls	3	0	0	0	0
Joshua Rice	New York Knights	1(2)	0	0	0	0
Tui Samoa	Unattached	2(1)	0	0	0	0
Matthew Shipway	South Newcastle	2	1	0	0	4
Sam Tochterman-Talbott	Tweed Heads Seagulls	(2)	0	0	0	0
David Ulch	Tampa Mayhem	(2)	0	0	0	0
Junior Vaivai	Illawarra Wests Devils	3	1	0	0	4
Matthew Walsh	White Plains Wombats	0	0	0	0	0

153

GROUP C/D

Sunday 29th October 2017

IRELAND 36 ITALY 12

IRELAND: 1 Scott Grix (Wakefield Trinity); 2 Shannon McDonnell (Camden Rams); 3 Ed Chamberlain (Widnes Vikings); 4 Michael Morgan (Canterbury Bulldogs); 5 Liam Kay (Toronto Wolfpack); 6 Api Pewhairangi (London Broncos); 7 Liam Finn (Wakefield Trinity) (C); 8 Brad Singleton (Leeds Rhinos); 9 Michael McIlorum (Wigan Warriors); 10 Kyle Amor (St Helens); 11 Louie McCarthy-Scarsbrook (St Helens); 12 Oliver Roberts (Huddersfield Giants); 13 George King (Warrington Wolves). Subs (all used): 14 Tyrone McCarthy (Salford Red Devils); 15 James Hasson (Wakefield Trinity); 16 Joe Philbin (Warrington Wolves); 17 Anthony Mullally (Leeds Rhinos).
Tries: Kay (3, 30), King (10), Amor (55), Morgan (60), McCarthy-Scarsbrook (78); **Goals:** Finn 6/7.
ITALY: 1 James Tedesco (Wests Tigers); 2 Mason Cerruto (Penrith Panthers); 3 Justin Castellaro (Northern Pride); 4 Nathan Milone (Wests Tigers); 5 Josh Mantellato (Wyong Roos); 9 Ryan Ghietti (Northern Pride); 7 Jack Johns (Newcastle Knights); 8 Paul Vaughan (St George Illawarra Dragons); 14 Colin Wilkie (Northern Pride); 10 Daniel Alvaro (Parramatta Eels); 11 Joel Riethmuller (Northern Pride); 12 Mark Minichiello (Hull FC) (C); 13 Nathan Brown (Parramatta Eels). Subs (all used): 15 Brendan Santi (Sydney Roosters); 16 Shannon Wakeman (Huddersfield Giants); 17 Jayden Walker (Cronulla Sharks); 18 Joe Tramontana (Canterbury Bulldogs).
Tries: Castellaro (38), Milone (47); **Goals:** Mantellato 2/2.
Rugby Leaguer & League Express Men of the Match:
Ireland: Liam Finn; *Italy:* Justin Castellaro.
Penalty count: 6-8; **Half-time:** 20-6; **Referee:** Grant Atkins (Australia); **Attendance:** 9,216 *(at Barlow Park, Cairns)*.

Sunday 5th November 2017

FIJI 72 WALES 6

FIJI: 1 Kevin Naiqama (Wests Tigers) (C); 2 Suliasi Vunivalu (Melbourne Storm); 3 Taane Milne (St George Illawarra Dragons); 4 Akuila Uate (Manly Sea Eagles); 5 Marcelo Montoya (Canterbury Bulldogs); 6 Jarryd Hayne (Gold Coast Titans); 7 Henry Raiwalui (Blacktown Workers); 8 Ashton Sims (Warrington Wolves); 9 Apisai Koroisau (Manly Sea Eagles); 10 Eloni Vunakece (Sydney Roosters); 11 Viliame Kikau (Penrith Panthers); 20 Salesi Faingaa (Parramatta Eels); 13 Tui Kamikamica (Melbourne Storm). Subs (all used): 14 Joe Lovadua (St George Illawarra Dragons); 15 Jacob Saifiti (Newcastle Knights); 16 Junior Roqica (London Broncos); 17 Ben Nakubuwai (Gold Coast Titans).
Tries: Vunakece (6), Vunivalu (14, 52, 61), Raiwalui (17), Kikau (22, 40), Faingaa (27), Milne (31, 56), Montoya (33), Hayne (42), Lovadua (65), Nakubuwai (70); **Goals:** Koroisau 4/7, Milne 3/5, Vunivalu 1/2.
WALES: 1 Elliot Kear (London Broncos); 5 Regan Grace (St Helens); 3 Michael Channing (London Broncos); 4 Christiaan Roets (South Wales Ironmen); 2 Rhys Williams (London Broncos); 6 Courtney Davies (Gloucestershire All Golds); 17 Dalton Grant (London Broncos); 8 Craig Kopczak (Salford Red Devils) (C); 9 Steve Parry (Gloucestershire All Golds); 10 Phil Joseph (Workington Town); 11 Rhodri Lloyd (Swinton Lions); 12 Joe Burke (Oldham); 13 Morgan Knowles (St Helens). Subs (all used): 7 Danny Ansell (Hunslet); 14 Matty Fozard (Sheffield Eagles); 15 Matt Barron (Newcastle Thunder); 16 Ben Evans (London Broncos).
Try: Knowles (11); **Goals:** Davies 1/1.
Rugby Leaguer & League Express Men of the Match:
Fiji: Jarryd Hayne; *Wales:* Morgan Knowles.
Penalty count: 4-2; **Half-time:** 42-6; **Referee:** Chris Kendall (England); **Attendance:** 7,732 *(at Townsville Stadium)*.

Sunday 12th November 2017

PAPUA NEW GUINEA 64 USA 0

PAPUA NEW GUINEA: 1 David Mead (Brisbane Broncos) (C); 2 Justin Olam (Melbourne Storm); 4 Nene Macdonald (St George Illawarra Dragons); 3 Kato Ottio (Canberra Raiders); 5 Garry Lo (Sheffield Eagles); 6 Lachlan Lam (Sydney Roosters); 7 Watson Boas (PNG Hunters); 8 Moses Meninga (PNG Hunters); 9 James Segeyaro (Cronulla Sharks); 10 Luke Page (Burleigh Bears); 11 Rhyse Martin (Canterbury Bulldogs); 18 Rod Griffin (Canterbury Bulldogs); 13 Paul Aiton (Catalans Dragons). Subs (all used): 14 Kurt Baptiste (Canberra Raiders); 15 Stargroth Amean (PNG Hunters); 16 Nixon Putt (PNG Hunters); 17 Thompson Teteh (Redcliffe Dolphins).
Tries: Lam (8, 16), Olam (12, 66, 75), Segeyaro (14), Griffin (25), Amean (40), Mead (42), W Boas (61), Macdonald (63); **Goals:** Martin 10/11.
USA: 1 Corey Makelim (Mounties); 2 Ryan Burroughs (Toronto Wolfpack); 5 Bureta Faraimo (New Zealand Warriors); 3 Junior Vaivai (Illawarra Wests Devils); 17 Gabriel Farley (Philadelphia Fight); 6 Kristian Freed (White Plains Wombats); 7 Tui Samoa (Unattached); 8 Eddy Pettybourne (Tweed Heads Seagulls); 9 David Marando (Belrose Eagles); 10 Mark Offerdahl (London Broncos); 11 Daniel Howard (Wentworthville Magpies); 12 Joe Eichner (Toronto Wolfpack); 18 Stephen Howard (Mounties). Subs (all used): 14 Sam Tochterman-Talbott (Tweed Heads Seagulls); 16 Martwain Johnston (Delaware Black Foxes); 20 David Ulch (Tampa Mayhem); 21 Joshua Rice (New York Knights).
Rugby Leaguer & League Express Men of the Match:
Papua New Guinea: Lachlan Lam; *USA:* Ryan Burroughs.
Penalty count: 5-5; **Half-time:** 34-0; **Referee:** Adam Gee (Australia); **Attendance:** 14,800 *(at National Football Stadium, Port Moresby)*.

GROUP C - FINAL STANDINGS

	P	W	D	L	F	A	D	Pts
Papua New Guinea	3	3	0	0	128	12	116	6
Ireland	3	2	0	1	76	32	44	4
Wales	3	0	0	3	18	156	-138	0

GROUP D - FINAL STANDINGS

	P	W	D	L	F	A	D	Pts
Fiji	3	3	0	0	168	28	140	6
Italy	3	1	0	2	68	74	-6	2
USA	3	0	0	3	12	168	-156	0

QUARTER FINALS

Friday 17th November 2017

AUSTRALIA 46 SAMOA 0

AUSTRALIA: 1 Billy Slater (Melbourne Storm); 2 Dane Gagai (Newcastle Knights); 3 Will Chambers (Melbourne Storm); 4 Josh Dugan (St George Illawarra Dragons); 5 Valentine Holmes (Cronulla Sharks); 6 Michael Morgan (North Queensland Cowboys); 7 Cooper Cronk (Melbourne Storm); 8 Aaron Woods (Wests Tigers); 9 Cameron Smith (Melbourne Storm) (C); 10 David Klemmer (Canterbury Bulldogs); 11 Boyd Cordner (Sydney Roosters); 12 Matt Gillett (Brisbane Broncos); 13 Josh McGuire (Brisbane Broncos). Subs (all used): 14 Wade Graham (Cronulla Sharks); 15 Jordan McLean (Melbourne Storm); 16 Reagan Campbell-Gillard (Penrith Panthers); 17 Tyson Frizell (St George Illawarra Dragons).
Tries: Holmes (8, 17, 51, 57, 74), Slater (24), Morgan (31, 36);
Goals: Smith 7/8.
SAMOA: 1 Young Tonumaipea (Melbourne Storm); 2 Matthew Wright (Manly Sea Eagles); 4 Joseph Leilua (Canberra Raiders); 3 Ricky Leutele (Cronulla Sharks); 5 Tim Lafai (St George Illawarra Dragons); 6 Jarome Luai (Penrith Panthers); 7 Ben Roberts (Castleford Tigers); 8 Junior Paulo (Canberra Raiders); 9 Jazz Tevaga (New Zealand Warriors); 15 Bunty Afoa (New Zealand Warriors); 11 Josh Papalii (Canberra Raiders); 12 Frank Pritchard (Parramatta Eels) (C); 13 Leeson Ah Mau (St George Illawarra Dragons). Subs (all used): 10 Herman Ese'ese (Brisbane Broncos); 14 Fa'amanu Brown (Cronulla Sharks); 16 Suaia Matagi (Parramatta Eels); 17 Joseph Paulo (Cronulla Sharks).
Rugby Leaguer & League Express Men of the Match:
Australia: Valentine Holmes; *Samoa:* Matthew Wright.
Penalty count: 8-6; **Half-time:** 30-0; **Referee:** Phil Bentham (England); **Attendance:** 13,473 *(at Darwin Stadium)*.

Saturday 18th November 2017

NEW ZEALAND 2 FIJI 4

NEW ZEALAND: 1 Roger Tuivasa-Sheck (New Zealand Warriors); 5 Jordan Rapana (Canberra Raiders); 4 Brad Takairangi (Parramatta Eels); 3 Dean Whare (Penrith Panthers); 2 Dallin Watene-Zelezniak (Penrith Panthers); 6 Te Maire Martin (North Queensland Cowboys); 7 Shaun Johnson (New Zealand Warriors); 8 Martin Taupau (Manly Sea Eagles); 9 Danny Levi (Newcastle Knights); 10 Jared Waerea-Hargreaves (Sydney Roosters); 11 Simon Mannering (New Zealand Warriors); 12 Joseph Tapine (Canberra Raiders); 13 Adam Blair (Brisbane Broncos) (C). Subs (all used): 14 Nelson Asofa-Solomona (Melbourne Storm); 15 Russell Packer (St George Illawarra Dragons); 16 Isaac Liu (Sydney Roosters); 17 Kodi Nikorima (Brisbane Broncos).
Goals: Johnson 1/1.
Sin bin: Rapana (47) - professional foul.
FIJI: 1 Kevin Naiqama (Wests Tigers) (C); 2 Suliasi Vunivalu (Melbourne Storm); 3 Taane Milne (St George Illawarra Dragons); 4 Akuila Uate (Manly Sea Eagles); 5 Marcelo Montoya (Canterbury Bulldogs); 6 Jarryd Hayne (Gold Coast Titans); 7 Henry Raiwalui (Blacktown Workers); 8 Ashton Sims (Warrington Wolves); 9 Apisai Koroisau (Manly Sea Eagles); 10 Eloni Vunakece (Sydney Roosters); 11 Viliame Kikau (Penrith Panthers); 12 Brayden Wiliame (Catalans Dragons); 13 Tui Kamikamica (Melbourne Storm). Subs (all used): 14 Joe Lovadua (St George Illawarra Dragons); 15 Jacob Saifiti (Newcastle Knights); 16 Junior Roqica (London Broncos); 17 Ben Nakubuwai (Gold Coast Titans).
Goals: Koroisau 1/1, Milne 1/1.
Rugby Leaguer & League Express Men of the Match:
New Zealand: Roger Tuivasa-Sheck; *Fiji:* Kevin Naiqama.
Penalty count: 8-7; **Half-time:** 0-2; **Referee:** Matt Cecchin (Australia); **Attendance:** 12,000 *(at Christchurch Stadium)*.

LEBANON 22 TONGA 24

LEBANON: 1 Anthony Layoun (Parramatta Eels); 5 Abbas Miski (North Sydney Bears); 3 James Elias (Wests Newcastle); 4 Adam Doueihi (South Sydney Rabbitohs); 2 Travis Robinson (Newtown Jets); 6 Mitchell Moses (Parramatta Eels); 7 Robbie Farah (South Sydney Rabbitohs) (C); 8 Tim Mannah (Parramatta Eels); 9 Michael Lichaa (Canterbury Bulldogs); 10 Alex Twal (Wests Tigers); 11 Nick Kassis (Blacktown Workers); 12 Ahmad Ellaz (Auburn Warriors); 14 Mitchell Mamary (Wentworthville Magpies). Subs (all used): 13 Jamie Clark (Auburn Warriors); 15 Ray Moujalli (Canterbury Bulldogs); 16 Elias Sukkar (Wentworthville Magpies); 17 Jason Wehbe (Unattached).
Tries: Doueihi (9), Elias (30), Miski (40, 69); **Goals:** Moses 3/4.
TONGA: 1 Will Hopoate (Canterbury Bulldogs); 5 David Fusitu'a (New Zealand Warriors); 4 Konrad Hurrell (Gold Coast Titans); 3 Michael Jennings (Parramatta Eels); 2 Daniel Tupou (Sydney Roosters); 6 Tuimoala Lolohea (Wests Tigers); 7 Ata Hingano (New Zealand Warriors); 8 Andrew Fifita (Cronulla Sharks); 14 Siliva Havili (St George Illawarra Dragons); 19 Joe Ofahengaue (Brisbane Broncos); 11 Manu Ma'u (Parramatta Eels); 12 Sika Manu (Hull FC) (C); 13 Jason Taumalolo (North Queensland Cowboys). Subs (all used): 9 Sione Katoa (Penrith Panthers); 16 Tevita Pangai Jnr (Brisbane Broncos); 17 Ben Murdoch-Masila (Salford Red Devils); 18 Ukuma Ta'ai (Huddersfield Giants).
Tries: Lolohea (4), Fusitu'a (19, 33), Hopoate (22); **Goals:** Hingano 4/5.
Rugby Leaguer & League Express Men of the Match:
Lebanon: Adam Doueihi; *Tonga:* David Fusitu'a.
Penalty count: 10-7; **Half-time:** 16-22; **Referee:** Gerard Sutton (Australia); **Attendance:** 8,309 *(at Wellington Regional Stadium)*.

Sunday 19th November 2017

ENGLAND 36 PAPUA NEW GUINEA 6

ENGLAND: 1 Gareth Widdop (St George Illawarra Dragons); 2 Jermaine McGillvary (Huddersfield Giants); 3 Kallum Watkins (Leeds Rhinos); 4 John Bateman (Wigan Warriors); 5 Ryan Hall (Leeds Rhinos); 6 Kevin Brown (Warrington Wolves); 7 Luke Gale (Castleford Tigers); 8 Chris Hill (Warrington Wolves); 9 Josh Hodgson (Canberra Raiders); 10 James Graham (Canterbury Bulldogs); 11 Sam Burgess (South Sydney Rabbitohs); 12 Elliott Whitehead (Canberra Raiders); 13 Sean O'Loughlin (Wigan Warriors) (C). Subs (all used): 14 Alex Walmsley (St Helens); 15 Tom Burgess (South Sydney Rabbitohs); 16 Ben Currie (Warrington Wolves); 17 James Roby (St Helens).
Tries: McGillvary (13, 19), Walmsley (33), Currie (56), Watkins (68, 72), Hall (78); **Goals:** Widdop 4/7.
PAPUA NEW GUINEA: 1 David Mead (Brisbane Broncos) (C); 2 Justin Olam (Melbourne Storm); 4 Nene Macdonald (St George Illawarra Dragons); 3 Kato Ottio (Canberra Raiders); 5 Garry Lo (Sheffield Eagles); 6 Ase Boas (PNG Hunters); 7 Watson Boas (PNG Hunters); 8 Moses Meninga (PNG Hunters); 9 James Segeyaro (Cronulla Sharks); 10 Luke Page (Burleigh Bears); 11 Rhyse Martin (Canterbury Bulldogs); 12 Willie Minoga (PNG Hunters); 13 Paul Aiton (Catalans Dragons). Subs (all used): 14 Kurt Baptiste (Canberra Raiders); 15 Stargroth Amean (PNG Hunters); 16 Stanton Albert (PNG Hunters); 17 Rod Griffin (Canterbury Bulldogs).
Try: Lo (60); **Goals:** Martin 1/1.
Rugby Leaguer & League Express Men of the Match:
England: Luke Gale; *Papua New Guinea:* Watson Boas.
Penalty count: 7-5; **Half-time:** 14-0; **Referee:** James Child (England); **Attendance:** 10,563 *(at Melbourne Rectangular Stadium)*.

SEMI-FINALS

Friday 24th November 2017

AUSTRALIA 54 FIJI 6

AUSTRALIA: 1 Billy Slater (Melbourne Storm); 2 Dane Gagai (Newcastle Knights); 3 Will Chambers (Melbourne Storm); 4 Josh Dugan (St George Illawarra Dragons); 5 Valentine Holmes (Cronulla Sharks); 6 Michael Morgan (North Queensland Cowboys); 7 Cooper Cronk (Melbourne Storm); 8 Aaron Woods (Wests Tigers); 9 Cameron Smith (Melbourne Storm) (C); 10 David Klemmer (Canterbury Bulldogs); 11 Boyd Cordner (Sydney Roosters); 12 Matt Gillett (Brisbane Broncos); 13 Josh McGuire (Brisbane Broncos). Subs (all used): 14 Wade Graham (Cronulla Sharks); 15 Jordan McLean (Melbourne Storm); 16 Reagan Campbell-Gillard (Penrith Panthers); 17 Tyson Frizell (St George Illawarra Dragons).
Tries: Slater (14, 48), Holmes (18, 25, 42, 52, 66, 76), Gagai (32, 70); **Goals:** Smith 7/10.
FIJI: 1 Kevin Naiqama (Wests Tigers) (C); 2 Suliasi Vunivalu (Melbourne Storm); 3 Taane Milne (St George Illawarra Dragons); 4 Akuila Uate (Manly Sea Eagles); 5 Marcelo Montoya (Canterbury Bulldogs); 6 Jarryd Hayne (Gold Coast Titans); 7 Henry Raiwalui (Blacktown Workers); 8 Ashton Sims (Warrington Wolves); 9 Apisai Koroisau (Manly Sea Eagles); 10 Eloni Vunakece (Sydney Roosters); 11 Viliame Kikau (Penrith Panthers); 12 Brayden Wiliame (Catalans Dragons); 13 Tui Kamikamica (Melbourne Storm). Subs (all used): 14 Joe Lovadua (St George Illawarra Dragons); 15 Jacob Saifiti (Newcastle Knights); 16 Junior Roqica (London Broncos); 17 Ben Nakubuwai (Gold Coast Titans).
Try: Vunivalu (60); **Goals:** Koroisau 1/2.
Rugby Leaguer & League Express Men of the Match:
Australia: Valentine Holmes; *Fiji:* Apisai Koroisau.
Penalty count: 6-4; **Half-time:** 22-2; **Referee:** Gerard Sutton (Australia); **Attendance:** 22,073 *(at Brisbane Stadium)*.

ENGLAND 20 TONGA 18

ENGLAND: 1 Gareth Widdop (St George Illawarra Dragons); 2 Jermaine McGillvary (Huddersfield Giants); 3 Kallum Watkins (Leeds Rhinos); 4 John Bateman (Wigan Warriors); 5 Ryan Hall (Leeds Rhinos); 6 Kevin Brown (Warrington Wolves); 7 Luke Gale (Castleford Tigers); 8 Chris Hill (Warrington Wolves); 9 Josh Hodgson (Canberra Raiders); 10 James Graham (Canterbury Bulldogs); 11 Sam Burgess (South Sydney Rabbitohs); 12 Elliott Whitehead (Canberra Raiders); 13 Sean O'Loughlin (Wigan Warriors) (C). Subs (all used): 14 Alex Walmsley (St Helens); 15 Tom Burgess (South Sydney Rabbitohs); 16 Ben Currie (Warrington Wolves); 17 James Roby (St Helens).
Tries: McGillvary (10), Widdop (16), Bateman (67); **Goals:** Widdop 4/4.
TONGA: 1 Will Hopoate (Canterbury Bulldogs); 5 David Fusitu'a (New Zealand Warriors); 4 Konrad Hurrell (Gold Coast Titans); 3 Michael Jennings (Parramatta Eels); 2 Daniel Tupou (Sydney Roosters); 6 Tuimoala Lolohea (Wests Tigers); 7 Ata Hingano (New Zealand Warriors); 8 Andrew Fifita (Cronulla Sharks); 9 Siliva Havili (St George Illawarra Dragons); 10 Sio Siua Taukeiaho (Sydney Roosters); 11 Manu Ma'u (Parramatta Eels); 12 Sika Manu (Hull FC) (C); 13 Jason Taumalolo (North Queensland Cowboys). Subs (all used): 14 Sione Katoa (Penrith Panthers); 15 Peni Terepo (Parramatta Eels); 16 Tevita Pangai Jnr (Brisbane Broncos); 17 Ben Murdoch-Masila (Salford Red Devils).
Tries: Pangai Jnr (73), Havili (77), Lolohea (78); **Goals:** Taukeiaho 3/3.
Rugby Leaguer & League Express Men of the Match:
England: Gareth Widdop; *Tonga:* Siliva Havili.
Penalty count: 8-6; **Half-time:** 12-0; **Referee:** Matt Cecchin (Australia); **Attendance:** 30,003 *(at Mount Smart Stadium, Auckland)*.

FINAL

Saturday 2nd December 2017

AUSTRALIA 6 ENGLAND 0

AUSTRALIA: 1 Billy Slater (Melbourne Storm); 2 Dane Gagai (Newcastle Knights); 3 Will Chambers (Melbourne Storm); 4 Josh Dugan (St George Illawarra Dragons); 5 Valentine Holmes (Cronulla Sharks); 6 Michael Morgan (North Queensland Cowboys); 7 Cooper Cronk (Melbourne Storm); 8 Aaron Woods (Wests Tigers); 9 Cameron Smith (Melbourne Storm) (C); 10 David Klemmer (Canterbury Bulldogs); 11 Boyd Cordner (Sydney Roosters); 12 Matt Gillett (Brisbane Broncos); 13 Josh McGuire (Brisbane Broncos). Subs (all used): 14 Wade Graham (Cronulla Sharks); 15 Jordan McLean (Melbourne Storm); 16 Reagan Campbell-Gillard (Penrith Panthers); 17 Tyson Frizell (St George Illawarra Dragons).
Try: Cordner (15); **Goals:** Smith 1/1.
ENGLAND: 1 Gareth Widdop (St George Illawarra Dragons); 2 Jermaine McGillvary (Huddersfield Giants); 3 Kallum Watkins (Leeds Rhinos); 4 John Bateman (Wigan Warriors); 5 Ryan Hall (Leeds Rhinos); 6 Kevin Brown (Warrington Wolves); 7 Luke Gale (Castleford Tigers); 8 Chris Hill (Warrington Wolves); 9 James Roby (St Helens); 10 James Graham (Canterbury Bulldogs); 16 Ben Currie (Warrington Wolves); 12 Elliott Whitehead (Canberra Raiders); 11 Sam Burgess (South Sydney Rabbitohs) (C). Subs (all used): 14 Alex Walmsley (St Helens); 15 Tom Burgess (South Sydney Rabbitohs); 17 Chris Heighington (Cronulla Sharks); 18 Jonny Lomax (St Helens).
Rugby Leaguer & League Express Men of the Match:
Australia: Cooper Cronk; *England:* James Graham.
Penalty count: 6-7; **Half-time:** 6-0; **Referee:** Gerard Sutton (Australia); **Attendance:** 40,033 *(at Brisbane Stadium)*.

LEADING SCORERS

TRIES

1	Valentine Holmes	Australia	12
2	Suliasi Vunivalu	Fiji	9
3	Jermaine McGillvary	England	7
4	Billy Slater	Australia	5
	David Fusitu'a	Tonga	5
	Michael Jennings	Tonga	5

GOALS

1	Cameron Smith	Australia	25
2	Shaun Johnson	New Zealand	18
3	Rhyse Martin	Papua New Guinea	16
	Sio Siua Taukeiaho	Tonga	16
	Gareth Widdop	England	16

POINTS

			T	G	FG	Pts
1	Cameron Smith	Australia	0	25	0	50
2	Valentine Holmes	Australia	12	0	0	48
3	Shaun Johnson	New Zealand	2	18	0	44
4	Gareth Widdop	England	2	16	1	41
5	Rhyse Martin	Papua New Guinea	2	16	0	40

TEST SERIES
England progress

England's Josh Hodgson and James Graham
show off the Albert Baskerville Shield

England won the end-of-season Test series against New Zealand, beating the Kiwis in the first two games of the series despite missing several first-choice players ruled out through injury.

New Zealand got some degree of satisfaction in the third Test at Elland Road when they nilled England for the first time in the history of games between the two nations, running out 34-0 winners.

It was England however who lifted the Albert Baskerville Shield after the final whistle and winger Tommy Makinson who was awarded the George Smith Medal as man of the series.

England, coached by Wayne Bennett, were without 12 of the squad that reached the previous year's World Cup final. With the third Test being played on the 100th anniversary of Armistice Day, Bennett had taken the full England squad to the war graves of Belgium in the lead up to the series and the resolve and team spirit in his players shone through.

The Kiwis were coached by former Wigan coach Michael Maguire who conjured a brilliant team performance from his side in the last game. In the aftermath, both coaches spoke of the huge potential of their teams in the years to come.

First Test

A youthful, exuberant England side stood tall to draw first blood with an 18-16 win over the Kiwis at Hull's KCOM Stadium.

Three weeks before the first Test, Wigan's Oliver Gildart was preparing to tour Papua New Guinea with the England Knights. But it was the 22-year-old centre, in the squad after the injury withdrawal of Sam Burgess and a surprise inclusion in the starting thirteen, who effectively won the game for England with a stunning 50-metre try 14 minutes from the end of a tense game.

Prior to Gildart's try, New Zealand were seemingly well on their way to grinding out a victory, thanks largely to halfback Shaun Johnson. His two penalties, which made it 16-14, appeared for large periods to be Johnson's latest torment of England, before Gildart struck from nowhere.

With points, and indeed clear-cut chances, at a premium, Gildart capitalised

FIRST TEST

Saturday 27th October 2018

ENGLAND 18 NEW ZEALAND 16

ENGLAND: 1 Jonny Lomax (St Helens); 2 Tommy Makinson (St Helens); 3 Jake Connor (Hull FC); 4 Oliver Gildart (Wigan Warriors); 5 Jermaine McGillvary (Huddersfield Giants); 6 George Williams (Wigan Warriors); 7 Sam Tomkins (Wigan Warriors); 15 Tom Burgess (South Sydney Rabbitohs); 9 Josh Hodgson (Canberra Raiders); 10 James Graham (St George Illawarra Dragons); 11 John Bateman (Wigan Warriors); 12 Elliott Whitehead (Canberra Raiders); 13 Sean O'Loughlin (Wigan Warriors) (C). Subs (all used): 8 Chris Hill (Warrington Wolves); 14 Luke Thompson (St Helens); 16 George Burgess (South Sydney Rabbitohs); 17 Daryl Clark (Warrington Wolves).
Tries: Tomkins (3), Connor (39, pen), Gildart (66); **Goals:** Connor 3/4.
NEW ZEALAND: 1 Dallin Watene-Zelezniak (Penrith Panthers) (C); 2 Ken Maumalo (New Zealand Warriors); 3 Esan Marsters (Wests Tigers); 4 Joseph Manu (Sydney Roosters); 5 Jordan Rapana (Canberra Raiders); 6 Shaun Johnson (New Zealand Warriors); 7 Kodi Nikorima (Brisbane Broncos); 8 Jesse Bromwich (Melbourne Storm); 9 Brandon Smith (Melbourne Storm); 10 Jared Waerea-Hargreaves (Sydney Roosters); 11 Kevin Proctor (Gold Coast Titans); 12 Isaac Liu (Sydney Roosters); 13 James Fisher-Harris (Penrith Panthers). Subs (all used): 14 Kenny Bromwich (Melbourne Storm); 15 Leeson Ah Mau (St George Illawarra Dragons); 16 Martin Taupau (Manly Sea Eagles); 17 Joseph Tapine (Canberra Raiders).
Tries: Marsters (12), Watene-Zelezniak (32); **Goals:** Johnson 4/4.
Rugby Leaguer & League Express Men of the Match:
England: John Bateman; *New Zealand:* Shaun Johnson.
Penalty count: 9-5; **Half-time:** 12-12; **Referee:** Robert Hicks (England); **Attendance:** 17,649 *(at KCOM Stadium, Hull)*.

on a superb offload from John Bateman out of a three-man tackle before racing downfield and stepping and swerving around New Zealand captain Dallin Watene-Zelezniak to put the hosts back ahead. From there, the nerve displayed by England to repel the Kiwis was impressive.

There was a negative in that captain Sean O'Loughlin withdrew after only 14 minutes, with the England skipper suffering a calf injury that would rule him out of the rest of the series.

England got off to a dream start after just three minutes. George Williams' towering bomb was pinched out of Jordan Rapana's hands by Tommy Makinson, who was outstanding throughout, before Elliott Whitehead and Jonny Lomax kept the ball alive to allow Sam Tomkins, playing at halfback, to cross unchallenged.

Jake Connor converted, before beginning his usual on-field antics of trying to get under the skin of the opposition. But as the half wore on, and O'Loughlin departed, the Kiwis began to assert their dominance. And they were rewarded after twelve minutes when a magnificent inside pass from Johnson was hit at speed by Esan Marsters and the Wests Tigers centre strode through a huge gap to level the scores.

As half-time approached the Kiwi forwards began to get on top and they went ahead on 32 minutes. This time, straight from a scrum, Kodi Nikorima's skip and delayed pass sent Watene-Zelezniak through a gap to make it 12-6.

There was just enough time for England to level. With seconds remaining before the break, Connor appeared to have squeezed over in the corner. The video referee deemed that Connor had not grounded the ball but Watene-Zelezniak had used his knees in the act of tackling him, resulting in a penalty try. That gave Connor a simple kick from in front of the posts to make it 12-12 at the break.

As the game wore on into the second half it became clear it would take something special to unlock either defence again. That was emphasised when the teams exchanged penalties; first, Johnson kicked the Kiwis back ahead before Connor levelled it once more at 14-14.

James Graham feels the force of the New Zealand defence at the KCOM Stadium

Johnson then repeated the trick on 62 minutes to put New Zealand in front for a third time. But four minutes later, the game's decisive moment arrived.

With England camped in their own half, the outstanding Bateman managed to wriggle the ball free to Gildart from a three-man tackle. Winger Ken Maumalo was one of the defenders and had committed to tackling Bateman, meaning Gildart had rare space, touching down after rounding Watene-Zelezniak to produce the loudest roar of the afternoon.

As the seconds ticked down, New Zealand, with Johnson at the heart of their attack, threw the kitchen sink at England to test their resolve. But they stood up to everything hurled at them.

Dallin Watene-Zelezniak splits the England defence to score the opening try of the Second Test

Second Test

England wrapped up the series to ensure they would lift the Albert Baskerville Shield with a 20-14 win in a superb second Test played at Liverpool's Anfield.

St Helens winger Tommy Makinson, playing on the left wing because of injury to Ryan Hall, won the game with his hat-trick try in the 74th minute, capping a superb all-round display that led to him being awarded the RLIF Golden Boot.

England made one change to the 17 that won the previous weekend's opening Test, with Adam Milner coming in for injured captain Sean O'Loughlin. Milner started on the bench, which meant Luke Thompson was elevated to the starting line-up after a strong performance in Hull.

For the Kiwis, Adam Blair returned from injury, moving him into outright

SECOND TEST

Sunday 4th November 2018

ENGLAND 20 NEW ZEALAND 14

ENGLAND: 1 Jonny Lomax (St Helens); 2 Tommy Makinson (St Helens); 3 Jake Connor (Hull FC); 4 Oliver Gildart (Wigan Warriors); 5 Jermaine McGillvary (Huddersfield Giants); 6 George Williams (Wigan Warriors); 7 Sam Tomkins (Wigan Warriors); 15 Tom Burgess (South Sydney Rabbitohs); 9 Josh Hodgson (Canberra Raiders); 10 James Graham (St George Illawarra Dragons) (C); 11 John Bateman (Wigan Warriors); 12 Elliott Whitehead (Canberra Raiders); 13 Luke Thompson (St Helens). Subs (all used): 8 Chris Hill (Warrington Wolves); 14 Adam Milner (Castleford Tigers); 16 George Burgess (South Sydney Rabbitohs); 17 Daryl Clark (Warrington Wolves).
Tries: Makinson (38, 58, 74), Connor (64); **Goals:** Connor 1/4, Tomkins 1/1.
NEW ZEALAND: 1 Dallin Watene-Zelezniak (Penrith Panthers) (C); 2 Ken Maumalo (New Zealand Warriors); 3 Esan Marsters (Wests Tigers); 4 Joseph Manu (Sydney Roosters); 5 Jordan Rapana (Canberra Raiders); 6 Shaun Johnson (New Zealand Warriors); 7 Kodi Nikorima (Brisbane Broncos); 8 Jesse Bromwich (Melbourne Storm); 9 Brandon Smith (Melbourne Storm); 10 Jared Waerea-Hargreaves (Sydney Roosters); 11 Kevin Proctor (Gold Coast Titans); 12 Isaac Liu (Sydney Roosters); 13 Adam Blair (New Zealand Warriors). Subs (all used): 14 Kenny Bromwich (Melbourne Storm); 15 Leeson Ah Mau (St George Illawarra Dragons); 16 Martin Taupau (Manly Sea Eagles); 17 James Fisher-Harris (Penrith Panthers).
Tries: Watene-Zelezniak (9), Maumalo (45); **Goals:** Johnson 3/3.
Rugby Leaguer & League Express Men of the Match:
England: Tommy Makinson; *New Zealand:* Dallin Watene-Zelezniak.
Penalty count: 6-5; **Half-time:** 6-6; **Referee:** Gerard Sutton (Australia); **Attendance:** 26,234 *(at Anfield, Liverpool).*

159

England celebrate their Second Test victory after an Anfield thriller

second on the list of all-time appearances for New Zealand with 47 caps. Only Ruben Wiki had made more Test appearances for the Kiwis than Blair.

England were handed a chance to open the scoring as early as the first set of the game, as Jesse Bromwich's error gave the hosts an early opportunity. They were, however, bundled into touch as the chance passed. However, after Bromwich was again in the wrong, this time for a late hit on Sam Tomkins, Jake Connor kicked England ahead with a penalty.

It did not take the tourists too long to respond. Three minutes later they were ahead and it was captain Dallin Watene-Zelezniak who did the damage. A constant danger with the ball in the first Test at Hull, the fullback stormed through a big gap between Sam Tomkins and Oliver Gildart to put New Zealand ahead, with Shaun Johnson making no mistake with the conversion.

And from there, it was the Kiwis who began to assume a position of dominance. Their power and ferocity through the middle was on display on several occasions. Had it not been for some inspired defending from Makinson, England may have fallen further behind.

On three separate occasions, the St Helens winger was on hand to deny New Zealand attacks. First, he did just about enough to stop Jordan Rapana as he reached out to touch down, before the Canberra winger was again halted by Makinson.

His best defensive effort came three minutes later though. With New Zealand creating a two-on-one overlap on the right, Makinson produced a superb ball-and-all hit to deny Kevin Proctor as he stormed for the line, allowing England to survive a period of intense pressure without conceding any further points.

Then, two minutes before the break, Makinson took centre stage once more, this time finishing a free-flowing move that resulted in a looping pass from George Williams that found the winger unmarked and he dived with a one-handed put-down into the corner. Connor missed the conversion, leaving it nicely poised at 6-6 at the break.

However, New Zealand came out after half-time much the stronger of the two sides, offloading the ball at will. Within five minutes, they were ahead once again. Another searing break from Watene-Zelezniak off a delayed pass from Kodi Nikorima cut through the England defence, before the fullback found Ken Maumalo with a long pass and the winger finished superbly.

Johnson converted, before tagging on a penalty five minutes later to make it 14-6.

As the hour mark approached, that was how it remained before England regained the offensive.

On 58 minutes, Makinson claimed his second after great handling from Connor and Jonny Lomax in the build-up. And while Connor again missed with the goal attempt, he was on hand to profit from a fine piece of play from the always-outstanding Elliott Whitehead to make it 14-14.

Connor's conversion again missed, setting up an incredible finale as the game awaited a hero to settle matters.

Makinson was that hero. The winger collected a pass wide on the left 25 metres out before surging infield with blistering pace and stretching over to produce a huge roar from the crowd, although it needed the video-referee Ben Thaler to closely examine whether he had lost control of the ball whilst touching it down. Referee Gerard Sutton's on-field call of 'try' proved crucial. Sam Tomkins converted to make it 20-14 and the outcome of the series was decided, the Kiwis' last effort ending when Whitehead, another top performer, stole the ball from Martin Tapau in midfield.

Third Test

New Zealand played to their potential in the Armistice Day Test at Elland Road in Leeds as they ran away with the third game of the series, nilling England for the first time in history while scoring six tries in their 34-0 win.

Test Series

Halfbacks Kodi Nikorima and Shaun Johnson ran riot on the back of a dominant pack display, with Nikorima having a hand or foot in four tries and Johnson's kicking game continually pinning England back in their own territory.

For England, there was no Sam Tomkins or Daryl Clark, both injured the week before, and George Burgess was serving the first of a four-match ban after being caught gouging Dallin Watene-Zelezniak. It meant a start for Richie Myler and a bench place for Stefan Ratchford, with Joe Greenwood making his debut off the bench.

Brisbane winger Jamayne Isaako made his debut in place of the injured Jordan Rapana, with the Warriors' Isaiah Papalii coming onto the field late on for his first cap. Canberra backrower Joseph Tapine was recalled on the bench.

The Kiwis settled the quickest, taking the lead on five minutes when a fine offload from Jared Waerea-Hargreaves and a sideways dart from Brandon Smith allowed Dallin Watene-Zelezniak to juggle the ball to Ken Maumalo, who cut inside and forced his way over to break the deadlock.

England played some expansive football and appeared to have struck on 19 minutes when Tommy Makinson finished in the corner with trademark aplomb. The score was, however, harshly ruled out when sent upstairs, with Tom Burgess adjudged to have caused an obstruction as the ball went wide. And there was further frustration 12 minutes later when, after Oliver Gildart crossed, Jermaine McGillvary's kick was ruled as a knock-on after it rebounded off a Kiwi player before he got his foot to the ball.

Those two plays would be crucial as, in seven destructive minutes before half-time, the momentum swung firmly in the Kiwis' favour.

Nikorima was at the heart of it all; first, his last-tackle skip and offload to Isaac Liu saw the forward stride through under the posts, before Nikorima ducked under Chris Hill's tackle and did a one-two with Johnson to touch down, allowing Johnson the simplest of conversions to make it 18-0 at the break.

England had to score next to stand a chance. But within four minutes of the restart, Maumalo again proved a pivotal influence, this time out-jumping McGillvary to claim a kick from the outstanding Nikorima and make it 22-0.

England continued to rally. But a frustrating afternoon was summed up when Waerea-Hargreaves was sin-binned for a flop and, two tackles later, Makinson again had a try ruled out by the video referee, this time because the winger had a toe on the touchline.

With the Kiwis surviving the 10-minute period without Waerea-Hargreaves, the hosts would not be as resolute when McGillvary was sin-binned for a professional foul.

Within two tackles, Jesse Bromwich strode through off Nikorima's disguised flat pass to touch down. Then, four minutes later, Tapine scored New Zealand's sixth try as he barged his way over off a short ball from Jesse Bromwich.

It was a resounding New Zealand win but it could only take away some of the gloss from a fine series win by England.

THIRD TEST

Sunday 11th November 2018

ENGLAND 0 NEW ZEALAND 34

ENGLAND: 1 Jonny Lomax (St Helens); 2 Tommy Makinson (St Helens); 3 Jake Connor (Hull FC); 4 Oliver Gildart (Wigan Warriors); 5 Jermaine McGillvary (Huddersfield Giants); 6 George Williams (Wigan Warriors); 7 Richie Myler (Leeds Rhinos); 15 Tom Burgess (South Sydney Rabbitohs); 9 Josh Hodgson (Canberra Raiders); 10 James Graham (St George Illawarra Dragons) (C); 11 John Bateman (Wigan Warriors); 12 Elliott Whitehead (Canberra Raiders); 13 Luke Thompson (St Helens). Subs (all used): 8 Chris Hill (Warrington Wolves); 14 Adam Milner (Castleford Tigers); 16 Joe Greenwood (Wigan Warriors); 17 Stefan Ratchford (Warrington Wolves). **Sin bin:** McGillvary (69) - professional foul.
NEW ZEALAND: 1 Dallin Watene-Zelezniak (Penrith Panthers) (C); 2 Ken Maumalo (New Zealand Warriors); 3 Esan Marsters (Wests Tigers); 4 Joseph Manu (Sydney Roosters); 5 Jamayne Isaako (Brisbane Broncos); 6 Shaun Johnson (New Zealand Warriors); 7 Kodi Nikorima (Brisbane Broncos); 8 Jesse Bromwich (Melbourne Storm); 9 Brandon Smith (Melbourne Storm); 10 Jared Waerea-Hargreaves (Sydney Roosters); 11 Kevin Proctor (Gold Coast Titans); 12 Isaac Liu (Sydney Roosters); 13 Adam Blair (New Zealand Warriors). Subs (all used): 14 Kenny Bromwich (Melbourne Storm); 15 Leeson Ah Mau (St George Illawarra Dragons); 16 Isaiah Papalii (New Zealand Warriors); 17 Joseph Tapine (Canberra Raiders). **Tries:** Maumalo (5, 44), Nikorima (39), J Bromwich (69), Tapine (73); **Goals:** Johnson 4/5, Papalii 1/1. **Sin bin:** Waerea-Hargreaves (57) - flop.
Rugby Leaguer & League Express Men of the Match: *England:* Luke Thompson; *New Zealand:* Kodi Nikorima.
Penalty count: 9-4; **Half-time:** 0-18; **Referee:** Gerard Sutton (Australia); **Attendance:** 32,186 *(at Elland Road, Leeds).*

Ken Maumalo and Jermaine McGillvary compete for a high ball during the Third Test *(above)* and *(below)* the teams line up for a minute's silence before kick-off, to commemorate the 100th anniversary of Armistice Day

England debutant Jake Connor touches down in Denver

In June, England came from behind to ease past New Zealand by 36-18 in a Test match that was played in Denver, Colorado, with a crowd of 19,320 turning out at Mile High Stadium.

In England's first match since the 2017 World Cup final loss to Australia, Esan Marsters and Dallin Watene-Zelezniak gave the Kiwis a 12-0 lead before Ryan Hall's brilliant try in the left corner cut the deficit.

Elliott Whitehead scored twice and debutants Jake Connor and Tommy Makinson, both starting on the bench, went over before John Bateman completed a resounding victory after Watene-Zelezniak scored his second try.

Connor played a vital role in giving the final passes for Hall's and Whitehead's tries that brought England back to 10-12 at the break. He then scored a superb try of his own in the second half that was decisive in ensuring an England victory, selling a superb dummy to Kiwi fullback Watene-Zelezniak in the process. Makinson, not to be outdone, gave the final pass for Whitehead's second try and then scored a fine try himself, this time taking the final pass from Whitehead and weaving his way to the line.

TEST MATCH

Saturday 23rd June 2018

ENGLAND 36 NEW ZEALAND 18

ENGLAND: 1 Stefan Ratchford (Warrington Wolves); 2 Jermaine McGillvary (Huddersfield Giants); 3 John Bateman (Wigan Warriors); 4 Mark Percival (St Helens); 5 Ryan Hall (Leeds Rhinos); 6 Jonny Lomax (St Helens); 7 Gareth Widdop (St George Illawarra Dragons); 8 Chris Hill (Warrington Wolves); 9 James Roby (St Helens); 10 James Graham (St George Illawarra Dragons); 11 Sam Burgess (South Sydney Rabbitohs); 12 Elliott Whitehead (Canberra Raiders); 13 Sean O'Loughlin (Wigan Warriors) (C). Subs (all used): 14 Jake Connor (Hull FC); 15 Tom Burgess (South Sydney Rabbitohs); 16 Tommy Makinson (St Helens); 17 Scott Taylor (Hull FC).
Tries: Hall (33), Whitehead (38, 53), Connor (60), Makinson (65), Bateman (80); **Goals:** Widdop 6/7, Graham 0/1.
NEW ZEALAND: 1 Dallin Watene-Zelezniak (Penrith Panthers); 2 Jamayne Isaako (Brisbane Broncos); 3 Esan Marsters (Wests Tigers); 4 Peta Hiku (New Zealand Warriors); 5 Ken Maumalo (New Zealand Warriors); 6 Te Maire Martin (North Queensland Cowboys); 7 Kodi Nikorima (Brisbane Broncos); 8 Jared Waerea-Hargreaves (Sydney Roosters); 9 Issac Luke (New Zealand Warriors); 10 Nelson Asofa-Solomona (Melbourne Storm); 11 Raymond Faitala-Mariner (Canterbury Bulldogs); 12 Joseph Tapine (Canberra Raiders); 13 Martin Taupau (Manly Sea Eagles). Subs (all used): 14 Slade Griffin (Newcastle Knights); 15 James Fisher-Harris (Penrith Panthers); 16 Herman Ese'ese (Newcastle Knights); 17 Leeson Ah Mau (St George Illawarra Dragons). *(No captain appointed).*
Tries: Marsters (10), Watene-Zelezniak (28, 69); **Goals:** Isaako 3/3.
Rugby Leaguer & League Express Men of the Match:
England: Jake Connor; *New Zealand:* Esan Marsters.
Penalty count: 3-10; **Half-time:** 10-12; **Referee:** Ben Thaler (England); **Attendance:** 19,320 *(at Sports Authority Field, Mile High, Denver).*

Tom Johnstone races over for his second try of the game against France

England beat France by 44-6 at Leigh Sports Village in a warm-up for the Kiwi Test series.

A team which left out players that had participated in the previous Saturday's Grand Final blitzed France in a first half after which England led 38-0. Wakefield winger Tom Johnstone scored a magnificent 12-minute hat-trick midway through the first half, although it wasn't enough to gain him a spot in the Test series ahead of St Helens' Tommy Makinson and Huddersfield's Jermaine McGillvary.

Hull's Jake Connor was man of the match against the Kiwis in Denver in June and he followed that up with another stellar display. Oliver Holmes, the Castleford second-rower, was also impressive.

Tom Burgess scored after one minute of the game, with Richie Myler, a late draft after the injury withdrawal of Luke Gale, Luke Thompson and Elliott Whitehead also crossing before the break. Connor scored England's only try of the second half. That was converted by Mark Percival, after Connor had kicked five previous goals, while Theo Fages added a consolation for France, who got up to speed after the break.

TEST MATCH

Wednesday 17th October 2018

ENGLAND 44 FRANCE 6

ENGLAND: 1 Jamie Shaul (Hull FC); 2 Tom Johnstone (Wakefield Trinity); 3 Reece Lyne (Wakefield Trinity); 4 Mark Percival (St Helens); 5 Jermaine McGillvary (Huddersfield Giants); 6 Richie Myler (Leeds Rhinos); 7 Jake Connor (Hull FC); 8 James Graham (St George Illawarra Dragons) (C); 9 Josh Hodgson (Canberra Raiders); 10 Tom Burgess (South Sydney Rabbitohs); 11 Oliver Holmes (Castleford Tigers); 12 Elliott Whitehead (Canberra Raiders); 13 George Burgess (South Sydney Rabbitohs). Subs (all used): 14 Adam Milner (Castleford Tigers); 15 Luke Thompson (St Helens); 16 Robbie Mulhern (Hull Kingston Rovers); 17 Liam Sutcliffe (Leeds Rhinos).
Tries: T Burgess (2), Johnstone (14, 19, 26), Myler (30), Thompson (33), Whitehead (40), Connor (59); **Goals:** Connor 5/7, Percival 1/1.
FRANCE: 1 Stan Robin (Toulouse Olympique); 25 Paul Marcon (Toulouse Olympique); 4 Tony Gigot (Catalans Dragons); 3 Bastien Ader (Toulouse Olympique); 5 Hakim Miloudi (Hull FC); 6 Theo Fages (St Helens) (C); 7 William Barthau (Toulouse Olympique); 10 Lambert Belmas (Catalans Dragons); 23 Alrix Da Costa (Catalans Dragons); 8 Bastien Canet (Toulouse Olympique); 12 Benjamin Jullien (Catalans Dragons); 13 Mickael Goudemand (Catalans Dragons); 24 Jason Baitieri (Catalans Dragons). Subs (all used): 22 Anthony Marion (Toulouse Olympique); 14 Thibaut Margalet (Catalans Dragons); 17 Valentin Yesa (Limoux); 16 Bastien Escamilla (Carcassonne).
Try: Fages (63); **Goals:** Barthau 1/1.
Rugby Leaguer & League Express Men of the Match:
England: Jake Connor; *France:* Theo Fages.
Penalty count: 8-7; **Half-time:** 38-0; **Referee:** Chris Kendall (England); **Attendance:** 5,144 *(at Leigh Sports Village)*.

INTERNATIONALS
Knight fever

England Knights

The England Knights feeder team was revived after a five-year hiatus and enjoyed a two-series tour of Papua New Guinea that ended all square.

Warrington halfback Declan Patton was a late call-up to the squad coached by former Huddersfield coach Paul Anderson, replacing injury victim Danny Richardson of St Helens. Hull fullback Jamie Shaul also withdrew for family reasons. Oliver Gildart (Wigan) was called into the full England squad and was replaced by Niall Evalds of Salford. Warrington's Tom Lineham was also called up to the Knights' squad to replace Castleford's Greg Minikin, who has also withdrawn through injury.

In the first game, played in Lae, PNG's second-largest city, the Knights held off a spirited second-half fightback by the Kumuls to claim a 16-12 victory.

A boisterous crowd created a fervent atmosphere for what turned out to be a physical, defence-dominated contest.

PNG struck first on 13 minutes after a crossfield kick was tapped back into the hands of winger Brendon Nima, who scored wide out. Featherstone-bound halfback Watson Boas was off target with the conversion attempt (he also missed his other two).

But after Nene Macdonald caught Warrington second row Joe Philbin with a late tackle, the Knights quickly shifted the ball to the left for Leeds centre Liam Sutcliffe to cross and Patton goaled to give England a 21st-minute lead.

The Kumuls hit back thanks to dominant defence which caused the Knights to spill

ENGLAND KNIGHTS SQUAD
Chris Atkin (Hull Kingston Rovers); James Batchelor (Wakefield Trinity); Tom Davies (Wigan Warriors); Niall Evalds (Salford Red Devils); Brad Fash (Hull FC); Dean Hadley (Hull FC); Ash Handley (Leeds Rhinos); Oliver Holmes (Castleford Tigers); Jack Hughes (Warrington Wolves) (C); Toby King (Warrington Wolves); Kruise Leeming (Huddersfield Giants); Matty Lees (St Helens); Tom Lineham (Warrington Wolves); Harvey Livett (Warrington Wolves); Robbie Mulhern (Hull Kingston Rovers); Mikolaj Oledzki (Leeds Rhinos); Declan Patton (Warrington Wolves); Joe Philbin (Warrington Wolves); Sam Powell (Wigan Warriors); Liam Sutcliffe (Leeds Rhinos); Danny Walker (Widnes Vikings); Jack Walker (Leeds Rhinos); Matt Whitley (Widnes Vikings).

Niall Evalds dragged down during England Knights' first clash with Papua New Guinea

possession and Moses Meninga crashed through by the posts. On the half hour, it was the Kumuls who coughed up the ball, which was moved left for Lineham to cross.

Huddersfield hooker Kruise Leeming made a difference on his introduction, livening up the speed of the play-the-ball and kicking an excellent 40/20. Off the back of it, England switched the ball to the right for Tom Davies to go over on 36 minutes and Patton converted to make it 16-8.

The Kumuls started the second half strongly, and England had to defend a string of sets on their own line. They eventually cracked when Edwin Ipape danced his way through a tiring defence on 50 minutes. But Paul Anderson's side showed real resolve and resilience to hold out for the victory. After the game he picked out Jack Hughes, the Warrington forward captaining the Knights, and Matty Lees, the St Helens prop who was one of the nominees for Super League's Young Player of the Year, for praise.

A week later, the Kumuls gained revenge with a 32-22 victory in the capital Port Moresby, 190 miles to the south of Lae.

The Knights struck first after ten minutes when Lineham, one of six Warrington players in the side, went in wide out after wonderful footwork from clubmate Hughes. Patton converted. The Knights capitalised after Catalans fullback David Mead knocked on in his own half and scored through Wigan winger Davies after 15 minutes. Patton, who had set up the score with a long cut-out pass, added the goal.

Nixon Putt and Justin Olam scored tries for PNG, with Leeds' Jack Walker getting one in between to make it 18-12 to the Knights at the break.

The home side started the second half with plenty of energy. Utility Ase Boas dummied and crashed over and the Kumuls went ahead for the first time when Mead grabbed a loose ball and powered over.

The Kumuls pack, led by Widnes prop Wellington Albert and Enock Maki, were setting the platform for the backs to fire. And Albert was getting under the skin of his opposite forwards, especially Lees, which caused a skirmish which referee John Stone quickly calmed.

The Kumuls added to their lead through centre Macdonald, who pounced on a grubber by Kyle Laybutt in the 58th minute.

Patton and Watson Boas were then sin-binned after clashing before a diving Lineham got one back. With Patton in the cooler, Danny Walker took on the kicking duties but could not convert, so the home side had an eight-point cushion with ten minutes remaining.

A late Watson Boas penalty, his sixth goal out of six attempts, sealed the win.

ENGLAND KNIGHTS IN PAPUA NEW GUINEA

Saturday 27th October 2018

PAPUA NEW GUINEA 12 ENGLAND KNIGHTS 16

PAPUA NEW GUINEA: 1 David Mead (Catalans Dragons) (C); 2 Junior Rau (PNG Hunters); 3 Justin Olam (Melbourne Storm); 4 Nene Macdonald (St George Illawarra Dragons); 5 Brendon Nima (Goroka Lahanis); 6 Edwin Ipape (Lea Snax Tigers); 7 Watson Boas (PNG Hunters); 8 Enock Maki (PNG Hunters); 9 Tom Butterfield (Easts Tigers); 10 Stanton Albert (PNG Hunters); 11 Moses Meninga (PNG Hunters); 12 Nixon Putt (PNG Hunters); 13 Wellington Albert (Widnes Vikings). Subs (all used): 14 Ase Boas (PNG Hunters); 15 Rhadley Brawa (PNG Hunters); 16 Dilbert Isaac (PNG Hunters); 17 Woods Kawage (Enga Mioks).
Tries: Nima (13), Meninga (26), Ipape (50); **Goals:** W Boas 0/3.
ENGLAND KNIGHTS: 1 Niall Evalds (Salford Red Devils); 2 Tom Davies (Wigan Warriors); 3 Toby King (Warrington Wolves); 4 Liam Sutcliffe (Leeds Rhinos); 5 Tom Lineham (Warrington Wolves); 6 Chris Atkin (Hull Kingston Rovers); 7 Declan Patton (Warrington Wolves); 8 Robbie Mulhern (Hull Kingston Rovers); 9 Sam Powell (Wigan Warriors); 10 Matty Lees (St Helens); 11 Oliver Holmes (Castleford Tigers); 12 Jack Hughes (Warrington Wolves); 13 Dean Hadley (Hull FC). Subs (all used): 14 Kruise Leeming (Huddersfield Giants); 15 Joe Philbin (Warrington Wolves); 16 James Batchelor (Wakefield Trinity); 17 Brad Fash (Hull FC).
Tries: Sutcliffe (21), Lineham (31), Davies (36); **Goals:** Patton 2/3.
Rugby Leaguer & League Express Men of the Match:
Papua New Guinea: Moses Meninga; *England Knights:* Matty Lees.
Half-time: 8-16; **Attendance:** 5,000 *(at Lae Oval).*

Saturday 3rd November 2018

PAPUA NEW GUINEA 32 ENGLAND KNIGHTS 22

PAPUA NEW GUINEA: 1 David Mead (Catalans Dragons) (C); 2 Junior Rau (PNG Hunters); 3 Justin Olam (Melbourne Storm); 4 Nene Macdonald (St George Illawarra Dragons); 5 Brendon Nima (Goroka Lahanis); 6 Kyle Laybutt (North Queensland Cowboys); 7 Watson Boas (PNG Hunters); 8 Moses Meninga (PNG Hunters); 9 Tom Butterfield (Easts Tigers); 10 Stanton Albert (PNG Hunters); 11 Rhadley Brawa (PNG Hunters); 12 Nixon Putt (PNG Hunters); 13 Wellington Albert (Widnes Vikings). Subs (all used): 15 Ase Boas (PNG Hunters); 16 Zev John (Melbourne Storm); 17 Dilbert Isaac (PNG Hunters); 19 Enock Maki (PNG Hunters).
Tries: Putt (30), Olam (40), A Boas (45), Mead (52), Macdonald (58); **Goals:** W Boas 6/6.
Sin bin: W Boas (65) - fighting.
ENGLAND KNIGHTS: 1 Jack Walker (Leeds Rhinos); 2 Tom Davies (Wigan Warriors); 3 Toby King (Warrington Wolves); 4 Ash Handley (Leeds Rhinos); 5 Tom Lineham (Warrington Wolves); 6 Declan Patton (Warrington Wolves); 7 Chris Atkin (Hull Kingston Rovers); 8 Mikolaj Oledzki (Leeds Rhinos); 9 Sam Powell (Wigan Warriors); 10 Matty Lees (St Helens); 11 Harvey Livett (Warrington Wolves); 12 Matt Whitley (Widnes Vikings); 13 Jack Hughes (Warrington Wolves) (C). Subs (all used): 14 Danny Walker (Widnes Vikings); 15 Oliver Holmes (Castleford Tigers); 16 Robbie Mulhern (Hull Kingston Rovers); 17 Joe Philbin (Warrington Wolves).
Tries: Lineham (10, 70), Davies (15), J Walker (35); **Goals:** Patton 3/3, J Walker 0/1.
Sin bin: Patton (65) - fighting.
Rugby Leaguer & League Express Men of the Match:
Papua New Guinea: Watson Boas; *England Knights:* Tom Lineham.
Half-time: 12-18;
Attendance: 5,686 *(at National Football Stadium, Port Moresby).*

Internationals

European Championship

France won the 2018 European Championship, winning all three games and earning qualification for the 2021 World Cup. Wales claimed their place alongside them by finishing second in the table.

France effectively topped the table with a 54-18 win over Wales in Carcassonne in week one.

James Olds, Connor and Curtis Davies, Sion Jones and Chris Vitalini all earned their first Wales caps in a side that fielded 12 Welsh-born players and had an average age of 23. France, on the other hand, were able to call on the likes of Tony Gigot, Morgan Escare, Theo Fages and Jason Baitieri and, by the half-hour mark, had established a 26-0 lead. Tries to Josh Ralph and Elliot Kear pulled it back to 26-12 at the break but Gigot crossed for a try in the 46th minute and the French held firm.

A 24-10 win over Ireland the following week in windy conditions at Santry, on the outskirts of Dublin, confirmed France's World Cup place. Ireland fought back in the second half but the damage had already been done in the first half as France, playing with the conditions in their favour, scored 18 points without reply, with St Helens halfback Fages involved in most French attacks.

Back in Carcassone the week after France were made to fight all the way in a feisty affair against Scotland.

A series of flare-ups between players in the second half demonstrated how much passion there was and referee Greg Dolan showed excellent international diplomacy by keeping a lid on simmering tempers.

Stade Albert Domec echoed to the sound of the Scottish national anthem before the game with 'Flower Of Scotland' sung loudly without accompanying music by every member of the team and support staff. It set the tone for a commited performance from both teams which was only separated by the star quality of France's Super League contingent.

Escare was pure box office from fullback, scoring two tries and kicking all of his six attempts on goal, some from difficult angles. His Wigan team-mate Romain Navarette led from the front as captain and Fages fizzed around the pack at scrum-half. Escare's dazzling footwork as he weaved through the Scottish defence to score in the 57th minute put France on 20 points and effectively sealed the game.

After their drubbing in France, Wales produced a stunning 50-12 win over Scotland in Galashiels, after being 12-0 down within eight minutes.

Nineteen-year-old Elliott Jenkins, who broke his jaw playing for Wales' under-19s in the summer and hadn't played for the best part of six months, was outstanding on his senior debut, as was halfback partner Josh Ralph.

While Wales' backline ran riot in the second half, Halifax prop Dan Fleming put in another outstanding display in the pack, playing the full 80 minutes.

The week after, Wales claimed a place at the 2021 World Cup with a fine 40-8 win over Ireland in Wrexham.

Tries from Chester Butler, Rhodri Lloyd, Gavin Bennion, Ben Evans, Rhys Williams and Ralph saw Wales finish second in the table. James Olds added eight goals.

Scott Grix and George King scored tries for Ireland, who along with Scotland could still make the World Cup.

The pair were to take on two from Italy, Greece, Spain, Norway or Russia in 2019 for another opportunity to obtain a berth.

EUROPEAN CHAMPIONSHIP

Saturday 27th October 2018

IRELAND 36 SCOTLAND 10

IRELAND: 1 Scott Grix (Wakefield Trinity); 2 Alan McMahon (Waterford Vikings); 3 James Bentley (St Helens); 4 Jack Higginson (Wigan Warriors); 5 Ethan Ryan (Bradford Bulls); 6 Gregg McNally (Bradford Bulls); 7 Liam Finn (Widnes Vikings) (C); 8 Liam Byrne (Wigan Warriors); 9 Declan O'Donnell (Wigan Warriors); 10 George King (Warrington Wolves); 11 Tyrone McCarthy (Salford Red Devils); 12 Will Hope (Swinton Lions); 13 Lewis Bienek (Hull FC). Subs (all used): 14 Peter Ryan (Coventry Bears); 15 Ronan Michael (Huddersfield Giants); 16 Gareth Gill (Longhorns); 17 Michael Ward (Batley Bulldogs).
Tries: McCarthy (14), E Ryan (17), O'Donnell (33), Bentley (37), McMahon (42), Higginson (61, 79); **Goals:** Finn 4/7.
SCOTLAND: 1 Dave Scott (Batley Bulldogs); 2 Davey Dixon (Keighley Cougars); 3 Murray Mitchell (Strathmore Silverbacks); 4 Will Oakes (Hull Kingston Rovers); 5 Finn Hutchison (Edinburgh Eagles); 6 Oscar Thomas (Sheffield Eagles); 7 Ryan Brierley (Toronto Wolfpack); 8 Ben Kavanagh (Hull Kingston Rovers) (C); 9 Kane Bentley (Toulouse Olympique); 10 Billy McConnachie (Ipswich Jets); 11 Frankie Mariano (Doncaster); 12 Nick Glohe (Lakes United Seagulls); 13 Sam Luckley (Newcastle Thunder). Subs: 14 Luke Westman (Berkeley Eagles); 15 Lewis Clarke (Edinburgh Eagles); 16 Kieran Moran (Keighley Cougars); 17 Lewis Tierney (Catalans Dragons) (not used).
Tries: Glohe (46), Kavanagh (56); **Goals:** Brierley 1/2.
Rugby Leaguer & League Express Men of the Match:
Ireland: Liam Finn; *Scotland:* Nick Glohe.
Penalty count: 1-7; **Half-time:** 20-0; **Referee:** Tom Grant (England); **Attendance:** 250 *(at Morton Stadium, Santry)*.

FRANCE 54 WALES 18

FRANCE: 1 Tony Gigot (Catalans Dragons); 20 Morgan Escare (Wigan Warriors); 3 Bastien Ader (Toulouse Olympique); 4 Hakim Miloudi (Hull FC); 5 Paul Marcon (Toulouse Olympique); 6 Lucas Albert (Catalans Dragons); 7 Theo Fages (St Helens) (C); 8 Romain Navarrete (Wigan Warriors); 9 Alrix Da Costa (Catalans Dragons); 24 Jason Baitieri (Catalans Dragons); 11 Benjamin Jullien (Catalans Dragons); 12 Rhys Curran (Toulouse Olympique); 13 Mickael Goudemand (Catalans Dragons). Subs (all used): 14 Thibaut Margalet (Catalans Dragons); 15 Bastien Canet (Toulouse Olympique); 16 Lambert Belmas (Catalans Dragons); 18 Stan Robin (Toulouse Olympique).
Tries: Marcon (8, 21), Miloudi (12), Ader (29), Gigot (53), Curran (53), Escare (58, 79), Navarrete (76); **Goals:** Gigot 7/8, Albert 2/2.
WALES: 1 Elliot Kear (London Broncos) (C); 5 Dalton Grant (Bradford Bulls); 4 James Olds (West Brisbane Panthers); 3 Ben Morris (St Helens); 2 Rhys Williams (London Broncos); 6 Courtney Davies (unattached); 7 Josh Ralph (Easts Tigers); 8 Ben Evans (London Broncos); 18 Steve Parry (West Wales Raiders); 13 Dan Fleming (Halifax); 11 Rhodri Lloyd (Swinton Lions); 12 Chester Butler (Halifax); 17 Gavin Bennion (Salford Red Devils). Subs (all used): 19 Curtis Davies (Halifax); 16 Sion Jones (Halifax); 21 Chris Vitalini (Coventry Bears); 15 Connor Davies (Halifax).
Tries: Ralph (36), Kear (39), Olds (70); **Goals:** Olds 3/3.
Rugby Leaguer & League Express Men of the Match:
France: Tony Gigot; *Wales:* Dan Fleming.
Penalty count: 9-8; **Half-time:** 26-12; **Referee:** James Child (England); **Attendance:** 4,055 *(at Stade Albert Domec, Carcassonne)*.

Friday 2nd November 2018

SCOTLAND 12 WALES 50

SCOTLAND: 1 Dave Scott (Batley Bulldogs); 5 Craig Robertson (Edinburgh Eagles); 4 Will Oakes (Hull Kingston Rovers); 3 Murray Mitchell (Strathmore Silverbacks); 2 Davey Dixon (Keighley Cougars); 6 Oscar Thomas (Sheffield Eagles); 7 Ryan Brierley (Toronto Wolfpack); 8 Ben Kavanagh (Hull Kingston Rovers) (C); 9 Kane Bentley (Toulouse Olympique); 10 Oliver Wilkes (Workington Town); 15 Nick Glohe (Lakes United Seagulls); 20 Frankie Mariano (Doncaster); 13 James Bell (New Zealand Warriors). Subs (all used): 17 Billy McConnachie (Ipswich Jets); 16 Sam Luckley (Newcastle Thunder); - Craig Borthwick (Edinburgh Eagles); 14 Lewis Clarke (Edinburgh Eagles).
Tries: Dixon (3), Bell (8); **Goals:** Brierley 2/2.
WALES: 1 Elliot Kear (London Broncos) (C); 22 Mike Butt (Swinton Lions); 4 James Olds (West Brisbane Panthers); 3 Ben Morris (St Helens); 2 Rhys Williams (London Broncos); 14 Elliott Jenkins (Rochdale Hornets); 7 Josh Ralph (Easts Tigers); 8 Ben Evans (London Broncos); 18 Steve Parry (West Wales Raiders); 13 Dan Fleming (Halifax); 11 Rhodri Lloyd (Swinton Lions); 12 Chester Butler (Halifax); 15 Connor Davies (Halifax). Subs (all used): 19 Curtis Davies (Halifax); 17 Gavin Bennion (Salford Red Devils); 5 Dalton Grant (Bradford Bulls); 20 Morgan Evans (West Wales Raiders).
Tries: Williams (20, 42, 74), Jenkins (33, 60), Butler (57), Ralph (67, 71), Evans (78); **Goals:** Olds 7/9.
Rugby Leaguer & League Express Men of the Match:
Scotland: James Bell; *Wales:* Dan Fleming.
Penalty count: 2-10; **Half-time:** 12-8; **Referee:** Ben Casty (France); **Attendance:** 600 *(at Netherdale, Galashiels)*.

Saturday 3rd November 2018

IRELAND 10 FRANCE 24

IRELAND: 1 Scott Grix (Wakefield Trinity); 2 Ed O'Keefe (Galway Tribesmen); 14 James Bentley (St Helens); 4 Jack Higginson (Wigan Warriors); 5 Ethan Ryan (Bradford Bulls); 6 Gregg McNally (Bradford Bulls); 7 Liam Finn (Widnes Vikings) (C); 8 George King (Warrington Wolves); 9 Declan O'Donnell (Wigan Warriors); 10 Liam Byrne (Wigan Warriors); 11 Tyrone McCarthy (Salford Red Devils); 12 Will Hope (Swinton Lions); 13 Lewis Bienek (Hull FC). Subs (all used): 19 Peter Ryan (Coventry Bears); 15 Ronan Michael (Huddersfield Giants); 16 Gareth Gill (Longhorns); 17 Michael Ward (Batley Bulldogs).
Tries: E Ryan (44), McNally (71); **Goals:** Finn 1/2.
FRANCE: 1 Tony Gigot (Catalans Dragons); 20 Morgan Escare (Wigan Warriors); 4 Hakim Miloudi (Hull FC); 3 Bastien Ader (Toulouse Olympique); 5 Paul Marcon (Toulouse Olympique); 6 Lucas Albert (Catalans Dragons); 7 Theo Fages (St Helens) (C); 24 Jason Baitieri (Catalans Dragons); 9 Alrix Da Costa (Catalans Dragons); 8 Romain Navarrete (Wigan Warriors); 11 Benjamin Jullien (Catalans Dragons); 12 Rhys Curran (Toulouse Olympique); 13 Mickael Goudemand (Catalans Dragons). Subs (all used): 14 William Barthau (Toulouse Olympique); 15 Lambert Belmas (Catalans Dragons); 18 Thibaut Margalet (Catalans Dragons); 17 Bastien Canet (Toulouse Olympique).
Tries: Da Costa (7, 65), Marcon (10), Ader (25); **Goals:** Gigot 4/5.
Rugby Leaguer & League Express Men of the Match:
Ireland: Scott Grix; *France:* Theo Fages.
Penalty count: 10-9; **Half-time:** 0-18; **Referee:** Scott Mikalauskas (England); **Attendance:** 300 *(at Morton Stadium, Santry)*.

Saturday 10th November 2018

FRANCE 28 SCOTLAND 10

FRANCE: 20 Morgan Escare (Wigan Warriors); 2 Paul Marcon (Toulouse Olympique); 3 Bastien Ader (Toulouse Olympique); 4 Hakim Miloudi (Hull FC); 5 Gavin Marguerite (Toulouse Olympique); 6 Stan Robin (Toulouse Olympique); 7 Theo Fages (St Helens) (C); 8 Romain Navarrete (Wigan Warriors); 9 Alrix Da Costa (Catalans Dragons); 16 Lambert Belmas (Catalans Dragons); 11 Rhys Curran (Toulouse Olympique); 12 Benjamin Jullien (Catalans Dragons); 13 Mickael Goudemand (Catalans Dragons). Subs (all used): 24 Anthony Marion (Toulouse Olympique); 19 Bastien Canet (Toulouse Olympique); 15 Valentin Yesa (Limoux); 18 Lucas Albert (Catalans Dragons).
Tries: Fages (19), Escare (32, 67), Marion (69); **Goals:** Escare 6/6.
SCOTLAND: 1 Oscar Thomas (Sheffield Eagles); 2 Davey Dixon (Keighley Cougars); 3 Dave Scott (Batley Bulldogs); 4 Craig Robertson (Edinburgh Eagles); 5 Niall Sidney (Newcastle Thunder); 6 Matt Hogg (Edinburgh Eagles); 7 Ryan Brierley (Toronto Wolfpack); 8 Joe McClean (West Wales Raiders); 16 Kane Bentley (Toulouse Olympique); 10 Oliver Wilkes (Workington Town) (C); 15 Nick Glohe (Lakes United Seagulls); 12 Frankie Mariano (Doncaster); 13 James Bell (New Zealand Warriors). Subs (all used): 14 Lewis Clarke (Edinburgh Eagles); 11 Dan Turland (Newcastle Thunder); 18 Hamish Bentley (Toulouse Olympique); 17 Kieran Moran (Keighley Cougars).
Tries: Dixon (26), Robertson (73); **Goals:** Thomas 1/2.
Rugby Leaguer & League Express Men of the Match: *France:* Morgan Escare; *Scotland:* Ryan Brierley.
Penalty count: 13-13; **Half-time:** 14-4; **Referee:** Greg Dolan (England); **Attendance:** 2,854 *(at Stade Albert Domec, Carcassonne)*.

Sunday 11th November 2018

WALES 40 IRELAND 8

WALES: 1 Elliot Kear (London Broncos) (C); 2 Rhys Williams (London Broncos); 3 Ben Morris (St Helens); 4 James Olds (West Brisbane Panthers); 5 Dalton Grant (Bradford Bulls); 14 Elliott Jenkins (Rochdale Hornets); 7 Josh Ralph (Easts Tigers); 8 Ben Evans (London Broncos); 18 Steve Parry (West Wales Raiders); 13 Dan Fleming (Halifax); 11 Rhodri Lloyd (Swinton Lions); 12 Chester Butler (Halifax); 15 Connor Davies (Halifax). Subs (all used): 19 Curtis Davies (Halifax); 17 Gavin Bennion (Salford Red Devils); 22 Mike Butt (Swinton Lions); 10 Jake Emmitt (Toronto Wolfpack).
Tries: Butler (4), Lloyd (18), Bennion (28), Evans (44), Williams (64), Ralph (69); **Goals:** Olds 8/10.
Sin bin: Morris (75) - dangerous challenge.
IRELAND: 1 Scott Grix (Wakefield Trinity); 24 Alan McMahon (Waterford Vikings); 14 James Bentley (St Helens); 4 Jack Higginson (Wigan Warriors); 5 Ethan Ryan (Bradford Bulls); 7 Liam Finn (Widnes Vikings) (C); 6 Gregg McNally (Bradford Bulls); 8 George King (Warrington Wolves); 9 Declan O'Donnell (Wigan Warriors); 10 Liam Byrne (Wigan Warriors); 11 Will Hope (Swinton Lions); 12 Tyrone McCarthy (Salford Red Devils); 13 Lewis Bienek (Hull FC). Subs (all used): 15 Ronan Michael (Huddersfield Giants); 16 Gareth Gill (Longhorns); 17 Michael Ward (Batley Bulldogs); 19 Peter Ryan (Coventry Bears).
Tries: Grix (34), King (66); **Goals:** Finn 0/2.
Rugby Leaguer & League Express Men of the Match:
Wales: Josh Ralph; *Ireland:* Gregg McNally.
Penalty count: 11-10; **Half-time:** 20-4; **Referee:** Gareth Hewer (England); **Attendance:** 1,257 *(at Racecourse Ground, Wrexham)*.

Internationals
Australia

Australia ended the season with two internationals, both played at Mount Smart Stadium, Auckland.

In the first, New Zealand prepared for their series in England with a shock 26-24 victory over the world champions.

With Roger Tuivasa-Sheck out injured, Penrith fullback Dallin Watene-Zelezniak captained New Zealand for the first time against a Kangaroos side that had seen the international retirement of its golden generation in Cameron Smith, Johnathan Thurston, Cooper Cronk and Billy Slater.

Valentine Holmes and Dane Gagai scored tries for the Kangaroos and Holmes added two conversions as they led 12-8 at half-time, with Shaun Johnson unable to convert tries from Ken Maumalo and Joseph Manu. But the Kiwis surged into a 26-12 lead by the 68th minute with converted tries from Brandon Smith, Esan Marsters and Jordan Rapana, before a late charge in the last five minutes from Australia with converted tries to Felise Kaufusi and James Tedesco led to a nerve-wracking last two minutes.

A week later the stadium was packed to the rafters with red and white as Tonga played their first ever Test against Australia. Tongan King George Tupou VI was among the supporters.

Australia prevailed on the day by 34-16 after a superb game packed with attacking football. In the end the result didn't really matter. It was a historic day for Tonga and that was far more important than the actual result.

Try-scoring doubles from Tom Trbojevic and Valentine Holmes gave Australia a 30-10 lead by half-time. Holmes' second was an eight-point try, the video referee harshly ruling that Tevita Pangai Jnr had fouled the winger as he touched down. Holmes missed the first kick from out wide and kicked the other, allowing the Aussies to go 20 points ahead at half-time.

Tonga won the second half 6-4, Solomone Kate getting their try before stand-out Roosters fullback James Tedesco scored a classic fullback's try.

Saturday 13th October 2018

NEW ZEALAND 26 AUSTRALIA 24

NEW ZEALAND: 1 Dallin Watene-Zelezniak (Penrith Panthers) (C); 2 Ken Maumalo (New Zealand Warriors); 3 Esan Marsters (Wests Tigers); 4 Joseph Manu (Sydney Roosters); 5 Jordan Rapana (Canberra Raiders); 6 Shaun Johnson (New Zealand Warriors); 7 Kodi Nikorima (Brisbane Broncos); 8 Jesse Bromwich (Melbourne Storm); 9 Brandon Smith (Melbourne Storm); 10 Jared Waerea-Hargreaves (Sydney Roosters); 11 Kevin Proctor (Gold Coast Titans); 12 Isaac Liu (Sydney Roosters); 13 James Fisher-Harris (Penrith Panthers). Subs (all used): 14 Kenny Bromwich (Melbourne Storm); 15 Leeson Ah Mau (St George Illawarra Dragons); 16 Martin Taupau (Manly Sea Eagles); 17 Adam Blair (New Zealand Warriors). **Tries:** Maumalo (28), Manu (35), Smith (54), Marsters (62), Rapana (68); **Goals:** Johnson 3/5.
AUSTRALIA: 1 James Tedesco (Sydney Roosters); 2 Dane Gagai (South Sydney Rabbitohs); 3 Tom Trbojevic (Manly Sea Eagles); 4 Latrell Mitchell (Sydney Roosters); 5 Valentine Holmes (Cronulla Sharks); 6 Luke Keary (Sydney Roosters); 7 Daly Cherry-Evans (Manly Sea Eagles); 8 David Klemmer (Canterbury Bulldogs); 9 Damien Cook (South Sydney Rabbitohs); 10 Jordan McLean (North Queensland Cowboys); 11 Boyd Cordner (Sydney Roosters) (C); 12 Felise Kaufusi (Melbourne Storm); 13 Josh McGuire (Brisbane Broncos). Subs (all used): 14 Ben Hunt (St George Illawarra Dragons); 15 Jake Trbojevic (Manly Sea Eagles); 16 Tyson Frizell (St George Illawarra Dragons); 17 Aaron Woods (Cronulla Sharks). **Tries:** Holmes (3), Gagai (40), Kaufusi (75), Tedesco (77); **Goals:** Holmes 4/4.
Rugby Leaguer & League Express Men of the Match:
New Zealand: Joseph Manu; *Australia:* Latrell Mitchell.
Penalty count: 5-5; **Half-time:** 8-12; **Referee:** Ashley Klein (Australia); **Attendance:** 12,763 *(at Mt Smart Stadium, Auckland).*

Saturday 20th October 2018

AUSTRALIA 34 TONGA 16

AUSTRALIA: 1 James Tedesco (Sydney Roosters); 2 Dane Gagai (South Sydney Rabbitohs); 3 Tom Trbojevic (Manly Sea Eagles); 4 Latrell Mitchell (Sydney Roosters); 5 Valentine Holmes (Cronulla Sharks); 6 Luke Keary (Sydney Roosters); 7 Daly Cherry-Evans (Manly Sea Eagles); 8 David Klemmer (Canterbury Bulldogs); 9 Damien Cook (South Sydney Rabbitohs); 10 Jordan McLean (North Queensland Cowboys); 11 Boyd Cordner (Sydney Roosters) (C); 12 Felise Kaufusi (Melbourne Storm); 13 Josh McGuire (Brisbane Broncos). Subs (all used): 14 Ben Hunt (St George Illawarra Dragons); 15 Jake Trbojevic (Manly Sea Eagles); 16 Tyson Frizell (St George Illawarra Dragons); 17 Aaron Woods (Cronulla Sharks). **Tries:** Cherry-Evans (6), T Trbojevic (11, 29), Holmes (26, 40), Tedesco (64); **Goals:** Holmes 5/7.
Sin bin: Cook (79) - professional foul.
TONGA: 1 Will Hopoate (Canterbury Bulldogs); 2 Daniel Tupou (Sydney Roosters); 3 Michael Jennings (Parramatta Eels); 4 Solomone Kata (New Zealand Warriors); 5 David Fusitu'a (New Zealand Warriors); 6 Tuimoala Lolohea (Wests Tigers); 7 Ata Hingano (Canberra Raiders); 8 Andrew Fifita (Cronulla Sharks); 9 Siliva Havili (Canberra Raiders); 10 Sio Siua Taukeiaho (Sydney Roosters); 11 Tevita Pangai Jnr (Brisbane Broncos); 12 Sika Manu (Hull FC) (C); 13 Jason Taumalolo (North Queensland Cowboys). Subs (all used): 14 Sione Katoa (Penrith Panthers); 15 Addin Fonua-Blake (Manly Sea Eagles); 16 Joe Ofahengaue (Brisbane Broncos); 21 Ben Murdoch-Masila (Warrington Wolves). **Tries:** Pangai Jnr (16), Tupou (34), Kata (50); **Goals:** Taukeiaho 1/2, Lolohea 1/1.
On report: Pangai Jnr (40) - alleged contact with the head on Holmes.
Rugby Leaguer & League Express Men of the Match:
Australia: James Tedesco; *Tonga:* Sio Siua Taukeiaho.
Penalty count: 6-8; **Half-time:** 30-10; **Referee:** Gerard Sutton (Australia); **Attendance:** 26,214 *(at Mt Smart Stadium, Auckland).*

Emerging Nations World Cup

Malta won the Emerging Nations World Championship played in Sydney in October 2018.

Just six days after starring as his club London Broncos defeated Toronto in Canada to earn promotion to Super League, 31-year-old scrum-half Jarrod Sammut was in Australia to score a try and kick two goals as Malta beat Niue 24-16 in the ENWC final at St Marys, Western Sydney.

The final was the culmination of a two-week tournament also involving Greece, Hong Kong, Hungary, Japan, Philippines, Poland, Solomon Islands, Turkey and Vanuatu.

It was designed to develop international Rugby League, with the ultimate aim of growing two or three nations to a level where they can win their way through World Cup qualification to join the well-established teams on the big stage.

Malta were beaten 26-16 by Niue during the group stages but in the final gained revenge over the South Pacific nation with a population of less than 2,000.

Nathan Benson (2), Jono Dallas and Jake Attard also scored tries while Justice Utatao, Christian Ulukita and George Lolo crossed for Niue, with Eddy Paea kicking two goals.

Malta beat Hungary in the semi-finals while Niue defeated Greece.

Poland were 14-10 winners over Philippines to lift the Trophy to claim fifth spot in the overall tournament.

Turkey and Vanuatu were the beaten semi-finalists.

Solomon Islands defeated Japan and Hong Kong to win the Bowl, which was run on a mini-league basis.

In addition, Mediterranean-Middle East won the regional Confederations Cup, defeating African United 32-6.

The Association of South-East Asian Nations beat Latin Heat 18-14 in the third-place play-off.

EMERGING NATIONS WORLD CUP

CUP
Semi-finals: Niue 16 Greece 8;
Hungary 10 Malta 20.
Final: Niue 16 Malta 24.
Third Place Play-off: Greece 26 Hungary 18.
TROPHY
Semi-finals: Philippines 29 Turkey 16;
Vanuatu 4 Poland 44.
Final/Fifth Place Play-off:
Philippines 10 Poland 14.
Seventh Place Play-off:
Turkey 27 Vanuatu 26.
BOWL MINI-LEAGUE
Solomon Islands 44 Japan 22;
Hong Kong 30 Japan 32;
Solomon Islands 56 Hong Kong 14.

FINAL RANKINGS:
Emerging Nations World Championship:
1 Malta; 2 Niue; 3 Greece; 4 Hungary;
5 Poland; 6 Philippines; 7 Turkey;
8 Vanuatu; 9 Solomon Islands;
10 Hong Kong; 11 Japan.
Confederations Cup:
1 Mediterranean-Middle East;
2 Africa United; 3 ASEAN; 4 Latin Heat.

Women's World Cup

The 2017 Women's Rugby League World Cup was the fifth staging of the competition and was held in Australia between 16th November and 2nd December 2017. Pool and semi-final matches were held at Southern Cross Group Stadium in Sydney with the final held at Suncorp Stadium, Brisbane. The final was played as a double-header with the men's final and Australia beat New Zealand 23-16 to win their second consecutive World Cup.

New Zealand had won the 2008 World Cup defeating Australia 34-0 at the same venue, having won the two previous tournaments in 2000 and 2005.

Six nations contested the 2017 Women's World Cup - Australia, Canada, Cook Islands, England, New Zealand and Papua Guinea. France withdrew before the tournament because of funding issues.

WOMEN'S WORLD CUP FINAL

Saturday 2nd December 2017

AUSTRALIA 23 NEW ZEALAND 16

AUSTRALIA: 1 Nakia Davis-Welsh; 2 Karina Brown; 3 Corban McGregor; 4 Isabelle Kelly; 5 Chelsea Baker; 6 Ali Brigginshaw; 7 Caitlin Moran; 8 Stephanie Hancock; 9 Brittany Breayley; 10 Heather Ballinger; 11 Renae Kunst (C); 12 Kezie Apps; 13 Simiana Taufa-Kautai. Subs (all used): 14 Lavina O'Mealey; 15 Ruan Sims; 16 Elianna Walton; 17 Zahara Temara. **Tries:** Kelly (8, 53), Moran (36), Walton (57); **Goals:** Moran 3/4; **Field goal:** Moran (80).
NEW ZEALAND: 1 Apii Nicholls-Pualau; 2 Atawhai Tupaea; 3 Maitua Feterika; 4 Shontelle Woodman; 5 Honey Hireme; 6 Raecene McGregor; 7 Kimiora Nati; 8 Lilieta Maumau; 9 Krystal Rota; 10 Aieshaleigh Smalley; 11 Teuila Fotu-Moala; 12 Hilda Peters; 13 Laura Mariu (C). Subs (all used): 14 Nita Maynard; 15 Krystal Murray; 16 Ngatokotoru Arakua; 17 Amber Kani. **Tries:** Hireme (12, 20), McGregor (69); **Goals:** Nati 2/3.
Rugby Leaguer & League Express Women of the Match:
Australia: Ali Brigginshaw; *New Zealand:* Apii Nicholls-Pualau
Penalty count: 10-7; **Half-time:** 12-10; **Referee:** Adam Gee (Australia). *(at Brisbane Stadium).*

The Australian Jillaroos celebrate winning the World Cup

New Zealand beat England in the semi-finals by 52-4 while Australia accounted for Canada by 58-6.

In the final, Australia fullback Ali Brigginshaw controlled the game from start to finish with a superb display of kicking and accurate passing. Two tries in the first 17 minutes of the second half from Isabelle Kelly and Elianna Walton pushed Australia out to a twelve-point advantage and it was a lead they didn't relinquish.

England Women

England Lionesses beat France 54-4 in Carcassonne with a new-look team of youngsters and debutants.

The French fought bravely to the end in Carcassonne but were outplayed in every department by the dominant visitors. Castleford's Tara Stanley excelled at fullback, scoring two tries and five goals while Woman of Steel Georgia Roche and St Helens' Faye Gaskin dictated everything. Bradford prop Shona Hoyle and Leeds loose forward Rhiannon Marshall ran riot in the middle of the pitch creating the space for Roche and Stanley to unleash their fellow backs.

It was a fitting end for a fine display from Roche, who had recently been nominated for BBC Young Sports Personality of the Year.

OTHER INTERNATIONALS

Saturday 3rd February 2018
Hungary 30 Philippines 12
(at Tugun, Australia)
Saturday 23rd June 2018
Fiji 14 Papua New Guinea 26
Samoa 22 Tonga 38
(both at Campbelltown Stadium, Sydney)
Sunday 24th June 2018
Malta 24 South Africa 30
(at St Marys Stadium, Sydney)
Saturday 30th June 2018
Hungary 0 Ireland 70
(at NKE Sportpalya, Budapest)
Saturday 1st September 2018
Norway 76 Poland 0
(at Stavanger Stadium, Norway)
Netherlands 38 Germany 22
(in Rotterdam)
Saturday 22nd September 2018
Sweden 4 Netherlands 24
(in Partille, Sweden)
Friday 28th September 2018
Hungary 0 Poland 32
(at Norford Park, Sydney)
Saturday 6th October 2018
Serbia 4 Wales 50
(in Belgrade)
Sunday 21st October 2018
Sweden 6 Norway 46
(in Partille, Sweden)
El Salvador 48 Colombia 10
(in Rochedale, Brisbane)
Saturday 27th October 2018
Niue 32 Italy 36
(at Marconi Stadium, Sydney)

7
STATISTICAL REVIEW

SUPER LEAGUE PLAYERS
1996-2018

Super League Players 1996-2018

PLAYER	CLUB	YEAR	APP	TRIES	GOALS	FG	PTS
Jordan Abdull	Hull	2014-16, 2018	32(20)	9	7	0	50
Carl Ablett	Leeds	2004,					
		2006-18	238(37)	63	0	0	252
	London	2005	3(2)	0	0	0	0
Darren Abram	Oldham	1996-97	25(2)	11	0	0	44
Mitch Achurch	Leeds	2013-16	25(50)	14	0	0	56
Jamie Acton	Leigh	2017	11(4)	4	0	0	16
Brad Adams	Bradford	2014	1(1)	0	0	0	0
Darren Adams	Paris	1996	9(1)	1	0	0	4
Guy Adams	Huddersfield	1998	1(2)	0	0	0	0
Luke Adamson	Salford	2006-07,					
		2009-12	73(39)	11	1	0	46
Matt Adamson	Leeds	2002-04	54(8)	9	0	0	36
Phil Adamson	St Helens	1999	(1)	0	0	0	0
Toby Adamson	Salford	2010	(1)	0	0	0	0
Danny Addy	Bradford	2010-14	49(42)	13	7	0	66
Ade Adebisi	London	2004	(1)	0	0	0	0
Patrick Ah Van	Widnes	2012-18	99	73	56	0	404
	Bradford	2011	26	9	87	0	210
Jamie Ainscough	Wigan	2002-03	30(2)	18	0	0	72
Shaun Ainscough	Bradford	2011-12	27	15	0	0	60
	Wigan	2009-10	12	13	0	0	52
	Castleford	2010	7	4	0	0	16
Glen Air	London	1998-2001	57(13)	27	0	1	109
Paul Aiton	Catalans	2016-18	30(11)	3	0	0	12
	Leeds	2014-15	36(6)	2	0	0	8
	Wakefield	2012-13	43(2)	7	0	0	28
Makali Aizue	Hull KR	2007-09	18(32)	4	0	0	16
Sitaleki Akauola	Warrington	2018	4(17)	3	0	0	12
Darren Albert	St Helens	2002-05	105	77	0	0	308
Lucas Albert	Catalans	2015-18	28(2)	5	23	0	66
Wellington Albert	Widnes	2018	(11)	2	0	0	8
Paul Alcock	Widnes	2003, 2005	1(7)	1	0	0	4
Neil Alexander	Salford	1998	(1)	0	0	0	0
Malcolm Alker	Salford	1997-2002,					
		2004-07,					
		2009-10	271(2)	40	0	1	161
Danny Allan	Leeds	2008-09	2(5)	0	0	0	0
Chris Allen	Castleford	1996	(1)	0	0	0	0
Dave Allen	Widnes	2012-14	50(13)	5	0	0	20
	Wigan	2003, 2005	6(15)	2	0	0	8
Gavin Allen	London	1996	10	0	0	0	0
John Allen	Workington	1996	20(1)	6	0	0	24
Ray Allen	London	1996	5(3)	3	0	0	12
Mitch Allgood	Wakefield	2017	6(2)	1	0	0	4
	Hull KR	2015-16	27(2)	5	0	0	20
Richard Allwood	Gateshead	1999	(4)	0	0	0	0
Sean Allwood	Gateshead	1999	3(17)	1	0	0	4
David Alstead	Warrington	2000-02	23(10)	3	0	0	12
Luke Ambler	Harlequins	2011	5(17)	1	0	0	4
	Leeds	2010	1(8)	1	0	0	4
Asa Amone	Halifax	1996-97	32(7)	10	0	0	40
Kyle Amor	St Helens	2014-18	99(27)	15	0	0	60
	Wakefield	2011-13	51(23)	9	0	0	36
	Leeds	2010	(3)	0	0	0	0
Thibaut Ancely	Catalans	2011	(2)	0	0	0	0
Grant Anderson	Castleford	1996-97	15(6)	3	0	0	12
Louis Anderson	Catalans	2012-18	86(41)	32	0	0	128
	Warrington	2008-11	92	18	0	0	72
Paul Anderson	St Helens	2005-06	48(5)	7	1	0	30
	Bradford	1997-2004	74(104)	30	0	0	120
	Halifax	1996	5(1)	1	0	0	4
Paul Anderson	Sheffield	1999	3(7)	1	0	0	4
	St Helens	1996-98	2(28)	4	1	0	18
Scott Anderson	Wakefield	2014-16	25(18)	2	0	0	8
Vinnie Anderson	Salford	2011-12	33(3)	14	0	0	56
	Warrington	2007-10	57(19)	22	0	0	88
	St Helens	2005-06	28(14)	17	0	0	68
Phil Anderton	St Helens	2004	1	0	0	0	0
Chris Annakin	Wakefield	2013-18	6(56)	1	0	0	4
Eric Anselme	Leeds	2008	2(2)	2	0	0	8
	Halifax	1997	(2)	0	0	0	0
Mark Applegarth	Wakefield	2004-07	20(5)	3	0	0	12
Graham Appo	Warrington	2002-05	60(13)	35	80	0	300
	Huddersfield	2001	7	4	0	0	16
Anthony Armour	London	2005	11(7)	1	0	0	4
Colin Armstrong	Workington	1996	11(2)	1	0	0	4
Tom Armstrong	Widnes	2017	1	0	0	0	4
	St Helens	2009-11	10(5)	9	0	0	36
Richard Armswood	Workington	1996	5(1)	1	0	0	4
Danny Arnold	Salford	2001-02	26(13)	13	0	0	52
	Huddersfield	1998-2000	55(7)	26	0	0	104
	Castleford	2000	(4)	0	0	0	0
	St Helens	1996-97	40(1)	33	0	0	132
Tinirau Arona	Wakefield	2016-18	52(33)	4	0	0	16
Joe Arundel	Wakefield	2015-18	60(8)	16	4	0	72
	Bradford	2014	9(3)	5	0	0	20
	Hull	2013-14	16	7	1	0	30
	Castleford	2008,					
		2010-12	35(4)	14	2	0	60
Craig Ashall	St Helens	2006	1	1	0	0	4
Olly Ashall-Bott	Widnes	2018	5	1	0	0	4
Nathan Ashe	St Helens	2011-13	6(4)	0	0	0	0
Chris Ashton	Wigan	2005-07	44(2)	25	2	0	104
Matty Ashurst	Wakefield	2015-18	85(3)	15	0	0	60
	Salford	2012-14	65(7)	11	0	0	44
	St Helens	2009-11	12(39)	8	0	0	32
Jack Ashworth	St Helens	2015-16, 2018	5(10)	2	0	0	8
Roy Asotasi	Warrington	2014-15	16(37)	5	1	0	22
Peter Aspinall	Huddersfield	2013	1(1)	0	0	0	0
Martin Aspinwall	Hull	2012	12(15)	0	0	0	0
	Castleford	2011	12(6)	2	0	0	8
	Huddersfield	2006-10	72(8)	22	0	0	88
	Wigan	2001-05	85(13)	27	0	0	108
Mark Aston	Sheffield	1996-99	67(6)	6	243	6	516
Paul Atcheson	Widnes	2002-04	16(35)	4	0	0	16
	St Helens	1998-2000	58(4)	18	0	0	72
	Oldham	1996-97	40	21	0	0	84
Chris Atkin	Hull KR	2018	17(5)	4	1	3	21
David Atkins	Huddersfield	2001	26(1)	4	0	0	16
Jordan Atkins	London	2014	1(1)	4	0	0	16
Ryan Atkins	Warrington	2010-18	224(2)	135	0	0	540
	Wakefield	2006-09	86(2)	45	0	0	180
Josh Atkinson	Castleford	2012	2	0	0	0	0
Brad Attwood	Halifax	2003	(3)	0	0	0	0
Warren Ayres	Salford	1999	2(9)	1	2	0	8
Jerome Azema	Paris	1997	(1)	0	0	0	0
Marcus Bai	Bradford	2006	24	9	0	0	36
	Leeds	2004-05	57	42	0	0	168
David Baildon	Hull	1998-99	26(2)	4	0	0	16
Jean-Philippe Baile	Catalans	2008-14	62(16)	23	0	0	92
Andy Bailey	Hull	2004-05	2(8)	1	0	0	4
Chris Bailey	Huddersfield	2014-15	17(17)	5	0	0	20
	London	2012-13	41	14	0	0	56
	Harlequins	2011	24	3	0	0	12
Julian Bailey	Huddersfield	2003-04	47	13	0	0	52
Phil Bailey	Wigan	2007-10	84(4)	13	0	0	52
Ricky Bailey	St Helens	2015, 2017	2	0	0	0	0
Ryan Bailey	Warrington	2016	1(11)	0	0	0	0
	Castleford	2015	3(2)	0	0	0	0
	Hull KR	2015	(1)	1	0	0	4
	Leeds	2002-14	171(102)	17	0	0	68
Jason Baitieri	Catalans	2011-18	132(49)	18	0	0	72
Simon Baldwin	Salford	2004-06	20(29)	3	0	0	12
	Sheffield	1999	7(15)	2	0	0	8
	Halifax	1996-98	41(15)	16	0	1	65
Jordan Baldwinson	Wakefield	2018	(4)	0	0	0	0
	Leeds	2013, 2016-17	4(9)	1	0	0	4
	Bradford	2014	2(4)	0	0	0	0
Rob Ball	Wigan	1998-2000	3(4)	0	0	0	0
Paul Ballard	Celtic	2009	2	0	0	0	0
	Widnes	2005	3(1)	2	0	0	8
Darren Bamford	Salford	2005	2(1)	0	0	0	0
Michael Banks	Bradford	1998	(1)	0	0	0	0
Steve Bannister	Harlequins	2007	(6)	0	0	0	0
	St Helens	2006-07	(3)	0	0	0	0
Frederic Banquet	Paris	1996	16(2)	7	4	0	36
Ben Barba	St Helens	2017-18	31	31	0	0	124
Lee Bardauskas	Castleford	1996-97	(2)	0	0	0	0
Craig Barker	Workington	1996	(2)	0	0	0	0
Dwayne Barker	Harlequins	2008	5(5)	1	0	0	4
	London	2004	3	1	0	0	4
	Hull	2003	(1)	0	0	0	0
Mark Barlow	Wakefield	2002	(1)	0	0	0	0
Danny Barnes	Halifax	1999	2	0	0	0	0
Richie Barnett	Salford	2007	7	4	0	0	16
	Warrington	2006-07	26(10)	15	0	0	60
	Hull	2004-05	21(5)	21	0	0	84
	Widnes	2005	4	2	0	0	8
Richie Barnett	Hull	2003-04	31(1)	17	0	0	68
	London	2001-02	31(4)	13	0	0	52
David Barnhill	Leeds	2000	20(8)	5	0	0	20
Trent Barrett	Wigan	2007-08	53(1)	22	0	4	92
Paul Barrow	Warrington	1996-97	1(10)	1	0	0	4
Scott Barrow	St Helens	1997-2000	9(13)	1	0	0	4
Steve Barrow	London	2000	2	0	0	0	0
	Hull	1998-99	4(17)	1	0	0	4
	Wigan	1996	3	0	0	0	0
William Barthau	Catalans	2010, 2012-14	13(3)	2	15	0	38
Ben Barton	Huddersfield	1998	1(6)	1	0	0	4
Danny Barton	Salford	2001	2	0	0	0	0
Wayne Bartrim	Castleford	2002-03	41(2)	9	157	0	350
Greg Barwick	London	1996-97	30(4)	21	110	2	306
David Bastian	Halifax	1996	(2)	0	0	0	0
James Batchelor	Wakefield	2016-18	15(12)	4	13	0	42
Ashley Bateman	Celtic	2009	2	0	0	0	0
John Bateman	Wigan	2014-18	110(8)	31	0	0	124
	Bradford	2011-13	25(5)	7	0	0	28

PLAYER	CLUB	YEAR	APP	TRIES	GOALS	FG	PTS
David Bates	Castleford	2001-02	(4)	0	0	0	0
	Warrington	2001	1(2)	0	0	0	0
Sam Bates	Bradford	2014	(2)	0	0	0	0
Nathan Batty	Wakefield	2001	1(1)	0	0	0	0
Andreas Bauer	Hull KR	2007	10(2)	5	0	0	20
Russell Bawden	London	1996-97, 2002-04	50(49)	15	0	0	60
Neil Baxter	Salford	2001	1	0	0	0	0
Neil Baynes	Salford	1999-2002, 2004	84(19)	10	0	0	40
	Wigan	1996-98	(10)	1	0	0	4
Chris Beasley	Celtic	2009	15(5)	2	0	0	8
Chris Beattie	Catalans	2006	22(5)	3	0	0	12
Richard Beaumont	Hull KR	2011-13	1(16)	1	0	0	4
Robbie Beazley	London	1997-99	48(15)	13	0	0	52
Robbie Beckett	Halifax	2002	27	15	0	0	60
Matty Beharrell	Hull KR	2013	1	0	0	0	0
Dean Bell	Leeds	1996	1	1	0	0	4
Ian Bell	Hull	2003	(1)	0	0	0	0
Mark Bell	Wigan	1998	22	12	0	0	48
Paul Bell	Leeds	2000	1	0	0	0	0
Steven Bell	Catalans	2009-10	43	14	0	0	56
Troy Bellamy	Paris	1997	5(10)	0	0	0	0
Adrian Belle	Huddersfield	1998	10(2)	0	0	0	0
	Oldham	1996	19	8	0	0	32
Lambert Belmas	Catalans	2017-18	3(5)	0	0	0	0
Jamie Benn	Castleford	1998, 2000	3(8)	1	15	0	34
Andy Bennett	Warrington	1996	6(5)	1	0	0	4
Mike Bennett	St Helens	2000-08	74(70)	15	0	0	60
Gavin Bennion	Salford	2018	1(1)	0	0	0	0
Andrew Bentley	Catalans	2007-10	9(15)	1	0	0	4
James Bentley	St Helens	2018	2(1)	0	0	0	0
John Bentley	Huddersfield	1999	13(4)	3	0	0	12
	Halifax	1996, 1998	22(3)	24	0	0	96
Kane Bentley	Catalans	2007-10	11(19)	5	0	0	20
Phil Bergman	Paris	1997	20(1)	14	0	0	56
Shaun Berrigan	Hull	2008-10	60(8)	12	0	0	48
Joe Berry	Huddersfield	1998-99	25(14)	3	0	0	12
David Berthezene	Salford	2007	9(1)	0	0	0	0
	Catalans	2006-07	5(14)	0	0	0	0
Colin Best	Hull	2003-04	57	34	0	0	136
Roger Best	London	1997-98	1(5)	1	0	0	4
Bob Beswick	Wigan	2004-05	5(14)	2	0	0	8
Monty Betham	Wakefield	2006	26	2	0	0	8
Mike Bethwaite	Workington	1996	17(3)	1	0	0	4
Denis Betts	Wigan	1998-2001	82(24)	33	0	0	132
Cliff Beverley	Salford	2004-05	47(1)	14	0	0	56
Kyle Bibb	Wakefield	2008-10	1(24)	0	0	0	0
	Harlequins	2010	(2)	0	0	0	0
	Hull KR	2009	(2)	0	0	0	0
Jake Bibby	Salford	2016-18	40(2)	17	0	0	68
Adam Bibey	Widnes	2004	(1)	0	0	0	0
Ricky Bibey	Wakefield	2007-09	32(25)	1	0	0	4
	St Helens	2004	4(14)	0	0	0	0
	Wigan	2001-03	5(29)	0	0	0	0
Lewis Bienek	Hull	2018	(7)	0	0	0	0
Chris Birchall	Halifax	2002-03	24(22)	4	0	0	16
	Bradford	2000	(1)	0	0	0	0
Deon Bird	Castleford	2006	17(6)	5	0	0	20
	Widnes	2003-04	39(6)	9	0	0	36
	Wakefield	2002	10(1)	1	0	0	4
	Hull	2000-02	37(22)	20	0	0	80
	Gateshead	1999	19(3)	13	0	0	52
	Paris	1996-97	30	12	2	0	52
Greg Bird	Catalans	2009, 2017-18	56(3)	9	3	0	42
Mike Bishay	London	2013-14	7(11)	2	2	0	12
Nathan Blacklock	Hull	2005-06	44(3)	33	0	0	132
Ben Blackmore	Huddersfield	2013-14	3	4	0	0	16
	Castleford	2012	1	0	0	0	0
Richie Blackmore	Leeds	1997-2000	63	25	0	0	100
Anthony Blackwood	Crusaders	2010	1	0	0	0	0
	Celtic	2009	25	5	0	0	20
Jack Blagbrough	Huddersfield	2013	(1)	0	0	0	0
Maurice Blair	Hull KR	2015-16, 2018	62(3)	10	1	0	42
Luke Blake	Wakefield	2009	(2)	0	0	0	0
Matthew Blake	Wakefield	2003-04	1(5)	0	0	0	0
Steve Blakeley	Salford	1997-2002	103(5)	26	241	2	588
	Warrington	2000	4(3)	1	9	0	22
Richard Blakeway	Castleford	2002-04	1(14)	0	0	0	0
Damien Blanch	Catalans	2011-13	70	42	0	0	168
	Wakefield	2008-10	44(3)	31	0	0	124
	Castleford	2006	3(2)	0	0	0	0
Matt Blaymire	Wakefield	2007-11	96(3)	26	0	1	105
Ian Blease	Salford	1997	(1)	0	0	0	0
Jamie Bloem	Huddersfield	2003	18(4)	3	11	0	34
	Halifax	1998-2002	82(25)	25	100	2	302

PLAYER	CLUB	YEAR	APP	TRIES	GOALS	FG	PTS
Vea Bloomfield	Paris	1996	4(14)	3	0	0	12
Matty Blythe	Warrington	2007-12, 2017	30(28)	12	0	0	48
	Bradford	2013-14	24(6)	8	0	0	32
Ben Bolger	London	2012	2(7)	1	0	0	4
	Harlequins	2010-11	4(15)	0	0	0	0
Pascal Bomati	Paris	1996	17(1)	10	0	0	40
Simon Booth	Hull	1998-99	15(9)	2	0	0	8
	St Helens	1996-97	10(4)	1	0	0	4
Steve Booth	Huddersfield	1998-99	16(4)	2	3	0	14
Alan Boothroyd	Halifax	1997	2(3)	0	0	0	0
Thomas Bosc	Catalans	2006-17	199(21)	48	483	12	1170
John Boslem	Paris	1996	(5)	0	0	0	0
Liam Bostock	St Helens	2004	1	0	0	0	0
Liam Botham	Wigan	2005	5	0	0	0	0
	Leeds	2003-05	2(11)	4	0	0	16
	London	2004	6(2)	3	7	0	26
Frano Botica	Castleford	1996	21	5	84	2	190
Matthew Bottom	Leigh	2005	(1)	0	0	0	0
Hadj Boudebza	Paris	1996	(2)	0	0	0	0
John Boudebza	Hull KR	2015-16	13(17)	2	0	0	8
David Boughton	Huddersfield	1999	26(1)	4	0	0	16
Julian Bousquet	Catalans	2012-18	37(97)	13	0	0	52
David Bouveng	Halifax	1997-99	66(2)	19	0	0	76
Josh Bowden	Hull	2012-18	53(68)	11	0	0	44
Matt Bowen	Wigan	2014-15	43	21	31	0	146
Tony Bowes	Huddersfield	1998	3(2)	0	0	0	0
Radney Bowker	London	2004	3	1	0	0	4
	St Helens	2001	1	0	0	0	0
David Boyle	Bradford	1999-2000	36(13)	15	0	1	61
Ryan Boyle	Castleford	2006, 2008-09, 2013-16	12(60)	5	0	0	20
	Salford	2010-13	57(14)	3	0	0	12
Andy Bracek	Crusaders	2011	(2)	0	0	0	0
	Warrington	2005-08	7(49)	7	0	0	28
	St Helens	2004	(1)	0	0	0	0
David Bradbury	Hudds-Sheff	2000	21(2)	1	0	0	4
	Salford	1997-99	23(10)	6	0	0	24
	Oldham	1996-97	19(6)	9	0	0	36
John Braddish	St Helens	2001-02	1(1)	0	3	0	6
Graeme Bradley	Bradford	1996-98	62(1)	29	0	0	116
Nick Bradley-Qalilawa	Harlequins	2006	27	6	0	0	24
	London	2005	28	19	0	0	76
Darren Bradstreet	London	1999-2000	1(3)	0	0	0	0
Dominic Brambani	Castleford	2004	2(2)	0	0	0	0
Keanan Brand	Widnes	2018	1	0	0	0	0
Joe Bretherton	Wigan	2016-17	2(13)	1	0	0	4
Liam Bretherton	Wigan	1999	(5)	2	0	0	8
	Warrington	1997	(2)	0	0	0	0
Johnny Brewer	Halifax	1996	4(2)	2	0	0	8
Chris Bridge	Widnes	2016-17	28(1)	4	11	0	38
	Warrington	2005-15	186(17)	89	248	1	853
	Bradford	2003-04	2(14)	4	6	0	28
Danny Bridge	Bradford	2014	4(4)	0	0	0	0
	Warrington	2013	(2)	0	0	0	0
Ryan Brierley	Huddersfield	2016-17	19(1)	6	2	0	28
Lee Briers	Warrington	1997-2013	365(12)	130	810	70	2210
	St Helens	1997	3	0	11	0	22
Carl Briggs	Salford	1999	8(5)	3	0	1	13
	Halifax	1996	5(3)	1	0	0	4
Kyle Briggs	Bradford	2011	6	4	0	0	16
	Harlequins	2011	3	0	0	0	0
Mike Briggs	Widnes	2002	1(2)	1	0	0	4
Kriss Brining	Salford	2017	2(20)	4	0	0	16
Luke Briscoe	Leeds	2014, 2016, 2018	9(4)	4	0	0	16
	Wakefield	2014	2	0	0	0	0
Shaun Briscoe	Widnes	2012-13	11(2)	4	0	0	16
	Hull KR	2008-11	92	27	0	0	108
	Hull	2004-07	83(9)	50	0	0	200
	Wigan	2002-03	23(5)	11	0	0	44
Tom Briscoe	Leeds	2014-18	100	43	0	0	172
	Hull	2008-13	131(3)	83	0	0	332
Darren Britt	St Helens	2002-03	41	3	0	0	12
Gary Broadbent	Salford	1997-2002	117(2)	22	0	0	88
Paul Broadbent	Wakefield	2002	16(5)	0	0	0	0
	Hull	2000-01	40(9)	3	0	0	12
	Halifax	1999	26(1)	2	0	0	8
	Sheffield	1996-98	63(1)	6	0	0	24
Robin Brochon	Catalans	2018	1	0	0	0	0
Andrew Brocklehurst	Salford	2004-07	34(23)	5	0	0	20
	London	2004	12(6)	2	0	0	8
	Halifax	2001-03	37(8)	2	0	0	8
Justin Brooker	Wakefield	2001	25	9	0	0	36
	Bradford	2000	17(4)	11	0	0	44
Sam Brooks	Widnes	2016-17	1(3)	1	0	0	4

Super League Players 1996-2018

PLAYER	CLUB	YEAR	APP	TRIES	GOALS	FG	PTS
Danny Brough	Huddersfield	2010-18	220(4)	45	721	20	1642
	Wakefield	2008-10	50(1)	14	174	4	408
	Castleford	2006	10	1	31	2	68
	Hull	2005-06	25(12)	3	85	1	183
Jodie Broughton	Catalans	2016-18	45	29	0	0	116
	Huddersfield	2014-15	30	16	0	0	64
	Salford	2010-13	93	53	0	0	212
	Hull	2008-09	9(3)	6	0	0	24
Alex Brown	Hull KR	2013	16	9	0	0	36
	Huddersfield	2009	1	0	0	0	0
Darren Brown	Salford	1999-2001	47(9)	11	6	0	56
Gavin Brown	Leeds	1996-97	5(2)	1	2	0	8
Kevin Brown	Warrington	2017-18	41(1)	9	0	0	36
	Widnes	2013-16	80	37	1	1	151
	Huddersfield	2006-12	156	43	0	1	173
	Wigan	2003-06	46(18)	27	0	0	108
Lee Brown	Hull	1999	(1)	0	0	0	0
Michael Brown	Huddersfield	2008	(1)	0	0	0	0
Michael Brown	London	1996	(2)	0	0	0	0
Mitch Brown	Warrington	2018	10(1)	2	0	0	8
	Leigh	2017	21	4	0	0	16
Todd Brown	Paris	1996	8(1)	2	0	0	8
Adrian Brunker	Wakefield	1999	17	6	0	0	24
Lamont Bryan	Harlequins	2008-11	9(22)	2	0	0	8
Justin Bryant	Paris	1996	4(1)	0	0	0	0
	London	1996	7(8)	1	0	0	4
Mark Bryant	London	2012-13	16(36)	3	1	0	14
	Crusaders	2010-11	42(8)	1	0	0	4
	Celtic	2009	23(3)	0	0	0	0
Austin Buchanan	Wakefield	2005-06	6	2	0	0	8
	London	2003	3(1)	2	0	0	8
Jack Buchanan	Widnes	2016-17	29(2)	2	0	0	8
Owen Buckley	Widnes	2018	4	3	0	0	12
Danny Buderus	Leeds	2009-11	57(14)	14	0	0	56
Neil Budworth	Celtic	2009	8(19)	0	0	0	0
	Harlequins	2006	2(19)	0	0	0	0
	London	2002-05	59(11)	4	1	0	18
James Bunyan	Huddersfield	1998-99	8(7)	2	0	0	8
Andy Burgess	Salford	1997	3(12)	0	0	0	0
Joe Burgess	Wigan	2013-15, 2017-18	81	71	0	0	284
Luke Burgess	Salford	2018	3(8)	0	0	0	0
	Catalans	2017	3(2)	0	0	0	0
	Leeds	2008-11	10(63)	6	0	0	24
	Harlequins	2007	(3)	0	0	0	0
Sam Burgess	Bradford	2006-09	46(34)	14	5	0	66
Tom Burgess	Bradford	2011-12	1(41)	3	0	0	12
Greg Burke	Salford	2018	2(3)	1	0	0	4
	Widnes	2016-18	21(12)	1	0	0	4
	Wigan	2013-14, 2016	13(26)	1	0	0	4
	Hull KR	2015	9(5)	0	0	0	0
	Bradford	2014	(1)	0	0	0	0
Joe Burke	Crusaders	2011	(1)	0	0	0	0
Mike Burnett	Harlequins	2011	16(4)	1	0	0	4
	Hull	2008-10	13(21)	3	0	0	12
Darren Burns	Warrington	2002-04	66(6)	19	0	0	76
Gary Burns	Oldham	1996	6	1	0	0	4
Paul Burns	Workington	1996	5(2)	1	0	0	4
Travis Burns	St Helens	2015-16	27(2)	4	28	0	72
	Hull KR	2013-14	46	8	81	2	196
Lachlan Burr	Leigh	2017	5(14)	1	0	0	4
Rob Burrow	Leeds	2001-17	313(116)	168	131	5	939
Dean Busby	Warrington	1999-2002	34(34)	7	0	0	28
	Hull	1998	8(6)	0	0	0	0
	St Helens	1996-98	1(7)	0	0	0	0
Tom Bush	Leeds	2010	3(1)	1	0	0	4
Ikram Butt	London	1996	5(1)	0	0	0	0
Shane Byrne	Huddersfield	1998-99	1(5)	0	0	0	0
Todd Byrne	Hull	2008-09	20	4	0	0	16
Didier Cabestany	Paris	1996-97	20(6)	2	0	0	8
Hep Cahill	Widnes	2012-18	106(13)	4	0	0	16
	Crusaders	2011	16	2	0	0	8
Joel Caine	Salford	2004	24	8	13	0	58
	London	2003	6	4	1	0	18
Mark Calderwood	Harlequins	2011	13	2	0	0	8
	Hull	2009-10	23	6	0	0	24
	Wigan	2006-08	64	23	0	0	92
	Leeds	2001-05	117(9)	88	0	0	352
Mike Callan	Warrington	2002	(4)	0	0	0	0
Matt Calland	Huddersfield	2003	2	0	0	0	0
	Hull	1999	1	0	0	0	0
	Bradford	1996-98	44(5)	24	0	0	96
Dean Callaway	London	1999-2000	26(24)	12	0	0	48
Laurent Cambres	Paris	1996	(1)	0	0	0	0
Chris Campbell	Warrington	2000	7(1)	2	0	0	8
Liam Campbell	Wakefield	2005	(1)	0	0	0	0
Logan Campbell	Hull	1998-99, 2001	70(13)	14	0	0	56
	Castleford	2000	14(2)	3	0	0	12
	Workington	1996	7(1)	1	0	0	4

PLAYER	CLUB	YEAR	APP	TRIES	GOALS	FG	PTS
Terry Campese	Hull KR	2015-16	19(1)	2	4	0	16
Blake Cannova	Widnes	2002	(1)	0	0	0	0
Phil Cantillon	Widnes	2002-03	27(21)	18	0	0	72
	Leeds	1997	(1)	0	0	0	0
Liam Carberry	Widnes	2014-15	2(5)	0	0	0	0
Damien Cardace	Catalans	2012, 2014-15	23	14	0	0	56
Daryl Cardiss	Warrington	2003-04	23(2)	3	4	0	20
	Halifax	1999-2003	91(8)	39	4	0	164
	Wigan	1996-98	12(6)	4	0	0	16
Dale Cardoza	Warrington	2002	5	1	0	0	4
	Halifax	2001	3	1	0	0	4
	Huddersfield	2000-01	20(9)	11	0	0	44
	Sheffield	1998-99	11(7)	3	0	0	12
Paul Carige	Salford	1999	24(1)	7	0	0	28
Dane Carlaw	Catalans	2008-10	58(15)	9	0	0	36
Keal Carlile	Hull KR	2012-15	6(28)	1	0	0	4
	Huddersfield	2009, 2011	2(1)	1	0	0	4
	Bradford	2008	(1)	0	0	0	0
Jim Carlton	Huddersfield	1999	3(11)	2	0	0	8
George Carmont	Wigan	2008-12	136	71	0	0	284
Brian Carney	Warrington	2009	4	2	0	0	8
	Wigan	2001-05	91(10)	42	1	0	170
	Hull	2000	13(3)	7	0	0	28
	Gateshead	1999	3(2)	2	0	0	8
Justin Carney	Hull KR	2018	14	3	0	0	12
	Salford	2016-17	28	12	0	0	48
	Castleford	2013-15	58	56	0	0	224
Martin Carney	Warrington	1997	(1)	0	0	0	0
Todd Carney	Hull KR	2018	(1)	0	0	0	0
	Salford	2017	9(5)	0	7	0	14
	Catalans	2015-16	32	9	4	1	45
Omari Caro	Hull KR	2013-14	21	20	0	0	80
	London	2012	11	4	0	0	16
Paul Carr	Sheffield	1996-98	45(5)	15	0	0	60
Bernard Carroll	London	1996	2(1)	1	0	0	4
Mark Carroll	London	1998	15(3)	1	0	0	4
Tonie Carroll	Leeds	2001-02	42(2)	30	0	0	120
Darren Carter	Workington	1996	10(3)	0	1	0	2
Steve Carter	Widnes	2002	14(7)	4	0	0	16
John Cartwright	Salford	1997	9	0	0	0	0
Garreth Carvell	Castleford	2014	1(4)	1	0	0	4
	Hull	2001-08, 2014	75(84)	22	0	0	88
	Warrington	2009-13	77(40)	13	0	0	52
	Leeds	1997-2000	(4)	0	0	0	0
	Gateshead	1999	4(4)	1	0	0	4
Garen Casey	Salford	1999	13(5)	3	23	0	58
Ray Cashmere	Salford	2009-11	63(3)	5	0	0	20
Mick Cassidy	Widnes	2005	24	0	0	0	0
	Wigan	1996-2004	184(36)	30	0	0	120
Remi Casty	Catalans	2006-13, 2015-18	167(96)	25	0	0	100
Ned Catic	Castleford	2008	7(7)	3	0	0	12
	Wakefield	2006-07	17(29)	4	0	0	16
Mason Caton-Brown	Wakefield	2017-18	24	21	0	0	84
	Salford	2014-16	28	10	0	0	40
	London	2013-14	19	15	0	0	60
Joe Cator	Hull KR	2016, 2018	2(3)	0	0	0	0
Chris Causey	Warrington	1997-99	(18)	1	0	0	4
Jason Cayless	St Helens	2006-09	62(9)	7	0	0	28
Arnaud Cervello	Paris	1996	4	4	0	0	16
Marshall Chalk	Celtic	2009	13	4	0	0	16
Ed Chamberlain	Salford	2018	4(1)	1	10	0	24
	Widnes	2016-18	15(1)	2	7	0	22
Gary Chambers	Warrington	1996-2000	65(28)	2	0	0	8
Pierre Chamorin	Paris	1996-97	27(3)	8	3	0	38
Alex Chan	Catalans	2006-08	59(11)	11	0	0	44
Jason Chan	Hull KR	2014	5(1)	3	0	0	12
	Huddersfield	2012-16	46(12)	9	0	0	36
	Crusaders	2010-11	48(1)	10	0	0	40
	Celtic	2009	17(6)	3	0	0	12
Joe Chandler	Leeds	2008	(1)	0	0	0	0
Michael Channing	Castleford	2013-15	27(2)	8	0	0	32
	London	2012-13	15(3)	2	0	0	8
Jay Chapelhow	Widnes	2016-18	23(15)	4	0	0	16
Ted Chapelhow	Widnes	2016-18	7(13)	0	0	0	0
Chris Chapman	Leeds	1999	(1)	0	0	0	0
Damien Chapman	London	1998	6(2)	3	4	1	21
David Chapman	Castleford	1996-98	24(6)	8	0	0	32
Jaymes Chapman	Halifax	2002-03	5(8)	1	0	0	4
Richard Chapman	Sheffield	1996	1	2	0	0	8
Chris Charles	Salford	2004-06	59(16)	6	140	0	304
	Castleford	2001	1(4)	1	0	0	4
Olivier Charles	Catalans	2007	2	2	0	0	8
Josh Charnley	Warrington	2018	23	16	0	0	64
	Wigan	2010-16	151(2)	141	77	0	718
	Hull KR	2010	5	5	0	0	20

PLAYER	CLUB	YEAR	APP	TRIES	GOALS	FG	PTS
Lewis Charnock	St Helens	2013, 2015	4(1)	2	6	0	20
Rangi Chase	Widnes	2017	6	0	0	0	0
	Castleford	2009-13,					
		2016-17	122(12)	39	0	3	159
	Salford	2014-15	37	10	13	2	68
Andy Cheetham	Huddersfield	1998-99	30	11	0	0	44
Kris Chesney	London	1998	1(2)	0	0	0	0
Chris Chester	Hull KR	2007-08	28(6)	4	0	0	16
	Hull	2002-06	67(25)	13	0	0	52
	Wigan	1999-2001	21(22)	5	0	0	20
	Halifax	1996-99	47(14)	16	15	1	95
Lee Chilton	Workington	1996	10(3)	6	0	0	24
Dane Chisholm	Hull KR	2015	1	0	0	0	0
Gary Christie	Bradford	1996-97	4(7)	1	0	0	4
James Clare	Castleford	2012-15, 2018	51	29	0	0	116
Daryl Clark	Warrington	2015-18	96(9)	23	0	0	92
	Castleford	2011-14	34(51)	31	0	0	124
Dean Clark	Leeds	1996	11(2)	3	0	0	12
Des Clark	St Helens	1999	4	0	0	0	0
	Halifax	1998-99	35(13)	6	0	0	24
Mitch Clark	Castleford	2018	(15)	2	0	0	8
Greg Clarke	Halifax	1997	1(1)	0	0	0	0
John Clarke	Oldham	1996-97	27(4)	5	0	0	20
Jon Clarke	Widnes	2012-14	59(1)	5	0	0	20
	Warrington	2001-11	217(25)	56	2	0	228
	London	2000-01	19(11)	2	0	0	8
	Wigan	1997-99	13(10)	3	0	0	12
Chris Clarkson	Hull KR	2016, 2018	38(2)	4	0	0	16
	Widnes	2015	17(1)	4	0	0	16
	Leeds	2010-14	61(39)	9	0	0	36
Adam Clay	Salford	2011	2	3	0	0	12
Ryan Clayton	Castleford	2004,					
		2008-10	36(24)	5	0	0	20
	Salford	2006	3(8)	2	0	0	8
	Huddersfield	2005	4(6)	0	0	0	0
	Halifax	2000,					
		2002-03	28(12)	6	0	0	24
Gavin Clinch	Salford	2004	21(1)	1	0	1	5
	Halifax	1998-99,					
		2001-02	88(2)	26	45	5	199
	Hudds-Sheff	2000	18(2)	5	0	1	21
	Wigan	1999	10(2)	4	12	0	40
Joel Clinton	Hull KR	2010-12	42(14)	2	0	0	8
John Clough	Salford	2004-06	1(16)	0	0	0	0
Paul Clough	Huddersfield	2017-18	25(33)	2	0	0	8
	Widnes	2014	4(8)	1	0	0	4
	St Helens	2005-13	53(113)	16	0	0	64
Tony Clubb	Wigan	2014-18	48(62)	17	0	0	68
	London	2012-13	24(8)	7	0	0	28
	Harlequins	2006-11	100(11)	29	0	0	116
Bradley Clyde	Leeds	2001	7(5)	1	0	0	4
Michael Coady	Leeds	2010	1	0	0	0	0
Evan Cochrane	London	1996	5(1)	1	0	0	4
Ben Cockayne	Hull KR	2007-11,					
		2014-16	125(30)	38	18	0	188
	Wakefield	2012-13	54	28	2	0	116
Liam Colbon	Hull	2014	8	1	0	0	4
	London	2012-13	22	5	0	0	20
	Hull KR	2009-11	51	20	0	0	80
	Wigan	2004-05,					
		2007-08	37(14)	15	0	0	60
Anthony Colella	Huddersfield	2003	5(1)	2	0	0	8
Liam Coleman	Leigh	2005	1(4)	0	0	0	0
Andy Coley	Wigan	2008-11	100(10)	8	0	0	32
	Salford	2001-02,					
		2004-07	112(34)	34	0	0	136
Richard Colley	Bradford	2004	1	0	0	0	0
Steve Collins	Hull	2000	28	17	0	0	68
	Gateshead	1999	20(4)	13	0	0	52
Wayne Collins	Leeds	1997	21	3	0	0	12
Dean Collis	Wakefield	2012-15	64	28	0	0	112
Aurelien Cologni	Catalans	2006	4(1)	3	0	0	12
Gary Connolly	Widnes	2005	20	4	1	0	18
	Wigan	1996-2002,					
		2004	168(10)	70	5	0	290
	Leeds	2003-04	27	6	0	0	24
Jake Connor	Hull	2017-18	42(10)	16	60	2	186
	Huddersfield	2013-16	47(1)	21	2	0	88
Nathan Conroy	Bradford	2013-14	(4)	0	0	0	0
Matt Cook	Castleford	2008,					
		2015-18	22(66)	10	0	0	40
	London	2012-14	50(7)	8	0	0	32
	Hull KR	2010-11	9(16)	7	0	0	28
	Bradford	2005-09	11(52)	4	0	0	16
Mick Cook	Sheffield	1996	9(10)	2	0	0	8
Paul Cook	Huddersfield	1998-99	11(6)	2	13	0	34
	Bradford	1996-97	14(8)	7	38	1	105
Peter Cook	St Helens	2004	(1)	0	0	0	0

PLAYER	CLUB	YEAR	APP	TRIES	GOALS	FG	PTS
Paul Cooke	Wakefield	2010	16(1)	3	36	1	85
	Hull KR	2007-10	54(5)	8	76	2	186
	Hull	1999-2007	177(27)	32	333	4	798
Ben Cooper	Leigh	2005	25(1)	5	0	0	20
	Huddersfield	2000-01,					
		2003-04	28(12)	3	0	0	12
Mike Cooper	Warrington	2006-13,					
		2017-18	74(88)	11	0	0	44
	Castleford	2010	1(5)	2	0	0	8
Ged Corcoran	Halifax	2003	1(11)	0	0	0	0
Wayne Corcoran	Halifax	2003	4(2)	0	0	0	0
Jamie Cording	Huddersfield	2011-13	4(21)	5	0	0	20
Josh Cordoba	Hull	2009	8	1	0	0	4
Mark Corvo	Salford	2002	7(5)	0	0	0	0
Matthew Costello	St Helens	2018	7	0	0	0	0
Neville Costigan	Hull KR	2014	24	3	0	0	12
Brandon Costin	Huddersfield	2001,					
		2003-04	69	42	93	3	357
	Bradford	2002	20(1)	8	0	0	32
Wes Cotton	London	1997-98	12	3	0	0	12
Phil Coussons	Salford	1997	7(2)	3	0	0	12
Alex Couttet	Paris	1997	1	0	0	0	0
Nick Couttet	Paris	1997	1	0	0	0	0
Jamie Coventry	Castleford	1996	1	0	0	0	0
Jimmy Cowan	Oldham	1996-97	2(8)	0	0	0	0
Will Cowell	Warrington	1998-2000	6(8)	1	0	0	4
Neil Cowie	Wigan	1996-2001	116(27)	10	0	1	41
Danny Cowling	Wakefield	2012-13	2	0	0	0	0
Jordan Cox	Warrington	2016	(16)	0	0	0	0
	Hull KR	2011-15	17(44)	4	0	0	16
	Huddersfield	2015	(2)	0	0	0	0
Mark Cox	London	2003	(3)	0	0	0	0
James Coyle	Wigan	2005	2(3)	1	0	0	4
Thomas Coyle	Wigan	2008	2(1)	0	0	0	0
Eorl Crabtree	Huddersfield	2001,					
		2003-16	180(167)	52	0	0	208
Andy Craig	Halifax	1999	13(7)	1	3	0	10
	Wigan	1996	5(5)	2	0	0	8
Owen Craigie	Widnes	2005	15	7	0	2	30
Scott Cram	London	1999-2002	65(7)	4	0	0	16
Danny Craven	Widnes	2012-15,					
		2017-18	52(17)	13	6	3	67
Steve Craven	Hull	1998-2003	53(42)	4	0	0	16
Nicky Crellin	Workington	1996	(2)	0	0	0	0
Jason Critchley	Wakefield	2000	7(1)	4	0	0	16
	Castleford	1997-98	27(3)	11	0	0	44
Jason Croker	Catalans	2007-09	56(2)	11	0	1	45
Martin Crompton	Salford	1998-2000	30(6)	11	6	2	58
	Oldham	1996-97	36(1)	16	0	3	67
Paul Crook	Widnes	2005	2(2)	0	5	1	11
Paul Crook	Oldham	1996	4(9)	0	3	0	6
Jason Crookes	Hull	2013-14	15(1)	5	0	0	20
	Bradford	2009-12	25(1)	7	0	0	28
Ben Crooks	Hull KR	2018	1	0	0	0	0
	Leigh	2017	19	6	0	0	24
	Castleford	2016	24(2)	5	1	0	22
	Hull	2012-14	42(3)	30	23	0	166
Lee Crooks	Castleford	1996-97	27(2)	2	14	0	36
Dominic Crosby	Leeds	2018	(2)	0	0	0	0
	Warrington	2017-18	(16)	0	0	0	0
	Wigan	2012-16	57(35)	6	0	0	24
Alan Cross	St Helens	1997	(2)	0	0	0	0
Ben Cross	Widnes	2012-13	27(1)	2	0	0	8
	Wigan	2011	(4)	0	0	0	0
	Leeds	2011	1(9)	0	0	0	0
Steve Crossley	Castleford	2015	(6)	0	0	0	0
	Bradford	2010-11	(9)	1	0	0	4
Garret Crossman	Hull KR	2008	8(18)	1	0	0	4
Steve Crouch	Castleford	2004	4(1)	2	0	0	8
Kevin Crouthers	Warrington	2001-03	12(1)	4	0	0	16
	London	2000	6(4)	1	0	0	4
	Wakefield	1999	4(4)	1	0	0	4
	Bradford	1997-98	3(9)	2	0	0	8
Jordan Crowther	Wakefield	2014-18	8(10)	1	0	0	4
Matt Crowther	Hull	2001-03	48	20	166	0	412
	Hudds-Sheff	2000	10(4)	5	22	0	64
	Sheffield	1996-99	43(43)	22	10	0	108
Heath Cruckshank	Halifax	2003	19(1)	0	0	0	0
	St Helens	2001	1(12)	0	0	0	0
Leroy Cudjoe	Huddersfield	2008-18	248(1)	100	57	1	515
Paul Cullen	Warrington	1996	19	3	0	0	12
Francis Cummins	Leeds	1996-2005	217(13)	120	26	2	534
James Cunningham	Hull	2012, 2014-15	(9)	0	0	0	0
	London	2014	10(7)	2	0	0	8
Keiron Cunningham	St Helens	1996-2010	357(24)	138	0	0	552
Liam Cunningham	Hull	2010	(1)	0	0	0	0

Super League Players 1996-2018

PLAYER	CLUB	YEAR	APP	TRIES	GOALS	FG	PTS
Ben Currie	Warrington	2012-18	84(31)	50	0	0	200
Andy Currier	Warrington	1996-97	(2)	1	0	0	4
Peter Cusack	Hull	2008-10	34(22)	3	0	0	12
Adam Cuthbertson	Leeds	2015-18	77(18)	24	0	0	96
Alrix Da Costa	Catalans	2016-18	9(27)	2	0	0	8
Will Dagger	Hull KR	2018	3(2)	0	0	0	0
	Warrington	2017	3	0	0	0	0
Joe Dakuitoga	Sheffield	1996	6(3)	0	0	0	0
Matty Dale	Hull	2006, 2008	(7)	1	0	0	4
	Wakefield	2008	1(1)	0	0	0	0
Brett Dallas	Wigan	2000-06	156	89	0	0	356
Mark Dalle Cort	Celtic	2009	23	4	0	0	16
Paul Darbyshire	Warrington	1997	(6)	0	0	0	0
James Davey	Wakefield	2009-11	3(14)	1	0	0	4
Maea David	Hull	1998	1	0	0	0	0
Alex Davidson	Salford	2011, 2013	(3)	0	0	0	0
Paul Davidson	Halifax	2001-03	22(30)	10	0	0	40
	London	2000	6(10)	4	0	0	16
	St Helens	1998-99	27(16)	7	0	0	28
	Oldham	1996-97	17(18)	14	0	1	57
Ben Davies	Castleford	2011, 2013	3(4)	2	0	0	8
	Widnes	2012-13	10(15)	3	0	0	12
	Wigan	2010	(5)	0	0	0	0
Gareth Davies	Warrington	1996-97	1(6)	0	0	0	0
Geraint Davies	Celtic	2009	(7)	0	0	0	0
John Davies	Castleford	2010-12	1(6)	1	0	0	4
Jordan Davies	Salford	2013	2(3)	0	0	0	0
Macauley Davies	Wigan	2016	(1)	0	0	0	0
Olly Davies	St Helens	2016	(1)	0	0	0	0
Tom Davies	Wigan	2017-18	50	26	0	0	104
Wes Davies	Wigan	1998-2001	22(22)	11	0	0	44
Brad Davis	Castleford	1997-2000, 2004, 2006	102(3)	31	43	10	220
	Wakefield	2001-03	51(12)	15	22	5	109
Matty Dawson	Leigh	2017	23	12	0	0	48
	St Helens	2014-16	46(1)	15	0	0	60
	Huddersfield	2012-13	4	0	0	0	0
Brad Day	Castleford	2014	(1)	0	0	0	0
Matt Daylight	Hull	2000	17(1)	7	0	0	28
	Gateshead	1999	30	25	0	0	100
Michael De Vere	Huddersfield	2005-06	36	6	74	0	172
Paul Deacon	Wigan	2010-11	32(11)	4	14	0	44
	Bradford	1998-2009	258(43)	72	1029	23	2369
	Oldham	1997	(2)	0	0	0	0
Chris Dean	Widnes	2012-18	114(6)	23	0	0	92
	Wakefield	2011	20	8	0	0	32
	St Helens	2007-10	18(3)	9	0	0	36
Craig Dean	Halifax	1996-97	25(11)	12	1	1	51
Gareth Dean	London	2002	(4)	0	0	0	0
Yacine Dekkiche	Hudds-Sheff	2000	11(3)	3	0	0	12
Brett Delaney	Leeds	2010-18	151(30)	23	0	0	92
Jason Demetriou	Wakefield	2004-10	174(3)	50	2	0	204
	Widnes	2002-03	47(1)	15	1	0	62
Martin Dermott	Warrington	1997	1	0	0	0	0
David Despin	Paris	1996	(1)	0	0	0	0
Fabien Devecchi	Paris	1996-97	17(10)	2	0	0	8
Paul Devlin	Widnes	2002-04	32	16	0	0	64
Jordan Dezaria	Catalans	2016-17	3(2)	0	0	0	0
Stuart Dickens	Salford	2005	4(5)	0	4	0	8
Tyler Dickinson	Huddersfield	2016-18	(17)	1	0	0	4
Matt Diskin	Bradford	2011-14	64(16)	11	0	0	44
	Leeds	2001-10	195(37)	40	0	0	160
Andrew Dixon	Salford	2013-14	34(2)	8	0	0	32
	St Helens	2009-12	19(41)	12	0	0	48
Kieran Dixon	Hull KR	2015-16	23(4)	21	9	0	102
	London	2012-14	49(1)	32	2	0	132
Kirk Dixon	Castleford	2008-14	143(2)	63	267	0	786
	Hull	2004-06	13(4)	7	4	0	36
Paul Dixon	Sheffield	1996-97	5(9)	1	0	0	4
Nabil Djalout	Catalans	2017	1	0	0	0	0
Gareth Dobson	Castleford	1998-2000	(10)	0	0	0	0
Michael Dobson	Salford	2015-17	58(1)	14	77	1	211
	Hull KR	2008-13	142	51	500	11	1215
	Wigan	2006	14	5	61	0	142
	Catalans	2006	10	4	31	1	79
Michael Docherty	Hull	2000-01	(6)	0	0	0	0
Mitchell Dodds	Warrington	2016	(2)	0	0	0	0
Erjon Dollapi	London	2013-14	(18)	4	0	0	16
Sid Domic	Hull	2006-07	39(4)	15	0	0	60
	Wakefield	2004-05	48	30	0	0	120
	Warrington	2002-03	41(4)	17	0	0	68
Scott Donald	Leeds	2006-10	131	77	0	0	308
James Donaldson	Hull KR	2015-16, 2018	12(30)	4	0	0	16
	Bradford	2009-14	38(35)	4	0	0	16
Glen Donkin	Hull	2002-03	(10)	1	0	0	4
Stuart Donlan	Castleford	2008	20	8	0	0	32
	Huddersfield	2004-06	59(3)	15	0	0	60
	Halifax	2001-03	65(2)	22	0	0	88
Jason Donohue	Bradford	1996	(4)	0	0	0	0
Jeremy Donougher	Bradford	1996-99	40(21)	13	0	0	52
Justin Dooley	London	2000-01	37(18)	2	0	0	8
Dane Dorahy	Halifax	2003	20	7	45	0	118
	Wakefield	2000-01	16(2)	4	19	1	55
Jamie Doran	Wigan	2014	(2)	0	0	0	0
Luke Dorn	Castleford	2008, 2014-16	78(2)	60	0	0	240
	London	2005, 2012-13	58(8)	42	0	0	168
	Harlequins	2006, 2009-11	83(1)	57	0	0	228
	Salford	2007	19(8)	11	0	0	44
Brandon Douglas	Castleford	2016	(1)	0	0	0	0
Luke Douglas	St Helens	2017-18	23(32)	5	0	0	20
Ewan Dowes	Hull	2003-11	169(51)	10	0	0	40
	Leeds	2001-03	1(9)	0	0	0	0
Jack Downs	Hull	2015-18	5(15)	1	0	0	4
Adam Doyle	Warrington	1998	9(3)	4	0	0	16
Rod Doyle	Sheffield	1997-99	52(10)	10	0	0	40
Brad Drew	Huddersfield	2005-07, 2010	78(13)	18	13	1	99
	Wakefield	2008-09	27(9)	7	14	1	57
Josh Drinkwater	Catalans	2018	17	7	53	0	134
	Leigh	2017	19	1	12	1	29
	London	2014	23(1)	5	54	0	128
Damien Driscoll	Salford	2001	23(1)	1	0	0	4
James Duckworth	London	2014	3	0	0	0	0
	Leeds	2013	2	1	0	0	4
Gil Dudson	Widnes	2015-18	57(11)	1	0	0	4
	Wigan	2012-14	26(16)	2	0	0	8
	Crusaders	2011	3(7)	0	0	0	0
	Celtic	2009	(1)	0	0	0	0
Jason Duffy	Leigh	2005	3(1)	0	0	0	0
John Duffy	Leigh	2005	21	6	0	0	24
	Salford	2000	3(11)	0	1	1	3
	Warrington	1997-99	12(12)	0	0	0	0
Tony Duggan	Celtic	2009	4	3	0	0	12
Andrew Duncan	London	1997	2(4)	2	0	0	8
	Warrington	1997	(1)	0	0	0	0
Andrew Dunemann							
	Salford	2006	25	1	0	2	6
	Leeds	2003-05	76(4)	11	0	2	46
	Halifax	1999-2002	68	19	0	1	77
Matt Dunford	London	1997-98	18(20)	3	0	1	13
Vincent Duport	Catalans	2007-09, 2011-18	156(16)	75	0	0	300
Jamie Durbin	Widnes	2005	1	0	0	0	0
	Warrington	2003	(1)	0	0	0	0
Scott Dureau	Catalans	2011-15	88(1)	29	315	10	756
James Durkin	Paris	1997	(5)	0	0	0	0
Bernard Dwyer	Bradford	1996-2000	65(10)	14	0	0	56
Brad Dwyer	Leeds	2018	5(8)	4	0	0	16
	Warrington	2012-17	12(63)	11	0	0	44
	Huddersfield	2013	(6)	0	0	0	0
Luke Dyer	Crusaders	2010	23(1)	5	0	0	20
	Celtic	2009	21	6	0	0	24
	Hull KR	2007	26	13	0	0	52
	Castleford	2006	17(2)	5	0	0	20
Adam Dykes	Hull	2008	12	1	0	2	6
Jim Dymock	London	2001-04	94(1)	15	0	1	61
Leo Dynevor	London	1996	8(11)	5	7	0	34
Jason Eade	Paris	1997	9	4	0	0	16
Michael Eagar	Hull	2004-05	12	4	0	0	16
	Castleford	1999-2003	130(2)	60	0	0	240
	Wigan	1998	21	6	0	0	24
Kyle Eastmond	St Helens	2007-11	46(20)	35	117	3	377
Greg Eastwood	Leeds	2010	5(12)	1	0	0	4
Barry Eaton	Widnes	2002	25	2	49	4	110
	Castleford	2000	1(4)	0	3	0	6
Greg Ebrill	Salford	2002	15(6)	1	0	0	4
Cliff Eccles	Salford	1997-98	30(5)	1	0	0	4
Chris Eckersley	Warrington	1996	1	0	0	0	0
Greg Eden	Castleford	2011, 2017-18	46	57	0	0	228
	Hull KR	2013-14	37	23	0	0	92
	Salford	2014	4	1	0	0	4
	Huddersfield	2012	24	8	0	0	32
Steve Edmed	Sheffield	1997	15(1)	0	0	0	0
Mark Edmondson	Salford	2007	10(2)	0	0	0	0
	St Helens	1999-2005	27(75)	10	0	0	40
Diccon Edwards	Castleford	1996-97	10(5)	1	0	0	4
Grant Edwards	Castleford	2006	(2)	0	0	0	0
Kenny Edwards	Catalans	2018	3(10)	8	0	0	32
Max Edwards	Harlequins	2010	1	0	0	0	0
Peter Edwards	Salford	1997-98	35(2)	4	0	0	16
Shaun Edwards	London	1997-2000	82(8)	16	1	0	66
	Bradford	1998	8(2)	4	0	0	16
	Wigan	1996	17(3)	12	1	0	50
Tuoyo Egodo	Castleford	2017-18	2(1)	3	0	0	12

PLAYER	CLUB	YEAR	APP	TRIES	GOALS	FG	PTS
Danny Ekis	Halifax	2001	(1)	0	0	0	0
Abi Ekoku	Bradford	1997-98	21(4)	6	0	0	24
	Halifax	1996	15(1)	5	0	0	20
Shane Elford	Huddersfield	2007-08	26(1)	7	0	0	28
Olivier Elima	Catalans	2008-10, 2013-16	99(35)	34	0	0	136
	Bradford	2011-12	37(3)	12	0	0	48
	Wakefield	2003-07	40(47)	13	0	0	52
	Castleford	2002	(1)	1	0	0	4
Abderazak Elkhalouki	Paris	1997	(1)	0	0	0	0
George Elliott	Leeds	2011	1	0	0	0	0
Andy Ellis	Wakefield	2012	10	0	0	0	0
	Harlequins	2010-11	26(11)	8	0	0	32
Gareth Ellis	Hull	2013-17	82(5)	19	0	0	76
	Leeds	2005-08	109	24	1	0	98
	Wakefield	1999-2004	86(17)	21	2	0	88
Jamie Ellis	Castleford	2012-14, 2018	53(8)	12	134	2	318
	Huddersfield	2015-16	37(3)	14	31	3	121
	Hull	2012	4(5)	1	0	0	4
	St Helens	2009	1(2)	0	1	0	2
Danny Ellison	Castleford	1998-99	7(16)	6	0	0	24
	Wigan	1996-97	15(1)	13	0	0	52
Andrew Emelio	Widnes	2005	22(2)	8	0	0	32
Jake Emmitt	Salford	2013	5(10)	0	0	0	0
	Castleford	2011-13	32(17)	0	0	0	0
	St Helens	2008-10	1(16)	1	0	0	4
Anthony England	Wakefield	2016-18	52(9)	2	0	0	8
	Warrington	2014-15	12(21)	3	0	0	12
Matty English	Huddersfield	2017-18	2(13)	0	0	0	0
Patrick Entat	Paris	1996	22	2	0	0	8
Jason Erba	Sheffield	1997	1(4)	0	0	0	0
Morgan Escare	Wigan	2017-18	18(21)	12	37	2	124
	Catalans	2013-16	83	58	1	2	236
Ryan Esders	Harlequins	2009-10	9(11)	3	0	0	12
	Hull KR	2009	(1)	0	0	0	0
Sonny Esslemont	Hull KR	2014-15	(5)	0	0	0	0
Niall Evalds	Salford	2013-18	75(11)	56	0	0	224
Ben Evans	Warrington	2014-15	3(16)	2	0	0	8
	Bradford	2013	3(12)	1	0	0	4
James Evans	Castleford	2009-10	26(1)	13	0	0	52
	Bradford	2007-08	43(5)	20	0	0	80
	Wakefield	2006	6	3	0	0	12
	Huddersfield	2004-06	51	22	0	0	88
Paul Evans	Paris	1997	18	8	0	0	32
Rhys Evans	Warrington	2010-17	87(7)	37	0	0	148
Wayne Evans	London	2002	11(6)	2	0	0	8
Toby Everett	London	2014	(2)	0	0	0	0
Richie Eyres	Warrington	1997	2(5)	0	0	0	0
	Sheffield	1997	2(3)	0	0	0	0
Henry Fa'afili	Warrington	2004-07	90(1)	70	0	0	280
David Fa'alogo	Huddersfield	2010-12	38(16)	13	0	0	52
Sala Fa'alogo	Widnes	2004-05	8(15)	2	0	0	8
Richard Fa'aoso	Castleford	2006	10(15)	5	0	0	20
Maurie Fa'asavalu	St Helens	2004-10	5(137)	29	0	0	116
Bolouagi Fagborun	Huddersfield	2004-06	4(2)	1	0	0	4
Theo Fages	St Helens	2016-18	49(25)	21	0	0	84
	Salford	2013-15	57(5)	18	4	0	80
Esene Faimalo	Salford	1997-99	23(25)	2	0	0	8
	Leeds	1996	3(3)	0	0	0	0
Joe Faimalo	Salford	1998-2000	23(47)	7	0	0	28
	Oldham	1996-97	37(5)	7	0	0	28
Jacob Fairbank	Huddersfield	2011-15	12(3)	0	0	0	0
	Wakefield	2014	1(3)	0	0	0	0
	London	2013	4(1)	1	0	0	4
	Bradford	2013	(2)	0	0	0	0
Karl Fairbank	Bradford	1996	17(2)	4	0	0	16
David Fairleigh	St Helens	2001	26(1)	8	0	0	32
David Faiumu	Huddersfield	2008-14	38(108)	13	0	0	52
Jamal Fakir	Bradford	2014	5(8)	1	0	0	4
	Catalans	2006-14	55(100)	13	0	0	52
Jim Fallon	Leeds	1996	10	5	0	0	20
Beau Falloon	Leeds	2016	8(2)	0	0	0	0
Bureta Faraimo	Hull	2018	26	17	4	0	76
Owen Farnworth	Widnes	2017-18	1(4)	0	0	0	0
Ben Farrar	London	2014	22	1	0	0	4
	Catalans	2011	13	3	0	0	12
Danny Farrar	Warrington	1998-2000	76	13	0	0	52
Andy Farrell	Wigan	1996-2004	230	77	1026	16	2376
Anthony Farrell	Widnes	2002-03	24(22)	4	1	0	18
	Leeds	1997-2001	99(23)	18	0	0	72
	Sheffield	1996	14(5)	5	0	0	20
Connor Farrell	Widnes	2016	3(9)	3	0	0	12
	Wigan	2014-15	1(8)	1	0	0	4
Craig Farrell	Hull	2000-01	1(3)	0	0	0	0
Liam Farrell	Wigan	2010-18	154(50)	77	0	0	308
Brad Fash	Hull	2015, 2017-18	2(45)	2	0	0	8
Abraham Fatnowna	London	1997-98	7(2)	2	0	0	8
	Workington	1996	5	2	0	0	8
Sione Faumuina	Castleford	2009	18	1	0	0	4
	Hull	2005	3	1	0	0	4
Vince Fawcett	Wakefield	1999	13(1)	2	0	0	8
	Warrington	1998	4(7)	1	0	0	4
	Oldham	1997	5	3	0	0	12
Danny Fearon	Huddersfield	2001	(1)	0	0	0	0
	Halifax	1999-2000	5(6)	0	0	0	0
Chris Feather	Castleford	2009	1(23)	0	0	0	0
	Bradford	2007-08	7(20)	1	0	0	4
	Leeds	2003-04, 2006	16(35)	6	0	0	24
	Wakefield	2001-02, 2004-05	29(32)	9	0	0	36
Dom Feaunati	Leigh	2005	4	1	0	0	4
	St Helens	2004	10(7)	7	0	0	28
Adel Fellous	Hull	2008	1(2)	0	0	0	0
	Catalans	2006-07	16(22)	4	0	0	16
Luke Felsch	Hull	2000-01	46(6)	7	0	0	28
	Gateshead	1999	28(1)	2	0	0	8
Leon Felton	Warrington	2002	4(2)	0	0	0	0
	St Helens	2001	1(1)	0	0	0	0
Dale Ferguson	Huddersfield	2011-13, 2017-18	61(22)	16	0	0	64
	Bradford	2014	3(3)	0	0	0	0
	Hull KR	2013	3(1)	1	0	0	4
	Wakefield	2007-11	40(14)	12	0	0	48
Brett Ferres	Leeds	2016-18	31(12)	9	0	0	36
	Huddersfield	2012-15	72	27	0	0	108
	Castleford	2009-12	78(5)	26	0	0	104
	Wakefield	2007-08	36(2)	6	5	0	34
	Bradford	2005-06	18(17)	11	2	0	48
David Ferriol	Catalans	2007-12	72(55)	8	0	0	32
Jason Ferris	Leigh	2005	4	1	0	0	4
Callum Field	Wigan	2017-18	(8)	0	0	0	0
Jamie Field	Wakefield	1999-2006	133(59)	19	0	0	76
	Huddersfield	1998	15(5)	0	0	0	0
	Leeds	1996-97	3(11)	0	0	0	0
Mark Field	Wakefield	2003-07	28(7)	3	0	0	12
Jamie Fielden	London	2003	(1)	0	0	0	0
	Huddersfield	1998-2000	4(8)	0	0	0	0
Stuart Fielden	Huddersfield	2013	8(1)	0	0	0	0
	Wigan	2006-12	105(24)	2	0	0	8
	Bradford	1998-2006	142(78)	41	0	0	164
David Fifita	Wakefield	2016-18	33(25)	7	0	0	28
Lafaele Filipo	Workington	1996	15(4)	3	0	0	12
Salesi Finau	Warrington	1996-97	16(15)	8	0	0	32
Brett Finch	Wigan	2011-12	49(3)	16	0	0	64
Vinny Finigan	Bradford	2010	4(1)	4	0	0	16
Liam Finn	Widnes	2018	1	0	0	0	0
	Wakefield	2004, 2016-18	70(4)	5	219	0	458
	Castleford	2014-15	45(2)	8	5	2	44
	Halifax	2002-03	16(5)	2	30	1	69
Lee Finnerty	Halifax	2003	18(2)	5	2	0	24
Phil Finney	Warrington	1998	1	0	0	0	0
Simon Finnigan	Widnes	2003-05, 2012	56(24)	21	0	0	84
	Huddersfield	2009-10	22(5)	6	0	0	24
	Bradford	2008	14(13)	8	0	0	32
	Salford	2006-07	50	17	0	0	68
Matt Firth	Halifax	2000-01	12(2)	0	0	0	0
Andy Fisher	Wakefield	1999-2000	31(8)	4	0	0	16
Ben Fisher	London	2013	8(12)	1	0	0	4
	Catalans	2012	9(5)	1	0	0	4
	Hull KR	2007-11	78(46)	18	0	0	72
Craig Fitzgibbon	Hull	2010-11	42(1)	9	8	0	52
Daniel Fitzhenry	Hull KR	2008-09	36(11)	14	0	0	56
Karl Fitzpatrick	Salford	2004-07, 2009-10	89(11)	33	2	0	136
Conor Fitzsimmons	Castleford	2016	(2)	0	0	0	0
Mark Flanagan	Salford	2016-18	46(9)	5	0	0	20
	St Helens	2012-15	40(39)	9	0	0	36
	Wigan	2009	3(7)	1	0	0	4
Chris Flannery	St Helens	2007-12	108(11)	32	0	0	128
Darren Fleary	Leigh	2005	24	1	0	0	4
	Huddersfield	2003-04	43(8)	4	0	0	16
	Leeds	1997-2002	98(9)	3	0	0	12
Daniel Fleming	Castleford	2013-14	(15)	1	0	0	4
Greg Fleming	London	1999-2001	64(1)	40	2	0	164
Matty Fleming	Leigh	2017	5	1	0	0	4
	St Helens	2015-17	17	7	0	0	28
Adam Fletcher	Castleford	2006, 2008	16(7)	11	0	0	44
Bryan Fletcher	Wigan	2006-07	47(2)	14	0	0	56
Richard Fletcher	Castleford	2006	13(5)	3	4	0	20
	Hull	1999-2004	11(56)	5	0	0	20
Greg Florimo	Halifax	2000	26	6	4	0	32
	Wigan	1999	18(2)	7	1	0	30
Ben Flower	Wigan	2012-18	117(24)	17	0	0	68
	Crusaders	2010-11	10(23)	2	0	0	8
	Celtic	2009	2(15)	0	0	0	0

181

Super League Players 1996-2018

PLAYER	CLUB	YEAR	APP	TRIES	GOALS	FG	PTS
Jason Flowers	Salford	2004	6(1)	0	0	0	0
	Halifax	2002	24(4)	4	0	0	16
	Castleford	1996-2001	119(19)	33	0	1	133
Stuart Flowers	Castleford	1996	(3)	0	0	0	0
Adrian Flynn	Castleford	1996-97	19(2)	10	0	0	40
Paddy Flynn	Castleford	2016	9(1)	6	0	0	24
	Widnes	2012-15	72	41	0	0	164
Wayne Flynn	Sheffield	1997	3(5)	0	0	0	0
Adam Fogerty	Warrington	1998	4	0	0	0	0
	St Helens	1996	13	1	0	0	4
Mahe Fonua	Hull	2016-17	50	25	0	0	100
Liam Foran	Salford	2013	10(3)	1	0	0	4
Carl Forber	Leigh	2005	4	1	0	0	4
	St Helens	2004	1(1)	0	6	0	12
Paul Forber	Salford	1997-98	19(12)	4	0	0	16
Byron Ford	Hull KR	2007	13	6	0	0	24
James Ford	Castleford	2009	3(5)	1	0	0	4
Mike Ford	Castleford	1997-98	25(12)	5	0	3	23
	Warrington	1996	3	0	0	0	0
Jim Forshaw	Salford	1999	(1)	0	0	0	0
Mike Forshaw	Warrington	2004	20(1)	5	0	0	20
	Bradford	1997-2003	162(7)	32	0	0	128
	Leeds	1996	11(3)	5	0	0	20
Carl Forster	Salford	2015-16	5(7)	1	0	0	4
	St Helens	2011-12, 2014	(4)	0	0	0	0
	London	2014	2(3)	0	0	0	0
Mark Forster	Warrington	1996-2000	102(1)	40	0	0	160
Liam Forsyth	Wigan	2017-18	11(2)	3	0	0	12
Alex Foster	Castleford	2017-18	24(9)	7	0	0	28
	London	2014	20	3	0	0	12
	Leeds	2013	(8)	1	0	0	4
David Foster	Halifax	2000-01	4(9)	0	0	0	0
Jamie Foster	Huddersfield	2016	3	2	5	0	18
	Bradford	2013-14	32	12	111	0	270
	Hull	2012	9	5	45	0	110
	St Helens	2010-12	44(3)	30	201	0	522
Peter Fox	Wakefield	2007, 2012-14	85	44	0	0	176
	Hull KR	2008-11	95	52	0	0	208
Matty Fozard	St Helens	2014	1	0	0	0	0
Nick Fozzard	Castleford	2011	7(10)	0	0	0	0
	St Helens	2004-08, 2010	100(25)	7	0	0	28
	Hull KR	2009	18(4)	1	0	0	4
	Warrington	2002-03	43(11)	2	0	0	8
	Huddersfield	1998-2000	24(8)	2	0	0	8
	Leeds	1996-97	6(16)	3	0	0	12
David Fraisse	Workington	1996	8	0	0	0	0
Daniel Frame	Widnes	2002-05	100(6)	24	0	0	96
Paul Franze	Castleford	2006	2(1)	0	0	0	0
Laurent Frayssinous	Catalans	2006	14(2)	3	32	0	76
Andrew Frew	Halifax	2003	17	5	0	0	20
	Wakefield	2002	21	8	0	0	32
	Huddersfield	2001	26	15	0	0	60
Dale Fritz	Castleford	1999-2003	120(4)	9	0	0	36
Gareth Frodsham	St Helens	2008-09	1(9)	0	0	0	0
Liam Fulton	Huddersfield	2009	12(3)	4	0	0	16
David Furner	Leeds	2003-04	45	8	23	0	78
	Wigan	2001-02	51(2)	21	13	0	110
David Furness	Castleford	1996	(1)	0	0	0	0
Matt Gafa	Harlequins	2006-09	81	26	16	0	136
Luke Gale	Castleford	2015-18	100	32	402	15	947
	Bradford	2012-14	56(2)	13	108	4	272
	Harlequins	2009-11	56(12)	18	86	3	247
Ben Galea	Hull	2013	12(2)	3	0	0	12
	Hull KR	2008-12	115(2)	33	0	0	132
Danny Galea	Widnes	2014-15	38(4)	5	0	0	20
Tommy Gallagher	Hull KR	2007	1(7)	0	0	0	0
	Widnes	2004	(6)	0	0	0	0
	London	2003	1(9)	1	0	0	4
Keith Galloway	Leeds	2016-17	28(4)	1	0	0	4
Mark Gamson	Sheffield	1996	3	0	0	0	0
Jim Gannon	Hull KR	2007	7(16)	1	0	0	4
	Huddersfield	2003-06	79(14)	11	0	0	44
	Halifax	1999-2002	83(4)	14	0	0	56
Josh Ganson	Wigan	2017-18	1(6)	2	0	0	8
Mitch Garbutt	Leeds	2015-18	36(25)	7	0	0	28
Steve Garces	Salford	2001	(1)	0	0	0	0
Benjamin Garcia	Catalans	2013-18	54(43)	16	0	0	64
Jean-Marc Garcia	Sheffield	1996-97	35(3)	22	0	0	88
Ade Gardner	Hull KR	2014	18	7	0	0	28
	St Helens	2002-13	236(12)	146	0	0	584
Matt Gardner	Harlequins	2009	6(3)	2	0	0	8
	Huddersfield	2006-07	22(3)	7	0	0	28
	Castleford	2004	1	1	0	0	4
Steve Gartland	Oldham	1996	1(1)	0	0	1	2
Daniel Gartner	Bradford	2001-03	74(1)	26	0	0	104
Dean Gaskell	Warrington	2002-05	58(1)	10	0	0	40
Lee Gaskell	Huddersfield	2017-18	51	17	0	0	68
	Bradford	2014	21	5	0	0	20
	Salford	2013	17	8	2	0	36
	St Helens	2010-13	33(9)	14	12	1	81
George Gatis	Huddersfield	2008	5(5)	1	0	0	4
Richard Gay	Castleford	1996-2002	94(16)	39	0	0	156
Andrew Gee	Warrington	2000-01	33(1)	4	0	0	16
Matty Gee	Salford	2015	(2)	0	0	0	0
Anthony Gelling	Wigan	2012-17	101(1)	52	0	0	208
Stanley Gene	Hull KR	2007-09	37(17)	9	0	0	36
	Bradford	2006	5(16)	8	0	0	32
	Huddersfield	2001, 2003-05	70(6)	27	0	0	108
	Hull	2000-01	5(23)	6	0	0	24
Steve Georgallis	Warrington	2001	5(1)	2	0	0	8
Luke George	Bradford	2014	9(1)	3	0	0	12
	Huddersfield	2012-13	28(2)	18	0	0	72
	Hull KR	2013	4	2	0	0	8
	Wakefield	2007-11	38(3)	24	0	0	96
Shaun Geritas	Warrington	1997	(5)	1	0	0	4
Alex Gerrard	Widnes	2012-18	48(40)	4	0	0	16
Anthony Gibbons	Leeds	1996	9(4)	2	0	1	9
David Gibbons	Leeds	1996	3(4)	2	0	0	8
Scott Gibbs	St Helens	1996	9	3	0	0	12
Ashley Gibson	Wakefield	2016-17	9	4	0	0	16
	Castleford	2014-15	27	9	0	0	36
	Salford	2010-13	77(4)	41	0	0	164
	Leeds	2005-09	25(7)	13	9	0	70
Damian Gibson	Castleford	2003-04	40(3)	5	0	0	20
	Salford	2002	28	3	0	0	12
	Halifax	1998-2001	104(1)	39	0	0	156
	Leeds	1997	18	3	0	0	12
Kurt Gidley	Warrington	2016-17	44	11	97	0	238
Matt Gidley	St Helens	2007-10	105	40	6	0	172
Tony Gigot	Catalans	2010-11, 2015-18	93(13)	35	38	7	223
	London	2014	2	0	4	0	8
Ian Gildart	Oldham	1996-97	31(7)	0	0	0	0
Oliver Gildart	Wigan	2015-18	74(2)	38	0	0	152
	Salford	2015	3	1	0	0	4
Chris Giles	Widnes	2003-04	35	12	0	0	48
	St Helens	2002	(1)	0	0	0	0
Kieran Gill	Castleford	2017-18	4	4	0	0	16
Peter Gill	London	1996-99	75(6)	20	0	0	80
Carl Gillespie	Halifax	1996-99	47(36)	13	0	0	52
Michael Gillett	London	2001-02	23(2)	12	2	0	52
Simon Gillies	Warrington	1999	28	6	0	0	24
Tom Gilmore	Widnes	2012-18	38(1)	11	51	3	149
Lee Gilmour	Wakefield	2014	10(3)	2	0	0	8
	Castleford	2013	10(2)	0	0	0	0
	Huddersfield	2010-12	71(1)	17	0	0	68
	St Helens	2004-09	149(3)	41	0	0	164
	Bradford	2001-03	44(31)	20	0	0	80
	Wigan	1997-2000	44(39)	22	0	0	88
Marc Glanville	Leeds	1998-99	44(3)	5	0	0	20
Eddie Glaze	Castleford	1996	1	0	0	0	0
Paul Gleadhill	Leeds	1996	4	0	0	0	0
Ben Gledhill	Salford	2012-13	3(10)	1	0	0	4
	Wakefield	2010-11	(16)	0	0	0	0
Mark Gleeson	Warrington	2000-08	38(102)	12	0	0	48
Martin Gleeson	Salford	2013-14	26(1)	4	0	0	16
	Hull	2011	6	4	0	0	16
	Wigan	2009-11	46(1)	19	0	0	76
	Warrington	2005-09	110(1)	44	0	0	176
	St Helens	2002-04	56(1)	25	0	0	100
	Huddersfield	1999-2001	47(9)	18	0	0	72
Sean Gleeson	Hull KR	2013	6	0	0	0	0
	Salford	2011-12	35	14	0	0	56
	Wakefield	2007-10	67(6)	20	0	0	80
	Wigan	2005-06	3(3)	0	0	0	0
Jon Goddard	Hull KR	2007	20	2	0	0	8
	Castleford	2000-01	(2)	0	0	0	0
Richard Goddard	Castleford	1996-97	11(3)	2	10	0	28
Brad Godden	Leeds	1998-99	47	15	0	0	60
Pita Godinet	Wakefield	2014-15	18(19)	10	0	0	40
Wayne Godwin	Salford	2011-13, 2015	43(8)	6	0	0	24
	Bradford	2008-10	16(44)	9	0	0	36
	Hull	2007	3(13)	1	0	0	4
	Wigan	2005-06	9(38)	6	0	0	24
	Castleford	2001-04	30(18)	46	0	0	184
Jason Golden	London	2012	7(2)	1	0	0	4
	Harlequins	2009-11	34(12)	3	0	0	12
	Wakefield	2007-08	26(5)	1	0	0	4
Marvin Golden	Widnes	2003	4	1	0	0	4
	London	2001	17(2)	1	0	0	4
	Halifax	2000	20(2)	5	0	0	20
	Leeds	1996-99	43(11)	19	0	0	76
Ashton Golding	Leeds	2014-18	42(9)	5	14	0	48

PLAYER	CLUB	YEAR	APP	TRIES	GOALS	FG	PTS
Brett Goldspink	Halifax	2000-02	64(5)	2	0	0	8
	Wigan	1999	6(16)	1	0	0	4
	St Helens	1998	19(4)	2	0	0	8
	Oldham	1997	13(2)	0	0	0	0
Lee Gomersall	Hull KR	2008	1	0	0	0	0
Bryson Goodwin	Warrington	2018	28	12	29	0	106
Luke Goodwin	London	1998	9(2)	3	1	1	15
	Oldham	1997	16(4)	10	17	2	76
Grant Gore	Widnes	2012-15	6(11)	1	0	0	4
Aaron Gorrell	Catalans	2007-08	23	6	14	0	52
Andy Gorski	Salford	2001-02	(2)	0	0	0	0
Cyrille Gossard	Catalans	2006-12	54(30)	5	0	0	20
Mickael Goudemand							
	Catalans	2018	2(7)	0	0	0	0
Bobbie Goulding	Salford	2001-02	31(1)	2	56	4	124
	Wakefield	2000	12	3	25	3	65
	Huddersfield	1998-99	27(1)	3	65	4	146
	St Helens	1996-98	42(2)	9	210	4	460
Bobbie Goulding (Jnr)							
	Wakefield	2013	1(2)	0	1	0	2
Darrell Goulding	Hull KR	2015	8	1	0	0	4
	Wigan	2005-14	129(24)	68	0	0	272
	Salford	2009	9	5	0	0	20
Mick Govin	Leigh	2005	5(6)	4	0	0	16
Craig Gower	London	2012-13	40	7	24	0	76
David Gower	Salford	2006-07	(16)	0	0	0	0
Regan Grace	St Helens	2017-18	53	26	0	0	104
Shane Grady	London	2013	5(4)	1	2	0	8
James Graham	St Helens	2003-11	132(63)	47	0	0	188
Nathan Graham	Bradford	1996-98	17(28)	4	0	1	17
Nick Graham	Wigan	2003	13(1)	2	0	0	8
Dalton Grant	Crusaders	2011	(1)	0	0	0	0
Jon Grayshon	Harlequins	2007-09	10(32)	4	0	0	16
	Huddersfield	2003-06	7(43)	5	0	0	20
Blake Green	Wigan	2013-14	42(1)	15	0	0	60
	Hull KR	2011-12	35	14	0	0	56
Brett Green	Gateshead	1999	10(2)	0	0	0	0
Chris Green	Hull	2012-18	28(86)	7	0	0	28
James Green	Castleford	2018	1(3)	0	0	0	0
	Leigh	2017	4(5)	0	0	0	0
	Hull KR	2012-16	8(64)	3	0	0	12
Toby Green	Huddersfield	2001	3(1)	1	0	0	4
Craig Greenhill	Castleford	2004	21(4)	1	0	0	4
	Hull	2002-03	56	3	2	0	16
Clint Greenshields	Catalans	2007-12	137	81	0	0	324
Brandon Greenwood							
	Halifax	1996	1	0	0	0	0
Gareth Greenwood	Huddersfield	2003	(1)	0	0	0	0
	Halifax	2002	1	0	0	0	0
James Greenwood	Hull KR	2015-16, 2018	28(19)	7	0	0	28
	Salford	2015	1(1)	1	0	0	4
	Wigan	2013, 2015	(2)	0	0	0	0
	London	2014	10(5)	3	0	0	12
Joe Greenwood	Wigan	2018	8(3)	4	0	0	16
	St Helens	2012-17	40(28)	26	0	0	104
Lee Greenwood	Huddersfield	2005	7	3	0	0	12
	London	2004-05	30(2)	19	0	0	76
	Halifax	2000-03	38(2)	17	0	0	68
	Sheffield	1999	1(1)	0	0	0	0
Nick Gregson	Wigan	2016-17	5(9)	1	0	0	4
James Grehan	Castleford	2012	2(2)	1	0	0	4
Maxime Gresesque	Wakefield	2007	2(1)	0	0	0	0
Mathieu Griffi	Catalans	2006-08	1(25)	0	0	0	0
Darrell Griffin	Salford	2013-15	31(27)	1	0	0	4
	Leeds	2012	8(19)	2	0	0	8
	Huddersfield	2007-11	65(60)	13	0	0	52
	Wakefield	2003-06	55(37)	9	3	0	42
George Griffin	Salford	2015-18	52(16)	12	0	0	48
	Wakefield	2015	5	0	0	0	0
	London	2014	(19)	1	0	0	4
	Hull KR	2012-13	11(7)	0	0	0	0
Josh Griffin	Hull	2017-18	43(5)	10	0	0	40
	Salford	2014-16	42	23	77	0	246
	Castleford	2012	20	13	1	0	54
	Wakefield	2011	17	5	21	0	62
	Huddersfield	2009	2	0	0	0	0
Jonathan Griffiths	Paris	1996	(4)	1	0	0	4
Andrew Grima	Workington	1996	2(9)	2	0	0	8
Tony Grimaldi	Hull	2000-01	56(1)	14	0	0	56
	Gateshead	1999	27(2)	10	0	0	40
Danny Grimley	Sheffield	1996	4(1)	1	0	0	4
Scott Grix	Wakefield	2008-09,					
		2017-18	80(3)	32	0	0	128
	Huddersfield	2010-16	137(11)	52	32	0	272
Simon Grix	Warrington	2006-14	133(25)	42	0	0	168
	Halifax	2003	2(4)	0	0	0	0
Brett Grogan	Gateshead	1999	14(7)	3	0	0	12
Brent Grose	Warrington	2003-07	134(1)	55	0	0	220

PLAYER	CLUB	YEAR	APP	TRIES	GOALS	FG	PTS
David Guasch	Catalans	2010	1	0	0	0	0
Joan Guasch	Catalans	2014-15	(6)	0	0	0	0
Renaud Guigue	Catalans	2006	14(4)	3	0	0	12
Jerome Guisset	Catalans	2006-10	102(23)	9	0	0	36
	Wigan	2005	20(2)	3	0	0	12
	Warrington	2000-04	59(65)	21	0	0	84
Awen Guttenbeil	Castleford	2008	19	0	0	0	0
Reece Guy	Oldham	1996	3(4)	0	0	0	0
Josh Guzdek	Hull KR	2013, 2015	2	1	0	0	4
Tom Haberecht	Castleford	2008	2(2)	1	0	0	4
Dean Hadley	Hull	2013-16, 2018	47(20)	9	0	0	36
	Wakefield	2017	14(7)	2	0	0	8
Gareth Haggerty	Harlequins	2008-09	8(28)	6	0	0	24
	Salford	2004-07	1(93)	15	0	0	60
	Widnes	2002	1(2)	1	0	0	4
Kurt Haggerty	Widnes	2012	6(8)	2	0	0	8
Andy Haigh	St Helens	1996-98	20(16)	11	0	0	44
Scott Hale	St Helens	2011	(3)	1	0	0	4
Michael Haley	Leeds	2008	(1)	0	0	0	0
Carl Hall	Leeds	1996	7(2)	3	0	0	12
Craig Hall	Hull KR	2011-14, 2018	75(3)	40	42	2	246
	Wakefield	2015-16	35	14	30	0	116
	Hull	2007-10	59(9)	39	11	0	178
Glenn Hall	Bradford	2010	7(18)	2	0	0	8
Martin Hall	Halifax	1998	2(10)	0	0	0	0
	Hull	1999	7	0	0	0	0
	Castleford	1998	4	0	0	0	0
	Wigan	1996-97	31(5)	7	6	0	40
Ryan Hall	Leeds	2007-18	278(3)	196	0	0	784
Steve Hall	Widnes	2004	1	0	0	0	0
	London	2002-03	35(3)	10	0	0	40
	St Helens	1999-2001	36(22)	19	0	0	76
Graeme Hallas	Huddersfield	2001	1	0	0	0	0
	Hull	1998-99	30(10)	6	39	1	103
	Halifax	1996	11(4)	5	0	0	20
Sam Hallas	Leeds	2016	(2)	0	0	0	0
Macauley Hallett	Hull KR	2014	2	3	0	0	12
Dave Halley	Bradford	2007-10	63(12)	20	0	0	80
	Wakefield	2009	5	4	0	0	16
Danny Halliwell	Salford	2007	2(3)	0	0	0	0
	Leigh	2005	5	3	0	0	12
	Halifax	2000-03	17(8)	4	0	0	16
	Warrington	2002	9(1)	8	0	0	32
	Wakefield	2002	3	0	0	0	0
Colum Halpenny	Wakefield	2003-06	103(1)	36	0	0	144
	Halifax	2002	22	12	0	0	48
Jon Hamer	Bradford	1996	(1)	0	0	0	0
Andrew Hamilton	London	1997, 2003	1(20)	3	0	0	12
John Hamilton	St Helens	1998	3	0	0	0	0
Gabe Hamlin	Wigan	2018	6(12)	3	0	0	12
Karle Hammond	Halifax	2002	10(2)	2	14	0	36
	Salford	2001	2(3)	1	0	0	4
	London	1999-2000	47	23	2	3	99
	St Helens	1996-98	58(8)	28	0	4	116
Ryan Hampshire	Wakefield	2018	20(5)	5	61	1	143
	Leigh	2017	12(1)	3	0	0	12
	Castleford	2016	19(2)	8	0	0	32
	Wigan	2013-15	20(5)	8	24	0	80
Rhys Hanbury	Widnes	2012-18	152	71	99	1	483
	Crusaders	2010-11	26(1)	14	0	0	56
Anthony Hancock	Paris	1997	8(6)	1	0	0	4
Michael Hancock	Salford	2001-02	12(24)	7	0	0	28
Jordan Hand	Wakefield	2015	(2)	0	0	0	0
	St Helens	2013-14	(3)	0	0	0	0
Gareth Handford	Castleford	2001	7(2)	0	0	0	0
	Bradford	2000	1(1)	0	0	0	0
Paul Handforth	Castleford	2006	2(15)	2	1	0	10
	Wakefield	2000-04	17(44)	10	13	0	66
Ash Handley	Leeds	2014-18	61(3)	29	0	0	116
Paddy Handley	Leeds	1996	1(1)	2	0	0	8
Dean Hanger	Warrington	1999	7(11)	3	0	0	12
	Huddersfield	1998	20(1)	5	0	0	20
Chris Hankinson	Wigan	2018	2	1	0	0	4
Josh Hannay	Celtic	2009	17	2	24	0	56
Harrison Hansen	Widnes	2018	1	1	0	0	4
	Leigh	2017	19(2)	1	0	0	4
	Salford	2014-15	4(2)	7	0	0	28
	Wigan	2004-13	155(62)	39	0	0	156
Lee Hansen	Wigan	1997	10(5)	0	0	0	0
Shontayne Hape	Bradford	2003-08	123(2)	79	0	0	316
Lionel Harbin	Wakefield	2001	(1)	0	0	0	0
Zak Hardaker	Castleford	2017	28	12	1	0	50
	Leeds	2011-16	135	57	43	1	315
Ian Hardman	Hull KR	2007	18	4	0	0	16
	St Helens	2003-07	32(11)	9	5	0	46
Jeff Hardy	Hudds-Sheff	2000	20(5)	6	0	1	25
	Sheffield	1999	22(4)	7	0	0	28
Spencer Hargrave	Castleford	1996-99	(6)	0	0	0	0

183

Super League Players 1996-2018

PLAYER	CLUB	YEAR	APP	TRIES	GOALS	FG	PTS
Bryn Hargreaves	Bradford	2011-12	45(5)	1	0	0	4
	St Helens	2007-10	53(44)	7	0	0	28
	Wigan	2004-06	16(12)	1	0	0	4
Lee Harland	Castleford	1996-2004	148(35)	20	0	0	80
Neil Harmon	Halifax	2003	13(3)	0	0	0	0
	Salford	2001	6(5)	0	0	0	0
	Bradford	1998-2000	15(13)	2	0	0	8
	Huddersfield	1998	12	1	0	0	4
	Leeds	1996	10	1	0	0	4
Ben Harris	Bradford	2005-07	70(4)	24	0	0	96
Iestyn Harris	Bradford	2004-08	109(11)	35	87	2	316
	Leeds	1997-2001	111(7)	57	490	6	1214
	Warrington	1996	16	4	63	2	144
Liam Harris	Hull	2018	9(2)	3	0	0	12
Ben Harrison	Wakefield	2016	3	0	0	0	0
	Warrington	2007-15	125(59)	14	0	0	56
Karl Harrison	Hull	1999	26	2	0	0	8
	Halifax	1996-98	60(2)	2	0	0	8
Andrew Hart	London	2004	12(1)	2	0	0	8
Tim Hartley	Harlequins	2006	2	1	0	0	4
	Salford	2004-05	6(7)	5	0	0	20
Carlos Hassan	Bradford	1996	6(4)	2	0	0	8
Phil Hassan	Wakefield	2002	9(1)	0	0	0	0
	Halifax	2000-01	25(4)	3	0	0	12
	Salford	1998	15	2	0	0	8
	Leeds	1996-97	38(4)	12	0	0	48
James Hasson	Wakefield	2017	(4)	0	0	0	0
	Salford	2017	4(1)	0	0	0	0
Jackson Hastings	Salford	2018	1	1	0	0	4
Tom Haughey	Castleford	2006	1(3)	1	0	0	4
	London	2003-04	10(8)	1	0	0	4
	Wakefield	2001-02	5(11)	0	0	0	0
Simon Haughton	Wigan	1996-2002	63(46)	32	0	0	128
Solomon Haumono							
	Harlequins	2006	10(9)	6	0	0	24
	London	2005	24(5)	8	0	0	32
Weller Hauraki	Widnes	2018	7	0	0	0	0
	Salford	2015-18	45(12)	8	0	0	32
	Castleford	2013-14	50(2)	9	0	0	36
	Leeds	2011-12	18(17)	6	0	0	24
	Crusaders	2010	26(1)	11	0	0	44
Richie Hawkyard	Bradford	2007	1(2)	1	0	0	4
Andy Hay	Widnes	2003-04	50(2)	7	0	0	28
	Leeds	1997-2002	112(27)	43	0	0	172
	Sheffield	1996-97	17(3)	5	0	0	20
Adam Hayes	Hudds-Sheff	2000	2(1)	0	0	0	0
Joey Hayes	Salford	1999	9	2	0	0	8
	St Helens	1996-98	11(6)	7	0	0	28
James Haynes	Hull KR	2009	1	0	0	0	0
Mathew Head	Hull	2007	9(1)	1	0	1	5
Mitch Healey	Castleford	2001-03	68(1)	10	16	0	72
Daniel Heckenberg	Harlequins	2006-09	31(39)	4	0	0	16
Andrew Heffernan	Hull KR	2018	7	2	0	0	8
Chris Heil	Hull KR	2012-13	4	2	0	0	8
Ricky Helliwell	Salford	1997-99	2(3)	0	0	0	0
Tom Hemingway	Huddersfield	2005-09	7(7)	1	17	0	38
Bryan Henare	St Helens	2000-01	4(12)	1	0	0	4
Richard Henare	Warrington	1996-97	28(2)	24	0	0	96
Andrew Henderson	Castleford	2006, 2008	44(11)	4	0	0	16
Ian Henderson	Catalans	2011-15	118(9)	12	0	0	48
	Bradford	2005-07	33(37)	13	0	0	52
Kevin Henderson	Wakefield	2005-11	52(68)	9	0	0	36
	Leigh	2005	(1)	0	0	0	0
Adam Henry	Bradford	2014	23(1)	5	0	0	20
Mark Henry	Salford	2009-11	87	22	0	0	88
Brad Hepi	Castleford	1999, 2001	9(21)	3	0	0	12
	Salford	2000	3(5)	0	0	0	0
	Hull	1998	15(1)	3	0	0	12
Tyla Hepi	Hull KR	2013	(4)	0	0	0	0
Jon Hepworth	Castleford	2003-04	19(23)	7	8	0	44
	Leeds	2003	(1)	0	0	0	0
	London	2002	(2)	0	0	0	0
Marc Herbert	Bradford	2011	20	4	2	0	20
Aaron Heremaia	Widnes	2015-18	43(41)	7	0	0	28
	Hull	2012-14	27(37)	12	0	0	48
Maxime Herold	London	2014	(2)	0	0	0	0
Ian Herron	Hull	2000	9	1	17	0	38
	Gateshead	1999	25	4	105	0	226
Jason Hetherington	London	2001-02	37	9	0	2	36
Gareth Hewitt	Salford	1999	2(1)	0	0	0	0
Sam Hewitt	Huddersfield	2018	(1)	0	0	0	0
Andrew Hick	Hull	2000	9(9)	1	0	0	4
	Gateshead	1999	12(5)	2	0	0	8
Jarrad Hickey	Wakefield	2011	(8)	2	0	0	8
Chris Hicks	Warrington	2008-10	72	56	119	0	462
Paul Hicks	Wakefield	1999	(1)	0	0	0	0
Darren Higgins	London	1998	5(6)	2	0	0	8
Iain Higgins	London	1997-98	1(7)	2	0	0	8

PLAYER	CLUB	YEAR	APP	TRIES	GOALS	FG	PTS
Liam Higgins	Wakefield	2011	4(12)	0	0	0	0
	Castleford	2008-10	42(32)	2	0	0	8
	Hull	2003-06	1(34)	0	0	0	0
Jack Higginson	Wigan	2016	2(1)	1	0	0	4
Micky Higham	Leigh	2017	11(1)	2	0	0	8
	Warrington	2009-15	73(78)	34	0	0	136
	Wigan	2006-08	61(28)	13	0	0	52
	St Helens	2001-05	43(56)	32	0	0	128
Chris Highton	Warrington	1997	1(1)	0	0	0	0
David Highton	London	2004-05	21(24)	2	0	0	8
	Salford	2002	4(5)	2	0	0	8
	Warrington	1998-2001	18(14)	2	0	0	8
Paul Highton	Salford	1998-2002, 2004-07	114(80)	14	0	0	56
	Halifax	1996-97	12(18)	2	0	0	8
Adam Higson	Leigh	2017	13	2	0	0	8
Peta Hiku	Warrington	2017	4	1	0	0	4
Andy Hill	Huddersfield	1999	(4)	0	0	0	0
	Castleford	1999	4(4)	0	0	0	0
Chris Hill	Warrington	2012-18	185(10)	21	0	0	84
	Leigh	2005	(1)	0	0	0	0
Danny Hill	Wigan	2006-07	1(10)	0	0	0	0
	Hull KR	2007	2	0	0	0	0
	Hull	2004-06	4(6)	0	0	0	0
Howard Hill	Oldham	1996-97	22(12)	4	0	0	16
John Hill	St Helens	2003	(1)	0	0	0	0
	Halifax	2003	1(2)	0	0	0	0
	Warrington	2001-02	(4)	0	0	0	0
Scott Hill	Harlequins	2007-08	41(2)	13	0	0	52
Mark Hilton	Warrington	1996-2000, 2002-06	141(40)	7	0	0	28
Ryan Hinchcliffe	Huddersfield	2016-18	70(11)	11	0	0	44
Ian Hindmarsh	Catalans	2006	25	3	0	0	12
Keegan Hirst	Wakefield	2017-18	15(30)	1	0	0	4
Jy Hitchcox	Castleford	2016-18	25(1)	21	0	0	84
Brendan Hlad	Castleford	2008	(3)	0	0	0	0
Andy Hobson	Widnes	2004	5(13)	0	0	0	0
	Halifax	1998-2003	51(85)	8	0	0	32
Gareth Hock	Leigh	2017	12(1)	3	0	0	12
	Salford	2014-15	15(1)	4	0	0	16
	Widnes	2013	15(2)	9	1	0	38
	Wigan	2003-09, 2011-12	126(43)	38	0	0	152
Tommy Hodgkinson	St Helens	2006	(1)	0	0	0	0
Andy Hodgson	Wakefield	1999	14(2)	2	1	0	10
	Bradford	1997-98	8(2)	4	0	0	16
Brett Hodgson	Warrington	2011-13	66	33	268	1	669
	Huddersfield	2009-10	45	13	166	0	384
David Hodgson	Hull KR	2012-14	51	31	0	0	124
	Huddersfield	2008-11	84	59	0	0	236
	Salford	2005-07	81	30	47	0	214
	Wigan	2000-04	90(19)	43	0	0	172
	Halifax	1999	10(3)	5	0	0	20
Elliot Hodgson	Huddersfield	2009	1	0	0	0	0
Josh Hodgson	Hull KR	2010-14	98(29)	35	0	0	140
	Hull	2009	(2)	0	0	0	0
Ryan Hoffman	Wigan	2011	28(1)	11	0	0	44
Darren Hogg	London	1996	(1)	0	0	0	0
Michael Hogue	Paris	1997	5(7)	0	0	0	0
Lance Hohaia	St Helens	2012-15	67(9)	21	0	1	85
Chris Holden	Warrington	1996-97	2(1)	0	0	0	0
Daniel Holdsworth	Hull	2013	19	2	28	2	66
	Salford	2010-12	71	18	183	1	439
Stephen Holgate	Halifax	2000	1(10)	0	0	0	0
	Hull	1999	1	0	0	0	0
	Wigan	1997-98	11(26)	2	0	0	8
	Workington	1996	19	3	0	0	12
Stephen Holker	Hull KR	2015-16	(4)	0	0	0	0
Martyn Holland	Wakefield	2000-03	52(3)	6	0	0	24
Oliver Holmes	Castleford	2010-18	139(30)	32	0	0	128
Tim Holmes	Widnes	2004-05	15(4)	0	0	0	0
Tom Holmes	Castleford	2015-17	7(8)	3	0	0	12
Graham Holroyd	Huddersfield	2003	3(5)	0	0	0	0
	Salford	2000-02	40(11)	8	75	5	187
	Halifax	1999	24(2)	3	74	5	165
	Leeds	1996-98	40(26)	22	101	8	298
Tom Holroyd	Leeds	2018	1	0	0	0	0
Dallas Hood	Wakefield	2003-04	18(9)	1	0	0	4
Liam Hood	Leigh	2017	8(5)	3	0	0	12
	Salford	2015	2(15)	0	0	0	0
	Leeds	2012	1(4)	3	0	0	12
Jason Hooper	St Helens	2003-07	89(6)	35	30	0	200
Will Hope	Salford	2013	1(2)	0	0	0	0
Lee Hopkins	Harlequins	2006-09	44(3)	11	0	0	44
	London	2005	29	6	0	0	24
Sam Hopkins	Leigh	2017	3(17)	6	0	0	24
Sean Hoppe	St Helens	1999-2002	69(16)	32	0	0	128

184

PLAYER	CLUB	YEAR	APP	TRIES	GOALS	FG	PTS
Graeme Horne	Hull KR	2012-16	81(18)	21	0	0	84
	Huddersfield	2010-11	23(17)	11	0	0	44
	Hull	2003-09	49(74)	24	0	0	96
Richard Horne	Hull	1999-2014	341(16)	115	12	6	490
Justin Horo	Wakefield	2018	17(6)	5	0	0	20
	Catalans	2016-17	34(1)	12	0	0	48
John Hough	Warrington	1996-97	9	2	0	0	8
Danny Houghton	Hull	2007-18	245(47)	38	0	0	152
Sylvain Houles	Wakefield	2003, 2005	8(1)	1	0	0	4
	London	2001-02	17(10)	11	0	0	44
	Hudds-Sheff	2000	5(2)	1	0	0	4
Chris Houston	Widnes	2016-18	57(1)	5	0	0	20
Harvey Howard	Wigan	2001-02	25(27)	1	0	0	4
	Bradford	1998	4(2)	1	0	0	4
	Leeds	1996	8	0	0	0	0
Kim Howard	London	1997	4(5)	0	0	0	0
Stuart Howarth	Wakefield	2011, 2015-16	30(5)	4	0	0	16
	Hull	2015	2(3)	0	0	0	0
	Salford	2012-14	25(12)	1	0	0	4
	St Helens	2013	14(1)	0	0	0	0
Stuart Howarth	Workington	1996	(2)	0	0	0	0
David Howell	London	2012-13	24	5	0	0	20
	Harlequins	2008-11	76	26	0	0	104
Phil Howlett	Bradford	1999	5(1)	2	0	0	8
Craig Huby	Wakefield	2017-18	24(25)	3	0	0	12
	Huddersfield	2015-16	37(2)	2	0	0	8
	Castleford	2003-04, 2006, 2008-14	130(57)	27	41	0	190
Ryan Hudson	Castleford	2002-04, 2009-12	138(12)	31	0	0	124
	Huddersfield	1998-99, 2007-08	51(22)	10	0	0	40
	Wakefield	2000-01	42(9)	11	0	1	45
Adam Hughes	Widnes	2002-05	89(2)	45	51	0	282
	Halifax	2001	8(8)	8	0	0	32
	Wakefield	1999-2000	43(3)	21	34	0	152
	Leeds	1996-97	4(5)	4	0	0	16
Ian Hughes	Sheffield	1996	9(8)	4	0	0	16
Jack Hughes	Warrington	2016-18	81	15	0	0	60
	Huddersfield	2015	30(1)	5	0	0	20
	Wigan	2011-14	31(33)	9	0	0	36
Mark Hughes	Catalans	2006	23	9	0	0	36
Steffan Hughes	London	1999-2001	1(13)	1	0	0	4
David Hulme	Salford	1997-99	53(1)	5	0	0	20
	Leeds	1996	8(1)	2	0	0	8
Declan Hulme	Widnes	2013-15	5	2	0	0	8
Paul Hulme	Warrington	1996-97	23(1)	2	0	0	8
Gary Hulse	Widnes	2005	12(5)	2	0	0	8
	Warrington	2001-04	20(28)	8	0	1	33
Alan Hunte	Salford	2002	19(2)	9	0	0	36
	Warrington	1999-2001	83	49	0	0	196
	Hull	1998	21	7	0	0	28
	St Helens	1996-97	30(2)	28	0	0	112
Alex Hurst	London	2013	8(2)	2	0	0	8
Kieran Hyde	Wakefield	2010-11	11	4	4	0	24
Nick Hyde	Paris	1997	5(5)	1	0	0	4
Chaz I'Anson	Hull KR	2007-10	17(13)	3	0	0	12
Sebastine Ikahihifo	Huddersfield	2016-18	37(13)	0	0	0	0
Ryan Ince	Widnes	2016-18	19	11	0	0	44
Krisnan Inu	Widnes	2018	13	6	21	0	66
	Catalans	2015-17	39	11	3	0	50
Andy Ireland	Hull	1998-99	22(15)	0	0	0	0
	Bradford	1996	1	0	0	0	0
Kevin Iro	St Helens	1999-2001	76	39	0	0	156
	Leeds	1996	16	9	0	0	36
Willie Isa	Wigan	2016-18	66(17)	6	0	0	24
	Widnes	2012-15	44(33)	3	0	0	12
	Castleford	2011	7(2)	6	0	0	24
Andrew Isherwood	Wigan	1998-99	(5)	0	0	0	0
Olu Iwenofu	London	2000-01	2(1)	0	0	0	0
Chico Jackson	Hull	1999	(4)	0	0	0	0
Lee Jackson	Hull	2001-02	37(9)	12	1	0	50
	Leeds	1999-2000	28(24)	7	0	0	28
Michael Jackson	Sheffield	1998-99	17(17)	2	0	0	8
	Halifax	1996-97	27(6)	11	0	0	44
Paul Jackson	Castleford	2003-04, 2010-12	44(30)	5	0	0	20
	Huddersfield	1998, 2005-09	50(73)	4	0	0	16
	Wakefield	1999-2002	57(42)	2	0	0	8
Rob Jackson	Leigh	2005	20(3)	5	0	0	20
	London	2002-04	26(14)	9	0	0	36
Wayne Jackson	Halifax	1996-97	17(5)	2	0	0	8
Aled James	Crusaders	2011	1	0	0	0	0
	Celtic	2009	3(3)	0	0	0	0
	Widnes	2003	3	0	0	0	0
Andy James	Halifax	1996	(4)	0	0	0	0
Jordan James	Wigan	2006, 2014	3(18)	4	0	0	16
	Salford	2012-13	1(40)	6	0	0	24
	Crusaders	2010-11	5(24)	3	0	0	12
	Celtic	2009	17(4)	1	0	0	4
Matt James	Wakefield	2012	(4)	0	0	0	0
	Harlequins	2010	(2)	0	0	0	0
	Bradford	2006-09	1(23)	0	0	0	0
Pascal Jampy	Catalans	2006	4(7)	0	0	0	0
	Paris	1996-97	3(2)	0	0	0	0
Adam Janowski	Harlequins	2008	(1)	0	0	0	0
Ben Jeffries	Bradford	2008-09, 2011-12	76(3)	20	0	0	80
	Wakefield	2003-07, 2010-11	151(10)	70	20	6	326
Mick Jenkins	Hull	2000	24	2	0	0	8
	Gateshead	1999	16	3	0	0	12
Ed Jennings	London	1998-99	1(2)	0	0	0	0
Rod Jensen	Huddersfield	2007-08	26(3)	13	0	0	52
Anthony Jerram	Warrington	2007		0	0	0	0
Lee Jewitt	Hull KR	2018	7(2)	0	0	0	0
	Castleford	2014-16	22(12)	0	0	0	0
	Salford	2007, 2009-13	32(62)	4	0	0	16
	Wigan	2005	(2)	0	0	0	0
Isaac John	Wakefield	2012	13	1	19	0	42
Andrew Johns	Warrington	2005	3	1	12	1	29
Matthew Johns	Wigan	2001	24	3	0	1	13
Andy Johnson	Salford	2004-05	8(26)	7	0	0	28
	Castleford	2002-03	32(16)	11	0	0	44
	London	2000-01	24(21)	12	0	0	48
	Huddersfield	1999	5	1	0	0	4
	Wigan	1996-99	24(20)	19	0	0	76
Bruce Johnson	Widnes	2004-05	(4)	0	0	0	0
Dallas Johnson	Catalans	2010	26	1	0	0	4
Greg Johnson	Salford	2014-18	85	36	1	0	146
	Wakefield	2011	12	2	0	0	8
Jack Johnson	Warrington	2015-17	13	4	0	0	16
	Widnes	2017	3	1	0	0	4
Jason Johnson	St Helens	1997-99	2	0	0	0	0
Josh Johnson	Hull KR	2018	2(2)	0	0	0	0
	Huddersfield	2013-16	14(17)	0	0	0	0
Luis Johnson	Warrington	2018	(1)	0	0	0	0
Mark Johnson	Salford	1999-2000	22(9)	16	0	0	64
	Hull	1998	10(1)	4	0	0	16
	Workington	1996	12	4	0	0	16
Nick Johnson	Hull KR	2012	1	0	0	0	0
Nick Johnson	London	2003	(1)	0	0	0	0
Paul Johnson	Crusaders	2011	6(4)	0	0	0	0
	Wakefield	2010	12(3)	4	0	0	16
	Warrington	2007-09	37(9)	17	0	0	68
	Bradford	2004-06	46(8)	19	0	0	76
	Wigan	1996-2003	74(46)	54	0	0	216
Paul Johnson	Widnes	2014	5(11)	0	0	0	0
	Hull	2013	3(16)	0	0	0	0
	Wakefield	2011-12	25(21)	6	0	0	24
	St Helens	2010	(2)	0	0	0	0
Richard Johnson	Bradford	2008	(2)	0	0	0	0
Ben Johnston	Castleford	2012	2	0	0	0	0
Jordan Johnstone	Widnes	2016-18	16(13)	1	0	0	4
Tom Johnstone	Wakefield	2015-18	67	54	0	0	216
Ben Jones	Harlequins	2010	(2)	0	0	0	0
Chris Jones	Leigh	2005	1(1)	0	0	0	0
Danny Jones	Halifax	2003	1	0	0	0	0
David Jones	Oldham	1997	14(1)	5	0	0	20
Josh Jones	Salford	2016-18	60(4)	11	0	0	44
	St Helens	2012-15	88(9)	22	0	0	88
Mark Jones	Warrington	1996	8(11)	2	0	0	8
Phil Jones	Leigh	2005	16	8	31	0	94
	Wigan	1999-2001	14(7)	6	25	0	74
Stacey Jones	Catalans	2006-07	39	11	43	3	133
Stephen Jones	Huddersfield	2005	(1)	0	0	0	0
Stuart Jones	Castleford	2009-12	69(27)	14	0	0	56
	Huddersfield	2004-08	96(22)	17	0	0	68
	St Helens	2003	(18)	2	0	0	8
	Wigan	2002	5(3)	1	0	0	4
Ben Jones-Bishop	Wakefield	2016-18	73	48	0	0	192
	Salford	2015	17	12	0	0	48
	Leeds	2008-09, 2011-14	70(2)	46	0	0	184
	Harlequins	2010	17	10	0	0	40
Jamie Jones-Buchanan	Leeds	1999-2018	289(69)	69	0	0	276
Tim Jonkers	Wigan	2006	3(1)	0	0	0	0
	Salford	2004-06	5(11)	0	0	0	0
	St Helens	1999-2004	41(64)	12	0	0	48
Darren Jordan	Wakefield	2003	(1)	0	0	0	0
Josh Jordan-Roberts	Leeds	2017	(1)	0	0	0	0

PLAYER	CLUB	YEAR	APP	TRIES	GOALS	FG	PTS
Phil Joseph	Salford	2016	(12)	0	0	0	0
	Widnes	2013-15	11(38)	1	0	0	4
	Bradford	2012	(6)	0	0	0	0
	Huddersfield	2004	7(6)	0	0	0	0
Max Jowitt	Wakefield	2014-18	38(2)	8	0	0	32
Warren Jowitt	Hull	2003	(2)	0	0	0	0
	Salford	2001-02	17(4)	2	0	0	8
	Wakefield	2000	19(3)	8	0	0	32
	Bradford	1996-99	13(25)	5	0	0	20
Chris Joynt	St Helens	1996-2004	201(14)	68	0	0	272
Benjamin Jullien	Catalans	2018	23(2)	7	0	0	28
	Warrington	2016-17	19(7)	4	0	0	16
Gregory Kacala	Paris	1996	7	1	0	0	4
Andy Kain	Castleford	2004, 2006	9(7)	3	10	0	32
Antonio Kaufusi	Huddersfield	2014	15(2)	1	0	0	4
	Bradford	2014	4	0	0	0	0
	London	2012-13	44(5)	5	0	0	20
Mal Kaufusi	London	2004	1(3)	0	0	0	0
Ben Kavanagh	Hull KR	2018	13(8)	0	0	0	0
	Wakefield	2015	6(3)	0	0	0	0
	Widnes	2012-15	18(33)	0	0	0	0
Liam Kay	Wakefield	2012-13	4	4	0	0	16
Ben Kaye	Harlequins	2009-10	2(13)	0	0	0	0
	Leeds	2008	2(2)	1	0	0	4
Elliot Kear	Bradford	2012-14	53(2)	17	0	0	68
	Crusaders	2010-11	16(1)	4	0	0	16
	Celtic	2009	3	0	0	0	0
Brett Kearney	Bradford	2010-14	107	55	0	0	220
Stephen Kearney	Hull	2005	22(2)	5	0	0	20
Damon Keating	Wakefield	2002	7(17)	1	0	0	4
Kris Keating	Hull KR	2014	23	5	0	0	20
Shaun Keating	London	1996	1(3)	0	0	0	0
Mark Keenan	Workington	1996	3(4)	1	0	0	4
Jimmy Keinhorst	Leeds	2012-18	46(23)	25	0	0	100
	Widnes	2018	3	1	0	0	4
	Wakefield	2014	7	1	0	0	4
Albert Kelly	Hull	2017-18	39	24	0	1	97
	Hull KR	2015-16	37	21	3	0	90
Tony Kemp	Wakefield	1999-2000	15(5)	2	0	1	9
	Leeds	1996-98	23(2)	5	0	2	22
Damien Kennedy	London	2003	5(11)	1	0	0	4
Ian Kenny	St Helens	2004	(1)	0	0	0	0
Sean Kenny	Salford	2016	(4)	0	0	0	0
Jason Kent	Leigh	2005	23	1	0	0	4
Liam Kent	Hull	2012-13	1(5)	0	0	0	0
Shane Kenward	Wakefield	1999	28	6	0	0	24
	Salford	1998	1	0	0	0	0
Jason Keough	Paris	1997	2	1	0	0	4
Keiran Kerr	Widnes	2005	6	2	0	0	8
Martin Ketteridge	Halifax	1996	7(5)	0	0	0	0
Ronnie Kettlewell	Warrington	1996	(1)	0	0	0	0
Joe Keyes	London	2014	7	5	0	0	20
Younes Khattabi	Catalans	2006-08	24(4)	10	0	0	40
Samy Kibula	Wigan	2018	(1)	0	0	0	0
David Kidwell	Warrington	2001-02	14(12)	9	0	0	36
Andrew King	London	2003	23(1)	15	0	0	60
Dave King	Huddersfield	1998-99	11(17)	2	0	0	8
George King	Warrington	2014-18	12(68)	1	0	0	4
James King	Leigh	2005	5(7)	0	0	0	0
Kevin King	Wakefield	2005	8(1)	2	0	0	8
	Castleford	2004	(1)	0	0	0	0
Matt King	Warrington	2008-11	91	58	0	0	232
Paul King	Wakefield	2010-11	10(19)	0	0	1	1
	Hull	1999-2009	136(93)	20	0	1	81
Toby King	Warrington	2014-18	42(7)	17	0	0	68
Andy Kirk	Wakefield	2005	6(3)	1	0	0	4
	Salford	2004	20	5	0	0	20
	Leeds	2001-02	4(4)	0	0	0	0
Ian Kirke	Wakefield	2015	2(2)	1	0	0	4
	Leeds	2006-14	52(132)	10	0	0	40
John Kirkpatrick	London	2004-05	18(1)	5	0	0	20
	St Helens	2001-03	10(11)	10	0	0	40
	Halifax	2003	4	1	0	0	4
Danny Kirmond	Wakefield	2010, 2012-18	131(11)	41	0	0	164
	Huddersfield	2008-11	18(31)	9	0	0	36
Wayne Kitchin	Workington	1996	11(6)	3	17	1	47
Sione Kite	Widnes	2012	6(8)	1	0	0	4
Ian Knott	Leigh	2005	8(1)	2	0	0	8
	Wakefield	2002-03	34(5)	7	79	0	186
	Warrington	1996-2001	68(41)	24	18	0	132
Matt Knowles	Wigan	1996	(3)	0	0	0	0
Michael Knowles	Castleford	2006	(1)	0	0	0	0
Morgan Knowles	St Helens	2016-18	30(48)	12	0	0	48
Phil Knowles	Salford	1997	1	0	0	0	0
Simon Knox	Halifax	1999	(6)	0	0	0	0
	Salford	1998	1(1)	0	0	0	0
	Bradford	1996-98	9(19)	7	0	0	28

PLAYER	CLUB	YEAR	APP	TRIES	GOALS	FG	PTS
Toa Kohe-Love	Warrington	1996-2001, 2005-06	166(3)	90	0	0	360
	Bradford	2004	1(1)	0	0	0	0
	Hull	2002-03	42	19	0	0	76
Paul Koloi	Wigan	1997	1(2)	1	0	0	4
Craig Kopczak	Salford	2016-18	39(27)	11	0	0	44
	Huddersfield	2013-15	48(37)	6	0	0	24
	Bradford	2006-12	32(83)	10	0	0	40
Michael Korkidas	Wakefield	2003-06, 2009-11	133(36)	15	0	0	60
	Huddersfield	2009	4(1)	1	0	0	4
	Castleford	2008	15(6)	1	0	0	4
	Salford	2007	26(1)	1	0	0	4
Nick Kouparitsas	Harlequins	2011	2(13)	1	0	0	4
Olsi Krasniqi	Salford	2015-17	8(29)	1	0	0	4
	London	2012-14	28(34)	3	0	0	12
	Harlequins	2010-11	3(20)	1	0	0	4
David Krause	London	1996-97	22(1)	7	0	0	28
Ben Kusto	Huddersfield	2001	21(4)	9	0	1	37
Anthony Laffranchi	St Helens	2012-14	50(18)	19	0	0	76
James Laithwaite	Warrington	2013-15	23(22)	1	0	0	4
	Hull KR	2012	1(2)	1	0	0	4
Adrian Lam	Wigan	2001-04	105(2)	40	1	9	171
Callum Lancaster	Hull	2014-16	7	9	0	0	36
Jordan Lane	Hull	2018	6(10)	1	0	0	4
Mark Lane	Paris	1996	(2)	0	0	0	0
Allan Langer	Warrington	2000-01	47	13	4	0	60
Kevin Langer	London	1996	12(4)	2	0	0	8
Junior Langi	Salford	2005-06	27(7)	7	0	0	28
Samisoni Langi	Catalans	2018	18	1	0	0	4
	Leigh	2017	3	1	0	0	4
Chris Langley	Huddersfield	2000-01	18(1)	3	0	0	12
Gareth Langley	St Helens	2006	1	1	3	0	10
Jamie Langley	Hull KR	2014	6(5)	1	0	0	4
	Bradford	2002-13	182(57)	36	0	0	144
Ryan Lannon	Salford	2015-18	20(23)	5	0	0	20
Kevin Larroyer	Castleford	2017	2(4)	0	0	0	0
	Hull KR	2014-16	34(13)	9	0	0	36
	Catalans	2012-13	9(10)	6	0	0	24
Andy Last	Hull	1999-2005	16(10)	4	0	0	16
Sam Latus	Hull KR	2010-13	34(3)	13	0	0	52
Epalahame Lauaki	Wigan	2012-13	14(16)	2	0	0	8
	Hull	2009-11	3(50)	4	0	0	16
Dale Laughton	Warrington	2002	15(1)	0	0	0	0
	Huddersfield	2000-01	36(2)	4	0	0	16
	Sheffield	1996-99	48(22)	5	0	0	20
Ali Lauitiiti	Wakefield	2012-15	46(31)	16	0	0	64
	Leeds	2004-11	64(117)	58	0	0	232
Quentin Laulu-Togagae	Castleford	2018	8(1)	6	0	0	24
Jason Laurence	Salford	1997	1	0	0	0	0
Graham Law	Wakefield	1999-2002	34(30)	6	40	0	104
Neil Law	Wakefield	1999-2002	83	39	0	0	156
	Sheffield	1998	1(1)	1	0	0	4
Dean Lawford	Widnes	2003-04	17(1)	5	2	4	28
	Halifax	2001	1(1)	0	0	0	0
	Leeds	1997-2000	15(8)	2	3	0	14
	Huddersfield	1999	6(1)	0	6	1	13
	Sheffield	1996	9(5)	2	1	1	11
George Lawler	Hull KR	2016, 2018	14(6)	2	0	0	8
Johnny Lawless	Halifax	2001-03	73(1)	10	0	0	40
	Hudds-Sheff	2000	19(6)	3	0	0	12
	Sheffield	1996-99	76(4)	11	0	0	44
Michael Lawrence	Huddersfield	2007-18	188(41)	45	0	0	180
Adam Lawton	Widnes	2013-14	2(10)	5	0	0	20
Charlie Leaeno	Wakefield	2010	7(3)	2	0	0	8
Mark Leafa	Castleford	2008	5(9)	1	0	0	4
	Leigh	2005	28	2	0	0	8
Leroy Leapai	London	1996	2	0	0	0	0
Jim Leatham	Hull	1998-99	20(18)	4	0	0	16
	Leeds	1997	(1)	0	0	0	0
Andy Leathem	Warrington	1999	2(8)	0	0	0	0
	St Helens	1996-98	20(1)	1	0	0	4
Danny Lee	Gateshead	1999	16(2)	0	0	0	0
Jason Lee	Halifax	2001	10(1)	2	0	0	8
Mark Lee	Salford	1997-2000	25(11)	1	0	4	8
Robert Lee	Hull	1999	4(3)	0	0	0	0
Tommy Lee	Hull KR	2018	15(2)	1	0	0	4
	St Helens	2017	9(9)	0	0	0	0
	Salford	2014-16	37(5)	4	0	0	16
	London	2013	16(4)	2	0	0	8
	Huddersfield	2012	11(7)	3	0	0	12
	Wakefield	2011	25	6	0	0	24
	Crusaders	2010	3(9)	0	0	0	0
	Hull	2005-09	44(27)	6	0	0	24
Kruise Leeming	Huddersfield	2013-18	35(53)	9	0	0	36
Matty Lees	St Helens	2017-18	3(16)	1	0	0	4
Matthew Leigh	Salford	2000	(6)	0	0	0	0

PLAYER	CLUB	YEAR	APP	TRIES	GOALS	FG	PTS
Chris Leikvoll	Warrington	2004-07	72(18)	4	0	0	16
Jim Lenihan	Huddersfield	1999	19(1)	10	0	0	40
Mark Lennon	Celtic	2009	10(3)	1	8	0	20
	Hull KR	2007	11(4)	5	7	0	34
	Castleford	2001-03	30(21)	10	21	0	82
Tevita Leo-Latu	Wakefield	2006-10	28(49)	10	0	0	40
Gary Lester	Hull	1998-99	46	17	0	0	68
Stuart Lester	Wigan	1997	1(3)	0	0	0	0
Heath L'Estrange	Bradford	2010-13	56(35)	7	0	0	28
Afi Leuila	Oldham	1996-97	17(3)	2	0	0	8
Kylie Leuluai	Leeds	2007-15	182(45)	20	0	0	80
Macgraff Leuluai	Widnes	2012-18	52(64)	5	0	0	20
Phil Leuluai	Salford	2007, 2009-10	7(47)	3	0	0	12
Thomas Leuluai	Wigan	2007-12, 2017-18	223(1)	58	0	1	233
	Harlequins	2006	15(2)	6	0	0	24
	London	2005	20	13	0	0	52
Simon Lewis	Castleford	2001	4	3	0	0	12
Paul Leyland	St Helens	2006	1	0	0	0	0
Jon Liddell	Leeds	2001	1	0	0	0	0
Jason Lidden	Castleford	1997	15(1)	7	0	0	28
Jordan Lilley	Leeds	2015-18	21(11)	2	42	0	92
Danny Lima	Wakefield	2007	(3)	0	0	0	0
	Salford	2006	7(2)	0	0	0	0
	Warrington	2004-06	15(47)	9	0	0	36
Jeff Lima	Catalans	2014-15	37(7)	3	1	0	14
	Wigan	2011-12	24(29)	4	0	0	16
Tom Lineham	Warrington	2016-18	70	49	0	0	196
	Hull	2012-15	61(1)	50	0	0	200
Jez Litten	Hull	2017-18	(11)	0	0	0	0
Harry Little	London	2013	2	0	0	0	0
Jack Littlejohn	Salford	2018	15(3)	3	1	0	14
Craig Littler	St Helens	2006	1	1	0	0	4
Stuart Littler	Salford	1998-2002, 2004-07, 2009-10	217(30)	65	0	0	260
Harvey Livett	Warrington	2017-18	17(10)	11	21	0	86
Peter Livett	Workington	1996	3(1)	0	0	0	0
Rhodri Lloyd	Wigan	2012-13, 2015	3(4)	0	0	0	0
	Widnes	2014	(4)	0	0	0	0
	London	2013	2	0	0	0	0
Garry Lo	Castleford	2018	1	1	0	0	4
Kevin Locke	Wakefield	2015	3	0	0	0	0
	Salford	2014-15	13	6	11	0	46
Jack Logan	Hull	2014-16, 2018	29(2)	11	0	0	44
Scott Logan	Wigan	2006	10(11)	0	0	0	0
	Hull	2001-03	27(20)	5	0	0	20
Jamahl Lolesi	Huddersfield	2007-10	75(9)	27	0	0	108
Filimone Lolohea	Harlequins	2006	3(6)	0	0	0	0
	London	2005	8(15)	0	0	0	0
David Lomax	Huddersfield	2000-01	45(9)	4	0	0	16
	Paris	1997	19(2)	1	0	0	4
Jonny Lomax	St Helens	2009-18	173(2)	83	84	2	502
Dave Long	London	1999	(1)	0	0	0	0
Karl Long	London	2003	(1)	0	0	0	0
	Widnes	2002	4	1	0	0	4
Sean Long	Hull	2010-11	22	6	0	0	24
	St Helens	1997-2009	263(8)	126	826	20	2176
	Wigan	1996-97	1(5)	0	0	0	0
Davide Longo	Bradford	1996	1(3)	0	0	0	0
Gary Lord	Oldham	1996-97	28(12)	3	0	0	12
Paul Loughlin	Huddersfield	1998-99	34(2)	4	4	0	24
	Bradford	1996-97	36(4)	15	8	0	76
Rhys Lovegrove	Hull KR	2007-14	75(74)	19	0	0	76
Karl Lovell	Hudds-Sheff	2000	14	5	0	0	20
	Sheffield	1999	22(4)	8	0	0	32
Will Lovell	London	2012-14	16(16)	4	0	0	16
James Lowes	Bradford	1996-2003	205	84	2	2	342
Laurent Lucchese	Paris	1996	13(5)	2	0	0	8
Robert Lui	Salford	2016-18	66(3)	20	33	0	146
Zebastian Luisi	Harlequins	2006-07	23(2)	4	0	0	16
	London	2004-05	21(1)	7	0	0	28
Keith Lulia	Bradford	2012-13	50	19	0	0	76
Shaun Lunt	Hull KR	2015-16, 2018	24(12)	11	0	0	44
	Huddersfield	2009-15	73(39)	60	0	0	240
	Leeds	2012	10(9)	7	0	0	28
Peter Lupton	Crusaders	2010-11	37(9)	10	0	0	40
	Celtic	2009	16(4)	4	0	0	16
	Castleford	2006, 2008	40	11	0	0	44
	Hull	2003-06	19(26)	10	3	0	46
	London	2000-02	10(15)	2	2	0	12
Andy Lynch	Castleford	1999-2004, 2014-17	157(54)	17	0	0	68
	Hull	2012-13	39(14)	3	0	0	12
	Bradford	2005-11	159(29)	46	0	0	184
Reece Lyne	Wakefield	2013-18	121(1)	44	0	0	176
	Hull	2010-11	11(1)	2	0	0	8

PLAYER	CLUB	YEAR	APP	TRIES	GOALS	FG	PTS
Jamie Lyon	St Helens	2005-06	54(1)	39	172	0	500
Iliess Macani	London	2013-14	12(3)	4	0	0	16
Duncan MacGillivray	Wakefield	2004-08	75(18)	6	0	0	24
Brad Mackay	Bradford	2000	24(2)	8	0	0	32
Graham Mackay	Hull	2002	27	18	24	0	120
	Bradford	2001	16(3)	12	1	0	50
	Leeds	2000	12(8)	10	2	0	44
Keiron Maddocks	Leigh	2005	1(3)	0	0	0	0
Steve Maden	Leigh	2005	23	9	0	0	36
	Warrington	2002	3	0	0	0	0
Mateaki Mafi	Warrington	1996-97	7(8)	7	0	0	28
Shaun Magennis	St Helens	2010-12	7(19)	3	0	0	12
Brendan Magnus	London	2000	3	1	0	0	4
Mark Maguire	London	1996-97	11(4)	7	13	0	54
Adam Maher	Hull	2000-03	88(4)	24	0	0	96
	Gateshead	1999	21(5)	3	0	0	12
Lee Maher	Leeds	1996	4(1)	0	0	0	0
Will Maher	Castleford	2014-18	2(25)	1	0	0	4
Shaun Mahony	Paris	1997	5	0	0	0	0
Hutch Maiava	Hull	2007	(19)	1	0	0	4
David Maiden	Hull	2000-01	32(10)	11	0	0	44
	Gateshead	1999	5(16)	8	0	0	32
Craig Makin	Salford	1999-2001	24(20)	2	0	0	8
Tommy Makinson	St Helens	2011-18	179(5)	97	102	0	592
Brady Malam	Wigan	2000	5(20)	1	0	0	4
Dominic Maloney	Hull	2009	(7)	0	0	0	0
Francis Maloney	Castleford	1998-99, 2003-04	71(7)	24	33	3	165
	Salford	2001-02	45(1)	26	5	0	114
	Wakefield	2000	11	1	1	0	6
	Oldham	1996-97	39(2)	12	91	2	232
Jake Mamo	Huddersfield	2017-18	23	17	0	0	68
Dom Manfredi	Wigan	2013-16, 2018	57	51	0	0	204
	Salford	2014	1	2	0	0	8
George Mann	Warrington	1997	14(5)	1	0	0	4
	Leeds	1996	11(4)	2	0	0	8
Dane Manning	Leeds	2009	(1)	0	0	0	0
Josh Mantellato	Hull KR	2015-16	26	16	88	0	240
Misili Manu	Widnes	2005	1	0	0	0	0
Sika Manu	Hull	2016-18	69(2)	8	0	0	32
Willie Manu	St Helens	2013-14	35(11)	9	0	0	36
	Hull	2007-12	133(18)	33	0	0	132
	Castleford	2006	19(4)	9	0	0	36
Manase Manuokafoa	Widnes	2015-17	3(54)	3	0	0	12
	Bradford	2012-14	49(21)	3	0	0	12
Darren Mapp	Celtic	2009	9(2)	1	0	0	4
David March	Wakefield	1999-2007	164(23)	34	126	0	388
Paul March	Wakefield	1999-2001, 2007	42(31)	17	23	0	114
	Huddersfield	2003-06	71(19)	17	36	1	141
Nick Mardon	London	1997-98	14	2	0	0	8
Thibaut Margalet	Catalans	2013-18	1(22)	0	0	0	0
Remy Marginet	Catalans	2011	2	0	9	0	18
Antoni Maria	Catalans	2012-16, 2018	7(42)	0	0	0	0
	Leigh	2017	2(6)	0	0	0	0
Frankie Mariano	Castleford	2014-16	14(21)	8	0	0	32
	Wakefield	2011-13	41(12)	20	0	0	80
	Hull KR	2010	(3)	0	0	0	0
Oliver Marns	Halifax	1996-2002	54(19)	23	0	0	92
Paul Marquet	Warrington	2002	23(2)	0	0	0	0
Callum Marriott	Salford	2011	(1)	0	0	0	0
Iain Marsh	Salford	1998-2001	1(4)	0	0	0	0
Lee Marsh	Salford	2001-02	3(4)	0	0	0	0
Matty Marsh	Hull KR	2015-16, 2018	18(4)	3	0	0	12
Stefan Marsh	Widnes	2012-18	121	56	21	0	266
	Wigan	2010-11	12	3	0	0	12
Liam Marshall	Wigan	2017-18	41	37	5	0	158
Richard Marshall	Leigh	2005	4(16)	1	0	0	4
	London	2002-03	33(11)	1	0	0	4
	Huddersfield	2000-01	35(14)	1	0	0	4
	Halifax	1996-99	38(34)	2	0	0	8
Charlie Martin	Castleford	2013	(6)	0	0	0	0
Jason Martin	Paris	1997	15(2)	3	0	0	12
Scott Martin	Salford	1997-99	32(18)	8	0	0	32
Tony Martin	Hull	2012	10	1	0	0	4
	Crusaders	2010-11	40(1)	14	1	0	58
	Wakefield	2008-09	33	10	33	0	106
	London	1996-97, 2001-03	97(1)	36	170	1	485
Ugo Martin	Catalans	2018	1	0	0	0	0
Mick Martindale	Halifax	1996	(4)	0	0	0	0
Sebastien Martins	Catalans	2006, 2009-11	(21)	2	0	0	8
Tommy Martyn	St Helens	1996-2003	125(20)	87	63	12	486
Dean Marwood	Workington	1996	9(6)	0	22	0	44
Martin Masella	Warrington	2001	10(14)	5	0	0	20
	Wakefield	2000	14(8)	4	0	0	16
	Leeds	1997-1999	59(5)	1	0	0	4

Super League Players 1996-2018

PLAYER	CLUB	YEAR	APP	TRIES	GOALS	FG	PTS
Colin Maskill	Castleford	1996	8	1	1	0	6
Mose Masoe	Hull KR	2018	11(11)	3	0	0	12
	St Helens	2014-15	17(39)	10	0	0	40
Keith Mason	Castleford	2006, 2013	11(6)	0	0	0	0
	Huddersfield	2006-12	118(14)	4	0	0	16
	St Helens	2003-05	33(23)	4	0	0	16
	Wakefield	2000-01	5(17)	0	0	0	0
Nathan Mason	Huddersfield	2013, 2015-17	3(26)	3	0	0	12
Willie Mason	Catalans	2016	6(8)	1	0	0	4
	Hull KR	2011	6	1	0	0	4
Samy Masselot	Wakefield	2011	(1)	0	0	0	0
Nathan Massey	Castleford	2008-18	123(63)	8	0	0	32
Suaia Matagi	Huddersfield	2018	7	0	0	0	0
Nesiasi Mataitonga	London	2014	11(1)	1	0	0	4
Peter Mata'utia	Castleford	2018	8	1	0	0	4
Vila Matautia	St Helens	1996-2001	73(68)	9	0	0	36
Feleti Mateo	London	2005	4(10)	1	0	0	4
Barrie-Jon Mather	Castleford	1998, 2000-02	50(12)	21	0	0	84
Richard Mathers	Wakefield	2012-14	71	24	0	0	96
	Castleford	2011	21(1)	7	0	0	28
	Warrington	2002, 2009-10	42(3)	11	0	0	44
	Wigan	2008-09	23(1)	2	0	0	8
	Leeds	2002-06	85(2)	26	0	0	104
Jamie Mathiou	Leeds	1997-2001	31(82)	3	0	0	12
Masi Matongo	Hull	2015, 2017-18	7(26)	1	0	0	4
Terry Matterson	London	1996-98	46	15	90	6	246
Vic Mauro	Salford	2013	1(7)	1	0	0	4
Luke May	Harlequins	2009-10	(3)	0	0	0	0
Casey Mayberry	Halifax	2000	1(1)	0	0	0	0
Chris Maye	Halifax	2003	3(4)	0	0	0	0
Judah Mazive	Wakefield	2016	2	1	0	0	4
Joe Mbu	Harlequins	2006-09	33(20)	3	0	0	12
	London	2003-05	29(19)	4	0	0	16
Danny McAllister	Gateshead	1999	3(3)	1	0	0	4
	Sheffield	1996-97	33(7)	10	0	0	40
John McAtee	St Helens	1996	2(1)	0	0	0	0
Nathan McAvoy	Bradford	1998-2002, 2007	83(31)	46	0	0	184
	Wigan	2006	15(2)	5	0	0	20
	Salford	1997-98, 2004-05	57(4)	18	0	0	72
Tyrone McCarthy	Salford	2017-18	16(7)	4	2	0	20
	Hull KR	2015	20(1)	4	0	0	16
	Warrington	2009-13	12(24)	2	0	0	8
	Wakefield	2011	2(5)	1	0	0	4
Louie McCarthy-Scarsbrook	St Helens	2011-18	122(106)	45	0	0	180
	Harlequins	2006-10	41(50)	17	0	0	68
Dave McConnell	London	2003	(4)	0	0	0	0
	St Helens	2001-02	3(2)	4	0	0	16
Robbie McCormack	Wigan	1998	24	2	0	0	8
Steve McCurrie	Leigh	2005	7(3)	1	0	0	4
	Widnes	2002-04	55(22)	10	0	0	40
	Warrington	1998-2001	69(26)	31	0	0	124
Barrie McDermott	Leeds	1996-2005	163(69)	28	0	0	112
Brian McDermott	Bradford	1996-2002	138(32)	33	0	0	132
Ryan McDonald	Widnes	2002-03	6(4)	0	0	0	0
Wayne McDonald	Huddersfield	2005-06	11(23)	1	0	0	4
	Wigan	2005	(4)	0	0	0	0
	Leeds	2002-05	34(47)	14	0	0	56
	St Helens	2001	7(11)	4	0	0	16
	Hull	2000	5(8)	4	0	0	16
	Wakefield	1999	9(17)	8	0	0	32
Shannon McDonnell	St Helens	2014-16	28	15	0	0	60
	Hull	2013	19	2	0	0	8
	Hull KR	2012	21	6	0	0	24
Craig McDowell	Huddersfield	2003	(1)	0	0	0	0
	Warrington	2002	(1)	0	0	0	0
	Bradford	2000	(1)	0	0	0	0
Wes McGibbon	Halifax	1999	1	0	0	0	0
Jermaine McGillvary	Huddersfield	2010-18	204	144	0	0	576
Dean McGilvray	Salford	2009-10	14	4	0	0	16
	St Helens	2006-08	5(1)	1	0	0	4
Billy McGinty	Workington	1996	1	0	0	0	0
Ryan McGoldrick	Salford	2013	19(1)	3	0	1	13
	Hull	2012	8	1	0	0	4
	Castleford	2006, 2008-12	129(5)	24	11	0	118
Kevin McGuinness	Salford	2004-07	63(3)	11	0	0	44
Casey McGuire	Catalans	2007-10	87(4)	27	0	0	108
Danny McGuire	Hull KR	2018	14	5	0	1	21
	Leeds	2001-17	331(39)	238	0	6	958
Gary McGuirk	Workington	1996	(4)	0	0	0	0
Michael McIlorum	Catalans	2018	24	2	0	0	8
	Wigan	2007-17	156(54)	22	0	0	88
Darnell McIntosh	Huddersfield	2017-18	42(1)	26	2	0	108
Richard McKell	Castleford	1997-98	22(7)	2	0	0	8
Chris McKenna	Bradford	2006-07	40(7)	7	0	0	28
	Leeds	2003-05	65(4)	18	0	0	72
Phil McKenzie	Workington	1996	4	0	0	0	0
Chris McKinney	Oldham	1996-97	4(9)	2	0	0	8
Wade McKinnon	Hull	2012	10	4	0	0	16
Mark McLinden	Harlequins	2006-08	46(1)	20	0	1	81
	London	2005	22(3)	8	0	0	32
Mike McMeeken	Castleford	2015-18	84(11)	23	0	0	92
	London	2012-14	25(9)	5	0	0	20
Shayne McMenemy	Hull	2003-07	80(8)	12	0	0	48
	Halifax	2001-03	63	11	0	0	44
Andy McNally	London	2004	5(3)	0	0	0	0
	Castleford	2001, 2003	2(5)	1	0	0	4
Gregg McNally	Leigh	2017	9	3	0	0	12
	Huddersfield	2011	1	0	6	0	12
Steve McNamara	Huddersfield	2001, 2003	41(9)	3	134	1	281
	Wakefield	2000	15(2)	2	32	0	72
	Bradford	1996-99	90(3)	14	348	7	759
Paul McNicholas	Hull	2004-05	28(12)	4	0	0	16
Neil McPherson	Salford	1997	(1)	0	0	0	0
Shannan McPherson	Salford	2012-14	20(11)	0	0	0	0
Duncan McRae	London	1996	11(2)	3	0	1	13
Paul McShane	Castleford	2015-18	77(20)	17	27	0	122
	Wakefield	2014-15	39(9)	5	0	0	20
	Leeds	2009-13	17(38)	12	0	0	48
	Widnes	2012	6(5)	3	4	0	20
	Hull	2010	(4)	0	0	0	0
Derek McVey	St Helens	1996-97	28(4)	6	1	0	26
Dallas Mead	Warrington	1997	2	0	0	0	0
David Mead	Catalans	2018	27	15	0	0	60
Robbie Mears	Leigh	2005	8(6)	0	0	0	0
	Leeds	2001	23	6	0	0	24
Paul Medley	Bradford	1996-98	6(35)	9	0	0	36
Francis Meli	Salford	2014	16	11	0	0	44
	St Helens	2006-13	194(1)	122	0	0	488
Vince Mellars	Wakefield	2012-13	21(5)	4	0	0	16
	Crusaders	2010-11	46	17	0	0	68
Chris Melling	London	2012-13	25(12)	5	2	0	24
	Harlequins	2007-11	100(11)	33	6	0	144
	Wigan	2004-05	8(2)	1	3	0	10
Alex Mellor	Huddersfield	2017-18	39(10)	10	0	0	40
	Bradford	2013-14	(10)	0	0	0	0
Joe Mellor	Widnes	2012-18	133(1)	46	0	1	185
	Wigan	2012	1(1)	1	0	0	4
	Harlequins	2011	(1)	0	0	0	0
Paul Mellor	Castleford	2003-04	36(3)	18	0	0	72
James Mendeika	London	2013	4(2)	2	0	0	8
Craig Menkins	Paris	1997	4(5)	0	0	0	0
Luke Menzies	Hull KR	2008	(1)	0	0	0	0
Steve Menzies	Catalans	2011-13	61(6)	30	0	0	120
	Bradford	2009-10	52(1)	24	1	0	98
Gary Mercer	Castleford	2002	(1)	0	0	0	0
	Leeds	1996-97, 2001	40(2)	9	0	0	36
	Warrington	2001	18	2	0	0	8
	Halifax	1998-2001	73(2)	16	0	0	64
Tony Mestrov	London	1996-97, 2001	59(8)	4	0	0	16
	Wigan	1998-2000	39(39)	3	0	0	12
Keiran Meyer	London	1996	4	1	0	0	4
Brad Meyers	Bradford	2005-06	40(11)	13	0	0	52
Steve Michaels	Hull	2015-17	68(1)	26	0	0	104
Gary Middlehurst	Widnes	2004	(2)	0	0	0	0
Simon Middleton	Castleford	1996-97	19(3)	8	0	0	32
Constantine Mika	Hull KR	2012-13	45(4)	9	0	0	36
Daryl Millard	Catalans	2011-14	91	38	1	0	154
	Wakefield	2010-11	21(1)	11	0	0	44
Shane Millard	Wigan	2007	19(6)	3	0	0	12
	Leeds	2006	6(21)	3	0	0	12
	Widnes	2003-05	69	23	0	0	92
	London	1998-2001	72(14)	11	1	0	46
Jack Miller	Huddersfield	2013	1	0	1	0	2
Jacob Miller	Wakefield	2015-18	96(3)	35	17	4	178
	Hull	2013-14	20	6	9	0	42
Grant Millington	Castleford	2012-18	124(55)	26	0	0	104
David Mills	Harlequins	2006-07, 2010	25(32)	2	0	0	8
	Hull KR	2008-09	20(11)	1	0	0	4
	Widnes	2002-05	17(77)	8	0	0	32
Lewis Mills	Celtic	2009	(4)	0	0	0	0
Adam Milner	Castleford	2010-18	138(63)	31	1	0	126
Lee Milner	Halifax	1999	(1)	0	0	0	0
Hakim Miloudi	Hull	2018	11(2)	5	1	0	22
Elliot Minchella	Leeds	2013-14	(6)	1	0	0	4
Mark Minichiello	Hull	2015-18	95(3)	18	0	0	72
Greg Minikin	Castleford	2016-18	60(2)	30	0	0	120

PLAYER	CLUB	YEAR	APP	TRIES	GOALS	FG	PTS
Thomas Minns	Hull KR	2016, 2018	24(1)	14	0	0	56
	London	2014	23	6	0	0	24
	Leeds	2013	2(1)	1	0	0	4
John Minto	London	1996	13	4	0	0	16
Lee Mitchell	Castleford	2012	13(10)	2	0	0	8
	Warrington	2007-11	8(27)	4	0	0	16
	Harlequins	2011	11(1)	1	0	0	4
Sam Moa	Catalans	2017-18	42(4)	6	0	0	24
	Hull	2009-12	29(44)	6	0	0	24
Martin Moana	Salford	2004	6(3)	1	0	0	4
	Halifax	1996-2001, 2003	126(22)	62	0	1	249
	Wakefield	2002	19(2)	10	0	0	40
	Huddersfield	2001	3(3)	2	0	0	8
Adam Mogg	Catalans	2007-10	74	19	0	1	77
Jon Molloy	Wakefield	2013-16	25(18)	5	0	0	20
	Huddersfield	2011-12	2(1)	0	0	0	0
Steve Molloy	Huddersfield	2000-01	26(20)	3	0	0	12
	Sheffield	1998-99	32(17)	3	0	0	12
Chris Molyneux	Huddersfield	2000-01	1(18)	0	0	0	0
	Sheffield	1999	1(2)	0	0	0	0
Joel Monaghan	Castleford	2016-17	29(3)	13	0	0	52
	Warrington	2011-15	127	125	2	0	504
Michael Monaghan	Warrington	2008-14	143(28)	31	0	4	128
Joel Moon	Leeds	2013-18	136(1)	61	0	0	244
	Salford	2012	17	9	0	0	36
Adrian Moore	Huddersfield	1998-99	1(4)	0	0	0	0
Danny Moore	London	2000	7	0	0	0	0
	Wigan	1998-99	49(3)	18	0	0	72
Gareth Moore	Wakefield	2011	5	1	14	1	33
Jason Moore	Workington	1996	(5)	0	0	0	0
Richard Moore	Wakefield	2007-10, 2014	52(57)	10	0	0	40
	Leeds	2012-13	3(27)	1	0	0	4
	Crusaders	2011	11(10)	1	0	0	4
	Leigh	2005	2(5)	0	0	0	0
	Bradford	2002-04	1(26)	0	0	0	0
	London	2002, 2004	5(9)	2	0	0	8
Scott Moore	Wakefield	2015-16	12(2)	0	0	0	0
	Castleford	2008, 2015	24(6)	2	0	0	8
	London	2014	26	3	0	0	12
	Huddersfield	2009, 2012	29(7)	9	0	0	36
	Widnes	2012	3(3)	0	0	0	0
	St Helens	2004-07, 2010-11	29(37)	9	0	0	36
Junior Moors	Castleford	2015-18	39(51)	15	0	0	60
Dennis Moran	Wigan	2005-06	39	17	1	1	71
	London	2001-04	107(2)	74	2	5	305
Kieran Moran	Hull KR	2016	(5)	0	0	0	0
Ryan Morgan	St Helens	2017-18	46	22	0	0	88
Willie Morganson	Sheffield	1997-98	18(12)	5	3	0	26
Paul Moriarty	Halifax	1996	3(2)	1	0	0	4
Adrian Morley	Salford	2014-15	31(14)	2	0	0	8
	Warrington	2007-13	135(21)	8	0	0	32
	Bradford	2005	2(4)	0	0	0	0
	Leeds	1996-2000	95(14)	25	0	0	100
Chris Morley	Salford	1999	3(5)	0	0	0	0
	Warrington	1998	2(8)	0	0	0	0
	St Helens	1996-97	21(16)	4	0	0	16
Frazer Morris	Wakefield	2016	(1)	0	0	0	0
Glenn Morrison	Wakefield	2010-11	43(1)	9	0	0	36
	Bradford	2007-09	48(2)	19	0	0	76
Iain Morrison	Hull KR	2007	5(6)	1	0	0	4
	Huddersfield	2003-05	11(23)	0	0	0	0
	London	2001	(1)	0	0	0	0
Daniel Mortimer	Leigh	2017	3	0	0	0	0
Dale Morton	Wakefield	2009-11	22(3)	8	5	0	42
Gareth Morton	Hull KR	2007	7(4)	3	23	0	58
	Leeds	2001-02	1(1)	0	0	0	0
Kieren Moss	Hull KR	2018	2(1)	4	0	0	16
Lee Mossop	Salford	2017-18	26(1)	0	0	0	0
	Wigan	2008-13, 2015-16	80(65)	11	0	0	44
	Huddersfield	2009	1(4)	1	0	0	4
Aaron Moule	Salford	2006-07	45	17	0	0	68
	Widnes	2004-05	29	12	0	0	48
Bradley Moules	Wakefield	2016	(1)	0	0	0	0
Wilfried Moulinec	Paris	1996	1	0	0	0	0
Gregory Mounis	Catalans	2006-16	149(105)	27	19	0	146
Arthur Mourgue	Catalans	2018	1	0	0	0	0
Mark Moxon	Salford	1998-2001	20(5)	1	0	1	5
Robbie Mulhern	Hull KR	2016, 2018	21(14)	3	0	0	12
	Leeds	2014-15	(5)	0	0	0	0
Anthony Mullally	Leeds	2016-18	10(48)	9	0	0	36
	Wakefield	2015	(2)	0	0	0	0
	Huddersfield	2013-15	12(24)	5	0	0	20
	Bradford	2014	1(5)	0	0	0	0
	Widnes	2012	(9)	0	0	0	0
Jake Mullaney	Salford	2014	12	2	24	0	56

PLAYER	CLUB	YEAR	APP	TRIES	GOALS	FG	PTS
Craig Mullen	Wigan	2018	1(1)	0	0	0	0
Brett Mullins	Leeds	2001	5(3)	1	0	0	4
Damian Munro	Widnes	2002	8(2)	1	0	0	4
	Halifax	1996-97	9(6)	8	0	0	32
Matt Munro	Oldham	1996-97	26(5)	8	0	0	32
Ben Murdoch-Masila	Warrington	2018	8(14)	6	0	0	24
	Salford	2016-17	46(1)	15	0	0	60
Craig Murdock	Salford	2000	(2)	0	0	0	0
	Hull	1998-99	21(6)	8	0	2	34
	Wigan	1996-98	18(17)	14	0	0	56
Aaron Murphy	Huddersfield	2012-18	148	69	0	0	276
	Wakefield	2008-11	57(2)	12	0	0	48
Jack Murphy	Wigan	2012, 2014	3	1	0	0	4
	Salford	2013	10	3	1	0	14
Jamie Murphy	Crusaders	2011	(2)	0	0	0	0
Jobe Murphy	Bradford	2013	(4)	0	0	0	0
Justin Murphy	Catalans	2006-08	59	49	0	0	196
	Widnes	2004	5	1	0	0	4
Daniel Murray	Salford	2017-18	9(8)	0	0	0	0
Doc Murray	Warrington	1997	(2)	0	0	0	0
	Wigan	1997	6(2)	0	0	0	0
Scott Murrell	Hull KR	2007-12	114(24)	24	26	1	149
	Leeds	2005	(1)	0	0	0	0
	London	2004	3(3)	2	0	0	8
David Mycoe	Sheffield	1996-97	12(13)	1	0	0	4
Richie Myler	Leeds	2018	20	4	6	0	28
	Catalans	2016-17	40	21	2	0	88
	Warrington	2010-15	127(4)	69	1	1	279
	Salford	2009	18	11	0	0	44
Rob Myler	Oldham	1996-97	19(2)	6	0	0	24
Stephen Myler	Salford	2006	4(8)	1	15	0	34
	Widnes	2003-05	35(14)	8	74	0	180
Vinny Myler	Salford	2004	(4)	0	0	0	0
	Bradford	2003	(1)	0	0	0	0
Matt Nable	London	1997	2(2)	1	0	0	4
Brad Nairn	Workington	1996	14	4	0	0	16
Ben Nakubuwai	Salford	2018	5(13)	2	0	0	8
Frank Napoli	London	2000	14(6)	2	0	0	8
Carlo Napolitano	Salford	2000	(3)	1	0	0	4
Stephen Nash	Castleford	2012	3(4)	0	0	0	0
	Salford	2007, 2009	2(18)	1	0	0	4
	Widnes	2005	4(1)	0	0	0	0
Curtis Naughton	Leigh	2017	5	3	0	0	12
	Hull	2015-16	26	13	1	0	54
	Bradford	2013	1	0	0	0	0
Romain Navarrete	Wigan	2017-18	20(14)	0	0	0	0
	Catalans	2016-17	1(12)	0	0	0	0
Jim Naylor	Halifax	2000	7(6)	2	0	0	8
Scott Naylor	Salford	1997-98, 2004	30(1)	9	0	0	36
	Bradford	1999-2003	127(1)	51	0	0	204
Adam Neal	Salford	2010-13	17(28)	0	0	0	0
Mike Neal	Salford	1998	(1)	0	0	0	0
	Oldham	1996-97	6(4)	3	0	0	12
Jonathan Neill	Huddersfield	1998-99	20(11)	0	0	0	0
	St Helens	1996	1	0	0	0	0
Chris Nero	Salford	2011-13	31(16)	7	0	0	28
	Bradford	2008-10	65(5)	24	0	0	96
	Huddersfield	2004-07	97(8)	38	0	0	152
Jason Netherton	Hull KR	2007-14	60(74)	4	0	0	16
	London	2003-04	6	0	0	0	0
	Halifax	2002	2(3)	0	0	0	0
	Leeds	2001	(3)	0	0	0	0
Kirk Netherton	Castleford	2009-10	5(23)	3	0	0	12
	Hull KR	2007-08	9(15)	2	0	0	8
Paul Newlove	Castleford	2004	5	1	0	0	4
	St Helens	1996-2003	162	106	0	0	424
Richard Newlove	Wakefield	2003	17(5)	8	0	0	32
Harry Newman	Leeds	2017-18	4	0	0	0	0
Clint Newton	Hull KR	2008-11	90(3)	37	0	0	148
Terry Newton	Wakefield	2010	(2)	0	0	0	0
	Bradford	2006-09	83(6)	26	0	0	104
	Wigan	2000-05	157(9)	62	0	0	248
	Leeds	1996-1999	55(14)	4	0	0	16
Gene Ngamu	Huddersfield	1999-2000	29(2)	9	67	0	170
Danny Nicklas	Hull	2010, 2012	2(8)	0	0	0	0
Sonny Nickle	St Helens	1999-2002	86(18)	14	0	0	56
	Bradford	1996-98	25(16)	9	0	0	36
Jason Nicol	Salford	2000-02	32(7)	11	0	0	44
Tawera Nikau	Warrington	2000-01	51	7	0	0	28
Rob Nolan	Hull	1998-99	20(11)	6	0	0	24
Paul Noone	Harlequins	2006	5(2)	0	0	0	0
	Warrington	2000-06	60(59)	12	20	0	88
Chris Norman	Halifax	2003	13(3)	2	0	0	8
Dan Norman	Widnes	2018	(1)	0	0	0	0
Paul Norman	Oldham	1996	(1)	0	0	0	0
Andy Northey	St Helens	1996-97	8(17)	2	0	0	8

Super League Players 1996-2018

PLAYER	CLUB	YEAR	APP	TRIES	GOALS	FG	PTS
Danny Nutley	Castleford	2006	28	3	0	0	12
	Warrington	1998-2001	94(1)	3	0	0	12
Tony Nuttall	Oldham	1996-97	1(7)	0	0	0	0
Frank-Paul Nuuausala							
	Wigan	2016-18	34(8)	2	0	0	8
Levy Nzoungou	Salford	2018	(3)	0	0	0	0
Will Oakes	Hull KR	2016, 2018	5	2	0	0	8
Adam O'Brien	Huddersfield	2017-18	25(20)	8	0	0	32
	Bradford	2011-14	12(29)	6	0	0	24
Clinton O'Brien	Wakefield	2003	(2)	0	0	0	0
Gareth O'Brien	Salford	2016-18	49(3)	12	105	2	260
	Warrington	2011-15	48(3)	16	69	3	205
	St Helens	2013	7	0	25	0	50
	Castleford	2013	2	0	0	1	1
	Widnes	2012	4	0	15	0	30
Sam Obst	Hull	2011	17(6)	6	0	0	24
	Wakefield	2005-11	100(28)	40	7	0	174
Jamie O'Callaghan	London	2012-14	44(2)	4	0	0	16
	Harlequins	2008-11	54(3)	12	0	0	48
Eamon O'Carroll	Widnes	2012-17	58(11)	3	0	0	12
	Hull	2012	1(9)	0	0	0	0
	Wigan	2006-11	2(59)	3	0	0	12
Matt O'Connor	Paris	1997	11(4)	1	26	2	58
Terry O'Connor	Widnes	2005	2	0	0	0	8
	Wigan	1996-2004	177(45)	9	0	0	36
Jarrod O'Doherty	Huddersfield	2003	26	3	0	0	12
David O'Donnell	Paris	1997	21	3	0	0	12
Luke O'Donnell	Huddersfield	2011-13	22(2)	2	0	0	8
Martin Offiah	Salford	2000-01	41	20	0	2	82
	London	1996-99	29(3)	21	0	0	84
	Wigan	1996	8	7	0	0	28
Mark O'Halloran	London	2004-05	34(3)	10	0	0	40
Ryan O'Hara	Hull KR	2012	8(7)	1	0	0	4
	Crusaders	2010-11	41(8)	3	0	0	12
	Celtic	2009	27	3	0	0	12
Hefin O'Hare	Huddersfield	2001, 2003-05	72(10)	27	0	0	108
Edwin Okanga-Ajwang							
	Salford	2013	2	0	0	0	0
Hitro Okesene	Hull	1998	21(1)	0	0	0	0
Anderson Okiwe	Sheffield	1997	1	0	0	0	0
Tom Olbison	Widnes	2017-18	17(22)	4	0	0	16
	Bradford	2009-14	55(26)	11	0	0	44
Michael Oldfield	Catalans	2014-15	41	28	0	0	112
Mikolaj Oledzki	Leeds	2017-18	6(13)	1	0	0	4
Jamie Olejnik	Paris	1997	11	8	0	0	32
Aaron Ollett	Hull KR	2013-15	5(16)	1	0	0	4
Kevin O'Loughlin	Halifax	1997-98	2(4)	0	0	0	0
	St Helens	1997	(3)	0	0	0	0
Sean O'Loughlin	Wigan	2002-18	354(22)	70	3	2	288
Derrell Olpherts	Salford	2018	13	2	0	0	8
Mark O'Meley	Hull	2010-13	70(13)	13	0	0	52
Jules O'Neill	Widnes	2003-05	57(3)	14	158	7	379
	Wakefield	2005	10(2)	2	4	0	16
	Wigan	2002-03	29(1)	12	72	0	192
Julian O'Neill	Widnes	2002-03	57(39)	3	0	0	12
	Wakefield	2001	24(1)	2	0	0	8
	St Helens	1997-2000	95(8)	5	0	0	20
Mark O'Neill	Hull KR	2007	17	5	0	0	20
	Leeds	2006	1(8)	0	0	0	0
Steve O'Neill	Gateshead	1999	1(1)	0	0	0	0
Tom O'Reilly	Warrington	2001-02	8(6)	1	0	0	4
Matt Orford	Bradford	2010	12	3	31	2	76
Jack Ormondroyd	Leeds	2017-18	3(9)	0	0	0	0
Gene Ormsby	Huddersfield	2016-17	8	4	0	0	16
	Warrington	2014-16	37	26	0	0	104
Chris Orr	Huddersfield	1998	19(3)	2	0	0	8
Danny Orr	Castleford	1997-2003, 2011-12	197(23)	75	308	3	919
	Harlequins	2007-10	90(4)	13	96	0	244
	Wigan	2004-06	66(2)	18	12	0	96
Gareth Owen	Salford	2010, 2012-13	4(32)	6	0	0	24
Nick Owen	Leigh	2005	8(1)	1	11	0	26
Richard Owen	Wakefield	2014-15	29(1)	9	0	0	36
	Castleford	2008-14	109(3)	57	0	0	228
Jack Owens	St Helens	2016-17	31	8	14	0	60
	Widnes	2012-15	53(1)	26	103	0	310
Lopini Paea	Wakefield	2015	1(3)	0	0	0	0
	Catalans	2011-14	41(41)	9	0	0	36
Mickey Paea	Hull	2014-15, 2018	57(16)	5	0	0	20
	Hull KR	2012-13	34(17)	5	0	0	20
Liam Paisley	Wigan	2018	2(2)	1	0	0	4
Mathias Pala	Catalans	2011-15	28(1)	4	0	0	16
Iafeta Palea'aesina	Hull	2014-16	(47)	1	0	0	4
	Salford	2011-12	4(37)	3	0	0	12
	Wigan	2006-10	55(77)	16	0	0	64
Jason Palmada	Workington	1996	12	2	0	0	8
Junior Paramore	Castleford	1996	5(5)	3	0	0	12

PLAYER	CLUB	YEAR	APP	TRIES	GOALS	FG	PTS
Matt Parcell	Leeds	2017-18	46(5)	22	0	0	88
Paul Parker	Hull	1999-2002	23(18)	9	0	0	36
Rob Parker	Castleford	2011	4(2)	2	0	0	8
	Salford	2009-11	23(14)	4	0	0	16
	Warrington	2006-08	10(56)	6	0	0	24
	Bradford	2000, 2002-05	19(76)	14	0	0	56
	London	2001	9	1	0	0	4
Wayne Parker	Halifax	1996-97	12(1)	0	0	0	0
Ian Parry	Warrington	2001	(1)	0	0	0	0
Jules Parry	Paris	1996	10(2)	0	0	0	0
Oliver Partington	Wigan	2018	(5)	0	0	0	0
Regis Pastre-Courtine							
	Paris	1996	4(3)	4	0	0	16
Cory Paterson	Leigh	2017	13	2	0	0	8
	Salford	2015	14(1)	7	6	0	40
	Hull KR	2013	15	7	0	0	28
Andrew Patmore	Oldham	1996	8(5)	3	0	0	12
Larne Patrick	Castleford	2016-17	14(7)	1	0	0	4
	Huddersfield	2009-14, 2016	30(107)	30	0	0	120
	Wigan	2015	7(20)	4	0	0	16
Luke Patten	Salford	2011-12	53	16	0	0	64
Declan Patton	Warrington	2015-18	39(17)	9	64	4	168
Henry Paul	Harlequins	2006-08	60(1)	8	94	2	222
	Bradford	1999-2001	81(5)	29	350	6	822
	Wigan	1996-98	60	37	23	0	194
Junior Paul	London	1996	3	1	0	0	4
Robbie Paul	Salford	2009	2(24)	2	0	0	8
	Huddersfield	2006-07	44(8)	7	0	0	28
	Bradford	1996-2005	198(31)	121	3	0	490
Pauli Pauli	Wakefield	2018	5(22)	8	0	0	32
Jason Payne	Castleford	2006	1(1)	0	0	0	0
Danny Peacock	Bradford	1997-99	32(2)	15	0	0	60
Jamie Peacock	Leeds	2006-15	234(16)	24	0	0	96
	Bradford	1999-2005	163(25)	38	0	0	152
Martin Pearson	Wakefield	2001	21(1)	3	60	3	135
	Halifax	1997-98, 2000	55(6)	24	181	0	458
	Sheffield	1999	17(6)	9	36	2	110
Jacques Pech	Paris	1996	16	0	0	0	0
Mike Pechey	Warrington	1998	6(3)	2	0	0	8
Bill Peden	London	2003	21(3)	7	0	0	28
Adam Peek	Crusaders	2010-11	5(22)	1	0	0	4
	Celtic	2009	5(12)	3	0	0	12
Eloi Pelissier	Leigh	2017	4(16)	0	0	0	0
	Catalans	2011-16	38(104)	23	0	1	93
Dimitri Pelo	Catalans	2007-10	79	37	0	0	148
Sean Penkywicz	Huddersfield	2004-05	21(11)	7	0	0	28
	Halifax	2000-03	29(27)	8	0	0	32
Julian Penni	Salford	1998-99	4	0	0	0	0
Kevin Penny	Warrington	2006-09, 2014-17	83(1)	52	0	0	208
	Wakefield	2011	5	1	0	0	4
	Harlequins	2010	5	3	0	0	12
Lee Penny	Warrington	1996-2003	140(5)	54	0	0	216
Paul Penrice	Workington	1996	11(2)	2	0	0	8
Chris Percival	Widnes	2002-03	26	6	0	0	24
Mark Percival	St Helens	2013-18	119(2)	65	205	0	670
Apollo Perelini	St Helens	1996-2000	103(16)	27	0	0	108
Ugo Perez	Catalans	2015, 2017-18	2(5)	0	0	0	0
Mark Perrett	Halifax	1996-97	15(4)	4	0	0	16
Josh Perry	St Helens	2011-13	32(9)	2	0	0	8
Shane Perry	Catalans	2009	8(8)	1	0	0	4
Adam Peters	Paris	1997	16(3)	0	0	0	0
Dominic Peters	London	1998-2003	58(11)	12	0	0	48
Mike Peters	Warrington	2000	2(12)	1	0	0	4
	Halifax	2000	1	0	0	0	0
Willie Peters	Widnes	2004	9	3	0	2	14
	Wigan	2000	29	15	5	6	76
	Gateshead	1999	27	11	1	6	52
Dave Petersen	Hull KR	2012	2(2)	1	0	0	4
Matt Petersen	Wakefield	2008-09	14	3	0	0	12
Nathaniel Peteru	Leeds	2018	1(3)	0	0	0	0
Adrian Petrie	Workington	1996	(1)	0	0	0	0
Eddy Pettybourne	Wigan	2014	1(15)	0	0	0	0
Dominique Peyroux	St Helens	2016-18	54(16)	8	0	0	32
Cameron Phelps	Widnes	2012-15	66(1)	23	2	0	96
	Hull	2011	19	2	0	0	8
	Wigan	2008-10	43(1)	14	4	0	64
Joe Philbin	Warrington	2014-18	10(63)	8	0	0	32
Rowland Phillips	Workington	1996	22	1	0	0	4
Nathan Picchi	Leeds	1996	(1)	0	0	0	0
Ian Pickavance	Hull	1999	4(2)	2	0	0	8
	Huddersfield	1999	3(14)	0	0	0	0
	St Helens	1996-98	12(44)	6	0	0	24
James Pickering	Castleford	1999	1(19)	0	0	0	0
Steve Pickersgill	Widnes	2012-13	27(8)	1	0	0	4
	Warrington	2005-09	1(36)	0	0	0	0

190

PLAYER	CLUB	YEAR	APP	TRIES	GOALS	FG	PTS
Nick Pinkney	Salford	2000-02	64	29	0	0	116
	Halifax	1999	26(2)	13	0	0	52
	Sheffield	1997-98	33	10	0	0	40
Mikhail Piskunov	Paris	1996	1(1)	1	0	0	4
Darryl Pitt	London	1996	2(16)	4	0	1	17
Jay Pitts	Bradford	2014	15(1)	3	0	0	12
	Hull	2012-14	18(30)	1	0	0	4
	Leeds	2009-12	10(15)	2	0	0	8
	Wakefield	2008-09	9(8)	2	0	0	8
Andy Platt	Salford	1997-98	20(3)	1	0	0	4
Michael Platt	Salford	2001-02, 2014	4(1)	1	0	0	4
	Bradford	2007-13	121(6)	44	0	0	176
	Castleford	2006	26	7	0	0	28
Willie Poching	Leeds	2002-06	58(73)	44	0	0	176
	Wakefield	1999-2001	65(4)	20	0	0	80
Ben Pomeroy	Warrington	2017-18	3(7)	1	0	0	4
	Catalans	2014-15	44	10	0	0	40
Quentin Pongia	Wigan	2003-04	15(10)	0	0	0	0
Justin Poore	Hull KR	2014	7	0	0	0	0
	Wakefield	2013	23	1	0	0	4
Dan Potter	Widnes	2002-03	34(2)	6	0	0	24
	London	2001	1(3)	1	0	0	4
Craig Poucher	Hull	1999-2002	31(5)	5	0	0	20
Andy Powell	Wigan	2013	2(3)	1	0	0	4
Bryn Powell	Salford	2004	1(1)	0	0	0	0
Daio Powell	Sheffield	1999	13(1)	2	0	0	8
	Halifax	1997-98	30(3)	17	0	0	68
Daryl Powell	Leeds	1998-2000	49(30)	12	0	2	50
Sam Powell	Wigan	2012-18	102(46)	19	4	2	86
Karl Pratt	Bradford	2003-05	35(19)	18	0	0	72
	Leeds	1999-2002	62(12)	33	0	0	132
Paul Prescott	Wigan	2004-12	49(75)	4	0	0	16
Steve Prescott	Hull	1998-99, 2001-03	99	46	191	3	569
	Wakefield	2000	22(1)	3	13	0	38
	St Helens	1996-97	32	15	17	0	94
Lee Prest	Workington	1996	(1)	0	0	0	0
Gareth Price	Salford	2002	(2)	0	0	0	0
	London	2002	2(2)	3	0	0	12
	St Helens	1999	(11)	2	0	0	8
Gary Price	Wakefield	1999-2001	55(13)	11	0	0	44
Richard Price	Sheffield	1996	1(2)	0	0	0	0
Tony Priddle	Paris	1997	11(7)	3	0	0	12
Frank Pritchard	Hull	2016	10(13)	4	0	0	16
Karl Pryce	Bradford	2003-06, 2012	47(19)	46	1	0	186
	Harlequins	2011	11(7)	12	0	0	48
	Wigan	2009-10	11(2)	12	0	0	48
Leon Pryce	Hull	2015-16	32(2)	8	0	0	32
	Catalans	2012-14	72(2)	15	0	0	60
	St Helens	2006-11	133(3)	64	0	0	256
	Bradford	1998-2005	159(29)	86	0	0	344
Waine Pryce	Wakefield	2007	10(2)	4	0	0	16
	Castleford	2000-06	97(12)	49	0	0	196
Tony Puletua	Hull KR	2015	7	0	0	0	0
	Salford	2014	16(9)	3	0	0	12
	St Helens	2009-13	108(18)	39	0	0	156
Andrew Purcell	Castleford	2000	15(5)	3	0	0	12
	Hull	1999	27	4	0	0	16
Rob Purdham	Harlequins	2006-11	112(3)	18	131	1	335
	London	2002-05	53(15)	16	2	1	69
Adrian Purtell	Bradford	2012-14	45(1)	16	0	0	64
Luke Quigley	Catalans	2007	16(1)	1	0	0	4
Adam Quinlan	Hull KR	2018	21	10	0	0	40
	St Helens	2015	11	6	0	0	24
Damien Quinn	Celtic	2009	20(1)	4	12	0	40
Scott Quinnell	Wigan	1996	5(3)	1	0	0	4
Florian Quintilla	Catalans	2008-09	1(4)	0	0	0	0
Lee Radford	Hull	1998, 2006-12	138(30)	23	1	0	94
	Bradford	1999-2005	79(65)	18	12	0	96
Kris Radlinski	Wigan	1996-2006	236(1)	134	1	0	538
Sebastien Raguin	Catalans	2007-12	103(22)	28	0	0	112
Adrian Rainey	Castleford	2002	4(7)	1	0	0	4
Andy Raleigh	Wakefield	2012-14	42(21)	9	0	0	36
	Huddersfield	2006-11	74(46)	13	0	0	52
Jean-Luc Ramondou	Paris	1996	1(1)	1	0	0	4
Chad Randall	London	2012-13	29(9)	4	0	0	16
	Harlequins	2006-11	141(2)	37	0	1	149
Craig Randall	Halifax	1999	8(11)	4	0	0	16
	Salford	1997-98	12(18)	4	0	0	16
Tyler Randell	Wakefield	2017-18	26(3)	6	1	0	26
Jordan Rankin	Huddersfield	2018	3	3	9	0	30
	Hull	2014-15	41(6)	20	43	0	166
Scott Ranson	Oldham	1996-97	19(2)	7	0	0	28
Aaron Raper	Castleford	1999-2001	48(4)	4	2	1	21

PLAYER	CLUB	YEAR	APP	TRIES	GOALS	FG	PTS
Sam Rapira	Huddersfield	2016-17	29(19)	3	0	0	12
Steve Rapira	Salford	2014	5(13)	0	0	0	0
Stefan Ratchford	Warrington	2012-18	173(10)	67	191	2	652
	Salford	2007,2009-11	65(5)	23	20	0	132
Mike Ratu	Hull KR	2010	5	1	0	0	4
	Leeds	2007,2009	1(5)	1	0	0	4
Paul Rauhihi	Warrington	2006-09	67(20)	10	0	0	40
Ben Rauter	Wakefield	2001	15(6)	4	0	0	16
Nick Rawsthorne	Leigh	2017	1	1	0	0	4
	Hull	2017	3	2	2	0	12
Gareth Raynor	Bradford	2011	18	4	0	0	16
	Crusaders	2010	7	4	0	0	16
	Hull	2001-09	186	102	0	0	408
	Leeds	2000	(3)	0	0	0	0
Tony Rea	London	1996	22	4	0	0	16
Stuart Reardon	Crusaders	2011	25	11	0	0	44
	Bradford	2003-05, 2010	78(11)	37	0	0	148
	Warrington	2006-08	48	12	0	0	48
	Salford	2002	7(1)	3	0	0	12
Mark Reber	Wigan	1999-2000	9(9)	5	0	0	20
Alan Reddicliffe	Warrington	2001	1	0	0	0	0
Tahi Reihana	Bradford	1997-98	17(21)	0	0	0	0
Paul Reilly	Wakefield	2008	5(2)	1	0	0	4
	Huddersfield	1999-2001, 2003-07	150(8)	35	1	0	142
Robert Relf	Widnes	2002-04	68(2)	5	0	0	20
Steve Renouf	Wigan	2000-01	55	40	0	0	160
Steele Retchless	London	1998-2004	177(6)	13	0	0	52
Ben Reynolds	Leigh	2017	16	6	48	0	120
	Castleford	2013-14	1(3)	0	0	0	0
Scott Rhodes	Hull	2000	2	0	0	0	0
Phillipe Ricard	Paris	1996-97	2	0	0	0	0
Andy Rice	Huddersfield	2000-01	2(13)	1	0	0	4
Basil Richards	Huddersfield	1998-99	28(17)	1	0	0	4
Craig Richards	Oldham	1996	1	0	0	0	0
Greg Richards	Leigh	2017	(1)	0	0	0	0
	St Helens	2013-17	19(49)	1	0	0	4
Pat Richards	Catalans	2016	19	9	69	0	174
	Wigan	2006-13	199	147	759	4	2110
Andy Richardson	Hudds-Sheff	2000	(2)	0	0	0	0
Danny Richardson	St Helens	2017-18	42(2)	7	135	8	306
Sean Richardson	Widnes	2002	2(18)	1	0	0	4
	Wakefield	1999	5(1)	0	0	0	0
	Castleford	1996-97	3(8)	1	0	0	4
Mark Riddell	Wigan	2009-10	45(11)	5	2	0	24
Martyn Ridyard	Huddersfield	2017	7	1	26	0	56
	Leigh	2017	4	0	2	0	4
Neil Rigby	St Helens	2006	(1)	0	0	0	0
Shane Rigon	Bradford	2001	14(11)	12	0	0	48
Craig Rika	Halifax	1996	2	0	0	0	0
Chris Riley	Wakefield	2014-15	44	16	0	0	64
	Warrington	2005-14	146(10)	102	0	0	408
	Harlequins	2011	3	2	0	0	8
Glenn Riley	Warrington	2013-14	(15)	0	0	0	0
Peter Riley	Workington	1996	7(5)	0	0	0	0
Julien Rinaldi	London	2012	4(16)	1	0	0	4
	Wakefield	2002,2010-11	27(9)	6	0	0	24
	Bradford	2009	(7)	1	0	0	4
	Harlequins	2007-08	4(43)	9	0	0	36
	Catalans	2006	16(6)	3	1	0	14
Dean Ripley	Castleford	2004	3(4)	1	0	0	4
Leroy Rivett	Warrington	2002	9	1	0	0	4
	Hudds-Sheff	2000	5(1)	1	0	0	4
	Leeds	1996-2000	39(15)	21	0	0	84
Jason Roach	Warrington	1998-99	29(7)	15	0	0	60
	Castleford	1997	7	4	0	0	16
Ben Roarty	Castleford	2006	11(6)	2	0	0	8
	Huddersfield	2003-05	52	5	0	0	20
Amos Roberts	Wigan	2009-11	47(2)	27	5	0	118
Ben Roberts	Castleford	2015-18	60(14)	20	0	2	82
Mark Roberts	Wigan	2003	(3)	0	0	0	0
Oliver Roberts	Huddersfield	2016-18	38(32)	11	0	0	44
	Bradford	2013-14	(5)	0	0	0	0
Robert Roberts	Huddersfield	2001	(1)	0	0	0	0
	Halifax	2000	(3)	0	0	0	0
	Hull	1999	24(2)	4	13	4	46
Tyrone Roberts	Warrington	2018	28	5	32	1	85
Michael Robertson	London	2012-13	35	17	0	0	68
Stan Robin	Catalans	2015-16	5(2)	1	0	0	4
Chad Robinson	Harlequins	2009	13(1)	2	0	0	8
Connor Robinson	Hull KR	2014-15	(2)	0	0	0	0
Craig Robinson	Wakefield	2005	(1)	0	0	0	0
Jason Robinson	Wigan	1996-2000	126(1)	87	0	1	349
Jeremy Robinson	Paris	1997	10(3)	1	21	0	46
John Robinson	Widnes	2003-04	7	1	0	0	4
Luke Robinson	Huddersfield	2008-15	191(18)	45	4	0	188
	Salford	2005-07	79	28	10	2	134
	Wigan	2002-04	17(25)	9	6	1	49
	Castleford	2004	9	4	3	0	22

191

Super League Players 1996-2018

PLAYER	CLUB	YEAR	APP	TRIES	GOALS	FG	PTS
Will Robinson	Hull	2000	22	4	0	0	16
	Gateshead	1999	28	9	0	0	36
Ash Robson	Castleford	2015	3	1	0	0	4
James Roby	St Helens	2004-18	263(123)	93	1	0	374
Mike Roby	St Helens	2004	(1)	0	0	0	0
Colton Roche	Huddersfield	2018	1(6)	0	0	0	0
Carl Roden	Warrington	1997	1	0	0	0	0
Shane Rodney	London	2012-13	28	3	12	0	36
Matt Rodwell	Warrington	2002	10	3	0	0	12
Darren Rogers	Castleford	1999-2004	162(1)	81	0	0	324
	Salford	1997-98	42	16	0	0	64
Arthur Romano	Catalans	2017	2	0	0	0	0
Jamie Rooney	Wakefield	2003-09	113(7)	60	321	21	903
	Castleford	2001	2(1)	0	6	0	12
Jonathan Roper	Castleford	2001	13	7	12	0	52
	Salford	2000	1(4)	1	3	0	10
	London	2000	4	0	0	0	0
	Warrington	1996-2000	75(8)	33	71	0	274
Scott Roskell	London	1996-97	30(2)	16	0	0	64
Steve Rosolen	London	1996-98	25(9)	10	0	0	40
Adam Ross	London	1996	(1)	0	0	0	0
Paul Round	Castleford	1996	(3)	0	0	0	0
Steve Rowlands	Widnes	2004-05	18(3)	2	15	0	38
	St Helens	2003	(1)	0	0	0	0
Paul Rowley	Leigh	2005	15(7)	3	0	0	12
	Huddersfield	2001	24	3	0	0	12
	Halifax	1996-2000	107(3)	27	1	3	113
Nigel Roy	London	2001-04	100	39	0	0	156
Nicky Royle	Widnes	2004	13	7	0	0	28
Shad Royston	Bradford	2011	17(1)	10	0	0	40
Chris Rudd	Warrington	1996-98	31(17)	10	16	0	72
Sean Rudder	Catalans	2006	22(1)	6	0	0	24
	Castleford	2004	9(3)	2	0	0	8
Charly Runciman	Widnes	2016-18	67	9	0	0	36
James Rushforth	Halifax	1997	(4)	0	0	0	0
Danny Russell	Huddersfield	1998-2000	50(13)	8	0	0	32
Ian Russell	Oldham	1997	1(3)	1	0	0	4
	Paris	1996	3	0	0	0	0
Matthew Russell	Warrington	2014-18	77(4)	22	0	0	88
	Hull	2012	6	0	0	0	0
	Wigan	2012	2	3	0	0	12
Oliver Russell	Huddersfield	2018	6	0	8	1	17
Richard Russell	Castleford	1996-98	37(4)	2	0	0	8
Robert Russell	Salford	1998-99	2(1)	0	1	0	2
Sean Rutgerson	Salford	2004-06	60(9)	4	0	0	16
Chris Ryan	London	1998-99	44(3)	17	10	0	88
Matt Ryan	Wakefield	2014-15	28(12)	7	0	0	28
Sean Ryan	Castleford	2004	11(5)	2	0	0	8
	Hull	2002-03	53	8	0	0	32
Justin Ryder	Wakefield	2004	19(3)	11	0	0	44
Jason Ryles	Catalans	2009	19(2)	2	0	0	8
Setaimata Sa	Widnes	2016	7(5)	3	0	0	12
	Hull	2014-15	18(6)	6	0	0	24
	Catalans	2010-12	58(5)	21	0	0	84
Teddy Sadaoui	Catalans	2006	7	0	0	0	0
Liam Salter	Hull KR	2012-16, 2018	83(3)	17	0	0	68
Matt Salter	London	1997-99	14(34)	0	0	0	0
Ben Sammut	Hull	2000	20	4	67	0	150
	Gateshead	1999	26(2)	6	17	0	58
Jarrod Sammut	Wakefield	2014-15	19(1)	9	52	0	140
	Bradford	2012-13	35(3)	28	47	1	207
	Crusaders	2010-11	17(16)	17	0	0	68
Dean Sampson	Castleford	1996-2003	124(28)	24	0	0	96
Paul Sampson	London	2004	1(2)	1	0	0	4
	Wakefield	2000	17	8	0	0	32
Lee Sanderson	London	2004	1(5)	1	7	0	18
Chris Sandow	Warrington	2015-16	27(1)	11	26	1	97
Jason Sands	Paris	1996-97	28	0	0	0	0
Mitchell Sargent	Castleford	2008-10	37(21)	6	0	0	24
Dan Sarginson	Wigan	2014-16, 2018	91(2)	27	0	0	108
	London	2012-13	35(1)	10	0	0	40
	Harlequins	2011	8	5	0	0	20
Matt Sarsfield	Salford	2016	2(2)	1	0	0	4
Junior Sa'u	Salford	2014-18	108	45	0	0	180
Andre Savelio	Warrington	2017	3(14)	4	0	0	16
	Castleford	2016	6(1)	1	0	0	4
	St Helens	2014-16	12(25)	2	0	0	8
Lokeni Savelio	Halifax	2000	2(11)	0	0	0	0
	Salford	1997-98	18(20)	0	0	0	0
Tom Saxton	Salford	2007	5	0	0	0	0
	Wakefield	2006	9(6)	2	0	0	8
	Hull	2005	19(8)	3	0	0	12
	Castleford	2002-04	37(12)	11	0	0	44
Jonathan Scales	Halifax	2000	1	0	0	0	0
	Bradford	1996-98	46(4)	24	0	0	96
Andrew Schick	Castleford	1996-98	45(13)	10	0	0	40
Clinton Schifcofske	Crusaders	2010-11	44	5	115	0	250
Garry Schofield	Huddersfield	1998	(2)	0	0	0	0
Gary Schubert	Workington	1996	(1)	0	0	0	0
Matt Schultz	Hull	1998-99	23(9)	2	0	0	8
	Leeds	1996	2(4)	0	0	0	0
John Schuster	Halifax	1996-97	31	9	127	3	293
Cameron Scott	Hull	2018	6	0	0	0	0
Nick Scruton	Hull KR	2018	7(10)	0	0	0	0
	Wakefield	2014-16	62(3)	9	0	0	36
	Bradford	2009-14	70(27)	5	0	0	20
	Leeds	2002, 2004-08	11(53)	3	0	0	12
	Hull	2004	2(16)	3	0	0	12
Danny Sculthorpe	Huddersfield	2009	5(8)	0	0	0	0
	Wakefield	2007-09	14(28)	1	0	0	4
	Castleford	2006	18(1)	4	0	1	17
	Wigan	2002-05	13(49)	7	0	0	28
Paul Sculthorpe	St Helens	1998-2008	223(4)	94	356	7	1095
	Warrington	1996-97	40	6	0	0	24
Mick Seaby	London	1997	3(2)	1	0	0	4
Danny Seal	Halifax	1996-99	8(17)	3	0	0	12
Matt Seers	Wakefield	2003	11(1)	2	0	0	8
James Segeyaro	Leeds	2016	3	1	0	0	4
Paul Seguier	Catalans	2016-17	(7)	0	0	0	0
Anthony Seibold	London	1999-2000	33(19)	5	0	0	20
Jesse Sene-Lefao	Castleford	2017-18	37(16)	8	0	0	32
Innes Senior	Huddersfield	2018	8	4	0	0	16
Keith Senior	Leeds	1999-2011	319(2)	159	0	0	636
	Sheffield	1996-99	90(2)	40	0	0	160
Louis Senior	Huddersfield	2018	3	1	0	0	4
Fili Seru	Hull	1998-99	37(1)	13	0	0	52
Anthony Seuseu	Halifax	2003	1(11)	1	0	0	4
Jerry Seuseu	Wigan	2005-06	29(9)	1	0	0	4
Brett Seymour	Hull	2012-13	26(1)	7	0	0	28
Will Sharp	Hull	2011-12	27(8)	10	0	0	40
	Harlequins	2008-10	65(1)	19	0	0	76
Jamie Shaul	Hull	2013-18	129	73	0	0	292
Darren Shaw	Salford	2002	5(1)	1	0	0	4
	London	1996, 2002	22(8)	3	0	0	12
	Castleford	2000-01	50(6)	1	0	0	4
	Sheffield	1998-99	51(1)	3	0	1	13
Mick Shaw	Halifax	1999	5	1	0	0	4
	Leeds	1996	12(2)	7	0	0	28
Ryan Shaw	Hull KR	2016, 2018	25(1)	15	62	0	184
	London	2013	2	1	2	0	8
Phil Shead	Paris	1996	3(2)	0	0	0	0
Richard Sheil	St Helens	1997	(1)	0	0	0	0
Kelly Shelford	Warrington	1996-97	25(3)	4	0	2	18
Kyle Shelford	Wigan	2016	(1)	0	0	0	0
Michael Shenton	Castleford	2004, 2006, 2008-10, 2013-18	233(2)	98	0	0	392
	St Helens	2011-12	51	15	0	0	60
Ryan Sheridan	Castleford	2004	2	0	0	0	0
	Widnes	2003	14(3)	2	0	0	8
	Leeds	1997-2002	123(7)	46	0	1	185
	Sheffield	1996	9(3)	5	0	1	21
Louis Sheriff	Hull KR	2011-12	8	3	0	0	12
Rikki Sheriffe	Bradford	2009-10	51	14	0	0	56
	Harlequins	2006-08	35(1)	16	0	0	64
	Halifax	2003	6(1)	3	0	0	12
Ian Sherratt	Oldham	1996	5(3)	1	0	0	4
Brent Sherwin	Catalans	2010	12	1	0	1	5
	Castleford	2008-10	48(1)	4	0	3	19
Peter Shiels	St Helens	2001-02	44(3)	11	0	0	44
Gary Shillabeer	Huddersfield	1999	(2)	0	0	0	0
Mark Shipway	Salford	2004-05	30(12)	3	0	0	12
Jake Shorrocks	Salford	2018	10	0	1	0	2
	Wigan	2016-17	2(11)	0	8	0	16
Ian Sibbit	Bradford	2011-12	11(7)	0	0	0	0
	Salford	2005-07, 2009-10	64(17)	11	0	0	44
	Warrington	1999-2001, 2003-04	63(18)	24	0	0	96
Mark Sibson	Huddersfield	1999	2	2	0	0	8
Adam Sidlow	Bradford	2013-14	20(22)	8	0	0	32
	Salford	2009-12	34(44)	14	0	0	56
Harry Siejka	Wakefield	2014	6(3)	1	0	0	4
Jordan Sigismeau	Catalans	2015-16	11	3	0	0	12
Jon Simms	St Helens	2002	(1)	0	0	0	0
Craig Simon	Hull	2000	23(2)	8	0	0	32
	Gateshead	1999	25(4)	6	0	0	24
Mickael Simon	Catalans	2010-14, 2017-18	44(63)	3	0	0	12
	Wakefield	2015-16	15(22)	3	0	0	12
Darren Simpson	Huddersfield	1998-99	17(1)	5	0	0	20
Jamie Simpson	Huddersfield	2011	8(1)	0	0	0	0
Jared Simpson	Huddersfield	2015-18	12	4	0	0	16
Robbie Simpson	London	1999	6(7)	0	0	0	0
Ashton Sims	Warrington	2015-17	69(11)	5	0	0	20

PLAYER	CLUB	YEAR	APP	TRIES	GOALS	FG	PTS
Kevin Sinfield	Leeds	1997-2015	425(29)	70	1566	31	3443
Matt Sing	Hull	2007-08	41	14	0	0	56
Wayne Sing	Paris	1997	18(1)	2	0	0	8
Brad Singleton	Leeds	2011-18	84(46)	15	0	0	60
	Wakefield	2013	(1)	0	0	0	0
Fata Sini	Salford	1997	22	7	0	0	28
Ken Sio	Hull KR	2015-16	42	23	13	0	118
Michael Sio	Wakefield	2015-17	25(14)	6	0	0	24
John Skandalis	Huddersfield	2007-08	37(5)	4	0	0	16
Dylan Skee	Harlequins	2008-09	(3)	0	0	0	0
Ben Skerrett	Castleford	2003	(1)	0	0	0	0
Kelvin Skerrett	Halifax	1997-99	31(6)	2	0	0	8
	Wigan	1996	1(8)	0	0	0	0
Troy Slattery	Wakefield	2002-03	33(5)	4	0	0	16
	Huddersfield	1999	3	1	0	0	4
Mick Slicker	Huddersfield	2001, 2003-05	17(48)	2	0	0	8
	Sheffield	1999	(3)	1	0	0	4
	Halifax	1997	2(5)	0	0	0	0
Nick Slyney	London	2014	20(4)	3	0	0	12
Ian Smales	Castleford	1996-97	10(8)	5	0	0	20
Aaron Smith	St Helens	2018	(1)	0	0	0	0
	Hull KR	2018	3(1)	0	0	0	0
Aaron Smith	Castleford	2006	(2)	0	0	0	0
	Bradford	2003-04	12(1)	3	0	0	12
Andy Smith	Harlequins	2007	6(3)	3	0	0	12
	Bradford	2004-06	9(9)	4	0	0	16
	Salford	2005	4	1	0	0	4
Byron Smith	Castleford	2004	(9)	0	0	0	0
	Halifax	2003	6(1)	0	0	0	0
Cameron Smith	Leeds	2016-18	3(14)	2	0	0	8
Chris Smith	Hull	2001-02	12	3	0	0	12
	St Helens	1998-2000	62(9)	26	0	0	104
	Castleford	1996-97	36(1)	12	0	0	48
Craig Smith	Wigan	2002-04	77(3)	10	0	0	40
Damien Smith	St Helens	1998	21(1)	8	0	0	32
Daniel Smith	Huddersfield	2015-18	9(38)	5	0	0	20
	Wakefield	2014-15	21(15)	6	0	0	24
Danny Smith	Paris	1996	10(2)	1	15	0	34
	London	1996	2(1)	1	0	0	4
Darren Smith	St Helens	2003	25(1)	14	0	0	56
Gary Smith	Castleford	2001	(1)	0	0	0	0
Hudson Smith	Bradford	2000	8(22)	2	0	0	8
	Salford	1999	23(2)	5	0	0	20
James Smith	Salford	2000	23(3)	6	0	0	24
Jamie Smith	Hull	1998-99	24(6)	6	12	0	48
	Workington	1996	5(3)	0	1	0	2
Jason Smith	Hull	2001-04	61(3)	17	0	1	69
Jeremy Smith	Wakefield	2011	9(1)	1	0	0	4
	Salford	2009-10	27(17)	2	0	0	8
Kris Smith	London	2001	(1)	0	0	0	0
	Halifax	2001	(1)	0	0	0	0
Lee Smith	Wakefield	2012-13, 2015	30(4)	16	54	2	174
	Leeds	2005-12	125(10)	60	34	1	309
Leigh Smith	Workington	1996	9	4	0	0	16
Mark Smith	Widnes	2005	12(15)	4	0	0	16
	Wigan	1999-2004	35(77)	8	0	0	32
Martyn Smith	Harlequins	2010	(2)	0	0	0	0
Matty Smith	St Helens	2006-08, 2010, 2017-18	38(9)	5	10	4	44
	Wigan	2012-16	122(3)	17	279	25	651
	Salford	2010-12	67(4)	13	6	1	65
	Celtic	2009	15(1)	3	2	1	17
Michael Smith	Hull KR	2007	(3)	1	0	0	4
	Castleford	1998, 2001-04	86(33)	32	0	0	128
	Hull	1999	12(6)	3	0	0	12
Morgan Smith	Warrington	2016-18	(18)	1	1	0	6
Paul Smith	Huddersfield	2004-06	52(17)	13	0	0	52
Paul Smith	Warrington	2001	(1)	0	0	0	0
	Castleford	1997-2000	6(37)	3	0	0	12
Paul Smith	London	1997	7(1)	2	0	0	8
Peter Smith	Oldham	1996	2	0	0	0	0
Richard Smith	Wakefield	2001	8(1)	1	0	0	4
	Salford	1997	1(1)	1	0	0	4
Tim Smith	Wakefield	2012-15	79	11	0	0	44
	Salford	2014	12	2	7	0	22
	Wigan	2008-09	13(8)	2	0	0	8
Tony Smith	Hull	2001-03	43(5)	26	0	0	104
	Wigan	1997-2000	66(5)	46	0	0	184
	Castleford	1996-97	18(2)	10	0	0	40
Tony Smith	Workington	1996	9	1	0	0	4
Tyrone Smith	Harlequins	2006-07	49(3)	13	0	0	52
	London	2005	20(4)	11	0	0	44
Rob Smyth	Leigh	2005	15(1)	4	0	0	16
	Warrington	2000-03	65	35	20	0	180
	London	1998-2000	32(2)	9	15	0	66
	Wigan	1996	11(5)	16	0	0	64

PLAYER	CLUB	YEAR	APP	TRIES	GOALS	FG	PTS
Marc Sneyd	Hull	2015-18	98	15	338	19	755
	Castleford	2014	25(1)	6	100	2	226
	Salford	2010-13	33(12)	4	61	3	141
Steve Snitch	Castleford	2010-12	38(18)	10	0	0	40
	Wakefield	2002-05, 2009	33(55)	9	0	0	36
	Huddersfield	2006-08	24(35)	12	0	0	48
Bright Sodje	Wakefield	2000	15	4	0	0	16
	Sheffield	1996-99	54	34	0	0	136
Iosia Soliola	St Helens	2010-14	83(24)	27	0	0	108
David Solomona	Warrington	2010-12	8(49)	16	1	0	66
	Bradford	2007-09	44(9)	19	0	0	76
	Wakefield	2004-06	73(3)	26	0	0	104
Denny Solomona	Castleford	2015-16	42	58	0	0	232
	London	2014	19(1)	8	0	0	32
Alfred Songoro	Wakefield	1999	8(5)	4	0	0	16
Romain Sort	Paris	1997	(1)	0	0	0	0
Paul Southern	Salford	1997-2002	79(33)	6	13	0	50
	St Helens	2002	1(1)	0	0	0	0
Steve Southern	Wakefield	2012	7(8)	3	0	0	12
Cain Southernwood							
	Bradford	2010	2	0	0	0	0
Roy Southernwood							
	Wakefield	1999	1	0	0	0	0
	Halifax	1996	2	0	0	0	0
Jason Southwell	Huddersfield	2004	(1)	0	0	0	0
Waisale Sovatabua	Wakefield	2001-03	44(3)	19	0	0	76
	Hudds-Sheff	2000	23(1)	8	0	0	32
	Sheffield	1996-99	56(17)	19	0	1	77
Jamie Soward	London	2013	6(1)	4	21	0	58
Yusef Sozi	London	2000-01	(5)	0	0	0	0
Scott Spaven	Hull KR	2010	(2)	0	0	0	0
Andy Speak	Castleford	2001	4(4)	0	0	0	0
	Wakefield	2000	6(5)	2	0	0	8
	Leeds	1999	4	1	0	0	4
Dom Speakman	St Helens	2013	(1)	0	0	0	0
Tim Spears	Castleford	2003	(3)	0	0	0	0
Jake Spedding	St Helens	2016-18	3(1)	0	0	0	0
Ady Spencer	London	1996-99	8(36)	5	0	0	20
Jack Spencer	Salford	2009-11	(7)	0	0	0	0
Tom Spencer	Wigan	2012-13	(7)	0	0	0	0
Rob Spicer	Wakefield	2002-05	28(18)	4	0	0	16
Russ Spiers	Wakefield	2011	(2)	0	0	0	0
Gadwin Springer	Castleford	2015-18	15(41)	3	0	0	12
	Catalans	2014-15	(3)	1	0	0	4
Stuart Spruce	Widnes	2002-03	45(4)	19	0	0	76
	Bradford	1996-2001	107(2)	57	0	0	228
Lee St Hilaire	Castleford	1997	4(2)	0	0	0	0
Marcus St Hilaire	Bradford	2006-07	34(1)	12	0	0	48
	Huddersfield	2003-05	72(2)	30	0	0	120
	Leeds	1996-2002	59(33)	31	0	0	124
Cyril Stacul	Catalans	2007-12	61(1)	18	0	0	72
Dylan Stainton	Workington	1996	2(3)	0	0	0	0
Mark Stamper	Workington	1996	(1)	0	0	0	0
John Stankevitch	Widnes	2005	17(5)	0	0	0	0
	St Helens	2000-04	74(40)	25	0	0	100
Gareth Stanley	Bradford	2000	1	1	0	0	4
Craig Stapleton	Salford	2009	24	2	0	0	8
	Leigh	2005	27(1)	4	0	0	16
Graham Steadman	Castleford	1996-97	11(17)	5	0	0	20
Jon Steel	Hull KR	2007-08	18	6	0	0	24
Jamie Stenhouse	Warrington	2000-01	9(3)	3	0	0	12
Gareth Stephens	Sheffield	1997-99	23(6)	2	0	0	8
David Stephenson	Hull	1998	11(7)	3	0	0	12
	Oldham	1997	10(8)	2	0	0	8
Francis Stephenson	London	2002-05	42(34)	5	0	0	20
	Wigan	2001	2(9)	0	0	0	0
	Wakefield	1999-2000	50(1)	6	0	0	24
Paul Sterling	Leeds	1997-2000	79(12)	50	0	0	200
Paul Stevens	Oldham	1996	2(1)	0	0	0	0
	London	1996	(1)	0	0	0	0
Warren Stevens	Leigh	2005	4(14)	1	0	0	4
	Warrington	1996-99, 2002-05	17(66)	1	0	0	4
	Salford	2001	(8)	0	0	0	0
Anthony Stewart	Harlequins	2006	4	0	0	0	0
	Salford	2004-06	51(2)	15	0	0	60
	St Helens	1997-2003	93(23)	44	0	0	176
Glenn Stewart	Leigh	2017	15	0	0	0	0
	Catalans	2016	28	3	0	0	12
Troy Stone	Widnes	2002	18(6)	1	0	0	4
	Huddersfield	2001	12(1)	1	0	0	4
James Stosic	Wakefield	2009	8(10)	1	0	0	4
Lynton Stott	Wakefield	1999	21	4	6	1	29
	Sheffield	1996-98	40(4)	15	0	0	60
Mitchell Stringer	Salford	2005-06	12(4)	0	0	0	0
	London	2004-05	10(19)	0	0	0	0
Graham Strutton	London	1996	9(1)	2	0	0	8

Super League Players 1996-2018

PLAYER	CLUB	YEAR	APP	TRIES	GOALS	FG	PTS
Matt Sturm	Leigh	2005	8(19)	3	0	0	12
	Warrington	2002-04	1(18)	0	0	0	0
	Huddersfield	1998-99	46	8	0	0	32
Anthony Sullivan	St Helens	1996-2001	137(2)	105	0	0	420
Michael Sullivan	Warrington	2006-07	21(16)	8	1	0	34
Phil Sumner	Warrington	1996	(5)	0	0	0	0
Alex Sutcliffe	Leeds	2017	1	0	0	0	0
Liam Sutcliffe	Leeds	2013-18	87(27)	38	126	2	406
	Bradford	2014	3(1)	1	0	0	4
Ryan Sutton	Wigan	2014-18	38(65)	10	0	0	40
Simon Svabic	Salford	1998-2000	13(5)	3	19	0	50
Luke Swain	Salford	2009-10	54	3	0	0	12
Richard Swain	Hull	2004-07	89	5	0	0	20
Anthony Swann	Warrington	2001	3	1	0	0	4
Logan Swann	Warrington	2005-06	49(1)	17	0	0	68
	Bradford	2004	25	6	0	0	24
Willie Swann	Warrington	1996-97	25(2)	6	0	0	24
Adam Swift	St Helens	2012-18	113	76	0	0	304
Nathan Sykes	Castleford	1996-2004	158(52)	3	0	0	12
Paul Sykes	Wakefield	2012-14	59(1)	12	135	6	324
	Bradford	1999-2002, 2008-12	99(4)	35	64	2	270
	Harlequins	2006-07	31(2)	15	47	1	155
	London	2001-05	95(1)	26	219	3	545
Wayne Sykes	London	1999	(2)	0	0	0	0
Tom Symonds	Huddersfield	2016-18	6(1)	3	0	0	12
Ukuma Ta'ai	Huddersfield	2013-18	100(45)	41	0	0	164
Semi Tadulala	Wakefield	2004-07, 2011	92	37	0	0	148
	Bradford	2008-09	49	30	0	0	120
Whetu Taewa	Sheffield	1997-98	33(7)	8	0	0	32
Zeb Taia	St Helens	2017-18	56(1)	14	0	0	56
	Catalans	2013-15	75	35	0	0	140
Alan Tait	Leeds	1996	3(3)	1	0	0	4
Fetuli Talanoa	Hull	2014-18	115(1)	54	0	0	216
Willie Talau	Salford	2009-10	22	4	0	0	16
	St Helens	2003-08	130(1)	50	0	0	200
Ian Talbot	Wakefield	1999	9(5)	2	31	0	70
	Wigan	1997	3	1	0	0	4
Albert Talipeau	Wakefield	2004	2(3)	0	0	0	0
Gael Tallec	Halifax	2000	5(19)	3	0	0	12
	Castleford	1998-99	19(21)	3	0	0	12
	Wigan	1996-97	8(12)	3	0	0	12
Joe Tamani	Bradford	1996	11(3)	4	0	0	16
Ryan Tandy	Hull KR	2007	8(4)	2	0	0	8
Andrew Tangata-Toa	Huddersfield	1999	15	2	0	0	8
David Tangata-Toa	Celtic	2009	1(18)	4	0	0	16
	Hull KR	2007	(17)	3	0	0	12
Jordan Tansey	Huddersfield	2016	2	1	1	0	6
	Wakefield	2015	4	1	0	0	4
	Castleford	2013-15	44(1)	15	0	0	60
	Crusaders	2011	14(4)	5	0	0	20
	Hull	2009-10	30	9	0	0	36
	Leeds	2006-08	18(32)	19	3	0	82
Lama Tasi	Salford	2014-15, 2017-18	55(26)	4	0	0	16
	St Helens	2016	9(8)	0	0	0	0
Kris Tassell	Wakefield	2002	24	10	0	0	40
	Salford	2000-01	35(10)	12	0	0	48
Shem Tatupu	Wigan	1996	(3)	0	0	0	0
Tony Tatupu	Wakefield	2000-01	20	2	0	0	8
	Warrington	1997	21(1)	6	0	0	24
Taulima Tautai	Wigan	2015-18	7(99)	4	0	0	16
	Wakefield	2013-14	6(19)	2	0	0	8
Dave Taylor	Catalans	2016	20(4)	8	0	0	32
James Taylor	Leigh	2005	(4)	0	0	0	0
Joe Taylor	Paris	1997	9(5)	2	0	0	8
Lawrence Taylor	Sheffield	1996	(1)	0	0	0	0
Scott Taylor	Hull	2016-18	77(5)	12	0	0	48
	Salford	2015	23	5	0	0	20
	Wigan	2013-14	18(29)	6	0	0	24
	Hull KR	2009-12	21(29)	8	0	0	32
Frederic Teixido	Sheffield	1999	(4)	0	0	0	0
	Paris	1996-97	2(3)	1	0	0	4
Lionel Teixido	Catalans	2006-07	11(13)	3	0	0	12
Karl Temata	London	2005, 2012	1(8)	1	0	0	4
	Harlequins	2006-11	94(22)	7	0	0	28
Jason Temu	Hull	1998	13(2)	1	0	0	4
	Oldham	1996-97	25(3)	1	0	0	4
Paul Terry	London	1997	(1)	0	0	0	0
Anthony Thackeray	Castleford	2008	3(6)	0	0	0	0
	Hull	2007	2	0	0	0	0
Jamie Thackray	Crusaders	2010	1(16)	2	0	0	8
	Hull	2005-06, 2008-09	37(45)	6	0	0	24
	Leeds	2006-07	5(27)	7	0	0	28
	Castleford	2003-04	7(11)	3	0	0	12
	Halifax	2000-02	10(38)	3	0	0	12

PLAYER	CLUB	YEAR	APP	TRIES	GOALS	FG	PTS
Adam Thaler	Castleford	2002	(1)	0	0	0	0
Gareth Thomas	Crusaders	2010-11	27(1)	6	0	0	24
Giles Thomas	London	1997-99	1(2)	0	0	0	0
Oscar Thomas	London	2014	4(2)	0	1	0	2
Rob Thomas	Harlequins	2011	(2)	0	0	0	0
Steve Thomas	London	2004	4(2)	0	0	0	0
	Warrington	2001	2	0	0	0	0
Alex Thompson	Warrington	2009	(1)	1	0	0	4
Alex Thompson	Sheffield	1997	4(11)	0	0	0	0
Bobby Thompson	Salford	1999	28	5	2	0	24
Bodene Thompson	Warrington	2018	7	0	0	0	0
Corey Thompson	Widnes	2016-17	48	36	9	0	162
David Thompson	Leigh	2017	1	0	0	0	0
	Hull KR	2016	1	0	0	0	0
Jordan Thompson	Leeds	2018	1	0	0	0	0
	Hull	2014-17	25(71)	11	0	0	44
	Castleford	2009-13	47(24)	25	0	0	100
Luke Thompson	St Helens	2013-18	68(54)	17	0	0	68
Sam Thompson	Harlequins	2009	(2)	0	0	0	0
	St Helens	2008	(5)	0	0	0	0
Chris Thorman	Hull	2009	19(2)	1	0	0	4
	Huddersfield	2000-01, 2005-08	126(20)	51	320	3	847
	London	2003	26(1)	7	81	1	191
	Sheffield	1999	5(13)	2	8	1	25
Tony Thorniley	Warrington	1997	(5)	0	0	0	0
Andy Thornley	Salford	2009	(1)	1	0	0	4
Iain Thornley	Catalans	2017-18	31(1)	7	0	0	28
	Hull KR	2016	21	10	0	0	40
	Wigan	2012-14	40	25	0	0	100
Danny Tickle	Hull KR	2018	14(3)	4	20	0	56
	Leigh	2017	10(13)	4	0	0	16
	Castleford	2016	6(3)	0	1	0	2
	Widnes	2014-15	33(1)	3	88	0	188
	Hull	2007-13	159(5)	45	528	1	1237
	Wigan	2002-06	94(36)	34	200	2	538
	Halifax	2000-02	25(17)	10	91	2	224
Kris Tickle	Warrington	2001	(1)	0	0	0	0
Lewis Tierney	Catalans	2017-18	27	5	0	0	20
	Wigan	2013-17	35	17	0	0	68
James Tilley	St Helens	2013-14	(3)	0	0	0	0
Dane Tilse	Hull KR	2015-16	29(1)	1	0	0	4
John Timu	London	1998-2000	57(3)	11	0	0	44
Kerrod Toby	London	1997	2(2)	0	0	0	0
Tulsen Tollett	London	1996-2001	105(5)	38	49	1	251
Joel Tomkins	Hull KR	2018	3	2	0	0	8
	Wigan	2005-11, 2014-18	161(51)	60	0	0	240
Logan Tomkins	Salford	2014-18	69(23)	5	0	0	20
	Wigan	2012-15	9(32)	1	0	0	4
Sam Tomkins	Wigan	2009-13, 2016-18	177(6)	129	125	7	773
Glen Tomlinson	Wakefield	1999-2000	41(5)	8	0	0	32
	Hull	1998	5	1	0	0	4
	Bradford	1996-97	27(13)	12	0	0	48
Willie Tonga	Leigh	2017	3	0	0	0	0
	Catalans	2015	18	6	0	0	24
Ryan Tongia	Wakefield	2011	4	2	0	0	8
Ian Tonks	Castleford	1996-2001	32(50)	11	13	0	70
Tony Tonks	Huddersfield	2012	(1)	0	0	0	0
Motu Tony	Wakefield	2011-12	7(3)	1	0	0	4
	Hull	2005-09	76(20)	25	0	0	100
	Castleford	2004	8(1)	1	0	0	4
Mark Tookey	Harlequins	2006	12(14)	1	0	0	4
	London	2005	13(14)	5	0	0	20
	Castleford	2004	2(8)	1	0	0	4
Clinton Toopi	Leeds	2006-08	40(3)	9	0	0	36
David Tootill	Harlequins	2006	1	0	0	0	0
Paul Topping	Oldham	1996-97	23(10)	1	19	0	42
Patrick Torreilles	Paris	1996	9(1)	1	25	0	54
Albert Torrens	Huddersfield	2006	7	5	0	0	20
Mat Toshack	London	1998-2004	120(21)	24	0	0	96
Julien Touxagas	Catalans	2006-11	14(45)	4	0	0	16
Darren Treacy	Salford	2002	24(1)	6	1	0	26
Dean Treister	Hull	2003	16(1)	3	0	0	12
Rocky Trimarchi	Crusaders	2010	16(8)	2	0	0	8
Steve Trindall	London	2003-05	40(20)	3	0	0	12
Shane Tronc	Wakefield	2010	8(3)	2	0	0	8
Kyle Trout	Wakefield	2012-15	6(17)	3	0	0	12
George Truelove	Wakefield	2002	2	1	0	0	4
	London	2000	5	1	0	0	4
Jake Trueman	Castleford	2017-18	28(2)	10	0	0	40
Va'aiga Tuigamala	Wigan	1996	21	10	3	0	46
Fereti Tuilagi	St Helens	1999-2000	43(15)	21	0	0	84
	Halifax	1996-98	55(3)	27	0	0	108
Carlos Tuimavave	Hull	2016-18	66(4)	24	0	0	96
Evarn Tuimavave	Hull KR	2013	11(12)	2	0	0	8
Sateki Tuipulotu	Leeds	1996	6(3)	1	2	0	8

PLAYER	CLUB	YEAR	APP	TRIES	GOALS	FG	PTS
Anthony Tupou	Wakefield	2016	12(9)	4	0	0	16
Bill Tupou	Wakefield	2015-18	70(3)	30	0	0	120
Tame Tupou	Bradford	2007-08	10(7)	8	0	0	32
Jansin Turgut	Hull	2015-18	10(18)	3	0	0	12
Neil Turley	Leigh	2005	6(3)	2	20	1	49
Calum Turner	Castleford	2018	2(3)	2	8	0	24
Darren Turner	Huddersfield	2000-01, 2003-04	42(13)	13	0	0	52
	Sheffield	1996-99	41(29)	15	0	0	60
Ian Turner	Paris	1996	1(1)	1	0	0	4
Jordan Turner	Huddersfield	2017-18	36	4	0	0	16
	St Helens	2013-16	106(4)	44	13	3	205
	Hull	2010-12	62(5)	28	0	0	112
	Salford	2006-07, 2009	22(10)	4	1	0	18
Chris Tuson	Hull	2014	10(1)	0	0	0	0
	Wigan	2008, 2010-13	24(49)	13	0	0	52
	Castleford	2010	3(5)	0	0	0	0
Gregory Tutard	Paris	1996	1(1)	0	0	0	0
Brendon Tuuta	Warrington	1998	18(2)	4	0	0	16
	Castleford	1996-97	41(1)	3	0	0	12
Steve Tyrer	Salford	2010	20	6	9	0	42
	Celtic	2009	8	2	5	0	18
	St Helens	2006-08	17(3)	12	42	0	132
Bobby Tyson-Wilson	Hull	2015	(1)	0	0	0	0
Harry Tyson-Wilson	Hull	2014	(1)	0	0	0	0
Wayne Ulugia	Hull KR	2014	3	1	0	0	4
Mike Umaga	Halifax	1996-97	38(1)	16	5	0	74
Kava Utoikamanu	Paris	1996	6(3)	0	0	0	0
Frederic Vaccari	Catalans	2010-11, 2013-14	50	26	0	0	104
David Vaealiki	Wigan	2005-07	67(1)	17	0	0	68
Joe Vagana	Bradford	2001-08	176(44)	17	0	0	68
Nigel Vagana	Warrington	1997	20	17	0	0	68
Tevita Vaikona	Bradford	1998-2004	145(2)	89	0	0	356
Lesley Vainikolo	Bradford	2002-07	132(4)	136	1	0	546
Junior Vaivai	Hull KR	2018	11	6	0	0	24
Eric Van Brussell	Paris	1996	2	0	0	0	0
Jace Van Dijk	Celtic	2009	19	1	1	0	6
Richard Varkulis	Warrington	2004	4(1)	3	0	0	12
Marcus Vassilakopoulos	Sheffield	1997-99	15(11)	3	10	2	34
	Leeds	1996-97	1(3)	0	0	0	0
Manu Vatuvei	Salford	2017	7	5	0	0	20
Atelea Vea	Leigh	2017	19(1)	5	0	0	20
	St Helens	2015-16	19(17)	10	0	0	40
	London	2014	19(3)	2	0	0	8
Josh Veivers	Salford	2012	5	2	0	0	8
	Wakefield	2011	10(2)	2	22	0	52
Phil Veivers	Huddersfield	1998	7(6)	1	0	0	4
	St Helens	1996	(1)	1	0	0	4
Michael Vella	Hull KR	2007-11	111(5)	13	0	0	52
Bruno Verges	Catalans	2006	25	6	0	0	24
Eric Vergniol	Paris	1996	14(1)	6	0	0	24
Gray Viane	Salford	2007	9	2	0	0	8
	Castleford	2006	20(7)	14	0	0	56
	Widnes	2005	20	13	0	0	52
	St Helens	2004	4	1	0	0	4
Joe Vickery	Leeds	2013	9	1	0	0	4
Daniel Vidot	Salford	2016	5(1)	5	0	0	20
Adrian Vowles	Castleford	1997-2001, 2003	125(1)	29	1	1	119
	Wakefield	2002-03	24(3)	6	1	0	26
	Leeds	2002	14(3)	2	0	0	8
Michael Wainwright	Castleford	2008-10	70	22	0	0	88
	Wakefield	2004-05	21(10)	8	0	0	32
Mike Wainwright	Salford	2000-02, 2007	75(3)	9	0	0	36
	Warrington	1996-99, 2003-07	168(14)	23	0	0	92
Shannon Wakeman	Huddersfield	2017-18	16(13)	3	0	0	12
Adam Walker	Wakefield	2017	5(1)	0	0	0	0
	St Helens	2017	(9)	1	0	0	4
	Hull KR	2013-16	60(27)	6	0	0	24
	Huddersfield	2010-12	1(5)	0	0	0	0
Alex Walker	London	2014	1	0	0	0	0
Anthony Walker	Wakefield	2015-17	1(11)	1	0	0	4
	St Helens	2013-14	9(7)	2	0	0	8
Ben Walker	Leeds	2002	23(1)	8	100	0	232
Brad Walker	Widnes	2016-18	3(5)	0	0	0	0
Chev Walker	Bradford	2011-14	44(22)	5	0	0	20
	Hull KR	2008-09	24(7)	5	0	0	20
	Leeds	1999-2006	142(19)	77	0	0	308
Chris Walker	Catalans	2010	11	6	2	0	28
Danny Walker	Widnes	2017-18	3(16)	2	0	0	8
Jack Walker	Leeds	2017-18	20(4)	4	0	0	16
Jonathan Walker	Hull KR	2014	2(6)	0	0	0	0
	Castleford	2010-13	17(31)	4	0	0	16
Jonny Walker	Wigan	2010	(1)	0	0	0	0
Matt Walker	Huddersfield	2001	3(6)	0	0	0	0
Anthony Wall	Paris	1997	9	3	3	0	18
Jon Wallace	London	2014	4(12)	0	0	0	0
Mark Wallace	Workington	1996	14(1)	3	0	0	12
Elliot Wallis	Hull KR	2018	4	2	0	0	8
Alex Walmsley	St Helens	2013-18	72(71)	23	0	0	92
Adam Walne	Huddersfield	2018	1(4)	0	0	0	0
	Salford	2012-17	15(50)	2	0	0	8
Jordan Walne	Hull KR	2018	(6)	0	0	0	0
	Salford	2013-17	20(32)	3	0	0	12
Joe Walsh	Huddersfield	2009	1(1)	1	0	0	4
	Harlequins	2007-08	1(4)	0	0	0	0
Liam Walsh	Widnes	2017	(1)	0	0	0	0
Luke Walsh	Catalans	2017-18	23	2	71	4	154
	St Helens	2014-16	56(2)	14	188	9	441
Lucas Walshaw	Wakefield	2011-14	15(6)	3	0	0	12
Josh Walters	Leeds	2014-18	15(36)	9	0	0	36
Kerrod Walters	Gateshead	1999	10(12)	2	1	0	10
Kevin Walters	Warrington	2001	1	0	0	0	0
Jason Walton	Wakefield	2016	7(8)	0	0	0	0
	Salford	2009, 2014-15	7(19)	1	0	0	4
Barry Ward	St Helens	2002-03	20(30)	4	0	0	16
Danny Ward	Harlequins	2008-11	89(7)	4	0	0	16
	Hull KR	2007	11(9)	0	0	0	0
	Castleford	2006	18(7)	2	0	0	8
	Leeds	1999-2005	70(48)	9	0	1	37
Robbie Ward	Leeds	2014-15	5(3)	1	0	0	4
Stevie Ward	Leeds	2012-18	80(28)	18	0	0	72
Joe Wardill	Hull KR	2016, 2018	6(2)	1	0	0	4
Jake Wardle	Huddersfield	2018	4	3	0	0	12
Joe Wardle	Castleford	2018	15(2)	1	0	0	4
	Huddersfield	2011-16	125	58	0	0	232
	Bradford	2010	1(1)	0	0	0	0
Phil Waring	Salford	1997-99	6(8)	2	0	0	8
Brett Warton	London	1999-2001	49(7)	14	133	0	322
Kyle Warren	Castleford	2002	13(14)	3	0	0	12
Danny Washbrook	Hull	2005-11, 2016-18	133(68)	19	0	0	76
	Wakefield	2012-15	93(8)	12	0	0	48
Adam Watene	Wakefield	2006-08	45(8)	5	0	0	20
	Bradford	2006	(4)	0	0	0	0
Frank Watene	Wakefield	1999-2001	24(37)	6	0	0	24
Trent Waterhouse	Warrington	2012-14	65(5)	15	0	0	60
Luke Waterworth	Wigan	2016	1	0	0	0	0
Kallum Watkins	Leeds	2008-18	198(7)	108	85	0	602
Dave Watson	Sheffield	1998-99	41(4)	4	0	0	16
Ian Watson	Salford	1997, 2002	24(17)	8	3	5	43
	Workington	1996	4(1)	1	15	0	34
Kris Watson	Warrington	1996	11(2)	2	0	0	8
Anthony Watts	Widnes	2012	(1)	0	0	0	0
Brad Watts	Widnes	2005	6	3	0	0	12
Liam Watts	Castleford	2018	22	0	0	0	0
	Hull	2012-18	116(19)	9	0	0	36
	Hull KR	2008, 2010-12	31(26)	6	0	0	24
Michael Watts	Warrington	2002	3	0	0	0	0
Brent Webb	Catalans	2013-14	10	2	0	0	8
	Leeds	2007-12	137(1)	73	0	0	292
Jason Webber	Salford	2000	25(1)	10	0	0	40
Ian Webster	St Helens	2006	1	0	0	0	0
Jake Webster	Castleford	2013-18	103(12)	45	0	0	180
	Hull KR	2008-12	95(1)	34	7	0	150
James Webster	Hull	2008	1	0	0	0	0
	Hull KR	2007-08	36	2	0	2	10
Pat Weisner	Hull KR	2007	(2)	0	0	0	0
	Harlequins	2006	10(6)	3	0	0	12
Taylor Welch	Warrington	2008	1	0	0	0	0
Kris Welham	Salford	2017-18	42	17	0	0	68
	Hull KR	2007-15	164(2)	90	1	0	362
Paul Wellens	St Helens	1998-2015	399(40)	199	34	1	865
Calvin Wellington	St Helens	2016	1	0	0	0	0
Jack Wells	Wigan	2016-17	4(11)	1	0	0	4
Jon Wells	Harlequins	2006-09	66	10	0	0	40
	London	2004-05	42(2)	19	0	0	76
	Wakefield	2003	22(1)	1	0	0	4
	Castleford	1996-2002	114(14)	49	0	0	196
Jack Welsby	St Helens	2018	(1)	0	0	0	0
Dwayne West	St Helens	2000-02	8(16)	6	0	0	24
	Wigan	1999	1(1)	0	0	0	0
Joe Westerman	Hull	2011-15, 2018	114(11)	26	52	1	209
	Warrington	2016-17	45(1)	12	0	0	48
	Castleford	2008-10	68(7)	29	151	0	418

Super League Players 1996-2018

PLAYER	CLUB	YEAR	APP	TRIES	GOALS	FG	PTS
Craig Weston	Widnes	2002, 2004	23(9)	2	1	2	12
	Huddersfield	1998-99	46(1)	15	15	0	90
Dayne Weston	Leigh	2017	6(5)	1	0	0	4
Ben Westwood	Warrington	2002-18	359(23)	112	64	0	576
	Wakefield	1999-2002	31(7)	8	1	0	34
Michael Weyman	Hull KR	2014	22(1)	7	0	0	28
Andrew Whalley	Workington	1996	(2)	0	0	0	0
Paul Whatuira	Huddersfield	2008-10	59	23	0	0	92
Scott Wheeldon	Castleford	2014-15	14(23)	5	0	0	20
	London	2012-13	27(4)	3	0	0	12
	Hull KR	2009-12	30(42)	4	0	0	16
	Hull	2006-08	2(60)	4	0	0	16
Gary Wheeler	Warrington	2015-16	6(4)	4	0	0	16
	St Helens	2008-14	48(10)	17	13	0	94
Matt Whitaker	Castleford	2006	8(2)	0	0	0	0
	Widnes	2004-05	10(20)	9	0	0	36
	Huddersfield	2003-04	3(14)	0	0	0	0
Ben White	Leeds	2014	1	0	0	0	0
David White	Wakefield	2000	(1)	0	0	0	0
Josh White	Salford	1998	18(3)	5	5	1	31
	London	1997	14(2)	8	0	1	33
Lloyd White	Widnes	2012-18	72(43)	27	24	1	157
	Crusaders	2010-11	13(11)	8	0	0	32
	Celtic	2009	6	1	0	0	4
Paul White	Salford	2009	1	1	0	0	4
	Wakefield	2006-07	24(12)	12	0	0	48
	Huddersfield	2003-05	11(32)	17	16	0	100
Elliott Whitehead	Catalans	2013-16	64(1)	30	0	0	120
	Bradford	2009-13	90(10)	30	0	0	120
Harvey Whiteley	Leeds	2017	(1)	0	0	0	0
Richard Whiting	Hull	2004-15	163(72)	69	19	2	316
Matt Whitley	Widnes	2015-18	49(27)	13	0	0	52
Emmerson Whittel	Bradford	2014	(1)	0	0	0	0
Danny Whittle	Warrington	1998	(2)	0	0	0	0
David Whittle	St Helens	2002	1(2)	0	0	0	0
	Warrington	2001	1(2)	0	0	0	0
Jon Whittle	Wakefield	2006	8(2)	3	0	0	12
	Widnes	2005	13	2	0	0	8
	Wigan	2003	1	0	0	0	0
Joel Wicks	London	2013-14	3(10)	0	0	0	0
Dean Widders	Castleford	2009-11	25(32)	23	0	0	92
Stephen Wild	Salford	2011-13	71	4	0	0	16
	Huddersfield	2006-10	116(2)	33	0	0	132
	Wigan	2001-05	67(20)	24	0	0	96
Sam Wilde	Widnes	2017-18	14(7)	2	0	0	8
	Warrington	2015-17	3(15)	1	0	0	4
Matty Wildie	Wakefield	2010-14	13(26)	3	0	0	12
Brayden Wiliame	Catalans	2017-18	39	15	0	0	60
Oliver Wilkes	Wakefield	2008-09, 2012-13	55(47)	10	0	0	40
	Harlequins	2010-11	39(13)	4	0	0	16
	Wigan	2006	1(5)	0	0	0	0
	Leigh	2005	13(1)	1	0	0	4
	Huddersfield	2000-01	1(6)	0	0	0	0
	Sheffield	1998	1	0	0	0	0
Jon Wilkin	St Helens	2003-18	350(30)	78	0	2	314
Alex Wilkinson	Hull	2003-04	11(4)	1	0	0	4
	Huddersfield	2003	8	4	0	0	16
	London	2002	5(1)	0	0	0	0
	Bradford	2000-01	3(3)	1	0	0	4
Bart Williams	London	1998	5(3)	1	0	0	4
Connor Williams	Salford	2016	1	0	0	0	0
Daley Williams	Salford	2006-07	9(2)	4	0	0	16
Danny Williams	Harlequins	2006	9(13)	4	0	0	16
	London	2005	1(16)	0	0	0	0
Danny Williams	Bradford	2014	7	2	0	0	8
	Salford	2011-14	54	31	0	0	124
	Leeds	2006, 2008	13(2)	7	0	0	28
	Hull	2008	3	0	0	0	0
Dave Williams	Harlequins	2008-11	1(17)	0	0	0	0
Desi Williams	Wigan	2004	2	0	0	0	0
George Williams	Wigan	2013-18	117(13)	40	56	1	273
Jonny Williams	London	2004	(4)	0	0	0	0
Lee Williams	Crusaders	2011	1(7)	0	0	0	0
Rhys Williams	Warrington	2010-13	23(1)	15	0	0	60
	Salford	2013	4	0	0	0	0
	Castleford	2012	8	4	0	0	16
	Crusaders	2011	6	3	0	0	12
Sam Williams	Wakefield	2017	17(5)	4	26	0	68
	Catalans	2014	11(1)	4	21	0	58
Luke Williamson	Harlequins	2009-10	39	6	0	0	24
John Wilshere	Salford	2006-07, 2009	72(2)	32	142	0	412
	Leigh	2005	26	8	6	0	44
	Warrington	2004	5	2	0	0	8
Craig Wilson	Hull	2000	2(16)	1	0	1	5
	Gateshead	1999	17(11)	5	0	1	21
George Wilson	Paris	1996	7(2)	3	0	0	12
John Wilson	Catalans	2006-08	69	23	0	0	92
Richard Wilson	Hull	1998-99	(13)	0	0	0	0
Scott Wilson	Warrington	1998-99	23(2)	6	0	0	24
Johan Windley	Hull	1999	2(2)	1	0	0	4
Paul Wingfield	Warrington	1997	5(3)	6	1	0	26
Frank Winterstein	Widnes	2012-13	37(9)	16	0	0	64
	Crusaders	2010-11	26(19)	4	0	0	16
	Wakefield	2009	(5)	0	0	0	0
Lincoln Withers	Hull KR	2012-13	18(22)	10	0	0	40
	Crusaders	2010-11	47	4	0	0	16
	Celtic	2009	21	6	0	0	24
Michael Withers	Wigan	2007	6(1)	1	0	0	4
	Bradford	1999-2006	156(6)	94	15	4	410
Michael Witt	London	2012-13	37	10	89	1	219
	Crusaders	2010-11	39	13	47	4	150
Jeff Wittenberg	Huddersfield	1998	18(1)	1	0	0	4
	Bradford	1997	8(9)	4	0	0	16
Josh Wood	Salford	2015-18	18(15)	2	0	0	8
Kyle Wood	Wakefield	2012-13, 2017-18	36(60)	17	0	0	68
	Huddersfield	2011, 2013-16	39(33)	7	0	0	28
	Castleford	2010	1(4)	0	0	0	0
Martin Wood	Sheffield	1997-98	24(11)	4	18	2	54
Mikey Wood	Huddersfield	2016-17	1(1)	0	0	0	0
Nathan Wood	Warrington	2002-05	90	38	0	3	155
	Wakefield	2002	11	2	0	0	8
Paul Wood	Warrington	2000-14	138(171)	40	0	0	160
Phil Wood	Widnes	2004	2(1)	0	0	0	0
Sam Wood	Bradford	2013-14	7(1)	0	0	0	0
Sam Wood	Huddersfield	2016-18	18	6	4	0	32
James Woodburn-Hall	London	2013-14	9(4)	2	0	0	8
Darren Woods	Widnes	2005	(1)	0	0	0	0
David Woods	Halifax	2002	18(2)	8	0	0	32
Josh Woods	Wigan	2017-18	10(1)	1	4	1	13
Simon Worrall	Leeds	2008-09	5(16)	1	0	0	4
Michael Worrincy	Bradford	2009-10	12(34)	12	0	0	48
	Harlequins	2006-08	20(12)	10	0	0	40
Rob Worrincy	Castleford	2004	1	0	0	0	0
James Worthington	Wigan	2017	1	2	0	0	8
Troy Wozniak	Widnes	2004	13(7)	1	0	0	4
Matthew Wray	Wakefield	2002-03	13(3)	2	0	0	8
David Wrench	Wakefield	2002-06	28(52)	6	0	0	24
	Leeds	1999-2001	7(17)	0	0	0	0
Callum Wright	Wigan	2014	(2)	0	0	0	0
Craig Wright	Castleford	2000	1(9)	0	0	0	0
Nigel Wright	Huddersfield	1999	4(6)	1	0	0	4
	Wigan	1996-97	5(5)	2	0	1	9
Ricky Wright	Sheffield	1997-99	2(13)	0	0	0	0
Vincent Wulf	Paris	1996	13(4)	4	0	0	16
Andrew Wynyard	London	1999-2000	34(6)	4	0	0	16
Bagdad Yaha	Paris	1996	4(4)	2	4	0	16
Fouad Yaha	Catalans	2015-18	57	30	0	0	120
Malakai Yasa	Sheffield	1996	1(3)	0	0	0	0
Andy Yates	Wakefield	2016	(7)	0	0	0	0
	Leeds	2015	(9)	1	0	0	4
Kirk Yeaman	Hull	2001-16, 2018	322(18)	159	0	0	636
Grant Young	London	1998-99	22(2)	2	0	0	8
Nick Youngquest	Castleford	2011-12	37	28	0	0	112
	Crusaders	2010	26(1)	9	0	0	36
Ronel Zenon	Paris	1996	(4)	0	0	0	0
Nick Zisti	Bradford	1999	6(1)	0	0	0	0
Freddie Zitter	Catalans	2006	1	0	0	0	0

All totals in 'Super League Players 1996-2018' include play-off games & Super League Super 8s from 2015. 2015-2018 Super 8s (Qualifiers) not included.

NEW FACES - Players making their Super League debuts in 2018

PLAYER	CLUB	DEBUT vs	ROUND	DATE
Sitaleki Akauola	Warrington	Wigan (h)	3	23/2/18
Wellington Albert	Widnes	Catalans (h)	1	4/2/18
Olly Ashall-Bott	Widnes	Castleford (a)	2	11/2/18
Chris Atkin	Hull KR	Leeds (a)	2	8/2/18
		(club debut: Halifax (a), Ch23, 23/7/17)		
Gavin Bennion	Salford	Wigan (a)	14	4/5/18
James Bentley	St Helens	Hull (h)	S85	14/9/18
Lewis Bienek	Hull	Wakefield (h)	S81	10/8/18
Keanan Brand	Widnes	Hull KR (a)	10	7/4/18
Robin Brochon	Catalans	Warrington (a)	S81	10/8/18
Owen Buckley	Widnes	Hull (a)	19	29/6/18
Mitch Clark	Castleford	Warrington (a)	17	8/6/18
Matthew Costello	St Helens	Huddersfield (h)	12	20/4/18
Kenny Edwards	Catalans	Widnes (h)	17	9/6/18
		(club debut: Huddersfield (a), CCQF, 31/5/18)		
Bureta Faraimo	Hull	Huddersfield (h)	1	1/2/18
Bryson Goodwin	Warrington	Leeds (h)	1	1/2/18
Mickael Goudemand				
	Catalans	Leeds (a)	16	26/5/18
		(club debut: Whitehaven (h), CC6, 12/5/18)		
Gabe Hamlin	Wigan	Hull KR (h)	9	2/4/18
Chris Hankinson	Wigan	St Helens (h)	22	19/7/18
Liam Harris	Hull	Hull KR (MW)	15	20/5/18
Jackson Hastings	Salford	Leeds (h)	23	27/7/18
Andrew Heffernan	Hull KR	Wakefield (h)	1	2/2/18
		(club debut: Bradford (h), Ch1, 5/2/17)		
Sam Hewitt	Huddersfield	Leeds (h)	8	30/3/18
Tom Holroyd	Leeds	Catalans (h)	4	20/6/18
Luis Johnson	Warrington	Wigan (a)	S85	14/9/18
Samy Kibula	Wigan	Huddersfield (a)	21	12/7/18
Jordan Lane	Hull	Leeds (a)	5	8/3/18
Quentin Laulu-Togagae				
	Castleford	Warrington (a)	17	8/6/18
Jack Littlejohn	Salford	Wigan (h)	1	2/2/18
Garry Lo	Castleford	Wigan (a)	12	20/4/18
Ugo Martin	Catalans	Warrington (a)	S81	10/8/18
Suaia Matagi	Huddersfield	St Helens (a)	S81	10/8/18
Peter Mata'utia	Castleford	Widnes (a)	23	29/7/18
David Mead	Catalans	Widnes (h)	1	4/2/18
Hakim Miloudi	Hull	Wakefield (h)	9	2/4/18
Kieren Moss	Hull KR	Wakefield (h)	14	6/5/18
		(club debut: Bradford (h), Ch1, 5/2/17)		
Arthur Mourgue	Catalans	Warrington (a)	S81	10/8/18
Craig Mullen	Wigan	Wakefield (a)	17	7/6/18
Ben Nakubuwai	Salford	Wakefield (a)	2	9/2/18
Dan Norman	Widnes	Salford (a)	18	14/6/18
Levy Nzoungou	Salford	Wigan (a)	14	4/5/18
Derrell Olpherts	Salford	Widnes (a)	7	22/3/18
Liam Paisley	Wigan	Castleford (a)	6	22/6/18
Oliver Partington	Wigan	Castleford (h)	S81	10/8/18
Pauli Pauli	Wakefield	Hull KR (a)	1	2/2/18
Nathaniel Peteru	Leeds	Warrington (a)	1	1/2/18
Tyrone Roberts	Warrington	Leeds (h)	1	1/2/18
Colton Roche	Huddersfield	Catalans (a)	9	2/4/18
Oliver Russell	Huddersfield	Widnes (h)	14	4/5/18
Cameron Scott	Hull	Hull KR (MW)	15	20/5/18
Innes Senior	Huddersfield	Catalans (a)	9	2/4/18
Louis Senior	Huddersfield	Leeds (h)	8	30/3/18
Aaron Smith	Hull KR	Wakefield (a)	14	6/5/18
Bodene Thompson	Warrington	Catalans (h)	S81	10/8/18
Calum Turner	Castleford	Hull (a)	14	5/5/18
Junior Vaivai	Hull KR	Warrington (a)	11	14/4/18
Elliot Wallis	Hull KR	Wigan (h)	16	25/5/18
		(club debut: Wigan (h), CC6, 13/5/18)		
Jake Wardle	Huddersfield	Widnes (h)	14	4/5/18
Jack Welsby	St Helens	Hull (h)	S85	14/9/18

Players making their club debuts in other competitions in 2018

Stanton Albert	Widnes	Coventry (h)	CC5	21/4/18
Charlie Gubb	Widnes	London Broncos (h)	S8Q1	9/8/18
Joey Lussick	Salford	Hull KR (a)	S8Q1	10/8/18
Joe Lyons	Widnes	Leeds (h)	S8Q4	9/9/18
Pat Moran	Warrington	Bradford (h)	CC5	21/4/18
Jansin Turgut	Salford	Leeds (a)	S8Q5	14/9/18

OLD FACES - Players making their Super League debuts for new clubs in 2018

PLAYER	CLUB	DEBUT vs	ROUND	DATE
Jordan Baldwinson	Wakefield	Catalans (a)	3	24/2/18
Luke Briscoe	Leeds	Catalans (h) (D2)	4	20/6/18
Mitch Brown	Warrington	Wigan (a)	3	23/2/18
Luke Burgess	Salford	Wigan (h) (D2)	1	2/2/18
Greg Burke	Salford	Widnes (h)	18	14/6/18
Justin Carney	Hull KR	Wakefield (h)	1	2/2/18
		(club debut: Sheffield (a), Ch19, 25/6/17)		
Todd Carney	Hull KR	Hull (a)	23	27/7/18
Ed Chamberlain	Salford	Widnes (h)	18	14/6/18
Josh Charnley	Warrington	Widnes (h)	8	30/3/18
James Clare	Castleford	Salford (h) (D2)	5	11/3/18
Ben Crooks	Hull KR	Hull (a)	23	27/7/18
Dominic Crosby	Leeds	Widnes (h)	22	20/7/18
Will Dagger	Hull KR	Catalans (h)	12	15/2/18
Josh Drinkwater	Catalans	Hull (h)	13	28/4/18
Brad Dwyer	Leeds	Warrington (a)	1	1/2/18
Jamie Ellis	Castleford	Widnes (h) (D2)	2	11/2/18
Liam Finn	Widnes	Castleford (h)	23	29/7/18
James Green	Castleford	St Helens (a)	1	2/2/18
Joe Greenwood	Wigan	Leeds (h)	19	28/6/18
Craig Hall	Hull KR	Hull (a) (D2)	23	27/7/18
Ryan Hampshire	Wakefield	Hull KR (a)	1	2/2/18
Harrison Hansen	Widnes	Castleford (h)	23	29/7/18
Weller Hauraki	Widnes	Catalans (a)	17	9/6/18
Justin Horo	Wakefield	Hull KR (a)	1	2/2/18
Krisnan Inu	Widnes	Catalans (h)	1	4/2/18
Lee Jewitt	Hull KR	Wakefield (h)	1	2/2/18
		(club debut: Dewsbury (h), Ch18, 18/6/17)		
Josh Johnson	Hull KR	Wigan (a)	9	2/4/18
		(club debut: Batley (h), Ch8, 2/4/18)		
Benjamin Jullien	Catalans	Widnes (a)	1	4/2/18
Ben Kavanagh	Hull KR	Wakefield (h)	1	2/2/18
		(club debut: Rochdale (a), Ch3, 19/2/17)		
Jimmy Keinhorst	Widnes	Wigan (h)	13	27/4/18
Samisoni Langi	Catalans	Widnes (a)	1	4/2/18
Tommy Lee	Hull KR	Wakefield (h)	1	2/2/18
Antoni Maria	Catalans	Widnes (a) (D2)	1	4/2/18
Mose Masoe	Hull KR	Wakefield (h)	1	2/2/18
		(club debut: Halifax (h), S8Q1, 6/8/17)		
Danny McGuire	Hull KR	Wakefield (h)	1	2/2/18
Michael McIlorum	Catalans	Widnes (a)	1	4/2/18
Ben Murdoch-Masila				
	Warrington	Leeds (h)	1	1/2/18
Richie Myler	Leeds	Warrington (a)	1	1/2/18
Mickey Paea	Hull	Huddersfield (h) (D2)	1	1/2/18
Ben Pomeroy	Warrington	Hull (h) (D2)	16	25/5/18
Adam Quinlan	Hull KR	Wakefield (h)	1	2/2/18
		(club debut: Bradford (h), Ch1, 5/2/17)		
Dan Sarginson	Wigan	Salford (a) (D2)	1	2/2/18
Nick Scruton	Hull KR	Salford (a)	3	23/2/18
		(club debut: Bradford (h), Ch1, 5/2/17)		
Jake Shorrocks	Salford	Warrington (h)	10	7/4/18
Aaron Smith	St Helens	Catalans (a)	S84	8/9/18
Jordan Thompson	Leeds	Salford (a)	23	27/7/18
Danny Tickle	Hull KR	Catalans (h)	12	15/2/18
Joel Tomkins	Hull KR	Castleford (a)	18	17/6/18
Adam Walne	Huddersfield	Hull (a)	1	1/2/18
Jordan Walne	Hull KR	Leeds (a)	2	8/2/18
Joe Wardle	Castleford	Hull (h)	3	24/2/18
Liam Watts	Castleford	Warrington (h) (D2)	9	2/4/18
Joe Westerman	Hull	Castleford (h) (D2)	14	5/5/18
Sam Wilde	Widnes	Castleford (a) (D2)	2	11/2/18

SUPER LEAGUE RECORDS
1996-2018

COMPETITION
Includes play-off games & Super League Super 8s (2015-2018)

TRIES
Danny McGuire (Hull Kingston Rovers/Leeds Rhinos)
(2001-2018) 243

GOALS
Kevin Sinfield (Leeds Rhinos) (1997-2015) 1,566

FIELD GOALS
Lee Briers (Warrington Wolves/St Helens) (1997-2013) 70

POINTS
Kevin Sinfield (Leeds Rhinos) (1997-2015) 3,443

APPEARANCES
Kevin Sinfield (Leeds Rhinos) (1997-2015) 454

SEASON
Includes play-off games & Super League Super 8s (2015-2018)
(Play-offs in brackets)

TRIES
Denny Solomona (Castleford Tigers) (2016) 40 (-)

GOALS
Henry Paul (Bradford Bulls) (2001) 178 (13)

FIELD GOALS
Lee Briers (Warrington Wolves) (2002) 11 (-)

POINTS
Pat Richards (Wigan Warriors) (2010) 434 (46)

MATCH RECORDS

Includes play-off games & Super League Super 8s (2015-2018)

TRIES
Lesley Vainikolo (Bradford Bulls) 6
(v Hull FC (h), 2/9/05)

GOALS
Henry Paul (Bradford Bulls) 14
(v Salford City Reds (h), 25/6/00)

FIELD GOALS
Lee Briers (Warrington Wolves) 5
(v Halifax Blue Sox (a), 25/5/02)

POINTS
Iestyn Harris (Leeds Rhinos) 42
(v Huddersfield Giants (h), 16/7/99)

TEAM RECORDS

Includes play-off games & Super League Super 8s (2015-2018)

HIGHEST SCORE
Bradford Bulls 96 Salford City Reds 16 (25/6/00)

WIDEST MARGIN
Leeds Rhinos 86 Huddersfield Giants 6 (16/7/99)
Bradford Bulls 96 Salford City Reds 16 (25/6/00)
Warrington Wolves 80 Wakefield Trinity Wildcats 0 (11/4/15)

ATTENDANCE RECORDS

GRAND FINAL
73,512 Leeds Rhinos v Wigan Warriors (10/10/15)

PLAY-OFFS
21,790 Wigan Warriors v St Helens (3/10/03)

REGULAR SEASON *(includes Super League Super 8s (2015-2018)*
25,004 Wigan Warriors v St Helens (25/3/05)

SUPER LEAGUE XXIII
Club by Club

17th October 2017 - Larne Patrick, with two years left on contract, signs for Leigh.

18th October 2017 - halfback Jamie Ellis returns on three-year contract.

19th October 2017 - front-rower Mitch Clark signs from Hull KR on two-year deal.

3rd November 2017 - prop James Green signs from Leigh on one-year deal.

9th November 2017 - prop Will Maher joins Halifax on season-long loan.

5th December 2017 - James Clare returns on one-year deal.

8th December 2017 - halfback Jake Trueman signs new three-year deal to end of 2020; teenage back-rower Luis Johnson transferred to Warrington for £45,000 fee.

11th December 2017 - halfback Cory Aston signs from Leeds on two-year contract. Prop Brandon Douglas joins Halifax on season-long loan.

26th December 2017 - 32-16 home friendly defeat to Featherstone.

9th January 2018 - hooker Paul McShane signs new five-year contract extension.

21st January 2018 - 16-4 home, pre-season win over Leeds.

30th January 2018 - Mitch Clark goes to Featherstone on month's loan.

31st January 2018 - Cory Aston and Garry Lo join Sheffield Eagles on month's loan.

2nd February 2018 - 46-6 defeat at St Helens in round one.

11th February 2018 - second-half Luke Gale field goal crucial in 13-12 home round-two win over Widnes.

21st February 2018 - Zak Hardaker dismissed from contract.

24th February 2018 - Greg Eden and debutant Joe Wardle injured in 28-18 home win over Hull FC.

1st March 2018 - big freeze causes postponement of Thursday-night fixture at Hull KR.

11th March 2018 - 22-18 home win over Salford.

12th March 2018 - Jon Wells joins as director of rugby.

14th March 2018 - Liam Watts signs with immediate effect from Hull FC on three-year deal until end of 2020 season.

18th March 2018 - home fixture with Wigan postponed because of snow.

23rd March 2018 - Luke Gale field goal on half-time hooter edges 25-24 win over Leeds at Elland Road, after leading 24-0 on 23 minutes.

28th March 2018 - Matt Cook agrees one-year contract extension to end of 2019 season.

29th March 2018 - forward Oliver Holmes signs new two-year deal to end of 2020 season, with option for further year.

29th March 2018 - three Luke Gale goals and field goal edge 11-6 win in the mud at Wakefield.

2nd April 2018 - Liam Watts makes debut as 18-6 home defeat by Warrington in wastersplash ends five-match winning run.

5th April 2018 - Greg Eden signs three-year contract extension to end of 2021 season.

8th April 2018 - 40-28 win at Huddersfield.

KEY DATES

10th April 2018 - prop Mitch Clark returns to Featherstone on loan on indefinite basis.

13th April 2018 - wingers Jy Hitchcox goes to Bradford and Kieran Gill to Oldham on month loans.

15th April 2018 - Paul McShane and Oliver Holmes score try-doubles in 41-0 home thrashing of Catalans.

20th April 2018 - winger Garry Lo scores try on debut in 28-12 defeat at Wigan.

23rd April 2018 - forward Jesse Sene-Lefao signs three-year contract extension to end of 2021 season.

27th April 2018 - Luke Gale sustains knee injury in hard-fought 24-4 home win over Wakefield. Garry Lo stood down before game to voluntarily assist the police with an inquiry.

30th April 2018 - Zak Hardaker banned for 14 months from all sport from 8th September 2017.

5th May 2018 - debutant Calum Turner scores try in 36-12 defeat at Hull FC.

6th May 2018 - club allows Garry Lo's release from contract to allow him to focus on personal matter.

12th May 2018 - 36-18 round-six home defeat to St Helens means Challenge Cup exit at first hurdle.

20th May 2018 - 38-10 win over Leeds at Magic Weekend in Newcastle.

24th May 2018 - 40-18 defeat at league leaders St Helens.

31st May 2018 - fullback Quentin Laulu-Togaga'e joins until end of 2018 season from dual registration partners Halifax.

1st June 2018 - options taken on Tuoyo Egodo and Kieran Gill's contracts to end of 2019 season.

1st June 2018 - Kieran Gill scores two tries on return from injury in 42-14 win at Hull KR in re-arranged round-four game to win inaugural Roger Millward Trophy.

8th June 2018 - Quentin Laulu-Togaga'e proves gamebreaker at stand-off in shock 34-30 win at Warrington. Matt Cook makes 250th career appearance.

17th June 2018 - Jy Hitchcox scores four tries in 24-all home draw with Hull KR.

19th June 2018 - utility Alex Foster signs new contract to end of 2021.

23rd June 2018 - last-gasp Jamie Ellis field goal seals 19-18 home win over Wigan in game postponed from round six.

30th June 2018 - 44-16 defeat to Catalans in baking-hot Perpignan.

5th July 2018 - Ben Roberts tears pectoral muscle in training. Greg Minikin undergoes ankle surgery. Alex Foster out for season after foot surgery.

8th July 2018 - Jake Trueman scores two tries among 38 unanswered points in 42-10 home win over Leeds.

10th July 2018 - winger James Clare signs two-year contract extension to end of 2020.

13th July 2018 - Jake Webster scores two tries in 24-6 win at Salford.

20th July 2018 - Adam Milner turns down NRL offers to sign three-year contract extension to end of 2021.

20th July 2018 - 32-18 home defeat to Huddersfield.

25th July 2018 - 19 year old fullback Calum Turner signs two-year contract extension to end of 2020.

26th July 2018 - Peter Matautia signs from Leigh on three-year deal.

26th July 2018 - Jy Hitchcox and Tuoyo Egodo to spend rest of season on loan at Bradford.

29th July 2018 - Greg Eden scores hat-trick in final regular-season 52-24 win at Widnes.

10th August 2018 - 24-22 defeat at Wigan in first Super 8s game.

17th August 2018 - 28-18 home win over Warrington.

21st August 2018 - Jake Webster to join Bradford at end of season.

1st September 2018 - Luke Gale returns from injury as Greg Eden scores hat-trick in 36-4 win over Challenge Cup winners Catalans.

7th September 2018 - 28-8 win at Hull FC confirms top-four finish.

13th September 2018 - Junior Moors leads dominant second half in 44-12 home win over Huddersfield.

21st September 2018 - Greg Eden scores four tries as semi-final trip to Wigan confirmed with 42-10 defeat of Wakefield.

28th September 2018 - 26-0 last round defeat at St Helens.

5th October 2018 - 14-0 semi-final defeat at Wigan.

18th October 2018 - French prop Gadwin Springer joins Toronto Wolfpack.

CLUB RECORDS

Highest score:
106-0 v Rochdale, 9/9/2007
Highest score against:
12-76 v Leeds, 14/8/2009
Record attendance:
25,449 v Hunslet, 9/3/35

MATCH RECORDS

Tries:
5 Derek Foster v Hunslet, 10/11/72
John Joyner v Millom, 16/9/73
Steve Fenton v Dewsbury, 27/1/78
Ian French v Hunslet, 9/2/86
St John Ellis v Whitehaven, 10/12/89
Greg Eden v Warrington, 11/6/2017
Goals: 17 Sammy Lloyd v Millom, 16/9/73
Points: 43 Sammy Lloyd v Millom, 16/9/73

SEASON RECORDS

Tries: 42 Denny Solomona 2016
Goals: 158 Sammy Lloyd 1976-77
Points: 355 Luke Gale 2017

CAREER RECORDS

Tries: 206 Alan Hardisty 1958-71
Goals: 875 Albert Lunn 1951-63
Points: 1,870 Albert Lunn 1951-63
Appearances: 613 John Joyner 1973-92

CASTLEFORD TIGERS

DATE	FIXTURE	RESULT	SCORERS	LGE	ATT
2/2/18	St Helens (a)	L46-6	t:McShane g:Gale	12th	13,108
11/2/18	Widnes (h)	W13-12	t:Minikin,Hitchcox g:Gale(2) fg:Gale	8th	7,106
24/2/18	Hull FC (h)	W28-18	t:Minikin,Webster,McMeeken,Shenton(2) g:Gale(4)	7th	9,365
11/3/18	Salford (h)	W22-8	t:Shenton,Clare,Gale g:Gale(5)	5th	7,480
23/3/18	Leeds (a) ●	W24-25	t:Ellis,Clare,Foster,Moors g:Gale(4) fg:Gale	6th	23,246
29/3/18	Wakefield (a)	W6-11	t:McMeeken g:Gale(3) fg:Gale	4th	7,020
2/4/18	Warrington (h)	L6-18	t:Holmes g:Gale	6th	6,881
8/4/18	Huddersfield (a)	W28-40	t:McShane,Minikin,Foster(2),Webster,Eden,Shenton g:Ellis(6)	5th	5,946
15/4/18	Catalans Dragons (h)	W41-0	t:McShane(2),Shenton,Holmes(2),Clare,Wardle g:Gale(6) fg:Gale	4th	7,137
20/4/18	Wigan (a)	L28-12	t:Holmes,Lo g:Gale(2)	5th	11,866
27/4/18	Wakefield (h)	W24-4	t:Minikin,Milner,McShane g:Gale(3),Ellis(3)	4th	7,485
5/5/18	Hull FC (a)	L36-12	t:McShane,Turner g:Ellis(2)	5th	14,623
12/5/18	St Helens (h) (CCR6)	L18-36	t:Trueman,Minikin,McMeeken g:Ellis(3)	N/A	5,342
19/5/18	Leeds (MW) ●●	W38-10	t:Hitchcox,Foster,Moors,Shenton,Milner,Holmes g:Ellis(7)	5th	N/A
24/5/18	St Helens (h)	L18-40	t:McMeeken,Hitchcox,Trueman,Holmes g:Ellis	5th	6,969
1/6/18	Hull KR (a)	W14-42	t:Gill(2),Eden,Foster,Cook,Shenton,Hitchcox g:Ellis(5)	4th	7,074
8/6/18	Warrington (a)	W30-34	t:McMeeken,Turner,Hitchcox,Laulu-Togagae,Holmes g:Turner(6),Milner	4th	9,198
17/6/18	Hull KR (h)	D24-24	t:McMeeken,Hitchcox(4) g:Turner(2)	4th	9,022
22/6/18	Wigan (h)	W19-18	t:Laulu-Togagae,Hitchcox,Cook g:Ellis(3) fg:Ellis	3rd	7,714
30/6/18	Catalans Dragons (a)	L44-16	t:Clare,Laulu-Togagae,McShane g:Ellis(2)	4th	10,236
8/7/18	Leeds (h)	W42-10	t:Eden,Laulu-Togagae,Cook,Trueman(2),Sene-Lefao(2) g:Ellis(7)	3rd	9,557
13/7/18	Salford (a)	W6-24	t:Webster(2),Shenton,Gill g:McShane(4)	3rd	2,681
20/7/18	Huddersfield (h)	L18-32	t:Ellis,Trueman,Moors g:Ellis(3)	4th	5,406
29/7/18	Widnes (a)	W24-52	t:Eden(3),Trueman,Laulu-Togagae(2),Holmes,Clark,Milner g:Ellis(8)	3rd	4,218
10/8/18	Wigan (a) (S8)	L24-22	t:Trueman,Clare,McShane,Clark g:Ellis(3)	4th	10,293
17/8/18	Warrington (h) (S8)	W28-18	t:Clare,Moors,Eden(2),McMeeken g:Ellis(4)	3rd	7,142
1/9/18	Catalans Dragons (h) (S8)	W36-4	t:Shenton,Eden(3),Trueman,Holmes g:Gale(6)	3rd	7,658
7/9/18	Hull FC (a) (S8)	W8-28	t:McMeeken,Moors,Eden(2),Clare g:Gale(4)	3rd	10,570
13/9/18	Huddersfield (h) (S8)	W44-12	t:Eden,Webster,Moors(2),Clare,McMeeken,Mata'utia,Millington g:McShane(6)	3rd	7,279
21/9/18	Wakefield (h) (S8)	W42-10	t:Eden(4),Minikin,Millington,Moors g:Gale(7)	3rd	7,860
28/9/18	St Helens (a) (S8)	L26-0		3rd	9,813
5/10/18	Wigan (a) (SF)	L14-0		N/A	13,461

● *Played at Elland Road*
●● *Played at St James' Park, Newcastle*

		APP		TRIES		GOALS		FG		PTS	
	D.O.B.	ALL	SL	ALL	SL	ALL	SL	ALL	SL	ALL	SL
James Clare	13/4/91	18	18	8	8	0	0	0	0	32	32
Mitch Clark	13/3/93	(15)	(15)	2	2	0	0	0	0	8	8
Matt Cook	14/11/86	6(14)	6(13)	3	3	0	0	0	0	12	12
Greg Eden	14/11/90	15	15	18	18	0	0	0	0	72	72
Tuoyo Egodo	16/2/97	1(1)	1(1)	0	0	0	0	0	0	0	0
Jamie Ellis	4/10/89	18	17	2	2	57	54	1	1	123	117
Alex Foster	25/9/93	14(2)	13(2)	5	5	0	0	0	0	20	20
Luke Gale	22/6/88	15	15	1	1	48	48	4	4	104	104
Kieran Gill	4/12/95	3	3	3	3	0	0	0	0	12	12
James Green	29/11/90	1(3)	1(3)	0	0	0	0	0	0	0	0
Jy Hitchcox	18/8/89	9	8	11	11	0	0	0	0	44	44
Oliver Holmes	7/8/92	20(7)	19(7)	9	9	0	0	0	0	36	36
Quentin Laulu-Togagae	1/12/84	8(1)	8(1)	6	6	0	0	0	0	24	24
Garry Lo	1/11/93	1	1	1	1	0	0	0	0	4	4
Will Maher	4/11/95	1(1)	1(1)	0	0	0	0	0	0	0	0
Nathan Massey	11/7/89	18(8)	18(8)	0	0	0	0	0	0	0	0
Peter Mata'utia	2/11/90	8	8	1	1	0	0	0	0	4	4
Mike McMeeken	10/5/94	23(3)	22(3)	9	8	0	0	0	0	36	32
Paul McShane	19/11/89	30(1)	29(1)	8	8	10	10	0	0	52	52
Grant Millington	1/11/86	18(11)	18(10)	2	2	0	0	0	0	8	8
Adam Milner	19/12/91	17(12)	16(12)	3	3	1	1	0	0	14	14
Greg Minikin	29/3/95	19(1)	18(1)	6	5	0	0	0	0	24	20
Junior Moors	30/7/86	7(18)	7(17)	8	8	0	0	0	0	32	32
Ben Roberts	8/7/85	14(3)	14(3)	0	0	0	0	0	0	0	0
Jesse Sene-Lefao	8/12/89	13(9)	12(9)	2	2	0	0	0	0	8	8
Michael Shenton	22/7/86	30	29	9	9	0	0	0	0	36	36
Gadwin Springer	4/4/93	(6)	(6)	0	0	0	0	0	0	0	0
Jake Trueman	16/2/99	26(2)	26(1)	8	7	0	0	0	0	32	28
Calum Turner	29/4/99	2(3)	2(3)	2	2	8	8	0	0	24	24
Joe Wardle	22/9/91	16(2)	15(2)	1	1	0	0	0	0	4	4
Liam Watts	8/7/90	23	22	0	0	0	0	0	0	0	0
Jake Webster	29/10/83	22(3)	21(3)	5	5	0	0	0	0	20	20

Paul McShane

LEAGUE RECORD
P30-W20-D1-L9
(3rd, SL/Semi-Finalists)
F767, A582, Diff+185
41 points.

CHALLENGE CUP
Round Six

ATTENDANCES
Best - v Leeds (SL - 9,557)
Worst - v St Helens (CC - 5,342)
Total (SL/S8s only) - 114,061
Average (SL/S8s only) - 7,604
(Down by 1,341 on 2017)

'SL' totals include Super 8s & semi-final; 'All' totals also include Challenge Cup

18th October 2017 - Louis Anderson signs one-year contract extension; prop Lambert Belmas, 20, signs two-year deal to end of 2019.

19th October 2017 - Lewis Tierney signs two-year contract.

20th October 2017 - hooker Alrix Da Costa signs new two-year deal; centre Arthur Romano, two years, and winger Georgy Gambaro, one year, sign full-time contracts.

2nd November 2017 - Tonga International Samisoni Langi signs two-year contract.

8th November 2017 - England Head of Performance Richard Hunwicks appointed Head of performance.

13th November 2017 - halfback Luke Walsh signs new one-year contract. Prop Luke Burgess released.

17th November 2017 - Krisnan Inu released.

20th November 2017 - Benjamin Jullien signs from Warrington on two-year contract.

12th December 2017 - PNG captain David Mead signs from Gold Coast on three-year contract.

2nd January 2018 - hooker Michael McIlorum signs from Wigan on two-year contract.

18th January 2018 - Academy back-rowers Sébastien Bled, Corentin Le Cam and centre Mathieu Laguerre sign two-year full-time contracts.

21st January 2018 - 24-10 pre-season defeat at snowy Hull FC.

30th January 2018 - Remi Casty appointed captain.

1st February 2018 - Thomas Bosc appointed assistant coach.

4th February 2018 - 40-12 round-one defeat at Widnes. Sam Moa suspended for two matches for late tackle.

9th February 2018 - Tony Gigot's two-year suspension by French Doping Control Agency ended on appeal.

10th February 2018 - 21-12 home defeat by St Helens. Benjamin Jullien suspended for one game for dangerous tackle. Appeal fails.

13th February 2018 - Tony Gigot signs two-year contract until end of 2019.

15th February 2018 - 23-4 round-11 defeat at promoted Hull KR.

24th February 2018 - 16-14 home defeat by Wakefield.

1st March 2018 - round-4 fixture at Leeds postponed a day early because of heavy snow.

10th March 2018 - late Lucas Albert penalty secures first win of season, by 18-16 at home to Hull KR.

12th March 2018 - Jason Baitieri gets one-match penalty notice for dangerous contact in Hull KR win. Tony Gigot given formal caution for dangerous throw.

17th March 2018 - 26-0 defeat to Warrington in cold and rain is first ever nilling at home.

23rd March 2018 - 42-16 defeat at Hull FC.

30th March 2018 - 32-16 Good Friday defeat at Salford.

2nd April 2018 - Jodie Broughton and David Mead score two tries each in 27-6 home win over Huddersfield.

7th April 2018 - 32-22 home defeat to Wigan, despite leading 21-0 early in second half. Greg Bird withdrawn early with hip injury.

15th April 2018 - 41-0 humiliation at Castleford.

22nd April 2018 - 34-22 win at League 1 York in fifth round of Challenge Cup.

24th April 2018 - Luke Walsh retires from playing after suffering ankle injury at Hull KR.

24th April 2018 - former London and Leigh Australian scrum-half Josh Drinkwater signs until end of season with immediate effect.

KEY DATES

28th April 2018 - Josh Drinkwater scores try and kicks six goals on debut as Tony Gigot kicks late field goal to seal 25-24 home win over Hull FC.

3rd May 2018 - 26-12 defeat at St Helens.

12th May 2018 - Mickael Goudemand scores two tries on debut and Jodie Broughton scores hat-trick in 56-10 Challenge Cup sixth round home win over Whitehaven.

14th May 2018 - Wigan's Sam Tomkins signs from 2019 on three-year contract, with option of further year.

20th May 2018 - Jodie Broughton scores second-half hat-trick as 26-12 Magic Weekend win over Salford at St James' Park lifts Dragons off bottom of table.

22nd May 2018 - Paul Aiton announces retirement from playing.

25th May 2018 - Parramatta backrower Kenny Edwards signs with immediate effect.

26th May 2018 - 33-20 home win over Leeds moves Dragons to within point of top eight.

31st May 2018 - Kenny Edwards makes strong debut as 20-6 win at Huddersfield takes Dragons into Challenge Cup semi-finals.

9th June 2018 - 32-12 home win over Widnes takes Dragons within a point of top eight. Fouad Yaha gets one-match ban for shoulder charge.

15th June 2018 - controversial late penalty means 26-25 defeat at Huddersfield. Sam Moa banned for two games for high tackle on Matty English.

20th June 2018 - late Kenny Edwards try seals 28-25 comeback win at Leeds in game postponed from round 4.

29th June 2018 - utility Ben Garcia signs new three-year contract to end of 2021 campaign.

30th June 2018 - Josh Drinkwater scores hat-trick and kicks six goals in 44-16 home win over Castleford.

7th July 2018 - Brayden Wiliame scores two tries in 35-18 win at Wakefield.

9th July 2018 - young prop Paul Séguier joins Toulouse on loan until end of season.

12th July 2018 - late Josh Drinkwater penalty earns 22-22 draw at Warrington.

21st July 2018 - Fouad Yaha scores four tries and Kenny Edwards two as 44-10 home win over Salford secures top-eight spot.

27th July 2018 - young centre Arthur Romano joins Toulouse on loan until end of season.

27th July 2018 - Kenny Edwards dismissed for late, high tackle in 25-20 defeat at Wigan. Jodie Broughton suffers season-ending ACL injury.

30th July 2018 - captain Rémi Casty signs two-year contract extension to end of 2020.

1st August 2018 - Greg Bird suspended for four games for dangerous contact on Gabe Hamlin in defeat at Wigan. Edwards gets sending off sufficient.

5th August 2018 - 35-16 win over St Helens in Challenge Cup semi-final at Bolton means first return to Wembley since 2007.

8th August 2018 - Greg Bird to miss Wembley final after appeal against four-match ban fails.

10th August 2018 - three under-19s make debut in 56-6 defeat at Warrington.

17th August 2018 - Sam Moa signs new two-year contract to end of 2020.

18th August 2018 - 35-6 home defeat to Wigan.

21st August 2018 - centre Brayden Wiliame signs new two-year contract to end of 2020.

25th August 2018 - Dragons make history as Tony Gigot wins Lance Todd Trophy in 20-14 Wembley win over Warrington.

31st August 2018 - Generalitat de Catalunya President Quim Torra visits Gilbert Brutus to congratulate the Dragons.

31st August 2018 - Vincent Duport announces retirement from professional game at end of season.

1st September 2018 - 36-4 defeat at Castleford.

3rd September 2018 - Louis Anderson announces he will retire at end of season.

8th September 2018 - last gasp converted Morgan Knowles try gives St Helens 26-22 win in Perpignan.

13th September 2018 - Fouad Yaha to join rugby union club Agen.

15th September 2018 - Mickael Simon dismissed for fighting in 34-22 defeat at Wakefield and banned for one game.

22nd September 2018 - 26-20 win at Hull FC.

24th September 2018 - Dragons present Challenge Cup to crowd at Nou Camp in Barcelona.

29th September 2018 - David Mead scores four second-half tries as comeback 22-12 home win over Huddersfield confirms seventh-placed finish.

2nd October 2018 - Lambert Belmas takes one-match penalty notice for dangerous tackle on Jermaine McGillvary.

4th October 2018 - halfback Matty Smith signs from St Helens on two-year contract.

10th October 2018 - forward Jason Baitieri signs new two-year contract to end of 2020.

12th October 2018 - Vincent Duport moves to Lezignan. Iain Thornley and Josh Drinkwater also depart.

22nd October 2018 - Matt Whitley signs from Widnes on two-year contract.

CLUB RECORDS

Highest score: 92-8 v York, 12/5/2013
Highest score against:
0-62 v Hull FC, 12/5/2017
Record attendance: 18,150 v Warrington, 20/6/2009 *(Barcelona)*
11,856 v Wigan, 2/7/2016
(Stade Gilbert Brutus)

MATCH RECORDS

Tries:
4 Justin Murphy v Warrington, 13/9/2008
Damien Cardace v Widnes, 31/3/2012
Kevin Larroyer v York, 12/5/2013
Jodie Broughton v St Helens, 14/4/2016
Fouad Yaha v Salford, 21/7/2018
David Mead v Huddersfield, 29/9/2018
Goals:
11 Thomas Bosc v Featherstone, 31/3/2007
Thomas Bosc v Batley, 29/5/2010
Scott Dureau v Widnes, 31/3/2012
Points:
26 Thomas Bosc v Featherstone, 31/3/2007

SEASON RECORDS

Tries: 29 Morgan Escare 2014
Goals: 134 Scott Dureau 2012
Points: 319 Scott Dureau 2012

CAREER RECORDS

Tries: 87 Vincent Duport
2007-2009; 2011-2018
Goals:
579 *(inc 14fg)* Thomas Bosc 2006-2017
Points: 1,380 Thomas Bosc 2006-2017
Appearances:
293 Remi Casty 2006-2013; 2015-2018

CATALANS DRAGONS

DATE	FIXTURE	RESULT	SCORERS	LGE	ATT
4/2/18	Widnes (a)	L40-12	t:Mead,Jullien g:Walsh(2)	10th	4,568
10/2/18	St Helens (h)	L12-21	t:Mead,Da Costa g:Albert(2)	12th	8,103
15/2/18	Hull KR (a)	L23-4	t:Mead	12th	6,711
24/2/18	Wakefield (h)	L14-16	t:Garcia,Tierney g:Albert(3)	12th	6,872
10/3/18	Hull KR (h)	W18-16	t:Tierney,Yaha g:Albert(5)	12th	7,342
17/3/18	Warrington (h)	L0-26		12th	6,585
23/3/18	Hull FC (a)	L42-16	t:Moa,Albert,Gigot g:Albert(2)	12th	10,347
30/3/18	Salford (a)	L32-16	t:Yaha(2),Bird g:Gigot(2)	12th	2,328
2/4/18	Huddersfield (h)	W27-6	t:Broughton(2),Jullien,Mead(2) g:Gigot(3) fg:Gigot	12th	8,853
7/4/18	Wigan (h)	L23-32	t:Jullien,Mead,Garcia g:Gigot(5) fg:Gigot	12th	8,640
15/4/18	Castleford (a)	L41-0		12th	7,137
22/4/18	York (a) (CCR5)	W22-34	t:Yaha,Baitieri,Simon,Albert,Broughton,Bird g:Albert(5)	N/A	3,081
28/4/18	Hull FC (h)	W25-24	t:Wiliame,Drinkwater,Gigot g:Drinkwater(6) fg:Gigot	11th	8,823
3/5/18	St Helens (a)	L26-12	t:Wiliame,Broughton,Tierney	12th	9,138
12/5/18	Whitehaven (h) (CCR6)	W56-10	t:Broughton(3),McIlorum,Drinkwater,Goudemand(2),Maria,Bousquet, Duport,Gigot g:Drinkwater(6)	N/A	2,533
20/5/18	Salford (MW) ●	W26-12	t:Garcia,Bousquet,Broughton(3) g:Gigot(3)	10th	N/A
26/5/18	Leeds (h)	W33-20	t:Jullien,Garcia,McIlorum,Gigot,Drinkwater,Broughton g:Drinkwater(4) fg:Gigot	10th	8,779
31/5/18	Huddersfield (a) (CCQF)	W6-20	t:Mead,Bird g:Drinkwater(6)	N/A	2,151
9/6/18	Widnes (h)	W32-12	t:Gigot,Wiliame,Casty,Edwards,Yaha g:Drinkwater(6)	9th	9,239
15/6/18	Huddersfield (a)	L26-25	t:Wiliame,Duport,Mead,Casty g:Drinkwater(4) fg:Gigot	9th	9,121
20/6/18	Leeds (a)	W25-28	t:Langi,Drinkwater,Yaha,Tierney,Edwards(2) g:Drinkwater(2)	8th	10,366
30/6/18	Castleford (h)	W44-16	t:Drinkwater(3),Bird,Anderson,Bousquet,Edwards,Tierney g:Drinkwater(6)	7th	10,236
7/7/18	Wakefield (a)	W18-35	t:Bird,Jullien,Mead,Wiliame(2),Yaha g:Drinkwater(5) fg:Gigot	7th	5,079
12/7/18	Warrington (a)	D22-22	t:Jullien,McIlorum,Gigot g:Drinkwater(5)	7th	8,807
21/7/18	Salford (h)	W44-10	t:Yaha(4),Drinkwater,Baitieri,Edwards(2) g:Drinkwater(6)	7th	8,672
27/7/18	Wigan (a)	L25-20	t:Broughton,Da Costa,Yaha g:Albert(4)	8th	10,656
5/8/18	St Helens (CCSF) ●●	W35-16	t:Tierney,Garcia(2),Gigot,Moa g:Drinkwater(7) fg:Gigot	N/A	26,086
10/8/18	Warrington (a) (S8)	L56-6	t:Mead g:Albert	8th	8,032
18/8/18	Wigan (h) (S8)	L6-35	t:Yaha g:Drinkwater	8th	6,739
25/8/18	Warrington (CCF) ●●●	W20-14	t:Tierney,Garcia,Wiliame g:Drinkwater(4)	N/A	50,672
1/9/18	Castleford (a) (S8)	L36-4	t:Wiliame	8th	7,658
8/9/18	St Helens (h) (S8)	L22-26	t:Mead,Casty,Thornley,Edwards g:Drinkwater(3)	8th	7,810
14/9/18	Wakefield (a) (S8)	L34-22	t:Jullien,Thornley,Mead,Wiliame g:Drinkwater(3)	8th	4,030
22/9/18	Hull FC (a) (S8)	W20-26	t:Moa,Gigot,Thornley,Wiliame,Edwards g:Drinkwater(2),Albert	7th	10,467
29/9/18	Huddersfield (h) (S8)	W22-12	t:Mead(4) g:Albert(3)	7th	7,340

● *Played at St James' Park, Newcastle* ●● *Played at University of Bolton Stadium* ●●● *Played at Wembley Stadium*

			APP		TRIES		GOALS		FG		PTS	
	D.O.B.		ALL	SL	ALL	SL	ALL	SL	ALL	SL	ALL	SL
Paul Aiton	29/5/85		2(6)	2(5)	0	0	0	0	0	0	0	0
Lucas Albert	4/7/98		14(1)	13(1)	2	1	26	21	0	0	60	46
Louis Anderson	27/6/85		4(14)	4(12)	1	1	0	0	0	0	4	4
Jason Baitieri	2/7/89		14(16)	12(14)	2	1	0	0	0	0	8	4
Lambert Belmas	11/8/97		1(4)	1(4)	0	0	0	0	0	0	0	0
Greg Bird	10/2/84		27	25	5	3	0	0	0	0	20	12
Julian Bousquet	18/7/91		2(28)	2(23)	3	2	0	0	0	0	12	8
Robin Brochon	21/9/00		1	1	0	0	0	0	0	0	0	0
Jodie Broughton	9/1/88		15	12	12	8	0	0	0	0	48	32
Remi Casty	5/2/85		25(4)	22(4)	3	3	0	0	0	0	12	12
Alrix Da Costa	2/10/97		4(11)	4(10)	2	2	0	0	0	0	8	8
Josh Drinkwater	15/6/92		21	17	8	7	76	53	0	0	184	134
Vincent Duport	15/12/87		6(1)	4(1)	2	1	0	0	0	0	8	4
Kenny Edwards	13/9/89		3(13)	3(10)	8	8	0	0	0	0	32	32
Benjamin Garcia	5/4/93		27(1)	22(1)	7	4	0	0	0	0	28	16
Tony Gigot	27/12/90		28	23	8	6	13	13	7	6	65	56
Mickael Goudemand	9/3/96		2(9)	2(7)	2	0	0	0	0	0	8	0
Benjamin Jullien	1/3/95		27(2)	23(2)	7	7	0	0	0	0	28	28
Samisoni Langi	11/6/93		22	18	1	1	0	0	0	0	4	4
Thibaut Margalet	3/1/93		(6)	(5)	0	0	0	0	0	0	0	0
Antoni Maria	21/3/87		4(11)	3(9)	1	0	0	0	0	0	4	0
Ugo Martin	5/11/98		1	1	0	0	0	0	0	0	0	0
Michael McIlorum	10/1/88		29	24	3	2	0	0	0	0	12	8
David Mead	4/11/88		31	27	16	15	0	0	0	0	64	60
Sam Moa	14/6/86		26(4)	21(4)	3	2	0	0	0	0	12	8
Arthur Mourgue	2/5/99		1	1	0	0	0	0	0	0	0	0
Ugo Perez	30/11/94		1	1	0	0	0	0	0	0	0	0
Mickael Simon	2/4/87		22(8)	18(7)	1	0	0	0	0	0	4	0
Iain Thornley	11/9/91		14(1)	13(1)	3	3	0	0	0	0	12	12
Lewis Tierney	20/10/94		29	25	7	5	0	0	0	0	28	20
Luke Walsh	12/5/87		2	2	0	0	2	2	0	0	4	4
Brayden Wiliame	17/12/92		31	28	10	9	0	0	0	0	40	36
Fouad Yaha	19/8/96		19	16	13	12	0	0	0	0	52	48

David Mead

LEAGUE RECORD
P30-W12-D1-L17
(7th, SL)
F596, A750, Diff-154
25 points.

CHALLENGE CUP
Winners

ATTENDANCES
Best - v Castleford (SL - 10,236)
Worst - v Whitehaven (CC - 2,533)
Total (SL/S8s only) - 114,033
Average (SL/S8s only) - 8,145
(Down by 467 on 2017)

'SL' totals include Super 8s; 'All' totals also include Challenge Cup

15th October 2017 - forward Mikey Wood joins Bradford on loan for 2018 season.

18th October 2017 - Jamie Ellis signs for Castleford after season on loan at Hull KR.

18th October 2017 - halfback Isaac Farrell joins Batley on loan for 2018.

23rd October 2017 - prop Nathan Mason joins Leigh on loan for 2018 season.

13th November 2017 - centre/backrower Liam Johnson goes on loan to Bradford for 2018 season.

14th January 2018 - 32-22 win over Dewsbury in Leroy Cudjoe testimonial.

20th January 2018 - Jake Mamo returns from injury in 26-22 pre-season defeat at Wakefield.

1st February 2018 - dominant first half ends in 38-12 round-one defeat at Hull FC.

2nd February 2018 - winger Gene Ormsby leaves the club.

8th February 2018 - 20-6 home victory over Warrington.

14th February 2018 - forward Oliver Roberts signs new five-year contract until end of 2023.

20th February 2018 - 2017 player of the year, prop Sebastine Ikahihifo signs three-year contract extension to end of 2021.

23rd February 2018 - 26-12 round-three home defeat to St Helens.

1st March 2018 - prop Colton Roche joins York on month's loan.

2nd March 2018 - round four, Friday night fixture at Wakefield postponed to following Sunday because of heavy snow.

4th March 2018 - 22-4 defeat at Wakefield in cold conditions. Daniel Smith gets one-match penalty for dangerous contact, doubled to two games on appeal.

5th March 2018 - prop Paul Clough signs two-year contract extension to end of 2020 season.

8th March 2018 - 20-year-old centre Sam Wood signs new contract to end of 2021.

9th March 2018 - 28-16 home win over Widnes after leading 24-0 after 60 minutes.

12th March 2018 - Danny Brough signs one-year contract extension.

15th March 2018 - Jake Mamo absent with injury in 38-6 home televised defeat to Hull KR.

21st March 2018 - 2017 Academy Player of the Year Sam Hewitt signs two-year contract.

23rd March 2018 - 48-10 defeat at Wigan.

27th March 2018 - Rick Stone sacked. Chris Thorman steps up as interim head coach.

30th March 2018 - Louis Senior and Sam Hewitt make first team debuts as threadbare side through injury holds Leeds to 22-all home Good Friday draw.

2nd April 2018 - Innes Senior makes debut on wing in 27-6 defeat at Catalans.

5th April 2018 - back-rower Tom Symonds released from contract which ran to end of 2019 to return to Australia.

8th April 2018 - 17-year-old twins, Louis and Innes Senior both start as Innes scores two tries in spirited 40-28 home defeat by Castleford.

15th April 2018 - Danny Brough red-carded for dissent near end of 30-12 home defeat by Salford and gets three-match ban.

KEY DATES

20th April 2018 - Lee Gaskell and Seb Ikahihifo both injured in training in build up to 66-4 defeat at leaders St Helens.

27th April 2018 - Aaron Murphy tears adductor muscle in 38-4 defeat at Warrington.

30th April 2018 - Newcastle Knights assistant Simon Woolford appointed head coach on two-and-a-half-year contract.

4th May 2018 - Jake Wardle, who scores two tries, and Oliver Russell make debuts in 28-18 home win over Widnes as Giants move off bottom to ninth spot. Wardle gets three-match ban for dangerous tackle.

11th May 2018 - Danny Brough returns from suspension in 24-14 home Challenge Cup sixth-round win over Wakefield.

20th May 2018 - Aaron Murphy is man of match in second-row in 25-22 Magic Weekend win over Wakefield.

23rd May 2018 - prop Matthew English signs contract extension to end of 2022 season.

25th May 2018 - 24-16 win at Salford as new head coach Simon Woolford lands just in time for game.

31st May 2018 - Leroy Cudjoe returns from nine-month injury absence in 20-6 home Challenge Cup quarter-final defeat by Catalans.

5th June 2018 - Danny Brough gets two-match penalty notice for crusher tackle on Kenny Edwards, and an extra match for unreasonably challenging the notice.

8th June 2018 - halfback Oliver Russell kicks late field goal to secure 25-18 win at Leeds.

15th June 2018 - late Oliver Russell penalty goal seals 26-25 home win over Catalans in front of over 9,000 people.

21st June 2018 - Jake Wardle signs contract extension to 2020.

29th June 2018 - 37-10 defeat at Hull KR ends winning league run at five games.

1st July 2018 - Samoa international prop Suaia Matagi signs for 2019.

2nd July 2018 - prop Shannon Wakeman out for season and not offered new contract.

4th July 2018 - prop Adam Walne joins Leigh on loan.

5th July 2018 - Danny Brough returns from suspension in dominant 29-18 home win over Hull FC.

12th July 2018 - Darnell McIntosh scores twice as 20-12 home win over Wigan moves Giants into seventh spot.

16th July 2018 - halfback Oliver Russell signs new two-year contract to end of 2020 season.

20th July 2018 - top eight finish guaranteed as Jermaine McGillvary scores hat-trick in 32-18 win at Castleford

26th July 2018 - Sam Wood joins Halifax on loan to end of season.

27th July 2018 - 40-28 home win over Wakefield in last game of regular season moves Giants into fifth spot.

27th July 2018 - Suaia Matagi given immediate release by Parramatta to join Giants early.

10th August 2018 - Suaia Matagi makes debut in opening Super 8s 16-12 win at runaway leaders St Helens.

17th August 2018 - 26-6 home win over Hull FC after scoreless first half.

27th August 2018 - former Castleford halfback Tom Holmes signs from Featherstone on three-year contract from 2019 season.

31st August 2018 - Giants' top four hopes ended with 42-16 home defeat by Wakefield.

4th September 2018 - Ryan Hinchcliffe announces he will retire at end of season.

7th September 2018 - long-range Danny Brough penalty goal attempt after final hooter falls short in 26-24 defeat at Warrington.

13th September 2018 - Jordan Turner suffers knee injury in 44-12 defeat at Castleford.

20th September 2018 - 13-6 home defeat to Wigan.

25th September 2018 - Sam Wood to join Batley on loan for 2019.

29th September 2018 - 22-12 last-round defeat at Catalans means sixth-placed finish.

1st October 2018 - Jermaine McGillvary signs new, extended deal to end of 2023 season.

5th October 2018 - 19-year-old hooker Reiss Butterworth signs from Bradford for undisclosed fee on three-year contract.

24th October 2018 - Aaron Murphy and Dale Ferguson sign two-year contract extensions. Tyler Dickinson leaves the club.

29th October 2018 - halfback Matthew Frawley joins on two-year contract from Canterbury Bulldogs.

CLUB RECORDS

Highest score:
142-4 v Blackpool, 26/11/94
Highest score against:
12-94 v Castleford, 18/9/88
Record attendance:
32,912 v Wigan, 4/3/50 *(Fartown)*
15,629 v Leeds, 10/2/2008
*(McAlpine/Galpharm/
John Smith's Stadium)*

MATCH RECORDS

Tries:
10 Lionel Cooper v Keighley, 17/11/51
Goals: 18 Major Holland
v Swinton Park, 28/2/1914
Points: 39 Major Holland
v Swinton Park, 28/2/1914

SEASON RECORDS

Tries: 80 Albert Rosenfeld 1913-14
Goals: 156 *(inc 2fg)* Danny Brough 2013
Points: 346 Danny Brough 2013

CAREER RECORDS

Tries: 420 Lionel Cooper 1947-55
Goals: 958 Frank Dyson 1949-63
Points: 2,072 Frank Dyson 1949-63
Appearances: 485 Douglas Clark 1909-29

HUDDERSFIELD GIANTS

DATE	FIXTURE	RESULT	SCORERS	LGE	ATT
1/2/18	Hull FC (a)	L38-12	t:Hinchcliffe,Ta'ai g:Brough(2)	9th	13,704
8/2/18	Warrington (h)	W20-6	t:Ferguson,McIntosh,Turner g:Brough(4)	7th	5,104
23/2/18	St Helens (h)	L12-26	t:Brough,Roberts g:Brough(2)	10th	5,915
4/3/18	Wakefield (a)	L22-4	t:Gaskell	11th	4,055
9/3/18	Widnes (a)	W16-28	t:Hinchcliffe,Mamo,Roberts,McGillvary g:Brough(6)	9th	4,298
15/3/18	Hull KR (h)	L6-38	t:Roberts g:Brough	11th	4,612
23/3/18	Wigan (a)	L48-10	t:McGillvary,Hinchcliffe g:Brough	11th	10,641
30/3/18	Leeds (h)	D22-22	t:Simpson(2),O'Brien g:Brough(5)	10th	7,544
2/4/18	Catalans Dragons (a)	L27-6	t:Murphy g:McIntosh	10th	8,853
8/4/18	Castleford (h)	L28-40	t:Ta'ai,Smith,I Senior(2),Wakeman g:Rankin(4)	11th	5,946
15/4/18	Salford (h)	L12-30	t:I Senior,Roberts g:Brough(2)	11th	4,385
20/4/18	St Helens (a)	L66-4	t:Turner	11th	10,278
27/4/18	Warrington (a)	L38-4	t:McIntosh	12th	8,792
4/5/18	Widnes (h)	W28-18	t:Wardle(2),Wood,Ta'ai,Mellor g:Wood(4)	9th	4,645
11/5/18	Wakefield (h) (CCR6)	W24-14	t:O'Brien,English,Ta'ai,Gaskell g:Brough(4)	N/A	2,631
20/5/18	Wakefield (MW) ●	W25-22	t:Murphy,O'Brien,Mamo,McIntosh g:Brough(4) fg:Brough	9th	N/A
25/5/18	Salford (a)	W16-24	t:McIntosh,Smith,Turner,Leeming g:Brough(4)	8th	2,343
31/5/18	Catalans Dragons (h) (CCQF)	L6-20	t:Cudjoe g:Brough	N/A	2,151
8/6/18	Leeds (h)	W18-25	t:Leeming,Murphy,Mellor,O'Brien g:Russell(4) fg:Russell	8th	11,051
15/6/18	Catalans Dragons (h)	W26-25	t:Mellor,McIntosh,McGillvary(2),O'Brien g:Russell(3)	8th	9,121
29/6/18	Hull KR (a)	L37-10	t:McIntosh,Murphy g:Russell	9th	7,080
5/7/18	Hull FC (h)	W29-18	t:Smith,Murphy,Rankin,McIntosh(2) g:Brough(4) fg:Brough	8th	4,696
12/7/18	Wigan (h)	W20-12	t:McIntosh(2),Mellor,Cudjoe g:Brough(2)	8th	5,264
20/7/18	Castleford (a)	W18-32	t:McGillvary(3),Gaskell,Cudjoe,McIntosh g:Brough(4)	8th	5,406
27/7/18	Wakefield (h)	W40-28	t:Rankin,Mellor,McGillvary(3),McIntosh,Ta'ai g:Brough(6)	5th	5,697
10/8/18	St Helens (a) (S8)	W12-16	t:McIntosh(2),Mellor g:Brough(2)	5th	8,979
17/8/18	Hull FC (h) (S8)	W26-6	t:Mellor,Gaskell,Hinchcliffe,Ta'ai g:Brough(4),McIntosh	5th	4,499
31/8/18	Wakefield (h) (S8)	L16-42	t:McGillvary,Ta'ai,Murphy g:Brough(2)	5th	4,963
7/9/18	Warrington (a) (S8)	L26-24	t:Mamo(3),Gaskell,Wardle g:Brough(2)	5th	9,076
13/9/18	Castleford (a) (S8)	L44-12	t:O'Brien,Gaskell g:Brough(2)	6th	7,279
20/9/18	Wigan (h) (S8)	L6-13	t:Leeming g:Brough	6th	4,197
29/9/18	Catalans Dragons (a) (S8)	L22-12	t:L Senior,I Senior g:Brough(2)	6th	7,340

● *Played at St James' Park, Newcastle*

<table>
<tr><th rowspan="2"></th><th rowspan="2">D.O.B.</th><th colspan="2">APP</th><th colspan="2">TRIES</th><th colspan="2">GOALS</th><th colspan="2">FG</th><th colspan="2">PTS</th></tr>
<tr><th>ALL</th><th>SL</th><th>ALL</th><th>SL</th><th>ALL</th><th>SL</th><th>ALL</th><th>SL</th><th>ALL</th><th>SL</th></tr>
<tr><td>Danny Brough</td><td>15/1/83</td><td>24</td><td>22</td><td>1</td><td>1</td><td>67</td><td>62</td><td>2</td><td>2</td><td>140</td><td>130</td></tr>
<tr><td>Paul Clough</td><td>27/9/87</td><td>19(11)</td><td>17(11)</td><td>0</td><td>0</td><td>0</td><td>0</td><td>0</td><td>0</td><td>0</td><td>0</td></tr>
<tr><td>Leroy Cudjoe</td><td>7/4/88</td><td>10</td><td>9</td><td>3</td><td>2</td><td>0</td><td>0</td><td>0</td><td>0</td><td>12</td><td>8</td></tr>
<tr><td>Tyler Dickinson</td><td>18/8/96</td><td>(6)</td><td>(6)</td><td>0</td><td>0</td><td>0</td><td>0</td><td>0</td><td>0</td><td>0</td><td>0</td></tr>
<tr><td>Matty English</td><td>14/11/97</td><td>2(14)</td><td>2(12)</td><td>1</td><td>0</td><td>0</td><td>0</td><td>0</td><td>0</td><td>4</td><td>0</td></tr>
<tr><td>Dale Ferguson</td><td>13/4/88</td><td>10(4)</td><td>10(4)</td><td>1</td><td>1</td><td>0</td><td>0</td><td>0</td><td>0</td><td>4</td><td>4</td></tr>
<tr><td>Lee Gaskell</td><td>28/10/90</td><td>26</td><td>25</td><td>6</td><td>5</td><td>0</td><td>0</td><td>0</td><td>0</td><td>24</td><td>20</td></tr>
<tr><td>Sam Hewitt</td><td>29/4/99</td><td>(1)</td><td>(1)</td><td>0</td><td>0</td><td>0</td><td>0</td><td>0</td><td>0</td><td>0</td><td>0</td></tr>
<tr><td>Ryan Hinchcliffe</td><td>7/10/84</td><td>23(8)</td><td>21(8)</td><td>4</td><td>4</td><td>0</td><td>0</td><td>0</td><td>0</td><td>16</td><td>16</td></tr>
<tr><td>Sebastine Ikahihifo</td><td>27/1/91</td><td>10(10)</td><td>8(10)</td><td>0</td><td>0</td><td>0</td><td>0</td><td>0</td><td>0</td><td>0</td><td>0</td></tr>
<tr><td>Michael Lawrence</td><td>12/4/90</td><td>15(5)</td><td>15(4)</td><td>0</td><td>0</td><td>0</td><td>0</td><td>0</td><td>0</td><td>0</td><td>0</td></tr>
<tr><td>Kruise Leeming</td><td>7/9/95</td><td>6(18)</td><td>6(16)</td><td>3</td><td>3</td><td>0</td><td>0</td><td>0</td><td>0</td><td>12</td><td>12</td></tr>
<tr><td>Jake Mamo</td><td>6/6/94</td><td>16</td><td>14</td><td>5</td><td>5</td><td>0</td><td>0</td><td>0</td><td>0</td><td>20</td><td>20</td></tr>
<tr><td>Suaia Matagi</td><td>23/3/88</td><td>7</td><td>7</td><td>0</td><td>0</td><td>0</td><td>0</td><td>0</td><td>0</td><td>0</td><td>0</td></tr>
<tr><td>Jermaine McGillvary</td><td>16/5/88</td><td>20</td><td>18</td><td>11</td><td>11</td><td>0</td><td>0</td><td>0</td><td>0</td><td>44</td><td>44</td></tr>
<tr><td>Darnell McIntosh</td><td>5/7/97</td><td>22</td><td>20</td><td>14</td><td>14</td><td>2</td><td>2</td><td>0</td><td>0</td><td>60</td><td>60</td></tr>
<tr><td>Alex Mellor</td><td>24/9/94</td><td>19(5)</td><td>17(5)</td><td>7</td><td>7</td><td>0</td><td>0</td><td>0</td><td>0</td><td>28</td><td>28</td></tr>
<tr><td>Aaron Murphy</td><td>26/11/88</td><td>23</td><td>22</td><td>6</td><td>6</td><td>0</td><td>0</td><td>0</td><td>0</td><td>24</td><td>24</td></tr>
<tr><td>Adam O'Brien</td><td>11/7/93</td><td>26(5)</td><td>24(5)</td><td>6</td><td>5</td><td>0</td><td>0</td><td>0</td><td>0</td><td>24</td><td>20</td></tr>
<tr><td>Jordan Rankin</td><td>17/12/91</td><td>30</td><td>28</td><td>2</td><td>2</td><td>4</td><td>4</td><td>0</td><td>0</td><td>16</td><td>16</td></tr>
<tr><td>Oliver Roberts</td><td>24/12/94</td><td>16(8)</td><td>16(7)</td><td>4</td><td>4</td><td>0</td><td>0</td><td>0</td><td>0</td><td>16</td><td>16</td></tr>
<tr><td>Colton Roche</td><td>23/6/93</td><td>1(6)</td><td>1(6)</td><td>0</td><td>0</td><td>0</td><td>0</td><td>0</td><td>0</td><td>0</td><td>0</td></tr>
<tr><td>Oliver Russell</td><td>21/9/98</td><td>6</td><td>6</td><td>0</td><td>0</td><td>8</td><td>8</td><td>1</td><td>1</td><td>17</td><td>17</td></tr>
<tr><td>Innes Senior</td><td>30/5/00</td><td>8</td><td>8</td><td>4</td><td>4</td><td>0</td><td>0</td><td>0</td><td>0</td><td>16</td><td>16</td></tr>
<tr><td>Louis Senior</td><td>30/5/00</td><td>3</td><td>3</td><td>1</td><td>1</td><td>0</td><td>0</td><td>0</td><td>0</td><td>4</td><td>4</td></tr>
<tr><td>Jared Simpson</td><td>4/1/96</td><td>5</td><td>5</td><td>2</td><td>2</td><td>0</td><td>0</td><td>0</td><td>0</td><td>8</td><td>8</td></tr>
<tr><td>Daniel Smith</td><td>20/3/93</td><td>6(17)</td><td>6(15)</td><td>3</td><td>3</td><td>0</td><td>0</td><td>0</td><td>0</td><td>12</td><td>12</td></tr>
<tr><td>Tom Symonds</td><td>17/2/89</td><td>(1)</td><td>(1)</td><td>0</td><td>0</td><td>0</td><td>0</td><td>0</td><td>0</td><td>0</td><td>0</td></tr>
<tr><td>Ukuma Ta'ai</td><td>17/1/87</td><td>23(3)</td><td>22(3)</td><td>7</td><td>6</td><td>0</td><td>0</td><td>0</td><td>0</td><td>28</td><td>24</td></tr>
<tr><td>Jordan Turner</td><td>9/1/89</td><td>29</td><td>27</td><td>3</td><td>3</td><td>0</td><td>0</td><td>0</td><td>0</td><td>12</td><td>12</td></tr>
<tr><td>Shannon Wakeman</td><td>15/2/90</td><td>(2)</td><td>(2)</td><td>1</td><td>1</td><td>0</td><td>0</td><td>0</td><td>0</td><td>4</td><td>4</td></tr>
<tr><td>Adam Walne</td><td>3/10/90</td><td>1(4)</td><td>1(4)</td><td>0</td><td>0</td><td>0</td><td>0</td><td>0</td><td>0</td><td>0</td><td>0</td></tr>
<tr><td>Jake Wardle</td><td>18/11/98</td><td>4</td><td>4</td><td>3</td><td>3</td><td>0</td><td>0</td><td>0</td><td>0</td><td>12</td><td>12</td></tr>
<tr><td>Sam Wood</td><td>11/6/97</td><td>6</td><td>6</td><td>1</td><td>1</td><td>4</td><td>4</td><td>0</td><td>0</td><td>12</td><td>12</td></tr>
</table>

Ryan Hinchcliffe

LEAGUE RECORD
P30-W13-D1-L16
(6th, SL)
F539, A794, Diff-255
27 points.

CHALLENGE CUP
Quarter Finalists

ATTENDANCES
Best - v Catalans (SL - 9,121)
Worst - v Catalans (CC - 2,151)
Total (SL/S8s only) - 76,588
Average (SL/S8s only) - 5,471
(Down by 402 on 2017)

'SL' totals include Super 8s; 'All' totals also include Challenge Cup

Super League XXIII - Club by Club

19th October 2017 - Jez Litten, Jordan Lane, Ross Osborne and Jack Sanderson join Doncaster on loan for 2018 season.

26th October 2017 - utility back Jake Connor signs new deal to end of 2020.

14th January 2018 - 34-26 home defeat to Hull KR in Clive Sullivan Trophy match.

17th January 2018 - Danny Houghton named new captain.

21st January 2018 - 24-10 home pre-season win over Catalans.

26th January 2018 - Nick Rawsthorne granted release to join Toronto.

1st February 2018 - Fetuli Talanoa scores hat-trick in 38-12 round one home win over Huddersfield.

10th February 2018 - Bureta Faraimo suffers head injury in second minute and Danny Houghton tears calf in 24-10 round-two defeat to Wigan in Wollongong.

17th February 2018 - St George Illawarra edge friendly in Sydney 24-18.

24th February 2018 - Sika Manu misses 28-18 defeat at Castleford, as club permits him to visit cyclone-hit Tonga. Mickey Paea breaks hand.

2nd March 2018 - Liam Watts sent off for head butt late on in 21-12 home win over Warrington and gets three-match ban.

8th March 2018 - forward Jordan Lane makes impressive debut and Jack Logan returns after near two-year absence in 20-16 defeat at Leeds.

14th March 2018 - Liam Watts transferred to Castleford for 'significant' fee.

14th March 2018 - prop Masi Matongo signs three-year contract extension until end of 2021. Centre Carlos Tuimavave signs two-year contract extension to until end of 2020.

16th March 2018 - 24-8 defeat at Salford.

20th March 2018 - 22-year old prop Brad Fash signs three-year contract extension to end of 2021.

21st March 2018 - 19-year-old prop Lewis Bienek signs on immediate three-and-a-half year deal from London Broncos and is loaned back to the capital club for remainder of season

23rd March 2018 - Albert Kelly returns after three-game absence with head injury in 42-16 home win over Catalans.

30th March 2018 - 30-22 Good Friday win at Hull KR despite dismissal of Bureta Faraimo after ten minutes for late tackle.

2nd April 2018 - Marc Sneyd kicks last-minute 51-metre field goal to snatch 27-26 home win over Wakefield.

6th April 2018 - Danny Houghton plays 300th club game as young prop Brad Fash breaks jaw in 26-12 defeat at leaders St Helens.

12th April 2018 - Josh Griffin scores impressive try-double in 39-20 win at Widnes.

13th April 2018 - back-rower Jansin Turgut joins Featherstone on one-month loan deal.

20th April 2018 - Jake Connor gets two tries as late Marc Sneyd field goal secures hard-fought 19-18 victory over Leeds at KCOM Stadium.

20th April 2018 - Joe Westerman returns after signing from Toronto on deal to end of season.

28th April 2018 - Jordan Abdull breaks leg as late Tony Gigot field goal means 25-24 defeat at Catalans.

3rd May 2018 - 20-year-old forward Jordan Lane signs two-year contract extension. Academy centre Kieran Buchanan also signs full-time deal to end of 2020.

5th May 2018 - Albert Kelly signs two-year contract extension to end of 2020

5th May 2018 - Joe Westerman makes second debut as Bureta Faraimo and Sika Manu score try-doubles in 36-12 home win over Castleford. Albert Kelly absent with hamstring as Marc Sneyd leaves field with long-term knee injury.

10th May 2018 - six sin bins and Bureta Faraimo gets last-minute red card in 38-20 Challenge Cup sixth-round win at Featherstone. Faraimo gets two-match penalty notice for reckless high tackle. Josh Bowden suffers season-ending knee injury.

17th May 2018 - halfback Liam Harris, 21, signs from Doncaster on two-and-a-half year deal.

20th May 2018 - Kirk Yeaman comes out of retirement as Jake Connor and Jamie Shaul score try-braces in 34-22 Magic Weekend win over Hull KR at St James' Park. Youngsters Cameron Scott and new-signing Liam Harris make debuts.

25th May 2018 - 30-12 defeat at Halliwell Jones Stadium as Wolves score 30 unanswered points in second half. Brad Fash returns from broken jaw.

3rd June 2018 - St Helens score twice just before half-time with Danny Houghton and Danny Washbrook both in sin bin to lead 23-12 at half-time of Challenge Cup quarter-final and then hang on to win 25-22. Dean Hadley leaves field with knee injury in first minute.

8th June 2018 - Bureta Faraimo scores hat-trick in 45-14 home victory over Salford.

14th June 2018 - Fetuli Talanoa signs one-year contract extension to end of 2019.

16th June 2018 - 14-10 home defeat to Wigan.

29th June 2018 - utility back Jake Connor pens new three-year deal until end of 2021.

29th June 2018 - roller-coaster 31-24 home win over Widnes. Sika Manu gets three-match penalty notice for dangerous contact.

4th July 2018 - Mark Minichiello and Sika Manu sign one-year contract extensions for 2019.

5th July 2018 - 29-18 defeat at Huddersfield.

10th July 2018 - Josh Griffin signs new two-year contract to end of 2021.

13th July 2018 - Jake Connor suffers season-ending, or so it was thought, hamstring tear in 34-18 home defeat to St Helens.

22nd July 2018 - Joe Westerman suffers season-ending knee injury in 72-10 defeat at Wakefield.

25th July 2018 - vice-captain Scott Taylor signs new five-year deal to end of 2023 season; prop Josh Bowden signs two-year contract extension to end of 2021; Danny Washbrook signs one-year extension for 2019.

27th July 2018 - Jansin Turgut and Ross Osborne both released from remainder of contracts. Jack Logan joins Doncaster on loan.

27th July 2018 - 20-16 home defeat by Hull KR in torrential conditions.

10th August 2018 - Lewis Bienek makes debut in 31-13 home defeat to Wakefield in Super 8s opener.

17th August 2018 - Chris Green suffers long-term Achilles injury in 26-6 defeat at Huddersfield after scoreless first half.

31st August 2018 - 80-10 loss at Warrington is club record defeat.

8th September 2018 - 28-8 defeat to Castleford in Armed Forces Day fixture at KCOM Stadium

14th September 2018 - Jake Connor makes surprise early return in 38-12 defeat at League Leaders St Helens. Sika Manu suffers MCL knee injury.

21st September 2018 - Jack Downs signs for Batley on permanent deal.

22nd September 2018 - 26-20 home defeat to Catalans after late Kenny Edwards try.

26th September 2018 - Joe Westerman extends contract for 2019.

27th September 2018 - Congo-born Salford prop forward Levy Nzoungou and Oldham second-rower Danny Langtree sign on two-year contracts.

28th September 2018 - 14-12 last-round defeat at Wigan means eight-placed finish.

15th October 2018 - winger Matty Dawson-Jones joins from Leigh on two-year contract. Jordan Thompson returns on two-year deal.

18th October 2018 - Academy fullback Connor Wynne signs three-year deal.

CLUB RECORDS

Highest score: 88-0 v Sheffield, 2/3/2003
Highest score against:
10-80 v Warrington, 30/8/2018
Record attendance:
28,798 v Leeds, 7/3/36 *(The Boulevard)*
23,004 v Hull KR, 2/9/2007 *(KC Stadium)*

MATCH RECORDS

Tries: 7 Clive Sullivan v Doncaster, 15/4/68
Goals: 14 Jim Kennedy v Rochdale, 7/4/21
Sammy Lloyd v Oldham, 10/9/78
Matt Crowther v Sheffield, 2/3/2003
Points: 36 Jim Kennedy v Keighley, 29/1/21

SEASON RECORDS

Tries: 52 Jack Harrison 1914-15
Goals: 170 Sammy Lloyd 1978-79
Points: 369 Sammy Lloyd 1978-79

CAREER RECORDS

Tries: 250 Clive Sullivan 1961-74; 1981-85
Goals: 687 Joe Oliver 1928-37; 1943-45
Points: 1,842 Joe Oliver 1928-37; 1943-45
Appearances: 500 Edward Rogers 1906-25

HULL F.C.

DATE	FIXTURE	RESULT	SCORERS	LGE	ATT
1/2/18	Huddersfield (h)	W38-12	t:Kelly,Talanoa(3),Connor,Shaul g:Sneyd(7)	4th	13,704
10/2/18	Wigan (a) ●	L24-10	t:Talanoa,Abdull g:Sneyd	6th	12,416
24/2/18	Castleford (a)	L28-18	t:Sneyd,Faraimo,Paea g:Sneyd(3)	8th	9,365
2/3/18	Warrington (h)	W21-12	t:Faraimo,Tuimavave g:Sneyd(6) fg:Sneyd	5th	10,051
8/3/18	Leeds (a)	L20-16	t:Hadley,Abdull,Talanoa g:Sneyd(2)	7th	11,158
16/3/18	Salford (a)	L24-8	t:Hadley g:Sneyd(2)	9th	2,902
23/3/18	Catalans Dragons (h)	W42-16	t:Griffin(2),Talanoa(2),Shaul,Taylor,Connor g:Sneyd(6),Connor	7th	10,347
30/3/18	Hull KR (a)	W22-30	t:Houghton,Talanoa(2),Shaul,Connor g:Sneyd(5)	6th	12,090
2/4/18	Wakefield (h)	W27-26	t:Abdull,Kelly,Talanoa(2) g:Sneyd(5) fg:Sneyd	5th	11,529
6/4/18	St Helens (a)	L26-12	t:Kelly,Green g:Sneyd(2)	6th	10,408
12/4/18	Widnes (a)	W20-39	t:Washbrook,Faraimo,Matongo,Griffin(2),Talanoa,Shaul g:Sneyd(5) fg:Sneyd	6th	3,733
19/4/18	Leeds (h)	W19-18	t:Connor(2),Faraimo,Tuimavave g:Sneyd fg:Sneyd	4th	11,391
28/4/18	Catalans Dragons (a)	L25-24	t:Taylor(2),Miloudi g:Connor(6)	6th	8,823
5/5/18	Castleford (h)	W36-12	t:Manu(3),Shaul,Faraimo(2),Griffin g:Sneyd(2),Connor(4)	4th	14,623
10/5/18	Featherstone (a) (CCR6)	W20-38	t:Connor(2),Manu,Shaul,Griffin,Faraimo(2) g:Connor(5)	N/A	3,222
20/5/18	Hull KR (MW) ●●	W34-22	t:Taylor,Shaul(2),Harris,Logan,Connor g:Connor(5)	4th	N/A
25/5/18	Warrington (a)	L30-12	t:Hadley,Paea g:Connor(2)	4th	8,646
3/6/18	St Helens (a) (CCQF)	L25-22	t:Kelly,Green,Taylor,Miloudi g:Connor(3)	N/A	8,928
8/6/18	Salford (h)	W45-14	t:Faraimo(3),Downs,Logan,Miloudi,Shaul g:Connor(8) fg:Connor	5th	10,606
16/6/18	Wigan (h)	L10-14	t:Faraimo(2) g:Connor	5th	13,256
29/6/18	Widnes (h)	W31-24	t:Kelly,Miloudi,Harris,Tuimavave,Faraimo g:Connor(5) fg:Connor	5th	10,420
5/7/18	Huddersfield (a)	L29-18	t:Faraimo,Miloudi,Houghton g:Connor(3)	5th	4,696
13/7/18	St Helens (h)	L18-34	t:Faraimo(2),Turgut,Kelly g:Miloudi	5th	11,130
22/7/18	Wakefield (a)	L72-10	t:Harris,Faraimo g:Faraimo	5th	5,634
27/7/18	Hull KR (h)	L16-20	t:Abdull,Griffin,Minichiello g:Sneyd(2)	6th	17,564
10/8/18	Wakefield (h) (S8)	L13-31	t:Taylor,Shaul g:Sneyd(2) fg:Sneyd	7th	10,301
17/8/18	Huddersfield (a) (S8)	L26-6	t:Faraimo g:Faraimo	7th	4,499
30/8/18	Warrington (a) (S8)	L80-10	t:Talanoa,Griffin g:Faraimo	7th	8,101
7/9/18	Castleford (h) (S8)	L8-28	t:Tuimavave,Miloudi	7th	10,570
14/9/18	St Helens (a) (S8)	L38-12	t:Lane,Fash g:Faraimo,Connor	7th	9,348
22/9/18	Catalans Dragons (h) (S8)	L20-26	t:Griffin,Fash,Talanoa,Shaul g:Connor(2)	8th	10,467
28/9/18	Wigan (a) (S8)	L14-12	t:Tuimavave,Shaul g:Connor(2)	8th	11,189

● *Played at WIN Stadium, Wollongong*
●● *Played at St James' Park, Newcastle*

APP TRIES GOALS FG PTS

		ALL	SL	ALL	SL	ALL	SL	ALL	SL	ALL	SL
	D.O.B.										
Jordan Abdull	5/2/96	10(8)	10(8)	4	4	0	0	0	0	16	16
Lewis Bienek	11/4/98	(7)	(7)	0	0	0	0	0	0	0	0
Josh Bowden	14/1/92	7(7)	6(7)	0	0	0	0	0	0	0	0
Jake Connor	18/10/94	23(3)	21(3)	8	6	48	40	2	2	130	106
Jack Downs	10/11/95	3(4)	3(4)	1	1	0	0	0	0	4	4
Bureta Faraimo	16/7/90	28	26	19	17	4	4	0	0	84	76
Brad Fash	24/1/96	2(18)	2(17)	2	2	0	0	0	0	8	8
Chris Green	3/1/90	11(7)	9(7)	2	1	0	0	0	0	8	4
Josh Griffin	9/5/90	23	22	9	8	0	0	0	0	36	32
Dean Hadley	5/8/92	22(1)	20(1)	3	3	0	0	0	0	12	12
Liam Harris	20/4/97	9(2)	9(2)	3	3	0	0	0	0	12	12
Danny Houghton	25/9/88	24	22	2	2	0	0	0	0	8	8
Albert Kelly	21/3/91	15	14	6	5	0	0	0	0	24	20
Jordan Lane	20/10/97	6(11)	6(10)	1	1	0	0	0	0	4	4
Jez Litten	10/3/98	(9)	(8)	0	0	0	0	0	0	0	0
Jack Logan	8/9/95	9(2)	8(2)	2	2	0	0	0	0	8	8
Sika Manu	22/1/87	18	16	3	2	0	0	0	0	12	8
Masi Matongo	15/5/96	7(18)	7(16)	1	1	0	0	0	0	4	4
Hakim Miloudi	26/6/93	12(2)	11(2)	6	5	1	1	0	0	26	22
Mark Minichiello	30/1/82	23	21	1	1	0	0	0	0	4	4
Mickey Paea	25/3/86	13(12)	13(11)	2	2	0	0	0	0	8	8
Cameron Scott	7/10/99	6	6	0	0	0	0	0	0	0	0
Jamie Shaul	1/7/92	27	25	12	11	0	0	0	0	48	44
Marc Sneyd	9/2/91	16	16	1	1	51	51	5	5	111	111
Fetuli Talanoa	23/11/87	24	23	14	14	0	0	0	0	56	56
Scott Taylor	27/2/91	28(1)	27(1)	6	5	0	0	0	0	24	20
Carlos Tuimavave	10/1/92	22(3)	20(3)	5	5	0	0	0	0	20	20
Jansin Turgut	8/3/96	3(2)	3(2)	1	1	0	0	0	0	4	4
Danny Washbrook	18/9/85	17(8)	17(6)	1	1	0	0	0	0	4	4
Liam Watts	8/7/90	2(1)	2(1)	0	0	0	0	0	0	0	0
Joe Westerman	15/11/89	5(1)	4(1)	0	0	0	0	0	0	0	0
Kirk Yeaman	15/9/83	1	1	0	0	0	0	0	0	0	0

'SL' totals include Super 8s; 'All' totals also include Challenge Cup

Scott Taylor

LEAGUE RECORD
P30-W11-D0-L19
(8th, SL)
F615, A787, Diff-172
22 points.

CHALLENGE CUP
Quarter Finalists

ATTENDANCES
Best - v Hull KR (SL - 17,564)
Worst - v Warrington (SL - 10,051)
Total (SL/S8s only) - 165,959
Average (SL/S8s only) - 11,854
(Up by 395 on 2017)

11th July 2017 - Leeds Rhinos captain Danny McGuire signs two-year contract from 2018.

9th October 2017 - utility back Will Dagger signs from Warrington on three-year contract; outside back Connor Williams joins from Salford on one-year deal.

19th October 2017 - prop Mitch Clark released to join Castleford; forward George Milton released to join Bradford.

24th October 2017 - St Helens hooker Tommy Lee joins on two-year deal; Salford prop Jordan Walne on one-year.

14th November 2017 - young halfback Thibault Franck signs from Catalans on one-year contract.

9th November 2017 - hooker Zach Dockar-Clay released to play in Australia.

12th December 2017 - outside back Jake Butler-Fleming and hooker Will Jubb join partner club York City Knights for 2018 season.

7th January 2018 - 28-6 home victory over York City Knights in Ben Cockayne testimonial.

14th January 2018 - 34-26 win at Hull FC in Danny Houghton Testimonial game to retain Clive Sullivan Trophy. Danny Addy suffers long-term knee injury.

26th January 2018 - 24-18 home win over London Broncos in last warm-up game.

2nd February 2018 - USA international centre Junior Vaivai and Danny Tickle join on one-year deals.

2nd February 2018 - 26-8 round-one home defeat to Wakefield.

8th February 2018 - 20-11 round-two defeat by Leeds at Elland Road.

15th February 2018 - 23-4 round-eleven, home win over Catalans.

23rd February 2018 - Danny McGuire misses 36-12 defeat at Salford.

1st March 2018 - big freeze causes postponement of Thursday night, round-four home game with Castleford.

10th March 2018 - controversial late Catalans penalty means 18-16 defeat in Perpignan.

15th March 2018 - centre Andrew Heffernan stars in resounding 38-6 TV win at Huddersfield.

20th March 2018 - offers to sign Salford's Robert Lui and Leigh's Drew Hutchinson rejected.

23rd March 2018 - George Lawler suffers dislocated ankle and broken leg in 30-6 home defeat by St Helens.

30th March 2018 - Thomas Minns hat-trick not enough as 12-man Hull FC win Craven Park derby 30-22 in front of record crowd.

2nd April 2018 - 44-6 Easter Monday defeat at Wigan.

7th April 2018 - Justin Carney scores two tries as 31-12 home win over Widnes ends three-game losing streak.

14th April 2018 - second-half revival not enough as Shaun Lunt suffers early knee injury in 40-26 defeat at Warrington.

22nd April 2018 - Adam Quinlan scores hat-trick in 32-0 fifth-round Challenge Cup victory away at Oldham.

29th April 2018 - 20-18 home defeat to Leeds after leading 18-12 at half-time.

30th April 2018 - news released that Thomas Minns tested positive for banned, non-performance enhancing substance after win at Huddersfield in March.

1st May 2018 - prop Robbie Mulhern signs contract to end of 2021 season.

2nd May 2018 - 19-year-old winger Will Oakes signs deal until end of 2021 season. Young St Helens hooker Aaron Smith joins on one-month deal.

3rd May 2018 - Joe Wardill signs contract extension until end of 2021.

KEY DATES

4th May 2018 - forward George Lawler signs three-year extension until end of 2021.

6th May 2018 - Aaron Smith makes debut as injury-hit side goes down 54-18 at Wakefield.

10th May 2018 - halfback Thibault Franck joins Sheffield Eagles on one-month loan.

13th May 2018 - Danny Tickle sent off for punching just before half-time of 28-10 home Challenge Cup sixth-round defeat to Wigan. Elliot Wallis makes debut on wing. Tickle escapes ban.

13th May 2018 - Kieren Moss scores hat-trick in 34-22 Magic Weekend defeat to Hull FC in Newcastle.

25th May 2018 - Junior Vaivai scores two tries in 24-8 home win over Wigan. Josh Johnson gets one-match ban for tripping.

1st June 2018 - 42-14 home Roger Millward Trophy defeat to Castleford in re-arranged round four game.

7th June 2018 - Kieren Moss joins Halifax on loan for rest of season.

8th June 2018 - 26-4 defeat at St Helens.

11th June 2018 - forward Joel Tomkins signs from Wigan with immediate effect on 18 month contract. Academy winger Elliot Wallis signs three-year contract.

12th June 2018 - Academy winger Elliot Wallis signs three-year contract from 2019.

14th June 2018 - centre Andrew Heffernan ruled out for season with ongoing concussion injury.

17th June 2018 - 24-all draw at Castleford after trailing by 12 points going into last ten minutes.

26th June 2018 - prop Mose Masoe agrees new three-year contract to end of 2021 season.

29th June 2018 - Adam Quinlan and Ryan Shaw score try-braces in 37-10 home win over Huddersfield that revives top-eight hopes.

2nd July 2018 - centre Junior Vaivai signs new two-year contract to end of 2020 season.

4th July 2018 - Adam Quinlan signs two-year contract extension to end of 2020 with option for extra year.

7th July 2018 - halfback Todd Carney signs to end of season.

8th July 2018 - Danny McGuire scores hat-trick in 52-22 home win over Salford. Ryan Shaw suffers knee injury.

12th July 2018 - prop Lee Jewitt signs two-year contract extension to end of 2020 season

14th July 2018 - 26-24 win at Widnes.

20th July 2018 - Elliot Wallis scores brace in 34-20 home defeat by Warrington. James Greenwood, dangerous contact, and Danny McGuire, contact with match official, banned for one match. Mose Masoe gets two-match penalty notice for dangerous challenge.

24th July 2018 - young forwards Owen Harrison, three years, and Adam Rooks, two, sign professional contracts.

24th July 2018 - Craig Hall and Ben Crooks sign from Leigh for rest of season ahead of Qualifiers deadline. Will Dagger, Josh Johnson and Jordan Walne go to Leigh on loan.

28th July 2018 - Craig Hall scores two tries on second debut in 20-16 win at Hull FC. Todd Carney and Ben Crooks also make debuts. 10th placed finish means four home games in play-offs.

8th August 2018 - Maurice Blair cops two-match ban for reacting to crowd after sin-binning in Hull derby.

10th August 2018 - 28-10 home defeat to Salford in first Qualifiers game.

18th August 2018 - crucial 28-22 victory over Toronto Wolfpack in Canada.

22nd August 2018 - Andrew Heffernan released from contract to return to Australia to continue recovery from long-standing concussion.

1st September 2018 - Craig Hall scores try hat-trick and kicks five goals in 38-36 win at Leeds.

8th September 2018 - winger Justin Carney to return to Australia.

9th September 2018 - Craig Hall scores four tries in 38-24 home win over Halifax.

15th September 2018 - James Greenwood scores try double in 30-18 home win over London Broncos.

22nd September 2018 - 34-23 defeat in Toulouse after leading 19-0 means a win by more than 15 points against Widnes will avoid Million Pound game.

28th September 2018 - captain Shaun Lunt hospitalised with infection.

30th September 2018 - 30-0 home win over Widnes secures Super League place.

1st October 2018 - Jimmy Keinhorst, Ryan Lannon and Weller Hauraki signings confirmed for 2019 by Tim Sheens

10th October 2018 - Nick Scruton and Craig Hall sign one-year contract extensions. Chris Clarkson, Ben Kavanagh, Danny Tickle, James Donaldson, Matty Marsh and Liam Salter all depart.

22nd October 2018 - Head of Rugby Jamie Peacock leaves after three years.

24th October 2018 - centre Ben Crooks signs two-year contract extension.

CLUB RECORDS

Highest score:
100-6 v Nottingham City, 19/8/90
Highest score against:
6-84 v Wigan, 1/4/2013
Record attendance:
27,670 v Hull FC, 3/4/53 *(Boothferry Park)*
12,090 v Hull FC, 30/3/2018 *(Craven Park)*

MATCH RECORDS

Tries: 11 George West
v Brooklands Rovers, 4/3/1905
Goals:
14 Alf Carmichael v Merthyr, 8/10/1910
Mike Fletcher v Whitehaven, 18/3/90
Colin Armstrong v Nottingham City, 19/8/90
Damien Couturier v Halifax, 23/4/2006
Points: 53 George West
v Brooklands Rovers, 4/3/1905

SEASON RECORDS

Tries: 45 Gary Prohm 1984-85
Goals: 199 Mike Fletcher 1989-90
Points: 450 Mike Fletcher 1989-90

CAREER RECORDS

Tries: 207 Roger Millward 1966-80
Goals: 1,268 Mike Fletcher 1987-98
Points: 2,760 Mike Fletcher 1987-98
Appearances: 489 Mike Smith 1975-91

HULL KINGSTON ROVERS

DATE	FIXTURE	RESULT	SCORERS	LGE	ATT
2/2/18	Wakefield (h)	L6-28	t:Clarkson g:Shaw	8th	8,615
8/2/18	Leeds (a) ●	L20-11	t:Shaw,Quinlan g:Shaw fg:Atkin	11th	16,149
15/2/18	Catalans Dragons (h)	W23-4	t:Shaw,Masoe,Lunt,Tickle g:Shaw(3) fg:Atkin	8th	6,711
23/2/18	Salford (a)	L36-12	t:Minns,Quinlan g:Shaw(2)	11th	2,948
10/3/18	Catalans Dragons (a)	L18-16	t:Lawler,J Carney g:Shaw(4)	10th	7,342
15/3/18	Huddersfield (a)	W6-38	t:Heffernan,Quinlan,Shaw(2),Greenwood,McGuire g:Shaw(7)	8th	4,612
23/3/18	St Helens (h)	L6-30	t:Shaw g:Shaw	9th	7,724
30/3/18	Hull FC (h)	L22-30	t:Minns(3),Shaw g:Shaw(3)	11th	12,090
2/4/18	Wigan (a)	L44-6	t:Atkin g:Shaw	11th	10,977
7/4/18	Widnes (h)	W31-12	t:J Carney(2),Heffernan,Tickle,Greenwood g:Shaw(5) fg:McGuire	9th	7,260
14/4/18	Warrington (a)	L40-26	t:Blair,Donaldson,Atkin,McGuire g:Shaw(5)	10th	9,305
22/4/18	Oldham (a) (CCR5)	W0-32	t:Atkin,Quinlan(3),Oakes,Dagger g:Shaw(4)	N/A	1,064
29/4/18	Leeds (h)	L18-28	t:Mulhern,Masoe g:Shaw(5)	10th	9,095
6/5/18	Wakefield (a)	L54-18	t:Clarkson,Quinlan,Moss g:Shaw(3)	11th	5,331
13/5/18	Wigan (h) (CCR6)	L10-28	t:Atkin,Vaivai g:Shaw	N/A	3,524
20/5/18	Hull FC (MW) ●●	L34-22	t:Moss(3),Lee g:Shaw(3)	12th	N/A
25/5/18	Wigan (h)	W24-8	t:Vaivai(2),Quinlan,Atkin g:Tickle(4)	11th	7,222
1/6/18	Castleford (h)	L14-42	t:Shaw(2),Clarkson g:Shaw	11th	7,074
8/6/18	St Helens (a)	L26-4	t:Vaivai	11th	9,405
17/6/18	Castleford (a)	D24-24	t:Vaivai(2),Quinlan,Masoe g:Shaw(4)	11th	9,022
29/6/18	Huddersfield (h)	W37-10	t:Tomkins,Quinlan(2),Vaivai,Shaw(2) g:Shaw(6) fg:Atkin	11th	7,080
8/7/18	Salford (h)	W52-22	t:Shaw,Quinlan,Oakes(2),Greenwood,McGuire(3),Tomkins g:Shaw,Tickle(7)	10th	7,698
14/7/18	Widnes (a)	W24-26	t:Donaldson,Tickle,Quinlan,Salter g:Atkin,Tickle(4)	10th	4,469
20/7/18	Warrington (h)	L20-34	t:Wallis(2),Mulhern,Atkin g:Tickle(2)	10th	7,045
27/7/18	Hull FC (a)	W16-20	t:Hall(2),Tickle g:Tickle(3),Hall	10th	17,564
10/8/18	Salford (h) (S8-Q)	L10-28	t:Hall,Lunt g:Tickle	7th(S8-Q)	7,081
18/8/18	Toronto (a) (S8-Q)	W22-28	t:Vaivai,Hall,Atkin,Clarkson g:Tickle(4),Hall(2)	5th(S8-Q)	7,540
1/9/18	Leeds (a) (S8-Q)	W36-38	t:Hall(3),Quinlan,Mulhern,Atkin,Vaivai g:Hall(5)	5th(S8-Q)	11,468
9/9/18	Halifax (h) (S8-Q)	W38-24	t:Hall(4),Greenwood,Atkin,Lunt g:Hall(4),Tickle	3rd(S8-Q)	7,952
15/9/18	London Broncos (h) (S8-Q)	W30-18	t:Greenwood(2),Atkin,Lee,Vaivai g:Atkin(3),Tickle(2)	3rd(S8-Q)	7,210
22/9/18	Toulouse (a) (S8-Q)	L34-23	t:Mulhern,Hall(2),Atkin g:Tickle(3) fg:McGuire	4th(S8-Q)	4,127
30/9/18	Widnes (h) (S8-Q)	W30-0	t:Greenwood,Crooks,Atkin,Vaivai,Hall g:Hall(5)	3rd(S8-Q)	8,232

● *Played at Elland Road* ●● *Played at St James' Park, Newcastle*

APP TRIES GOALS FG PTS

	D.O.B.	ALL	SL	ALL	SL	ALL	SL	ALL	SL	ALL	SL
Chris Atkin	7/2/93	25(6)	17(5)	12	4	4	1	3	3	59	21
Maurice Blair	16/10/84	23(4)	21(1)	1	1	0	0	0	0	4	4
Justin Carney	16/6/88	16	14	3	3	0	0	0	0	12	12
Todd Carney	2/6/86	4(2)	(1)	0	0	0	0	0	0	0	0
Joe Cator	15/6/98	4(1)	2(1)	0	0	0	0	0	0	0	0
Chris Clarkson	7/4/90	24(3)	18(2)	4	3	0	0	0	0	16	12
Ben Crooks	15/6/93	6	1	1	0	0	0	0	0	4	0
Will Dagger	21/2/99	3(3)	3(2)	1	0	0	0	0	0	4	0
James Donaldson	14/9/91	5(16)	4(11)	2	2	0	0	0	0	8	8
James Greenwood	17/6/91	22(8)	15(6)	7	3	0	0	0	0	28	12
Craig Hall	21/2/88	8	1	14	2	17	1	0	0	90	10
Andrew Heffernan	24/1/91	7	7	2	2	0	0	0	0	8	8
Lee Jewitt	14/2/87	7(3)	7(2)	0	0	0	0	0	0	0	0
Josh Johnson	25/7/94	2(2)	2(2)	0	0	0	0	0	0	0	0
Ben Kavanagh	4/3/88	13(15)	13(8)	0	0	0	0	0	0	0	0
George Lawler	1/9/95	2(1)	2(1)	1	1	0	0	0	0	4	4
Tommy Lee	1/2/88	21(2)	15(2)	2	1	0	0	0	0	8	4
Shaun Lunt	15/4/86	6(10)	4(7)	3	1	0	0	0	0	12	4
Matty Marsh	21/4/95	6(3)	5(2)	0	0	0	0	0	0	0	0
Mose Masoe	17/5/89	15(14)	11(11)	3	3	0	0	0	0	12	12
Danny McGuire	6/12/82	20	14	5	5	0	0	2	1	22	21
Thomas Minns	4/9/94	10	10	4	4	0	0	0	0	16	16
Kieren Moss	6/8/93	2(1)	2(1)	4	4	0	0	0	0	16	16
Robbie Mulhern	18/10/94	19(4)	13(3)	4	2	0	0	0	0	16	8
Will Oakes	27/2/99	8	4	3	2	0	0	0	0	12	8
Adam Quinlan	13/11/92	27	21	14	10	0	0	0	0	56	40
Liam Salter	14/6/93	17(3)	12(3)	1	1	0	0	0	0	4	4
Nick Scruton	24/12/84	12(12)	7(10)	0	0	0	0	0	0	0	0
Ryan Shaw	27/2/92	21	19	11	11	61	56	0	0	166	156
Aaron Smith	12/10/96	3(1)	3(1)	0	0	0	0	0	0	0	0
Danny Tickle	10/3/83	21(5)	14(3)	4	4	31	20	0	0	78	56
Joel Tomkins	21/3/87	9	3	2	2	0	0	0	0	8	8
Junior Vaivai	18/1/90	19(1)	11	11	6	0	0	0	0	44	24
Elliot Wallis	10/5/00	5	4	2	2	0	0	0	0	8	8
Jordan Walne	28/12/92	1(7)	(6)	0	0	0	0	0	0	0	0
Joe Wardill	26/11/97	1(1)	(1)	0	0	0	0	0	0	0	0

Chris Atkin

LEAGUE RECORD
SL: P23-W8-D1-L14 (10th)
F476, A582, Diff-106, 17 points.

S8-Q: P7-W5-D0-L2 (3rd)
F197, A162, Diff+35, 10 points.

CHALLENGE CUP
Round Six

ATTENDANCES
Best - v Hull FC (SL - 12,090)
Worst - v Wigan (CC - 3,524)
Total (SL/S8s only) - 118,089
Average (SL/S8s only) - 7,873
(Up by 444 on 2017, Championship)

'SL' totals include regular season only; 'All' totals also include Super 8s (Qualifiers) & Challenge Cup

20th October 2017 - Kylie Leuluai leaves to take up head of rugby operations post at Warrington.

22nd October 2017 - Academy centre Harry Newman signs three-year first-team contract.

26th December 2017 - 17-10 win at Wakefield in Wetherby Whaler Challenge.

16th January 2018 - Kallum Watkins named captain for 2018.

21st January 2018 - 16-4 pre-season defeat at Castleford.

1st February 2018 - Richie Myler, Brad Dwyer and Nathan Peteru make debuts as Ryan Hall scores two tries in 16-12, round-one win at Warrington. Peteru suffers pectoral injury.

8th February 2018 - Jimmy Keinhorst scores hat-trick in comeback 20-11 win over Hull KR at Elland Road.

16th February 2018 - 38-4 World Club Challenge defeat in Melbourne.

25th February 2018 - twelve first-teamers missing in 23-6 defeat at Widnes.

28th February 2018 - prop Keith Galloway retires from top-level game after injury-hit 2017.

1st March 2018 - round-four home fixture with Catalans postponed a day early because of heavy snow.

8th March 2018 - 20-16 home victory over Hull FC on first appearance since September 2017 at partially-reconstructed Headingley. Mitch Garbutt injures knee which requires surgery.

13th March 2018 - forward Josh Jordan-Roberts goes to Hunslet on month's loan.

16th March 2018 - Ash Handley double inflicts first defeat of season on St Helens, by 28-20.

23rd March 2018 - Luke Gale field goal on half-time hooter means 25-24 defeat to Castleford at Elland Road, after trailing 24-0 on 23 minutes, in front of club record Super League crowd.

30th March 2018 - centre Ash Handley's second try after 76 minutes and Kallum Watkins' third goal rescues 22-all draw at Huddersfield. Brad Dwyer fractures bone in elbow but plays in next two games.

2nd April 2018 - wintry 20-0 home win over Salford.

8th April 2018 - Ash Handley stars at centre in 28-26 win at Wakefield.

12th April 2018 - Kallum Watkins signs two-year contract extension until end of 2021 season.

12th April 2018 - Jimmy Keinhorst joins Widnes on four-week loan.

13th April 2018 - Wigan score nine unanswered points in final eight minutes to win 9-8 at Headingley.

20th April 2018 - Jamie Jones-Buchanan makes 400th club appearance as late Marc Sneyd field goal means 19-18 defeat at Hull FC.

29th April 2018 - 55th minute Kallum Watkins penalty goal is last score of 20-18 win at Hull KR.

4th May 2018 - 33-22 home defeat to Warrington.

4th May 2018 - prop Brad Singleton signs contract extension to end of 2020 season.

11th May 2018 - 23-20 Challenge Cup sixth round win at Widnes after leading 23-4 at start of second half. Anthony Mullally banned for two games after four charges of raising knees while running into tacklers.

KEY DATES

15th May 2018 - Jimmy Keinhorst loan spell at Widnes extended with Leeds having right to recall.

19th May 2018 - Kallum Watkins suffers season-ending knee injury in 38-10 Magic Weekend defeat by Castleford in Newcastle.

21st May 2018 - Jimmy Keinhorst recalled from loan at Widnes.

26th May 2018 - 33-20 defeat at bottom side Catalans after trailing 16-0.

1st June 2018 - 52-22 home Challenge Cup quarter-final win over Championship Leigh in game played at Featherstone because of clash with cricket test.

8th June 2018 - prop Adam Cuthbertson agrees new two-year contract.

8th June 2018 - Mitch Garbutt returns from knee injury in 25-18 home defeat by Huddersfield.

12th June 2018 - winger Tom Briscoe signs new two-year contract to end of 2020.

15th June 2018 - Danny Richardson field goal two minutes from time means 23-22 home defeat to St Helens.

19th June 2018 - winger Luke Briscoe re-joins from Featherstone on loan.

20th June 2018 - late try means 28-25 home defeat to Catalans in game postponed from round four.

28th June 2018 - 46-8 defeat at Wigan is seventh in a row, the club's worst run in Super League history.

2nd July 2018 - Brian McDermott's run as longest serving coach in Super League ends after six-and-a-half years as he is sacked.

6th July 2018 - Kevin Sinfield returns as director of rugby with James Lowes as first team coach.

8th July 2018 - Rhinos concede 38 unanswered points in 42-10 defeat at Castleford.

10th July 2018 - Wests Tigers halfback Tuimoala Lolohea signs three-year deal from 2019.

13th July 2018 - 20-all home draw with Wakefield ends eight-match losing league run but leaves Rhinos three points adrift of top eight with two games to play.

16th July 2018 - Jordan Lilley signs for Bradford on loan until end of 2019 season.

17th July 2018 - Ryan Hall to leave for Sydney Roosters at end of season.

19th July 2018 - Warrington prop Dom Crosby signs on loan for rest of season.

20th July 2018 - 34-0 home win over Widnes but wins for Catalans, Huddersfield and Salford means second Middle Eights campaign in three years.

26th July 2018 - utility Jordan Thompson joins on loan from Leigh to end of season.

27th July 2018 - 38-22 defeat at Salford, who have Lee Mossop sent off on 20 minutes.

5th August 2018 - 48-12 defeat to Warrington in Challenge Cup semi-final at Bolton.

11th August 2018 - 48-22 home victory over Toulouse in Super 8s Qualifiers opener. Ryan Hall suffers season-ending knee injury.

14th August 2018 - young former Castleford halfback Callum McLelland signs from Scotland rugby union.

17th August 2018 - Mitch Garbutt undergoes knee surgery.

19th August 2018 - Joel Moon scores hat-trick in 48-32 win at London Broncos.

1st September 2018 - 38-36 home defeat by Danny McGuire-inspired Hull KR.

8th September 2018 - current South Sydney assistant David Furner to return in 2019 as head coach on three-year contract.

9th September 2018 - late Richie Myler try secures vital 16-6 win at Widnes.

14th September 2018 - last-minute Liam Sutcliffe penalty goal earns 18-16 home win over Salford.

23rd September 2018 - 34-6 win at Halifax secures Super League place.

28th September 2018 - late Gareth O'Brien field goal means 17-16 home defeat to Toronto Wolfpack.

18th October 2018 - Tongan centre Konrad Hurrell, 27, joins from NRL side Gold Coast Titans on three-year contract.

22nd October 2018 - Richard Agar appointed Head of Player and Coach Development.

24th October 2018 - prop Dom Crosby signs three-year contract to end of 2021 season.

CLUB RECORDS

Highest score:
106-10 v Swinton, 11/2/2001
Highest score against:
6-74 v Wigan, 20/5/92
Record attendance:
40,175 v Bradford, 21/5/47

MATCH RECORDS

Tries:
8 Fred Webster v Coventry, 12/4/1913
Eric Harris v Bradford, 14/9/31
Goals:
17 Iestyn Harris v Swinton, 11/2/2001
Points:
42 Iestyn Harris v Huddersfield, 16/7/99

SEASON RECORDS

Tries: 63 Eric Harris 1935-36
Goals: 173 *(inc 5fg)* Kevin Sinfield 2012
Points: 431 Lewis Jones 1956-57

CAREER RECORDS

Tries: 391 Eric Harris 1930-39
Goals:
1,831 *(inc 39fg)* Kevin Sinfield 1997-2015
Points: 3,967 Kevin Sinfield 1997-2015
Appearances: 625 John Holmes 1968-89

LEEDS RHINOS

DATE	FIXTURE	RESULT	SCORERS	LGE	ATT
1/2/18	Warrington (a)	W12-16	t:Jones-Buchanan,Hall(2) g:Watkins(2)	6th	11,241
8/2/18	Hull KR (h) ●	W20-11	t:Cuthbertson,Keinhorst(3) g:Myler(2)	4th	16,149
16/2/18	Melbourne (a) (WCC)	L38-4	t:Hall	N/A	19,062
25/2/18	Widnes (a)	L23-6	t:Dwyer g:Watkins	6th	5,519
8/3/18	Hull FC (h)	W20-16	t:Watkins(2),T Briscoe(2) g:Watkins(2)	4th	11,158
16/3/18	St Helens (a)	W20-28	t:Mullally,Myler,Handley(2),Parcell g:Watkins(3),Myler	4th	11,482
23/3/18	Castleford (h) ●	L24-25	t:Watkins(2),Handley(2),Hall g:Watkins(2)	4th	23,246
30/3/18	Huddersfield (a)	D22-22	t:Watkins,Hall,Handley(2) g:Watkins(3)	5th	7,544
2/4/18	Salford (h)	W20-0	t:T Briscoe,Handley,Walters g:Watkins(4)	4th	10,718
8/4/18	Wakefield (a)	W26-28	t:Watkins(2),Handley,Singleton,Walters g:Watkins(4)	4th	6,767
13/4/18	Wigan (h)	L8-9	t:T Briscoe g:Watkins(2)	5th	12,225
19/4/18	Hull FC (a)	L19-18	t:Hall,Moon,Parcell g:Watkins(3)	6th	11,391
29/4/18	Hull KR (a)	W18-20	t:Moon,Jones-Buchanan,Hall g:Watkins(4)	5th	9,095
4/5/18	Warrington (h)	L22-33	t:Golding,Moon,Hall,Ablett g:Watkins(3)	6th	11,749
11/5/18	Widnes (a) (CCR6)	W20-23	t:T Briscoe,Myler,Golding,Ward g:Watkins(3) fg:Myler	N/A	1,865
19/5/18	Castleford (MW) ●●	L38-10	t:Oledzki,Ferres g:Watkins	6th	N/A
26/5/18	Catalans Dragons (a)	L33-20	t:Handley,Ferres,Hall,Dwyer g:Lilley(2)	6th	8,779
1/6/18	Leigh (h) (CCQF) ●●●	W52-22	t:T Briscoe(2),Walker,Handley,Keinhorst,Golding,Myler,Smith,Cuthbertson g:Lilley(8)	N/A	3,277
8/6/18	Huddersfield (h)	L18-25	t:Parcell,Myler,Smith g:Lilley(3)	7th	11,051
15/6/18	St Helens (h)	L22-23	t:T Briscoe(2),Garbutt,Ferres g:Sutcliffe(3)	7th	12,106
20/6/18	Catalans Dragons (h)	L25-28	t:Walker,Sutcliffe,Smith,L Briscoe g:Sutcliffe(4) fg:Sutcliffe	7th	10,366
28/6/18	Wigan (a)	L46-8	t:Ferres,Moon	8th	10,645
8/7/18	Castleford (a)	L42-10	t:T Briscoe(2) g:Sutcliffe	9th	9,557
13/7/18	Wakefield (h)	D20-20	t:Hall,Myler,Handley g:Sutcliffe(4)	9th	11,140
20/7/18	Widnes (h)	W34-0	t:Dwyer,L Briscoe,Myler,Parcell,Moon,T Briscoe,Walker g:Myler(3)	9th	10,977
27/7/18	Salford (a)	L38-22	t:Dwyer,Sutcliffe,T Briscoe,Parcell g:Sutcliffe(3)	9th	2,387
5/8/18	Warrington (CCSF) ●●●●	L12-48	t:Hall,Cuthbertson g:Sutcliffe(2)	N/A	26,086
11/8/18	Toulouse (h) (S8-Q)	W48-22	t:Dwyer(2),Moon(2),Hall,Myler,Cuthbertson,Ablett,Golding g:Sutcliffe(6)	1st(S8-Q)	10,166
19/8/18	London Broncos (a) (S8-Q)	W32-48	t:Moon(3),L Briscoe,Ferres,Ablett,Golding(2) g:Sutcliffe(8)	2nd(S8-Q)	1,793
1/9/18	Hull KR (h) (S8-Q)	L36-38	t:Moon,T Briscoe(2),Myler,Peteru,Parcell g:Sutcliffe(6)	2nd(S8-Q)	11,468
9/9/18	Widnes (a) (S8-Q)	W6-16	t:L Briscoe,Parcell,Myler g:Sutcliffe(2)	2nd(S8-Q)	4,050
14/9/18	Salford (h) (S8-Q)	W18-16	t:T Briscoe(2),Keinhorst g:Sutcliffe(3)	2nd(S8-Q)	11,202
23/9/18	Halifax (a) (S8-Q)	W6-34	t:Myler,Dwyer(2),Sutcliffe,Smith,L Briscoe g:Sutcliffe(5)	1st(S8-Q)	4,507
28/9/18	Toronto (h) (S8-Q)	L16-17	t:T Briscoe,Sutcliffe,Keinhorst g:Sutcliffe(2)	2nd(S8-Q)	11,565

● Played at Elland Road   ●● Played at St James' Park, Newcastle
●●● Played at LD Nutrition Stadium, Featherstone   ●●●● Played at University of Bolton Stadium

APP TRIES GOALS FG PTS

		APP		TRIES		GOALS		FG		PTS	
	D.O.B.	ALL	SL	ALL	SL	ALL	SL	ALL	SL	ALL	SL
Carl Ablett	19/12/85	22	15	3	1	0	0	0	0	12	4
Luke Briscoe	11/3/94	10	4	5	2	0	0	0	0	20	8
Tom Briscoe	19/3/90	33	22	18	10	0	0	0	0	72	40
Dominic Crosby	11/12/90	5(2)	(2)	0	0	0	0	0	0	0	0
Adam Cuthbertson	24/2/85	19(6)	13(2)	4	1	0	0	0	0	16	4
Brett Delaney	26/10/85	12(4)	12(3)	0	0	0	0	0	0	0	0
Brad Dwyer	28/4/93	10(13)	5(8)	8	4	0	0	0	0	32	16
Brett Ferres	17/4/86	16(7)	8(6)	5	4	0	0	0	0	20	16
Mitch Garbutt	18/4/89	7(2)	7(2)	1	1	0	0	0	0	4	4
Ashton Golding	4/9/96	15(7)	12(5)	6	1	0	0	0	0	24	4
Ryan Hall	27/11/87	24	20	12	9	0	0	0	0	48	36
Ash Handley	16/2/96	22	19	11	10	0	0	0	0	44	40
Tom Holroyd	9/2/01	(1)	(1)	0	0	0	0	0	0	0	0
Jamie Jones-Buchanan	1/8/81	23	13	2	2	0	0	0	0	8	8
Jimmy Keinhorst	14/7/90	11(2)	4(1)	6	3	0	0	0	0	24	12
Jordan Lilley	4/9/96	4	3	0	0	13	5	0	0	26	10
Joel Moon	20/5/88	28	18	11	5	0	0	0	0	44	20
Anthony Mullally	28/6/91	4(15)	4(9)	1	1	0	0	0	0	4	4
Richie Myler	21/5/90	31	20	10	4	6	6	1	0	53	28
Harry Newman	19/2/00	3	3	0	0	0	0	0	0	0	0
Mikolaj Oledzki	8/11/98	8(14)	6(11)	1	1	0	0	0	0	4	4
Jack Ormondroyd	7/11/91	1(7)	1(6)	0	0	0	0	0	0	0	0
Matt Parcell	30/10/92	23(6)	17(3)	7	5	0	0	0	0	28	20
Nathaniel Peteru	1/1/92	4(9)	1(3)	1	0	0	0	0	0	4	0
Brad Singleton	29/10/92	24(1)	16(1)	1	1	0	0	0	0	4	4
Cameron Smith	7/11/98	3(17)	3(12)	4	2	0	0	0	0	16	8
Liam Sutcliffe	25/11/94	21	12	4	2	49	15	1	1	115	39
Jordan Thompson	4/9/91	5(1)	1	0	0	0	0	0	0	0	0
Jack Walker	8/8/99	19(3)	11(3)	3	2	0	0	0	0	12	8
Josh Walters	23/12/94	5(14)	5(10)	2	2	0	0	0	0	8	8
Stevie Ward	17/11/93	14(3)	10(2)	1	0	0	0	0	0	4	0
Kallum Watkins	12/3/91	16	14	7	7	37	34	0	0	102	96

Tom Briscoe

LEAGUE RECORD
SL: P23-W8-D2-L13 (9th)
F441, A527, Diff-86, 18 points.

S8-Q: P7-W5-D0-L2 (2nd)
F216, A137, Diff+79, 10 points.

CHALLENGE CUP
Semi-Finalists

ATTENDANCES
Best - v Castleford (SL - 23,246)
Worst - v Leigh (CC - 3,277)
Total (SL/S8s only) - 185,286
Average (SL/S8s only) - 12,352
(Down by 2,221 on 2017)

'SL' totals include regular season only; 'All' totals also include Super 8s (Qualifiers), Challenge Cup & World Club Challenge

Super League XXIII - Club by Club

24th October 2018 - Ben Murdoch-Masila leaves to join Warrington for £175,000 transfer fee.

17th November 2017 - halfback Jack Littlejohn signs from Wests Tigers on two-year contract.

28th November 2017 - Kris Welham extends contract by one year to end of 2019.

1st December 2017 - Fiji World Cup prop Ben Nakubuwai signs from Gold Coast Titans on unrevealed contract.

9th January 2018 - fans consortium, forming not-for-profit holding company, Salford RD Holdings, complete takeover from Marwan Koukash.

2nd February 2018 - 40-12 home, round-one defeat by Wigan.

3rd February 2018 - Levy Nzoungou joins Whitehaven on month's loan.

5th February 2018 - confirmation that Manu Vatuvei ruled out for season with Achilles training injury.

8th February 2018 - Daniel Murray joins Halifax on one-month loan deal.

10th February 2018 - Gareth O'Brien misses last-second touchline conversion in 14-12 defeat at Wakefield.

24th February 2018 - Two tries from Niall Evalds help earn first victory with 36-12 home win over Hull KR.

1st March 2018 - round-four game at St Helens postponed a day in advance because of heavy snow.

1st March 2018 - Ian Blease switches role to become Director of Rugby & Operations.

4th March 2018 - 34-2 defeat at league leaders St Helens in delayed round-four game.

11th March 2018 - 22-8 defeat at Castleford after trailing 20-nil at half-time.

12th March 2018 - Gareth O'Brien signs for Toronto Wolfpack with immediate effect.

16th March 2018 - gamestar Robert Lui scores decisive try to secure 24-8 home win over Hull FC.

17th March 2018 - other clubs block plans to play home Good Friday fixture with Catalans in New York.

20th March 2018 - six-figure offer from Hull KR to sign Robert Lui rejected.

22nd March 2018 - winger Derrell Olpherts makes debut in 24-16 defeat at Widnes.

29th March 2018 - Wigan halfback Jake Shorrocks joins on month's loan.

30th March 2018 - 32-16 home Good Friday win over Catalans.

2nd April 2018 - 20-0 defeat at Leeds on wintry Easter Monday afternoon.

7th April 2018 - Niall Evalds out with concussion and Logan Tomkins with illness for 22-6 home defeat to Warrington.

15th April 2018 - Jake Bibby scores double as 30-12 win at Huddersfield moves Red Devils into top eight.

KEY DATES

20th April 2018 - Jake Bibby scores try double as 38-4 home win over Wakefield moves Red Devils into seventh spot. Robert Lui suffers knee injury.

25th April 2018 - prop Daniel Murray signs new two-year contract.

26th April 2018 - 60-10 hammering at home to leaders St Helens.

4th May 2018 - Levy Nzoungou and Gavin Bennion make debuts in 30-0 defeat away at Wigan.

11th May 2018 - Cup exit in sixth round by 22-10 at Leigh.

20th May 2018 - 26-12 Magic Weekend defeat to Catalans in Newcastle.

23rd May 2018 - former owner Marwan Koukash writes off five million pound debt.

25th May 2018 - fullback Niall Evalds breaks leg as 24-16 defeat at Huddersfield drops Red Devils out of top eight.

4th June 2018 - Manu Vatuvei released from five months left on contract.

6th June 2018 - Greg Burke and Ed Chamberlain join on season-long loans from Widnes Vikings with Weller Hauraki heading the other way.

8th June 2018 - 45-14 defeat at Hull FC is sixth straight defeat.

12th June 2018 - forward Levy Nzoungou joins Swinton on one-month loan.

15th June 2018 - two tries from Kris Welham help secure 26-12 home win over Widnes.

27th June 2018 - Gavin Bennion joins Rochdale on loan.

30th June 2018 - Jack Littlejohn scores first-half try double, then ruptures biceps in 30-14 away defeat at Warrington.

8th July 2018 - 52-22 defeat at Hull KR.

12th July 2018 - released Manly halfback Jackson Hastings signs to end of season.

13th July 2018 - 24-6 home defeat by Castleford.

18th July 2018 - Widnes loanee Ed Chamberlain signs permanent two-year deal.

21st July 2018 - 44-10 defeat at Catalans guarantees Qualifiers place.

27th July 2018 - dummy-half Joey Lussick signs from Manly feeder for rest of season.

27th July 2018 - Jackson Hastings makes debut in 38-22 home win over Leeds. Lee Mossop is sent off for headbutt in 20th minute and escapes ban.

3rd August 2018 - former England Academy forward Jansin Turgut signs from Hull FC on short-term deal until end of season.

10th August 2018 - Joey Lussick makes debut in 28-10 win at Hull KR in first game of Qualifiers.

16th August 2018 - Widnes loanee Greg Burke signs permanent two-year contract.

18th August 2018 - Junior Sa'u scores two tries in 32-6 home win over Widnes.

2nd September 2018 - Derrell Olpherts scores hat-trick in 62-4 win at Halifax.

8th September 2018 - Luke Burgess and Jackson Hastings sent off in 28-16 home win over Toronto.

11th September 2018 - Jackson Hastings gets two matches, Luke Burgess one.

15th September 2018 - last-minute penalty in front of sticks means 18-16 defeat at Leeds.

22nd September 2018 - 11-8 defeat at London Broncos leaves Super League place unconfirmed.

27th September 2018 - Jackson Hastings back as 44-10 home win over Toulouse secures Super League place. Prop forward Levy Nzoungou signs for Hull FC.

2nd October 2018 - hooker Joey Lussick signs two-year deal.

3rd October 2018 - Jackson Hastings signs one-year contract.

19th October 2018 - prop Craig Kopczak leaves for Wakefield.

25th October 2018 - Jack Littlejohn to leave the club.

CLUB RECORDS

Highest score:
100-12 v Gateshead, 23/3/2003
Highest score against:
16-96 v Bradford, 25/6/2000
Record attendance:
26,470 v Warrington, 13/2/37
(The Willows)
7,102 v Wakefield, 16/2/2014
(AJ Bell Stadium)

MATCH RECORDS

Tries:
6 Frank Miles v Lees, 5/3/1898
Ernest Bone v Goole, 29/3/1902
Jack Hilton v Leigh, 7/10/39
Goals:
14 Steve Blakeley v Gateshead, 23/3/2003
Points:
39 Jim Lomas v Liverpool City, 2/2/1907

SEASON RECORDS

Tries: 46 Keith Fielding 1973-74
Goals: 221 David Watkins 1972-73
Points: 493 David Watkins 1972-73

CAREER RECORDS

Tries: 297 Maurice Richards 1969-83
Goals: 1,241 David Watkins 1967-79
Points: 2,907 David Watkins 1967-79
Appearances:
498 Maurice Richards 1969-83

SALFORD RED DEVILS

DATE	FIXTURE	RESULT	SCORERS	LGE	ATT
2/2/18	Wigan (h)	L12-40	t:Welham,Evalds g:O'Brien(2)	11th	5,506
9/2/18	Wakefield (a)	L14-12	t:Lui,Evalds,Welham	10th	4,262
23/2/18	Hull KR (h)	W36-12	t:O'Brien,Sa'u,Bibby,Lui,Evalds(2) g:O'Brien(6)	9th	2,948
4/3/18	St Helens (a)	L34-2	g:O'Brien	10th	10,008
11/3/18	Castleford (a)	L22-8	t:Sa'u,Bibby	11th	7,480
16/3/18	Hull FC (h)	W24-8	t:Nakubuwai,Littlejohn,Lui,Johnson g:Lui(4)	10th	2,902
22/3/18	Widnes (a)	L24-16	t:Kopczak,Hauraki g:Lui(4)	10th	4,007
30/3/18	Catalans Dragons (h)	W32-16	t:Bibby,Evalds,Johnson,Jones,Welham g:Lui(6)	9th	2,328
2/4/18	Leeds (a)	L20-0		9th	10,718
7/4/18	Warrington (h)	L6-22	t:Lui g:Lui	10th	3,428
15/4/18	Huddersfield (a)	W12-30	t:Flanagan,Nakubuwai,Hauraki,Bibby(2) g:Lui(5)	8th	4,385
20/4/18	Wakefield (h)	W38-4	t:Sa'u,McCarthy,Lannon,Bibby(2),Griffin,Johnson g:Lui(2),McCarthy(2),Littlejohn	7th	2,686
26/4/18	St Helens (h)	L10-60	t:McCarthy,Welham g:Shorrocks	8th	3,105
4/5/18	Wigan (a)	L30-0		8th	10,733
11/5/18	Leigh (a) (CCR6)	L22-10	t:Evalds,Griffin g:Shorrocks	N/A	4,024
20/5/18	Catalans Dragons (MW) ●	L26-12	t:Hauraki,Griffin g:Lui(2)	8th	N/A
25/5/18	Huddersfield (h)	L16-24	t:Sa'u(2),Evalds g:Lui(2)	9th	2,343
8/6/18	Hull FC (a)	L45-14	t:Johnson,Olpherts,Griffin g:Lui	10th	10,606
14/6/18	Widnes (h)	W26-12	t:Welham(2),Bibby,Burke,Lui g:Lui(3)	10th	2,248
29/6/18	Warrington (a)	L30-14	t:Littlejohn(2),Bibby g:Lui	10th	9,171
8/7/18	Hull KR (a)	L52-22	t:Johnson,Sa'u(2),Bibby g:Chamberlain(3)	11th	7,698
13/7/18	Castleford (h)	L6-24	t:Bibby g:Chamberlain	11th	2,681
21/7/18	Catalans Dragons (a)	L44-10	t:Olpherts,Wood g:Chamberlain	11th	8,672
27/7/18	Leeds (h)	W38-22	t:Lannon,Evalds(2),Hastings,Chamberlain,Lui,Jones g:Chamberlain(5)	11th	2,387
10/8/18	Hull KR (a) (S8-Q)	W10-28	t:Evalds,Lui,Lussick,Wood g:Chamberlain(2),Hastings(4)	2nd(S8-Q)	7,081
18/8/18	Widnes (h) (S8-Q)	W32-6	t:Sa'u(2),Lui,Evalds,Flanagan g:Chamberlain(6)	1st(S8-Q)	2,317
2/9/18	Halifax (a) (S8-Q)	W4-62	t:Hastings(2),Chamberlain,Olpherts(3),Nakubuwai,Welham,Tasi,Sa'u(2),Wood g:Chamberlain(7)	1st(S8-Q)	2,555
8/9/18	Toronto (h) (S8-Q)	W28-16	t:Chamberlain,Lui,Hastings,Lannon g:Chamberlain(6)	1st(S8-Q)	2,509
14/9/18	Leeds (a) (S8-Q)	L18-16	t:Evalds,Burke,Olpherts g:Chamberlain(2)	1st(S8-Q)	11,202
22/9/18	London Broncos (a) (S8-Q)	L11-8	t:Johnson(2)	2nd(S8-Q)	809
27/9/18	Toulouse (h) (S8-Q)	W44-10	t:Hastings,Lussick,Johnson,Evalds,Olpherts,Welham,McCarthy g:Hastings(7),Burgess	1st(S8-Q)	2,130

● *Played at St James' Park, Newcastle*

	D.O.B.	APP ALL	APP SL	TRIES ALL	TRIES SL	GOALS ALL	GOALS SL	FG ALL	FG SL	PTS ALL	PTS SL
Gavin Bennion	31/12/93	1(1)	1(1)	0	0	0	0	0	0	0	0
Jake Bibby	17/6/96	26	21	11	11	0	0	0	0	44	44
Luke Burgess	20/2/87	6(9)	3(8)	0	0	1	0	0	0	2	0
Greg Burke	12/2/93	3(8)	2(3)	2	1	0	0	0	0	8	4
Ed Chamberlain	8/2/96	10(1)	4(1)	3	1	33	10	0	0	78	24
Niall Evalds	26/8/93	23(1)	15(1)	13	8	0	0	0	0	52	32
Mark Flanagan	4/12/87	17(7)	12(4)	2	1	0	0	0	0	8	4
George Griffin	26/6/92	11(2)	9(1)	4	3	0	0	0	0	16	12
Jackson Hastings	14/1/96	6	1	5	1	11	0	0	0	42	4
Weller Hauraki	18/2/85	12(2)	11(2)	3	3	0	0	0	0	12	12
Greg Johnson	20/2/90	16	13	8	5	0	0	0	0	32	20
Josh Jones	12/5/93	22(1)	15(1)	2	2	0	0	0	0	8	8
Craig Kopczak	20/12/86	6(16)	6(10)	1	1	0	0	0	0	4	4
Ryan Lannon	11/1/96	14(5)	9(4)	3	2	0	0	0	0	12	8
Jack Littlejohn	8/11/91	17(3)	15(3)	3	3	1	1	0	0	14	14
Robert Lui	23/2/90	28	21	9	6	31	31	0	0	98	86
Joey Lussick	28/12/95	3(4)	0	2	0	0	0	0	0	8	0
Tyrone McCarthy	21/4/88	15(8)	10(7)	3	2	2	2	0	0	16	12
Lee Mossop	17/1/89	21(1)	17(1)	0	0	0	0	0	0	0	0
Daniel Murray	21/3/96	8(5)	6(4)	0	0	0	0	0	0	0	0
Ben Nakubuwai	15/3/96	6(17)	5(13)	3	2	0	0	0	0	12	8
Levy Nzoungou	22/1/98	(3)	(3)	0	0	0	0	0	0	0	0
Gareth O'Brien	31/10/91	4	4	1	1	9	9	0	0	22	22
Derrell Olpherts	7/1/92	19	13	7	2	0	0	0	0	28	8
Junior Sa'u	18/4/87	28	23	11	7	0	0	0	0	44	28
Jake Shorrocks	26/10/95	11	10	0	0	2	1	0	0	4	2
Lama Tasi	3/5/90	15(12)	11(10)	1	0	0	0	0	0	4	0
Logan Tomkins	1/8/91	13(6)	12(6)	0	0	0	0	0	0	0	0
Jansin Turgut	8/3/96	(2)	0	0	0	0	0	0	0	0	0
Kris Welham	12/5/87	24	17	8	6	0	0	0	0	32	24
Josh Wood	15/11/95	18(10)	13(9)	3	1	0	0	0	0	12	4

'SL' totals include regular season only; 'All' totals also include Super 8s (Qualifiers) & Challenge Cup

Robert Lui

LEAGUE RECORD
SL: P23-W7-D0-L16 (11th)
F384, A597, Diff-213, 14 points.

S8-Q: P7-W5-D0-L2 (1st)
F218, A75, Diff+143, 10 points.

CHALLENGE CUP
Round Six

ATTENDANCES
Best - v Wigan (SL - 5,506)
Worst - v Toulouse (S8 - 2,130)
Total (SL/S8s only) - 39,518
Average (SL/S8s only) - 2,823
(Down by 1,118 on 2017)

Super League XXIII - Club by Club

6th October 2017 - Matty Fleming joins London Broncos.

17th October 2017 - Morgan Knowles signs new four-year contract to end of 2021.

20th October 2017 - Ricky Bailey and Jonah Cunningham join Leigh on loan for 2018.

24th October 2017 - Tommy Lee leaves to join Hull KR.

2nd November 2017 - Dominique Peyroux signs new one-year deal for 2018. Calvin Wellington moves to rugby union for transfer fee.

20th January 2018 - 64-6 pre-season win over Sheffield at Ruskin Sports Village.

24th January 2018 - James Roby named new captain.

26th January 2018 - 24-20 home pre-season win over Leigh.

31st January 2018 - Jake Spedding, Jack Ashworth, James Bentley and Matty Lees dual-registered with Sheffield.

2nd February 2018 - Alex Walmsley signs new contract until end of 2022 season.

2nd February 2018 - Mark Percival scores hat-trick and Ben Barba stars in 46-6, round-one home win over Castleford.

10th February 2018 - Morgan Knowles sent off for dangerous tackle in 21-12 win at Catalans.

14th February 2018 - Morgan Knowles banned for four games.

23rd February 2018 - 26-12 win at Huddersfield makes it three wins from three.

1st March 2018 - round-four game at home to Salford postponed a day in advance because of heavy snow.

4th March 2018 - Luke Thompson scores try on 100th club appearance in 34-2 home win over Salford in delayed round-four game.

9th March 2018 - Mark Percival scores hat-trick and young halfback Danny Richardson shines in 30-12 win at Warrington. Alex Walmsley suffers neck injury.

14th March 2018 - Louie McCarthy-Scarsbrook signs one-year contract extension for 2019.

19th March 2018 - Ben Barba scores try double but 28-20 home defeat to Leeds is first of season.

23rd March 2018 - Ben Barba scores try-brace in 30-6 win at Hull KR.

30th March 2018 - late Regan Grace try secures 21-18 home win over Wigan, the first Good Friday win for nine years.

2nd April 2018 - Tommy Makinson crosses for his 100th try in try-double in 28-6 Easter Monday win at Widnes. Mark Percival also bags brace.

6th April 2018 - Ben Barba ruled out with illness before Zeb Taia scores twice in 26-12 home win over Hull FC.

15th April 2018 - Mark Percival scores twice and is sin-binned near end of 24-20 defeat at Wakefield. He gets one-match penalty notice.

20th April 2018 - Jonny Lomax scores try hat-trick in 66-4 home hammering of Huddersfield.

KEY DATES

26th April 2018 - Ben Barba scores hat-trick then suffers neck injury in 11-try 60-10 win at Salford, despite 38th minute dismissal of Matty Lees. Lees gets two-match penalty notice.

2nd May 2018 - young hooker Aaron Smith joins Hull KR on month's loan.

3rd May 2018 - James Roby signs one-year contract extension until end of 2019 season.

3rd May 2018 - Ben Barba absent as Regan Grace scores two second-half tries in 26-12 home win over Catalans.

12th May 2018 - Ben Barba scores hat-trick in 36-18 Challenge Cup sixth-round win at Castleford. Kyle Amor banned for one game for dangerous contact.

13th May 2018 - York City Knights second-rower Joe Batchelor signs three-year contract from 2019.

19th May 2018 - Regan Grace and Ryan Morgan score try-doubles in 38-18 win over Widnes at Magic Weekend in Newcastle.

22nd May 2018 - Fijian flyer Kevin Naiqama signs from Wests Tigers on three-year contract from 2019.

24th May 2018 - Ryan Morgan and Theo Fages both score braces as Jonny Lomax stars in 40-18 win at Castleford.

3rd June 2018 - Mark Percival and Regan Grace score braces in heart-stopping 25-22 Challenge Cup quarter-final win over Hull FC.

8th June 2018 - lead at the top of Super League extends to six points after 26-4 home win over Hull KR.

15th June 2018 - last-gasp Danny Richardson field goal seals 23-22 comeback win at Leeds.

29th June 2018 - three tries late in the second half secures 34-30 home comeback win over Wakefield.

6th July 2018 - Adam Swift scores hat-trick in 36-6 home win over Widnes.

13th July 2018 - Jonny Lomax and Ben Barba score try braces in 34-18 win at Hull FC to take home Steve Prescott Cup.

19th July 2018 - lead at top of table increased to 10 points with 14-6 win at Wigan.

25th July 2018 - Cronulla utility Joseph Paulo signs three-year contract from 2019.

26th July 2018 - Danny Richardson kicks 55-metre penalty goal after final hooter to secure 14-12 home win over Warrington.

5th August 2018 - 35-16 Challenge Cup semi-final defeat to Catalans in Bolton.

10th August 2018 - 16-12 home defeat to Huddersfield in Super 8s opener.

13th August 2018 - Luke Thompson gets one-match penalty notice for reckless contact with a match official.

16th August 2018 - Tommy Makinson scores try-brace as 36-16 win at Wakefield re-opens ten-point gap at top of table.

31st August 2018 - Tommy Makinson scores another brace in 30-10 defeat at Wigan that delays awarding of League Leaders Shield.

8th September 2018 - late Morgan Knowles try seals 26-22 comeback win at Catalans.

14th September 2018 - 38-12 home win over Hull FC seals League Leaders Shield.

20th September 2018 - Matty Smith to leave at end of season.

21st September 2018 - centre Matty Costello signs new two-year contract. Jack Ashworth pens one-year deal.

22nd September 2018 - early-season form recaptured in 34-14 win at play-off opponents Warrington.

25th September 2018 - Ben Barba to join North Queensland Cowboys at end of season for a transfer fee.

26th September 2018 - backrower Dominique Peyroux signs new contract to end of 2020 season.

28th September 2018 - fullback Lachlan Coote signs from North Queensland on three-year contract.

28th September 2018 - Ben Barba scores twice in 26-0 last-round win over Castleford.

1st October 2018 - seven Saints players named in Super League dream team.

4th October 2018 - late Tom Lineham try means 18-13 semi-final exit at home to Warrington.

8th October 2018 - Ben Barba wins Man of Steel award.

CLUB RECORDS
Highest score: 112-0 v Carlisle, 14/9/86 **Highest score against:** 6-78 v Warrington, 12/4/1909 **Record attendance:** 35,695 v Wigan, 26/12/49 *(Knowsley Road)* 17,980 v Wigan, 6/4/2012 v Wigan, 18/4/2014 v South Sydney, 22/2/2015 v Wigan, 30/3/2018 *(Langtree Park)*

MATCH RECORDS
Tries: 6 Alf Ellaby v Barrow, 5/3/32 Steve Llewellyn v Castleford, 3/3/56 Steve Llewellyn v Liverpool, 20/8/56 Tom van Vollenhoven v Wakefield, 21/12/57 Tom van Vollenhoven v Blackpool, 23/4/62 Frank Myler v Maryport, 1/9/69 Shane Cooper v Hull, 17/2/88 **Goals:** 16 Paul Loughlin v Carlisle, 14/9/86 **Points:** 40 Paul Loughlin v Carlisle, 14/9/86

SEASON RECORDS
Tries: 62 Tom van Vollenhoven 1958-59 **Goals:** 214 Kel Coslett 1971-72 **Points:** 452 Kel Coslett 1971-72

CAREER RECORDS
Tries: 392 Tom van Vollenhoven 1957-68 **Goals:** 1,639 Kel Coslett 1962-76 **Points:** 3,413 Kel Coslett 1962-76 **Appearances:** 531 Kel Coslett 1962-76

ST HELENS

DATE	FIXTURE	RESULT	SCORERS	LGE	ATT
2/2/18	Castleford (h)	W46-6	t:Barba(2),Taia(2),Lomax,Percival(3) g:Richardson(7)	1st	13,108
10/2/18	Catalans Dragons (a)	W12-21	t:Lomax,Grace,Swift g:Richardson(4) fg:Richardson	1st	8,103
23/2/18	Huddersfield (a)	W12-26	t:Wilkin,Roby,Taia,Percival g:Richardson(5)	1st	5,915
4/3/18	Salford (h)	W34-2	t:Makinson,Barba(2),McCarthy-Scarsbrook,Lomax,Thompson g:Richardson(5)	1st	10,008
9/3/18	Warrington (a)	W12-30	t:Percival(3),Roby,Richardson g:Richardson(5)	1st	12,268
16/3/18	Leeds (h)	L20-28	t:Barba(2),Swift g:Richardson(4)	1st	11,482
23/3/18	Hull KR (a)	W6-30	t:Thompson,Barba(2),Lomax,Peyroux g:Richardson(5)	1st	7,724
30/3/18	Wigan (h)	W21-18	t:Barba,Taia,Grace g:Richardson(4) fg:Richardson	1st	17,980
2/4/18	Widnes (a)	W6-28	t:Morgan,Percival(2),Barba,Makinson(2) g:Richardson(2)	1st	6,706
6/4/18	Hull FC (h)	W26-12	t:Taia(2),Percival,Thompson g:Richardson(5)	1st	10,408
15/4/18	Wakefield (a)	L24-20	t:Percival(2),Makinson,Douglas g:Richardson(2)	1st	5,231
20/4/18	Huddersfield (h)	W66-4	t:Lomax(3),Barba(2),McCarthy-Scarsbrook(2),Morgan(2),Richardson, Grace,Amor g:Richardson(9)	1st	10,278
26/4/18	Salford (a)	W10-60	t:Makinson,Peyroux,Barba(3),Morgan(2),Grace(2),Percival,Fages g:Richardson(8)	1st	3,105
3/5/18	Catalans Dragons (h)	W26-12	t:Lomax,Makinson,Knowles,Grace(2) g:Richardson(3)	1st	9,138
12/5/18	Castleford (a) (CCR6)	W18-36	t:Grace,Barba(3),Morgan,Richardson g:Richardson(6)	N/A	5,342
19/5/18	Widnes (MW) ●	W38-18	t:Richardson,Percival,Grace(2),Barba,Morgan(2) g:Richardson(5)	1st	N/A
24/5/18	Castleford (a)	W18-40	t:Amor,Barba,Lomax,Peyroux,Morgan(2),Fages(2) g:Richardson(4)	1st	6,969
3/6/18	Hull FC (h) (CCQF)	W25-22	t:Percival(2),Grace(2) g:Richardson(4) fg:Richardson	N/A	8,928
8/6/18	Hull KR (h)	W26-4	t:Morgan,Roby,Barba(2),Percival g:Richardson(3)	1st	9,405
15/6/18	Leeds (a)	W22-23	t:Barba,Lomax,Percival,Morgan g:Richardson(3) fg:Richardson	1st	12,106
29/6/18	Wakefield (h)	W34-30	t:Grace(2),Lomax,Richardson,Roby,Taia g:Richardson(5)	1st	10,008
6/7/18	Widnes (h)	W36-6	t:Taia,Percival,Swift(3),McCarthy-Scarsbrook,Fages g:Richardson(4)	1st	9,923
13/7/18	Hull FC (a)	W18-34	t:Makinson,Barba(2),Lomax(2),Swift,Thompson g:Richardson(3)	1st	11,130
19/7/18	Wigan (a)	W6-14	t:Peyroux,Knowles g:Richardson(3)	1st	16,047
26/7/18	Warrington (h)	W14-12	t:Barba,Lomax g:Richardson(3)	1st	12,454
5/8/18	Catalans Dragons (CCSF) ●●	L35-16	t:Percival(2),McCarthy-Scarsbrook g:Richardson(2)	N/A	26,086
10/8/18	Huddersfield (h) (S8)	L12-16	t:Barba,Thompson g:Richardson(2)	1st	8,979
16/8/18	Wakefield (a) (S8)	W16-36	t:Makinson(2),Lomax,Fages,Douglas,Grace g:Richardson(6)	1st	4,592
31/8/18	Wigan (h) (S8)	L10-30	t:Makinson g:Richardson	1st	14,061
8/9/18	Catalans Dragons (a) (S8)	W22-26	t:Percival,Fages,Lomax,Knowles g:Richardson(5)	1st	7,810
14/9/18	Hull FC (h) (S8)	W38-12	t:Percival(2),Knowles,Thompson,Grace(2) g:Richardson(7)	1st	9,348
22/9/18	Warrington (a) (S8)	W14-34	t:Douglas,Grace,Lomax,Richardson,Barba(2) g:Richardson(5)	1st	10,747
28/9/18	Castleford (a) (S8)	W26-0	t:Lees,Knowles,Barba(2) g:Richardson(5)	1st	9,813
4/10/18	Warrington (h) (SF)	L13-18	t:Douglas g:Richardson(3) fg:Richardson(3)	N/A	12,309

● *Played at St James' Park, Newcastle* ●● *Played at University of Bolton Stadium*

		APP		TRIES		GOALS		FG		PTS	
	D.O.B.	ALL	SL	ALL	SL	ALL	SL	ALL	SL	ALL	SL
Kyle Amor	26/5/87	27(1)	24(1)	2	2	0	0	0	0	8	8
Jack Ashworth	3/7/95	1(7)	1(7)	0	0	0	0	0	0	0	0
Ben Barba	13/6/89	29	26	31	28	0	0	0	0	124	112
James Bentley	19/10/97	2(1)	2(1)	0	0	0	0	0	0	0	0
Matthew Costello	9/4/98	7	7	0	0	0	0	0	0	0	0
Luke Douglas	12/5/86	6(26)	6(23)	4	4	0	0	0	0	16	16
Theo Fages	23/8/94	8(23)	8(20)	6	6	0	0	0	0	24	24
Regan Grace	12/12/96	33	30	18	15	0	0	0	0	72	60
Morgan Knowles	5/11/96	11(19)	10(17)	5	5	0	0	0	0	20	20
Matty Lees	4/2/98	3(16)	3(15)	1	1	0	0	0	0	4	4
Jonny Lomax	4/9/90	31	28	17	17	0	0	0	0	68	68
Tommy Makinson	10/10/91	32	29	11	11	0	0	0	0	44	44
Louie McCarthy-Scarsbrook	14/1/86	5(27)	5(24)	5	4	0	0	0	0	20	16
Ryan Morgan	4/5/90	21	19	12	11	0	0	0	0	48	44
Mark Percival	29/5/94	31	28	24	20	0	0	0	0	96	80
Dominique Peyroux	21/1/89	27(1)	25(1)	4	4	0	0	0	0	16	16
Danny Richardson	2/9/96	34	31	6	5	147	135	7	6	325	296
James Roby	22/11/85	27(1)	24(1)	4	4	0	0	0	0	16	16
Aaron Smith	12/10/96	(1)	(1)	0	0	0	0	0	0	0	0
Matty Smith	23/7/87	3(4)	3(4)	0	0	0	0	0	0	0	0
Jake Spedding	26/9/96	(1)	(1)	0	0	0	0	0	0	0	0
Adam Swift	20/2/93	12	11	6	6	0	0	0	0	24	24
Zeb Taia	11/10/84	31	28	8	8	0	0	0	0	32	32
Luke Thompson	27/4/95	32	29	6	6	0	0	0	0	24	24
Alex Walmsley	10/4/90	(5)	(5)	0	0	0	0	0	0	0	0
Jack Welsby	17/3/01	(1)	(1)	0	0	0	0	0	0	0	0
Jon Wilkin	11/1/83	29(2)	26(2)	1	1	0	0	0	0	4	4

'SL' totals include Super 8s & semi-final; 'All' totals also include Challenge Cup

Ben Barba

LEAGUE RECORD
P30-W26-D0-L4
(1st, SL/Semi-Finalists)
F895, A408, Diff+487
52 points.

CHALLENGE CUP
Semi-Finalists

ATTENDANCES
Best - v Wigan (SL - 17,980)
Worst - v Hull FC (CC - 8,928)
Total (SL/S8s/SF only) - 178,702
Average (SL/S8s/SF only) - 11,169
(Up by 223 on 2017)

Super League XXIII - Club by Club

KEY DATES

9th November 2017 - prop Keegan Hirst takes up contract option for 2018.

10th November 2017 - Matty Ashurst signs new four-year deal to end of 2021.

22nd November 2017 - Newcastle Knights forward Pauli Pauli joins on one-year deal with option of further year.

28th November 2017 - Mikey Sio leaves by mutual consent with a year to go on contract.

28th November 2017 - fullback Scott Grix signs one-year extension to end of 2019.

11th December 2017 - halfback Kyle Wood signs three-year deal to end of 2020.

12th December 2017 - head of rugby John Kear leaves to become head coach at Bradford.

18th December 2017 - Leigh halfback Ryan Hampshire joins on one-year deal.

26th December 2017 - Tyler Randell suffers knee injury in 17-10 defeat by Leeds in Wetherby Whaler Challenge.

7th January 2018 - 62-0 home pre-season home win over Halifax.

16th January 2018 - Michael Monaghan appointed assistant coach for 2018 season.

20th January 2018 - 26-22 home win over Huddersfield in final pre-season warm-up.

2nd February 2018 - Tom Johnstone scores spectacular hat-trick in 28-6 round-one win at Hull KR.

9th February 2018 - 14-12 home win over Salford despite scoring two tries against three.

24th February 2018 - Kyle Wood suffers ankle injury in 16-14 win at Catalans.

2nd March 2018 - round four, Friday night home fixture with Huddersfield postponed to following Sunday because of heavy snow.

4th March 2018 - 22-4 home win over Huddersfield in cold conditions makes it four wins from four, the best start to a season since 1945.

5th March 2018 - prop Keegan Hirst signs one-year contract extension until end of 2019 season.

11th March 2018 - 30-18 defeat at Wigan is first of season.

17th March 2018 - home game with Widnes abandoned after 26 minutes because of blizzards, with Trinity leading 2-0.

24th March 2018 - 34-24 defeat at Warrington.

29th March 2018 - 11-6 home defeat to Castleford in heavy mud and rain.

2nd April 2018 - last-minute 50-metre Marc Sneyd field goal means 27-26 Easter Monday defeat at Hull FC.

6th April 2018 - halfback Jacob Miller signs new four-and-a-half year deal.

8th April 2018 - Scott Grix and Liam Finn rested for 28-26 home defeat by Leeds.

15th April 2018 - two Liam Finn penalties the difference in thrilling 24-20 home win over leaders St Helens.

20th April 2018 - 38-4 defeat at Salford sees Red Devils leapfrog Trinity into seventh spot.

27th April 2018 - Chris Annakin carried off with ACL strain in hard-fought 24-4 defeat at Castleford.

1st May 2018 - 19-year-old Zimbabwean born Titus Tendei Gwaze joins on one-year contract.

6th May 2018 - Tom Johnstone scores hat-trick in 54-18 sun-soaked home win over Hull KR.

11th May 2018 - 24-14 sixth-round defeat at Huddersfield means Challenge Cup exit at first hurdle. Joe Arundel suffers ankle injury which needs surgery.

14th May 2018 - prop Jordan Baldwinson goes to Leigh on month's loan.

20th May 2018 - 25-22 defeat to Huddersfield at Magic Weekend in Newcastle.

25th May 2018 - 19-6 win at Widnes.

7th June 2018 - David Fifita stars in 32-16 home win over Wigan.

13th June 2018 - captain Danny Kirmond signs one-year contract extension for 2019.

17th June 2018 - late comeback not enough in 32-30 home defeat to Warrington.

17th June 2018 - Pauli Pauli signs new one-year contract extension to remain at Trinity until end of 2019.

18th June 2018 - young fullback Max Jowitt signs new three-year deal to end of 2021.

24th June 2018 - 44-22 home win over Widnes in re-run of round six abandoned game.

29th June 2018 - three late tries conceded to go down 34-30 at leaders St Helens.

7th July 2018 - 35-18 home defeat to Catalans pulls Trinity back into reach of bottom four.

13th July 2018 - comeback 20-all draw at Leeds leaves Trinity three points above bottom four with two games to play.

22nd July 2018 - stunning 72-10 home win over Hull FC secures top-eight spot.

25th July 2018 - Liam Finn joins Widnes on loan for remainder of season before joining the coaching staff at Wakefield for 2019.

27th July 2018 - 40-28 defeat at Huddersfield in last game of regular season.

10th August 2018 - 31-13 win at Hull FC in Super 8s opener.

12th August 2018 - Reece Lyne signs new four and half year contract.

16th August 2018 - 36-16 home defeat by St Helens.

24th August 2018 - 17-year-old Academy centre Jack Croft signs four-year deal

31st August 2018 - 36-unanswered points in second half seals 42-16 win at in-form Huddersfield.

6th September 2018 - Matty Ashurst and Scott Grix sin-binned in 25-10 defeat at Wigan.

14th September 2018 - Craig Huby sin-binned and Jacob Miller red-carded in 34-22 home win over Catalans.

21st September 2018 - 42-10 defeat at Castleford.

28th September 2018 - 36-23 home defeat by Warrington means fifth-placed finish for second successive yer.

1st October 2018 - Tom Johnstone, Bill Tupou and Matt Ashurst all named in Super League dream team.

10th October 2018 - Academy prop Yusuf Aydin signs four-year deal.

16th October 2018 - Jordan Crowther signs one-year contract extension.

18th October 2018 - prop George King joins from Warrington on two-year deal. Assistant coach Michael Monaghan leaves to go home to Australia.

18th October 2018 - Tom Johnstone scores hat-trick as he makes England debut alongside Reece Lyne in win over France.

22nd October 2018 - prop Craig Kopczak joins from Salford on one-year deal for undisclosed fee.

24th October 2018 - halfback Ben Reynolds joins from Leigh on two-year deal.

CLUB RECORDS

Highest score:
90-12 v Highfield, 27/10/92
Highest score against:
0-86 v Castleford, 17/4/95
Record attendance:
30,676 v Huddersfield, 26/2/21

MATCH RECORDS

Tries:
7 Fred Smith v Keighley, 25/4/59
Keith Slater v Hunslet, 6/2/71
Goals:
13 Mark Conway v Highfield, 27/10/92
Points:
36 Jamie Rooney v Chorley, 27/2/2004

SEASON RECORDS

Tries: 38 Fred Smith 1959-60
David Smith 1973-74
Goals: 163 Neil Fox 1961-62
Points: 407 Neil Fox 1961-62

CAREER RECORDS

Tries: 272 Neil Fox 1956-74
Goals: 1,836 Neil Fox 1956-74
Points: 4,488 Neil Fox 1956-74
Appearances:
605 Harry Wilkinson 1930-49

WAKEFIELD TRINITY

DATE	FIXTURE	RESULT	SCORERS	LGE	ATT
2/2/18	Hull KR (a)	W6-28	t:Johnstone(3),Tupou,Finn,Hampshire g:Finn(2)	5th	8,615
9/2/18	Salford (h)	W14-12	t:Grix,Miller g:Finn(3)	3rd	4,262
24/2/18	Catalans Dragons (a)	W14-16	t:Lyne,Johnstone,Fifita g:Finn(2)	2nd	6,872
4/3/18	Huddersfield (h)	W22-4	t:Jones-Bishop(2),Caton-Brown g:Finn(5)	2nd	4,055
11/3/18	Wigan (a)	L30-18	t:Jones-Bishop(2),Arona g:Finn(3)	3rd	11,455
23/3/18	Warrington (a)	L34-24	t:Lyne,Tupou,Finn,Johnstone,Jones-Bishop g:Finn,Randell	3rd	9,154
29/3/18	Castleford (h)	L6-11	t:Jones-Bishop g:Finn	7th	7,020
2/4/18	Hull FC (a)	L27-26	t:Tupou(2),Caton-Brown(2) g:Batchelor(5)	7th	11,529
8/4/18	Leeds (h)	L26-28	t:Miller,Wood,Ashurst,Jowitt g:Hampshire(5)	7th	6,767
15/4/18	St Helens (h)	W24-20	t:Jones-Bishop,Lyne,Horo,Tupou g:Finn(4)	7th	5,231
20/4/18	Salford (a)	L38-4	t:Arundel	8th	2,686
27/4/18	Castleford (a)	L24-4	t:Randell	7th	7,485
6/5/18	Hull KR (h)	W54-18	t:Ashurst,Johnstone(3),Randell,Grix(2),Jones-Bishop,England g:Finn(9)	7th	5,331
11/5/18	Huddersfield (a) (CCR6)	L24-14	t:Caton-Brown,Hampshire g:Finn(3)	N/A	2,631
20/5/18	Huddersfield (MW) ●	L25-22	t:Ashurst,Jones-Bishop(2),Lyne g:Finn(3)	7th	N/A
25/5/18	Widnes (a)	W6-19	t:Pauli,Johnstone,Fifita g:Batchelor(3) fg:Miller	7th	3,681
7/6/18	Wigan (h)	W32-16	t:Jones-Bishop(2),Tupou,Johnstone,Pauli g:Hampshire(6)	6th	4,681
17/6/18	Warrington (h)	L30-32	t:Arona,Wood(2),Johnstone,Pauli g:Hampshire(5)	6th	5,034
24/6/18	Widnes (h)	W44-22	t:Johnstone,Jones-Bishop,Tupou(2),Lyne(2),Batchelor,Arona g:Batchelor(5),Hampshire	6th	4,589
29/6/18	St Helens (a)	L34-30	t:Johnstone(2),Hampshire,Miller,Caton-Brown,Lyne g:Finn(3)	6th	10,008
7/7/18	Catalans Dragons (h)	L18-35	t:Horo(2),Johnstone g:Finn(3)	6th	5,079
13/7/18	Leeds (a)	D20-20	t:Tupou,Horo,Wood g:Hampshire(4)	6th	11,140
22/7/18	Hull FC (h)	W72-10	t:Johnstone,Fifita,Miller(2),Pauli(2),Lyne(2),Batchelor,Jones-Bishop(2),Jowitt g:Hampshire(12)	6th	5,634
27/7/18	Huddersfield (a)	L40-28	t:Jones-Bishop,Tupou,Pauli,Horo,Johnstone g:Hampshire(4)	7th	5,697
10/8/18	Hull FC (a) (S8)	W13-31	t:Huby,Tupou,Pauli,Johnstone g:Hampshire(7) fg:Miller	6th	10,301
16/8/18	St Helens (h) (S8)	L16-36	t:Wood,Pauli,Tupou g:Hampshire(2)	6th	4,592
31/8/18	Huddersfield (a) (S8)	W16-42	t:Johnstone(2),Hampshire,Grix(2),Jones-Bishop,Miller g:Hampshire(7)	6th	4,963
6/9/18	Wigan (a) (S8)	L25-10	t:Johnstone,Tupou g:Hampshire	6th	9,559
14/9/18	Catalans Dragons (h) (S8)	W34-22	t:Ashurst,Johnstone(3),Hampshire,Randell,Lyne g:Hampshire(3)	5th	4,030
21/9/18	Castleford (a) (S8)	L42-10	t:Tupou,Lyne g:Hampshire	5th	7,860
28/9/18	Warrington (h) (S8)	L23-36	t:Randell,Arundel,Hampshire,Jones-Bishop g:Hampshire(3) fg:Hampshire	5th	4,479

● *Played at St James' Park, Newcastle*

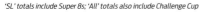

		APP		TRIES		GOALS		FG		PTS	
	D.O.B.	ALL	SL	ALL	SL	ALL	SL	ALL	SL	ALL	SL
Chris Annakin	30/1/91	3(8)	3(8)	0	0	0	0	0	0	0	0
Tinirau Arona	8/5/89	14(16)	14(15)	3	3	0	0	0	0	12	12
Joe Arundel	22/8/91	8(1)	7(1)	2	2	0	0	0	0	8	8
Matty Ashurst	1/11/89	30	29	4	4	0	0	0	0	16	16
Jordan Baldwinson	10/11/94	(4)	(4)	0	0	0	0	0	0	0	0
James Batchelor	9/4/98	13(3)	13(2)	2	2	13	13	0	0	34	34
Mason Caton-Brown	24/5/93	5	4	5	4	0	0	0	0	20	16
Jordan Crowther	19/2/97	5	5	0	0	0	0	0	0	0	0
Anthony England	19/10/86	20(2)	19(2)	1	1	0	0	0	0	4	4
David Fifita	28/6/89	16(4)	15(4)	3	3	0	0	0	0	12	12
Liam Finn	2/11/83	14	13	2	2	42	39	0	0	92	86
Scott Grix	1/5/84	14	14	5	5	0	0	0	0	20	20
Ryan Hampshire	29/12/94	20(6)	20(5)	6	5	61	61	1	1	147	143
Keegan Hirst	13/12/88	12(13)	12(12)	0	0	0	0	0	0	0	0
Justin Horo	7/9/86	18(6)	17(6)	5	5	0	0	0	0	20	20
Craig Huby	21/5/86	9(13)	9(13)	1	1	0	0	0	0	4	4
Tom Johnstone	13/8/95	24	23	24	24	0	0	0	0	96	96
Ben Jones-Bishop	24/8/88	27	27	18	18	0	0	0	0	72	72
Max Jowitt	6/5/97	14(1)	13(1)	2	2	0	0	0	0	8	8
Danny Kirmond	11/11/85	8(4)	8(4)	0	0	0	0	0	0	0	0
Reece Lyne	2/12/92	29	29	11	11	0	0	0	0	44	44
Jacob Miller	22/8/92	30	29	6	6	0	0	2	2	26	26
Pauli Pauli	4/8/94	6(22)	5(22)	8	8	0	0	0	0	32	32
Tyler Randell	31/8/92	23(3)	23(3)	4	4	1	1	0	0	18	18
Bill Tupou	2/7/90	31	30	14	14	0	0	0	0	56	56
Kyle Wood	18/6/89	9(19)	8(19)	5	5	0	0	0	0	20	20

'SL' totals include Super 8s; 'All' totals also include Challenge Cup

Tom Johnstone

LEAGUE RECORD
P30-W13-D1-L16
(5th, SL)
F747, A696, Diff+51
27 points.

CHALLENGE CUP
Round Six

ATTENDANCES
Best - v Castleford (SL - 7,020)
Worst - v Catalans (S8 - 4,030)
Total (SL/S8s only) - 70,784
Average (SL/S8s only) - 5,056
(Down by 227 on 2017)

9th October 2017 - Will Dagger signs for Hull KR.

17th October 2017 - Gold Coast halfback Tyrone Roberts becomes marquee signing on three-year deal.

20th October 2017 - former Leeds forward Kylie Leuluai becomes head of rugby operations.

24th October 2017 - Ben Murdoch-Masila signs from Salford on three-year deal for £175,000 transfer fee.

16th November 2017 - threequarter Mitch Brown signs from Leigh on one-year contract.

20th November 2017 - Benjamin Jullien leaves for Catalans for undisclosed fee.

8th December 2017 - teenage back-rower Luis Johnson transferred from Castleford for £45,000 fee on four-year contract.

29th December 2017 - 26-22 defeat at Widnes in Festive Friendly.

20th January 2018 - 18-6 home pre-season win over Salford.

1st February 2018 - 16-12 home round-one defeat to Leeds.

8th February 2018 - 20-6 round-two defeat at Huddersfield.

16th February 2018 - Ryan Atkins scores two tries as 18-10 round-11 win at Widnes gets season off the mark.

23rd February 2018 - Mitch Brown and Sitaleki Akauola make debuts in dominant 16-10 home win over Wigan.

2nd March 2018 - stand-off Declan Patton dismissed for high tackle early in second half of 21-12 defeat at Hull FC.

6th March 2018 - Declan Patton banned for five games. Sitaleki Akauola gets a game for dangerous contact.

17th March 2018 - Chris Hill makes 200th club appearance in comprehensive 26-0 win against Catalans in cold and rainy Perpignan.

19th March 2018 - winger Josh Charnley signs from rugby union on contract until end of 2020 season.

23rd March 2018 - Tom Lineham scores try hat-trick in 34-24 home win over Wakefield.

30th March 2018 - Josh Charnley scores two tries on debut in 32-18 home Good Friday win over Widnes.

2nd April 2018 - 18-6 watersplash win at Castleford.

7th April 2018 - Kevin Brown scores clinching try in 22-6 win at Salford.

11th April 2018 - centre Toby King signs contract extension until November 2019.

14th April 2018 - Jack Hughes scores two tries and Stefan Ratchford 16 points with try and six conversions in 40-26 home win over Hull KR.

22nd April 2018 - 54-6, 10-try home rout of League 1 Bradford Bulls in fifth round of Challenge Cup. Ben Currie ruled out for season with ACL injury.

27th April 2018 - Josh Charnley scores try hat-trick in 38-4 home win over Huddersfield.

1st May 2018 - Matty Russell leaves for Toronto Wolfpack.

KEY DATES

2nd May 2018 - Ben Pomeroy re-signs for rest of season.

4th May 2018 - Harvey Livett scores hat-trick as Wolves score four tries in last 20 minutes to snatch dramatic 33-22 win at Leeds.

9th May 2018 - Mike Cooper signs contract extension until end of 2020 season.

13th May 2018 - early 8-0 deficit ends in 66-10 Challenge Cup sixth round home win over Toronto Wolfpack.

19th May 2018 - 38-10 defeat by Wigan at Magic Weekend in Newcastle ends ten-match winning run. Sitaleki Akauola gets one match for dangerous contact.

23rd May 2018 - utility player Harvey Livett agrees two-year contract extension until November 2020.

25th May 2018 - 30-12 home win over Hull FC after trailing 12-0 at half-time.

2nd June 2018 - Josh Charnley scores 200th career try in 23-0 home Challenge Cup quarter-final victory over Wigan.

5th June 2018 - South Sydney forward Jason Clark signs two-year contract from 2019 season.

8th June 2018 - 34-30 home defeat to Castleford.

17th June 2018 - 32-30 win at Wakefield after leading 22-6 at half-time. Ryan Atkins tears biceps.

18th June 2018 - Tyrone Roberts announces he will take option of leaving his three-year contract after first year to return to NRL.

27th June 2018 - former Leicester Storm second row Matt Davis signs from London Broncos on two-year contract from 2019.

29th June 2018 - 30-14 home win over Salford.

6th July 2018 - last-minute Josh Woods field goal means 13-12 defeat at Wigan.

9th July 2018 - Canberra stand-off Blake Austin signs three-year deal from 2019.

12th July 2018 - late Josh Drinkwater penalty earns Catalans 22-22 draw at Warrington.

19th July 2018 - Dominic Crosby joins Leeds on loan until end of season.

20th July 2018 - 34-20 win at Hull KR moves Wolves into third spot.

25th July 2018 - forward Bodene Thompson signs from Leigh until end of season

26th July 2018 - 55-metre Danny Richardson penalty goal after final hooter means 14-12 defeat at St Helens.

5th August 2018 - wingers Josh Charnley and Tom Lineham each score two tries in 48-12 Challenge Cup semi-final win over Leeds.

10th August 2018 - Tom Lineham scores hat-trick in 56-6 home win over Wembley opponents Catalans.

17th August 2018 - Mitch Brown stretchered off with long-term knee injury in 28-18 defeat at Castleford. Sitaleki Akauola banned for one game for dangerous contact.

25th August 2018 - 20-14 defeat to Catalans in fifth Wembley appearance in ten seasons.

30th August 2018 - Bryson Goodwin scores five tries in 80-10 home win over Hull FC.

30th August 2018 - Wolves crowned first-ever Physical Disability Rugby League (PDRL) World Club Champions, beating South Sydney 34-12 in Sydney.

7th September 2018 - 26-24 home win over Huddersfield secures top-four finish.

14th September 2018 - Luis Johnson makes debut as late try-flurry leads to 26-6 defeat at Wigan. Tom Lineham banned for three games for high tackle.

21st September 2018 - Tyrone Roberts, Ben Pomeroy, George King, Mitch Brown, Bodene Thompson, Dominic Crosby and Taylor Prell all to leave at season end.

22nd September 2018 - 34-14 home defeat to St Helens.

26th September 2018 - Tom Lineham's three-match penalty notice reduced to two matches on appeal.

28th September 2018 - 36-23 last-round win at Wakefield.

1st October 2018 - Stefan Ratchford wins Albert Goldthorpe Medal.

2nd October 2018 - prop Lama Tasi joins from Salford on one-year deal.

4th October 2018 - late Tom Lineham try secures 18-13 semi-final win at St Helens.

13th October 2018 - Stefan Ratchford wins Harry Sunderland Trophy in 12-4 Grand Final defeat to Wigan.

22nd October 2018 - teenage hooker Danny Walker joins from Widnes on three-year deal.

CLUB RECORDS

Highest score:
112-0 v Swinton, 20/5/2011
Highest score against:
12-84 v Bradford, 9/9/2001
Record attendance:
34,404 v Wigan, 22/1/49 *(Wilderspool)*
15,008 v Widnes, 25/3/2016
(Halliwell Jones Stadium)

MATCH RECORDS

Tries:
7 Brian Bevan v Leigh, 29/3/48
Brian Bevan v Bramley, 22/4/53
Goals:
16 Lee Briers v Swinton, 20/5/2011
Points:
44 Lee Briers v Swinton, 20/5/2011

SEASON RECORDS

Tries: 66 Brian Bevan 1952-53
Goals: 170 Steve Hesford 1978-79
Points: 363 Harry Bath 1952-53

CAREER RECORDS

Tries: 740 Brian Bevan 1945-62
Goals: 1,159 Steve Hesford 1975-85
Points: 2,586 Lee Briers 1997-2013
Appearances: 620 Brian Bevan 1945-62

WARRINGTON WOLVES

DATE	FIXTURE	RESULT	SCORERS	LGE	ATT
1/2/18	Leeds (h)	L12-16	t:Goodwin,Lineham g:Goodwin(2)	7th	11,241
8/2/18	Huddersfield (a)	L20-6	t:Lineham g:Goodwin	9th	5,104
16/2/18	Widnes (a)	W10-18	t:Atkins(2),Ratchford g:Goodwin(3)	7th	7,009
23/2/18	Wigan (h)	W16-10	t:Lineham,Atkins g:Goodwin(4)	5th	12,012
2/3/18	Hull FC (a)	L21-12	t:Hughes,Atkins g:Ratchford(2)	7th	10,051
9/3/18	St Helens (h)	L12-30	t:T King,Livett g:Ratchford(2)	8th	12,268
17/3/18	Catalans Dragons (a)	W0-26	t:M Brown,Clark,Murdoch-Masila(2),Livett g:Goodwin(3)	5th	6,585
23/3/18	Wakefield (h)	W34-24	t:Lineham(3),Goodwin,Cooper,Murdoch-Masila g:Goodwin(2),Ratchford(3)	5th	9,154
30/3/18	Widnes (h)	W32-18	t:T King(2),Charnley(2),Akauola,Westwood g:Goodwin(4)	3rd	12,175
2/4/18	Castleford (a)	W6-18	t:T King,Clark g:Ratchford(5)	3rd	6,881
7/4/18	Salford (a)	W6-22	t:T King,Charnley,Roberts,K Brown g:Ratchford(3)	3rd	3,428
14/4/18	Hull KR (h)	W40-26	t:Cooper,Hughes(2),Currie,Lineham,Ratchford,Atkins g:Ratchford(6)	3rd	9,305
21/4/18	Bradford (h) (CCR5)	W54-6	t:Hill,Currie(2),Goodwin(3),Charnley(4) g:Ratchford(3),Goodwin(4)	N/A	4,710
27/4/18	Huddersfield (h)	W38-4	t:Charnley(3),Ratchford(2),Lineham,Livett,Philbin g:Goodwin,Ratchford,Livett	3rd	8,792
4/5/18	Leeds (a)	W22-33	t:K Brown,Livett(3),Atkins,Murdoch-Masila g:Goodwin,Ratchford(3) fg:Roberts	3rd	11,749
13/5/18	Toronto (a) (CCR6) ●	W10-66	t:Cooper,Charnley(2),Livett,Murdoch-Masila(2),Hughes,Westwood,Lineham(3),Roberts g:Goodwin(9)	N/A	6,507
19/5/18	Wigan (MW) ●●	L10-38	t:Livett,Ratchford g:Goodwin	3rd	N/A
25/5/18	Hull FC (h)	W30-12	t:Livett,Murdoch-Masila,Charnley,Atkins g:Livett(5)	3rd	8,646
2/6/18	Wigan (h) (CCQF)	W23-0	t:K Brown,Murdoch-Masila,Charnley,Patton g:Livett(2),Goodwin fg:Roberts	N/A	10,213
8/6/18	Castleford (h)	L30-34	t:Roberts,Ratchford,Clark,Akauola,Charnley(2) g:Livett(2),Goodwin	3rd	9,198
17/6/18	Wakefield (a)	W30-32	t:Ratchford(2),Lineham,K Brown g:Livett(5),Goodwin(3)	3rd	5,034
29/6/18	Salford (h)	W30-14	t:Akauola,Lineham,T King,Charnley,Clark,Cooper g:Goodwin(3)	3rd	9,171
6/7/18	Wigan (a)	L13-12	t:T King,Lineham,Charnley	4th	13,249
12/7/18	Catalans Dragons (h)	D22-22	t:Goodwin,Charnley,Livett g:Roberts(5)	4th	8,807
20/7/18	Hull KR (a)	W20-34	t:Cooper,Ratchford,Roberts,T King,K Brown,Patton g:Roberts(5)	3rd	7,045
26/7/18	St Helens (a)	L14-12	t:Clark g:Roberts(4)	4th	12,454
5/8/18	Leeds (CCSF) ●●●	W12-48	t:Lineham(2),Charnley(2),K Brown,Murdoch-Masila,T King,Goodwin g:Roberts(8)	N/A	26,086
10/8/18	Catalans Dragons (h) (S8)	W56-6	t:Charnley,Lineham(3),M Brown,K Brown,Roberts,T King,Patton,Philbin g:Patton(8)	3rd	8,032
17/8/18	Castleford (a) (S8)	L28-18	t:Ratchford(2),Goodwin g:Ratchford(2),Patton	4th	7,142
25/8/18	Catalans Dragons (CCF) ●●●●	L20-14	t:Murdoch-Masila,G King g:Roberts(3)	N/A	50,672
30/8/18	Hull FC (h) (S8)	W80-10	t:Charnley(2),T King(2),Goodwin(5),Hughes,Philbin,Roberts,Lineham,Ratchford g:Roberts(12)	4th	8,101
7/9/18	Huddersfield (h) (S8)	W26-24	t:Goodwin(2),Atkins,Ratchford,Lineham g:Roberts(3)	4th	9,076
14/9/18	Wigan (a) (S8)	L26-6	t:Ratchford g:Patton	4th	12,372
22/9/18	St Helens (h) (S8)	L14-34	t:K Brown,T King,Goodwin g:Patton	4th	10,747
28/9/18	Wakefield (a) (S8)	W23-36	t:Murdoch-Masila,T King,Ratchford,Hughes,Patton,Atkins g:Patton(6)	4th	4,479
4/10/18	St Helens (a) (SF)	W13-18	t:Hughes,Lineham(2) g:Roberts(3)	N/A	12,309
13/10/18	Wigan (GF) ●●●●●	L4-12	t:Charnley	N/A	64,892

● Played at Halliwell Jones Stadium ●● Played at St James' Park, Newcastle
●●● Played at University of Bolton Stadium ●●●● Played at Wembley Stadium ●●●●● Played at Old Trafford, Manchester

		APP		TRIES		GOALS		FG		PTS	
	D.O.B.	ALL	SL	ALL	SL	ALL	SL	ALL	SL	ALL	SL
Sitaleki Akauola	7/4/92	5(19)	4(17)	3	3	0	0	0	0	12	12
Ryan Atkins	7/10/85	21(1)	18(1)	9	9	0	0	0	0	36	36
Kevin Brown	2/10/84	33	29	9	7	0	0	0	0	36	28
Mitch Brown	7/11/87	11(1)	10(1)	2	2	0	0	0	0	8	8
Josh Charnley	26/6/91	28	23	25	16	0	0	0	0	100	64
Daryl Clark	10/2/93	34	30	5	5	0	0	0	0	20	20
Mike Cooper	15/9/88	31	27	5	4	0	0	0	0	20	16
Dominic Crosby	11/12/90	(10)	(10)	0	0	0	0	0	0	0	0
Ben Currie	15/7/94	9	8	3	1	0	0	0	0	12	4
Bryson Goodwin	30/12/85	33	28	16	12	43	29	0	0	150	106
Chris Hill	3/11/87	35	30	1	0	0	0	0	0	4	0
Jack Hughes	4/1/92	36	31	7	6	0	0	0	0	28	24
Luis Johnson	20/2/99	(1)		0		0		0		0	
George King	24/2/95	6(16)	5(14)	1	0	0	0	0	0	4	0
Toby King	9/7/96	22(1)	20(1)	14	13	0	0	0	0	56	52
Tom Lineham	21/9/91	34	30	23	18	0	0	0	0	92	72
Harvey Livett	4/1/97	17(5)	13(4)	10	9	15	13	0	0	70	62
Pat Moran	2/4/98	(1)	0	0	0	0	0	0	0	0	0
Ben Murdoch-Masila	7/2/91	8(18)	8(14)	11	6	0	0	0	0	44	24
Declan Patton	23/5/95	8(19)	7(15)	4	3	17	17	0	0	50	46
Joe Philbin	16/11/94	(35)	(30)	3	3	0	0	0	0	12	12
Ben Pomeroy	10/1/84	1(7)	1(7)	0	0	0	0	0	0	0	0
Stefan Ratchford	19/7/88	35	30	15	15	30	27	0	0	120	114
Tyrone Roberts	1/6/91	33	28	6	5	43	32	2	1	112	85
Matthew Russell	6/6/93	3	3	0	0	0	0	0	0	0	0
Morgan Smith	30/4/98	1(7)	(7)	0	0	0	0	0	0	0	0
Bodene Thompson	1/8/88	7	7	0	0	0	0	0	0	0	0
Ben Westwood	25/7/81	30(3)	26(2)	2	1	0	0	0	0	8	4

'SL' totals include Super 8s, semi-final & Grand Final; 'All' totals also include Challenge Cup

Stefan Ratchford

LEAGUE RECORD
P30-W18-D1-L11
(4th, SL/Grand Final Runners-Up)
F767, A561, Diff+206
37 points.

CHALLENGE CUP
Runners-Up

ATTENDANCES
Best – v St Helens (SL - 12,268)
Worst – v Bradford (CC - 4,710)
Total (SL/S8s only) - 146,725
Average (SL/S8s only) - 9,782
(Down by 382 on 2017)

219

16th November 2017 - centre Krisnan Inu signs from Catalans on two-year deal.

1st December 2017 - Papua New Guinea Rugby League World Cup centre Benkato 'Kato' Ottio joins from Canberra Raiders.

6th December 2017 - Will Matthews, signed from St George Illawarra in September, released from contract on compassionate grounds.

16th December 2017 - PNG World Cup prop Wellington Albert signs from PNG Hunters.

29th December 2017 - 26-22 home Festive Friendly win over Warrington.

8th January 2018 - Kato Ottio, 23, dies in Australia a week before his departure to the UK.

12th January 2018 - PNG World Cup prop Stanton Albert, brother of Wellington Albert joins on two-year deal.

4th February 2018 - Patrick Ah Van breaks arm as Chris Dean scores double in 40-12 round-one, home win over Catalans.

11th February 2018 - Olly Ashall-Bott makes debut in 13-12 defeat at Castleford.

15th February 2018 - back-rower Chris Dean signs new two-year deal until end of 2020 season.

16th February 2018 - 18-10 home defeat to Warrington. Chris Houston gets two-game 'penalty notice' for collision with referee.

26th February 2018 - Kristian Inu scores two tries as 19 unanswered second-half points secures 23-6 home win over Leeds.

2nd March 2018 - 32-16 defeat at Wigan despite leading 16-0 a minute before half-time.

8th March 2018 - forward Tom Olbison signs new deal until end of 2020 season.

9th March 2018 - prop Wellington Albert sent off on hour mark of rainy 28-16 home defeat to Huddersfield.

13th March 2018 - Wellington Albert receives two-match suspension for dangerous contact.

17th March 2018 - Saturday evening game at Wakefield abandoned after 22 minutes because of blizzards, with Trinity leading 2-0.

22nd March 2018 - 24-16 home win over Salford.

30th March 2018 - 32-18 Good Friday defeat at Warrington.

2nd April 2018 - weakened side suffers spirited 28-6 home, Easter Monday defeat by leaders St Helens.

5th April 2018 - Danny Craven signs new two-year contract extension to end of 2020.

7th April 2018 - young winger Keanan Brand suffers broken leg seven minutes into debut and Gil Dudson, Wellington Albert and Danny Craven all join injury list during 31-12 defeat at Hull KR.

12th April 2018 - Leeds centre Jimmy Keinhorst arrives on four-week loan.

12th April 2018 - 39-20 home defeat to Hull FC.

18th April 2018 - forward Matt Whitley signs new three-year deal to end of 2021 season.

19th April 2018 - Brad Walker signs new three-year deal to end of 2021 season.

WIDNES VIKINGS
KEY DATES

22nd April 2018 - 90-0 home defeat of League 1 Coventry Bears in fifth round of Challenge Cup sets record for biggest-ever victory.

27th April 2018 - 32-24 home defeat to Wigan after leading 18-4 at half-time. On-loan Jimmy Keinhorst makes debut.

30th April 2018 - Liam Walsh signs new three-year deal to end of 2021 season.

4th May 2018 - 28-18 defeat at Huddersfield.

11th May 2018 - comeback from 23-4 falls short in 23-20 sixth-round Challenge Cup defeat to Leeds.

13th May 2018 - Stanton Albert released from contract on compassionate grounds to return to PNG.

15th May 2018 - England Academy prop Owen Farnworth and Gil Dudson both sign new three-year contracts until end of 2021 season.

17th May 2018 - Chris Houston announces he will retire at end of season.

19th May 2018 - 38-18 defeat to St Helens at Magic Weekend in Newcastle.

21st May 2018 - Leeds recall Jimmy Keinhorst from loan.

22nd May 2018 - winger Ryan Ince signs new two year-deal to end of 2020 season.

25th May 2018 - 19-6 home defeat by Wakefield. Hep Cahill's season ended with Achilles injury.

31st May 2018 - head coach Denis Betts is sacked after eight seasons in charge. Assistant Francis Cummins appointed interim coach.

6th June 2018 - Salford forward Weller Hauraki joins on loan with Greg Burke and Ed Chamberlain going the other way on loan.

9th June 2018 - 32-12 defeat at Catalans after leading 10-0.

14th June 2018 - Chris Houston sent off for applauding his sin-binning ten minutes from end of 26-12 defeat at Salford and gets two-match ban.

24th June 2018 - 44-22 defeat at Wakefield in re-run of round six abandoned game.

29th June 2018 - late Bureta Faraimo try seals battling 31-24 defeat at Hull and ensures bottom-four finish. Owen Buckley scores try on debut.

4th July 2018 - former Wigan centre Anthony Gelling signs for 2019 from NZ Warriors on two-year deal.

6th July 2018 - Chris Houston, set for return from two-match suspension, misses 36-6 defeat at St Helens as his wife goes into labour prior to kick-off.

14th July 2018 - 26-24 Saturday afternoon defeat by Hull KR at sun-soaked Halton Stadium.

20th July 2018 - 34-0 defeat at Leeds.

25th July 2018 - Harrison Hansen signs from Leigh with immediate effect until end of 2019 season. Wakefield halfback Liam Finn signs until end of current season.

27th July 2018 - forward Charlie Gubb signs from Canberra Raiders for remainder of season

1st August 2018 - hooker Aaron Heremaia announces he will retire at end of season.

1st August 2018 - assistant coach Mick Cassidy to leave at end of season after ten years at the Vikings.

9th August 2018 - last minute Jarrod Sammut field goal means 21-20 home defeat to London Broncos in first Qualifiers match. Charlie Gubb injured.

18th August 2018 - 32-6 defeat at Salford in second Qualifiers match. Olly Ashall-Bott suffers season-ending knee injury.

22nd August 2018 - Academy graduate Dan Norman signs new one-year deal for 2019 season.

2nd September 2018 - 42-22 defeat in Toulouse leaves Vikings point-less in Qualifiers. Gil Dudson suffers ankle injury.

6th September 2018 - fullback Olly Ashall-Bott signs two-year contract extension to end of 2020.

9th September 2018 - 16-6 home defeat to Leeds.

15th September 2018 - 26-12 home win over Halifax keeps Super League survival hopes alive.

22nd September 2018 - 20-12 defeat at Toronto confirms relegation.

26th September 2018 - Hep Cahill named as new club captain.

30th September 2018 - 30-0 defeat at Hull KR ends season.

CLUB RECORDS

Highest score:
90-4 v Doncaster, 10/6/2007
90-0 v Coventry, 21/4/2018
Highest score against:
6-76 v Catalans Dragons, 31/3/2012
Record attendance:
24,205 v St Helens, 16/2/61

MATCH RECORDS

Tries: 7 Phil Cantillon v York, 18/2/2001
Goals: 14 Mark Hewitt v Oldham, 25/7/99
Tim Hartley v Saddleworth, 7/3/2009
Points:
38 Gavin Dodd v Doncaster, 10/6/2007

SEASON RECORDS

Tries: 58 Martin Offiah 1988-89
Goals: 161 Mick Nanyn 2007
Points: 434 Mick Nanyn 2007

CAREER RECORDS

Tries: 234 Mal Aspey 1964-80
Goals: 1,083 Ray Dutton 1966-78
Points: 2,195 Ray Dutton 1966-78
Appearances: 591 Keith Elwell 1970-86

WIDNES VIKINGS

WIDNES VIKINGS

DATE	FIXTURE	RESULT	SCORERS	LGE	ATT
4/2/18	Catalans Dragons (h)	W40-12	t:Dean(2),Mellor,Inu,Ah Van,Runciman,Marsh g:Gilmore(6)	2nd	4,568
11/2/18	Castleford (a)	L13-12	t:Whitley,J Chapelhow g:Gilmore(2)	5th	7,106
16/2/18	Warrington (h)	L10-18	t:Inu(2) g:Gilmore	5th	7,009
25/2/18	Leeds (h)	W23-6	t:Mellor,Inu(2),D Walker g:Inu(3) fg:Craven	3rd	5,519
2/3/18	Wigan (a)	L32-16	t:Whitley,Marsh g:Gilmore(4)	4th	10,815
9/3/18	Huddersfield (h)	L16-28	t:Mellor,Whitley,Marsh g:Gilmore(2)	6th	4,298
22/3/18	Salford (h)	W24-16	t:Dean,Inu,Burke,Heremaia g:Inu(4)	8th	4,007
30/3/18	Warrington (a)	L32-18	t:Chamberlain(2),Hanbury g:Inu(2),Gilmore	8th	12,175
2/4/18	St Helens (h)	L6-28	t:W Albert g:Gilmore	8th	6,706
7/4/18	Hull KR (a)	L31-12	t:Ince,Mellor g:Chamberlain(2)	8th	7,260
12/4/18	Hull FC (h)	L20-39	t:Wilde,Olbison(2) g:Gilmore(4)	9th	3,733
21/4/18	Coventry (h) (CCR5)	W90-0	t:Hanbury(3),Ah Van(3),White,Craven(4),B Walker,Whitley,Chamberlain,D Walker,J Chapelhow,Ince g:Gilmore(11)	N/A	1,438
27/4/18	Wigan (h)	L24-32	t:Olbison,J Chapelhow,Ince(2) g:Gilmore(4)	9th	5,668
4/5/18	Huddersfield (a)	L28-18	t:Craven,Ince,Gilmore g:Gilmore(3)	10th	4,645
11/5/18	Leeds (h) (CCR6)	L20-23	t:Whitley(2),Gerrard,Runciman g:Gilmore(2)	N/A	1,865
19/5/18	St Helens (MW) ●	L38-18	t:Whitley,W Albert,Keinhorst g:Marsh(3)	11th	N/A
25/5/18	Wakefield (h)	L6-19	t:Ah Van g:Marsh	12th	3,681
9/6/18	Catalans Dragons (a)	L32-12	t:J Chapelhow,Hanbury g:Craven,Ah Van	12th	9,239
14/6/18	Salford (a)	L26-12	t:Gilmore,Ah Van g:Gilmore(2)	12th	2,248
24/6/18	Wakefield (a)	L44-22	t:Marsh,D Walker,Gerrard,Ince g:Gilmore(3)	12th	4,589
29/6/18	Hull FC (h)	L31-24	t:Runciman,Buckley,Wilde,J Chapelhow g:Inu(4)	12th	10,420
6/7/18	St Helens (a)	L36-6	t:Craven g:Inu	12th	9,923
14/7/18	Hull KR (h)	L24-26	t:Ashall-Bott,Craven,Buckley(2) g:Inu(4)	12th	4,469
20/7/18	Leeds (a)	L34-0		12th	10,977
29/7/18	Castleford (h)	L24-52	t:Ah Van(2),Hanbury,Hansen g:Ah Van,Inu(3)	12th	4,218
9/8/18	London Broncos (h) (S8-Q)	L20-21	t:Ashall-Bott,Dean,Inu g:Inu(4)	5th(S8-Q)	3,432
18/8/18	Salford (a) (S8-Q)	L32-6	t:Runciman g:Inu	7th(S8-Q)	2,317
1/9/18	Toulouse (a) (S8-Q)	L42-22	t:Inu,Hansen,Hauraki,White g:Inu(3)	7th(S8-Q)	2,911
9/9/18	Leeds (h) (S8-Q)	L6-16	t:Olbison g:Inu	7th(S8-Q)	4,050
15/9/18	Halifax (h) (S8-Q)	W26-12	t:Hauraki,Inu(2),Ah Van(2) g:Inu(3)	7th(S8-Q)	3,372
22/9/18	Toronto (a) (S8-Q)	L20-12	t:Mellor,Dean g:Inu(2)	7th(S8-Q)	8,381
30/9/18	Hull KR (a) (S8-Q)	L30-0		7th(S8-Q)	8,232

● *Played at St James' Park, Newcastle*

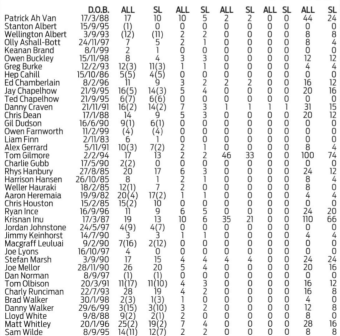

	D.O.B.	APP		TRIES		GOALS		FG		PTS	
		ALL	SL	ALL	SL	ALL	SL	ALL	SL	ALL	SL
Patrick Ah Van	17/3/88	17	10	10	5	2	2	0	0	44	24
Stanton Albert	15/9/95	(1)	0	0	0	0	0	0	0	0	0
Wellington Albert	3/9/93	(12)	(11)	2	2	0	0	0	0	8	8
Olly Ashall-Bott	24/11/97	7	5	2	1	0	0	0	0	8	4
Keanan Brand	8/1/99	2	1	0	0	0	0	0	0	0	0
Owen Buckley	15/11/98	8	4	3	3	0	0	0	0	12	12
Greg Burke	12/2/93	12(3)	11(3)	1	1	0	0	0	0	4	4
Hep Cahill	15/10/86	5(5)	4(5)	0	0	0	0	0	0	0	0
Ed Chamberlain	8/2/96	11	9	3	2	2	2	0	0	16	12
Jay Chapelhow	21/9/95	16(5)	14(3)	5	4	0	0	0	0	20	16
Ted Chapelhow	21/9/95	6(7)	6(6)	0	0	0	0	0	0	0	0
Danny Craven	21/11/91	16(2)	14(2)	7	3	1	1	1	1	31	15
Chris Dean	17/1/88	14	9	5	3	0	0	0	0	20	12
Gil Dudson	16/6/90	9(1)	6(1)	0	0	0	0	0	0	0	0
Owen Farnworth	11/2/99	(4)	(4)	0	0	0	0	0	0	0	0
Liam Finn	2/11/83	6	1	0	0	0	0	0	0	0	0
Alex Gerrard	5/11/91	10(3)	7(2)	2	1	0	0	0	0	8	4
Tom Gilmore	2/2/94	17	13	2	2	46	33	0	0	100	74
Charlie Gubb	17/5/90	2(2)	0	0	0	0	0	0	0	0	0
Rhys Hanbury	27/8/85	20	17	6	3	0	0	0	0	24	12
Harrison Hansen	26/10/85	8	1	2	1	0	0	0	0	8	4
Weller Hauraki	18/2/85	12(1)	7	2	0	0	0	0	0	8	0
Aaron Heremaia	19/9/82	20(4)	17(2)	1	1	0	0	0	0	4	4
Chris Houston	15/2/85	12(1)	10	0	0	0	0	0	0	0	0
Ryan Ince	16/9/96	11	9	6	5	0	0	0	0	24	20
Krisnan Inu	17/3/87	19	13	10	6	35	21	0	0	110	66
Jordan Johnstone	24/5/97	4(9)	4(7)	0	0	0	0	0	0	0	0
Jimmy Keinhorst	14/7/90	3	3	1	1	0	0	0	0	4	4
Macgraff Leuluai	9/2/90	7(16)	2(12)	0	0	0	0	0	0	0	0
Joe Lyons	16/10/97	4	0	0	0	0	0	0	0	0	0
Stefan Marsh	3/9/90	17	15	4	4	4	4	0	0	24	24
Joe Mellor	28/11/90	26	20	5	4	0	0	0	0	20	16
Dan Norman	8/9/97	(1)	(1)	0	0	0	0	0	0	0	0
Tom Olbison	20/3/91	11(17)	11(10)	4	3	0	0	0	0	16	12
Charly Runciman	22/7/93	28	19	4	2	0	0	0	0	16	8
Brad Walker	30/1/98	2(3)	1(3)	1	0	0	0	0	0	4	0
Danny Walker	29/6/99	3(15)	3(10)	3	2	0	0	0	0	12	8
Lloyd White	9/8/88	9(2)	9(2)	2	2	0	0	0	0	8	8
Matt Whitley	20/1/96	25(2)	19(2)	7	4	0	0	0	0	28	16
Sam Wilde	8/9/95	14(11)	12(7)	2	2	0	0	0	0	8	8

Krisnan Inu

LEAGUE RECORD
SL: P23-W3-D0-L20 (12th)
F387, A653, Diff-266, 6 points.

S8-Q: P7-W1-D0-L6 (7th)
F92, A173, Diff-81, 2 points.

CHALLENGE CUP
Round Six

ATTENDANCES
Best - v Warrington (SL - 7,009)
Worst - v Coventry (CC - 1,438)
Total (SL/S8s only) - 64,730
Average (SL/S8s only) - 4,624
(Down by 963 on 2017)

'SL' totals include regular season only; 'All' totals also include Super 8s (Qualifiers) & Challenge Cup

3rd October 2017 - Oliver Gildart named 2017 Super League Young Player of the Year.

11th October 2017 - prop Gabriel Hamlin joins from South Sydney on two-year deal

19th October 2017 - Lewis Tierney released to join Catalans. Nick Gregson joins Leigh.

24th October 2017 - Kyle Shelford released and joins Swinton Lions.

6th November 2017 - Gabe Fell released to join Swinton.

13th December 2017 - Dan Sarginson returns on two-year contract after one season in the NRL with Gold Coast Titans.

2nd January 2018 - Michael McIlorum granted early contract release and signs for Catalans. Anthony Gelling also released to return to New Zealand.

21st January 2018 - 22-14 pre-season win at Leigh.

2nd February 2018 - young prop Caine Barnes joins Workington Town on month's loan.

2nd February 2018 - Liam Marshall and Oliver Gildart both score braces in dominant 40-12 round-one win at Salford.

10th February 2018 - Liam Marshall scores two tries in historic 24-10, round-two win over Hull FC in Wollongong.

17th February 2018 - 18-8 defeat to South Sydney before 18,721 crowd at ANZ Stadium, Sydney.

21st February 2018 - prop Frank-Paul Nuuausala released to return to Australia.

23rd February 2018 - 16-10 defeat at Warrington flatters Warriors.

2nd March 2018 - 32-16 home win over Widnes after trailing 16-0 just before half-time.

11th March 2018 - Joe Burgess scores hat-trick as 30-18 home win over Wakefield moves Warriors to second in table.

29th March 2018 - halfback Jake Shorrocks joins Salford on month's loan.

30th March 2018 - Sam Tomkins late withdrawal with illness before 21-18 Good Friday away defeat at St Helens.

2nd April 2018 - winger Liam Marshall scores four tries and Gabe Hamlin makes debut in 44-6 Easter Monday home win over Hull KR.

7th April 2018 - comeback from 21-0 behind to win at Catalans 32-23.

13th April 2018 - late penalty and field goal from Sam Tomkins seal dramatic 9-8 win at Leeds.

17th April 2018 - winger Liam Marshall signs new four-year contract to end of 2022 season.

18th April 2018 - utility Willie Isa signs new three-year deal to end of 2021 season.

19th April 2018 - winger Tom Davies agrees terms on new five-year contract to the end of 2023 season.

20th April 2018 - Oliver Gildart scores two tries in 28-12 home win over Castleford.

27th April 2018 - Joe Burgess suffers season-ending knee injury in 32-24 comeback from 18-4 down win at Widnes.

4th May 2018 - Sam Tomkins scores try-brace in 30-0 home win over Salford.

11th May 2018 - former Wigan prop Danny Tickle sent off just before half-time in 28-10 sixth-round Challenge Cup win at Hull KR.

KEY DATES

14th May 2018 - Sam Tomkins to leave for Catalans Dragons at end of season.

16th May 2018 - Joe Bretherton and James Worthington join Toulouse Olympique on loan for one month.

17th May 2018 - Oliver Gildart agrees new three-year contract.

18th May 2018 - Zak Hardaker signs on four-year contract from November 8th 2018.

19th May 2018 - 38-10 Magic Weekend win over Warrington extends winning run to eight games.

21st May 2018 - head coach Shaun Wane announces he is to leave club at end of season.

25th May 2018 - eight-match unbeaten run comes to an end with 24-8 defeat at Hull KR.

30th May 2018 - prop Ryan Sutton to join Canberra at end of season.

2nd June 2018 - 23-0 quarter-final defeat at Warrington means Challenge Cup exit.

3rd June 2018 - Joel Tomkins suspended and fined £10,000 after video of abuse of bar staff emerges on social media. Brother Sam fined £5,000 but not suspended.

7th June 2018 - Craig Mullen makes debut in 32-16 defeat at Wakefield.

11th June 2018 - Joel Tomkins leaves to join Hull KR with immediate effect.

11th June 2018 - former St Helens backrower Joe Greenwood signs from Gold Coast Titans with immediate effect on three-and-a-half year deal.

16th June 2018 - Liam Marshall scores late winner in 14-10 win at Hull FC.

23rd June 2018 - last-gasp Jamie Ellis field goal seals 19-18 defeat at Castleford in game postponed from round six.

25th June 2018 - Shaun Wane to join Scotland rugby union team as new high performance coach at end of season.

28th June 2018 - Joe Greenwood makes debut as Liam Marshall scores hat-trick in 46-8 home hammering of Leeds. Romain Navarrete gets one-match ban for dangerous tackle.

6th July 2018 - Josh Woods kicks field goal in dying seconds to clinch 13-12 home win over Warrington. Liam Farrell suffers shoulder injury.

12th July 2018 - Samy Kibula makes debut in 20-12 defeat at Huddersfield.

17th July 2018 - Swinton centre Chris Hankinson signs until 2020 with immediate effect, with option of one-year extension.

19th July 2018 - Chris Hankinson makes debut in 14-6 Thursday-night defeat to St Helens at the DW Stadium.

27th July 2018 - late Joe Greenwood try seals 25-20 home win over Catalans.

31st July 2018 - 25-year-old Barrow Raiders prop Joe Bullock signs on three-year deal from 2019.

1st August 2018 - Mick Cassidy to return as head of youth at end of season.

8th August 2018 - John Bateman signs two-year contract with option for a third year with Canberra Raiders for an undisclosed fee. Also agrees three-year deal to become Wigan's marquee player should he return to Super League.

8th August 2018 - Shaun Edwards to return as head coach in 2020 on three-year contract, with Adrian Lam taking the role for 2019.

10th August 2018 - 24-22 home win over Castleford, after leading 20-0, in first Super 8s fixture. Oliver Partington makes debut off bench.

18th August 2018 - Joe Greenwood and Morgan Escare score twice in 35-6 win over Dragons in Perpignan.

31st August 2018 - St Helens' League Leaders Shield coronation delayed by 30-10 away win.

6th September 2018 - 25-10 home win over Wakefield.

14th September 2018 - Dom Manfredi makes first appearance in two years and scores two tries in 26-6 home win over Warrington.

21st September 2018 - 13-6 win at Huddersfield confirms home semi-final.

28th September 2018 - 14-12 home win over Hull FC in last Super 8s round.

1st October 2018 - John Bateman and Sean O'Loughlin named in Super League Dream Team.

5th October 2018 - 14-0 semi-final home win over Castleford.

9th October 2018 - Shaun Wane named coach of the year.

13th October 2018 - Dom Manfredi scores two tries in 12-4 Grand Final win over Warrington.

19th October 2018 - Zak Hardaker enters rehab after drink-driving conviction.

31st October 2018 - Sean O'Loughlin signs one-year contract extension.

CLUB RECORDS		
Highest score:		
116-0 v Flimby & Fothergill, 14/2/25		
Highest score against:		
0-75 v St Helens, 26/6/2005		
Record attendance:		
47,747 v St Helens, 27/3/59 *(Central Park)*		
25,004 v St Helens, 25/3/2005		
(JJB/DW Stadium)		

MATCH RECORDS		
Tries: 10 Martin Offiah v Leeds, 10/5/92		
Shaun Edwards v Swinton, 29/9/92		
Goals: 22 Jim Sullivan		
v Flimby & Fothergill, 14/2/25		
Points: 44 Jim Sullivan		
v Flimby & Fothergill, 14/2/25		

SEASON RECORDS		
Tries: 62 Johnny Ring 1925-26		
Goals: 186 Frano Botica 1994-95		
Points: 462 Pat Richards 2010		

CAREER RECORDS		
Tries: 478 Billy Boston 1953-68		
Goals: 2,317 Jim Sullivan 1921-46		
Points: 4,883 Jim Sullivan 1921-46		
Appearances: 774 Jim Sullivan 1921-46		

WIGAN WARRIORS

DATE	FIXTURE	RESULT	SCORERS	LGE	ATT
2/2/18	Salford (a)	W12-40	t:Davies,Gildart(2),Escare,Marshall(2),Clubb g:S Tomkins(6)	3rd	5,506
10/2/18	Hull FC (h) ●	W24-10	t:Marshall(2),Sutton,Flower g:S Tomkins(4)	2nd	12,416
23/2/18	Warrington (a)	L16-10	t:Marshall,Clubb g:S Tomkins	4th	12,012
2/3/18	Widnes (h)	W32-16	t:Burgess,Sutton,Leuluai,Farrell,S Tomkins,Davies g:S Tomkins(3),Escare	3rd	10,815
11/3/18	Wakefield (h)	W30-18	t:Burgess(3),Tautai,Davies g:S Tomkins(4),Escare	2nd	11,455
23/3/18	Huddersfield (h)	W48-10	t:Davies(2),Gildart,Burgess(2),Bateman,Williams,Sutton,Isa g:S Tomkins(5),Escare	2nd	10,641
30/3/18	St Helens (a)	L21-18	t:J Tomkins(2),Isa g:Escare(2),Williams	2nd	17,980
2/4/18	Hull KR (h)	W44-6	t:S Tomkins,Farrell(2),Williams,Marshall(4) g:S Tomkins(6)	2nd	10,977
7/4/18	Catalans Dragons (a)	W23-32	t:Sarginson,Gildart,Burgess,Farrell,S Tomkins,Clubb g:S Tomkins(4)	2nd	8,640
13/4/18	Leeds (a)	W8-9	t:Gildart g:S Tomkins(2) fg:S Tomkins	2nd	12,225
20/4/18	Castleford (h)	W28-12	t:Gildart(2),Farrell,Williams,Clubb g:S Tomkins(4)	2nd	11,866
27/4/18	Widnes (a)	W24-32	t:Gildart,Burgess,Escare,Isa,Sutton,Tautai g:Powell(4)	2nd	5,668
4/5/18	Salford (h)	W30-0	t:Gildart,Clubb,Williams,S Tomkins(2),Bateman g:S Tomkins(3)	2nd	10,733
13/5/18	Hull KR (a) (CCR6)	W10-28	t:Woods,Marshall,S Tomkins,Clubb,Davies g:S Tomkins(4)	N/A	3,524
19/5/18	Warrington (MW) ●●	W10-38	t:Powell,S Tomkins,Bateman,Williams,Marshall,Davies g:S Tomkins(7)	2nd	N/A
25/5/18	Hull KR (a)	L24-8	t:J Tomkins g:S Tomkins(2)	2nd	7,222
2/6/18	Warrington (a) (CCQF)	L23-0		N/A	10,213
7/6/18	Wakefield (a)	L32-16	t:Hamlin,Davies,Escare g:S Tomkins(2)	2nd	4,681
16/6/18	Hull FC (a)	W10-14	t:Sarginson,Marshall g:S Tomkins(3)	2nd	13,256
22/6/18	Castleford (a)	L19-18	t:S Tomkins,Marshall,Davies g:S Tomkins(3)	2nd	7,714
28/6/18	Leeds (h)	W46-8	t:Marshall(3),Woods,Farrell,Leuluai,Davies g:S Tomkins(9)	2nd	10,645
6/7/18	Warrington (h)	W13-12	t:Davies,Paisley g:S Tomkins(2) fg:Woods	2nd	13,249
12/7/18	Huddersfield (a)	L20-12	t:S Tomkins,Davies g:S Tomkins(2)	2nd	5,264
19/7/18	St Helens (h)	L6-14	t:S Tomkins g:S Tomkins	2nd	16,047
27/7/18	Catalans Dragons (h)	W25-20	t:Hankinson,Escare,S Tomkins,Greenwood g:S Tomkins(4) fg:S Tomkins	2nd	10,656
10/8/18	Castleford (h) (S8)	W24-22	t:Marshall,Hamlin,Sarginson,Sutton g:S Tomkins(2),Escare(2)	2nd	10,293
18/8/18	Catalans Dragons (a) (S8)	W6-35	t:Greenwood(2),Escare(2),Clubb,Williams g:S Tomkins(5) fg:S Tomkins	2nd	6,739
31/8/18	St Helens (a) (S8)	W10-30	t:Sarginson(2),Bateman,Davies,Gildart,O'Loughlin g:Williams(3)	2nd	14,061
6/9/18	Wakefield (h) (S8)	W25-10	t:Gildart,Powell,Escare,Greenwood g:S Tomkins(4) fg:S Tomkins	2nd	9,559
14/9/18	Warrington (h) (S8)	W26-6	t:Leuluai,Manfredi(2),Sutton g:S Tomkins(4),Williams	2nd	12,372
20/9/18	Huddersfield (a) (S8)	W6-13	t:Escare,Gildart g:S Tomkins(2) fg:Escare	2nd	4,197
28/9/18	Hull FC (h) (S8)	W14-12	t:Hamlin,Sarginson,Gildart g:Woods	2nd	11,189
5/10/18	Castleford (h) (SF)	W14-0	t:Leuluai,S Tomkins g:S Tomkins(2) fg:S Tomkins(2)	N/A	13,461
13/10/18	Warrington (GF) ●●●	W4-12	t:Manfredi(2),Davies	N/A	64,892

● *Played at WIN Stadium, Wollongong* ●● *Played at St James' Park, Newcastle* ●●● *Played at Old Trafford, Manchester*

		APP		TRIES		GOALS		FG		PTS	
	D.O.B.	ALL	SL	ALL	SL	ALL	SL	ALL	SL	ALL	SL
John Bateman	30/9/93	29	27	4	4	0	0	0	0	16	16
Joe Burgess	14/10/94	8	8	8	8	0	0	0	0	32	32
Tony Clubb	12/6/87	22(11)	20(11)	7	6	0	0	0	0	28	24
Tom Davies	11/1/97	30	28	14	13	0	0	0	0	56	52
Morgan Escare	18/10/91	6(22)	6(21)	8	8	7	7	1	1	47	47
Liam Farrell	2/7/90	18(3)	16(3)	6	6	0	0	0	0	24	24
Callum Field	7/10/97	(4)	(4)	0	0	0	0	0	0	0	0
Ben Flower	19/10/87	27	25	1	1	0	0	0	0	4	4
Liam Forsyth	23/3/96	1	1	0	0	0	0	0	0	0	0
Josh Ganson	19/2/98	(3)	(3)	0	0	0	0	0	0	0	0
Oliver Gildart	6/8/96	29	27	13	13	0	0	0	0	52	52
Joe Greenwood	2/4/93	8(3)	8(3)	4	4	0	0	0	0	16	16
Gabe Hamlin	4/1/97	6(12)	6(12)	3	3	0	0	0	0	12	12
Chris Hankinson	30/11/93	2	2	1	1	0	0	0	0	4	4
Willie Isa	1/1/89	24(6)	23(5)	3	3	0	0	0	0	12	12
Samy Kibula	7/8/99	(1)	(1)	0	0	0	0	0	0	0	0
Thomas Leuluai	22/6/85	31	29	4	4	0	0	0	0	16	16
Dom Manfredi	1/10/93	5	5	4	4	0	0	0	0	16	16
Liam Marshall	9/5/96	22	20	17	16	0	0	0	0	68	64
Craig Mullen	15/1/98	1(1)	1(1)	0	0	0	0	0	0	0	0
Romain Navarrete	30/6/94	20(5)	20(5)	0	0	0	0	0	0	0	0
Frank-Paul Nuuausala	13/2/87	(1)	(1)	0	0	0	0	0	0	0	0
Sean O'Loughlin	24/11/82	20	18	1	1	0	0	0	0	4	4
Liam Paisley	27/11/97	2(2)	2(2)	1	1	0	0	0	0	4	4
Oliver Partington	3/9/98	(5)	(5)	0	0	0	0	0	0	0	0
Sam Powell	3/7/92	33	31	2	2	4	4	0	0	16	16
Dan Sarginson	26/5/93	21(1)	20(1)	6	6	0	0	0	0	24	24
Ryan Sutton	2/8/95	4(22)	4(20)	6	6	0	0	0	0	24	24
Taulima Tautai	3/4/88	(24)	(22)	2	2	0	0	0	0	8	8
Joel Tomkins	21/3/87	7(8)	7(6)	3	3	0	0	0	0	12	12
Sam Tomkins	23/3/89	30	28	12	11	100	96	6	6	254	242
George Williams	31/10/94	27	26	6	6	5	5	0	0	34	34
Josh Woods	13/12/97	9(1)	8(1)	2	1	1	1	1	1	11	7

Sam Tomkins

LEAGUE RECORD
P30-W23-D0-L7
(2nd, SL/Grand Final Winners,
Champions)
F740, A417, Diff+323
46 points.

CHALLENGE CUP
Quarter Finalists

ATTENDANCES
Best - v St Helens (SL - 16,047)
Worst - v Wakefield (S8 - 9,559)
Total (SL/S8s/SF only) - 186,374
Average (SL/S8s/SF only) - 11,648
(Down by 2,021 on 2017)

'SL' totals include Super 8s, semi-final & Grand Final; 'All' totals also include Challenge Cup

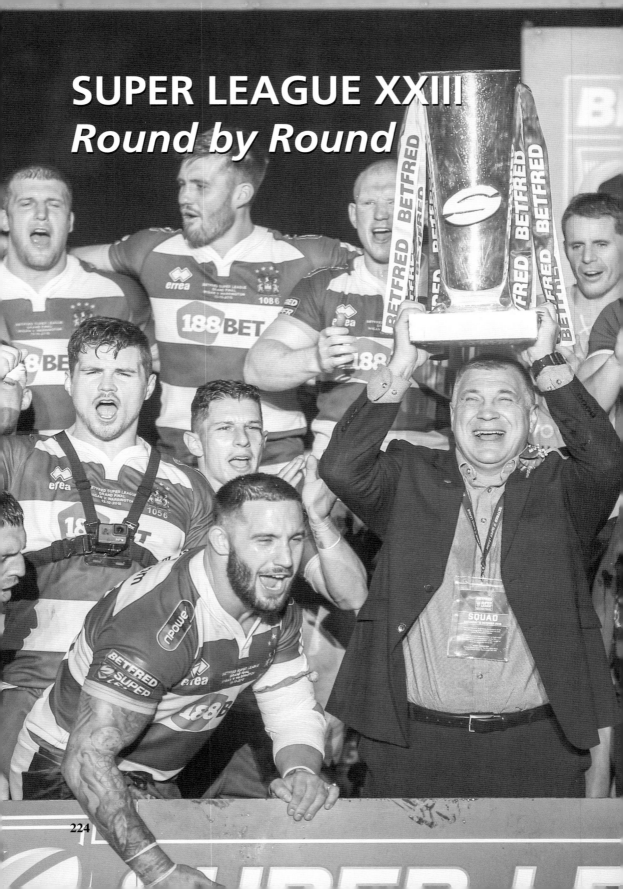

SUPER LEAGUE XXIII
Round by Round

ROUND 1

Thursday 1st February 2018

HULL FC 38 HUDDERSFIELD GIANTS 12

HULL FC: 1 Jamie Shaul; 2 Bureta Faraimo (D); 14 Jake Connor; 4 Josh Griffin; 5 Fetuli Talanoa; 6 Albert Kelly; 7 Marc Sneyd; 8 Scott Taylor; 9 Danny Houghton (C); 23 Mickey Paea (D2); 12 Mark Minichiello; 21 Sika Manu; 11 Dean Hadley. Subs (all used): 13 Josh Bowden; 16 Jordan Abdull; 25 Jansin Turgut; 29 Masi Matongo.
Tries: Kelly (37), Talanoa (45, 49, 61), Connor (57), Shaul (63); **Goals:** Sneyd 7/8.
GIANTS: 1 Jake Mamo; 23 Darnell McIntosh; 6 Lee Gaskell; 4 Jordan Turner; 5 Aaron Murphy; 15 Jordan Rankin; 7 Danny Brough; 20 Adam Walne (D); 21 Adam O'Brien; 17 Ukuma Ta'ai; 16 Oliver Roberts; 12 Michael Lawrence (C); 13 Ryan Hinchcliffe. Subs (all used): 8 Sebastine Ikahihifo; 9 Kruise Leeming; 18 Paul Clough; 19 Daniel Smith.
Tries: Hinchcliffe (14), Ta'ai (18); **Goals:** Brough 2/2.
Rugby Leaguer & League Express Men of the Match:
Hull FC: Marc Sneyd; *Giants:* Adam Walne.
Penalty count: 10-9; **Half-time:** 10-12;
Referee: Scott Mikalauskas; **Attendance:** 13,704.

WARRINGTON WOLVES 12 LEEDS RHINOS 16

WOLVES: 1 Stefan Ratchford; 2 Tom Lineham; 3 Bryson Goodwin (D); 4 Ryan Atkins; 5 Matthew Russell; 6 Kevin Brown; 7 Tyrone Roberts (D); 8 Chris Hill (C); 9 Daryl Clark; 10 Mike Cooper; 11 Ben Currie; 12 Jack Hughes; 13 Ben Murdoch-Masila (D). Subs (all used): 34 Ben Westwood; 17 Joe Philbin; 19 George King; 15 Declan Patton.
Tries: Goodwin (30), Lineham (78); **Goals:** Goodwin 2/2.
RHINOS: 24 Jack Walker; 2 Tom Briscoe; 3 Kallum Watkins (C); 4 Liam Sutcliffe; 5 Ryan Hall; 6 Joel Moon; 7 Richie Myler (D); 8 Adam Cuthbertson; 9 Matt Parcell; 10 Brad Singleton; 11 Jamie Jones-Buchanan; 12 Carl Ablett; 15 Brett Delaney. Subs (all used): 14 Brad Dwyer (D); 16 Anthony Mullally; 21 Nathaniel Peteru (D); 23 Jack Ormondroyd.
Tries: Jones-Buchanan (15), Hall (18, 55);
Goals: Watkins 2/4.
Rugby Leaguer & League Express Men of the Match:
Wolves: Bryson Goodwin; *Rhinos:* Jack Walker.
Penalty count: 7-5; **Half-time:** 6-12;
Referee: Phil Bentham; **Attendance:** 11,241.

Friday 2nd February 2018

SALFORD RED DEVILS 12 WIGAN WARRIORS 40

RED DEVILS: 5 Niall Evalds; 24 Jake Bibby; 3 Kris Welham; 4 Junior Sa'u; 2 Greg Johnson; 6 Robert Lui; 1 Gareth O'Brien; 23 Lee Mossop (C); 19 Josh Wood; 14 Lama Tasi; 11 Josh Jones; 12 Weller Hauraki; 17 Tyrone McCarthy. Subs (all used): 16 Luke Burgess (D2); 10 George Griffin; 7 Jack Littlejohn (D); 8 Craig Kopczak.
Tries: Welham (4), Evalds (75); **Goals:** O'Brien 2/2.
Sin bin: Griffin (35) - dangerous challenge.
WARRIORS: 1 Sam Tomkins (C); 2 Tom Davies; 3 Dan Sarginson (D2); 4 Oliver Gildart; 22 Liam Marshall; 6 George Williams; 7 Sam Powell; 10 Ben Flower; 9 Thomas Leuluai; 8 Tony Clubb; 11 Joel Tomkins; 12 Liam Farrell; 15 Ryan Sutton. Subs (all used): 20 Morgan Escare; 19 Willie Isa; 17 Taulima Tautai; 16 Frank-Paul Nuuausala.
Tries: Davies (12), Gildart (18, 64), Escare (43), Marshall (57, 62), Clubb (68); **Goals:** S Tomkins 6/7.
Rugby Leaguer & League Express Men of the Match:
Red Devils: Lee Mossop; *Warriors:* Oliver Gildart.
Penalty count: 5-6; **Half-time:** 6-10;
Referee: Robert Hicks; **Attendance:** 5,506.

ST HELENS 46 CASTLEFORD TIGERS 6

SAINTS: 23 Ben Barba; 2 Tommy Makinson; 3 Ryan Morgan; 4 Mark Percival; 19 Regan Grace; 1 Jonny Lomax; 18 Danny Richardson; 10 Kyle Amor; 9 James Roby (C); 16 Luke Thompson; 17 Dominique Peyroux; 11 Zeb Taia; 12 Jon Wilkin. Subs (all used): 6 Theo Fages; 8 Alex Walmsley; 13 Louie McCarthy-Scarsbrook; 15 Morgan Knowles.
Tries: Barba (4, 67), Taia (7, 77), Lomax (24), Percival (27, 55, 80); **Goals:** Richardson 7/8.
Sin bin: Amor (59) - kicking Roberts.
TIGERS: 1 Ben Roberts; 2 Greg Minikin; 3 Jake Webster; 4 Michael Shenton (C); 5 Greg Eden; 21 Jake Trueman; 7 Luke Gale; 8 Junior Moors; 9 Paul McShane; 22 James Green (D); 11 Oliver Holmes; 12 Mike McMeeken; 14 Nathan Massey. Subs (all used): 10 Grant Millington; 13 Adam Milner; 15 Jesse Sene-Lefao; 18 Matt Cook.
Try: McShane (60); **Goals:** Gale 1/1.
Rugby Leaguer & League Express Men of the Match:
Saints: Ben Barba; *Tigers:* Greg Minikin.
Penalty count: 9-5; **Half-time:** 22-0;
Referee: James Child; **Attendance:** 13,108.

HULL KINGSTON ROVERS 6 WAKEFIELD TRINITY 28

ROVERS: 1 Adam Quinlan; 5 Ryan Shaw; 4 Andrew Heffernan; 3 Thomas Minns; 36 Justin Carney; 7 Danny McGuire (D); 20 Matty Marsh; 14 Lee Jewitt; 19 Tommy Lee (D); 21 Robbie Mulhern; 11 Maurice Blair; 12 James Greenwood; 17 Chris Clarkson. Subs (all used): 13 Ben Kavanagh; 22 Liam Salter; 9 Shaun Lunt (C); 10 Mose Masoe.
Try: Clarkson (58); **Goals:** Shaw 1/1.
Sin bin: Marsh (13) - off the ball challenge.
TRINITY: 1 Scott Grix; 5 Ben Jones-Bishop; 4 Reece Lyne; 3 Bill Tupou; 2 Tom Johnstone; 6 Jacob Miller; 7 Liam Finn; 8 David Fifita; 9 Kyle Wood; 10 Anthony England; 11 Matty Ashurst; 14 Justin Horo (D); 16 Tinirau Arona. Subs (all used): 25 Ryan Hampshire (D); 12 Danny Kirmond (C); 15 Pauli Pauli (D); 20 Keegan Hirst.
Tries: Johnstone (14, 40, 68), Tupou (17), Finn (23), Hampshire (74); **Goals:** Finn 2/6.
Rugby Leaguer & League Express Men of the Match:
Rovers: Justin Carney; *Trinity:* Tom Johnstone.
Penalty count: 12-10; **Half-time:** 0-18;
Referee: Chris Kendall; **Attendance:** 8,615.

Sunday 4th February 2018

WIDNES VIKINGS 40 CATALANS DRAGONS 12

VIKINGS: 1 Rhys Hanbury; 5 Patrick Ah Van; 4 Charly Runciman; 3 Krisnan Inu (D); 2 Stefan Marsh; 6 Joe Mellor (C); 7 Tom Gilmore; 25 Jay Chapelhow; 33 Aaron Heremaia; 19 Greg Burke; 14 Chris Dean; 12 Matt Whitley; 11 Chris Houston (C). Subs (all used): 9 Lloyd White; 36 Wellington Albert (D); 13 Hep Cahill; 16 Tom Olbison.
Tries: Dean (13, 55), Mellor (35), Inu (49), Ah Van (71), Runciman (74), Marsh (79); **Goals:** Gilmore 6/7, Inu 0/1.
DRAGONS: 1 David Mead (D); 2 Jodie Broughton; 3 Iain Thornley; 4 Brayden Wiliame; 20 Lewis Tierney; 6 Samisoni Langi (D); 7 Luke Walsh; 10 Sam Moa; 19 Michael McIlorum (D); 14 Julian Bousquet; 21 Benjamin Jullien (D); 12 Benjamin Garcia; 8 Remi Casty (C). Subs (all used): 15 Mickael Simon; 23 Antoni Maria (D2); 17 Jason Baitieri; 22 Lucas Albert.
Tries: Mead (19), Jullien (24); **Goals:** Walsh 2/2.
Sin bin: Moa (7) - late challenge on Mellor.
Rugby Leaguer & League Express Men of the Match:
Vikings: Joe Mellor; *Dragons:* Michael McIlorum.
Penalty count: 15-4; **Half-time:** 12-12;
Referee: Ben Thaler; **Attendance:** 4,568.

ROUND 2

Thursday 8th February 2018

HUDDERSFIELD GIANTS 20 WARRINGTON WOLVES 6

GIANTS: 1 Jake Mamo; 23 Darnell McIntosh; 6 Lee Gaskell; 4 Jordan Turner; 5 Aaron Murphy; 15 Jordan Rankin; 7 Danny Brough; 18 Paul Clough; 21 Adam O'Brien; 17 Ukuma Ta'ai; 14 Dale Ferguson; 16 Oliver Roberts; 13 Ryan Hinchcliffe (C). Subs (all used): 9 Kruise Leeming; 8 Sebastine Ikahihifo; 19 Daniel Smith; 24 Tyler Dickinson.
Tries: Ferguson (14), McIntosh (18), Turner (63);
Goals: Brough 4/4.
WOLVES: 1 Stefan Ratchford; 2 Tom Lineham; 3 Bryson Goodwin; 4 Ryan Atkins; 5 Matthew Russell; 6 Kevin Brown; 15 Declan Patton; 8 Chris Hill (C); 9 Daryl Clark; 10 Mike Cooper; 11 Ben Currie; 12 Jack Hughes; 13 Ben Murdoch-Masila. Subs (all used): 19 George King; 34 Ben Westwood; 17 Joe Philbin; 22 Morgan Smith.
Try: Lineham (5); **Goals:** Goodwin 1/2.
Rugby Leaguer & League Express Men of the Match:
Giants: Jordan Rankin; *Wolves:* Chris Hill.
Penalty count: 14-10; **Half-time:** 14-6;
Referee: Ben Thaler; **Attendance:** 5,104.

LEEDS RHINOS 20 HULL KINGSTON ROVERS 11

RHINOS: 24 Jack Walker; 2 Tom Briscoe; 3 Kallum Watkins (C); 18 Jimmy Keinhorst; 5 Ryan Hall; 4 Liam Sutcliffe; 7 Richie Myler; 8 Adam Cuthbertson; 9 Matt Parcell; 10 Brad Singleton; 11 Jamie Jones-Buchanan; 12 Carl Ablett; 15 Brett Delaney. Subs (all used): 16 Anthony Mullally; 13 Stevie Ward; 14 Brad Dwyer; 23 Jack Ormondroyd.
Tries: Cuthbertson (33), Keinhorst (35, 67, 72);
Goals: Myler 2/4.
ROVERS: 1 Adam Quinlan; 5 Ryan Shaw; 4 Andrew Heffernan; 3 Thomas Minns; 36 Justin Carney; 7 Danny McGuire; 24 Chris Atkin; 14 Lee Jewitt; 19 Tommy Lee; 21 Robbie Mulhern; 11 Maurice Blair; 12 James Greenwood; 17 Chris Clarkson. Subs (all used): 13 Ben Kavanagh; 9 Shaun Lunt (C); 10 Mose Masoe; 29 Jordan Walne (D).
Tries: Shaw (19), Quinlan (22); **Goals:** Shaw 1/2;
Field goal: Atkin (42).
Rugby Leaguer & League Express Men of the Match:
Rhinos: Ryan Hall; *Rovers:* Robbie Mulhern.
Penalty count: 6-8; **Half time:** 10-10;
Referee: Robert Hicks; **Attendance:** 16,149
(at Elland Road).

Friday 9th February 2018

WAKEFIELD TRINITY 14 SALFORD RED DEVILS 12

TRINITY: 1 Scott Grix; 5 Ben Jones-Bishop; 4 Reece Lyne; 3 Bill Tupou; 2 Tom Johnstone; 6 Jacob Miller; 7 Liam Finn; 8 David Fifita; 9 Kyle Wood; 10 Anthony England; 11 Matty Ashurst; 14 Justin Horo; 16 Tinirau Arona. Subs (all used): 25 Ryan Hampshire; 12 Danny Kirmond (C); 15 Pauli Pauli; 17 Craig Huby.
Tries: Grix (6), Miller (64); **Goals:** Finn 3/3.
RED DEVILS: 1 Gareth O'Brien; 24 Jake Bibby; 3 Kris Welham; 4 Junior Sa'u; 5 Niall Evalds; 6 Robert Lui; 7 Jack Littlejohn; 23 Lee Mossop (C); 19 Josh Wood; 14 Lama Tasi; 11 Josh Jones; 12 Weller Hauraki; 17 Tyrone McCarthy. Subs (all used): 8 Craig Kopczak; 9 Logan Tomkins; 16 Luke Burgess; 18 Ben Nakubuwai (D).
Tries: Lui (47), Evalds (53), Welham (80);
Goals: O'Brien 0/3.
Rugby Leaguer & League Express Men of the Match:
Trinity: Scott Grix; *Red Devils:* Josh Jones.
Penalty count: 10-10; **Half-time:** 8-0;
Referee: James Child; **Attendance:** 4,262.

Saturday 10th February 2018

WIGAN WARRIORS 24 HULL FC 10

WARRIORS: 1 Sam Tomkins; 2 Tom Davies; 3 Dan Sarginson; 4 Oliver Gildart; 22 Liam Marshall; 6 George Williams; 7 Sam Powell; 8 Tony Clubb; 9 Thomas Leuluai; 10 Ben Flower; 11 Joel Tomkins; 12 Liam Farrell; 13 Sean O'Loughlin (C). Subs (all used): 15 Ryan Sutton; 17 Taulima Tautai; 19 Willie Isa; 20 Morgan Escare.
Tries: Marshall (4, 12), Sutton (45), Flower (70);
Goals: S Tomkins 4/5.
Sin bin: S Tomkins (76) - fighting.
HULL FC: 1 Jamie Shaul; 2 Bureta Faraimo; 14 Jake Connor; 4 Josh Griffin; 5 Fetuli Talanoa; 6 Albert Kelly; 7 Marc Sneyd; 8 Scott Taylor; 9 Danny Houghton (C); 23 Mickey Paea; 21 Sika Manu; 12 Mark Minichiello; 11 Dean Hadley. Subs (all used): 16 Jordan Abdull; 17 Danny Washbrook; 13 Josh Bowden; 10 Liam Watts.
Tries: Talanoa (24), Abdull (35); **Goals:** Sneyd 1/2.
Sin bin: Griffin (76) - fighting.
Rugby Leaguer & League Express Men of the Match:
Warriors: George Williams; *Hull FC:* Sika Manu.
Penalty count: 5-10; **Half-time:** 12-10;
Referee: Matt Cecchin; **Attendance:** 12,416
(at WIN Stadium, Wollongong).

CATALANS DRAGONS 12 ST HELENS 21

DRAGONS: 1 David Mead; 2 Jodie Broughton; 3 Iain Thornley; 4 Brayden Wiliame; 20 Lewis Tierney; 13 Greg Bird; 22 Lucas Albert; 8 Remi Casty (C); 19 Michael McIlorum; 15 Mickael Simon; 21 Benjamin Jullien; 12 Benjamin Garcia; 17 Jason Baitieri. Subs (all used): 14 Julian Bousquet; 18 Thibaut Margalet; 23 Antoni Maria; 24 Alrix Da Costa.
Tries: Mead (47), Da Costa (65); **Goals:** Albert 2/2.
Sin bin: Jullien (54) - dangerous challenge on Lomax.
SAINTS: 23 Ben Barba; 5 Adam Swift; 2 Tommy Makinson; 4 Mark Percival; 19 Regan Grace; 1 Jonny Lomax; 18 Danny Richardson; 14 Luke Douglas; 9 James Roby (C); 16 Luke Thompson; 17 Dominique Peyroux; 11 Zeb Taia; 12 Jon Wilkin. Subs (all used): 6 Theo Fages; 8 Alex Walmsley; 13 Louie McCarthy-Scarsbrook; 15 Morgan Knowles.
Tries: Lomax (1), Grace (23), Swift (58);
Goals: Richardson 4/5; **Field goal:** Richardson (79).
Dismissal:
Knowles (52) - dangerous challenge on Margalet.
Rugby Leaguer & League Express Men of the Match:
Dragons: Remi Casty; *Saints:* Ben Barba.
Penalty count: 5-5; **Half-time:** 0-12;
Referee: Phil Bentham; **Attendance:** 8,103.

Sunday 11th February 2018

CASTLEFORD TIGERS 13 WIDNES VIKINGS 12

TIGERS: 1 Ben Roberts; 2 Greg Minikin; 3 Jake Webster; 4 Michael Shenton (C); 24 Jy Hitchcox; 6 Jamie Ellis (D2); 7 Luke Gale; 10 Grant Millington; 9 Paul McShane; 17 Alex Foster; 11 Oliver Holmes; 12 Mike McMeeken; 13 Adam Milner. Subs (all used): 8 Junior Moors; 14 Nathan Massey; 15 Jesse Sene-Lefao; 18 Matt Cook.
Tries: Minikin (39), Hitchcox (63); **Goals:** Gale 2/3;
Field goal: Gale (72).
VIKINGS: 1 Rhys Hanbury; 27 Olly Ashall-Bott (D); 4 Charly Runciman; 3 Krisnan Inu; 2 Stefan Marsh; 6 Joe Mellor (C); 7 Tom Gilmore; 25 Jay Chapelhow; 23 Danny Walker; 19 Greg Burke; 14 Chris Dean; 12 Matt Whitley; 11 Chris Houston (C). Subs (all used): 17 Sam Wilde (D2); 36 Wellington Albert; 13 Hep Cahill; 16 Tom Olbison.
Try: Whitley (49), J Chapelhow (73); **Goals:** Gilmore 2/2.

Rugby Leaguer & League Express Men of the Match: *Tigers:* Oliver Holmes; *Vikings:* Danny Walker.
Penalty count: 5-4; **Half-time:** 4-0;
Referee: Chris Kendall; **Attendance:** 7,106.

ROUND 12

Thursday 15th February 2018

HULL KINGSTON ROVERS 23 CATALANS DRAGONS 4

ROVERS: 28 Will Dagger (D); 5 Ryan Shaw; 22 Liam Salter; 3 Thomas Minns; 36 Justin Carney; 7 Danny McGuire; 24 Chris Atkin; 14 Lee Jewitt; 19 Tommy Lee; 21 Robbie Mulhern; 11 Maurice Blair; 17 Chris Clarkson; 13 Ben Kavanagh. Subs (all used): 29 Jordan Walne; 9 Shaun Lunt (C); 10 Mose Masoe; 34 Danny Tickle (D).
Tries: Shaw (5), Masoe (34), Lunt (38), Tickle (50); **Goals:** Shaw 3/5; **Field goal:** Atkin (79).
DRAGONS: 1 David Mead; 2 Jodie Broughton; 3 Iain Thornley; 4 Brayden Wiliame; 20 Lewis Tierney; 22 Lucas Albert; 7 Luke Walsh; 8 Remi Casty (C); 9 Paul Aiton; 15 Mickael Simon; 12 Benjamin Garcia; 13 Greg Bird; 17 Jason Baitieri. Subs (all used): 14 Julian Bousquet; 16 Vincent Duport; 18 Thibaut Margalet; 24 Alrix Da Costa.
Try: Mead (61); **Goals:** Walsh 0/1.
Rugby Leaguer & League Express Men of the Match: *Rovers:* Shaun Lunt; *Dragons:* Remi Casty.
Penalty count: 8-6; **Half-time:** 16-0;
Referee: James Child; **Attendance:** 6,711.

Friday 16th February 2018

WIDNES VIKINGS 10 WARRINGTON WOLVES 18

VIKINGS: 1 Rhys Hanbury; 2 Stefan Marsh; 3 Krisnan Inu; 12 Matt Whitley; 27 Olly Ashall-Bott; 6 Joe Mellor (C); 7 Tom Gilmore; 25 Jay Chapelhow; 33 Aaron Heremaia; 13 Hep Cahill; 14 Chris Dean; 17 Sam Wilde; 11 Chris Houston (C). Subs (all used): 23 Danny Walker; 19 Greg Burke; 15 Danny Craven; 16 Tom Olbison.
Tries: Inu (22, 65); **Goals:** Gilmore 1/2.
On report: Houston (54) - contact with referee.
WOLVES: 1 Stefan Ratchford; 2 Tom Lineham; 3 Bryson Goodwin; 4 Ryan Atkins; 5 Matthew Russell; 6 Kevin Brown; 15 Declan Patton; 8 Chris Hill (C); 9 Daryl Clark; 10 Mike Cooper; 11 Ben Currie; 12 Jack Hughes; 34 Ben Westwood. Subs (all used): 14 Dominic Crosby; 22 Morgan Smith; 13 Ben Murdoch-Masila; 17 Joe Philbin.
Tries: Atkins (8, 45), Ratchford (14); **Goals:** Goodwin 3/4.
Sin bin: Cooper (72) - professional foul.
Rugby Leaguer & League Express Men of the Match: *Vikings:* Krisnan Inu; *Wolves:* Stefan Ratchford.
Penalty count: 9-5; **Half-time:** 4-10;
Referee: Phil Bentham *(replaced by Scott Mikalauskas, 54)*;
Attendance: 7,009.

ROUND 3

Friday 23rd February 2018

HUDDERSFIELD GIANTS 12 ST HELENS 26

GIANTS: 1 Jake Mamo; 2 Jermaine McGillvary; 6 Lee Gaskell; 4 Jordan Turner; 5 Aaron Murphy; 15 Jordan Rankin; 7 Danny Brough; 17 Ukuma Ta'ai; 21 Adam O'Brien; 18 Paul Clough; 16 Oliver Roberts; 14 Dale Ferguson; 13 Ryan Hinchcliffe (C). Subs (all used): 9 Kruise Leeming; 20 Adam Walne; 19 Daniel Smith; 8 Sebastine Ikahihifo.
Tries: Brough (20), Roberts (56); **Goals:** Brough 2/3.
SAINTS: 23 Ben Barba; 5 Adam Swift; 2 Tommy Makinson; 4 Mark Percival; 19 Regan Grace; 1 Jonny Lomax; 18 Danny Richardson; 10 Kyle Amor; 9 James Roby (C); 16 Luke Thompson; 11 Zeb Taia; 17 Dominique Peyroux; 12 Jon Wilkin. Subs (all used): 6 Theo Fages; 8 Alex Walmsley; 13 Louie McCarthy-Scarsbrook; 14 Luke Douglas.
Tries: Wilkin (8), Roby (38), Taia (49), Percival (52);
Goals: Richardson 5/5.
Rugby Leaguer & League Express Men of the Match: *Giants:* Kruise Leeming; *Saints:* Zeb Taia.
Penalty count: 8-10; **Half-time:** 8-14;
Referee: Liam Moore; **Attendance:** 5,915.

WARRINGTON WOLVES 16 WIGAN WARRIORS 10

WOLVES: 1 Stefan Ratchford; 2 Tom Lineham; 3 Bryson Goodwin; 4 Ryan Atkins; 21 Mitch Brown (D); 6 Kevin Brown; 7 Tyrone Roberts; 8 Chris Hill (C); 9 Daryl Clark; 10 Mike Cooper; 11 Ben Currie; 12 Jack Hughes; 34 Ben Westwood. Subs (all used): 13 Ben Murdoch-Masila; 14 Dominic Crosby; 15 Declan Patton; 16 Sitaleki Akauola (D).
Tries: Lineham (8), Atkins (55); **Goals:** Goodwin 4/5.
WARRIORS: 1 Sam Tomkins; 2 Tom Davies; 14 John Bateman; 4 Oliver Gildart; 22 Liam Marshall; 6 George Williams; 7 Sam Powell; 8 Tony Clubb; 9 Thomas Leuluai; 10 Ben Flower; 11 Joel Tomkins; 12 Liam Farrell; 13 Sean O'Loughlin (C). Subs (all used): 15 Ryan Sutton; 17 Taulima Tautai; 19 Willie Isa; 20 Morgan Escare.
Tries: Marshall (62), Clubb (80); **Goals:** S Tomkins 1/2.
Rugby Leaguer & League Express Men of the Match: *Wolves:* Bryson Goodwin; *Warriors:* John Bateman.
Penalty count: 8-7; **Half-time:** 8-0;
Referee: Ben Thaler; **Attendance:** 12,012.

SALFORD RED DEVILS 36 HULL KINGSTON ROVERS 12

RED DEVILS: 1 Gareth O'Brien; 5 Niall Evalds; 4 Junior Sa'u; 3 Kris Welham; 24 Jake Bibby; 6 Robert Lui; 7 Jack Littlejohn; 23 Lee Mossop; 19 Josh Wood; 14 Lama Tasi; 11 Josh Jones; 12 Weller Hauraki; 17 Tyrone McCarthy. Subs (all used): 16 Luke Burgess; 18 Ben Nakubuwai; 9 Logan Tomkins; 8 Craig Kopczak (C).
Tries: O'Brien (8), Sa'u (18), Bibby (31), Lui (41), Evalds (66, 71); **Goals:** O'Brien 6/8.
ROVERS: 1 Adam Quinlan; 5 Ryan Shaw; 4 Andrew Heffernan; 3 Thomas Minns; 36 Justin Carney; 24 Chris Atkin; 11 Maurice Blair; 14 Lee Jewitt; 19 Tommy Lee; 10 Mose Masoe; 13 Ben Kavanagh; 12 James Greenwood; 21 Robbie Mulhern. Subs (all used): 9 Shaun Lunt (C); 8 Nick Scruton; 34 Danny Tickle; 22 Liam Salter.
Tries: Minns (3), Quinlan (55); **Goals:** Shaw 2/2.
Rugby Leaguer & League Express Men of the Match: *Red Devils:* Junior Sa'u; *Rovers:* Chris Atkin.
Penalty count: 11-7; **Half-time:** 18-6;
Referee: James Child; **Attendance:** 2,948.

Saturday 24th February 2018

CASTLEFORD TIGERS 28 HULL FC 18

TIGERS: 1 Ben Roberts; 2 Greg Minikin; 3 Jake Webster; 4 Michael Shenton (C); 5 Greg Eden; 6 Jamie Ellis; 7 Luke Gale; 17 Alex Foster; 9 Paul McShane; 10 Grant Millington; 11 Oliver Holmes; 12 Mike McMeeken; 13 Adam Milner. Subs (all used): 8 Junior Moors; 14 Nathan Massey; 15 Jesse Sene-Lefao; 16 Joe Wardle (D).
Tries: Minikin (29), Webster (39), McMeeken (45), Shenton (47, 63); **Goals:** Gale 4/6.
HULL FC: 1 Jamie Shaul; 2 Bureta Faraimo; 14 Jake Connor; 4 Josh Griffin; 5 Fetuli Talanoa; 6 Albert Kelly; 7 Marc Sneyd (C); 23 Mickey Paea; 11 Dean Hadley; 10 Liam Watts; 17 Danny Washbrook; 12 Mark Minichiello; 13 Josh Bowden. Subs (all used): 3 Carlos Tuimavave; 16 Jordan Abdull; 20 Brad Fash; 29 Masi Matongo.
Tries: Sneyd (21), Faraimo (56), Paea (68);
Goals: Sneyd 3/4.
Rugby Leaguer & League Express Men of the Match: *Tigers:* Jamie Ellis; *Hull FC:* Mickey Paea.
Penalty count: 10-6; **Half-time:** 10-8;
Referee: Chris Kendall; **Attendance:** 9,365.

CATALANS DRAGONS 14 WAKEFIELD TRINITY 16

DRAGONS: 1 David Mead; 20 Lewis Tierney; 31 Tony Gigot; 4 Brayden Wiliame; 5 Fouad Yaha; 13 Greg Bird; 22 Lucas Albert; 8 Remi Casty (C); 24 Alrix Da Costa; 10 Sam Moa; 21 Benjamin Jullien; 12 Benjamin Garcia; 17 Jason Baitieri. Subs (all used): 11 Louis Anderson; 14 Julian Bousquet; 15 Mickael Simon; 3 Iain Thornley.
Tries: Garcia (25), Tierney (64); **Goals:** Albert 3/4.
TRINITY: 1 Scott Grix; 5 Ben Jones-Bishop; 4 Reece Lyne; 3 Bill Tupou; 2 Tom Johnstone; 6 Jacob Miller; 7 Liam Finn (C); 8 David Fifita; 9 Kyle Wood; 10 Anthony England; 11 Matty Ashurst; 14 Justin Horo; 16 Tinirau Arona. Subs (all used): 15 Pauli Pauli; 17 Craig Huby; 22 Jordan Baldwinson (D); 25 Ryan Hampshire.
Tries: Lyne (15), Johnstone (34), Fifita (51); **Goals:** Finn 2/4.
Rugby Leaguer & League Express Men of the Match: *Dragons:* Greg Bird; *Trinity:* David Fifita.
Penalty count: 8-8; **Half-time:** 10-8;
Referee: Gareth Hewer; **Attendance:** 6,872.

Sunday 25th February 2018

WIDNES VIKINGS 23 LEEDS RHINOS 6

VIKINGS: 1 Rhys Hanbury; 24 Ed Chamberlain; 15 Danny Craven; 3 Krisnan Inu; 2 Stefan Marsh; 6 Joe Mellor (C); 7 Tom Gilmore; 25 Jay Chapelhow; 33 Aaron Heremaia; 13 Hep Cahill; 14 Chris Dean; 12 Matt Whitley; 16 Tom Olbison. Subs (all used): 23 Danny Walker; 36 Wellington Albert; 26 Ted Chapelhow; 17 Sam Wilde.
Tries: Mellor (20), Inu (53, 78), D Walker (74);
Goals: Inu 3/4; **Field goal:** Craven (72).
Sin bin: Cahill (42) - punching.
RHINOS: 1 Ashton Golding; 26 Harry Newman; 3 Kallum Watkins (C); 18 Jimmy Keinhorst; 22 Ash Handley; 4 Liam Sutcliffe; 7 Richie Myler; 11 Jamie Jones-Buchanan; 9 Matt Parcell; 10 Brad Singleton; 30 Josh Walters; 15 Brett Delaney; 23 Jack Ormondroyd. Subs (all used): 27 Cameron Smith; 14 Brad Dwyer; 17 Mitch Garbutt; 28 Mikolaj Oledzki.
Try: Dwyer (32); **Goals:** Watkins 1/1.
Rugby Leaguer & League Express Men of the Match: *Vikings:* Krisnan Inu; *Rhinos:* Brad Singleton.
Penalty count: 9-6; **Half-time:** 4-6;
Referee: Robert Hicks; **Attendance:** 5,519.

ROUND 4

Friday 2nd March 2018

HULL FC 21 WARRINGTON WOLVES 12

HULL FC: 1 Jamie Shaul; 2 Bureta Faraimo; 3 Carlos Tuimavave; 4 Josh Griffin; 5 Fetuli Talanoa; 14 Jake Connor; 7 Marc Sneyd; 8 Scott Taylor (C); 17 Danny Washbrook; 10 Liam Watts; 12 Mark Minichiello; 21 Sika Manu; 11 Dean Hadley. Subs (all used): 20 Brad Fash; 25 Jansin Turgut; 16 Jordan Abdull; 13 Josh Bowden.
Tries: Faraimo (24), Tuimavave (53); **Goals:** Sneyd 6/6;
Field goal: Sneyd (80).
Dismissal: Watts (73) - headbutt on Crosby.
WOLVES: 1 Stefan Ratchford; 2 Tom Lineham; 3 Bryson Goodwin; 4 Ryan Atkins; 21 Mitch Brown; 15 Declan Patton; 7 Tyrone Roberts; 8 Chris Hill (C); 9 Daryl Clark; 10 Mike Cooper; 13 Ben Murdoch-Masila; 12 Jack Hughes; 34 Ben Westwood. Subs (all used): 14 Dominic Crosby; 16 Sitaleki Akauola; 17 Joe Philbin; 18 Toby King.
Tries: Hughes (57), Atkins (60); **Goals:** Ratchford 2/2.
Dismissal: Patton (48) - high tackle on Faraimo.
Rugby Leaguer & League Express Men of the Match: *Hull FC:* Carlos Tuimavave; *Wolves:* Daryl Clark.
Penalty count: 10-8; **Half-time:** 10-0;
Referee: Ben Thaler; **Attendance:** 10,051.

WIGAN WARRIORS 32 WIDNES VIKINGS 16

WARRIORS: 1 Sam Tomkins; 2 Tom Davies; 14 John Bateman; 4 Oliver Gildart; 5 Joe Burgess; 6 George Williams; 7 Sam Powell; 8 Tony Clubb; 9 Thomas Leuluai; 10 Ben Flower; 11 Joel Tomkins; 12 Liam Farrell; 13 Sean O'Loughlin (C). Subs (all used): 15 Ryan Sutton; 17 Taulima Tautai; 19 Willie Isa; 20 Morgan Escare.
Tries: Burgess (39), Sutton (52), Leuluai (60), Farrell (64), S Tomkins (74), Davies (79);
Goals: S Tomkins 3/5, Escare 1/1.
VIKINGS: 1 Rhys Hanbury; 24 Ed Chamberlain; 15 Danny Craven; 4 Charly Runciman; 2 Stefan Marsh; 6 Joe Mellor (C); 7 Tom Gilmore; 19 Greg Burke; 33 Aaron Heremaia; 10 Alex Gerrard; 17 Sam Wilde; 12 Matt Whitley; 16 Tom Olbison. Subs (all used): 13 Hep Cahill; 20 Macgraff Leuluai; 23 Danny Walker; 26 Ted Chapelhow.
Tries: Whitley (6), Marsh (27); **Goals:** Gilmore 4/4.
Rugby Leaguer & League Express Men of the Match: *Warriors:* Liam Farrell; *Vikings:* Matt Whitley.
Penalty count: 10-6; **Half-time:** 4-16;
Referee: Robert Hicks; **Attendance:** 10,815.

Sunday 4th March 2018

WAKEFIELD TRINITY 22 HUDDERSFIELD GIANTS 4

TRINITY: 1 Scott Grix; 5 Ben Jones-Bishop; 18 Joe Arundel; 3 Bill Tupou; 24 Mason Caton-Brown; 6 Jacob Miller; 7 Liam Finn; 8 David Fifita; 9 Kyle Wood; 10 Anthony England; 11 Matty Ashurst; 12 Danny Kirmond (C); 16 Tinirau Arona. Subs (all used): 25 Ryan Hampshire; 17 Craig Huby; 15 Pauli Pauli; 20 Keegan Hirst.
Tries: Jones-Bishop (23, 54), Caton-Brown (78);
Goals: Finn 5/5.
GIANTS: 1 Jake Mamo; 2 Jermaine McGillvary; 6 Lee Gaskell; 4 Jordan Turner; 5 Aaron Murphy; 15 Jordan Rankin; 7 Danny Brough; 18 Paul Clough; 21 Adam O'Brien; 17 Ukuma Ta'ai; 16 Oliver Roberts; 14 Dale Ferguson; 13 Ryan Hinchcliffe (C). Subs (all used): 9 Kruise Leeming; 8 Sebastine Ikahihifo; 19 Daniel Smith; 11 Tom Symonds.
Try: Gaskell (35); **Goals:** Brough 0/1.
Sin bin: Leeming (50) - persistent team offences.
Rugby Leaguer & League Express Men of the Match: *Trinity:* Liam Finn; *Giants:* Dale Ferguson.
Penalty count: 12-8; **Half-time:** 6-4;
Referee: Gareth Hewer; **Attendance:** 4,055.

ST HELENS 34 SALFORD RED DEVILS 2

SAINTS: 23 Ben Barba; 5 Adam Swift; 2 Tommy Makinson; 4 Mark Percival; 19 Regan Grace; 1 Jonny Lomax; 18 Danny Richardson; 10 Kyle Amor; 9 James Roby (C); 16 Luke Thompson; 17 Dominique Peyroux; 11 Zeb Taia; 12 Jon Wilkin. Subs (all used): 6 Theo Fages; 8 Alex Walmsley; 13 Louie McCarthy-Scarsbrook; 14 Luke Douglas.
Tries: Makinson (25), Barba (36, 45), McCarthy-Scarsbrook (70), Lomax (73), Thompson (80);
Goals: Richardson 5/7.
RED DEVILS: 1 Gareth O'Brien; 24 Jake Bibby; 3 Kris Welham; 4 Junior Sa'u; 5 Niall Evalds; 6 Robert Lui; 7 Jack Littlejohn; 23 Lee Mossop; 9 Logan Tomkins; 14 Lama Tasi; 17 Tyrone McCarthy; 11 Josh Jones; 13 Mark Flanagan.

Subs (all used): 8 Craig Kopczak (C); 16 Luke Burgess; 18 Ben Nakubuwai; 19 Josh Wood.
Goals: O'Brien 1/1.
Sin bin: Tasi (56) - high tackle.
Rugby Leaguer & League Express Men of the Match:
Saints: Ben Barba; *Red Devils:* Robert Lui.
Penalty count: 12-7; **Half-time:** 8-2;
Referee: Scott Mikalauskas; **Attendance:** 10,008.

ROUND 5

Thursday 8th March 2018

LEEDS RHINOS 20 HULL FC 16

RHINOS: 1 Ashton Golding; 2 Tom Briscoe; 3 Kallum Watkins (C); 22 Ash Handley; 5 Ryan Hall; 6 Joel Moon; 7 Richie Myler; 17 Mitch Garbutt; 9 Matt Parcell; 10 Brad Singleton; 11 Jamie Jones-Buchanan; 12 Carl Ablett; 15 Brett Delaney. Subs: 16 Anthony Mullally; 23 Jack Ormondroyd; 30 Josh Walters; 24 Jack Walker (not used).
Tries: Watkins (4, 55), T Briscoe (14, 59);
Goals: Watkins 2/4.
HULL FC: 1 Jamie Shaul; 24 Jack Logan; 4 Josh Griffin; 3 Carlos Tuimavave; 5 Fetuli Talanoa; 14 Jake Connor; 7 Marc Sneyd; 8 Scott Taylor (C); 17 Danny Washbrook; 29 Masi Matongo; 21 Sika Manu; 12 Mark Minichiello; 11 Dean Hadley. Subs (all used): 15 Chris Green; 16 Jordan Abdull; 20 Brad Fash; 26 Jordan Lane (D).
Tries: Hadley (28), Abdull (62), Talanoa (68);
Goals: Sneyd 2/3.
Rugby Leaguer & League Express Men of the Match:
Rhinos: Richie Myler; *Hull FC:* Dean Hadley.
Penalty count: 8-8; **Half time:** 10-6;
Referee: Robert Hicks; **Attendance:** 11,158.

Friday 9th March 2018

WARRINGTON WOLVES 12 ST HELENS 30

WOLVES: 1 Stefan Ratchford; 2 Tom Lineham; 18 Toby King; 4 Ryan Atkins; 21 Mitch Brown; 6 Kevin Brown; 7 Tyrone Roberts; 8 Chris Hill (C); 9 Daryl Clark; 10 Mike Cooper; 13 Ben Murdoch-Masila; 12 Jack Hughes; 34 Ben Westwood. Subs (all used): 17 Joe Philbin; 14 Dominic Crosby; 19 George King; 20 Harvey Livett.
Tries: T King (25), Livett (53); **Goals:** Ratchford 2/2.
SAINTS: 23 Ben Barba; 5 Adam Swift; 2 Tommy Makinson; 4 Mark Percival; 19 Regan Grace; 1 Jonny Lomax; 18 Danny Richardson; 10 Kyle Amor; 9 James Roby (C); 16 Luke Thompson; 11 Zeb Taia; 17 Dominique Peyroux; 13 Louie McCarthy-Scarsbrook. Subs (all used): 6 Theo Fages; 8 Alex Walmsley; 14 Luke Douglas; 20 Matty Lees.
Tries: Percival (6, 58, 67), Roby (41), Richardson (78);
Goals: Richardson 5/6.
Rugby Leaguer & League Express Men of the Match:
Wolves: Chris Hill; *Saints:* Danny Richardson.
Penalty count: 6-11; **Half-time:** 6-8;
Referee: James Child; **Attendance:** 12,268.

WIDNES VIKINGS 16 HUDDERSFIELD GIANTS 28

VIKINGS: 1 Rhys Hanbury; 2 Stefan Marsh; 3 Krisnan Inu; 4 Charly Runciman; 24 Ed Chamberlain; 6 Joe Mellor (C); 7 Tom Gilmore; 19 Greg Burke; 33 Aaron Heremaia; 25 Jay Chapelhow; 14 Chris Dean; 12 Matt Whitley; 11 Chris Houston (C). Subs (all used): 21 Jordan Johnstone; 16 Tom Olbison; 17 Sam Wilde; 36 Wellington Albert.
Tries: Mellor (64), Whitley (66), Marsh (73);
Goals: Gilmore 2/4.
Dismissal:
W Albert (61) - dangerous challenge on McGillvary.
GIANTS: 1 Jake Mamo; 2 Jermaine McGillvary; 6 Lee Gaskell; 26 Sam Wood; 5 Aaron Murphy; 15 Jordan Rankin; 7 Danny Brough; 8 Sebastine Ikahihifo; 21 Adam O'Brien; 17 Ukuma Ta'ai; 16 Oliver Roberts; 14 Dale Ferguson; 13 Ryan Hinchcliffe (C). Subs (all used): 9 Kruise Leeming; 18 Paul Clough; 22 Alex Mellor; 24 Tyler Dickinson.
Tries: Hinchcliffe (3), Mamo (12), Roberts (50), McGillvary (62); **Goals:** Brough 6/7.
Sin bin: Hinchcliffe (71) - dangerous contact.
Rugby Leaguer & League Express Men of the Match:
Vikings: Krisnan Inu; *Giants:* Danny Brough.
Penalty count: 10-7; **Half-time:** 0-14;
Referee: Ben Thaler; **Attendance:** 4,298.

Saturday 10th March 2018

CATALANS DRAGONS 18 HULL KINGSTON ROVERS 16

DRAGONS: 1 David Mead; 5 Fouad Yaha; 31 Tony Gigot; 4 Bradyen Wiliame; 20 Lewis Tierney; 13 Greg Bird; 22 Lucas Albert; 8 Remi Casty (C); 19 Michael McIlorum; 10 Sam Moa; 21 Benjamin Jullien; 12 Benjamin Garcia; 17 Jason Baitieri. Subs (all used): 9 Paul Aiton; 11 Louis Anderson; 14 Julian Bousquet; 15 Mickael Simon.
Tries: Tierney (34), Yaha (63); **Goals:** Albert 5/6.
ROVERS: 1 Adam Quinlan; 5 Ryan Shaw; 4 Andrew Heffernan; 3 Thomas Minns; 36 Justin Carney; 7 Danny McGuire (C); 24 Chris Atkin; 8 Nick Scruton; 19 Tommy Lee; 10 Mose Masoe; 12 James Greenwood; 13 Ben Kavanagh; 17 Chris Clarkson. Subs (all used): 11 Maurice Blair; 18 George Lawler; 21 Robbie Mulhern; 34 Danny Tickle.
Tries: Lawler (38), J Carney (66); **Goals:** Shaw 4/4.
Rugby Leaguer & League Express Men of the Match:
Dragons: Greg Bird; *Rovers:* Danny McGuire.
Penalty count: 12-6; **Half-time:** 8-8;
Referee: Scott Mikalauskas; **Attendance:** 7,342.

Sunday 11th March 2018

WIGAN WARRIORS 30 WAKEFIELD TRINITY 18

WARRIORS: 1 Sam Tomkins; 2 Tom Davies; 14 John Bateman; 4 Oliver Gildart; 5 Joe Burgess; 6 George Williams; 7 Sam Powell; 8 Tony Clubb; 9 Thomas Leuluai; 10 Ben Flower; 19 Willie Isa; 12 Liam Farrell; 13 Sean O'Loughlin (C). Subs (all used): 15 Ryan Sutton; 17 Taulima Tautai; 20 Morgan Escare; 25 Romain Navarrete.
Tries: Burgess (17, 46, 63), Tautai (32), Davies (58);
Goals: S Tomkins 4/5, Escare 1/1.
TRINITY: 1 Scott Grix; 5 Ben Jones-Bishop; 4 Reece Lyne; 3 Bill Tupou; 2 Tom Johnstone; 6 Jacob Miller; 7 Liam Finn; 8 David Fifita; 13 Tyler Randell; 10 Anthony England; 11 Matty Ashurst; 12 Danny Kirmond (C); 16 Tinirau Arona. Subs (all used): 17 Craig Huby; 9 Kyle Wood; 14 Justin Horo; 20 Keegan Hirst.
Tries: Jones-Bishop (4, 36), Arona (73); **Goals:** Finn 3/4.
Rugby Leaguer & League Express Men of the Match:
Warriors: Sam Tomkins; *Trinity:* Tyler Randell.
Penalty count: 10-10; **Half-time:** 10-12;
Referee: Chris Kendall; **Attendance:** 11,455.

CASTLEFORD TIGERS 22 SALFORD RED DEVILS 8

TIGERS: 1 Ben Roberts; 2 Greg Minikin; 3 Jake Webster; 4 Michael Shenton (C); 26 James Clare (D2); 6 Jamie Ellis; 7 Luke Gale; 14 Nathan Massey; 9 Paul McShane; 10 Grant Millington; 11 Oliver Holmes; 12 Mike McMeeken; 17 Alex Foster. Subs (all used): 13 Adam Milner; 18 Matt Cook; 15 Jesse Sene-Lefao; 22 James Green.
Tries: Shenton (5), Clare (13), Gale (29); **Goals:** Gale 5/5.
Sin bin: Holmes (19) - dangerous challenge on McCarthy; Millington (60) - fighting.
RED DEVILS: 5 Niall Evalds; 24 Jake Bibby; 3 Kris Welham; 4 Junior Sa'u; 2 Greg Johnson; 6 Robert Lui; 7 Jack Littlejohn; 10 George Griffin; 19 Josh Wood; 16 Luke Burgess; 11 Josh Jones; 12 Weller Hauraki; 17 Tyrone McCarthy. Subs (all used): 9 Logan Tomkins; 14 Lama Tasi; 18 Ben Nakubuwai; 13 Mark Flanagan (C).
Tries: Sa'u (50), Bibby (78); **Goals:** Lui 0/1, Littlejohn 0/1.
Sin bin: Tomkins (60) - fighting.
Rugby Leaguer & League Express Men of the Match:
Tigers: Luke Gale; *Red Devils:* Junior Sa'u.
Penalty count: 10-9; **Half-time:** 20-0;
Referee: Liam Moore; **Attendance:** 7,480.

ROUND 6

Thursday 15th March 2018

HUDDERSFIELD GIANTS 6
HULL KINGSTON ROVERS 38

GIANTS: 15 Jordan Rankin; 2 Jermaine McGillvary; 4 Jordan Turner; 26 Sam Wood; 5 Aaron Murphy; 6 Lee Gaskell; 7 Danny Brough; 8 Sebastine Ikahihifo; 21 Adam O'Brien; 17 Ukuma Ta'ai; 16 Oliver Roberts; 14 Dale Ferguson; 13 Ryan Hinchcliffe (C). Subs (all used): 9 Kruise Leeming; 18 Paul Clough; 24 Tyler Dickinson; 22 Alex Mellor.
Try: Roberts (8); **Goals:** Brough 1/1.
On report:
Hinchcliffe (17) - alleged dangerous contact on Masoe.
ROVERS: 1 Adam Quinlan; 5 Ryan Shaw; 4 Andrew Heffernan; 3 Thomas Minns; 36 Justin Carney; 7 Danny McGuire (C); 24 Chris Atkin; 21 Robbie Mulhern; 18 George Lawler; 10 Mose Masoe; 17 Chris Clarkson; 11 Maurice Blair; 13 Ben Kavanagh. Subs (all used): 8 Nick Scruton; 19 Tommy Lee; 15 James Donaldson; 12 James Greenwood.
Tries: Heffernan (13), Quinlan (15), Shaw (37, 73), Greenwood (64), McGuire (78); **Goals:** Shaw 7/7.
Rugby Leaguer & League Express Men of the Match:
Giants: Dale Ferguson; *Rovers:* Andrew Heffernan.
Penalty count: 10-6; **Half-time:** 6-20;
Referee: Ben Thaler; **Attendance:** 4,612.

Friday 16th March 2018

ST HELENS 20 LEEDS RHINOS 28

SAINTS: 23 Ben Barba; 5 Adam Swift; 2 Tommy Makinson; 4 Mark Percival; 19 Regan Grace; 1 Jonny Lomax; 18 Danny Richardson; 10 Kyle Amor; 9 James Roby (C); 16 Luke Thompson; 17 Dominique Peyroux; 11 Zeb Taia; 12 Jon Wilkin. Subs (all used): 6 Theo Fages; 13 Louie McCarthy-Scarsbrook; 14 Luke Douglas; 20 Matty Lees.
Tries: Barba (17, 71), Swift (28); **Goals:** Richardson 4/5.
RHINOS: 1 Ashton Golding; 2 Tom Briscoe; 3 Kallum Watkins (C); 22 Ash Handley; 5 Ryan Hall; 6 Joel Moon; 7 Richie Myler; 16 Anthony Mullally; 9 Matt Parcell; 10 Brad Singleton; 11 Jamie Jones-Buchanan; 12 Carl Ablett; 15 Brett Delaney. Subs (all used): 24 Jack Walker; 27 Cameron Smith; 28 Mikolaj Oledzki; 30 Josh Walters.
Tries: Mullally (10), Myler (36), Handley (61, 65), Parcell (73); **Goals:** Watkins 3/4, Myler 1/2.
Rugby Leaguer & League Express Men of the Match:
Saints: James Roby; *Rhinos:* Joel Moon.
Penalty count: 7-7; **Half-time:** 12-12;
Referee: James Child; **Attendance:** 11,482.

SALFORD RED DEVILS 24 HULL FC 8

RED DEVILS: 5 Niall Evalds; 2 Greg Johnson; 4 Junior Sa'u; 3 Kris Welham; 24 Jake Bibby; 6 Robert Lui; 7 Jack Littlejohn; 23 Lee Mossop (C); 9 Logan Tomkins; 8 Craig Kopczak; 11 Josh Jones; 12 Weller Hauraki; 13 Mark Flanagan. Subs (all used): 14 Lama Tasi; 18 Ben Nakubuwai; 19 Josh Wood; 17 Tyrone McCarthy.
Tries: Nakubuwai (35), Littlejohn (62), Lui (72), Johnson (75); **Goals:** Lui 4/6.
HULL FC: 1 Jamie Shaul; 2 Bureta Faraimo; 3 Carlos Tuimavave; 4 Josh Griffin; 5 Fetuli Talanoa; 14 Jake Connor; 7 Marc Sneyd; 8 Scott Taylor (C); 17 Danny Washbrook; 15 Chris Green; 11 Dean Hadley; 12 Mark Minichiello; 16 Jordan Abdull. Subs (all used): 29 Masi Matongo; 20 Brad Fash; 13 Josh Bowden; 26 Jordan Lane.
Try: Hadley (15); **Goals:** Sneyd 2/2.
Rugby Leaguer & League Express Men of the Match:
Red Devils: Robert Lui; *Hull FC:* Dean Hadley.
Penalty count: 5-7; **Half time:** 10-8;
Referee: Scott Mikalauskas; **Attendance:** 2,902.

Saturday 17th March 2018

CATALANS DRAGONS 0 WARRINGTON WOLVES 26

DRAGONS: 1 David Mead; 5 Fouad Yaha; 31 Tony Gigot; 3 Iain Thornley; 20 Lewis Tierney; 13 Greg Bird; 22 Lucas Albert; 8 Remi Casty (C); 19 Michael McIlorum; 10 Sam Moa; 11 Louis Anderson; 4 Brayden Wiliame; 12 Benjamin Garcia. Subs (all used): 9 Paul Aiton; 14 Julian Bousquet; 15 Mickael Simon; 21 Benjamin Jullien.
Sin bin: Yaha (31) - fighting; McIlorum (78) - fighting.
WOLVES: 1 Stefan Ratchford; 2 Tom Lineham; 3 Bryson Goodwin; 18 Toby King; 21 Mitch Brown; 6 Kevin Brown; 7 Tyrone Roberts; 8 Chris Hill (C); 9 Daryl Clark; 10 Mike Cooper; 34 Ben Westwood; 12 Jack Hughes; 19 George King. Subs (all used): 13 Ben Murdoch-Masila; 16 Sitaleki Akauola; 17 Joe Philbin; 20 Harvey Livett.
Tries: M Brown (4), Clark (18), Murdoch-Masila (26, 42), Livett (77); **Goals:** Goodwin 3/6.
Sin bin: Lineham (31) - fighting; G King (78) - fighting.
Rugby Leaguer & League Express Men of the Match:
Dragons: Greg Bird; *Wolves:* Chris Hill.
Penalty count: 10-9; **Half-time:** 0-14;
Referee: Chris Kendall; **Attendance:** 6,585.

ROUND 7

Thursday 22nd March 2018

WIDNES VIKINGS 24 SALFORD RED DEVILS 16

VIKINGS: 1 Rhys Hanbury; 2 Stefan Marsh; 3 Krisnan Inu; 4 Charly Runciman; 24 Ed Chamberlain; 6 Joe Mellor (C); 15 Danny Craven; 11 Chris Houston (C); 33 Aaron Heremaia; 19 Greg Burke; 14 Chris Dean; 12 Matt Whitley; 16 Tom Olbison. Subs (all used): 21 Jordan Johnstone; 28 Brad Walker; 26 Ted Chapelhow; 17 Sam Wilde.
Tries: Dean (27), Inu (49), Burke (70), Heremaia (76);
Goals: Inu 4/4.
RED DEVILS: 5 Niall Evalds; 24 Jake Bibby; 22 Derrell Olpherts (D); 4 Junior Sa'u; 2 Greg Johnson; 6 Robert Lui; 7 Jack Littlejohn; 23 Lee Mossop; 9 Logan Tomkins; 8 Craig Kopczak; 11 Josh Jones; 12 Weller Hauraki; 13 Mark Flanagan (C). Subs (all used): 19 Josh Wood; 14 Lama Tasi; 18 Ben Nakubuwai; 17 Tyrone McCarthy.
Tries: Kopczak (18), Hauraki (58); **Goals:** Lui 4/5.
Sin bin: Tasi (44) - high tackle on Heremaia.
Rugby Leaguer & League Express Men of the Match:
Vikings: Aaron Heremaia; *Red Devils:* Craig Kopczak.
Penalty count: 9-9; **Half-time:** 6-10;
Referee: Ben Thaler; **Attendance:** 4,007.

Friday 23rd March 2018

HULL FC 42 CATALANS DRAGONS 16

HULL FC: 1 Jamie Shaul; 2 Bureta Faraimo; 4 Josh Griffin; 3 Carlos Tuimavave; 5 Fetuli Talanoa; 6 Albert Kelly; 7

Marc Sneyd; 8 Scott Taylor (C); 17 Danny Washbrook; 15 Chris Green; 12 Mark Minichiello; 26 Jordan Lane; 11 Dean Hadley. Subs (all used): 13 Josh Bowden; 14 Jake Connor; 16 Jordan Abdull; 20 Brad Fash.
Tries: Griffin (11, 80), Talanoa (15, 55), Shaul (43), Taylor (59), Connor (62); **Goals:** Sneyd 6/6, Connor 1/1.
DRAGONS: 31 Tony Gigot; 20 Lewis Tierney; 1 David Mead; 4 Brayden Wiliame; 5 Fouad Yaha; 6 Samisoni Langi; 22 Lucas Albert; 8 Remi Casty (C); 9 Paul Aiton; 10 Sam Moa; 13 Greg Bird; 12 Benjamin Garcia; 17 Jason Baitieri. Subs (all used): 24 Alrix Da Costa; 14 Julian Bousquet; 15 Mickael Simon; 18 Thibaut Margalet.
Tries: Moa (20), Albert (73), Gigot (76); **Goals:** Albert 2/3.
Rugby Leaguer & League Express Men of the Match: *Hull FC:* Scott Taylor; *Dragons:* Lucas Albert.
Penalty count: 7-6; **Half-time:** 12-4;
Referee: Jack Smith; **Attendance:** 10,347.

LEEDS RHINOS 24 CASTLEFORD TIGERS 25

RHINOS: 1 Ashton Golding; 2 Tom Briscoe; 3 Kallum Watkins (C); 22 Ash Handley; 5 Ryan Hall; 6 Joel Moon; 7 Richie Myler; 16 Anthony Mullally; 9 Matt Parcell; 10 Brad Singleton; 11 Jamie Jones-Buchanan; 12 Carl Ablett; 15 Brett Delaney. Subs (all used): 28 Mikolaj Oledzki; 24 Jack Walker; 27 Cameron Smith; 30 Josh Walters.
Tries: Watkins (28, 69), Handley (32, 54), Hall (77);
Goals: Watkins 2/5.
Sin bin: Singleton (46) - high tackle on Moors.
TIGERS: 1 Ben Roberts; 24 Jy Hitchcox; 3 Jake Webster; 2 Greg Minikin; 26 James Clare; 6 Jamie Ellis; 7 Luke Gale (C); 14 Nathan Massey; 9 Paul McShane; 10 Grant Millington; 12 Mike McMeeken; 17 Alex Foster; 13 Adam Milner. Subs (all used): 8 Junior Moors; 18 Matt Cook; 22 James Green; 21 Jake Trueman.
Tries: Ellis (6), Clare (8), Foster (11), Moors (25);
Goals: Gale 4/4; **Field goal:** Gale (40).
On report: McShane (62) - alleged stamp on Myler.
Rugby Leaguer & League Express Men of the Match: *Rhinos:* Kallum Watkins; *Tigers:* Mike McMeeken.
Penalty count: 8-10; **Half time:** 10-25;
Referee: Chris Kendall; **Attendance:** 23,246
(at Elland Road).

WARRINGTON WOLVES 34 WAKEFIELD TRINITY 24

WOLVES: 1 Stefan Ratchford; 2 Tom Lineham; 3 Bryson Goodwin; 18 Toby King; 21 Mitch Brown; 6 Kevin Brown; 7 Tyrone Roberts; 8 Chris Hill (C); 9 Daryl Clark; 10 Mike Cooper; 34 Ben Westwood; 12 Jack Hughes; 19 George King. Subs (all used): 17 Joe Philbin; 13 Ben Murdoch-Masila; 16 Sitaleki Akauola; 20 Harvey Livett.
Tries: Lineham (2, 13, 77), Goodwin (41), Cooper (57), Murdoch-Masila (62); **Goals:** Goodwin 2/4, Ratchford 3/4.
TRINITY: 1 Scott Grix; 5 Ben Jones-Bishop; 4 Reece Lyne; 3 Bill Tupou; 2 Tom Johnstone; 6 Jacob Miller; 7 Liam Finn; 20 Keegan Hirst; 13 Tyler Randell; 10 Anthony England; 12 Danny Kirmond (C); 11 Matty Ashurst; 14 Justin Horo. Subs (all used): 25 Ryan Hampshire; 15 Pauli Pauli; 16 Tinirau Arona; 17 Craig Huby.
Tries: Lyne (10), Tupou (25), Finn (29), Johnstone (64), Jones-Bishop (80); **Goals:** Finn 1/4, Randell 1/1.
Rugby Leaguer & League Express Men of the Match: *Wolves:* Stefan Ratchford; *Trinity:* Bill Tupou.
Penalty count: 6-7; **Half-time:** 12-14;
Referee: James Child; **Attendance:** 9,154.

HULL KINGSTON ROVERS 6 ST HELENS 30

ROVERS: 1 Adam Quinlan; 5 Ryan Shaw; 4 Andrew Heffernan; 3 Thomas Minns; 36 Justin Carney; 7 Danny McGuire (C); 24 Chris Atkin; 21 Robbie Mulhern; 18 George Lawler; 10 Mose Masoe; 11 Maurice Blair; 17 Chris Clarkson; 13 Ben Kavanagh. Subs (all used): 19 Tommy Lee; 15 James Donaldson; 12 James Greenwood; 29 Jordan Walne.
Try: Shaw (40); **Goals:** Shaw 1/1.
SAINTS: 23 Ben Barba; 5 Adam Swift; 2 Tommy Makinson; 4 Mark Percival; 19 Regan Grace; 1 Jonny Lomax; 18 Danny Richardson; 10 Kyle Amor; 9 James Roby (C); 16 Luke Thompson; 17 Dominique Peyroux; 11 Zeb Taia; 12 Jon Wilkin. Subs (all used): 6 Theo Fages; 13 Louie McCarthy-Scarsbrook; 14 Luke Douglas; 15 Morgan Knowles.
Tries: Thompson (15), Barba (26, 56), Lomax (71), Peyroux (73); **Goals:** Richardson 5/6.
Rugby Leaguer & League Express Men of the Match: *Rovers:* Adam Quinlan; *Saints:* Ben Barba.
Penalty count: 10-9; **Half-time:** 6-14;
Referee: Liam Moore; **Attendance:** 7,724.

WIGAN WARRIORS 48 HUDDERSFIELD GIANTS 10

WARRIORS: 1 Sam Tomkins; 2 Tom Davies; 14 John Bateman; 4 Oliver Gildart; 5 Joe Burgess; 6 George Williams; 7 Sam Powell; 8 Tony Clubb; 9 Thomas Leuluai; 10 Ben Flower; 19 Willie Isa; 12 Liam Farrell; 13 Sean O'Loughlin (C). Subs (all used): 11 Joel Tomkins; 15 Ryan Sutton; 17 Taulima Tautai; 20 Morgan Escare.
Tries: Davies (2, 19), Gildart (24), Burgess (31, 76), Bateman (40), Williams (52), Sutton (61), Isa (67);
Goals: S Tomkins 5/6, Escare 1/3.
GIANTS: 15 Jordan Rankin; 2 Jermaine McGillvary; 4 Jordan Turner; 26 Sam Wood; 5 Aaron Murphy; 6 Lee Gaskell; 7 Danny Brough; 17 Ukuma Ta'ai; 9 Kruise Leeming; 18 Paul Clough; 12 Michael Lawrence; 14 Dale Ferguson; 13 Ryan Hinchcliffe (C). Subs (all used): 19 Daniel Smith; 20 Adam Walne; 21 Adam O'Brien; 22 Alex Mellor.
Tries: McGillvary (7), Hinchcliffe (73); **Goals:** Brough 1/2.
Rugby Leaguer & League Express Men of the Match: *Warriors:* Sam Powell; *Giants:* Kruise Leeming.
Penalty count: 11-6; **Half-time:** 28-4;
Referee: Scott Mikalauskas; **Attendance:** 10,641.

ROUND 8

Thursday 29th March 2018

WAKEFIELD TRINITY 6 CASTLEFORD TIGERS 11

TRINITY: 1 Scott Grix; 5 Ben Jones-Bishop; 4 Reece Lyne; 3 Bill Tupou; 2 Tom Johnstone; 6 Jacob Miller; 7 Liam Finn (C); 10 Anthony England; 13 Tyler Randell; 17 Craig Huby; 14 Justin Horo; 11 Matty Ashurst; 16 Tinirau Arona. Subs (all used): 9 Kyle Wood; 8 David Fifita; 15 Pauli Pauli; 20 Keegan Hirst.
Try: Jones-Bishop (60); **Goals:** Finn 1/1.
TIGERS: 21 Jake Trueman; 2 Greg Minikin; 3 Jake Webster; 4 Michael Shenton (C); 26 James Clare; 1 Ben Roberts; 7 Luke Gale; 18 Matt Cook; 9 Paul McShane; 10 Grant Millington; 11 Oliver Holmes; 12 Mike McMeeken; 13 Adam Milner. Subs: 6 Jamie Ellis (not used); 8 Junior Moors; 17 Alex Foster; 19 Gadwin Springer.
Try: McMeeken (17); **Goals:** Gale 3/3; **Field goal:** Gale (36).
Rugby Leaguer & League Express Men of the Match: *Trinity:* Kyle Wood; *Tigers:* Oliver Holmes.
Penalty count: 9-10; **Half-time:** 0-7;
Referee: James Child; **Attendance:** 7,020.

Friday 30th March 2018

SALFORD RED DEVILS 32 CATALANS DRAGONS 16

RED DEVILS: 5 Niall Evalds; 2 Greg Johnson; 4 Junior Sa'u; 3 Kris Welham; 24 Jake Bibby; 6 Robert Lui; 19 Josh Wood; 23 Lee Mossop (C); 9 Logan Tomkins; 8 Craig Kopczak; 11 Josh Jones; 12 Weller Hauraki; 13 Mark Flanagan. Subs (all used): 7 Jack Littlejohn; 18 Ben Nakubuwai; 14 Lama Tasi; 16 Luke Burgess.
Tries: Bibby (9), Evalds (12), Johnson (52), Jones (69), Welham (74); **Goals:** Lui 6/6.
Sin bin: Hauraki (21) - high tackle on Langi.
On report: Tasi (35) - alleged late challenge on Gigot.
DRAGONS: 20 Lewis Tierney; 2 Jodie Broughton; 1 David Mead; 4 Brayden Wiliame; 5 Fouad Yaha; 31 Tony Gigot; 6 Samisoni Langi; 8 Remi Casty (C); 19 Michael McIlorum; 10 Sam Moa; 13 Greg Bird; 12 Benjamin Garcia; 17 Jason Baitieri. Subs (all used): 9 Paul Aiton; 14 Julian Bousquet; 15 Mickael Simon; 21 Benjamin Jullien.
Tries: Yaha (27, 60), Bird (79); **Goals:** Gigot 2/3.
Rugby Leaguer & League Express Men of the Match: *Red Devils:* Lama Tasi; *Dragons:* Fouad Yaha.
Penalty count: 12-7; **Half-time:** 12-4;
Referee: Gareth Hewer; **Attendance:** 2,328.

HULL KINGSTON ROVERS 22 HULL FC 30

ROVERS: 1 Adam Quinlan; 5 Ryan Shaw; 22 Liam Salter; 3 Thomas Minns; 36 Justin Carney; 20 Matty Marsh; 24 Chris Atkin; 14 Lee Jewitt; 19 Tommy Lee; 10 Mose Masoe; 12 James Greenwood; 11 Maurice Blair (C); 13 Ben Kavanagh. Subs (all used): 8 Nick Scruton; 15 James Donaldson; 17 Chris Clarkson; 28 Will Dagger.
Tries: Minns (11, 31, 67), Shaw (46); **Goals:** Shaw 3/4.
HULL FC: 1 Jamie Shaul; 2 Bureta Faraimo; 4 Josh Griffin; 3 Carlos Tuimavave; 5 Fetuli Talanoa; 6 Albert Kelly; 7 Marc Sneyd; 8 Scott Taylor; 9 Danny Houghton (C); 23 Mickey Paea; 26 Jordan Lane; 12 Mark Minichiello; 15 Chris Green. Subs (all used): 13 Josh Bowden; 29 Masi Matongo; 14 Jake Connor; 17 Danny Washbrook.
Tries: Houghton (2), Talanoa (24, 39), Shaul (26), Connor (59); **Goals:** Sneyd 5/7.
Dismissal: Faraimo (8) - shoulder charge on Atkin.
Rugby Leaguer & League Express Men of the Match: *Rovers:* Adam Quinlan; *Hull FC:* Carlos Tuimavave.
Penalty count: 9-7; **Half-time:** 12-22;
Referee: Chris Kendall; **Attendance:** 12,090.

HUDDERSFIELD GIANTS 22 LEEDS RHINOS 22

GIANTS: 23 Darnell McIntosh; 28 Jared Simpson; 4 Jordan Turner; 5 Aaron Murphy; 31 Louis Senior (D); 15 Jordan Rankin; 7 Danny Brough; 8 Sebastine Ikahihifo; 21 Adam O'Brien; 18 Paul Clough; 16 Oliver Roberts; 12 Michael Lawrence; 13 Ryan Hinchcliffe (C). Subs (all used): 17 Ukuma Ta'ai; 19 Daniel Smith; 24 Tyler Dickinson; 32 Sam Hewitt (D).
Tries: Simpson (2, 17), O'Brien (64); **Goals:** Brough 5/5.
RHINOS: 24 Jack Walker; 2 Tom Briscoe; 3 Kallum Watkins (C); 22 Ash Handley; 5 Ryan Hall; 6 Joel Moon; 7 Richie Myler; 16 Anthony Mullally; 14 Brad Dwyer; 10 Brad Singleton; 11 Jamie Jones-Buchanan; 12 Carl Ablett; 15 Brett Delaney. Subs (all used): 19 Brett Ferres; 27 Cameron Smith; 28 Mikolaj Oledzki; 1 Ashton Golding.
Tries: Watkins (22), Hall (44), Handley (52, 76);
Goals: Watkins 3/4.
Rugby Leaguer & League Express Men of the Match: *Giants:* Sam Hewitt; *Rhinos:* Ash Handley.
Penalty count: 5-5; **Half-time:** 14-6;
Referee: Jack Smith; **Attendance:** 7,544.

WARRINGTON WOLVES 32 WIDNES VIKINGS 18

WOLVES: 1 Stefan Ratchford; 2 Tom Lineham; 3 Bryson Goodwin; 18 Toby King; 27 Josh Charnley (D); 6 Kevin Brown; 7 Tyrone Roberts; 8 Chris Hill (C); 9 Daryl Clark; 10 Mike Cooper; 11 Ben Currie; 12 Jack Hughes; 34 Ben Westwood. Subs (all used): 17 Joe Philbin; 13 Ben Murdoch-Masila; 16 Sitaleki Akauola; 22 Morgan Smith.
Tries: T King (28, 32), Charnley (42, 63), Akauola (54), Westwood (68); **Goals:** Goodwin 4/6.
VIKINGS: 1 Rhys Hanbury; 2 Stefan Marsh; 3 Krisnan Inu; 4 Charly Runciman; 24 Ed Chamberlain; 6 Joe Mellor (C); 7 Tom Gilmore; 26 Ted Chapelhow; 33 Aaron Heremaia; 19 Greg Burke; 14 Chris Dean; 17 Sam Wilde; 11 Chris Houston (C). Subs (all used): 21 Jordan Johnstone; 16 Tom Olbison; 28 Brad Walker; 8 Gil Dudson.
Tries: Chamberlain (12, 23), Hanbury (74);
Goals: Inu 2/3, Gilmore 1/1.
Rugby Leaguer & League Express Men of the Match: *Wolves:* Ben Westwood; *Vikings:* Charly Runciman.
Penalty count: 11-7; **Half-time:** 10-12;
Referee: Liam Moore; **Attendance:** 12,175.

ST HELENS 21 WIGAN WARRIORS 18

SAINTS: 23 Ben Barba; 2 Tommy Makinson; 3 Ryan Morgan; 4 Mark Percival; 19 Regan Grace; 1 Jonny Lomax; 18 Danny Richardson; 10 Kyle Amor; 9 James Roby (C); 16 Luke Thompson; 17 Dominique Peyroux; 11 Zeb Taia; 12 Jon Wilkin. Subs (all used): 6 Theo Fages; 13 Louie McCarthy-Scarsbrook; 14 Luke Douglas; 15 Morgan Knowles.
Tries: Barba (18), Taia (35), Grace (75);
Goals: Richardson 4/4; **Field goal:** Richardson (78).
WARRIORS: 20 Morgan Escare; 2 Tom Davies; 14 John Bateman; 4 Oliver Gildart; 5 Joe Burgess; 6 George Williams; 7 Sam Powell; 8 Tony Clubb; 9 Thomas Leuluai; 10 Ben Flower; 19 Willie Isa; 12 Liam Farrell; 13 Sean O'Loughlin (C). Subs (all used): 11 Joel Tomkins; 15 Ryan Sutton; 17 Taulima Tautai; 34 Josh Woods.
Tries: J Tomkins (46, 79), Isa (66);
Goals: Escare 2/2, Williams 1/2.
Rugby Leaguer & League Express Men of the Match: *Saints:* James Roby; *Warriors:* Joel Tomkins.
Penalty count: 11-6; **Half-time:** 12-2;
Referee: Robert Hicks; **Attendance:** 17,980.

ROUND 9

Monday 2nd April 2018

CASTLEFORD TIGERS 6 WARRINGTON WOLVES 18

TIGERS: 21 Jake Trueman; 2 Greg Minikin; 3 Jake Webster; 4 Michael Shenton (C); 26 James Clare; 1 Ben Roberts; 7 Luke Gale; 14 Nathan Massey; 9 Paul McShane; 32 Liam Watts (D2); 11 Oliver Holmes; 12 Mike McMeeken; 13 Adam Milner. Subs (all used): 8 Junior Moors; 10 Grant Millington; 17 Alex Foster; 18 Matt Cook.
Try: Holmes (52); **Goals:** Gale 1/1.
WOLVES: 1 Stefan Ratchford; 2 Tom Lineham; 4 Ryan Atkins; 18 Toby King; 27 Josh Charnley; 6 Kevin Brown; 7 Tyrone Roberts; 8 Chris Hill (C); 9 Daryl Clark; 10 Mike Cooper; 11 Ben Currie; 12 Jack Hughes; 34 Ben Westwood. Subs (all used): 13 Ben Murdoch-Masila; 17 Joe Philbin; 14 Dominic Crosby; 16 Sitaleki Akauola.
Tries: T King (40), Clark (79); **Goals:** Ratchford 5/5.
Rugby Leaguer & League Express Men of the Match: *Tigers:* Liam Watts; *Wolves:* Daryl Clark.
Penalty count: 5-4; **Half-time:** 0-10;
Referee: Robert Hicks; **Attendance:** 6,881.

HULL FC 27 WAKEFIELD TRINITY 26

HULL FC: 28 Hakim Miloudi (D); 2 Bureta Faraimo; 14 Jake Connor; 4 Josh Griffin; 5 Fetuli Talanoa; 6 Albert Kelly; 7 Marc Sneyd; 23 Mickey Paea; 17 Danny Washbrook; 13 Josh Bowden; 12 Mark Minichiello; 25 Jansin Turgut; 16 Jordan Abdull. Subs (all used): 8 Scott Taylor (C); 15 Chris Green; 20 Brad Fash; 22 Jez Litten.
Tries: Abdull (17), Kelly (46), Talanoa (52, 63);
Goals: Sneyd 5/5; **Field goal:** Sneyd (79).

TRINITY: 21 Max Jowitt; 24 Mason Caton-Brown; 4 Reece Lyne; 18 Joe Arundel; 3 Bill Tupou; 6 Jacob Miller (C); 25 Ryan Hampshire; 17 Craig Huby; 13 Tyler Randell; 20 Keegan Hirst; 11 Matty Ashurst; 19 James Batchelor; 14 Justin Horo. Subs (all used): 9 Kyle Wood; 15 Pauli Pauli; 16 Tinirau Arona; 22 Jordan Baldwinson.
Tries: Tupou (23, 31), Caton-Brown (37, 73);
Goals: Batchelor 5/5.
Rugby Leaguer & League Express Men of the Match: *Hull FC:* Marc Sneyd; *Trinity:* James Batchelor.
Penalty count: 8-7; **Half time:** 8-18;
Referee: Liam Moore; **Attendance:** 11,529.

LEEDS RHINOS 20 SALFORD RED DEVILS 0

RHINOS: 1 Ashton Golding; 2 Tom Briscoe; 3 Kallum Watkins (C); 22 Ash Handley; 5 Ryan Hall; 6 Joel Moon; 7 Richie Myler; 15 Brett Delaney; 9 Matt Parcell; 10 Brad Singleton; 13 Stevie Ward; 12 Carl Ablett; 30 Josh Walters. Subs (all used): 14 Brad Dwyer; 19 Brett Ferres; 27 Cameron Smith; 28 Mikolaj Oledzki.
Tries: T Briscoe (4), Handley (17), Walters (76);
Goals: Watkins 4/5.
RED DEVILS: 5 Niall Evalds; 24 Jake Bibby; 3 Kris Welham; 4 Junior Sa'u; 22 Derrell Olpherts; 6 Robert Lui; 19 Josh Wood; 18 Ben Nakubuwai; 9 Logan Tomkins; 14 Lama Tasi; 11 Josh Jones; 10 George Griffin; 26 Daniel Murray. Subs (all used): 7 Jack Littlejohn; 12 Weller Hauraki (C); 16 Luke Burgess; 15 Ryan Lannon.
Rugby Leaguer & League Express Men of the Match: *Rhinos:* Josh Walters; *Red Devils:* Josh Jones.
Penalty count: 10-8; **Half time:** 12-0;
Referee: Greg Dolan; **Attendance:** 10,718.

WIGAN WARRIORS 44 HULL KINGSTON ROVERS 6

WARRIORS: 1 Sam Tomkins; 2 Tom Davies; 3 Dan Sarginson; 4 Oliver Gildart; 22 Liam Marshall; 6 George Williams; 34 Josh Woods; 10 Ben Flower; 9 Thomas Leuluai (C); 25 Romain Navarrete; 19 Willie Isa; 12 Liam Farrell; 14 John Bateman. Subs (all used): 11 Joel Tomkins; 15 Ryan Sutton; 23 Josh Ganson; 30 Gabe Hamlin (D).
Tries: S Tomkins (25), Farrell (29, 37), Williams (31), Marshall (35, 50, 66, 72); **Goals:** S Tomkins 6/9.
ROVERS: 1 Adam Quinlan; 5 Ryan Shaw; 3 Thomas Minns; 22 Liam Salter; 36 Justin Carney; 24 Chris Atkin; 20 Matty Marsh; 14 Lee Jewitt; 19 Tommy Lee; 10 Mose Masoe; 11 Maurice Blair (C); 12 James Greenwood; 17 Chris Clarkson. Subs (all used): 8 Nick Scruton; 15 James Donaldson; 23 Josh Johnson; 28 Will Dagger.
Try: Atkin (45); **Goals:** Shaw 1/1.
Sin bin: Johnson (65) - interference.
Rugby Leaguer & League Express Men of the Match: *Warriors:* Gabe Hamlin; *Rovers:* Justin Carney.
Penalty count: 18-9; **Half time:** 26-0;
Referee: Ben Thaler; **Attendance:** 10,977.

WIDNES VIKINGS 6 ST HELENS 28

VIKINGS: 15 Danny Craven; 2 Stefan Marsh; 24 Ed Chamberlain; 4 Charly Runciman; 22 Ryan Ince; 33 Aaron Heremaia; 7 Tom Gilmore (C); 10 Alex Gerrard; 21 Jordan Johnstone; 26 Ted Chapelhow; 16 Tom Olbison; 17 Sam Wilde; 28 Brad Walker. Subs (all used): 23 Danny Walker; 36 Wellington Albert; 19 Greg Burke; 20 Macgraff Leuluai.
Try: W Albert (23); **Goals:** Gilmore 1/1.
SAINTS: 23 Ben Barba; 2 Tommy Makinson; 3 Ryan Morgan; 4 Mark Percival; 19 Regan Grace; 6 Theo Fages; 18 Danny Richardson; 10 Kyle Amor; 9 James Roby (C); 16 Luke Thompson; 17 Dominique Peyroux; 11 Zeb Taia; 12 Jon Wilkin. Subs (all used): 7 Matty Smith; 13 Louie McCarthy-Scarsbrook; 14 Luke Douglas; 15 Morgan Knowles.
Tries: Morgan (7), Percival (10, 28), Barba (43), Makinson (47, 59); **Goals:** Richardson 2/6.
Sin bin: Douglas (41) - dangerous contact.
Rugby Leaguer & League Express Men of the Match: *Vikings:* Tom Olbison; *Saints:* Ben Barba.
Penalty count: 9-8; **Half-time:** 6-16;
Referee: Chris Kendall; **Attendance:** 6,706.

CATALANS DRAGONS 27 HUDDERSFIELD GIANTS 6

DRAGONS: 1 David Mead; 2 Jodie Broughton; 3 Iain Thornley; 4 Brayden Wiliame; 5 Fouad Yaha; 31 Tony Gigot; 6 Samisoni Langi; 8 Remi Casty (C); 19 Michael McIlorum; 10 Sam Moa; 11 Louis Anderson; 21 Benjamin Jullien; 13 Greg Bird. Subs (all used): 9 Paul Aiton; 14 Julian Bousquet; 15 Mickael Simon; 17 Jason Baitieri.
Tries: Broughton (21, 69), Jullien (41), Mead (46, 53);
Goals: Gigot 3/6; **Field goal:** Gigot (77).
GIANTS: 23 Darnell McIntosh; 28 Jared Simpson; 22 Alex Mellor; 5 Aaron Murphy; 33 Innes Senior (D); 4 Jordan Turner; 15 Jordan Rankin; 8 Sebastine Ikahihifo; 21 Adam O'Brien; 18 Paul Clough; 14 Dale Ferguson; 12 Michael Lawrence; 19 Daniel Smith. Subs (all used): 13 Ryan Hinchcliffe (C); 17 Ukuma Ta'ai; 10 Shannon Wakeman; 25 Colton Roche (D).
Try: Murphy (18); **Goals:** McIntosh 1/1.
Rugby Leaguer & League Express Men of the Match: *Dragons:* Tony Gigot; *Giants:* Ukuma Ta'ai.
Penalty count: 7-9; **Half-time:** 4-6;
Referee: Scott Mikalauskas; **Attendance:** 8,853.

ROUND 10

Friday 6th April 2018

ST HELENS 26 HULL FC 12

SAINTS: 1 Jonny Lomax; 2 Tommy Makinson; 3 Ryan Morgan; 4 Mark Percival; 19 Regan Grace; 6 Theo Fages; 18 Danny Richardson; 10 Kyle Amor; 9 James Roby (C); 16 Luke Thompson; 17 Dominique Peyroux; 11 Zeb Taia; 12 Jon Wilkin. Subs (all used): 7 Matty Smith; 13 Louie McCarthy-Scarsbrook; 14 Luke Douglas; 15 Morgan Knowles.
Tries: Taia (8, 67), Percival (43), Thompson (72);
Goals: Richardson 5/5.
HULL FC: 1 Jamie Shaul; 24 Jack Logan; 4 Josh Griffin; 3 Carlos Tuimavave; 5 Fetuli Talanoa; 6 Albert Kelly; 7 Marc Sneyd; 8 Scott Taylor; 9 Danny Houghton (C); 23 Mickey Paea; 17 Danny Washbrook; 26 Jordan Lane; 20 Brad Fash. Subs (all used): 13 Josh Bowden; 14 Jake Connor; 15 Chris Green; 16 Jordan Abdull.
Tries: Kelly (57), Green (75); **Goals:** Sneyd 2/2.
On report:
Abdull (47) - alleged dangerous challenge on Richardson.
Rugby Leaguer & League Express Men of the Match: *Saints:* Tommy Makinson; *Hull FC:* Danny Houghton.
Penalty count: 5-5; **Half-time:** 6-0;
Referee: Robert Hicks; **Attendance:** 10,408.

Saturday 7th April 2018

SALFORD RED DEVILS 6 WARRINGTON WOLVES 22

RED DEVILS: 6 Robert Lui; 22 Derrell Olpherts; 4 Junior Sa'u; 3 Kris Welham; 24 Jake Bibby; 28 Jake Shorrocks (D); 7 Jack Littlejohn; 23 Lee Mossop; 19 Josh Wood; 8 Craig Kopczak (C); 11 Josh Jones; 12 Weller Hauraki; 13 Mark Flanagan. Subs (all used): 15 Ryan Lannon; 18 Ben Nakubuwai; 14 Lama Tasi; 16 Luke Burgess.
Try: Lui (27); **Goals:** Lui 1/1.
WOLVES: 1 Stefan Ratchford; 2 Tom Lineham; 3 Bryson Goodwin; 18 Toby King; 27 Josh Charnley; 6 Kevin Brown; 7 Tyrone Roberts; 8 Chris Hill (C); 9 Daryl Clark; 10 Mike Cooper; 11 Ben Currie; 12 Jack Hughes; 34 Ben Westwood. Subs (all used): 4 Ryan Atkins; 17 Joe Philbin; 14 Dominic Crosby; 16 Sitaleki Akauola.
Tries: T King (5), Charnley (12), Roberts (23), K Brown (73);
Goals: Ratchford 3/5.
Rugby Leaguer & League Express Men of the Match: *Red Devils:* Robert Lui; *Wolves:* Kevin Brown.
Penalty count: 5-6; **Half-time:** 6-14;
Referee: Gareth Hewer; **Attendance:** 3,428.

CATALANS DRAGONS 23 WIGAN WARRIORS 32

DRAGONS: 1 David Mead; 2 Jodie Broughton; 3 Iain Thornley; 4 Brayden Wiliame; 5 Fouad Yaha; 31 Tony Gigot; 6 Samisoni Langi; 15 Mickael Simon; 19 Michael McIlorum; 10 Sam Moa; 21 Benjamin Jullien; 12 Benjamin Garcia; 13 Greg Bird. Subs (all used): 8 Remi Casty (C); 9 Paul Aiton; 14 Julian Bousquet; 17 Jason Baitieri.
Tries: Jullien (13), Mead (38), Garcia (42);
Goals: Gigot 5/5; **Field goal:** Gigot (40).
Sin bin: Simon (73) - dangerous challenge on Bateman.
WARRIORS: 1 Sam Tomkins; 22 Liam Marshall; 3 Dan Sarginson; 4 Oliver Gildart; 5 Joe Burgess; 6 George Williams; 7 Sam Powell; 13 Sean O'Loughlin (C); 9 Thomas Leuluai; 10 Ben Flower; 19 Willie Isa; 12 Liam Farrell; 14 John Bateman. Subs (all used): 8 Tony Clubb; 15 Ryan Sutton; 25 Romain Navarrete; 30 Gabe Hamlin.
Tries: Sarginson (47), Gildart (53), Burgess (58), Farrell (60), S Tomkins (65), Clubb (78);
Goals: S Tomkins 4/6.
Rugby Leaguer & League Express Men of the Match: *Dragons:* Tony Gigot; *Warriors:* Sean O'Loughlin.
Penalty count: 8-14; **Half-time:** 15-0;
Referee: Liam Moore; **Attendance:** 8,640.

HULL KINGSTON ROVERS 31 WIDNES VIKINGS 12

ROVERS: 28 Will Dagger; 5 Ryan Shaw; 4 Andrew Heffernan; 3 Thomas Minns; 36 Justin Carney; 7 Danny McGuire; 19 Tommy Lee; 21 Robbie Mulhern; 9 Shaun Lunt (C); 10 Mose Masoe; 34 Danny Tickle; 11 Maurice Blair; 13 Ben Kavanagh. Subs (all used): 24 Chris Atkin; 17 Chris Clarkson; 12 James Greenwood; 15 James Donaldson.
Tries: J Carney (31, 80), Heffernan (33), Tickle (62), Greenwood (72); **Goals:** Shaw 5/6;
Field goal: McGuire (69).
Sin bin: Clarkson (45) - dangerous challenge.
VIKINGS: 1 Rhys Hanbury; 22 Ryan Ince; 24 Ed Chamberlain; 30 Keanan Brand (D); 4 Charly Runciman; 6 Joe Mellor (C); 15 Danny Craven; 10 Alex Gerrard; 33 Aaron Heremaia; 8 Gil Dudson; 12 Matt Whitley; 17 Sam Wilde; 11 Chris Houston (C). Subs (all used): 19 Greg Burke; 36 Wellington Albert; 16 Tom Olbison; 21 Jordan Johnstone.
Tries: Ince (47), Mellor (49); **Goals:** Chamberlain 2/3.
Sin bin: Houston (77) - holding down.
Rugby Leaguer & League Express Men of the Match: *Rovers:* Justin Carney; *Vikings:* Joe Mellor.
Penalty count: 8-9; **Half-time:** 10-2;
Referee: James Child; **Attendance:** 7,260.

Sunday 8th April 2018

HUDDERSFIELD GIANTS 28 CASTLEFORD TIGERS 40

GIANTS: 28 Jared Simpson; 31 Louis Senior; 4 Jordan Turner; 5 Aaron Murphy; 33 Innes Senior; 6 Lee Gaskell; 15 Jordan Rankin; 8 Sebastine Ikahihifo; 21 Adam O'Brien; 17 Ukuma Ta'ai; 14 Dale Ferguson; 12 Michael Lawrence (C); 19 Daniel Smith. Subs (all used): 18 Paul Clough; 10 Shannon Wakeman; 16 Oliver Roberts; 27 Matty English.
Tries: Ta'ai (35), Smith (46), I Senior (56, 67), Wakeman (74); **Goals:** Rankin 4/5.
Sin bin: Turner (26) - dissent.
TIGERS: 21 Jake Trueman; 2 Greg Minikin; 3 Jake Webster; 4 Michael Shenton (C); 5 Greg Eden; 1 Ben Roberts; 6 Jamie Ellis; 32 Liam Watts; 9 Paul McShane; 10 Grant Millington; 11 Oliver Holmes; 16 Joe Wardle; 17 Alex Foster. Subs (all used): 8 Junior Moors; 12 Mike McMeeken; 13 Adam Milner; 19 Gadwin Springer.
Tries: McShane (4), Minikin (12), Foster (24, 73), Webster (29), Eden (39), Shenton (79); **Goals:** Ellis 6/8.
Sin bin: Milner (66) - punching O'Brien.
Rugby Leaguer & League Express Men of the Match: *Giants:* Innes Senior; *Tigers:* Alex Foster.
Penalty count: 8-10; **Half-time:** 6-28;
Referee: Ben Thaler; **Attendance:** 5,946.

WAKEFIELD TRINITY 26 LEEDS RHINOS 28

TRINITY: 21 Max Jowitt; 5 Ben Jones-Bishop; 4 Reece Lyne; 3 Bill Tupou; 2 Tom Johnstone; 6 Jacob Miller; 25 Ryan Hampshire; 20 Keegan Hirst; 13 Tyler Randell; 17 Craig Huby; 11 Matty Ashurst; 19 James Batchelor; 14 Justin Horo. Subs (all used): 9 Kyle Wood; 16 Tinirau Arona; 15 Pauli Pauli; 12 Danny Kirmond (C).
Tries: Miller (24), Wood (30), Ashurst (55), Jowitt (79);
Goals: Hampshire 5/5.
RHINOS: 1 Ashton Golding; 2 Tom Briscoe; 3 Kallum Watkins (C); 22 Ash Handley; 5 Ryan Hall; 4 Liam Sutcliffe; 7 Richie Myler; 11 Jamie Jones-Buchanan; 9 Matt Parcell; 10 Brad Singleton; 13 Stevie Ward; 30 Josh Walters; 12 Carl Ablett. Subs (all used): 14 Brad Dwyer; 19 Brett Ferres; 28 Mikolaj Oledzki; 27 Cameron Smith.
Tries: Watkins (16, 62), Handley (47), Singleton (65), Walters (75); **Goals:** Watkins 4/5.
Rugby Leaguer & League Express Men of the Match: *Trinity:* Matty Ashurst; *Rhinos:* Kallum Watkins.
Penalty count: 5-4; **Half-time:** 12-6;
Referee: Chris Kendall; **Attendance:** 6,767.

ROUND 11

Thursday 12th April 2018

WIDNES VIKINGS 20 HULL FC 39

VIKINGS: 1 Rhys Hanbury; 4 Charly Runciman; 12 Matt Whitley; 14 Chris Dean; 22 Ryan Ince; 7 Tom Gilmore; 6 Joe Mellor (C); 19 Greg Burke; 33 Aaron Heremaia; 26 Ted Chapelhow; 17 Sam Wilde; 16 Tom Olbison; 11 Chris Houston (C). Subs (all used): 20 Macgraff Leuluai; 29 Owen Farnworth; 21 Jordan Johnstone; 25 Jay Chapelhow.
Tries: Wilde (21), Olbison (51, 72); **Goals:** Gilmore 4/4.
HULL FC: 1 Jamie Shaul; 2 Bureta Faraimo; 14 Jake Connor; 4 Josh Griffin; 5 Fetuli Talanoa; 6 Albert Kelly; 7 Marc Sneyd; 8 Scott Taylor; 9 Danny Houghton (C); 23 Mickey Paea; 17 Danny Washbrook; 27 Jack Downs; 13 Josh Bowden. Subs: 15 Chris Green; 29 Masi Matongo; 3 Carlos Tuimavave (not used); 22 Jez Litten.
Tries: Washbrook (9), Faraimo (14), Matongo (54), Griffin (57, 76), Talanoa (60), Shaul (78);
Goals: Sneyd 5/7; **Field goal:** Sneyd (66).
Rugby Leaguer & League Express Men of the Match: *Vikings:* Tom Olbison; *Hull FC:* Josh Griffin.
Penalty count: 9-7; **Half-time:** 8-12;
Referee: Chris Kendall; **Attendance:** 3,733.

Friday 13th April 2018

LEEDS RHINOS 8 WIGAN WARRIORS 9

RHINOS: 1 Ashton Golding; 2 Tom Briscoe; 3 Kallum Watkins (C); 22 Ash Handley; 5 Ryan Hall; 6 Joel Moon; 7 Richie Myler; 15 Brett Delaney; 9 Matt Parcell; 10 Brad Singleton; 11 Jamie Jones-Buchanan; 13 Stevie Ward; 12

Carl Ablett. Subs (all used): 8 Adam Cuthbertson; 28 Mikolaj Oledzki; 27 Cameron Smith; 16 Anthony Mullally.
Try: T Briscoe (21); **Goals:** Watkins 2/2.
WARRIORS: 1 Sam Tomkins; 22 Liam Marshall; 4 Oliver Gildart; 14 John Bateman; 5 Joe Burgess; 6 George Williams; 7 Sam Powell; 8 Tony Clubb; 9 Thomas Leuluai; 25 Romain Navarrete; 19 Willie Isa; 12 Liam Farrell; 13 Sean O'Loughlin (C). Subs (all used): 15 Ryan Sutton; 3 Dan Sarginson; 17 Taulima Tautai; 11 Joel Tomkins.
Try: Gildart (71); **Goals:** S Tomkins 2/2;
Field goal: S Tomkins (77).
Sin bin: Powell (42) - dangerous contact on Golding.
Rugby Leaguer & League Express Men of the Match: *Rhinos:* Ashton Golding; *Warriors:* John Bateman.
Penalty count: 11-13; **Half-time:** 6-0;
Referee: Ben Thaler; **Attendance:** 12,225.

Saturday 14th April 2018

WARRINGTON WOLVES 40
HULL KINGSTON ROVERS 26

WOLVES: 1 Stefan Ratchford; 2 Tom Lineham; 3 Bryson Goodwin; 4 Ryan Atkins; 27 Josh Charnley; 6 Kevin Brown; 7 Tyrone Roberts; 8 Chris Hill (C); 9 Daryl Clark; 10 Mike Cooper; 11 Ben Currie; 12 Jack Hughes; 34 Ben Westwood. Subs (all used): 17 Joe Philbin; 14 Dominic Crosby; 16 Sitaleki Akauola; 22 Morgan Smith.
Tries: Cooper (21), Hughes (25, 39), Currie (30), Lineham (64), Ratchford (68), Atkins (72);
Goals: Ratchford 6/7.
ROVERS: 1 Adam Quinlan; 5 Ryan Shaw; 22 Liam Salter; 2 Junior Vaivai (D); 36 Justin Carney; 7 Danny McGuire; 24 Chris Atkin; 21 Robbie Mulhern; 9 Shaun Lunt (C); 10 Mose Masoe; 11 Maurice Blair; 34 Danny Tickle; 13 Ben Kavanagh. Subs (all used): 8 Nick Scruton; 20 Matty Marsh; 12 James Greenwood; 15 James Donaldson.
Tries: Blair (42), Donaldson (46), Atkin (49), McGuire (76);
Goals: Shaw 5/5.
Rugby Leaguer & League Express Men of the Match: *Wolves:* Daryl Clark; *Rovers:* Junior Vaivai.
Penalty count: 8-7; **Half-time:** 22-2;
Referee: Jack Smith; **Attendance:** 9,305.

Sunday 15th April 2018

HUDDERSFIELD GIANTS 12 SALFORD RED DEVILS 30

GIANTS: 15 Jordan Rankin; 23 Darnell McIntosh; 4 Jordan Turner; 5 Aaron Murphy; 33 Innes Senior; 6 Lee Gaskell; 7 Danny Brough (C); 8 Sebastine Ikahihifo; 9 Kruise Leeming; 18 Paul Clough; 16 Oliver Roberts; 17 Ukuma Ta'ai; 19 Daniel Smith. Subs (all used): 13 Ryan Hinchcliffe; 20 Adam Walne; 27 Matty English; 22 Alex Mellor.
Tries: I Senior (22), Roberts (55); **Goals:** Brough 2/2.
Dismissal: Brough (75) - dissent.
RED DEVILS: 5 Niall Evalds; 24 Jake Bibby; 4 Junior Sa'u; 3 Kris Welham; 2 Greg Johnson; 6 Robert Lui; 7 Jack Littlejohn; 18 Ben Nakubuwai; 9 Logan Tomkins; 23 Lee Mossop; 12 Weller Hauraki; 11 Josh Jones; 13 Mark Flanagan. Subs (all used): 14 Lama Tasi; 8 Craig Kopczak (C); 15 Ryan Lannon; 19 Josh Wood.
Tries: Flanagan (12), Nakubuwai (14), Hauraki (50), Bibby (77, 79); **Goals:** Lui 5/7.
Rugby Leaguer & League Express Men of the Match: *Giants:* Aaron Murphy; *Red Devils:* Robert Lui.
Penalty count: 9-10; **Half-time:** 6-12;
Referee: James Child; **Attendance:** 4,385.

WAKEFIELD TRINITY 24 ST HELENS 20

TRINITY: 1 Scott Grix; 5 Ben Jones-Bishop; 4 Reece Lyne; 18 Joe Arundel; 3 Bill Tupou; 6 Jacob Miller; 7 Liam Finn; 17 Craig Huby; 13 Tyler Randell; 20 Keegan Hirst; 11 Matty Ashurst; 12 Danny Kirmond (C); 14 Justin Horo. Subs (all used): 9 Kyle Wood; 10 Anthony England; 16 Tinirau Arona; 22 Jordan Baldwinson.
Tries: Jones-Bishop (6), Lyne (13), Horo (18), Tupou (23);
Goals: Finn 4/5.
Sin bin: Randell (75) - high tackle on Lomax.
SAINTS: 23 Ben Barba; 2 Tommy Makinson; 3 Ryan Morgan; 4 Mark Percival; 19 Regan Grace; 1 Jonny Lomax; 18 Danny Richardson; 10 Kyle Amor; 7 Matty Smith; 16 Luke Thompson; 17 Dominique Peyroux; 11 Zeb Taia; 12 Jon Wilkin (C). Subs (all used): 6 Theo Fages; 13 Louie McCarthy-Scarsbrook; 14 Luke Douglas; 15 Morgan Knowles.
Tries: Percival (3, 40), Makinson (26), Douglas (47);
Goals: Richardson 2/4.
Sin bin: Percival (77) - dissent.
Rugby Leaguer & League Express Men of the Match: *Trinity:* Reece Lyne; *Saints:* Luke Thompson.
Penalty count: 9-7; **Half-time:** 22-14;
Referee: Gareth Hewer; **Attendance:** 5,231.

CASTLEFORD TIGERS 41 CATALANS DRAGONS 0

TIGERS: 21 Jake Trueman; 2 Greg Minikin; 3 Jake Webster; 4 Michael Shenton (C); 26 James Clare; 1 Ben Roberts; 7 Luke Gale; 32 Liam Watts; 9 Paul McShane; 14 Nathan Massey; 16 Joe Wardle; 11 Oliver Holmes; 17 Alex Foster. Subs (all used): 10 Grant Millington; 12 Mike McMeeken; 13 Adam Milner; 18 Matt Cook.
Tries: McShane (15, 46), Shenton (20), Holmes (24, 68), Clare (48), Wardle (65); **Goals:** Gale 6/7;
Field goal: Gale (40).
DRAGONS: 20 Lewis Tierney; 2 Jodie Broughton; 3 Iain Thornley; 1 David Mead; 5 Fouad Yaha; 31 Tony Gigot; 6 Samisoni Langi; 15 Mickael Simon; 19 Michael McIlorum; 10 Sam Moa; 21 Benjamin Jullien; 12 Benjamin Garcia; 17 Jason Baitieri. Subs (all used): 8 Remi Casty (C); 14 Julian Bousquet; 18 Thibaut Margalet; 24 Alrix Da Costa.
Rugby Leaguer & League Express Men of the Match: *Tigers:* Luke Gale; *Dragons:* Benjamin Garcia.
Penalty count: 7-5; **Half-time:** 19-0;
Referee: Scott Mikalauskas; **Attendance:** 7,137.

ROUND 12

Thursday 19th April 2018

HULL FC 19 LEEDS RHINOS 18

HULL FC: 1 Jamie Shaul; 2 Bureta Faraimo; 14 Jake Connor; 4 Josh Griffin; 5 Fetuli Talanoa; 6 Albert Kelly; 7 Marc Sneyd; 8 Scott Taylor; 9 Danny Houghton (C); 13 Josh Bowden; 12 Mark Minichiello; 21 Sika Manu; 11 Dean Hadley. Subs (all used): 3 Carlos Tuimavave; 23 Mickey Paea; 26 Jordan Lane; 29 Masi Matongo.
Tries: Connor (13, 44), Faraimo (34), Tuimavave (71);
Goals: Sneyd 1/4; **Field goal:** Sneyd (76).
RHINOS: 1 Ashton Golding; 2 Tom Briscoe; 3 Kallum Watkins (C); 22 Ash Handley; 5 Ryan Hall; 6 Joel Moon; 7 Richie Myler; 8 Adam Cuthbertson; 9 Matt Parcell; 15 Brett Delaney; 11 Jamie Jones-Buchanan; 13 Stevie Ward; 12 Carl Ablett. Subs (all used): 16 Anthony Mullally; 19 Brett Ferres; 27 Cameron Smith; 28 Mikolaj Oledzki.
Tries: Hall (51), Moon (60), Parcell (62);
Goals: Watkins 3/3.
Rugby Leaguer & League Express Men of the Match: *Hull FC:* Albert Kelly; *Rhinos:* Matt Parcell.
Penalty count: 10-11; **Half-time:** 8-0;
Referee: Ben Thaler; **Attendance:** 11,391.

Friday 20th April 2018

WIGAN WARRIORS 28 CASTLEFORD TIGERS 12

WARRIORS: 1 Sam Tomkins; 22 Liam Marshall; 14 John Bateman; 4 Oliver Gildart; 5 Joe Burgess; 6 George Williams; 7 Sam Powell; 8 Tony Clubb; 9 Thomas Leuluai; 10 Ben Flower; 19 Willie Isa; 12 Liam Farrell; 13 Sean O'Loughlin (C). Subs (all used): 11 Joel Tomkins; 15 Ryan Sutton; 17 Taulima Tautai; 25 Romain Navarrete.
Tries: Gildart (18, 42), Farrell (25), Williams (59), Clubb (77);
Goals: S Tomkins 4/7.
TIGERS: 21 Jake Trueman; 2 Greg Minikin; 3 Jake Webster; 4 Michael Shenton (C); 20 Garry Lo (D); 1 Ben Roberts; 7 Luke Gale; 32 Liam Watts; 9 Paul McShane; 14 Nathan Massey; 16 Joe Wardle; 11 Oliver Holmes; 17 Alex Foster. Subs (all used): 10 Grant Millington; 12 Mike McMeeken; 13 Adam Milner; 18 Matt Cook.
Tries: Holmes (33), Lo (38); **Goals:** Gale 2/3.
Rugby Leaguer & League Express Men of the Match: *Warriors:* Sam Tomkins; *Tigers:* Garry Lo.
Penalty count: 11-9; **Half-time:** 14-12;
Referee: Robert Hicks; **Attendance:** 11,866.

SALFORD RED DEVILS 38 WAKEFIELD TRINITY 4

RED DEVILS: 5 Niall Evalds; 2 Greg Johnson; 4 Junior Sa'u; 3 Kris Welham; 24 Jake Bibby; 6 Robert Lui; 7 Jack Littlejohn; 18 Ben Nakubuwai; 9 Logan Tomkins; 16 Luke Burgess; 10 George Griffin; 17 Tyrone McCarthy; 13 Mark Flanagan. Subs (all used): 15 Ryan Lannon; 8 Craig Kopczak (C); 26 Daniel Murray; 19 Josh Wood.
Tries: Sa'u (2), McCarthy (48), Lannon (51), Bibby (57, 74), Griffin (69), Johnson (76);
Goals: Lui 2/2, McCarthy 2/4, Littlejohn 1/3.
TRINITY: 1 Scott Grix; 5 Ben Jones-Bishop; 4 Reece Lyne; 18 Joe Arundel; 3 Bill Tupou; 6 Jacob Miller; 7 Liam Finn; 17 Craig Huby; 13 Tyler Randell; 20 Keegan Hirst; 11 Matty Ashurst; 12 Danny Kirmond (C); 14 Justin Horo. Subs (all used): 9 Kyle Wood; 10 Anthony England; 16 Tinirau Arona; 22 Jordan Baldwinson.
Try: Arundel (55); **Goals:** Finn 0/1.
Sin bin: Lyne (45) - professional foul.
Rugby Leaguer & League Express Men of the Match: *Red Devils:* George Griffin; *Trinity:* Matty Ashurst.
Penalty count: 8-7; **Half-time:** 8-0;
Referee: James Child; **Attendance:** 2,686.

ST HELENS 66 HUDDERSFIELD GIANTS 4

SAINTS: 23 Ben Barba; 2 Tommy Makinson; 3 Ryan Morgan; 30 Matthew Costello (D); 19 Regan Grace; 1 Jonny Lomax; 18 Danny Richardson; 10 Kyle Amor; 7 Matty Smith; 16 Luke Thompson; 17 Dominique Peyroux; 15 Morgan Knowles; 12 Jon Wilkin (C). Subs (all used): 6 Theo Fages; 13 Louie McCarthy-Scarsbrook; 14 Luke Douglas; 20 Matty Lees.
Tries: Lomax (13, 30, 70), Barba (17, 36), McCarthy-Scarsbrook (32, 38), Morgan (47, 53), Richardson (67), Grace (73), Amor (75);
Goals: Richardson 9/12.
GIANTS: 28 Jared Simpson; 23 Darnell McIntosh; 4 Jordan Turner; 5 Aaron Murphy; 33 Innes Senior; 26 Sam Wood; 15 Jordan Rankin; 25 Colton Roche; 9 Kruise Leeming; 18 Paul Clough; 16 Oliver Roberts; 17 Ukuma Ta'ai; 19 Daniel Smith. Subs (all used): 13 Ryan Hinchcliffe (C); 20 Adam Walne; 21 Adam O'Brien; 22 Alex Mellor.
Try: Turner (64); **Goals:** Rankin 0/1.
Rugby Leaguer & League Express Men of the Match: *Saints:* Jonny Lomax; *Giants:* Jordan Turner.
Penalty count: 2-4; **Half-time:** 34-0;
Referee: Scott Mikalauskas; **Attendance:** 10,278.

ROUND 13

Thursday 26th April 2018

SALFORD RED DEVILS 10 ST HELENS 60

RED DEVILS: 5 Niall Evalds; 2 Greg Johnson; 4 Junior Sa'u; 3 Kris Welham; 24 Jake Bibby; 28 Jake Shorrocks; 7 Jack Littlejohn; 23 Lee Mossop (C); 9 Logan Tomkins; 16 Luke Burgess; 10 George Griffin; 15 Ryan Lannon; 13 Mark Flanagan. Subs (all used): 14 Lama Tasi; 8 Craig Kopczak; 19 Josh Wood; 17 Tyrone McCarthy.
Tries: McCarthy (28), Welham (80); **Goals:** Shorrocks 1/2.
Sin bin: Sa'u (63) - use of the arm on Morgan.
SAINTS: 23 Ben Barba; 2 Tommy Makinson; 3 Ryan Morgan; 4 Mark Percival; 19 Regan Grace; 1 Jonny Lomax; 18 Danny Richardson; 10 Kyle Amor; 7 Matty Smith; 16 Luke Thompson; 17 Dominique Peyroux; 11 Zeb Taia; 12 Jon Wilkin (C). Subs (all used): 6 Theo Fages; 13 Louie McCarthy-Scarsbrook; 20 Matty Lees; 15 Morgan Knowles.
Tries: Makinson (4), Peyroux (14), Barba (16, 35, 60), Morgan (22, 77), Grace (40, 54), Percival (56), Fages (74);
Goals: Richardson 8/11.
Dismissal: Lees (38) - high tackle on Evalds.
Rugby Leaguer & League Express Men of the Match: *Red Devils:* Logan Tomkins; *Saints:* Ben Barba.
Penalty count: 7-6; **Half time:** 6-32;
Referee: Chris Kendall; **Attendance:** 3,105.

Friday 27th April 2018

CASTLEFORD TIGERS 24 WAKEFIELD TRINITY 4

TIGERS: 21 Jake Trueman; 2 Greg Minikin; 3 Jake Webster; 16 Joe Wardle; 4 Michael Shenton (C); 6 Jamie Ellis; 7 Luke Gale; 32 Liam Watts; 9 Paul McShane; 15 Jesse Sene-Lefao; 11 Oliver Holmes; 12 Mike McMeeken; 13 Adam Milner. Subs (all used): 8 Junior Moors; 10 Grant Millington; 18 Matt Cook; 19 Gadwin Springer.
Tries: Minikin (27), Milner (55), McShane (76);
Goals: Gale 3/3, Ellis 3/5.
TRINITY: 21 Max Jowitt; 5 Ben Jones-Bishop; 4 Reece Lyne; 3 Bill Tupou; 2 Tom Johnstone; 6 Jacob Miller (C); 25 Ryan Hampshire; 10 Anthony England; 9 Kyle Wood; 20 Keegan Hirst; 11 Matty Ashurst; 15 Pauli Pauli; 23 Chris Annakin. Subs (all used): 13 Tyler Randell; 16 Tinirau Arona; 17 Craig Huby; 19 James Batchelor.
Try: Randell (36); **Goals:** Hampshire 0/1.
Rugby Leaguer & League Express Men of the Match: *Tigers:* Paul McShane; *Trinity:* Tyler Randell.
Penalty count: 9-7; **Half-time:** 10-4;
Referee: Robert Hicks; **Attendance:** 7,485.

WARRINGTON WOLVES 38 HUDDERSFIELD GIANTS 4

WOLVES: 1 Stefan Ratchford; 2 Tom Lineham; 3 Bryson Goodwin; 4 Ryan Atkins; 27 Josh Charnley; 6 Kevin Brown; 7 Tyrone Roberts; 8 Chris Hill (C); 9 Daryl Clark; 16 Sitaleki Akauola; 20 Harvey Livett; 12 Jack Hughes; 34 Ben Westwood. Subs (all used): 17 Joe Philbin; 13 Ben Murdoch-Masila; 15 Declan Patton; 19 George King.
Tries: Charnley (22, 58, 63), Ratchford (32, 68), Lineham (38), Livett (70), Philbin (74);
Goals: Goodwin 1/3, Ratchford 1/3, Livett 1/2.
GIANTS: 1 Jake Mamo; 23 Darnell McIntosh; 4 Jordan Turner; 5 Aaron Murphy; 28 Jared Simpson; 26 Sam Wood; 15 Jordan Rankin; 8 Sebastine Ikahihifo; 21 Adam O'Brien; 18 Paul Clough; 17 Ukuma Ta'ai; 12 Michael Lawrence; 13 Ryan Hinchcliffe (C). Subs (all used): 9 Kruise Leeming; 16 Oliver Roberts; 19 Daniel Smith; 24 Tyler Dickinson.
Try: McIntosh (26); **Goals:** Rankin 0/1.

Catalans' Tony Gigot *(right)* celebrates his late winning field goal against Hull FC, flanked by Benjamin Garcia

Rugby Leaguer & League Express Men of the Match:
Wolves: Stefan Ratchford; *Giants:* Ukuma Ta'ai.
Penalty count: 7-5; **Half-time:** 14-4.
Referee: Tom Grant; **Attendance:** 8,792.

WIDNES VIKINGS 24 WIGAN WARRIORS 32

VIKINGS: 1 Rhys Hanbury; 22 Ryan Ince; 38 Jimmy Keinhorst (D); 24 Ed Chamberlain; 5 Patrick Ah Van; 7 Tom Gilmore (C); 15 Danny Craven; 10 Alex Gerrard; 9 Lloyd White; 19 Greg Burke; 12 Matt Whitley; 17 Sam Wilde; 16 Tom Olbison. Subs (all used): 20 Macgraff Leuluai; 13 Hep Cahill; 25 Jay Chapelhow; 21 Jordan Johnstone.
Tries: Olbison (17), J Chapelhow (34), Ince (36, 74);
Goals: Gilmore 4/5.
WARRIORS: 20 Morgan Escare; 22 Liam Marshall; 3 Dan Sarginson; 4 Oliver Gildart; 5 Joe Burgess; 6 George Williams; 7 Sam Powell; 8 Tony Clubb; 9 Thomas Leuluai; 25 Romain Navarrete; 15 Ryan Sutton; 19 Willie Isa; 13 Sean O'Loughlin (C). Subs (all used): 23 Josh Ganson; 11 Joel Tomkins; 30 Gabe Hamlin; 17 Taulima Tautai.
Tries: Gildart (12), Burgess (50), Escare (52), Isa (55), Sutton (72), Tautai (79); **Goals:** Escare 0/2, Powell 4/4.
Sin bin: Leuluai (36) - professional foul.
Rugby Leaguer & League Express Men of the Match:
Vikings: Tom Gilmore; *Warriors:* Ryan Sutton.
Penalty count: 9-7; **Half-time:** 18-4;
Referee: Ben Thaler; **Attendance:** 5,668.

Saturday 28th April 2018

CATALANS DRAGONS 25 HULL FC 24

DRAGONS: 31 Tony Gigot; 2 Jodie Broughton; 1 David Mead; 4 Brayden Wiliame; 20 Lewis Tierney; 6 Samisoni Langi; 33 Josh Drinkwater (D); 8 Remi Casty (C); 19 Michael McIlorum; 15 Mickael Simon; 21 Benjamin Jullien; 12 Benjamin Garcia; 13 Greg Bird. Subs (all used): 10 Sam Moa; 11 Jason Baitieri; 23 Antoni Maria.
Tries: Wiliame (19), Drinkwater (42), Gigot (44);
Goals: Drinkwater 6/6; **Field goal:** Gigot (79).
Sin bin: McIlorum (64) - fighting.
HULL FC: 28 Hakim Miloudi; 2 Bureta Faraimo; 14 Jake Connor; 4 Josh Griffin; 5 Fetuli Talanoa; 6 Albert Kelly; 16 Jordan Abdull; 8 Scott Taylor; 9 Danny Houghton (C); 13 Josh Bowden; 21 Sika Manu; 12 Mark Minichiello; 11

Dean Hadley. Subs (all used): 26 Jordan Lane; 29 Masi Matongo; 23 Mickey Paea; 3 Carlos Tuimavave.
Tries: Taylor (4, 50), Miloudi (21); **Goals:** Connor 6/6.
Sin bin: Connor (64) - fighting.
Rugby Leaguer & League Express Men of the Match:
Dragons: Tony Gigot; *Hull FC:* Scott Taylor.
Penalty count: 9-12; **Half-time:** 8-14;
Referee: James Child; **Attendance:** 8,823.

Sunday 29th April 2018

HULL KINGSTON ROVERS 18 LEEDS RHINOS 20

ROVERS: 1 Adam Quinlan; 5 Ryan Shaw; 12 James Greenwood; 2 Junior Vaivai; 36 Justin Carney; 7 Danny McGuire (C); 19 Tommy Lee; 21 Robbie Mulhern; 24 Chris Atkin; 10 Mose Masoe; 17 Chris Clarkson; 34 Danny Tickle; 13 Ben Kavanagh. Subs (all used): 8 Nick Scruton; 15 James Donaldson; 20 Matty Marsh; 30 Joe Cator.
Tries: Mulhern (12), Masoe (30); **Goals:** Shaw 5/5.
Sin bin: Masoe (43) - high tackle.
RHINOS: 1 Ashton Golding; 2 Tom Briscoe; 3 Kallum Watkins (C); 22 Ash Handley; 5 Ryan Hall; 6 Joel Moon; 7 Richie Myler; 8 Adam Cuthbertson; 9 Matt Parcell; 10 Brad Singleton; 11 Jamie Jones-Buchanan; 13 Stevie Ward; 12 Carl Ablett. Subs (all used): 15 Brett Delaney; 16 Anthony Mullally; 19 Brett Ferres; 28 Mikolaj Oledzki.
Tries: Moon (20), Jones-Buchanan (25), Hall (48);
Goals: Watkins 4/4.
Rugby Leaguer & League Express Men of the Match:
Rovers: Robbie Mulhern; *Rhinos:* Anthony Mullally.
Penalty count: 9-4; **Half-time:** 18-12;
Referee: Scott Mikalauskas; **Attendance:** 9,095.

ROUND 14

Thursday 3rd May 2018

ST HELENS 26 CATALANS DRAGONS 12

SAINTS: 1 Jonny Lomax; 2 Tommy Makinson; 3 Ryan Morgan; 4 Mark Percival; 19 Regan Grace; 6 Theo Fages; 18 Danny Richardson; 10 Kyle Amor; 9 James Roby (C); 16 Luke Thompson; 17 Dominique Peyroux; 11 Zeb Taia; 12 Jon Wilkin. Subs (all used): 7 Matty Smith; 13 Louie McCarthy-Scarsbrook; 14 Luke Douglas; 15 Morgan Knowles.

Tries: Lomax (10), Makinson (14), Knowles (33), Grace (44, 69); **Goals:** Richardson 3/5.
DRAGONS: 31 Tony Gigot; 2 Jodie Broughton; 16 Vincent Duport; 4 Brayden Wiliame; 20 Lewis Tierney; 6 Samisoni Langi; 33 Josh Drinkwater; 8 Remi Casty (C); 19 Michael McIlorum; 14 Julian Bousquet; 11 Louis Anderson; 21 Benjamin Jullien; 13 Greg Bird. Subs (all used): 10 Sam Moa; 17 Jason Baitieri; 23 Antoni Maria; 24 Alrix Da Costa.
Tries: Wiliame (31), Broughton (45), Tierney (76);
Goals: Drinkwater 0/3.
Rugby Leaguer & League Express Men of the Match:
Saints: Jonny Lomax; *Dragons:* Tony Gigot.
Penalty count: 11-7; **Half time:** 16-4;
Referee: Robert Hicks; **Attendance:** 9,138.

Friday 4th May 2018

HUDDERSFIELD GIANTS 28 WIDNES VIKINGS 18

GIANTS: 15 Jordan Rankin; 23 Darnell McIntosh; 26 Sam Wood; 29 Jake Wardle (D); 1 Jake Mamo; 4 Jordan Turner; 34 Oliver Russell (D); 8 Sebastine Ikahihifo; 21 Adam O'Brien; 18 Paul Clough; 22 Alex Mellor; 17 Ukuma Ta'ai; 13 Ryan Hinchcliffe (C). Subs (all used): 9 Kruise Leeming; 12 Michael Lawrence; 19 Daniel Smith; 27 Matty English.
Tries: Wardle (13, 44), Wood (34), Ta'ai (62), Mellor (73);
Goals: Wood 4/5.
Sin bin: Wardle (68) - dangerous challenge on Hanbury.
VIKINGS: 1 Rhys Hanbury; 22 Ryan Ince; 38 Jimmy Keinhorst; 4 Charly Runciman; 5 Patrick Ah Van; 7 Tom Gilmore (C); 15 Danny Craven; 10 Alex Gerrard; 9 Lloyd White; 19 Greg Burke; 12 Matt Whitley; 17 Sam Wilde; 16 Tom Olbison. Subs (all used): 13 Hep Cahill; 20 Macgraff Leuluai; 33 Aaron Heremaia; 36 Wellington Albert.
Tries: Craven (28), Ince (53), Gilmore (70);
Goals: Gilmore 3/3.
Rugby Leaguer & League Express Men of the Match:
Giants: Jake Wardle; *Vikings:* Tom Gilmore.
Penalty count: 5-8; **Half-time:** 10-6;
Referee: Liam Moore; **Attendance:** 4,645.

LEEDS RHINOS 22 WARRINGTON WOLVES 33

RHINOS: 1 Ashton Golding; 2 Tom Briscoe; 3 Kallum Watkins (C); 22 Ash Handley; 5 Ryan Hall; 6 Joel Moon; 7 Richie Myler; 8 Adam Cuthbertson; 19 Brett Ferres; 10

Brad Singleton; 11 Jamie Jones-Buchanan; 13 Stevie Ward; 12 Carl Ablett. Subs (all used): 9 Matt Parcell; 16 Anthony Mullally; 21 Nathaniel Peteru; 30 Josh Walters.
Tries: Golding (32), Moon (46), Hall (55), Ablett (59);
Goals: Watkins 3/4.
WOLVES: 1 Stefan Ratchford; 2 Tom Lineham; 3 Bryson Goodwin; 4 Ryan Atkins; 27 Josh Charnley; 6 Kevin Brown; 7 Tyrone Roberts; 8 Chris Hill (C); 9 Daryl Clark; 10 Mike Cooper; 12 Jack Hughes; 20 Harvey Livett; 34 Ben Westwood. Subs: 17 Joe Philbin; 13 Ben Murdoch-Masila; 16 Sitaleki Akauola; 15 Declan Patton (not used).
Tries: K Brown (6), Livett (18, 69, 72), Atkins (63), Murdoch-Masila (79); **Goals:** Goodwin 1/3, Ratchford 3/4;
Field goal: Roberts (39).
Rugby Leaguer & League Express Men of the Match:
Rhinos: Stevie Ward; *Wolves:* Harvey Livett.
Penalty count: 7-4; **Half time:** 4-11;
Referee: Ben Thaler; **Attendance:** 11,749.

WIGAN WARRIORS 30 SALFORD RED DEVILS 0

WARRIORS: 1 Sam Tomkins (C); 2 Tom Davies; 3 Dan Sarginson; 4 Oliver Gildart; 22 Liam Marshall; 6 George Williams; 7 Sam Powell; 25 Romain Navarrete; 9 Thomas Leuluai; 10 Ben Flower; 19 Willie Isa; 14 John Bateman; 11 Joel Tomkins. Subs (all used): 8 Tony Clubb; 15 Ryan Sutton; 17 Taulima Tautai; 20 Morgan Escare.
Tries: Gildart (22), Clubb (24), Williams (29), S Tomkins (57, 69), Bateman (75); **Goals:** S Tomkins 3/6.
RED DEVILS: 22 Derrell Olpherts; 2 Greg Johnson; 4 Junior Sa'u; 3 Kris Welham; 24 Jake Bibby; 28 Jake Shorrocks; 7 Jack Littlejohn; 8 Craig Kopczak; 9 Logan Tomkins; 27 Gavin Bennion (D); 12 Weller Hauraki (C); 15 Ryan Lannon; 26 Daniel Murray. Subs (all used): 14 Lama Tasi; 16 Luke Burgess; 17 Tyrone McCarthy; 25 Levy Nzoungou (D).
Rugby Leaguer & League Express Men of the Match:
Warriors: Sam Tomkins; *Red Devils:* Logan Tomkins.
Penalty count: 7-8; **Half-time:** 18-0;
Referee: Chris Kendall; **Attendance:** 10,733.

Saturday 5th May 2018

HULL FC 36 CASTLEFORD TIGERS 12

HULL FC: 1 Jamie Shaul; 2 Bureta Faraimo; 4 Josh Griffin; 3 Carlos Tuimavave; 5 Fetuli Talanoa; 14 Jake Connor; 7 Marc Sneyd; 8 Scott Taylor; 9 Danny Houghton (C); 13 Josh Bowden; 21 Sika Manu; 12 Mark Minichiello; 11 Dean Hadley. Subs (all used): 15 Chris Green; 23 Mickey Paea; 29 Masi Matongo; 33 Joe Westerman (D2).
Tries: Manu (12, 26), Shaul (19), Faraimo (31, 65), Griffin (77); **Goals:** Sneyd 2/4, Connor 4/4.
TIGERS: 21 Jake Trueman; 2 Greg Minikin; 17 Alex Foster; 16 Joe Wardle; 4 Michael Shenton (C); 6 Jamie Ellis; 9 Paul McShane; 32 Liam Watts; 13 Adam Milner; 15 Jesse Sene-Lefao; 11 Oliver Holmes; 12 Mike McMeeken; 18 Matt Cook. Subs (all used): 8 Junior Moors; 10 Grant Millington; 19 Gadwin Springer; 33 Calum Turner (D).
Tries: McShane (16), Turner (50); **Goals:** Ellis 2/2.
Rugby Leaguer & League Express Men of the Match:
Hull FC: Jake Connor; *Tigers:* Paul McShane.
Penalty count: 10-6; **Half-time:** 20-6;
Referee: Gareth Hewer; **Attendance:** 14,623.

Sunday 6th May 2018

WAKEFIELD TRINITY 54 HULL KINGSTON ROVERS 18

TRINITY: 1 Scott Grix; 2 Tom Johnstone; 3 Bill Tupou; 4 Reece Lyne; 5 Ben Jones-Bishop; 6 Jacob Miler (C); 7 Liam Finn; 10 Anthony England; 13 Tyler Randell; 20 Keegan Hirst; 15 Pauli Pauli; 11 Matty Ashurst; 16 Tinirau Arona. Subs (all used): 9 Kyle Wood; 19 James Batchelor; 8 David Fifita; 17 Craig Huby.
Tries: Ashurst (8), Johnstone (12, 54, 77), Randell (29), Grix (47, 64), Jones-Bishop (52), England (74);
Goals: Finn 9/10.
ROVERS: 1 Adam Quinlan; 5 Ryan Shaw; 11 Maurice Blair; 2 Junior Vaivai; 22 Liam Salter; 7 Danny McGuire (C); 19 Tommy Lee; 21 Robbie Mulhern; 24 Chris Atkin; 10 Mose Masoe; 17 Chris Clarkson; 34 Danny Tickle; 13 Ben Kavanagh. Subs (all used): 38 Aaron Smith (D); 12 James Greenwood; 29 Jordan Walne; 25 Kieren Moss.
Tries: Clarkson (18), Quinlan (21), Moss (68);
Goals: Shaw 3/3.
Rugby Leaguer & League Express Men of the Match:
Trinity: Jacob Miller; *Rovers:* Adam Quinlan.
Penalty count: 11-6; **Half-time:** 18-12;
Referee: James Child; **Attendance:** 5,331.

ROUND 15 - MAGIC WEEKEND

Saturday 19th May 2018

ST HELENS 38 WIDNES VIKINGS 18

SAINTS: 23 Ben Barba; 2 Tommy Makinson; 3 Ryan Morgan; 4 Mark Percival; 19 Regan Grace; 1 Jonny Lomax; 18 Danny Richardson; 14 Luke Douglas; 9 James Roby (C); 16 Luke Thompson; 17 Dominique Peyroux; 11 Zeb Taia; 12 Jon Wilkin. Subs (all used): 6 Theo Fages; 13 Louie McCarthy-Scarsbrook; 15 Morgan Knowles; 20 Matty Lees.
Tries: Richardson (9), Percival (14), Grace (19, 78), Barba (30), Morgan (55, 63); **Goals:** Richardson 5/8.
Sin bin: Peyroux (38) - professional foul.
VIKINGS: 1 Rhys Hanbury; 5 Patrick Ah Van; 4 Charly Runciman; 38 Jimmy Keinhorst; 2 Stefan Marsh; 6 Joe Mellor (C); 33 Aaron Heremaia; 25 Jay Chapelhow; 21 Jordan Johnstone; 19 Greg Burke; 12 Matt Whitley; 17 Sam Wilde; 13 Hep Cahill. Subs (all used): 16 Tom Olbison; 20 Macgraff Leuluai; 23 Danny Walker; 36 Wellington Albert.
Tries: Whitley (6), W Albert (26), Keinhorst (40);
Goals: Marsh 3/3.
Rugby Leaguer & League Express Men of the Match:
Saints: Danny Richardson; *Vikings:* Jordan Johnstone.
Penalty count: 6-5; **Half-time:** 22-18;
Referee: Liam Moore.

WARRINGTON WOLVES 10 WIGAN WARRIORS 38

WOLVES: 1 Stefan Ratchford; 2 Tom Lineham; 3 Bryson Goodwin; 4 Ryan Atkins; 27 Josh Charnley; 6 Kevin Brown; 7 Tyrone Roberts; 8 Chris Hill (C); 9 Daryl Clark; 16 Sitaleki Akauola; 20 Harvey Livett; 12 Jack Hughes; 34 Ben Westwood. Subs (all used): 13 Ben Murdoch-Masila; 15 Declan Patton; 17 Joe Philbin; 19 George King.
Tries: Livett (12), Ratchford (35); **Goals:** Goodwin 1/2.
WARRIORS: 1 Sam Tomkins (C); 2 Tom Davies; 14 John Bateman; 4 Oliver Gildart; 22 Liam Marshall; 6 George Williams; 7 Sam Powell; 8 Tony Clubb; 9 Thomas Leuluai; 10 Ben Flower; 19 Willie Isa; 12 Liam Farrell; 11 Joel Tomkins. Subs (all used): 20 Morgan Escare; 15 Ryan Sutton; 25 Romain Navarrete; 17 Taulima Tautai.
Tries: Powell (27), S Tomkins (30), Bateman (51), Williams (53), Marshall (74), Davies (77);
Goals: S Tomkins 7/9.
Rugby Leaguer & League Express Men of the Match:
Wolves: Ben Murdoch-Masila; *Warriors:* Sam Tomkins.
Penalty count: 7-11; **Half-time:** 10-16;
Referee: Robert Hicks.

CASTLEFORD TIGERS 38 LEEDS RHINOS 10

TIGERS: 4 Michael Shenton (C); 2 Greg Minikin; 3 Jake Webster; 16 Joe Wardle; 24 Jy Hitchcox; 6 Jamie Ellis; 21 Jake Trueman; 32 Liam Watts; 9 Paul McShane; 15 Jesse Sene-Lefao; 17 Alex Foster; 12 Mike McMeeken; 13 Adam Milner. Subs (all used): 10 Grant Millington; 11 Oliver Holmes; 14 Nathan Massey; 8 Junior Moors.
Tries: Hitchcox (11), Foster (18), Moors (38), Shenton (42), Milner (62), Holmes (66); **Goals:** Ellis 7/8.
Sin bin: McMeeken (76) - professional foul.
RHINOS: 24 Jack Walker; 2 Tom Briscoe; 3 Kallum Watkins (C); 22 Ash Handley; 5 Ryan Hall; 6 Joel Moon; 7 Richie Myler; 28 Mikolaj Oledzki; 9 Matt Parcell; 21 Nathaniel Peteru; 13 Stevie Ward; 11 Jamie Jones-Buchanan; 15 Brett Delaney. Subs (all used): 8 Adam Cuthbertson; 19 Brett Ferres; 27 Cameron Smith; 14 Brad Dwyer.
Tries: Oledzki (57), Ferres (79);
Goals: Watkins 1/1, Myler 0/1.
Rugby Leaguer & League Express Men of the Match:
Tigers: Alex Foster; *Rhinos:* Jack Walker.
Penalty count: 7-8; **Half time:** 22-0;
Referee: Chris Kendall.

Attendance: 38,881 *(at St James' Park, Newcastle)*.

Sunday 20th May 2018

CATALANS DRAGONS 26 SALFORD RED DEVILS 12

DRAGONS: 31 Tony Gigot; 2 Jodie Broughton; 1 David Mead; 4 Brayden Wiliame; 20 Lewis Tierney; 13 Greg Bird; 33 Josh Drinkwater; 15 Mickael Simon; 19 Michael Mcllorum; 10 Sam Moa; 21 Benjamin Jullien; 12 Benjamin Garcia; 8 Remi Casty (C). Subs (all used): 11 Louis Anderson; 14 Julian Bousquet; 23 Antoni Maria; 17 Jason Baitieri.
Tries: Garcia (14), Bousquet (23), Broughton (50, 61, 62);
Goals: Gigot 3/6.
RED DEVILS: 5 Niall Evalds; 2 Greg Johnson; 3 Kris Welham; 4 Junior Sa'u; 22 Derrell Olpherts; 6 Robert Lui; 7 Jack Littlejohn; 8 Craig Kopczak (C); 9 Logan Tomkins; 23 Lee Mossop; 10 George Griffin; 12 Weller Hauraki; 13 Mark Flanagan. Subs (all used): 14 Lama Tasi; 26 Daniel Murray; 19 Josh Wood; 17 Tyrone McCarthy.
Tries: Hauraki (9), Griffin (76); **Goals:** Lui 2/2.
Rugby Leaguer & League Express Men of the Match:
Dragons: Jodie Broughton; *Red Devils:* Weller Hauraki.
Penalty count: 9-6; **Half-time:** 10-6;
Referee: Gareth Hewer.

HUDDERSFIELD GIANTS 25 WAKEFIELD TRINITY 22

GIANTS: 15 Jordan Rankin; 2 Jermaine McGillvary; 6 Lee Gaskell; 1 Jake Mamo; 23 Darnell McIntosh; 4 Jordan Turner; 7 Danny Brough; 17 Ukuma Ta'ai; 21 Adam O'Brien; 18 Paul Clough (C); 22 Alex Mellor; 5 Aaron Murphy; 13 Ryan Hinchcliffe. Subs (all used): 9 Kruise Leeming; 24 Tyler Dickinson; 27 Matty English; 8 Sebastine Ikahihifo.
Tries: Murphy (11), O'Brien (19), Mamo (24), McIntosh (50);
Goals: Brough 4/4; **Field goal:** Brough (39).
Sin bin: Leeming (44) - repeated team offences.
TRINITY: 25 Ryan Hampshire; 5 Ben Jones-Bishop; 3 Bill Tupou; 4 Reece Lyne; 24 Mason Caton-Brown; 6 Jacob Miller; 7 Liam Finn; 8 David Fifita; 13 Tyler Randell; 20 Keegan Hirst; 12 Danny Kirmond (C); 11 Matty Ashurst; 16 Tinirau Arona. Subs (all used): 9 Kyle Wood; 17 Craig Huby; 15 Pauli Pauli; 14 Justin Horo.
Tries: Ashurst (32), Jones-Bishop (46, 57), Lyne (73);
Goals: Finn 3/4.
Rugby Leaguer & League Express Men of the Match:
Giants: Danny Brough; *Trinity:* Jacob Miller.
Penalty count: 7-11; **Half-time:** 19-6; **Referee:** James Child.

HULL FC 34 HULL KINGSTON ROVERS 22

HULL FC: 1 Jamie Shaul; 4 Josh Griffin; 30 Cameron Scott (D); 34 Kirk Yeaman; 24 Jack Logan; 14 Jake Connor; 35 Liam Harris (D); 8 Scott Taylor; 9 Danny Houghton (C); 15 Chris Green; 21 Sika Manu; 12 Mark Minichiello; 33 Joe Westerman. Subs (all used): 29 Masi Matongo; 23 Mickey Paea; 11 Dean Hadley; 28 Hakim Miloudi.
Tries: Taylor (19), Shaul (24, 38), Harris (31), Logan (68), Connor (69); **Goals:** Connor 5/6.
ROVERS: 1 Adam Quinlan; 5 Ryan Shaw; 22 Liam Salter; 2 Junior Vaivai; 25 Kieren Moss; 11 Maurice Blair (C); 19 Tommy Lee; 10 Mose Masoe; 38 Aaron Smith; 8 Nick Scruton; 34 Danny Tickle; 17 Chris Clarkson; 15 James Donaldson. Subs (all used): 12 James Greenwood; 24 Chris Atkin; 29 Jordan Walne; 13 Ben Kavanagh.
Tries: Moss (14, 28, 56), Lee (74); **Goals:** Shaw 3/4.
Sin bin: Scruton (51) - dangerous challenge.
Rugby Leaguer & League Express Men of the Match:
Hull FC: Jake Connor; *Rovers:* Chris Atkin.
Penalty count: 9-9; **Half-time:** 24-10; **Referee:** Ben Thaler.

Attendance: 25,438 *(at St James' Park, Newcastle)*.

ROUND 16

Thursday 24th May 2018

CASTLEFORD TIGERS 18 ST HELENS 40

TIGERS: 4 Michael Shenton (C); 2 Greg Minikin; 1 Ben Roberts; 17 Alex Foster; 24 Jy Hitchcox; 6 Jamie Ellis; 21 Jake Trueman; 32 Liam Watts; 9 Paul McShane; 15 Jesse Sene-Lefao; 11 Oliver Holmes; 12 Mike McMeeken; 13 Adam Milner. Subs (all used): 8 Junior Moors; 10 Grant Millington; 14 Nathan Massey; 18 Matt Cook.
Tries: McMeeken (7), Hitchcox (63), Trueman (68), Holmes (73); **Goals:** Ellis 1/4.
SAINTS: 23 Ben Barba; 5 Adam Swift; 3 Ryan Morgan; 4 Mark Percival; 19 Regan Grace; 1 Jonny Lomax; 18 Danny Richardson; 10 Kyle Amor; 9 James Roby (C); 16 Luke Thompson; 17 Dominique Peyroux; 11 Zeb Taia; 12 Jon Wilkin. Subs (all used): 6 Theo Fages; 13 Louie McCarthy-Scarsbrook; 14 Luke Douglas; 15 Morgan Knowles.
Tries: Amor (3), Barba (14), Lomax (26), Peyroux (30), Morgan (44, 51), Fages (59, 75); **Goals:** Richardson 4/8.
Rugby Leaguer & League Express Men of the Match:
Tigers: Mike McMeeken; *Saints:* Jonny Lomax.
Penalty count: 4-5; **Half-time:** 4-22;
Referee: Chris Kendall; **Attendance:** 6,969.

Friday 25th May 2018

WARRINGTON WOLVES 30 HULL FC 12

WOLVES: 1 Stefan Ratchford; 2 Tom Lineham; 21 Mitch Brown; 4 Ryan Atkins; 27 Josh Charnley; 6 Kevin Brown; 7 Tyrone Roberts; 8 Chris Hill (C); 9 Daryl Clark; 13 Ben Murdoch-Masila; 20 Harvey Livett; 12 Jack Hughes; 34 Ben Westwood. Subs (all used): 17 Joe Philbin; 19 George King; 15 Declan Patton; 29 Ben Pomeroy (D2).
Tries: Livett (46), K Brown (53), Murdoch-Masila (59), Charnley (62), Atkins (70); **Goals:** Livett 5/5.
HULL FC: 1 Jamie Shaul; 24 Jack Logan; 11 Dean Hadley; 30 Cameron Scott; 28 Hakim Miloudi; 14 Jake Connor; 35 Liam Harris; 15 Chris Green; 9 Danny Houghton (C); 23 Mickey Paea; 21 Sika Manu; 12 Mark Minichiello; 33 Joe Westerman. Subs (all used): 17 Danny Washbrook; 26 Jordan Lane; 20 Brad Fash; 29 Masi Matongo.
Tries: Hadley (6), Paea (13); **Goals:** Connor 2/2.
On report: Miloudi (39) - alleged bite on Hill.
Rugby Leaguer & League Express Men of the Match:
Wolves: Harvey Livett; *Hull FC:* Danny Houghton.
Penalty count: 3-6; **Half-time:** 0-12;
Referee: Gareth Hewer; **Attendance:** 8,646.

HULL KINGSTON ROVERS 24 WIGAN WARRIORS 8

ROVERS: 1 Adam Quinlan; 37 Elliot Wallis; 22 Liam Salter; 2 Junior Vaivai; 36 Justin Carney; 28 Will Dagger; 11 Maurice Blair (C); 23 Josh Johnson; 19 Tommy Lee; 12 James Greenwood; 34 Danny Tickle; 17 Chris Clarkson; 15 James Donaldson. Subs (all used): 10 Mose Masoe; 8 Nick Scruton; 24 Chris Atkin; 13 Ben Kavanagh.
Tries: Vaivai (23, 74), Quinlan (27), Atkin (51);
Goals: Tickle 4/5.
Sin bin: Johnson (77) - kicking out.
WARRIORS: 1 Sam Tomkins (C); 2 Tom Davies; 14 John Bateman; 28 Liam Forsyth; 22 Liam Marshall; 6 George Williams; 20 Morgan Escare; 25 Romain Navarrete; 7 Sam Powell; 10 Ben Flower; 19 Willie Isa; 12 Liam Farrell; 11 Joel Tomkins. Subs (all used): 23 Josh Ganson; 8 Tony Clubb; 15 Ryan Sutton; 17 Taulima Tautai.
Try: J Tomkins (7); **Goals:** S Tomkins 2/2.
Sin bin: J Tomkins (70) - dissent.
On report:
S Tomkins (69) - alleged use of the knees on Atkin.
Rugby Leaguer & League Express Men of the Match:
Rovers: Maurice Blair; *Warriors:* George Williams.
Penalty count: 8-8; **Half-time:** 10-8;
Referee: Ben Thaler; **Attendance:** 7,222.

SALFORD RED DEVILS 16 HUDDERSFIELD GIANTS 24

RED DEVILS: 5 Niall Evalds; 2 Greg Johnson; 4 Junior Sa'u; 24 Jake Bibby; 22 Derrell Olpherts; 6 Robert Lui; 28 Jake Shorrocks; 23 Lee Mossop; 9 Logan Tomkins; 26 Daniel Murray; 10 George Griffin; 15 Ryan Lannon; 13 Mark Flanagan. Subs (all used): 8 Craig Kopczak (C); 12 Weller Hauraki; 18 Ben Nakubuwai; 19 Josh Wood.
Tries: Sa'u (3, 77), Evalds (29); **Goals:** Lui 2/4.
GIANTS: 15 Jordan Rankin; 2 Jermaine McGillvary; 6 Lee Gaskell; 1 Jake Mamo; 23 Darnell McIntosh; 4 Jordan Turner; 7 Danny Brough; 17 Ukuma Ta'ai; 21 Adam O'Brien; 18 Paul Clough; 22 Alex Mellor; 16 Oliver Roberts; 13 Ryan Hinchcliffe (C). Subs (all used): 8 Sebastine Ikahihifo; 9 Kruise Leeming; 19 Daniel Smith; 27 Matty English.
Tries: McIntosh (19), Smith (51), Turner (64), Leeming (74);
Goals: Brough 4/5.
Rugby Leaguer & League Express Men of the Match:
Red Devils: Junior Sa'u; *Giants:* Daniel Smith.
Penalty count: 10-8; **Half-time:** 10-6;
Referee: Liam Moore; **Attendance:** 2,343.

WIDNES VIKINGS 6 WAKEFIELD TRINITY 19

VIKINGS: 15 Danny Craven; 5 Patrick Ah Van; 4 Charly Runciman; 24 Ed Chamberlain; 2 Stefan Marsh; 6 Joe Mellor (C); 33 Aaron Heremaia; 25 Jay Chapelhow; 21 Jordan Johnstone; 19 Greg Burke; 12 Matt Whitley; 17 Sam Wilde; 13 Hep Cahill. Subs (all used): 20 Macgraff Leuluai; 16 Tom Olbison; 36 Wellington Albert; 23 Danny Walker.
Try: Ah Van (45); **Goals:** Marsh 1/2.
TRINITY: 21 Max Jowitt; 5 Ben Jones-Bishop; 3 Bill Tupou; 4 Reece Lyne; 2 Tom Johnstone; 6 Jacob Miller (C); 25 Ryan Hampshire; 10 Anthony England; 13 Tyler Randell; 20 Keegan Hirst; 14 Justin Horo; 15 Pauli Pauli; 19 James Batchelor. Subs (all used): 23 Chris Annakin; 16 Tinirau Arona; 8 David Fifita; 9 Kyle Wood.
Tries: Pauli (14), Johnstone (27), Fifita (31);
Goals: Batchelor 3/4; **Field goal:** Miller (78).
Rugby Leaguer & League Express Men of the Match:
Vikings: Matt Whitley; *Trinity:* Jacob Miller.
Penalty count: 8-7; **Half-time:** 2-16;
Referee: Robert Hicks; **Attendance:** 3,681.

Saturday 26th May 2018

CATALANS DRAGONS 33 LEEDS RHINOS 20

DRAGONS: 31 Tony Gigot; 2 Jodie Broughton; 1 David Mead; 4 Brayden Wiliame; 20 Lewis Tierney; 13 Greg Bird; 33 Josh Drinkwater; 15 Mickael Simon; 19 Michael McIlorum; 10 Sam Moa; 21 Benjamin Jullien; 12 Benjamin Garcia; 8 Remi Casty (C). Subs (all used): 11 Louis Anderson; 14 Julian Bousquet; 23 Antoni Maria; 32 Mickael Goudemand.
Tries: Jullien (4), Garcia (8), McIlorum (18), Gigot (65), Drinkwater (67), Broughton (74); **Goals:** Drinkwater 4/6;
Field goal: Gigot (35).
Sin bin: Moa (25) - late challenge on Myler.
RHINOS: 24 Jack Walker; 2 Tom Briscoe; 18 Jimmy Keinhorst; 22 Ash Handley; 5 Ryan Hall; 25 Jordan Lilley; 7 Richie Myler; 8 Adam Cuthbertson; 14 Brad Dwyer; 28 Mikolaj Oledzki; 19 Brett Ferres; 13 Stevie Ward (C); 15 Brett Delaney. Subs (all used): 1 Ashton Golding; 23 Jack Ormondroyd; 27 Cameron Smith; 30 Josh Walters.
Tries: Handley (31), Ferres (44), Hall (53), Dwyer (79);
Goals: Lilley 2/4.
Rugby Leaguer & League Express Men of the Match:
Dragons: Remi Casty; *Rhinos:* Adam Cuthbertson.
Penalty count: 11-5; **Half-time:** 17-4;
Referee: James Child; **Attendance:** 8,779.

ROUND 4

Friday 1st June 2018

HULL KINGSTON ROVERS 14 CASTLEFORD TIGERS 42

ROVERS: 1 Adam Quinlan; 5 Ryan Shaw; 22 Liam Salter; 2 Junior Vaivai; 25 Kieren Moss; 19 Tommy Lee; 11 Maurice Blair (C); 13 Ben Kavanagh; 38 Aaron Smith; 12 James Greenwood; 17 Chris Clarkson; 34 Danny Tickle; 15 James Donaldson. Subs (all used): 10 Mose Masoe; 8 Nick Scruton; 24 Chris Atkin; 29 Jordan Walne.
Tries: Shaw (28, 77), Clarkson (64); **Goals:** Shaw 1/3.
TIGERS: 5 Greg Eden; 28 Kieran Gill; 17 Alex Foster; 4 Michael Shenton (C); 24 Jy Hitchcox; 6 Jamie Ellis; 21 Jake Trueman; 32 Liam Watts; 9 Paul McShane; 18 Matt Cook; 16 Joe Wardle; 12 Mike McMeeken; 13 Adam Milner. Subs (all used): 10 Grant Millington; 11 Oliver Holmes; 14 Nathan Massey; 15 Jesse Sene-Lefao.
Tries: Gill (6, 51), Eden (8), Foster (14), Cook (19), Shenton (34), Hitchcox (61, 80); **Goals:** Ellis 5/8.
Rugby Leaguer & League Express Men of the Match:
Rovers: Adam Quinlan; *Tigers:* Paul McShane.
Penalty count: 6-5; **Half-time:** 4-28;
Referee: James Child; **Attendance:** 7,074.

ROUND 17

Thursday 7th June 2018

WAKEFIELD TRINITY 32 WIGAN WARRIORS 16

TRINITY: 21 Max Jowitt; 5 Ben Jones-Bishop; 4 Reece Lyne; 3 Bill Tupou; 2 Tom Johnstone; 6 Jacob Miller; 25 Ryan Hampshire; 8 David Fifita; 13 Tyler Randell; 10 Anthony England; 11 Matty Ashurst; 12 Danny Kirmond (C); 14 Justin Horo. Subs (all used): 9 Kyle Wood; 20 Keegan Hirst; 15 Pauli Pauli; 16 Tinirau Arona.
Tries: Jones-Bishop (7, 42), Tupou (20), Johnstone (58), Pauli (77); **Goals:** Hampshire 6/8.
WARRIORS: 1 Sam Tomkins; 2 Tom Davies; 3 Dan Sarginson; 4 Oliver Gildart; 38 Craig Mullen (D); 6 George Williams; 7 Sam Powell; 8 Tony Clubb; 9 Thomas Leuluai; 25 Romain Navarrete; 14 John Bateman; 12 Liam Farrell; 13 Sean O'Loughlin (C). Subs (all used): 19 Willie Isa; 20 Morgan Escare; 27 Callum Field; 30 Gabe Hamlin.
Tries: Hamlin (35), Davies (72), Escare (74);
Goals: S Tomkins 2/3.
Sin bin: Leuluai (20) - dangerous contact on Horo.
Rugby Leaguer & League Express Men of the Match:
Trinity: David Fifita; *Warriors:* John Bateman.
Penalty count: 11-7; **Half-time:** 14-6;
Referee: James Child; **Attendance:** 4,681.

Friday 8th June 2018

HULL FC 45 SALFORD RED DEVILS 14

HULL FC: 1 Jamie Shaul; 2 Bureta Faraimo; 24 Jack Logan; 3 Carlos Tuimavave; 28 Hakim Miloudi; 14 Jake Connor; 35 Liam Harris; 8 Scott Taylor (C); 17 Danny Washbrook; 15 Chris Green; 12 Mark Minichiello; 27 Jack Downs; 33 Joe Westerman. Subs (all used): 20 Brad Fash; 22 Jez Litten; 23 Mickey Paea; 29 Masi Matongo.
Tries: Faraimo (5, 12, 50), Downs (15), Logan (19), Miloudi (34), Shaul (40); **Goals:** Connor 8/8;
Field goal: Connor (39).
Sin bin: Faraimo (54) - high tackle on Flanagan.
RED DEVILS: 7 Jack Littlejohn; 2 Greg Johnson; 3 Kris Welham; 4 Junior Sa'u; 22 Derrell Olpherts; 6 Robert Lui; 28 Jake Shorrocks; 14 Lama Tasi; 9 Logan Tomkins; 23 Lee Mossop (C); 10 George Griffin; 11 Josh Jones; 13 Mark Flanagan. Subs (all used): 8 Craig Kopczak; 17 Tyrone McCarthy; 18 Ben Nakubuwai; 19 Josh Wood.
Tries: Johnson (57), Olpherts (65), Griffin (72);
Goals: Lui 1/2, Littlejohn 0/1.
Rugby Leaguer & League Express Men of the Match:
Hull FC: Jake Connor; *Red Devils:* Kris Welham.
Penalty count: 10-5; **Half-time:** 37-0;
Referee: Robert Hicks; **Attendance:** 10,606.

LEEDS RHINOS 18 HUDDERSFIELD GIANTS 25

RHINOS: 24 Jack Walker; 2 Tom Briscoe; 4 Liam Sutcliffe; 22 Ash Handley; 5 Ryan Hall; 25 Jordan Lilley; 7 Richie Myler; 8 Adam Cuthbertson; 9 Matt Parcell; 28 Mikolaj Oledzki; 19 Brett Ferres; 13 Stevie Ward (C); 30 Josh Walters. Subs (all used): 15 Brett Delaney; 17 Mitch Garbutt; 27 Cameron Smith; 1 Ashton Golding.
Tries: Parcell (12), Myler (16), Smith (41); **Goals:** Lilley 3/3.
Sin bin: Ferres (73) - fighting.
GIANTS: 15 Jordan Rankin; 2 Jermaine McGillvary; 3 Leroy Cudjoe (C); 6 Lee Gaskell; 23 Darnell McIntosh; 4 Jordan Turner; 34 Oliver Russell; 12 Michael Lawrence; 9 Kruise Leeming; 18 Paul Clough; 22 Alex Mellor; 5 Aaron Murphy; 13 Ryan Hinchcliffe. Subs (all used): 19 Daniel Smith; 8 Sebastine Ikahihifo; 21 Adam O'Brien; 27 Matty English.
Tries: Leeming (7), Murphy (30), Mellor (36), O'Brien (49);
Goals: Russell 4/5; **Field goal:** Russell (75).
Sin bin: McGillvary (73) - fighting.
Rugby Leaguer & League Express Men of the Match:
Rhinos: Stevie Ward; *Giants:* Alex Mellor.
Penalty count: 8-6; **Half time:** 12-18;
Referee: Liam Moore; **Attendance:** 11,051.

WARRINGTON WOLVES 30 CASTLEFORD TIGERS 34

WOLVES: 1 Stefan Ratchford; 2 Tom Lineham; 3 Bryson Goodwin; 4 Ryan Atkins; 27 Josh Charnley; 6 Kevin Brown; 7 Tyrone Roberts; 8 Chris Hill (C); 9 Daryl Clark; 10 Mike Cooper; 20 Harvey Livett; 12 Jack Hughes; 34 Ben Westwood. Subs (all used): 13 Ben Murdoch-Masila; 15 Declan Patton; 16 Sitaleki Akauola; 17 Joe Philbin.
Tries: Roberts (12), Ratchford (17), Clark (21), Akauola (31), Charnley (53, 70); **Goals:** Livett 2/5, Goodwin 1/1.
TIGERS: 33 Calum Turner; 2 Greg Minikin; 17 Alex Foster; 4 Michael Shenton (C); 24 Jy Hitchcox; 34 Quentin Laulu-Togagae (D); 21 Jake Trueman; 18 Matt Cook; 13 Adam Milner; 10 Grant Millington; 16 Joe Wardle; 12 Mike McMeeken; 15 Jesse Sene-Lefao. Subs: 11 Oliver Holmes; 14 Nathan Massey; 23 Mitch Clark (D); 25 Will Maher (not used).
Tries: McMeeken (5), Turner (7), Hitchcox (35), Laulu-Togagae (62), Holmes (66);
Goals: Turner 6/6, Milner 1/1.
Sin bin: Milner (47) - late challenge on Roberts.
Rugby Leaguer & League Express Men of the Match:
Wolves: Daryl Clark; *Tigers:* Adam Milner.
Penalty count: 10-6; **Half-time:** 20-20;
Referee: Ben Thaler; **Attendance:** 9,198.

ST HELENS 26 HULL KINGSTON ROVERS 4

SAINTS: 23 Ben Barba; 2 Tommy Makinson; 3 Ryan Morgan; 4 Mark Percival; 19 Regan Grace; 6 Theo Fages; 18 Danny Richardson; 10 Kyle Amor; 9 James Roby (C); 16 Luke Thompson; 17 Dominique Peyroux; 11 Zeb Taia; 13 Louie McCarthy-Scarsbrook. Subs (all used): 7 Matty Smith; 14 Luke Douglas; 15 Morgan Knowles; 20 Matty Lees.
Tries: Morgan (2), Roby (8), Barba (28, 80), Percival (47);
Goals: Richardson 3/5.
ROVERS: 1 Adam Quinlan; 5 Ryan Shaw; 22 Liam Salter; 2 Junior Vaivai; 37 Elliot Wallis; 20 Matty Marsh; 11 Maurice Blair (C); 23 Josh Johnson; 30 Joe Cator; 12 James Greenwood; 17 Chris Clarkson; 34 Danny Tickle; 15 James Donaldson. Subs (all used): 8 Nick Scruton; 10 Mose Masoe; 13 Ben Kavanagh; 24 Chris Atkin.
Try: Vaivai (42); **Goals:** Shaw 0/1.
Rugby Leaguer & League Express Men of the Match:
Saints: James Roby; *Rovers:* Chris Atkin.
Penalty count: 11-7; **Half-time:** 18-0;
Referee: Gareth Hewer; **Attendance:** 9,405.

Saturday 9th June 2018

CATALANS DRAGONS 32 WIDNES VIKINGS 12

DRAGONS: 31 Tony Gigot; 20 Lewis Tierney; 1 David Mead; 4 Brayden Wiliame; 5 Fouad Yaha; 13 Greg Bird; 33 Josh Drinkwater; 15 Mickael Simon; 19 Michael McIlorum; 10 Sam Moa; 21 Benjamin Jullien; 12 Benjamin Garcia; 8 Remi Casty (C). Subs (all used): 11 Louis Anderson; 14 Julian Bousquet; 23 Antoni Maria; 34 Kenny Edwards.
Tries: Gigot (25), Wiliame (31), Casty (60), Edwards (73), Yaha (77); **Goals:** Drinkwater 6/7.
Sin bin:
Bousquet (45) - off-the-ball challenge on J Chapelhow.
VIKINGS: 1 Rhys Hanbury; 22 Ryan Ince; 2 Stefan Marsh; 4 Charly Runciman; 5 Patrick Ah Van; 6 Joe Mellor (C); 15 Danny Craven; 25 Jay Chapelhow; 33 Aaron Heremaia; 26 Ted Chapelhow; 12 Matt Whitley; 39 Weller Hauraki (D); 16 Tom Olbison. Subs (all used): 17 Sam Wilde; 20 Macgraff Leuluai; 21 Jordan Johnstone; 29 Owen Farnworth.
Tries: J Chapelhow (10), Hanbury (16);
Goals: Craven 1/2, Ah Van 1/1.
Rugby Leaguer & League Express Men of the Match:
Dragons: Tony Gigot; *Vikings:* Aaron Heremaia.
Penalty count: 8-6; **Half-time:** 12-10;
Referee: Chris Kendall; **Attendance:** 9,239.

ROUND 18

Thursday 14th June 2018

SALFORD RED DEVILS 26 WIDNES VIKINGS 12

RED DEVILS: 7 Jack Littlejohn; 22 Derrell Olpherts; 3 Kris Welham; 4 Junior Sa'u; 24 Jake Bibby; 6 Robert Lui; 28 Jake Shorrocks; 14 Lama Tasi; 19 Josh Wood; 30 Greg Burke (D); 17 Tyrone McCarthy; 10 George Griffin; 15 Ryan Lannon. Subs (all used): 8 Craig Kopczak (C); 9 Logan Tomkins; 18 Ben Nakubuwai; 29 Ed Chamberlain (D).

Junior Moors fends off Mose Masoe as Castleford and Hull KR fight out a summer stalemate

Tries: Welham (11, 16), Bibby (50), Burke (62), Lui (77);
Goals: Lui 3/6.
Sin bin: Welham (23) - late challenge on Mellor.
VIKINGS: 15 Danny Craven; 5 Patrick Ah Van; 4 Charly Runciman; 16 Tom Olbison; 22 Ryan Ince; 6 Joe Mellor (C); 7 Tom Gilmore; 25 Jay Chapelhow; 21 Jordan Johnstone; 26 Ted Chapelhow; 12 Matt Whitley; 39 Weller Hauraki; 11 Chris Houston (C). Subs (all used): 10 Alex Gerrard; 34 Dan Norman (D); 33 Aaron Heremaia; 29 Owen Farnworth.
Tries: Gilmore (5), Ah Van (24); **Goals:** Gilmore 2/2.
Dismissal: Houston (69) - dissent.
Sin bin: Houston (69) - late challenge.
Rugby Leaguer & League Express Men of the Match:
Red Devils: Robert Lui; *Vikings:* Tom Gilmore.
Penalty count: 7-6; **Half-time:** 8-12;
Referee: James Child; **Attendance:** 2,248.

Friday 15th June 2018

HUDDERSFIELD GIANTS 26 CATALANS DRAGONS 25

GIANTS: 15 Jordan Rankin; 2 Jermaine McGillvary; 3 Leroy Cudjoe (C); 6 Lee Gaskell; 23 Darnell McIntosh; 4 Jordan Turner; 34 Oliver Russell; 12 Michael Lawrence; 9 Kruise Leeming; 27 Matty English; 22 Alex Mellor; 5 Aaron Murphy; 13 Ryan Hinchcliffe. Subs (all used): 8 Sebastine Ikahihifo; 14 Dale Ferguson; 19 Daniel Smith; 21 Adam O'Brien.
Tries: Mellor (21), McIntosh (31), McGillvary (37, 64), O'Brien (56); **Goals:** Russell 3/6.
DRAGONS: 31 Tony Gigot; 16 Vincent Duport; 1 David Mead; 4 Brayden Wiliame; 20 Lewis Tierney; 13 Greg Bird; 33 Josh Drinkwater; 15 Mickael Simon; 19 Michael Mcllorum; 10 Sam Moa; 21 Benjamin Jullien; 12 Benjamin Garcia; 8 Remi Casty (C). Subs (all used): 11 Louis Anderson; 14 Julian Bousquet; 34 Kenny Edwards; 17 Jason Baitieri.
Tries: Wiliame (5), Duport (7), Mead (17), Casty (28);
Goals: Drinkwater 4/4; **Field goal:** Gigot (74).
Rugby Leaguer & League Express Men of the Match:
Giants: Alex Mellor; *Dragons:* Josh Drinkwater.
Penalty count: 13-4; **Half-time:** 14-24;
Referee: Gareth Hewer; **Attendance:** 9,121.

LEEDS RHINOS 22 ST HELENS 23

RHINOS: 24 Jack Walker; 2 Tom Briscoe; 26 Harry Newman; 22 Ash Handley; 5 Ryan Hall; 4 Liam Sutcliffe; 6 Joel Moon; 17 Mitch Garbutt; 9 Matt Parcell; 16 Anthony Mullally; 19 Brett Ferres; 30 Josh Walters; 8 Adam Cuthbertson (C). Subs: 23 Jack Ormondroyd; 27 Cameron Smith; 14 Brad Dwyer; 32 Tom Holroyd (not used).
Tries: T Briscoe (12, 43), Garbutt (54), Ferres (71);
Goals: Sutcliffe 3/6.
SAINTS: 23 Ben Barba; 2 Tommy Makinson; 3 Ryan Morgan; 4 Mark Percival; 19 Regan Grace; 1 Jonny Lomax; 18 Danny Richardson; 14 Luke Douglas; 9 James Roby (C); 16 Luke Thompson; 11 Zeb Taia; 17 Dominique Peyroux; 12 Jon Wilkin. Subs (all used): 13 Louie McCarthy-Scarsbrook; 15 Morgan Knowles; 20 Matty Lees; 6 Theo Fages.
Tries: Barba (23), Lomax (31), Percival (51), Morgan (73);
Goals: Richardson 3/4; **Field goal:** Richardson (78).
Rugby Leaguer & League Express Men of the Match:
Rhinos: Matt Parcell; *Saints:* James Roby.
Penalty count: 9-4; **Half-time:** 6-10;
Referee: Ben Thaler; **Attendance:** 12,106.

Saturday 16th June 2018

HULL FC 10 WIGAN WARRIORS 14

HULL FC: 1 Jamie Shaul; 2 Bureta Faraimo; 14 Jake Connor; 3 Carlos Tuimavave; 28 Hakim Miloudi; 6 Albert Kelly; 35 Liam Harris; 8 Scott Taylor; 9 Danny Houghton (C); 15 Chris Green; 12 Mark Minichiello; 27 Jack Downs; 17 Danny Washbrook. Subs (all used): 20 Brad Fash; 23 Mickey Paea; 24 Jack Logan; 29 Masi Matongo.
Try: Faraimo (36, 53); **Goals:** Connor 1/2.
WARRIORS: 1 Sam Tomkins; 2 Tom Davies; 3 Dan Sarginson; 4 Oliver Gildart; 22 Liam Marshall; 6 George Williams; 7 Sam Powell; 8 Tony Clubb; 9 Thomas Leuluai; 10 Ben Flower; 14 John Bateman; 19 Willie Isa; 13 Sean O'Loughlin (C); Subs (all used): 20 Morgan Escare; 25 Romain Navarrete; 27 Callum Field; 30 Gabe Hamlin.
Tries: Sarginson (23), Marshall (75); **Goals:** S Tomkins 3/4.

Rugby Leaguer & League Express Men of the Match:
Hull FC: Albert Kelly; *Warriors:* Sean O'Loughlin.
Penalty count: 4-3; **Half-time:** 6-8;
Referee: Robert Hicks; **Attendance:** 13,256.

Sunday 17th June 2018

WAKEFIELD TRINITY 30 WARRINGTON WOLVES 32

TRINITY: 21 Max Jowitt; 5 Ben Jones-Bishop; 3 Bill Tupou; 4 Reece Lyne; 2 Tom Johnstone; 6 Jacob Miller; 25 Ryan Hampshire; 8 David Fifita; 13 Tyler Randell; 10 Anthony England; 15 Pauli Pauli; 11 Matty Ashurst; 14 Justin Horo. Subs (all used): 9 Kyle Wood; 12 Danny Kirmond (C); 16 Tinirau Arona; 20 Keegan Hirst.
Tries: Arona (27), Wood (45, 47), Johnstone (77), Pauli (78);
Goals: Hampshire 5/5.
WOLVES: 1 Stefan Ratchford; 2 Tom Lineham; 3 Bryson Goodwin; 4 Ryan Atkins; 27 Josh Charnley; 6 Kevin Brown; 7 Tyrone Roberts; 8 Chris Hill (C); 9 Daryl Clark; 10 Mike Cooper; 20 Harvey Livett; 12 Jack Hughes; 34 Ben Westwood. Subs: 13 Ben Murdoch-Masila; 15 Declan Patton (not used); 16 Sitaleki Akauola; 14 Dominic Crosby.
Tries: Ratchford (4, 10), Lineham (23), K Brown (65);
Goals: Livett 5/5, Goodwin 3/3.
Sin bin: Akauola (76) - high tackle.
Rugby Leaguer & League Express Men of the Match:
Trinity: Kyle Wood; *Wolves:* Stefan Ratchford.
Penalty count: 14-9; **Half-time:** 6-22;
Referee: Chris Kendall; **Attendance:** 5,034.

CASTLEFORD TIGERS 24
HULL KINGSTON ROVERS 24

TIGERS: 33 Calum Turner; 2 Greg Minikin; 17 Alex Foster; 4 Michael Shenton (C); 24 Jy Hitchcox; 34 Quentin Laulu-Togagae; 21 Jake Trueman; 18 Matt Cook; 13 Adam Milner; 14 Nathan Massey; 16 Joe Wardle; 12 Mike McMeeken; 15 Jesse Sene-Lefao. Subs (all used): 3 Jake Webster; 8 Junior Moors; 9 Paul McShane; 11 Oliver Holmes.
Tries: McMeeken (2), Hitchcox (10, 24, 45, 70);
Goals: Turner 2/6.

ROVERS: 1 Adam Quinlan; 5 Ryan Shaw; 11 Maurice Blair; 2 Junior Vaivai; 37 Elliot Wallis; 20 Matty Marsh; 24 Chris Atkin; 8 Nick Scruton; 38 Aaron Smith; 34 Danny Tickle; 39 Joel Tomkins (D); 12 James Greenwood; 17 Chris Clarkson. Subs (all used): 10 Mose Masoe; 14 Lee Jewitt; 9 Shaun Lunt (C); 15 James Donaldson.
Tries: Vaivai (37, 77), Quinlan (41), Masoe (74);
Goals: Shaw 4/4.
Rugby Leaguer & League Express Men of the Match:
Tigers: Jy Hitchcox; *Rovers:* Adam Quinlan.
Penalty count: 5-7; **Half-time:** 14-6;
Referee: Liam Moore; **Attendance:** 9,022.

ROUND 4

Wednesday 20th June 2018

LEEDS RHINOS 25 CATALANS DRAGONS 28

RHINOS: 24 Jack Walker; 2 Tom Briscoe; 26 Harry Newman; 22 Ash Handley; 34 Luke Briscoe (D2); 6 Joel Moon; 4 Liam Sutcliffe; 28 Mikolaj Oledzki; 9 Matt Parcell; 17 Mitch Garbutt; 19 Brett Ferres; 27 Cameron Smith; 8 Adam Cuthbertson (C). Subs (all used): 16 Anthony Mullally; 32 Tom Holroyd (D); 14 Brad Dwyer; 30 Josh Walters.
Tries: Walker (8), Sutcliffe (10), Smith (15), L Briscoe (35);
Goals: Sutcliffe 4/4; **Field goal:** Sutcliffe (72).
Sin bin: Parcell (76) - dangerous challenge.
On report:
Cuthbertson (78) - alleged dangerous contact on Edwards.
DRAGONS: 31 Tony Gigot; 20 Lewis Tierney; 1 David Mead; 4 Brayden Wiliame; 5 Fouad Yaha; 6 Samisoni Langi; 33 Josh Drinkwater; 8 Remi Casty (C); 19 Michael Mcllorum; 15 Mickael Simon; 21 Benjamin Jullien; 12 Benjamin Garcia; 13 Greg Bird. Subs (all used): 14 Julian Bousquet; 17 Jason Baitieri; 34 Kenny Edwards; 11 Louis Anderson.
Tries: Langi (2), Drinkwater (19), Yaha (45), Tierney (54), Edwards (56, 74); **Goals:** Drinkwater 2/6.
Sin bin: Bird (25) - high tackle on Oledzki;
Yaha (79) - professional foul.
Rugby Leaguer & League Express Men of the Match:
Rhinos: Tom Briscoe; *Dragons:* Kenny Edwards.
Penalty count: 8-7; **Half time:** 24-10;
Referee: Scott Mikalauskas; **Attendance:** 10,366.

ROUND 6

Friday 22nd June 2018

CASTLEFORD TIGERS 19 WIGAN WARRIORS 18

TIGERS: 34 Quentin Laulu-Togagae; 26 James Clare; 3 Jake Webster; 4 Michael Shenton (C); 24 Jy Hitchcox; 6 Jamie Ellis; 21 Jake Trueman; 18 Matt Cook; 9 Paul McShane; 14 Nathan Massey; 8 Junior Moors; 10 Grant Millington; 25 Will Maher. Subs (all used): 19 Gadwin Springer; 22 James Green; 23 Mitch Clark; 29 Tuoyo Egodo.
Tries: Laulu-Togagae (25), Hitchcox (49), Cook (62);
Goals: Ellis 3/4; **Field goal:** Ellis (79).
Sin bin: Cook (69) - dangerous contact on Navarrete.
WARRIORS: 1 Sam Tomkins (C); 2 Tom Davies; 3 Dan Sarginson; 4 Oliver Gildart; 22 Liam Marshall; 34 Josh Woods; 7 Sam Powell; 25 Romain Navarrete; 9 Thomas Leuluai; 10 Ben Flower; 39 Liam Paisley (D); 19 Willie Isa; 30 Gabe Hamlin. Subs (all used): 20 Morgan Escare; 27 Callum Field; 8 Tony Clubb; 17 Taulima Tautai.
Tries: S Tomkins (16), Marshall (30), Davies (70);
Goals: S Tomkins 3/4.
Rugby Leaguer & League Express Men of the Match:
Tigers: Junior Moors; *Warriors:* Gabe Hamlin.
Penalty count: 5-7; **Half-time:** 4-12;
Referee: James Child; **Attendance:** 7,714.

Sunday 24th June 2018

WAKEFIELD TRINITY 44 WIDNES VIKINGS 22

TRINITY: 21 Max Jowitt; 5 Ben Jones-Bishop; 3 Bill Tupou; 4 Reece Lyne; 2 Tom Johnstone; 6 Jacob Miller; 25 Ryan Hampshire; 20 Keegan Hirst; 13 Tyler Randell; 10 Anthony England; 12 Danny Kirmond (C); 11 Matty Ashurst; 19 James Batchelor. Subs (all used): 8 David Fifita; 9 Kyle Wood; 15 Pauli Pauli; 16 Tinirau Arona.
Tries: Johnstone (17), Jones-Bishop (21), Tupou (27, 44), Lyne (35, 77), Batchelor (56), Arona (71);
Goals: Batchelor 5/7, Hampshire 1/1.
VIKINGS: 27 Olly Ashall-Bott; 2 Stefan Marsh; 4 Charly Runciman; 3 Krisnan Inu; 22 Ryan Ince; 6 Joe Mellor (C); 7 Tom Gilmore; 25 Jay Chapelhow; 33 Aaron Heremaia; 8 Gil Dudson; 12 Matt Whitley; 39 Weller Hauraki; 10 Alex Gerrard. Subs (all used): 20 Macgraff Leuluai; 17 Sam Wilde; 23 Danny Walker; 26 Ted Chapelhow.
Tries: Marsh (48), D Walker (58), Gerrard (67), Ince (73);
Goals: Gilmore 3/4.
Rugby Leaguer & League Express Men of the Match:
Trinity: Bill Tupou; *Vikings:* Danny Walker.
Penalty count: 5-6; **Half-time:** 22-0;
Referee: Liam Moore; **Attendance:** 4,589.

ROUND 19

Thursday 28th June 2018

WIGAN WARRIORS 46 LEEDS RHINOS 8

WARRIORS: 1 Sam Tomkins; 2 Tom Davies; 14 John Bateman; 4 Oliver Gildart; 22 Liam Marshall; 34 Josh Woods; 7 Sam Powell; 25 Romain Navarrete; 9 Thomas Leuluai; 8 Tony Clubb; 19 Willie Isa; 12 Liam Farrell; 13 Sean O'Loughlin (C). Subs (all used): 17 Taulima Tautai; 20 Morgan Escare; 30 Gabe Hamlin; 40 Joe Greenwood (D).
Tries: Marshall (13, 15, 80), Woods (31), Farrell (50), Leuluai (65), Davies (77); **Goals:** S Tomkins 9/10.
Sin bin: Navarrete (72) - dangerous contact on Ormondroyd.
RHINOS: 24 Jack Walker; 2 Tom Briscoe; 4 Liam Sutcliffe; 34 Luke Briscoe; 5 Ryan Hall; 6 Joel Moon; 7 Richie Myler; 28 Mikolaj Oledzki; 9 Matt Parcell; 17 Mitch Garbutt; 19 Brett Ferres; 27 Cameron Smith; 8 Adam Cuthbertson (C). Subs (all used): 1 Ashton Golding; 10 Brad Singleton; 23 Jack Ormondroyd; 30 Josh Walters.
Tries: Ferres (5), Moon (70); **Goals:** Sutcliffe 0/2.
Rugby Leaguer & League Express Men of the Match:
Warriors: Josh Woods; *Rhinos:* Brett Ferres.
Penalty count: 6-3; **Half-time:** 22-4;
Referee: Ben Thaler; **Attendance:** 10,645.

Friday 29th June 2018

ST HELENS 34 WAKEFIELD TRINITY 30

SAINTS: 23 Ben Barba; 2 Tommy Makinson; 3 Ryan Morgan; 4 Mark Percival; 19 Regan Grace; 1 Jonny Lomax; 18 Danny Richardson; 14 Luke Douglas; 9 James Roby (C); 16 Luke Thompson; 17 Dominique Peyroux; 11 Zeb Taia; 12 Jon Wilkin. Subs (all used): 6 Theo Fages; 13 Louie McCarthy-Scarsbrook; 15 Morgan Knowles; 20 Matty Lees.
Tries: Grace (13, 65), Lomax (24), Richardson (34), Roby (68), Taia (72); **Goals:** Richardson 5/7.
TRINITY: 25 Ryan Hampshire; 24 Mason Caton-Brown; 3 Bill Tupou; 4 Reece Lyne; 2 Tom Johnstone; 6 Jacob Miller; 7 Liam Finn; 8 David Fifita; 13 Tyler Randell; 10 Anthony England; 19 James Batchelor; 11 Matty Ashurst (C); 16 Tinirau Arona. Subs (all used): 9 Kyle Wood; 15 Pauli Pauli; 20 Keegan Hirst; 23 Chris Annakin.
Tries: Johnstone (18, 61), Hampshire (43), Miller (52), Caton-Brown (55), Lyne (79);
Goals: Finn 3/5 *(last conversion attempt declined)*.
Rugby Leaguer & League Express Men of the Match:
Saints: James Roby; *Trinity:* Kyle Wood.
Penalty count: 5-9; **Half-time:** 20-6;
Referee: James Child; **Attendance:** 10,008.

WARRINGTON WOLVES 30 SALFORD RED DEVILS 14

WOLVES: 21 Mitch Brown; 2 Tom Lineham; 3 Bryson Goodwin; 18 Toby King; 27 Josh Charnley; 6 Kevin Brown; 7 Tyrone Roberts; 16 Sitaleki Akauola; 9 Daryl Clark; 10 Mike Cooper; 29 Ben Pomeroy; 12 Jack Hughes; 34 Ben Westwood (C). Subs (all used): 17 Joe Philbin; 15 Declan Patton; 14 Dominic Crosby; 19 George King.
Tries: Akauola (7), Lineham (16), T King (23), Charnley (53), Clark (70), Cooper (78); **Goals:** Goodwin 3/6.
RED DEVILS: 7 Jack Littlejohn; 22 Derrell Olpherts; 3 Kris Welham; 4 Junior Sa'u; 24 Jake Bibby; 6 Robert Lui; 28 Jake Shorrocks; 14 Lama Tasi; 19 Josh Wood; 23 Lee Mossop (C); 10 George Griffin; 15 Ryan Lannon; 30 Greg Burke. Subs (all used): 13 Mark Flanagan; 9 Logan Tomkins; 18 Ben Nakubuwai; 26 Daniel Murray.
Tries: Littlejohn (13, 35), Bibby (45); **Goals:** Lui 1/3.
Sin bin: Lannon (26) - holding down.
Rugby Leaguer & League Express Men of the Match:
Wolves: Mitch Brown; *Red Devils:* Robert Lui.
Penalty count: 6-3; **Half-time:** 14-10;
Referee: Chris Kendall; **Attendance:** 9,171.

HULL FC 31 WIDNES VIKINGS 24

HULL FC: 1 Jamie Shaul; 2 Bureta Faraimo; 14 Jake Connor; 3 Carlos Tuimavave; 28 Hakim Miloudi; 6 Albert Kelly; 35 Liam Harris; 8 Scott Taylor; 9 Danny Houghton (C); 23 Mickey Paea; 21 Sika Manu; 12 Mark Minichiello; 11 Dean Hadley. Subs (all used): 17 Danny Washbrook; 20 Brad Fash; 24 Jack Logan; 29 Masi Matongo.
Tries: Kelly (6), Miloudi (20), Harris (28), Tuimavave (48), Faraimo (72); **Goals:** Connor 5/6; **Field goal:** Connor (68).
VIKINGS: 1 Rhys Hanbury; 5 Patrick Ah Van; 4 Charly Runciman; 3 Krisnan Inu; 40 Owen Buckley (D); 6 Joe Mellor (C); 15 Danny Craven; 25 Jay Chapelhow; 33 Aaron Heremaia; 8 Gil Dudson; 17 Sam Wilde; 39 Weller Hauraki; 16 Tom Olbison. Subs (all used): 20 Macgraff Leuluai; 12 Matt Whitley; 23 Danny Walker; 10 Alex Gerrard.
Tries: Runciman (35), Buckley (39), Wilde (45), J Chapelhow (55); **Goals:** Inu 4/4.
Rugby Leaguer & League Express Men of the Match:
Hull FC: Jake Connor; *Vikings:* Danny Walker.
Penalty count: 8-3; **Half-time:** 16-12;
Referee: Greg Dolan; **Attendance:** 10,420.

HULL KINGSTON ROVERS 37 HUDDERSFIELD GIANTS 10

ROVERS: 1 Adam Quinlan; 5 Ryan Shaw; 11 Maurice Blair; 2 Junior Vaivai; 22 Liam Salter; 7 Danny McGuire; 24 Chris Atkin; 8 Nick Scruton; 19 Tommy Lee; 34 Danny Tickle; 12 James Greenwood; 39 Joel Tomkins; 17 Chris Clarkson. Subs (all used): 9 Shaun Lunt (C); 10 Mose Masoe; 13 Ben Kavanagh; 21 Robbie Mulhern.
Tries: Tomkins (32), Quinlan (36, 48), Vaivai (44), Shaw (55, 58); **Goals:** Shaw 6/6; **Field goal:** Atkin (80).
GIANTS: 15 Jordan Rankin; 2 Jermaine McGillvary; 3 Leroy Cudjoe (C); 6 Lee Gaskell; 23 Darnell McIntosh; 4 Jordan Turner; 34 Oliver Russell; 12 Michael Lawrence; 9 Kruise Leeming; 27 Matty English; 22 Alex Mellor; 5 Aaron Murphy; 13 Ryan Hinchcliffe. Subs (all used): 21 Adam O'Brien; 8 Sebastine Ikahihifo; 19 Daniel Smith; 16 Oliver Roberts.
Tries: McIntosh (16), Murphy (72); **Goals:** Russell 1/2.
Rugby Leaguer & League Express Men of the Match:
Rovers: Junior Vaivai; *Giants:* Jordan Rankin.
Penalty count: 10-6; **Half-time:** 12-4;
Referee: Scott Mikalauskas; **Attendance:** 7,080.

Saturday 30th June 2018

CATALANS DRAGONS 44 CASTLEFORD TIGERS 16

DRAGONS: 31 Tony Gigot; 20 Lewis Tierney; 1 David Mead; 4 Brayden Wiliame; 5 Fouad Yaha; 6 Samisoni Langi; 33 Josh Drinkwater; 8 Remi Casty (C); 19 Michael Mcllorum; 15 Mickael Simon; 21 Benjamin Jullien; 12 Benjamin Garcia; 13 Greg Bird. Subs (all used): 11 Louis Anderson; 14 Julian Bousquet; 17 Jason Baitieri; 34 Kenny Edwards.
Tries: Drinkwater (4, 28, 68), Bird (23), Anderson (34), Bousquet (36), Edwards (50), Tierney (77);
Goals: Drinkwater 6/9.
TIGERS: 34 Quentin Laulu-Togagae; 29 Tuoyo Egodo; 3 Jake Webster; 4 Michael Shenton (C); 26 James Clare; 6 Jamie Ellis; 21 Jake Trueman; 32 Liam Watts; 9 Paul McShane; 15 Jesse Sene-Lefao; 8 Junior Moors; 11 Oliver Holmes; 14 Nathan Massey. Subs (all used): 10 Grant Millington; 18 Matt Cook; 19 Gadwin Springer; 23 Mitch Clark.
Tries: Clare (12), Laulu-Togagae (19), McShane (60);
Goals: Ellis 2/3.
Rugby Leaguer & League Express Men of the Match:
Dragons: Josh Drinkwater; *Tigers:* Mitch Clark.
Penalty count: 8-7; **Half-time:** 30-10;
Referee: Robert Hicks; **Attendance:** 10,236.

ROUND 20

Thursday 5th July 2018

HUDDERSFIELD GIANTS 29 HULL FC 18

GIANTS: 15 Jordan Rankin; 2 Jermaine McGillvary; 6 Lee Gaskell; 29 Jake Wardle; 23 Darnell McIntosh; 4 Jordan Turner; 7 Danny Brough; 17 Ukuma Ta'ai; 21 Adam O'Brien; 12 Michael Lawrence; 22 Alex Mellor; 5 Aaron Murphy; 19 Daniel Smith. Subs (all used): 13 Ryan Hinchcliffe (C); 8 Sebastine Ikahihifo; 18 Paul Clough; 16 Oliver Roberts.
Tries: Smith (15), Murphy (29), Rankin (33), McIntosh (51, 72); **Goals:** Brough 4/5;
Field goal: Brough (40).
HULL FC: 28 Hakim Miloudi; 2 Bureta Faraimo; 30 Cameron Scott; 3 Carlos Tuimavave; 24 Jack Logan; 6 Albert Kelly; 14 Jake Connor; 23 Mickey Paea; 9 Danny Houghton (C); 8 Scott Taylor; 11 Dean Hadley; 12 Mark Minichiello; 15 Chris Green. Subs (all used): 29 Masi Matongo; 17 Danny Washbrook; 20 Brad Fash; 27 Jack Downs.
Tries: Faraimo (21), Miloudi (53), Houghton (77);
Goals: Connor 3/3.
Rugby Leaguer & League Express Men of the Match:
Giants: Jordan Turner; *Hull FC:* Chris Green.
Penalty count: 7-5; **Half-time:** 19-6;
Referee: Robert Hicks; **Attendance:** 4,696.

Friday 6th July 2018

WIGAN WARRIORS 13 WARRINGTON WOLVES 12

WARRIORS: 1 Sam Tomkins (C); 2 Tom Davies; 14 John Bateman; 4 Oliver Gildart; 22 Liam Marshall; 34 Josh Woods; 7 Sam Powell; 8 Tony Clubb; 9 Thomas Leuluai; 10 Ben Flower; 19 Willie Isa; 12 Liam Farrell; 30 Gabe Hamlin. Subs (all used): 17 Taulima Tautai; 20 Morgan Escare; 27 Callum Field; 39 Liam Paisley.
Tries: Davies (13), Paisley (29); **Goals:** S Tomkins 2/2.
Field goal: Woods (79).
On report:
Powell (56) - alleged dangerous contact on Clark.
WOLVES: 1 Stefan Ratchford; 2 Tom Lineham; 3 Bryson Goodwin; 18 Toby King; 27 Josh Charnley; 6 Kevin Brown; 7 Tyrone Roberts; 8 Chris Hill; 9 Daryl Clark; 10 Mike Cooper; 16 Sitaleki Akauola; 12 Jack Hughes; 34 Ben Westwood (C). Subs (all used): 14 Dominic Crosby; 15 Declan Patton; 17 Joe Philbin; 21 Mitch Brown.

Tries: T King (22), Lineham (62), Charnley (77);
Goals: Goodwin 0/1, Ratchford 0/2.
Rugby Leaguer & League Express Men of the Match:
Warriors: Liam Paisley; *Wolves:* Daryl Clark.
Penalty count: 7-5; **Half-time:** 12-4;
Referee: Chris Kendall; **Attendance:** 13,249.

ST HELENS 36 WIDNES VIKINGS 6

SAINTS: 1 Jonny Lomax; 5 Adam Swift; 30 Matthew Costello; 4 Mark Percival; 19 Regan Grace; 6 Theo Fages; 18 Danny Richardson; 10 Kyle Amor; 9 James Roby (C); 16 Luke Thompson; 17 Dominique Peyroux; 11 Zeb Taia; 12 Jon Wilkin. Subs (all used): 13 Louie McCarthy-Scarsbrook; 14 Luke Douglas; 15 Morgan Knowles; 20 Matty Lees.
Tries: Taia (7), Percival (11), Swift (22, 60, 71), McCarthy-Scarsbrook (38), Fages (51);
Goals: Richardson 4/7.
VIKINGS: 1 Rhys Hanbury; 2 Stefan Marsh; 4 Charly Runciman; 3 Krisnan Inu; 40 Owen Buckley; 6 Joe Mellor (C); 15 Danny Craven; 25 Jay Chapelhow; 33 Aaron Heremaia; 8 Gil Dudson; 17 Sam Wilde; 39 Weller Hauraki; 10 Alex Gerrard. Subs (all used): 12 Matt Whitley; 16 Tom Olbison; 20 Macgraff Leuluai; 23 Danny Walker.
Try: Craven (43); **Goals:** Inu 1/1.
Rugby Leaguer & League Express Men of the Match:
Saints: Jonny Lomax; *Vikings:* Matt Whitley.
Penalty count: 10-7; **Half-time:** 20-0;
Referee: Scott Mikalauskas; **Attendance:** 9,923.

Saturday 7th July 2018

WAKEFIELD TRINITY 18 CATALANS DRAGONS 35

TRINITY: 25 Ryan Hampshire; 2 Tom Johnstone; 4 Reece Lyne; 3 Bill Tupou; 5 Ben Jones-Bishop; 6 Jacob Miller; 7 Liam Finn; 8 David Fifita; 13 Tyler Randell; 10 Anthony England; 11 Matty Ashurst (C); 14 Justin Horo; 16 Tinirau Arona. Subs (all used): 9 Kyle Wood; 15 Pauli Pauli; 20 Keegan Hirst; 23 Chris Annakin.
Tries: Horo (5, 53), Johnstone (40); **Goals:** Finn 3/3.
DRAGONS: 31 Tony Gigot; 20 Lewis Tierney; 1 David Mead; 4 Brayden Wiliame; 5 Fouad Yaha; 6 Samisoni Langi; 33 Josh Drinkwater; 15 Mickael Simon; 19 Michael McIlorum; 8 Remi Casty (C); 21 Benjamin Jullien; 12 Benjamin Garcia; 13 Greg Bird. Subs (all used): 14 Julian Bousquet; 10 Sam Moa; 34 Kenny Edwards; 17 Jason Baitieri.
Tries: Bird (15), Jullien (26), Mead (28), Wiliame (32, 69), Yaha (76); **Goals:** Drinkwater 5/8; **Field goal:** Gigot (66).
Sin bin: Tierney (52) - dangerous challenge on Johnstone.
Rugby Leaguer & League Express Men of the Match:
Trinity: Justin Horo; *Dragons:* Brayden Wiliame.
Penalty count: 6-6; **Half-time:** 12-22;
Referee: Ben Thaler; **Attendance:** 5,079.

Sunday 8th July 2018

HULL KINGSTON ROVERS 52 SALFORD RED DEVILS 22

ROVERS: 1 Adam Quinlan; 5 Ryan Shaw; 11 Maurice Blair; 2 Junior Vaivai; 27 Will Oakes; 7 Danny McGuire; 24 Chris Atkin; 8 Nick Scruton; 19 Tommy Lee; 34 Danny Tickle; 12 James Greenwood; 39 Joel Tomkins; 13 Ben Kavanagh. Subs (all used): 9 Shaun Lunt (C); 10 Mose Masoe; 15 James Donaldson; 21 Robbie Mulhern.
Tries: Shaw (17), Quinlan (23), Oakes (27, 56), Greenwood (33), McGuire (36, 51, 58), Tomkins (39);
Goals: Shaw 1/1, Tickle 7/8.
RED DEVILS: 29 Ed Chamberlain; 2 Greg Johnson; 24 Jake Bibby; 4 Junior Sa'u; 22 Derrell Olpherts; 6 Robert Lui; 28 Jake Shorrocks; 14 Lama Tasi; 19 Josh Wood; 23 Lee Mossop (C); 15 Ryan Lannon; 17 Tyrone McCarthy; 13 Mark Flanagan. Subs (all used): 9 Logan Tomkins; 30 Greg Burke; 26 Daniel Murray; 11 Josh Jones.
Tries: Johnson (8), Sa'u (45, 61), Bibby (78);
Goals: Chamberlain 3/4.
Rugby Leaguer & League Express Men of the Match:
Rovers: Danny McGuire; *Red Devils:* Robert Lui.
Penalty count: 7-7; **Half-time:** 36-6;
Referee: Gareth Hewer; **Attendance:** 7,698.

CASTLEFORD TIGERS 42 LEEDS RHINOS 10

TIGERS: 34 Quentin Laulu-Togagae; 26 James Clare; 3 Jake Webster; 4 Michael Shenton (C); 5 Greg Eden; 6 Jamie Ellis; 21 Jake Trueman; 32 Liam Watts; 9 Paul McShane; 15 Jesse Sene-Lefao; 8 Junior Moors; 10 Grant Millington; 13 Adam Milner. Subs (all used): 11 Oliver Holmes; 14 Nathan Massey; 18 Matt Cook; 23 Mitch Clark.
Tries: Eden (7), Laulu-Togagae (25), Cook (30), Trueman (45, 55), Sene-Lefao (69, 75); **Goals:** Ellis 7/8.
RHINOS: 1 Ashton Golding; 2 Tom Briscoe; 4 Liam Sutcliffe; 6 Joel Moon; 5 Ryan Hall; 25 Jordan Lilley; 7 Richie Myler; 28 Mikolaj Oledzki; 9 Matt Parcell; 10 Brad Singleton; 13 Stevie Ward (C); 19 Brett Ferres; 8 Adam Cuthbertson. Subs (all used): 24 Jack Walker; 15 Brett Delaney; 16 Anthony Mullally; 30 Josh Walters.
Tries: T Briscoe (3, 17); **Goals:** Sutcliffe 1/2.
Rugby Leaguer & League Express Men of the Match:
Tigers: Jake Trueman; *Rhinos:* Matt Parcell.
Penalty count: 4-5; **Half-time:** 16-10;
Referee: Liam Moore; **Attendance:** 9,557.

ROUND 21

Thursday 12th July 2018

HUDDERSFIELD GIANTS 20 WIGAN WARRIORS 12

GIANTS: 1 Jake Mamo; 2 Jermaine McGillvary; 3 Leroy Cudjoe (C); 4 Jordan Turner; 23 Darnell McIntosh; 6 Lee Gaskell; 7 Danny Brough; 12 Michael Lawrence; 21 Adam O'Brien; 18 Paul Clough; 22 Alex Mellor; 5 Aaron Murphy; 19 Daniel Smith. Subs (all used): 13 Ryan Hinchcliffe; 27 Matty English; 14 Dale Ferguson; 16 Oliver Roberts.
Tries: McIntosh (12, 42), Mellor (25), Cudjoe (65);
Goals: Brough 2/6.
Sin bin: Lawrence (58) - professional foul.
WARRIORS: 1 Sam Tomkins; 2 Tom Davies; 39 Liam Paisley; 4 Oliver Gildart; 22 Liam Marshall; 34 Josh Woods; 7 Sam Powell; 25 Romain Navarrete; 9 Thomas Leuluai; 10 Ben Flower; 19 Willie Isa; 30 Gabe Hamlin; 13 Sean O'Loughlin (C). Subs (all used): 20 Morgan Escare; 8 Tony Clubb; 36 Samy Kibula (D); 17 Taulima Tautai.
Tries: S Tomkins (5), Davies (75); **Goals:** S Tomkins 2/2.
Rugby Leaguer & League Express Men of the Match:
Giants: Lee Gaskell; *Warriors:* Romain Navarrete.
Penalty count: 12-12; **Half-time:** 12-6;
Referee: Gareth Hewer; **Attendance:** 5,264.

WARRINGTON WOLVES 22 CATALANS DRAGONS 22

WOLVES: 1 Stefan Ratchford; 2 Tom Lineham; 3 Bryson Goodwin; 18 Toby King; 27 Josh Charnley; 6 Kevin Brown; 7 Tyrone Roberts; 8 Chris Hill (C); 9 Daryl Clark; 10 Mike Cooper; 20 Harvey Livett; 12 Jack Hughes; 34 Ben Westwood. Subs (all used): 17 Joe Philbin; 29 Ben Pomeroy; 15 Declan Patton; 16 Sitaleki Akauola.
Tries: Goodwin (16), Charnley (21), Livett (25);
Goals: Roberts 5/6.
DRAGONS: 31 Tony Gigot; 20 Lewis Tierney; 1 David Mead; 4 Brayden Wiliame; 5 Fouad Yaha; 6 Samisoni Langi; 33 Josh Drinkwater; 8 Remi Casty (C); 19 Michael McIlorum; 15 Mickael Simon; 21 Benjamin Jullien; 12 Benjamin Garcia; 13 Greg Bird. Subs (all used): 14 Julian Bousquet; 10 Sam Moa; 34 Kenny Edwards; 17 Jason Baitieri.
Tries: Jullien (5), McIlorum (28), Gigot (38);
Goals: Drinkwater 5/5.
Sin bin: Simon (69) - retaliation.
Rugby Leaguer & League Express Men of the Match:
Wolves: Stefan Ratchford; *Dragons:* Remi Casty.
Penalty count: 9-8; **Half-time:** 18-20;
Referee: Ben Thaler; **Attendance:** 8,807.

Friday 13th July 2018

HULL FC 18 ST HELENS 34

HULL FC: 28 Hakim Miloudi; 2 Bureta Faraimo; 14 Jake Connor; 3 Carlos Tuimavave; 24 Jack Logan; 6 Albert Kelly; 16 Jordan Abdull; 8 Scott Taylor; 9 Danny Houghton (C); 15 Chris Green; 25 Jansin Turgut; 12 Mark Minichiello; 11 Dean Hadley. Subs (all used): 23 Mickey Paea; 26 Jordan Lane; 27 Jack Downs; 29 Masi Matongo.
Tries: Faraimo (1, 37), Turgut (49), Kelly (52);
Goals: Connor 0/1, Miloudi 1/3.
SAINTS: 23 Ben Barba; 5 Adam Swift; 2 Tommy Makinson; 4 Mark Percival; 19 Regan Grace; 1 Jonny Lomax; 18 Danny Richardson; 16 Luke Thompson; 9 James Roby (C); 10 Kyle Amor; 11 Zeb Taia; 17 Dominique Peyroux; 12 Jon Wilkin. Subs (all used): 6 Theo Fages; 13 Louie McCarthy-Scarsbrook; 14 Luke Douglas; 15 Morgan Knowles.
Tries: Makinson (17), Barba (29, 56), Lomax (60, 66), Swift (69), Thompson (77); **Goals:** Richardson 3/7.
Rugby Leaguer & League Express Men of the Match:
Hull FC: Albert Kelly; *Saints:* Jonny Lomax.
Penalty count: 5-3; **Half-time:** 8-10;
Referee: Liam Moore; **Attendance:** 11,130.

LEEDS RHINOS 20 WAKEFIELD TRINITY 20

RHINOS: 24 Jack Walker; 2 Tom Briscoe; 4 Liam Sutcliffe; 22 Ash Handley; 5 Ryan Hall; 6 Joel Moon; 7 Richie Myler; 17 Mitch Garbutt; 14 Brad Dwyer; 10 Brad Singleton; 12 Carl Ablett (C); 19 Brett Ferres; 8 Adam Cuthbertson. Subs (all used): 13 Stevie Ward; 28 Mikolaj Oledzki; 1 Ashton Golding; 30 Josh Walters.
Tries: Hall (4), Myler (22), Handley (24);
Goals: Sutcliffe 4/4.
TRINITY: 21 Max Jowitt; 5 Ben Jones-Bishop; 4 Reece Lyne; 3 Bill Tupou; 2 Tom Johnstone; 6 Jacob Miller; 25 Ryan Hampshire; 8 David Fifita; 13 Tyler Randell; 10 Anthony England; 11 Matty Ashurst (C); 14 Justin Horo; 23 Chris Annakin. Subs (all used): 9 Kyle Wood; 16 Tinirau Arona; 20 Keegan Hirst; 15 Pauli Pauli.
Tries: Tupou (11), Horo (32), Wood (71);
Goals: Hampshire 4/4.
Rugby Leaguer & League Express Men of the Match:
Rhinos: Brad Dwyer; *Trinity:* Kyle Wood.
Penalty count: 6-8; **Half time:** 18-12;
Referee: Robert Hicks; **Attendance:** 11,140.

SALFORD RED DEVILS 6 CASTLEFORD TIGERS 24

RED DEVILS: 29 Ed Chamberlain; 22 Derrell Olpherts; 4 Junior Sa'u; 11 Josh Jones; 24 Jake Bibby; 6 Robert Lui; 28 Jake Shorrocks; 14 Lama Tasi; 19 Josh Wood; 18 Ben Nakubuwai; 15 Ryan Lannon; 17 Tyrone McCarthy; 26 Daniel Murray. Subs (all used): 13 Mark Flanagan; 30 Greg Burke; 23 Lee Mossop (C); 25 Levy Nzoungou.
Try: Bibby (25); **Goals:** Chamberlain 1/1.
TIGERS: 5 Greg Eden; 28 Kieran Gill; 3 Jake Webster; 4 Michael Shenton (C); 26 James Clare; 34 Quentin Laulu-Togagae; 21 Jake Trueman; 32 Liam Watts; 9 Paul McShane; 15 Jesse Sene-Lefao; 8 Junior Moors; 10 Grant Millington; 13 Adam Milner. Subs (all used): 11 Oliver Holmes; 16 Joe Wardle; 18 Matt Cook; 23 Mitch Clark.
Tries: Webster (18, 52), Shenton (47), Gill (72);
Goals: McShane 4/4.
Rugby Leaguer & League Express Men of the Match:
Red Devils: Josh Wood; *Tigers:* Jake Webster.
Penalty count: 6-3; **Half-time:** 6-6;
Referee: Chris Kendall; **Attendance:** 2,681.

Saturday 14th July 2018

WIDNES VIKINGS 24 HULL KINGSTON ROVERS 26

VIKINGS: 27 Olly Ashall-Bott; 2 Stefan Marsh; 4 Charly Runciman; 3 Krisnan Inu; 40 Owen Buckley; 6 Joe Mellor (C); 15 Danny Craven; 25 Jay Chapelhow; 33 Aaron Heremaia; 8 Gil Dudson; 12 Matt Whitley; 11 Chris Houston (C); 20 Macgraff Leuluai. Subs (all used): 16 Tom Olbison; 23 Danny Walker; 26 Ted Chapelhow; 36 Wellington Albert.
Tries: Ashall-Bott (50), Craven (56), Buckley (64, 78);
Goals: Inu 4/5.
ROVERS: 1 Adam Quinlan; 36 Justin Carney; 11 Maurice Blair; 22 Liam Salter; 27 Will Oakes; 7 Danny McGuire; 24 Chris Atkin; 8 Nick Scruton; 9 Shaun Lunt (C); 21 Robbie Mulhern; 34 Danny Tickle; 12 James Greenwood; 17 Chris Clarkson. Subs (all used): 23 Josh Johnson; 10 Mose Masoe; 13 Ben Kavanagh; 15 James Donaldson.
Tries: Donaldson (31), Tickle (43), Quinlan (59), Salter (68);
Goals: Atkin 1/1, Tickle 4/4.
Sin bin: Tickle (14) - professional foul.
Rugby Leaguer & League Express Men of the Match:
Vikings: Olly Ashall-Bott; *Rovers:* Shaun Lunt.
Penalty count: 8-8; **Half-time:** 2-8;
Referee: Tom Grant; **Attendance:** 4,469.

ROUND 22

Thursday 19th July 2018

WIGAN WARRIORS 6 ST HELENS 14

WARRIORS: 1 Sam Tomkins (C); 2 Tom Davies; 41 Chris Hankinson (D); 3 Dan Sarginson; 22 Liam Marshall; 34 Josh Woods; 7 Sam Powell; 8 Tony Clubb; 9 Thomas Leuluai; 10 Ben Flower; 19 Willie Isa; 14 John Bateman; 25 Romain Navarrete. Subs (all used): 17 Taulima Tautai; 30 Gabe Hamlin; 39 Liam Paisley; 40 Joe Greenwood.
Try: S Tomkins (71); **Goals:** S Tomkins 1/1.
SAINTS: 1 Jonny Lomax; 5 Adam Swift; 2 Tommy Makinson; 3 Ryan Morgan; 19 Regan Grace; 6 Theo Fages; 18 Danny Richardson; 10 Kyle Amor; 9 James Roby (C); 16 Luke Thompson; 17 Dominique Peyroux; 15 Morgan Knowles; 12 Jon Wilkin. Subs (all used): 13 Louie McCarthy-Scarsbrook; 14 Luke Douglas; 20 Matty Lees; 21 Jack Ashworth.
Tries: Peyroux (10), Knowles (50); **Goals:** Richardson 3/3.
Rugby Leaguer & League Express Men of the Match:
Warriors: Chris Hankinson; *Saints:* James Roby.
Penalty count: 6-5; **Half-time:** 0-8;
Referee: Robert Hicks; **Attendance:** 16,047.

Friday 20th July 2018

CASTLEFORD TIGERS 18 HUDDERSFIELD GIANTS 32

TIGERS: 34 Quentin Laulu-Togagae; 26 James Clare; 3 Jake Webster; 4 Michael Shenton (C); 5 Greg Eden; 6 Jamie Ellis; 21 Jake Trueman; 32 Liam Watts; 9 Paul McShane; 15 Jesse Sene-Lefao; 11 Oliver Holmes; 10 Grant Millington; 13 Adam Milner. Subs (all used): 8 Junior Moors; 14 Nathan Massey; 18 Matt Cook; 23 Mitch Clark.

Tries: Ellis (7), Trueman (9), Moors (34); **Goals:** Ellis 3/3.
GIANTS: 15 Jordan Rankin; 2 Jermaine McGillvary; 3 Leroy Cudjoe (C); 4 Jordan Turner; 23 Darnell McIntosh; 6 Lee Gaskell; 7 Danny Brough; 18 Paul Clough; 21 Adam O'Brien; 12 Michael Lawrence; 22 Alex Mellor; 5 Aaron Murphy; 17 Ukuma Ta'ai. Subs (all used): 13 Ryan Hinchcliffe; 14 Dale Ferguson; 16 Oliver Roberts; 19 Daniel Smith.
Tries: McGillvary (18, 23, 52), Gaskell (40), Cudjoe (44), McIntosh (47); **Goals:** Brough 4/8.
Rugby Leaguer & League Express Men of the Match: *Tigers:* Paul McShane; *Giants:* Danny Brough.
Penalty count: 6-6; **Half-time:** 18-18;
Referee: Chris Kendall; **Attendance:** 5,406.

HULL KINGSTON ROVERS 20 WARRINGTON WOLVES 34

ROVERS: 1 Adam Quinlan; 37 Elliot Wallis; 11 Maurice Blair; 2 Junior Vaivai; 27 Will Oakes; 7 Danny McGuire; 24 Chris Atkin; 8 Nick Scruton; 9 Shaun Lunt (C); 21 Robbie Mulhern; 34 Danny Tickle; 12 James Greenwood; 17 Chris Clarkson. Subs (all used): 10 Mose Masoe; 13 Ben Kavanagh; 14 Lee Jewitt; 22 Liam Salter.
Tries: Wallis (13, 24), Mulhern (43), Atkin (59);
Goals: Tickle 2/4.
WOLVES: 1 Stefan Ratchford; 2 Tom Lineham; 21 Mitch Brown; 18 Toby King; 27 Josh Charnley; 6 Kevin Brown; 7 Tyrone Roberts; 8 Chris Hill (C); 9 Daryl Clark; 10 Mike Cooper; 20 Harvey Livett; 12 Jack Hughes; 19 George King. Subs (all used): 15 Declan Patton; 16 Sitaleki Akauola; 17 Joe Philbin; 29 Ben Pomeroy.
Tries: Cooper (8), Ratchford (28), Roberts (50), T King (54), K Brown (69), Patton (73); **Goals:** Roberts 5/6.
Rugby Leaguer & League Express Men of the Match: *Rovers:* Chris Atkin; *Wolves:* Stefan Ratchford.
Penalty count: 5-8; **Half-time:** 8-12;
Referee: Liam Moore; **Attendance:** 7,045.

LEEDS RHINOS 34 WIDNES VIKINGS 0

RHINOS: 24 Jack Walker; 2 Tom Briscoe; 22 Ash Handley; 5 Ryan Hall; 34 Luke Briscoe; 6 Joel Moon; 7 Richie Myler; 17 Mitch Garbutt; 14 Brad Dwyer; 10 Brad Singleton (C); 4 Liam Sutcliffe; 12 Carl Ablett; 8 Adam Cuthbertson. Subs (all used): 36 Dominic Crosby (D); 9 Matt Parcell; 28 Mikolaj Oledzki; 18 Jimmy Keinhorst.
Tries: Dwyer (18), L Briscoe (22), Myler (37), Parcell (39), Moon (42), T Briscoe (47), Walker (70); **Goals:** Myler 3/7.
VIKINGS: 27 Olly Ashall-Bott; 5 Patrick Ah Van; 4 Charly Runciman; 3 Krisnan Inu; 40 Owen Buckley; 6 Joe Mellor (C); 15 Danny Craven; 26 Ted Chapelhow; 23 Danny Walker; 8 Gil Dudson; 12 Matt Whitley; 39 Weller Hauraki; 20 Macgraff Leuluai. Subs (all used): 25 Jay Chapelhow; 36 Wellington Albert; 28 Brad Walker; 17 Sam Wilde.
Sin bin: D Walker (14) - dangerous challenge on Handley; Hauraki (79) - punching.
Rugby Leaguer & League Express Men of the Match: *Rhinos:* Jack Walker; *Vikings:* Charly Runciman.
Penalty count: 12-6; **Half time:** 20-0;
Referee: James Child; **Attendance:** 10,977.

Saturday 21st July 2018

CATALANS DRAGONS 44 SALFORD RED DEVILS 10

DRAGONS: 31 Tony Gigot; 20 Lewis Tierney; 1 David Mead; 4 Brayden Wiliame; 5 Fouad Yaha; 6 Samisoni Langi; 33 Josh Drinkwater; 15 Mickael Simon; 19 Michael McIlorum; 10 Sam Moa; 21 Benjamin Jullien; 12 Benjamin Garcia; 8 Remi Casty (C). Subs (all used): 11 Louis Anderson; 14 Julian Bousquet; 17 Jason Baitieri; 34 Kenny Edwards.
Tries: Yaha (6, 38, 44, 47), Drinkwater (17), Baitieri (31), Edwards (33, 69); **Goals:** Drinkwater 6/9.
RED DEVILS: 29 Ed Chamberlain; 24 Jake Bibby; 11 Josh Jones; 4 Junior Sa'u; 22 Derrell Olpherts; 6 Robert Lui; 28 Jake Shorrocks; 14 Lama Tasi; 19 Josh Wood; 23 Lee Mossop (C); 15 Ryan Lannon; 18 Ben Nakubuwai; 26 Daniel Murray. Subs (all used): 5 Niall Evalds; 17 Tyrone McCarthy; 25 Levy Nzoungou; 30 Greg Burke.
Tries: Olpherts (20), Wood (63); **Goals:** Chamberlain 1/2.
Rugby Leaguer & League Express Men of the Match: *Dragons:* Fouad Yaha; *Red Devils:* Robert Lui.
Penalty count: 4-4; **Half-time:** 28-4;
Referee: Scott Mikalauskas; **Attendance:** 8,672.

Sunday 22nd July 2018

WAKEFIELD TRINITY 72 HULL FC 10

TRINITY: 21 Max Jowitt; 5 Ben Jones-Bishop; 4 Reece Lyne; 3 Bill Tupou; 2 Tom Johnstone; 6 Jacob Miller (C); 25 Ryan Hampshire; 20 Keegan Hirst; 13 Tyler Randell; 8 David Fifita; 11 Matty Ashurst; 19 James Batchelor; 14 Justin Horo. Subs (all used): 9 Kyle Wood; 15 Pauli Pauli; 17 Craig Huby; 16 Tinirau Arona.
Tries: Johnstone (11), Fifita (16), Miller (25, 50), Pauli (35, 65), Lyne (38, 56), Batchelor (39), Jones-Bishop (44, 62), Jowitt (47); **Goals:** Hampshire 12/13.
HULL FC: 1 Jamie Shaul; 2 Bureta Faraimo; 24 Jack Logan; 3 Carlos Tuimavave; 5 Fetuli Talanoa; 16 Jordan Abdull; 7 Marc Sneyd; 29 Masi Matongo; 9 Danny Houghton (C); 8 Scott Taylor; 11 Dean Hadley; 25 Jansin Turgut; 33 Joe Westerman. Subs (all used): 23 Mickey Paea; 27 Jack Downs; 20 Brad Fash; 35 Liam Harris.
Tries: Harris (68), Faraimo (70); **Goals:** Faraimo 1/2.
Rugby Leaguer & League Express Men of the Match: *Trinity:* Ryan Hampshire; *Hull FC:* Liam Harris.
Penalty count: 5-5; **Half-time:** 38-0;
Referee: Ben Thaler; **Attendance:** 5,634.

ROUND 23

Thursday 26th July 2018

ST HELENS 14 WARRINGTON WOLVES 12

SAINTS: 23 Ben Barba; 2 Tommy Makinson; 3 Ryan Morgan; 4 Mark Percival; 19 Regan Grace; 1 Jonny Lomax; 18 Danny Richardson; 10 Kyle Amor; 9 James Roby (C); 16 Luke Thompson; 17 Dominique Peyroux; 11 Zeb Taia; 12 Jon Wilkin. Subs (all used): 6 Theo Fages; 13 Louie McCarthy-Scarsbrook; 14 Luke Douglas; 15 Morgan Knowles.
Tries: Barba (41), Lomax (65); **Goals:** Richardson 3/3.
WOLVES: 1 Stefan Ratchford; 2 Tom Lineham; 3 Bryson Goodwin; 18 Toby King; 27 Josh Charnley; 6 Kevin Brown; 7 Tyrone Roberts; 8 Chris Hill (C); 9 Daryl Clark; 10 Mike Cooper; 20 Harvey Livett; 12 Jack Hughes; 34 Ben Westwood. Subs (all used): 17 Joe Philbin; 13 Ben Murdoch-Masila; 15 Declan Patton; 16 Sitaleki Akauola.
Try: Clark (11); **Goals:** Roberts 4/4.
Rugby Leaguer & League Express Men of the Match: *Saints:* Jonny Lomax; *Wolves:* Mike Cooper.
Penalty count: 6-7; **Half-time:** 0-8;
Referee: James Child; **Attendance:** 12,454.

Friday 27th July 2018

HUDDERSFIELD GIANTS 40 WAKEFIELD TRINITY 28

GIANTS: 15 Jordan Rankin; 2 Jermaine McGillvary; 3 Leroy Cudjoe; 4 Jordan Turner; 23 Darnell McIntosh; 6 Lee Gaskell; 7 Danny Brough; 18 Paul Clough; 21 Adam O'Brien; 12 Michael Lawrence; 22 Alex Mellor; 5 Aaron Murphy; 14 Dale Ferguson. Subs (all used): 13 Ryan Hinchcliffe (C); 16 Oliver Roberts; 17 Ukuma Ta'ai; 27 Matty English.
Tries: Rankin (5), Mellor (17), McGillvary (20, 37, 43), McIntosh (34), Ta'ai (52); **Goals:** Brough 6/7.
TRINITY: 21 Max Jowitt; 5 Ben Jones-Bishop; 4 Reece Lyne; 3 Bill Tupou; 2 Tom Johnstone; 6 Jacob Miller (C); 25 Ryan Hampshire; 20 Keegan Hirst; 13 Tyler Randell; 8 David Fifita; 19 James Batchelor; 11 Matty Ashurst; 14 Justin Horo. Subs (all used): 15 Pauli Pauli; 16 Tinirau Arona; 17 Craig Huby; 23 Chris Annakin.
Tries: Jones-Bishop (8), Tupou (24), Pauli (57), Horo (59), Johnstone (79); **Goals:** Hampshire 4/5.
Sin bin: Ashurst (11) - dissent.
Rugby Leaguer & League Express Men of the Match: *Giants:* Leroy Cudjoe; *Trinity:* Pauli Pauli.
Penalty count: 11-11; **Half-time:** 30-10;
Referee: Robert Hicks; **Attendance:** 5,697.

HULL FC 16 HULL KINGSTON ROVERS 20

HULL FC: 1 Jamie Shaul; 2 Bureta Faraimo; 4 Josh Griffin; 3 Carlos Tuimavave; 5 Fetuli Talanoa; 16 Jordan Abdull; 7 Marc Sneyd; 8 Scott Taylor; 9 Danny Houghton (C); 29 Masi Matongo; 12 Mark Minichiello; 17 Danny Washbrook; 21 Sika Manu. Subs (all used): 20 Brad Fash; 35 Liam Harris; 26 Jordan Lane; 23 Mickey Paea.
Tries: Abdull (44), Griffin (50), Minichiello (57);
Goals: Sneyd 2/3.
ROVERS: 1 Adam Quinlan; 27 Will Oakes; 22 Liam Salter; 42 Ben Crooks (D); 41 Craig Hall (D2); 11 Maurice Blair (C); 24 Chris Atkin; 14 Lee Jewitt; 30 Joe Cator; 21 Robbie Mulhern; 34 Danny Tickle; 17 Chris Clarkson; 13 Ben Kavanagh. Subs (all used): 8 Nick Scruton; 15 James Donaldson; 26 Joe Wardill; 40 Todd Carney (D).
Tries: Hall (2, 24), Tickle (38); **Goals:** Tickle 3/5, Hall 1/1.
Sin bin: Blair (44) - dissent.
Rugby Leaguer & League Express Men of the Match: *Hull FC:* Danny Houghton; *Rovers:* Danny Tickle.
Penalty count: 11-6; **Half-time:** 0-16;
Referee: Gareth Hewer; **Attendance:** 17,564.

SALFORD RED DEVILS 38 LEEDS RHINOS 22

RED DEVILS: 5 Niall Evalds; 24 Jake Bibby; 29 Ed Chamberlain; 4 Junior Sa'u; 22 Derrell Olpherts; 6 Robert Lui; 31 Jackson Hastings (D); 23 Lee Mossop (C); 19 Josh Wood; 26 Daniel Murray; 11 Josh Jones; 17 Tyrone McCarthy; 15 Ryan Lannon. Subs (all used): 27 Gavin Bennion; 13 Mark Flanagan; 14 Lama Tasi; 18 Ben Nakubuwai.
Tries: Lannon (8), Evalds (10, 62), Hastings (15), Chamberlain (17), Lui (40), Jones (69);
Goals: Chamberlain 5/8.
Dismissal: Mossop (19) - headbutt.
RHINOS: 1 Ashton Golding; 2 Tom Briscoe; 18 Jimmy Keinhorst; 22 Ash Handley; 34 Luke Briscoe; 6 Joel Moon; 4 Liam Sutcliffe; 17 Mitch Garbutt; 14 Brad Dwyer; 10 Brad Singleton (C); 12 Carl Ablett; 37 Jordan Thompson (D); 27 Cameron Smith. Subs (all used): 9 Matt Parcell; 21 Nathaniel Peteru; 30 Josh Walters; 36 Dominic Crosby.
Tries: Dwyer (2), Sutcliffe (21), T Briscoe (55), Parcell (75);
Goals: Sutcliffe 3/4.
Rugby Leaguer & League Express Men of the Match: *Red Devils:* Robert Lui; *Rhinos:* Dominic Crosby.
Penalty count: 8-4; **Half-time:** 26-12;
Referee: Tom Grant; **Attendance:** 2,387.

WIGAN WARRIORS 25 CATALANS DRAGONS 20

WARRIORS: 1 Sam Tomkins (C); 2 Tom Davies; 41 Chris Hankinson; 3 Dan Sarginson; 22 Liam Marshall; 34 Josh Woods; 7 Sam Powell; 8 Tony Clubb; 9 Thomas Leuluai; 10 Ben Flower; 19 Willie Isa; 14 John Bateman; 25 Romain Navarrete. Subs (all used): 17 Taulima Tautai; 20 Morgan Escare; 30 Gabe Hamlin; 40 Joe Greenwood.
Tries: Hankinson (15), Escare (41), S Tomkins (46), Greenwood (78); **Goals:** S Tomkins 4/6;
Field goal: S Tomkins (73).
DRAGONS: 31 Tony Gigot; 2 Jodie Broughton; 3 Iain Thornley; 4 Brayden Wiliame; 5 Fouad Yaha; 6 Samisoni Langi; 22 Lucas Albert; 11 Louis Anderson; 19 Michael McIlorum; 10 Sam Moa; 13 Greg Bird (C); 34 Kenny Edwards; 17 Jason Baitieri. Subs (all used): 14 Julian Bousquet; 23 Antoni Maria; 24 Alrix Da Costa; 32 Mickael Goudemand.
Tries: Broughton (7), Da Costa (54), Yaha (58);
Goals: Albert 4/4.
Dismissal: Edwards (40) - late challenge on Bateman.
Rugby Leaguer & League Express Men of the Match: *Warriors:* Sam Tomkins; *Dragons:* Lucas Albert.
Penalty count: 11-8; **Half-time:** 8-6;
Referee: Scott Mikalauskas; **Attendance:** 10,656.

Sunday 29th July 2018

WIDNES VIKINGS 24 CASTLEFORD TIGERS 52

VIKINGS: 1 Rhys Hanbury; 5 Patrick Ah Van; 12 Matt Whitley; 3 Krisnan Inu; 22 Ryan Ince; 6 Joe Mellor (C); 42 Liam Finn (D); 25 Jay Chapelhow; 23 Danny Walker; 16 Tom Olbison; 14 Chris Dean; 41 Harrison Hansen (D); 39 Weller Hauraki. Subs (all used): 20 Macgraff Leuluai; 29 Owen Farnworth; 15 Danny Craven; 26 Ted Chapelhow.
Tries: Ah Van (10, 75), Hanbury (17), Hansen (38);
Goals: Ah Van 1/1, Inu 3/3.
Sin bin: Inu (3) - dissent.
TIGERS: 34 Quentin Laulu-Togagae; 26 James Clare; 36 Peter Mata'utia (D); 4 Michael Shenton (C); 5 Greg Eden; 6 Jamie Ellis; 21 Jake Trueman; 32 Liam Watts; 9 Paul McShane; 14 Nathan Massey; 11 Oliver Holmes; 12 Mike McMeeken; 13 Adam Milner. Subs (all used): 8 Junior Moors; 15 Jesse Sene-Lefao; 23 Mitch Clark; 33 Calum Turner.
Tries: Eden (4, 23, 59), Trueman (26), Laulu-Togagae (28, 30), Holmes (45), Clark (48), Milner (78); **Goals:** Ellis 8/9.
Rugby Leaguer & League Express Men of the Match: *Vikings:* Liam Finn; *Tigers:* Quentin Laulu-Togagae.
Penalty count: 8-6; **Half-time:** 18-28;
Referee: Liam Moore; **Attendance:** 4,218.

SUPER 8s

ROUND 1

Friday 10th August 2018

HULL FC 13 WAKEFIELD TRINITY 31

HULL FC: 1 Jamie Shaul; 2 Bureta Faraimo; 4 Josh Griffin; 3 Carlos Tuimavave; 5 Fetuli Talanoa; 16 Jordan Abdull; 7 Marc Sneyd; 8 Scott Taylor; 9 Danny Houghton (C); 23 Mickey Paea; 26 Jordan Lane; 17 Danny Washbrook; 21 Sika Manu. Subs (all used): 15 Chris Green; 20 Brad Fash; 27 Jack Downs; 36 Lewis Bienek (D).
Tries: Taylor (10), Shaul (56); **Goals:** Sneyd 2/3;
Field goal: Sneyd (40).
TRINITY: 21 Max Jowitt; 5 Ben Jones-Bishop; 4 Reece Lyne; 3 Bill Tupou; 2 Tom Johnstone; 6 Jacob Miller (C); 25 Ryan Hampshire; 10 Anthony England; 13 Tyler Randell; 8 David Fifita; 14 Justin Horo; 11 Matty Ashurst; 23 Chris Annakin. Subs (all used): 9 Kyle Wood; 15 Pauli Pauli; 16 Tinirau Arona; 17 Craig Huby.
Tries: Huby (33), Tupou (67), Pauli (73), Johnstone (75);
Goals: Hampshire 7/7; **Field goal:** Miller (39).
Sin bin: Jowitt (50) - professional foul.

Rugby Leaguer & League Express Men of the Match:
Hull FC: Jamie Shaul; *Trinity:* Jacob Miller.
Penalty count: 7-9; **Half-time:** 7-7;
Referee: Jack Smith; **Attendance:** 10,301.

ST HELENS 12 HUDDERSFIELD GIANTS 16

SAINTS: 23 Ben Barba; 2 Tommy Makinson; 30 Matthew Costello; 4 Mark Percival; 5 Adam Swift; 1 Jonny Lomax; 18 Danny Richardson; 10 Kyle Amor; 9 James Roby (C); 16 Luke Thompson; 15 Morgan Knowles; 11 Zeb Taia; 12 Jon Wilkin. Subs (all used): 6 Theo Fages; 13 Louie McCarthy-Scarsbrook; 14 Luke Douglas; 20 Matty Lees.
Tries: Barba (35), Thompson (59); **Goals:** Richardson 2/2.
GIANTS: 15 Jordan Rankin; 2 Jermaine McGillvary; 3 Leroy Cudjoe (C); 4 Jordan Turner; 23 Darnell McIntosh; 6 Lee Gaskell; 7 Danny Brough; 35 Suaia Matagi (D); 21 Adam O'Brien; 17 Ukuma Ta'ai; 22 Alex Mellor; 16 Oliver Roberts; 14 Dale Ferguson. Subs (all used): 13 Ryan Hinchcliffe; 18 Paul Clough; 25 Colton Roche; 27 Matty English.
Tries: McIntosh (4, 21), Mellor (10); **Goals:** Brough 2/3.
Rugby Leaguer & League Express Men of the Match:
Saints: Luke Thompson; *Giants:* Ukuma Ta'ai.
Penalty count: 8-4; **Half-time:** 6-16;
Referee: Scott Mikalauskas; **Attendance:** 8,979.

WARRINGTON WOLVES 56 CATALANS DRAGONS 6

WOLVES: 21 Mitch Brown; 2 Tom Lineham; 18 Toby King; 3 Bryson Goodwin; 27 Josh Charnley; 6 Kevin Brown; 7 Tyrone Roberts; 8 Chris Hill (C); 15 Declan Patton; 34 Ben Westwood; 20 Harvey Livett; 12 Jack Hughes; 30 Bodene Thompson (D). Subs: 9 Daryl Clark (not used); 16 Sitaleki Akauola; 17 Joe Philbin; 19 George King.
Tries: Charnley (5), Lineham (28, 36, 79), M Brown (32), K Brown (44), Roberts (54), T King (58), Patton (65), Philbin (67); **Goals:** Livett 0/1, Patton 8/8, Goodwin 0/1.
DRAGONS: 35 Robin Brochon (D); 3 Iain Thornley; 16 Vincent Duport; 1 David Mead; 36 Ugo Martin (D); 30 Arthur Mourgue (D); 22 Lucas Albert; 15 Mickael Simon; 24 Alrix Da Costa; 23 Antoni Maria; 27 Ugo Perez; 32 Mickael Goudemand; 17 Jason Baitieri. Subs (all used): 8 Remi Casty (C); 12 Benjamin Garcia; 18 Thibaut Margalet; 26 Lambert Belmas.
Try: Mead (73); **Goals:** Albert 1/1.
Rugby Leaguer & League Express Men of the Match:
Wolves: Kevin Brown; *Dragons:* Benjamin Garcia.
Penalty count: 6-7; **Half-time:** 22-0;
Referee: Ben Thaler; **Attendance:** 8,032.

WIGAN WARRIORS 24 CASTLEFORD TIGERS 22

WARRIORS: 1 Sam Tomkins (C); 2 Tom Davies; 19 Willie Isa; 3 Dan Sarginson; 22 Liam Marshall; 6 George Williams; 9 Thomas Leuluai; 25 Romain Navarrete; 7 Sam Powell; 10 Ben Flower; 40 Joe Greenwood; 14 John Bateman; 30 Gabe Hamlin. Subs (all used): 8 Tony Clubb; 15 Ryan Sutton; 20 Morgan Escare; 35 Oliver Partington (D).
Tries: Marshall (5), Hamlin (15), Sarginson (28), Sutton (32); **Goals:** S Tomkins 2/3, Escare 2/3.
TIGERS: 5 Greg Eden; 28 Kieran Gill; 16 Joe Wardle; 4 Michael Shenton (C); 26 James Clare; 6 Jamie Ellis; 21 Jake Trueman; 32 Liam Watts; 9 Paul McShane; 15 Jesse Sene-Lefao; 11 Oliver Holmes; 12 Mike McMeeken; 14 Nathan Massey. Subs (all used): 3 Jake Webster; 8 Junior Moors; 13 Adam Milner; 23 Mitch Clark.
Tries: Trueman (43), Clare (52), McShane (63), Clark (80); **Goals:** Ellis 3/4.
Rugby Leaguer & League Express Men of the Match:
Warriors: Romain Navarrete; *Tigers:* Jamie Ellis.
Penalty count: 11-10; **Half-time:** 20-0;
Referee: James Child; **Attendance:** 10,293.

ROUND 2

Thursday 16th August 2018

WAKEFIELD TRINITY 16 ST HELENS 36

TRINITY: 21 Max Jowitt; 5 Ben Jones-Bishop; 4 Reece Lyne; 3 Bill Tupou; 2 Tom Johnstone; 6 Jacob Miller (C); 25 Ryan Hampshire; 8 David Fifita; 13 Tyler Randell; 10 Anthony England; 11 Matty Ashurst; 19 James Batchelor; 14 Justin Horo. Subs (all used): 9 Kyle Wood; 15 Pauli Pauli; 16 Tinirau Arona; 17 Craig Huby.
Tries: Wood (45), Pauli (56), Tupou (66);
Goals: Hampshire 2/3.
Sin bin: Huby (52) - high tackle on Amor.
SAINTS: 23 Ben Barba; 2 Tommy Makinson; 30 Matthew Costello; 4 Mark Percival; 19 Regan Grace; 1 Jonny Lomax; 18 Danny Richardson; 10 Kyle Amor; 9 James Roby (C); 14 Luke Douglas; 11 Zeb Taia; 15 Morgan Knowles; 13 Louie McCarthy-Scarsbrook. Subs (all used): 6 Theo Fages; 12 Jon Wilkin; 20 Matty Lees; 21 Jack Ashworth.
Tries: Makinson (27, 34), Lomax (31), Fages (60), Douglas (71), Grace (75); **Goals:** Richardson 6/7.
Rugby Leaguer & League Express Men of the Match:
Trinity: Bill Tupou; *Saints:* Louie McCarthy-Scarsbrook.
Penalty count: 8-7; **Half-time:** 0-16;
Referee: Liam Moore; **Attendance:** 4,592.

Friday 17th August 2018

CASTLEFORD TIGERS 28 WARRINGTON WOLVES 18

TIGERS: 36 Peter Mata'utia; 26 James Clare; 3 Jake Webster; 4 Michael Shenton (C); 5 Greg Eden; 6 Jamie Ellis; 21 Jake Trueman; 32 Liam Watts; 9 Paul McShane; 10 Grant Millington; 16 Joe Wardle; 12 Mike McMeeken; 14 Nathan Massey. Subs (all used): 8 Junior Moors; 11 Oliver Holmes; 23 Mitch Clark; 33 Calum Turner.
Tries: Clare (7), Moors (27), Eden (40, 62), McMeeken (66);
Goals: Ellis 4/6.
WOLVES: 1 Stefan Ratchford; 2 Tom Lineham; 18 Toby King; 3 Bryson Goodwin; 21 Mitch Brown; 6 Kevin Brown; 7 Tyrone Roberts; 8 Chris Hill (C); 9 Daryl Clark; 10 Mike Cooper; 30 Bodene Thompson; 12 Jack Hughes; 19 George King. Subs (all used): 17 Joe Philbin; 16 Sitaleki Akauola; 15 Declan Patton; 29 Ben Pomeroy.
Tries: Ratchford (44, 79), Goodwin (47);
Goals: Ratchford 2/2, Patton 1/1.
Rugby Leaguer & League Express Men of the Match:
Tigers: Paul McShane; *Wolves:* Stefan Ratchford.
Penalty count: 6-7; **Half-time:** 16-0;
Referee: Gareth Hewer; **Attendance:** 7,142.

HUDDERSFIELD GIANTS 26 HULL FC 6

GIANTS: 15 Jordan Rankin; 2 Jermaine McGillvary; 3 Leroy Cudjoe (C); 4 Jordan Turner; 23 Darnell McIntosh; 6 Lee Gaskell; 7 Danny Brough; 35 Suaia Matagi; 21 Adam O'Brien; 17 Ukuma Ta'ai; 22 Alex Mellor; 16 Oliver Roberts; 13 Ryan Hinchcliffe. Subs (all used): 14 Dale Ferguson; 18 Paul Clough; 9 Kruise Leeming; 25 Colton Roche.
Tries: Mellor (43), Gaskell (46), Hinchcliffe (72), Ta'ai (76);
Goals: Brough 4/4, McIntosh 1/1.
HULL FC: 1 Jamie Shaul; 2 Bureta Faraimo; 4 Josh Griffin; 3 Carlos Tuimavave; 5 Fetuli Talanoa; 16 Jordan Abdull; 35 Liam Harris; 8 Scott Taylor; 9 Danny Houghton (C); 23 Mickey Paea; 21 Sika Manu; 12 Mark Minichiello; 11 Dean Hadley. Subs (all used): 15 Chris Green; 36 Lewis Bienek; 17 Danny Washbrook; 26 Jordan Lane.
Try: Faraimo (54); **Goals:** Faraimo 1/1.
Rugby Leaguer & League Express Men of the Match:
Giants: Ukuma Ta'ai; *Hull FC:* Scott Taylor.
Penalty count: 7-5; **Half-time:** 0-0;
Referee: Robert Hicks; **Attendance:** 4,499.

Saturday 18th August 2018

CATALANS DRAGONS 6 WIGAN WARRIORS 35

DRAGONS: 22 Lucas Albert; 20 Lewis Tierney; 3 Iain Thornley; 4 Brayden Wiliame; 5 Fouad Yaha; 6 Samisoni Langi; 33 Josh Drinkwater; 10 Sam Moa; 19 Michael Mcllorum; 23 Antoni Maria; 21 Benjamin Jullien (C); 34 Kenny Edwards; 17 Jason Baitieri. Subs (all used): 11 Louis Anderson; 14 Julian Bousquet; 24 Alrix Da Costa; 32 Mickael Goudemand.
Try: Yaha (48); **Goals:** Drinkwater 1/1.
WARRIORS: 1 Sam Tomkins (C); 2 Tom Davies; 19 Willie Isa; 3 Dan Sarginson; 22 Liam Marshall; 6 George Williams; 9 Thomas Leuluai; 25 Romain Navarrete; 7 Sam Powell; 10 Ben Flower; 14 John Bateman; 40 Joe Greenwood; 30 Gabe Hamlin. Subs (all used): 15 Ryan Sutton; 8 Tony Clubb; 20 Morgan Escare; 35 Oliver Partington.
Tries: Greenwood (10, 67), Escare (36, 39), Clubb (42), Williams (58); **Goals:** S Tomkins 5/6;
Field goal: S Tomkins (80).
Rugby Leaguer & League Express Men of the Match:
Dragons: Benjamin Jullien; *Warriors:* Sam Tomkins.
Penalty count: 4-7; **Half-time:** 0-18;
Referee: Greg Dolan; **Attendance:** 6,739.

ROUND 3

Thursday 30th August 2018

WARRINGTON WOLVES 80 HULL FC 10

WOLVES: 1 Stefan Ratchford; 2 Tom Lineham; 3 Bryson Goodwin; 18 Toby King; 27 Josh Charnley; 6 Kevin Brown; 7 Tyrone Roberts; 8 Chris Hill (C); 9 Daryl Clark; 10 Mike Cooper; 13 Ben Murdoch-Masila; 30 Bodene Thompson; 12 Jack Hughes. Subs (all used): 15 Declan Patton; 17 Joe Philbin; 19 George King; 29 Ben Pomeroy.
Tries: Charnley (3, 69), T King (14, 29), Goodwin (16, 23, 42, 45, 80), Hughes (32), Philbin (65), Roberts (72), Lineham (75), Ratchford (77);
Goals: Roberts 12/14.
HULL FC: 1 Jamie Shaul; 2 Bureta Faraimo; 4 Josh Griffin; 3 Carlos Tuimavave; 5 Fetuli Talanoa; 35 Liam Harris; 16 Jordan Abdull; 23 Mickey Paea; 9 Danny Houghton (C); 8 Scott Taylor; 11 Dean Hadley; 17 Danny Washbrook; 21 Sika Manu. Subs (all used): 22 Jez Litten; 26 Jordan Lane; 29 Masi Matongo; 36 Lewis Bienek.
Tries: Talanoa (10), Griffin (49); **Goals:** Faraimo 1/2.
Rugby Leaguer & League Express Men of the Match:
Wolves: Bryson Goodwin; *Hull FC:* Danny Houghton.
Penalty count: 10-7; **Half-time:** 34-6;
Referee: Liam Moore; **Attendance:** 8,101.

Friday 31st August 2018

HUDDERSFIELD GIANTS 16 WAKEFIELD TRINITY 42

GIANTS: 15 Jordan Rankin; 2 Jermaine McGillvary; 3 Leroy Cudjoe (C); 4 Jordan Turner; 23 Darnell McIntosh; 6 Lee Gaskell; 7 Danny Brough; 17 Ukuma Ta'ai; 21 Adam O'Brien; 35 Suaia Matagi; 22 Alex Mellor; 5 Aaron Murphy; 13 Ryan Hinchcliffe. Subs (all used): 9 Kruise Leeming; 12 Michael Lawrence; 18 Paul Clough; 25 Colton Roche.
Tries: McGillvary (12), Ta'ai (17), Murphy (43);
Goals: Brough 2/3.
TRINITY: 1 Scott Grix; 5 Ben Jones-Bishop; 4 Reece Lyne; 3 Bill Tupou; 2 Tom Johnstone; 6 Jacob Miller (C); 25 Ryan Hampshire; 17 Craig Huby; 9 Kyle Wood; 16 Tinirau Arona; 11 Matty Ashurst; 19 James Batchelor; 27 Jordan Crowther. Subs (all used): 13 Tyler Randell; 15 Pauli Pauli; 20 Keegan Hirst; 23 Chris Annakin.
Tries: Johnstone (23, 46), Hampshire (55), Grix (58, 74), Jones-Bishop (68), Miller (72); **Goals:** Hampshire 7/7.
Rugby Leaguer & League Express Men of the Match:
Giants: Jordan Rankin; *Trinity:* Ryan Hampshire.
Penalty count: 9-5; **Half-time:** 12-6;
Referee: Gareth Hewer; **Attendance:** 4,963.

ST HELENS 10 WIGAN WARRIORS 30

SAINTS: 23 Ben Barba; 2 Tommy Makinson; 3 Ryan Morgan; 4 Mark Percival; 19 Regan Grace; 1 Jonny Lomax; 18 Danny Richardson; 14 Luke Douglas; 9 James Roby (C); 16 Luke Thompson; 13 Louie McCarthy-Scarsbrook; 11 Zeb Taia; 15 Morgan Knowles. Subs (all used): 10 Kyle Amor; 12 Jon Wilkin; 20 Matty Lees; 21 Jack Ashworth.
Tries: Makinson (40, 51); **Goals:** Richardson 1/2.
WARRIORS: 20 Morgan Escare; 2 Tom Davies; 19 Willie Isa; 3 Dan Sarginson; 4 Oliver Gildart; 6 George Williams; 9 Thomas Leuluai; 25 Romain Navarrete; 7 Sam Powell; 10 Ben Flower; 40 Joe Greenwood; 14 John Bateman; 13 Sean O'Loughlin (C). Subs (all used): 8 Tony Clubb; 15 Ryan Sutton; 30 Gabe Hamlin; 35 Oliver Partington.
Tries: Sarginson (4, 32), Bateman (37), Davies (42), Gildart (64), O'Loughlin (70);
Goals: Escare 0/2, Williams 3/4.
Rugby Leaguer & League Express Men of the Match:
Saints: James Roby; *Warriors:* Joe Greenwood.
Penalty count: 5-4; **Half-time:** 4-14;
Referee: Chris Kendall; **Attendance:** 14,061.

Saturday 1st September 2018

CASTLEFORD TIGERS 36 CATALANS DRAGONS 4

TIGERS: 36 Peter Mata'utia; 26 James Clare; 16 Joe Wardle; 4 Michael Shenton (C); 5 Greg Eden; 21 Jake Trueman; 7 Luke Gale; 32 Liam Watts; 9 Paul McShane; 10 Grant Millington; 11 Oliver Holmes; 12 Mike McMeeken; 14 Nathan Massey. Subs (all used): 1 Ben Roberts; 8 Junior Moors; 13 Adam Milner; 23 Mitch Clark.
Tries: Shenton (14), Eden (29, 42, 70), Trueman (36), Holmes (73); **Goals:** Gale 6/7.
On report: Holmes (35) - alleged high tackle on Langi.
DRAGONS: 1 David Mead; 16 Vincent Duport; 6 Samisoni Langi; 4 Brayden Wiliame; 20 Lewis Tierney; 22 Lucas Albert; 33 Josh Drinkwater; 26 Lambert Belmas; 24 Alrix Da Costa; 10 Sam Moa; 21 Benjamin Jullien; 12 Benjamin Garcia; 13 Greg Bird. Subs (all used): 8 Remi Casty (C); 14 Julian Bousquet; 32 Mickael Goudemand; 34 Kenny Edwards.
Try: Wiliame (51); **Goals:** Drinkwater 0/1.
Sin bin: Bousquet (60) - late challenge;
Wiliame (70) - delaying restart.
Rugby Leaguer & League Express Men of the Match:
Tigers: Luke Gale; *Dragons:* Benjamin Jullien.
Penalty count: 8-9; **Half-time:** 18-0;
Referee: Greg Dolan; **Attendance:** 7,658.

ROUND 4

Thursday 6th September 2018

WIGAN WARRIORS 25 WAKEFIELD TRINITY 10

WARRIORS: 1 Sam Tomkins; 2 Tom Davies; 19 Willie Isa; 3 Dan Sarginson; 4 Oliver Gildart; 6 George Williams; 9 Thomas Leuluai; 25 Romain Navarrete; 7 Sam Powell;

10 Ben Flower; 40 Joe Greenwood; 14 John Bateman; 13 Sean O'Loughlin (C). Subs (all used): 8 Tony Clubb; 15 Ryan Sutton; 20 Morgan Escare; 30 Gabe Hamlin.
Tries: Gildart (1), Powell (19), Escare (68), Greenwood (77); **Goals:** S Tomkins 4/5; **Field goal:** S Tomkins (40).
TRINITY: 1 Scott Grix; 5 Ben Jones-Bishop; 4 Reece Lyne; 3 Bill Tupou; 2 Tom Johnstone; 6 Jacob Miller (C); 25 Ryan Hampshire; 17 Craig Huby; 13 Tyler Randell; 16 Tinirau Arona; 19 James Batchelor; 11 Matty Ashurst; 27 Jordan Crowther. Subs (all used): 15 Pauli Pauli; 18 Joe Arundel; 20 Keegan Hirst; 23 Chris Annakin.
Tries: Johnstone (34), Tupou (57); **Goals:** Hampshire 1/2.
Sin bin: Ashurst (33) - dangerous contact on Hamlin; Grix (63) - dangerous challenge on Greenwood.
Rugby Leaguer & League Express Men of the Match: *Warriors:* Gabe Hamlin; *Trinity:* Tyler Randell.
Penalty count: 13-4; **Half-time:** 11-6;
Referee: Ben Thaler; **Attendance:** 9,559.

Friday 7th September 2018

HULL FC 8 CASTLEFORD TIGERS 28

HULL FC: 1 Jamie Shaul; 2 Bureta Faraimo; 3 Carlos Tuimavave; 30 Cameron Scott; 5 Fetuli Talanoa; 28 Hakim Miloudi; 35 Liam Harris; 8 Scott Taylor; 9 Danny Houghton (C); 29 Masi Matongo; 17 Danny Washbrook; 11 Dean Hadley; 21 Sika Manu. Subs (all used): 20 Brad Fash; 22 Jez Litten; 26 Jordan Lane; 36 Lewis Bienek.
Tries: Tuimavave (59), Miloudi (69); **Goals:** Faraimo 0/2.
TIGERS: 36 Peter Mata'utia; 26 James Clare; 16 Joe Wardle; 4 Michael Shenton (C); 5 Greg Eden; 21 Jake Trueman; 7 Luke Gale; 32 Liam Watts; 9 Paul McShane; 10 Grant Millington; 11 Oliver Holmes; 12 Mike McMeeken; 14 Nathan Massey. Subs (all used): 1 Ben Roberts; 8 Junior Moors; 13 Adam Milner; 23 Mitch Clark.
Tries: McMeeken (18), Moors (29), Eden (37, 43), Clare (51); **Goals:** Gale 4/5.
Rugby Leaguer & League Express Men of the Match: *Hull FC:* Jamie Shaul; *Tigers:* Jake Trueman.
Penalty count: 12-3; **Half-time:** 0-18;
Referee: Gareth Hewer; **Attendance:** 10,570.

WARRINGTON WOLVES 26 HUDDERSFIELD GIANTS 24

WOLVES: 1 Stefan Ratchford; 2 Tom Lineham; 3 Bryson Goodwin; 18 Toby King; 27 Josh Charnley; 6 Kevin Brown; 7 Tyrone Roberts; 8 Chris Hill (C); 9 Daryl Clark; 10 Mike Cooper; 12 Jack Hughes; 4 Ryan Atkins; 20 Harvey Livett. Subs (all used): 17 Joe Philbin; 15 Declan Patton; 19 George King; 29 Ben Pomeroy.
Tries: Goodwin (23, 68), Atkins (36), Ratchford (49), Lineham (52); **Goals:** Roberts 3/5.
Sin bin: Cooper (15) - high tackle on O'Brien.
GIANTS: 15 Jordan Rankin; 1 Jake Mamo; 4 Jordan Turner; 29 Jake Wardle; 33 Innes Senior; 6 Lee Gaskell; 7 Danny Brough; 17 Ukuma Ta'ai; 21 Adam O'Brien; 35 Suaia Matagi; 22 Alex Mellor; 16 Oliver Roberts; 13 Ryan Hinchcliffe (C). Subs (all used): 9 Kruise Leeming; 12 Michael Lawrence; 18 Paul Clough; 19 Daniel Smith.
Tries: Mamo (16, 33, 38), Gaskell (61), Wardle (77); **Goals:** Brough 2/7.
Rugby Leaguer & League Express Men of the Match: *Wolves:* Bryson Goodwin; *Giants:* Jake Mamo.
Penalty count: 8-10; **Half-time:** 12-14;
Referee: James Child; **Attendance:** 9,076.

Saturday 8th September 2018

CATALANS DRAGONS 22 ST HELENS 26

DRAGONS: 31 Tony Gigot; 20 Lewis Tierney; 1 David Mead; 4 Brayden Wiliame; 3 Iain Thornley; 6 Samisoni Langi; 33 Josh Drinkwater; 15 Mickael Simon; 19 Michael McIlorum; 10 Sam Moa; 13 Greg Bird; 34 Kenny Edwards; 8 Remi Casty (C). Subs (all used): 14 Julian Bousquet; 17 Jason Baitieri; 24 Alrix Da Costa; 32 Mickael Goudemand.
Tries: Mead (8), Casty (13), Thornley (45), Edwards (52); **Goals:** Drinkwater 3/5.
Sin bin: Moa (32) - high tackle on A Smith.
SAINTS: 1 Jonny Lomax; 2 Tommy Makinson; 30 Matthew Costello; 4 Mark Percival; 19 Regan Grace; 6 Theo Fages; 18 Danny Richardson; 10 Kyle Amor; 15 Morgan Knowles; 16 Luke Thompson; 11 Zeb Taia; 13 Louie McCarthy-Scarsbrook; 12 Jon Wilkin (C). Subs (all used): 14 Luke Douglas; 20 Matty Lees; 21 Jack Ashworth; 25 Aaron Smith (D).
Tries: Percival (17), Fages (30), Lomax (71), Knowles (78); **Goals:** Richardson 5/5.
Rugby Leaguer & League Express Men of the Match: *Dragons:* David Mead; *Saints:* Jonny Lomax.
Penalty count: 8-8; **Half-time:** 12-14;
Referee: Liam Moore; **Attendance:** 7,810.

ROUND 5

Thursday 13th September 2018

CASTLEFORD TIGERS 44 HUDDERSFIELD GIANTS 12

TIGERS: 36 Peter Mata'utia; 26 James Clare; 3 Jake Webster; 4 Michael Shenton (C); 5 Greg Eden; 1 Ben Roberts; 21 Jake Trueman; 32 Liam Watts; 9 Paul McShane; 10 Grant Millington; 8 Junior Moors; 12 Mike McMeeken; 14 Nathan Massey. Subs (all used): 2 Greg Minikin; 13 Adam Milner; 15 Jesse Sene-Lefao; 23 Mitch Clark.
Tries: Eden (5), Webster (24), Moors (35, 71), Clare (58), McMeeken (67), Mata'utia (75), Millington (79); **Goals:** McShane 6/7, Webster 0/1.
GIANTS: 15 Jordan Rankin; 1 Jake Mamo; 4 Jordan Turner; 29 Jake Wardle; 33 Innes Senior; 6 Lee Gaskell; 7 Danny Brough; 12 Michael Lawrence; 21 Adam O'Brien; 35 Suaia Matagi; 17 Ukuma Ta'ai; 16 Oliver Roberts; 13 Ryan Hinchcliffe (C). Subs (all used): 9 Kruise Leeming; 18 Paul Clough; 19 Daniel Smith; 27 Matty English.
Tries: O'Brien (2), Gaskell (19); **Goals:** Brough 2/2.
Rugby Leaguer & League Express Men of the Match: *Tigers:* Jake Trueman; *Giants:* Suaia Matagi.
Penalty count: 6-8; **Half-time:** 16-12;
Referee: Ben Thaler; **Attendance:** 7,279.

Friday 14th September 2018

ST HELENS 38 HULL FC 12

SAINTS: 23 Ben Barba; 2 Tommy Makinson; 30 Matthew Costello; 4 Mark Percival; 19 Regan Grace; 1 Jonny Lomax; 18 Danny Richardson; 10 Kyle Amor; 15 Morgan Knowles; 16 Luke Thompson; 24 James Bentley (D); 21 Jack Ashworth; 12 Jon Wilkin (C). Subs (all used): 14 Luke Douglas; 20 Matty Lees; 22 Jake Spedding; 31 Jack Welsby (D).
Tries: Percival (11, 54), Knowles (14), Thompson (39), Grace (60, 73); **Goals:** Richardson 7/7.
HULL FC: 28 Hakim Miloudi; 2 Bureta Faraimo; 30 Cameron Scott; 4 Josh Griffin; 5 Fetuli Talanoa; 35 Liam Harris; 14 Jake Connor; 29 Masi Matongo; 17 Danny Washbrook; 8 Scott Taylor (C); 11 Dean Hadley; 26 Jordan Lane; 21 Sika Manu. Subs (all used): 16 Jordan Abdull; 20 Brad Fash; 22 Jez Litten; 36 Lewis Bienek.
Tries: Lane (22), Fash (36); **Goals:** Faraimo 1/1, Connor 1/1.
Rugby Leaguer & League Express Men of the Match: *Saints:* Luke Thompson; *Hull FC:* Masi Matongo.
Penalty count: 5-9; **Half-time:** 18-12;
Referee: Chris Kendall; **Attendance:** 9,348.

WAKEFIELD TRINITY 34 CATALANS DRAGONS 22

TRINITY: 1 Scott Grix; 3 Bill Tupou; 4 Reece Lyne; 18 Joe Arundel; 2 Tom Johnstone; 6 Jacob Miller (C); 25 Ryan Hampshire; 17 Craig Huby; 9 Kyle Wood; 10 Anthony England; 11 Matty Ashurst; 19 James Batchelor; 27 Jordan Crowther. Subs (all used): 13 Tyler Randell; 15 Pauli Pauli; 14 Justin Horo; 20 Keegan Hirst.
Tries: Ashurst (8), Johnstone (18, 31, 49), Hampshire (22), Randell (35), Lyne (37); **Goals:** Hampshire 3/7.
Dismissal: Miller (77) - fighting.
Sin bin: Huby (65) - punching Simon.
DRAGONS: 31 Tony Gigot; 20 Lewis Tierney; 1 David Mead; 4 Brayden Wiliame; 3 Iain Thornley; 22 Lucas Albert; 33 Josh Drinkwater; 15 Mickael Simon; 24 Alrix Da Costa; 10 Sam Moa; 21 Benjamin Jullien; 12 Benjamin Garcia; 13 Greg Bird (C). Subs (all used): 34 Kenny Edwards; 32 Mickael Goudemand; 26 Lambert Belmas; 17 Jason Baitieri.
Tries: Jullien (13), Thornley (26), Mead (56), Wiliame (66); **Goals:** Drinkwater 3/4.
Dismissal: Simon (77) - fighting.
Rugby Leaguer & League Express Men of the Match: *Trinity:* Tom Johnstone; *Dragons:* Lucas Albert.
Penalty count: 6-5; **Half-time:** 30-12;
Referee: Scott Mikalauskas; **Attendance:** 4,030.

WIGAN WARRIORS 26 WARRINGTON WOLVES 6

WARRIORS: 1 Sam Tomkins (C); 21 Dom Manfredi; 4 Oliver Gildart; 3 Dan Sarginson; 2 Tom Davies; 6 George Williams; 9 Thomas Leuluai; 25 Romain Navarrete; 7 Sam Powell; 8 Tony Clubb; 19 Willie Isa; 14 John Bateman; 30 Gabe Hamlin. Subs (all used): 15 Ryan Sutton; 20 Morgan Escare; 17 Taulima Tautai; 35 Oliver Partington.
Tries: Leuluai (38), Manfredi (71, 74), Sutton (77); **Goals:** S Tomkins 4/4, Williams 1/1.
Sin bin: S Tomkins (53) - dissent.
WOLVES: 1 Stefan Ratchford (C); 2 Tom Lineham; 3 Bryson Goodwin; 4 Ryan Atkins; 27 Josh Charnley; 20 Harvey Livett; 15 Declan Patton; 19 George King; 9 Daryl Clark; 34 Ben Westwood; 30 Bodene Thompson; 18 Toby King; 12 Jack Hughes. Subs (all used): 17 Joe Philbin; 24 Luis Johnson (D); 22 Morgan Smith; 29 Ben Pomeroy.
Try: Ratchford (54); **Goals:** Patton 1/1.
Sin bin: Lineham (68) - high tackle on Manfredi.
Rugby Leaguer & League Express Men of the Match: *Warriors:* Dom Manfredi; *Wolves:* Stefan Ratchford.
Penalty count: 9-9; **Half-time:** 6-0;
Referee: Robert Hicks; **Attendance:** 12,372.

ROUND 6

Thursday 20th September 2018

HUDDERSFIELD GIANTS 6 WIGAN WARRIORS 13

GIANTS: 6 Lee Gaskell; 15 Jordan Rankin; 22 Alex Mellor; 1 Jake Mamo; 33 Innes Senior; 34 Oliver Russell; 7 Danny Brough; 12 Michael Lawrence; 21 Adam O'Brien; 35 Suaia Matagi; 17 Ukuma Ta'ai; 16 Oliver Roberts; 13 Ryan Hinchcliffe (C). Subs (all used): 9 Kruise Leeming; 18 Paul Clough; 27 Matty English; 25 Colton Roche.
Try: Leeming (71); **Goals:** Brough 1/1.
Sin bin: Brough (77) - high tackle on Escare.
WARRIORS: 20 Morgan Escare; 21 Dom Manfredi; 4 Oliver Gildart; 3 Dan Sarginson; 2 Tom Davies; 6 George Williams; 1 Sam Tomkins (C); 8 Tony Clubb; 7 Sam Powell; 25 Romain Navarrete; 40 Joe Greenwood; 14 John Bateman; 15 Ryan Sutton. Subs: 30 Gabe Hamlin; 35 Oliver Partington; 34 Josh Woods (not used); 17 Taulima Tautai.
Tries: Escare (16), Gildart (78); **Goals:** S Tomkins 2/3; **Field goal:** Escare (59).
Rugby Leaguer & League Express Men of the Match: *Giants:* Matty English; *Warriors:* Morgan Escare.
Penalty count: 7-11; **Half-time:** 0-6;
Referee: Greg Dolan; **Attendance:** 4,197.

Friday 21st September 2018

CASTLEFORD TIGERS 42 WAKEFIELD TRINITY 10

TIGERS: 36 Peter Mata'utia; 2 Greg Minikin; 3 Jake Webster; 4 Michael Shenton (C); 5 Greg Eden; 21 Jake Trueman; 7 Luke Gale; 32 Liam Watts; 9 Paul McShane; 10 Grant Millington; 8 Junior Moors; 12 Mike McMeeken; 14 Nathan Massey. Subs (all used): 1 Ben Roberts; 13 Adam Milner; 15 Jesse Sene-Lefao; 23 Mitch Clark.
Tries: Eden (1, 10, 59, 63), Minikin (15), Millington (53), Moors (76); **Goals:** Gale 7/7.
TRINITY: 1 Scott Grix; 5 Ben Jones-Bishop; 4 Reece Lyne; 18 Joe Arundel; 3 Bill Tupou; 9 Kyle Wood; 25 Ryan Hampshire; 17 Craig Huby; 13 Tyler Randell; 16 Tinirau Arona; 11 Matty Ashurst (C); 19 James Batchelor; 27 Jordan Crowther. Subs (all used): 21 Max Jowitt; 15 Pauli Pauli; 23 Chris Annakin; 14 Justin Horo.
Tries: Tupou (48), Lyne (57); **Goals:** Hampshire 1/2.
Sin bin: Randell (14) - dangerous challenge on Massey.
Rugby Leaguer & League Express Men of the Match: *Tigers:* Luke Gale; *Trinity:* Reece Lyne.
Penalty count: 8-9; **Half-time:** 18-0;
Referee: Gareth Hewer; **Attendance:** 7,860.

Saturday 22nd September 2018

WARRINGTON WOLVES 14 ST HELENS 34

WOLVES: 1 Stefan Ratchford; 3 Bryson Goodwin; 18 Toby King; 4 Ryan Atkins; 27 Josh Charnley; 6 Kevin Brown; 7 Tyrone Roberts; 8 Chris Hill (C); 15 Declan Patton; 10 Mike Cooper; 13 Ben Murdoch-Masila; 30 Bodene Thompson; 34 Ben Westwood. Subs (all used): 19 George King; 17 Joe Philbin; 20 Harvey Livett; 22 Morgan Smith.
Tries: K Brown (23), T King (65), Goodwin (79); **Goals:** Patton 1/3.
Sin bin: Atkins (13) - fighting.
SAINTS: 23 Ben Barba; 2 Tommy Makinson; 3 Ryan Morgan; 4 Mark Percival; 19 Regan Grace; 1 Jonny Lomax; 18 Danny Richardson; 16 Luke Thompson; 15 Morgan Knowles; 20 Matty Lees; 11 Zeb Taia; 24 James Bentley; 12 Jon Wilkin (C). Subs (all used): 6 Theo Fages; 14 Luke Douglas; 17 Dominique Peyroux; 21 Jack Ashworth.
Tries: Douglas (32), Grace (40), Lomax (51), Richardson (53), Barba (58, 76); **Goals:** Richardson 5/7.
Sin bin: Lees (13) - dangerous challenge on Roberts; Percival (13) - fighting.
Rugby Leaguer & League Express Men of the Match: *Wolves:* Mike Cooper; *Saints:* Ben Barba.
Penalty count: 10-6; **Half-time:** 6-12;
Referee: Chris Kendall; **Attendance:** 10,747.

HULL FC 20 CATALANS DRAGONS 26

HULL FC: 1 Jamie Shaul; 2 Bureta Faraimo; 4 Josh Griffin; 3 Carlos Tuimavave; 5 Fetuli Talanoa; 28 Hakim Miloudi; 14 Jake Connor; 8 Scott Taylor; 9 Danny Houghton (C); 29 Masi Matongo; 26 Jordan Lane; 17 Danny Washbrook; 11 Dean Hadley. Subs (all used): 20 Brad Fash; 22 Jez Litten; 23 Mickey Paea; 36 Lewis Bienek.
Tries: Griffin (36), Fash (50), Talanoa (62), Shaul (71); **Goals:** Connor 2/4.

DRAGONS: 31 Tony Gigot; 20 Lewis Tierney; 1 David Mead; 4 Brayden Wiliame; 3 Iain Thornley; 22 Lucas Albert; 33 Josh Drinkwater; 23 Antoni Maria; 19 Michael McIlorum; 10 Sam Moa; 13 Greg Bird (C); 21 Benjamin Jullien; 17 Jason Baitieri. Subs (all used): 26 Lambert Belmas; 24 Alrix Da Costa; 34 Kenny Edwards; 32 Mickael Goudemand.
Tries: Moa (14), Gigot (34), Thornley (58), Wiliame (75), Edwards (77); **Goals:** Drinkwater 2/5, Albert 1/1.
On report: Baitieri (3) - alleged dangerous contact.
Rugby Leaguer & League Express Men of the Match: Hull FC: Jake Connor; Dragons: Kenny Edwards.
Penalty count: 9-6; **Half-time:** 4-10;
Referee: Marcus Griffiths; **Attendance:** 10,467.

ROUND 7

Friday 28th September 2018

ST HELENS 26 CASTLEFORD TIGERS 0

SAINTS: 23 Ben Barba; 2 Tommy Makinson; 3 Ryan Morgan; 30 Matthew Costello; 19 Regan Grace; 6 Theo Fages; 18 Danny Richardson; 10 Kyle Amor; 9 James Roby (C); 20 Matty Lees; 11 Zeb Taia; 17 Dominique Peyroux; 15 Morgan Knowles. Subs (all used): 13 Louie McCarthy-Scarsbrook; 14 Luke Douglas; 21 Jack Ashworth; 24 James Bentley.
Tries: Lees (8), Knowles (25), Barba (35, 45);
Goals: Richardson 5/5.
TIGERS: 36 Peter Mata'utia; 2 Greg Minikin; 3 Jake Webster; 1 Ben Roberts; 26 James Clare; 21 Jake Trueman; 7 Luke Gale; 32 Liam Watts; 9 Paul McShane; 10 Grant Millington; 16 Joe Wardle; 15 Jesse Sene-Lefao; 14 Nathan Massey. Subs (all used): 13 Adam Milner; 23 Mitch Clark; 25 Will Maher; 34 Quentin Laulu-Togagae.
Sin bin: Wardle (21) - professional foul.
Rugby Leaguer & League Express Men of the Match: Saints: Morgan Knowles; Tigers: Jake Webster.
Penalty count: 7-5; **Half-time:** 18-0;
Referee: Scott Mikalauskas; **Attendance:** 9,813.

WAKEFIELD TRINITY 23 WARRINGTON WOLVES 36

TRINITY: 21 Max Jowitt; 3 Bill Tupou; 4 Reece Lyne; 18 Joe Arundel; 5 Ben Jones-Bishop; 6 Jacob Miller (C); 25 Ryan Hampshire; 15 Pauli Pauli; 13 Tyler Randell; 16 Tinirau Arona; 11 Matty Ashurst; 19 James Batchelor; 27 Jordan Crowther. Subs (all used): 9 Kyle Wood; 17 Craig Huby; 14 Justin Horo; 23 Chris Annakin.
Tries: Randell (5), Arundel (25), Hampshire (59), Jones-Bishop (74); **Goals:** Hampshire 3/4;
Field goal: Hampshire (38).
WOLVES: 1 Stefan Ratchford; 4 Ryan Atkins; 3 Bryson Goodwin; 18 Toby King; 27 Josh Charnley; 20 Harvey Livett; 15 Declan Patton; 8 Chris Hill (C); 9 Daryl Clark; 10 Mike Cooper; 12 Jack Hughes; 13 Ben Murdoch-Masila; 34 Ben Westwood. Subs (all used): 17 Joe Philbin; 19 George King; 16 Sitaleki Akauola; 22 Morgan Smith.
Tries: Murdoch-Masila (18), T King (40), Ratchford (47), Hughes (52), Patton (69), Atkins (76);
Goals: Patton 6/6.
Rugby Leaguer & League Express Men of the Match: Trinity: Ryan Hampshire; Wolves: Ben Murdoch-Masila.
Penalty count: 9-6; **Half-time:** 13-12;
Referee: Marcus Griffiths; **Attendance:** 4,479.

WIGAN WARRIORS 14 HULL FC 12

WARRIORS: 20 Morgan Escare; 21 Dom Manfredi; 4 Oliver Gildart; 3 Dan Sarginson; 2 Tom Davies; 6 George Williams; 34 Josh Woods; 15 Ryan Sutton; 7 Sam Powell; 25 Romain Navarrete; 40 Joe Greenwood; 14 John Bateman (C); 8 Tony Clubb. Subs (all used): 12 Liam Farrell; 17 Taulima Tautai; 30 Gabe Hamlin; 38 Craig Mullen.
Tries: Hamlin (32), Sarginson (53), Gildart (61);
Goals: Woods 1/3.
On report: Tautai (48) - alleged use of the knees on Shaul.
HULL FC: 1 Jamie Shaul; 2 Bureta Faraimo; 3 Carlos Tuimavave; 30 Cameron Scott; 5 Fetuli Talanoa; 16 Jordan Abdull; 14 Jake Connor; 29 Masi Matongo; 9 Danny Houghton (C); 8 Scott Taylor; 17 Danny Washbrook; 4 Josh Griffin; 20 Brad Fash. Subs (all used): 36 Lewis Bienek; 22 Jez Litten; 28 Hakim Miloudi; 23 Mickey Paea.
Tries: Tuimavave (20), Shaul (29); **Goals:** Connor 2/2.
Rugby Leaguer & League Express Men of the Match: Warriors: Oliver Gildart; Hull FC: Jamie Shaul.
Penalty count: 9-5; **Half-time:** 6-12;
Referee: Liam Moore; **Attendance:** 11,189.

Saturday 29th September 2018

CATALANS DRAGONS 22 HUDDERSFIELD GIANTS 12

DRAGONS: 22 Lucas Albert; 1 David Mead; 21 Benjamin Jullien; 6 Samisoni Langi; 4 Brayden Wiliame; 13 Greg Bird;

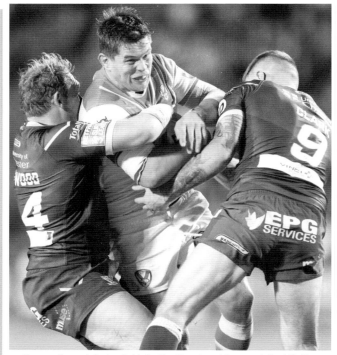

No way through for Louie McCarthy-Scarsbrook in a semi-final thriller

33 Josh Drinkwater; 15 Mickael Simon; 19 Michael McIlorum; 10 Sam Moa; 8 Remi Casty (C); 32 Mickael Goudemand; 17 Jason Baitieri. Subs (all used): 11 Louis Anderson; 23 Antoni Maria; 24 Alrix Da Costa; 26 Lambert Belmas.
Tries: Mead (50, 59, 73, 75); **Goals:** Albert 3/6.
Sin bin: Belmas (55) - high tackle; Simon (64) - fighting.
GIANTS: 6 Lee Gaskell; 2 Jermaine McGillvary; 31 Louis Senior; 1 Jake Mamo; 33 Innes Senior; 34 Oliver Russell; 7 Danny Brough; 18 Paul Clough; 21 Adam O'Brien; 35 Suaia Matagi; 16 Oliver Roberts; 22 Alex Mellor; 13 Ryan Hinchcliffe (C). Subs (all used): 9 Kruise Leeming; 12 Michael Lawrence; 25 Colton Roche; 27 Matty English.
Tries: L Senior (2), I Senior (23); **Goals:** Brough 2/3.
Sin bin: Hinchcliffe (64) - fighting.
Rugby Leaguer & League Express Men of the Match: Dragons: David Mead; Giants: Danny Brough.
Penalty count: 7-7; **Half-time:** 0-12;
Referee: Greg Dolan; **Attendance:** 7,340.

SEMI-FINALS

Thursday 4th October 2018

ST HELENS 13 WARRINGTON WOLVES 18

SAINTS: 23 Ben Barba; 2 Tommy Makinson; 3 Ryan Morgan; 4 Mark Percival; 19 Regan Grace; 1 Jonny Lomax; 18 Danny Richardson; 20 Matty Lees; 15 Morgan Knowles; 16 Luke Thompson; 11 Zeb Taia; 17 Dominique Peyroux; 12 Jon Wilkin. Subs (all used): 9 James Roby (C); 13 Louie McCarthy-Scarsbrook; 14 Luke Douglas; 21 Jack Ashworth.
Try: Douglas (42); **Goals:** Richardson 3/4;
Field goals: Richardson (37, 69, 71).
WOLVES: 1 Stefan Ratchford; 2 Tom Lineham; 3 Bryson Goodwin; 18 Toby King; 27 Josh Charnley; 6 Kevin Brown; 7 Tyrone Roberts; 8 Chris Hill (C); 9 Daryl Clark; 10 Mike Cooper; 30 Bodene Thompson; 12 Jack Hughes; 34 Ben Westwood. Subs: 13 Ben Murdoch-Masila; 15 Declan Patton (not used); 17 Joe Philbin; 19 George King.
Tries: Hughes (45), Lineham (58, 74); **Goals:** Roberts 3/4.
Rugby Leaguer & League Express Men of the Match: Saints: Luke Thompson; Wolves: Tom Lineham.
Penalty count: 12-7; **Half-time:** 3-2;
Referee: Robert Hicks; **Attendance:** 12,309.

Friday 5th October 2018

WIGAN WARRIORS 14 CASTLEFORD TIGERS 0

WARRIORS: 1 Sam Tomkins; 21 Dom Manfredi; 4 Oliver Gildart; 3 Dan Sarginson; 2 Tom Davies; 6 George Williams; 9 Thomas Leuluai; 25 Romain Navarrete; 7 Sam Powell; 10 Ben Flower; 40 Joe Greenwood; 14 John Bateman; 13 Sean O'Loughlin (C). Subs (all used): 8 Tony Clubb; 12 Liam Farrell; 15 Ryan Sutton; 20 Morgan Escare.
Tries: Leuluai (11), S Tomkins (48); **Goals:** S Tomkins 2/3;
Field goal: S Tomkins (39, 80).
TIGERS: 36 Peter Mata'utia; 26 James Clare; 16 Joe Wardle; 4 Michael Shenton (C); 5 Greg Eden; 1 Ben Roberts; 7 Luke Gale; 32 Liam Watts; 9 Paul McShane; 10 Grant Millington; 11 Oliver Holmes; 12 Mike McMeeken; 14 Nathan Massey. Subs (all used): 3 Jake Webster; 13 Adam Milner; 15 Jesse Sene-Lefao; 23 Mitch Clark.
Rugby Leaguer & League Express Men of the Match: Warriors: Sam Tomkins; Tigers: Michael Shenton.
Penalty count: 9-4; **Half-time:** 7-0;
Referee: Ben Thaler; **Attendance:** 13,461.

GRAND FINAL

Saturday 13th October 2018

WARRINGTON WOLVES 4 WIGAN WARRIORS 12

WOLVES: 1 Stefan Ratchford; 2 Tom Lineham; 3 Bryson Goodwin; 18 Toby King; 27 Josh Charnley; 6 Kevin Brown; 7 Tyrone Roberts; 8 Chris Hill (C); 9 Daryl Clark; 10 Mike Cooper; 30 Bodene Thompson; 12 Jack Hughes; 34 Ben Westwood. Subs (all used): 17 Joe Philbin; 13 Ben Murdoch-Masila; 19 George King; 15 Declan Patton.
Try: Charnley (12); **Goals:** Roberts 0/1.
WARRIORS: 1 Sam Tomkins; 21 Dom Manfredi; 4 Oliver Gildart; 3 Dan Sarginson; 2 Tom Davies; 6 George Williams; 9 Thomas Leuluai; 25 Romain Navarrete; 7 Sam Powell; 10 Ben Flower; 40 Joe Greenwood; 14 John Bateman; 13 Sean O'Loughlin (C). Subs (all used): 20 Morgan Escare; 15 Ryan Sutton; 12 Liam Farrell; 8 Tony Clubb.
Tries: Manfredi (25, 77), Davies (31); **Goals:** S Tomkins 0/4.
Rugby Leaguer & League Express Men of the Match: Wolves: Stefan Ratchford; Warriors: Dom Manfredi.
Penalty count: 7-4; **Half-time:** 4-8;
Referee: Robert Hicks; **Attendance:** 64,892
(at Old Trafford, Manchester).

Wigan's Oliver Gildart takes on Warrington's Kevin Brown and Bryson Goodwin during the Super League Grand Final

SUPER 8s -
THE QUALIFIERS
2018 Round by Round

ROUND 1

Thursday 9th August 2018

WIDNES VIKINGS 20 LONDON BRONCOS 21

VIKINGS: 27 Olly Ashall-Bott; 5 Patrick Ah Van; 3 Krisnan Inu; 12 Matt Whitley; 4 Charly Runciman; 6 Joe Mellor (C); 42 Liam Finn; 11 Chris Houston (C); 33 Aaron Heremaia; 8 Gil Dudson; 14 Chris Dean; 41 Harrison Hansen; 39 Weller Hauraki. Subs (all used): 16 Tom Olbison; 20 Macgraff Leuluai; 23 Danny Walker; 43 Charlie Gubb (D).
Tries: Ashall-Bott (31), Dean (55), Inu (75); **Goals:** Inu 4/4.
BRONCOS: 14 Alex Walker; 5 Kieran Dixon; 3 Ben Hellewell; 1 Elliot Kear; 2 Rhys Williams; 6 Api Pewhairangi; 9 James Cunningham; 15 Eddie Battye; 30 Eloi Pelissier; 18 Ben Evans; 12 Jay Pitts; 26 Daniel Hindmarsh; 13 Matt Davis. Subs (all used): 7 Jarrod Sammut; 8 Tom Spencer; 10 Mark Ioane; 11 Daniel Harrison.
Tries: Ioane (43), Harrison (59), Dixon (62, 67);
Goals: Sammut 2/4; **Field goal:** Sammut (80).
Rugby Leaguer & League Express Men of the Match:
Vikings: Olly Ashall-Bott; *Broncos:* Jarrod Sammut.
Penalty count: 7-3; **Half-time:** 6-0;
Referee: Liam Moore; **Attendance:** 3,432.

Friday 10th August 2018

**HULL KINGSTON ROVERS 10
SALFORD RED DEVILS 28**

ROVERS: 1 Adam Quinlan; 27 Will Oakes; 42 Ben Crooks; 2 Junior Vaivai; 41 Craig Hall; 40 Todd Carney; 7 Danny McGuire; 8 Nick Scruton; 9 Shaun Lunt (C); 21 Robbie Mulhern; 34 Danny Tickle; 39 Joel Tomkins; 17 Chris Clarkson. Subs (all used): 12 James Greenwood; 13 Ben Kavanagh; 15 James Donaldson; 24 Chris Atkin.
Tries: Hall (32), Lunt (74); **Goals:** Tickle 1/2.
RED DEVILS: 5 Niall Evalds; 24 Jake Bibby; 29 Ed Chamberlain; 4 Junior Sa'u; 22 Derrell Olpherts; 6 Robert Lui; 31 Jackson Hastings; 23 Lee Mossop (C); 19 Josh Wood; 26 Daniel Murray; 11 Josh Jones; 17 Tyrone McCarthy; 15 Ryan Lannon. Subs (all used): 32 Joey Lussick (D); 13 Mark Flanagan; 14 Lama Tasi; 18 Ben Nakubuwai.
Tries: Evalds (20), Lui (56), Lussick (67), Wood (78);
Goals: Chamberlain 2/4, Hastings 4/4.
On report: Lussick (39) - alleged high tackle.
Rugby Leaguer & League Express Men of the Match:
Rovers: Robbie Mulhern; *Red Devils:* Jackson Hastings.
Penalty count: 7-8; **Half-time:** 4-6;
Referee: Robert Hicks; **Attendance:** 7,081.

Saturday 11th August 2018

LEEDS RHINOS 48 TOULOUSE OLYMPIQUE 22

RHINOS: 4 Liam Sutcliffe; 2 Tom Briscoe; 18 Jimmy Keinhorst; 6 Joel Moon; 5 Ryan Hall; 12 Carl Ablett (C); 7 Richie Myler; 36 Dominic Crosby; 14 Brad Dwyer; 10 Brad Singleton; 11 Jamie Jones-Buchanan; 19 Brett Ferres; 8 Adam Cuthbertson. Subs (all used): 21 Nathaniel Peteru; 16 Anthony Mullally; 1 Ashton Golding; 28 Mikolaj Oledzki.
Tries: Dwyer (4, 55), Moon (13, 22), Hall (28), Myler (64), Cuthbertson (67), Ablett (70), Golding (79);
Goals: Sutcliffe 6/9.
OLYMPIQUE: 1 Mark Kheirallah; 20 Paul Marcon; 22 Chris Centrone; 3 Bastien Ader; 2 Tony Maurel; 6 Johnathon Ford; 30 William Barthau; 24 Joe Bretherton; 9 Anthony Marion; 18 Sam Rapira; 10 Bastien Canet; 26 Constantine Mika; 8 Clement Boyer. Subs (all used): 16 Tyla Hepi; 15 Maxime Puech; 7 Stan Robin; 17 Eddy Pettybourne.
Tries: Canet (7), Ader (31), Puech (39), Centrone (76);
Goals: Kheirallah 3/4.
Rugby Leaguer & League Express Men of the Match:
Rhinos: Richie Myler; *Olympique:* Johnathon Ford.
Penalty count: 6-6; **Half time:** 20-16;
Referee: Gareth Hewer; **Attendance:** 10,166.

Sunday 12th August 2018

HALIFAX 0 TORONTO WOLFPACK 14

HALIFAX: 24 Kieren Moss; 5 James Saltonstall; 3 Steve Tyrer; 2 Ben Heaton; 1 Will Sharp; 6 Scott Murrell; 7 Ben Johnston; 17 Will Maher; 9 Ben Kaye; 13 Jacob Fairbank; 11 Shane Grady; 18 Chester Butler; 4 Ed Barber. Subs (all used): 28 Sam Wood; 14 Brandon Moore; 8 Elliot Morris; 27 Jordan Baldwinson.
WOLFPACK: 31 Gareth O'Brien; 30 Matthew Russell; 33 Chase Stanley; 4 Gary Wheeler; 5 Liam Kay; 6 Josh McCrone; 17 Blake Wallace; 10 Ashton Sims; 9 Bob Beswick; 32 Darcy Lussick; 11 Andrew Dixon; 24 Cory Paterson; 29 Jake Emmitt. Subs (all used): 8 Jack Buchanan; 13 Jack Bussey; 14 Andy Ackers; 15 Adam Sidlow.
Tries: Ackers (35), Dixon (77); **Goals:** O'Brien 3/3.
Rugby Leaguer & League Express Men of the Match:
Halifax: James Saltonstall; *Wolfpack:* Ashton Sims.
Penalty count: 7-7; **Half-time:** 0-6;
Referee: Chris Kendall; **Attendance:** 1,774.

ROUND 2

Saturday 18th August 2018

SALFORD RED DEVILS 32 WIDNES VIKINGS 6

RED DEVILS: 5 Niall Evalds; 29 Ed Chamberlain; 3 Kris Welham; 4 Junior Sa'u; 22 Derrell Olpherts; 6 Robert Lui; 31 Jackson Hastings; 23 Lee Mossop (C); 19 Josh Wood; 14 Lama Tasi; 11 Josh Jones; 15 Ryan Lannon; 13 Mark Flanagan. Subs (all used): 8 Craig Kopczak; 30 Greg Burke; 32 Joey Lussick; 18 Ben Nakubuwai.
Tries: Sa'u (16, 21), Lui (45), Evalds (61), Flanagan (73);
Goals: Chamberlain 6/6.
Sin bin: Lussick (37) - dangerous challenge on Inu.
VIKINGS: 27 Olly Ashall-Bott; 5 Patrick Ah Van; 3 Krisnan Inu; 12 Matt Whitley; 4 Charly Runciman; 6 Joe Mellor (C); 42 Liam Finn; 41 Harrison Hansen; 33 Aaron Heremaia; 8 Gil Dudson; 14 Chris Dean; 11 Chris Houston (C); 39 Weller Hauraki. Subs (all used): 20 Macgraff Leuluai; 10 Alex Gerrard; 16 Tom Olbison; 9 Lloyd White.
Try: Runciman (3); **Goals:** Inu 1/1.
Rugby Leaguer & League Express Men of the Match:
Red Devils: Jackson Hastings; *Vikings:* Olly Ashall-Bott.
Penalty count: 9-4; **Half-time:** 12-6;
Referee: Ben Thaler; **Attendance:** 2,317.

TOULOUSE OLYMPIQUE 28 HALIFAX 6

OLYMPIQUE: 1 Mark Kheirallah; 20 Paul Marcon; 31 Arthur Romano; 3 Bastien Ader; 22 Chris Centrone; 6 Johnathon Ford; 7 Stan Robin; 24 Joe Bretherton; 9 Anthony Marion; 15 Maxime Puech; 10 Bastien Canet; 11 Sebastien Planas; 18 Sam Rapira. Subs (all used): 16 Tyla Hepi; 8 Clement Boyer; 30 William Barthau; 29 Paul Seguier.
Tries: Centrone (13, 33), Marcon (38), Robin (60), Marion (67); **Goals:** Kheirallah 4/5.
On report: Hepi (31) - alleged dangerous contact.
HALIFAX: 24 Kieren Moss; 1 Will Sharp; 16 James Woodburn-Hall; 3 Steve Tyrer; 5 James Saltonstall; 6 Scott Murrell; 7 Ben Johnston; 27 Jordan Baldwinson; 9 Ben Kaye; 29 Dan Fleming; 2 Ben Heaton; 11 Shane Grady; 12 Simon Grix. Subs (all used): 30 Brandon Douglas; 14 Brandon Moore; 32 Liam Cooper; 13 Jacob Fairbank.
Try: Fleming (75); **Goals:** Grady 1/1.
Rugby Leaguer & League Express Men of the Match:
Olympique: Mark Kheirallah; *Halifax:* Ben Johnston.
Penalty count: 6-8; **Half-time:** 16-0;
Referee: Scott Mikalauskas; **Attendance:** 1,899.

**TORONTO WOLFPACK 22
HULL KINGSTON ROVERS 28**

WOLFPACK: 31 Gareth O'Brien; 23 Nick Rawsthorne; 4 Gary Wheeler; 33 Chase Stanley; 34 Mason Caton-Brown; 6 Josh McCrone; 17 Blake Wallace; 32 Darcy Lussick; 9 Bob Beswick; 10 Ashton Sims; 11 Andrew Dixon; 24 Cory Paterson; 29 Jake Emmitt. Subs (all used): 14 Andy Ackers; 8 Jack Buchanan; 15 Adam Sidlow; 22 Richard Whiting.
Tries: Rawsthorne (11), Dixon (43, 74); **Goals:** O'Brien 5/5.
ROVERS: 1 Adam Quinlan; 41 Craig Hall; 42 Ben Crooks; 2 Junior Vaivai; 26 Joe Wardill; 7 Danny McGuire (C); 24 Chris Atkin; 8 Nick Scruton; 19 Tommy Lee; 21 Robbie Mulhern; 39 Joel Tomkins; 12 James Greenwood; 34 Danny Tickle. Subs (all used): 15 James Donaldson; 10 Mose Masoe; 13 Ben Kavanagh; 17 Chris Clarkson.
Tries: Vaivai (21), Hall (25), Atkin (62), Clarkson (64);
Goals: Tickle 4/4, Hall 2/2.
Rugby Leaguer & League Express Men of the Match:
Wolfpack: Andrew Dixon; *Rovers:* Craig Hall.
Penalty count: 11-14; **Half-time:** 6-14;
Referee: James Child; **Attendance:** 7,540.

Sunday 19th August 2018

LONDON BRONCOS 32 LEEDS RHINOS 48

BRONCOS: 14 Alex Walker; 5 Kieran Dixon; 3 Ben Hellewell; 1 Elliot Kear; 2 Rhys Williams; 6 Api Pewhairangi; 9 James Cunningham; 15 Eddie Battye; 30 Eloi Pelissier; 18 Ben Evans; 12 Jay Pitts; 26 Daniel Hindmarsh; 13 Matt Davis. Subs (all used): 8 Tom Spencer; 10 Mark Ioane; 11 Daniel Harrison; 7 Jarrod Sammut.
Tries: Dixon (21), Williams (47, 73), Hindmarsh (64), Evans (69), Hellewell (75); **Goals:** Sammut 4/6.
RHINOS: 1 Ashton Golding; 2 Tom Briscoe; 18 Jimmy Keinhorst; 6 Joel Moon; 34 Luke Briscoe; 4 Liam Sutcliffe; 7 Richie Myler; 21 Nathaniel Peteru; 14 Brad Dwyer; 10 Brad Singleton; 19 Brett Ferres; 12 Carl Ablett (C); 11 Jamie Jones-Buchanan. Subs (all used): 28 Mikolaj Oledzki; 8 Adam Cuthbertson; 16 Anthony Mullally; 13 Stevie Ward.
Tries: Moon (3, 5, 14), L Briscoe (29), Ferres (31), Ablett (52), Golding (57, 62); **Goals:** Sutcliffe 8/9.
Rugby Leaguer & League Express Men of the Match:
Broncos: James Cunningham; *Rhinos:* Brad Dwyer.
Penalty count: 10-10; **Half-time:** 6-28;
Referee: Chris Kendall; **Attendance:** 1,793.

ROUND 3

Saturday 1st September 2018

LEEDS RHINOS 36 HULL KINGSTON ROVERS 38

RHINOS: 24 Jack Walker; 2 Tom Briscoe; 13 Stevie Ward; 6 Joel Moon; 34 Luke Briscoe; 4 Liam Sutcliffe; 7 Richie Myler; 10 Brad Singleton; 14 Brad Dwyer; 8 Adam Cuthbertson; 12 Carl Ablett (C); 19 Brett Ferres; 11 Jamie Jones-Buchanan. Subs (all used): 37 Jordan Thompson; 21 Nathaniel Peteru; 9 Matt Parcell; 16 Anthony Mullally.
Tries: Moon (4), T Briscoe (28, 53), Myler (37), Peteru (39), Parcell (51); **Goals:** Sutcliffe 6/7.
ROVERS: 1 Adam Quinlan; 41 Craig Hall; 42 Ben Crooks; 2 Junior Vaivai; 36 Justin Carney; 7 Danny McGuire; 24 Chris Atkin; 10 Mose Masoe; 19 Tommy Lee; 21 Robbie Mulhern; 34 Danny Tickle; 12 James Greenwood; 17 Chris Clarkson. Subs (all used): 8 Nick Scruton; 9 Shaun Lunt (C); 13 Ben Kavanagh; 11 Maurice Blair.
Tries: Hall (12, 44, 48), Quinlan (14), Mulhern (24), Atkin (61), Vaivai (67); **Goals:** Tickle 0/2, Hall 5/6.
Rugby Leaguer & League Express Men of the Match:
Rhinos: Tom Briscoe; *Rovers:* Adam Quinlan.
Penalty count: 7-8; **Half time:** 22-16;
Referee: Ben Thaler; **Attendance:** 11,468.

TOULOUSE OLYMPIQUE 42 WIDNES VIKINGS 22

OLYMPIQUE: 1 Mark Kheirallah; 22 Chris Centrone; 3 Bastien Ader; 31 Arthur Romano; 20 Paul Marcon; 6 Johnathon Ford; 7 Stan Robin; 15 Maxime Puech; 9 Anthony Marion; 24 Joe Bretherton; 11 Sebastien Planas; 12 Rhys Curran; 18 Sam Rapira. Subs (all used): 30 William Barthau; 10 Bastien Canet; 16 Tyla Hepi; 29 Paul Seguier.
Tries: Kheirallah (9, 29), Centrone (36, 64), Ford (58), Robin (68), Barthau (75); **Goals:** Kheirallah 7/7.
VIKINGS: 15 Danny Craven; 5 Patrick Ah Van; 3 Krisnan Inu; 12 Matt Whitley; 4 Charly Runciman; 6 Joe Mellor (C); 7 Tom Gilmore; 8 Gil Dudson; 9 Lloyd White; 10 Alex Gerrard; 41 Harrison Hansen; 14 Chris Dean; 20 Macgraff Leuluai. Subs (all used): 11 Chris Houston (C); 16 Tom Olbison; 33 Aaron Heremaia; 39 Weller Hauraki.
Tries: Inu (13), Hansen (26), Hauraki (43), White (74);
Goals: Inu 3/4.
Rugby Leaguer & League Express Men of the Match:
Olympique: Johnathon Ford; *Vikings:* Lloyd White.
Penalty count: 5-5; **Half-time:** 18-10;
Referee: Robert Hicks; **Attendance:** 2,911.

TORONTO WOLFPACK 34 LONDON BRONCOS 22

WOLFPACK: 31 Gareth O'Brien; 34 Mason Caton-Brown; 33 Chase Stanley; 4 Gary Wheeler; 30 Matthew Russell; 6 Josh McCrone; 17 Blake Wallace; 8 Jack Buchanan; 9 Bob Beswick; 32 Darcy Lussick; 11 Andrew Dixon; 22 Richard Whiting; 29 Jake Emmitt. Subs (all used): 10 Ashton Sims; 14 Andy Ackers; 15 Adam Sidlow; 21 Olsi Krasniqi.
Tries: Wallace (4), O'Brien (12), Stanley (17), McCrone (41), Caton-Brown (52); **Goals:** O'Brien 7/7.
Sin bin: Whiting (78) - fighting.
BRONCOS: 14 Alex Walker; 5 Kieran Dixon; 3 Ben Hellewell; 1 Elliot Kear; 2 Rhys Williams; 7 Jarrod Sammut; 9 James Cunningham; 15 Eddie Battye; 30 Eloi Pelissier; 18 Ben Evans; 12 Jay Pitts; 26 Daniel Hindmarsh; 13 Matt Davis. Subs (all used): 10 Mark Ioane; 8 Tom Spencer; 11 Daniel Harrison; 16 Matty Gee.
Tries: Williams (59), Walker (62), Evans (66), Matt Davis (68); **Goals:** Sammut 3/4.
Sin bin: Sammut (78) - fighting.
Rugby Leaguer & League Express Men of the Match:
Wolfpack: Gareth O'Brien; *Broncos:* Rhys Williams.
Penalty count: 8-7; **Half-time:** 20-0;
Referee: Scott Mikalauskas; **Attendance:** 7,557.

Sunday 2nd September 2018

HALIFAX 4 SALFORD RED DEVILS 62

HALIFAX: 24 Kieren Moss; 2 Ben Heaton; 28 Sam Wood; 18 Chester Butler; 1 Will Sharp; 6 Scott Murrell; 7 Ben Johnston; 29 Dan Fleming; 9 Ben Kaye; 27 Jordan Baldwinson; 10 Adam Tangata; 11 Shane Grady; 12 Simon Grix. Subs (all used): 17 Will Maher; 14 Brandon Moore; 32 Liam Cooper; 13 Jacob Fairbank.
Try: Wood (8); **Goals:** Grady 0/1.
RED DEVILS: 5 Niall Evalds; 22 Derrell Olpherts; 3 Kris Welham; 4 Junior Sa'u; 29 Ed Chamberlain; 6 Robert Lui; 31 Jackson Hastings; 26 Daniel Murray; 19 Josh Wood; 14 Lama Tasi; 11 Josh Jones; 17 Tyrone McCarthy; 13 Mark Flanagan (C). Subs (all used): 16 Luke Burgess; 18 Ben Nakubuwai; 30 Greg Burke; 32 Joey Lussick.
Tries: Hastings (12, 65), Chamberlain (18), Olpherts (23, 35, 44), Nakubuwai (27), Welham (40), Tasi (48), Sa'u (54, 79), Wood (72); **Goals:** Chamberlain 7/12.
Rugby Leaguer & League Express Men of the Match:
Halifax: Sam Wood; *Red Devils:* Jackson Hastings.
Penalty count: 7-7; **Half-time:** 4-30;
Referee: Tom Grant; **Attendance:** 2,555.

Super 8s - The Qualifiers - 2018 Round by Round

ROUND 4

Saturday 8th September 2018

SALFORD RED DEVILS 28 TORONTO WOLFPACK 16

RED DEVILS: 5 Niall Evalds; 29 Ed Chamberlain; 3 Kris Welham; 4 Junior Sa'u; 24 Jake Bibby; 6 Robert Lui; 31 Jackson Hastings; 16 Luke Burgess; 19 Josh Wood; 14 Lama Tasi; 11 Josh Jones; 10 George Griffin; 15 Ryan Lannon. Subs (all used): 8 Craig Kopczak; 30 Greg Burke; 32 Joey Lussick; 13 Mark Flanagan (C).
Tries: Chamberlain (6), Lui (16), Hastings (34), Lannon (62);
Goals: Chamberlain 6/6.
Dismissals: Burgess (53) - high tackle on Emmitt; Hastings (80) - swinging arm on O'Brien.
Sin bin: Tasi (14) - high tackle on O'Brien.
WOLFPACK: 31 Gareth O'Brien; 30 Matthew Russell; 33 Chase Stanley; 4 Gary Wheeler; 34 Mason Caton-Brown; 6 Josh McCrone; 17 Blake Wallace; 32 Darcy Lussick; 9 Bob Beswick; 10 Ashton Sims; 11 Andrew Dixon; 24 Cory Paterson; 8 Jack Buchanan. Subs (all used): 14 Andy Ackers; 15 Adam Sidlow; 21 Olsi Krasniqi; 29 Jake Emmitt.
Tries: Sidlow (47), Russell (50), Ackers (57);
Goals: O'Brien 2/3.
Sin bin: Stanley (60) - dangerous challenge.
Rugby Leaguer & League Express Men of the Match:
Red Devils: Robert Lui; *Wolfpack:* Adam Sidlow.
Penalty count: 8-8; **Half-time:** 20-0;
Referee: Robert Hicks; **Attendance:** 2,509.

Sunday 9th September 2018

HULL KINGSTON ROVERS 38 HALIFAX 24

ROVERS: 1 Adam Quinlan; 41 Craig Hall; 22 Liam Salter; 11 Maurice Blair; 36 Justin Carney; 7 Danny McGuire; 24 Chris Atkin; 10 Mose Masoe; 9 Shaun Lunt (C); 34 Danny Tickle; 12 James Greenwood; 39 Joel Tomkins; 17 Chris Clarkson. Subs (all used): 2 Junior Vaivai; 13 Ben Kavanagh; 14 Lee Jewitt; 40 Todd Carney.
Tries: Hall (7, 10, 18, 27), Greenwood (16), Atkin (69), Lunt (72); **Goals:** Hall 4/6, Tickle 1/2.
HALIFAX: 16 James Woodburn-Hall; 5 James Saltonstall; 2 Ben Heaton; 18 Chester Butler; 1 Will Sharp; 6 Scott Murrell; 7 Ben Johnston; 29 Dan Fleming; 9 Ben Kaye; 25 Sion Jones; 10 Adam Tangata; 11 Shane Grady; 13 Jacob Fairbank. Subs (all used): 14 Brandon Moore; 17 Will Maher; 32 Liam Cooper; 33 Connor Davies.
Tries: Saltonstall (44, 64), Fleming (76), Sharp (78);
Goals: Grady 1/1, Fleming 3/3.
Rugby Leaguer & League Express Men of the Match:
Rovers: Adam Quinlan; *Halifax:* Will Sharp.
Penalty count: 11-8; **Half-time:** 24-0;
Referee: Marcus Griffiths; **Attendance:** 7,952.

LONDON BRONCOS 34 TOULOUSE OLYMPIQUE 8

BRONCOS: 14 Alex Walker; 5 Kieran Dixon; 1 Elliot Kear; 3 Ben Hellewell; 2 Rhys Williams; 7 Jarrod Sammut; 9 James Cunningham; 10 Mark Ioane; 13 Matt Davis; 18 Ben Evans; 12 Jay Pitts; 26 Daniel Hindmarsh; 15 Eddie Battye. Subs (all used): 16 Matty Gee; 19 Sadiq Adebiyi; 11 Daniel Harrison; 30 Eloi Pelissier.
Tries: Cunningham (7), Dixon (28), Walker (34, 37), Hellewell (71); **Goals:** Sammut 7/8.
OLYMPIQUE: 1 Mark Kheirallah; 20 Paul Marcon; 31 Arthur Romano; 3 Bastien Ader; 22 Chris Centrone; 6 Johnathon Ford; 7 Stan Robin; 24 Joe Bretherton; 9 Anthony Marion; 15 Maxime Puech; 11 Sebastien Planas; 12 Rhys Curran; 18 Sam Rapira. Subs (all used): 30 William Barthau; 10 Bastien Canet; 16 Tyla Hepi; 29 Paul Seguier.
Tries: Romano (17), Robin (75); **Goals:** Kheirallah 0/2.
Sin bin: Canet (57) - dangerous challenge.
Rugby Leaguer & League Express Men of the Match:
Broncos: Jarrod Sammut; *Olympique:* Stan Robin.
Penalty count: 8-8; **Half-time:** 26-4;
Referee: Tom Grant; **Attendance:** 696.

WIDNES VIKINGS 6 LEEDS RHINOS 16

VIKINGS: 6 Joe Mellor (C); 5 Patrick Ah Van; 3 Krisnan Inu; 4 Charly Runciman; 40 Owen Buckley; 35 Joe Lyons (D); 42 Liam Finn; 25 Jay Chapelhow; 9 Lloyd White; 11 Chris Houston (C); 39 Weller Hauraki; 41 Harrison Hansen; 20 Macgraff Leuluai. Subs (all used): 23 Danny Walker; 43 Charlie Gubb; 16 Tom Olbison; 17 Sam Wilde.
Try: Olbison (37); **Goals:** Inu 1/1.
RHINOS: 24 Jack Walker; 2 Tom Briscoe; 18 Jimmy Keinhorst; 6 Joel Moon; 34 Luke Briscoe; 4 Liam Sutcliffe; 7 Richie Myler; 36 Dominic Crosby; 14 Brad Dwyer; 10 Brad Singleton; 11 Jamie Jones-Buchanan; 19 Brett Ferres (C); 37 Jordan Thompson. Subs (all used): 9 Matt Parcell; 21 Nathaniel Peteru; 27 Cameron Smith; 30 Josh Walters.
Tries: L Briscoe (33), Parcell (55), Myler (77);
Goals: Sutcliffe 2/3.
Rugby Leaguer & League Express Men of the Match:
Vikings: Tom Olbison; *Rhinos:* Jack Walker.
Penalty count: 9-7; **Half-time:** 6-4;
Referee: Chris Kendall; **Attendance:** 4,050.

ROUND 5

Friday 14th September 2018

LEEDS RHINOS 18 SALFORD RED DEVILS 16

RHINOS: 24 Jack Walker; 2 Tom Briscoe; 18 Jimmy Keinhorst; 6 Joel Moon; 34 Luke Briscoe; 4 Liam Sutcliffe; 7 Richie Myler; 36 Dominic Crosby; 14 Brad Dwyer; 10 Brad Singleton; 19 Brett Ferres (C); 11 Jamie Jones-Buchanan; 37 Jordan Thompson. Subs (all used): 21 Nathaniel Peteru; 9 Matt Parcell; 8 Adam Cuthbertson; 27 Cameron Smith.
Tries: T Briscoe (9, 70), Keinhorst (38); **Goals:** Sutcliffe 3/5.
Sin bin: Ferres (56) - dangerous contact.
RED DEVILS: 5 Niall Evalds; 24 Jake Bibby; 29 Ed Chamberlain; 3 Kris Welham; 22 Derrell Olpherts; 6 Robert Lui; 19 Josh Wood; 14 Lama Tasi; 32 Joey Lussick; 15 Ryan Lannon; 11 Josh Jones; 17 Tyrone McCarthy; 13 Mark Flanagan (C). Subs (all used): 8 Craig Kopczak; 26 Daniel Murray; 30 Greg Burke; 33 Jansin Turgut (D).
Tries: Evalds (14), Burke (56), Olpherts (74);
Goals: Chamberlain 2/3.
Rugby Leaguer & League Express Men of the Match:
Rhinos: Dominic Crosby; *Red Devils:* Ryan Lannon.
Penalty count: 10-10; **Half-time:** 8-4;
Referee: James Child; **Attendance:** 11,202.

Saturday 15th September 2018

WIDNES VIKINGS 26 HALIFAX 12

VIKINGS: 6 Joe Mellor (C); 5 Patrick Ah Van; 3 Krisnan Inu; 4 Charly Runciman; 40 Owen Buckley; 35 Joe Lyons; 42 Liam Finn; 43 Charlie Gubb; 9 Lloyd White; 11 Chris Houston (C); 39 Weller Hauraki; 41 Harrison Hansen; 20 Macgraff Leuluai. Subs (all used): 23 Danny Walker; 25 Jay Chapelhow; 16 Tom Olbison; 17 Sam Wilde.
Tries: Hauraki (10), Inu (14, 62), Ah Van (48, 80);
Goals: Inu 3/5.
HALIFAX: 1 Will Sharp; 5 James Saltonstall; 2 Ben Heaton; 18 Chester Butler; 16 James Woodburn-Hall; 6 Scott Murrell; 7 Ben Johnston; 29 Dan Fleming; 9 Ben Kaye; 13 Jacob Fairbank; 10 Adam Tangata; 11 Shane Grady; 33 Connor Davies. Subs (all used): 25 Sion Jones; 14 Brandon Moore; 32 Liam Cooper; 17 Will Maher.
Tries: Woodburn-Hall (35), Saltonstall (75);
Goals: Grady 1/1, Murrell 1/1.
Rugby Leaguer & League Express Men of the Match:
Vikings: Krisnan Inu; *Halifax:* Brandon Moore.
Penalty count: 7-10; **Half-time:** 10-6;
Referee: Gareth Hewer; **Attendance:** 3,372.

TORONTO WOLFPACK 13 TOULOUSE OLYMPIQUE 12

WOLFPACK: 31 Gareth O'Brien; 23 Nick Rawsthorne; 33 Chase Stanley; 4 Gary Wheeler; 34 Mason Caton-Brown; 6 Josh McCrone; 17 Blake Wallace; 29 Jake Emmitt; 9 Bob Beswick; 10 Ashton Sims; 11 Andrew Dixon; 24 Cory Paterson; 13 Jack Bussey. Subs (all used): 14 Andy Ackers; 15 Adam Sidlow; 8 Jack Buchanan; 32 Darcy Lussick.
Tries: Caton-Brown (19), Rawsthorne (28), Stanley (44);
Goals: O'Brien 0/3; **Field goal:** O'Brien (77).
On report: Bussey (13) - alleged bite on Ader.
OLYMPIQUE: 1 Mark Kheirallah; 20 Paul Marcon; 4 Gavin Marguerite; 3 Bastien Ader; 22 Chris Centrone; 6 Johnathon Ford; 7 Stan Robin; 24 Joe Bretherton; 9 Anthony Marion; 15 Maxime Puech; 11 Sebastien Planas; 12 Rhys Curran; 18 Sam Rapira. Subs (all used): 30 William Barthau; 23 Justin Sangare; 16 Tyla Hepi; 8 Clement Boyer.
Tries: Marcon (39), Robin (72);
Goals: Kheirallah 2/3, Barthau 0/1.
Sin bin: Robin (26) - dissent.
On report: Bretherton (10) - alleged dangerous challenge on Rawsthorne.
Rugby Leaguer & League Express Men of the Match:
Wolfpack: Mason Caton-Brown; *Olympique:* Paul Marcon.
Penalty count: 6-10; **Half-time:** 8-8;
Referee: Tom Grant; **Attendance:** 7,923.

HULL KINGSTON ROVERS 30 LONDON BRONCOS 18

ROVERS: 41 Craig Hall; 22 Liam Salter; 42 Ben Crooks; 2 Junior Vaivai; 27 Will Oakes; 40 Todd Carney; 24 Chris Atkin; 8 Nick Scruton; 19 Tommy Lee; 21 Robbie Mulhern; 12 James Greenwood; 39 Joel Tomkins; 17 Chris Clarkson. Subs (all used): 9 Shaun Lunt (C); 13 Ben Kavanagh; 15 James Donaldson; 34 Danny Tickle.
Tries: Greenwood (7, 71), Atkin (21), Lee (26), Vaivai (78);
Goals: Atkin 3/4, Tickle 2/3.
Sin bin: Crooks (4) - delaying restart.
BRONCOS: 14 Alex Walker; 17 Michael Channing; 3 Ben Hellewell; 1 Elliot Kear; 2 Rhys Williams; 9 James Cunningham; 7 Jarrod Sammut; 10 Mark Ioane; 13 Matt Davis; 18 Ben Evans; 12 Jay Pitts; 26 Daniel Hindmarsh; 15 Eddie Battye. Subs (all used): 30 Eloi Pelissier; 16 Matty Gee; 19 Sadiq Adebiyi; 21 Will Lovell.
Tries: Sammut (14), Evans (55), Channing (67);
Goals: Sammut 3/3.
On report: Pelissier (73) - alleged high tackle on Crooks.
Rugby Leaguer & League Express Men of the Match:
Rovers: Robbie Mulhern; *Broncos:* Jarrod Sammut.
Penalty count: 13-6; **Half-time:** 20-6;
Referee: Greg Dolan; **Attendance:** 7,210.

ROUND 6

Saturday 22nd September 2018

LONDON BRONCOS 11 SALFORD RED DEVILS 8

BRONCOS: 14 Alex Walker; 5 Kieran Dixon; 1 Elliot Kear; 3 Ben Hellewell; 2 Rhys Williams; 12 Jay Pitts; 7 Jarrod Sammut; 10 Mark Ioane; 13 Matt Davis; 18 Ben Evans; 16 Matty Gee; 26 Daniel Hindmarsh; 15 Eddie Battye. Subs (all used): 23 Rob Butler; 19 Sadiq Adebiyi; 8 Tom Spencer; 30 Eloi Pelissier.
Try: Pitts (13); **Goals:** Sammut 3/3;
Field goal: Sammut (34).
Sin bin: Battye (24) - repeated team offences.
RED DEVILS: 5 Niall Evalds; 2 Greg Johnson; 3 Kris Welham; 29 Ed Chamberlain; 24 Jake Bibby; 6 Robert Lui; 7 Jack Littlejohn; 30 Greg Burke; 32 Joey Lussick; 16 Luke Burgess; 11 Josh Jones; 17 Tyrone McCarthy; 15 Ryan Lannon. Subs (all used): 13 Mark Flanagan (C); 18 Ben Nakubuwai; 8 Craig Kopczak; 33 Jansin Turgut.
Tries: Johnson (56, 76); **Goals:** Lussick 0/1, Chamberlain 0/1.
Rugby Leaguer & League Express Men of the Match:
Broncos: Alex Walker; *Red Devils:* Greg Johnson.
Penalty count: 8-12; **Half-time:** 9-0;
Referee: Scott Mikalauskas; **Attendance:** 809.

TOULOUSE OLYMPIQUE 34
HULL KINGSTON ROVERS 23

OLYMPIQUE: 1 Mark Kheirallah; 22 Chris Centrone; 3 Bastien Ader; 4 Gavin Marguerite; 20 Paul Marcon; 6 Johnathon Ford; 7 Stan Robin; 15 Maxime Puech; 30 William Barthau; 24 Joe Bretherton; 26 Constantine Mika; 12 Rhys Curran; 9 Anthony Marion. Subs (all used): 8 Clement Boyer; 11 Sebastien Planas; 14 Mourad Kriouache; 16 Tyla Hepi.
Tries: Curran (30), Centrone (33, 55), Robin (35), Marguerite (52), Ader (66); **Goals:** Kheirallah 5/8.
Sin bin: Barthau (17) - dissent; Hepi (39) - fighting.
ROVERS: 24 Chris Atkin; 41 Craig Hall; 39 Joel Tomkins; 2 Junior Vaivai; 22 Liam Salter; 7 Danny McGuire; 40 Todd Carney; 10 Mose Masoe; 19 Tommy Lee; 21 Robbie Mulhern; 34 Danny Tickle; 12 James Greenwood; 17 Chris Clarkson. Subs (all used): 9 Shaun Lunt (C); 13 Ben Kavanagh; 15 James Donaldson; 8 Nick Scruton.
Tries: Mulhern (6), Hall (10, 72), Atkin (24);
Goals: Tickle 3/3, Hall 0/1; **Field goal:** McGuire (20).
Sin bin: Greenwood (39) - fighting.
Rugby Leaguer & League Express Men of the Match:
Olympique: Johnathon Ford; *Rovers:* Craig Hall.
Penalty count: 10-17; **Half time:** 18-19;
Referee: Ben Thaler; **Attendance:** 4,127.

TORONTO WOLFPACK 20 WIDNES VIKINGS 12

WOLFPACK: 31 Gareth O'Brien; 34 Mason Caton-Brown; 33 Chase Stanley; 4 Gary Wheeler; 30 Matthew Russell; 6 Josh McCrone; 17 Blake Wallace; 32 Darcy Lussick; 9 Bob Beswick; 10 Ashton Sims; 11 Andrew Dixon; 24 Cory Paterson; 29 Jake Emmitt. Subs (all used): 14 Andy Ackers; 15 Adam Sidlow; 8 Jack Buchanan; 21 Olsi Krasniqi.
Tries: Paterson (17), Russell (32), Wallace (57);
Goals: O'Brien 4/7.
Sin bin: Stanley (25) - high tackle on Buckley.
VIKINGS: 6 Joe Mellor (C); 5 Patrick Ah Van; 3 Krisnan Inu; 4 Charly Runciman; 40 Owen Buckley; 35 Joe Lyons; 42 Liam Finn; 43 Charlie Gubb; 9 Lloyd White; 41 Harrison Hansen; 39 Weller Hauraki; 14 Chris Dean; 20 Macgraff Leuluai. Subs (all used): 23 Danny Walker; 11 Chris Houston (C); 16 Tom Olbison; 17 Sam Wilde.
Tries: Mellor (13), Dean (43); **Goals:** Inu 2/3.
Rugby Leaguer & League Express Men of the Match:
Wolfpack: Blake Wallace; *Vikings:* Chris Dean.
Penalty count: 10-9; **Half-time:** 10-8;
Referee: Robert Hicks; **Attendance:** 8,381.

Sunday 23rd September 2018

HALIFAX 6 LEEDS RHINOS 34

HALIFAX: 24 Kieren Moss; 16 James Woodburn-Hall; 3 Steve Tyrer; 18 Chester Butler; 1 Will Sharp; 6 Scott

London Broncos' Alex Walker beats Toronto's Josh McCrone to a high ball during the Million Pound Game

Murrell; 7 Ben Johnston; 29 Dan Fleming; 9 Ben Kaye; 13 Jacob Fairbank; 10 Adam Tangata; 11 Shane Grady; 14 Brandon Moore. Subs (all used): 25 Sion Jones; 2 Ben Heaton; 33 Connor Davies; 17 Will Maher.
Try: Tyrer (30); **Goals:** Tyrer 1/1.
Sin bin: Heaton (77) - high tackle on T Briscoe.
RHINOS: 24 Jack Walker; 2 Tom Briscoe; 18 Jimmy Keinhorst; 6 Joel Moon; 34 Luke Briscoe; 4 Liam Sutcliffe; 7 Richie Myler; 36 Dominic Crosby; 9 Matt Parcell; 10 Brad Singleton (C); 11 Jamie Jones-Buchanan; 21 Nathaniel Peteru; 37 Jordan Thompson. Subs (all used): 8 Adam Cuthbertson; 14 Brad Dwyer; 27 Cameron Smith; 30 Josh Walters.
Tries: Myler (5), Dwyer (42, 48), Sutcliffe (54), Smith (68), L Briscoe (71); **Goals:** Sutcliffe 5/6.
Rugby Leaguer & League Express Men of the Match: *Halifax:* James Woodburn-Hall; *Rhinos:* Jack Walker.
Penalty count: 7-13; **Half-time:** 6-6;
Referee: Liam Moore; **Attendance:** 4,507.

ROUND 7

Thursday 27th September 2018

SALFORD RED DEVILS 44 TOULOUSE OLYMPIQUE 10

RED DEVILS: 5 Niall Evalds; 2 Greg Johnson; 24 Jake Bibby; 3 Kris Welham; 22 Derrell Olpherts; 6 Robert Lui; 31 Jackson Hastings; 23 Lee Mossop; 32 Joey Lussick; 16 Luke Burgess; 11 Josh Jones; 17 Tyrone McCarthy; 13 Mark Flanagan (C). Subs (all used): 8 Craig Kopczak; 30 Greg Burke; 10 George Griffin; 15 Ryan Lannon.
Tries: Hastings (14), Lussick (26), Johnson (59), Evalds (64), Olpherts (66), Welham (75), McCarthy (78); **Goals:** Hastings 7/8, Burgess 1/2.
OLYMPIQUE: 1 Mark Kheirallah; 20 Paul Marcon; 4 Gavin Marguerite; 3 Bastien Ader; 22 Chris Centrone; 6 Johnathon Ford; 7 Stan Robin; 24 Joe Bretherton; 30 William Barthau; 15 Maxime Puech; 26 Constantine Mika; 12 Rhys Curran; 9 Anthony Marion. Subs (all used): 14 Mourad Kriouache; 8 Clement Boyer; 16 Tyla Hepi; 11 Sebastien Planas.
Tries: Centrone (36), Robin (42); **Goals:** Kheirallah 1/2.
Rugby Leaguer & League Express Men of the Match: *Red Devils:* Jackson Hastings; *Olympique:* Stan Robin.
Penalty count: 7-9; **Half-time:** 14-4;
Referee: Ben Thaler; **Attendance:** 2,130.

Friday 28th September 2018

LEEDS RHINOS 16 TORONTO WOLFPACK 17

RHINOS: 1 Ashton Golding; 2 Tom Briscoe; 18 Jimmy Keinhorst; 6 Joel Moon; 34 Luke Briscoe; 4 Liam Sutcliffe; 7

Richie Myler; 21 Nathaniel Peteru; 9 Matt Parcell; 36 Dominic Crosby; 11 Jamie Jones-Buchanan; 19 Brett Ferres (C); 37 Jordan Thompson. Subs (all used): 8 Adam Cuthbertson; 14 Brad Dwyer; 16 Anthony Mullally; 27 Cameron Smith.
Tries: T Briscoe (18), Sutcliffe (28), Keinhorst (54); **Goals:** Sutcliffe 2/3.
Sin bin: Crosby (68) - dangerous contact on Lussick.
WOLFPACK: 31 Gareth O'Brien; 34 Mason Caton-Brown; 23 Nick Rawsthorne; 4 Gary Wheeler; 30 Matthew Russell; 6 Josh McCrone; 17 Blake Wallace; 32 Darcy Lussick; 9 Bob Beswick; 10 Ashton Sims; 11 Andrew Dixon; 24 Cory Paterson; 29 Jake Emmitt. Subs (all used): 8 Jack Buchanan; 15 Adam Sidlow; 14 Andy Ackers; 21 Olsi Krasniqi.
Tries: Paterson (12), Rawsthorne (39), Russell (65); **Goals:** O'Brien 2/4; **Field goal:** O'Brien (75).
Rugby Leaguer & League Express Men of the Match: *Rhinos:* Tom Briscoe; *Wolfpack:* Josh McCrone.
Penalty count: 10-10; **Half-time:** 10-12;
Referee: Robert Hicks; **Attendance:** 11,565.

Saturday 29th September 2018

LONDON BRONCOS 23 HALIFAX 16

BRONCOS: 14 Alex Walker; 5 Kieran Dixon; 1 Elliot Kear; 3 Ben Hellewell; 2 Rhys Williams; 12 Jay Pitts; 7 Jarrod Sammut; 10 Mark Ioane; 30 Eloi Pelissier; 18 Ben Evans; 16 Matty Gee; 26 Daniel Hindmarsh; 15 Eddie Battye. Subs (all used): 21 Will Lovell; 19 Sadiq Adebiyi; 8 Tom Spencer; 25 Matthew Davies.
Tries: Sammut (20), Pelissier (23), Dixon (59), Kear (66); **Goals:** Sammut 3/4; **Field goal:** Sammut (80).
HALIFAX: 16 James Woodburn-Hall; 24 Kieren Moss; 3 Steve Tyrer; 2 Ben Heaton; 1 Will Sharp; 6 Scott Murrell; 7 Ben Johnston; 29 Dan Fleming; 9 Ben Kaye; 13 Jacob Fairbank; 10 Adam Tangata; 18 Chester Butler; 14 Brandon Moore. Subs (all used): - Curtis Davies; 33 Connor Davies; 32 Liam Cooper; 30 Brandon Douglas.
Tries: Kaye (11), Tyrer (14), Tangata (27); **Goals:** Tyrer 2/3.
Sin bin: Moore (73) - dissent.
Rugby Leaguer & League Express Men of the Match: *Broncos:* Jarrod Sammut; *Halifax:* Ben Johnston.
Penalty count: 7-6; **Half-time:** 12-16;
Referee: Gareth Hewer; **Attendance:** 869.

Sunday 30th September 2018

HULL KINGSTON ROVERS 30 WIDNES VIKINGS 0

ROVERS: 24 Chris Atkin; 41 Craig Hall; 42 Ben Crooks; 2 Junior Vaivai; 27 Will Oakes; 40 Todd Carney; 7 Danny McGuire (C); 10 Mose Masoe; 19 Tommy Lee; 8 Nick

Scruton; 12 James Greenwood; 39 Joel Tomkins; 17 Chris Clarkson. Subs (all used): 21 Robbie Mulhern; 11 Maurice Blair; 13 Ben Kavanagh; 34 Danny Tickle.
Tries: Greenwood (8), Crooks (16), Atkin (37), Vaivai (57), Hall (67); **Goals:** Hall 5/7.
VIKINGS: 1 Rhys Hanbury; 2 Stefan Marsh; 30 Keanan Brand; 4 Charly Runciman; 40 Owen Buckley; 35 Joe Lyons; 7 Tom Gilmore; 11 Chris Houston (C); 9 Lloyd White; 41 Harrison Hansen; 12 Matt Whitley; 14 Chris Dean; 20 Macgraff Leuluai. Subs (all used): 33 Aaron Heremaia; 17 Sam Wilde; 25 Jay Chapelhow; 26 Ted Chapelhow.
Sin bin: Gilmore (77) - dissent.
Rugby Leaguer & League Express Men of the Match: *Rovers:* Danny McGuire; *Vikings:* Joe Lyons.
Penalty count: 8-5; **Half-time:** 20-0;
Referee: Chris Kendall; **Attendance:** 8,232.

MILLION POUND GAME

Sunday 7th October 2018

TORONTO WOLFPACK 2 LONDON BRONCOS 4

WOLFPACK: 31 Gareth O'Brien; 34 Mason Caton-Brown; 23 Nick Rawsthorne; 4 Gary Wheeler; 30 Matthew Russell; 6 Josh McCrone; 17 Blake Wallace; 32 Darcy Lussick; 9 Bob Beswick; 10 Ashton Sims; 11 Andrew Dixon; 22 Richard Whiting; 29 Jake Emmitt. Subs (all used): 8 Jack Buchanan; 14 Andy Ackers; 15 Adam Sidlow; 19 Adam Higson.
Goals: O'Brien 1/2.
Sin bin: Ackers (32) - late challenge on Pelissier.
BRONCOS: 14 Alex Walker; 2 Rhys Williams; 1 Elliot Kear; 3 Ben Hellewell; 5 Kieran Dixon; 12 Jay Pitts; 7 Jarrod Sammut; 16 Matty Gee; 21 Will Lovell; 26 Daniel Hindmarsh. Subs (all used): 8 Tom Spencer; 15 Eddie Battye; 23 Rob Butler; 25 Matthew Davies.
Goals: Sammut 2/2.
Rugby Leaguer & League Express Men of the Match: *Wolfpack:* Gareth O'Brien; *Broncos:* Alex Walker.
Penalty count: 8-7; **Half-time:** 0-2;
Referee: Chris Kendall; **Attendance:** 9,266.

245

SUPER LEAGUE XXIII
Opta Analysis

SUPER LEAGUE XXIII TOP PERFORMERS

TACKLES

Daryl Clark	Warrington	882
Paul McShane	Castleford	880
Matty Ashurst	Wakefield	813
James Roby	St Helens	813
Ryan Hinchcliffe	Huddersfield	763
Danny Houghton	Hull FC	747
Tinirau Arona	Wakefield	738
Chris Hill	Warrington	715
Willie Isa	Wigan	708
Jack Hughes	Warrington	698

OFFLOADS

John Bateman	Wigan	47
Mike Cooper	Warrington	42
Julian Bousquet	Catalans	39
Adam Cuthbertson	Leeds	37
Bryson Goodwin	Warrington	34
Joel Moon	Leeds	34
Sebastine Ikahihifo	Huddersfield	32
Tom Lineham	Warrington	32
David Fifita	Wakefield	29
Zeb Taia	St Helens	28

CARRIES

Luke Thompson	St Helens	370
Bill Tupou	Wakefield	359
Tom Davies	Wigan	334
Chris Hill	Warrington	329
Louie McCarthy-Scarsbrook	St Helens	329
Stefan Ratchford	Warrington	329
Ryan Hall	Leeds	326
John Bateman	Wigan	324
Zeb Taia	St Helens	322
Tom Briscoe	Leeds	320

CLEAN BREAKS

Tom Johnstone	Wakefield	32
Mark Percival	St Helens	31
Adam Quinlan	Hull KR	26
Ben Barba	St Helens	25
Tom Davies	Wigan	23
Bureta Faraimo	Hull FC	23
Liam Marshall	Wigan	23
Ben Jones-Bishop	Wakefield	21
Regan Grace	St Helens	20
Josh Charnley	Warrington	19

OFFENSIVE MISS *

Mark Percival	St Helens	140
Ben Barba	St Helens	115
David Fifita	Wakefield	104
Reece Lyne	Wakefield	92
Daryl Clark	Warrington	90
Tommy Makinson	St Helens	85
Bill Tupou	Wakefield	85
John Bateman	Wigan	84
Bureta Faraimo	Hull FC	84
Adam Quinlan	Hull KR	84

ERRORS

Ben Jones-Bishop	Wakefield	36
Jake Bibby	Salford	35
Tom Briscoe	Leeds	32
Adam Quinlan	Hull KR	30
Mark Percival	St Helens	29
Danny Richardson	St Helens	28
Regan Grace	St Helens	27
Ash Handley	Leeds	27
Richie Myler	Leeds	27
Jake Connor	Hull FC	24

METRES

Bill Tupou	Wakefield	3126
Luke Thompson	St Helens	3006
Tom Davies	Wigan	2913
Ryan Hall	Leeds	2844
Reece Lyne	Wakefield	2740
Stefan Ratchford	Warrington	2690
Tom Lineham	Warrington	2581
Chris Hill	Warrington	2496
Louie McCarthy-Scarsbrook	St Helens	2415
Daryl Clark	Warrington	2382

MISSED TACKLES

Jacob Miller	Wakefield	83
Dominique Peyroux	St Helens	76
Aaron Heremaia	Widnes	71
Danny Richardson	St Helens	68
Robert Lui	Salford	66
Paul McShane	Castleford	66
Matt Whitley	Widnes	65
Adam Milner	Castleford	64
Daryl Clark	Warrington	63
Tyrone Roberts	Warrington	61

KICKS IN GENERAL PLAY

Danny Richardson	St Helens	220
Richie Myler	Leeds	210
Robert Lui	Salford	189
Tyrone Roberts	Warrington	180
Danny Brough	Huddersfield	167
Jacob Miller	Wakefield	147
Kevin Brown	Warrington	145
Marc Sneyd	Hull FC	141
Sam Tomkins	Wigan	138
Danny McGuire	Hull KR	132

QUICK PLAY-THE-BALLS

Ryan Hall	Leeds	73
Tom Briscoe	Leeds	66
Tom Lineham	Warrington	54
Bill Tupou	Wakefield	54
Julian Bousquet	Catalans	52
Luke Thompson	St Helens	52
Liam Marshall	Wigan	51
Carlos Tuimavave	Hull FC	49
Matt Whitley	Widnes	48
Tony Gigot	Catalans	44

PENALTIES CONCEDED

Chris Houston	Widnes	23
James Greenwood	Hull KR	22
Matty Ashurst	Wakefield	20
Pauli Pauli	Wakefield	20
Greg Bird	Catalans	19
Jay Chapelhow	Widnes	19
Paul McShane	Castleford	19
Ben Westwood	Warrington	19
George Griffin	Salford	18
Adam Milner	Castleford	17

TRY ASSISTS

Richie Myler	Leeds	23
Ben Barba	St Helens	22
Jacob Miller	Wakefield	20
George Williams	Wigan	17
Albert Kelly	Hull FC	16
Paul McShane	Castleford	16
Stefan Ratchford	Warrington	16
Jake Trueman	Castleford	16
Sam Tomkins	Wigan	15
Josh Drinkwater	Catalans	14

All statistics in Opta Analysis include Super League regular season (Rounds 1-23) only

* Offensive miss equates to a defender beaten

SUPER LEAGUE XXIII TRIES SCORED/CONCEDED

TOTAL TRIES SCORED

St Helens	127
Wakefield Trinity	100
Wigan Warriors	99
Castleford Tigers	95
Warrington Wolves	92
Hull FC	89
Catalans Dragons	83
Leeds Rhinos	80
Hull Kingston Rovers	79
Huddersfield Giants	74
Salford Red Devils	69
Widnes Vikings	65

TOTAL TRIES CONCEDED

Widnes Vikings	115
Huddersfield Giants	109
Salford Red Devils	104
Hull Kingston Rovers	103
Hull FC	92
Catalans Dragons	90
Leeds Rhinos	88
Castleford Tigers	87
Wakefield Trinity	85
Warrington Wolves	68
Wigan Warriors	57
St Helens	54

SCORED FROM KICKS

Catalans Dragons	20
Castleford Tigers	18
Wakefield Trinity	16
Leeds Rhinos	15
Widnes Vikings	15
St Helens	14
Warrington Wolves	14
Hull FC	12
Hull Kingston Rovers	12
Wigan Warriors	12
Huddersfield Giants	9
Salford Red Devils	5

St Helens' Regan Grace crosses to score against Wakefield. The Saints scored the most tries in Super League XXIII

CONCEDED FROM KICKS

Huddersfield Giants	20
Salford Red Devils	20
Catalans Dragons	18
Widnes Vikings	17
Hull Kingston Rovers	15
Castleford Tigers	14
Warrington Wolves	13
Leeds Rhinos	11
Hull FC	10
Wigan Warriors	10
Wakefield Trinity	8
St Helens	6

TRIES SCORED FROM OWN HALF

St Helens	23
Wigan Warriors	16
Hull Kingston Rovers	14
Wakefield Trinity	12
Catalans Dragons	9
Leeds Rhinos	9
Hull FC	9
Castleford Tigers	8
Salford Red Devils	7
Warrington Wolves	6
Widnes Vikings	2
Huddersfield Giants	1

TRIES CONCEDED FROM OVER 50M

Widnes Vikings	18
Salford Red Devils	16
Catalans Dragons	11
Castleford Tigers	11
Hull Kingston Rovers	10
Leeds Rhinos	10
Huddersfield Giants	10
Wakefield Trinity	7
Warrington Wolves	7
Hull FC	6
St Helens	5
Wigan Warriors	5

TRIES SCORED FROM UNDER 10M

Wakefield Trinity	50
St Helens	50
Castleford Tigers	45
Warrington Wolves	44
Wigan Warriors	44
Salford Red Devils	42
Leeds Rhinos	42
Huddersfield Giants	42
Hull FC	42
Widnes Vikings	40
Catalans Dragons	38
Hull Kingston Rovers	37

TRIES CONCEDED FROM UNDER 10M

Hull Kingston Rovers	55
Huddersfield Giants	54
Hull FC	50
Salford Red Devils	49
Widnes Vikings	47
Castleford Tigers	44
Leeds Rhinos	44
Wakefield Trinity	39
Catalans Dragons	39
Warrington Wolves	35
St Helens	33
Wigan Warriors	27

SUPER LEAGUE XXIII AVERAGES PER MATCH

TACKLES

Widnes Vikings	349.1
Salford Red Devils	349.0
Leeds Rhinos	347.7
Huddersfield Giants	342.1
Hull FC	331.0
St Helens	329.9
Wakefield Trinity	325.3
Catalans Dragons	324.5
Castleford Tigers	323.1
Wigan Warriors	320.8
Hull Kingston Rovers	317.3
Warrington Wolves	316.6

MISSED TACKLES

Widnes Vikings	35.2
Leeds Rhinos	34.2
Catalans Dragons	33.3
Hull Kingston Rovers	33.3
Salford Red Devils	30.7
Hull FC	30.6
Wakefield Trinity	29.5
Huddersfield Giants	28.5
Castleford Tigers	28.4
St Helens	27.5
Wigan Warriors	25.3
Warrington Wolves	23.2

OFFLOADS

Leeds Rhinos	13.3
Warrington Wolves	12.1
Catalans Dragons	9.9
Castleford Tigers	9.8
St Helens	9.7
Salford Red Devils	9.6
Hull FC	9.5
Wakefield Trinity	9.2
Widnes Vikings	8.8
Wigan Warriors	8.8
Hull Kingston Rovers	8.5
Huddersfield Giants	7.5

METRES

St Helens	1419.0
Warrington Wolves	1356.0
Wigan Warriors	1336.9
Leeds Rhinos	1285.9
Catalans Dragons	1258.0
Castleford Tigers	1239.8
Wakefield Trinity	1231.4
Hull FC	1227.1
Hull Kingston Rovers	1151.5
Salford Red Devils	1126.0
Widnes Vikings	1119.0
Huddersfield Giants	1107.7

CLEAN BREAKS

St Helens	8.1
Wigan Warriors	6.6
Hull Kingston Rovers	6.4
Wakefield Trinity	6.3
Hull FC	6.0
Castleford Tigers	5.7
Warrington Wolves	5.6
Leeds Rhinos	5.3
Catalans Dragons	5.0
Salford Red Devils	4.8
Huddersfield Giants	4.4
Widnes Vikings	4.3

PASSES

St Helens	248.2
Wigan Warriors	244.0
Wakefield Trinity	219.1
Warrington Wolves	213.5
Castleford Tigers	210.2
Hull FC	209.3
Hull Kingston Rovers	209.0
Huddersfield Giants	208.8
Widnes Vikings	204.4
Catalans Dragons	202.7
Leeds Rhinos	201.6
Salford Red Devils	198.2

ERRORS

Leeds Rhinos	12.6
St Helens	12.3
Hull Kingston Rovers	12.2
Widnes Vikings	12.1
Hull FC	11.7
Salford Red Devils	11.7
Warrington Wolves	11.2
Castleford Tigers	11.1
Catalans Dragons	10.9
Wakefield Trinity	10.7
Huddersfield Giants	10.0
Wigan Warriors	9.7

KICKS IN GENERAL PLAY

Wigan Warriors	19.8
Catalans Dragons	19.0
Castleford Tigers	18.8
Warrington Wolves	18.8
Hull Kingston Rovers	18.3
Hull FC	18.0
Huddersfield Giants	17.7
Leeds Rhinos	17.7
Widnes Vikings	17.7
Salford Red Devils	17.5
Wakefield Trinity	17.0
St Helens	16.8

247

SUPER LEAGUE XXIII PENALTIES

TOTAL PENALTIES AWARDED
Wakefield Trinity.................... 205
Wigan Warriors 203
Huddersfield Giants 187
Widnes Vikings........................187
Hull FC 180
Hull Kingston Rovers 179
Catalans Dragons 174
St Helens 173
Salford Red Devils..................171
Warrington Wolves 170
Leeds Rhinos 167
Castleford Tigers 164

TOTAL PENALTIES CONCEDED
Huddersfield Giants 207
Catalans Dragons 204
Hull Kingston Rovers 195
Warrington Wolves 183
Wigan Warriors 183
Widnes Vikings........................179
Salford Red Devils..................177
Wakefield Trinity.....................177
Leeds Rhinos 173
Castleford Tigers 171
St Helens 163
Hull FC 148

FOUL PLAY - AWARDED
Widnes Vikings..........................55
Huddersfield Giants 51
Wakefield Trinity.......................46
St Helens 43
Warrington Wolves 43
Hull Kingston Rovers 41
Leeds Rhinos 39
Wigan Warriors 39
Catalans Dragons 37
Salford Red Devils....................37
Castleford Tigers 28
Hull FC 26

FOUL PLAY - CONCEDED
Catalans Dragons 54
Warrington Wolves 53
Salford Red Devils....................48
Hull Kingston Rovers 47
Wakefield Trinity.......................45
St Helens 41
Wigan Warriors 41
Castleford Tigers 32
Hull FC 32
Huddersfield Giants 31
Widnes Vikings..........................31
Leeds Rhinos 30

OFFSIDE - AWARDED
Huddersfield Giants 18
Salford Red Devils....................18
Wakefield Trinity.......................15
Hull Kingston Rovers 14
Warrington Wolves 13
Catalans Dragons 12
Castleford Tigers 9
Leeds Rhinos 9
Widnes Vikings............................9
Wigan Warriors 9
Hull FC 6
St Helens 6

OFFSIDE - CONCEDED
Wakefield Trinity.......................16
Huddersfield Giants 15
Catalans Dragons 14
Castleford Tigers 13
Salford Red Devils....................13
Leeds Rhinos 12
Hull Kingston Rovers 11
St Helens 11
Wigan Warriors 11
Widnes Vikings............................9
Warrington Wolves 8
Hull FC 5

INTERFERENCE - AWARDED
Wigan Warriors 99
Hull FC 83
Wakefield Trinity.......................81
Hull Kingston Rovers 75
Warrington Wolves 75
St Helens 73
Castleford Tigers 71
Salford Red Devils....................66
Huddersfield Giants 65
Leeds Rhinos 65
Widnes Vikings..........................65
Catalans Dragons 58

INTERFERENCE - CONCEDED
Huddersfield Giants 101
Widnes Vikings..........................83
Catalans Dragons 76
Hull Kingston Rovers 75
Salford Red Devils....................73
Warrington Wolves 73
Leeds Rhinos 72
Hull FC 68
Wigan Warriors 68
Castleford Tigers 65
Wakefield Trinity.......................63
St Helens 59

OBSTRUCTION - AWARDED
Widnes Vikings..........................21
Wigan Warriors 19
Castleford Tigers 14
Wakefield Trinity.......................14
Hull FC 13
Hull Kingston Rovers 13
Warrington Wolves 13
Leeds Rhinos 12
Salford Red Devils....................10
St Helens 10
Catalans Dragons 9
Huddersfield Giants 5

OBSTRUCTION - CONCEDED
Huddersfield Giants 16
Hull Kingston Rovers 16
Wigan Warriors 16
Catalans Dragons 15
Castleford Tigers 14
St Helens 14
Wakefield Trinity.......................13
Leeds Rhinos 12
Warrington Wolves 11
Salford Red Devils....................10
Hull FC 8
Widnes Vikings............................8

BALL STEALING - AWARDED
Catalans Dragons 20
Hull FC 20
Castleford Tigers 17
Wigan Warriors 16
Wakefield Trinity.......................15
Leeds Rhinos 13
Salford Red Devils....................12
Huddersfield Giants 11
St Helens 10
Widnes Vikings..........................10
Hull Kingston Rovers 5
Warrington Wolves 5

BALL STEALING - CONCEDED
Castleford Tigers 21
Catalans Dragons 15
Hull Kingston Rovers 14
Leeds Rhinos 14
Wigan Warriors 14
Wakefield Trinity.......................13
Huddersfield Giants 12
St Helens 11
Warrington Wolves 11
Hull FC 10
Widnes Vikings..........................10
Salford Red Devils......................9

OFFSIDE MARKERS - AWARDED
Hull Kingston Rovers 11
Catalans Dragons 10
Huddersfield Giants 9
Hull FC 9
Salford Red Devils......................9
Warrington Wolves 8
Leeds Rhinos 6
Castleford Tigers 5
Wakefield Trinity.........................5
St Helens 4
Widnes Vikings............................4
Wigan Warriors 4

OFFSIDE MARKERS - CONCEDED
Warrington Wolves 11
Hull Kingston Rovers 9
Catalans Dragons 8
Leeds Rhinos 8
Widnes Vikings............................8
Castleford Tigers 7
Huddersfield Giants 7
St Helens 7
Wakefield Trinity.........................6
Salford Red Devils......................5
Hull FC 4
Wigan Warriors 3

OFFSIDE FROM KICK - AWARDED
Hull FC 14
St Helens 9
Catalans Dragons 7
Huddersfield Giants 6
Wakefield Trinity.........................6
Leeds Rhinos 5
Hull Kingston Rovers 4
Widnes Vikings............................4
Salford Red Devils......................3
Castleford Tigers 2
Warrington Wolves 1
Wigan Warriors 1

OFFSIDE FROM KICK - CONCEDED
Widnes Vikings............................9
Huddersfield Giants 8
Salford Red Devils......................8
Catalans Dragons 7
Wigan Warriors 7
Leeds Rhinos 5
Wakefield Trinity.........................5
Warrington Wolves 5
Castleford Tigers 3
Hull FC 2
St Helens 2
Hull Kingston Rovers 1

DISSENT - AWARDED
Wakefield Trinity.........................6
Huddersfield Giants 4
Salford Red Devils......................4
Leeds Rhinos 3
Widnes Vikings............................3
Castleford Tigers 2
Catalans Dragons 2
Hull FC 2
Wigan Warriors 2
Hull Kingston Rovers 1
St Helens 1
Warrington Wolves 0

DISSENT - CONCEDED
Catalans Dragons 5
Wigan Warriors 5
Hull Kingston Rovers 4
Huddersfield Giants 3
Hull FC 2
Leeds Rhinos 2
St Helens 2
Wakefield Trinity.........................2
Widnes Vikings............................2
Castleford Tigers 1
Salford Red Devils......................1
Warrington Wolves 1

CASTLEFORD TIGERS
SUPER LEAGUE XXIII LEADERS

CARRIES
Grant Millington	282
Michael Shenton	248
Mike McMeeken	247
Liam Watts	240
Oliver Holmes	237

OFFLOADS
Jesse Sene-Lefao	27
Grant Millington	23
Mike McMeeken	20
Liam Watts	18
Junior Moors	15

METRES
Liam Watts	1857
Grant Millington	1821
Michael Shenton	1737
Mike McMeeken	1705
Oliver Holmes	1689

TACKLES
Paul McShane	880
Oliver Holmes	626
Adam Milner	611
Grant Millington	525
Mike McMeeken	512

CLEAN BREAKS
Greg Minikin	13
James Clare	12
Greg Eden	11
Michael Shenton	11
Quentin Lalu-Togagae	9

OFFENSIVE MISS
Junior Moors	52
Michael Shenton	46
Jake Trueman	42
Jesse Sene-Lefao	37
Mike McMeeken	35

MARKER TACKLES
Paul McShane	169
Oliver Holmes	108
Adam Milner	100
Mike McMeeken	99
Matt Cook	94

TRY ASSISTS
Paul McShane	16
Jake Trueman	16
Michael Shenton	12
Jamie Ellis	9
Luke Gale	7

TOTAL OPTA INDEX
Paul McShane	12228.1
Oliver Holmes	10018.8
Mike McMeeken	8427.8
Jake Trueman	8232.0
Junior Moors	8020.9

CATALANS DRAGONS
SUPER LEAGUE XXIII LEADERS

CARRIES
Lewis Tierney	274
Greg Bird	273
Julian Bousquet	273
Brayden Wiliame	257
Mickael Simon	246

OFFLOADS
Julian Bousquet	39
Mickael Simon	27
Greg Bird	23
Tony Gigot	18
David Mead	18

METRES
Julian Bousquet	2260
Greg Bird	2104
Brayden Wiliame	2068
Lewis Tierney	2056
David Mead	1825

TACKLES
Benjamin Jullien	657
Benjamin Garcia	628
Jason Baitieri	611
Remi Casty	594
Michael McIlorum	510

CLEAN BREAKS
Jodie Broughton	14
Brayden Wiliame	14
Fouad Yaha	10
Benjamin Garcia	9
Tony Gigot	9

OFFENSIVE MISS
Tony Gigot	74
Greg Bird	60
Benjamin Garcia	58
Brayden Wiliame	43
Lewis Tierney	41

MARKER TACKLES
Benjamin Jullien	126
Jason Baitieri	125
Remi Casty	112
Benjamin Garcia	112
Mickael Simon	94

TRY ASSISTS
Josh Drinkwater	14
Michael McIlorum	12
Tony Gigot	8
Greg Bird	7
Samisoni Langi	7

TOTAL OPTA INDEX
Benjamin Garcia	10088.6
Tony Gigot	9427.6
Remi Casty	8969.4
Greg Bird	8578.1
Julian Bousquet	8317.5

HUDDERSFIELD GIANTS
SUPER LEAGUE XXIII LEADERS

CARRIES
Jordan Rankin	268
Aaron Murphy	234
Paul Clough	227
Daniel Smith	221
Jermaine McGillvary	216

OFFLOADS
Sebastine Ikahihifo	32
Daniel Smith	20
Aaron Murphy	12
Lee Gaskell	11
Jermaine McGillvary	9

METRES
Jermaine McGillvary	1783
Jordan Rankin	1715
Paul Clough	1676
Ukuma Ta'ai	1531
Daniel Smith	1504

TACKLES
Ryan Hinchcliffe	763
Paul Clough	619
Adam O'Brien	572
Daniel Smith	470
Ukuma Ta'ai	452

CLEAN BREAKS
Jermaine McGillvary	16
Darnell McIntosh	11
Jordan Turner	9
Lee Gaskell	8
Jordan Rankin	8

OFFENSIVE MISS
Sebastine Ikahihifo	75
Jordan Rankin	51
Jermaine McGillvary	48
Dale Ferguson	34
Darnell McIntosh	34

MARKER TACKLES
Ryan Hinchcliffe	135
Adam O'Brien	127
Paul Clough	120
Oliver Roberts	75
Daniel Smith	69

TRY ASSISTS
Danny Brough	9
Lee Gaskell	9
Jordan Turner	7
Leroy Cudjoe	6
Jordan Rankin	6

TOTAL OPTA INDEX
Ryan Hinchcliffe	9920.7
Jordan Rankin	9044.6
Paul Clough	8876.5
Sebastine Ikahihifo	7742.4
Ukuma Ta'ai	7742.4

HULL F.C.
SUPER LEAGUE XXIII LEADERS

CARRIES

Scott Taylor	257
Mark Minichiello	244
Bureta Faraimo	239
Carlos Tuimavave	227
Jamie Shaul	222

OFFLOADS

Jake Connor	26
Carlos Tuimavave	23
Albert Kelly	21
Mark Minichiello	19
Bureta Faraimo	18

METRES

Scott Taylor	2108
Bureta Faraimo	2060
Josh Griffin	1922
Carlos Tuimavave	1857
Jamie Shaul	1741

TACKLES

Danny Houghton	747
Dean Hadley	593
Scott Taylor	590
Mark Minichiello	487
Danny Washbrook	444

CLEAN BREAKS

Bureta Faraimo	23
Josh Griffin	16
Fetuli Talanoa	14
Jake Connor	12
Albert Kelly	10

OFFENSIVE MISS

Bureta Faraimo	84
Jamie Shaul	79
Hakim Miloudi	57
Mark Minichiello	53
Carlos Tuimavave	50

MARKER TACKLES

Danny Houghton	139
Dean Hadley	101
Scott Taylor	96
Mickey Paea	72
Danny Washbrook	71

TRY ASSISTS

Albert Kelly	16
Jake Connor	11
Marc Sneyd	7
Jamie Shaul	6
Jordan Abdull	5

TOTAL OPTA INDEX

Danny Houghton	9754.1
Scott Taylor	9662.5
Bureta Faraimo	9495.5
Jamie Shaul	8748.6
Jake Connor	8306.2

HULL KINGSTON ROVERS
SUPER LEAGUE XXIII LEADERS

CARRIES

Adam Quinlan	266
Ryan Shaw	254
Justin Carney	246
Robbie Mulhern	235
Mose Masoe	223

OFFLOADS

Mose Masoe	23
James Greenwood	20
Danny Tickle	18
Maurice Blair	16
Danny McGuire	15

METRES

Justin Carney	1984
Adam Quinlan	1834
Ryan Shaw	1692
Mose Masoe	1675
Robbie Mulhern	1600

TACKLES

Chris Clarkson	622
Danny Tickle	549
James Greenwood	546
Robbie Mulhern	514
Ben Kavanagh	474

CLEAN BREAKS

Adam Quinlan	26
Ryan Shaw	17
Chris Atkin	11
Justin Carney	11
Junior Vaivai	10

OFFENSIVE MISS

Adam Quinlan	84
Justin Carney	64
Junior Vaivai	47
Ryan Shaw	45
Maurice Blair	43

MARKER TACKLES

Chris Clarkson	139
Danny Tickle	99
Robbie Mulhern	96
Nick Scruton	90
James Greenwood	85

TRY ASSISTS

Adam Quinlan	12
Chris Atkin	11
Danny McGuire	11
Maurice Blair	5
Junior Vaivai	5

TOTAL OPTA INDEX

Adam Quinlan	9795.8
Maurice Blair	8129.8
James Greenwood	8042.0
Chris Atkin	7647.1
Chris Clarkson	7524.0

LEEDS RHINOS
SUPER LEAGUE XXIII LEADERS

CARRIES

Ryan Hall	326
Tom Briscoe	320
Ash Handley	259
Adam Cuthbertson	232
Kallum Watkins	214

OFFLOADS

Adam Cuthbertson	38
Joel Moon	35
Tom Briscoe	25
Ash Handley	23
Ryan Hall	22

METRES

Ryan Hall	2844
Tom Briscoe	2201
Ash Handley	1951
Matt Parcell	1647
Kallum Watkins	1556

TACKLES

Matt Parcell	662
Brad Singleton	621
Adam Cuthbertson	549
Jamie Jones-Buchanan	508
Stevie Ward	473

CLEAN BREAKS

Ryan Hall	18
Tom Briscoe	15
Ash Handley	13
Joel Moon	8
Kallum Watkins	8

OFFENSIVE MISS

Tom Briscoe	81
Ryan Hall	78
Ash Handley	68
Ashton Golding	64
Joel Moon	54

MARKER TACKLES

Brad Singleton	155
Matt Parcell	128
Stevie Ward	106
Adam Cuthbertson	101
Brett Delaney	93

TRY ASSISTS

Richie Myler	23
Ash Handley	8
Joel Moon	8
Matt Parcell	6
Liam Sutcliffe	5

TOTAL OPTA INDEX

Ryan Hall	10152.2
Matt Parcell	10099.2
Tom Briscoe	9802.5
Ashton Golding	8791.8
Richie Myler	8315.3

SALFORD RED DEVILS
SUPER LEAGUE XXIII LEADERS

CARRIES
Junior Sa'u	280
Robert Lui	254
Lama Tasi	211
Derrell Olpherts	207
Jake Bibby	199

OFFLOADS
Robert Lui	26
Tyrone McCarthy	26
Josh Jones	25
Kris Welham	14
Jack Littlejohn	11

METRES
Junior Sa'u	1930
Jake Bibby	1575
Lama Tasi	1569
Derrell Olpherts	1558
Lee Mossop	1530

TACKLES
Logan Tomkins	630
Tyrone McCarthy	537
Lama Tasi	530
Josh Wood	477
Lee Mossop	476

CLEAN BREAKS
Jake Bibby	18
Niall Evalds	12
Kris Welham	11
Robert Lui	10
Junior Sa'u	9

OFFENSIVE MISS
Josh Jones	62
Junior Sa'u	60
Robert Lui	49
Derrell Olpherts	44
Kris Welham	35

MARKER TACKLES
Logan Tomkins	123
Tyrone McCarthy	104
Lee Mossop	90
Lama Tasi	73
Craig Kopczak	70

TRY ASSISTS
Robert Lui	9
Jack Littlejohn	6
Logan Tomkins	6
Niall Evalds	5
Josh Wood	4

TOTAL OPTA INDEX
Robert Lui	9637.0
Junior Sa'u	7836.6
Josh Jones	7362.7
Lama Tasi	7231.6
Tyrone McCarthy	6757.9

ST HELENS
SUPER LEAGUE XXIII LEADERS

CARRIES
Luke Thompson	370
Louie McCarthy-Scarsbrook	329
Zeb Taia	322
Mark Percival	302
Jonny Lomax	292

OFFLOADS
Zeb Taia	28
Louie McCarthy-Scarsbrook	27
Mark Percival	23
Tommy Makinson	20
Ben Barba	18

METRES
Luke Thompson	3006
Louie McCarthy-Scarsbrook	2415
Zeb Taia	2312
Tommy Makinson	2232
Mark Percival	2198

TACKLES
James Roby	813
Jon Wilkin	657
Luke Thompson	653
Dominique Peyroux	652
Zeb Taia	588

CLEAN BREAKS
Mark Percival	31
Ben Barba	25
Regan Grace	20
Jonny Lomax	15
Tommy Makinson	15

OFFENSIVE MISS
Mark Percival	140
Ben Barba	115
Tommy Makinson	85
Jonny Lomax	66
Regan Grace	64

MARKER TACKLES
James Roby	147
Jon Wilkin	139
Luke Thompson	130
Morgan Knowles	115
Dominique Peyroux	115

TRY ASSISTS
Ben Barba	22
Jonny Lomax	13
Danny Richardson	13
Mark Percival	12
James Roby	10

TOTAL OPTA INDEX
James Roby	13156.8
Mark Percival	13093.9
Ben Barba	12719.0
Luke Thompson	11641.6
Zeb Taia	10667.3

WAKEFIELD TRINITY
SUPER LEAGUE XXIII LEADERS

CARRIES
Bill Tupou	359
Reece Lyne	320
Tinirau Arona	268
Jacob Miller	259
David Fifita	255

OFFLOADS
David Fifita	29
Bill Tupou	28
Craig Huby	27
Pauli Pauli	18
Tinirau Arona	15

METRES
Bill Tupou	3126
Reece Lyne	2740
Tom Johnstone	2138
David Fifita	1961
Ben Jones-Bishop	1935

TACKLES
Matty Ashurst	813
Tinirau Arona	738
Tyler Randell	555
Keegan Hirst	451
Kyle Wood	442

CLEAN BREAKS
Tom Johnstone	32
Ben Jones-Bishop	21
Bill Tupou	18
Reece Lyne	16
Jacob Miller	11

OFFENSIVE MISS
David Fifita	104
Reece Lyne	92
Bill Tupou	85
Tom Johnstone	77
Pauli Pauli	66

MARKER TACKLES
Matty Ashurst	170
Tinirau Arona	134
Tyler Randell	110
Keegan Hirst	82
Anthony England	77

TRY ASSISTS
Jacob Miller	20
Ryan Hampshire	13
Tyler Randell	6
Kyle Wood	6
Reece Lyne	5

TOTAL OPTA INDEX
Bill Tupou	12236.0
Reece Lyne	12043.8
Matty Ashurst	11066.5
Tinirau Arona	10554.2
David Fifita	9738.5

| WARRINGTON WOLVES | WIDNES VIKINGS | WIGAN WARRIORS |
| *SUPER LEAGUE XXIII LEADERS* | *SUPER LEAGUE XXIII LEADERS* | *SUPER LEAGUE XXIII LEADERS* |

CARRIES

WARRINGTON WOLVES		WIDNES VIKINGS		WIGAN WARRIORS	
Chris Hill	329	Matt Whitley	246	Tom Davies	334
Stefan Ratchford	329	Rhys Hanbury	235	John Bateman	324
Tom Lineham	309	Joe Mellor	228	Willie Isa	281
Ben Westwood	273	Tom Olbison	217	George Williams	240
Jack Hughes	259	Charly Runciman	216	Liam Farrell	237

OFFLOADS

Mike Cooper	43	Matt Whitley	20	John Bateman	47
Bryson Goodwin	34	Wellington Albert	18	George Williams	27
Tom Lineham	32	Krisnan Inu	18	Sean O'Loughlin	20
Chris Hill	19	Chris Houston	16	Oliver Gildart	13
Jack Hughes	18	Charly Runciman	16	Willie Isa	13

METRES

Stefan Ratchford	2690	Matt Whitley	1614	Tom Davies	2913
Tom Lineham	2581	Rhys Hanbury	1607	John Bateman	2277
Chris Hill	2496	Charly Runciman	1519	Oliver Gildart	2023
Daryl Clark	2382	Tom Olbison	1397	Liam Marshall	1946
Bryson Goodwin	2040	Joe Mellor	1319	Willie Isa	1872

TACKLES

Daryl Clark	882	Matt Whitley	650	Willie Isa	708
Chris Hill	715	Sam Wilde	600	Sam Powell	618
Jack Hughes	698	Tom Olbison	598	Thomas Leuluai	525
Mike Cooper	627	Jay Chapelhow	587	Liam Farrell	495
Ben Westwood	596	Weller Hauraki	587	Ben Flower	476

CLEAN BREAKS

Josh Charnley	19	Joe Mellor	12	Tom Davies	23
Tom Lineham	16	Rhys Hanbury	10	Liam Marshall	23
Bryson Goodwin	14	Krisnan Inu	7	Oliver Gildart	14
Daryl Clark	12	Charly Runciman	6	Joe Burgess	13
Stefan Ratchford	12	Sam Wilde	6	George Williams	13

OFFENSIVE MISS

Daryl Clark	90	Rhys Hanbury	68	John Bateman	84
Stefan Ratchford	74	Joe Mellor	64	Sam Tomkins	66
Bryson Goodwin	67	Krisnan Inu	34	Liam Marshall	59
Tom Lineham	54	Matt Whitley	29	Tom Davies	56
Mike Cooper	40	Weller Hauraki	28	George Williams	52

MARKER TACKLES

Daryl Clark	153	Matt Whitley	124	Willie Isa	128
Chris Hill	133	Jay Chapelhow	109	Sam Powell	110
Jack Hughes	122	Sam Wilde	109	Liam Farrell	106
Ben Westwood	121	Tom Olbison	101	Ryan Sutton	77
Mike Cooper	108	Hep Cahill	78	Taulima Tautai	77

TRY ASSISTS

Stefan Ratchford	16	Joe Mellor	11	George Williams	17
Kevin Brown	11	Tom Gilmore	8	Sam Tomkins	15
Daryl Clark	6	Aaron Heremaia	6	Thomas Leuluai	12
Toby King	6	Danny Craven	4	Sam Powell	8
Tyrone Roberts	6	Rhys Hanbury	4	Liam Marshall	7

TOTAL OPTA INDEX

Daryl Clark	13379.2	Matt Whitley	9637.0	Sam Tomkins	11235.6
Stefan Ratchford	12388.6	Joe Mellor	9431.1	John Bateman	10770.5
Chris Hill	12220.6	Sam Wilde	8659.2	Liam Farrell	10157.8
Jack Hughes	10600.7	Tom Olbison	8286.7	Willie Isa	10094.0
Mike Cooper	9928.6	Jay Chapelhow	7038.0	Tom Davies	9346.5

CHAMPIONSHIP 2018
Club by Club

BARROW RAIDERS

DATE	FIXTURE	RESULT	SCORERS	LGE	ATT
4/2/18	London Broncos (a)	L56-12	t:Dallimore,Fieldhouse g:Charnock,Dallimore	12th	801
11/2/18	Toronto (h)	D8-8	t:D Toal g:Dallimore(2)	8th	1,266
18/2/18	Leigh (h)	W24-20	t:S Toal(3),Fieldhouse g:Dallimore(4)	6th	1,991
25/2/18	Batley (a)	L32-12	t:Fieldhouse,Susino g:Dallimore(2)	8th	657
11/3/18	Rochdale (a)	L24-12	t:Cresswell,Hulme g:Marwood(2)	8th	414
18/3/18	Sheffield (h) (CCR4)	W28-16	t:Fieldhouse,Bullock,Stack,Ormsby,Litherland g:Carter(4)	N/A	936
25/3/18	Sheffield (h)	W36-22	t:Litherland,D Toal,Duffy,S Toal(3),Bullock g:Carter(4)	7th	1,210
30/3/18	Halifax (a)	L30-4	t:Ormsby	9th	1,298
2/4/18	Swinton (h)	D16-16	t:S Toal (2) g:Dallimore(4)	9th	1,133
7/4/18	Toulouse (a)	L50-4	t:Susino	9th	1,177
15/4/18	Featherstone (h)	L26-38	t:Smith,Duffy,Parata,Ormsby g:Dallimore(5)	9th	1,231
22/4/18	Toronto (a) (CCR5) ●	L16-12	t:Mossop,Aspinwall g:Dallimore(2)	N/A	1,140
29/4/18	Leigh (a)	L46-18	t:Bullock,Stack,Carter g:Dallimore(3)	9th	3,228
6/5/18	Batley (h)	W20-18	t:Bullock,Parata,Johnston g:Dallimore(4)	8th	1,211
13/5/18	Dewsbury (h)	W58-32	t:Bullock,Smith,Ormsby,Duffy,Dallimore,Stack(2),Parata,Fieldhouse,Morrow g:Dallimore(9)	8th	1,061
20/5/18	Swinton (a)	D22-22	t:Fieldhouse,S Toal,Parata g:Dallimore(5)	8th	656
26/5/18	Sheffield (SB) ●●	L22-38	t:S Toal,Stack,Dallimore,Ormsby g:Dallimore(3)	8th	N/A
10/6/18	Rochdale (h)	W20-6	t:Hulme,Fieldhouse,Bullock(2) g:Dallimore(2)	8th	1,212
17/6/18	Featherstone (a)	L52-4	t:Johnston	8th	1,880
23/6/18	Toronto (a)	L64-0		8th	5,287
1/7/18	Halifax (h)	L22-48	t:D Toal,S Toal(2),Johnston g:Dallimore(3)	8th	1,293
8/7/18	Dewsbury (a)	L22-20	t:While,Parata g:Dallimore(6)	8th	635
15/7/18	Toulouse (a)	L6-72	t:Harrison g:Dallimore	8th	981
22/7/18	Sheffield (a)	L28-10	t:Carter,Mossop g:Dallimore	10th	702
29/7/18	London Broncos (h)	L6-72	t:Dallimore g:Dallimore	10th	1,044
12/8/18	Rochdale (h) (CS)	W17-10	t:Smith,Susino g:Dallimore(4) fg:Johnston	5th(CS)	1,033
19/8/18	Leigh (a) (CS)	L38-0		6th(CS)	2,646
2/9/18	Batley (h) (CS)	L16-36	t:Gambaro,Charnock,Holmes g:Dallimore(2)	6th(CS)	1,103
9/9/18	Dewsbury (a) (CS)	L32-12	t:Gambaro,Mossop g:Dallimore(2)	6th(CS)	807
16/9/18	Swinton (h) (CS)	W34-18	t:Dallimore,Burroughs(2),Carter(2),Barthes g:Dallimore(5)	5th(CS)	1,357
23/9/18	Sheffield (a) (CS)	W22-24	t:Carter(2),Fieldhouse,Burroughs g:Dallimore(4)	5th(CS)	404
30/9/18	Featherstone (a) (CS)	L34-6	t:Dallimore g:Dallimore	5th(CS)	1,125

● *Played at Craven Park*
●● *Played at Bloomfield Road, Blackpool*

		APP		TRIES		GOALS		FG		PTS	
	D.O.B.	ALL	Ch	ALL	Ch	ALL	Ch	ALL	Ch	ALL	Ch
Karl Ashall	3/11/89	12	11	0	0	0	0	0	0	0	0
Martin Aspinwall	21/10/81	18(3)	13(1)	1	0	0	0	0	0	4	0
Arnaud Barthes	13/8/90	7(2)	2	1	0	0	0	0	0	4	0
Joe Bullock	27/11/92	20(2)	17(2)	7	6	0	0	0	0	28	24
Ryan Burroughs	26/8/91	12	5	3	0	0	0	0	0	12	0
Brett Carter	9/7/88	21	14	6	2	8	4	0	0	40	16
Lewis Charnock	2/9/94	6	1	1	0	1	1	0	0	6	2
Bradd Crellin	2/7/89	12(5)	9(3)	0	0	0	0	0	0	0	0
Luke Cresswell	5/5/95	3	2	1	1	0	0	0	0	4	4
Jamie Dallimore	20/8/88	28	20	6	4	76	56	0	0	176	128
Ryan Duffy	13/5/93	8(17)	7(12)	3	3	0	0	0	0	12	12
Ryan Fieldhouse	10/4/81	27	18	8	6	0	0	0	0	32	24
Chris Fleming	11/1/91	1	1	0	0	0	0	0	0	0	0
Georgy Gambaro	2/7/98	8	2	2	0	0	0	0	0	8	0
Ben Garner	22/12/93	1	1	0	0	0	0	0	0	0	0
Liam Harrison	3/12/82	1	1	1	1	0	0	0	0	4	4
Matthew Holmes	24/4/94	5(2)	4	1	1	0	0	0	0	4	0
Declan Hulme	14/1/93	19	16	2	2	0	0	0	0	8	8
Ryan Johnston	16/3/98	15(1)	12	3	3	0	0	1	0	13	12
Andy Litherland	15/5/90	7	6	2	1	0	0	0	0	8	4
Tom Loxam	27/1/92	15	11	0	0	0	0	0	0	0	0
Brad Marwood	4/11/93	2	2	0	0	2	2	0	0	4	4
Saloty Mendy	30/7/97	(4)	(1)	0	0	0	0	0	0	0	0
Danny Morrow	30/4/90	11(2)	6(2)	1	1	0	0	0	0	4	4
Nathan Mossop	21/2/88	16(14)	13(10)	3	1	0	0	0	0	12	4
Gene Ormsby	12/9/92	9	7	5	4	0	0	0	0	20	16
Dean Parata	4/10/91	16(14)	10(11)	5	5	0	0	0	0	20	20
Jonny Pownall	22/8/91	4(1)	4(1)	0	0	0	0	0	0	0	0
Glenn Riley	29/1/92	5(18)	2(15)	0	0	0	0	0	0	0	0
Jono Smith	12/11/88	24(1)	16(1)	3	2	0	0	0	0	12	8
Jarrad Stack	13/2/88	21	18	5	4	0	0	0	0	20	16
Alec Susino	24/5/95	26(2)	20(2)	3	2	0	0	0	0	12	8
Dan Toal	22/9/89	12(12)	9(7)	3	3	0	0	0	0	12	12
Shane Toal	11/11/95	19	17	12	12	0	0	0	0	48	48
Tom Walker	25/12/94	4(11)	1(9)	0	0	0	0	0	0	0	0
Matty While	25/11/96	1(10)	1(9)	1	1	0	0	0	0	4	4

Jamie Dallimore

LEAGUE RECORD
Championship, before Super 8 split:
P23-W5-D3-L15 (10th)
F382, A816, Diff-434, 13 points.

After Championship Shield:
P30-W8-D3-L19 (5th)
F491, A1006, Diff-515, 19 points.

CHALLENGE CUP
Round Five

ATTENDANCES
Best - v Leigh (Ch - 1,991)
Worst - v Sheffield (CC - 936)
Total (Championship/
Championship Shield only) - 17,126
Average (Championship/
Championship Shield only) - 1,223
(Up by 181 on 2017, League 1)

'Ch' totals include Championship regular season only; 'All' totals also include Championship Shield & Challenge Cup

CLUB RECORDS **MATCH RECORDS**	Highest score: 138-0 v Nottingham City, 27/11/94 Highest score against: 0-90 v Leeds, 11/2/90 Record attendance: 21,651 v Salford, 15/4/38
	Tries: 6 Val Cumberbatch v Batley, 21/11/36; Jim Thornburrow v Maryport, 19/2/38; Steve Rowan v Nottingham City, 15/11/92
	Goals: 17 Darren Carter v Nottingham City, 27/11/94 Points: 42 Darren Carter v Nottingham City, 27/11/94
SEASON RECORDS **CAREER RECORDS**	Tries: 50 Jim Lewthwaite 1956-57 Goals: 135 Joe Ball 1956-57 Points: 323 Jamie Rooney 2010
	Tries: 352 Jim Lewthwaite 1943-57 Goals: 1,099 *(inc 63fg)* Darren Holt 1998-2002; 2004-2009; 2012
	Points: 2,403 Darren Holt 1998-2002; 2004-2009; 2012 Appearances: 500 Jim Lewthwaite 1943-57

BATLEY BULLDOGS

DATE	FIXTURE	RESULT	SCORERS	LGE	ATT
11/2/18	Leigh (a)	L34-6	t:Rowe g:Walker	11th	3,216
18/2/18	Swinton (a) ●	W28-48	t:Galbraith(2),Reittie,Gledhill,Ward(2),Day,Scott,Leak g:Walker(6)	8th	588
25/2/18	Barrow (h)	W32-12	t:Day(2),Manning,Reittie,Scott(2) g:Walker(4)	6th	657
11/3/18	London Broncos (a)	L68-12	t:Brown(2) g:Walker(2)	7th	526
18/3/18	Leigh (h) (CCR4)	L4-8	g:Walker(2)	N/A	606
25/3/18	Featherstone (h)	L14-40	t:Scott(2) g:Walker(3)	9th	1,273
30/3/18	Dewsbury (h)	W18-10	t:Reittie,Day,Crookes g:Walker(3)	8th	1,117
2/4/18	Sheffield (a)	W14-28	t:Scott,Manning,Walker,Reittie,Hemingway g:Walker(4)	7th	597
8/4/18	Toronto (a)	L18-26	t:Harrison,Reittie,Day g:Walker(3)	7th	1,157
14/4/18	Toulouse (h)	W46-22	t:Crookes(3),Leak,Ainscough,Ward,Day(2) g:I Farrell(7)	7th	662
29/4/18	Featherstone (a)	L50-12	t:Scott,Brambani g:I Farrell(2)	7th	2,225
6/5/18	Barrow (a)	L20-18	t:Scott,Brambani,Leak g:Walker(3)	7th	1,211
12/5/18	Rochdale (a)	W10-48	t:Ward,Crookes,Galbraith,Day,Ainscough,I Farrell,Gledhill,Brambani g:Walker(6),I Farrell(2)	7th	408
20/5/18	Rochdale (h)	W23-14	t:Brambani,Harrison,Bretherton,I Farrell g:Walker(3) fg:I Farrell	7th	743
27/5/18	Dewsbury (SB) ●●	L18-20	t:Harrison,Butterworth,I Farrell g:I Farrell(3)	7th	N/A
2/6/18	Halifax (h)	L18-32	t:J Farrell(2),Harrison g:Walker(3)	7th	1,002
9/6/18	Toulouse (a)	L42-26	t:Scott,Tomlinson,Galbraith,Harrison g:I Farrell(3)	7th	2,250
17/6/18	Sheffield (h)	L20-38	t:Crookes,Butterworth,Davey g:Scott(4)	7th	2,328
24/6/18	Halifax (a)	L50-12	t:Brown,Gledhill g:Scott(2)	7th	1,561
1/7/18	London Broncos (h)	L16-38	t:Smeaton,Davey,Galbraith g:Walker(2)	7th	889
8/7/18	Leigh (h)	L12-30	t:Tomlinson,Campbell g:Walker(2)	7th	1,223
14/7/18	Toronto (a)	L64-18	t:Brambani,Davey,Ward g:I Farrell(3)	7th	6,088
22/7/18	Dewsbury (a)	L23-20	t:Day,Leak,Bretherton,Walker g:Walker(2)	7th	1,501
29/7/18	Swinton (h)	W40-18	t:Day,Crookes,Harrison(2),Reittie,Scott,Campbell g:Scott(2)	7th	856
12/8/18	Featherstone (a) (CS)	L26-12	t:Smeaton,Manning g:Walker(2)	3rd(CS)	1,236
19/8/18	Dewsbury (h) (CS)	W42-22	t:Gledhill,Tomlinson,Reittie(2),Harrison,Manning,Day g:Scott(2),Walker(5)	3rd(CS)	1,485
2/9/18	Barrow (a) (CS)	W16-36	t:Campbell(3),Brambani,Day(2),Scott g:Scott(3),Walker	3rd(CS)	1,103
9/9/18	Rochdale (h) (CS)	W26-12	t:Rowe,Campbell,Gledhill,Reittie,Smeaton g:Scott,Walker(2)	3rd(CS)	616
16/9/18	Sheffield (h) (CS)	W44-4	t:Brambani,Smeaton,Galbraith,Campbell,Day,Brown g:Scott(6)	3rd(CS)	607
23/9/18	Leigh (a) (CS)	W16-30	t:Galbraith,Campbell(2),Scott,Jouffret g:Scott(5)	3rd(CS)	1,730
30/9/18	Swinton (h) (CS)	W40-6	t:Gledhill,Smeaton,Reittie,Scott,Jouffret(2),Brambani g:Brambani,Walker(4),Rowe	3rd(CS)	817

● Played at AJ Bell Stadium, Salford ●● Played at Bloomfield Road, Blackpool

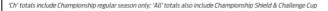

		APP		TRIES		GOALS		FG		PTS	
	D.O.B.	ALL	Ch	ALL	Ch	ALL	Ch	ALL	Ch	ALL	Ch
Shaun Ainscough	27/11/89	9	9	2	2	0	0	0	0	8	8
Dominic Brambani	10/5/85	22(2)	14(2)	8	5	1	0	0	0	34	20
Alex Bretherton	5/12/82	4(14)	2(11)	2	2	0	0	0	0	8	8
James Brown	6/5/88	6(15)	3(10)	4	3	0	0	0	0	16	12
Reiss Butterworth	7/12/98	1(3)	1(3)	2	2	0	0	0	0	8	8
Johnny Campbell	17/7/87	10	3	11	2	0	0	0	0	44	8
Joe Chandler	2/11/88	3(7)	2(7)	0	0	0	0	0	0	0	0
Danny Cowling	20/12/92	8	7	0	0	0	0	0	0	0	0
Jason Crookes	21/4/90	21	20	7	7	0	0	0	0	28	28
James Davey	21/8/89	7(14)	5(12)	3	3	0	0	0	0	12	12
Brad Day	23/9/94	25(1)	18(1)	14	10	0	0	0	0	56	40
Izaac Farrell	30/1/98	9(1)	9(1)	2	2	20	20	1	1	49	49
Joel Farrell	15/3/94	17(3)	15(2)	3	3	0	0	0	0	12	12
Lewis Galbraith	1/2/95	29	21	7	5	0	0	0	0	28	20
Adam Gledhill	15/2/93	21	14	6	3	0	0	0	0	24	12
James Harrison	15/6/96	22(4)	16(4)	7	6	0	0	0	0	28	24
Tom Hemingway	6/12/86	4(4)	4(3)	1	1	0	0	0	0	4	4
Tommy Holland	28/8/95	10(7)	10(7)	1	1	0	0	0	0	4	4
Louis Jouffret	24/5/95	9	2	3	0	0	0	0	0	12	0
Alistair Leak	5/4/92	25	19	4	4	0	0	0	0	16	16
Tom Lillycrop	29/11/91	2	2	0	0	0	0	0	0	0	0
Dane Manning	15/4/89	18(2)	13(2)	4	2	0	0	0	0	16	8
Danny Maun	5/1/81	(1)	(1)	0	0	0	0	0	0	0	0
Wayne Reittie	21/1/88	15	8	10	6	0	0	0	0	40	24
Alex Rowe	11/3/85	19(9)	14(6)	2	1	1	0	0	0	10	4
Dave Scott	8/6/93	31	23	13	10	29	12	0	0	110	64
Sam Smeaton	26/10/88	19(3)	13(2)	5	1	0	0	0	0	20	4
Danny Sowerby	13/9/96	4	4	0	0	0	0	0	0	0	0
Keenen Tomlinson	22/5/97	12(5)	9(1)	4	3	0	0	0	0	16	12
Pat Walker	24/3/86	16	15	2	2	63	47	0	0	134	102
Michael Ward	10/2/91	5(22)	4(16)	5	5	0	0	0	0	20	20

'Ch' totals include Championship regular season only; 'All' totals also include Championship Shield & Challenge Cup

Dave Scott

LEAGUE RECORD
Championship, before Super 8 split:
P23-W8-D0-L15 (7th)
F523, A703, Diff-180, 16 points.

After Championship Shield:
P30-W14-D0-L16 (3rd)
F753, A805, Diff-52, 28 points.

CHALLENGE CUP
Round Four

ATTENDANCES
Best - v Sheffield (Ch - 2,328)
Worst - v Leigh (CC - 606)
Total (Championship/
Championship Shield only) - 15,432
Average (Championship/
Championship Shield only) - 1,029
(Up by 31 on 2017)

CLUB RECORDS MATCH RECORDS	**Highest score:** 100-4 v Gateshead, 17/3/2010 **Highest score against:** 9-78 v Wakefield, 26/8/67 **Record attendance:** 23,989 v Leeds, 14/3/25 **Tries:** 5 Joe Oakland v Bramley, 19/12/1908; Tommy Brannan v Swinton, 17/1/20; Jim Wale v Bramley, 4/12/26; Jim Wale v Cottingham, 12/2/27; Tommy Oldroyd v Highfield, 6/3/94; Ben Feehan v Halifax, 10/8/2008; Jermaine McGillvary v Whitehaven, 24/5/2009 **Goals:** 16 Gareth Moore v Gateshead, 17/3/2010 **Points:** 40 Gareth Moore v Gateshead, 17/3/2010
SEASON RECORDS CAREER RECORDS	**Tries:** 30 Johnny Campbell 2010 **Goals:** 144 Barry Eaton 2004 **Points:** 308 Richard Price 1997 **Tries:** 142 Craig Lingard 1998-2008 **Goals:** 463 Wharton 'Wattie' Davies 1897-1912 **Points:** 1,297 Wharton 'Wattie' Davies 1897-1912 **Appearances:** 421 Wharton 'Wattie' Davies 1897-1912

DEWSBURY RAMS

DATE	FIXTURE	RESULT	SCORERS	LGE	ATT
2/2/18	Sheffield (h)	W20-18	t:Glover,Worrincy,Speakman,Morton g:Sykes(2)	5th	808
11/2/18	London Broncos (h)	L0-12		7th	795
19/2/18	Rochdale (a)	W6-38	t:Morton,Glover,Worrincy(2),Brown(2),Guzdek g:Sykes(5)	4th	427
25/2/18	Swinton (h)	W20-0	t:Spicer,Brown,Hallett g:Sykes(4)	4th	961
11/3/18	Toulouse (h)	L20-40	t:Ward,Morton,Spicer,Knowles g:Sykes(2)	5th	720
18/3/18	Whitehaven (a) (CCR4)	L25-18	t:Reilly,Teanby,Glover g:Glover(3)	N/A	414
25/3/18	Leigh (a)	L36-0		5th	3,136
30/3/18	Batley (a)	L18-10	t:Morton,Worrincy g:Sykes	7th	1,117
8/4/18	Featherstone (a)	L46-18	t:Sheriffe,Brown,Hallett g:Sykes(3)	8th	2,031
15/4/18	Toronto (h)	L12-23	t:Speakman,Crowther g:Sykes(2)	8th	932
22/4/18	Halifax (h)	L18-46	t:Morton,Speakman,Sykes g:Sykes(3)	8th	1,394
28/4/18	London Broncos (a)	L64-6	t:Ansell g:Glover	8th	733
6/5/18	Rochdale (h)	W27-32	t:Scott,Brown,Speakman,Guzdek,Moore g:Glover(3) fg:Moore	9th	649
13/5/18	Barrow (h)	L58-32	t:Brown,Guzdek(3),Hallett,Day g:Glover(4)	9th	1,061
20/5/18	Halifax (a)	D22-22	t:Crowther,Knowles,Worrincy g:Sykes(5)	9th	1,739
27/5/18	Batley (SB) ●	W18-20	t:Brown,Day,Igbinedion g:Sykes(4)	9th	N/A
10/6/18	Featherstone (h)	L18-42	t:Crowther,Potts,Trout g:Sykes(2),Morton	9th	1,268
16/6/18	Toronto (a)	L64-12	t:Everett,Guzdek g:Glover(2)	10th	5,937
24/6/18	Leigh (h)	L12-58	t:Ward(2) g:Sykes(2)	10th	1,351
1/7/18	Swinton (a)	L29-28	t:Brown,Walshaw,Morton(2),Potts,Igbinedion g:Sykes(2)	10th	555
8/7/18	Barrow (h)	W22-20	t:Teanby,Day,Potts,Walshaw g:Sykes(2),Glover	9th	635
15/7/18	Sheffield (a)	L30-28	t:Morton,Igbinedion,Speakman,Ryder,Knowles g:Sykes(4)	10th	425
22/7/18	Batley (h)	W23-20	t:Walshaw(2),Ryder,Potts g:Sykes(3) fg:Knowles	9th	1,501
28/7/18	Toulouse (a)	L44-18	t:Glover(2),Brown g:Sykes(3)	9th	1,914
12/8/18	Swinton (h) (CS)	W40-7	t:Ward,Speakman,Ryder,Brown,Potts,Knowles,Guzdek g:Sykes(6)	4th(CS)	752
19/8/18	Batley (a) (CS)	L42-22	t:Walshaw,Richardson,Glover,Speakman g:Sykes(3)	5th(CS)	1,485
31/8/18	Sheffield (a) (CS)	W20-30	t:Ryder,Delaney(2),Igbinedion,Ward g:Sykes(5)	4th(CS)	638
9/9/18	Barrow (h) (CS)	W32-12	t:Worrincy,Delaney,Walshaw,Brown,Ryder(2) g:Sykes(4)	4th(CS)	807
16/9/18	Featherstone (a) (CS)	L40-28	t:Sykes,Glover(2),Igbinedion,Morton g:Sykes(3),Glover	4th(CS)	1,380
23/9/18	Rochdale (a) (CS)	L26-22	t:Knowles,Delaney(2),Worrincy g:Sykes(3)	4th(CS)	651
30/9/18	Leigh (h) (CS)	W52-6	t:Brown(2),Sykes,Guzdek(2),Glover,Ryder,Worrincy,Igbinedion g:Sykes(8)	4th(CS)	999

● *Played at Bloomfield Road, Blackpool*

			APP		TRIES		GOALS		FG		PTS	
	D.O.B.		ALL	Ch	ALL	Ch	ALL	Ch	ALL	Ch	ALL	Ch
Chris Annakin	30/1/91		1(1)	1(1)	0	0	0	0	0	0	0	0
Danny Ansell	9/10/91		5(1)	4(1)	1	1	0	0	0	0	4	4
Joe Arundel	22/8/91		1	1	0	0	0	0	0	0	0	0
Aaron Brown	27/7/92		28(1)	22(1)	13	9	0	0	0	0	52	36
Jordan Crowther	19/2/97		20	19	3	3	0	0	0	0	12	12
Sam Day	12/6/94		1(11)	1(10)	3	3	0	0	0	0	12	12
Brad Delaney	25/5/95		6(1)		5	0	0	0	0	0	20	0
Matty English	14/11/97		(5)	(5)	0	0	0	0	0	0	0	0
Toby Everett	22/12/95		6(18)	4(15)	1	1	0	0	0	0	4	4
James Glover	2/12/93		26(3)	18(3)	9	4	15	11	0	0	66	38
Jamel Goodall	7/9/97		(1)	(1)	0	0	0	0	0	0	0	0
Josh Guzdek	22/4/95		30	23	9	6	0	0	0	0	36	24
Macauley Hallett	27/11/95		16	15	3	3	0	0	0	0	12	12
Billy Hayes	12/4/98		1	1	0	0	0	0	0	0	0	0
Lewis Heckford	25/9/97		4	4	0	0	0	0	0	0	0	0
Daniel Igbinedion	26/1/95		2(13)	2(6)	6	3	0	0	0	0	24	12
Michael Knowles	2/5/87		20(1)	13(1)	5	3	0	0	1	1	21	13
Gareth Moore	3/6/89		10	7	1	1	0	0	1	1	5	5
Dale Morton	31/10/90		27	20	9	8	1	1	0	0	38	34
Gareth Potts	25/7/90		13(1)	10(1)	5	4	0	0	0	0	20	16
Martyn Reilly	5/1/96		3(8)	2(8)	1	0	0	0	0	0	4	0
Toby Richardson	5/6/96		1(7)		1	0	0	0	0	0	4	0
Adam Ryder	20/10/89		11	4	7	2	0	0	0	0	28	8
Cameron Scott	7/10/99		2	2	1	1	0	0	0	0	4	4
Jode Sheriffe	4/7/86		20(5)	16(4)	1	1	0	0	0	0	4	4
Jared Simpson	4/1/96		4	3	0	0	0	0	0	0	0	0
Dom Speakman	22/3/94		7(18)	6(12)	7	5	0	0	0	0	28	20
Rob Spicer	22/9/84		7	7	2	2	0	0	0	0	8	8
Paul Sykes	11/8/81		26	19	3	1	81	49	0	0	174	102
Jack Teanby	14/5/96		23(7)	21(1)	2	1	0	0	0	0	8	4
Kyle Trout	1/3/91		16(10)	8(10)	1	1	0	0	0	0	4	4
Shannon Wakeman	15/2/90		3(2)	3(2)	0	0	0	0	0	0	0	0
Lucas Walshaw	4/8/92		21(6)	13(6)	6	4	0	0	0	0	24	16
Robbie Ward	27/10/95		24(2)	17(1)	5	3	0	0	0	0	20	12
Harry Woollard	13/9/97		2(1)	1(1)	0	0	0	0	0	0	0	0
Rob Worrincy	9/7/85		16	11	8	5	0	0	0	0	32	20

'Ch' totals include Championship regular season only; 'All' totals also include Championship Shield & Challenge Cup

Dale Morton

LEAGUE RECORD
Championship, before Super 8 split:
P23-W6-D1-L16 (9th)
F424, A746, Diff-322, 13 points.

After Championship Shield:
P30-W10-D1-L19 (4th)
F650, A899, Diff-249, 21 points.

CHALLENGE CUP
Round Four

ATTENDANCES
Best - v Batley (Ch - 1,501)
Worst - v Barrow (Ch - 635)
Total (Championship/
Championship Shield only) - 13,572
Average (Championship/
Championship Shield only) - 969
(Down by 59 on 2017)

CLUB RECORDS	
	Highest score: 90-5 v Blackpool, 4/4/93 **Highest score against:** 0-82 v Widnes, 30/11/86
MATCH RECORDS	**Record attendance:** 26,584 v Halifax, 30/10/20 *(Crown Flatt)*; 4,068 v Bradford, 6/4/2015 *(Tetley's Stadium)*
	Tries: 8 Dai Thomas v Liverpool, 13/4/1907
SEASON RECORDS	**Goals:** 13 Greg Pearce v Blackpool Borough, 4/4/93; Francis Maloney v Hunslet, 25/3/2007 **Points:** 32 Les Holliday v Barrow, 11/9/94
	Tries: 40 Dai Thomas 1906-07 **Goals:** 169 Barry Eaton 2000 **Points:** 394 Barry Eaton 2000
CAREER RECORDS	**Tries:** 144 Joe Lyman 1913-31 **Goals:** 863 Nigel Stephenson 1967-78; 1984-86 **Points:** 2,082 Nigel Stephenson 1967-78; 1984-86
	Appearances: 454 Joe Lyman 1913-31

FEATHERSTONE ROVERS

DATE	FIXTURE	RESULT	SCORERS	LGE	ATT
4/2/18	Halifax (h)	W20-4	t:Briscoe,Robinson,Ridyard,Thackeray g:Ridyard(2)	4th	2,743
11/2/18	Toulouse (h)	W36-18	t:Briscoe(2),Thackeray,Clark,Davies,Hardcastle g:Ridyard(6)	2nd	2,033
18/2/18	London Broncos (a)	L44-24	t:Taulapapa,Hardcastle(2),Briscoe,Lockwood g:Ridyard(2)	5th	1,085
25/2/18	Sheffield (h)	W58-14	t:Robinson(2),Ridyard,Briscoe,Brooks,Mariano,Hardman,Thackeray(2),Wildie, Hardcastle g:Hardman(7)	3rd	2,048
4/3/18	Leigh (a)	W30-38	t:Briscoe(2),Robinson,Farrell,Ridyard(2),Clark g:Hardman,Ridyard(4)	3rd	3,594
11/3/18	Swinton (h)	W32-18	t:Briscoe,Carlile,Mariano,Ridyard,Robinson(2) g:Ridyard(4)	3rd	2,082
20/3/18	North Wales (a) (CCR4) ●	W6-66	t:Carlile(2),Wildie(2),Knowles,Briscoe(4),Hardman,Hardcastle,Davies,Holmes g:Hardman(7)	N/A	1,098
25/3/18	Batley (a)	W14-40	t:Lockwood,Briscoe(3),Newman,Holmes,Wildie g:Ridyard(6)	3rd	1,273
30/3/18	Toronto (h)	L16-24	t:Briscoe(2),Taulapapa g:Ridyard(2)	4th	3,131
2/4/18	Rochdale (a)	W0-42	t:Newman(3),Hardcastle,Ridyard,Briscoe(3) g:Ridyard(5)	3rd	659
8/4/18	Dewsbury (a)	W46-18	t:Farrell,Newman(2),Wildie(3),Briscoe g:Ridyard(7)	3rd	2,031
15/4/18	Barrow (a)	W26-38	t:Farrell,Briscoe,Newman(2),Hardman,Ridyard,Carlile g:Ridyard(5)	2nd	1,231
22/4/18	Doncaster (a) (CCR5)	W16-26	t:Briscoe(2),Holmes,Robinson(2) g:Ridyard(3)	N/A	1,076
29/4/18	Batley (h)	W50-12	t:Robinson(3),Briscoe,Hardcastle(2),Hock,Holmes(2),Walters g:Ridyard(5)	2nd	2,225
5/5/18	Toulouse (a)	L36-10	t:Briscoe,Newman g:Ridyard	3rd	2,876
10/5/18	Hull FC (h) (CCR6)	L20-38	t:Thackeray,Briscoe(2),Hock g:Ridyard(2)	N/A	3,222
19/5/18	Leigh (h)	L20-42	t:Walters(2),Wildie,Hardcastle g:Hardman(2)	4th	2,854
26/5/18	Halifax (SB) ●●	L18-24	t:Hock,Thackeray,Wildie g:Hardman(3)	4th	N/A
10/6/18	Dewsbury (a)	W18-42	t:Cooper,Wildie,Ormondroyd(2),Thackeray(2),Hock g:Hardman(7)	3rd	1,268
17/6/18	Barrow (h)	W52-4	t:Cooper(2),Hock,Thackeray,Briscoe,Davies,Hardcastle,Lockwood,Walton g:Hardman(8)	3rd	1,880
23/6/18	Sheffield (a)	W6-40	t:Thackeray,Hardman(2),Briscoe,Hardcastle(2) g:Hardman(6)	3rd	917
1/7/18	Rochdale (h)	W80-4	t:Lockwood(3),Walton(2),Dwyer(6),Knowles,Thackeray,Davies g:Hardman(12)	3rd	1,820
8/7/18	Halifax (a)	L34-20	t:Hardman,Hardcastle,Briscoe g:Hardman(4)	4th	2,356
15/7/18	Swinton (a)	W4-60	t:Robinson,Briscoe(2),Hardman(2),A Smith,Taulapapa(2),Thackeray,Hardcastle g:Hardman(10)	3rd	610
22/7/18	London Broncos (h)	L7-14	t:A Smith g:Hardman fg:Hardman	5th	2,434
28/7/18	Toronto (a)	W12-30	t:Carlile,Walton,Hardcastle,Wildie g:Hardman(7)	5th	8,217
12/8/18	Batley (h) (CS)	W26-12	t:Briscoe,Thackeray,Cooper,Maskill g:Hardman(4),Cooper	1st(CS)	1,236
19/8/18	Rochdale (a) (CS)	W24-33	t:Thackeray,Davies(2),Newman(2) g:Hardman(6) fg:Thackeray	2nd(CS)	586
2/9/18	Leigh (h) (CS)	W22-4	t:Hardcastle,Davies,Thackeray,Wildie g:Hardman(3)	1st(CS)	2,194
7/9/18	Sheffield (a) (CS)	W12-32	t:Knowles,Thackeray,Newman(2),Whylie,Hardman g:Hardman(4)	1st(CS)	689
16/9/18	Dewsbury (h) (CS)	W40-28	t:Robinson,Newman,Whylie,Davies,Taulapapa,Farrell(2),Ridyard g:Hardman,Ridyard(3)	1st(CS)	1,380
23/9/18	Swinton (a) (CS)	W18-34	t:Davies,Taulapapa,Thackeray,Maskill,Farrell,Hardcastle g:Hardman(5)	1st(CS)	606
30/9/18	Barrow (h) (CS)	W34-6	t:Cooper,Hardcastle,Farrell,Davies(2),Robinson g:Ridyard(2),Hardman(3)	1st(CS)	1,125
7/10/18	Leigh (h) (CSF)	W42-10	t:Carlile,Dupree,Newman(2),Farrell,Robinson(2) g:Hardman(7)	N/A	2,123

● *Played at LD Nutrition Stadium* ●● *Played at Bloomfield Road, Blackpool*

		APP		TRIES		GOALS		FG		PTS	
	D.O.B.	ALL	Ch	ALL	Ch	ALL	Ch	ALL	Ch	ALL	Ch
James Barraclough	22/9/99	(1)	0	0	0	0	0	0	0	0	0
Luke Briscoe	11/3/94	24	20	33	24	0	0	0	0	132	96
Sam Brooks	29/9/93	8(22)	(19)	1	1	0	0	0	0	4	4
Keal Carlile	20/3/90	28(4)	23	6	3	0	0	0	0	24	12
Mitch Clark	13/3/93	6(5)	6(5)	2	2	0	0	0	0	8	8
Luke Cooper	28/7/94	21(6)	11(5)	5	3	1	0	0	0	22	12
John Davies	8/1/91	25(1)	16	11	3	0	0	0	0	44	12
Tyler Dupree	8/2/00	(1)	0	1	0	0	0	0	0	4	0
Brad Dwyer	28/4/93	(3)	(3)	6	6	0	0	0	0	24	24
Connor Farrell	6/11/93	23(2)	14	9	4	0	0	0	0	36	16
Ash Handley	16/2/96	1	1	0	0	0	0	0	0	0	0
Josh Hardcastle	28/8/92	26(4)	17(2)	18	14	0	0	0	0	72	56
Ian Hardman	8/12/84	27(1)	19	9	7	108	68	1	1	253	165
Gareth Hock	5/9/83	7(13)	7(11)	5	4	0	0	0	0	20	16
Tom Holmes	2/3/96	18	15	5	3	0	0	0	0	20	12
Bradley Knowles	31/7/93	12(12)	10(6)	3	1	0	0	0	0	12	4
Jordan Lilley	4/9/96	2	2	0	0	0	0	0	0	0	0
James Lockwood	21/3/86	25(2)	15(1)	6	6	0	0	0	0	24	24
Frankie Mariano	10/5/87	3(4)	3(3)	2	2	0	0	0	0	8	8
Danny Maskill	28/6/95	5(4)	0	2	0	0	0	0	0	8	0
Richard Moore	2/2/81	7(9)	6(9)	0	0	0	0	0	0	0	0
Muizz Mustapha	3/4/00	(1)	0	0	0	0	0	0	0	0	0
Harry Newman	19/2/00	12	8	16	9	0	0	0	0	64	36
Mikolaj Oledzki	8/11/98	3	3	0	0	0	0	0	0	0	0
Jack Ormondroyd	7/11/91	2(6)	2(6)	2	2	0	0	0	0	8	8
Nathaniel Peteru	1/1/92	(1)	0	0	0	0	0	0	0	0	0
Martyn Ridyard	25/7/86	18(2)	14	8	7	59	49	0	0	150	126
Shaun Robinson	13/7/89	31	28	17	11	0	0	0	0	68	44
Aaron Smith	12/10/96	(3)	(3)	2	2	0	0	0	0	8	8
Cameron Smith	7/11/98	1(1)	1(1)	0	0	0	0	0	0	0	0
Misi Taulapapa	25/1/82	28(1)	17(1)	6	4	0	0	0	0	24	16
Anthony Thackeray	19/2/86	22(1)	13(1)	18	12	0	0	1	0	73	48
James Thornton	30/9/95	(1)	(1)	0	0	0	0	0	0	0	0
Jansin Turgut	8/3/96	2	2	0	0	0	0	0	0	0	0
Josh Walters	23/12/94	2(1)	2(1)	3	3	0	0	0	0	12	12
Jason Walton	13/6/90	9	7	4	4	0	0	0	0	16	16
Scott Wheeldon	23/2/86	18(1)	16	0	0	0	0	0	0	0	0
Dakota Whylie	28/7/99	8	1	2	0	0	0	0	0	8	0
Matty Wildie	25/10/90	18(13)	8(12)	12	9	0	0	0	0	48	36

'Ch' totals include Championship regular season only; 'All' totals also include Championship Shield & Challenge Cup

Luke Briscoe

LEAGUE RECORD
Championship, before Super 8 split:
P23-W16-D0-L7 (5th)
F819, A420, Diff+399, 32 points.

After Championship Shield:
P30-W23-D0-L7 (1st/Winners)
F1040, A524, Diff+516, 46 points.

CHALLENGE CUP
Round Six

ATTENDANCES
Best - v Hull FC (CC - 3,222)
Worst - v North Wales (CC - 1,098)
Total (Championship/
Championship Shield only) - 33,339
Average (Championship/
Championship Shield only) - 2,084
(Down by 540 on 2017)

CLUB RECORDS MATCH RECORDS	**Highest score:** 96-0 v Castleford Lock Lane, 8/2/2004 **Highest score against:** 14-80 v Bradford, 3/4/2005 **Record attendance:** 17,531 v St Helens, 21/3/59
	Tries: 6 Mike Smith v Doncaster, 13/4/68; Chris Bibb v Keighley, 17/9/89; Brad Dwyer v Rochdale, 1/7/2018
	Goals: 13 Mark Knapper v Keighley, 17/9/89; Liam Finn v Hunslet Old Boys, 25/3/2012; Liam Finn v Swinton, 12/8/2012
	Points: 40 Martin Pearson v Whitehaven, 26/11/95
SEASON RECORDS	**Tries:** 48 Paul Newlove 1992-93 **Goals:** 183 *(inc 2fg)* Liam Finn 2012 **Points:** 436 Liam Finn 2012
CAREER RECORDS	**Tries:** 162 Don Fox 1953-66 **Goals:** 1,210 Steve Quinn 1975-88 **Points:** 2,654 Steve Quinn 1975-88 **Appearances:** 440 Jim Denton 1921-34

HALIFAX

DATE	FIXTURE	RESULT	SCORERS	LGE	ATT
4/2/18	Featherstone (a)	L20-4	t:Heaton	9th	2,743
11/2/18	Sheffield (h)	W30-10	t:Murray(2),Woodburn-Hall,Barber,Fleming g:Tyrer(5)	6th	1,513
18/2/18	Toronto (h)	L6-20	t:Butler g:Tyrer	9th	2,036
25/2/18	Rochdale (a)	W20-26	t:Kaye,Sharp(2),Grix,Barber g:Tyrer(3)	7th	703
11/3/18	Leigh (h)	W38-18	t:Grady(2),Moore,Heaton,Tyrer(2) g:Tyrer(5)	6th	2,119
20/3/18	Oldham (h) (CCR4)	L6-27	t:Heaton g:Tyrer	N/A	688
24/3/18	Toulouse (a)	L38-6	t:Fleming g:Tyrer	6th	2,137
30/3/18	Barrow (h)	W30-4	t:Morris,Tyrer,Jones,McGrath g:Tyrer(7)	5th	1,298
8/4/18	London Broncos (h)	W26-16	t:Tyrer(2),Grady,Grix,McGrath g:Tyrer(3)	6th	1,595
15/4/18	Swinton (h)	W18-12	t:Butler,Tyrer(2),McGrath g:Tyrer	6th	1,399
22/4/18	Dewsbury (a)	W18-46	t:Butler(2),Moore,Saltonstall,Kaye,Tyrer,Laulu-Togagae,Sharp g:Tyrer(7)	5th	1,394
28/4/18	Toronto (a) ●	L42-10	t:McGrath,Heaton g:Grady	6th	1,658
6/5/18	Sheffield (a)	W6-42	t:Kaye,Butler(2),Laulu-Togagae(2),Barber,Johnston g:Tyrer(7)	6th	891
20/5/18	Dewsbury (h)	D22-22	t:Laulu-Togagae,Tyrer(2),Barber g:Tyrer(3)	6th	1,739
26/5/18	Featherstone (SB) ●●	W18-24	t:Murrell(2),Tyrer,Johnston g:Tyrer(3),Grady	5th	N/A
2/6/18	Batley (a)	W18-32	t:Butler,Johnston,Saltonstall,Heaton(2),Tyrer g:Tyrer(4)	3rd	1,002
10/6/18	Leigh (a)	L36-30	t:Murrell,Moss,Johnston(2),Heaton g:Grady(5)	4th	3,891
17/6/18	Swinton (a)	W4-46	t:Butler,Moss(2),Johnston(2),Fleming,Tyrer,Murrell g:Tyrer(7)	4th	953
24/6/18	Batley (h)	W50-12	t:Grady,Sharp,Moore(2),Woodburn-Hall,Saltonstall,Murrell,Johnston,Morris g:Tyrer(7)	4th	1,561
1/7/18	Barrow (a)	W22-48	t:Fairbank,Johnston(2),Murrell,Grady,Butler,Moss,Tangata g:Tyrer(8)	4th	1,293
8/7/18	Featherstone (h)	W34-20	t:Sharp(2),Johnston,Tangata,Kaye,Moss g:Tyrer(5)	3rd	2,356
15/7/18	London Broncos (a)	L20-18	t:Moss,Grady,Fairbank g:Tyrer(3)	5th	754
22/7/18	Toulouse (h)	W19-14	t:Tyrer,Kaye,Grady g:Tyrer(3) fg:Murrell	4th	1,794
29/7/18	Rochdale (h)	W38-6	t:Grix,Fairbank,Butler,Tyrer,Moss,Kaye g:Tyrer(7)	4th	1,866
12/8/18	Toronto (h) (S8-Q)	L0-14		6th(S8-Q)	1,774
18/8/18	Toulouse (a) (S8-Q)	L28-6	t:Fleming g:Grady	8th(S8-Q)	1,899
2/9/18	Salford (h) (S8-Q)	L4-62	t:Wood	8th(S8-Q)	2,555
9/9/18	Hull KR (a) (S8-Q)	L38-24	t:Saltonstall(2),Fleming,Sharp g:Grady,Fleming(3)	8th(S8-Q)	7,952
15/9/18	Widnes (a) (S8-Q)	L26-12	t:Woodburn-Hall,Saltonstall g:Grady,Murrell	8th(S8-Q)	3,372
23/9/18	Leeds (h) (S8-Q)	L6-34	t:Tyrer g:Tyrer	8th(S8-Q)	4,507
29/9/18	London Broncos (a) (S8-Q)	L23-16	t:Kaye,Tyrer,Tangata g:Tyrer(2)	8th(S8-Q)	869

● Played at New River Stadium, London
●● Played at Bloomfield Road, Blackpool

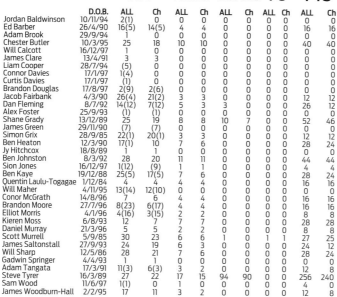

	D.O.B.	APP ALL	APP Ch	TRIES ALL	TRIES Ch	GOALS ALL	GOALS Ch	FG ALL	FG Ch	PTS ALL	PTS Ch
Jordan Baldwinson	10/11/94	2(1)	0	0	0	0	0	0	0	0	0
Ed Barber	26/4/90	16(5)	14(5)	4	4	0	0	0	0	16	16
Adam Brook	29/9/94	1	0	0	0	0	0	0	0	0	0
Chester Butler	10/3/95	25	18	10	10	0	0	0	0	40	40
Will Calcott	16/12/97	1	0	0	0	0	0	0	0	0	0
James Clare	13/4/91	3	3	0	0	0	0	0	0	0	0
Liam Cooper	28/7/94	(5)	0	0	0	0	0	0	0	0	0
Connor Davies	17/1/97	1(4)	0	0	0	0	0	0	0	0	0
Curtis Davies	17/1/97	(1)	0	0	0	0	0	0	0	0	0
Brandon Douglas	17/8/97	2(9)	2(6)	0	0	0	0	0	0	0	0
Jacob Fairbank	4/3/90	26(4)	21(2)	3	3	0	0	0	0	12	12
Dan Fleming	8/7/92	14(12)	7(12)	5	3	3	0	0	0	26	12
Alex Foster	25/9/93	(1)	(1)	0	0	0	0	0	0	0	0
Shane Grady	13/12/89	25	19	8	8	10	7	0	0	52	46
James Green	29/11/90	(7)	(7)	0	0	0	0	0	0	0	0
Simon Grix	28/9/85	22(1)	20(1)	3	3	0	0	0	0	12	12
Ben Heaton	12/3/90	17(1)	10	7	6	0	0	0	0	28	24
Jy Hitchcox	18/8/89	1	1	0	0	0	0	0	0	0	0
Ben Johnston	8/3/92	28	20	11	11	0	0	0	0	44	44
Sion Jones	16/12/97	1(12)	(9)	1	1	0	0	0	0	4	4
Ben Kaye	19/12/88	25(5)	17(5)	7	6	0	0	0	0	28	24
Quentin Laulu-Togagae	1/12/84	4	4	4	4	0	0	0	0	16	16
Will Maher	4/11/95	13(14)	12(10)	0	0	0	0	0	0	0	0
Conor McGrath	14/8/96	7	6	4	4	0	0	0	0	16	16
Brandon Moore	27/7/96	8(23)	6(17)	4	4	0	0	0	0	16	16
Elliot Morris	4/1/96	4(16)	3(15)	2	2	0	0	0	0	8	8
Kieren Moss	6/8/93	12	7	7	7	0	0	0	0	28	28
Daniel Murray	21/3/96	5	5	2	2	0	0	0	0	8	8
Scott Murrell	5/9/85	30	23	6	6	1	0	1	1	27	25
James Saltonstall	27/9/93	24	19	6	3	0	0	0	0	24	12
Will Sharp	12/5/86	28	21	7	6	0	0	0	0	28	24
Gadwin Springer	4/4/93	1	1	0	0	0	0	0	0	0	0
Adam Tangata	17/3/91	11(3)	6(3)	3	2	0	0	0	0	12	8
Steve Tyrer	16/3/89	27	22	17	15	94	90	0	0	256	240
Sam Wood	11/6/97	1(1)	0	1	0	0	0	0	0	4	0
James Woodburn-Hall	2/2/95	17	11	3	2	0	0	0	0	12	8

Brandon Moore

LEAGUE RECORD
Championship, before Super 8 split:
P23-W16-D1-L6 (4th)
F643, A416, Diff+227, 33 points.

S8-Q: P7-W0-D0-L7 (8th)
F68, A225, Diff-157, 0 points.

CHALLENGE CUP
Round Four

ATTENDANCES
Best - v Leeds (S8 - 4,507)
Worst - v Oldham (CC - 688)
Total (Championship/S8s only) - 28,112
Average (Championship/
S8s only) - 2,008
(Up by 212 on 2017)

'Ch' totals include Championship regular season only; 'All' totals also include Super 8s (Qualifiers) & Challenge Cup

CLUB RECORDS	
MATCH RECORDS	**Highest score:** 94-4 v Myton, 25/3/2012 **Highest score against:** 6-88 v Hull KR, 23/4/2006 **Record attendance:** 29,153 v Wigan, 21/3/59 *(Thrum Hall)*; 9,827 v Bradford, 12/3/2000 *(The Shay)* **Tries:** 8 Keith Williams v Dewsbury, 9/11/57 **Goals:** 14 Bruce Burton v Hunslet, 27/8/72 **Points:** 32 John Schuster v Doncaster, 9/10/94; Steve Tyrer v Whitehaven, 7/2/2016
SEASON RECORDS	**Tries:** 48 Johnny Freeman 1956-57 **Goals:** 156 Graham Holroyd 2008 **Points:** 362 John Schuster 1994-95
CAREER RECORDS	**Tries:** 290 Johnny Freeman 1954-67 **Goals:** 1,028 Ronnie James 1961-71 **Points:** 2,191 Ronnie James 1961-71 **Appearances:** 482 Stan Kielty 1946-58

LEIGH CENTURIONS

DATE	FIXTURE	RESULT	SCORERS	LGE	ATT
4/2/18	Toronto (h)	L12-34	t:Hansen,Dawson-Jones g:Reynolds(2)	10th	5,452
11/2/18	Batley (h)	W34-6	t:Crooks(2),Mason,Larroyer,Dawson-Jones,Acton g:Reynolds(5)	5th	3,216
18/2/18	Barrow (a)	L24-20	t:Bergal(2),Mata'utia,Patrick g:Reynolds(2)	7th	1,991
25/2/18	Toulouse (h)	L26-32	t:Dawson-Jones(2),Hood(2),Bergal g:Owens(3)	9th	3,143
4/3/18	Featherstone (h)	L30-38	t:Evans,Crooks(3),B Thompson,Dawson-Jones g:Hall(3)	9th	3,594
11/3/18	Halifax (a)	L38-18	t:Hall(2),Evans g:Lilley(3)	9th	2,119
18/3/18	Batley (a) (CCR4)	W4-8	t:Ricky Bailey g:Owens(2)	N/A	606
25/3/18	Dewsbury (h)	W36-0	t:Mata'utia(2),Hansen,Lovett(2),Crooks g:Reynolds(4),Owens(2)	8th	3,136
30/3/18	Swinton (a)	W10-40	t:Hood,Mason,Hall(2),B Thompson,Mata'utia,Dawson-Jones g:Hall(6)	6th	1,345
2/4/18	London Broncos (h)	W31-18	t:Hood(2),J Thompson,Hansen,Hutchison g:Reynolds(5) fg:Reynolds	5th	3,328
8/4/18	Rochdale (h)	W68-10	t:Hall(2),Reynolds(2),Acton(2),Evans,Hansen,Ricky Bailey(2),Hood,Owens g:Reynolds(10)	5th	3,144
15/4/18	Sheffield (h)	W20-72	t:Dawson-Jones,Mata'utia(2),Hall(4),Lovett,Owens(2),Hood,Hutchison,Larroyer g:Reynolds(10)	5th	982
22/4/18	London Broncos (h) (CCR5)	W40-0	t:Dawson-Jones,Hood,Hall,Owens,Crooks(2),Hansen g:Reynolds(6)	N/A	2,507
29/4/18	Barrow (h)	W46-18	t:Hutchison(3),Reynolds,Ryan Bailey,Dawson-Jones,Hood,Hall g:Reynolds(7)	5th	3,228
6/5/18	London Broncos (a)	W30-40	t:Evans,Hansen,Hall(2),Higham,Hood,Mata'utia g:Reynolds(6)	5th	1,340
11/5/18	Salford (h) (CCR6)	W22-10	t:Reynolds,Hansen,Mortimer,Hutchison g:Reynolds(3)	N/A	4,024
19/5/18	Featherstone (a)	W20-42	t:Owens,Hood,Crooks(2),Mason,Hansen,Reynolds g:Reynolds(7)	5th	2,854
26/5/18	Toronto (SB) ●	L26-28	t:Mason,Crooks(2),Acton,Owens g:Reynolds(3)	6th	N/A
1/6/18	Leeds (a) (CCQF) ●●	L52-22	t:Mason,Hutchison,Crooks,Hood g:Reynolds(3)	N/A	3,277
10/6/18	Halifax (a)	W36-30	t:Hood(2),Acton,Gregson,Hall g:Reynolds(6)	6th	3,891
16/6/18	Toulouse (a) ●●●	W16-18	t:Larroyer,Acton,Ricky Bailey g:Reynolds(2)	6th	5,373
24/6/18	Dewsbury (a)	W12-58	t:Hutchison(2),Hood,Hall(2),Ricky Bailey,Mortimer,B Thompson,Hansen,Larroyer g:Reynolds(9)	6th	1,351
30/6/18	Toronto (a)	L46-28	t:Crooks(2),Mortimer(2),Lovett g:Reynolds(4)	6th	6,844
8/7/18	Batley (a)	W12-30	t:Bergal(2),Ricky Bailey,Hansen(2),Reynolds g:Reynolds(3)	6th	1,223
14/7/18	Rochdale (a)	W32-54	t:Larroyer,Hall(2),Crooks,Ricky Bailey,Mata'utia,Mortimer(2),Hansen,Dawson-Jones g:Reynolds(7)	6th	1,080
22/7/18	Swinton (h)	W50-24	t:Hansen,Dawson-Jones(2),B Thompson,Hall(2),Hood,Mata'utia,Hutchison g:Reynolds(7)	6th	3,680
29/7/18	Sheffield (h)	W34-10	t:Ryan Bailey,Bergal(3),Dawson-Jones(2),Dagger g:Owens(3)	6th	3,112
12/8/18	Sheffield (h) (CS)	W68-6	t:Bergal(4),Mason,Hutchison(2),Cox,Ricky Bailey,Hood,Owens,Dawson-Jones g:Owens(10)	2nd(CS)	2,647
19/8/18	Barrow (a) (CS)	W38-0	t:Larroyer,Ricky Bailey,Richards,Owens,Dawson-Jones,J Walne,Reynolds g:Reynolds(5)	1st(CS)	2,646
2/9/18	Featherstone (a) (CS)	L22-4	t:Dawson-Jones	2nd(CS)	2,194
9/9/18	Swinton (h) (CS)	W54-10	t:Larroyer(2),Reynolds,J Walne,Peet,Hutchison,Richards(2),Whelan g:Reynolds(6),Gregson(3)	2nd(CS)	2,757
16/9/18	Rochdale (a) (CS)	W16-24	t:J Walne,Ricky Bailey,Bergal,Larroyer g:Reynolds(4)	2nd(CS)	834
23/9/18	Batley (h) (CS)	L16-30	t:Ricky Bailey,Owens,Reynolds g:Reynolds(2)	2nd(CS)	1,730
30/9/18	Dewsbury (a) (CS)	L52-6	t:Acton g:Owens	2nd(CS)	999
7/10/18	Featherstone (a) (CSF)	L42-10	t:Dawson-Jones,Owens g:Owens	N/A	2,123

● *Played at Bloomfield Road, Blackpool* ●● *Played at LD Nutrition Stadium, Featherstone* ●●● *Played at Stadium Municipal, Albi*

		APP		TRIES		GOALS		FG		PTS	
	D.O.B.	ALL	Ch	ALL	Ch	ALL	Ch	ALL	Ch	ALL	Ch
Jamie Acton	4/4/92	15(8)	9(8)	7	6	0	0	0	0	28	24
Ricky Bailey	25/4/97	18	9	11	6	0	0	0	0	44	24
Ryan Bailey	11/11/83	6(5)	3(4)	2	2	0	0	0	0	8	8
Jordan Baldwinson	10/11/94	2(4)	2(3)	0	0	0	0	0	0	0	0
Kurt Baptiste	15/3/91	(1)	(1)	0	0	0	0	0	0	0	0
James Barran	26/10/98	1		0		0		0		0	
Ilias Bergal	6/4/96	11	6	13	8	0	0	0	0	52	32
Jack Blagbrough	18/1/94	4(9)	(5)	0	0	0	0	0	0	0	0
Kevin Brown	27/11/98	1		0		0		0		0	
Liam Byrne	18/8/99	1		0		0		0		0	
Mitch Cox	15/11/93	2(4)	0	1	0	0	0	0	0	4	0
Ben Crooks	15/6/93	25	21	16	13	0	0	0	0	64	52
Jonah Cunningham	20/8/97	(2)	(2)	0	0	0	0	0	0	0	0
Will Dagger	21/2/99	4	1	1	1	0	0	0	0	4	4
Matty Dawson-Jones	2/10/90	28	17	18	13	0	0	0	0	72	52
Jordan Dezaria	6/11/96	2(10)	(4)	0	0	0	0	0	0	0	0
Rhys Evans	30/10/92	17	11	4	4	0	0	0	0	16	16
Chris Follin	26/10/98	(1)		0		0		0		0	
Sam Grant	24/3/99	1		0		0		0		0	
Nick Gregson	17/12/95	8(6)	3(4)	2	2	3	0	0	0	14	8
Craig Hall	21/2/88	20	17	21	20	11	11	0	0	106	102
Harrison Hansen	26/10/85	22(3)	19(2)	13	11	0	0	0	0	52	44
Micky Higham	18/9/80	12(10)	9(10)	1	1	0	0	0	0	4	4
Liam Hood	6/1/92	22(4)	18(4)	17	14	0	0	0	0	68	56
Drew Hutchison	26/4/95	35	23	13	8	0	0	0	0	52	32
Josh Johnson	25/7/94	1(6)	0	0	0	0	0	0	0	0	0
Ben Kilner	11/5/99	(1)		0		0		0		0	
Kevin Larroyer	19/6/89	19(7)	11(4)	9	5	0	0	0	0	36	20
Jordan Lilley	4/9/96	1		0		3		0		6	6
Kyle Lovett	23/3/93	4(6)	3(6)	4	4	0	0	0	0	16	16
Nathan Mason	8/9/93	14(8)	12(4)	6	4	0	0	0	0	24	16
Peter Mata'utia	2/11/90	20	16	9	9	0	0	0	0	36	36
Daniel Mortimer	13/6/89	1(11)	1(10)	6	5	0	0	0	0	24	20
Jacques O'Neill	8/5/99	1	0	0	0	0	0	0	0	0	0
Jack Owens	3/6/94	26	17	10	5	22	8	0	0	84	36
Larne Patrick	3/11/88	1(5)	1(5)	1	1	0	0	0	0	4	4
Sam Peet	21/2/94	1(2)		1		0		0		4	0
Ben Reynolds	15/1/94	28	20	9	5	127	98	1	1	291	217
Greg Richards	12/7/95	6(20)	2(16)	3	0	0	0	0	0	12	0
Bodene Thompson	1/8/88	24	20	4	4	0	0	0	0	16	16
Jordan Thompson	4/9/91	23(3)	20(2)	1	1	0	0	0	0	4	4
Paterika Vaivai	14/2/92	8(1)	7(1)	0	0	0	0	0	0	0	0
Adam Walne	3/10/90	7(1)	3(1)	0	0	0	0	0	0	0	0
Jordan Walne	28/12/92	8	1	3	0	0	0	0	0	12	0
Brad Whelan	20/1/99	1(2)		0		0		0		4	0

Ben Reynolds

LEAGUE RECORD
Championship, before Super 8 split:
P23-W16-D0-L7 (6th)
F849, A508, Diff+341, 32 points.

After Championship Shield:
P30-W20-D0-L10 (2nd/Runners-Up)
F1059, A644, Diff+415, 40 points.

CHALLENGE CUP
Quarter Finalists

ATTENDANCES
Best - v Toronto (Ch - 5,452)
Worst - v Batley (CS - 1,730)
Total (Championship/
Championship Shield only) - 48,704
Average (Championship/
Championship Shield only) - 3,247
(Down by 3,054 on 2017, Super League)

*'Ch' totals include Championship
regular season only; 'All' totals also include
Championship Shield & Challenge Cup*

CLUB RECORDS
Highest score: 92-2 v Keighley, 30/4/86 **Highest score against:** 4-94 v Workington, 26/2/95
Record attendance: 31,326 v St Helens, 14/3/53 *(Hilton Park)*; 10,556 v Batley, 17/9/2016 *(Leigh Sports Village)*
MATCH RECORDS **Tries:** 6 Jack Wood v York, 4/10/47; Neil Turley v Workington, 31/1/2001 **Goals:** 15 Mick Stacey v Doncaster, 28/3/76 **Points:** 42 Neil Turley v Chorley, 4/4/2004
SEASON RECORDS **Tries:** 55 Neil Turley 2001 **Goals:** 187 Neil Turley 2004 **Points:** 468 Neil Turley 2004
CAREER RECORDS **Tries:** 189 Mick Martyn 1954-67 **Goals:** 1,043 Jimmy Ledgard 1948-58 **Points:** 2,492 John Woods 1976-85; 1990-92 **Appearances:** 503 Albert Worrall 1920-38

LONDON BRONCOS

DATE	FIXTURE	RESULT	SCORERS	LGE	ATT
4/2/18	Barrow (h)	W56-12	t:Meadows,Williams,Harrison,Dixon(2),Battye,Sammut,Ioane,Matt Davis,Walker g:Sammut(8)	1st	801
11/2/18	Dewsbury (a)	W0-12	t:Battye,Sammut g:Sammut(2)	1st	795
18/2/18	Featherstone (h)	W44-24	t:Sammut(3),Pitts,Walker,Dixon(2) g:Sammut(7),Dixon	1st	1,085
25/2/18	Toronto (a)	W47-16	t:Pewhairangi,Matt Davis,Williams,Johnstone,Walker(2),Cunningham g:Sammut(9) fg:Sammut	1st	1,000
11/3/18	Batley (h)	W68-12	t:Dixon(4),Lovell,Cunningham,Pewhairangi(2),Williams(2),S Davis,Gee g:Sammut(6),Dixon(4)	1st	526
18/3/18	Workington (a) (CCR4)	W20-22	t:Pewhairangi,Williams(2),Spencer g:Dixon(3)	N/A	548
25/3/18	Swinton (a)	W18-64	t:Dixon(2),Walker(3),Lovell,Cunningham(2),Meadows,Bienek,Hellewell,Spencer g:Dixon(8)	1st	518
30/3/18	Toulouse (h)	L16-36	t:Pitts,Hellewell,Pewhairangi g:Sammut(2)	3rd	891
2/4/18	Leigh (a)	L31-18	t:Kear,Cunningham,Gee g:Sammut(3)	4th	3,328
8/4/18	Halifax (a)	L26-16	t:Williams,Kear,Lovell g:Sammut,Dixon	4th	1,595
13/4/18	Rochdale (a)	W15-30	t:Dixon(3),Adebiyi(2) g:Sammut(3),Dixon(2)	4th	312
22/4/18	Leigh (a) (CCR5)	L40-0		N/A	2,507
28/4/18	Dewsbury (h)	W64-6	t:Pitts,Sammut(3),Matthew Davies,Evans,Lovell,Williams(2),Kear,Matt Davis g:Sammut(10)	4th	733
6/5/18	Leigh (h)	L30-40	t:Williams,Walker,Evans,Meadows,Adebiyi g:Sammut(5)	4th	1,340
13/5/18	Sheffield (a)	W14-66	t:Pitts,Sammut(3),Pewhairangi,Dixon(2),Ioane,Adebiyi,Walker,Cunningham g:Sammut(11)	4th	517
20/5/18	Sheffield (h)	W46-12	t:Williams(2),Ioane,Gee(2),Sammut,Matt Davis,Dixon g:Sammut(7)	2nd	771
27/5/18	Toulouse (SB) ●	L28-40	t:Sammut,Pitts,Evans,Williams(2) g:Sammut(4)	3rd	N/A
9/6/18	Toronto (a)	L32-12	t:Sammut,Kear g:Sammut(2)	5th	7,384
17/6/18	Rochdale (h)	W68-0	t:Pitts(2),Dixon(2),Pewhairangi(3),Cunningham(2),Evans,Walker(2) g:Dixon(10)	5th	684
24/6/18	Swinton (h)	W58-22	t:Williams,Dixon,Cunningham,Sammut(2),Kear,Pewhairangi,Matt Davis,Pitts,Walker g:Dixon(9)	5th	684
1/7/18	Batley (a)	W16-38	t:Pewhairangi,Williams(2),Gee,Pitts,Dixon,Spencer g:Dixon(5)	5th	889
7/7/18	Toulouse (a)	D20-20	t:Cunningham,Matthew Davies,Battye g:Dixon(4)	5th	2,528
15/7/18	Halifax (h)	W20-18	t:Williams(2),Walker,Evans g:Dixon(2)	4th	754
22/7/18	Featherstone (a)	W7-14	t:Dixon,Walker,Sammut g:Sammut	3rd	2,434
29/7/18	Barrow (a)	W6-72	t:Pewhairangi,Walker(3),Williams(3),Cunningham(2),Dixon,Harrison,Sammut(2) g:Dixon(4),Sammut(6)	2nd	1,044
9/8/18	Widnes (a) (S8-Q)	W20-21	t:Ioane,Harrison,Dixon(2) g:Sammut(2) fg:Sammut	4th(S8-Q)	3,432
19/8/18	Leeds (h) (S8-Q)	L32-48	t:Dixon,Williams(2),Hindmarsh,Evans,Hellewell g:Sammut(4)	6th(S8-Q)	1,793
1/9/18	Toronto (a) (S8-Q)	L34-22	t:Williams,Walker,Evans,Matt Davis g:Sammut(3)	6th(S8-Q)	7,557
9/9/18	Toulouse (h) (S8-Q)	W34-8	t:Cunningham,Dixon,Walker(2),Hellewell g:Sammut(7)	5th(S8-Q)	696
15/9/18	Hull KR (a) (S8-Q)	L30-18	t:Sammut,Evans,Channing g:Sammut(3)	6th(S8-Q)	7,210
22/9/18	Salford (h) (S8-Q)	W11-8	t:Pitts g:Sammut fg:Sammut	6th(S8-Q)	809
29/9/18	Halifax (h) (S8-Q)	W23-16	t:Sammut,Pelissier,Dixon,Kear g:Sammut(3) fg:Sammut	5th(S8-Q)	869
7/10/18	Toronto (a) (MPG)	W2-4	g:Sammut(2)	N/A	9,266

● *Played at Bloomfield Road, Blackpool*

		APP		TRIES		GOALS		FG		PTS	
	D.O.B.	ALL	Ch	ALL	Ch	ALL	Ch	ALL	Ch	ALL	Ch
Sadiq Adebiyi	8/1/97	4(16)	4(11)	4	4	0	0	0	0	16	16
Eddie Battye	24/7/91	20(12)	12(10)	3	3	0	0	0	0	12	12
Lewis Bienek	11/4/98	2(6)	1(5)	1	1	0	0	0	0	4	4
Rob Butler	15/5/98	(11)	(7)	0	0	0	0	0	0	0	0
Michael Channing	30/6/92	9	7	1	0	0	0	0	0	4	0
James Cunningham	3/4/94	23(4)	17(4)	13	12	0	0	0	0	52	48
Matthew Davies	9/4/98	2(6)	2(4)	2	2	0	0	0	0	8	8
Matt Davis	5/7/96	29	22	6	5	0	0	0	0	24	20
Sam Davis	11/11/98	(10)	(8)	1	1	0	0	0	0	4	4
Kieran Dixon	22/8/92	29	20	27	22	53	50	0	0	214	188
Ben Evans	30/10/92	16(4)	8(4)	8	5	0	0	0	0	32	20
Matty Fleming	13/1/96	10	8	0	0	0	0	0	0	0	0
Matty Gee	12/12/94	9(14)	4(11)	5	5	0	0	0	0	20	20
Daniel Harrison	15/4/88	6(9)	6(5)	3	2	0	0	0	0	12	8
Ben Hellewell	30/1/92	22	14	4	2	0	0	0	0	16	8
Daniel Hindmarsh	8/8/98	16(2)	8(1)	1	0	0	0	0	0	4	0
Mark Ioane	3/2/90	16(12)	11(9)	4	3	0	0	0	0	16	12
Jordan Johnstone	24/5/97	(3)	(3)	1	1	0	0	0	0	4	4
Elliot Kear	29/11/88	26	16	6	5	0	0	0	0	24	20
Will Lovell	10/5/93	12(5)	10(3)	4	4	0	0	0	0	16	16
James Meadows	15/6/99	11	9	3	3	0	0	0	0	12	12
Jake Ogden	23/1/98	2	1	0	0	0	0	0	0	0	0
Eloi Pelissier	18/6/91	8(3)	3	1	0	0	0	0	0	4	0
Api Pewhairangi	19/3/92	19	15	12	11	0	0	0	0	48	44
Jay Pitts	9/12/89	33	23	10	9	0	0	0	0	40	36
Jarrod Sammut	15/2/87	23(6)	16(4)	21	19	114	87	4	1	316	251
Tom Spencer	2/1/91	19(9)	17(3)	3	2	0	0	0	0	12	8
Alex Walker	4/9/95	30	22	20	17	0	0	0	0	80	68
Rhys Williams	8/12/89	33	23	25	20	0	0	0	0	100	80

'Ch' totals include Championship regular season only;
'All' totals also include Super 8s (Qualifiers), Million Pound Game & Challenge Cup

Kieran Dixon

LEAGUE RECORD
Championship, before Super 8 split:
P23-W16-D1-L6 (2nd)
F907, A423, Diff+484, 33 points.

S8-Q: P7-W4-D0-L3 (5th)
F161, A164, Diff-3, 8 points.
(Winners, Million Pound Game)

CHALLENGE CUP
Round Five

ATTENDANCES
Best - v Leeds (S8 - 1,793)
Worst - v Batley (Ch - 526)
Total (Championship/S8s only) - 13,436
Average (Championship/S8s only) - 896
(Up by 5 on 2017)

CLUB RECORDS	
	Highest score: 82-0 v Highfield, 12/11/95; 82-2 v Barrow, 20/5/2006 **Highest score against:** 6-82 v Warrington, 20/3/2011; 10-82 v Warrington, 8/6/2013
MATCH RECORDS	**Record attendance:** 15,013 v Wakefield, 15/2/81 *(Craven Cottage)*; 1,845 v Leeds, 20/8/2016 *(Trailfinders Sports Ground)* **Tries:** 5 Martin Offiah v Whitehaven, 14/3/99; Sean Morris v Batley, 13/9/2015 **Goals:** 13 Rob Purdham v Barrow, 20/5/2006 **Points:** 34 Rob Purdham v Barrow, 20/5/2006; Jarrod Sammut v Sheffield, 13/5/2018
SEASON RECORDS	**Tries:** 43 Mark Johnson 1993-94 **Goals:** 159 John Gallagher 1993-94 **Points:** 384 John Gallagher 1993-94
CAREER RECORDS	**Tries:** 109 Luke Dorn 2005-2006; 2009-2013 **Goals:** 309 Steve Diamond 1981-84 **Points:** 772 Paul Sykes 2001-2007 **Appearances:** 202 Steele Retchless 1998-2004

ROCHDALE HORNETS

DATE	FIXTURE	RESULT	SCORERS	LGE	ATT
19/2/18	Dewsbury (h)	L6-38	t:L Adamson g:Livett	10th	427
25/2/18	Halifax (h)	L20-26	t:Massam,Moran,Livett g:Livett(4)	10th	703
3/3/18	Toulouse (a)	L54-6	t:Gregory g:Livett	10th	1,747
11/3/18	Barrow (h)	W24-12	t:Palfrey,Moran,Cross,Mitchell,Massam g:Palfrey(2)	10th	414
17/3/18	Normanton (a) (CCR4) ●	W8-20	t:Massam(2),Yates,Kay g:Palfrey(2)	N/A	N/A
23/3/18	Toronto (h)	L17-18	t:Hurst,Middlehurst,Massam g:Palfrey(2) fg:Smith	10th	504
30/3/18	Sheffield (a)	L38-20	t:Yates,Massam,Moores,Cross g:Palfrey(2)	10th	516
2/4/18	Featherstone (h)	L0-42		10th	659
8/4/18	Leigh (a)	L68-18	t:Hatton,Kay g:Patton	11th	3,144
13/4/18	London Broncos (h)	L15-30	t:Moores,Kay g:Livett(3) fg:Patton	11th	312
22/4/18	Whitehaven (a) (CCR5)	L38-0		N/A	604
29/4/18	Sheffield (h)	L16-38	t:Mitchell,Brickhill,Hadden g:Whittaker(2)	11th	459
6/5/18	Dewsbury (a)	W27-32	t:Whittaker,Tala(2),Hadden,Kay g:Whittaker(6)	11th	649
12/5/18	Batley (h)	L10-48	t:Kay(2) g:Whittaker	11th	408
20/5/18	Batley (a)	L23-14	t:Massam(2),Cross g:Whittaker	11th	743
27/5/18	Swinton (SB) ●●	L12-38	t:Lepori,Cunningham g:Whittaker(2)	12th	N/A
3/6/18	Swinton (h)	W18-25	t:Yates,Middlehurst,Massam,Cross g:Whittaker(4) fg:Whittaker	11th	631
10/6/18	Barrow (a)	L20-6	t:Tala g:Whittaker	12th	1,212
17/6/18	London Broncos (a)	L68-0		12th	684
24/6/18	Toulouse (h)	L14-70	t:Fox,Hatton g:Whittaker(3)	12th	304
1/7/18	Featherstone (a)	L80-4	t:Massam	12th	1,820
8/7/18	Swinton (h)	W28-26	t:Tala,Lepori,Taira,G King,Smith g:Smith(4)	12th	676
14/7/18	Leigh (h)	L32-54	t:Massam(2),Lepori(2),Moores,Taira g:Smith(4)	12th	1,080
21/7/18	Toronto (a)	L52-10	t:Cross,Taira g:Whittaker	12th	7,144
29/7/18	Halifax (a)	L38-6	t:Hatton g:Whittaker	12th	1,866
12/8/18	Barrow (a) (CS)	L17-10	t:Cross g:Smith(3)	8th(CS)	1,033
19/8/18	Featherstone (h) (CS)	L24-33	t:Mitchell,Massam(2),Tala g:Whittaker(4)	8th(CS)	586
2/9/18	Swinton (a) (CS)	L23-18	t:Smith,Fox,Lepori g:Whittaker(3)	8th(CS)	541
9/9/18	Batley (a) (CS)	L26-12	t:Fox,Cross(2)	8th(CS)	616
16/9/18	Leigh (h) (CS)	L16-24	t:Lepori,Yates g:Whittaker(4)	8th(CS)	834
23/9/18	Dewsbury (h) (CS)	W26-22	t:Tala,Cross(2),Gregory,Hatton g:Whittaker(3)	8th(CS)	651
30/9/18	Sheffield (a) (CS)	W22-32	t:T Adamson,Cross,Mitchell,Fox,Taira,Whittaker g:Whittaker(4)	7th(CS)	789

● Played at LD Nutrition Stadium, Featherstone
●● Played at Bloomfield Road, Blackpool

		APP		TRIES		GOALS		FG		PTS	
	D.O.B.	ALL	Ch	ALL	Ch	ALL	Ch	ALL	Ch	ALL	Ch
Luke Adamson	17/11/87	22(3)	14(3)	1	1	0	0	0	0	4	4
Toby Adamson	28/5/90	18(6)	11(6)	1	0	0	0	0	0	4	0
Dave Allen	15/9/85	13	11	0	0	0	0	0	0	0	0
Gavin Bennion	31/12/93	4	4	0	0	0	0	0	0	0	0
Billy Brickhill	30/4/97	14(10)	10(5)	1	1	0	0	0	0	4	4
Will Calcott	16/12/97	2	2	0	0	0	0	0	0	0	0
Deon Cross	30/7/96	29	20	11	5	0	0	0	0	44	20
Jonah Cunningham	20/8/97	1(6)	1(6)	1	1	0	0	0	0	4	4
Jack Fox	9/1/98	6(1)	4	4	1	0	0	0	0	16	4
Alex Gaskell	9/9/96	1(4)	1(3)	0	0	0	0	0	0	0	0
Miles Greenwood	30/7/87	1(1)	0	0	0	0	0	0	0	0	0
Declan Gregory	18/1/97	2(15)	2(10)	2	1	0	0	0	0	8	4
Matty Hadden	7/6/90	1(6)	1(5)	2	2	0	0	0	0	8	8
Lewis Hatton	14/1/97	17(7)	10(6)	4	3	0	0	0	0	16	12
Earl Hurst	21/4/89	14(1)	12(1)	1	1	0	0	0	0	4	4
Jack Johnson	25/4/96	1	1	0	0	0	0	0	0	0	0
Luis Johnson	20/2/99	2(1)	2(1)	0	0	0	0	0	0	0	0
Declan Kay	24/11/96	23	20	6	5	0	0	0	0	24	20
George King	24/2/95	5	5	1	1	0	0	0	0	4	4
Toby King	9/7/96	1	1	0	0	0	0	0	0	0	0
Richard Lepori	22/10/91	27	18	6	4	0	0	0	0	24	16
Harvey Livett	4/1/97	4	4	1	1	9	9	0	0	22	22
Ryan Maneely	19/10/94	(4)	(4)	0	0	0	0	0	0	0	0
Rob Massam	29/11/87	26	20	14	10	0	0	0	0	56	40
Gary Middlehurst	24/10/83	12	10	2	2	0	0	0	0	8	8
Ryan Millington	14/1/87	1(5)	0	0	0	0	0	0	0	0	0
Lee Mitchell	8/9/88	30	21	4	2	0	0	0	0	16	8
Ben Moores	6/12/93	24	17	3	3	0	0	0	0	12	12
Pat Moran	2/4/98	10(18)	3(18)	2	2	0	0	0	0	8	8
Callum Mulkeen	10/12/90	(2)	(1)	0	0	0	0	0	0	0	0
Lewis Palfrey	25/2/90	8	7	1	1	8	6	0	0	20	16
Declan Patton	23/5/95	2	2	0	0	1	1	1	1	3	3
Ben Pomeroy	10/1/84	1	1	0	0	0	0	0	0	0	0
Joe Ryan	27/9/95	(11)	(4)	0	0	0	0	0	0	0	0
Morgan Smith	30/4/98	8(2)	6(1)	2	1	11	8	1	1	31	21
Jordan Syme	14/11/96	4(5)	4(5)	0	0	0	0	0	0	0	0
Jovili Taira	30/3/89	17(9)	11(6)	4	3	0	0	0	0	16	12
Seta Tala	22/7/91	15(4)	9(3)	6	4	0	0	0	0	24	16
Blake Turner	29/9/98	3(2)	3(2)	0	0	0	0	0	0	0	0
Taylor Welch	1/11/89	2	1	0	0	0	0	0	0	0	0
Tyler Whittaker	12/11/95	18(1)	12	2	1	40	22	1	1	89	49
Danny Yates	28/5/94	27	18	4	2	0	0	0	0	16	8

Declan Kay

LEAGUE RECORD
Championship, before Super 8 split:
P23-W4-D0-L19 (12th)
F327, A926, Diff-599, 8 points.

After Championship Shield:
P30-W6-D0-L24 (7th)
F465, A1093, Diff-628, 12 points.

CHALLENGE CUP
Round Five

ATTENDANCES
Best - v Leigh (Ch - 1,080)
Worst - v Toulouse (Ch - 304)
Total (Championship/
Championship Shield only) - 8,017
Average (Championship/
Championship Shield only) - 573
(Down by 259 on 2017)

*'Ch' totals include Championship
regular season only; 'All' totals also include
Championship Shield & Challenge Cup*

CLUB RECORDS	**Highest score:** 120-4 v Illingworth, 13/3/2005 **Highest score against:** 0-106 v Castleford, 9/9/2007
	Record attendance: 26,664 v Oldham, 25/3/22 *(Athletic Grounds)*; 8,061 v Oldham, 26/12/89 *(Spotland)*
MATCH RECORDS	**Tries:** 5 Jack Corsi v Barrow, 31/12/21; Jack Corsi v Broughton Moor, 25/2/22; Jack Williams v St Helens, 4/4/33; Norman Brelsford v Whitehaven, 3/9/73; Marlon Billy v York, 8/4/2001 **Goals:** 18 Lee Birdseye v Illingworth, 13/3/2005 **Points:** 44 Lee Birdseye v Illingworth, 13/3/2005
SEASON RECORDS	**Tries:** 31 Marlon Billy 2001 **Goals:** 150 Martin Strett 1994-95 **Points:** 350 Mick Nanyn 2003
CAREER RECORDS	**Tries:** 103 Jack Williams 1931-37 **Goals:** 741 Walter Gowers 1922-36
	Points: 1,497 Walter Gowers 1922-36; Paul Crook 2010-2016 **Appearances:** 456 Walter Gowers 1922-36

SHEFFIELD EAGLES

DATE	FIXTURE	RESULT	SCORERS	LGE	ATT
2/2/18	Dewsbury (a)	L20-18	t:Offerdahl,Toole,Spedding g:Thomas(3)	8th	808
11/2/18	Halifax (a)	L30-10	t:Ashworth,James g:Thomas	10th	1,513
17/2/18	Toulouse (a)	L50-6	t:Aston g:Thomas	12th	1,533
25/2/18	Featherstone (a)	L58-14	t:Macani(2),Fozard g:Thomas	12th	2,048
11/3/18	Toronto (h)	L10-44	t:James,Macani g:Thomas	12th	863
18/3/18	Barrow (a) (CCR4)	L28-16	t:Fozard,Macani,Millar g:Thomas,Brown	N/A	936
25/3/18	Barrow (a)	L36-22	t:Blackmore,Fozard,Lo(2) g:Aston(2),Brown	11th	1,210
30/3/18	Rochdale (h)	W38-20	t:Pick,Millar,Lo(2),Igbinedion,Thomas,Fozard g:Thomas(4),Brown	11th	516
2/4/18	Batley (h)	L14-28	t:Toole,Davies,Millar g:Thomas	11th	597
8/4/18	Swinton (a)	W18-19	t:Blackmore(2),Macani g:Thomas(3) fg:Brown	10th	532
15/4/18	Leigh (h)	L20-72	t:Millar,Bentley,Thomas,Broadbent g:Thomas(2)	10th	982
29/4/18	Rochdale (a)	W16-38	t:Millar,G Burns,Makelim,Offerdahl,Ashworth,Fozard,Toole g:Brown(3),Fozard(2)	10th	459
6/5/18	Halifax (h)	L6-42	t:Costello g:Thomas	10th	891
13/5/18	London Broncos (h)	L14-66	t:Costello(2),Spedding g:Thomas	10th	517
20/5/18	London Broncos (a)	L46-12	t:Fozard,Davies g:Fozard(2)	10th	771
26/5/18	Barrow (SB) ●	W22-38	t:Aston(3),Yere,Toole,Spedding,Makelim g:Aston(4),Thomas	10th	N/A
10/6/18	Swinton (h)	L18-29	t:Ashworth,Aston,Spedding g:Aston(3)	10th	872
17/6/18	Batley (a)	W20-38	t:James,Fozard,Swift,Millar,Blackmore,Spedding g:Aston(7)	9th	2,328
23/6/18	Featherstone (h)	L6-40	t:Pick g:Aston	9th	917
1/7/18	Toulouse (h)	L24-46	t:Millar(2),Swift(2),Toole g:Aston(2)	9th	458
7/7/18	Toronto (a)	L68-4	t:Spedding	10th	6,329
15/7/18	Dewsbury (h)	W30-28	t:Magrin,Costello,Fozard,Spedding,Ashworth g:Aston(5)	9th	425
22/7/18	Barrow (h)	W28-10	t:James,Blackmore,Aston(2),Yere g:Aston(4)	8th	702
29/7/18	Leigh (a)	L34-10	t:Bentley,Aston g:Thomas	8th	3,112
12/8/18	Leigh (a) (CS)	L68-6	t:Toole g:Thomas	6th(CS)	2,647
19/8/18	Swinton (a) (CS)	W18-26	t:Yere,Brown(2),Bentley,Magrin g:Brown(3)	4th(CS)	420
31/8/18	Dewsbury (h) (CS)	L20-30	t:Toole,Macani(2),Thomas g:Thomas(2)	5th(CS)	638
7/9/18	Featherstone (h) (CS)	L12-32	t:Broadbent(2) g:Thomas(2)	5th(CS)	689
16/9/18	Batley (a) (CS)	L44-4	t:Macani	6th(CS)	607
23/9/18	Barrow (h) (CS)	L22-24	t:G Burns,Toole(2),Offerdahl g:Thomas(3)	6th(CS)	404
30/9/18	Rochdale (h) (CS)	L22-32	t:Broadbent,G Burns,Aston,Spedding g:Thomas(3)	6th(CS)	789

● Played at Bloomfield Road, Blackpool

		APP		TRIES		GOALS		FG		PTS	
	D.O.B.	ALL	Ch	ALL	Ch	ALL	Ch	ALL	Ch	ALL	Ch
Jack Ashworth	3/7/95	15	15	4	4	0	0	0	0	16	16
Cory Aston	1/3/95	23	16	9	8	28	28	0	0	92	88
James Bentley	19/10/97	14(2)	11(2)	3	2	0	0	0	0	12	8
Ben Blackmore	19/2/93	22(1)	16(1)	5	5	0	0	0	0	20	20
Blake Broadbent	11/12/98	1(5)	(1)	4	1	0	0	0	0	16	4
Simon Brown	23/6/89	14(1)	6(1)	2	0	9	5	1	1	27	11
Greg Burns	25/3/95	12(13)	8(9)	3	1	0	0	0	0	12	4
Paddy Burns	15/3/98	6(9)	3(5)	0	0	0	0	0	0	0	0
Matthew Costello	9/4/98	15	15	4	4	0	0	0	0	16	16
Olly Davies	30/11/95	11(12)	8(7)	2	2	0	0	0	0	8	8
Nabil Djalout	28/3/89	1(5)	1(4)	0	0	0	0	0	0	0	0
Matty Fozard	3/3/95	30	22	8	7	4	4	0	0	40	36
Thibault Franck	26/1/99	2	2	0	0	0	0	0	0	0	0
Max Garcia	15/1/98	1(16)	1(12)	0	0	0	0	0	0	0	0
Daniel Igbinedion	26/1/95	2(5)	1(5)	1	1	0	0	0	0	4	4
Matt James	26/3/87	22(2)	16(1)	4	4	0	0	0	0	16	16
Matty Lees	4/2/98	5(1)	5(1)	0	0	0	0	0	0	0	0
Garry Lo	1/11/93	6	6	4	4	0	0	0	0	16	16
Iliess Macani	6/12/93	15(2)	9(2)	8	4	0	0	0	0	32	16
Jon Magrin	8/10/94	14(13)	12(9)	2	1	0	0	0	0	8	4
Corey Makelim	6/1/94	14(1)	12(1)	2	2	0	0	0	0	8	8
Ryan Millar	12/5/94	21	20	8	7	0	0	0	0	32	28
Kieran Moran	2/11/96	2(7)	1(7)	0	0	0	0	0	0	0	0
Ben Morris	1/8/97	(1)	0	0	0	0	0	0	0	0	0
Mark Offerdahl	15/10/87	21(8)	14(8)	3	2	0	0	0	0	12	8
Shaun Pick	21/9/93	27(3)	19(3)	2	2	0	0	0	0	8	8
Matty Smith	23/7/87	1	1	0	0	0	0	0	0	0	0
Jake Spedding	26/9/96	18	16	8	7	0	0	0	0	32	28
Adam Swift	20/2/93	4	4	3	3	0	0	0	0	12	12
Oscar Thomas	3/1/94	21(3)	13(3)	3	2	33	21	0	0	78	50
Joshua Toole	11/9/89	22(1)	14(1)	9	5	0	0	0	0	36	20
Mike Weldon	10/4/98	4(11)	2(7)	0	0	0	0	0	0	0	0
Menzie Yere	24/10/83	17(1)	10(1)	3	2	0	0	0	0	12	8

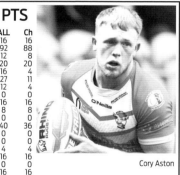

Cory Aston

LEAGUE RECORD
Championship, before Super 8 split:
P23-W7-D0-L16 (8th)
F437, A843, Diff-406, 14 points.

After Championship Shield:
P30-W8-D0-L22 (6th)
F549, A1091, Diff-542, 16 points.

CHALLENGE CUP
Round Four

ATTENDANCES
Best - v Leigh (Ch - 982)
Worst - v Barrow (CS - 404)
Total (Championship/
Championship Shield only) - 10,260
Average (Championship/
Championship Shield only) - 684
(Up by 47 on 2017)

'Ch' totals include Championship regular season only; 'All' totals also include Championship Shield & Challenge Cup

CLUB RECORDS	
	Highest score: 112-6 v Leigh East, 7/4/2013 **Highest score against:** 0-88 v Hull, 2/3/2003
	Record attendance: 10,603 v Bradford, 16/8/97 *(Don Valley Stadium)*; 982 v Leigh, 15/4/2018 *(Olympic Legacy Park)*
MATCH RECORDS	**Tries:** 5 Daryl Powell v Mansfield, 2/1/89; Menzie Yere v Leigh East, 7/4/2013; Quentin Laulu-Togagae v Rochdale, 7/9/2014; Garry Lo v Rochdale, 4/6/2017
	Goals: 14 Dominic Brambani v Leigh East, 7/4/2013 **Points:** 32 Roy Rafferty v Fulham, 21/9/86
SEASON RECORDS	**Tries:** 46 Menzie Yere 2013 **Goals:** 169 *(inc 1fg)* Dominic Brambani 2013 **Points:** 361 Dominic Brambani 2013
CAREER RECORDS	**Tries:** 193 Menzie Yere 2009-2018 **Goals:** 986 Mark Aston 1986-2004 **Points:** 2,142 Mark Aston 1986-2004 **Appearances:** 389 Mark Aston 1986-2004

SWINTON LIONS

DATE	FIXTURE	RESULT	SCORERS	LGE	ATT
3/2/18	Toulouse (a)	L46-14	t:Shelford,Butt g:Hankinson(3)	11th	1,740
18/2/18	Batley (h) ●	L28-48	t:Fell,J Hansen,Hankinson,Waterworth,Sarsfield g:Hankinson(4)	11th	588
25/2/18	Dewsbury (a)	L20-0		11th	961
4/3/18	Toronto (h)	L12-52	t:Butt,Waterworth g:Woods(2)	12th	701
11/3/18	Featherstone (a) ●●	L32-18	t:Sarsfield(2),Tyson(2) g:Woods	11th	2,082
18/3/18	York (a) (CCR4) ●●	L26-12	t:Tyson,Lloyd g:Hankinson(2)	N/A	525
25/3/18	London Broncos (h)	L18-64	t:Caine,H Hansen,Hankinson g:Hankinson(3)	12th	518
30/3/18	Leigh (h)	L10-40	t:Tyson,Shelford g:Hankinson	12th	1,345
2/4/18	Barrow (a)	D16-16	t:Forsyth,H Hansen(2) g:Hankinson(2)	12th	1,133
8/4/18	Sheffield (h)	L18-19	t:Webb,Mullen,Hankinson g:Hankinson(3)	12th	532
15/4/18	Halifax (a)	L18-12	t:Thornley,Webb g:Hankinson(2)	12th	1,399
28/4/18	Toulouse (h)	L8-62	t:Hope g:Hankinson(2)	12th	2,155
5/5/18	Toronto (a) ●●●	L62-14	t:Austin,Butt g:Hankinson(3)	12th	2,917
20/5/18	Barrow (h)	D22-22	t:Tyson(2),Lloyd,Paisley(2) g:Hankinson	12th	656
27/5/18	Rochdale (SB) ●●●●	W12-38	t:Waterworth,Tyson,Hope,Woods,Paisley g:Hankinson(7)	11th	N/A
3/6/18	Rochdale (h)	L18-25	t:Lloyd(2),Hankinson(2) g:Hankinson	12th	631
10/6/18	Sheffield (a)	W18-29	t:Lloyd,Tyson(2),Butt,Hope g:Hankinson(4) fg:Woods	11th	872
17/6/18	Halifax (h)	L4-46	t:Butt	11th	953
24/6/18	London Broncos (a)	L58-22	t:Hankinson,Brown(3) g:Hankinson(3)	11th	684
1/7/18	Dewsbury (h)	W29-28	t:Tyson(2),Fell,Ganson,Lloyd g:Hankinson(4) fg:Hankinson	11th	555
8/7/18	Rochdale (a)	L28-26	t:Tyson,Brown,Jones g:Hankinson(7)	11th	676
15/7/18	Featherstone (h)	L4-60	t:Butt	11th	610
22/7/18	Leigh (a)	L50-24	t:Barlow,Fairclough,Lloyd,Shelford g:J Hansen(3),Fairclough	11th	3,680
29/7/18	Batley (a)	L40-18	t:Barlow,Hall,Butt g:Billsborough,J Hansen(2)	11th	856
12/8/18	Dewsbury (a) (CS)	L40-7	t:Waterworth g:Fairclough fg:Woods	7th(CS)	752
19/8/18	Sheffield (h) (CS)	L18-26	t:Brown,Fairclough,Butt g:Fairclough(3)	7th(CS)	420
2/9/18	Rochdale (h) (CS)	W23-18	t:Brown(3),Tyson g:Fairclough(3) fg:Woods	7th(CS)	541
9/9/18	Leigh (a) (CS)	L54-10	t:Shelford,Thornley g:Fairclough	7th(CS)	2,757
16/9/18	Barrow (a) (CS)	L34-18	t:J Hansen,Butt(2) g:Fairclough(3)	7th(CS)	1,357
23/9/18	Featherstone (h) (CS)	L18-34	t:Thornley,Gray,Mullen g:J Hansen(3)	7th(CS)	606
30/9/18	Batley (a) (CS)	L40-6	t:Hall g:J Hansen	8th(CS)	817
14/10/18	Workington (h) (CP/RPO)	W33-20	t:Waterworth(2),Lloyd(2),Woods,Shelford g:J Hansen(4) fg:Woods	N/A	703

● Played at AJ Bell Stadium, Salford ●● Played at LD Nutrition Stadium, Featherstone ●●● Played at Fletcher's Fields ●●●● Played at Bloomfield Road, Blackpool

		APP		TRIES		GOALS		FG		PTS	
	D.O.B.	ALL	Ch	ALL	Ch	ALL	Ch	ALL	Ch	ALL	Ch
Danny Ansell	9/10/91	1	1	0	0	0	0	0	0	0	0
Ben Austin	3/5/95	14(10)	9(6)	1	1	0	0	0	0	4	4
Josh Barlow	15/5/91	5(13)	4(12)	2	2	0	0	0	0	8	8
Gavin Bennion	31/12/93	7	7	0	0	0	0	0	0	0	0
Ilias Bergal	6/4/96	4	4	0	0	0	0	0	0	0	0
Brad Billsborough	4/8/98	7(3)	7(1)	0	0	1	1	0	0	2	2
Andy Bracek	21/3/84	28	21	0	0	0	0	0	0	0	0
Joe Brown	14/1/99	12	7	8	4	0	0	0	0	32	16
Mike Butt	6/5/95	27	19	10	7	0	0	0	0	40	28
Elliott Caine	3/7/98	4	3	1	1	0	0	0	0	4	4
Macauley Davies	4/9/96	5(1)	5(1)	0	0	0	0	0	0	0	0
Rob Fairclough	10/9/97	13	4	2	1	12	1	0	0	32	6
Gabriel Fell	12/9/95	22	20	2	2	0	0	0	0	8	8
Callum Field	7/10/97	(1)	(1)	0	0	0	0	0	0	0	0
Liam Forsyth	23/3/96	5	5	1	1	0	0	0	0	4	4
Tommy Gallagher	10/9/83	(3)	(2)	0	0	0	0	0	0	0	0
Josh Ganson	19/2/98	6(9)	6(2)	1	1	0	0	0	0	4	4
Ryan Gray	2/3/98	4	0	1	0	0	0	0	0	4	0
Aaron Hall	19/2/93	2(14)	(11)	2	1	0	0	0	0	8	4
Gabe Hamlin	4/1/97	1	1	0	0	0	0	0	0	0	0
Chris Hankinson	30/11/93	20	19	6	6	52	50	1	1	129	125
Hayden Hansen	25/1/94	11(20)	6(17)	3	3	0	0	0	0	12	12
Jack Hansen	12/1/97	31	22	2	1	13	5	0	0	34	14
Jack Higginson	4/4/97	1	1	0	0	0	0	0	0	0	0
Will Hope	2/6/93	17(1)	14(1)	3	3	0	0	0	0	12	12
Paddy Jones	7/2/97	(12)	(4)	1	1	0	0	0	0	4	4
Samy Kibula	7/8/99	(1)	(1)	0	0	0	0	0	0	0	0
Rhodri Lloyd	22/7/93	31	23	9	6	0	0	0	0	36	24
Craig Mullen	15/1/98	7	5	2	1	0	0	0	0	8	4
Romain Navarrete	30/6/94	(1)	(1)	0	0	0	0	0	0	0	0
Mark Nicholson	29/1/95	3(3)	3(3)	0	0	0	0	0	0	0	0
Levy Nzoungou	22/1/98	2(3)	2(3)	0	0	0	0	0	0	0	0
Liam Paisley	27/11/97	6	5	3	3	0	0	0	0	12	12
Oliver Partington	3/9/98	(2)	(2)	0	0	0	0	0	0	0	0
Matt Sarsfield	10/9/91	8	7	3	3	0	0	0	0	12	12
Kyle Shelford	13/9/96	19(11)	11(10)	5	3	0	0	0	0	20	12
Conor Taylor	11/8/98	(4)	(3)	0	0	0	0	0	0	0	0
Andy Thornley	1/3/89	23(3)	15(3)	3	1	0	0	0	0	12	4
George Tyson	1/10/93	24	17	14	12	0	0	0	0	56	48
Luke Waterworth	20/6/96	20(4)	12(3)	6	3	0	0	0	0	24	12
Marcus Webb	11/1/97	6	5	2	2	0	0	0	0	8	8
Paul Wood	10/10/81	4	0	0	0	0	0	0	0	0	0
Josh Woods	13/12/97	13	7	2	1	3	3	4	1	18	11
Chris Worrell	11/10/96	2(9)	1(5)	0	0	0	0	0	0	0	0
James Worthington	21/5/99	1	1	0	0	0	0	0	0	0	0

George Tyson

LEAGUE RECORD
Championship, before Super 8 split:
P23-W3-D2-L18 (11th)
F402, A866, Diff-464, 8 points.

After Championship Shield:
P30-W4-D2-L24 (8th)
F502, A1112, Diff-610, 10 points.
(Winners, Promotion/Relegation play-off)

CHALLENGE CUP
Round Four

ATTENDANCES
Best - v Toulouse (Ch - 2,155)
Worst - v Sheffield (CS - 420)
Total (all home games included) - 11,514
Average (all home games included) - 768
(Down by 7 on 2017)

'Ch' totals include Championship regular season only; 'All' totals also include Championship Shield, Championship Promotion/Relegation play-off & Challenge Cup

CLUB RECORDS

MATCH RECORDS
SEASON RECORDS
CAREER RECORDS

Highest score: 96-4 v Oxford, 12/7/2015 **Highest score against:** 0-112 v Warrington, 20/5/2011
Record attendance: 26,891 v Wigan, 12/2/64 *(Station Road)*; 2,155 v Toulouse, 28/4/2018 *(Heywood Road)*
Tries: 6 Mark Riley v Prescot, 11/8/96 **Goals:** 14 Ian Mort v Oxford, 12/7/2015 **Points:** 48 Ian Mort v Oxford, 12/7/2015
Tries: 42 John Stopford 1963-64 **Goals:** 128 Albert Blan 1960-61 **Points:** 338 Ian Mort 2011
Tries: 197 Frank Evans 1921-31 **Goals:** 970 Ken Gowers 1954-73 **Points:** 2,105 Ken Gowers 1954-73 **Appearances:** 601 Ken Gowers 1954-73

TORONTO
WOLFPACK

TORONTO WOLFPACK

DATE	FIXTURE	RESULT	SCORERS	LGE	ATT
4/2/18	Leigh (a)	W12-34	t:Sidlow,Kay(3),Paterson,Brierley g:Brierley(5)	3rd	5,452
11/2/18	Barrow (a)	D8-8	t:Dixon,Rawsthorne	3rd	1,266
18/2/18	Halifax (a)	W6-20	t:Worthington,Rawsthorne,Higson(2) g:Brierley(2)	2nd	2,036
25/2/18	London Broncos (a)	L47-16	t:Whiting,Dixon,Kay g:Brierley(2)	5th	1,000
4/3/18	Swinton (a)	W12-52	t:Butler-Fleming(2),Brierley(2),Laulu-Togagae,Wallace(2),Ackers,Pownall g:Brierley(8)	4th	701
11/3/18	Sheffield (a)	W10-44	t:Kay,Whiting(2),Sidlow,Rawsthorne,Wallace,Pownall(2) g:Brierley(6)	4th	863
16/3/18	Kells (a) (CCR4) ●	W6-56	t:Wallace,Kay(3),Rawsthorne(2),Laulu-Togagae,Pownall,Brierley,Ackers g:Brierley(8)	N/A	1,000
23/3/18	Rochdale (a)	W17-18	t:Kay,McCrone,Maitua g:Brierley(3)	4th	504
30/3/18	Featherstone (a)	W16-24	t:Brierley(2),Whiting(2) g:Brierley(4)	2nd	3,131
2/4/18	Toulouse (a)	W22-24	t:Pownall,Kay,Rawsthorne(2),Ackers g:Brierley(2)	1st	3,313
8/4/18	Batley (a)	W18-26	t:McCrone,O'Brien(3),Bussey g:Brierley(3)	1st	1,157
15/4/18	Dewsbury (a)	W12-23	t:Maitua,Higson(2),Stanley,Brierley g:Brierley fg:Brierley	1st	932
22/4/18	Barrow (h) (CCR5) ●●	W16-12	t:O'Brien,Beswick,Rawsthorne g:Brierley(2)	N/A	1,140
28/4/18	Halifax (h) ●●●	W42-10	t:Lussick,Kay(2),Beswick,Brierley,Ackers,Paterson g:Brierley(7)	1st	1,658
5/5/18	Swinton (h) ●●●●	W62-14	t:Kay(3),Stanley,O'Brien(2),Krasniqi,Rawsthorne,Wallace,Sidlow,Dixon,Higson g:Brierley(7)	1st	2,917
13/5/18	Warrington (h) (CCR6) ●●●●●	L10-66	t:Higson,Kay g:Brierley	N/A	6,507
19/5/18	Toulouse (h) ●●●●●●	W43-30	t:Kay(3),Russell,Dixon,Brierley,Stanley,Hopkins g:Brierley(5) fg:Brierley	1st	N/A
26/5/18	Leigh (SB) ●●●●●●●	W26-28	t:McCrone,O'Brien,Rawsthorne,Krasniqi,Paterson g:Brierley(4)	1st	N/A
9/6/18	London Broncos (h)	W32-12	t:Paterson(2),Kay,McCrone,Brierley g:Brierley(6)	1st	7,384
16/6/18	Dewsbury (h)	W64-12	t:Kay,Lussick,Ackers,Russell(2),Paterson,O'Brien(2),Wallace,Buchanan,Rawsthorne g:O'Brien(10)	1st	5,937
23/6/18	Barrow (h)	W64-0	t:Kay(2),O'Brien,Wallace(2),Paterson,Beswick,Rawsthorne(2),Russell,Sidlow,Ackers g:O'Brien(8)	1st	5,287
30/6/18	Leigh (h)	W46-28	t:Wallace(3),Russell(2),Ackers(2),Kay g:O'Brien(7)	1st	6,844
7/7/18	Sheffield (h)	W68-4	t:Stanley(2),Brierley,Beswick,Whiting,Higson(2),Rawsthorne,Wallace,O'Brien,Kay,Dixon g:O'Brien(10)	1st	6,329
14/7/18	Batley (h)	W64-18	t:Wallace(3),Worthington,Stanley,Rawsthorne,Beswick,Paterson,Higson,Ackers(2),Brierley g:O'Brien(4),Brierley(4)	1st	6,088
21/7/18	Rochdale (h)	W52-10	t:Ackers,Buchanan,Wheeler(2),Sidlow,Whiting,Paterson,Stanley,Hopkins,Kay g:O'Brien(6)	1st	7,144
28/7/18	Featherstone (h)	L12-30	t:Sims,Sidlow g:Brierley(2)	1st	8,217
12/8/18	Halifax (a) (S8-Q)	W0-14	t:Ackers,Dixon g:O'Brien(3)	6th(S8-Q)	1,774
18/8/18	Hull KR (h) (S8-Q)	L22-28	t:Rawsthorne,Dixon g:O'Brien(5)	3rd(S8-Q)	7,540
1/9/18	London Broncos (h) (S8-Q)	W34-22	t:Wallace,O'Brien,Stanley,McCrone,Caton-Brown g:O'Brien(7)	3rd(S8-Q)	7,557
8/9/18	Salford (a) (S8-Q)	L28-16	t:Sidlow,Russell,Ackers g:O'Brien(2)	4th(S8-Q)	2,509
15/9/18	Toulouse (h) (S8-Q)	W13-12	t:Caton-Brown,Rawsthorne,Stanley fg:O'Brien	4th(S8-Q)	7,923
22/9/18	Widnes (h) (S8-Q)	W20-12	t:Paterson,Russell,Wallace g:O'Brien(4)	3rd(S8-Q)	8,381
28/9/18	Leeds (a) (S8-Q)	W16-17	t:Paterson,Rawsthorne,Russell g:O'Brien(2) fg:O'Brien	4th(S8-Q)	11,565
7/10/18	London Broncos (h) (MPG)	L2-4	g:O'Brien	N/A	9,266

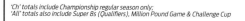

● *Played at Recreation Ground, Whitehaven* ●● *Played at Craven Park* ●●● *Played at New River Stadium, London* ●●●● *Played at Fletcher's Fields*
●●●●● *Played at Halliwell Jones Stadium* ●●●●●● *Played at St James' Park, Newcastle* ●●●●●●● *Played at Bloomfield Road, Blackpool*

APP   TRIES GOALS FG   PTS

	D.O.B.	ALL	Ch	ALL	Ch	ALL	Ch	ALL	Ch	ALL	Ch
Andy Ackers	25/12/93	12(19)	10(10)	13	10	0	0	0	0	52	40
Bob Beswick	8/12/84	23(3)	14(2)	5	4	0	0	0	0	20	16
Ryan Brierley	12/3/92	23	20	12	11	82	71	2	2	214	188
Jack Buchanan	10/4/92	13(16)	10(9)	2	2	0	0	0	0	8	8
Jack Bussey	17/8/92	12(4)	9(2)	1	1	0	0	0	0	4	4
Jake Butler-Fleming	8/1/92	1	1	2	2	0	0	0	0	8	8
Mason Caton-Brown	24/5/93	7	0	2	0	0	0	0	0	8	0
Andrew Dixon	28/2/90	24(2)	15(2)	8	5	0	0	0	0	32	20
Jake Emmitt	4/10/88	25(3)	16(1)	0	0	0	0	0	0	0	0
Adam Higson	19/5/87	10(1)	8	9	8	0	0	0	0	36	32
Sam Hopkins	17/2/90	7(12)	6(10)	2	2	0	0	0	0	8	8
Liam Kay	17/12/91	26	22	26	22	0	0	0	0	104	88
Olsi Krasniqi	26/6/92	5(14)	5(10)	2	2	0	0	0	0	8	8
James Laithwaite	23/9/91	(2)	(1)	0	0	0	0	0	0	0	0
Quentin Laulu-Togagae	1/12/84	9	8	2	1	0	0	0	0	8	4
Darcy Lussick	6/6/89	16(2)	8	2	2	0	0	0	0	8	8
Reni Maitua	11/6/82	5(3)	4(3)	2	2	0	0	0	0	8	8
Josh McCrone	12/4/97	29(1)	18(1)	5	4	0	0	0	0	20	16
Quinn Ngawati	15/6/99	1	1	0	0	0	0	0	0	0	0
Gareth O'Brien	31/10/91	24	14	12	10	69	45	2	0	188	130
Cory Paterson	14/7/87	18	11	11	9	0	0	0	0	44	36
Jonny Pownall	22/8/91	8	7	5	4	0	0	0	0	20	16
Nick Rawsthorne	30/9/95	18(2)	12(2)	18	12	0	0	0	0	72	48
Matthew Russell	6/6/93	13	7	9	6	0	0	0	0	36	24
Adam Sidlow	25/10/87	3(31)	2(21)	7	6	0	0	0	0	28	24
Ashton Sims	26/2/85	24(3)	15(2)	1	1	0	0	0	0	4	4
Chase Stanley	31/5/89	19	11	9	7	0	0	0	0	36	28
Blake Wallace	18/6/92	18(7)	9(7)	17	14	0	0	0	0	68	56
Joe Westerman	15/11/89	5	5	0	0	0	0	0	0	0	0
Gary Wheeler	30/9/89	10(1)	2(1)	2	2	0	0	0	0	8	8
Richard Whiting	20/12/84	13(9)	9(8)	7	7	0	0	0	0	28	28
Greg Worthington	17/7/90	21	20	2	2	0	0	0	0	8	8

Liam Kay

'Ch' totals include Championship regular season only;
'All' totals also include Super 8s (Qualifiers), Million Pound Game & Challenge Cup

LEAGUE RECORD
Championship, before Super 8 split:
P23-W20-D1-L2 (1st)
F866, A374, Diff+492, 41 points.

S8-Q: P7-W5-D0-L2 (4th)
F136, A118, Diff+18, 10 points.
(Losers, Million Pound Game)

CHALLENGE CUP
Round Six

ATTENDANCES
Best - v London Broncos (MPG - 9,266)
Worst - v Halifax (Ch - 1,658)
Total (Championship/
S8s/MPG only) - 98,472
Average (Championship/
S8s/MPG only) - 6,565
(Down by 395 on 2017, League 1)

CLUB RECORDS	**Highest score:** 82-6 v Doncaster, 9/4/2017 **Highest score against:** 10-66 v Warrington, 13/5/2018 **Record attendance:** 9,266 v London Broncos, 7/10/2018
MATCH RECORDS	**Tries:** 5 Liam Kay v York, 1/7/2017 **Goals:** 13 Craig Hall v Doncaster, 9/4/2017 **Points:** 38 Craig Hall v Hemel, 15/7/2017
SEASON RECORDS	**Tries:** 27 Liam Kay 2017 **Goals:** 171 Craig Hall 2017 **Points:** 442 Craig Hall 2017
CAREER RECORDS	**Tries:** 53 Liam Kay 2017-2018 **Goals:** 171 Craig Hall 2017 **Points:** 442 Craig Hall 2017 **Appearances:** 56 Adam Sidlow 2017-2018

TOULOUSE OLYMPIQUE

DATE	FIXTURE	RESULT	SCORERS	LGE	ATT
3/2/18	Swinton (h)	W46-14	t:Barthau,Maurel(2),Curran,Marcon,Robin,Marguerite,Ader,Kheirallah g:Kheirallah(5)	2nd	1,740
11/2/18	Featherstone (a)	L36-18	t:Marcon(2),Curran,Marguerite g:Kheirallah	4th	2,033
17/2/18	Sheffield (h)	W50-6	t:Marcon,Kriouache,Mika,Sangare(2),Robin,Barthau(2),Kheirallah g:Kheirallah(7)	3rd	1,533
25/2/18	Leigh (a)	W26-32	t:Curran,Marguerite(2),Canet,Kheirallah,Robin g:Kheirallah(4)	2nd	3,143
3/3/18	Rochdale (h)	W54-6	t:Barthau(2),Ader,Maurel,Marcon(2),Mika,Kriouache,Canet(2) g:Kheirallah(7)	1st	1,747
11/3/18	Dewsbury (a)	W20-40	t:Curran(2),Robin,Hepi(2),Maurel,Kheirallah g:Kheirallah(6)	2nd	720
24/3/18	Halifax (h)	W38-6	t:Maurel(2),Curran,Kheirallah,Marguerite,Ader,Marcon g:Kheirallah(5)	2nd	2,137
30/3/18	London Broncos (a)	W16-36	t:Maurel,Curran,Ader,Marion,Hepi,Kheirallah g:Kheirallah(6)	1st	891
2/4/18	Toronto (h)	L22-24	t:Curran,Boyer,Robin,Maurel g:Kheirallah(3)	2nd	3,313
7/4/18	Barrow (h)	W50-4	t:Curran,Ford,Canet,Barthau,Sangare,Boyer,Planas,Pettybourne,Kheirallah g:Kheirallah(7)	2nd	1,177
14/4/18	Batley (a)	L46-22	t:Ader(2),Kheirallah,Barthau g:Kheirallah(2),Barthau	3rd	662
28/4/18	Swinton (a)	W8-62	t:Ford(2),Robin(2),Kheirallah(2),Marion(2),Maurel,Bouzinac,Kriouache g:Kheirallah(9)	3rd	2,155
5/5/18	Featherstone (h)	W36-10	t:Kheirallah,Marion,Hepi,Barthau,Canet,Ader g:Kheirallah(6)	2nd	2,876
19/5/18	Toronto (a) ●	L43-30	t:Kriouache,Marion,Bouzinac,Curran,Ford g:Kheirallah(5)	3rd	N/A
27/5/18	London Broncos (SB) ●●	W28-40	t:Maurel(2),Worthington,Curran,Bouzinac,Kheirallah(2) g:Kheirallah(6)	2nd	N/A
9/6/18	Batley (h)	W42-26	t:Ader(2),Marguerite,Mika,Kheirallah,Maurel,Bouscayrol g:Kheirallah(7)	2nd	2,250
16/6/18	Leigh (h) ●●●	L16-18	t:Marguerite,Canet,Mika g:Kheirallah(2)	2nd	5,373
24/6/18	Rochdale (h)	W14-70	t:Mika(2),Kheirallah(2),Kriouache(2),Bouzinac,Barthau(3),Puech,Canet,Ader g:Kheirallah(9)	2nd	304
1/7/18	Sheffield (a)	W24-46	t:Barthau,Maurel,Bretherton,Curran,Kheirallah(2),Marguerite,Centrone g:Kheirallah(7)	2nd	458
7/7/18	London Broncos (h)	D20-20	t:Mika,Ader,Centrone g:Kheirallah(4)	2nd	2,528
15/7/18	Barrow (a)	W6-72	t:Marion,Ader(3),Centrone(2),Seguier(2),Kheirallah,Curran,Marcon,Sangare,Barthau g:Kheirallah(10)	2nd	981
22/7/18	Halifax (a)	L19-14	t:Canet,Bretherton g:Kheirallah(3)	2nd	1,794
28/7/18	Dewsbury (h)	W44-18	t:Centrone(3),Kheirallah,Planas,Puech,Marion,Marcon g:Kheirallah(6)	3rd	1,914
11/8/18	Leeds (a) (S8-Q)	L48-22	t:Canet,Ader,Puech,Centrone g:Kheirallah(3)	8th(S8-Q)	10,166
18/8/18	Halifax (h) (S8-Q)	W28-6	t:Centrone(2),Marcon,Robin,Marion g:Kheirallah(4)	4th(S8-Q)	1,899
1/9/18	Widnes (h) (S8-Q)	W42-22	t:Kheirallah(2),Centrone(2),Ford,Robin,Barthau g:Kheirallah(7)	4th(S8-Q)	2,911
9/9/18	London Broncos (a) (S8-Q)	L34-8	t:Romano,Robin	6th(S8-Q)	696
15/9/18	Toronto (a) (S8-Q)	L13-12	t:Marcon,Robin g:Kheirallah(2)	5th(S8-Q)	7,923
22/9/18	Hull KR (h) (S8-Q)	W34-23	t:Curran,Centrone(2),Robin,Marguerite,Ader g:Kheirallah(5)	5th(S8-Q)	4,127
27/9/18	Salford (a) (S8-Q)	L44-10	t:Centrone,Robin g:Kheirallah	6th(S8-Q)	2,130

● *Played at St James' Park, Newcastle*
●● *Played at Bloomfield Road, Blackpool*
●●● *Played at Stadium Municipal, Albi*

		APP		TRIES		GOALS		FG		PTS	
	D.O.B.	ALL	Ch	ALL	Ch	ALL	Ch	ALL	Ch	ALL	Ch
Bastien Ader	6/6/91	28	21	16	14	0	0	0	0	64	56
William Barthau	30/1/90	22(6)	19(2)	14	13	1	1	0	0	58	54
Andrew Bentley	13/5/85	12(1)	12(1)	0	0	0	0	0	0	0	0
Justin Bouscayrol	15/12/97	(2)	(2)	1	1	0	0	0	0	4	4
Charles Bouzinac	10/1/94	3(11)	3(11)	4	4	0	0	0	0	16	16
Clement Boyer	27/7/94	12(13)	11(9)	2	2	0	0	0	0	8	8
Joe Bretherton	5/10/95	11(1)	8(1)	2	2	0	0	0	0	8	8
Bastien Canet	26/6/93	20(3)	18(1)	9	8	0	0	0	0	36	32
Chris Centrone	24/7/91	16	9	15	7	0	0	0	0	60	28
Rhys Curran	7/7/89	23	18	14	13	0	0	0	0	56	52
Johnathon Ford	17/8/89	26	19	5	4	0	0	0	0	20	16
Tyla Hepi	15/6/93	1(28)	1(21)	4	4	0	0	0	0	16	16
Mark Kheirallah	15/2/90	30	23	22	20	149	127	0	0	386	334
Mourad Kriouache	10/5/91	10(9)	10(7)	6	6	0	0	0	0	24	24
Pierre-Jean Lima	13/10/00	1	1	0	0	0	0	0	0	0	0
Paul Marcon	10/7/95	20	13	11	9	0	0	0	0	44	36
Gavin Marguerite	12/8/96	20	17	9	8	0	0	0	0	36	32
Anthony Marion	12/1/94	23(5)	16(5)	8	7	0	0	0	0	32	28
Tony Maurel	21/4/93	21	20	13	13	0	0	0	0	52	52
Constantine Mika	14/9/89	23	20	7	7	0	0	0	0	28	28
Eddy Pettybourne	13/2/88	2(8)	2(7)	1	1	0	0	0	0	4	4
Sebastien Planas	5/5/84	13(6)	9(4)	2	2	0	0	0	0	8	8
Maxime Puech	16/3/94	13(10)	7(9)	3	2	0	0	0	0	12	8
Sam Rapira	8/4/87	14(1)	9(1)	0	0	0	0	0	0	0	0
Stan Robin	21/10/90	15(2)	9(1)	13	7	0	0	0	0	52	28
Arthur Romano	17/8/97	3	0	1	0	0	0	0	0	4	0
Justin Sangare	7/3/98	(9)	(8)	4	4	0	0	0	0	16	16
Paul Seguier	8/9/97	(5)	(2)	2	2	0	0	0	0	8	8
Joseph Therond	17/8/98	2	2	0	0	0	0	0	0	0	0
James Worthington	21/5/99	2	2	1	1	0	0	0	0	4	4

'Ch' totals include Championship regular season only; 'All' totals also include Super 8s (Qualifiers)

Mark Kheirallah

LEAGUE RECORD
Championship, before Super 8 split:
P23-W16-D1-L6 (3rd)
F900, A438, Diff+462, 33 points.

S8-Q: P7-W3-D0-L4 (6th)
F156, A190, Diff-34, 6 points.

CHALLENGE CUP
Not entered

ATTENDANCES
Best - v Leigh (Ch - 5,373)
Worst - v Barrow (Ch - 1,177)
Total (all home games included) - 35,525
Average (all home games included) - 2,538
(Up by 724 on 2017)

CLUB RECORDS	
	Highest score: 84-6 v Keighley, 18/6/2016 **Highest score against:** 10-90 v Featherstone, 3/7/2011
MATCH RECORDS	**Record attendance:** 5,373 v Leigh, 16/6/2018 *(Albi)*; 4,127 v Hull KR, 22/9/2018 *(Stade Ernest Argeles)*
	Tries: 4 Mark Kheirallah v Wath Brow, 27/2/2016; Danny Hulme v Coventry, 5/3/2016; Kuni Minga v South Wales, 10/4/2016; Mark Kheirallah v Keighley, 18/6/2016; Mark Kheirallah v London Skolars, 26/8/2016; Tony Maurel v Rochdale, 2/4/2017
	Goals: 12 Mark Kheirallah v Keighley, 18/6/2016 **Points:** 40 Mark Kheirallah v Keighley, 18/6/2016
SEASON RECORDS	**Tries:** 36 Kuni Minga 2016 **Goals:** 171 Mark Kheirallah 2016 **Points:** 466 Mark Kheirallah 2016
CAREER RECORDS	**Tries:** 73 Mark Kheirallah 2016-2018 **Goals:** 440 Mark Kheirallah 2016-2018
	Points: 1,173 Mark Kheirallah 2016-2018 **Appearances:** 128 Sebastien Planas 2009-2011; 2016-2018

● *Records only include seasons when the club competed in the British game (2009-2011 & 2016-2018)*

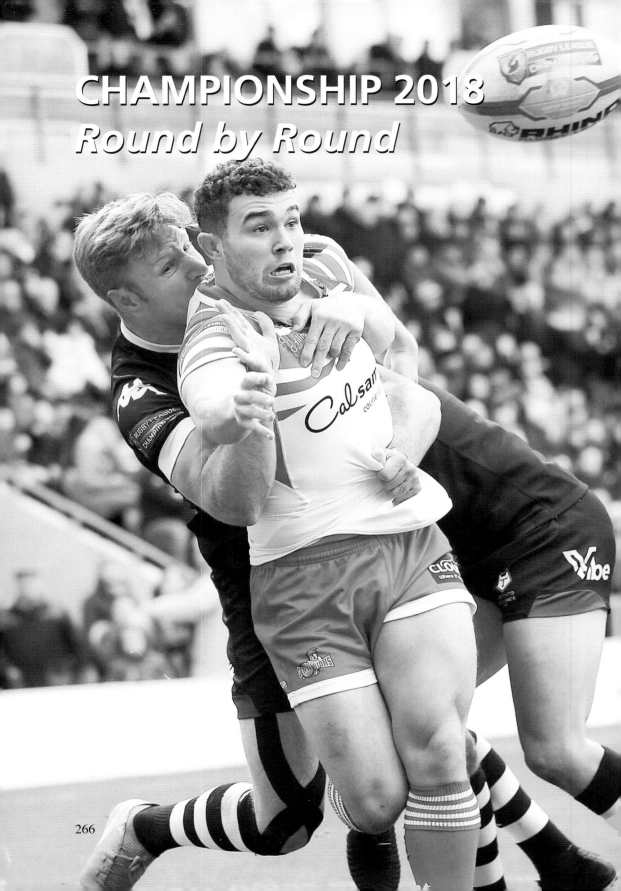

CHAMPIONSHIP 2018
Round by Round

ROUND 1

Friday 2nd February 2018

DEWSBURY RAMS 20 SHEFFIELD EAGLES 18

RAMS: 1 Josh Guzdek; 2 Rob Worrincy; 3 James Glover; 4 Macauley Hallett; 5 Dale Morton; 6 Paul Sykes; 7 Gareth Moore; 8 Jode Sheriffe; 9 Robbie Ward; 10 Jack Teanby; 15 Lucas Walshaw; 12 Michael Knowles; 13 Aaron Brown. Subs (all used): 14 Dom Speakman; 17 Toby Everett; 24 Kyle Trout; 22 Martyn Reilly.
Tries: Glover (8), Worrincy (20), Speakman (35), Morton (61); **Goals:** Sykes 2/4.
EAGLES: 1 Ryan Millar; 2 Iliess Macani; 25 Jake Spedding; 4 Joshua Toole; 5 Ben Blackmore; 23 Cory Aston; 6 Oscar Thomas; 28 Matty Lees; 9 Matty Fozard; 10 Jon Magrin; 27 Jack Ashworth; 12 Shaun Pick; 13 Matt James. Subs (all used): 11 Nabil Djalout; 26 James Bentley; 16 Kieran Moran; 8 Mark Offerdahl.
Tries: Offerdahl (47), Toole (50), Spedding (57); **Goals:** Thomas 3/3.
Rugby Leaguer & League Express Men of the Match: *Rams:* James Glover; *Eagles:* Jack Ashworth.
Penalty count: 8-11; **Half-time:** 14-0;
Referee: Greg Dolan; **Attendance:** 808.

Saturday 3rd February 2018

TOULOUSE OLYMPIQUE 46 SWINTON LIONS 14

OLYMPIQUE: 1 Mark Kheirallah; 2 Tony Maurel; 3 Bastien Ader; 4 Gavin Marguerite; 20 Paul Marcon; 30 William Barthau; 7 Stan Robin; 15 Maxime Puech; 9 Anthony Marion; 10 Bastien Canet; 26 Constantine Mika; 12 Rhys Curran; 13 Andrew Bentley. Subs (all used): 11 Sebastien Planas; 14 Mourad Kriouache; 16 Tyla Hepi; 23 Justin Sangare.
Tries: Barthau (7), Maurel (10, 70), Curran (17), Marcon (37), Robin (65), Marguerite (73), Ader (75), Kheirallah (79); **Goals:** Kheirallah 5/9.
LIONS: 1 Gabriel Fell; 5 Mike Butt; 3 Chris Hankinson; 4 George Tyson; 19 James Worthington; 6 Danny Ansell; 7 Jack Hansen; 8 Andy Bracek; 14 Hayden Hansen; 17 Kyle Shelford; 11 Rhodri Lloyd; 12 Matt Sarsfield; 13 Josh Barlow. Subs (all used): - Oliver Partington; 16 Macauley Davies; 21 Chris Worrell; 22 Conor Taylor.
Tries: Shelford (22), Butt (30); **Goals:** Hankinson 3/4.
Rugby Leaguer & League Express Men of the Match: *Olympique:* Stan Robin; *Lions:* Danny Ansell.
Penalty count: 9-9; **Half-time:** 20-12;
Referee: Tom Grant; **Attendance:** 1,740.

Sunday 4th February 2018

FEATHERSTONE ROVERS 20 HALIFAX 4

ROVERS: 1 Ian Hardman; 5 Luke Briscoe; 20 Josh Hardcastle; 4 Misi Taulapapa; 2 Shaun Robinson; 6 Martyn Ridyard; 19 Tom Holmes; 17 Luke Cooper; 9 Keal Carlile; 8 Scott Wheeldon; 11 Connor Farrell; 12 John Davies; 10 Richard Moore. Subs (all used): 7 Anthony Thackeray; 15 Gareth Hock; 16 Frankie Mariano; 25 Mitch Clark.
Tries: Briscoe (5), Robinson (10), Ridyard (63), Thackeray (71); **Goals:** Ridyard 2/4.
HALIFAX: 1 Will Sharp; 2 Ben Heaton; 16 James Woodburn-Hall; 3 Steve Tyrer; 25 Jy Hitchcox; 6 Scott Murrell; 7 Ben Johnston; 17 Will Maher; 9 Ben Kaye; 8 Elliot Morris; 4 Ed Barber; 12 Simon Grix; 13 Jacob Fairbank. Subs (all used): 29 Dan Fleming; 30 Brandon Douglas; 14 Brandon Moore; 27 Alex Foster.
Try: Heaton (37); **Goals:** Tyrer 0/1.
Rugby Leaguer & League Express Men of the Match: *Rovers:* Martyn Ridyard; *Halifax:* Will Sharp.
Penalty count: 10-8; **Half-time:** 8-4;
Referee: Gareth Hewer; **Attendance:** 2,743.

LEIGH CENTURIONS 12 TORONTO WOLFPACK 34

CENTURIONS: 1 Craig Hall; 2 Matty Dawson-Jones; 3 Ben Crooks; 4 Peter Mata'utia; 19 Jack Owens; 6 Ben Reynolds; 7 Drew Hutchison; 8 Paterika Vaivai; 14 Liam Hood; 10 Jamie Acton; 13 Harrison Hansen; 12 Bodene Thompson; 15 Jordan Thompson. Subs (all used): 9 Daniel Mortimer; 16 Larne Patrick; 17 Kyle Lovett; 18 Nathan Mason.
Tries: Hansen (2), Dawson-Jones (8); **Goals:** Reynolds 2/2.
WOLFPACK: 1 Quentin Laulu-Togagae; 19 Adam Higson; 3 Greg Worthington; 23 Nick Rawsthorne; 5 Liam Kay; 6 Josh McCrone; 7 Ryan Brierley; 29 Jake Emmitt; 9 Bob Beswick; 28 Sam Hopkins; 11 Andrew Dixon; 24 Cory Paterson; 12 Joe Westerman. Subs (all used): 14 Andy Ackers; 15 Adam Sidlow; 8 Jack Buchanan; 13 Jack Bussey.
Tries: Sidlow (20), Kay (30, 54, 79), Paterson (48), Brierley (57); **Goals:** Brierley 5/7.
Sin bin: Higson (23) - high tackle on Mason.
Rugby Leaguer & League Express Men of the Match: *Centurions:* Paterika Vaivai; *Wolfpack:* Quentin Laulu-Togagae.
Penalty count: 10-14; **Half-time:** 12-10;
Referee: Liam Moore; **Attendance:** 5,452.

LONDON BRONCOS 56 BARROW RAIDERS 12

BRONCOS: 14 Alex Walker; 2 Rhys Williams; 21 Will Lovell; 3 Ben Hellewell; 5 Kieran Dixon; 27 James Meadows; 7 Jarrod Sammut; 8 Tom Spencer; 9 James Cunningham; 10 Mark Ioane; 11 Daniel Harrison; 12 Jay Pitts; 13 Matt Davis. Subs (all used): 19 Sadiq Adebiyi; 16 Matty Gee; 15 Eddie Battye; 29 Sam Davis.
Tries: Meadows (10), Williams (20), Harrison (35), Dixon (49, 75), Battye (52), Sammut (65), Ioane (69), Matt Davis (77), Walker (78); **Goals:** Sammut 8/10.
RAIDERS: 1 Ryan Fieldhouse; 2 Shane Toal; 3 Declan Hulme; 4 Andy Litherland; 5 Brett Carter; 6 Jamie Dallimore; 7 Lewis Charnock; 8 Joe Bullock; 22 Dean Parata; 17 Alec Susino; 25 Jono Smith; 12 Jarrad Stack; 13 Martin Aspinwall. Subs (all used): 9 Nathan Mossop; 10 Tom Walker; 15 Glenn Riley; 11 Dan Toal.
Tries: Dallimore (30), Fieldhouse (80);
Goals: Charnock 1/1, Dallimore 1/1.
Rugby Leaguer & League Express Men of the Match: *Broncos:* Daniel Harrison; *Raiders:* Jamie Dallimore.
Penalty count: 11-8; **Half-time:** 18-6;
Referee: John McMullen; **Attendance:** 801.

ROUND 2

Sunday 11th February 2018

BARROW RAIDERS 8 TORONTO WOLFPACK 8

RAIDERS: 1 Ryan Fieldhouse; 5 Brett Carter; 3 Declan Hulme; 23 Tom Loxam; 2 Shane Toal; 6 Jamie Dallimore; 14 Karl Ashall; 8 Joe Bullock; 22 Dean Parata; 17 Alec Susino; 12 Jarrad Stack; 25 Jono Smith; 13 Martin Aspinwall. Subs (all used): 9 Nathan Mossop; 10 Tom Walker; 15 Glenn Riley; 11 Dan Toal.
Try: D Toal (55); **Goals:** Dallimore 2/2.
WOLFPACK: 1 Quentin Laulu-Togagae; 5 Liam Kay; 3 Greg Worthington; 23 Nick Rawsthorne; 19 Adam Higson; 6 Josh McCrone; 7 Ryan Brierley; 8 Jack Buchanan; 9 Bob Beswick; 13 Jack Bussey; 11 Andrew Dixon; 22 Richard Whiting; 29 Jake Emmitt. Subs (all used): 14 Andy Ackers; 21 Olsi Krasniqi; 15 Adam Sidlow; 17 Blake Wallace.
Tries: Dixon (24), Rawsthorne (42); **Goals:** Brierley 0/2.
Rugby Leaguer & League Express Men of the Match: *Raiders:* Tom Walker; *Wolfpack:* Jack Bussey.
Penalty count: 9-9; **Half-time:** 2-4;
Referee: Gareth Hewer; **Attendance:** 1,266.

DEWSBURY RAMS 0 LONDON BRONCOS 12

RAMS: 1 Josh Guzdek; 25 Jared Simpson; 3 James Glover; 4 Macauley Hallett; 5 Dale Morton; 6 Paul Sykes; 7 Gareth Moore; 8 Jode Sheriffe; 9 Robbie Ward; 10 Jack Teanby; 20 Jordan Crowther; 16 Billy Hayes; 13 Aaron Brown. Subs (all used): 14 Dom Speakman; 24 Kyle Trout; 15 Lucas Walshaw; 26 Matty English.
BRONCOS: 14 Alex Walker; 2 Rhys Williams; 21 Will Lovell; 3 Ben Hellewell; 5 Kieran Dixon; 27 James Meadows; 7 Jarrod Sammut; 8 Tom Spencer; 9 James Cunningham; 10 Mark Ioane; 16 Matty Gee; 12 Jay Pitts; 13 Matt Davis. Subs (all used): 15 Eddie Battye; 19 Sadiq Adebiyi; 11 Daniel Harrison; 28 Jordan Johnstone.
Tries: Battye (23), Sammut (68); **Goals:** Sammut 2/3.
Rugby Leaguer & League Express Men of the Match: *Rams:* Jack Teanby; *Broncos:* Alex Walker.
Penalty count: 10-9; **Half-time:** 0-6;
Referee: Tom Crashley; **Attendance:** 795.

FEATHERSTONE ROVERS 36 TOULOUSE OLYMPIQUE 18

ROVERS: 7 Anthony Thackeray; 5 Luke Briscoe; 20 Josh Hardcastle; 26 Ash Handley; 4 Misi Taulapapa; 6 Martyn Ridyard; 19 Tom Holmes; 10 Richard Moore; 9 Keal Carlile; 8 Scott Wheeldon; 11 Connor Farrell; 12 John Davies; 13 James Lockwood. Subs (all used): 14 Matty Wildie; 21 Bradley Knowles; 15 Gareth Hock; 25 Mitch Clark.
Tries: Briscoe (29, 75), Thackeray (45), Clark (54), Davies (57), Hardcastle (67); **Goals:** Ridyard 6/8.
OLYMPIQUE: 1 Mark Kheirallah; 20 Paul Marcon; 4 Gavin Marguerite; 3 Bastien Ader; 2 Tony Maurel; 30 William Barthau; 7 Stan Robin; 15 Maxime Puech; 19 Charles Bouzinac; 10 Bastien Canet; 12 Rhys Curran; 26 Constantine Mika; 9 Anthony Marion. Subs (all used): 14 Mourad Kriouache; 13 Andrew Bentley; 16 Tyla Hepi; 17 Eddy Pettybourne.
Tries: Marcon (18, 42), Curran (38), Marguerite (78); **Goals:** Kheirallah 1/4.
Sin bin: Hepi (23) - punching Handley.
Rugby Leaguer & League Express Men of the Match: *Rovers:* Mitch Clark; *Olympique:* Stan Robin.
Penalty count: 10-9; **Half-time:** 8-10;
Referee: Scott Mikalauskas; **Attendance:** 2,033.

HALIFAX 30 SHEFFIELD EAGLES 10

HALIFAX: 1 Will Sharp; 26 James Clare; 3 Steve Tyrer; 4 Ed Barber; 5 James Saltonstall; 6 Scott Murrell; 16 James Woodburn-Hall; 29 Dan Fleming; 14 Brandon Moore; 27 Daniel Murray; 12 Simon Grix; 11 Shane Grady; 13 Jacob Fairbank. Subs (all used): 8 Elliot Morris; 30 Brandon Douglas; 9 Ben Kaye; 17 Will Maher.
Tries: Murray (2, 71), Woodburn-Hall (19), Barber (44), Fleming (75); **Goals:** Tyrer 5/5.
EAGLES: 1 Ryan Millar; 24 Garry Lo; 25 Jake Spedding; 4 Joshua Toole; 5 Ben Blackmore; 6 Oscar Thomas; 23 Cory Aston; 28 Matty Lees; 9 Matty Fozard; 8 Mark Offerdahl; 13 Matt James; 27 Jack Ashworth; 16 Kieran Moran. Subs (all used): 14 Greg Burns; 10 Jon Magrin; 11 Nabil Djalout; 12 Shaun Pick.
Tries: Ashworth (13), James (62);
Goals: Thomas 1/1, Aston 0/1.
Rugby Leaguer & League Express Men of the Match: *Halifax:* Daniel Murray; *Eagles:* Cory Aston.
Penalty count: 8-9; **Half-time:** 12-6;
Referee: John McMullen; **Attendance:** 1,513.

LEIGH CENTURIONS 34 BATLEY BULLDOGS 6

CENTURIONS: 19 Jack Owens; 2 Matty Dawson-Jones; 3 Ben Crooks; 4 Peter Mata'utia; 25 Ilias Bergal; 6 Ben Reynolds; 7 Drew Hutchison; 8 Paterika Vaivai; 14 Liam Hood; 18 Nathan Mason; 11 Kevin Larroyer; 12 Bodene Thompson; 15 Jordan Thompson. Subs (all used): 27 Kurt Baptiste; 10 Jamie Acton; 16 Larne Patrick; 13 Harrison Hansen.
Tries: Crooks (7, 30), Mason (20), Larroyer (49), Dawson-Jones (54), Acton (65); **Goals:** Reynolds 5/6.
BULLDOGS: 1 Dave Scott; 2 Wayne Reittie; 4 Jason Crookes; 29 Lewis Galbraith; 5 Shaun Ainscough; 6 Pat Walker; 7 Dominic Brambani; 8 Adam Gledhill; 9 Alistair Leak; 20 Alex Rowe; 11 Dane Manning; 15 James Harrison; 21 James Brown. Subs (all used): 14 James Davey; 13 Brad Day; 24 Tommy Holland; 16 Michael Ward.
Try: Rowe (39); **Goals:** Walker 1/1.
Rugby Leaguer & League Express Men of the Match: *Centurions:* Jack Owens; *Bulldogs:* Dave Scott.
Penalty count: 11-8; **Half-time:** 18-6;
Referee: Greg Dolan; **Attendance:** 3,216.

ROUND 3

Saturday 17th February 2018

TOULOUSE OLYMPIQUE 50 SHEFFIELD EAGLES 6

OLYMPIQUE: 1 Mark Kheirallah; 2 Tony Maurel; 3 Bastien Ader; 4 Gavin Marguerite; 20 Paul Marcon; 30 William Barthau; 7 Stan Robin; 16 Tyla Hepi; 19 Charles Bouzinac; 10 Bastien Canet; 26 Constantine Mika; 12 Rhys Curran; 13 Andrew Bentley. Subs (all used): 8 Clement Boyer; 14 Mourad Kriouache; 17 Eddy Pettybourne; 23 Justin Sangare.
Tries: Marcon (12), Kriouache (30), Mika (44), Sangare (49, 65), Robin (51), Barthau (56, 60), Kheirallah (69); **Goals:** Kheirallah 7/9.
Sin bin: Canet (18) - dangerous challenge.
EAGLES: 1 Ryan Millar; 24 Garry Lo; 5 Ben Blackmore; 25 Jake Spedding; 2 Iliess Macani; 6 Oscar Thomas; 23 Cory Aston; 28 Matty Lees; 9 Matty Fozard; 10 Jon Magrin; 15 Olly Davies; 26 James Bentley; 12 Shaun Pick. Subs (all used): 8 Mark Offerdahl; 14 Greg Burns; 17 Daniel Igbinedion; 20 Max Garcia.
Try: Aston (9); **Goals:** Thomas 1/1.
Rugby Leaguer & League Express Men of the Match: *Olympique:* William Barthau; *Eagles:* Matty Fozard.
Penalty count: 7-5; **Half-time:** 8-6;
Referee: Liam Moore; **Attendance:** 1,533.

Sunday 18th February 2018

BARROW RAIDERS 24 LEIGH CENTURIONS 20

RAIDERS: 1 Ryan Fieldhouse; 2 Shane Toal; 12 Jarrad Stack; 3 Declan Hulme; 5 Brett Carter; 6 Jamie Dallimore; 14 Karl Ashall; 27 Ryan Duffy; 22 Dean Parata; 17 Alec Susino; 11 Dan Toal; 19 Bradd Crellin; 13 Martin Aspinwall. Subs (all used): 9 Nathan Mossop; 8 Joe Bullock; 15 Glenn Riley; 10 Tom Walker.
Tries: S Toal (17, 26, 71), Fieldhouse (56);
Goals: Dallimore 4/5.
CENTURIONS: 19 Jack Owens; 2 Matty Dawson-Jones; 3 Ben Crooks; 4 Peter Mata'utia; 25 Ilias Bergal; 6 Ben Reynolds; 7 Drew Hutchison; 8 Paterika Vaivai; 14 Liam Hood; 18 Nathan Mason; 11 Kevin Larroyer; 12 Bodene Thompson; 15 Jordan Thompson. Subs (all used): 9 Daniel Mortimer; 10 Jamie Acton; 13 Harrison Hansen; 16 Larne Patrick.
Tries: Bergal (8, 40), Mata'utia (24), Patrick (36);
Goals: Reynolds 2/4.
Rugby Leaguer & League Express Men of the Match: *Raiders:* Shane Toal; *Centurions:* Ilias Bergal.
Penalty count: 7-7; **Half-time:** 12-20;
Referee: John McMullen; **Attendance:** 1,991.

Championship 2018 - Round by Round

HALIFAX 6 TORONTO WOLFPACK 20

HALIFAX: 1 Will Sharp; 5 James Saltonstall; 4 Ed Barber; 3 Steve Tyrer; 23 James Clare; 6 Scott Murrell; 16 James Woodburn-Hall; 17 Will Maher; 14 Brandon Moore; 27 Daniel Murray; 12 Simon Grix; 18 Chester Butler; 13 Jacob Fairbank. Subs (all used): 8 Elliot Morris; 9 Ben Kaye; 28 James Green; 30 Brandon Douglas.
Try: Butler (39); **Goals:** Tyrer 1/1.
WOLFPACK: 1 Quentin Laulu-Togagae; 5 Liam Kay; 3 Greg Worthington; 23 Nick Rawsthorne; 19 Adam Higson; 7 Ryan Brierley; 6 Josh McCrone; 10 Ashton Sims; 9 Bob Beswick; 8 Jack Buchanan; 11 Andrew Dixon; 22 Richard Whiting; 12 Joe Westerman. Subs (all used): 29 Jake Emmitt; 21 Olsi Krasniqi; 15 Adam Sidlow; 14 Andy Ackers.
Tries: Worthington (31), Rawsthorne (45), Higson (72, 80); **Goals:** Brierley 2/5.
Sin bin: McCrone (50) - dangerous challenge.
Rugby League & League Express Men of the Match: *Halifax:* Elliot Morris; *Wolfpack:* Adam Higson.
Penalty count: 12-10; **Half-time:** 6-4;
Referee: Jack Smith; **Attendance:** 2,036.

LONDON BRONCOS 44 FEATHERSTONE ROVERS 24

BRONCOS: 14 Alex Walker; 5 Kieran Dixon; 4 Matty Fleming; 3 Ben Hellewell; 2 Rhys Williams; 27 James Meadows; 7 Jarrod Sammut; 8 Tom Spencer; 9 James Cunningham; 10 Mark Ioane; 12 Jay Pitts; 16 Matty Gee; 13 Matt Davis. Subs (all used): 15 Eddie Battye; 20 Lewis Bienek; 19 Sadiq Adebiyi; 28 Jordan Johnstone.
Tries: Sammut (8, 24, 59), Pitts (12), Walker (36), Dixon (55, 57); **Goals:** Sammut 7/7, Dixon 1/1.
Sin bin: Sammut (45) - high tackle.
ROVERS: 7 Anthony Thackeray; 5 Luke Briscoe; 20 Josh Hardcastle; 1 Ian Hardman; 4 Misi Taulapapa; 6 Martyn Ridyard; 19 Tom Holmes; 8 Scott Wheeldon; 9 Keal Carlile; 17 Luke Cooper; 11 Connor Farrell; 12 John Davies; 13 James Lockwood. Subs (all used): 14 Matty Wildie; 10 Richard Moore; 25 Mitch Clark; 22 Sam Brooks.
Tries: Taulapapa (18), Hardcastle (38, 63), Briscoe (69), Lockwood (73); **Goals:** Ridyard 2/5.
Dismissal: Moore (43) - swinging arm on Cunningham.
Rugby League & League Express Men of the Match: *Broncos:* Jarrod Sammut; *Rovers:* Josh Hardcastle.
Penalty count: 14-15; **Half-time:** 26-10;
Referee: Tom Grant; **Attendance:** 1,085.

SWINTON LIONS 28 BATLEY BULLDOGS 48

LIONS: 1 Gabriel Fell; 5 Mike Butt; 3 Chris Hankinson; 11 Rhodri Lloyd; 16 Liam Forsyth; 31 Josh Woods; 7 Jack Hansen; 8 Andy Bracek; 9 Luke Waterworth; 17 Kyle Shelford; 32 Macauley Davies; 12 Matt Sarsfield; 33 Gavin Bennion. Subs (all used): 13 Josh Barlow; 14 Hayden Hansen; - Samy Kibula; 22 Conor Taylor.
Tries: Fell (3), J Hansen (33), Hankinson (36), Waterworth (63), Sarsfield (67); **Goals:** Hankinson 4/5.
Sin bin: Barlow (49) - punching.
On report:
H Hansen (44) - alleged late challenge on Walker.
BULLDOGS: 1 Dave Scott; 2 Wayne Reittie; 4 Jason Crookes; 29 Lewis Galbraith; 5 Shaun Ainscough; 6 Pat Walker; 7 Dominic Brambani; 8 Adam Gledhill; 9 Alistair Leak; 20 Alex Rowe; 11 Dane Manning; 13 Brad Day; 21 James Brown. Subs (all used): 17 Joe Chandler; 14 James Davey; 24 Tommy Holland; 16 Michael Ward.
Tries: Galbraith (11, 30), Reittie (23), Gledhill (27), Ward (50, 53), Day (55), Scott (61), Leak (71);
Goals: Walker 6/9.
Rugby League & League Express Men of the Match: *Lions:* Chris Hankinson; *Bulldogs:* Lewis Galbraith.
Penalty count: 7-10; **Half-time:** 16-20;
Referee: Gareth Hewer; **Attendance:** 588
(at AJ Bell Stadium, Salford).

Monday 19th February 2018

ROCHDALE HORNETS 6 DEWSBURY RAMS 38

HORNETS: 2 Declan Kay; 31 Deon Cross; 30 Luis Johnson; 3 Earl Hurst; 5 Rob Massam; 6 Lewis Palfrey; 7 Danny Yates; 13 Luke Adamson; 9 Ben Moores; 10 Matty Hadden; 23 Gary Middlehurst; 19 Lee Mitchell; 26 Harvey Livett. Subs (all used): 14 Ryan Maneely; 15 Lewis Hatton; 8 Jovili Taira; 16 Pat Moran.
Try: L Adamson (63); **Goals:** Livett 1/1.
Sin bin: Middlehurst (24) - fighting.
RAMS: 1 Josh Guzdek; 2 Rob Worrincy; 3 James Glover; 4 Macauley Hallett; 5 Dale Morton; 6 Paul Sykes; 12 Michael Knowles; 8 Jode Sheriffe; 9 Robbie Ward; 10 Jack Teanby; 11 Rob Spicer; 20 Jordan Crowther; 13 Aaron Brown. Subs (all used): 14 Dom Speakman; 15 Lucas Walshaw; 26 Matty English; 17 Toby Everett.
Tries: Morton (8), Glover (13), Worrincy (16, 40), Brown (26, 35), Guzdek (59); **Goals:** Sykes 5/7.
Rugby League & League Express Men of the Match: *Hornets:* Lewis Palfrey; *Rams:* James Glover.
Penalty count: 9-5; **Half-time:** 0-32;
Referee: Nick Bennett; **Attendance:** 427.

ROUND 4

Sunday 25th February 2018

BATLEY BULLDOGS 32 BARROW RAIDERS 12

BULLDOGS: 1 Dave Scott; 2 Wayne Reittie; 22 Danny Cowling; 4 Jason Crookes; 5 Shaun Ainscough; 6 Pat Walker; 7 Dominic Brambani; 8 Adam Gledhill; 9 Alistair Leak; 20 Alex Rowe; 11 Dane Manning; 13 Brad Day; 24 Tommy Holland. Subs (all used): 18 Tom Hemingway; 17 Joe Chandler; 16 Michael Ward; 21 James Brown.
Tries: Day (13, 43), Manning (27), Reittie (36), Scott (49, 59); **Goals:** Walker 4/6.
Sin bin: Chandler (79) - fighting.
RAIDERS: 1 Ryan Fieldhouse; 2 Shane Toal; 12 Jarrad Stack; 3 Declan Hulme; 5 Brett Carter; 6 Jamie Dallimore; 14 Karl Ashall; 27 Ryan Duffy; 22 Dean Parata; 17 Alec Susino; 24 Danny Morrow; 19 Bradd Crellin; 13 Martin Aspinwall. Subs (all used): 9 Nathan Mossop; 8 Joe Bullock; 10 Tom Walker; 15 Glenn Riley.
Tries: Fieldhouse (5), Susino (9); **Goals:** Dallimore 2/2.
Sin bin: Parata (79) - fighting.
Rugby League & League Express Men of the Match: *Bulldogs:* Brad Day; *Raiders:* Joe Bullock.
Penalty count: 10-12; **Half-time:** 16-12;
Referee: Greg Dolan; **Attendance:** 657.

DEWSBURY RAMS 20 SWINTON LIONS 0

RAMS: 1 Josh Guzdek; 2 Rob Worrincy; 3 James Glover; 4 Macauley Hallett; 25 Jared Simpson; 6 Paul Sykes; 12 Michael Knowles; 8 Jode Sheriffe; 9 Robbie Ward; 10 Jack Teanby; 20 Jordan Crowther; 11 Rob Spicer; 13 Aaron Brown. Subs (all used): 14 Dom Speakman; 15 Lucas Walshaw; 26 Matty English; 17 Toby Everett.
Tries: Spicer (25), Brown (46), Hallett (69);
Goals: Sykes 4/5.
LIONS: 1 Gabriel Fell; 5 Mike Butt; 3 Chris Hankinson; 4 George Tyson; 16 Liam Forsyth; 31 Josh Woods; 7 Jack Hansen; 8 Andy Bracek; 9 Luke Waterworth; 17 Kyle Shelford; 11 Rhodri Lloyd; 12 Matt Sarsfield; 33 Gavin Bennion. Subs (all used): 13 Josh Barlow; 14 Hayden Hansen; 18 Mark Nicholson; 22 Conor Taylor.
Rugby League & League Express Men of the Match: *Rams:* Michael Knowles; *Lions:* Gavin Bennion.
Penalty count: 10-7; **Half-time:** 10-0;
Referee: Jon Roberts; **Attendance:** 961.

FEATHERSTONE ROVERS 58 SHEFFIELD EAGLES 14

ROVERS: 1 Ian Hardman; 5 Luke Briscoe; 20 Josh Hardcastle; 7 Anthony Thackeray; 2 Shaun Robinson; 6 Martyn Ridyard; 19 Tom Holmes; 10 Richard Moore; 9 Keal Carlile; 8 Scott Wheeldon; 11 Connor Farrell; 16 Frankie Mariano; 25 Mitch Clark. Subs (all used): 14 Matty Wildie; 21 Bradley Knowles; 15 Gareth Hock; 22 Sam Brooks.
Tries: Robinson (2, 5), Ridyard (20), Briscoe (26), Brooks (36), Mariano (46), Hardman (53), Thackeray (55, 79), Wildie (58), Hardcastle (67);
Goals: Ridyard 0/1, Hardman 7/10.
EAGLES: 6 Oscar Thomas; 2 Iliess Macani; 17 Daniel Igbinedion; 25 Jake Spedding; 1 Ryan Millar; 9 Matty Fozard; 23 Cory Aston; 28 Matty Lees; 14 Greg Burns; 12 Shaun Pick; 15 Olly Davies; 26 James Bentley; 13 Matt James. Subs (all used): 16 Kieran Moran; 8 Mark Offerdahl; 11 Nabil Djalout; 10 Jon Magrin.
Tries: Macani (22, 50), Fozard (64); **Goals:** Thomas 1/3.
Rugby League & League Express Men of the Match: *Rovers:* Ian Hardman; *Eagles:* Matty Fozard.
Penalty count: 7-6; **Half-time:** 24-4;
Referee: John McMullen; **Attendance:** 2,048.

LONDON BRONCOS 47 TORONTO WOLFPACK 16

BRONCOS: 14 Alex Walker; 5 Kieran Dixon; 3 Ben Hellewell; 4 Matty Fleming; 2 Rhys Williams; 6 Api Pewhairangi; 7 Jarrod Sammut; 8 Tom Spencer; 9 James Cunningham; 10 Mark Ioane; 12 Jay Pitts; 21 Will Lovell; 13 Matt Davis. Subs (all used): 15 Eddie Battye; 23 Rob Butler; 19 Sadiq Adebiyi; 28 Jordan Johnstone.
Tries: Pewhairangi (6), Matt Davis (15), Williams (26), Johnstone (52), Walker (65, 79), Cunningham (71);
Goals: Sammut 9/10; **Field goal:** Sammut (39).
WOLFPACK: 1 Quentin Laulu-Togagae; 2 Jonny Pownall; 3 Greg Worthington; 23 Nick Rawsthorne; 5 Liam Kay; 6 Josh McCrone; 7 Ryan Brierley; 29 Jake Emmitt; 9 Bob Beswick; 10 Ashton Sims; 11 Andrew Dixon; 22 Richard Whiting; 12 Joe Westerman. Subs (all used): 15 Adam Sidlow; 8 Jack Buchanan; 21 Olsi Krasniqi; 14 Andy Ackers.
Tries: Whiting (19), Dixon (33), Kay (54); **Goals:** Brierley 2/3.
Sin bin: Dixon (58) - professional foul.
Rugby League & League Express Men of the Match: *Broncos:* Jarrod Sammut; *Wolfpack:* Liam Kay.
Penalty count: 6-4; **Half-time:** 21-12;
Referee: Matt Rossleigh; **Attendance:** 1,000.

ROCHDALE HORNETS 20 HALIFAX 26

HORNETS: 21 Richard Lepori; 30 Deon Cross; 3 Earl Hurst; - Toby King; 5 Rob Massam; 6 Lewis Palfrey; 7 Danny Yates; 8 Jovili Taira; 9 Ben Moores; 13 Luke Adamson; 11 Dave Allen; 19 Lee Mitchell; - Harvey Livett. Subs (all used): 12 Toby Adamson; 14 Ryan Maneely; 16 Pat Moran; 26 Luis Johnson.
Tries: Massam (11), Moran (44), Livett (79);
Goals: Livett 4/4.
HALIFAX: 1 Will Sharp; 25 James Clare; 2 Ben Heaton; 3 Steve Tyrer; 5 James Saltonstall; 6 Scott Murrell; 16 James Woodburn-Hall; 17 Will Maher; 14 Brandon Moore; 27 Daniel Murray; 4 Ed Barber; 12 Simon Grix; 13 Jacob Fairbank. Subs (all used): 29 Dan Fleming; 9 Ben Kaye; 26 Sion Jones; 8 Elliot Morris.
Tries: Kaye (38), Sharp (51, 63), Grix (58), Barber (78);
Goals: Tyrer 3/6.
On report:
Woodburn-Hall (55) - alleged dangerous challenge.
Rugby League & League Express Men of the Match: *Hornets:* Harvey Livett; *Halifax:* Will Sharp.
Penalty count: 5-13; **Half-time:** 8-6;
Referee: Tom Grant; **Attendance:** 703.

LEIGH CENTURIONS 26 TOULOUSE OLYMPIQUE 32

CENTURIONS: 19 Jack Owens; 2 Matty Dawson-Jones; 3 Ben Crooks; 4 Peter Mata'utia; 25 Ilias Bergal; 9 Daniel Mortimer; 7 Drew Hutchison; 8 Paterika Vaivai; 14 Liam Hood; 13 Harrison Hansen; 11 Kevin Larroyer; 12 Bodene Thompson; 15 Jordan Thompson. Subs (all used): 23 Jonah Cunningham; 10 Jamie Acton; 18 Nathan Mason; 20 Greg Richards.
Tries: Dawson-Jones (22, 33), Hood (24, 45), Bergal (67);
Goals: Owens 3/5.
OLYMPIQUE: 1 Mark Kheirallah; 20 Paul Marcon; 4 Gavin Marguerite; 3 Bastien Ader; 21 Joseph Therond; 30 William Barthau; 7 Stan Robin; 15 Maxime Puech; 9 Anthony Marion; 10 Bastien Canet; 26 Constantine Mika; 12 Rhys Curran; 13 Andrew Bentley. Subs (all used): 19 Charles Bouzinac; 8 Clement Boyer; 16 Tyla Hepi; 17 Eddy Pettybourne.
Tries: Curran (3), Marguerite (48, 74), Canet (54), Kheirallah (72), Robin (78); **Goals:** Kheirallah 4/6.
Dismissal: Pettybourne (37) - high tackle on Acton.
Rugby League & League Express Men of the Match: *Centurions:* Liam Hood; *Olympique:* Mark Kheirallah.
Penalty count: 7-6; **Half-time:** 14-6;
Referee: Jack Smith; **Attendance:** 3,143.

ROUND 5

Saturday 3rd March 2018

TOULOUSE OLYMPIQUE 54 ROCHDALE HORNETS 6

OLYMPIQUE: 1 Mark Kheirallah; 2 Tony Maurel; 3 Bastien Ader; 11 Sebastien Planas; 20 Paul Marcon; 6 Johnathon Ford; 30 William Barthau; 18 Sam Rapira; 9 Anthony Marion; 10 Bastien Canet; 26 Constantine Mika; 12 Rhys Curran; 17 Eddy Pettybourne. Subs (all used): 8 Clement Boyer; 14 Mourad Kriouache; 15 Maxime Puech; 23 Justin Sangare.
Tries: Barthau (3, 35), Ader (17), Maurel (24), Marcon (31, 62), Mika (39), Kriouache (54), Canet (57, 75);
Goals: Kheirallah 7/10.
Sin bin: Puech (49) - fighting.
HORNETS: 4 Jack Johnson; 21 Richard Lepori; 3 Earl Hurst; 31 Deon Cross; 5 Rob Massam; - Harvey Livett; 7 Danny Yates; 20 Blake Turner; 24 Declan Gregory; 13 Luke Adamson; 11 Dave Allen; 19 Lee Mitchell; 9 Ben Moores. Subs (all used): 12 Toby Adamson; 14 Ryan Maneely; 16 Pat Moran; 18 Billy Brickhill.
Try: Gregory (20); **Goals:** Livett 1/1.
Sin bin: L Adamson (49) - fighting.
Rugby League & League Express Men of the Match: *Olympique:* William Barthau; *Hornets:* Declan Gregory.
Penalty count: 4-8; **Half-time:** 34-6;
Referee: Matt Rossleigh; **Attendance:** 1,747.

Sunday 4th March 2018

LEIGH CENTURIONS 30 FEATHERSTONE ROVERS 38

CENTURIONS: 1 Craig Hall; 2 Matty Dawson-Jones; 3 Ben Crooks; 4 Peter Mata'utia; 5 Rhys Evans; 6 Ben Reynolds; 7 Drew Hutchison; 20 Greg Richards; 14 Liam Hood; 13 Harrison Hansen; 16 Larne Patrick; 12 Bodene Thompson; 15 Jordan Thompson. Subs (all used): 30 Micky Higham; 8 Paterika Vaivai; 10 Jamie Acton; 11 Kevin Larroyer.
Tries: Evans (8), Crooks (16, 31, 61), B Thompson (28), Dawson-Jones (56); **Goals:** Reynolds 0/1, Hall 3/6.

ROVERS: 1 Ian Hardman; 5 Luke Briscoe; 20 Josh Hardcastle; 7 Anthony Thackeray; 2 Shaun Robinson; 6 Martyn Ridyard; 19 Tom Holmes; 25 Mitch Clark; 9 Keal Carlile; 28 Mikolaj Oledzki; 11 Connor Farrell; 16 Frankie Mariano; 21 Bradley Knowles. Subs (all used): 14 Matty Wildie; 15 Gareth Hock; 27 Jack Ormondroyd; 22 Sam Brooks.
Tries: Briscoe (3, 78), Robinson (19), Farrell (25), Ridyard (53, 64), Clark (74);
Goals: Hardman 1/4, Ridyard 4/4.
Rugby Leaguer & League Express Men of the Match: *Centurions:* Ben Crooks; *Rovers:* Martyn Ridyard.
Penalty count: 9-5; **Half-time:** 20-14;
Referee: Chris Kendall; **Attendance:** 3,594.

SWINTON LIONS 12 TORONTO WOLFPACK 52

LIONS: 1 Gabriel Fell; 5 Mike Butt; 11 Rhodri Lloyd; 4 George Tyson; 23 Elliott Caine; 31 Josh Woods; 7 Jack Hansen; 8 Andy Bracek; 9 Luke Waterworth; 33 Gavin Bennion; 18 Mark Nicholson; 12 Matt Sarsfield; 17 Kyle Shelford. Subs (all used): 15 Ben Austin; 13 Josh Barlow; 14 Hayden Hansen; - Romain Navarrete.
Tries: Butt (6), Waterworth (76); **Goals:** Woods 2/2.
WOLFPACK: 1 Quentin Laulu-Togagae; 2 Jonny Pownall; 3 Greg Worthington; 25 Jake Butler-Fleming; 5 Liam Kay; 17 Blake Wallace; 7 Ryan Brierley; 8 Jack Buchanan; 9 Bob Beswick; 10 Ashton Sims; 11 Andrew Dixon; 16 Reni Maitua; 12 Joe Westerman. Subs (all used): 15 Adam Sidlow; 18 James Laithwaite; 21 Olsi Krasniqi; 14 Andy Ackers.
Tries: Butler-Fleming (2, 63), Brierley (18, 47), Laulu-Togagae (21), Wallace (30, 61), Ackers (40), Pownall (51); **Goals:** Brierley 8/9.
Rugby Leaguer & League Express Men of the Match: *Lions:* George Tyson; *Wolfpack:* Blake Wallace.
Penalty count: 10-6; **Half-time:** 6-30;
Referee: Jack Smith; **Attendance:** 701.

ROUND 6

Sunday 11th March 2018

DEWSBURY RAMS 20 TOULOUSE OLYMPIQUE 40

RAMS: 1 Josh Guzdek; 25 Jared Simpson; 3 James Glover; 4 Macauley Hallett; 5 Dale Morton; 6 Paul Sykes; 12 Michael Knowles; 8 Jode Sheriffe; 9 Robbie Ward; 10 Jack Teanby; 20 Jordan Crowther; 11 Rob Spicer; 13 Aaron Brown. Subs (all used): 14 Dom Speakman; 15 Lucas Walshaw; 26 Matty English; 17 Toby Everett.
Tries: Ward (15), Morton (45), Spicer (48), Knowles (65);
Goals: Sykes 2/4.
Sin bin: Speakman (77) - punching.
OLYMPIQUE: 1 Mark Kheirallah; 20 Paul Marcon; 11 Sebastien Planas; 3 Bastien Ader; 2 Tony Maurel; 6 Johnathon Ford; 7 Stan Robin; 18 Sam Rapira; 9 Anthony Marion; 10 Bastien Canet; 26 Constantine Mika; 12 Rhys Curran; 13 Andrew Bentley. Subs (all used): 30 William Barthau; 8 Clement Boyer; 16 Tyla Hepi; 23 Justin Sangare.
Tries: Curran (18, 67), Robin (21), Hepi (37, 40), Maurel (57), Kheirallah (79); **Goals:** Kheirallah 6/8.
Sin bin: Mika (14) - dangerous challenge.
On report: Hepi (44) - alleged dangerous challenge.
Rugby Leaguer & League Express Men of the Match: *Rams:* Rob Spicer; *Olympique:* Tyla Hepi.
Penalty count: 10-9; **Half-time:** 6-22;
Referee: Jack Smith; **Attendance:** 720.

FEATHERSTONE ROVERS 32 SWINTON LIONS 18

ROVERS: 1 Ian Hardman; 5 Luke Briscoe; 20 Josh Hardcastle; 4 Misi Taulapapa; 2 Shaun Robinson; 6 Martyn Ridyard; 19 Tom Holmes; 28 Mikolaj Oledzki; 9 Keal Carlile; 25 Mitch Clark; 11 Connor Farrell; 16 Frankie Mariano; 21 Bradley Knowles. Subs (all used): 14 Matty Wildie; 15 Gareth Hock; 22 Sam Brooks; 13 James Lockwood.
Tries: Briscoe (7), Carlile (21), Mariano (35), Ridyard (45), Robinson (64, 79); **Goals:** Ridyard 4/4, Hardman 0/2.
Dismissal: Taulapapa (72) - fighting.
Sin bin: Holmes (66) - fighting.
LIONS: 1 Gabriel Fell; 5 Mike Butt; 3 Chris Hankinson; 4 George Tyson; 34 Jack Higginson; 31 Josh Woods; 35 Rob Fairclough; 8 Andy Bracek; 14 Hayden Hansen; 33 Gavin Bennion; 11 Rhodri Lloyd; 12 Matt Sarsfield; 13 Josh Barlow. Subs (all used): 15 Ben Austin; 36 Oliver Partington; 17 Kyle Shelford; 9 Luke Waterworth.
Tries: Sarsfield (30, 75), Tyson (49, 56);
Goals: Hankinson 0/3, Woods 1/1.
Sin bin: Lloyd (66) - fighting; Fairclough (72) - fighting.
Rugby Leaguer & League Express Men of the Match: *Rovers:* Martyn Ridyard; *Lions:* Matt Sarsfield.
Penalty count: 13-15; **Half-time:** 18-4;
Referee: Tom Grant; **Attendance:** 2,082.

HALIFAX 38 LEIGH CENTURIONS 18

HALIFAX: 16 James Woodburn-Hall; 5 James Saltonstall; 2 Ben Heaton; 3 Steve Tyrer; 1 Will Sharp; 6 Scott Murrell; 7 Ben Johnston; - Gadwin Springer; 9 Ben Kaye; 27 Daniel Murray; 12 Simon Grix; 11 Shane Grady; 13 Jacob Fairbank. Subs (all used): 14 Brandon Moore; 4 Ed Barber; 26 Sion Jones; 17 Will Maher.
Tries: Grady (12, 30, 38), Moore (26), Heaton (34), Tyrer (60, 72); **Goals:** Tyrer 5/7.
CENTURIONS: 1 Craig Hall; 2 Matty Dawson-Jones; 3 Ben Crooks; 4 Peter Mata'utia; 5 Rhys Evans; 7 Drew Hutchison; 28 Jordan Lilley; 20 Greg Richards; 30 Micky Higham; 13 Harrison Hansen; 11 Kevin Larroyer; 12 Bodene Thompson; 15 Jordan Thompson. Subs (all used): 14 Liam Hood; 10 Jamie Acton; 16 Larne Patrick; 17 Kyle Lovett.
Tries: Hall (47, 57), Evans (65); **Goals:** Lilley 3/3.
Sin bin: Dawson-Jones (60) - dissent.
On report: Acton (25) - alleged late challenge.
Rugby Leaguer & League Express Men of the Match: *Halifax:* Shane Grady; *Centurions:* Rhys Evans.
Penalty count: 10-5; **Half-time:** 28-0;
Referee: Gareth Hewer; **Attendance:** 2,119.

LONDON BRONCOS 68 BATLEY BULLDOGS 12

BRONCOS: 14 Alex Walker; 5 Kieran Dixon; 3 Ben Hellewell; 4 Matty Fleming; 2 Rhys Williams; 6 Api Pewhairangi; 7 Jarrod Sammut; 8 Tom Spencer; 9 James Cunningham; 10 Mark Ioane; 12 Jay Pitts; 21 Will Lovell; 13 Matt Davis. Subs (all used): 16 Matty Gee; 23 Rob Butler; 19 Sadiq Adebiyi; 29 Sam Davis.
Tries: Dixon (5, 13, 34, 44), Lovell (19), Cunningham (27), Pewhairangi (40, 77), Williams (63, 70), S Davis (74), Gee (80); **Goals:** Sammut 6/7, Dixon 4/5.
BULLDOGS: 1 Dave Scott; 2 Wayne Reittie; 4 Jason Crookes; 29 Lewis Galbraith; 5 Shaun Ainscough; 18 Tom Hemingway; 7 Dominic Brambani; 13 Brad Day; 14 James Davey; 20 Alex Rowe; 15 James Harrison; 12 Joel Farrell; 6 Pat Walker. Subs (all used): 25 Izaac Farrell; 24 Tommy Holland; 17 Joe Chandler; 21 James Brown.
Tries: Brown (36, 58); **Goals:** Walker 2/2.
Dismissal: Brambani (69) - dissent.
Rugby Leaguer & League Express Men of the Match: *Broncos:* Kieran Dixon; *Bulldogs:* James Brown.
Penalty count: 7-6; **Half-time:** 36-6;
Referee: John McMullen; **Attendance:** 526.

ROCHDALE HORNETS 24 BARROW RAIDERS 12

HORNETS: 21 Richard Lepori; 2 Declan Kay; 3 Earl Hurst; 30 Deon Cross; 5 Rob Massam; 6 Lewis Palfrey; 7 Danny Yates; 8 Jovili Taira; 9 Ben Moores; 19 Lee Mitchell; 23 Gary Middlehurst; 11 Dave Allen; 13 Luke Adamson. Subs (all used): 24 Declan Gregory; 12 Toby Adamson; 16 Pat Moran; 18 Billy Brickhill.
Tries: Palfrey (45), Moran (49), Cross (52), Mitchell (60), Massam (66); **Goals:** Palfrey 2/5.
Sin bin: Lepori (29) - fighting.
RAIDERS: 1 Ryan Fieldhouse; 2 Shane Toal; 3 Declan Hulme; 23 Tom Lomax; 18 Luke Cresswell; 26 Brad Marwood; 14 Karl Ashall; 27 Ryan Duffy; 22 Dean Parata; 8 Joe Bullock; 19 Bradd Crellin; 12 Jarrad Stack; 13 Martin Aspinwall. Subs (all used): 9 Nathan Mossop; 10 Tom Walker; 11 Dan Toal; 17 Alec Susino.
Tries: Cresswell (15), Hulme (18); **Goals:** Marwood 2/3.
Dismissal:
Stack (29) - dangerous challenge on Middlehurst.
Rugby Leaguer & League Express Men of the Match: *Hornets:* Lewis Palfrey; *Raiders:* Joe Bullock.
Penalty count: 7-8; **Half-time:** 0-12;
Referee: Matt Rossleigh; **Attendance:** 414.

SHEFFIELD EAGLES 10 TORONTO WOLFPACK 44

EAGLES: 1 Ryan Millar; 24 Garry Lo; 30 Matthew Costello; 25 Jake Spedding; 2 Iliess Macani; 6 Oscar Thomas; 23 Cory Aston; 8 Mark Offerdahl; 14 Greg Burns; 12 Shaun Pick; 13 Matt James; 26 James Bentley; 9 Matty Fozard. Subs (all used): 4 Joshua Toole; 11 Nabil Djalout; 16 Kieran Moran; 10 Jon Magrin.
Tries: James (39), Macani (78);
Goals: Thomas 1/2, Aston 0/1.
Sin bin: James (71) - professional foul.
WOLFPACK: 1 Quentin Laulu-Togagae; 2 Jonny Pownall; 3 Greg Worthington; 23 Nick Rawsthorne; 5 Liam Kay; 7 Ryan Brierley; 6 Josh McCrone; 8 Jack Buchanan; 9 Bob Beswick; 10 Ashton Sims; 11 Andrew Dixon; 16 Reni Maitua; 12 Joe Westerman. Subs (all used): 13 Jack Bussey; 17 Blake Wallace; 15 Adam Sidlow; 22 Richard Whiting.
Tries: Kay (21), Whiting (29, 74), Sidlow (33), Rawsthorne (45), Wallace (55), Pownall (60, 66);
Goals: Brierley 6/8.
Rugby Leaguer & League Express Men of the Match: *Eagles:* Matt James; *Wolfpack:* Richard Whiting.
Penalty count: 8-11; **Half-time:** 6-16;
Referee: Greg Dolan; **Attendance:** 863.

ROUND 7

Friday 23rd March 2018

ROCHDALE HORNETS 17 TORONTO WOLFPACK 18

HORNETS: 2 Declan Kay; 30 Deon Cross; 3 Earl Hurst; 18 Billy Brickhill; 5 Rob Massam; 6 Lewis Palfrey; - Morgan Smith; 8 Jovili Taira; 9 Ben Moores; 19 Lee Mitchell; 23 Gary Middlehurst; 11 Dave Allen; 13 Luke Adamson. Subs (all used): 24 Declan Gregory; 12 Toby Adamson; 16 Pat Moran; - Seta Tala.
Tries: Hurst (2), Middlehurst (20), Massam (50);
Goals: Palfrey 2/4; **Field goal:** Smith (68).
Sin bin: Palfrey (64) - fighting.
WOLFPACK: 31 Gareth O'Brien; 1 Quentin Laulu-Togagae; 3 Greg Worthington; 4 Gary Wheeler; 5 Liam Kay; 6 Josh McCrone; 7 Ryan Brierley; 29 Jake Emmitt; 14 Andy Ackers; 10 Ashton Sims; 11 Andrew Dixon; 16 Reni Maitua; 13 Jack Bussey. Subs (all used): 15 Adam Sidlow; 22 Richard Whiting; 28 Sam Hopkins; 8 Jack Buchanan.
Tries: Kay (9), McCrone (53), Maitua (65);
Goals: Brierley 3/4.
Sin bin: Kay (64) - fighting; O'Brien (64) - fighting.
On report:
McCrone (45) - alleged dangerous challenge on T Adamson.
Rugby Leaguer & League Express Men of the Match: *Hornets:* Morgan Smith; *Wolfpack:* Ryan Brierley.
Penalty count: 7-6; **Half-time:** 12-6;
Referee: Matt Rossleigh; **Attendance:** 504.

Saturday 24th March 2018

TOULOUSE OLYMPIQUE 38 HALIFAX 6

OLYMPIQUE: 1 Mark Kheirallah; 2 Tony Maurel; 3 Bastien Ader; 4 Gavin Marguerite; 20 Paul Marcon; 6 Johnathon Ford; 7 Stan Robin; 18 Sam Rapira; 9 Anthony Marion; 10 Bastien Canet; 26 Constantine Mika; 12 Rhys Curran; 13 Andrew Bentley. Subs (all used): 8 Clement Boyer; 15 Maxime Puech; 16 Tyla Hepi; 30 William Barthau.
Tries: Maurel (3, 6), Curran (12), Kheirallah (53), Marguerite (64), Ader (71), Marcon (80);
Goals: Kheirallah 5/7.
HALIFAX: 1 Will Sharp; 2 Ben Heaton; 4 Ed Barber; 3 Steve Tyrer; 5 James Saltonstall; 6 Scott Murrell; 7 Ben Johnston; 9 Ben Kaye; - Daniel Murray; 17 Will Maher; 13 Jacob Fairbank; 11 Shane Grady; 12 Simon Grix. Subs (all used): 14 Brandon Moore; 26 Sion Jones; 29 Dan Fleming; 30 Brandon Douglas.
Try: Fleming (38); **Goals:** Tyrer 1/1.
Sin bin: Jones (78) - punching.
On report: Fleming (58) - alleged high tackle.
Rugby Leaguer & League Express Men of the Match: *Olympique:* Johnathon Ford; *Halifax:* Will Sharp.
Penalty count: 3-7; **Half-time:** 16-6;
Referee: John McMullen; **Attendance:** 2,137.

Sunday 25th March 2018

BARROW RAIDERS 36 SHEFFIELD EAGLES 22

RAIDERS: 18 Luke Cresswell; 2 Shane Toal; 3 Declan Hulme; 4 Andy Litherland; 5 Brett Carter; 1 Ryan Fieldhouse; 22 Dean Parata; 8 Joe Bullock; 14 Karl Ashall; 10 Tom Walker; 25 Jono Smith; 24 Danny Morrow; 17 Alec Susino. Subs (all used): 9 Nathan Mossop; 27 Ryan Duffy; 15 Glenn Riley; 11 Dan Toal.
Tries: Litherland (28), D Toal (42), Duffy (51), S Toal (59, 66, 74), Bullock (68); **Goals:** Carter 4/7.
Sin bin: Carter (13) - holding down.
EAGLES: 1 Ryan Millar; 24 Garry Lo; 4 Joshua Toole; 25 Jake Spedding; 5 Ben Blackmore; 23 Cory Aston; 19 Simon Brown; 13 Matt James; 9 Matty Fozard; 10 Jon Magrin; 26 James Bentley; 15 Olly Davies; 27 Jack Ashworth. Subs (all used): 14 Greg Burns; 8 Mark Offerdahl; 6 Oscar Thomas; 12 Shaun Pick.
Tries: Blackmore (10), Fozard (16), Lo (22, 80);
Goals: Aston 2/2, Brown 1/1, Thomas 0/1.
Rugby Leaguer & League Express Men of the Match: *Raiders:* Nathan Mossop; *Eagles:* Jack Ashworth.
Penalty count: 9-7; **Half-time:** 4-18;
Referee: Marcus Griffiths; **Attendance:** 1,210.

BATLEY BULLDOGS 14 FEATHERSTONE ROVERS 40

BULLDOGS: 1 Dave Scott; 28 Keenen Tomlinson; 22 Danny Cowling; 29 Lewis Galbraith; 4 Jason Crookes; 6 Pat Walker; 25 Izaac Farrell; 20 Alex Rowe; 9 Alistair Leak; 16 Michael Ward; 3 Sam Smeaton; 15 James Harrison; 17 Joe Chandler. Subs (all used): 7 Dominic Brambani; 21 James Brown; 14 James Davey; 24 Tommy Holland.
Tries: Scott (6, 8); **Goals:** Walker 3/3.
Sin bin: Crookes (30) - dangerous challenge.

ROVERS: 19 Tom Holmes; 5 Luke Briscoe; 20 Josh Hardcastle; 29 Harry Newman; 2 Shaun Robinson; 6 Martyn Ridyard; 14 Matty Wildie; 21 Bradley Knowles; 9 Keal Carlile; 25 Mitch Clark; 11 Connor Farrell; 12 John Davies; 13 James Lockwood. Subs (all used): 17 Luke Cooper; 22 Sam Brooks; 16 Frankie Mariano; 27 Jack Ormondroyd.
Tries: Lockwood (15), Briscoe (35, 59, 70), Newman (52), Holmes (62), Wildie (76); **Goals:** Ridyard 6/7.
Rugby Leaguer & League Express Men of the Match:
Bulldogs: Dave Scott; *Rovers:* Luke Briscoe.
Penalty count: 7-10; **Half-time:** 14-10;
Referee: Nick Bennett; **Attendance:** 1,273.

LEIGH CENTURIONS 36 DEWSBURY RAMS 0

CENTURIONS: 4 Peter Mata'utia; 2 Matty Dawson-Jones; 3 Ben Crooks; 5 Rhys Evans; 19 Jack Owens; 6 Ben Reynolds; 7 Drew Hutchison; 8 Paterika Vaivai; 14 Liam Hood; 18 Nathan Mason; 13 Harrison Hansen; 17 Kyle Lovett; 21 Nick Gregson. Subs (all used): 30 Micky Higham; 26 Jordan Dezaria; 20 Greg Richards; 15 Jordan Thompson.
Tries: Mata'utia (14, 21), Hansen (18), Lovett (49, 53), Crooks (56); **Goals:** Reynolds 4/4, Owens 2/2.
Sin bin: Reynolds (44) - fighting;
Dawson-Jones (44) - fighting.
RAMS: 1 Josh Guzdek; 2 Rob Worrincy; 3 James Glover; 4 Macauley Hallett; 5 Dale Morton; 6 Paul Sykes; 7 Gareth Moore; 8 Jode Sheriffe; 9 Robbie Ward; 10 Jack Teanby; 20 Jordan Crowther; 12 Michael Knowles; - Chris Annakin. Subs (all used): 19 Sam Day; 13 Aaron Brown; 26 Matty English; - Shannon Wakeman.
Sin bin: Moore (44) - fighting;
Annakin (51) - professional foul.
Rugby Leaguer & League Express Men of the Match:
Centurions: Peter Mata'utia; *Rams:* Chris Annakin.
Penalty count: 12-8; **Half-time:** 18-0;
Referee: Gareth Hewer; **Attendance:** 3,136.

SWINTON LIONS 18 LONDON BRONCOS 64

LIONS: 1 Gabriel Fell; 23 Elliott Caine; 11 Rhodri Lloyd; 4 George Tyson; 2 Marcus Webb; 3 Chris Hankinson; 7 Jack Hansen; 8 Andy Bracek; 9 Luke Waterworth; 33 Gavin Bennion; 21 Chris Worrell; 10 Andy Thornley; 15 Ben Austin. Subs (all used): 13 Josh Barlow; 14 Hayden Hansen; 31 Will Hope; 24 Aaron Hall.
Tries: Caine (8), H Hansen (64), Hankinson (80);
Goals: Hankinson 3/3.
Dismissal: Barlow (40) - headbutt on Battye.
BRONCOS: 14 Alex Walker; 5 Kieran Dixon; 21 Will Lovell; 3 Ben Hellewell; 2 Rhys Williams; 6 Api Pewhairangi; 27 James Meadows; 8 Tom Spencer; 9 James Cunningham; 10 Mark Ioane; 12 Jay Pitts; 16 Matty Gee; 13 Matt Davis. Subs (all used): 29 Sam Davis; 23 Rob Butler; 20 Lewis Bienek; 15 Eddie Battye.
Tries: Dixon (15, 43), Walker (18, 36, 74), Lovell (24), Cunningham (45, 70), Meadows (48), Bienek (55), Hellewell (58), Spencer (67); **Goals:** Dixon 8/13.
Rugby Leaguer & League Express Men of the Match:
Lions: Gavin Bennion; *Broncos:* Api Pewhairangi.
Penalty count: 13-11; **Half-time:** 6-24;
Referee: Liam Staveley; **Attendance:** 518.

ROUND 8

Friday 30th March 2018

LONDON BRONCOS 16 TOULOUSE OLYMPIQUE 36

BRONCOS: 14 Alex Walker; 2 Rhys Williams; 4 Matty Fleming; 3 Ben Hellewell; 5 Kieran Dixon; 6 Api Pewhairangi; 7 Jarrod Sammut; 8 Tom Spencer; 9 James Cunningham; 10 Mark Ioane; 12 Jay Pitts; 21 Will Lovell; 13 Matt Davis. Subs (all used): 20 Lewis Bienek; 15 Eddie Battye; 23 Rob Butler; 29 Sam Davis.
Tries: Pitts (5), Hellewell (20), Pewhairangi (41);
Goals: Sammut 2/3.
Sin bin: Fleming (50) - use of the elbow.
OLYMPIQUE: 1 Mark Kheirallah; 20 Paul Marcon; 4 Gavin Marguerite; 3 Bastien Ader; 2 Tony Maurel; 6 Johnathon Ford; 30 William Barthau; 18 Sam Rapira; 9 Anthony Marion; 10 Bastien Canet; 26 Constantine Mika; 12 Rhys Curran; 13 Andrew Bentley. Subs (all used): 8 Clement Boyer; 14 Mourad Kriouache; 16 Tyla Hepi; 17 Eddy Pettybourne.
Tries: Maurel (12), Curran (16), Ader (23), Marion (31), Hepi (34), Kheirallah (45); **Goals:** Kheirallah 6/6.
Rugby Leaguer & League Express Men of the Match:
Broncos: Sam Davis; *Olympique:* Johnathon Ford.
Penalty count: 5-7; **Half-time:** 10-30;
Referee: Matt Rossleigh; **Attendance:** 891.

SHEFFIELD EAGLES 38 ROCHDALE HORNETS 20

EAGLES: 30 Matthew Costello; 24 Garry Lo; 11 Nabil Djalout; 4 Joshua Toole; 1 Ryan Millar; 19 Simon Brown; 6 Oscar Thomas; 12 Shaun Pick; 14 Greg Burns; 13 Matt James; 26 James Bentley; 15 Olly Davies; 9 Matty Fozard. Subs (all used): 17 Daniel Igbinedion; 8 Mark Offerdahl; 20 Max Garcia; 10 Jon Magrin.
Tries: Pick (1), Millar (17), Lo (30, 79), Igbinedion (34), Thomas (40), Fozard (76); **Goals:** Thomas 4/6, Brown 1/1.
HORNETS: 21 Richard Lepori; 2 Declan Kay; 30 Deon Cross; 3 Earl Hurst; 5 Rob Massam; 6 Lewis Palfrey; 7 Danny Yates; 8 Jovili Taira; 9 Ben Moores; 19 Lee Mitchell; 23 Gary Middlehurst; 11 Dave Allen; 13 Luke Adamson. Subs: 24 Declan Gregory; 12 Toby Adamson; 16 Pat Moran; 18 Billy Brickhill (not used).
Tries: Yates (15), Massam (19), Moores (26), Cross (67);
Goals: Palfrey 2/4.
Rugby Leaguer & League Express Men of the Match:
Eagles: Simon Brown; *Hornets:* Deon Cross.
Penalty count: 5-3; **Half-time:** 28-16;
Referee: Tom Grant; **Attendance:** 516.

SWINTON LIONS 10 LEIGH CENTURIONS 40

LIONS: 4 George Tyson; 23 Elliott Caine; 11 Rhodri Lloyd; 16 Liam Forsyth; 2 Marcus Webb; 3 Chris Hankinson; 7 Jack Hansen; 8 Andy Bracek; 9 Luke Waterworth; 10 Andy Thornley; 32 Macauley Davies; 12 Matt Sarsfield; 31 Will Hope. Subs (all used): 13 Josh Barlow; 24 Aaron Hall; 14 Hayden Hansen; 17 Kyle Shelford.
Tries: Tyson (26), Shelford (32); **Goals:** Hankinson 1/2.
CENTURIONS: 4 Peter Mata'utia; 2 Matty Dawson-Jones; 3 Ben Crooks; 5 Rhys Evans; 22 Ricky Bailey; 1 Craig Hall; 7 Drew Hutchison; 8 Paterika Vaivai; 14 Liam Hood; 18 Nathan Mason; 17 Kyle Lovett; 12 Bodene Thompson; 15 Jordan Thompson. Subs (all used): 23 Jonah Cunningham; 20 Greg Richards; 10 Jamie Acton; 21 Nick Gregson.
Tries: Hood (14), Mason (19), Hall (37, 40), B Thompson (48), Mata'utia (50), Dawson-Jones (68);
Goals: Hall 6/7.
Rugby Leaguer & League Express Men of the Match:
Lions: Jack Hansen; *Centurions:* Craig Hall.
Penalty count: 10-6; **Half-time:** 10-24;
Referee: Greg Dolan; **Attendance:** 1,345.

**FEATHERSTONE ROVERS 16
TORONTO WOLFPACK 24**

ROVERS: 1 Ian Hardman; 5 Luke Briscoe; 20 Josh Hardcastle; 29 Harry Newman; 4 Misi Taulapapa; 6 Martyn Ridyard; 19 Tom Holmes; 15 Gareth Hock; 9 Keal Carlile; 21 Bradley Knowles; 11 Connor Farrell; 12 John Davies; 13 James Lockwood. Subs (all used): 14 Matty Wildie; 17 Luke Cooper; 22 Sam Brooks; 16 Frankie Mariano.
Tries: Briscoe (50, 76), Taulapapa (74); **Goals:** Ridyard 2/6.
WOLFPACK: 31 Gareth O'Brien; 2 Jonny Pownall; 33 Chase Stanley; 3 Greg Worthington; 5 Liam Kay; 6 Josh McCrone; 7 Ryan Brierley; 29 Jake Emmitt; 14 Andy Ackers; 10 Ashton Sims; 13 Jack Bussey; 22 Richard Whiting; 28 Sam Hopkins. Subs (all used): 16 Reni Maitua; 17 Blake Wallace; 15 Adam Sidlow; 8 Jack Buchanan.
Tries: Brierley (18, 60), Whiting (25, 28); **Goals:** Brierley 4/6.
Rugby Leaguer & League Express Men of the Match:
Rovers: Luke Briscoe; *Wolfpack:* Richard Whiting.
Penalty count: 18-11; **Half-time:** 4-16;
Referee: Marcus Griffiths; **Attendance:** 3,131.

BATLEY BULLDOGS 18 DEWSBURY RAMS 10

BULLDOGS: 1 Dave Scott; 2 Wayne Reittie; 3 Sam Smeaton; 29 Lewis Galbraith; 4 Jason Crookes; 6 Pat Walker; 7 Dominic Brambani; 16 Michael Ward; 9 Alistair Leak; 20 Alex Rowe; 15 James Harrison; 13 Brad Day; 12 Joel Farrell. Subs (all used): 18 Tom Hemingway; 21 James Brown; 11 Dane Manning; 24 Tommy Holland.
Tries: Reittie (23), Day (28), Crookes (60);
Goals: Walker 3/4.
RAMS: 1 Josh Guzdek; 2 Rob Worrincy; 21 Harry Woollard; 4 Macauley Hallett; 5 Dale Morton; 6 Paul Sykes; 14 Dom Speakman; 17 Toby Everett; 9 Robbie Ward; 22 Martyn Reilly; 15 Lucas Walshaw; 11 Rob Spicer; 13 Aaron Brown. Subs (all used): 19 Sam Day; 29 Danny Ansell; 8 Jode Sheriffe; 24 Kyle Trout.
Tries: Morton (7), Worrincy (74); **Goals:** Sykes 1/3.
Rugby Leaguer & League Express Men of the Match:
Bulldogs: Pat Walker; *Rams:* Dale Morton.
Penalty count: 10-10; **Half-time:** 10-6;
Referee: Tom Crashley; **Attendance:** 1,117.

HALIFAX 30 BARROW RAIDERS 4

HALIFAX: 1 Will Sharp; 21 Conor McGrath; 3 Steve Tyrer; 4 Ed Barber; 5 James Saltonstall; 6 Scott Murrell; 7 Ben Johnston; 8 Elliot Morris; 9 Ben Kaye; 17 Will Maher; 18 Chester Butler; 11 Shane Grady; 13 Jacob Fairbank. Subs (all used): 14 Brandon Moore; 25 Sion Jones; 30 Brandon Douglas; 29 Dan Fleming.
Tries: Morris (13), Tyrer (17), Jones (52), McGrath (67);
Goals: Tyrer 7/7.
On report: Tyrer (55) - alleged dangerous contact.
RAIDERS: 5 Brett Carter; 23 Tom Loxam; 3 Declan Hulme; 29 Gene Ormsby; 2 Shane Toal; 1 Ryan Fieldhouse; 26 Brad Marwood; 15 Glenn Riley; 22 Dean Parata; 17 Alec Susino; 24 Danny Morrow; 28 Matthew Holmes; 20 Matty While. Subs (all used): 9 Nathan Mossop; 19 Bradd Crellin; 27 Ryan Duffy; 10 Tom Walker.
Try: Ormsby (25); **Goals:** Carter 0/1.
Rugby Leaguer & League Express Men of the Match:
Halifax: Sion Jones; *Raiders:* Gene Ormsby.
Penalty count: 12-6; **Half-time:** 16-4;
Referee: Liam Staveley; **Attendance:** 1,298.

ROUND 9

Monday 2nd April 2018

TOULOUSE OLYMPIQUE 22 TORONTO WOLFPACK 24

OLYMPIQUE: 1 Mark Kheirallah; 2 Tony Maurel; 3 Bastien Ader; 11 Sebastien Planas; 20 Paul Marcon; 6 Johnathon Ford; 7 Stan Robin; 10 Bastien Canet; 9 Anthony Marion; 18 Sam Rapira; 26 Constantine Mika; 12 Rhys Curran; 13 Andrew Bentley. Subs (all used): 8 Clement Boyer; 14 Mourad Kriouache; 16 Tyla Hepi; 17 Eddy Pettybourne.
Tries: Curran (25), Boyer (55), Robin (65), Maurel (75);
Goals: Kheirallah 3/4.
WOLFPACK: 1 Quentin Laulu-Togagae; 2 Jonny Pownall; 3 Greg Worthington; 23 Nick Rawsthorne; 5 Liam Kay; 17 Blake Wallace; 7 Ryan Brierley; 29 Jake Emmitt; 14 Andy Ackers; 8 Jack Buchanan; 13 Jack Bussey; 22 Richard Whiting; 28 Sam Hopkins. Subs (all used): 6 Josh McCrone; 10 Ashton Sims; 15 Adam Sidlow; 16 Reni Maitua.
Tries: Pownall (18), Kay (21), Rawsthorne (35, 51), Ackers (40); **Goals:** Brierley 2/5.
Rugby Leaguer & League Express Men of the Match:
Olympique: Tyla Hepi; *Wolfpack:* Liam Kay.
Penalty count: 8-6; **Half-time:** 4-20;
Referee: Jack Smith; **Attendance:** 3,313.

BARROW RAIDERS 16 SWINTON LIONS 16

RAIDERS: 1 Ryan Fieldhouse; 5 Brett Carter; 29 Gene Ormsby; 3 Declan Hulme; 2 Shane Toal; 6 Jamie Dallimore; 14 Karl Ashall; 8 Joe Bullock; 22 Dean Parata; 17 Alec Susino; 25 Jono Smith; 12 Jarrad Stack; 13 Martin Aspinwall. Subs (all used): 9 Nathan Mossop; 11 Dan Toal; 15 Glenn Riley; 10 Tom Walker.
Tries: S Toal (18, 26); **Goals:** Dallimore 4/4.
On report: D Toal (32) - alleged shoulder charge.
LIONS: 30 Craig Mullen; 2 Marcus Webb; 11 Rhodri Lloyd; 4 George Tyson; 16 Liam Forsyth; 3 Chris Hankinson; 7 Jack Hansen; 15 Ben Austin; 9 Luke Waterworth; 10 Andy Thornley; 31 Will Hope; 33 Liam Paisley; 13 Josh Barlow. Subs (all used): 17 Kyle Shelford; 24 Aaron Hall; 14 Hayden Hansen; 18 Mark Nicholson.
Tries: Forsyth (5), H Hansen (31, 65); **Goals:** Hankinson 2/3.
Rugby Leaguer & League Express Men of the Match:
Raiders: Jamie Dallimore; *Lions:* Hayden Hansen.
Penalty count: 9-8; **Half-time:** 12-10;
Referee: Tom Grant; **Attendance:** 1,133.

LEIGH CENTURIONS 31 LONDON BRONCOS 18

CENTURIONS: 4 Peter Mata'utia; 2 Matty Dawson-Jones; 3 Ben Crooks; 1 Craig Hall; 5 Rhys Evans; 6 Ben Reynolds; 7 Drew Hutchison; 8 Paterika Vaivai; 30 Micky Higham; 18 Nathan Mason; 13 Harrison Hansen; 12 Bodene Thompson; 15 Jordan Thompson. Subs (all used): 14 Liam Hood; 10 Jamie Acton; 17 Kyle Lovett; 26 Jordan Dezaria.
Tries: Hood (27, 63), J Thompson (43), Hansen (52), Hutchison (72); **Goals:** Reynolds 5/5, Hall 0/1;
Field goal: Reynolds (77).
BRONCOS: 14 Alex Walker; 1 Elliot Kear; 21 Will Lovell; 3 Ben Hellewell; 2 Rhys Williams; 27 James Meadows; 7 Jarrod Sammut; 8 Tom Spencer; 9 James Cunningham; 15 Eddie Battye; 16 Matty Gee; 12 Jay Pitts; 13 Matt Davis. Subs (all used): 29 Sam Davis; 10 Mark Ioane; 23 Rob Butler; 20 Lewis Bienek.
Tries: Kear (36), Cunningham (57), Gee (78);
Goals: Sammut 3/3.
Rugby Leaguer & League Express Men of the Match:
Centurions: Liam Hood; *Broncos:* James Cunningham.
Penalty count: 6-6; **Half-time:** 6-6;
Referee: John McMullen; **Attendance:** 3,328.

ROCHDALE HORNETS 0 FEATHERSTONE ROVERS 42

HORNETS: 21 Richard Lepori; 32 Deon Cross; 3 Earl Hurst; 18 Billy Brickhill; 5 Rob Massam; 6 Lewis Palfrey; 24 Declan Gregory; 15 Lewis Hatton; 9 Ben Moores; 19 Lee Mitchell; 23 Gary Middlehurst; 11 Dave Allen; 13 Luke Adamson. Subs (all used): 14 Ryan Maneely; 12 Toby Adamson; - Pat Moran; 25 Callum Mulkeen.
ROVERS: 1 Ian Hardman; 5 Luke Briscoe; 20 Josh Hardcastle; 29 Harry Newman; 2 Shaun Robinson; 6 Martyn Ridyard; 19 Tom Holmes; 17 Luke Cooper; 9 Keal

Carlile; 21 Bradley Knowles; 11 Connor Farrell; 12 John Davies; 13 James Lockwood. Subs (all used): 14 Matty Wildie; 15 Gareth Hock; 22 Sam Brooks; 4 Misi Taulapapa.
Tries: Newman (7, 12, 24), Hardcastle (21), Ridyard (65), Briscoe (68, 72, 76); **Goals:** Ridyard 5/8.
Rugby Leaguer & League Express Men of the Match: *Hornets:* Dave Allen; *Rovers:* Luke Briscoe.
Penalty count: 10-9; **Half-time:** 0-22;
Referee: Gareth Hewer; **Attendance:** 659.

SHEFFIELD EAGLES 14 BATLEY BULLDOGS 28

EAGLES: 30 Matthew Costello; 24 Garry Lo; 26 James Bentley; 4 Joshua Toole; 1 Ryan Millar; 19 Simon Brown; 6 Oscar Thomas; 13 Matt James; 14 Greg Burns; 12 Shaun Pick; 27 Jack Ashworth; 15 Olly Davies; 9 Matty Fozard. Subs (all used): 17 Daniel Igbinedion; 5 Ben Blackmore; 20 Max Garcia; 10 Jon Magrin.
Tries: Toole (8), Davies (19), Millar (61); **Goals:** Thomas 1/3.
BULLDOGS: 1 Dave Scott; 2 Wayne Reittie; 22 Danny Cowling; 29 Lewis Galbraith; 4 Jason Crookes; 6 Pat Walker; 7 Dominic Brambani; 16 Michael Ward; 14 James Davey; 24 Tommy Holland; 11 Dane Manning; 12 Joel Farrell; 17 Joe Chandler. Subs (all used): 18 Tom Hemingway; 19 Alex Bretherton; 21 James Brown; 28 Keenen Tomlinson.
Tries: Scott (36), Manning (50), Walker (55), Reittie (58), Hemingway (78); **Goals:** Walker 4/6.
Rugby Leaguer & League Express Men of the Match: *Eagles:* Matt James; *Bulldogs:* Dane Manning.
Penalty count: 7-7; **Half-time:** 10-4;
Referee: Matt Rossleigh; **Attendance:** 597.

ROUND 10

Saturday 7th April 2018

TOULOUSE OLYMPIQUE 50 BARROW RAIDERS 4

OLYMPIQUE: 1 Mark Kheirallah; 2 Tony Maurel; 12 Rhys Curran; 11 Sebastien Planas; 21 Joseph Therond; 6 Johnathon Ford; 30 William Barthau; 15 Maxime Puech; 14 Mourad Kriouache; 18 Sam Rapira; 10 Bastien Canet; 26 Constantine Mika; 17 Eddy Pettybourne. Subs (all used): 8 Clement Boyer; 16 Tyla Hepi; 23 Justin Sangare; 19 Charles Bouzinac.
Tries: Curran (2), Ford (16), Canet (25), Barthau (31), Sangare (45), Boyer (51), Planas (67), Pettybourne (72), Kheirallah (79); **Goals:** Kheirallah 7/9.
RAIDERS: 5 Brett Carter; 2 Shane Toal; 11 Dan Toal; 4 Andy Litherland; 3 Declan Hulme; 6 Jamie Dallimore; 14 Karl Ashall; 8 Joe Bullock; 22 Dean Parata; 15 Glenn Riley; 25 Jono Smith; 28 Matthew Holmes; 13 Martin Aspinwall. Subs (all used): 9 Nathan Mossop; 10 Tom Walker; 17 Alec Susino; 27 Ryan Duffy.
Try: Susino (65); **Goals:** Dallimore 0/1.
Sin bin: D Toal (72) - high tackle.
On report: Walker (21) - alleged use of the elbow.
Rugby Leaguer & League Express Men of the Match: *Olympique:* Charles Bouzinac; *Raiders:* Joe Bullock.
Penalty count: 14-9; **Half-time:** 22-0;
Referee: Matt Rossleigh; **Attendance:** 1,177.

Sunday 8th April 2018

BATLEY BULLDOGS 18 TORONTO WOLFPACK 26

BULLDOGS: 1 Dave Scott; 2 Wayne Reittie; 3 Sam Smeaton; 29 Lewis Galbraith; 4 Jason Crookes; 6 Pat Walker; 7 Dominic Brambani; 24 Tommy Holland; 9 Alistair Leak; 20 Alex Rowe; 15 James Harrison; 13 Brad Day; 12 Joel Farrell. Subs (all used): 14 James Davey; 21 James Brown; 11 Dane Manning; 16 Michael Ward.
Tries: Harrison (11), Reittie (40), Day (79);
Goals: Walker 3/3.
WOLFPACK: 31 Gareth O'Brien; 2 Jonny Pownall; 33 Chase Stanley; 3 Greg Worthington; 5 Liam Kay; 6 Josh McCrone; 7 Ryan Brierley; 29 Jake Emmitt; 14 Andy Ackers; 10 Ashton Sims; 13 Jack Bussey; 22 Richard Whiting; 8 Jack Buchanan. Subs (all used): 16 Reni Maitua; 15 Adam Sidlow; 28 Sam Hopkins; 17 Blake Wallace.
Tries: McCrone (7), O'Brien (49, 53, 62), Bussey (69);
Goals: Brierley 3/5.
Sin bin: Hopkins (80) - dangerous challenge.
Rugby Leaguer & League Express Men of the Match: *Bulldogs:* Joel Farrell; *Wolfpack:* Gareth O'Brien.
Penalty count: 8-8; **Half-time:** 12-6;
Referee: Tom Grant; **Attendance:** 1,157.

FEATHERSTONE ROVERS 46 DEWSBURY RAMS 18

ROVERS: 1 Ian Hardman; 5 Luke Briscoe; 4 Misi Taulapapa; 29 Harry Newman; 2 Shaun Robinson; 6 Martyn Ridyard; 19 Tom Holmes; 27 Jack Ormondroyd; 9 Keal Carlile; 21 Bradley Knowles; 11 Connor Farrell; 12 John Davies; 13 James Lockwood. Subs (all used): 14 Matty Wildie; 15 Gareth Hock; 17 Luke Cooper; 22 Sam Brooks.
Tries: Farrell (15, 26), Newman (33, 69), Wildie (36, 44, 62), Briscoe (65); **Goals:** Ridyard 7/8.
RAMS: 1 Josh Guzdek; 2 Rob Worrincy; 15 Lucas Walshaw; 4 Macauley Hallett; 5 Dale Morton; 6 Paul Sykes; 29 Danny Ansell; 8 Jode Sheriffe; 9 Robbie Ward; 10 Jack Teanby; 20 Jordan Crowther; 11 Rob Spicer; 13 Aaron Brown. Subs (all used): 14 Dom Speakman; 21 Harry Woollard; 24 Kyle Trout; 22 Martyn Reilly.
Tries: Sheriffe (9), Brown (21), Hallett (31);
Goals: Sykes 3/3.
Rugby Leaguer & League Express Men of the Match: *Rovers:* Tom Holmes; *Rams:* Josh Guzdek.
Penalty count: 8-8; **Half-time:** 22-18;
Referee: Greg Dolan; **Attendance:** 2,031.

HALIFAX 26 LONDON BRONCOS 16

HALIFAX: 1 Will Sharp; 21 Conor McGrath; 3 Steve Tyrer; 18 Chester Butler; 5 James Saltonstall; 6 Scott Murrell; 7 Ben Johnston; 30 Brandon Douglas; 14 Brandon Moore; 17 Will Maher; 12 Simon Grix; 11 Shane Grady; 13 Jacob Fairbank. Subs (all used): 8 Elliot Morris; 25 Sion Jones; 29 Dan Fleming; - James Green.
Tries: Tyrer (21, 45), Grady (33), Grix (36), McGrath (40);
Goals: Tyrer 3/6.
Sin bin: Moore (16) - dissent; Johnston (25) - fighting.
BRONCOS: 14 Alex Walker; 5 Kieran Dixon; 1 Elliot Kear; 3 Ben Hellewell; 2 Rhys Williams; 6 Api Pewhairangi; 7 Jarrod Sammut; 8 Tom Spencer; 9 James Cunningham; 20 Lewis Bienek; 21 Will Lovell; 12 Jay Pitts; 13 Matt Davis. Subs (all used): 29 Sam Davis; 15 Eddie Battye; 23 Rob Butler; 19 Sadiq Adebiyi.
Tries: Williams (10), Kear (29), Lovell (68);
Goals: Sammut 1/2, Dixon 1/2.
Sin bin: Pewhairangi (25) - fighting.
Rugby Leaguer & League Express Men of the Match: *Halifax:* Scott Murrell; *Broncos:* Kieran Dixon.
Penalty count: 6-12; **Half-time:** 20-10;
Referee: Scott Mikalauskas; **Attendance:** 1,595.

LEIGH CENTURIONS 68 ROCHDALE HORNETS 10

CENTURIONS: 19 Jack Owens; 22 Ricky Bailey; 3 Ben Crooks; 1 Craig Hall; 5 Rhys Evans; 6 Ben Reynolds; 7 Drew Hutchison; 18 Nathan Mason; 14 Liam Hood; 10 Jamie Acton; 13 Harrison Hansen; 12 Bodene Thompson; 15 Jordan Thompson. Subs (all used): 30 Micky Higham; 20 Greg Richards; 17 Kyle Lovett; 16 Larne Patrick.
Tries: Hall (7, 67), Reynolds (13, 70), Acton (17, 65), Evans (25), Hansen (30), Ricky Bailey (38, 58), Hood (73), Owens (79); **Goals:** Reynolds 10/12.
HORNETS: 2 Declan Kay; 22 Alex Gaskell; 3 Earl Hurst; 31 Deon Cross; 5 Rob Massam; 6 Lewis Palfrey; 26 Declan Patton; 8 Jovili Taira; 9 Ben Moores; 13 Luke Adamson; 12 Toby Adamson; 19 Lee Mitchell; 23 Gary Middlehurst. Subs (all used): 15 Lewis Hatton; 16 Pat Moran; 18 Billy Brickhill; 24 Declan Gregory.
Tries: Hatton (35), Kay (45); **Goals:** Patton 1/1, Palfrey 0/1.
Sin bin: Taira (65) - holding down.
Rugby Leaguer & League Express Men of the Match: *Centurions:* Ben Reynolds; *Hornets:* Declan Kay.
Penalty count: 13-10; **Half-time:** 36-6;
Referee: Jack Smith; **Attendance:** 3,144.

SWINTON LIONS 18 SHEFFIELD EAGLES 19

LIONS: 30 Craig Mullen; 16 Liam Forsyth; 3 Chris Hankinson; 11 Rhodri Lloyd; 2 Marcus Webb; 31 Josh Woods; 7 Jack Hansen; 33 Gavin Bennion; 9 Luke Waterworth; 8 Andy Bracek; 18 Mark Nicholson; 25 Will Hope; 10 Andy Thornley. Subs (all used): 15 Ben Austin; 32 Callum Field; 14 Hayden Hansen; 17 Kyle Shelford.
Tries: Webb (47), Mullen (63), Hankinson (74);
Goals: Hankinson 3/4.
EAGLES: 30 Matthew Costello; 2 Iliess Macani; 26 James Bentley; 5 Ben Blackmore; 1 Ryan Millar; 6 Oscar Thomas; 19 Simon Brown; 8 Mark Offerdahl; 14 Greg Burns; 12 Shaun Pick; 27 Jack Ashworth; 28 Matty Lees; 9 Matty Fozard. Subs: 17 Daniel Igbinedion; 20 Max Garcia; 21 Blake Broadbent (not used); 10 Jon Magrin.
Tries: Blackmore (12, 39), Macani (51); **Goals:** Thomas 3/3;
Field goal: Brown (78).
Rugby Leaguer & League Express Men of the Match: *Lions:* Liam Forsyth; *Eagles:* Oscar Thomas.
Penalty count: 10-3; **Half-time:** 2-12;
Referee: John McMullen; **Attendance:** 532.

ROUND 11

Friday 13th April 2018

ROCHDALE HORNETS 15 LONDON BRONCOS 30

HORNETS: 2 Declan Kay; 21 Richard Lepori; 4 Taylor Welch; 3 Earl Hurst; 30 Deon Cross; 26 Declan Patton; 7 Danny Yates; 8 Jovili Taira; 9 Ben Moores; 13 Luke Adamson; 12 Toby Adamson; 11 Dave Allen; - Harvey Livett. Subs: 15 Lewis Hatton; 16 Pat Moran; 18 Billy Brickhill; 20 Blake Turner (not used).
Tries: Moores (6), Kay (73); **Goals:** Livett 3/4;
Field goal: Patton (40).
BRONCOS: 5 Kieran Dixon; 1 Elliot Kear; 17 Michael Channing; 3 Ben Hellewell; 2 Rhys Williams; 6 Api Pewhairangi; 27 James Meadows; 8 Tom Spencer; 7 Jarrod Sammut; 15 Eddie Battye; 21 Will Lovell; 12 Jay Pitts; 13 Matt Davis. Subs (all used): 29 Sam Davis; 20 Lewis Bienek; 19 Sadiq Adebiyi; 26 Daniel Hindmarsh.
Tries: Dixon (34, 45, 66), Adebiyi (54, 58);
Goals: Sammut 3/4, Dixon 2/2.
Rugby Leaguer & League Express Men of the Match: *Hornets:* Declan Kay; *Broncos:* Kieran Dixon.
Penalty count: 13-11; **Half-time:** 9-6;
Referee: John McMullen; **Attendance:** 312.

Saturday 14th April 2018

BATLEY BULLDOGS 46 TOULOUSE OLYMPIQUE 22

BULLDOGS: 1 Dave Scott; 5 Shaun Ainscough; 3 Sam Smeaton; 29 Lewis Galbraith; 4 Jason Crookes; 25 Izaac Farrell; 7 Dominic Brambani; 24 Tommy Holland; 9 Alistair Leak; 20 Alex Rowe; 15 James Harrison; 13 Brad Day; 11 Dane Manning. Subs (all used): 14 James Davey; 21 James Brown; 12 Joel Farrell; 16 Michael Ward.
Tries: Crookes (6, 29, 74), Leak (10), Ainscough (35), Ward (45), Day (60, 77); **Goals:** I Farrell 7/9.
OLYMPIQUE: 1 Mark Kheirallah; 24 Pierre-Jean Lima; 11 Sebastien Planas; 3 Bastien Ader; 2 Tony Maurel; 6 Johnathon Ford; 30 William Barthau; 8 Clement Boyer; 14 Mourad Kriouache; 18 Sam Rapira; 26 Constantine Mika; 12 Rhys Curran; 13 Andrew Bentley. Subs (all used): 7 Stan Robin; 15 Maxime Puech; 16 Tyla Hepi; 9 Anthony Marion.
Tries: Ader (2, 23), Kheirallah (54), Barthau (70);
Goals: Kheirallah 2/3, Barthau 1/1.
Rugby Leaguer & League Express Men of the Match: *Bulldogs:* Jason Crookes; *Olympique:* Johnathon Ford.
Penalty count: 5-4; **Half-time:** 20-10;
Referee: Liam Moore; **Attendance:** 662.

Sunday 15th April 2018

BARROW RAIDERS 26 FEATHERSTONE ROVERS 38

RAIDERS: 1 Ryan Fieldhouse; 5 Brett Carter; 3 Declan Hulme; 12 Jarrad Stack; 29 Gene Ormsby; 6 Jamie Dallimore; 21 Ryan Johnston; 8 Joe Bullock; 9 Nathan Mossop; 17 Alec Susino; 25 Jono Smith; 19 Bradd Crellin; 13 Martin Aspinwall. Subs (all used): 27 Ryan Duffy; 22 Dean Parata; 15 Glenn Riley; 10 Tom Walker.
Tries: Smith (18), Duffy (46), Parata (54), Ormsby (76);
Goals: Dallimore 5/6.
ROVERS: 1 Ian Hardman; 5 Luke Briscoe; 4 Misi Taulapapa; 29 Harry Newman; 2 Shaun Robinson; 6 Martyn Ridyard; 19 Tom Holmes; 25 Mitch Clark; 9 Keal Carlile; 21 Bradley Knowles; 11 Connor Farrell; 30 Jansin Turgut; 13 James Lockwood. Subs (all used): 14 Matty Wildie; 15 Gareth Hock; 10 Richard Moore; 17 Luke Cooper.
Tries: Farrell (10), Briscoe (28), Newman (33, 56), Hardman (65), Ridyard (67), Carlile (73); **Goals:** Ridyard 5/7.
Sin bin: Lockwood (77) - dangerous contact.
Rugby Leaguer & League Express Men of the Match: *Raiders:* Dean Parata; *Rovers:* Martyn Ridyard.
Penalty count: 13-13; **Half-time:** 8-16;
Referee: Tom Crashley; **Attendance:** 1,231.

DEWSBURY RAMS 12 TORONTO WOLFPACK 23

RAMS: 1 Josh Guzdek; 18 Gareth Potts; 3 James Glover; 4 Macauley Hallett; 2 Rob Worrincy; 6 Paul Sykes; 7 Gareth Moore; 17 Toby Everett; 14 Dom Speakman; 22 Martyn Reilly; 20 Jordan Crowther; 15 Lucas Walshaw; 13 Aaron Brown. Subs (all used): 19 Sam Day; 28 Kyle Trout; 10 Jack Teanby; 9 Robbie Ward.
Tries: Speakman (25), Crowther (79, pen);
Goals: Sykes 2/2.
WOLFPACK: 31 Gareth O'Brien; 19 Adam Higson; 33 Chase Stanley; 3 Greg Worthington; 5 Liam Kay; 6 Josh McCrone; 7 Ryan Brierley; 15 Adam Sidlow; 14 Andy Ackers; 10 Ashton Sims; 16 Reni Maitua; 13 Jack Bussey; 8 Jack Buchanan. Subs (all used): 21 Olsi Krasniqi; 9 Bob Beswick; 22 Richard Whiting; 28 Sam Hopkins.
Tries: Maitua (12), Higson (14, 53), Stanley (17), Brierley (77);
Goals: Brierley 1/6; **Field goal:** Brierley (72).
Sin bin: O'Brien (79) - dissent.
Rugby Leaguer & League Express Men of the Match: *Rams:* Jack Teanby; *Wolfpack:* Ryan Brierley.
Penalty count: 12-8; **Half-time:** 6-14;
Referee: Robert Hicks; **Attendance:** 932.

HALIFAX 18 SWINTON LIONS 12

HALIFAX: 1 Will Sharp; 21 Conor McGrath; 3 Steve Tyrer; 18 Chester Butler; 5 James Saltonstall; 6 Scott Murrell; 7 Ben Johnston; 30 Brandon Douglas; 9 Ben Kaye; 17 Will Maher; 12 Simon Grix; 11 Shane Grady; 13 Jacob Fairbank. Subs (all used): 14 Brandon Moore; 25 Sion Jones; 29 Dan Fleming; 31 James Green.

Barrow's Joe Bullock bursts through the Batley defence

Tries: Butler (28), Tyrer (61, 77), McGrath (75);
Goals: Tyrer 1/4.
On report: Grady (66) - alleged kicking.
LIONS: 1 Gabriel Fell; 2 Marcus Webb; 3 Chris Hankinson; 11 Rhodri Lloyd; 5 Mike Butt; 6 Brad Billsborough; 7 Jack Hansen; 8 Andy Bracek; 9 Luke Waterworth; 33 Gavin Bennion; 10 Andy Thornley; 18 Mark Nicholson; 34 Levy Nzoungou. Subs (all used): 14 Hayden Hansen; 15 Ben Austin; 17 Kyle Shelford; 24 Aaron Hall.
Tries: Thornley (4), Webb (51); **Goals:** Hankinson 2/3.
Rugby Leaguer & League Express Men of the Match:
Halifax: Will Sharp; *Lions:* Chris Hankinson.
Penalty count: 8-9; **Half-time:** 4-6;
Referee: Matt Rossleigh; **Attendance:** 1,399.

SHEFFIELD EAGLES 20 LEIGH CENTURIONS 72

EAGLES: 29 Corey Makelim; 2 Iliess Macani; 26 James Bentley; 5 Ben Blackmore; 1 Ryan Millar; 6 Oscar Thomas; 19 Simon Brown; 8 Mark Offerdahl; 14 Greg Burns; 10 Jon Magrin; 27 Jack Ashworth; 15 Olly Davies; 9 Matty Fozard. Subs (all used): 17 Daniel Igbinedion; 16 Kieran Moran; 20 Max Garcia; 21 Blake Broadbent.
Tries: Millar (40), Bentley (48), Thomas (51), Broadbent (65); **Goals:** Thomas 2/4.
CENTURIONS: 4 Peter Mata'utia; 2 Matty Dawson-Jones; 3 Ben Crooks; 1 Craig Hall; 19 Jack Owens; 6 Ben Reynolds; 7 Drew Hutchison; 18 Nathan Mason; 14 Liam Hood; 10 Jamie Acton; 13 Harrison Hansen; 12 Bodene Thompson; 15 Jordan Thompson. Subs (all used): 30 Micky Higham; 20 Greg Richards; 11 Kevin Larroyer; 17 Kyle Lovett.
Tries: Dawson-Jones (4), Mata'utia (9, 14), Hall (18, 21, 23, 54), Lovett (29), Owens (35, 68), Hood (37), Hutchison (56), Larroyer (73); **Goals:** Reynolds 10/13.
Sin bin: Acton (63) - dangerous contact.
Rugby Leaguer & League Express Men of the Match:
Eagles: Daniel Igbinedion; *Centurions:* Craig Hall.
Penalty count: 6-7; **Half-time:** 4-50;
Referee: Tom Grant; **Attendance:** 982.

ROUND 9

Sunday 22nd April 2018

DEWSBURY RAMS 18 HALIFAX 46

RAMS: 1 Josh Guzdek; 2 Rob Worrincy; 3 James Glover; 4 Macauley Hallett; 5 Dale Morton; 6 Paul Sykes; 7 Gareth Moore; 8 Jode Sheriffe; 9 Robbie Ward; 10 Jack Teanby; 20 Dom Crowther; 11 Rob Spicer; 13 Aaron Brown. Subs (all used): 14 Dom Speakman; 15 Lucas Walshaw; 26 Chris Annakin; 28 Kyle Trout.

Tries: Morton (12), Speakman (37), Sykes (48);
Goals: Sykes 3/3.
Sin bin: Walshaw (57) - interference.
HALIFAX: 26 Quentin Laulu-Togagae; 21 Conor McGrath; 3 Steve Tyrer; 5 James Saltonstall; 1 Will Sharp; 6 Scott Murrell; 7 Ben Johnston; 13 Jacob Fairbank; 14 Brandon Moore; 17 Will Maher; 18 Chester Butler; 11 Shane Grady; 12 Simon Grix. Subs (all used): 9 Ben Kaye; 8 Elliot Morris; 29 Dan Fleming; 31 James Green.
Tries: Butler (10, 50), Moore (22), Saltonstall (27), Kaye (33), Tyrer (65), Laulu-Togagae (68), Sharp (73);
Goals: Tyrer 7/8.
Rugby Leaguer & League Express Men of the Match:
Rams: Gareth Moore; *Halifax:* Quentin Laulu-Togagae.
Penalty count: 14-7; **Half-time:** 12-22;
Referee: Marcus Griffiths; **Attendance:** 1,394.

ROUND 12

Saturday 28th April 2018

LONDON BRONCOS 64 DEWSBURY RAMS 6

BRONCOS: 14 Alex Walker; 2 Rhys Williams; 17 Michael Channing; 1 Elliot Kear; 24 Jake Ogden; 27 James Meadows; 7 Jarrod Sammut; 8 Tom Spencer; 13 Matt Davis; 15 Eddie Battye; 12 Jay Pitts; 11 Daniel Harrison; 19 Sadiq Adebiyi. Subs (all used): 25 Matthew Davies; 21 Will Lovell; 18 Ben Evans; 16 Matty Gee.
Tries: Pitts (20), Sammut (30, 40, 74), Matthew Davies (37), Evans (48), Lovell (53), Williams (57, 61), Kear (72), Matt Davis (76);
Goals: Sammut 10/11.
RAMS: 1 Josh Guzdek; 2 Rob Worrincy; 3 James Glover; 31 Cameron Scott; 5 Dale Morton; 30 Danny Ansell; 33 Lewis Heckford; 8 Jode Sheriffe; 20 Jordan Crowther; 10 Jack Teanby; 28 Kyle Trout; 15 Lucas Walshaw; 13 Aaron Brown. Subs (all used): 19 Sam Day; 22 Martyn Reilly; 17 Toby Everett; 18 Gareth Potts.
Try: Ansell (67); **Goals:** Glover 1/2.
Rugby Leaguer & League Express Men of the Match:
Broncos: Jarrod Sammut; *Rams:* Josh Guzdek.
Penalty count: 3-5; **Half-time:** 24-0;
Referee: Matt Rossleigh; **Attendance:** 733.

SWINTON LIONS 8 TOULOUSE OLYMPIQUE 62

LIONS: 1 Gabriel Fell; 16 Ilias Bergal; 3 Chris Hankinson; 11 Rhodri Lloyd; 5 Mike Butt; 6 Brad Billsborough; 7 Jack Hansen; 8 Andy Bracek; 9 Luke Waterworth; 10 Andy Thornley; 12 Matt Sarsfield; 25 Will Hope; 35 Levy Nzoungou. Subs (all used): 15 Ben Austin; 14 Hayden Hansen; 17 Kyle Shelford; 24 Aaron Hall.

Try: Hope (10); **Goals:** Hankinson 2/2.
OLYMPIQUE: 1 Mark Kheirallah; 20 Paul Marcon; 4 Gavin Marguerite; 3 Bastien Ader; 2 Tony Maurel; 6 Johnathon Ford; 7 Stan Robin; 8 Clement Boyer; 14 Mourad Kriouache; 18 Sam Rapira; 11 Sebastien Planas; 12 Rhys Curran; 13 Andrew Bentley. Subs (all used): 19 Charles Bouzinac; 10 Bastien Canet; 16 Tyla Hepi; 9 Anthony Marion.
Tries: Ford (5, 73), Robin (29, 44), Kheirallah (34, 77), Marion (36, 75), Maurel (52), Bouzinac (57), Kriouache (67);
Goals: Kheirallah 9/11.
Rugby Leaguer & League Express Men of the Match:
Lions: Chris Hankinson; *Olympique:* Stan Robin.
Penalty count: 5-2; **Half-time:** 8-22;
Referee: Greg Dolan; **Attendance:** 2,155.

TORONTO WOLFPACK 42 HALIFAX 10

WOLFPACK: 17 Blake Wallace; 2 Jonny Pownall; 19 Adam Higson; 23 Nick Rawsthorne; 5 Liam Kay; 6 Josh McCrone; 7 Ryan Brierley; 29 Jake Emmitt; 9 Bob Beswick; 10 Ashton Sims; 24 Cory Paterson; 13 Jack Bussey; 32 Darcy Lussick. Subs (all used): 14 Andy Ackers; 15 Adam Sidlow; 22 Richard Whiting; 28 Sam Hopkins.
Tries: Lussick (5), Kay (9, 77), Beswick (16), Brierley (34), Ackers (37), Paterson (48); **Goals:** Brierley 7/7.
HALIFAX: 1 Will Sharp; 5 James Saltonstall; 3 Steve Tyrer; 2 Ben Heaton; 21 Conor McGrath; 6 Scott Murrell; 7 Ben Johnston; 13 Jacob Fairbank; 14 Brandon Moore; 17 Will Maher; 18 Chester Butler; 11 Shane Grady; 12 Simon Grix. Subs (all used): 8 Elliot Morris; 9 Ben Kaye; 30 Brandon Douglas; 31 James Green.
Tries: McGrath (39), Heaton (68); **Goals:** Grady 1/2.
Rugby Leaguer & League Express Men of the Match:
Wolfpack: Cory Paterson; *Halifax:* Chester Butler.
Penalty count: 10-8; **Half-time:** 30-4;
Referee: Liam Moore; **Attendance:** 1,658
(at New River Stadium, London).

Sunday 29th April 2018

FEATHERSTONE ROVERS 50 BATLEY BULLDOGS 12

ROVERS: 19 Tom Holmes; 5 Luke Briscoe; 20 Josh Hardcastle; 4 Misi Taulapapa; 2 Shaun Robinson; 6 Martyn Ridyard; 31 Jordan Lilley; 8 Scott Wheeldon; 9 Keal Carlile; 25 Mitch Clark; 11 Connor Farrell; 32 Josh Walters; 10 Richard Moore. Subs (all used): 14 Matty Wildie; 15 Gareth Hock; 22 Sam Brooks; 33 Nathaniel Peteru.
Tries: Robinson (15, 45, 72), Briscoe (24), Hardcastle (28, 79), Hock (36), Holmes (52, 67), Walters (62); **Goals:** Ridyard 5/10.

BULLDOGS: 1 Dave Scott; 5 Shaun Ainscough; 3 Sam Smeaton; 29 Lewis Galbraith; 4 Jason Crookes; 25 Izaac Farrell; 7 Dominic Brambani; 24 Tommy Holland; 9 Alistair Leak; 20 Alex Rowe; 15 James Harrison; 13 Brad Day; 11 Dane Manning. Subs (all used): 16 Michael Ward; 14 James Davey; 12 Joel Farrell; 21 James Brown.
Tries: Scott (50), Brambani (75); **Goals:** I Farrell 2/2.
Rugby Leaguer & League Express Men of the Match: *Rovers:* Tom Holmes; *Bulldogs:* Lewis Galbraith.
Penalty count: 8-9; **Half-time:** 18-0;
Referee: John McMullen; **Attendance:** 2,225.

LEIGH CENTURIONS 46 BARROW RAIDERS 18

CENTURIONS: 4 Peter Mata'utia; 2 Matty Dawson-Jones; 5 Rhys Evans; 1 Craig Hall; 19 Jack Owens; 6 Ben Reynolds; 7 Drew Hutchison; 18 Nathan Mason; 14 Liam Hood; 10 Jamie Acton; 13 Harrison Hansen; 12 Bodene Thompson; 15 Jordan Thompson. Subs (all used): 30 Micky Higham; 29 Ryan Bailey; 20 Greg Richards; 11 Kevin Larroyer.
Tries: Hutchison (3, 68, 73), Reynolds (9), Ryan Bailey (31), Dawson-Jones (35), Hood (76), Hall (80);
Goals: Reynolds 7/8.
RAIDERS: 1 Ryan Fieldhouse; 5 Brett Carter; 3 Declan Hulme; 4 Andy Litherland; 29 Gene Ormsby; 6 Jamie Dallimore; 21 Ryan Johnston; 8 Joe Bullock; 9 Nathan Mossop; 17 Alec Susino; 25 Jono Smith; 12 Jarrad Stack; 13 Martin Aspinwall. Subs (all used): 22 Dean Parata; 19 Bradd Crellin; 11 Dan Toal; 27 Ryan Duffy.
Tries: Bullock (18), Stack (46), Carter (54);
Goals: Dallimore 3/3.
Rugby Leaguer & League Express Men of the Match: *Centurions:* Drew Hutchison; *Raiders:* Alec Susino.
Penalty count: 13-14; **Half-time:** 22-6;
Referee: Marcus Griffiths; **Attendance:** 3,228.

ROCHDALE HORNETS 16 SHEFFIELD EAGLES 38

HORNETS: 2 Declan Kay; 21 Richard Lepori; 25 Seta Tala; 12 Toby Adamson; 31 Deon Cross; 30 Tyler Whittaker; 7 Danny Yates; 8 Jovili Taira; 18 Billy Brickhill; 13 Luke Adamson; 19 Lee Mitchell; 11 Dave Allen; 23 Gary Middlehurst. Subs (all used): 3 Earl Hurst; 10 Matty Hadden; 16 Pat Moran; 20 Blake Turner.
Tries: Mitchell (31), Brickhill (38), Hadden (42);
Goals: Whittaker 2/3.
EAGLES: 29 Corey Makelim; 1 Ryan Millar; 26 James Bentley; 30 Matthew Costello; 5 Ben Blackmore; 23 Cory Aston; 19 Simon Brown; 12 Shaun Pick; 14 Greg Burns; 13 Matt James; 27 Jack Ashworth; 4 Joshua Toole; 9 Matty Fozard. Subs (all used): 16 Kieran Moran; 8 Mark Offerdahl; 15 Olly Davies; 10 Jon Magrin.
Tries: Millar (4), G Burns (15), Makelim (28), Offerdahl (35), Ashworth (46), Fozard (71), Toole (78);
Goals: Brown 3/4, Fozard 2/3.
Rugby Leaguer & League Express Men of the Match: *Hornets:* Billy Brickhill; *Eagles:* Matt James.
Penalty count: 6-8; **Half-time:** 10-22;
Referee: Gareth Hewer; **Attendance:** 459.

ROUND 13

Saturday 5th May 2018

TOULOUSE OLYMPIQUE 36 FEATHERSTONE ROVERS 10

OLYMPIQUE: 1 Mark Kheirallah; 2 Tony Maurel; 3 Bastien Ader; 30 William Barthau; 4 Gavin Marguerite; 6 Johnathon Ford; 7 Stan Robin; 8 Clement Boyer; 14 Mourad Kriouache; 10 Bastien Canet; 11 Sebastien Planas; 26 Constantine Mika; 13 Andrew Bentley. Subs (all used): 9 Anthony Marion; 15 Maxime Puech; 16 Tyla Hepi; 19 Charles Bouzinac.
Tries: Kheirallah (31), Marion (34), Hepi (45), Barthau (50), Canet (59), Ader (78); **Goals:** Kheirallah 6/6.
ROVERS: 19 Tom Holmes; 5 Luke Briscoe; 4 Misi Taulapapa; 29 Harry Newman; 2 Shaun Robinson; 6 Martyn Ridyard; 31 Jordan Lilley; 8 Scott Wheeldon; 9 Keal Carlile; 28 Mikolaj Oledzki; 11 Connor Farrell; 30 Jansin Turgut; 21 Bradley Knowles. Subs (all used): 10 Richard Moore; 15 Gareth Hock; 22 Sam Brooks; 25 Mitch Clark.
Tries: Briscoe (4), Newman (23); **Goals:** Ridyard 1/2.
Rugby Leaguer & League Express Men of the Match: *Olympique:* Johnathon Ford; *Rovers:* Tom Holmes.
Penalty count: 9-13; **Half-time:** 12-10;
Referee: Liam Staveley; **Attendance:** 2,876.

TORONTO WOLFPACK 62 SWINTON LIONS 14

WOLFPACK: 31 Gareth O'Brien; 19 Adam Higson; 33 Chase Stanley; 23 Nick Rawsthorne; 5 Liam Kay; 6 Josh McCrone; 7 Ryan Brierley; 29 Jake Emmitt; 9 Bob Beswick; 32 Darcy Lussick; 24 Cory Paterson; 13 Jack Bussey; 15 Adam Sidlow. Subs (all used): 28 Sam Hopkins; 17 Blake Wallace; 21 Olsi Krasniqi; 11 Andrew Dixon.
Tries: Kay (4, 42, 69), Stanley (9), O'Brien (22, 47), Krasniqi (25), Rawsthorne (50), Wallace (53), Sidlow (59), Dixon (75), Higson (80); **Goals:** Brierley 7/12.
LIONS: 1 Gabriel Fell; 5 Mike Butt; 3 Chris Hankinson; 4 George Tyson; 16 Ilias Bergal; 6 Brad Billsborough; 7 Jack Hansen; 15 Ben Austin; 9 Luke Waterworth; 17 Kyle Shelford; 11 Rhodri Lloyd; 10 Andy Thornley; 25 Will Hope. Subs (all used): 14 Hayden Hansen; 21 Chris Worrell; 18 Mark Nicholson; - Tommy Gallagher.
Tries: Austin (15), Butt (66); **Goals:** Hankinson 3/3.
Rugby Leaguer & League Express Men of the Match: *Wolfpack:* Liam Kay; *Lions:* George Tyson.
Penalty count: 10-7; **Half-time:** 22-8;
Referee: Tom Grant; **Attendance:** 2,917
(at Fletcher's Fields).

Sunday 6th May 2018

BARROW RAIDERS 20 BATLEY BULLDOGS 18

RAIDERS: 1 Ryan Fieldhouse; 29 Gene Ormsby; 3 Declan Hulme; 4 Andy Litherland; 2 Shane Toal; 6 Jamie Dallimore; 21 Ryan Johnston; 8 Joe Bullock; 9 Nathan Mossop; 17 Alec Susino; 25 Jono Smith; 12 Jarrad Stack; 13 Martin Aspinwall. Subs (all used): 24 Danny Morrow; 22 Dean Parata; 15 Glenn Riley; 19 Bradd Crellin.
Tries: Bullock (37), Parata (51), Johnston (79);
Goals: Dallimore 4/4.
BULLDOGS: 1 Dave Scott; 5 Shaun Ainscough; 22 Danny Cowling; 29 Lewis Galbraith; 28 Keenen Tomlinson; 6 Pat Walker; 7 Dominic Brambani; 8 Adam Gledhill; 9 Alistair Leak; 20 Alex Rowe; 15 James Harrison; 13 Brad Day; 11 Dane Manning. Subs (all used): 16 Michael Ward; 14 James Davey; 17 Joe Chandler; 19 Alex Bretherton.
Tries: Scott (12), Brambani (46), Leak (57);
Goals: Walker 3/3.
Rugby Leaguer & League Express Men of the Match: *Raiders:* Joe Bullock; *Bulldogs:* Pat Walker.
Penalty count: 9-5; **Half-time:** 8-6;
Referee: Marcus Griffiths; **Attendance:** 1,211.

DEWSBURY RAMS 27 ROCHDALE HORNETS 32

RAMS: 1 Josh Guzdek; 2 Rob Worrincy; 3 James Glover; 31 Cameron Scott; 5 Dale Morton; 12 Michael Knowles; 7 Gareth Moore; 17 Toby Everett; 9 Robbie Ward; 10 Jack Teanby; 20 Jordan Crowther; 11 Rob Spicer; 13 Aaron Brown. Subs (all used): 14 Dom Speakman; 27 Jamel Goodall; 28 Kyle Trout; 8 Jode Sheriffe.
Tries: Scott (10), Brown (30), Speakman (43), Guzdek (47), Moore (74); **Goals:** Glover 3/5; **Field goal:** Moore (76).
HORNETS: 2 Declan Kay; 21 Richard Lepori; 3 Earl Hurst; 25 Seta Tala; 31 Deon Cross; 30 Tyler Whittaker; 7 Danny Yates; 15 Lewis Hatton; 26 Morgan Smith; 20 Blake Turner; 19 Lee Mitchell; 23 Gary Middlehurst; 18 Billy Brickhill. Subs (all used): 17 Jonah Cunningham; 10 Matty Hadden; 16 Pat Moran; 22 Alex Gaskell.
Tries: Whittaker (7), Tala (35, 56), Hadden (64), Kay (79);
Goals: Whittaker 6/6.
Rugby Leaguer & League Express Men of the Match: *Rams:* Dom Speakman; *Hornets:* Tyler Whittaker.
Penalty count: 9-9; **Half-time:** 10-14;
Referee: Scott Mikalauskas; **Attendance:** 649.

LONDON BRONCOS 30 LEIGH CENTURIONS 40

BRONCOS: 14 Alex Walker; 5 Kieran Dixon; 17 Michael Channing; 1 Elliot Kear; 2 Rhys Williams; 27 James Meadows; 7 Jarrod Sammut; 18 Ben Evans; 13 Matt Davis; 15 Eddie Battye; 12 Jay Pitts; 11 Daniel Harrison; 19 Sadiq Adebiyi. Subs (all used): 10 Mark Ioane; 9 James Cunningham; 21 Will Lovell; 16 Matty Gee.
Tries: Williams (7), Walker (33), Evans (44), Meadows (58), Adebiyi (68); **Goals:** Sammut 5/5.
CENTURIONS: 4 Peter Mata'utia; 2 Matty Dawson-Jones; 3 Ben Crooks; 1 Craig Hall; 5 Rhys Evans; 6 Ben Reynolds; 7 Drew Hutchison; 18 Nathan Mason; 14 Liam Hood; 10 Jamie Acton; 13 Harrison Hansen; 12 Bodene Thompson; 15 Jordan Thompson. Subs (all used): 17 Kyle Lovett; 20 Greg Richards; 29 Ryan Bailey; 30 Micky Higham.
Tries: Evans (11), Hansen (18), Hall (39, 51), Higham (54), Hood (71), Mata'utia (73); **Goals:** Reynolds 6/8.
Sin bin: Hutchison (58) - holding down.
Rugby Leaguer & League Express Men of the Match: *Broncos:* James Meadows; *Centurions:* Harrison Hansen.
Penalty count: 12-12; **Half-time:** 12-18;
Referee: Greg Dolan; **Attendance:** 1,340.

SHEFFIELD EAGLES 6 HALIFAX 42

EAGLES: 29 Corey Makelim; 1 Ryan Millar; 24 Adam Swift; 25 Jake Spedding; 5 Ben Blackmore; 6 Oscar Thomas; 30 Matthew Costello; 12 Shaun Pick; 9 Matty Fozard; 10 Jon Magrin; 13 Matt James; 27 Jack Ashworth; 22 Paddy Burns. Subs (all used): 14 Greg Burns; 15 Olly Davies; 20 Max Garcia; 8 Mark Offerdahl.
Try: Costello (60); **Goals:** Thomas 1/1.
HALIFAX: 26 Quentin Laulu-Togagae; 5 James Saltonstall; 3 Steve Tyrer; 4 Ed Barber; 1 Will Sharp; 6 Scott Murrell; 7 Ben Johnston; 13 Jacob Fairbank; 9 Ben Kaye; 29 Dan Fleming; 18 Chester Butler; 11 Shane Grady; 12 Simon Grix. Subs (all used): 14 Brandon Moore; 8 Elliot Morris; 17 Will Maher; 25 Sion Jones.
Tries: Kaye (4), Butler (7, 20), Laulu-Togagae (16, 39), Barber (68), Johnston (76); **Goals:** Tyrer 7/7.
Rugby Leaguer & League Express Men of the Match: *Eagles:* Corey Makelim; *Halifax:* Quentin Laulu-Togagae.
Penalty count: 5-8; **Half-time:** 0-30;
Referee: Billy Pearson; **Attendance:** 891.

ROUND 1

Saturday 12th May 2018

ROCHDALE HORNETS 10 BATLEY BULLDOGS 48

HORNETS: 2 Declan Kay; 25 Seta Tala; 31 Deon Cross; 4 Jordan Syme; 5 Rob Massam; 14 Tyler Whittaker; 7 Danny Yates; 20 Blake Turner; 17 Jonah Cunningham; 16 Pat Moran; 19 Lee Mitchell; - Luis Johnson; 18 Billy Brickhill. Subs (all used): 26 Morgan Smith; 8 Jovili Taira; 10 Matty Hadden; 22 Alex Gaskell.
Tries: Kay (11, 67); **Goals:** Whittaker 1/3.
Sin bin: Cunningham (75) - holding down.
BULLDOGS: 1 Dave Scott; 5 Shaun Ainscough; 22 Danny Cowling; 29 Lewis Galbraith; 4 Jason Crookes; 6 Pat Walker; 25 Izaac Farrell; 8 Adam Gledhill; 9 Alistair Leak; 20 Alex Rowe; 15 James Harrison; 12 Joel Farrell; 13 Brad Day. Subs (all used): 16 Michael Ward; 3 Sam Smeaton; 7 Dominic Brambani; 17 Joe Chandler.
Tries: Ward (21), Crookes (29), Galbraith (37), Day (39), Ainscough (52), I Farrell (55), Gledhill (73), Brambani (77);
Goals: Walker 6/6, I Farrell 2/2.
Sin bin: Galbraith (49) - dissent.
Rugby Leaguer & League Express Men of the Match: *Hornets:* Declan Kay; *Bulldogs:* Alistair Leak.
Penalty count: 9-3; **Half-time:** 4-24;
Referee: Liam Staveley; **Attendance:** 408.

ROUND 5

Sunday 13th May 2018

BARROW RAIDERS 58 DEWSBURY RAMS 32

RAIDERS: 1 Ryan Fieldhouse; 29 Gene Ormsby; 3 Declan Hulme; 4 Andy Litherland; 2 Shane Toal; 6 Jamie Dallimore; 21 Ryan Johnston; 8 Joe Bullock; 9 Nathan Mossop; 17 Alec Susino; 25 Jono Smith; 12 Jarrad Stack; 13 Martin Aspinwall. Subs (all used): 27 Ryan Duffy; 22 Dean Parata; 15 Glenn Riley; 24 Danny Morrow.
Tries: Bullock (10), Smith (24), Ormsby (27), Duffy (35), Dallimore (38), Stack (45, 49), Parata (47), Fieldhouse (54), Morrow (70); **Goals:** Dallimore 9/10.
RAMS: 1 Josh Guzdek; 18 Gareth Potts; 3 James Glover; 4 Macauley Hallett; 5 Dale Morton; 13 Aaron Brown; 7 Gareth Moore; 8 Jode Sheriffe; 9 Robbie Ward; 10 Jack Teanby; 15 Lucas Walshaw; 12 Michael Knowles; 20 Jordan Crowther. Subs (all used): 19 Sam Day; 22 Martyn Reilly; 28 Kyle Trout; 17 Toby Everett.
Tries: Brown (15), Guzdek (18, 57, 78), Hallett (64), Day (72);
Goals: Glover 4/6.
Rugby Leaguer & League Express Men of the Match: *Raiders:* Jarrad Stack; *Rams:* Josh Guzdek.
Penalty count: 8-11; **Half-time:** 28-12;
Referee: John McMullen; **Attendance:** 1,061.

SHEFFIELD EAGLES 14 LONDON BRONCOS 66

EAGLES: 30 Matthew Costello; 1 Ryan Millar; 3 Menzie Yere; 25 Jake Spedding; 5 Ben Blackmore; 6 Oscar Thomas; 7 Thibault Franck; 12 Shaun Pick; 14 Greg Burns; 10 Jon Magrin; 20 Max Garcia; 15 Olly Davies; 27 Jack Ashworth. Subs (all used): 22 Paddy Burns; 2 Iliess Macani; 16 Kieran Moran; 8 Mark Offerdahl.
Tries: Costello (16, 80), Spedding (50);
Goals: Thomas 1/1, Franck 0/2.
BRONCOS: 14 Alex Walker; 5 Kieran Dixon; 17 Michael Channing; 1 Elliot Kear; 2 Rhys Williams; 6 Api Pewhairangi; 7 Jarrod Sammut; 15 Eddie Battye; 13 Matt Davis; 18 Ben Evans; 12 Jay Pitts; 11 Daniel Harrison; 19 Sadiq Adebiyi. Subs (all used): 16 Matty Gee; 21 Will Lovell; 10 Mark Ioane; 9 James Cunningham.
Tries: Pitts (3), Sammut (7, 25, 47), Pewhairangi (10), Dixon (34, 76), Ioane (43), Adebiyi (60), Walker (61), Cunningham (68); **Goals:** Sammut 11/11.
Rugby Leaguer & League Express Men of the Match: *Eagles:* Matthew Costello; *Broncos:* Jarrod Sammut.
Penalty count: 5-6; **Half-time:** 6-30;
Referee: Tom Grant; **Attendance:** 517.

Championship 2018 - Round by Round

ROUND 14

Saturday 19th May 2018

TORONTO WOLFPACK 43 TOULOUSE OLYMPIQUE 30

WOLFPACK: 31 Gareth O'Brien; 30 Matthew Russell; 33 Chase Stanley; 3 Greg Worthington; 5 Liam Kay; 6 Josh McCrone; 7 Ryan Brierley; 29 Jake Emmitt; 9 Bob Beswick; 10 Ashton Sims; 11 Andrew Dixon; 24 Cory Paterson; 28 Sam Hopkins. Subs (all used): 15 Adam Sidlow; 21 Olsi Krasniqi; 22 Richard Whiting; 17 Blake Wallace.
Tries: Kay (5, 43, 53), Russell (12), Dixon (30), Brierley (50), Stanley (61), Hopkins (66); **Goals:** Brierley 5/8;
Field goal: Brierley (65).
Sin bin: Beswick (75) - dangerous challenge.
OLYMPIQUE: 1 Mark Kheirallah; 22 Chris Centrone; 4 Gavin Marguerite; 3 Bastien Ader; 21 James Worthington; 6 Johnathon Ford; 30 William Barthau; 8 Clement Boyer; 14 Mourad Kriouache; 15 Maxime Puech; 11 Sebastien Planas; 12 Rhys Curran; 13 Andrew Bentley. Subs (all used): 19 Charles Bouzinac; 23 Justin Sangare; 16 Tyla Hepi; 9 Anthony Marion.
Tries: Kriouache (18), Marion (39), Bouzinac (56), Curran (76), Ford (80); **Goals:** Kheirallah 5/5.
Rugby Leaguer & League Express Men of the Match: *Wolfpack:* Ryan Brierley; *Olympique:* Johnathon Ford.
Penalty count: 5-11; **Half-time:** 16-12;
Referee: Scott Mikalauskas. *(at St James' Park, Newcastle).*

FEATHERSTONE ROVERS 20 LEIGH CENTURIONS 42

ROVERS: 1 Ian Hardman; 5 Luke Briscoe; 20 Josh Hardcastle; 29 Harry Newman; 2 Shaun Robinson; 6 Martyn Ridyard; 19 Tom Holmes; 8 Scott Wheeldon; 9 Keal Carlile; 21 Bradley Knowles; 11 Connor Farrell; 32 Josh Walters; 13 James Lockwood. Subs (all used): 14 Matty Wildie; 17 Luke Cooper; 22 Sam Brooks; 27 Jack Ormondroyd.
Tries: Walters (7, 56), Wildie (44), Hardcastle (59);
Goals: Ridyard 0/1, Hardman 2/3.
CENTURIONS: 4 Peter Mata'utia; 2 Matty Dawson-Jones; 3 Ben Crooks; 1 Craig Hall; 19 Jack Owens; 6 Ben Reynolds; 7 Drew Hutchison; 18 Nathan Mason; 30 Micky Higham; 10 Jamie Acton; 13 Harrison Hansen; 12 Bodene Thompson; 15 Jordan Thompson. Subs (all used): 14 Liam Hood; 31 Jordan Baldwinson; 20 Greg Richards; 11 Kevin Larroyer.
Tries: Owens (16), Hood (27), Crooks (31, 52), Mason (49), Hansen (70), Reynolds (79); **Goals:** Reynolds 7/8.
Rugby Leaguer & League Express Men of the Match: *Rovers:* Ian Hardman; *Centurions:* Jamie Acton.
Penalty count: 12-13; **Half-time:** 4-18;
Referee: Matt Rossleigh; **Attendance:** 2,854.

Sunday 20th May 2018

BATLEY BULLDOGS 23 ROCHDALE HORNETS 14

BULLDOGS: 1 Dave Scott; 5 Shaun Ainscough; 22 Danny Cowling; 29 Lewis Galbraith; 4 Jason Crookes; 25 Izaac Farrell; 7 Dominic Brambani; 8 Adam Gledhill; 14 James Davey; 20 Alex Rowe; 15 James Harrison; 12 Joel Farrell; 6 Pat Walker. Subs (all used): 16 Michael Ward; 3 Sam Smeaton; 19 Alex Bretherton; 17 Joe Chandler.
Tries: Brambani (13), Harrison (15), Bretherton (32), I Farrell (49); **Goals:** Walker 3/4; **Field goal:** I Farrell (70).
HORNETS: 2 Declan Kay; 21 Richard Lepori; 3 Earl Hurst; 30 Deon Cross; 5 Rob Massam; 14 Tyler Whittaker; 7 Danny Yates; 16 Pat Moran; 18 Billy Brickhill; 15 Lewis Hatton; 25 Seta Tala; 19 Lee Mitchell; 11 Dave Allen. Subs (all used): 17 Jonah Cunningham; 4 Jordan Syme; 10 Matty Hadden; 22 Alex Gaskell.
Tries: Massam (5, 73), Cross (27);
Goals: Whittaker 1/2, Syme 0/1.
Rugby Leaguer & League Express Men of the Match: *Bulldogs:* Izaac Farrell; *Hornets:* Rob Massam.
Penalty count: 5-6; **Half-time:** 18-10;
Referee: Greg Dolan; **Attendance:** 743.

HALIFAX 22 DEWSBURY RAMS 22

HALIFAX: 26 Quentin Laulu-Togagae; 21 Conor McGrath; 3 Steve Tyrer; 4 Ed Barber; 1 Will Sharp; 6 Scott Murrell; 7 Ben Johnston; 13 Jacob Fairbank; 9 Ben Kaye; 29 Dan Fleming; 18 Chester Butler; 11 Shane Grady; 12 Simon Grix. Subs (all used): 8 Elliot Morris; 14 Brandon Moore; 17 Will Maher; 25 Sion Jones.
Tries: Laulu-Togagae (47), Tyrer (52, 58), Barber (74);
Goals: Tyrer 3/4.
Sin bin: Johnston (35) - fighting.
RAMS: 1 Josh Guzdek; 2 Rob Worrincy; 3 James Glover; 4 Macauley Hallett; 5 Dale Morton; 6 Paul Sykes; 13 Aaron Brown; 24 Shannon Wakeman; 9 Robbie Ward; 10 Jack Teanby; 15 Lucas Walshaw; 12 Michael Knowles; 20 Jordan Crowther. Subs (all used): 8 Jode Sheriffe; 14 Dom Speakman; 17 Toby Everett; 31 Daniel Igbinedion.
Tries: Crowther (9), Knowles (26), Worrincy (60);
Goals: Sykes 5/5.
Sin bin: Everett (35) - fighting.
Rugby Leaguer & League Express Men of the Match: *Halifax:* Quentin Laulu-Togagae; *Rams:* Shannon Wakeman.
Penalty count: 12-8; **Half-time:** 0-14;
Referee: Billy Pearson; **Attendance:** 1,739.

LONDON BRONCOS 46 SHEFFIELD EAGLES 12

BRONCOS: 14 Alex Walker; 5 Kieran Dixon; 21 Will Lovell; 1 Elliot Kear; 2 Rhys Williams; 17 Michael Channing; 7 Jarrod Sammut; 8 Tom Spencer; 13 Matt Davis; 15 Eddie Battye; 12 Jay Pitts; 26 Daniel Hindmarsh; 19 Sadiq Adebiyi. Subs (all used): 9 James Cunningham; 10 Mark Ioane; 18 Ben Evans; 16 Matty Gee.
Tries: Williams (30, 80), Ioane (34), Gee (38, 40), Sammut (69), Matt Davis (74), Dixon (78);
Goals: Sammut 7/9.
Dismissal: Evans (56) - punching P Burns.
EAGLES: 30 Matthew Costello; 1 Ryan Millar; 3 Menzie Yere; 25 Jake Spedding; 5 Ben Blackmore; 29 Corey Makelim; 7 Thibault Franck; 8 Mark Offerdahl; 9 Matty Fozard; 10 Jon Magrin; 27 Jack Ashworth; 12 Shaun Pick; 22 Paddy Burns. Subs (all used): 2 Iliess Macani; 15 Olly Davies; 16 Kieran Moran; 20 Max Garcia.
Tries: Fozard (10), Davies (46); **Goals:** Fozard 2/2.
Sin bin: Costello (37) - holding down; Millar (38) - dissent.
Rugby Leaguer & League Express Men of the Match: *Broncos:* Alex Walker; *Eagles:* Matty Fozard.
Penalty count: 9-5; **Half-time:** 20-6;
Referee: Liam Staveley; **Attendance:** 771.

SWINTON LIONS 22 BARROW RAIDERS 22

LIONS: 1 Gabriel Fell; 5 Mike Butt; 3 Chris Hankinson; 4 George Tyson; 16 Ilias Bergal; 6 Brad Billsborough; 7 Jack Hansen; 8 Andy Bracek; 9 Luke Waterworth; 15 Ben Austin; 11 Rhodri Lloyd; 33 Liam Paisley; - Will Hope. Subs (all used): 13 Josh Barlow; 14 Hayden Hansen; 10 Andy Thornley; 17 Kyle Shelford.
Tries: Tyson (19, 69), Lloyd (31), Paisley (35, 55);
Goals: Hankinson 1/4, Billsborough 0/1.
Sin bin: Tyson (58) - high tackle on D Toal.
RAIDERS: 1 Ryan Fieldhouse; 5 Brett Carter; 3 Declan Hulme; 23 Tom Loxam; 2 Shane Toal; 6 Jamie Dallimore; 21 Ryan Johnston; 17 Alec Susino; 9 Nathan Mossop; 13 Martin Aspinwall; 25 Jono Smith; 12 Jarrad Stack; 19 Bradd Crellin. Subs (all used): 22 Dean Parata; 11 Dan Toal; 20 Matty While; 27 Ryan Duffy.
Tries: Fieldhouse (14), S Toal (38), Parata (60);
Goals: Dallimore 5/5.
Sin bin: D Toal (27) - dangerous challenge on Billsborough.
Rugby Leaguer & League Express Men of the Match: *Lions:* George Tyson; *Raiders:* Jamie Dallimore.
Penalty count: 10-9; **Half-time:** 14-12;
Referee: Steve Race; **Attendance:** 656.

ROUND 15 - SUMMER BASH

Saturday 26th May 2018

BARROW RAIDERS 22 SHEFFIELD EAGLES 38

RAIDERS: 1 Ryan Fieldhouse; 5 Brett Carter; 3 Declan Hulme; 29 Gene Ormsby; 2 Shane Toal; 6 Jamie Dallimore; 14 Karl Ashall; 8 Joe Bullock; 9 Nathan Mossop; 13 Martin Aspinwall; 25 Jono Smith; 12 Jarrad Stack; 11 Dan Toal. Subs (all used): 22 Dean Parata; 20 Matty While; 15 Glenn Riley; 27 Ryan Duffy.
Tries: S Toal (31), Stack (36), Dallimore (71), Ormsby (73);
Goals: Dallimore 3/4.
EAGLES: 30 Matthew Costello; 1 Ryan Millar; 3 Menzie Yere; 25 Jake Spedding; 5 Ben Blackmore; 23 Cory Aston; 29 Corey Makelim; 8 Mark Offerdahl; 9 Matty Fozard; 10 Jon Magrin; 27 Jack Ashworth; 12 Shaun Pick; 4 Joshua Toole. Subs (all used): 6 Oscar Thomas; 15 Olly Davies; 19 Mike Weldon; 28 Matty Lees.
Tries: Aston (5, 43, 58), Yere (45), Toole (56), Spedding (64), Makelim (77); **Goals:** Aston 4/7, Thomas 1/1.
Rugby Leaguer & League Express Men of the Match: *Raiders:* Jamie Dallimore; *Eagles:* Cory Aston.
Penalty count: 7-8; **Half-time:** 12-8;
Referee: Liam Staveley.

FEATHERSTONE ROVERS 18 HALIFAX 24

ROVERS: 1 Ian Hardman; 5 Luke Briscoe; 20 Josh Hardcastle; 29 Harry Newman; 2 Shaun Robinson; 19 Tom Holmes; 7 Anthony Thackeray; 8 Scott Wheeldon; 9 Keal Carlile; 21 Bradley Knowles; 13 James Lockwood; 12 John Davies; 10 Richard Moore. Subs (all used): 14 Matty Wildie; 15 Gareth Hock; 22 Sam Brooks; 25 Mitch Clark.
Tries: Hock (53), Thackeray (57), Wildie (59);
Goals: Hardman 3/3.
Sin bin: Clark (42) - fighting.
HALIFAX: 26 Quentin Laulu-Togagae; 5 James Saltonstall; 4 Ed Barber; 3 Steve Tyrer; 1 Will Sharp; 6 Scott Murrell; 7 Ben Johnston; 13 Jacob Fairbank; 9 Ben Kaye; 10 Adam Tangata; 11 Shane Grady; 18 Chester Butler; 12 Simon Grix. Subs (all used): 14 Brandon Moore; 8 Elliot Morris; 29 Dan Fleming; 17 Will Maher.
Tries: Murrell (9, 78), Tyrer (23), Johnston (75);
Goals: Tyrer 3/4, Grady 1/1.
Sin bin: Fleming (42) - fighting; Tyrer (67) - trip on Carlile.
Rugby Leaguer & League Express Men of the Match: *Rovers:* Gareth Hock; *Halifax:* Shane Grady.
Penalty count: 11-11; **Half-time:** 0-14; **Referee:** Tom Grant.

LEIGH CENTURIONS 26 TORONTO WOLFPACK 28

CENTURIONS: 4 Peter Mata'utia; 2 Matty Dawson-Jones; 3 Ben Crooks; 1 Craig Hall; 19 Jack Owens; 6 Ben Reynolds; 7 Drew Hutchison; 29 Ryan Bailey; 30 Micky Higham; 18 Nathan Mason; 13 Harrison Hansen; 12 Bodene Thompson; 15 Jordan Thompson. Subs (all used): 14 Liam Hood; 20 Greg Richards; 31 Jordan Baldwinson; 10 Jamie Acton.
Tries: Mason (3), Crooks (21, 46), Acton (31), Owens (56);
Goals: Reynolds 3/6.
Sin bin: Mata'utia (71) - high tackle on Russell.
WOLFPACK: 31 Gareth O'Brien; 30 Matthew Russell; 3 Greg Worthington; 23 Nick Rawsthorne; 5 Liam Kay; 6 Josh McCrone; 7 Ryan Brierley; 29 Jake Emmitt; 9 Bob Beswick; 28 Sam Hopkins; 11 Andrew Dixon; 24 Cory Paterson; 21 Olsi Krasniqi. Subs (all used): 10 Ashton Sims; 8 Jack Buchanan; 15 Adam Sidlow; 14 Andy Ackers.
Tries: McCrone (10), O'Brien (41), Rawsthorne (63), Krasniqi (66), Paterson (75); **Goals:** Brierley 4/5.
Rugby Leaguer & League Express Men of the Match: *Centurions:* Ben Reynolds; *Wolfpack:* Matthew Russell.
Penalty count: 8-10; **Half-time:** 16-6;
Referee: Scott Mikalauskas.

Attendance: 7,877 *(at Bloomfield Road, Blackpool).*

Sunday 27th May 2018

LONDON BRONCOS 28 TOULOUSE OLYMPIQUE 40

BRONCOS: 14 Alex Walker; 5 Kieran Dixon; 4 Matty Fleming; 1 Elliot Kear; 2 Rhys Williams; 17 Michael Channing; 7 Jarrod Sammut; 8 Tom Spencer; 13 Matt Davis; 10 Mark Ioane; 11 Daniel Harrison; 12 Jay Pitts; 15 Eddie Battye. Subs (all used): 16 Matty Gee; 9 James Cunningham; 18 Ben Evans; 19 Sadiq Adebiyi.
Tries: Sammut (26), Pitts (40), Evans (49), Williams (65, 78); **Goals:** Sammut 4/5.
Sin bin: Dixon (59) - high tackle.
OLYMPIQUE: 1 Mark Kheirallah; 21 James Worthington; 4 Gavin Marguerite; 3 Bastien Ader; 2 Tony Maurel; 6 Johnathon Ford; 30 William Barthau; 8 Clement Boyer; 14 Mourad Kriouache; 10 Bastien Canet; 26 Constantine Mika; 12 Rhys Curran; 13 Andrew Bentley. Subs (all used): 19 Charles Bouzinac; 24 Joe Bretherton; 16 Tyla Hepi; 9 Anthony Marion.
Tries: Maurel (13, 36), Worthington (23), Curran (54), Bouzinac (61), Kheirallah (75, 80); **Goals:** Kheirallah 6/7.
Rugby Leaguer & League Express Men of the Match: *Broncos:* Jay Pitts; *Olympique:* Mark Kheirallah.
Penalty count: 7-6; **Half-time:** 12-18; **Referee:** Greg Dolan.

ROCHDALE HORNETS 12 SWINTON LIONS 38

HORNETS: 2 Declan Kay; 21 Richard Lepori; 3 Earl Hurst; 31 Deon Cross; 5 Rob Massam; 14 Tyler Whittaker; 7 Danny Yates; 8 Jovili Taira; 18 Billy Brickhill; 15 Lewis Hatton; 25 Seta Tala; 19 Lee Mitchell; 11 Dave Allen. Subs (all used): 17 Jonah Cunningham; 16 Pat Moran; 10 Matty Hadden; 4 Jordan Syme.
Tries: Lepori (8), Cunningham (74); **Goals:** Whittaker 2/2.
LIONS: 1 Gabriel Fell; 5 Mike Butt; 3 Chris Hankinson; 4 George Tyson; 16 Ilias Bergal; 31 Josh Woods; 7 Jack Hansen; 8 Andy Bracek; 9 Luke Waterworth; 15 Ben Austin; 11 Rhodri Lloyd; 34 Liam Paisley; 25 Will Hope. Subs (all used): 13 Josh Barlow; 14 Hayden Hansen; 10 Andy Thornley; 6 Brad Billsborough.
Tries: Waterworth (5), Tyson (36, 47), Hope (43), Woods (54), Paisley (61); **Goals:** Hankinson 7/7.
Rugby Leaguer & League Express Men of the Match: *Hornets:* Declan Kay; *Lions:* Josh Woods.
Penalty count: 5-7; **Half-time:** 6-12;
Referee: Matt Rossleigh.

BATLEY BULLDOGS 18 DEWSBURY RAMS 20

BULLDOGS: 1 Dave Scott; 28 Keenen Tomlinson; 3 Sam Smeaton; 29 Lewis Galbraith; 4 Jason Crookes; 27 Danny Sowerby; 25 Izaac Farrell; 8 Adam Gledhill; 9 Alistair Leak; 20 Alex Rowe; 19 Alex Bretherton; 12 Joel Farrell; 13 Brad Day. Subs (all used): 30 Reiss Butterworth; 24 Tommy Holland; 16 Michael Ward; 15 James Harrison.
Tries: Harrison (32), Butterworth (38), J Farrell (48);
Goals: I Farrell 3/4.

RAMS: 1 Josh Guzdek; 18 Gareth Potts; 3 James Glover; 4 Macauley Hallett; 5 Dale Morton; 6 Paul Sykes; 13 Aaron Brown; 24 Shannon Wakeman; 14 Dom Speakman; 10 Jack Teanby; 28 Kyle Trout; 12 Michael Knowles; 20 Jordan Crowther. Subs (all used): 19 Sam Day; 22 Martyn Reilly; 17 Toby Everett; 31 Daniel Igbinedion.
Tries: Brown (14), Day (43), Igbinedion (55);
Goals: Sykes 4/4.
Rugby Leaguer & League Express Men of the Match: *Bulldogs:* Izaac Farrell; *Rams:* Daniel Igbinedion.
Penalty count: 8-11; **Half-time:** 12-6; **Referee:** Jack Smith.

Attendance: 3,928 *(at Bloomfield Road, Blackpool).*

ROUND 5

Saturday 2nd June 2018

BATLEY BULLDOGS 18 HALIFAX 32

BULLDOGS: 25 Izaac Farrell; 1 Dave Scott; 3 Sam Smeaton; 29 Lewis Galbraith; 4 Jason Crookes; 6 Pat Walker; 27 Danny Sowerby; 8 Adam Gledhill; 9 Alistair Leak; 24 Tommy Holland; 15 James Harrison; 12 Joel Farrell; 13 Brad Day. Subs (all used): 16 Michael Ward; 20 Alex Rowe; 30 Reiss Butterworth; 19 Alex Bretherton.
Tries: J Farrell (40, 51), Harrison (57); **Goals:** Walker 3/3.
HALIFAX: 16 James Woodburn-Hall; 5 James Saltonstall; 3 Steve Tyrer; 4 Ed Barber; 2 Ben Heaton; 6 Scott Murrell; 7 Ben Johnston; 29 Dan Fleming; 9 Ben Kaye; 8 Elliot Morris; 18 Chester Butler; 11 Shane Grady; 13 Jacob Fairbank. Subs (all used): 14 Brandon Moore; 10 Adam Tangata; 31 James Green; 17 Will Maher.
Tries: Butler (6), Johnston (10), Saltonstall (14), Heaton (29, 53), Tyrer (74); **Goals:** Tyrer 4/6.
Rugby Leaguer & League Express Men of the Match: *Bulldogs:* Joel Farrell; *Halifax:* Chester Butler.
Penalty count: 7-5; **Half-time:** 6-22;
Referee: John McMullen; **Attendance:** 1,002.

ROUND 2

Sunday 3rd June 2018

SWINTON LIONS 18 ROCHDALE HORNETS 25

LIONS: 1 Gabriel Fell; 5 Mike Butt; 3 Chris Hankinson; 11 Rhodri Lloyd; 4 George Tyson; 6 Brad Billsborough; 7 Jack Hansen; 8 Andy Bracek; 14 Hayden Hansen; 15 Ben Austin; 10 Andy Thornley; 33 Liam Paisley; - Gabe Hamlin. Subs (all used): 13 Josh Barlow; 17 Kyle Shelford; 21 Chris Worrell; 35 Tommy Gallagher.
Tries: Lloyd (18, 73), Hankinson (54, 80);
Goals: Hankinson 1/3, J Hansen 0/1.
Dismissal: Barlow (75) - dissent.
Sin bin: Barlow (33) - punching.
HORNETS: 2 Declan Kay; 21 Richard Lepori; 25 Jack Fox; 31 Deon Cross; 5 Rob Massam; 14 Tyler Whittaker; 7 Danny Yates; 8 Jovili Taira; 9 Ben Moores; 23 Gary Middlehurst; 12 Toby Adamson; 19 Lee Mitchell; 11 Dave Allen. Subs (all used): 17 Jonah Cunningham; 15 Lewis Hatton; 16 Pat Moran; 13 Luke Adamson.
Tries: Yates (15), Middlehurst (22), Massam (30), Cross (46); **Goals:** Whittaker 4/5;
Field goal: Whittaker (78).
Rugby Leaguer & League Express Men of the Match: *Lions:* Rhodri Lloyd; *Hornets:* Tyler Whittaker.
Penalty count: 9-7; **Half-time:** 4-18;
Referee: Tom Grant; **Attendance:** 631.

ROUND 16

Saturday 9th June 2018

TOULOUSE OLYMPIQUE 42 BATLEY BULLDOGS 26

OLYMPIQUE: 1 Mark Kheirallah; 2 Tony Maurel; 3 Bastien Ader; 4 Gavin Marguerite; 22 Chris Centrone; 30 William Barthau; 6 Johnathon Ford; 10 Bastien Canet; 19 Charles Bouzinac; 24 Joe Bretherton; 26 Constantine Mika; 12 Rhys Curran; 9 Anthony Marion. Subs (all used): 16 Tyla Hepi; 17 Eddy Pettybourne; 23 Justin Sangare; 28 Justin Bouscayrol.
Tries: Ader (3, 19), Marguerite (24), Mika (29), Kheirallah (32), Maurel (35), Bouscayrol (50);
Goals: Kheirallah 7/8.
Sin bin: Canet (4) - fighting.
BULLDOGS: 1 Dave Scott; 28 Keenen Tomlinson; 3 Sam Smeaton; 29 Lewis Galbraith; 4 Jason Crookes; 25 Izaac Farrell; 27 Danny Sowerby; 8 Adam Gledhill; 9 Alistair Leak; 24 Tommy Holland; 15 James Harrison; 12 Joel Farrell; 13 Brad Day. Subs (all used): 16 Michael Ward; 20 Alex Rowe; 14 James Davey; 19 Alex Bretherton.
Tries: Scott (23), Tomlinson (48, 66), Galbraith (59), Holland (75); **Goals:** I Farrell 3/5.
Sin bin: J Farrell (4) - fighting.
Rugby Leaguer & League Express Men of the Match: *Olympique:* Mark Kheirallah; *Bulldogs:* Dave Scott.
Penalty count: 13-8; **Half-time:** 34-6;
Referee: Billy Pearson; **Attendance:** 2,250.

TORONTO WOLFPACK 32 LONDON BRONCOS 12

WOLFPACK: 31 Gareth O'Brien; 30 Matthew Russell; 33 Chase Stanley; 3 Greg Worthington; 5 Liam Kay; 6 Josh McCrone; 7 Ryan Brierley; 29 Jake Emmitt; 14 Andy Ackers; 10 Ashton Sims; 11 Andrew Dixon; 24 Cory Paterson; 21 Olsi Krasniqi. Subs (all used): 8 Jack Buchanan; 15 Adam Sidlow; 28 Sam Hopkins; 17 Blake Wallace.
Tries: Paterson (3, 43), Kay (13), McCrone (46), Brierley (80); **Goals:** Brierley 6/6.
BRONCOS: 14 Alex Walker; 1 Elliot Kear; 4 Matty Fleming; 6 Api Pewhairangi; 2 Rhys Williams; 27 James Meadows; 7 Jarrod Sammut; 8 Tom Spencer; 9 James Cunningham; 10 Mark Ioane; 12 Jay Pitts; 11 Daniel Harrison; 13 Matt Davis. Subs (all used): 19 Sadiq Adebiyi; 16 Matty Gee; 15 Eddie Battye; 25 Matthew Davies.
Tries: Sammut (19), Kear (59); **Goals:** Sammut 2/2.
Rugby Leaguer & League Express Men of the Match: *Wolfpack:* Cory Paterson; *Broncos:* Jarrod Sammut.
Penalty count: 9-9; **Half-time:** 14-6;
Referee: Tom Crashley; **Attendance:** 7,384.

Sunday 10th June 2018

BARROW RAIDERS 20 ROCHDALE HORNETS 6

RAIDERS: 1 Ryan Fieldhouse; 2 Shane Toal; 3 Declan Hulme; 12 Jarrad Stack; 23 Tom Loxam; 6 Jamie Dallimore; 21 Ryan Johnston; 8 Joe Bullock; 14 Karl Ashall; 17 Alec Susino; 25 Jono Smith; 19 Bradd Crellin; 11 Dan Toal. Subs (all used): 27 Ryan Duffy; 9 Nathan Mossop; 15 Glenn Riley; 20 Matty While.
Tries: Hulme (43), Fieldhouse (51), Bullock (62, 78);
Goals: Dallimore 2/6.
HORNETS: 2 Declan Kay; 21 Richard Lepori; 25 Seta Tala; 31 Deon Cross; 5 Rob Massam; 14 Tyler Whittaker; 7 Danny Yates; 8 Jovili Taira; 9 Ben Moores; 26 George King; 12 Toby Adamson; 19 Lee Mitchell; 23 Gary Middlehurst. Subs (all used): 17 Jonah Cunningham; 15 Lewis Hatton; 16 Pat Moran; 13 Luke Adamson.
Try: Tala (67); **Goals:** Whittaker 1/1.
Rugby Leaguer & League Express Men of the Match: *Raiders:* Dan Toal; *Hornets:* Seta Tala.
Penalty count: 9-6; **Half-time:** 4-0;
Referee: Jack Smith; **Attendance:** 1,212.

DEWSBURY RAMS 18 FEATHERSTONE ROVERS 42

RAMS: 1 Josh Guzdek; 18 Gareth Potts; 3 James Glover; 4 Macauley Hallett; 5 Dale Morton; 6 Paul Sykes; 13 Aaron Brown; 8 Jode Sheriffe; 9 Robbie Ward; 10 Jack Teanby; 28 Kyle Trout; 31 Daniel Igbinedion; 20 Jordan Crowther. Subs (all used): 14 Dom Speakman; 17 Toby Everett; 24 Shannon Wakeman; 15 Lucas Walshaw.
Tries: Crowther (47), Potts (50), Trout (65);
Goals: Sykes 2/2, Morton 1/1.
Sin bin: Sykes (60) - dissent.
ROVERS: 1 Ian Hardman; 5 Luke Briscoe; 4 Misi Taulapapa; 18 Jason Walton; 2 Shaun Robinson; 7 Anthony Thackeray; 14 Matty Wildie; 8 Scott Wheeldon; 9 Keal Carlile; 17 Luke Cooper; 13 James Lockwood; 12 John Davies; 15 Gareth Hock. Subs (all used): 10 Richard Moore; 22 Sam Brooks; 27 Jack Ormondroyd; 34 Brad Dwyer.
Tries: Cooper (6), Wildie (18), Ormondroyd (29, 73), Thackeray (38, 58), Hock (54); **Goals:** Hardman 7/7.
Rugby Leaguer & League Express Men of the Match: *Rams:* Jordan Crowther; *Rovers:* Anthony Thackeray.
Penalty count: 7-5; **Half-time:** 0-24;
Referee: Tom Grant; **Attendance:** 1,268.

LEIGH CENTURIONS 36 HALIFAX 30

CENTURIONS: 19 Jack Owens; 22 Ricky Bailey; 3 Ben Crooks; 1 Craig Hall; 5 Rhys Evans; 6 Ben Reynolds; 7 Drew Hutchison; 18 Nathan Mason; 14 Liam Hood; 10 Jamie Acton; 13 Harrison Hansen; 12 Bodene Thompson; 21 Nick Gregson. Subs (all used): 9 Daniel Mortimer; 29 Ryan Bailey; 20 Greg Richards; 15 Jordan Thompson.
Tries: Hood (17, 63), Acton (50), Gregson (57, 65), Hall (78);
Goals: Reynolds 6/6.
HALIFAX: 24 Kieren Moss; 5 James Saltonstall; 4 Ed Barber; 18 Chester Butler; 2 Ben Heaton; 6 Scott Murrell; 7 Ben Johnston; 29 Dan Fleming; 9 Ben Kaye; 13 Jacob Fairbank; 10 Adam Tangata; 11 Shane Grady; 12 Simon Grix. Subs (all used): 8 Elliot Morris; 14 Brandon Moore; 17 Will Maher; 31 James Green.
Tries: Murrell (25), Moss (41), Johnston (46, 70), Heaton (73); **Goals:** Grady 5/5.
Sin bin: Barber (29) - holding down.
Rugby Leaguer & League Express Men of the Match: *Centurions:* Liam Hood; *Halifax:* Scott Murrell.
Penalty count: 3-7; **Half-time:** 6-6;
Referee: Scott Mikalauskas; **Attendance:** 3,891.

SHEFFIELD EAGLES 18 SWINTON LIONS 29

EAGLES: 30 Matthew Costello; 1 Ryan Millar; 3 Menzie Yere; 25 Jake Spedding; 5 Ben Blackmore; 23 Cory Aston; 29 Corey Makelim; 8 Mark Offerdahl; 9 Matty Fozard; 10 Jon Magrin; 27 Jack Ashworth; 12 Shaun Pick; 4 Joshua Toole. Subs (all used): 14 Greg Burns; 18 Mike Weldon; 22 Paddy Burns; 13 Matt James.
Tries: Ashworth (6), Aston (22), Spedding (58);
Goals: Aston 3/3.
LIONS: 1 Gabriel Fell; 5 Mike Butt; 3 Chris Hankinson; 4 George Tyson; 32 Joe Brown; 31 Josh Woods; 7 Jack Hansen; 8 Andy Bracek; - Josh Ganson; 15 Ben Austin; 11 Rhodri Lloyd; 33 Liam Paisley; 25 Will Hope. Subs (all used): 13 Josh Barlow; 14 Hayden Hansen; 17 Kyle Shelford; 10 Andy Thornley.
Tries: Lloyd (19), Tyson (29, 78), Butt (45), Hope (50);
Goals: Hankinson 4/5; **Field goal:** Woods (69).
Rugby Leaguer & League Express Men of the Match: *Eagles:* Matty Fozard; *Lions:* George Tyson.
Penalty count: 4-4; **Half-time:** 12-12;
Referee: John McMullen; **Attendance:** 872.

ROUND 17

Saturday 16th June 2018

TOULOUSE OLYMPIQUE 16 LEIGH CENTURIONS 18

OLYMPIQUE: 1 Mark Kheirallah; 2 Tony Maurel; 3 Bastien Ader; 4 Gavin Marguerite; 22 Chris Centrone; 6 Johnathon Ford; 30 William Barthau; 8 Clement Boyer; 14 Mourad Kriouache; 24 Joe Bretherton; 10 Bastien Canet; 26 Constantine Mika; 9 Anthony Marion. Subs (all used): 15 Maxime Puech; 16 Tyla Hepi; 19 Charles Bouzinac; 17 Eddy Pettybourne.
Tries: Marguerite (2), Canet (29), Mika (47);
Goals: Kheirallah 2/3.
CENTURIONS: 19 Jack Owens; 22 Ricky Bailey; 3 Ben Crooks; 1 Craig Hall; 5 Rhys Evans; 6 Ben Reynolds; 7 Drew Hutchison; 13 Harrison Hansen; 14 Liam Hood; 10 Jamie Acton; 11 Kevin Larroyer; 12 Bodene Thompson; 15 Jordan Thompson. Subs (all used): 9 Daniel Mortimer; 31 Jordan Baldwinson; 26 Jordan Dezaria; 21 Nick Gregson.
Tries: Larroyer (6), Acton (14), Ricky Bailey (25);
Goals: Reynolds 1/3, Hall 2/2.
Rugby Leaguer & League Express Men of the Match: *Olympique:* Johnathon Ford; *Centurions:* Jordan Thompson.
Penalty count: 6-5; **Half-time:** 10-14;
Referee: Tom Grant; **Attendance:** 5,373 *(at Stadium Municipal, Albi).*

TORONTO WOLFPACK 64 DEWSBURY RAMS 12

WOLFPACK: 31 Gareth O'Brien; 30 Matthew Russell; 3 Greg Worthington; 33 Chase Stanley; 5 Liam Kay; 6 Josh McCrone; 17 Blake Wallace; 32 Darcy Lussick; 14 Andy Ackers; 8 Jack Buchanan; 11 Andrew Dixon; 24 Cory Paterson; 21 Olsi Krasniqi. Subs (all used): 28 Sam Hopkins; 15 Adam Sidlow; 22 Richard Whiting; 23 Nick Rawsthorne.
Tries: Kay (7), Lussick (13), Ackers (17), Russell (20, 78), Paterson (25), O'Brien (28, 67), Wallace (39), Buchanan (62), Rawsthorne (73); **Goals:** O'Brien 10/11.
RAMS: 1 Josh Guzdek; 18 Gareth Potts; 3 James Glover; 4 Macauley Hallett; 5 Dale Morton; 25 Lewis Heckford; 30 Danny Ansell; 24 Shannon Wakeman; 14 Dom Speakman; 10 Jack Teanby; 28 Kyle Trout; 20 Jordan Crowther; 13 Aaron Brown. Subs (all used, only three named): 8 Jode Sheriffe; 17 Toby Everett; 22 Martyn Reilly.
Tries: Everett (36), Guzdek (43); **Goals:** Glover 2/2.
Rugby Leaguer & League Express Men of the Match: *Wolfpack:* Gareth O'Brien; *Rams:* Dom Speakman.
Penalty count: 2-11; **Half-time:** 40-6;
Referee: Nick Bennett; **Attendance:** 5,937.

Sunday 17th June 2018

BATLEY BULLDOGS 20 SHEFFIELD EAGLES 38

BULLDOGS: 1 Dave Scott; 28 Keenen Tomlinson; 22 Danny Cowling; 29 Lewis Galbraith; 4 Jason Crookes; 30 Reiss Butterworth; 27 Danny Sowerby; 8 Adam Gledhill; 9 Alistair Leak; 24 Tommy Holland; 15 James Harrison; 12 Joel Farrell; 13 Brad Day. Subs (all used): 16 Michael Ward; 20 Alex Rowe; 14 James Davey; 19 Alex Bretherton.
Tries: Crookes (6), Butterworth (26), Davey (63);
Goals: Scott 4/4.
EAGLES: 30 Matthew Costello; 1 Ryan Millar; 24 Adam Swift; 25 Jake Spedding; 5 Ben Blackmore; 23 Cory Aston; 29 Corey Makelim; 8 Mark Offerdahl; 9 Matty Fozard; 10 Jon Magrin; 13 Matt James; 27 Jack Ashworth; 12 Shaun Pick. Subs (all used): 14 Greg Burns; 19 Simon Brown; 3 Menzie Yere; 18 Mike Weldon.

Championship 2018 - Round by Round

Tries: James (3), Fozard (12), Swift (31), Millar (58), Blackmore (70), Spedding (75); **Goals:** Aston 7/8.
Rugby Leaguer & League Express Men of the Match: *Bulldogs:* Joel Farrell; *Eagles:* Adam Swift.
Penalty count: 11-8; **Half-time:** 14-20;
Referee: Scott Mikalauskas; **Attendance:** 2,328.

FEATHERSTONE ROVERS 52 BARROW RAIDERS 4

ROVERS: 1 Ian Hardman; 5 Luke Briscoe; 18 Jason Walton; 4 Misi Taulapapa; 2 Shaun Robinson; 14 Matty Wildie; 7 Anthony Thackeray; 8 Scott Wheeldon; 9 Keal Carlile; 17 Luke Cooper; 12 John Davies; 13 James Lockwood; 15 Gareth Hock. Subs (all used): 10 Richard Moore; 20 Josh Hardcastle; 21 Bradley Knowles; 22 Sam Brooks.
Tries: Cooper (8, 68), Hock (12), Thackeray (19), Briscoe (22), Davies (25), Hardcastle (54), Lockwood (59), Walton (70); **Goals:** Hardman 8/9.
Sin bin: Moore (46) - fighting.
RAIDERS: 30 Jonny Pownall; 2 Shane Toal; 12 Jarrad Stack; 24 Danny Morrow; 23 Tom Loxam; 6 Jamie Dallimore; 21 Ryan Johnston; 27 Ryan Duffy; 14 Karl Ashall; 17 Alec Susino; 11 Dan Toal; 25 Jono Smith; 9 Nathan Mossop. Subs (both used, only two named): 22 Dean Parata; 20 Matty While.
Try: Johnston (49); **Goals:** Dallimore 0/1.
Sin bin: Duffy (46) - fighting.
Rugby Leaguer & League Express Men of the Match: *Rovers:* John Davies; *Raiders:* Matty While.
Penalty count: 13-9; **Half-time:** 30-0;
Referee: Greg Dolan; **Attendance:** 1,880.

LONDON BRONCOS 68 ROCHDALE HORNETS 0

BRONCOS: 14 Alex Walker; 5 Kieran Dixon; 4 Matty Fleming; 1 Elliot Kear; 2 Rhys Williams; 6 Api Pewhairangi; 9 James Cunningham; 8 Tom Spencer; 25 Matthew Davies; 10 Mark Ioane; 12 Jay Pitts; 26 Daniel Hindmarsh; 13 Matt Davis. Subs (all used): 15 Eddie Battye; 18 Ben Evans; 19 Sadiq Adebiyi; 29 Sam Davis.
Tries: Pitts (8, 24), Dixon (15, 21), Pewhairangi (27, 39, 60), Cunningham (31, 67), Evans (42), Walker (49, 71);
Goals: Dixon 10/12.
HORNETS: 2 Declan Kay; - Jack Fox; 31 Ben Pomeroy; 25 Seta Tala; 5 Rob Massam; 30 Jordan Syme; 14 Tyler Whittaker; 8 Jovili Taira; 9 Ben Moores; 15 Lee Mitchell; 26 George King; 12 Toby Adamson; 18 Billy Brickhill. Subs (all used): 15 Lewis Hatton; 16 Pat Moran; 24 Declan Gregory; 13 Luke Adamson.
Rugby Leaguer & League Express Men of the Match: *Broncos:* Api Pewhairangi; *Hornets:* Ben Pomeroy.
Penalty count: 8-5; **Half-time:** 38-0;
Referee: Jack Smith; **Attendance:** 684.

SWINTON LIONS 4 HALIFAX 46

LIONS: 30 Craig Mullen; 5 Mike Butt; 3 Chris Hankinson; 4 George Tyson; 1 Gabriel Fell; 6 Brad Billsborough; 7 Jack Hansen; 8 Andy Bracek; - Josh Ganson; 15 Ben Austin; 11 Rhodri Lloyd; 10 Andy Thornley; 25 Will Hope. Subs (all used): 24 Aaron Hall; 14 Hayden Hansen; 33 Levy Nzoungou; 17 Kyle Shelford.
Try: Butt (19); **Goals:** Hankinson 0/1.
HALIFAX: 24 Kieren Moss; 4 Ed Barber; 3 Steve Tyrer; 2 Ben Heaton; 1 Will Sharp; 6 Scott Murrell; 7 Ben Johnston; 17 Will Maher; 9 Ben Kaye; 13 Jacob Fairbank; 18 Chester Butler; 11 Shane Grady; 12 Simon Grix. Subs (all used): 8 Elliot Morris; 14 Brandon Moore; 29 Dan Fleming; 10 Adam Tangata.
Tries: Butler (13), Moss (27, 32), Johnston (37, 58), Fleming (40), Tyrer (46), Murrell (54); **Goals:** Tyrer 7/8.
Rugby Leaguer & League Express Men of the Match: *Lions:* Craig Mullen; *Halifax:* Ben Johnston.
Penalty count: 10-7; **Half-time:** 4-30;
Referee: Marcus Griffiths; **Attendance:** 953.

ROUND 18

Saturday 23rd June 2018

SHEFFIELD EAGLES 6 FEATHERSTONE ROVERS 40

EAGLES: 30 Matthew Costello; 1 Ryan Millar; 3 Menzie Yere; 25 Jake Spedding; 24 Adam Swift; 29 Corey Makelim; 23 Cory Aston; 8 Mark Offerdahl; 9 Matty Fozard; 10 Jon Magrin; 4 Joshua Toole; 12 Shaun Pick; 13 Matt James. Subs (all used): 6 Oscar Thomas; 15 Olly Davies; 20 Max Garcia; 18 Mike Weldon.
Try: Pick (59); **Goals:** Aston 1/1.
ROVERS: 1 Ian Hardman; 5 Luke Briscoe; 4 Misi Taulapapa; 20 Josh Hardcastle; 2 Shaun Robinson; 7 Anthony Thackeray; 14 Matty Wildie; 8 Scott Wheeldon; 9 Keal Carlile; 17 Luke Cooper; 13 James Lockwood; 12 John Davies; 15 Gareth Hock. Subs (all used): 10 Richard Moore; 21 Bradley Knowles; 22 Sam Brooks; 27 Jack Ormondroyd.
Tries: Thackeray (8, 34), Hardman (16, 71), Briscoe (29), Hardcastle (44, 49); **Goals:** Hardman 6/7.
Rugby Leaguer & League Express Men of the Match: *Eagles:* Shaun Pick; *Rovers:* Anthony Thackeray.
Penalty count: 7-7; **Half-time:** 0-24;
Referee: Greg Dolan; **Attendance:** 917.

TORONTO WOLFPACK 64 BARROW RAIDERS 0

WOLFPACK: 31 Gareth O'Brien; 30 Matthew Russell; 3 Greg Worthington; 23 Nick Rawsthorne; 5 Liam Kay; 6 Josh McCrone; 17 Blake Wallace; 32 Darcy Lussick; 14 Andy Ackers; 8 Jack Buchanan; 11 Andrew Dixon; 24 Cory Paterson; 29 Jake Emmitt. Subs (all used): 9 Bob Beswick; 15 Adam Sidlow; 22 Richard Whiting; 21 Olsi Krasniqi.
Tries: Kay (11, 78), O'Brien (17), Wallace (21, 44), Paterson (24), Beswick (38), Rawsthorne (42, 68), Russell (50), Sidlow (53), Ackers (80); **Goals:** O'Brien 8/12.
RAIDERS: 2 Shane Toal; - Ben Garner; 12 Jarrad Stack; 24 Danny Morrow; - Chris Fleming; 6 Jamie Dallimore; 21 Ryan Johnston; 8 Joe Bullock; 14 Karl Ashall; 27 Ryan Duffy; 17 Alec Susino; 25 Jono Smith; 9 Nathan Mossop. Sub (used, only one named): 20 Matty While.
Rugby Leaguer & League Express Men of the Match: *Wolfpack:* Blake Wallace; *Raiders:* Nathan Mossop.
Penalty count: 8-3; **Half-time:** 24-0;
Referee: John McMullen; **Attendance:** 5,287.

Sunday 24th June 2018

DEWSBURY RAMS 12 LEIGH CENTURIONS 58

RAMS: 1 Josh Guzdek; 18 Gareth Potts; 3 James Glover; 13 Aaron Brown; 5 Dale Morton; 6 Paul Sykes; 30 Danny Ansell; 8 Jode Sheriffe; 9 Robbie Ward; 10 Jack Teanby; 15 Lucas Walshaw; 28 Kyle Trout; 20 Jordan Crowther. Subs (all used): 19 Sam Day; 31 Daniel Igbinedion; 17 Toby Everett; 22 Martyn Reilly.
Tries: Ward (23, 67); **Goals:** Sykes 2/2.
CENTURIONS: 19 Jack Owens; 22 Ricky Bailey; 3 Ben Crooks; 1 Craig Hall; 5 Rhys Evans; 6 Ben Reynolds; 7 Drew Hutchison; 13 Harrison Hansen; 14 Liam Hood; 31 Jordan Baldwinson; 11 Kevin Larroyer; 12 Bodene Thompson; 15 Jordan Thompson. Subs (all used): 9 Daniel Mortimer; 20 Greg Richards; 21 Nick Gregson; 26 Jordan Dezaria.
Tries: Hutchison (10, 38), Hood (17), Hall (19, 59), Ricky Bailey (31), Mortimer (52), B Thompson (54), Hansen (62), Larroyer (74); **Goals:** Reynolds 9/10.
Rugby Leaguer & League Express Men of the Match: *Rams:* Robbie Ward; *Centurions:* Drew Hutchison.
Penalty count: 7-4; **Half-time:** 6-28;
Referee: Jack Smith; **Attendance:** 1,351.

HALIFAX 50 BATLEY BULLDOGS 12

HALIFAX: 16 James Woodburn-Hall; 5 James Saltonstall; 3 Steve Tyrer; 2 Ben Heaton; 1 Will Sharp; 6 Scott Murrell; 7 Ben Johnston; 29 Dan Fleming; 9 Ben Kaye; 13 Jacob Fairbank; 18 Chester Butler; 11 Shane Grady; 12 Simon Grix. Subs (all used): 8 Elliot Morris; 14 Brandon Moore; 10 Adam Tangata; 4 Ed Barber.
Tries: Grady (2), Sharp (20), Moore (35, 48), Woodburn-Hall (39), Saltonstall (53), Murrell (65), Johnston (71), Morris (77); **Goals:** Tyrer 7/9.
BULLDOGS: 28 Keenen Tomlinson; 3 Sam Smeaton; 19 Alex Bretherton; 29 Lewis Galbraith; 4 Jason Crookes; 1 Dave Scott; 14 James Davey; 8 Adam Gledhill; 18 Tom Hemingway; 16 Michael Ward; 11 Dane Manning; 12 Joel Farrell; 13 Brad Day. Subs (all used): 15 James Harrison; 20 Alex Rowe; 21 James Brown; 30 Reiss Butterworth.
Tries: Brown (31), Gledhill (50); **Goals:** Scott 2/2.
Rugby Leaguer & League Express Men of the Match: *Halifax:* Chester Butler; *Bulldogs:* Michael Ward.
Penalty count: 2-4; **Half-time:** 20-6;
Referee: Tom Grant; **Attendance:** 1,561.

LONDON BRONCOS 58 SWINTON LIONS 22

BRONCOS: 14 Alex Walker; 5 Kieran Dixon; 4 Matty Fleming; 1 Elliot Kear; 2 Rhys Williams; 6 Api Pewhairangi; 9 James Cunningham; 10 Mark Ioane; 25 Matthew Davies; 18 Ben Evans; 12 Jay Pitts; 26 Daniel Hindmarsh; 13 Matt Davis. Subs (all used): 15 Eddie Battye; 16 Matty Gee; 19 Sadiq Adebiyi; 7 Jarrod Sammut.
Tries: Williams (4), Dixon (15), Cunningham (19), Sammut (40, 63), Kear (50), Pewhairangi (55), Matt Davis (66), Pitts (70), Walker (73); **Goals:** Dixon 9/10.
Sin bin: Battye (46) - punching.
LIONS: 1 Gabriel Fell; 5 Mike Butt; 11 Rhodri Lloyd; 30 Craig Mullen; 32 Joe Brown; 3 Chris Hankinson; 7 Jack Hansen; 8 Andy Bracek; - Josh Ganson; 15 Ben Austin; 10 Andy Thornley; 25 Will Hope; 17 Kyle Shelford. Subs (all used): 33 Levy Nzoungou; 21 Chris Worrell; 14 Hayden Hansen; 24 Aaron Hall.
Tries: Hankinson (9), Brown (12, 34, 78);
Goals: Hankinson 3/4.
Rugby Leaguer & League Express Men of the Match: *Broncos:* Jay Pitts; *Lions:* Rhodri Lloyd.
Penalty count: 6-9; **Half-time:** 22-16;
Referee: Scott Mikalauskas; **Attendance:** 684.

ROCHDALE HORNETS 14 TOULOUSE OLYMPIQUE 70

HORNETS: 2 Declan Kay; 21 Richard Lepori; 26 Jack Fox; 31 Deon Cross; 5 Rob Massam; 14 Tyler Whittaker; 7 Danny Yates; 18 Billy Brickhill; 9 Ben Moores; 15 Lewis Hatton; 12 Toby Adamson; 4 Jordan Syme; - Will Calcott. Subs (all used): 17 Jonah Cunningham; - Joe Ryan; 20 Blake Turner; 25 Seta Tala.
Tries: Fox (46), Hatton (66); **Goals:** Whittaker 3/3.
Sin bin: Moores (70) - dissent.
OLYMPIQUE: 1 Mark Kheirallah; 22 Chris Centrone; 4 Gavin Marguerite; 3 Bastien Ader; 2 Tony Maurel; 6 Johnathon Ford; 30 William Barthau; 8 Clement Boyer; 14 Mourad Kriouache; 24 Joe Bretherton; 10 Bastien Canet; 26 Constantine Mika; 9 Anthony Marion. Subs (all used): 19 Charles Bouzinac; 15 Maxime Puech; 16 Tyla Hepi; 11 Sebastien Planas.
Tries: Mika (12, 14), Kheirallah (16, 79), Kriouache (25, 73), Bouzinac (36), Barthau (39, 46, 56), Puech (41), Canet (70), Ader (77); **Goals:** Kheirallah 9/15.
Sin bin: Bretherton (2) - dangerous challenge.
Rugby Leaguer & League Express Men of the Match: *Hornets:* Jack Fox; *Olympique:* Mark Kheirallah.
Penalty count: 7-4; **Half-time:** 2-30;
Referee: Gareth Hewer; **Attendance:** 304.

ROUND 19

Saturday 30th June 2018

TORONTO WOLFPACK 46 LEIGH CENTURIONS 28

WOLFPACK: 31 Gareth O'Brien; 30 Matthew Russell; 33 Chase Stanley; 3 Greg Worthington; 5 Liam Kay; 17 Blake Wallace; 7 Ryan Brierley; 32 Darcy Lussick; 9 Bob Beswick; 29 Jake Emmitt; 24 Cory Paterson; 22 Richard Whiting; 21 Olsi Krasniqi. Subs (all used): 8 Jack Buchanan; 15 Adam Sidlow; 28 Sam Hopkins; 14 Andy Ackers.
Tries: Wallace (9, 29, 58), Russell (16, 40), Ackers (54, 61), Kay (80); **Goals:** O'Brien 7/9.
Sin bin: Paterson (32) - shoulder charge; Emmitt (73) - fighting.
CENTURIONS: 19 Jack Owens; 22 Ricky Bailey; 3 Ben Crooks; 17 Kyle Lovett; 25 Ilias Bergal; 6 Ben Reynolds; 7 Drew Hutchison; 13 Harrison Hansen; 14 Liam Hood; 31 Jordan Baldwinson; 11 Kevin Larroyer; 12 Bodene Thompson; 15 Jordan Thompson. Subs (all used): 9 Daniel Mortimer; 20 Greg Richards; 21 Nick Gregson; 24 Jack Blagbrough.
Tries: Crooks (42, 74), Mortimer (65, 79), Lovett (69);
Goals: Reynolds 4/5.
Sin bin: Richards (73) - fighting.
Rugby Leaguer & League Express Men of the Match: *Wolfpack:* Blake Wallace; *Centurions:* Ben Crooks.
Penalty count: 14-10; **Half-time:** 24-0;
Referee: Gareth Hewer; **Attendance:** 6,844.

Sunday 1st July 2018

BARROW RAIDERS 22 HALIFAX 48

RAIDERS: 31 Ryan Burroughs; 2 Shane Toal; 12 Jarrad Stack; 23 Tom Loxam; 30 Jonny Pownall; 6 Jamie Dallimore; 21 Ryan Johnston; 8 Joe Bullock; 9 Nathan Mossop; 17 Alec Susino; 25 Jono Smith; 24 Danny Morrow; 11 Dan Toal. Subs (all used): 27 Ryan Duffy; 22 Dean Parata; 15 Glenn Riley; 20 Matty While.
Tries: D Toal (5), S Toal (30, 57), Johnston (43);
Goals: Dallimore 3/4.
Sin bin: D Toal (40) - dissent.
HALIFAX: 24 Kieren Moss; 5 James Saltonstall; 3 Steve Tyrer; 16 James Woodburn-Hall; 1 Will Sharp; 6 Scott Murrell; 7 Ben Johnston; 10 Adam Tangata; 9 Ben Kaye; 13 Jacob Fairbank; 18 Chester Butler; 11 Shane Grady; 12 Simon Grix. Subs (all used): 17 Will Maher; 14 Brandon Moore; 29 Dan Fleming; 4 Ed Barber.
Tries: Fairbank (2), Johnston (19, 78), Murrell (22), Grady (25), Butler (37), Moss (62), Tangata (72);
Goals: Tyrer 8/9.
Sin bin: Fleming (44) - high tackle on Dallimore.
Rugby Leaguer & League Express Men of the Match: *Raiders:* Jono Smith; *Halifax:* Ben Johnston.
Penalty count: 5-9; **Half-time:** 10-30;
Referee: Liam Staveley; **Attendance:** 1,293.

BATLEY BULLDOGS 16 LONDON BRONCOS 38

BULLDOGS: 1 Dave Scott; 28 Keenen Tomlinson; 3 Sam Smeaton; 29 Lewis Galbraith; 4 Jason Crookes; 6 Pat

Walker; 18 Tom Hemingway; 8 Adam Gledhill; 9 Alistair Leak; 10 Tom Lillycrop; 11 Dane Manning; 13 Brad Day; 12 Joel Farrell. Subs (all used): 15 James Harrison; 21 James Brown; 14 James Davey; 19 Alex Bretherton.
Tries: Smeaton (7), Davey (40), Galbraith (75);
Goals: Walker 2/3.
BRONCOS: 14 Alex Walker; 5 Kieran Dixon; 17 Michael Channing; 1 Elliot Kear; 2 Rhys Williams; 6 Api Pewhairangi; 9 James Cunningham; 15 Eddie Battye; 7 Jarrod Sammut; 18 Ben Evans; 12 Jay Pitts; 26 Daniel Hindmarsh; 13 Matt Davis. Subs (all used): 10 Mark Ioane; 16 Matty Gee; 8 Tom Spencer; 25 Matthew Davies.
Tries: Pewhairangi (28), Williams (36, 71), Gee (45), Pitts (50), Dixon (52), Spencer (62); **Goals:** Dixon 5/7.
Rugby Leaguer & League Express Men of the Match:
Bulldogs: Lewis Galbraith; *Broncos:* Kieran Dixon.
Penalty count: 4-4; **Half-time:** 12-12;
Referee: John McMullen; **Attendance:** 889.

FEATHERSTONE ROVERS 80 ROCHDALE HORNETS 4

ROVERS: 1 Ian Hardman; 4 Misi Taulapapa; 20 Josh Hardcastle; 18 Jason Walton; 2 Shaun Robinson; 14 Matty Wildie; 7 Anthony Thackeray; 8 Scott Wheeldon; 9 Keal Carlile; 17 Luke Cooper; 12 John Davies; 13 James Lockwood; 10 Richard Moore. Subs (all used): 21 Bradley Knowles; 22 Sam Brooks; 27 Jack Ormondroyd; 34 Brad Dwyer.
Tries: Lockwood (6, 33, 49), Walton (15, 67), Dwyer (21, 26, 30, 40, 55, 58), Knowles (38), Thackeray (74), Davies (80); **Goals:** Hardman 12/14.
Sin bin: Wheeldon (70) - late challenge.
HORNETS: 2 Declan Kay; 21 Richard Lepori; 28 Jack Fox; 31 Deon Cross; 5 Rob Massam; 14 Tyler Whittaker; 27 Morgan Smith; 15 Lewis Hatton; 9 Ben Moores; 10 Gavin Bennion; 4 Jordan Syme; 19 Lee Mitchell; - Will Calcott. Subs (all used): 24 Declan Gregory; - Joe Ryan; 16 Pat Moran; 18 Billy Brickhill.
Try: Massam (42); **Goals:** Whittaker 0/1.
Sin bin: Moores (72) - dissent.
Rugby Leaguer & League Express Men of the Match:
Rovers: Brad Dwyer; *Hornets:* Declan Kay.
Penalty count: 5-5; **Half-time:** 44-0;
Referee: Jack Smith; **Attendance:** 1,820.

SHEFFIELD EAGLES 24 TOULOUSE OLYMPIQUE 46

EAGLES: 30 Matthew Costello; 24 Adam Swift; 25 Jake Spedding; 3 Menzie Yere; 1 Ryan Millar; 23 Cory Aston; - Matty Smith; 8 Mark Offerdahl; 9 Matty Fozard; 12 Shaun Pick; 18 Mike Weldon; 4 Joshua Toole; 13 Matt James. Subs (all used): 29 Corey Makelim; 15 Olly Davies; 20 Max Garcia; 22 Paddy Burns.
Tries: Millar (29, 77), Swift (43, 67), Toole (61);
Goals: Aston 2/5.
OLYMPIQUE: 1 Mark Kheirallah; 20 Paul Marcon; 4 Gavin Marguerite; 22 Chris Centrone; 2 Tony Maurel; 6 Johnathon Ford; 30 William Barthau; 8 Clement Boyer; 14 Mourad Kriouache; 24 Joe Bretherton; 26 Constantine Mika; 12 Rhys Curran; 9 Anthony Marion. Subs (all used): 28 Justin Bouscayrol; 15 Maxime Puech; 16 Tyla Hepi; 11 Sebastien Planas.
Tries: Barthau (6), Maurel (16), Bretherton (20), Curran (24), Kheirallah (35, 50), Marguerite (59), Centrone (72); **Goals:** Kheirallah 7/8.
Rugby Leaguer & League Express Men of the Match:
Eagles: Adam Swift; *Olympique:* Johnathon Ford.
Penalty count: 7-3; **Half-time:** 4-30;
Referee: Marcus Griffiths; **Attendance:** 458.

SWINTON LIONS 29 DEWSBURY RAMS 28

LIONS: 1 Gabriel Fell; 5 Mike Butt; 30 Craig Mullen; 4 George Tyson; 32 Joe Brown; 3 Chris Hankinson; 7 Jack Hansen; 8 Andy Bracek; - Josh Ganson; 10 Andy Thornley; 11 Rhodri Lloyd; 25 Will Hope; 17 Kyle Shelford. Subs (all used): 24 Aaron Hall; 14 Hayden Hansen; 33 Paddy Jones; 35 Levy Nzoungou.
Tries: Tyson (12, 55), Fell (30), Ganson (49), Lloyd (53);
Goals: Hankinson 4/5; **Field goal:** Hankinson (59).
Dismissal: Hankinson (66) - dangerous challenge on Glover.
RAMS: 1 Josh Guzdek; 18 Gareth Potts; 3 James Glover; 15 Lucas Walshaw; 5 Dale Morton; 6 Paul Sykes; 13 Aaron Brown; 8 Jode Sheriffe; 9 Robbie Ward; 10 Jack Teanby; 28 Kyle Trout; 12 Michael Knowles; 20 Jordan Crowther. Subs (all used): 14 Dom Speakman; 17 Toby Everett; 22 Martyn Reilly; 31 Daniel Igbinedion.
Tries: Brown (3), Walshaw (6), Morton (15, 71), Potts (64), Igbinedion (68); **Goals:** Sykes 2/6.
Sin bin: Igbinedion (47) - dangerous challenge.
Rugby Leaguer & League Express Men of the Match:
Lions: George Tyson; *Rams:* Michael Knowles.
Penalty count: 11-8; **Half-time:** 10-16;
Referee: Michael Mannifield; **Attendance:** 555.

ROUND 20

Saturday 7th July 2018

TOULOUSE OLYMPIQUE 20 LONDON BRONCOS 20

OLYMPIQUE: 1 Mark Kheirallah; 2 Tony Maurel; 3 Bastien Ader; 4 Gavin Marguerite; 22 Chris Centrone; 6 Johnathon Ford; 30 William Barthau; 10 Bastien Canet; 14 Mourad Kriouache; 24 Joe Bretherton; 26 Constantine Mika; 12 Rhys Curran; 9 Anthony Marion. Subs (all used): 8 Clement Boyer; 15 Maxime Puech; 16 Tyla Hepi; 19 Charles Bouzinac.
Tries: Mika (8), Ader (18), Centrone (63);
Goals: Kheirallah 4/4.
Sin bin: Curran (30) - high tackle.
BRONCOS: 14 Alex Walker; 2 Rhys Williams; 1 Elliot Kear; 3 Ben Hellewell; 5 Kieran Dixon; 6 Api Pewhairangi; 9 James Cunningham; 15 Eddie Battye; 8 Tom Spencer; 18 Ben Evans; 12 Jay Pitts; 26 Daniel Hindmarsh; 13 Matt Davis. Subs (all used): 10 Mark Ioane; 16 Matty Gee; 11 Daniel Harrison; 25 Matthew Davies.
Tries: Cunningham (14), Matthew Davies (54), Battye (70);
Goals: Dixon 4/4.
Sin bin: Walker (58) - professional foul.
Rugby Leaguer & League Express Men of the Match:
Olympique: Chris Centrone; *Broncos:* Api Pewhairangi.
Penalty count: 3-10; **Half-time:** 12-6;
Referee: Matt Rossleigh; **Attendance:** 2,528.

TORONTO WOLFPACK 68 SHEFFIELD EAGLES 4

WOLFPACK: 31 Gareth O'Brien; 19 Adam Higson; 3 Greg Worthington; 33 Chase Stanley; 5 Liam Kay; 17 Blake Wallace; 7 Ryan Brierley; 32 Darcy Lussick; 9 Bob Beswick; 10 Ashton Sims; 11 Andrew Dixon; 22 Richard Whiting; 29 Jake Emmitt. Subs (all used): 14 Andy Ackers; 15 Adam Sidlow; 21 Olsi Krasniqi; 23 Nick Rawsthorne.
Tries: Stanley (5, 69), Brierley (9), Beswick (26), Whiting (28), Higson (38, 44), Rawsthorne (49), Wallace (52), O'Brien (61), Kay (74), Dixon (80);
Goals: O'Brien 10/12.
EAGLES: 29 Corey Makelim; 1 Ryan Millar; 3 Menzie Yere; 4 Joshua Toole; 25 Jake Spedding; 6 Oscar Thomas; 23 Cory Aston; 8 Mark Offerdahl; 9 Matty Fozard; 12 Shaun Pick; 27 Jack Ashworth; 15 Olly Davies; 13 Matt James. Subs (all used): 20 Max Garcia; 14 Greg Burns; 22 Paddy Burns; 18 Mike Weldon.
Try: Spedding (20); **Goals:** Thomas 0/1.
Sin bin: James (33) - high tackle.
Rugby Leaguer & League Express Men of the Match:
Wolfpack: Gareth O'Brien; *Eagles:* Jake Spedding.
Penalty count: 9-8; **Half-time:** 28-4;
Referee: Steve Race; **Attendance:** 6,329.

Sunday 8th July 2018

BATLEY BULLDOGS 12 LEIGH CENTURIONS 30

BULLDOGS: 1 Dave Scott; 28 Keenen Tomlinson; 3 Sam Smeaton; 29 Lewis Galbraith; 23 Johnny Campbell; 6 Pat Walker; 18 Tom Hemingway; 20 Alex Rowe; 9 Alistair Leak; 10 Tom Lillycrop; 11 Dane Manning; 15 James Harrison; 12 Joel Farrell. Subs (all used): 16 Michael Ward; 17 Joe Chandler; 14 James Davey; 19 Alex Bretherton.
Tries: Tomlinson (1), Campbell (20); **Goals:** Walker 2/3.
CENTURIONS: 19 Jack Owens; 22 Ricky Bailey; 3 Ben Crooks; 1 Craig Hall; 25 Ilias Bergal; 6 Ben Reynolds; 7 Drew Hutchison; 29 Ryan Bailey; 14 Liam Hood; 10 Jamie Acton; 11 Kevin Larroyer; 13 Harrison Hansen; 15 Jordan Thompson. Subs (all used): 9 Daniel Mortimer; 20 Greg Richards; 24 Jack Blagbrough; 32 Adam Walne.
Tries: Bergal (23, 79), Ricky Bailey (44), Hansen (49, 62), Reynolds (57); **Goals:** Reynolds 3/6.
Dismissal: Acton (6) - late challenge on Hemingway.
Rugby Leaguer & League Express Men of the Match:
Bulldogs: Dane Manning; *Centurions:* Harrison Hansen.
Penalty count: 8-7; **Half-time:** 12-4;
Referee: James Child; **Attendance:** 1,223.

DEWSBURY RAMS 22 BARROW RAIDERS 20

RAMS: 1 Josh Guzdek; 18 Gareth Potts; 15 Lucas Walshaw; 40 Adam Ryder; 5 Dale Morton; 6 Paul Sykes; 25 Lewis Heckford; 8 Jode Sheriffe; 14 Dom Speakman; 10 Jack Teanby; 28 Kyle Trout; 12 Michael Knowles; 13 Aaron Brown. Subs (all used): 19 Sam Day; 31 Daniel Igbinedion; 17 Toby Everett; 3 James Glover.
Tries: Teanby (21), Day (42), Potts (54), Walshaw (73);
Goals: Sykes 2/3, Glover 1/1.
RAIDERS: 1 Ryan Fieldhouse; 30 Jonny Pownall; 12 Jarrad Stack; 23 Tom Loxam; 31 Ryan Burroughs; 6 Jamie Dallimore; 21 Ryan Johnston; 8 Joe Bullock; 9 Nathan Mossop; 17 Alec Susino; 25 Jono Smith; 19 Bradd Crellin; 11 Dan Toal. Subs: 22 Dean Parata; 27 Ryan Duffy; 20 Matty While; - Ben Garner (not used).
Tries: While (25), Parata (62); **Goals:** Dallimore 6/6.
Rugby Leaguer & League Express Men of the Match:
Rams: Dom Speakman; *Raiders:* Jamie Dallimore.
Penalty count: 7-9; **Half-time:** 6-12;
Referee: Jack Smith; **Attendance:** 635.

HALIFAX 34 FEATHERSTONE ROVERS 20

HALIFAX: 24 Kieren Moss; 5 James Saltonstall; 3 Steve Tyrer; 16 James Woodburn-Hall; 1 Will Sharp; 6 Scott Murrell; 7 Ben Johnston; 10 Adam Tangata; 9 Ben Kaye; 17 Will Maher; 18 Chester Butler; 11 Shane Grady; 12 Simon Grix. Subs (all used): 13 Jacob Fairbank; 14 Brandon Moore; 29 Dan Fleming; 4 Ed Barber.
Tries: Sharp (8, 26), Johnston (30), Tangata (54), Kaye (66), Moss (76); **Goals:** Tyrer 5/6.
Sin bin: Johnston (45) - fighting;
Fairbank (69) - professional foul; Sharp (73) - fighting.
ROVERS: 1 Ian Hardman; 5 Luke Briscoe; 4 Misi Taulapapa; 18 Jason Walton; 2 Shaun Robinson; 7 Anthony Thackeray; 14 Matty Wildie; 8 Scott Wheeldon; 9 Keal Carlile; 17 Luke Cooper; 27 Jack Ormondroyd; 12 John Davies; 15 Gareth Hock. Subs (all used): 20 Josh Hardcastle; 21 Bradley Knowles; 22 Sam Brooks; 34 Brad Dwyer.
Tries: Hardman (20), Hardcastle (61), Robinson (79);
Goals: Hardman 4/4.
Sin bin: Ormondroyd (45) - fighting;
Wildie (67) - dissent; Hock (73) - fighting.
Rugby Leaguer & League Express Men of the Match:
Halifax: James Saltonstall; *Rovers:* Misi Taulapapa.
Penalty count: 7-6; **Half-time:** 16-8;
Referee: Tom Grant; **Attendance:** 2,356.

ROCHDALE HORNETS 28 SWINTON LIONS 26

HORNETS: 2 Declan Kay; 21 Richard Lepori; 25 Seta Tala; 12 Toby Adamson; 5 Rob Massam; - Morgan Smith; 7 Danny Yates; 15 Lewis Hatton; 9 Ben Moores; 10 Gavin Bennion; 26 George King; 19 Lee Mitchell; 13 Luke Adamson. Subs (all used): 24 Declan Gregory; 8 Jovili Taira; 16 Pat Moran; 4 Jordan Syme.
Tries: Tala (13), Lepori (25), Taira (35), G King (75), Smith (79); **Goals:** Smith 4/5.
LIONS: 1 Gabriel Fell; 5 Mike Butt; 11 Rhodri Lloyd; 4 George Tyson; 32 Joe Brown; 3 Chris Hankinson; 7 Jack Hansen; 8 Andy Bracek; 34 Josh Ganson; 10 Andy Thornley; 17 Kyle Shelford; 25 Will Hope; 14 Hayden Hansen. Subs (all used): 13 Josh Barlow; 24 Aaron Hall; 9 Luke Waterworth; - Paddy Jones.
Tries: Tyson (3), Brown (8), Jones (68);
Goals: Hankinson 7/8.
Rugby Leaguer & League Express Men of the Match:
Hornets: Morgan Smith; *Lions:* Jack Hansen.
Penalty count: 6-10; **Half-time:** 16-18;
Referee: Greg Dolan; **Attendance:** 676.

ROUND 21

Saturday 14th July 2018

ROCHDALE HORNETS 32 LEIGH CENTURIONS 54

HORNETS: 2 Declan Kay; 21 Richard Lepori; 25 Seta Tala; 12 Toby Adamson; 5 Rob Massam; - Morgan Smith; 7 Danny Yates; 26 George King; 9 Ben Moores; 15 Lewis Hatton; 19 Lee Mitchell; 13 Luke Adamson; 10 Gavin Bennion. Subs (all used): 24 Declan Gregory; 8 Jovili Taira; 16 Pat Moran; 4 Jordan Syme.
Tries: Massam (18, 50), Lepori (25, 70), Moores (30), Taira (32); **Goals:** Smith 4/6.
Sin bin: Moores (44) - dissent.
CENTURIONS: 4 Peter Mata'utia; 22 Ricky Bailey; 3 Ben Crooks; 1 Craig Hall; 2 Matty Dawson-Jones; 6 Ben Reynolds; 7 Drew Hutchison; 13 Harrison Hansen; 14 Liam Hood; 32 Adam Walne; 11 Kevin Larroyer; 12 Bodene Thompson; 15 Jordan Thompson. Subs (all used): 9 Daniel Mortimer; 20 Greg Richards; 29 Ryan Bailey; 24 Jack Blagbrough.
Tries: Larroyer (3), Hall (7, 60), Crooks (14), Ricky Bailey (35), Mata'utia (42), Mortimer (46, 78), Hansen (64), Dawson-Jones (80); **Goals:** Reynolds 7/10.
On report:
Larroyer (57) - alleged dangerous challenge on Moores.
Rugby Leaguer & League Express Men of the Match:
Hornets: Morgan Smith; *Centurions:* Craig Hall.
Penalty count: 6-8; **Half-time:** 22-22;
Referee: Steve Race; **Attendance:** 1,080.

TORONTO WOLFPACK 64 BATLEY BULLDOGS 18

WOLFPACK: 31 Gareth O'Brien; 19 Adam Higson; 3 Greg Worthington; 33 Chase Stanley; 23 Nick Rawsthorne; 17 Blake Wallace; 7 Ryan Brierley; 10 Ashton Sims; 9 Bob Beswick; 32 Darcy Lussick; 11 Andrew Dixon; 24 Cory Paterson; 28 Sam Hopkins. Subs (all used): 14 Andy Ackers; 8 Jack Buchanan; 21 Olsi Krasniqi; 15 Adam Sidlow.

Tries: Wallace (7, 16, 77), Worthington (11), Stanley (14), Rawsthorne (21), Beswick (25), Paterson (34), Higson (45), Ackers (63, 66), Brierley (68);
Goals: O'Brien 4/8, Brierley 4/4.
Sin bin: Krasniqi (55) - dissent.
BULLDOGS: 25 Izaac Farrell; 28 Keenen Tomlinson; 4 Jason Crookes; 29 Lewis Galbraith; 1 Dave Scott; 9 Alistair Leak; 7 Dominic Brambani; 24 Tommy Holland; 14 James Davey; 15 James Harrison; 11 Dane Manning; 13 Brad Day; 12 Joel Farrell. Subs (all used, only three named): 44 Danny Maun; 16 Michael Ward; 19 Alex Bretherton.
Tries: Brambani (30), Davey (50), Ward (72);
Goals: I Farrell 3/3.
Rugby Leaguer & League Express Men of the Match: *Wolfpack:* Blake Wallace; *Bulldogs:* Izaac Farrell.
Penalty count: 6-10; **Half-time:** 36-6;
Referee: Michael Mannifield; **Attendance:** 6,088.

Sunday 15th July 2018

SHEFFIELD EAGLES 30 DEWSBURY RAMS 28

EAGLES: 30 Matthew Costello; 2 Iliess Macani; 3 Menzie Yere; 25 Jake Spedding; 5 Ben Blackmore; 23 Cory Aston; 29 Corey Makelim; 8 Mark Offerdahl; 9 Matty Fozard; 10 Jon Magrin; 27 Jack Ashworth; 4 Joshua Toole; 13 Matt James. Subs (all used): 22 Paddy Burns; 18 Mike Weldon; 26 James Bentley; 12 Shaun Pick.
Tries: Magrin (7), Costello (28), Fozard (37), Spedding (54), Ashworth (75); **Goals:** Aston 5/6.
RAMS: 1 Josh Guzdek; 18 Gareth Potts; 15 Lucas Walshaw; 40 Adam Ryder; 5 Dale Morton; 6 Paul Sykes; 13 Aaron Brown; 8 Jode Sheriffe; 14 Dom Speakman; 10 Jack Teanby; 28 Kyle Trout; 12 Michael Knowles; 20 Jordan Crowther. Subs (all used): 19 Sam Day; 17 Toby Everett; 31 Daniel Igbinedion; 3 James Glover.
Tries: Morton (11), Igbinedion (20), Speakman (66), Ryder (70), Knowles (79); **Goals:** Sykes 4/5.
Rugby Leaguer & League Express Men of the Match: *Eagles:* Jack Ashworth; *Rams:* Jack Teanby.
Penalty count: 5-7; **Half-time:** 18-12;
Referee: Greg Dolan; **Attendance:** 425.

LONDON BRONCOS 20 HALIFAX 18

BRONCOS: 14 Alex Walker; 5 Kieran Dixon; 3 Ben Hellewell; 1 Elliot Kear; 2 Rhys Williams; 6 Api Pewhairangi; 9 James Cunningham; 15 Eddie Battye; 30 Eloi Pelissier; 18 Ben Evans; 12 Jay Pitts; 26 Daniel Hindmarsh; 13 Matt Davis. Subs (all used): 8 Tom Spencer; 10 Mark Ioane; 11 Daniel Harrison; 7 Jarrod Sammut.
Tries: Williams (10, 48), Walker (25), Evans (72);
Goals: Dixon 2/4.
HALIFAX: 24 Kieren Moss; 5 James Saltonstall; 3 Steve Tyrer; 16 James Woodburn-Hall; 1 Will Sharp; 6 Scott Murrell; 7 Ben Johnston; 10 Adam Tangata; 9 Ben Kaye; 13 Jacob Fairbank; 18 Chester Butler; 11 Shane Grady; 12 Simon Grix. Subs (all used): 17 Will Maher; 14 Brandon Moore; 8 Elliot Morris; 4 Ed Barber.
Tries: Moss (52), Grady (68), Fairbank (79);
Goals: Tyrer 3/3.
Rugby Leaguer & League Express Men of the Match: *Broncos:* Rhys Williams; *Halifax:* Scott Murrell.
Penalty count: 6-8; **Half-time:** 10-0;
Referee: James Child; **Attendance:** 754.

SWINTON LIONS 4 FEATHERSTONE ROVERS 60

LIONS: 1 Gabriel Fell; 5 Mike Butt; 11 Rhodri Lloyd; 4 George Tyson; 32 Joe Brown; 30 Rob Fairclough; 7 Jack Hansen; 8 Andy Bracek; 33 Josh Ganson; 10 Andy Thornley; - Macauley Davies; 17 Kyle Shelford; 25 Will Hope. Subs (all used): 13 Josh Barlow; 14 Hayden Hansen; 35 Paddy Jones; 9 Luke Waterworth.
Try: Butt (76); **Goals:** Fairclough 0/1.
Sin bin: J Hansen (66) - punching; Bracek (66) - dissent.
ROVERS: 1 Ian Hardman; 5 Luke Briscoe; 4 Misi Taulapapa; 18 Jason Walton; 2 Shaun Robinson; 7 Anthony Thackeray; 14 Matty Wildie; 8 Scott Wheeldon; 9 Keal Carlile; 17 Luke Cooper; 20 Josh Hardcastle; 12 John Davies; 15 Gareth Hock. Subs (all used): 10 Richard Moore; 35 James Thornton; 36 Aaron Smith; 37 Cameron Smith.
Tries: Robinson (7), Briscoe (27, 62), Hardman (36, 72), A Smith (43), Taulapapa (48, 52), Thackeray (58), Hardcastle (74); **Goals:** Hardman 10/10.
Dismissal: Hock (65) - dangerous contact on Barlow.
Sin bin: Wheeldon (30) - dissent.
On report: Hock (13) - alleged dangerous challenge.
Rugby Leaguer & League Express Men of the Match: *Lions:* Andy Bracek; *Rovers:* Ian Hardman.
Penalty count: 10-10; **Half-time:** 0-18;
Referee: Matt Rossleigh; **Attendance:** 610.

BARROW RAIDERS 6 TOULOUSE OLYMPIQUE 72

RAIDERS: 5 Brett Carter; 31 Ryan Burroughs; 34 Liam Harrison; 23 Tom Loxam; 30 Jonny Pownall; 1 Ryan Fieldhouse; 6 Jamie Dallimore; 27 Ryan Duffy; 9 Nathan Mossop; 17 Alec Susino; 19 Bradd Crellin; 12 Jarrad Stack; 11 Dan Toal. Subs (all used): 20 Matty While; 22 Dean Parata; 15 Glenn Riley; 25 Jono Smith.
Try: Harrison (47); **Goals:** Dallimore 1/1.
Sin bin: Dallimore (50) - high tackle.
OLYMPIQUE: 1 Mark Kheirallah; 20 Paul Marcon; 4 Gavin Marguerite; 3 Bastien Ader; 22 Chris Centrone; 6 Johnathon Ford; 30 William Barthau; 24 Joe Bretherton; 9 Anthony Marion; 15 Maxime Puech; 11 Sebastien Planas; 12 Rhys Curran; 8 Clement Boyer. Subs (all used): 19 Charles Bouzinac; 29 Paul Seguier; 16 Tyla Hepi; 23 Justin Sangare.
Tries: Marion (2), Ader (11, 17, 63), Centrone (26, 28), Seguier (34, 42), Kheirallah (38), Curran (51), Marcon (56), Sangare (69), Barthau (74); **Goals:** Kheirallah 10/13.
Rugby Leaguer & League Express Men of the Match: *Raiders:* Liam Harrison; *Olympique:* Anthony Marion.
Penalty count: 7-12; **Half-time:** 0-38;
Referee: Scott Mikalauskas; **Attendance:** 981.

ROUND 22

Saturday 21st July 2018

TORONTO WOLFPACK 52 ROCHDALE HORNETS 10

WOLFPACK: 31 Gareth O'Brien; 30 Matthew Russell; 3 Greg Worthington; 33 Chase Stanley; 5 Liam Kay; 6 Josh McCrone; 17 Blake Wallace; 32 Darcy Lussick; 14 Andy Ackers; 10 Ashton Sims; 11 Andrew Dixon; 24 Cory Paterson; 8 Jack Buchanan. Subs (all used): 28 Sam Hopkins; 15 Adam Sidlow; 4 Gary Wheeler; 22 Richard Whiting.
Tries: Ackers (6), Buchanan (9), Wheeler (26, 76), Sidlow (31), Whiting (36), Paterson (43), Stanley (52), Hopkins (60), Kay (71); **Goals:** O'Brien 6/10.
Sin bin: Lussick (22) - punching; Stanley (64) - fighting.
HORNETS: 2 Declan Kay; 21 Richard Lepori; 31 Deon Cross; 12 Toby Adamson; 5 Rob Massam; 14 Tyler Whittaker; 7 Danny Yates; 15 Lewis Hatton; 9 Ben Moores; 10 Gavin Bennion; 13 Luke Adamson; 19 Lee Mitchell; 18 Billy Brickhill. Subs (all used): 24 Declan Gregory; 8 Jovili Taira; 16 Joe Ryan; 4 Jordan Syme.
Tries: Cross (47), Taira (68); **Goals:** Whittaker 1/2.
Sin bin: T Adamson (64) - fighting.
Rugby Leaguer & League Express Men of the Match: *Wolfpack:* Cory Paterson; *Hornets:* Deon Cross.
Penalty count: 10-7; **Half-time:** 26-0;
Referee: Liam Staveley; **Attendance:** 7,144.

Sunday 22nd July 2018

DEWSBURY RAMS 23 BATLEY BULLDOGS 20

RAMS: 1 Josh Guzdek; 18 Gareth Potts; 27 Joe Arundel; 40 Adam Ryder; 5 Dale Morton; 6 Paul Sykes; 13 Aaron Brown; 8 Jode Sheriffe; 9 Robbie Ward; 10 Jack Teanby; 15 Lucas Walshaw; 12 Michael Knowles; 20 Jordan Crowther. Subs (all used): 19 Sam Day; 17 Toby Everett; 28 Kyle Trout; 3 James Glover.
Tries: Walshaw (13, 61), Ryder (46), Potts (52);
Goals: Sykes 3/4; **Field goal:** Knowles (73).
BULLDOGS: 31 Louis Jouffret; 1 Dave Scott; 3 Sam Smeaton; 29 Lewis Galbraith; 23 Johnny Campbell; 6 Pat Walker; 7 Dominic Brambani; 8 Adam Gledhill; 9 Alistair Leak; 15 James Harrison; 11 Dane Manning; 13 Brad Day; 12 Joel Farrell. Subs (all used): 24 Tommy Holland; 16 Michael Ward; 20 Alex Rowe; 19 Alex Bretherton.
Tries: Day (9), Leak (17), Bretherton (74), Walker (77);
Goals: Walker 2/4.
Sin bin: Leak (45) - professional foul.
Rugby Leaguer & League Express Men of the Match: *Rams:* Lucas Walshaw; *Bulldogs:* Alex Rowe.
Penalty count: 9-8; **Half-time:** 6-10;
Referee: John McMullen; **Attendance:** 1,501.

FEATHERSTONE ROVERS 7 LONDON BRONCOS 14

ROVERS: 1 Ian Hardman; 4 Misi Taulapapa; 20 Josh Hardcastle; 18 Jason Walton; 2 Shaun Robinson; 7 Anthony Thackeray; 9 Keal Carlile; 8 Scott Wheeldon; 12 John Davies; 17 Luke Cooper; 13 James Lockwood; 37 Cameron Smith; 15 Gareth Hock. Subs (all used): 10 Richard Moore; 36 Aaron Smith; 32 Josh Walters; 22 Sam Brooks.
Try: A Smith (37); **Goals:** Hardman 1/2;
Field goal: Hardman (40).
Sin bin: Hock (78) - dissent.
BRONCOS: 14 Alex Walker; 5 Kieran Dixon; 3 Ben Hellewell; 1 Elliot Kear; 2 Rhys Williams; 6 Api Pewhairangi; 9 James Cunningham; 15 Eddie Battye; 30 Eloi Pelissier; 18 Ben Evans; 12 Jay Pitts; 26 Daniel Hindmarsh; 13 Matt Davis. Subs (all used): 8 Tom Spencer; 10 Mark Ioane; 11 Daniel Harrison; 7 Jarrod Sammut.
Tries: Dixon (49), Walker (63), Sammut (68);
Goals: Dixon 0/2, Sammut 1/1.
Rugby Leaguer & League Express Men of the Match: *Rovers:* Scott Wheeldon; *Broncos:* Kieran Dixon.
Penalty count: 5-9; **Half-time:** 7-0;
Referee: Jack Smith; **Attendance:** 2,434.

HALIFAX 19 TOULOUSE OLYMPIQUE 14

HALIFAX: 24 Kieren Moss; 5 James Saltonstall; 3 Steve Tyrer; 18 Chester Butler; 1 Will Sharp; 6 Scott Murrell; 7 Ben Johnston; 10 Adam Tangata; 9 Ben Kaye; 29 Dan Fleming; 4 Ed Barber; 11 Shane Grady; 13 Jacob Fairbank. Subs (all used): 12 Simon Grix; 14 Brandon Moore; 8 Elliot Morris; 17 Will Maher.
Tries: Tyrer (6), Kaye (21), Grady (74); **Goals:** Tyrer 3/4;
Field goal: Murrell (62).
OLYMPIQUE: 1 Mark Kheirallah; 22 Chris Centrone; 4 Gavin Marguerite; 3 Bastien Ader; 2 Tony Maurel; 6 Johnathon Ford; 30 William Barthau; 24 Joe Bretherton; 9 Anthony Marion; 15 Maxime Puech; 10 Bastien Canet; 26 Constantine Mika; 8 Clement Boyer. Subs (all used): 16 Tyla Hepi; 18 Sam Rapira; 19 Charles Bouzinac; 29 Paul Seguier.
Tries: Canet (13), Bretherton (65); **Goals:** Kheirallah 3/3.
Rugby Leaguer & League Express Men of the Match: *Halifax:* Brandon Moore; *Olympique:* Chris Centrone.
Penalty count: 4-5; **Half-time:** 12-6;
Referee: Greg Dolan; **Attendance:** 1,794.

LEIGH CENTURIONS 50 SWINTON LIONS 24

CENTURIONS: 4 Peter Mata'utia; 2 Matty Dawson-Jones; 3 Ben Crooks; 1 Craig Hall; 19 Jack Owens; 6 Ben Reynolds; 7 Drew Hutchison; 32 Adam Walne; 14 Liam Hood; 13 Harrison Hansen; 11 Kevin Larroyer; 12 Bodene Thompson; 15 Jordan Thompson. Subs (all used): 9 Daniel Mortimer; 18 Nathan Mason; 20 Greg Richards; 24 Jack Blagbrough.
Tries: Hansen (11), Dawson-Jones (13, 27), B Thompson (16), Hall (20, 52), Hood (37), Mata'utia (64), Hutchison (71); **Goals:** Reynolds 7/9.
LIONS: 1 Gabriel Fell; 32 Joe Brown; 11 Rhodri Lloyd; 4 George Tyson; 5 Mike Butt; 30 Rob Fairclough; 7 Jack Hansen; 8 Andy Bracek; 14 Hayden Hansen; 10 Andy Thornley; 35 Macauley Davies; 17 Kyle Shelford; 25 Will Hope. Subs (all used): 34 Josh Ganson; 13 Josh Barlow; 24 Aaron Hall; 36 Paddy Jones.
Tries: Barlow (30), Fairclough (42), Lloyd (45), Shelford (68); **Goals:** J Hansen 3/3, Fairclough 1/1.
Rugby Leaguer & League Express Men of the Match: *Centurions:* Adam Walne; *Lions:* Rob Fairclough.
Penalty count: 7-9; **Half-time:** 34-6;
Referee: Marcus Griffiths; **Attendance:** 3,680.

SHEFFIELD EAGLES 28 BARROW RAIDERS 10

EAGLES: 30 Matthew Costello; 2 Iliess Macani; 3 Menzie Yere; 4 Joshua Toole; 5 Ben Blackmore; 23 Cory Aston; 29 Corey Makelim; 8 Mark Offerdahl; 9 Matty Fozard; 12 Shaun Pick; 26 James Bentley; 13 Matt James; 22 Paddy Burns. Subs (all used): 14 Greg Burns; 20 Max Garcia; 18 Mike Weldon; 10 Jon Magrin.
Tries: James (10), Blackmore (17), Aston (41, 62), Yere (80);
Goals: Aston 4/6.
RAIDERS: 1 Ryan Fieldhouse; 36 Georgy Gambaro; 31 Ryan Burroughs; 23 Tom Loxam; 5 Brett Carter; 6 Jamie Dallimore; 21 Ryan Johnston; 8 Joe Bullock; 9 Nathan Mossop; 35 Arnaud Barthes; 28 Matthew Holmes; 11 Dan Toal; 17 Alec Susino. Subs (all used): 22 Dean Parata; 27 Ryan Duffy; 15 Glenn Riley; 30 Jonny Pownall.
Tries: Carter (36), Mossop (57); **Goals:** Dallimore 1/2.
Rugby Leaguer & League Express Men of the Match: *Eagles:* Cory Aston; *Raiders:* Nathan Mossop.
Penalty count: 7-5; **Half-time:** 10-4;
Referee: Nick Bennett; **Attendance:** 702.

ROUND 23

Saturday 28th July 2018

TOULOUSE OLYMPIQUE 44 DEWSBURY RAMS 18

OLYMPIQUE: 1 Mark Kheirallah; 2 Tony Maurel; 3 Bastien Ader; 22 Chris Centrone; 20 Paul Marcon; 30 William Barthau; 6 Johnathon Ford; 18 Sam Rapira; 9 Anthony Marion; 24 Joe Bretherton; 26 Constantine Mika; 10 Bastien Canet; 8 Clement Boyer. Subs (all used): 11 Sebastien Planas; 14 Mourad Kriouache; 15 Maxime Puech; 16 Tyla Hepi.
Tries: Centrone (4, 8, 59), Kheirallah (21), Planas (45), Puech (57), Marion (62), Marcon (79);
Goals: Kheirallah 6/9.
Sin bin: Bretherton (77) - fighting.
On report: Mika (17) - alleged dangerous contact; Puech (68) - alleged use of the elbow.

Dakota Whylie on the charge as Featherstone become the first team to win in Toronto

RAMS: 1 Josh Guzdek; 19 Sam Day; 3 James Glover; 40 Adam Ryder; 27 Brad Delaney; 6 Paul Sykes; 25 Lewis Heckford; 17 Toby Everett; 9 Robbie Ward; 10 Jack Teanby; 15 Lucas Walshaw; 31 Daniel Igbinedion; 13 Aaron Brown. Subs (all used): 12 Michael Knowles; 14 Dom Speakman; 28 Kyle Trout; 32 Toby Richardson.
Tries: Glover (27, 29), Brown (52); **Goals:** Sykes 3/3.
Sin bin: Ward (77) - fighting.
Rugby Leaguer & League Express Men of the Match: *Olympique:* Johnathon Ford; *Rams:* Lewis Heckford.
Penalty count: 8-5; **Half-time:** 14-12;
Referee: Nick Bennett; **Attendance:** 1,914.

TORONTO WOLFPACK 12
FEATHERSTONE ROVERS 30

WOLFPACK: 4 Gary Wheeler; 23 Nick Rawsthorne; 27 Quinn Ngawati; 22 Richard Whiting; 5 Liam Kay; 6 Josh McCrone; 7 Ryan Brierley; 29 Jake Emmitt; 14 Andy Ackers; 10 Ashton Sims; 9 Bob Beswick; 13 Jack Bussey; 21 Olsi Krasniqi. Subs (all used): 11 Andrew Dixon; 15 Adam Sidlow; 8 Jack Buchanan; 28 Sam Hopkins.
Tries: Sims (23), Sidlow (43); **Goals:** Brierley 2/2.
ROVERS: 1 Ian Hardman; 38 Dakota Whylie; 4 Misi Taulapapa; 20 Josh Hardcastle; 2 Shaun Robinson; 7 Anthony Thackeray; 14 Matty Wildie; 8 Scott Wheeldon; 9 Keal Carlile; 17 Luke Cooper; 18 Jason Walton; 12 John Davies; 13 James Lockwood. Subs (all used, only three named): 10 Richard Moore; 22 Sam Brooks; 36 Aaron Smith.
Tries: Carlile (9), Walton (29), Hardcastle (47), Wildie (67);
Goals: Hardman 7/8.
Rugby Leaguer & League Express Men of the Match: *Wolfpack:* Ashton Sims; *Rovers:* Ian Hardman.
Penalty count: 15-12; **Half-time:** 6-16;
Referee: Greg Dolan; **Attendance:** 8,217.

Sunday 29th July 2018

BARROW RAIDERS 6 LONDON BRONCOS 72

RAIDERS: 21 Ryan Johnston; 36 Georgy Gambaro; 19 Bradd Crellin; 23 Tom Loxam; 31 Ryan Burroughs; 6 Jamie Dallimore; 22 Dean Parata; 27 Ryan Duffy; 9 Nathan Mossop; 35 Arnaud Barthes; 8 Joe Bullock; 28 Matthew

Holmes; 17 Alec Susino. Subs (all used): 20 Matty While; 13 Martin Aspinwall; 15 Glenn Riley; 37 Saloty Mendy.
Try: Dallimore (73); **Goals:** Dallimore 1/1.
Sin bin: While (33) - use of the knees.
BRONCOS: 14 Alex Walker; 5 Kieran Dixon; 3 Ben Hellewell; 1 Elliot Kear; 2 Rhys Williams; 6 Api Pewhairangi; 9 James Cunningham; 15 Eddie Battye; 30 Eloi Pelissier; 18 Ben Evans; 12 Jay Pitts; 26 Daniel Hindmarsh; 8 Tom Spencer. Subs (all used): 23 Rob Butler; 10 Mark Ioane; 7 Jarrod Sammut; 11 Daniel Harrison.
Tries: Pewhairangi (11), Walker (19, 62, 67), Williams (23, 57, 78), Cunningham (27, 60), Dixon (32), Harrison (33), Sammut (39, 70);
Goals: Dixon 4/6, Sammut 6/7.
Rugby Leaguer & League Express Men of the Match: *Raiders:* Arnaud Barthes; *Broncos:* James Cunningham.
Penalty count: 7-9; **Half-time:** 0-38;
Referee: Ben Thaler; **Attendance:** 1,044.

BATLEY BULLDOGS 40 SWINTON LIONS 18

BULLDOGS: 1 Dave Scott; 2 Wayne Reittie; 3 Sam Smeaton; 4 Jason Crookes; 23 Johnny Campbell; 31 Louis Jouffret; 7 Dominic Brambani; 8 Adam Gledhill; 9 Alistair Leak; 24 Tommy Holland; 11 Dane Manning; 13 Brad Day; 21 James Brown. Subs (all used): 20 Alex Rowe; 14 James Davey; 15 James Harrison; 19 Alex Bretherton.
Tries: Day (11), Crookes (22), Harrison (28, 41), Reittie (36), Scott (54), Campbell (60); **Goals:** Scott 6/7.
Sin bin: Gledhill (72) - fighting;
Rowe (75) - late challenge on Worrell.
LIONS: 7 Jack Hansen; 5 Mike Butt; 11 Rhodri Lloyd; 32 Joe Brown; 1 Gabriel Fell; 6 Brad Billsborough; 30 Rob Fairclough; 8 Andy Bracek; 14 Hayden Hansen; 10 Andy Thornley; 35 Macauley Davies; 17 Kyle Shelford; 13 Josh Barlow. Subs (all used): 15 Ben Austin; 33 Josh Ganson; 24 Aaron Hall; 21 Chris Worrell.
Tries: Barlow (63), Hall (76), Butt (79);
Goals: Billsborough 1/1, J Hansen 2/3.
Sin bin: Fairclough (72) - fighting.
Rugby Leaguer & League Express Men of the Match: *Bulldogs:* James Harrison; *Lions:* Rhodri Lloyd.
Penalty count: 8-11; **Half-time:** 24-2;
Referee: Matt Rossleigh; **Attendance:** 856.

HALIFAX 38 ROCHDALE HORNETS 6

HALIFAX: 24 Kieren Moss; 2 Ben Heaton; 3 Steve Tyrer; 16 James Woodburn-Hall; 1 Will Sharp; 6 Scott Murrell; 7 Ben Johnston; 17 Will Maher; 9 Ben Kaye; 13 Jacob Fairbank; 4 Ed Barber; 18 Chester Butler; 12 Simon Grix. Subs (all used): 25 Sion Jones; 14 Brandon Moore; 8 Elliot Morris; 29 Dan Fleming.
Tries: Grix (15), Fairbank (19), Butler (21), Tyrer (32), Moss (60), Kaye (70); **Goals:** Tyrer 7/8.
HORNETS: 2 Declan Kay; 21 Richard Lepori; 31 Deon Cross; 12 Toby Adamson; 5 Rob Massam; - Morgan Smith; 7 Danny Yates; 26 George King; 14 Tyler Whittaker; 16 Pat Moran; 13 Luke Adamson; 19 Lee Mitchell; 15 Lewis Hatton. Subs (all used): 8 Jovili Taira; 10 Joe Ryan; 24 Declan Gregory; 25 Seta Tala.
Try: Hatton (43); **Goals:** Whittaker 1/1.
Rugby Leaguer & League Express Men of the Match: *Halifax:* Jacob Fairbank; *Hornets:* Rob Massam.
Penalty count: 6-4; **Half-time:** 22-0;
Referee: Jack Smith; **Attendance:** 1,866.

LEIGH CENTURIONS 34 SHEFFIELD EAGLES 10

CENTURIONS: 34 Will Dagger; 22 Ricky Bailey; 19 Jack Owens; 2 Matty Dawson-Jones; 25 Ilias Bergal; 6 Ben Reynolds; 7 Drew Hutchison; 32 Adam Walne; 30 Micky Higham; 29 Ryan Bailey; 11 Kevin Larroyer; 21 Nick Gregson; 35 Jordan Walne. Subs (all used): 9 Daniel Mortimer; 18 Nathan Mason; 20 Greg Richards; 24 Jack Blagbrough.
Tries: Ryan Bailey (39), Bergal (48, 58, 65), Dawson-Jones (51, 75), Dagger (70);
Goals: Reynolds 0/1, Owens 3/6.
EAGLES: 6 Oscar Thomas; 2 Iliess Macani; 3 Menzie Yere; 4 Joshua Toole; 15 Ben Blackmore; 23 Cory Aston; 29 Corey Makelim; 8 Mark Offerdahl; 9 Matty Fozard; 12 Shaun Pick; 26 James Bentley; 11 Mike Weldon; 13 Matt James. Subs (all used): 14 Greg Burns; 20 Max Garcia; 15 Olly Davies; 10 Jon Magrin.
Tries: Bentley (18), Aston (33); **Goals:** Thomas 1/2.
Rugby Leaguer & League Express Men of the Match: *Centurions:* Matty Dawson-Jones; *Eagles:* Cory Aston.
Penalty count: 8-8; **Half-time:** 4-10;
Referee: Chris Kendall; **Attendance:** 3,112.

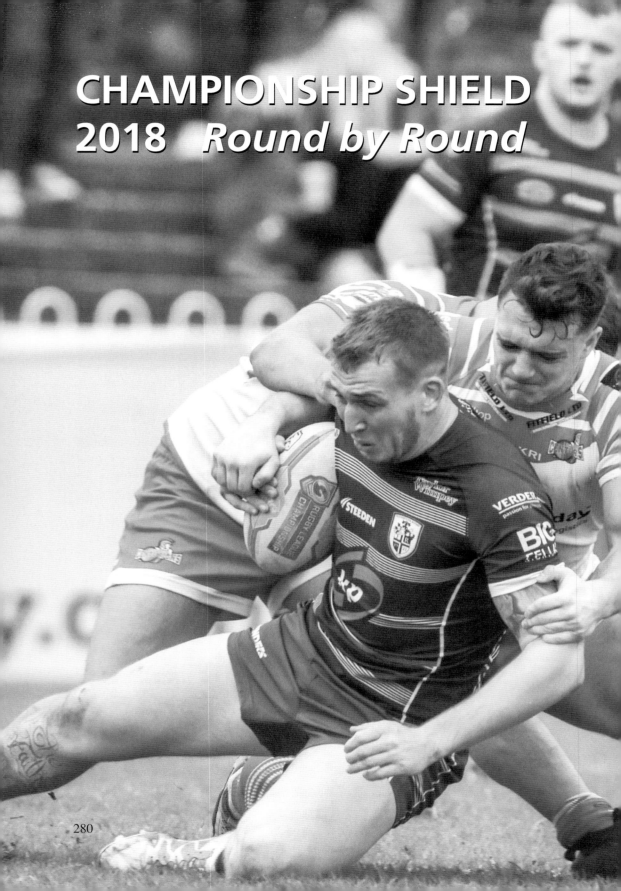

CHAMPIONSHIP SHIELD
2018 *Round by Round*

ROUND 1

Sunday 12th August 2018

BARROW RAIDERS 17 ROCHDALE HORNETS 10

RAIDERS: 1 Ryan Fieldhouse; 5 Brett Carter; 12 Jarrad Stack; 31 Ryan Burroughs; 23 Tom Loxam; 6 Jamie Dallimore; 21 Ryan Johnston; 8 Joe Bullock; 22 Dean Parata; 17 Alec Susino; 25 Jono Smith; 11 Dan Toal; 35 Arnaud Barthes. Subs (all used): 27 Ryan Duffy; 13 Martin Aspinwall; 15 Glenn Riley; 9 Nathan Mossop.
Tries: Smith (60), Susino (76); **Goals:** Dallimore 4/4;
Field goal: Johnston (74).
HORNETS: 2 Declan Kay; 21 Richard Lepori; 31 Deon Cross; 25 Seta Tala; 5 Rob Massam; - Morgan Smith; 7 Danny Yates; 30 Ryan Millington; 18 Billy Brickhill; 16 Pat Moran; 13 Luke Adamson; 19 Lee Mitchell; 15 Lewis Hatton. Subs (all used): 1 Miles Greenwood; 14 Tyler Whittaker; 10 Joe Ryan; 8 Jovili Taira.
Try: Cross (79); **Goals:** Smith 3/3.
Sin bin: Tala (25) - high tackle on Carter.
Rugby Leaguer & League Express Men of the Match:
Raiders: Arnaud Barthes; *Hornets:* Morgan Smith.
Penalty count: 14-12; **Half-time:** 0-4;
Referee: Marcus Griffiths; **Attendance:** 1,033.

DEWSBURY RAMS 40 SWINTON LIONS 7

RAMS: 1 Josh Guzdek; 18 Gareth Potts; 3 James Glover; 40 Adam Ryder; 5 Dale Morton; 6 Paul Sykes; 7 Gareth Moore; 8 Jode Sheriffe; 9 Robbie Ward; 28 Kyle Trout; 15 Lucas Walshaw; 12 Michael Knowles; 13 Aaron Brown. Subs (all used): 14 Dom Speakman; 10 Jack Teanby; 31 Daniel Igbinedion; 32 Toby Richardson.
Tries: Ward (24), Speakman (45), Ryder (51), Brown (57), Potts (66), Knowles (72), Guzdek (75); **Goals:** Sykes 6/7.
LIONS: 7 Jack Hansen; 32 Joe Brown; 4 George Tyson; 11 Rhodri Lloyd; 5 Mike Butt; 30 Rob Fairclough; 31 Josh Woods; 8 Andy Bracek; 9 Luke Waterworth; 15 Ben Austin; 10 Andy Thornley; 17 Kyle Shelford; 33 Paul Wood. Subs (all used): 14 Hayden Hansen; 13 Josh Barlow; 34 Paddy Jones; 21 Chris Worrell.
Tries: Waterworth (16); **Goals:** Fairclough 1/1;
Field goal: Woods (37).
Sin bin: Barlow (46) - dissent.
Rugby Leaguer & League Express Men of the Match:
Rams: Adam Ryder; *Lions:* Josh Woods.
Penalty count: 6-7; **Half-time:** 6-7;
Referee: Tom Grant; **Attendance:** 752.

FEATHERSTONE ROVERS 26 BATLEY BULLDOGS 12

ROVERS: 1 Ian Hardman; 2 Shaun Robinson; 5 Luke Briscoe; 4 Misi Taulapapa; 38 Dakota Whylie; 7 Anthony Thackeray; 14 Matty Wildie; 8 Scott Wheeldon; 24 Danny Maskill; 17 Luke Cooper; 20 Josh Hardcastle; 18 Jason Walton; 13 James Lockwood. Subs (all used): 22 Sam Brooks; 21 Bradley Knowles; 11 Connor Farrell; 12 John Davies.
Tries: Briscoe (39), Thackeray (61), Cooper (65), Maskill (68); **Goals:** Hardman 4/4, Cooper 1/1.
Sin bin: Hardcastle (31) - professional foul.
BULLDOGS: 1 Dave Scott; 2 Wayne Reittie; 3 Sam Smeaton; 29 Lewis Galbraith; 23 Johnny Campbell; 31 Louis Jouffret; 7 Dominic Brambani; 8 Adam Gledhill; 9 Alistair Leak; 20 Alex Rowe; 11 Dane Manning; 15 James Harrison; 13 Brad Day. Subs (all used): 16 Michael Ward; 6 Pat Walker; 19 Alex Bretherton; 21 James Brown.
Tries: Smeaton (33), Manning (58); **Goals:** Walker 2/2.
Sin bin: Reittie (35) - professional foul.
Rugby Leaguer & League Express Men of the Match:
Rovers: Anthony Thackeray; *Bulldogs:* Alistair Leak.
Penalty count: 13-10; **Half-time:** 6-6;
Referee: Matt Rossleigh; **Attendance:** 1,236.

LEIGH CENTURIONS 68 SHEFFIELD EAGLES 6

CENTURIONS: 34 Will Dagger; 22 Ricky Bailey; 5 Rhys Evans; 2 Matty Dawson-Jones; 25 Ilias Bergal; 19 Jack Owens; 7 Drew Hutchison; 32 Adam Walne; 14 Liam Hood; 18 Nathan Mason; 11 Kevin Larroyer; 35 Jordan Walne; 26 Jordan Dezaria. Subs (all used): 30 Micky Higham; 20 Greg Richards; 24 Jack Blagbrough; 36 Mitch Cox.
Tries: Bergal (4, 25, 35, 42), Mason (23), Hutchison (27, 74), Cox (38), Ricky Bailey (50), Hood (64), Owens (71), Dawson-Jones (78); **Goals:** Owens 10/12.
EAGLES: 6 Oscar Thomas; 2 Iliess Macani; 3 Menzie Yere; 4 Joshua Toole; 29 Corey Makelim; 23 Cory Aston; 19 Simon Brown; 8 Mark Offerdahl; 9 Matty Fozard; 12 Shaun Pick; 26 James Bentley; 18 Mike Weldon; 13 Matt James. Subs (all used): 14 Greg Burns; 20 Max Garcia; 15 Olly Davies; 22 Paddy Burns.
Try: Toole (55); **Goals:** Thomas 1/1.
Rugby Leaguer & League Express Men of the Match:
Centurions: Drew Hutchison; *Eagles:* James Bentley.
Penalty count: 5-5; **Half-time:** 34-0;
Referee: Nick Bennett; **Attendance:** 2,647.

ROUND 2

Sunday 19th August 2018

BATLEY BULLDOGS 42 DEWSBURY RAMS 22

BULLDOGS: 1 Dave Scott; 2 Wayne Reittie; 28 Keenen Tomlinson; 29 Lewis Galbraith; 23 Johnny Campbell; 31 Louis Jouffret; 7 Dominic Brambani; 8 Adam Gledhill; 9 Alistair Leak; 15 James Harrison; 11 Dane Manning; 12 Joel Farrell; 13 Brad Day. Subs (all used): 6 Pat Walker; 21 James Brown; 20 Alex Rowe; 19 Alex Bretherton.
Tries: Gledhill (2), Tomlinson (13), Reittie (55, 73), Harrison (60), Manning (62), Day (79);
Goals: Scott 2/3, Walker 5/5.
RAMS: 1 Josh Guzdek; 40 Adam Ryder; 3 James Glover; 4 Macauley Hallett; 5 Dale Morton; 6 Paul Sykes; 7 Gareth Moore; 17 Toby Everett; 9 Robbie Ward; 28 Kyle Trout; 15 Lucas Walshaw; 32 Toby Richardson; 20 Jordan Crowther. Subs (all used): 14 Dom Speakman; 25 Brad Delaney; 10 Jack Teanby; 31 Daniel Igbinedion.
Tries: Walshaw (16), Richardson (19), Glover (27), Speakman (38); **Goals:** Sykes 3/4.
Sin bin: Igbinedion (36) - kicking Farrell.
Rugby Leaguer & League Express Men of the Match:
Bulldogs: James Harrison; *Rams:* Dale Morton.
Penalty count: 11-7; **Half-time:** 12-22;
Referee: Jack Smith; **Attendance:** 1,485.

LEIGH CENTURIONS 38 BARROW RAIDERS 0

CENTURIONS: 34 Will Dagger; 22 Ricky Bailey; 5 Rhys Evans; 2 Matty Dawson-Jones; 19 Jack Owens; 6 Ben Reynolds; 7 Drew Hutchison; 20 Greg Richards; 30 Micky Higham; 18 Nathan Mason; 11 Kevin Larroyer; 35 Jordan Walne; 26 Jordan Dezaria. Subs (all used): 21 Nick Gregson; 24 Jack Blagbrough; 33 Josh Johnson; 36 Mitch Cox.
Tries: Larroyer (10), Ricky Bailey (19), Richards (22), Owens (26), Dawson-Jones (38), J Walne (45), Reynolds (79); **Goals:** Reynolds 5/7.
Sin bin: Dagger (7) - dangerous challenge on Gambaro.
RAIDERS: 1 Ryan Fieldhouse; 36 Georgy Gambaro; 31 Ryan Burroughs; 23 Tom Loxam; 5 Brett Carter; 6 Jamie Dallimore; 21 Ryan Johnston; 17 Alec Susino; 22 Dean Parata; 35 Arnaud Barthes; 25 Jono Smith; 19 Bradd Crellin; 13 Martin Aspinwall. Subs (all used): 9 Nathan Mossop; 37 Saloty Mendy; 11 Dan Toal; 15 Glenn Riley.
Rugby Leaguer & League Express Men of the Match:
Centurions: Jack Owens; *Raiders:* Alec Susino.
Penalty count: 9-8; **Half-time:** 26-0;
Referee: Tom Grant; **Attendance:** 2,646.

ROCHDALE HORNETS 24 FEATHERSTONE ROVERS 33

HORNETS: 21 Richard Lepori; 1 Miles Greenwood; 25 Seta Tala; 31 Deon Cross; 5 Rob Massam; 14 Tyler Whittaker; 7 Danny Yates; 8 Jovili Taira; 9 Ben Moores; 16 Pat Moran; 13 Luke Adamson; 19 Lee Mitchell; 15 Lewis Hatton. Subs (all used, only three named): 18 Billy Brickhill; 30 Ryan Millington; 10 Joe Ryan.
Tries: Mitchell (7), Massam (38, 45), Tala (72);
Goals: Whittaker 4/5.
ROVERS: 1 Ian Hardman; 38 Dakota Whylie; 4 Misi Taulapapa; 29 Harry Newman; 2 Shaun Robinson; 7 Anthony Thackeray; 14 Matty Wildie; 17 Luke Cooper; 24 Danny Maskill; 22 Sam Brooks; 12 John Davies; 20 Josh Hardcastle; 18 Jason Walton. Subs: 13 James Lockwood; 21 Bradley Knowles; 11 Connor Farrell; 9 Keal Carlile (not used).
Tries: Thackeray (25), Davies (33, 79), Newman (52, 55);
Goals: Hardman 6/6; **Field goal:** Thackeray (71).
Rugby Leaguer & League Express Men of the Match:
Hornets: Rob Massam; *Rovers:* John Davies.
Penalty count: 6-8; **Half-time:** 14-12;
Referee: Nick Bennett; **Attendance:** 586.

SWINTON LIONS 18 SHEFFIELD EAGLES 26

LIONS: 7 Jack Hansen; 5 Mike Butt; 11 Rhodri Lloyd; 4 George Tyson; 32 Joe Brown; 30 Rob Fairclough; 31 Josh Woods; 8 Andy Bracek; 9 Luke Waterworth; 15 Ben Austin; 10 Andy Thornley; 17 Kyle Shelford; 14 Hayden Hansen. Subs (all used): 33 Josh Ganson; 21 Chris Worrell; 34 Paddy Jones; 24 Aaron Hall.
Tries: Brown (12), Fairclough (38), Butt (64);
Goals: Fairclough 3/4.
EAGLES: 29 Corey Makelim; 6 Oscar Thomas; 3 Menzie Yere; 4 Joshua Toole; 5 Ben Blackmore; 19 Simon Brown; 23 Cory Aston; 8 Mark Offerdahl; 14 Greg Burns; 12 Shaun Pick; 13 Matt James; 26 James Bentley; 9 Matty Fozard. Subs (all used): 22 Paddy Burns; 15 Olly Davies; 18 Mike Weldon; 10 Jon Magrin.
Tries: Yere (18), Brown (46, 56), Bentley (70), Magrin (73);
Goals: Brown 3/4, Aston 0/1.
Sin bin: Thomas (39) - holding down.
Rugby Leaguer & League Express Men of the Match:
Lions: Andy Thornley; *Eagles:* Simon Brown.
Penalty count: 5-4; **Half-time:** 14-4;
Referee: Matt Rossleigh; **Attendance:** 420.

ROUND 3

Friday 31st August 2018

SHEFFIELD EAGLES 20 DEWSBURY RAMS 30

EAGLES: 6 Oscar Thomas; 2 Iliess Macani; 3 Menzie Yere; 4 Joshua Toole; 5 Ben Blackmore; 19 Simon Brown; 23 Cory Aston; 8 Mark Offerdahl; 9 Matty Fozard; 12 Shaun Pick; 26 James Bentley; 13 Matt James; 22 Paddy Burns. Subs (all used): 14 Greg Burns; 21 Blake Broadbent; 15 Olly Davies; 10 Jon Magrin.
Tries: Toole (30), Macani (37, 80), Thomas (68);
Goals: Thomas 2/4.
Sin bin: Macani (21) - punching.
On report: Offerdahl (4) - alleged late challenge.
RAMS: 1 Josh Guzdek; 2 Rob Worrincy; 3 James Glover; 40 Adam Ryder; 5 Dale Morton; 6 Paul Sykes; 25 Brad Delaney; 8 Jode Sheriffe; 9 Robbie Ward; 28 Kyle Trout; 15 Lucas Walshaw; 12 Michael Knowles; 13 Aaron Brown. Subs (all used): 14 Dom Speakman; 32 Toby Richardson; 10 Jack Teanby; 31 Daniel Igbinedion.
Tries: Ryder (24), Delaney (43, 77), Igbinedion (46), Ward (72); **Goals:** Sykes 5/5.
Rugby Leaguer & League Express Men of the Match:
Eagles: Joshua Toole; *Rams:* Dom Speakman.
Penalty count: 7-9; **Half-time:** 10-6;
Referee: Nick Bennett; **Attendance:** 638.

Sunday 2nd September 2018

BARROW RAIDERS 16 BATLEY BULLDOGS 36

RAIDERS: 1 Ryan Fieldhouse; 36 Georgy Gambaro; 24 Danny Morrow; 31 Ryan Burroughs; 23 Tom Loxam; 6 Jamie Dallimore; 7 Lewis Charnock; 35 Arnaud Barthes; 9 Nathan Mossop; 17 Alec Susino; 25 Jono Smith; 19 Bradd Crellin; 13 Martin Aspinwall. Subs (all used): 11 Dan Toal; 28 Matthew Holmes; 37 Saloty Mendy; 22 Dean Parata.
Tries: Gambaro (4), Charnock (47), Holmes (74);
Goals: Dallimore 2/3.
BULLDOGS: 1 Dave Scott; 28 Keenen Tomlinson; 3 Sam Smeaton; 29 Lewis Galbraith; 23 Johnny Campbell; 31 Louis Jouffret; 7 Dominic Brambani; 8 Adam Gledhill; 9 Alistair Leak; 15 James Harrison; 11 Dane Manning; 13 Brad Day; 21 James Brown. Subs (all used): 16 Michael Ward; 20 Alex Rowe; 12 Joel Farrell; 6 Pat Walker.
Tries: Campbell (7, 15, 63), Brambani (24), Day (37, 70), Scott (55); **Goals:** Scott 3/6, Walker 1/1.
Rugby Leaguer & League Express Men of the Match:
Raiders: Arnaud Barthes; *Bulldogs:* Louis Jouffret.
Penalty count: 7-9; **Half-time:** 4-20;
Referee: James Child; **Attendance:** 1,103.

FEATHERSTONE ROVERS 22 LEIGH CENTURIONS 4

ROVERS: 1 Ian Hardman; 4 Misi Taulapapa; 20 Josh Hardcastle; 12 John Davies; 2 Shaun Robinson; 7 Anthony Thackeray; 14 Matty Wildie; 22 Sam Brooks; 9 Keal Carlile; 17 Luke Cooper; 13 James Lockwood; 11 Connor Farrell; 21 Bradley Knowles. Sub (used, only one named): 24 Danny Maskill.
Tries: Hardcastle (10), Davies (24), Thackeray (38), Wildie (76); **Goals:** Hardman 3/4.
Sin bin: Hardcastle (40) - fighting.
CENTURIONS: 22 Ricky Bailey; 25 Ilias Bergal; 2 Matty Dawson-Jones; 36 Mitch Cox; 5 Rhys Evans; 6 Ben Reynolds; 7 Drew Hutchison; 20 Greg Richards; 30 Micky Higham; 18 Nathan Mason; 11 Kevin Larroyer; 35 Jordan Walne; 32 Adam Walne. Subs (all used): 21 Nick Gregson; 33 Josh Johnson; 24 Jack Blagbrough; 26 Jordan Dezaria.
Try: Dawson-Jones (64); **Goals:** Reynolds 0/1.
Sin bin: Bergal (40) - fighting.
Rugby Leaguer & League Express Men of the Match:
Rovers: Josh Hardcastle; *Centurions:* Greg Richards.
Penalty count: 7-10; **Half-time:** 16-0;
Referee: Matt Rossleigh; **Attendance:** 2,194.

SWINTON LIONS 23 ROCHDALE HORNETS 18

LIONS: 7 Jack Hansen; 5 Mike Butt; 11 Rhodri Lloyd; 4 George Tyson; 32 Joe Brown; 30 Rob Fairclough; 31 Josh Woods; 8 Andy Bracek; 9 Luke Waterworth; 33 Paul Wood; 10 Andy Thornley; 17 Kyle Shelford; 25 Will Hope. Subs (all used): 34 Josh Ganson; 15 Ben Austin; 35 Paddy Jones; 14 Hayden Hansen.
Tries: Brown (9, 12, 62), Tyson (15); **Goals:** Fairclough 3/5;
Field goal: Woods (37).
HORNETS: 14 Tyler Whittaker; 21 Richard Lepori; 31 Deon Cross; 12 Toby Adamson; 5 Rob Massam; 30 Morgan Smith; 7 Danny Yates; 8 Jovili Taira; 9 Ben Moores; 16 Pat Moran; 13 Luke Adamson; 19 Lee Mitchell; 15 Lewis Hatton. Subs: 18 Billy Brickhill; 26 Jack Fox; 10 Joe Ryan; 25 Seta Tala (not used).
Tries: Smith (20), Fox (45), Lepori (68);
Goals: Whittaker 3/3.
Sin bin: L Adamson (28) - high tackle.

Championship Shield 2018 - Round by Round

Rugby Leaguer & League Express Men of the Match: *Lions:* Joe Brown; *Hornets:* Lewis Hatton.
Penalty count: 9-7; **Half-time:** 19-6;
Referee: Jack Smith; **Attendance:** 541.

ROUND 4

Friday 7th September 2018

SHEFFIELD EAGLES 12 FEATHERSTONE ROVERS 32

EAGLES: 6 Oscar Thomas; 2 Iliess Macani; 3 Menzie Yere; 4 Joshua Toole; 5 Ben Blackmore; 19 Simon Brown; 23 Cory Aston; 8 Mark Offerdahl; 14 Greg Burns; 12 Shaun Pick; 15 Olly Davies; 13 Matt James; 9 Matty Fozard. Subs (all used): 22 Paddy Burns; 18 Mike Weldon; 21 Blake Broadbent; 20 Max Garcia.
Tries: Broadbent (26, 78); **Goals:** Thomas 2/2.
ROVERS: 1 Ian Hardman; 38 Dakota Whylie; 4 Misi Taulapapa; 29 Harry Newman; 2 Shaun Robinson; 7 Anthony Thackeray; 14 Matty Wildie; 17 Luke Cooper; 9 Keal Carlile; 22 Sam Brooks; 11 Connor Farrell; 12 John Davies; 13 James Lockwood. Subs (all used, only three named): 20 Josh Hardcastle; 24 Danny Maskill; 21 Bradley Knowles.
Tries: Knowles (29), Thackeray (33), Newman (37, 57), Whylie (43), Hardman (50); **Goals:** Hardman 4/7.
Sin bin: Newman (69) - dissent.
On report: Farrell (15) - alleged high tackle on Aston.
Rugby Leaguer & League Express Men of the Match: *Eagles:* Blake Broadbent; *Rovers:* John Davies.
Penalty count: 13-7; **Half-time:** 6-16;
Referee: Greg Dolan; **Attendance:** 689.

Sunday 9th September 2018

BATLEY BULLDOGS 26 ROCHDALE HORNETS 12

BULLDOGS: 1 Dave Scott; 2 Wayne Reittie; 3 Sam Smeaton; 29 Lewis Galbraith; 23 Johnny Campbell; 31 Louis Jouffret; 7 Dominic Brambani; 8 Adam Gledhill; 9 Alistair Leak; 20 Alex Rowe; 11 Dane Manning; 28 Keenen Tomlinson; 12 Joel Farrell. Subs (all used): 6 Pat Walker; 19 Alex Bretherton; 21 James Brown; 16 Michael Ward.
Tries: Rowe (4), Campbell (9), Gledhill (70), Reittie (74), Smeaton (79); **Goals:** Scott 1/2, Walker 2/4.
Sin bin: Manning (56) - shoulder charge.
HORNETS: 21 Richard Lepori; 31 Deon Cross; 12 Toby Adamson; 25 Seta Tala; 26 Jack Fox; 14 Tyler Whittaker; 7 Danny Yates; 15 Lewis Hatton; 9 Ben Moores; 16 Pat Moran; 19 Lee Mitchell; 13 Luke Adamson; 18 Billy Brickhill. Subs (all used): - Morgan Smith; 8 Jovili Taira; 10 Joe Ryan; 30 Ryan Millington.
Tries: Fox (38), Cross (56, 61); **Goals:** Whittaker 0/3.
Rugby Leaguer & League Express Men of the Match: *Bulldogs:* James Brown; *Hornets:* Jovili Taira.
Penalty count: 9-9; **Half-time:** 10-4;
Referee: Nick Bennett; **Attendance:** 616.

DEWSBURY RAMS 32 BARROW RAIDERS 12

RAMS: 1 Josh Guzdek; 2 Rob Worrincy; 3 James Glover; 40 Adam Ryder; 5 Dale Morton; 6 Paul Sykes; 25 Brad Delaney; 8 Jode Sheriffe; 9 Robbie Ward; 28 Kyle Trout; 15 Lucas Walshaw; 12 Michael Knowles; 13 Aaron Brown. Subs (all used): 14 Dom Speakman; 32 Toby Richardson; 31 Daniel Igbinedion; 10 Jack Teanby.
Tries: Worrincy (12), Delaney (30), Walshaw (37), Brown (42), Ryder (45, 70); **Goals:** Sykes 4/7.
Sin bin: Sheriffe (55) - high tackle.
RAIDERS: 1 Ryan Fieldhouse; 31 Ryan Burroughs; 23 Tom Loxam; 36 Georgy Gambaro; 5 Brett Carter; 6 Jamie Dallimore; 7 Lewis Charnock; 27 Ryan Duffy; 22 Dean Parata; 35 Arnaud Barthes; 17 Alec Susino; 19 Bradd Crellin; 13 Martin Aspinwall. Subs (all used): 9 Nathan Mossop; 37 Saloty Mendy; 11 Dan Toal; 10 Tom Walker.
Tries: Gambaro (34), Mossop (54); **Goals:** Dallimore 2/2.
Sin bin: Duffy (66) - dissent; Aspinwall (80) - high tackle.
Rugby Leaguer & League Express Men of the Match: *Rams:* Dale Morton; *Raiders:* Jamie Dallimore.
Penalty count: 13-10; **Half-time:** 16-6;
Referee: Liam Staveley; **Attendance:** 807.

LEIGH CENTURIONS 54 SWINTON LIONS 10

CENTURIONS: 6 Ben Reynolds; 22 Ricky Bailey; 5 Rhys Evans; 2 Matty Dawson-Jones; 25 Ilias Bergal; 21 Nick Gregson; 7 Drew Hutchison; 20 Greg Richards; 30 Micky Higham; 32 Adam Walne; 11 Kevin Larroyer; 24 Jack Blagbrough; 35 Jordan Walne. Subs (all used): 33 Josh Johnson; 37 Sam Peet; 26 Jordan Dezaria; 38 Brad Whelan.
Tries: Larroyer (5, 62), Reynolds (8), J Walne (10), Peet (33), Hutchison (47), Richards (58, 68), Whelan (77);
Goals: Reynolds 6/6, Gregson 3/3.
LIONS: 7 Jack Hansen; 5 Mike Butt; 32 Joe Brown; 4 George Tyson; 16 Ryan Gray; 30 Rob Fairclough; 31 Josh Woods; 8 Andy Bracek; 9 Luke Waterworth; 35 Paul Wood; 17 Kyle Shelford; 10 Andy Thornley; 25 Will Hope. Subs (all used): 15 Ben Austin; 34 Josh Ganson; 14 Hayden Hansen; 36 Paddy Jones.
Tries: Shelford (15), Thornley (17); **Goals:** Fairclough 1/2.
Sin bin: Fairclough (56) - interference.
Rugby Leaguer & League Express Men of the Match: *Centurions:* Adam Walne; *Lions:* Josh Woods.
Penalty count: 5-7; **Half-time:** 24-10;
Referee: Scott Mikalauskas; **Attendance:** 2,757.

ROUND 5

Sunday 16th September 2018

BARROW RAIDERS 34 SWINTON LIONS 18

RAIDERS: 1 Ryan Fieldhouse; 36 Georgy Gambaro; 3 Declan Hulme; 31 Ryan Burroughs; 5 Brett Carter; 6 Jamie Dallimore; 7 Lewis Charnock; 10 Tom Walker; 9 Nathan Mossop; 15 Glenn Riley; 25 Jono Smith; 24 Danny Morrow; 13 Martin Aspinwall. Subs (all used): 11 Dan Toal; 27 Ryan Duffy; 35 Arnaud Barthes; 22 Dean Parata.
Tries: Dallimore (7), Burroughs (28, 58), Carter (51, 80), Barthes (56); **Goals:** Dallimore 5/6.
Sin bin: Duffy (61) - late challenge;
Aspinwall (75) - dangerous contact.
LIONS: 7 Jack Hansen; 5 Mike Butt; 11 Rhodri Lloyd; 4 George Tyson; 32 Joe Brown; 30 Rob Fairclough; 31 Josh Woods; 8 Andy Bracek; 9 Luke Waterworth; 35 Paul Wood; 10 Andy Thornley; 17 Kyle Shelford; 14 Hayden Hansen. Subs (all used): 15 Ben Austin; 34 Josh Ganson; 36 Paddy Jones; 21 Chris Worrell.
Tries: J Hansen (1), Butt (37, 76); **Goals:** Fairclough 3/4.
Sin bin: Tyson (51) - dissent.
Rugby Leaguer & League Express Men of the Match: *Raiders:* Ryan Burroughs; *Lions:* Rob Fairclough.
Penalty count: 9-7; **Half-time:** 12-14;
Referee: Liam Moore; **Attendance:** 1,357.

BATLEY BULLDOGS 44 SHEFFIELD EAGLES 4

BULLDOGS: 1 Dave Scott; 2 Wayne Reittie; 3 Sam Smeaton; 29 Lewis Galbraith; 23 Johnny Campbell; 31 Louis Jouffret; 7 Dominic Brambani; 8 Adam Gledhill; 14 James Davey; 15 James Harrison; 13 Brad Day; 11 Dane Manning; 20 Alex Rowe. Subs (all used): 6 Pat Walker; 28 Keenen Tomlinson; 21 James Brown; 16 Michael Ward.
Tries: Brambani (12), Smeaton (31), Galbraith (36), Campbell (49, 57, 72), Day (54), Brown (76);
Goals: Scott 6/8.
EAGLES: 6 Oscar Thomas; 2 Iliess Macani; 3 Menzie Yere; 4 Joshua Toole; 5 Ben Blackmore; 19 Simon Brown; 23 Cory Aston; 12 Shaun Pick; 14 Greg Burns; 10 Jon Magrin; 13 Matt James; 15 Olly Davies; 9 Matty Fozard. Subs (all used): 22 Paddy Burns; 21 Blake Broadbent; 18 Mike Weldon; 20 Max Garcia.
Try: Macani (66); **Goals:** Thomas 0/1.
Rugby Leaguer & League Express Men of the Match: *Bulldogs:* James Davey; *Eagles:* Ben Blackmore.
Penalty count: 7-5; **Half-time:** 18-0;
Referee: Marcus Griffiths; **Attendance:** 607.

FEATHERSTONE ROVERS 40 DEWSBURY RAMS 28

ROVERS: 1 Ian Hardman; 38 Dakota Whylie; 4 Misi Taulapapa; 29 Harry Newman; 2 Shaun Robinson; 7 Anthony Thackeray; 14 Matty Wildie; 22 Sam Brooks; 9 Keal Carlile; 17 Luke Cooper; 12 John Davies; 11 Connor Farrell; 13 James Lockwood. Subs (all used): 24 Danny Maskill; 21 Bradley Knowles; 20 Josh Hardcastle; 6 Martyn Ridyard.
Tries: Robinson (9), Newman (16), Whylie (33), Davies (37), Taulapapa (39), Farrell (47, 64), Ridyard (72);
Goals: Hardman 1/2, Ridyard 3/6.
RAMS: 1 Josh Guzdek; 18 Gareth Potts; 3 James Glover; 40 Adam Ryder; 5 Dale Morton; 6 Paul Sykes; 25 Brad Delaney; 8 Jode Sheriffe; 9 Robbie Ward; 28 Kyle Trout; 15 Lucas Walshaw; 12 Michael Knowles; 13 Aaron Brown. Subs (all used): 32 Toby Richardson; 17 Toby Everett; 10 Jack Teanby; 31 Daniel Igbinedion.
Tries: Sykes (12), Glover (30, 53), Igbinedion (43), Morton (70); **Goals:** Sykes 3/4, Glover 1/1.
Rugby Leaguer & League Express Men of the Match: *Rovers:* Martyn Ridyard; *Rams:* Josh Guzdek.
Penalty count: 8-6; **Half-time:** 24-12;
Referee: Nick Bennett; **Attendance:** 1,380.

ROCHDALE HORNETS 16 LEIGH CENTURIONS 24

HORNETS: 21 Richard Lepori; 31 Deon Cross; 12 Toby Adamson; 25 Seta Tala; 5 Rob Massam; 14 Tyler Whittaker; 7 Danny Yates; 15 Lewis Hatton; 18 Billy Brickhill; 16 Pat Moran; 19 Lee Mitchell; 13 Luke Adamson; 8 Jovili Taira. Subs (all used): 24 Declan Gregory; 22 Alex Gaskell; 10 Joe Ryan; 30 Ryan Millington.
Tries: Lepori (6), Yates (8); **Goals:** Whittaker 4/4.
Sin bin: T Adamson (49) - fighting;
Lepori (57) - high tackle on Dawson-Jones.
CENTURIONS: 6 Ben Reynolds; 22 Ricky Bailey; 19 Jack Owens; 2 Matty Dawson-Jones; 25 Ilias Bergal; 21 Nick Gregson; 7 Drew Hutchison; 20 Greg Richards; 30 Micky Higham; 32 Adam Walne; 11 Kevin Larroyer; 24 Jack Blagbrough; 35 Jordan Walne. Subs (all used): 33 Josh Johnson; 37 Sam Peet; 26 Jordan Dezaria; 36 Mitch Cox.
Tries: J Walne (14), Ricky Bailey (18), Bergal (20), Larroyer (64); **Goals:** Reynolds 4/5.
Sin bin: Larroyer (49) - fighting;
Bergal (57) - punching Lepori.
Rugby Leaguer & League Express Men of the Match: *Hornets:* Richard Lepori; *Centurions:* Ben Reynolds.
Penalty count: 11-11; **Half-time:** 16-16;
Referee: John McMullen; **Attendance:** 834.

ROUND 6

Sunday 23rd September 2018

LEIGH CENTURIONS 16 BATLEY BULLDOGS 30

CENTURIONS: 19 Jack Owens; 22 Ricky Bailey; 37 Sam Peet; 2 Matty Dawson-Jones; 25 Ilias Bergal; 6 Ben Reynolds; 7 Drew Hutchison; 29 Ryan Bailey; 30 Micky Higham; 10 Jamie Acton; 11 Kevin Larroyer; 36 Mitch Cox; 35 Jordan Walne. Subs (all used): 33 Josh Johnson; 24 Jack Blagbrough; 26 Jordan Dezaria; 38 Brad Whelan.
Tries: Ricky Bailey (26), Owens (33), Reynolds (45);
Goals: Reynolds 2/3.
Sin bin: Johnson (65) - dissent; Ryan Bailey (73) - fighting.
BULLDOGS: 1 Dave Scott; 2 Wayne Reittie; 3 Sam Smeaton; 29 Lewis Galbraith; 23 Johnny Campbell; 31 Louis Jouffret; 7 Dominic Brambani; 8 Adam Gledhill; 9 Alistair Leak; 15 James Harrison; 13 Brad Day; 19 Alex Bretherton; 21 James Brown. Subs (all used): 14 James Davey; 20 Alex Rowe; 28 Keenen Tomlinson; 16 Michael Ward.
Tries: Galbraith (5), Campbell (14, 51), Scott (48), Jouffret (69); **Goals:** Scott 5/8.
Sin bin: Galbraith (73) - fighting.
Rugby Leaguer & League Express Men of the Match: *Centurions:* Micky Higham; *Bulldogs:* Louis Jouffret.
Penalty count: 6-12; **Half-time:** 10-8;
Referee: Billy Pearson; **Attendance:** 1,730.

ROCHDALE HORNETS 26 DEWSBURY RAMS 22

HORNETS: 21 Richard Lepori; 31 Deon Cross; 12 Toby Adamson; 25 Seta Tala; 5 Rob Massam; 14 Tyler Whittaker; 7 Danny Yates; 15 Lewis Hatton; 9 Ben Moores; 16 Pat Moran; 19 Lee Mitchell; 13 Luke Adamson; 8 Jovili Taira. Subs (all used): 24 Declan Gregory; 10 Joe Ryan; 30 Ryan Millington; 18 Billy Brickhill
Tries: Tala (10), Cross (19, 33), Gregory (37), Hatton (45);
Goals: Whittaker 3/6.
RAMS: 1 Josh Guzdek; 2 Rob Worrincy; 3 James Glover; 40 Adam Ryder; 5 Dale Morton; 6 Paul Sykes; 25 Brad Delaney; 28 Kyle Trout; 9 Robbie Ward; 10 Jack Teanby; 15 Lucas Walshaw; 12 Michael Knowles; 13 Aaron Brown. Subs (all used): 14 Dom Speakman; 32 Toby Richardson; 17 Toby Everett; 31 Daniel Igbinedion.
Tries: Knowles (4), Delaney (6, 75), Worrincy (71);
Goals: Sykes 3/4.
Rugby Leaguer & League Express Men of the Match: *Hornets:* Pat Moran; *Rams:* Adam Ryder.
Penalty count: 6-8; **Half-time:** 20-10;
Referee: James Child; **Attendance:** 651.

SHEFFIELD EAGLES 22 BARROW RAIDERS 24

EAGLES: 6 Oscar Thomas; 25 Jake Spedding; 3 Menzie Yere; 4 Joshua Toole; 5 Ben Blackmore; 19 Simon Brown; 23 Cory Aston; 8 Mark Offerdahl; 14 Greg Burns; 10 Jon Magrin; 22 Paddy Burns; 12 Shaun Pick; 9 Matty Fozard. Subs (all used): 21 Blake Broadbent; 20 Max Garcia; 15 Olly Davies; 18 Mike Weldon.
Tries: G Burns (22), Toole (38, 65), Offerdahl (75);
Goals: Thomas 3/4.
RAIDERS: 1 Ryan Fieldhouse; 5 Brett Carter; 31 Ryan Burroughs; 3 Declan Hulme; 36 Georgy Gambaro; 6 Jamie Dallimore; 7 Lewis Charnock; 15 Glenn Riley; 22 Dean Parata; 10 Tom Walker; 25 Jono Smith; 24 Danny Morrow; 11 Dan Toal. Subs: 13 Martin Aspinwall; 35 Arnaud Barthes; 28 Matthew Holmes; 21 Ryan Johnston (not used).
Tries: Carter (26, 35), Fieldhouse (58), Burroughs (77);
Goals: Dallimore 4/5.
Rugby Leaguer & League Express Men of the Match: *Eagles:* Oscar Thomas; *Raiders:* Jamie Dallimore.
Penalty count: 7-7; **Half-time:** 10-10;
Referee: Andrew Sweet; **Attendance:** 404.

Featherstone celebrate winning the Championship Shield

SWINTON LIONS 18 FEATHERSTONE ROVERS 34

LIONS: 1 Gabriel Fell; 5 Mike Butt; 11 Rhodri Lloyd; 31 Craig Mullen; 16 Ryan Gray; 30 Rob Fairclough; 7 Jack Hansen; 15 Ben Austin; 9 Luke Waterworth; 24 Aaron Hall; 10 Andy Thornley; 17 Kyle Shelford; 14 Hayden Hansen. Subs (all used): 21 Chris Worrell; 34 Paddy Jones; 33 Josh Ganson; 6 Brad Billsborough.
Tries: Thornley (10), Gray (13), Mullen (19);
Goals: Fairclough 0/2, J Hansen 3/3.
Sin bin: Fairclough (60) - fighting.
ROVERS: 1 Ian Hardman; 38 Dakota Whylie; 4 Misi Taulapapa; 20 Josh Hardcastle; 2 Shaun Robinson; 7 Anthony Thackeray; 14 Matty Wildie; 17 Luke Cooper; 24 Danny Maskill; 22 Sam Brooks; 12 John Davies; 11 Connor Farrell; 13 James Lockwood. Subs (only three named): 9 Keal Carlile; 21 Bradley Knowles (not used); 6 Martyn Ridyard.
Tries: Davies (6), Taulapapa (27), Thackeray (56), Maskill (64), Farrell (68), Hardcastle (72);
Goals: Hardman 5/6.
Sin bin: Davies (9) - high tackle on Fairclough; Taulapapa (60) - fighting.
Rugby Leaguer & League Express Men of the Match:
Lions: Mike Butt; *Rovers:* Luke Cooper.
Penalty count: 13-11; **Half-time:** 16-12;
Referee: Tom Grant; **Attendance:** 606.

ROUND 7

Sunday 30th September 2018

BATLEY BULLDOGS 40 SWINTON LIONS 6

BULLDOGS: 1 Dave Scott; 2 Wayne Reittie; 3 Sam Smeaton; 29 Lewis Galbraith; 23 Johnny Campbell; 31 Louis Jouffret; 7 Dominic Brambani; 8 Adam Gledhill; 9 Alistair Leak; 20 Alex Rowe; 13 Brad Day; 19 Alex Bretherton; 21 James Brown. Subs (all used): 6 Pat Walker; 14 James Davey; 28 Keenen Tomlinson; 16 Michael Ward.
Tries: Gledhill (8), Smeaton (35), Reittie (46), Scott (49), Jouffret (55, 75), Brambani (80);
Goals: Brambani 1/1, Walker 4/5, Rowe 1/1.
LIONS: 23 Elliott Caine; 5 Mike Butt; 11 Rhodri Lloyd; 10 Andy Thornley; 16 Ryan Gray; 30 Rob Fairclough; 7 Jack Hansen; 24 Aaron Hall; 9 Luke Waterworth; 15 Ben Austin; 21 Chris Worrell; 17 Kyle Shelford; 14 Hayden Hansen. Subs (all used): 34 Paddy Jones; 35 Tommy Gallagher; 6 Brad Billsborough; 33 Josh Ganson.
Try: Hall (16); **Goals:** J Hansen 1/1.
Rugby Leaguer & League Express Men of the Match:
Bulldogs: Louis Jouffret; *Lions:* Jack Hansen.
Penalty count: 7-5; **Half-time:** 12-6;
Referee: John McMullen; **Attendance:** 817.

DEWSBURY RAMS 52 LEIGH CENTURIONS 6

RAMS: 1 Josh Guzdek; 2 Rob Worrincy; 3 James Glover; 40 Adam Ryder; 5 Dale Morton; 6 Paul Sykes; 25 Brad Delaney; 28 Kyle Trout; 9 Robbie Ward; 10 Jack Teanby; 12 Michael Knowles; 15 Lucas Walshaw; 13 Aaron Brown. Subs (all used): 14 Dom Speakman; 17 Toby Everett; 31 Daniel Igbinedion; 32 Toby Richardson.
Tries: Brown (13, 20), Sykes (30), Guzdek (32, 41), Glover (44), Ryder (47), Worrincy (51), Igbinedion (73);
Goals: Sykes 8/10.
CENTURIONS: 34 Will Dagger; 38 Brad Whelan; 21 Nick Gregson; 11 Kevin Larroyer; 22 Ricky Bailey; 19 Jack Owens; 7 Drew Hutchison; 29 Ryan Bailey; 30 Micky Higham; 33 Josh Johnson; 35 Jordan Walne; 24 Jack Blagbrough; 10 Jamie Acton. (Only thirteen players named).
Try: Acton (64); **Goals:** Owens 1/1.
Rugby Leaguer & League Express Men of the Match:
Rams: Josh Guzdek; *Centurions:* Micky Higham.
Penalty count: 9-5; **Half-time:** 26-0;
Referee: Andrew Sweet; **Attendance:** 999.

FEATHERSTONE ROVERS 34 BARROW RAIDERS 6

ROVERS: 6 Martyn Ridyard; 38 Dakota Whylie; 4 Misi Taulapapa; 20 Josh Hardcastle; 2 Shaun Robinson; 7 Anthony Thackeray; 14 Matty Wildie; 22 Sam Brooks; 24 Danny Maskill; 17 Luke Cooper; 12 John Davies; 11 Connor Farrell; 13 James Lockwood. Subs (only three named): 9 Keal Carlile; 21 Bradley Knowles (not used); 1 Ian Hardman.
Tries: Cooper (10), Hardcastle (28), Farrell (35), Davies (45, 55), Robinson (78);
Goals: Ridyard 2/3, Hardman 3/3.
Sin bin: Thackeray (7) - dangerous challenge; Hardcastle (75) - holding down.
RAIDERS: 1 Ryan Fieldhouse; 5 Brett Carter; 24 Danny Morrow; 31 Ryan Burroughs; 36 Georgy Gambaro; 6 Jamie Dallimore; 7 Lewis Charnock; 15 Glenn Reilly; 22 Dean Parata; 35 Arnaud Barthes; 25 Jono Smith; 28 Matthew Holmes; 11 Dan Toal. Subs (all used): 21 Ryan Johnston; 27 Ryan Duffy; 19 Bradd Crellin; 20 Matty While.
Try: Dallimore (19); **Goals:** Dallimore 1/1.
Sin bin: Parata (54) - high tackle on Whylie.
Rugby Leaguer & League Express Men of the Match:
Rovers: Josh Hardcastle; *Raiders:* Dan Toal.
Penalty count: 14-10; **Half-time:** 16-6;
Referee: Tom Crashley; **Attendance:** 1,125.

SHEFFIELD EAGLES 22 ROCHDALE HORNETS 32

EAGLES: 6 Oscar Thomas; 2 Iliess Macani; 3 Menzie Yere; 4 Joshua Toole; 25 Jake Spedding; 19 Simon Brown; 23 Cory Aston; 8 Mark Offerdahl; 9 Matty Fozard; 21 Blake Broadbent; 18 Mike Weldon; 12 Shaun Pick; 22 Paddy Burns. Subs (all used): 14 Greg Burns; 13 Matt James; 15 Olly Davies; 10 Jon Magrin.
Tries: Broadbent (3), G Burns (45), Aston (51), Spedding (63); **Goals:** Thomas 3/4.
HORNETS: 21 Richard Lepori; 31 Deon Cross; 12 Toby Adamson; 25 Seta Tala; 26 Jack Fox; 14 Tyler Whittaker; 7 Danny Yates; 15 Lewis Hatton; 9 Ben Moores; 16 Pat Moran; 19 Lee Mitchell; 13 Luke Adamson; 8 Jovili Taira. Subs (all used): 24 Declan Gregory; 10 Joe Ryan; 30 Ryan Millington; 18 Billy Brickhill.
Tries: T Adamson (6), Cross (21), Mitchell (24), Fox (47), Taira (65), Whittaker (78); **Goals:** Whittaker 4/7.
Rugby Leaguer & League Express Men of the Match:
Eagles: Jon Magrin; *Hornets:* Jovili Taira.
Penalty count: 9-7; **Half-time:** 6-16;
Referee: Tom Grant; **Attendance:** 789.

FINAL

Sunday 7th October 2018

FEATHERSTONE ROVERS 42 LEIGH CENTURIONS 10

ROVERS: 1 Ian Hardman; 38 Dakota Whylie; 4 Misi Taulapapa; 29 Harry Newman; 2 Shaun Robinson; 6 Martyn Ridyard; 14 Matty Wildie; 17 Luke Cooper; 24 Danny Maskill; 22 Sam Brooks; 12 John Davies; 11 Connor Farrell; 20 Josh Hardcastle; 13 James Lockwood. Subs (all used): 9 Keal Carlile; 39 Tyler Dupree; 40 Muizz Mustapha; 41 James Barraclough.
Tries: Carlile (16), Dupree (44), Newman (51, 73), Farrell (57), Robinson (60, 68); **Goals:** Hardman 7/8.
CENTURIONS: 19 Jack Owens; 42 Kevin Brown; 2 Matty Dawson-Jones; 43 Sam Grant; 22 Ricky Bailey; 45 James Barran; 7 Drew Hutchison; 10 Jamie Acton; 39 Jacques O'Neill; 24 Jack Blagbrough; 11 Kevin Larroyer; 21 Nick Gregson; 41 Liam Byrne. Subs (all used): 40 Ben Kilner; 33 Josh Johnson; 52 Chris Follin; 36 Mitch Cox.
Tries: Dawson-Jones (5), Owens (54); **Goals:** Owens 1/2.
Sin bin: Larroyer (34) - delaying restart; Acton (76) - late challenge on Brooks.
Rugby Leaguer & League Express Men of the Match:
Rovers: Ian Hardman; *Centurions:* Kevin Brown.
Penalty count: 11-8; **Half-time:** 8-6;
Referee: John McMullen; **Attendance:** 2,123.

LEAGUE 1 2018
Club by Club

BRADFORD BULLS

DATE	FIXTURE	RESULT	SCORERS	LGE	ATT
18/2/18	York (a)	W20-22	t:Gibson,Minchella,Crossley g:Keyes(5)	5th	4,221
25/2/18	West Wales (h) (CCR3)	W82-6	t:Johnson(2),Crossley,Ryan,McNally(2),Minchella(5),Bustin,Gibson(2),Chisholm g:Keyes(11)	N/A	1,505
11/3/18	Keighley (a)	W6-54	t:Minchella(2),Peltier,Flanagan(2),Keyes,Grant,Hallas,Ryan g:Keyes(9)	2nd	2,912
25/3/18	Hunslet (h)	W32-12	t:Hallas(2),Grant(3),Chisholm g:Keyes(4)	2nd	3,688
30/3/18	Oldham (h)	W30-12	t:Minchella,Chisholm,Grant(2) g:Keyes(4),Smith(2),Chisholm	1st	4,036
2/4/18	Hunslet (a) (CCR4)	W10-34	t:Garside,Ryan,Johnson,Minchella,Rickett g:Chisholm(7)	N/A	1,081
8/4/18	Workington (a)	L17-16	t:Peltier,Butler-Fleming g:Keyes(4)	2nd	1,366
15/4/18	Coventry (h)	W52-6	t:Johnson(2),Gibson,Hitchcox(2),Flanagan(2),Ryan,Keyes,Minchella g:Keyes(6)	2nd	3,545
21/4/18	Warrington (a) (CCR5)	L54-6	t:Keyes g:Keyes	N/A	4,710
29/4/18	Doncaster (a)	W6-32	t:Ryan,Minchella(2),Wood,Flanagan g:Keyes(6)	2nd	2,780
6/5/18	West Wales (h)	W124-0	t:Bustin,Grant(2),Ryan(2),Hallas,Chisholm(2),Laithwaite,Smith,Garside(3),Pickersgill(2),Minchella(3),Peltier,Halafihi,Flanagan g:Chisholm(20)	1st	3,398
12/5/18	London Skolars (h)	W54-16	t:Pickersgill,Ryan(4),Grant(2),Peltier,Smith,Gibson,Bustin g:Chisholm(5)	1st	3,041
18/5/18	Newcastle (a)	W16-26	t:Minchella,Ryan,Flanagan,Chisholm g:Chisholm(5)	2nd	4,137
27/5/18	Hemel (a)	W0-68	t:Chisholm,Garside,Peltier,Flanagan,Ryan,Minchella(2),Pickersgill,Grant(2),Laithwaite,Halafihi g:Chisholm(10)	1st	736
9/6/18	North Wales (h)	W50-12	t:Chisholm,Smith(2),Pickersgill,Ryan(2),Garside(2),Keyes g:Chisholm(7)	1st	3,112
17/6/18	Whitehaven (a)	W20-27	t:Crossley,Keyes(2),Halafihi g:Chisholm(5) fg:Keyes	1st	1,476
24/6/18	Doncaster (h)	W56-14	t:Ryan(4),Crossley,Pickersgill(2),Chisholm,Laithwaite,Bustin g:Chisholm(8)	1st	4,060
30/6/18	Coventry (a)	W12-62	t:Ryan,Milton,Minchella(3),Peltier,Laithwaite,Keyes,Johnson,Hallas(2) g:Chisholm(9)	1st	1,465
6/7/18	Newcastle (h)	W24-4	t:Chisholm,Pickersgill,Ryan g:Chisholm(6)	1st	3,029
15/7/18	Hunslet (a)	W16-36	t:Gibson(2),Crossley,Keyes,Flanagan(2) g:Chisholm(6)	1st	1,536
22/7/18	York (h)	L28-30	t:Grant(2),McNally,Peltier,Ryan g:Chisholm(4)	1st	6,441
28/7/18	London Skolars (a)	W12-58	t:Green,Chisholm(2),Ryan(3),Peltier,Halafihi,Lilley,Pickersgill,Minchella g:Chisholm(7)	1st	1,178
4/8/18	Whitehaven (h)	W46-0	t:Hallas,Ryan(3),Lilley,Pickersgill,Minchella(2) g:Chisholm(6),Lilley	1st	2,818
12/8/18	North Wales (a)	W0-48	t:Ryan,Minchella,Egodo,Chisholm(2),Garside,Pownall,Keyes g:Chisholm(8)	1st	886
19/8/18	Workington (h)	L18-24	t:Minchella,Chisholm,Garside g:Lilley(3)	2nd	3,320
2/9/18	Keighley (h)	W54-4	t:Keyes,Egodo(3),Ryan(3),Flanagan(2),Minchella g:Keyes(7)	2nd	3,119
9/9/18	West Wales (a)	W0-104	t:Grant(2),Minchella(3),Bustin(2),Ryan(2),Hitchcox(3),Crossley,Peltier,McNally,Storton,Egodo,Chisholm g:Keyes(14)	2nd	826
16/9/18	Oldham (a)	W16-24	t:Storton,Hitchcox,Flanagan,Peltier g:Keyes(4)	2nd	1,038
23/9/18	Hemel (h)	W52-7	t:Grant(2),Bustin,Pownall(2),Hitchcox,Pickersgill,Storton(2),Oakes g:Chisholm(6)	2nd	2,855
30/9/18	Oldham (h) (SF)	W47-0	t:Ryan(2),Keyes,Peltier,Minchella(2),Hitchcox,Gibson g:Keyes(7) fg:Chisholm	N/A	2,788
7/10/18	Workington (h) (PF)	W27-8	t:Hitchcox(3),Flanagan,Keyes,Chisholm g:Chisholm fg:Chisholm	N/A	6,011

		APP		TRIES		GOALS		FG		PTS	
	D.O.B.	ALL	L1	ALL	L1	ALL	L1	ALL	L1	ALL	L1
Jordan Andrade	24/1/92	(1)	0	0	0	0	0	0	0	0	0
Callum Bustin	12/8/97	16(4)	16(2)	7	6	0	0	0	0	28	24
Jake Butler-Fleming	8/1/92	2	2	1	1	0	0	0	0	4	4
Dane Chisholm	4/7/90	26(2)	25(1)	17	16	121	114	2	2	312	294
Steve Crossley	28/11/89	26(2)	24(1)	6	5	0	0	0	0	24	20
Tuoyo Egodo	16/2/97	8	8	5	5	0	0	0	0	20	20
George Flanagan	8/10/86	4(16)	4(14)	14	14	0	0	0	0	56	56
Matt Garside	1/10/90	24(2)	22(2)	9	8	0	0	0	0	36	32
Ashley Gibson	25/9/86	24	21	8	6	0	0	0	0	32	24
Dalton Grant	21/4/90	25	23	18	18	0	0	0	0	72	72
James Green	29/11/90	5(6)	5(6)	1	1	0	0	0	0	4	4
Vila Halafihi	24/1/94	7(10)	5(9)	4	4	0	0	0	0	16	16
Sam Hallas	18/10/96	19(4)	18(4)	7	7	0	0	0	0	28	28
Jy Hitchcox	18/8/89	8	8	11	11	0	0	0	0	44	44
Liam Johnson	12/5/97	7(7)	4(7)	6	3	0	0	0	0	24	12
Joe Keyes	17/9/95	21(2)	19(2)	12	11	82	70	1	1	213	185
Liam Kirk	26/3/97	13(9)	11(9)	0	0	0	0	0	0	0	0
James Laithwaite	23/9/91	11(1)	11(1)	4	4	0	0	0	0	16	16
Jordan Lilley	4/9/96	10	10	2	2	4	4	0	0	16	16
Gregg McNally	2/1/91	12(1)	10(1)	5	3	0	0	0	0	20	12
Rowan Milnes	1/9/97	1(1)	1(1)	0	0	0	0	0	0	0	0
George Milton	4/9/95	11(2)	9(2)	1	1	0	0	0	0	4	4
Elliot Minchella	28/1/96	26(3)	24(2)	33	27	0	0	0	0	132	108
Ross Oakes	12/10/96	12(1)	10(1)	1	1	0	0	0	0	4	4
Ross Peltier	24/4/92	2(28)	(27)	11	11	0	0	0	0	44	44
Brandon Pickersgill	29/3/97	22(3)	19(3)	11	11	0	0	0	0	44	44
Jonny Pownall	22/8/91	2(2)	2(2)	3	3	0	0	0	0	12	12
Josh Rickett	20/10/97	1	0	1	0	0	0	0	0	4	0
Ethan Ryan	12/5/96	30	27	36	34	0	0	0	0	144	136
Lee Smith	8/8/86	12	11	4	4	2	2	0	0	20	20
Matthew Storton	10/3/99	4(1)	4(1)	4	4	0	0	0	0	16	16
Oliver Wilson	22/3/99	(1)	(1)	0	0	0	0	0	0	0	0
Mikey Wood	18/4/96	12(15)	11(13)	1	1	0	0	0	0	4	4

'L1' totals include play-offs; 'All' totals also include Challenge Cup

Elliot Minchella

LEAGUE RECORD
P26-W23-D0-L3
(2nd/Winners, Promotion Final)
F1197, A282, Diff+915, 46 points.

CHALLENGE CUP
Round Five

ATTENDANCES
Best - v York (L1 - 6,441)
Worst - v West Wales (CC - 1,505)
Total (excluding Challenge Cup) - 55,261
Average (excluding Challenge Cup) - 3,684
(Down by 193 on 2017, Championship)

CLUB RECORDS	
MATCH RECORDS	**Highest score:** 124-0 v West Wales, 6/5/2018 **Highest score against:** 6-84 v Wigan, 21/4/2014 **Record attendance:** 69,429 v Huddersfield, 14/3/53
	Tries: 6 Eric Batten v Leeds, 15/9/45; Trevor Foster v Wakefield, 10/4/48; Steve McGowan v Barrow, 8/11/92; Lesley Vainikolo v Hull, 2/9/2005
	Goals: 20 Dane Chisholm v West Wales, 6/5/2018 **Points:** 48 Dane Chisholm v West Wales, 6/5/2018
SEASON RECORDS	**Tries:** 63 Jack McLean 1951-52 **Goals:** 213 *(inc 5fg)* Henry Paul 2001 **Points:** 457 Henry Paul 2001
CAREER RECORDS	**Tries:** 261 Jack McLean 1950-56 **Goals:** 1,165 *(inc 25fg)* Paul Deacon 1998-2009 **Points:** 2,605 Paul Deacon 1998-2009
	Appearances: 588 Keith Mumby 1973-90; 1992-93

COVENTRY BEARS

DATE	FIXTURE	RESULT	SCORERS	LGE	ATT
18/2/18	Doncaster (a)	L70-10	t:Freeman,Lord g:Stead	14th	787
25/2/18	Distington (h) (CCR3)	W42-12	t:Chapman(2),Bass(2),Barratt,Lord,Freeman g:Stead(7)	N/A	267
11/3/18	Hemel (a)	W16-22	t:Carter(2),Morley-Samuels,Beddows g:Stead(3)	9th	110
25/3/18	Pilkington Recs (h) (CCR4)	W31-20	t:Mason(2),Emanuelli,Freeman,Bass g:Stead(5) fg:Emanuelli	N/A	395
30/3/18	Newcastle (h)	L18-32	t:Mason,Carter,Stead g:Stead(3)	12th	343
8/4/18	Whitehaven (h)	L12-44	t:Chapman(2) g:Emanuelli(2)	12th	279
15/4/18	Bradford (a)	L52-6	t:Chapman g:Stead	12th	3,545
21/4/18	Widnes (a) (CCR5)	L90-0		N/A	1,438
29/4/18	London Skolars (h)	L20-28	t:Morley-Samuels(2),Pearce-Paul,Freeman g:Stead(2)	12th	266
6/5/18	Keighley (a)	L98-6	t:Gant g:Stead	12th	446
12/5/18	York (h)	L18-58	t:Ogden,Hughes,Ryan g:Stead(3)	12th	252
20/5/18	Workington (h)	L4-52	t:Pearce-Paul	12th	264
27/5/18	North Wales (a)	L42-6	t:Rance g:Stead	12th	301
10/6/18	Oldham (h)	L0-60		12th	337
17/6/18	Hunslet (a)	L40-16	t:Cator,Barratt,Mason g:Stead(2)	12th	511
24/6/18	Newcastle (a)	L46-12	t:Clavering,Barratt g:Stead(2)	12th	903
30/6/18	Bradford (h)	L12-62	t:Pearce-Paul,Barratt g:Stead(2)	12th	1,465
7/7/18	London Skolars (a)	W20-24	t:Vitalini,Pearce-Paul,Freeman(2) g:Stead(4)	12th	160
15/7/18	Hemel (h)	W20-18	t:Bass(2),Sherratt,Chapman g:Stead(2)	12th	281
21/7/18	Keighley (h)	W30-20	t:M Russell(3),Barratt,Ogden g:Emanuelli(5)	12th	303
25/7/18	West Wales (h)	W64-6	t:Barratt,Bass,Freeman(3),Geurtjens,Pearce-Paul(3),Stead,Sherratt,Chapman g:Stead(8)	11th	272
29/7/18	York (a)	L68-6	t:Bass g:Stead	11th	1,104
5/8/18	Doncaster (h)	L4-46	t:M Russell	11th	300
12/8/18	Workington (a)	L40-16	t:Stead,Freeman,Bass g:Stead(2)	11th	556
19/8/18	West Wales (a)	W18-28	t:Freeman(2),Rice-Wilson,Bateman,Sherratt g:Stead,Emanuelli(3)	11th	409
2/9/18	Oldham (a)	L58-6	t:Morley-Samuels g:Stead	11th	373
9/9/18	North Wales (h)	L12-36	t:Rance,Bass g:Stead(2)	12th	288
16/9/18	Whitehaven (a)	L24-20	t:Pearce-Paul,Freeman,Rance g:Stead(4)	12th	691
22/9/18	Hunslet (h)	W14-4	t:Barratt,Gray g:Stead(3)	11th	380

		APP		TRIES		GOALS		FG		PTS	
	D.O.B.	ALL	L1	ALL	L1	ALL	L1	ALL	L1	ALL	L1
John Aldred	3/10/89	2(6)	1(5)	0	0	0	0	0	0	0	0
Chris Barratt	7/2/93	19	18	7	6	0	0	0	0	28	24
Jason Bass	10/5/96	24(1)	21(1)	9	6	0	0	0	0	36	24
Ashley Bateman	11/2/90	10(3)	10(3)	1	1	0	0	0	0	4	4
Alex Beddows	1/8/94	1(3)	1(2)	1	1	0	0	0	0	4	4
Callum Bradbury	3/8/96	1	1	0	0	0	0	0	0	0	0
Rob Butler	15/5/98	(1)	(1)	0	0	0	0	0	0	0	0
Errol Carter	22/1/96	11(3)	8(3)	3	3	0	0	0	0	12	12
Joe Cator	15/6/98	2	1	1	1	0	0	0	0	4	4
Harry Chapman	15/7/97	12	11	7	5	0	0	0	0	28	20
Charles Clarke	5/2/98	1	1	0	0	0	0	0	0	0	0
Brad Clavering	14/3/98	2	2	1	1	0	0	0	0	4	4
Sam Davis	11/11/98	2(2)	2(2)	0	0	0	0	0	0	0	0
Brad Delaney	25/5/95	1	1	0	0	0	0	0	0	0	0
Paul Emanuelli	3/1/84	19	16	1	0	10	10	1	0	25	20
Hayden Freeman	20/8/97	23	21	13	11	0	0	0	0	52	44
Rhys Gant	15/11/95	3	2	1	1	0	0	0	0	4	4
James Geurtjens	28/4/86	14(12)	13(10)	1	1	0	0	0	0	4	4
Dan Gover	23/9/93	8(11)	7(10)	0	0	0	0	0	0	0	0
Ben Gray	12/11/95	10(2)	9(1)	1	1	0	0	0	0	4	4
Richard Hughes	28/3/93	3(4)	2(4)	1	1	0	0	0	0	4	4
Jamahl Hunte	27/4/94	3	3	0	0	0	0	0	0	0	0
Jacob Jones	15/2/99	1	1	0	0	0	0	0	0	0	0
Harry Kaufman	20/12/91	3(6)	3(4)	0	0	0	0	0	0	0	0
Malikhi Lloyd-Jones	29/8/94	7(13)	7(13)	0	0	0	0	0	0	0	0
Lewis Lord	29/11/95	3(6)	2(6)	2	1	0	0	0	0	8	4
James Mason	27/1/95	8(11)	6(11)	4	2	0	0	0	0	16	8
Dante Morley-Samuels	22/11/98	20(1)	17(1)	4	4	0	0	0	0	16	16
Jake Ogden	23/1/98	12	12	2	2	0	0	0	0	8	8
Kameron Pearce-Paul	28/2/97	24	22	8	8	0	0	0	0	32	32
Reece Rance	17/7/93	11	11	3	3	0	0	0	0	12	12
Liam Rice-Wilson	16/3/96	13(8)	13(6)	1	1	0	0	0	0	4	4
Lewis Russell	12/5/97	(1)	(1)	0	0	0	0	0	0	0	0
Mikey Russell	29/8/94	1(1)	1(1)	4	4	0	0	0	0	16	16
Peter Ryan	25/2/95	10(3)	10(3)	1	1	0	0	0	0	4	4
Brad Sheridan	24/3/94	3(4)	3(4)	0	0	0	0	0	0	0	0
Kieran Sherratt	15/11/95	19	17	3	3	0	0	0	0	12	12
Ben Stead	13/10/92	27	24	3	3	61	49	0	0	134	110
Cameron Stewart	1/3/99	1(4)	1(4)	0	0	0	0	0	0	0	0
Joel Thomas	11/11/94	4(4)	3(3)	0	0	0	0	0	0	0	0
Chris Vitalini	5/5/87	23(1)	20(1)	1	1	0	0	0	0	4	4
Zak Williams	17/9/96	16(5)	14(5)	0	0	0	0	0	0	0	0

'L1' totals include League 1 regular season only; 'All' totals also include Challenge Cup

Ben Stead

LEAGUE RECORD
P26-W7-D0-L19 (11th)
F406, A1058, Diff-652, 14 points.

CHALLENGE CUP
Round Five

ATTENDANCES
Best - v Bradford (L1 - 1,465)
Worst - v York (L1 - 252)
Total (excluding Challenge Cup) - 5,030
Average (excluding Challenge Cup) - 387
(Up by 21 on 2017)

CLUB RECORDS   **Highest score:** 64-6 v West Wales, 25/7/2018   **Highest score against:** 6-98 v Keighley, 6/5/2018   **Record attendance:** 1,465 v Bradford, 30/6/2018
MATCH RECORDS   **Tries:** 3 *(10 players)* **Goals:** 8 Connor Robinson v Hemel, 19/4/2015; Ben Stead v West Wales, 25/7/2018   **Points:** 22 Dan Parker v London Skolars, 7/6/2015
SEASON RECORDS   **Tries:** 13 Jamahl Hunte 2017; Hayden Freeman 2017; Jamahl Hunte 2017; Mikey Russell 2017; Hayden Freeman 2018
   Goals: 61 Ben Stead 2018   **Points:** 138 Brad Delaney 2017
CAREER RECORDS   **Tries:** 30 Jamahl Hunte 2015-2018   **Goals:** 61 Ben Stead 2018   **Points:** 138 Brad Delaney 2017-2018   **Appearances:** 87 Chris Barratt 2015-2018

DONCASTER

DATE	FIXTURE	RESULT	SCORERS	LGE	ATT
18/2/18	Coventry (h)	W70-10	t:Tali(2),England,Spiers(2),Harris(2),Braham,Miloudi(4) g:Miller(3),Miloudi(8)	1st	787
25/2/18	Myton (h) (CCR3)	W82-6	t:Harris,Kesik,Tali(4),Doherty,Cross,Howden,Jones-Bishop,Martin,Hedges, Boyle,Bower(2),Connor Scott g:Harris(9)	N/A	388
11/3/18	Whitehaven (h)	W44-6	t:Howden(2),Harris,Sanderson(2),Doherty,Bower(2),Litten g:Harris(4)	1st	782
16/3/18	Newcastle (h) (CCR4)	W34-0	t:Owen,Harris,Sanderson,Welham,Jones-Bishop,Doherty g:Harris(5)	N/A	398
25/3/18	Newcastle (a)	W20-22	t:Martin,Downs,Doherty,Miloudi g:Miloudi(3)	1st	818
30/3/18	York (h)	L14-16	t:Cross,Cameron Scott g:Harris(3)	2nd	906
8/4/18	North Wales (h)	W28-20	t:Wilkinson,Connor Scott,Tali,Owen,England g:Miloudi(4)	1st	668
15/4/18	Hemel (h)	W60-0	t:Kesik,Tali(2),Owen(2),Welham,Braham,Muranka,Jones-Bishop,Harris,Miloudi g:Miller(8)	1st	580
22/4/18	Featherstone (h) (CCR5)	L16-26	t:Jones-Bishop,England,Tali g:Miller(2)	N/A	1,076
29/4/18	Bradford (h)	L6-32	t:Jones-Bishop g:Miller	3rd	2,780
5/5/18	London Skolars (a)	W18-42	t:Wilkinson,Miloudi(2),Cross(2),Braham,Jones-Bishop,Welham g:Miloudi(5)	3rd	186
13/5/18	West Wales (a)	W18-70	t:Connor Scott,Downs,Miller,Osborne(2),Mariano,Kesik,Jones-Bishop,Tali(2), Muranka(2),Doherty g:Miller(9)	3rd	188
20/5/18	Hunslet (h)	L16-35	t:Doherty,Osborne,Kesik g:Miller(2)	4th	597
3/6/18	Oldham (a)	L32-12	t:Wilkinson,Tali g:Howden,Sanderson	4th	453
10/6/18	Keighley (h)	W29-20	t:Sanderson,Martin,Doherty,Cross g:Hedges(5),Howden fg:Howden	4th	678
17/6/18	Workington (a)	L34-6	t:Cameron Scott g:Hedges	7th	550
24/6/18	Bradford (a)	L56-14	t:Hedges,Tali,Cameron Scott g:Hedges	9th	4,060
1/7/18	Hemel (a)	W10-74	t:Turgut(2),Sanderson(4),Downs,Tali,Kesik,Hedges(2),Jones-Bishop(2),Litten g:Hedges(2),Sanderson(3),Howden(4)	6th	108
8/7/18	York (a)	L31-16	t:Owen(2),Howden g:Sanderson(2)	8th	1,311
15/7/18	West Wales (h) ●	W102-6	t:Owen,Harris(2),Howden,Mariano(2),Kesik(2),Doherty,Litten(3),England, Hedges,Cameron Scott,Spiers,Muranka,Jones-Bishop g:Harris(15)	7th	306
22/7/18	Hunslet (a)	W14-30	t:Connor Scott,Martin,Beharrell,Tali,Sanderson g:Sanderson(4),Beharrell	6th	517
29/7/18	Oldham (h)	W26-22	t:Doherty,England,Jones-Bishop,Logan g:Beharrell(5)	6th	647
5/8/18	Coventry (a)	W4-46	t:Howden,Owen,Bower(2),Mariano,Jones-Bishop,Boyle,Spiers,England g:Beharrell(5)	5th	300
12/8/18	London Skolars (h)	W38-6	t:Tali,Owen,Miloudi,Logan(2),Connor Scott,Kesik g:Beharrell(5)	5th	589
19/8/18	Whitehaven (a)	W14-23	t:Miloudi,Bower,Logan,England g:Beharrell(3) fg:Miloudi	4th	871
2/9/18	Newcastle (h)	W38-21	t:Miloudi,Beharrell,Sanderson,Tali(2),Howden,Logan g:Beharrell(5)	3rd	741
9/9/18	Keighley (a)	W6-50	t:Mariano,Spiers(2),Owen,Logan,Tali,Doherty,Muranka(2) g:Beharrell(7)	3rd	596
16/9/18	North Wales (a)	W12-36	t:Spiers,Tali(2),Owen,Jones-Bishop,Doherty,Martin g:Hedges(3),Sanderson	3rd	296
23/9/18	Workington (h)	W44-32	t:Logan(2),Sanderson(2),Beharrell,Jones-Bishop,Muranka,Harris g:Beharrell(6)	3rd	689
30/9/18	Workington (h) (SF)	L18-30	t:Harris,England,Tali g:Beharrell(3)	N/A	542

● Played at LD Nutrition Stadium, Featherstone

APP TRIES GOALS FG PTS

	D.O.B.	ALL	L1	ALL	L1	ALL	L1	ALL	L1	ALL	L1
Matty Beharrell	29/3/94	11	11	3	3	40	40	0	0	92	92
Lewis Bienek	11/4/98	2(2)	2(2)	0	0	0	0	0	0	0	0
Connor Bower	18/1/97	14(2)	12(2)	7	5	0	0	0	0	28	20
Ryan Boyle	17/10/87	17(6)	15(6)	2	1	0	0	0	0	8	4
Zac Braham	14/1/95	(11)	(8)	3	3	0	0	0	0	12	12
Kieran Cross	18/2/95	4(11)	3(9)	5	4	0	0	0	0	20	16
Sam Doherty	14/11/93	24(1)	21(1)	11	9	0	0	0	0	44	36
Jack Downs	10/11/95	9(1)	9(1)	3	3	0	0	0	0	12	12
Brad England	20/11/94	23	20	8	7	0	0	0	0	32	28
Liam Harris	20/4/97	14	12	10	8	36	22	0	0	112	76
Jordie Hedges	4/8/95	10(14)	10(12)	5	4	12	12	0	0	44	40
Jordan Howden	6/5/96	21	18	7	6	6	6	1	1	41	37
Aaron Jones-Bishop	18/1/90	15(2)	13(1)	14	11	0	0	0	0	56	44
Kyle Kesik	3/6/93	27	25	8	7	0	0	0	0	32	28
Jordan Lane	20/10/97	5	5	0	0	0	0	0	0	0	0
Jez Litten	10/3/98	(13)	(13)	5	5	0	0	0	0	20	20
Jack Logan	8/9/95	7	7	8	8	0	0	0	0	32	32
Karim Madani	4/1/94	(3)	(3)	0	0	0	0	0	0	0	0
Frankie Mariano	10/5/87	13(3)	13(3)	5	5	0	0	0	0	20	20
Charlie Martin	2/12/92	14(6)	11(6)	5	4	0	0	0	0	20	16
Jack Miller	28/11/94	7	6	1	1	25	23	0	0	54	50
Hakim Miloudi	26/6/93	8(1)	8(1)	11	11	20	20	1	1	85	85
Jason Muranka	4/8/89	7(13)	7(11)	7	7	0	0	0	0	28	28
Ross Osborne	7/7/97	2(10)	2(10)	3	3	0	0	0	0	12	12
Richard Owen	25/4/90	24	22	11	10	0	0	0	0	44	40
Jack Sanderson	18/3/98	20(1)	18(1)	12	11	11	11	0	0	70	66
Cameron Scott	7/10/99	5(1)	5(1)	4	4	0	0	0	0	16	16
Connor Scott	27/5/93	21(8)	18(8)	5	4	0	0	0	0	20	16
Russ Spiers	28/4/91	18(8)	17(6)	7	7	0	0	0	0	28	28
Jason Tali	7/7/89	27(1)	25(1)	23	18	0	0	0	0	92	72
Jansin Turgut	8/3/96	2	2	2	2	0	0	0	0	8	8
Liam Welham	11/11/88	6(1)	4(1)	3	2	0	0	0	0	12	8
Brandan Wilkinson	7/9/97	13(1)	10(1)	3	3	0	0	0	0	12	12

'L1' totals include play-offs; 'All' totals also include Challenge Cup

Connor Scott

LEAGUE RECORD
P26-W19-D0-L7 (3rd/Semi-Finalists)
F956, A495, Diff+461, 38 points.

CHALLENGE CUP
Round Five

ATTENDANCES
Best - v Bradford (L1 - 2,780)
Worst - v West Wales (L1 - 306)
Total (excluding Challenge Cup) - 11,292
Average (excluding Challenge Cup) - 807
(Up by 235 on 2017)

CLUB RECORDS	
	Highest score: 102-6 v West Wales, 15/7/2018 Highest score against: 4-90 v Widnes, 10/6/2007
	Record attendance: 10,000 v Bradford, 16/2/52 (York Road); 6,528 v Castleford, 12/4/2007 (Keepmoat Stadium)
MATCH RECORDS	Tries: 6 Kane Epati v Oldham, 30/7/2006; Lee Waterman v Sharlston, 24/3/2012
	Goals: 15 Liam Harris v West Wales, 15/7/2018 Points: 38 Liam Harris v West Wales, 15/7/2018
SEASON RECORDS	Tries: 36 Lee Waterman 2012 Goals: 129 Jonny Woodcock 2002 Points: 306 Jonny Woodcock 2002
CAREER RECORDS	Tries: 112 Mark Roache 1985-97 Goals: 850 David Noble 1976-77; 1980-89; 1992 Points: 1,751 David Noble 1976-77; 1980-89; 1992
	Appearances: 327 Audley Pennant 1980-83; 1985-97

HEMEL STAGS

DATE	FIXTURE	RESULT	SCORERS	LGE	ATT
18/2/18	Hunslet (h)	L14-28	t:K Williams,Darville(2) g:Coe	12th	220
25/2/18	Newcastle (h) (CCR3)	L0-74		N/A	115
11/3/18	Coventry (h)	L16-22	t:Stock,Hunter,Heil g:Hunter,Hough	12th	110
25/3/18	Whitehaven (a)	L30-6	t:J Burns g:Hunter	13th	438
30/3/18	London Skolars (h)	L12-18	t:Fitzpatrick-Parry,J Burns g:Hunter(2)	13th	155
8/4/18	Keighley (a)	L80-10	t:Elliott,J Burns g:Smith	13th	529
15/4/18	Doncaster (a)	L60-0		13th	580
29/4/18	North Wales (a)	L40-16	t:Reece Williams,Smith,Mitchell g:Smith(2)	13th	215
6/5/18	Workington (h)	L12-60	t:Moran,Taylor g:Smith,Hough	13th	110
13/5/18	Oldham (a)	L74-6	t:Forde g:Mitchell	13th	411
20/5/18	York (a)	L90-0		13th	987
27/5/18	Bradford (h)	L0-68		13th	736
9/6/18	West Wales (a)	W12-48	t:Thornton(2),Fitzpatrick-Parry,Sheriff(2),Stamp(3),A Williams g:Smith(6)	13th	319
17/6/18	Newcastle (h)	L8-56	t:Forde(2)	13th	109
24/6/18	Workington (a)	L60-12	t:Welham,Stock g:Smith(2)	13th	444
1/7/18	Doncaster (h)	L10-74	t:Forde,Welham g:Smith	13th	108
8/7/18	Keighley (h)	L16-32	t:J Burns,Welham,Forde g:Smith(2)	13th	136
15/7/18	Coventry (a)	L20-18	t:Broadbent,A Williams,Smith g:Smith(3)	13th	281
22/7/18	Newcastle (a)	L42-14	t:D Roberts(2),Jowett g:S Roberts	13th	676
29/7/18	West Wales (h)	W30-22	t:Decaro,Welham(2),Hanson(2),Sheriff g:Mitchell(3)	13th	118
5/8/18	Oldham (a)	L28-60	t:D Roberts,Hanson,Smith,Taylor,Stock g:Mitchell(4)	13th	109
12/8/18	Hunslet (a)	L54-6	t:Hanson g:Mitchell	13th	610
19/8/18	North Wales (h)	L0-50		13th	110
2/9/18	Whitehaven (h)	L13-50	t:Taylor,Esslemont g:Smith(2) fg:Smith	13th	109
8/9/18	London Skolars (a)	L76-6	t:Howieson g:Sheriff	13th	172
16/9/18	York (h)	L6-56	t:Howieson g:Smith	13th	175
23/9/18	Bradford (a)	L52-7	t:Barlow g:Jowett fg:Sheriff	13th	2,855

		APP		TRIES		GOALS		FG		PTS	
	D.O.B.	ALL	L1	ALL	L1	ALL	L1	ALL	L1	ALL	L1
Brad Adams	31/3/95	1(3)	(3)	0	0	0	0	0	0	0	0
Mark Barlow	16/2/84	2(5)	2(5)	1	1	0	0	0	0	4	4
Joe Barron	6/5/98	1	1	0	0	0	0	0	0	0	0
Stefanos Bastas	22/12/93	5(7)	5(7)	0	0	0	0	0	0	0	0
Austin Bell	6/9/91	2(6)	2(6)	0	0	0	0	0	0	0	0
Tom Bonillo	27/2/98	2	2	0	0	0	0	0	0	0	0
Blake Broadbent	11/12/98	10(4)	10(4)	1	1	0	0	0	0	4	4
Jono Burns	22/8/92	11(6)	10(6)	4	4	0	0	0	0	16	16
Paddy Burns	15/3/98	1	1	0	0	0	0	0	0	0	0
Liam Coe	19/4/94	2	1	0	0	1	1	0	0	2	2
Chris Cullimore	13/2/93	2(2)	2(2)	0	0	0	0	0	0	0	0
Liam Darville	7/7/94	3	2	2	2	0	0	0	0	8	8
Santino Decaro	2/2/95	7(5)	7(5)	1	1	0	0	0	0	4	4
Rory Dixon	17/10/97	8	8	0	0	0	0	0	0	0	0
Marcus Elliott	8/3/94	8	8	1	1	0	0	0	0	4	4
Sonny Esslemont	29/12/93	22	21	1	1	0	0	0	0	4	4
Jordan Fitzpatrick-Parry	26/7/92	15	15	2	2	0	0	0	0	8	8
Darren Forde	8/1/96	21	20	5	5	0	0	0	0	20	20
Munashe Fumhanda	18/3/97	(1)	(1)	0	0	0	0	0	0	0	0
Max Garcia	15/1/98	(1)	(1)	0	0	0	0	0	0	0	0
Corey Hanson	11/8/92	5(7)	5(6)	4	4	0	0	0	0	16	16
Chris Heil	18/8/92	9	9	1	1	0	0	0	0	4	4
Ricky Hough	22/8/85	10(1)	9(1)	0	0	2	2	0	0	4	4
Jack Howieson	28/7/81	5(5)	5(5)	2	2	0	0	0	0	8	8
Braden Hunter	6/6/96	5	5	1	1	4	4	0	0	12	12
Wayne Jowett	13/2/84	6(13)	5(13)	1	1	1	1	0	0	6	6
Jack Mitchell	16/3/95	15(4)	15(3)	1	1	9	9	0	0	22	22
Kieran Moran	2/11/96	5	5	1	1	0	0	0	0	4	4
Dean Roberts	19/8/96	10(1)	10(1)	3	3	0	0	0	0	12	12
Shaun Roberts	26/2/93	10(1)	10(1)	0	0	1	1	0	0	2	2
Danny Samuel	8/8/85	(1)	(1)	0	0	0	0	0	0	0	0
Louis Sheriff	6/9/92	21	20	3	3	1	1	1	1	15	15
Kieran Smith	28/6/96	19	19	3	3	21	21	1	1	55	55
Paul Stamp	25/1/89	11(7)	11(7)	3	3	0	0	0	0	12	12
Marcus Stock	1/5/96	19(4)	19(3)	3	3	0	0	0	0	12	12
Lewis Taylor	15/4/97	6(12)	6(11)	3	3	0	0	0	0	12	12
James Thornton	30/9/95	13	12	2	2	0	0	0	0	8	8
Mitch Vincent	14/3/94	2	1	0	0	0	0	0	0	0	0
Matt Welham	1/2/93	11	11	5	5	0	0	0	0	20	20
Alex Williams	8/8/93	14	14	2	2	0	0	0	0	8	8
Kadeem Williams	23/3/95	16	15	1	1	0	0	0	0	4	4
Reece Williams	28/2/95	9(8)	8(8)	1	1	0	0	0	0	4	4
Ricky Williams	4/8/92	7	7	0	0	0	0	0	0	0	0

Jack Mitchell

'L1' totals include League 1 regular season only; 'All' totals also include Challenge Cup

LEAGUE RECORD
P26-W2-D0-L24 (13th)
F314, A1286, Diff-972, 4 points.

CHALLENGE CUP
Round Three

ATTENDANCES
Best - v Bradford (L1 - 736)
Worst - v Doncaster (L1 - 108)
Total (excluding Challenge Cup) - 2,305
Average (excluding Challenge Cup) - 177
(Up by 61 on 2017)

CLUB RECORDS		
MATCH RECORDS	**Highest score:** 52-24 v South Wales, 26/5/2013 **Highest score against:** 0-90 v York, 20/5/2018 **Record attendance:** 736 v Bradford, 27/5/2018	
	Tries: 3 *(5 players)* **Goals:** 8 Mike Bishay v South Wales, 26/5/2013; Jy-mel Coleman v Oldham, 8/6/2014	
	Points: 16 Mike Bishay v South Wales, 26/5/2013; Jy-mel Coleman v Oldham, 8/6/2014; Mitch Vincent v Oxford, 30/7/2017	
SEASON RECORDS	**Tries:** 14 Alex Anthony 2015 **Goals:** 62 Barry-John Swindells 2014 **Points:** 160 Barry-John Swindells 2014	
CAREER RECORDS	**Tries:** 19 Barry-John Swindells 2013-2016 **Goals:** 138 Barry-John Swindells 2013-2016	
	Points: 352 Barry-John Swindells 2013-2016 **Appearances:** 76 Barry-John Swindells 2013-2016	

HUNSLET

DATE	FIXTURE	RESULT	SCORERS	LGE	ATT
18/2/18	Hemel (a)	W14-28	t:Foggin-Johnston,Gibson,Flanagan,Straugheir,Lee g:Southernwood(4)	2nd	220
25/2/18	Oulton (h) (CCR3)	W72-16	t:Cooke,Lee,Foster,Southernwood,Watson,Flynn(2),Chappell,Mallinder,Ashton, Gibson,Mackay g:Sanderson(10),Southernwood(2)	N/A	896
11/3/18	North Wales (h)	W26-10	t:Lee(2),Sanderson,Gibson,Ashton g:Sanderson(3)	3rd	465
25/3/18	Bradford (a)	L32-12	t:Gibson,D Roberts g:Sanderson(2)	6th	3,688
30/3/18	Keighley (h)	L22-38	t:Sanderson,Chappell,Watson,Reed g:Sanderson(3)	7th	471
2/4/18	Bradford (h) (CCR4)	L10-34	t:Halmshaw g:Sanderson(3)	N/A	1,081
8/4/18	Oldham (a)	W16-24	t:Walker(2),Straugheir,Blagbrough g:Sanderson(4)	7th	544
15/4/18	Workington (h)	W27-20	t:Haley,Ashton,Blagbrough,Foggin-Johnston g:Sanderson(5) fg:Southernwood	5th	561
29/4/18	Newcastle (a)	L28-10	t:Lee,Mackay g:Sanderson	9th	837
6/5/18	York (h)	L24-26	t:Jordan-Roberts,Chappell(2),Walton g:Sanderson(4)	9th	729
20/5/18	Doncaster (a)	W16-35	t:Southernwood,Walton,Chappell,Sanderson,Straugheir g:Sanderson(7) fg:Southernwood	8th	597
27/5/18	West Wales (h)	W86-0	t:Straugheir,Watson(2),Lee(2),Chappell,Foggin-Johnston,Walton,Mvududu, Southernwood,Ashton(2),Hema(2),Sanderson g:Sanderson(13)	8th	415
2/6/18	Whitehaven (h)	W39-32	t:Sanderson,Ashton,Foggin-Johnston(2),Watson,Mvududu g:Sanderson(7) fg:Southernwood	8th	576
9/6/18	London Skolars (a)	W30-37	t:Lee,Haley,Southernwood(2),Halmshaw,Cooke g:Sanderson(6) fg:Southernwood	5th	389
17/6/18	Coventry (h)	W40-16	t:Lee,Foggin-Johnston(2),Chappell(3),Watson g:Sanderson(6)	4th	511
24/6/18	Oldham (h)	W16-12	t:Braham,Mvududu,Southernwood g:Sanderson(2)	4th	605
1/7/18	North Wales (a)	W18-19	t:Straugheir,Sanderson,Mvududu g:Sanderson(3) fg:Southernwood	3rd	317
8/7/18	Workington (a)	L28-18	t:Straugheir,Mvududu(2) g:Sanderson(3)	5th	601
15/7/18	Bradford (h)	L16-36	t:Duffy,Straugheir g:Sanderson(4)	6th	1,536
22/7/18	Doncaster (h)	L14-30	t:Lee,Chappell g:Sanderson(3)	7th	517
29/7/18	Keighley (a)	W16-24	t:Watson,Mackay,Mvududu,Haley g:Sanderson(4)	7th	793
4/8/18	West Wales (a)	W6-86	t:Foggin-Johnston,Lee,Williams,Tonks(4),Mvududu(2),Duffy,Flynn,Chappell,Cooke, Hema,Nicholson g:Sanderson(13)	6th	258
12/8/18	Hemel (h)	W54-6	t:Nicholson,Duffy(3),Straugheir,Walton(2),Mackay,Foggin-Johnston,Cooke g:Sanderson(7)	6th	610
19/8/18	York (a)	L48-6	t:Brierley g:Sanderson	6th	1,491
2/9/18	London Skolars (h)	W48-12	t:Watson,Southernwood(2),Wright(2),Tonks,Nicholson,Foster g:Sanderson(8)	6th	453
9/9/18	Whitehaven (a)	L46-10	t:Mvududu,Grimshaw g:Sanderson	7th	672
16/9/18	Newcastle (h)	L10-46	t:Foggin-Johnston,Williams g:Sanderson	7th	560
22/9/18	Coventry (a)	L14-4	t:Williams	7th	380

		APP		TRIES		GOALS		FG		PTS	
	D.O.B.	ALL	L1	ALL	L1	ALL	L1	ALL	L1	ALL	L1
Tom Ashton	20/6/92	19(1)	18(1)	6	5	0	0	0	0	24	20
Jake Barnett	30/4/95	(5)	(3)	0	0	0	0	0	0	0	0
Jack Blagbrough	18/1/94	5	4	2	2	0	0	0	0	8	8
Zac Braham	14/1/95	(4)	(4)	1	1	0	0	0	0	4	4
Alex Bretherton	5/12/82	(1)	(1)	0	0	0	0	0	0	0	0
Tommy Brierley	8/9/96	4	4	1	1	0	0	0	0	4	4
Joe Chandler	2/11/88	1(1)	1(1)	0	0	0	0	0	0	0	0
Nathan Chappell	4/12/89	15	14	11	10	0	0	0	0	44	40
Will Cooke	22/12/96	6(4)	4(4)	4	3	0	0	0	0	16	12
Jack Coventry	5/3/94	(8)	(7)	0	0	0	0	0	0	0	0
Danny Cowling	20/12/92	1	1	0	0	0	0	0	0	0	0
Sam Crowther	21/10/86	(1)	(1)	0	0	0	0	0	0	0	0
Gavin Duffy	9/4/87	7	7	5	5	0	0	0	0	20	20
Marcus Elliott	8/3/94	1	1	0	0	0	0	0	0	0	0
George Flanagan	8/10/86	(1)	(1)	1	1	0	0	0	0	4	4
Nyle Flynn	27/7/97	1(9)	1(8)	3	1	0	0	0	0	12	4
David Foggin-Johnston	19/8/96	24	24	10	10	0	0	0	0	40	40
Brad Foster	28/8/95	17	16	2	1	0	0	0	0	8	4
Joel Gibson	8/9/90	5	4	3	0	0	0	0	0	16	12
Jordan Gill	2/5/94	1	0	0	0	0	0	0	0	0	0
Danny Grimshaw	25/2/86	6	6	1	1	0	0	0	0	4	4
Michael Haley	19/9/87	1(19)	(18)	3	3	0	0	0	0	12	12
Daniel Halmshaw	17/8/97	(15)	(14)	2	1	0	0	0	0	8	4
Aiden Hema	27/10/95	12(1)	12(1)	3	3	0	0	0	0	12	12
Josh Jordan-Roberts	26/8/98	14(1)	13(1)	1	1	0	0	0	0	4	4
Jack Lee	1/11/88	28	26	11	10	0	0	0	0	44	40
Liam Mackay	26/10/90	16(6)	15(6)	4	3	0	0	0	0	16	12
Ryan Mallinder	17/7/88	1(2)	1(1)	1	0	0	0	0	0	4	0
Luke Million	28/12/97	(1)	(1)	0	0	0	0	0	0	0	0
Mufaro Mvududu	29/8/91	20	20	10	10	0	0	0	0	40	40
Matt Nicholson	11/9/91	22(2)	21(1)	3	3	0	0	0	0	12	12
Lewis Reed	24/3/91	16(9)	14(9)	1	1	0	0	0	0	4	4
Dean Roberts	19/8/96	(3)	(3)	1	1	0	0	0	0	4	4
Shaun Roberts	26/2/93	1	1	0	0	0	0	0	0	0	0
Joe Sanderson	17/3/97	26	24	6	6	124	111	0	0	272	246
Cain Southernwood	4/5/92	25	23	8	7	6	4	5	5	49	41
Duane Straugheir	29/9/89	23(1)	22(1)	8	8	0	0	0	0	32	32
Josh Tonks	14/8/91	10	10	5	5	0	0	0	0	20	20
Harry Tyson-Wilson	29/12/96	1	1	0	0	0	0	0	0	0	0
Niall Walker	21/4/97	4	3	2	2	0	0	0	0	8	8
Jack Walton	7/5/95	1(9)	(9)	5	5	0	0	0	0	20	20
Jimmy Watson	9/9/91	24	22	8	7	0	0	0	0	32	28
Daley Williams	15/5/86	5(1)	5(1)	3	3	0	0	0	0	12	12
Ryan Wright	28/10/91	1(7)	1(7)	2	2	0	0	0	0	8	8

Jack Lee

'L1' totals include League 1 regular season only; 'All' totals also include Challenge Cup

LEAGUE RECORD
P26-W15-D0-L11 (7th)
F735, A596, Diff+139, 30 points.

CHALLENGE CUP
Round Four

ATTENDANCES
Best - v Bradford (L1 - 1,536)
Worst - v West Wales (L1 - 415)
Total (excluding Challenge Cup) - 8,009
Average (excluding Challenge Cup) - 616
(Up by 193 on 2017)

CLUB RECORDS	
MATCH RECORDS	**Highest score:** 86-0 v West Wales, 27/5/2018; 86-6 v West Wales, 4/8/2018 **Highest score against:** 0-82 v Bradford, 2/3/2003 **Record attendance:** 24,700 v Wigan, 15/3/24 *(Parkside)*; 2,454 v Wakefield, 13/4/98 *(South Leeds Stadium)* **Tries:** 7 George Dennis v Bradford, 20/1/34 **Goals:** 13 Joe Sanderson v West Wales, 27/5/2018; Joe Sanderson v West Wales, 4/8/2018 **Points:** 30 Simon Wilson v Highfield, 21/1/96; Joe Sanderson v West Wales, 27/5/2018
SEASON RECORDS	**Tries:** 34 Alan Snowden 1956-57 **Goals:** 181 Billy Langton 1958-59 **Points:** 380 Billy Langton 1958-59
CAREER RECORDS	**Tries:** 154 Fred Williamson 1943-55 **Goals:** 1,044 Billy Langton 1955-66 **Points:** 2,202 Billy Langton 1955-66 **Appearances:** 579 Geoff Gunney 1951-73

KEIGHLEY COUGARS

DATE	FIXTURE	RESULT	SCORERS	LGE	ATT
18/2/18	Workington (h)	W44-34	t:Aaronson,Bailey,Lynam,Beharrell,Gabriel(2),Hardcastle g:Hardcastle(8)	4th	707
25/2/18	North Wales (a) (CCR3)	L28-24	t:Rawlins(2),Tonks,Hawkyard g:Hardcastle(4)	N/A	281
11/3/18	Bradford (h)	L6-54	t:Nicholson g:Hardcastle	8th	2,912
25/3/18	York (a)	L26-12	t:Whiteley,Barnes g:Hardcastle(2)	9th	1,481
30/3/18	Hunslet (a)	W22-38	t:Fairhurst,Wright,Conroy(2),Nicholson,Ryder g:Hardcastle(7)	9th	471
8/4/18	Hemel (h)	W80-10	t:Hallas,Fairhurst(2),Hawkyard(2),Ryder(2),Gabriel,Conroy,Tonks(2),Morris, Beharrell,Emmett g:Hardcastle(12)	5th	529
15/4/18	Oldham (a)	L32-18	t:Nicholson,Tonks,Ryder g:Hardcastle(3)	9th	530
22/4/18	Newcastle (a)	W14-34	t:Griffin,Wright,Ryder,Gabriel(2),Tonks g:Hardcastle(5)	6th	623
29/4/18	Whitehaven (h)	L24-30	t:Lynam,Beharrell,Aaronson,Leeming g:Hardcastle(4)	8th	648
6/5/18	Coventry (h)	W98-6	t:Hardcastle,Bailey,Ryder(3),Aaronson(2),Gabriel(2),Tonks,Parker,Law, Nicholson,Hawkyard,Beharrell,Rawlins(2) g:Hardcastle(14),Beharrell	4th	446
20/5/18	North Wales (a)	W28-46	t:Parker(2),Whiteley(2),Ryder(2),Conroy,Law g:Hardcastle(6),Beharrell	6th	337
27/5/18	London Skolars (h)	W26-18	t:Ryder,Gabriel(2),Nicholson,Whiteley g:Beharrell(3)	6th	521
10/6/18	Doncaster (a)	L29-20	t:Bailey,Nicholson,Ryder g:Hardcastle(4)	6th	678
17/6/18	West Wales (h)	W94-0	t:Ryder(3),Parker(2),Hawkyard(4),Law,Whiteley(3),Gabriel(3),Griffin g:Hardcastle(13)	5th	470
24/6/18	York (h)	L14-46	t:Whiteley,Gabriel,Nicholson g:Hardcastle	6th	698
1/7/18	Whitehaven (a)	L28-14	t:Hardcastle(2) g:Hardcastle(3)	8th	592
8/7/18	Hemel (a)	W16-32	t:Cullimore,Leeming,Dixon,Levy,Gabriel,Rawlins g:Hardcastle(4)	7th	136
13/7/18	Oldham (h)	W15-8	t:Emmett g:Hardcastle(5) fg:Hardcastle	8th	510
21/7/18	Coventry (a)	L30-20	t:Conroy,Aaronson,Hallas,Parker g:Hardcastle(2)	8th	303
29/7/18	Hunslet (h)	L16-24	t:Lynam,Hardcastle g:Hardcastle(4)	8th	793
5/8/18	Workington (a)	L34-12	t:Levy g:Hardcastle(4)	9th	607
12/8/18	Newcastle (h)	W24-16	t:Dixon,Lynam,Seeley,Hawkyard g:Hardcastle(4)	8th	732
24/8/18	London Skolars (a)	L20-6	t:Feather g:Aaronson	9th	1,043
2/9/18	Bradford (a)	L54-4	t:Leeming	9th	3,119
9/9/18	Doncaster (h)	L6-50	t:Gabriel g:Hardcastle	9th	596
15/9/18	West Wales (a)	W6-112	t:Gabriel(3),Leeming(3),Parker(2),Whittel,Hawkyard(3),Kenga,Feather, Seeley(3),Gaylor,Hardcastle,Cullimore g:Hardcastle(14),Gaylor(2)	9th	218
23/9/18	North Wales (h)	W24-22	t:Lynam,Gabriel,Rawlins,Seeley g:Hardcastle(4)	9th	592

		APP		TRIES		GOALS		FG		PTS	
	D.O.B.	ALL	L1	ALL	L1	ALL	L1	ALL	L1	ALL	L1
Harry Aaronson	28/3/98	19	18	5	5	1	1	0	0	22	22
Matthew Bailey	1/12/91	24	23	3	3	0	0	0	0	12	12
Hamish Barnes	22/5/92	10	9	1	1	0	0	0	0	4	4
Matty Beharrell	29/3/94	10(2)	9(2)	4	4	5	5	0	0	26	26
Anthony Bowman	18/3/92	1	1	0	0	0	0	0	0	0	0
Nathan Conroy	6/3/95	3(19)	2(19)	5	5	0	0	0	0	20	20
Chris Cullimore	13/2/93	3(4)	3(4)	2	2	0	0	0	0	8	8
Davey Dixon	31/5/97	12	12	2	2	0	0	0	0	8	8
Mike Emmett	13/5/87	26	25	2	2	0	0	0	0	8	8
Lewis Fairhurst	24/12/96	4	4	3	3	0	0	0	0	12	12
James Feather	15/4/84	7	7	2	2	0	0	0	0	8	8
Andy Gabriel	21/12/93	22	21	19	19	0	0	0	0	76	76
Billy Gaylor	30/4/97	5(1)	5(1)	1	1	2	2	0	0	8	8
Darrell Griffin	19/6/81	12(2)	12(2)	2	2	0	0	0	0	8	8
Harvey Hallas	14/11/97	7(5)	7(4)	2	2	0	0	0	0	8	8
Benn Hardcastle	4/1/90	24	23	6	6	129	125	1	1	283	275
Ritchie Hawkyard	21/1/86	23	22	12	11	0	0	0	0	48	44
James Haynes	22/3/89	3	3	0	0	0	0	0	0	0	0
Jose Kenga	3/5/93	3(9)	3(9)	1	1	0	0	0	0	4	4
Scott Law	19/2/85	1(25)	1(24)	3	3	0	0	0	0	12	12
Cameron Leeming	3/7/95	15(2)	15(2)	6	6	0	0	0	0	24	24
Aaron Levy	19/12/95	3(3)	3(3)	2	2	0	0	0	0	8	8
Joe Lumb	21/8/96	1	1	0	0	0	0	0	0	0	0
Josh Lynam	16/2/93	11(2)	11(2)	5	5	0	0	0	0	20	20
Kieran Moran	2/11/96	2(4)	2(4)	0	0	0	0	0	0	0	0
Ben Morris	1/8/97	3	3	1	1	0	0	0	0	4	4
Brad Nicholson	20/8/95	2(16)	2(15)	7	7	0	0	0	0	28	28
Trae O'Sullivan	7/9/96	(3)	(3)	0	0	0	0	0	0	0	0
Dan Parker	11/3/93	17	17	8	8	0	0	0	0	32	32
Brendon Rawlins	28/1/86	13(6)	12(6)	6	4	0	0	0	0	24	16
Adam Ryder	20/10/89	16	15	15	15	0	0	0	0	60	60
Alfie Seeley	30/12/96	4(1)	4(1)	5	5	0	0	0	0	20	20
Samir Tahraoui	28/12/90	2(2)	1(2)	0	0	0	0	0	0	0	0
Josh Tonks	14/8/91	13	12	6	5	0	0	0	0	24	20
Perry Whiteley	22/2/93	12	12	8	8	0	0	0	0	32	32
Emmerson Whittel	13/9/94	5	5	1	1	0	0	0	0	4	4
Ryan Wright	28/10/91	13(2)	13(1)	2	2	0	0	0	0	8	8

Scott Law

'L1' totals include League 1 regular season only; 'All' totals also include Challenge Cup

LEAGUE RECORD
P26-W13-D0-L13 (9th)
F839, A657, Diff+182, 26 points.

CHALLENGE CUP
Round Three

ATTENDANCES
Best - v Bradford (L1 - 2,912)
Worst - v Coventry (L1 - 446)
Total (all home games included) - 10,154
Average (all home games included) - 781
(Down by 3 on 2017)

CLUB RECORDS MATCH RECORDS	Highest score: 112-6 v West Wales, 15/9/2018 Highest score against: 2-92 v Leigh, 30/4/86 Record attendance: 14,500 v Halifax, 3/3/51 Tries: 6 Jason Critchley v Widnes, 18/8/96 Goals: 15 John Wasyliw v Nottingham City, 1/11/92; Martyn Wood v Lancashire Lynx, 1/5/2000 Points: 36 John Wasyliw v Nottingham City, 1/11/92
SEASON RECORDS CAREER RECORDS	Tries: 45 Nick Pinkney 1994-95 Goals: 187 John Wasyliw 1992-93 Points: 490 John Wasyliw 1992-93 Tries: 155 Sam Stacey 1904-20 Goals: 967 Brian Jefferson 1965-77 Points: 2,116 Brian Jefferson 1965-77 Appearances: 372 Hartley Tempest 1902-15; David McGoun 1925-38

LONDON SKOLARS

DATE	FIXTURE	RESULT	SCORERS	LGE	ATT
18/2/18	North Wales (a)	D24-24	t:Caro,Bryan,Butler,Hall g:C Lawrence,Jy-mel Coleman(3)	6th	306
24/2/18	Whitehaven (a) (CCR3)	L16-14	t:Melling(2),Driver g:Lyon	N/A	439
10/3/18	Newcastle (h)	L16-60	t:Field,Mullen,Driver g:Thorman(2)	11th	273
24/3/18	Workington (h)	L26-42	t:Jy-mel Coleman,Hall,C Lawrence(2),Finigan g:Thorman(3)	12th	328
30/3/18	Hemel (a)	W12-18	t:Jy-mel Coleman,Mbaraga g:Thorman(5)	11th	155
7/4/18	West Wales (h)	W76-8	t:Martin,Melling(2),Finigan(3),Ogden,Driver,Bryan,Nash(2),Mbaraga,Ngawati g:Thorman(12)	8th	198
15/4/18	York (a)	L66-6	t:Hall g:Thorman	10th	916
29/4/18	Coventry (a)	W20-28	t:Driver,Bryan,Thorman,Finigan,Chester g:Thorman(4)	10th	266
5/5/18	Doncaster (h)	L18-42	t:Bryan,Hall(2) g:Thorman(3)	11th	186
12/5/18	Bradford (a)	L54-16	t:Burroughs,Mbaraga,Lyon g:Thorman(2)	11th	3,041
19/5/18	Whitehaven (h)	L26-44	t:Caro,Butler,Hall,Fleming,Burroughs g:Thorman(3)	11th	346
27/5/18	Keighley (a)	L26-18	t:Thorman,Burroughs g:Thorman(5)	11th	521
9/6/18	Hunslet (h)	L30-37	t:Brown,Juma,Bryan,Burroughs,Thorman g:Thorman(5)	11th	389
17/6/18	Oldham (a)	L44-12	t:Macani,Mbaraga g:Thorman(2)	11th	419
23/6/18	North Wales (h)	L28-36	t:M Greenhalgh,Kibula(2),Juma,Bryan g:Thorman(4)	11th	275
30/6/18	West Wales (a)	W12-62	t:Bryan(3),Hall,Macani(3),Finigan(2),Juma(2),Mbaraga g:Thorman(5),Bishay(2)	11th	224
7/7/18	Coventry (h)	L20-24	t:C Lawrence,Bryan,Bishay g:Thorman(4)	11th	160
14/7/18	York (h)	L20-22	t:Finigan,Meadows,Bishay g:Bishay(4)	11th	258
22/7/18	Whitehaven (a)	L28-18	t:Juma(2),Jy-mel Coleman g:Thorman(3)	11th	661
28/7/18	Bradford (h)	L12-58	t:Juma(2) g:Thorman(2)	12th	1,178
5/8/18	Newcastle (a)	L46-14	t:Brown,Pelo,Williams g:Thorman	12th	554
12/8/18	Doncaster (a)	L38-6	t:Juma g:Thorman	12th	589
24/8/18	Keighley (a)	W20-6	t:Bishay,Pelo,Nash,Caro g:Thorman(2)	12th	1,043
2/9/18	Hunslet (a)	L48-12	t:Bryan,Driver g:Lyon(2)	12th	453
8/9/18	Hemel (h)	W76-6	t:Pelo,Juma,Finigan(2),Caro(2),Lyon,Bishay,Nash(2),Bryan,Fleming(2),Thorman g:Thorman(8),Lyon(2)	11th	172
16/9/18	Workington (a)	L38-6	t:Fleming g:C Lawrence	11th	545
22/9/18	Oldham (h)	L18-46	t:Mbaraga(2),Caro g:Thorman,Lyon(2)	12th	402

		APP		TRIES		GOALS		FG		PTS	
	D.O.B.	ALL	L1	ALL	L1	ALL	L1	ALL	L1	ALL	L1
Sadiq Adebiyi	8/1/97	1	1	0	0	0	0	0	0	0	0
Mike Bishay	8/2/93	12(1)	11(1)	4	4	6	6	0	0	28	28
Michael Brown	9/9/86	15	14	2	2	0	0	0	0	8	8
Lamont Bryan	12/4/88	22	21	12	12	0	0	0	0	48	48
Ryan Burroughs	26/8/91	5	5	4	4	0	0	0	0	16	16
Rob Butler	15/5/98	2(12)	2(12)	2	2	0	0	0	0	8	8
Omari Caro	7/3/91	9(1)	8(1)	6	6	0	0	0	0	24	24
Ryan Chester	19/3/92	23(1)	22(1)	1	1	0	0	0	0	4	4
Jermaine Coleman	17/6/82	4	4	0	0	0	0	0	0	0	0
Jy-mel Coleman	13/10/88	11(1)	10(1)	3	3	3	3	0	0	18	18
Matthew Davies	9/4/98	(8)	(8)	0	0	0	0	0	0	0	0
Billy Driver	18/9/90	15(10)	15(9)	5	4	0	0	0	0	20	16
Callum Field	7/10/97	1(1)	1(1)	1	1	0	0	0	0	4	4
Vinny Finigan	4/8/89	18	18	10	10	0	0	0	0	40	40
Matty Fleming	13/1/96	12	12	4	4	0	0	0	0	16	16
Josh Ganson	19/2/98	1	1	0	0	0	0	0	0	0	0
Judd Greenhalgh	16/1/93	1(5)	1(5)	0	0	0	0	0	0	0	0
Mike Greenhalgh	8/6/94	6(3)	6(3)	1	1	0	0	0	0	4	4
Elliot Hall	6/7/97	14	13	7	7	0	0	0	0	28	28
Lameck Juma	6/12/90	19	18	10	10	0	0	0	0	40	40
Samy Kibula	7/8/99	(2)	(2)	2	2	0	0	0	0	8	8
Alfie Lawrence	5/10/97	(1)	(1)	0	0	0	0	0	0	0	0
Charlie Lawrence	6/10/94	8(4)	8(4)	3	3	2	2	0	0	16	16
Phil Lyon	21/3/92	12(2)	11(2)	2	2	7	6	0	0	22	20
Iliess Macani	6/12/93	5	5	4	4	0	0	0	0	16	16
Will Martin	28/12/93	16	15	1	1	0	0	0	0	4	4
Eddie Mbaraga	9/9/87	10(12)	9(12)	7	7	0	0	0	0	28	28
James Meadows	15/6/99	2	2	1	1	0	0	0	0	4	4
Jake Melling	25/6/94	8	7	4	2	0	0	0	0	16	8
Craig Mullen	15/1/98	1	1	1	1	0	0	0	0	4	4
Sam Nash	1/5/89	22(1)	21(1)	5	5	0	0	0	0	20	20
Quinn Ngawati	15/6/99	6(3)	6(3)	1	1	0	0	0	0	4	4
Jake Ogden	23/1/98	3	3	1	1	0	0	0	0	4	4
Oliver Partington	3/9/98	1(1)	1(1)	0	0	0	0	0	0	0	0
Daymeric Pelo	24/7/96	9	9	3	3	0	0	0	0	12	12
Api Pewhairangi	19/3/92	1	1	0	0	0	0	0	0	0	0
Ollie Purslow	17/9/87	(3)	(2)	0	0	0	0	0	0	0	0
Louis Robinson	9/1/91	1(5)	1(5)	0	0	0	0	0	0	0	0
Matt Ross	2/9/92	5(8)	5(8)	0	0	0	0	0	0	0	0
Michael Sykes	10/12/86	8(12)	8(11)	0	0	0	0	0	0	0	0
Neil Thorman	4/6/84	25(1)	25(1)	4	4	78	78	0	0	172	172
Jordan Williams	4/6/97	12(8)	12(7)	1	1	0	0	0	0	4	4
James Worthington	21/5/99	1	1	0	0	0	0	0	0	0	0
Lewis Wray	6/5/98	(2)	(2)	0	0	0	0	0	0	0	0
Jerome Yates	31/10/97	4	4	0	0	0	0	0	0	0	0

Billy Driver

LEAGUE RECORD
P26-W6-D1-L19 (12th)
F626, A887, Diff-261, 13 points.

CHALLENGE CUP
Round Three

ATTENDANCES
Best - v Bradford (L1 - 1,178)
Worst - v Coventry (L1 - 160)
Total (all home games included) - 5,208
Average (all home games included) - 401
(Down by 50 on 2017)

'L1' totals include League 1 regular season only; 'All' totals also include Challenge Cup

CLUB RECORDS Highest score: 76-8 v West Wales, 7/4/2018; 76-6 v Hemel, 8/9/2018 Highest score against: 4-98 v Sheffield, 3/8/2003
Record attendance: 1,524 v Toronto, 4/3/2017
MATCH RECORDS Tries: 5 Mark Cantoni v Gateshead, 27/6/2004 Goals: 12 Neil Thorman v West Wales, 7/4/2018 Points: 28 Dylan Skee v South Wales, 29/7/2012
SEASON RECORDS Tries: 20 Mark Cantoni 2004; James Anthony 2013 Goals: 100 Dylan Skee 2013 Points: 248 Dylan Skee 2013
CAREER RECORDS Tries: 57 Austen Aggrey 2004-2012 Goals: 230 (inc 1fg) Dylan Skee 2011-2013 Points: 579 Dylan Skee 2011-2013 Appearances: 198 Gareth Honor 2003-2011

NEWCASTLE THUNDER

DATE	FIXTURE	RESULT	SCORERS	LGE	ATT
25/2/18	Hemel (a) (CCR3)	W0-74	t:Young(2),Agoro(2),Ollett(2),Ritson(3),Fitzsimmons,Calland,Blair,Rennie g:Shaw(11)	N/A	115
10/3/18	London Skolars (a)	W16-60	t:McAvoy,Young(2),Egodo,Agoro,Shaw,Ritson,Pointer,Ollett,Lloyd g:Shaw(10)	5th	273
16/3/18	Doncaster (a) (CCR4)	L34-0		N/A	398
25/3/18	Doncaster (h)	L20-22	t:Simons,Clarke,Fitzsimmons g:Shaw(4)	7th	818
30/3/18	Coventry (a)	W18-32	t:Ritson(3),Young,Ollett g:Shaw(6)	5th	343
8/4/18	York (h)	L16-26	t:Egodo(2),Simons g:Shaw(2)	9th	954
15/4/18	North Wales (a)	W10-30	t:Simons,Ollett,Nicklas,Rennie(2) g:Shaw(5)	6th	321
22/4/18	Keighley (h)	L14-34	t:Ollett,Calland g:Shaw(3)	8th	623
29/4/18	Hunslet (h)	W28-10	t:Young,Brown,Rennie,Agoro,Craig g:Shaw(4)	5th	837
6/5/18	Oldham (a)	L28-12	t:Blair,Young g:Shaw(2)	8th	455
18/5/18	Bradford (h)	L16-26	t:Ritson,Craig,Egodo g:Brook(2)	9th	4,137
27/5/18	Workington (a)	L38-18	t:Marginet(2),McAvoy g:Brook(3)	10th	696
3/6/18	West Wales (a)	W20-82	t:Clarke(2),Sidney(2),Fitzsimmons(2),Young(3),Calland,Morris,McAvoy, Ritson,Brook,Marginet g:Marginet(5),Brook(6)	9th	272
10/6/18	Whitehaven (h)	W30-22	t:Clarke,Egodo(2),Dent,Young(2) g:Marginet(2),Brook	9th	759
17/6/18	Hemel (a)	W8-56	t:Scott(2),Shaw(2),Brown,McGrath(2),Dent,Luckley,Pointer g:Shaw(8)	8th	109
24/6/18	Coventry (h)	W46-12	t:Young(4),Agoro(2),Ritson(2),Craig g:Marginet(5)	7th	903
1/7/18	York (a)	L24-6	t:Dent g:Shaw	9th	1,212
6/7/18	Bradford (a)	L24-4	t:Gill	9th	3,029
15/7/18	North Wales (h)	L20-24	t:Brown,Shaw(2) g:Shaw(4)	9th	637
22/7/18	Hemel (h)	W42-14	t:Blair,Agoro,Simons(2),Weetman,Ollett,Sidney(2) g:Shaw(5)	9th	676
29/7/18	Whitehaven (a)	L12-8	t:Young g:Marginet(2)	9th	551
5/8/18	London Skolars (h)	W46-14	t:Marginet,Blair,Ritson(2),Ollett,Young(2),Pointer g:Marginet(7)	8th	554
12/8/18	Keighley (a)	L24-16	t:Ollett,Ritson,Richmond g:Shaw(2)	9th	732
19/8/18	Oldham (h)	W24-18	t:Agoro,Ritson(2),Marginet g:Marginet(4)	8th	749
2/9/18	Doncaster (a)	L38-21	t:Weetman,Pointer,Rennie g:Marginet(4) fg:Marginet	8th	741
8/9/18	Workington (h)	W50-22	t:Pointer,Young,Calland,Ritson,H Aldous,Brook,Dent,Scott,Agoro g:Marginet(7)	8th	769
16/9/18	Hunslet (a)	W10-46	t:Marginet(2),Ritson,Young,Pointer(2),Blair,Agoro g:Marginet(7)	8th	560
23/9/18	West Wales (h)	W98-6	t:Craig(3),Sidney(4),Clegg,Marginet,Young,Nettleton(2),Blair(2),Gowing(2), Luckley,Fitzsimmons g:Shaw(10),Marginet(3)	8th	889

Theerapol Ritson

	D.O.B.	APP		TRIES		GOALS		FG		PTS	
		ALL	L1	ALL	L1	ALL	L1	ALL	L1	ALL	L1
Mo Agoro	29/1/93	25	23	10	8	0	0	0	0	40	32
Harry Aldous	19/11/95	14(10)	14(8)	1	1	0	0	0	0	4	4
Jack Aldous	3/4/91	24	22	0	0	0	0	0	0	0	0
Adam Bielby	13/10/98	(1)	(1)	0	0	0	0	0	0	0	0
Ali Blair	21/2/90	13	12	7	6	0	0	0	0	28	24
Sam Blake	5/5/98	(5)	(5)	0	0	0	0	0	0	0	0
Adam Brook	29/9/94	16	16	2	2	12	12	0	0	32	32
Joe Brown	24/4/87	20(1)	19(1)	3	3	0	0	0	0	12	12
Ben Calland	24/9/96	7(6)	5(6)	4	3	0	0	0	0	16	12
Tom Capper	10/10/92	1	1	0	0	0	0	0	0	0	0
Joe Cator	15/6/98	(3)	(3)	0	0	0	0	0	0	0	0
Jed Charlton	14/1/99	3	3	0	0	0	0	0	0	0	0
Rhys Clarke	12/3/91	10(4)	10(4)	4	4	0	0	0	0	16	16
Alex Clegg	9/7/99	1	1	1	1	0	0	0	0	4	4
Tyler Craig	4/7/93	13	12	6	6	0	0	0	0	24	24
Curtis Davies	17/1/97	(1)	(1)	0	0	0	0	0	0	0	0
Ben Dent	27/9/91	12	11	4	4	0	0	0	0	16	16
Tuoyo Egodo	16/2/97	7	7	6	6	0	0	0	0	24	24
Conor Fitzsimmons	7/5/98	7(18)	7(16)	5	4	0	0	0	0	20	16
Kieran Gill	4/12/95	1	1	1	1	0	0	0	0	4	4
Ollie Gowing	24/7/00	(3)	(3)	2	2	0	0	0	0	8	8
Kieran Hudson	13/6/00	1	1	0	0	0	0	0	0	0	0
Ryan Lloyd	5/6/97	2(2)	1(2)	1	1	0	0	0	0	4	4
Sam Luckley	29/11/95	20	19	2	2	0	0	0	0	8	8
Remy Marginet	27/5/89	11(1)	11(1)	8	8	46	46	1	1	125	125
Liam McAvoy	24/9/93	23(2)	21(2)	3	3	0	0	0	0	12	12
Conor McGrath	14/8/96	1	1	2	2	0	0	0	0	8	8
Frazer Morris	22/2/97	(2)	(2)	1	1	0	0	0	0	4	4
Rory Nettleton	26/2/00	(1)	(1)	2	2	0	0	0	0	8	8
Danny Nicklas	29/6/91	3	2	1	1	0	0	0	0	4	4
Aaron Ollett	19/11/92	23(1)	21(1)	9	7	0	0	0	0	36	28
Ben Pointer	25/5/96	8(13)	8(11)	7	7	0	0	0	0	28	28
Vincent Rennie	7/6/94	8(19)	6(19)	5	4	0	0	0	0	20	16
Liam Richmond	17/10/96	(5)	(5)	1	1	0	0	0	0	4	4
Theerapol Ritson	7/1/96	22	20	18	15	0	0	0	0	72	60
Liam Scott	24/9/94	2(4)	2(3)	3	3	0	0	0	0	12	12
Tom Shaw	19/11/93	16	15	5	5	77	66	0	0	174	152
Niall Sidney	3/8/98	3(1)	3(1)	8	8	0	0	0	0	32	32
Evan Simons	11/10/91	22(2)	20(2)	5	5	0	0	0	0	20	20
Dan Turland	11/1/94	(2)	(1)	0	0	0	0	0	0	0	0
David Weetman	24/5/98	(5)	(5)	2	2	0	0	0	0	8	8
Lewis Young	1/7/95	25	23	22	20	0	0	0	0	88	80

'L1' totals include League 1 regular season only; 'All' totals also include Challenge Cup

LEAGUE RECORD
P26-W14-D0-L12 (8th)
F841, A520, Diff+321, 28 points.

CHALLENGE CUP
Round Four

ATTENDANCES
Best - v Bradford (L1 - 4,137)
Worst - v London Skolars (L1 - 554)
Total (all home games included) - 13,305
Average (all home games included) - 1,023
(Up by 160 on 2017)

CLUB RECORDS
Highest score: 98-6 v West Wales, 23/9/2018 **Highest score against:** 0-132 v Blackpool Panthers, 16/5/2010
Record attendance: 6,631 v Bradford, 16/5/99 *(Gateshead International Stadium)*; 4,137 v Bradford, 18/5/2018 *(Kingston Park)*
Tries: 5 Andy Walker v London Skolars, 22/6/2003
MATCH RECORDS
Goals: 11 Ian Herron v Wakefield, 5/9/99; Tom Shaw v Hemel, 25/2/2018 **Points:** 28 Benn Hardcastle v Oxford, 18/6/2017
SEASON RECORDS **Tries:** 25 Matt Daylight 1999 **Goals:** 129 *(inc 1fg)* Dan Russell 2008 **Points:** 293 Dan Russell 2008
CAREER RECORDS **Tries:** 74 Kevin Neighbour 2001-2006; 2008-2010 **Goals:** 283 *(inc 8fg)* Benn Hardcastle 2013-2017 **Points:** 682 Benn Hardcastle 2013-2017
Appearances: 218 Robin Peers 2002-2016

NORTH WALES CRUSADERS

DATE	FIXTURE	RESULT	SCORERS	LGE	ATT
18/2/18	London Skolars (h)	D24-24	t:A Thompson,Conroy,Bloomfield,Smith g:Johnson(4)	6th	306
25/2/18	Keighley (h) (CCR3)	W28-24	t:Roper,Houghton,Atherton(2) g:Johnson(4)	N/A	281
11/3/18	Hunslet (a)	L26-10	t:Atherton,Bloomfield g:Johnson	10th	465
20/3/18	Featherstone (h) (CCR4) ●	L6-66	t:Johnson g:Johnson	N/A	1,098
25/3/18	Oldham (h)	L2-30	g:Johnson	11th	449
30/3/18	West Wales (a)	W6-54	t:Bloomfield(2),Houghton(2),Hudson,Moore,Atherton,Dandy,Price,Davidson g:Johnson(7)	10th	306
8/4/18	Doncaster (a)	L28-20	t:Case(2),Baker g:Johnson(4)	11th	668
15/4/18	Newcastle (h)	L10-30	t:Baker,Trumper g:Johnson	11th	321
22/4/18	Workington (a)	L20-12	t:Brennan,Knox g:Johnson(2)	11th	597
29/4/18	Hemel (h)	W40-16	t:Johnson,Buckley,Lyons,Moore,Atherton,Houghton,Dandy g:Johnson(6)	11th	215
6/5/18	Whitehaven (a)	W22-25	t:Roper,Conroy,Smith,Baker g:Johnson(4) fg:B Walker	10th	603
20/5/18	Keighley (h)	L28-46	t:Baker(2),B Walker,Brennan(2) g:B Walker(3),Roper	10th	337
27/5/18	Coventry (h)	W42-6	t:Johnson(2),Ashall-Bott(2),Lyons,Bloomfield,Moore g:Johnson(7)	9th	301
9/6/18	Bradford (a)	L50-12	t:Bloomfield,Atherton g:Baker(2)	10th	3,112
17/6/18	York (h)	L4-31	t:Bloomfield	10th	408
23/6/18	London Skolars (a)	W28-36	t:Houghton(2),Atherton,A Thompson,Johnson,Baker g:Johnson(6)	10th	275
1/7/18	Hunslet (h)	L18-19	t:W Thompson,B Walker,Bloomfield g:Johnson(3)	10th	317
8/7/18	Whitehaven (h)	L14-22	t:Ashall-Bott,Baker g:B Walker(3)	10th	321
15/7/18	Newcastle (a)	W20-24	t:Smith,Bloomfield,Norman,Baker g:Ah Van(3),Baker	10th	637
22/7/18	Oldham (a)	L50-6	t:Houghton g:Johnson	10th	466
29/7/18	Workington (h)	L22-36	t:Hurst,Trumper,Bloomfield g:Johnson(4),B Walker	10th	340
5/8/18	York (a)	L30-0		10th	981
12/8/18	Bradford (h)	L0-48		10th	886
19/8/18	Hemel (a)	W0-50	t:B Walker,Conroy(2),Bate,Smith,Moore,Hurst,Fairhurst,Baker g:B Walker(7)	10th	110
2/9/18	West Wales (a)	W66-0	t:Conroy(3),B Walker,Fairhurst(2),Hurst,J Walker,Brennan,Wild,Ashall,Bloomfield g:B Walker(3),Fairhurst(6)	10th	368
9/9/18	Coventry (a)	W12-36	t:Hurst,Ashall,Baker(2),Moore,Conroy,Bloomfield g:Johnson(4)	10th	288
16/9/18	Doncaster (h)	L12-36	t:Davies,Houghton g:Johnson(2)	10th	296
23/9/18	Keighley (a)	L24-22	t:Johnson,Bloomfield,Houghton,W Thompson g:Johnson(3)	10th	592

● *Played at LD Nutrition Stadium, Featherstone*

		APP		TRIES		GOALS		FG		PTS	
	D.O.B.	ALL	L1	ALL	L1	ALL	L1	ALL	L1	ALL	L1
Patrick Ah Van	17/3/88	1	1	0	0	3	3	0	0	6	6
Stanton Albert	15/9/95	2(2)	2(2)	0	0	0	0	0	0	0	0
Wellington Albert	3/9/93	(1)	(1)	0	0	0	0	0	0	0	0
Karl Ashall	3/11/89	7(1)	7(1)	2	2	0	0	0	0	8	8
Olly Ashall-Bott	24/11/97	3	3	3	3	0	0	0	0	12	12
Simon Atherton	8/11/90	21	19	8	5	0	0	0	0	32	20
Kenny Baker	1/3/92	24	23	11	11	3	3	0	0	50	50
Joe Bate	24/10/92	12(11)	12(10)	1	1	0	0	0	0	4	4
Callan Beckett	24/3/93	1	0	0	0	0	0	0	0	0	0
Dale Bloomfield	24/10/87	21	21	13	13	0	0	0	0	52	52
Brad Brennan	18/1/93	(22)	(20)	4	4	0	0	0	0	16	16
Owen Buckley	15/11/98	1	1	1	1	0	0	0	0	4	4
Jordan Case	10/4/93	13	11	2	2	0	0	0	0	8	8
Ted Chapelhow	21/9/95	(1)	(1)	0	0	0	0	0	0	0	0
Gavin Conroy	6/3/95	20	18	8	8	0	0	0	0	32	32
James Dandy	23/5/90	15(2)	15(1)	2	2	0	0	0	0	8	8
Alex Davidson	1/11/92	5(4)	4(4)	1	1	0	0	0	0	4	4
Aled Davies	7/3/96	1	1	1	1	0	0	0	0	4	4
Lewis Fairhurst	24/12/96	3(1)	3(1)	3	3	6	6	0	0	24	24
Alex Gerrard	5/11/91	1	1	0	0	0	0	0	0	0	0
Jack Houghton	10/1/97	26	24	9	8	0	0	0	0	36	32
Lee Hudson	28/9/90	14(6)	12(6)	1	1	0	0	0	0	4	4
Liam Hulme	28/10/91	1(5)	1(5)	0	0	0	0	0	0	0	0
Earl Hurst	21/4/89	13	13	4	4	0	0	0	0	16	16
Ryan Ince	16/9/96	1	1	0	0	0	0	0	0	0	0
Tommy Johnson	19/4/91	21	19	6	5	65	60	0	0	154	140
Jake Knox	2/12/97	7	7	1	1	0	0	0	0	4	4
Macgraff Leuluai	9/2/90	1	1	0	0	0	0	0	0	0	0
Joe Lyons	16/10/97	16	16	2	2	0	0	0	0	8	8
Ryan Millington	14/1/87	4(1)	2(1)	0	0	0	0	0	0	0	0
Aaron Moore	14/11/97	3(18)	3(17)	5	5	0	0	0	0	20	20
Dan Norman	8/9/97	2(15)	2(15)	1	1	0	0	0	0	4	4
Dan Price	5/10/92	2	1	1	1	0	0	0	0	4	4
Steve Roper	10/11/86	13(1)	11(1)	2	1	1	1	0	0	10	6
Billy Sheen	8/12/89	2	1	0	0	0	0	0	0	0	0
Ryan Smith	25/9/89	24(1)	23(1)	4	4	0	0	0	0	16	16
Samir Tahraoui	28/12/90	(1)	(1)	0	0	0	0	0	0	0	0
Alex Thompson	11/2/90	4(4)	3(4)	2	2	0	0	0	0	8	8
Warren Thompson	24/2/90	13(3)	13(3)	2	2	0	0	0	0	8	8
Alex Trumper	5/4/91	18(4)	18(2)	2	2	0	0	0	0	8	8
Brad Walker	30/1/98	11(1)	11(1)	4	4	17	17	1	1	51	51
Jonny Walker	26/9/86	12(5)	10(5)	1	1	0	0	0	0	4	4
Luke Warburton	4/8/94	(2)	(1)	0	0	0	0	0	0	0	0
Kash Watkins	20/6/88	1	0	0	0	0	0	0	0	0	0
Stephen Wild	26/4/81	4	4	1	1	0	0	0	0	4	4

Kenny Baker

LEAGUE RECORD
P26-W9-D1-L16 (10th)
F589, A660, Diff-71, 19 points.

CHALLENGE CUP
Round Four

ATTENDANCES
Best - v Bradford (L1 - 886)
Worst - v Hemel (L1 - 215)
Total (excluding Challenge Cup) - 4,865
Average (excluding Challenge Cup) - 374
(Up by 32 on 2017)

'L1' totals include League 1 regular season only;
'All' totals also include Challenge Cup

CLUB RECORDS	
	Highest score: 82-6 v West Hull, 6/4/2013 **Highest score against:** 4-98 v Wigan, 15/4/2012
	Record attendance: 1,562 v South Wales, 1/9/2013 *(Racecourse Ground)*; 886 v Bradford, 12/8/2018 *(Queensway Stadium)*
MATCH RECORDS	**Tries:** 5 Rob Massam v Rochdale, 30/6/2013; Jono Smith v Hemel, 16/5/2015
	Goals: 11 Tommy Johnson v West Hull, 6/4/2013; Ian Mort v Hemel, 16/5/2015 **Points:** 30 Tommy Johnson v West Hull, 6/4/2013
SEASON RECORDS	**Tries:** 29 Rob Massam 2015 **Goals:** 109 Tommy Johnson 2015 **Points:** 266 Tommy Johnson 2015
CAREER RECORDS	**Tries:** 97 Rob Massam 2012-2016 **Goals:** 542 Tommy Johnson 2012-2018 **Points:** 1,308 Tommy Johnson 2012-2018
	Appearances: 166 Tommy Johnson 2012-2018

OLDHAM

DATE	FIXTURE	RESULT	SCORERS	LGE	ATT
18/2/18	Whitehaven (a)	W0-14	t:Wilkinson g:Crook(5)	3rd	785
25/2/18	Featherstone Lions (h) (CCR3)	W42-0	t:Langtree(2),McComb,West,Joy,Eccleston,Bridge g:Crook(7)	N/A	364
11/3/18	York (h)	L22-24	t:Reid(2),Langtree,West g:Crook(3)	6th	703
20/3/18	Halifax (a) (CCR4)	W6-27	t:Langtree,West,Reid,Crook g:Crook(5) fg:Hewitt	N/A	688
25/3/18	North Wales (a)	W2-30	t:McComb,Martin,Bridge(2),Joy g:Crook(3)	4th	449
30/3/18	Bradford (a)	L30-12	t:Johnson,Briscoe g:Crook(2)	6th	4,036
8/4/18	Hunslet (h)	L16-24	t:Hewitt(2),Langtree g:Crook(2)	10th	544
15/4/18	Keighley (h)	W32-18	t:Eccleston,Kershaw(2),Gill,Bent g:Crook(6)	8th	530
22/4/18	Hull KR (h) (CCR5)	L0-32		N/A	1,064
29/4/18	Workington (a)	W10-32	t:Bent,Langtree,Kershaw,Hooley,Joy,Hewitt g:Crook(4)	7th	712
6/5/18	Newcastle (h)	W28-12	t:Gill,Bridge,Eccleston,Joy,Briscoe g:Crook(4)	7th	455
13/5/18	Hemel (h)	W74-6	t:Owen,West,Bridge(2),Nelmes(2),Johnson(2),McComb(3),Wilkinson,Bennion g:Crook(11)	4th	411
19/5/18	West Wales (a)	W0-74	t:Eccleston,McComb(3),Hughes,Bridge,Reid(2),West,Wilkinson,Rasool,Hewitt(2),Joy g:Hewitt(5),Johnson(4)	3rd	424
3/6/18	Doncaster (h)	W32-12	t:Langtree,Hooley,Nelmes,Kershaw,Joy g:Crook(6)	3rd	453
10/6/18	Coventry (a)	W0-60	t:Davies,West,Wilkinson,Briscoe(2),Langtree(2),Rasool,Crook,Johnson,Hewitt g:Crook(6),Hewitt(2)	3rd	337
17/6/18	London Skolars (h)	W44-12	t:Hewitt,McComb,Wilkinson,Langtree,Bridge(3),Holmes g:Crook(6)	3rd	419
24/6/18	Hunslet (h)	L16-12	t:Hooley,Wilkinson g:Crook(2)	3rd	605
1/7/18	Workington (h)	L14-16	t:Reid,West,Johnson g:Crook	4th	486
8/7/18	West Wales (h)	W102-6	t:Hooley(4),Holmes(3),Spencer,Cunningham(3),Dezaria,Hewitt(3),Kershaw,West,McComb g:Crook(7),Hewitt(8)	3rd	274
13/7/18	Keighley (a)	L15-8	t:Hooley g:Crook(2)	3rd	510
22/7/18	North Wales (h)	W50-6	t:Langtree(4),Nelmes,Cunningham(2),Reid,Joy g:Crook(7)	3rd	466
29/7/18	Doncaster (a)	L26-22	t:Langtree,Reid,Eccleston g:Crook(3),Hooley,Hewitt	5th	647
5/8/18	Hemel (a)	W28-60	t:Langtree(2),Reid,Hewitt,Crook(2),Spencer,Wilkinson,Kershaw(2) g:Crook(10)	4th	109
12/8/18	Whitehaven (h)	W20-0	t:Briscoe,Hewitt,Langtree g:Crook(4)	4th	413
19/8/18	Newcastle (a)	L24-18	t:Bent,Kershaw,Nelmes g:Crook(3)	5th	749
2/9/18	Coventry (h)	W58-6	t:Holmes(2),Briscoe,Langtree(2),Wilkinson(2),Hooley,West,Joy g:Crook(7),Hooley(2)	5th	373
9/9/18	York (a)	L10-6	t:Holmes g:Hooley	5th	1,692
16/9/18	Bradford (h)	L16-24	t:Hewitt,Reid,Briscoe g:Hooley(2)	6th	1,038
22/9/18	London Skolars (a)	W18-46	t:Crook,Kershaw(3),Langtree,Briscoe,Hughes,Reid g:Crook(6),Hooley	5th	402
30/9/18	Bradford (a) (SF)	L47-0		N/A	2,788

		APP		TRIES		GOALS		FG		PTS	
	D.O.B.	ALL	L1	ALL	L1	ALL	L1	ALL	L1	ALL	L1
Gavin Bennion	31/12/93	2	2	1	1	0	0	0	0	4	4
Liam Bent	11/10/97	23(2)	20(2)	3	3	0	0	0	0	12	12
Danny Bridge	4/1/93	20	17	10	9	0	0	0	0	40	36
Craig Briscoe	8/12/92	13(11)	13(9)	8	8	0	0	0	0	32	32
Paul Crook	28/8/86	28	25	5	4	122	110	0	0	264	236
Jonah Cunningham	20/8/97	(3)	(3)	5	5	0	0	0	0	20	20
Ben Davies	2/11/89	2(10)	2(10)	1	1	0	0	0	0	4	4
Jordan Dezaria	6/11/96	(1)	(1)	1	1	0	0	0	0	4	4
Dave Eccleston	12/9/96	20	17	5	4	0	0	0	0	20	16
Kieran Gill	4/12/95	3	3	2	2	0	0	0	0	8	8
Nick Gregson	17/12/95	(1)	(1)	0	0	0	0	0	0	0	0
Dave Hewitt	4/11/94	28	25	13	13	16	16	1	0	85	84
Jack Holmes	5/1/94	17	15	7	7	0	0	0	0	28	28
Luke Hooley	1/8/98	15	14	9	9	7	7	0	0	50	50
Kenny Hughes	30/3/90	7(8)	6(6)	2	2	0	0	0	0	8	8
Kyran Johnson	23/3/94	16	15	5	5	4	4	0	0	28	28
Adam Jones	13/4/97	(16)	(14)	0	0	0	0	0	0	0	0
Phil Joy	4/9/91	27	25	8	7	0	0	0	0	32	28
Lee Kershaw	2/5/99	20	19	11	11	0	0	0	0	44	44
Danny Langtree	18/2/91	26	23	21	18	0	0	0	0	84	72
Ryan Lannon	11/1/96	2	2	0	0	0	0	0	0	0	0
Joe Martin	28/3/95	2	1	2	2	0	0	0	0	8	8
Zack McComb	9/9/95	17(1)	15(1)	10	9	0	0	0	0	40	36
Daniel Murray	21/3/96	1	1	0	0	0	0	0	0	0	0
Adam Neal	21/5/90	12(3)	10(3)	0	0	0	0	0	0	0	0
Luke Nelmes	7/6/93	(27)	(24)	5	5	0	0	0	0	20	20
Steven Nield	20/11/90	3	3	0	0	0	0	0	0	0	0
Levy Nzoungou	22/1/98	2	2	0	0	0	0	0	0	0	0
Gareth Owen	3/7/92	22(2)	21(2)	1	1	0	0	0	0	4	4
Danny Rasool	25/10/95	2(8)	2(6)	2	2	0	0	0	0	8	8
Matt Reid	16/9/92	22	20	11	10	0	0	0	0	44	40
Jack Spencer	21/12/90	19(7)	17(7)	2	2	0	0	0	0	8	8
Ben West	10/5/96	14	12	9	7	0	0	0	0	36	28
Matt Wilkinson	13/6/96	5(20)	4(19)	9	9	0	0	0	0	36	36

'L1' totals include play-offs; 'All' totals also include Challenge Cup

Danny Langtree

LEAGUE RECORD
P26-W16-D0-L10 (5th/Semi-Finalists)
F902, A345, Diff+557, 32 points.

CHALLENGE CUP
Round Five

ATTENDANCES
Best - v Hull KR (CC - 1,064)
Worst - v West Wales (L1 - 274)
Total (excluding Challenge Cup) - 6,565
Average (excluding Challenge Cup) - 505
(Down by 272 on 2017, Championship)

CLUB RECORDS	
	Highest score: 102-6 v West Wales, 8/7/2018 Highest score against: 0-84 v Widnes, 25/7/99
	Record attendance: 28,000 v Huddersfield, 24/2/1912 (Watersheddings); 1,405 v Keighley, 20/9/2015 (Vestacare Stadium)
MATCH RECORDS	Tries: 7 James Miller v Barry, 31/10/1908 Goals: 14 Bernard Ganley v Liverpool City, 4/4/59
	Points: 34 Andy Ballard v London Skolars, 2/5/2009; Chris Baines v Hunslet, 20/9/2009; Lewis Palfrey v Hemel, 9/8/2015
SEASON RECORDS	Tries: 49 Reg Farrar 1921-22 Goals: 200 Bernard Ganley 1957-58 Points: 412 Bernard Ganley 1957-58
CAREER RECORDS	Tries: 174 Alan Davies 1950-61 Goals: 1,358 Bernard Ganley 1951-61 Points: 2,761 Bernard Ganley 1951-61 Appearances: 627 Joe Ferguson 1899-1923

WEST WALES RAIDERS

DATE	FIXTURE	RESULT	SCORERS	LGE	ATT
25/2/18	Bradford (a) (CCR3)	L82-6	t:Parry g:Stroud	N/A	1,505
11/3/18	Workington (a)	L74-6	t:Parry g:Tennant	14th	614
30/3/18	North Wales (h)	L6-54	t:Farrer g:Stroud	14th	306
7/4/18	London Skolars (a)	L76-8	t:Elliott,Tennant	14th	198
15/4/18	Whitehaven (a)	L84-6	t:Boots g:Stroud	14th	401
29/4/18	York (a)	L144-0		14th	1,089
6/5/18	Bradford (a)	L124-0		14th	3,398
13/5/18	Doncaster (h)	L18-70	t:Farrer,Silver,Parry g:Tennant(3)	14th	188
19/5/18	Oldham (h)	L0-74		14th	424
27/5/18	Hunslet (a)	L86-0		14th	415
3/6/18	Newcastle (h)	L20-82	t:Baker,Parry,Elliott,Kislingbury g:Williams(2)	14th	272
9/6/18	Hemel (h)	L12-48	t:Elliott,Cowburn g:Stroud(2)	14th	319
17/6/18	Keighley (a)	L94-0		14th	470
23/6/18	Whitehaven (h)	L6-66	t:Parry g:Stroud	14th	296
30/6/18	London Skolars (h)	L12-62	t:Walker,Cowburn g:Stroud(2)	14th	224
8/7/18	Oldham (a)	L102-6	t:Kislingbury g:Williams	14th	274
15/7/18	Doncaster (a) ●	L102-6	t:Parry g:Stroud	14th	306
21/7/18	Workington (h)	L6-46	t:A Pope g:Williams	14th	246
25/7/18	Coventry (a)	L64-6	t:Cowburn g:Williams	14th	272
29/7/18	Hemel (a)	L30-22	t:Cowburn,Williams,A Pope,McClean g:Stroud,Williams(2)	14th	118
4/8/18	Hunslet (h)	L6-86	t:Silver g:Williams	14th	258
11/8/18	York (h)	L0-130		14th	196
19/8/18	Coventry (h)	L18-28	t:Parry(2),Baker g:Williams(3)	14th	409
2/9/18	North Wales (a)	L66-0		14th	368
9/9/18	Bradford (h)	L0-104		14th	826
15/9/18	Keighley (h)	L6-112	t:A Pope g:Elliott	14th	218
23/9/18	Newcastle (a)	L98-6	t:Elliott g:Elliott	14th	889

● *Played at LD Nutrition Stadium, Featherstone*

APP TRIES GOALS FG PTS

	D.O.B.	ALL	L1	ALL	L1	ALL	L1	ALL	L1	ALL	L1
Sam Baker	8/10/92	11(1)	11(1)	2	2	0	0	0	0	8	8
Ashley Bateman	11/2/90	1	0	0	0	0	0	0	0	0	0
Dewi Billingham	9/11/98	3	3	0	0	0	0	0	0	0	0
Aseri Biutanaseva	21/2/83	2	2	0	0	0	0	0	0	0	0
Robert Bonehill	14/4/95	1(1)	1(1)	0	0	0	0	0	0	0	0
Harry Boots	15/12/96	6(8)	6(7)	1	1	0	0	0	0	4	4
Karlin Claridge	2/10/99	12	12	0	0	0	0	0	0	0	0
Phil Cowburn	15/10/90	13	13	4	4	0	0	0	0	16	16
Matt Davies	1/3/85	8	8	0	0	0	0	0	0	0	0
Dalton Desmond-Walker	25/4/93	6(10)	5(10)	0	0	0	0	0	0	0	0
Harrison Elliott	16/3/92	22	21	4	4	2	2	0	0	20	20
Morgan Evans	23/3/92	12	11	0	0	0	0	0	0	0	0
Connor Farrer	6/6/95	2(3)	2(3)	2	2	0	0	0	0	8	8
Louis Ford	20/8/95	4(1)	4(1)	0	0	0	0	0	0	0	0
Dan Fox	13/6/88	2	2	0	0	0	0	0	0	0	0
Sam Fraser	3/9/97	(1)	(1)	0	0	0	0	0	0	0	0
Kurtis Haile	11/10/90	21	20	0	0	0	0	0	0	0	0
Macauley Harris	27/2/99	10(8)	10(8)	0	0	0	0	0	0	0	0
Taine Hendy	3/3/00	(1)	(1)	0	0	0	0	0	0	0	0
Dean Higgs	2/2/87	7(5)	6(5)	0	0	0	0	0	0	0	0
Danny Hunter	11/9/90	1(2)	1(2)	0	0	0	0	0	0	0	0
Rowland Kaye	27/8/99	16(6)	16(5)	0	0	0	0	0	0	0	0
David Kearns	24/4/86	3(1)	3(1)	0	0	0	0	0	0	0	0
Craig Kelly	21/10/88	(3)	(3)	0	0	0	0	0	0	0	0
Brad Kislingbury	2/2/96	12	12	2	2	0	0	0	0	8	8
Craig Lewis	15/10/86	11(4)	10(4)	0	0	0	0	0	0	0	0
Joe McClean	10/8/89	8	8	1	1	0	0	0	0	4	4
Callum Mulkeen	10/12/90	4(1)	4(1)	0	0	0	0	0	0	0	0
Connor Parker	23/10/97	14(2)	13(2)	0	0	0	0	0	0	0	0
Steve Parry	19/10/88	23	22	8	7	0	0	0	0	32	28
Barrie Phillips	27/5/86	(1)	0	0	0	0	0	0	0	0	0
Dafydd Phillips	10/8/95	(2)	(2)	0	0	0	0	0	0	0	0
Alan Pope	1/4/85	10(3)	10(3)	3	3	0	0	0	0	12	12
Rhys Pope	5/7/91	2(2)	2(2)	0	0	0	0	0	0	0	0
Ross Price	14/12/92	4(2)	4(2)	0	0	0	0	0	0	0	0
Andrew Rees-Spowart	18/11/84	2	2	0	0	0	0	0	0	0	0
Liam Silver	9/12/97	15(1)	15(1)	2	2	0	0	0	0	8	8
Ellis Simon	15/10/99	2(8)	2(7)	0	0	0	0	0	0	0	0
James Smith	18/7/00	5	4	0	0	0	0	0	0	0	0
Liam Smith	11/4/96	1	1	0	0	0	0	0	0	0	0
Archie Snook	26/3/99	20(1)	19(1)	0	0	0	0	0	0	0	0
Frazer Stroud	12/4/99	13	12	0	0	10	9	0	0	20	18
Shaun Tennant	25/7/93	9(1)	8(1)	1	1	4	4	0	0	12	12
Aneurin Walker	16/1/00	15(4)	15(4)	1	1	0	0	0	0	4	4
James Walter	11/9/91	(2)	(2)	0	0	0	0	0	0	0	0
Mike Ward	22/2/92	3	3	0	0	0	0	0	0	0	0
Lewys Willacott	21/9/97	1	1	0	0	0	0	0	0	0	0
Luke Williams	4/10/96	13(2)	13(2)	1	1	11	11	0	0	26	26

'L1' totals include League 1 regular season only; 'All' totals also include Challenge Cup

Steve Parry

LEAGUE RECORD
P26-W0-D0-L26 (14th)
F176, A2106, Diff-1930, 0 points.

CHALLENGE CUP
Round Three

ATTENDANCES
Best - v Bradford (L1 - 826)
Worst - v Doncaster (L1 - 188)
Total (all home games included) - 4,182
Average (all home games included) - 322

WHITEHAVEN

DATE	FIXTURE	RESULT	SCORERS	LGE	ATT
18/2/18	Oldham (h)	L0-14		13th	785
24/2/18	London Skolars (h) (CCR3)	W16-14	t:Gillam,Abram,Tilley g:Billsborough(2)	N/A	439
11/3/18	Doncaster (a)	L44-6	t:Tilley g:Billsborough	13th	782
18/3/18	Dewsbury (h) (CCR4)	W25-18	t:Parker(2),Forster,Mossop g:Burns(4) fg:Howarth	N/A	414
25/3/18	Hemel (h)	W30-6	t:Brown,Parker,Billsborough,Bradley,Abram g:Abram(5)	8th	438
30/3/18	Workington (h)	W14-12	t:D Thompson,Taylor g:Billsborough,Abram(2)	8th	1,395
8/4/18	Coventry (a)	W12-44	t:Aiye,Green,Abram,Mossop,Forster(2),Cooper,Parker g:Abram(6)	6th	279
15/4/18	West Wales (h)	W84-6	t:D Thompson,Green(2),Taylor(2),Cooper,Reece(2),Abram(2),Holliday(2),Aiye,Parker,Eaves,Phillips,Shackley g:Abram(7),Parker	4th	401
22/4/18	Rochdale (h) (CCR5)	W38-0	t:Phillips(2),Abram,Holliday,Parker g:Abram(9)	N/A	604
29/4/18	Keighley (a)	W24-30	t:Abram(2),Aiye,Green,Eaves g:Abram(5)	4th	648
6/5/18	North Wales (h)	L22-25	t:Phillips,Taylor,D Thompson,Abram g:Abram(3)	6th	603
12/5/18	Catalans Dragons (a) (CCR6)	L56-10	t:Parker,D Thompson g:Abram	N/A	2,533
19/5/18	London Skolars (a)	W26-44	t:Forster,Aiye(2),Green,Holliday,D Thompson,Taylor,Phillips,Phillips g:Abram(6)	7th	346
27/5/18	York (h)	W26-18	t:Parker,Gillam,Phillips,D Thompson g:Abram(5)	7th	640
2/6/18	Hunslet (a)	L39-32	t:Aiye,Forster,Taylor,Parker,Cooper g:Abram(6)	7th	576
10/6/18	Newcastle (a)	L30-22	t:Cooper,Forster,Eaves,Burns g:Abram(3)	8th	759
17/6/18	Bradford (h)	L20-27	t:Gillam,Aiye,Eaves g:Abram(4)	9th	1,476
23/6/18	West Wales (a)	W6-66	t:Burns,Gillam(2),Phillips(2),Shackley,Aiye,D Thompson(3),Coward,McAvoy g:Burns(9)	8th	296
1/7/18	Keighley (h)	W28-14	t:Parker,D Thompson(2),Taylor g:Burns(6)	7th	592
8/7/18	North Wales (a)	W14-22	t:Burns(2),Aiye,Eaves g:Abram(3)	6th	321
15/7/18	Workington (a)	W22-24	t:Gillam(2),Green g:Abram(6)	5th	1,258
22/7/18	London Skolars (h)	W28-18	t:Burns(2),Eaves,Holliday,Taylor g:Abram(2),Burns(2)	5th	661
29/7/18	Newcastle (h)	W12-8	t:D Thompson,Parker g:Burns(2)	4th	551
4/8/18	Bradford (a)	L46-0		7th	2,818
12/8/18	Oldham (a)	L20-0		7th	413
19/8/18	Doncaster (h)	L14-23	t:McAvoy,Mossop g:Abram(3)	7th	871
2/9/18	Hemel (a)	W13-50	t:Green,Forster(3),Coward,Mossop,D Thompson,Eaves,Aiye g:Abram(5),Roper,Aiye	7th	109
9/9/18	Hunslet (h)	W46-10	t:McAvoy,Parker(2),Burns(3),Aiye(2) g:Abram(7)	6th	672
16/9/18	Coventry (h)	W24-20	t:Shackley,Forster(3) g:Abram(4)	5th	691
23/9/18	York (a)	L32-14	t:Eaves,Burns g:Abram(3)	6th	3,223

APP TRIES GOALS FG PTS

	D.O.B.	ALL	L1	ALL	L1	ALL	L1	ALL	L1	ALL	L1
Dan Abram	11/11/95	26(2)	22(2)	9	7	95	85	0	0	226	198
Dion Aiye	6/11/87	25(2)	21(2)	12	12	1	1	0	0	50	50
Brad Billsborough	4/8/98	3(3)	3(1)	1	1	4	2	0	0	12	8
Jake Bradley	29/4/01	1(1)	1(1)	1	1	0	0	0	0	4	4
Lewis Brown	29/11/98	8(7)	8(4)	1	1	0	0	0	0	4	4
Jordan Burns	2/9/95	19	18	10	10	23	19	0	0	86	78
Liam Cooper	28/7/94	10(8)	7(8)	4	4	0	0	0	0	16	16
Kris Coward	1/10/81	9(18)	7(16)	2	2	0	0	0	0	8	8
Josh Eaves	20/10/97	6(17)	6(16)	8	8	0	0	0	0	32	32
Carl Forster	4/6/92	28(1)	25	12	11	0	0	0	0	48	44
Ellis Gillam	6/10/97	24(4)	20(4)	7	6	0	0	0	0	28	24
Danny Green	21/6/92	16(1)	14(1)	7	7	0	0	0	0	28	28
Jordan Herve	23/8/90	(2)	(2)	0	0	0	0	0	0	0	0
Connor Holliday	9/6/95	8(16)	8(14)	5	4	0	0	0	0	20	16
Stuart Howarth	25/1/90	24(2)	22(1)	0	0	0	0	1	0	1	0
Phil Lister	28/11/87	1	1	0	0	0	0	0	0	0	0
Scott McAvoy	9/4/86	2(4)	2(4)	3	3	0	0	0	0	12	12
Jason Mossop	12/9/85	26(2)	22(2)	4	3	0	0	0	0	16	12
Levy Nzoungou	22/1/98	(2)	(2)	0	0	0	0	0	0	0	0
Karl Olstrom	21/9/91	1	0	0	0	0	0	0	0	0	0
Jessie Joe Parker	22/8/85	19(7)	16(6)	13	9	1	1	0	0	54	38
Callum Phillips	19/2/92	28	24	8	6	0	0	0	0	32	24
Lewis Reece	17/6/91	1(6)	1(4)	2	2	0	0	0	0	8	8
Steve Roper	10/11/86	5	5	0	0	1	1	0	0	2	2
Marc Shackley	14/1/89	25(3)	21(3)	3	3	0	0	0	0	12	12
Carl Sice	13/4/80	(1)	(1)	0	0	0	0	0	0	0	0
Chris Taylor	25/10/93	22(1)	20	8	8	0	0	0	0	32	32
Dave Thompson	13/9/95	27(1)	23(1)	13	12	0	0	0	0	52	48
Jordan Thompson	23/1/93	6(1)	6(1)	0	0	0	0	0	0	0	0
James Tilley	11/11/93	19(6)	15(6)	2	1	0	0	0	0	8	4
Matty While	25/11/96	1	0	0	0	0	0	0	0	0	0

'L1' totals include League 1 regular season only; 'All' totals also include Challenge Cup

Dan Abram

LEAGUE RECORD
P26-W16-D0-L10 (6th)
F702, A529, Diff+173, 32 points.

CHALLENGE CUP
Round Six

ATTENDANCES
Best - v Bradford (L1 - 1,476)
Worst - v West Wales (L1 - 401)
Total (excluding Challenge Cup) - 9,776
Average (excluding Challenge Cup) - 752
(Up by 49 on 2017)

CLUB RECORDS	Highest score: 86-6 v Highfield, 25/1/95 **Highest score against:** 8-106 v Wigan, 12/5/2008 **Record attendance:** 18,500 v Wakefield, 19/3/60
MATCH RECORDS	**Tries:** 6 Vince Gribbin v Doncaster, 18/11/84 **Goals:** 13 Lee Anderson v Highfield, 25/1/95 **Points:** 32 Mick Nanyn v Batley, 22/8/2004
SEASON RECORDS	**Tries:** 34 Mike Pechey 1994-95 **Goals:** 141 John McKeown 1956-57 **Points:** 398 Mick Nanyn 2004
CAREER RECORDS	**Tries:** 239 Craig Calvert 2004-2017 **Goals:** 1,050 John McKeown 1948-61 **Points:** 2,133 John McKeown 1948-61 **Appearances:** 417 John McKeown 1948-61

WORKINGTON TOWN

DATE	FIXTURE	RESULT	SCORERS	LGE	ATT
18/2/18	Keighley (a)	L44-34	t:G Maudling,Forber,K Maudling(2),Hambley,Penkywicz g:Foster(5)	11th	707
24/2/18	Hunslet Club Parkside (a) (CCR3) ●	W16-24	t:Doran,Forrester,Singleton,K Maudling,Penkywicz g:Forber,Leatherbarrow	N/A	285
11/3/18	West Wales (h)	W74-6	t:Forrester(5),G Maudling,Hambley,Ryan Bailey,Singleton(2),Akehurst(2),Barnes,Ryan g:Foster(9)	4th	614
18/3/18	London Broncos (h) (CCR4)	L20-22	t:Singleton,Doran(2) g:Foster(4)	N/A	548
24/3/18	London Skolars (a)	W26-42	t:Doran(2),Penkywicz,Forrester(2),K Maudling,Newton g:Foster(3),Tansey(4)	3rd	328
30/3/18	Whitehaven (a)	L14-12	t:Hambley g:Foster(4)	4th	1,395
8/4/18	Bradford (h)	W17-16	t:Barnes,Miller g:Tansey(4) fg:Tansey	4th	1,366
15/4/18	Hunslet (a)	L27-20	t:Doran,Forber,Dawson g:Tansey(4)	7th	561
22/4/18	North Wales (h)	W20-12	t:Doran,Barnes g:Forber(6)	5th	597
29/4/18	Oldham (h)	L10-32	t:Gregson,Miller g:Foster	6th	712
6/5/18	Hemel (a)	W12-60	t:Barnes(2),Miller(3),Wilkes,Hambley,Doran,Forrester,Olstrom,Forber g:Forber(8)	5th	110
20/5/18	Coventry (a)	W4-52	t:Miller,Singleton(2),Blagbrough,Doran,Scholey,Penkywicz,Forrester,Olstrom,Ricky Bailey g:Forber(6)	5th	264
27/5/18	Newcastle (h)	W38-18	t:Wilkes,Ricky Bailey,Penkywicz(3),Barnes,Blagbrough g:Forber(5)	5th	696
10/6/18	York (a)	L40-8	t:Dawson g:Forber(2)	7th	1,399
17/6/18	Doncaster (h)	W34-6	t:Miller(2),Moimoi(2),Singleton,Doran g:Forber(5)	6th	550
24/6/18	Hemel (h)	W60-12	t:Wilkes,Singleton,Moimoi,Miller,Rooke,Hambley,Scholey,Penkywicz,Forber(2),Blagbrough g:Forber(8)	5th	444
1/7/18	Oldham (a)	W14-16	t:Morris,Miller,Hambley g:Forber,Wood	5th	486
8/7/18	Hunslet (h)	W28-18	t:K Maudling,Scholey,Wilkes,Doran,Rooke g:Forber(4)	4th	601
15/7/18	Whitehaven (h)	L22-24	t:Rooke(2),Curwen g:Forber(5)	4th	1,258
21/7/18	West Wales (a)	W6-46	t:Bergal(4),Curwen,Hambley,Wilkes,Dawson g:Forber(7)	4th	246
29/7/18	North Wales (a)	W22-36	t:Forrester,Wilkes,Morris,Penkywicz(2),Curwen g:Forber(6)	3rd	340
5/8/18	Keighley (h)	W34-12	t:Forrester,Penkywicz,Mellor,Miller(3),Doran g:Forber(3)	3rd	607
12/8/18	Coventry (h)	W40-16	t:Newton,Doran,Hambley(2),Curwen,Wilkes,Morris g:Forber(6)	3rd	556
19/8/18	Bradford (h)	W18-24	t:Forrester,Miller,Doran,Penkywicz g:Forber(4)	3rd	3,320
2/9/18	York (h)	L14-18	t:Mellor,Moimoi,Miller g:Forber	4th	1,623
8/9/18	Newcastle (a)	L50-22	t:Hambley(2),Mellor,Dickinson g:Forber(2),Doran	4th	769
16/9/18	London Skolars (h)	W38-6	t:Mellor(2),Dickinson,Rooke(2),Wilkes,Moimoi g:Forber(5)	4th	545
23/9/18	Doncaster (h)	L44-32	t:Mellor,Moore(2),Penkywicz,Hambley,Moimoi g:Forber(4)	4th	689
30/9/18	Doncaster (a) (SF)	W18-30	t:G Maudling,Wilkes,Dickinson,Hambley g:Forber(7)	N/A	542
7/10/18	Bradford (a) (PF)	L27-8	t:Miller g:Forber(2)	N/A	6,011
14/10/18	Swinton (a) (CP/RPO)	L33-20	t:Hambley,Rooke,Mellor g:Forber(4)	N/A	703

● *Played at South Leeds Stadium*

APP TRIES GOALS FG PTS

	D.O.B.	ALL	L1	ALL	L1	ALL	L1	ALL	L1	ALL	L1
Scott Akehurst	10/8/92	7	5	2	2	0	0	0	0	8	8
Ricky Bailey	25/4/97	3	3	2	2	0	0	0	0	8	8
Ryan Bailey	11/11/83	6	6	1	1	0	0	0	0	4	4
Caine Barnes	22/2/99	6(6)	6(4)	6	6	0	0	0	0	24	24
Ilias Bergal	6/4/96	2	2	4	4	0	0	0	0	16	16
Jack Blagbrough	18/1/94	6(2)	6(2)	3	3	0	0	0	0	12	12
Jonah Cunningham	20/8/97	(2)	(2)	0	0	0	0	0	0	0	0
Tom Curwen	15/8/89	12(6)	11(6)	3	3	0	0	0	0	12	12
Andrew Dawson	12/3/89	2(26)	2(23)	3	3	0	0	0	0	12	12
Jordan Dezaria	6/11/96	(1)	(1)	0	0	0	0	0	0	0	0
Tyler Dickinson	18/8/96	6(4)	5(4)	4	4	0	0	0	0	16	16
Jamie Doran	8/12/94	28(1)	25(1)	14	11	1	1	0	0	58	46
Carl Forber	17/3/85	29	26	5	5	102	97	0	0	224	214
Sam Forrester	28/6/93	20	18	13	12	0	0	0	0	52	48
Jamie Foster	27/7/90	6	5	0	0	26	22	0	0	52	44
Nick Gregson	17/12/95	2(1)	2(1)	1	1	0	0	0	0	4	4
Joe Hambley	2/12/95	24(1)	22	14	13	0	0	0	0	56	52
Matthew Johnson	18/3/82	(1)	(1)	0	0	0	0	0	0	0	0
Scott Leatherbarrow	3/9/90	3(3)	3(2)	0	0	1	0	0	0	2	0
Kyle Lovett	23/3/93	1		0	0	0	0	0	0	0	0
Gordon Maudling	9/2/91	11(1)	9(1)	3	3	0	0	0	0	12	12
Kurt Maudling	5/2/89	13(8)	10(8)	5	4	0	0	0	0	20	16
Tyllar Mellor	21/4/99	10	9	7	6	0	0	0	0	28	24
Elliott Miller	14/9/90	24	23	16	16	0	0	0	0	64	64
Fuifui Moimoi	26/9/79	(17)	(17)	6	6	0	0	0	0	24	24
Jake Moore	6/9/96	12(9)	11(8)	2	2	0	0	0	0	8	8
Ben Morris	1/8/97	16	15	3	3	0	0	0	0	12	12
James Newton	20/6/97	12(15)	10(14)	2	2	0	0	0	0	8	8
Karl Olstrom	21/9/91	19	18	2	2	0	0	0	0	8	8
John Patrick	29/11/82	9(1)	9(1)	0	0	0	0	0	0	0	0
Larne Patrick	3/11/88	3	3	0	0	0	0	0	0	0	0
Sean Penkywicz	18/5/82	19(5)	18(4)	13	12	0	0	0	0	52	48
Scott Rooke	3/11/94	11(2)	10(2)	7	6	0	0	0	0	28	24
Joe Ryan	27/9/95	3(4)	1(4)	1	1	0	0	0	0	4	4
Stevie Scholey	7/1/96	23(4)	21(4)	3	3	0	0	0	0	12	12
Perry Singleton	5/1/94	17(2)	15(1)	8	6	0	0	0	0	32	24
Jordan Tansey	9/9/86	8	6	0	0	12	12	1	1	25	25
Oliver Wilkes	2/5/80	28(2)	26(1)	9	9	0	0	0	0	36	36
Sam Wood	11/6/97	2	2	0	0	1	1	0	0	2	2

'L1' totals include play-offs; 'All' totals also include Championship Promotion/Relegation play-off & Challenge Cup

Elliott Miller

LEAGUE RECORD
P26-W17-D0-L9
(4th/Losers, Promotion Final)
(Losers, Promotion/Relegation play-off)
F833, A517, Diff+316, 34 points.

CHALLENGE CUP
Round Four

ATTENDANCES
Best - v York (L1 - 1,623)
Worst - v Hemel (L1 - 444)
Total (excluding Challenge Cup) - 10,169
Average (excluding Challenge Cup) - 782
(Up by 151 on 2017)

CLUB RECORDS MATCH RECORDS	Highest score: 94-4 v Leigh, 26/2/95 Highest score against: 0-92 v Bradford, 14/2/99 Record attendance: 17,741 v Wigan, 3/3/65 Tries: 7 Ike Southward v Blackpool, 14/9/55 Goals: 14 Darren Holt v Gateshead, 12/6/2011 Points: 42 Dean Marwood v Highfield, 1/11/92; Dean Marwood v Leigh, 26/2/95
SEASON RECORDS CAREER RECORDS	Tries: 49 Johnny Lawrenson 1951-52 Goals: 186 Lyn Hopkins 1981-82 Points: 438 Lyn Hopkins 1981-82 Tries: 274 Ike Southward 1952-68 Goals: 809 Iain MacCorquodale 1972-80 Points: 1,800 Iain MacCorquodale 1972-80 Appearances: 419 Paul Charlton 1961-69; 1975-80

YORK CITY KNIGHTS

DATE	FIXTURE	RESULT	SCORERS	LGE	ATT
18/2/18	Bradford (h)	L20-22	t:Moss,Batchelor(2) g:C Robinson(3) fg:C Robinson(2)	10th	4,221
24/2/18	Askam (a) (CCR3)	W6-64	t:A Robinson,Siddons,Kelly,Batchelor,Moss,Mazive,Normington,Hey(3),Robson,Porter g:C Robinson(8)	N/A	750
11/3/18	Oldham (a)	W22-24	t:Marsh,Moss,Donaldson,Batchelor g:C Robinson(4)	7th	703
18/3/18	Swinton (h) (CCR4) ●	W26-12	t:Mazive(2),Cockayne,Spears g:C Robinson(5)	N/A	525
25/3/18	Keighley (h)	W26-12	t:Spears,Normington,Batchelor,Jubb g:C Robinson(5)	5th	1,481
30/3/18	Doncaster (a)	W14-16	t:Ronan Dixon,Jubb g:C Robinson(4)	3rd	906
8/4/18	Newcastle (a)	W16-26	t:Ellis,Batchelor,Mazive,Moss g:C Robinson(5)	3rd	954
15/4/18	London Skolars (h)	W66-6	t:Mazive(3),Ellis,Scott,Moss(2),Smith(2),Oakes,Ronan Dixon g:C Robinson(11)	3rd	916
22/4/18	Catalans Dragons (h) (CCR5)	L22-34	t:Porter(2),Moss,Batchelor g:C Robinson(3)	N/A	3,091
29/4/18	West Wales (h)	W144-0	t:Jackson,Moss(7),C Robinson(2),Hey,Porter,Robson(2),Batchelor,Ronan Dixon(2),Horne(3),Mazive,Smith(2),Kelly,A Robinson g:C Robinson(14),Robson(8)	1st	1,089
6/5/18	Hunslet (a)	W24-26	t:Mazive(2),Dagger,Cockayne g:C Robinson(5)	2nd	729
12/5/18	Coventry (a)	W18-58	t:A Robinson,Jubb,Spears,Hawksworth,Ronan Dixon,Robson,Mazive,Batchelor(2),Hey g:C Robinson(9)	2nd	252
20/5/18	Hemel (h)	W90-0	t:Dagger(2),Robson(3),C Robinson,Marsh(4),Siddons,Kelly(2),Maskill,Spears,Batchelor g:C Robinson(13)	1st	987
27/5/18	Whitehaven (a)	L26-18	t:C Robinson,Horne,A Robinson g:C Robinson(3)	2nd	640
10/6/18	Workington (h)	W40-8	t:Scott,Oakes,Kelly,Batchelor(2),Cockayne,Horne g:C Robinson(6)	2nd	1,399
17/6/18	North Wales (a)	W4-31	t:Robson,Oakes,Cockayne,Hawksworth,Ellis g:C Robinson(5) fg:C Robinson	2nd	408
24/6/18	Keighley (a)	W14-46	t:Spears,Jubb,C Robinson,Batchelor,Horne,Porter,Kelly g:C Robinson(4),Robson(5)	2nd	698
1/7/18	Newcastle (h)	W24-6	t:Robson,Scott,Oakes,Marsh g:Robson(4)	2nd	1,212
8/7/18	Doncaster (h)	W31-16	t:Mazive,Robson,Marsh,Horne,Cockayne g:C Robinson(5) fg:C Robinson	2nd	1,311
14/7/18	London Skolars (a)	W20-22	t:Mazive,C Robinson,Porter,Batchelor g:C Robinson(3)	2nd	258
22/7/18	Bradford (a)	W28-30	t:Johnson,Cockayne,Mazive(2),Batchelor g:C Robinson(5)	2nd	6,441
29/7/18	Coventry (h)	W68-6	t:Jordan-Roberts(2),Ronan Dixon,Horne,C Robinson,Batchelor(4),Kelly,Hey,Robson,Ormondroyd g:C Robinson(8)	2nd	1,104
5/8/18	North Wales (h)	W30-0	t:Scott(2),C Robinson,Mazive,Hey g:C Robinson(5)	2nd	981
11/8/18	West Wales (a)	W0-130	t:Robson(4),Scott,Jubb,Whiteley(3),Chilton(3),Porter,Carter(2),Jordan-Roberts,Cockayne,C Robinson,Edwards,Hawksworth,Batchelor(2) g:C Robinson(21)	2nd	196
19/8/18	Hunslet (h)	W48-6	t:Horne,Oakes(2),Cockayne,Ormondroyd,Marsh,Robson,C Robinson g:C Robinson(8)	1st	1,491
2/9/18	Workington (a)	W14-18	t:Robson,C Robinson,Batchelor g:C Robinson(3)	1st	1,623
9/9/18	Oldham (h)	W10-6	t:Scott,C Robinson g:C Robinson	1st	1,692
16/9/18	Hemel (a)	W6-56	t:Cockayne(3),Spears,C Robinson,Kelly,Carter,Marsh(2),Hey g:C Robinson(8)	1st	175
23/9/18	Whitehaven (h)	W32-14	t:Chilton(2),Scott,Edwards g:C Robinson(8)	1st	3,223

● Played at LD Nutrition Stadium, Featherstone

APP   TRIES   GOALS   FG   PTS

	D.O.B.	ALL	L1	ALL	L1	ALL	L1	ALL	L1	ALL	L1
Joe Batchelor	28/10/94	27	24	23	21	0	0	0	0	92	84
Jake Butler-Fleming	8/1/92	6	5	0	0	0	0	0	0	0	0
Harry Carter	10/2/94	(12)	(11)	3	3	0	0	0	0	12	12
Matt Chilton	27/4/98	5	5	5	5	0	0	0	0	20	20
Ben Cockayne	20/7/83	27	25	11	10	0	0	0	0	44	40
Will Dagger	21/2/99	4	4	3	3	0	0	0	0	12	12
Ronan Dixon	25/7/97	8(10)	8(9)	6	6	0	0	0	0	24	24
Rory Dixon	17/10/97	(2)	(0)	0	0	0	0	0	0	0	0
James Donaldson	14/9/91	(1)	(1)	1	1	0	0	0	0	4	4
Joel Edwards	17/7/88	3(4)	3(4)	2	2	0	0	0	0	8	8
Andy Ellis	15/12/84	19(1)	16(1)	3	3	0	0	0	0	12	12
Dan Hawksworth	30/3/93	8(6)	7(4)	3	3	0	0	0	0	12	12
Brad Hey	4/9/94	25	22	8	5	0	0	0	0	32	20
Graeme Horne	22/3/85	15(8)	14(8)	9	9	0	0	0	0	36	36
Liam Jackson	17/2/95	4(1)	3(1)	1	1	0	0	0	0	4	4
Josh Johnson	25/7/94	5(1)	5(1)	1	1	0	0	0	0	4	4
Josh Jordan-Roberts	26/8/98	8	8	3	3	0	0	0	0	12	12
Will Jubb	17/9/96	8(10)	8(9)	5	5	0	0	0	0	20	20
Mike Kelly	23/5/89	12(2)	11(2)	8	7	0	0	0	0	32	28
Matty Marsh	21/4/95	12	12	10	10	0	0	0	0	40	40
Danny Maskill	28/6/95	2(1)	2(1)	1	1	0	0	0	0	4	4
Judah Mazive	2/1/98	18	15	16	13	0	0	0	0	64	52
Kieren Moss	6/8/93	10	7	14	12	0	0	0	0	56	48
Jake Normington	11/10/91	6(1)	4	2	1	0	0	0	0	8	4
Will Oakes	27/2/99	10	10	6	6	0	0	0	0	24	24
Jack Ormondroyd	7/11/91	1(6)	1(6)	2	2	0	0	0	0	8	8
Joe Porter	26/1/93	2(26)	2(23)	7	4	0	0	0	0	28	16
Adam Robinson	8/4/87	14(9)	12(9)	4	3	0	0	0	0	16	12
Connor Robinson	23/10/94	28	25	13	13	182	166	4	4	420	388
Ash Robson	4/11/95	26	23	17	16	17	17	0	0	102	98
Colton Roche	23/6/93	(5)	(5)	0	0	0	0	0	0	0	0
Tom Saxton	3/10/83	2	2	0	0	0	0	0	0	0	0
Sam Scott	5/6/90	24	22	8	8	0	0	0	0	32	32
Chris Siddons	30/1/92	6(7)	4(6)	2	1	0	0	0	0	8	4
Aaron Smith	12/10/96	1(2)	1(2)	4	4	0	0	0	0	16	16
Tim Spears	27/7/84	24	21	6	5	0	0	0	0	24	20
Jordan Walne	28/12/92	5(1)	5(1)	0	0	0	0	0	0	0	0
Perry Whiteley	22/2/93	2	2	3	3	0	0	0	0	12	12

'L1' totals include League 1 regular season only; 'All' totals also include Challenge Cup

Connor Robinson

LEAGUE RECORD
P26-W24-D0-L2 (1st/Champions)
F1130, A308, Diff+822, 48 points.

CHALLENGE CUP
Round Five

ATTENDANCES
Best - v Bradford (L1 - 4,221)
Worst - v Swinton (CC - 525)
Total (excluding Challenge Cup) - 21,107
Average (excluding Challenge Cup) - 1,624
(Up by 569 on 2017)

CLUB RECORDS	
	Highest score: 144-0 v West Wales, 29/4/2018 **Highest score against:** 0-98 v Rochdale, 8/4/2001
	Record attendance: 14,689 v Swinton, 10/2/34 (Clarence Street); 4,221 v Bradford, 18/2/2018 (Bootham Crescent)
MATCH RECORDS	**Tries:** 7 Brad Davis v Highfield, 17/9/95; Kieren Moss v West Wales, 29/4/2018
	Goals: 21 Connor Robinson v West Wales, 11/8/2018 **Points:** 56 Chris Thorman v Northumbria University, 6/3/2011
SEASON RECORDS	**Tries:** 35 John Crossley 1980-81 **Goals:** 186 (inc 4fg) Connor Robinson 2018 **Points:** 420 Connor Robinson 2018
CAREER RECORDS	**Tries:** 167 Peter Foster 1955-67 **Goals:** 1,060 Vic Yorke 1954-67 **Points:** 2,159 Vic Yorke 1954-67 **Appearances:** 449 Willie Hargreaves 1952-65

299

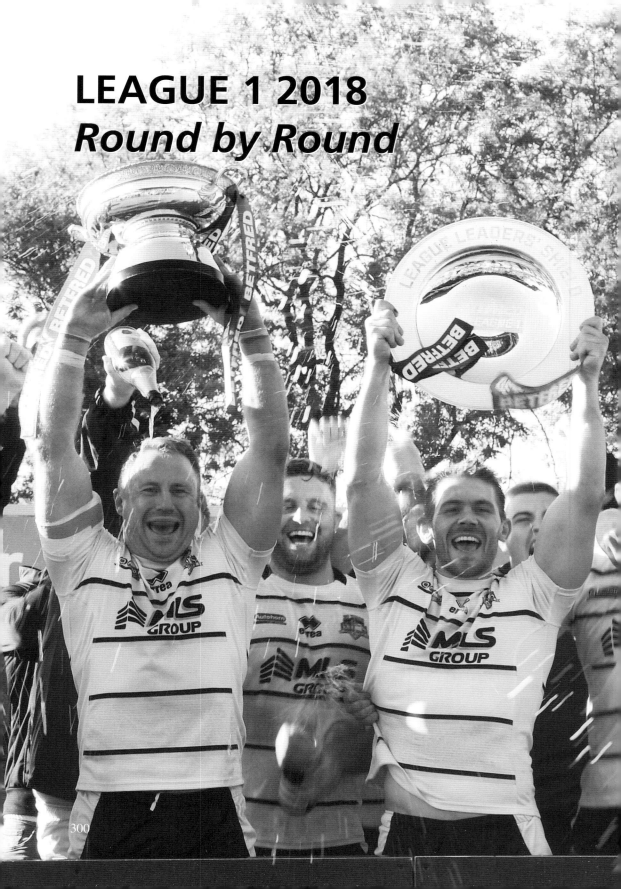

LEAGUE 1 2018
Round by Round

ROUND 1

Sunday 18th February 2018

HEMEL STAGS 14 HUNSLET 28

STAGS: 22 Louis Sheriff; 2 Darren Forde; 3 Kadeem Williams; 4 Chris Heil; 5 Mitch Vincent; 6 Liam Darville; 7 Liam Coe; 10 Wayne Jowett; 9 Jono Burns; 21 James Thornton; 11 Sonny Esslemont; 19 Marcus Stock; 18 Ricky Hough. Subs (all used): 14 Jack Mitchell; 15 Brad Adams; 17 Reece Williams; 8 Corey Hanson.
Tries: K Williams (43), Darville (67, 73);
Goals: Vincent 0/1, Coe 1/2.
Sin bin: K Williams (50) - high tackle.
HUNSLET: 1 Jimmy Watson; 2 David Foggin-Johnston; 4 Mufaro Mvududu; 23 Tom Ashton; 5 Joel Gibson; 18 Harry Tyson-Wilson; 7 Cain Southernwood; 10 Lewis Reed; 9 Jack Lee; 13 Matt Nicholson; 12 Duane Straugheir; 15 Brad Foster; 11 Liam Mackay. Subs (all used): 14 George Flanagan; 16 Ryan Mallinder; 25 Sam Crowther; 27 Dean Roberts.
Tries: Foggin-Johnston (4), Gibson (11), Flanagan (57), Straugheir (60), Lee (78); **Goals:** Southernwood 4/5.
Sin bin: Watson (64) - punching.
Rugby Leaguer & League Express Men of the Match: *Stags:* Liam Darville; *Hunslet:* Cain Southernwood.
Penalty count: 8-13; **Half-time:** 0-10;
Referee: Michael Mannifield; **Attendance:** 220.

NORTH WALES CRUSADERS 24 LONDON SKOLARS 24

CRUSADERS: 1 Tommy Johnson; 24 Gavin Conroy; 20 Alex Thompson; 12 Simon Atherton; 5 Dale Bloomfield; 6 Steve Roper; 7 Ryan Smith; 10 Warren Thompson; 9 Lee Hudson; 16 Alex Davidson; 11 Jack Houghton; 25 Jordan Case; 13 Ryan Millington. Subs (all used): 14 James Dandy; 15 Joe Bate; 8 Jonny Walker; - Luke Warburton.
Tries: A Thompson (25), Conroy (35), Bloomfield (37), Smith (55); **Goals:** Johnson 4/4.
SKOLARS: 1 Elliot Hall; 22 Sam Nash; 3 Michael Brown; 4 Api Pewhairangi; 5 Lameck Juma; 6 Jy-mel Coleman; 7 Mike Bishay; 8 Louis Robinson; 16 Charlie Lawrence; 10 Lamont Bryan; 11 Omari Caro; 12 Eddie Mbaraga; 13 Ryan Chester. Subs (all used): 9 Neil Thorman; 17 Rob Butler; 19 Michael Sykes; 14 Ollie Purslow.
Tries: Caro (19), Bryan (29), Butler (49), Hall (61);
Goals: C Lawrence 1/1, Jy-mel Coleman 3/4.
Sin bin: Bishay (18) - professional foul.
Rugby Leaguer & League Express Men of the Match: *Crusaders:* Ryan Millington; *Skolars:* Omari Caro.
Penalty count: 13-8; **Half-time:** 18-12;
Referee: Liam Staveley; **Attendance:** 306.

DONCASTER 70 COVENTRY BEARS 10

DONCASTER: 1 Richard Owen; 5 Sam Doherty; 19 Connor Bower; 4 Jason Tali; 2 Aaron Jones-Bishop; 17 Jack Miller; 7 Liam Harris; 10 Ryan Boyle; 9 Kyle Kesik; 14 Connor Scott; 11 Brad England; 18 Charlie Martin; 13 Jordie Hedges. Subs (all used): 8 Russ Spiers; 15 Kieran Cross; 16 Zac Braham; 31 Hakim Miloudi.
Tries: Tali (7, 52), England (11), Spiers (30, 36), Harris (34, 77), Braham (49), Miloudi (61, 66, 72, 80);
Goals: Miller 3/3, Miloudi 8/9.
BEARS: 1 Harry Chapman; 2 Hayden Freeman; 3 Dante Morley-Samuels; 4 Charles Clarke; 5 Errol Carter; 6 Paul Emanuelli; 7 Ben Stead; 8 James Geurtjens; 9 Lewis Lord; 10 Joel Thomas; 11 Kieran Sherratt; 12 Chris Barratt; 13 Chris Vitalini. Subs (all used): 14 Richard Hughes; 24 Jason Bass; 19 Alex Beddows; 18 Dan Gover.
Tries: Freeman (5), Lord (27);
Goals: Emanuelli 0/1, Stead 1/1.
Rugby Leaguer & League Express Men of the Match: *Doncaster:* Hakim Miloudi; *Bears:* Lewis Lord.
Penalty count: 11-12; **Half-time:** 30-10;
Referee: Billy Pearson; **Attendance:** 787.

KEIGHLEY COUGARS 44 WORKINGTON TOWN 34

COUGARS: 1 Ritchie Hawkyard; 28 Harry Aaronson; 3 Hamish Barnes; 4 Adam Ryder; 2 Andy Gabriel; 23 Benn Hardcastle; 7 Matty Beharrell; 27 Samir Tahraoui; 9 Nathan Conroy; 19 Matthew Bailey; 11 Josh Lynam; 12 Brendon Rawlins; 13 Mike Emmett. Subs (all used): 8 Scott Law; 15 Ryan Wright; 16 Harvey Hallas; 29 Brad Nicholson.
Tries: Aaronson (6), Bailey (9), Lynam (24), Beharrell (36), Gabriel (40, 80), Hardcastle (68);
Goals: Hardcastle 8/8.
TOWN: 7 Jamie Foster; 5 Joe Hambley; 4 Scott Akehurst; 3 Perry Singleton; 2 Sam Forrester; 24 Scott Leatherbarrow; - Carl Forber; 8 Oliver Wilkes; 20 Sean Penkywicz; 10 Stevie Scholey; 18 Gordon Maudling; 12 Kurt Maudling; 14 Ryan Bailey. Subs (all used): 9 James Newton; 19 Andrew Dawson; 13 Joe Ryan; 22 Caine Barnes.
Tries: G Maudling (2), Forber (17), K Maudling (30, 52), Hambley (46), Penkywicz (75);
Goals: Forber 0/1, Foster 5/5.
Rugby Leaguer & League Express Men of the Match: *Cougars:* Benn Hardcastle; *Town:* Gordon Maudling.
Penalty count: 7-6; **Half-time:** 30-16;
Referee: Marcus Griffiths; **Attendance:** 707.

WHITEHAVEN 0 OLDHAM 14

WHITEHAVEN: 1 Jordan Burns; 5 Dave Thompson; 3 Chris Taylor; 11 Connor Holliday; 23 Jason Mossop; 17 Brad Billsborough; 7 Callum Phillips; 16 Kris Coward; 14 Dan Abram; 8 Marc Shackley; 18 Ellis Gillam; 20 Lewis Reece; 10 Carl Forster. Subs (all used, only three named): 9 James Tilley; 28 Levy Nzoungou; 6 Dion Aiye.
Sin bin: Aiye (70) - persistent team offences.
OLDHAM: 5 Steven Nield; 2 Dave Eccleston; 4 Jack Holmes; 3 Matt Reid; 1 Kyran Johnson; 6 Paul Crook; 7 Dave Hewitt; 8 Phil Joy; 20 Matt Wilkinson; 10 Adam Neal; 25 Danny Bridge; 12 Danny Langtree; 16 Ryan Lannon. Subs (all used): 21 Kenny Hughes; 23 Luke Nelmes; 13 Jack Spencer; 19 Adam Jones.
Try: Wilkinson (23); **Goals:** Crook 5/6.
Sin bin: Eccleston (8) - holding down.
Rugby Leaguer & League Express Men of the Match: *Whitehaven:* Jordan Burns; *Oldham:* Paul Crook.
Penalty count: 9-16; **Half-time:** 0-6;
Referee: Brandon Robinson; **Attendance:** 785.

YORK CITY KNIGHTS 20 BRADFORD BULLS 22

CITY KNIGHTS: 1 Ash Robson; 2 Ben Cockayne; - Will Oakes; 4 Brad Hey; - Kieren Moss; 6 Connor Robinson; - Matty Marsh; 8 Adam Robinson; 9 Andy Ellis; 10 Graeme Horne; 11 Joe Batchelor; 12 Sam Scott; 13 Tim Spears. Subs (all used): 20 Will Jubb; 15 Chris Siddons; 16 Ronan Dixon; 17 Joe Porter.
Tries: Moss (3), Batchelor (51, 65); **Goals:** C Robinson 3/4;
Field goals: C Robinson (69, 78).
BULLS: 14 Gregg McNally; 5 Dalton Grant; 3 Ashley Gibson; 1 Lee Smith; 2 Ethan Ryan; 6 Joe Keyes; 12 Elliot Minchella; 10 Steve Crossley; 9 Sam Hallas; 8 Liam Kirk; 11 Matt Garside; 18 Liam Johnson; 13 George Milton. Subs (all used): 17 Ross Peltier; 26 Vila Halafihi; 19 Mikey Wood; 24 Brandon Pickersgill.
Tries: Gibson (18), Minchella (37), Crossley (48);
Goals: Keyes 5/6.
Rugby Leaguer & League Express Men of the Match: *City Knights:* Connor Robinson; *Bulls:* Steve Crossley.
Penalty count: 6-6; **Half-time:** 8-10;
Referee: Matt Rossleigh; **Attendance:** 4,221.

ROUND 3

Saturday 10th March 2018

LONDON SKOLARS 16 NEWCASTLE THUNDER 60

SKOLARS: 1 Craig Mullen; 2 Sam Nash; 3 Jake Melling; 4 Lameck Juma; 5 Elliot Hall; 6 Charlie Lawrence; 7 Neil Thorman; 20 Callum Field; 14 Josh Ganson; 18 Lamont Bryan; 12 Omari Caro; - Jordan Williams; 13 Ryan Chester. Subs (all used): 9 Billy Driver; 10 Michael Sykes; - Louis Robinson; - Eddie Mbaraga.
Tries: Field (20), Mullen (23), Driver (72);
Goals: Thorman 2/3.
Sin bin: Juma (34) - fighting; Caro (37) - tripping.
THUNDER: 1 Theerapol Ritson; 5 Mo Agoro; 4 Joe Brown; 33 Tuoyo Egodo; 2 Ali Blair; 6 Lewis Young; 16 Tom Shaw; 13 Jack Aldous; 9 Evan Simons; 14 Vincent Rennie; 26 Ryan Lloyd; 12 Aaron Ollett; 8 Liam McAvoy. Subs (all used): 11 Harry Aldous; 20 Conor Fitzsimmons; 21 Ben Pointer; 24 Ben Calland.
Tries: McAvoy (13), Young (30, 39), Egodo (35), Agoro (42), Shaw (47), Ritson (55), Pointer (60), Ollett (62), Lloyd (78); **Goals:** Shaw 10/10.
Sin bin: Simons (34) - fighting.
Rugby Leaguer & League Express Men of the Match: *Skolars:* Billy Driver; *Thunder:* Lewis Young.
Penalty count: 5-10; **Half-time:** 12-24;
Referee: Andrew Sweet; **Attendance:** 273.

Sunday 11th March 2018

HEMEL STAGS 16 COVENTRY BEARS 22

STAGS: 22 Louis Sheriff; 2 Darren Forde; 13 Braden Hunter; 4 Chris Heil; 5 Jordan Fitzpatrick-Parry; 6 Liam Darville; 7 Kieran Smith; 10 Wayne Jowett; 18 Ricky Hough; 16 Lewis Taylor; 3 Kadeem Williams; 21 James Thornton; 11 Sonny Esslemont. Subs (all used): 14 Jack Mitchell; 19 Marcus Stock; 17 Reece Williams; 8 Corey Hanson.
Tries: Stock (44), Hunter (75), Heil (77);
Goals: Hunter 1/1, Hough 1/2.
BEARS: 1 Harry Chapman; 2 Hayden Freeman; 3 Dante Morley-Samuels; 4 Jason Bass; 5 Errol Carter; 6 Liam Rice-Wilson; 7 Ben Stead; 8 James Geurtjens; 9 Zak Williams; 10 John Aldred; 11 Kieran Sherratt; 12 Chris Barratt; 13 Chris Vitalini. Subs (all used): 14 James Mason; 15 Ben Gray; 16 Dan Gover; 17 Alex Beddows.
Tries: Carter (1, 19), Morley-Samuels (10), Beddows (70);
Goals: Stead 3/4.
Rugby Leaguer & League Express Men of the Match: *Stags:* Liam Darville; *Bears:* Errol Carter.
Penalty count: 7-6; **Half-time:** 0-16;
Referee: Craig Field; **Attendance:** 110.

DONCASTER 44 WHITEHAVEN 6

DONCASTER: 1 Richard Owen; 5 Sam Doherty; 19 Connor Bower; 4 Jason Tali; 24 Jack Sanderson; 6 Jordan Howden; 7 Liam Harris; 10 Ryan Boyle; 15 Kieran Cross; 14 Connor Scott; 30 Jack Downs; 18 Charlie Martin; 26 Brandan Wilkinson. Subs (all used): 8 Russ Spiers; 21 Jez Litten; 16 Zac Braham; 13 Jordie Hedges.
Tries: Howden (10, 75), Harris (29), Sanderson (40, 70), Doherty (43), Bower (51, 57), Litten (63);
Goals: Harris 4/6, Sanderson 0/2, Howden 0/2.
Sin bin: Owen (7) - trip on Burns.
WHITEHAVEN: 14 Dan Abram; 1 Jordan Burns; 23 Jason Mossop; 3 Chris Taylor; 5 Dave Thompson; 7 Callum Phillips; 17 Brad Billsborough; 8 Marc Shackley; 22 Stuart Howarth; 16 Kris Coward; 18 Ellis Gillam; 6 Dion Aiye; 10 Carl Forster. Subs (all used): 27 Liam Cooper; 11 Connor Holliday; 28 Levy Nzoungou; 9 James Tilley.
Try: Tilley (35); **Goals:** Billsborough 1/2.
Sin bin: Tilley (37) - shoulder charge.
Rugby Leaguer & League Express Men of the Match: *Doncaster:* Liam Harris; *Whitehaven:* Dan Abram.
Penalty count: 13-10; **Half-time:** 20-6;
Referee: Liam Staveley; **Attendance:** 782.

HUNSLET 26 NORTH WALES CRUSADERS 10

HUNSLET: 1 Jimmy Watson; 2 David Foggin-Johnston; 23 Tom Ashton; 30 Nathan Chappell; 5 Joel Gibson; 6 Joe Sanderson; 26 Shaun Roberts; 13 Matt Nicholson; 9 Jack Lee; 10 Lewis Reed; 16 Ryan Mallinder; 12 Duane Straugheir; 11 Liam Mackay. Subs (all used): 29 Jake Barnett; 8 Michael Haley; 17 Nyle Flynn; 21 Jack Walton.
Tries: Lee (2, 71), Sanderson (21), Gibson (29), Ashton (73);
Goals: Sanderson 3/6.
CRUSADERS: 1 Tommy Johnson; 24 Gavin Conroy; 12 Simon Atherton; 17 Kenny Baker; 5 Dale Bloomfield; 6 Steve Roper; 7 Ryan Smith; 8 Jonny Walker; 9 Lee Hudson; 16 Alex Davidson; 11 Jack Houghton; 25 Jordan Case; 13 Ryan Millington. Subs (all used): 19 Aaron Moore; 22 Brad Brennan; - Stanton Albert; - Brad Walker.
Tries: Atherton (42), Bloomfield (75); **Goals:** Johnson 1/2.
Sin bin: Atherton (27) - kicking the ball away.
Rugby Leaguer & League Express Men of the Match: *Hunslet:* Jack Lee; *Crusaders:* Brad Brennan.
Penalty count: 13-13; **Half-time:** 16-0;
Referee: Michael Mannifield; **Attendance:** 465.

KEIGHLEY COUGARS 6 BRADFORD BULLS 54

COUGARS: 1 Ritchie Hawkyard; 28 Harry Aaronson; 3 Hamish Barnes; 4 Adam Ryder; 2 Andy Gabriel; 23 Benn Hardcastle; 7 Matty Beharrell; 8 Scott Law; 14 Joe Lumb; 19 Matthew Bailey; 29 Brad Nicholson; 18 Josh Tonks; 13 Mike Emmett. Subs (all used): 9 Nathan Conroy; 12 Brendon Rawlins; 16 Harvey Hallas; 27 Samir Tahraoui.
Try: Nicholson (55); **Goals:** Hardcastle 1/1.
Sin bin: Beharrell (4) - dangerous challenge on Minchella.
BULLS: 14 Gregg McNally; 5 Dalton Grant; 3 Ashley Gibson; 1 Lee Smith; 2 Ethan Ryan; 6 Joe Keyes; 24 Brandon Pickersgill; 10 Steve Crossley; 9 Sam Hallas; 15 Callum Bustin; 11 Matt Garside; 12 Elliot Minchella; 13 George Milton. Subs (all used): 7 Dane Chisholm; 17 Ross Peltier; 19 Mikey Wood; 21 George Flanagan.
Tries: Minchella (13, 60), Peltier (27), Flanagan (30, 63), Keyes (43), Grant (48), Hallas (69), Ryan (80);
Goals: Keyes 9/10.
Rugby Leaguer & League Express Men of the Match: *Cougars:* Samir Tahraoui; *Bulls:* Joe Keyes.
Penalty count: 10-11; **Half-time:** 0-18;
Referee: Billy Pearson; **Attendance:** 2,912.

OLDHAM 22 YORK CITY KNIGHTS 24

OLDHAM: 1 Kyran Johnson; 2 Dave Eccleston; 4 Jack Holmes; 3 Matt Reid; 30 Ben West; 6 Paul Crook; 7 Dave Hewitt; 8 Phil Joy; 21 Kenny Hughes; 10 Adam Neal; 12 Danny Langtree; 25 Danny Bridge; 28 Ryan Lannon. Subs (all used): 20 Matt Wilkinson; 23 Luke Nelmes; 13 Jack Spencer; 24 Liam Bent.
Tries: Reid (29, 54), Langtree (43), West (63);
Goals: Crook 3/4.

CITY KNIGHTS: 28 Kieren Moss; 1 Ash Robson; 11 Joe Batchelor; 4 Brad Hey; 2 Ben Cockayne; 6 Connor Robinson; 29 Matty Marsh; 8 Adam Robinson; 9 Andy Ellis; 15 Chris Siddons; 10 Graeme Horne; 12 Sam Scott; 13 Tim Spears. Subs (all used): - James Donaldson; 30 Colton Roche; 17 Joe Porter; 20 Will Jubb.
Tries: Marsh (11), Moss (37), Donaldson (52), Batchelor (60); **Goals:** C Robinson 4/4.
Rugby Leaguer & League Express Men of the Match: *Oldham:* Dave Hewitt; *City Knights:* James Donaldson.
Penalty count: 9-4; **Half-time:** 6-12;
Referee: Marcus Griffiths; **Attendance:** 703.

WORKINGTON TOWN 74 WEST WALES RAIDERS 6

TOWN: 1 Jordan Tansey; 2 Sam Forrester; 7 Jamie Foster; 4 Scott Akehurst; 5 Joe Hambley; 6 Jamie Doran; 24 Scott Leatherbarrow; 8 Oliver Wilkes; 9 James Newton; 10 Stevie Scholey; 18 Gordon Maudling; 3 Perry Singleton; 14 Ryan Bailey. Subs (all used): 12 Kurt Maudling; 13 Joe Ryan; 21 Jake Moore; 22 Caine Barnes.
Tries: Forrester (2, 3, 26, 37, 52), G Maudling (7), Hambley (9), Ryan Bailey (12), Singleton (23, 67), Akehurst (43, 62), Barnes (57), Ryan (73);
Goals: Foster 9/14.
RAIDERS: 25 James Smith; 26 Louis Ford; 3 Kurtis Haile; 16 Shaun Tennant; 1 Rowland Kaye; 23 Karlin Claridge; 21 Steve Parry; 14 Dalton Desmond-Walker; 15 Macauley Harris; 17 Harry Boots; 20 Archie Snook; 24 Ellis Simon; 10 Morgan Evans. Subs (used, only one named): 19 Taine Hendy.
Try: Parry (16); **Goals:** Tennant 1/1.
Rugby Leaguer & League Express Men of the Match: *Town:* Sam Forrester; *Raiders:* Morgan Evans.
Penalty count: 5-7; **Half-time:** 44-6;
Referee: Brandon Robinson; **Attendance:** 614.

ROUND 4

Saturday 24th March 2018

LONDON SKOLARS 26 WORKINGTON TOWN 42

SKOLARS: 1 Elliot Hall; 2 Vinny Finigan; 3 Michael Brown; 4 Lameck Juma; 5 Jake Ogden; 6 Jy-mel Coleman; 7 Neil Thorman; 8 Sadiq Adebiyi; 25 Charlie Lawrence; 10 Will Martin; 11 Sam Nash; 12 Lamont Bryan; 13 Ryan Chester. Subs (all used): 9 Phil Lyon; 16 Louis Robinson; 18 Mike Greenhalgh; 22 Quinn Ngawati.
Tries: Jy-mel Coleman (20), Hall (25), C Lawrence (33, 47), Finigan (44); **Goals:** Thorman 3/5.
TOWN: 1 Jordan Tansey; 5 Joe Hambley; 18 Elliott Miller; 7 Jamie Foster; 2 Sam Forrester; 6 Jamie Doran; - Carl Forber; 14 Ryan Bailey; 9 James Newton; 10 Stevie Scholey; 11 Larne Patrick; 12 Kurt Maudling; 13 Joe Ryan. Subs (all used): 8 Oliver Wilkes; 20 Sean Penkywicz; 21 Jake Moore; 19 Andrew Dawson.
Tries: Doran (2, 53), Penkywicz (27), Forrester (40, 57), K Maudling (66), Newton (68);
Goals: Foster 3/3, Tansey 4/4.
Sin bin: Scholey (23) - dangerous challenge.
Rugby Leaguer & League Express Men of the Match: *Skolars:* Charlie Lawrence; *Town:* Jamie Doran.
Penalty count: 5-14; **Half-time:** 16-18;
Referee: Michael Mannifield; **Attendance:** 328.

Sunday 25th March 2018

NEWCASTLE THUNDER 20 DONCASTER 22

THUNDER: 1 Theerapol Ritson; 5 Mo Agoro; 4 Joe Brown; 33 Tuoyo Egodo; 22 Tom Capper; 6 Lewis Young; 16 Tom Shaw; 8 Liam McAvoy; 9 Evan Simons; 14 Vincent Rennie; 15 Sam Luckley; 12 Aaron Ollett; 13 Jack Aldous. Subs (all used): 10 Rhys Clarke; 11 Harry Aldous; 20 Conor Fitzsimmons; 21 Ben Pointer.
Tries: Simons (29), Clarke (47), Fitzsimmons (78);
Goals: Shaw 4/4.
DONCASTER: 30 Hakim Miloudi; 5 Sam Doherty; 19 Connor Bower; 3 Liam Welham; 31 Jack Logan; 13 Jordie Hedges; 7 Liam Harris; 8 Russ Spiers; 9 Kyle Kesik; 14 Connor Scott; 11 Brad England; 18 Charlie Martin; 26 Brandan Wilkinson. Subs (all used): 16 Zac Braham; 12 Jason Muranka; 33 Jack Downs; 21 Jez Litten.
Tries: Martin (1), Downs (23), Doherty (65), Miloudi (68);
Goals: Harris 0/1, Miloudi 3/3.
Rugby Leaguer & League Express Men of the Match: *Thunder:* Lewis Young; *Doncaster:* Charlie Martin.
Penalty count: 11-8; **Half-time:** 6-10;
Referee: Billy Pearson; **Attendance:** 818.

NORTH WALES CRUSADERS 2 OLDHAM 30

CRUSADERS: 1 Tommy Johnson; 24 Gavin Conroy; 12 Simon Atherton; 17 Kenny Baker; 5 Dale Bloomfield; 6 Steve Roper; 29 Billy Sheen; 8 Jonny Walker; 9 Lee Hudson; - Macgraff Leuluai; 11 Jack Houghton; 16 Alex Davidson; 25 Jordan Case. Subs (all used): 19 Aaron Moore; 22 Brad Brennan; - Stanton Albert; 26 Alex Trumper.
Goals: Johnson 1/1.
OLDHAM: 27 Joe Martin; 2 Dave Eccleston; 4 Jack Holmes; 29 Zack McComb; 30 Ben West; 6 Paul Crook; 7 Dave Hewitt; 8 Phil Joy; 20 Matt Wilkinson; 28 Levy Nzoungou; 25 Danny Bridge; 12 Danny Langtree; 24 Liam Bent. Subs (all used): 21 Kenny Hughes; 13 Jack Spencer; 23 Luke Nelmes; 11 Craig Briscoe.
Tries: McComb (21), Martin (36, 77), Bridge (56, 65), Joy (71);
Goals: Crook 3/6.
Rugby Leaguer & League Express Men of the Match: *Crusaders:* Kenny Baker; *Oldham:* Danny Bridge.
Penalty count: 5-10; **Half-time:** 2-8;
Referee: Andrew Sweet; **Attendance:** 449.

BRADFORD BULLS 32 HUNSLET 12

BULLS: 14 Gregg McNally; 2 Ethan Ryan; 23 Jake Butler-Fleming; 3 Ashley Gibson; 5 Dalton Grant; 6 Joe Keyes; 7 Dane Chisholm; 15 Callum Bustin; 9 Sam Hallas; 10 Steve Crossley; 11 Matt Garside; 12 Elliot Minchella; 13 George Milton. Subs (all used): 21 George Flanagan; 19 Mikey Wood; 17 Ross Peltier; 18 Liam Johnson.
Tries: Hallas (11, 17), Grant (28, 45, 68), Chisholm (53);
Goals: Keyes 4/7.
HUNSLET: 1 Jimmy Watson; 2 David Foggin-Johnston; 23 Tom Ashton; 30 Nathan Chappell; 5 Joel Gibson; 6 Joe Sanderson; 7 Cain Southernwood; 38 Jack Blagbrough; 9 Jack Lee; 13 Matt Nicholson; 39 Josh Jordan-Roberts; 12 Duane Straugheir; 11 Liam Mackay. Subs (all used): 8 Michael Haley; 10 Lewis Reed; 29 Jake Barnett; 27 Dean Roberts.
Tries: Gibson (7), D Roberts (63); **Goals:** Sanderson 2/2.
Rugby Leaguer & League Express Men of the Match: *Bulls:* Steve Crossley; *Hunslet:* Jimmy Watson.
Penalty count: 8-5; **Half-time:** 16-6;
Referee: Brandon Robinson; **Attendance:** 3,688.

WHITEHAVEN 30 HEMEL STAGS 6

WHITEHAVEN: 14 Dan Abram; 5 Dave Thompson; 23 Jason Mossop; 4 Jessie Joe Parker; 25 Jake Bradley; 6 Dion Aiye; 7 Callum Phillips; 19 Lewis Brown; 9 James Tilley; 8 Marc Shackley; 18 Ellis Gillam; 27 Liam Cooper; 22 Stuart Howarth. Subs (all used): 16 Kris Coward; 17 Brad Billsborough; 20 Lewis Reece; 11 Connor Holliday.
Tries: Brown (5), Parker (18), Billsborough (32), Bradley (57), Abram (76); **Goals:** Abram 5/5.
STAGS: 22 Louis Sheriff; 2 Marcus Elliott; 13 Braden Hunter; 4 Chris Heil; 5 Jordan Fitzpatrick-Parry; 14 Jack Mitchell; 7 Kieran Smith; 21 James Thornton; 18 Ricky Hough; 17 Reece Williams; 3 Kadeem Williams; 11 Sonny Esslemont; 19 Marcus Stock. Subs (all used): 9 Jono Burns; 15 Brad Adams; 16 Lewis Taylor; 10 Wayne Jowett.
Try: J Burns (75); **Goals:** Hunter 1/1.
Rugby Leaguer & League Express Men of the Match: *Whitehaven:* Dan Abram; *Stags:* Wayne Jowett.
Penalty count: 10-8; **Half-time:** 18-0;
Referee: Jon Roberts; **Attendance:** 438.

YORK CITY KNIGHTS 26 KEIGHLEY COUGARS 12

CITY KNIGHTS: 1 Ash Robson; 5 Judah Mazive; 22 Jake Normington; 4 Brad Hey; 28 Kieren Moss; 2 Ben Cockayne; 6 Connor Robinson; 10 Graeme Horne; 20 Will Jubb; - Josh Johnson; 11 Joe Batchelor; 12 Sam Scott; 13 Tim Spears. Subs (all used): 8 Adam Robinson; 15 Chris Siddons; - Colton Roche; 27 Liam Jackson.
Tries: Spears (7), Normington (26), Batchelor (42), Jubb (53); **Goals:** C Robinson 5/6.
COUGARS: 1 Ritchie Hawkyard; 28 Harry Aaronson; 3 Hamish Barnes; 4 Adam Ryder; 2 Andy Gabriel; 23 Benn Hardcastle; 20 Lewis Fairhurst; 31 Jose Kenga; 15 Ryan Wright; 19 Matthew Bailey; 24 Perry Whiteley; 18 Josh Tonks; 13 Mike Emmett. Subs (all used): 8 Scott Law; 11 Josh Lynam; 27 Samir Tahraoui; 30 Billy Gaylor.
Tries: Whiteley (17), Barnes (63); **Goals:** Hardcastle 2/2.
Rugby Leaguer & League Express Men of the Match: *City Knights:* Graeme Horne; *Cougars:* Benn Hardcastle.
Penalty count: 11-8; **Half-time:** 12-6;
Referee: Tom Grant; **Attendance:** 1,481.

ROUND 5

Friday 30th March 2018

HEMEL STAGS 12 LONDON SKOLARS 18

STAGS: 22 Louis Sheriff; 2 Marcus Elliott; 13 Braden Hunter; 4 Chris Heil; 5 Jordan Fitzpatrick-Parry; 14 Jack Mitchell; 7 Kieran Smith; 21 James Thornton; 18 Ricky Hough; 16 Lewis Taylor; 3 Kadeem Williams; 11 Sonny Esslemont; 19 Marcus Stock. Subs (all used): 9 Jono Burns; 15 Brad Adams; - Santino Decaro; 10 Wayne Jowett.
Tries: Fitzpatrick-Parry (15), J Burns (79); **Goals:** Hunter 2/2.
Sin bin: Heil (67) - dissent.
SKOLARS: 1 Elliot Hall; 5 Jake Ogden; 4 Jake Melling; 3 Michael Brown; 2 Vinny Finigan; 6 Jy-mel Coleman; 7 Neil Thorman; 8 Will Martin; 25 Charlie Lawrence; 10 Lamont Bryan; 11 Quinn Ngawati; 22 Sam Nash; 13 Ryan Chester. Subs (all used): 9 Billy Driver; 16 Louis Robinson; 14 Eddie Mbaraga; 17 Omari Caro.
Tries: Jy-mel Coleman (23), Mbaraga (55);
Goals: Thorman 5/5.
Rugby Leaguer & League Express Men of the Match: *Stags:* Lewis Taylor; *Skolars:* Neil Thorman.
Penalty count: 7-12; **Half-time:** 6-10;
Referee: Cameron Worsley; **Attendance:** 155.

HUNSLET 22 KEIGHLEY COUGARS 38

HUNSLET: 1 Jimmy Watson; 2 David Foggin-Johnston; 4 Mufaro Mvududu; 30 Nathan Chappell; 23 Tom Ashton; 6 Joe Sanderson; 7 Cain Southernwood; 38 Jack Blagbrough; 9 Jack Lee; 13 Matt Nicholson; 39 Josh Jordan-Roberts; 12 Duane Straugheir; 11 Liam Mackay. Subs (all used): 8 Michael Haley; 10 Lewis Reed; 27 Dean Roberts; 29 Jake Barnett.
Tries: Sanderson (5), Chappell (9), Watson (45), Reed (56);
Goals: Sanderson 3/4.
COUGARS: 1 Ritchie Hawkyard; 28 Harry Aaronson; 17 Perry Whiteley; 4 Adam Ryder; 2 Andy Gabriel; 23 Benn Hardcastle; 20 Lewis Fairhurst; 12 Brendon Rawlins; 15 Ryan Wright; 19 Matthew Bailey; 11 Josh Lynam; 18 Josh Tonks; 13 Mike Emmett. Subs (all used): 9 Nathan Conroy; 29 Brad Nicholson; 8 Scott Law; 31 Jose Kenga.
Tries: Fairhurst (14), Wright (24), Conroy (31, 46), Nicholson (39), Ryder (60); **Goals:** Hardcastle 7/7.
Rugby Leaguer & League Express Men of the Match: *Hunslet:* Jimmy Watson; *Cougars:* Benn Hardcastle.
Penalty count: 7-7; **Half-time:** 12-24;
Referee: Andrew Sweet; **Attendance:** 471.

WEST WALES RAIDERS 6
NORTH WALES CRUSADERS 54

RAIDERS: 3 Kurtis Haile; 26 Louis Ford; 16 Shaun Tennant; 5 Dan Fox; 25 James Smith; 19 Fraser Stroud; 21 Steve Parry; 12 Harrison Elliott; 9 Connor Farrer; 17 Harry Boots; 20 Archie Snook; 18 Craig Lewis; 8 Connor Parker. Subs (all used): 14 Dalton Desmond-Walker; 15 Dean Higgs; 11 Ross Price; 29 Ellis Simon.
Try: Farrer (27); **Goals:** Stroud 1/1.
CRUSADERS: 1 Tommy Johnson; 24 Gavin Conroy; 12 Simon Atherton; 2 Dan Price; 5 Dale Bloomfield; 6 Steve Roper; 7 Ryan Smith; 16 Alex Davidson; 9 Lee Hudson; - Stanton Albert; 11 Jack Houghton; 14 James Dandy; 25 Jordan Case. Subs (all used): 19 Aaron Moore; 15 Joe Bate; 22 Brad Brennan; - Dan Norman.
Tries: Bloomfield (8, 65), Houghton (15, 53), Hudson (20), Moore (40), Atherton (44), Dandy (48), Price (73), Davidson (78); **Goals:** Johnson 7/10.
Rugby Leaguer & League Express Men of the Match: *Raiders:* Steve Parry; *Crusaders:* Tommy Johnson.
Penalty count: 9-9; **Half-time:** 6-22;
Referee: Steve Race; **Attendance:** 306.

COVENTRY BEARS 18 NEWCASTLE THUNDER 32

BEARS: 1 Jason Bass; 2 Hayden Freeman; 3 Kameron Pearce-Paul; 4 Dante Morley-Samuels; 5 Jamahl Hunte; 6 Paul Emanuelli; 7 Ben Stead; 8 James Geurtjens; 9 Zak Williams; 10 Dan Gover; 11 Kieran Sherratt; 12 James Mason; 13 Chris Vitalini. Subs (all used): 14 Liam Rice-Wilson; 19 Joel Thomas; 16 Malikhi Lloyd-Jones; 17 Errol Carter.
Tries: Mason (48), Carter (56), Stead (78);
Goals: Stead 3/3.
Sin bin: Vitalini (70) - fighting.
THUNDER: 1 Theerapol Ritson; 2 Ali Blair; 33 Tuoyo Egodo; 4 Joe Brown; 5 Mo Agoro; 6 Lewis Young; 16 Tom Shaw; 8 Liam McAvoy; 9 Evan Simons; 14 Vincent Rennie; 15 Sam Luckley; 12 Aaron Ollett; 13 Jack Aldous. Subs (all used): 10 Rhys Clarke; 11 Harry Aldous; 20 Conor Fitzsimmons; 21 Ben Pointer.
Tries: Ritson (7, 13, 75), Young (36), Ollett (49);
Goals: Shaw 6/6.
Sin bin: J Aldous (70) - fighting.
Rugby Leaguer & League Express Men of the Match: *Bears:* Ben Stead; *Thunder:* Theerapol Ritson.
Penalty count: 11-7; **Half-time:** 0-18;
Referee: Brandon Robinson; **Attendance:** 343.

DONCASTER 14 YORK CITY KNIGHTS 16

DONCASTER: 1 Richard Owen; 5 Sam Doherty; 19 Connor Bower; 4 Jason Tali; 24 Jack Sanderson; 13 Jordie Hedges; 7 Liam Harris; 8 Russ Spiers; 9 Kyle Kesik; 14 Connor Scott; 11 Brad England; 30 Jack Downs; 26 Brandan Wilkinson. Subs (all used): 16 Zac Braham; 12 Jason Muranka; 15 Kieran Cross; 33 Cameron Scott.
Tries: Cross (23), Cameron Scott (74); **Goals:** Harris 3/3.
Sin bin: Hedges (12) - fighting.

CITY KNIGHTS: 30 Kieren Moss; 25 Tom Saxton; 22 Jake Normington; 11 Joe Batchelor; 5 Judah Mazive; 2 Ben Cockayne; 6 Connor Robinson; 8 Adam Robinson; 9 Andy Ellis; 10 Graeme Horne; 20 Will Jubb; 12 Sam Scott; 13 Tim Spears. Subs (all used): 29 Aaron Smith; 15 Chris Siddons; 16 Ronan Dixon; 17 Joe Porter.
Tries: Ronan Dixon (29), Jubb (55); **Goals:** C Robinson 4/4.
Sin bin: A Robinson (12) - fighting; Scott (12) - fighting.
Rugby Leaguer & League Express Men of the Match:
Doncaster: Jason Tali; *City Knights:* Connor Robinson.
Penalty count: 10-7; **Half-time:** 6-8;
Referee: Billy Pearson; **Attendance:** 906.

WHITEHAVEN 14 WORKINGTON TOWN 12

WHITEHAVEN: 14 Dan Abram; 23 Jason Mossop; 3 Chris Taylor; 4 Jessie Joe Parker; 5 Dave Thompson; 17 Brad Billsborough; 7 Callum Phillips; 10 Carl Forster; 9 James Tilley; 8 Marc Shackley; 18 Ellis Gillam; 6 Dion Aiye; 22 Stuart Howarth. Subs: 16 Kris Coward; 19 Lewis Brown; 15 Danny Green (not used); 11 Connor Holliday.
Tries: D Thompson (74), Taylor (79);
Goals: Billsborough 1/1, Abram 2/2.
TOWN: 1 Jordan Tansey; 5 Joe Hambley; 4 Elliott Miller; 7 Jamie Foster; 2 Sam Forrester; 6 Jamie Doran; 24 Scott Leatherbarrow; 8 Oliver Wilkes; 9 James Newton; 10 Stevie Scholey; 18 Gordon Maudling; 12 Kurt Maudling; 14 Ryan Bailey. Subs (all used): 22 Caine Barnes; 20 Sean Penkywicz; 21 Jake Moore; 19 Andrew Dawson.
Try: Hambley (78); **Goals:** Foster 4/4.
Rugby Leaguer & League Express Men of the Match:
Whitehaven: Dan Abram; *Town:* Oliver Wilkes.
Penalty count: 15-13; **Half-time:** 2-6;
Referee: Michael Mannifield; **Attendance:** 1,395.

BRADFORD BULLS 30 OLDHAM 12

BULLS: 14 Gregg McNally; 2 Ethan Ryan; 1 Lee Smith; 3 Ashley Gibson; 5 Dalton Grant; 6 Joe Keyes; 7 Dane Chisholm; 15 Callum Bustin; 9 Sam Hallas; 10 Steve Crossley; 11 Matt Garside; 12 Elliot Minchella; 13 George Milton. Subs (all used): 21 George Flanagan; 19 Mikey Wood; 17 Ross Peltier; 18 Liam Johnson.
Tries: Minchella (18), Chisholm (47), Grant (74, 77);
Goals: Keyes 4/4, Smith 2/3, Chisholm 1/1.
OLDHAM: 1 Kyran Johnson; 2 Dave Eccleston; 4 Jack Holmes; 3 Matt Reid; 30 Ben West; 6 Paul Crook; 7 Dave Hewitt; 10 Adam Neal; 21 Kenny Hughes; 8 Phil Joy; 25 Danny Bridge; 12 Danny Langtree; 13 Jack Spencer. Subs (all used): 23 Luke Nelmes; 20 Matt Wilkinson; 24 Liam Bent; 11 Craig Briscoe.
Tries: Johnson (42), Briscoe (53); **Goals:** Crook 2/2.
Rugby Leaguer & League Express Men of the Match:
Bulls: Dane Chisholm; *Oldham:* Matt Wilkinson.
Penalty count: 14-10; **Half-time:** 12-0;
Referee: Nick Bennett; **Attendance:** 4,036.

ROUND 6

Saturday 7th April 2018

LONDON SKOLARS 76 WEST WALES RAIDERS 8

SKOLARS: 1 Elliot Hall; 2 Vinny Finigan; 3 Jake Melling; 4 Michael Brown; 5 Jake Ogden; 6 Jy-mel Coleman; 7 Neil Thorman; 8 Will Martin; 9 Billy Driver; 10 Lamont Bryan; 11 Quinn Ngawati; 22 Sam Nash; 13 Ryan Chester. Subs (all used): 24 Alfie Lawrence; 16 Louis Robinson; 14 Eddie Mbaraga; 17 Jordan Williams.
Tries: Martin (2), Melling (10, 60), Finigan (14, 67, 77), Ogden (16), Driver (19), Bryan (28), Nash (45, 62), Mbaraga (55), Ngawati (65); **Goals:** Thorman 12/13.
Sin bin: Brown (70) - punching;
Jy-mel Coleman (72) - fighting.
RAIDERS: 25 James Smith; 3 Kurtis Haile; 5 Dan Fox; 10 Morgan Evans; 2 Liam Silver; 19 Fraser Stroud; 16 Shaun Tennant; 12 Harrison Elliott; 15 Dean Higgs; 17 Harry Boots; 11 Ross Price; 18 Craig Lewis; 8 Connor Parker. Subs (all used): 9 Connor Farrer; 14 Dalton Desmond-Walker; 20 Archie Snook; 1 Rowland Kaye.
Tries: Elliott (34), Tennant (80); **Goals:** Stroud 0/2.
Dismissal: Evans (55) - high tackle on Jy-mel Coleman.
Sin bin: Desmond-Walker (72) - fighting.
Rugby Leaguer & League Express Men of the Match:
Skolars: Neil Thorman; *Raiders:* Harrison Elliott.
Penalty count: 11-8; **Half-time:** 36-4;
Referee: Brandon Robinson; **Attendance:** 198.

Sunday 8th April 2018

COVENTRY BEARS 12 WHITEHAVEN 44

BEARS: 1 Jason Bass; 2 Harry Chapman; 3 Kameron Pearce-Paul; 4 Dante Morley-Samuels; 5 Hayden Freeman; 6 Paul Emanuelli; 7 Liam Rice-Wilson; 8 James Geurtjens; 9 Zak Williams; 10 Alex Beddows; 11 Ben Gray; 12 James Mason; 13 Chris Vitalini. Subs (all used): 14 Lewis Lord; 15 Harry Kaufman; 16 John Aldred; 17 Joel Thomas.
Tries: Chapman (47, 69); **Goals:** Emanuelli 2/2.
WHITEHAVEN: 14 Dan Abram; 5 Dave Thompson; 23 Jason Mossop; 3 Chris Taylor; 15 Danny Green; 22 Stuart Howarth; 6 Dion Aiye; 8 Marc Shackley; 9 James Tilley; 16 Kris Coward; 11 Connor Holliday; 18 Ellis Gillam; 10 Carl Forster. Subs (all used): 19 Lewis Brown; - Liam Cooper; - Josh Eaves; 4 Jessie Joe Parker.
Tries: Aiye (7), Green (23), Abram (36), Mossop (53), Forster (57, 72), Cooper (63), Parker (65); **Goals:** Abram 6/8.
Rugby Leaguer & League Express Men of the Match:
Bears: Chris Vitalini; *Whitehaven:* Dan Abram.
Penalty count: 7-7; **Half-time:** 0-18;
Referee: Andrew Sweet; **Attendance:** 279.

DONCASTER 28 NORTH WALES CRUSADERS 20

DONCASTER: 30 Hakim Miloudi; 5 Sam Doherty; 19 Connor Bower; 4 Jason Tali; 1 Richard Owen; 15 Kieran Cross; 7 Liam Harris; 10 Ryan Boyle; 9 Kyle Kesik; 14 Connor Scott; 11 Brad England; 26 Brandan Wilkinson; 12 Jason Muranka. Subs (all used): 8 Russ Spiers; 21 Jez Litten; 23 Ross Osborne; 13 Jordie Hedges.
Tries: Wilkinson (13), Connor Scott (43), Tali (48), Owen (56), England (68); **Goals:** Miloudi 4/5.
Sin bin: England (79) - late challenge.
CRUSADERS: 1 Tommy Johnson; 24 Gavin Conroy; 12 Simon Atherton; 17 Kenny Baker; 5 Dale Bloomfield; 6 Steve Roper; 7 Ryan Smith; 15 Joe Bate; 14 James Dandy; - Stanton Albert; 11 Jack Houghton; 25 Jordan Case; - Brad Walker. Subs (all used): 19 Aaron Moore; 26 Alex Trumper; 16 Alex Davidson; - Dan Norman.
Tries: Case (29, 54), Baker (77); **Goals:** Johnson 4/4.
On report: Dandy (24) - alleged dangerous challenge.
Rugby Leaguer & League Express Men of the Match:
Doncaster: Brad England; *Crusaders:* Jordan Case.
Penalty count: 9-9; **Half-time:** 6-8;
Referee: Steve Race; **Attendance:** 668.

KEIGHLEY COUGARS 80 HEMEL STAGS 10

COUGARS: 1 Ritchie Hawkyard; 5 Davey Dixon; 34 Perry Whiteley; 4 Adam Ryder; 2 Andy Gabriel; 23 Benn Hardcastle; 20 Lewis Fairhurst; 16 Harvey Hallas; 15 Ryan Wright; 19 Matthew Bailey; 37 Ben Morris; 18 Josh Tonks; 13 Mike Emmett. Subs (all used): 7 Matty Beharrell; 8 Scott Law; 9 Nathan Conroy; 12 Brendon Rawlins.
Tries: Hallas (4), Fairhurst (10, 63), Hawkyard (13, 25), Ryder (22, 60), Gabriel (28), Conroy (32), Tonks (39, 55), Morris (46), Beharrell (49), Emmett (80);
Goals: Hardcastle 12/14.
STAGS: 13 Braden Hunter; 2 Marcus Elliott; 3 Kadeem Williams; 4 Chris Heil; 5 Jordan Fitzpatrick-Parry; 14 Jack Mitchell; 7 Kieran Smith; 21 James Thornton; 18 Ricky Hough; 16 Reece Williams; 17 Santino Decaro; 11 Sonny Esslemont; 19 Marcus Stock. Subs (all used): 9 Jono Burns; 10 Stefanos Bastas; 15 Danny Samuel; - Munashe Fumhanda.
Tries: Elliott (41), J Burns (78); **Goals:** Smith 1/2.
Rugby Leaguer & League Express Men of the Match:
Cougars: Josh Tonks; *Stags:* Kieran Smith.
Penalty count: 8-5; **Half-time:** 46-0;
Referee: Jon Roberts; **Attendance:** 529.

NEWCASTLE THUNDER 16 YORK CITY KNIGHTS 26

THUNDER: 1 Theerapol Ritson; 5 Mo Agoro; 4 Joe Brown; 33 Tuoyo Egodo; 24 Ben Calland; 6 Lewis Young; 16 Tom Shaw; 8 Liam McAvoy; 9 Evan Simons; 13 Jack Aldous; 15 Sam Luckley; 12 Aaron Ollett; 20 Conor Fitzsimmons. Subs (all used): 10 Rhys Clarke; 11 Harry Aldous; 14 Vincent Rennie; 21 Ben Pointer.
Tries: Egodo (24, 46), Simons (80); **Goals:** Shaw 2/3.
CITY KNIGHTS: 30 Kieren Moss; 2 Ben Cockayne; - Will Oakes; 22 Jake Normington; 5 Judah Mazive; 33 Matty Marsh; 6 Connor Robinson; 34 Josh Johnson; 9 Andy Ellis; 10 Graeme Horne; 11 Joe Batchelor; 12 Sam Scott; 13 Tim Spears. Subs (all used): 8 Adam Robinson; 16 Ronan Dixon; 17 Joe Porter; 20 Will Jubb.
Tries: Ellis (9), Batchelor (33), Mazive (47), Moss (75);
Goals: C Robinson 5/5.
Rugby Leaguer & League Express Men of the Match:
Thunder: Tuoyo Egodo; *City Knights:* Connor Robinson.
Penalty count: 8-8; **Half-time:** 6-14;
Referee: Billy Pearson; **Attendance:** 954.

OLDHAM 16 HUNSLET 24

OLDHAM: 1 Kyran Johnson; 2 Dave Eccleston; 4 Jack Holmes; 3 Matt Reid; 5 Steven Nield; 6 Paul Crook; 7 Dave Hewitt; 8 Phil Joy; 20 Matt Wilkinson; 10 Adam Neal; 12 Danny Langtree; 25 Danny Bridge; 13 Jack Spencer. Subs (all used): 23 Luke Nelmes; 11 Craig Briscoe; 19 Adam Jones; 9 Gareth Owen.
Tries: Hewitt (37, 50), Langtree (42); **Goals:** Crook 2/3.
HUNSLET: 1 Jimmy Watson; 2 David Foggin-Johnston; 32 Danny Cowling; 23 Tom Ashton; 22 Niall Walker; 6 Joe Sanderson; 7 Cain Southernwood; 38 Jack Blagbrough; 9 Jack Lee; 13 Matt Nicholson; 39 Josh Jordan-Roberts; 12 Duane Straugheir; 11 Liam Mackay. Subs (all used): 31 Daniel Halmshaw; 10 Lewis Reed; 19 Jack Coventry; 42 Joe Chandler.
Tries: Walker (47, 65), Straugheir (62), Blagbrough (77);
Goals: Sanderson 4/4.
Rugby Leaguer & League Express Men of the Match:
Oldham: Danny Langtree; *Hunslet:* Jimmy Watson.
Penalty count: 6-6; **Half-time:** 6-0;
Referee: Marcus Griffiths; **Attendance:** 544.

WORKINGTON TOWN 17 BRADFORD BULLS 16

TOWN: 1 Jordan Tansey; 5 Joe Hambley; 4 Scott Akehurst; 3 Elliott Miller; 24 John Patrick; 6 Jamie Doran; 7 Carl Forber; 8 Oliver Wilkes; 20 Sean Penkywicz; 14 Ryan Bailey; 18 Gordon Maudling; 12 Kurt Maudling; 22 Caine Barnes. Subs (all used): 9 James Newton; 19 Andrew Dawson; 21 Jake Moore; 13 Joe Ryan.
Tries: Barnes (34), Miller (76); **Goals:** Tansey 4/4;
Field goal: Tansey (78).
BULLS: 24 Brandon Pickersgill; 5 Dalton Grant; 23 Jake Butler-Fleming; 4 Ross Oakes; 2 Ethan Ryan; 6 Joe Keyes; 7 Dane Chisholm; 10 Steve Crossley; 9 Sam Hallas; 15 Callum Bustin; 11 Matt Garside; 12 Elliot Minchella; 13 George Milton. Subs (all used): 21 George Flanagan; 18 Liam Johnson; 17 Ross Peltier; 19 Mikey Wood.
Tries: Peltier (39), Butler-Fleming (54); **Goals:** Keyes 4/4.
Sin bin: Chisholm (34) - professional foul, (66) - high tackle.
Rugby Leaguer & League Express Men of the Match:
Town: Sean Penkywicz; *Bulls:* Ross Peltier.
Penalty count: 9-8; **Half-time:** 10-10;
Referee: Liam Staveley; **Attendance:** 1,366.

ROUND 7

Sunday 15th April 2018

BRADFORD BULLS 52 COVENTRY BEARS 6

BULLS: 24 Brandon Pickersgill; 2 Ethan Ryan; 3 Ashley Gibson; 35 Jy Hitchcox; 5 Dalton Grant; 6 Joe Keyes; 7 Dane Chisholm; 10 Steve Crossley; 26 Vila Halafihi; 8 Liam Kirk; 36 James Laithwaite; 18 Liam Johnson; 13 George Milton. Subs (all used): 9 Sam Hallas; 21 George Flanagan; 15 Callum Bustin; 12 Elliot Minchella.
Tries: Johnson (3, 40), Gibson (11), Hitchcox (21, 51), Flanagan (32, 65), Ryan (43), Keyes (72), Minchella (75);
Goals: Keyes 6/10.
BEARS: 1 Jason Bass; 2 Harry Chapman; 3 Kameron Pearce-Paul; 4 Dante Morley-Samuels; 5 Hayden Freeman; 6 Paul Emanuelli; 7 Ben Stead; 8 Chris Vitalini; 9 Zak Williams; 10 Joel Thomas; 11 Kieran Sherratt; 12 James Mason; 13 Ben Gray. Subs (all used): 14 Lewis Lord; 25 Richard Hughes; 16 Malikhi Lloyd-Jones; 17 James Geurtjens.
Try: Chapman (26); **Goals:** Stead 1/1.
Rugby Leaguer & League Express Men of the Match:
Bulls: Steve Crossley; *Bears:* Harry Chapman.
Penalty count: 7-4; **Half-time:** 28-6;
Referee: Billy Pearson; **Attendance:** 3,545.

DONCASTER 60 HEMEL STAGS 0

DONCASTER: 30 Hakim Miloudi; 2 Aaron Jones-Bishop; 19 Connor Bower; 4 Jason Tali; 1 Richard Owen; 17 Jack Miller; 7 Liam Harris; 10 Ryan Boyle; 9 Kyle Kesik; 14 Connor Scott; 11 Brad England; 18 Charlie Martin; 26 Brandan Wilkinson. Subs (all used): 3 Liam Welham; 16 Zac Braham; 12 Jason Muranka; 13 Jordie Hedges.
Tries: Kesik (3), Tali (7, 42), Owen (18, 76), Welham (38), Braham (49), Muranka (51), Jones-Bishop (61), Harris (66), Miloudi (70); **Goals:** Miller 8/11.
STAGS: 22 Louis Sheriff; 2 Marcus Elliott; 13 Braden Hunter; 4 Chris Heil; 5 Jordan Fitzpatrick-Parry; 14 Jack Mitchell; 7 Kieran Smith; 21 James Thornton; 18 Ricky Hough; 16 Reece Williams; 3 Kadeem Williams; 11 Sonny Esslemont; 19 Marcus Stock. Subs (all used): 9 Jono Burns; 1 Paul Stamp; 15 Jack Howieson; 10 Stefanos Bastas.
Sin bin: Elliott (7) - holding down.
On report: Sheriff (7) - alleged dangerous challenge.
Rugby Leaguer & League Express Men of the Match:
Doncaster: Kyle Kesik; *Stags:* Louis Sheriff.
Penalty count: 12-1; **Half-time:** 20-0;
Referee: Michael Mannifield; **Attendance:** 580.

HUNSLET 27 WORKINGTON TOWN 20

HUNSLET: 1 Jimmy Watson; 2 David Foggin-Johnston; 4 Mufaro Mvududu; 23 Tom Ashton; 22 Niall Walker; 6 Joe Sanderson; 7 Cain Southernwood; 38 Jack Blagbrough; 9 Jack Lee; 10 Lewis Reed; 39 Josh Jordan-Roberts; 12 Duane Straugheir; 11 Liam Mackay. Subs (all used): 19 Jack Coventry; 31 Daniel Halmshaw; 8 Michael Haley; 21 Jack Walton.

Tries: Haley (23), Ashton (62), Blagbrough (74), Foggin-Johnston (79); **Goals:** Sanderson 5/5;
Field goal: Southernwood (76).
TOWN: 1 Jordan Tansey; 5 Joe Hambley; 4 Scott Akehurst; 18 Elliott Miller; 24 John Patrick; 6 Jamie Doran; 7 Carl Forber; 8 Oliver Wilkes; 9 James Newton; 14 Ryan Bailey; 2 Karl Olstrom; 21 Jake Moore; 22 Caine Barnes. Subs (all used): - Nick Gregson; 19 Andrew Dawson; 13 Joe Ryan; 20 Scott Leatherbarrow.
Tries: Doran (4), Forber (39), Dawson (45);
Goals: Tansey 4/4.
Rugby Leaguer & League Express Men of the Match:
Hunslet: Jimmy Watson; *Town:* Jamie Doran.
Penalty count: 8-5; **Half-time:** 8-12;
Referee: Brandon Robinson; **Attendance:** 561.

NORTH WALES CRUSADERS 10
NEWCASTLE THUNDER 30

CRUSADERS: 1 Tommy Johnson; 24 Gavin Conroy; 12 Simon Atherton; 26 Alex Trumper; 17 Kenny Baker; 6 Steve Roper; 7 Ryan Smith; - Alex Gerrard; 14 James Dandy; 15 Joe Bate; 11 Jack Houghton; 25 Jordan Case; - Brad Walker. Subs (all used): 9 Lee Hudson; 16 Alex Davidson; 10 Warren Thompson; 27 Liam Hulme.
Tries: Baker (11), Trumper (50); **Goals:** Johnson 1/2.
THUNDER: 6 Lewis Young; 5 Mo Agoro; 4 Joe Brown; 24 Ben Calland; 1 Theerapol Ritson; 7 Danny Nicklas; 16 Tom Shaw; 8 Liam McAvoy; 9 Evan Simons; 13 Jack Aldous; 15 Sam Luckley; 12 Aaron Ollett; 20 Conor Fitzsimmons. Subs (all used): 21 Ben Pointer; 11 Harry Aldous; 14 Vincent Rennie; 26 Ryan Lloyd.
Tries: Simons (6), Ollett (14), Nicklas (25), Rennie (34, 76);
Goals: Shaw 5/6.
Rugby Leaguer & League Express Men of the Match:
Crusaders: Jordan Case; *Thunder:* Evan Simons.
Penalty count: 4-6; **Half-time:** 4-22;
Referee: Nick Bennett; **Attendance:** 321.

OLDHAM 32 KEIGHLEY COUGARS 18

OLDHAM: 15 Luke Hooley; 2 Dave Eccleston; 29 Zack McComb; 14 Kieran Gill; 28 Lee Kershaw; 6 Paul Crook; 7 Dave Hewitt; 17 Daniel Murray; 9 Gareth Owen; 10 Adam Neal; 25 Danny Bridge; 12 Danny Langtree; 24 Liam Bent. Subs (all used): 11 Craig Briscoe; 21 Kenny Hughes; 13 Jack Spencer; 23 Luke Nelmes.
Tries: Eccleston (3), Kershaw (7, 12), Gill (52), Bent (69);
Goals: Crook 6/7.
COUGARS: 1 Ritchie Hawkyard; 5 Davey Dixon; 3 Hamish Barnes; 4 Adam Ryder; 2 Andy Gabriel; 23 Benn Hardcastle; 20 Lewis Fairhurst; 19 Matthew Bailey; 15 Ryan Wright; 35 Darrell Griffin; 22 Ben Morris; 18 Josh Tonks; 13 Mike Emmett. Subs (all used): 7 Matty Beharrell; 8 Scott Law; 9 Nathan Conroy; 29 Brad Nicholson.
Tries: Nicholson (27), Tonks (33), Ryder (61);
Goals: Hardcastle 3/4.
Rugby Leaguer & League Express Men of the Match:
Oldham: Luke Hooley; *Cougars:* Benn Hardcastle.
Penalty count: 10-11; **Half-time:** 16-14;
Referee: Liam Staveley; **Attendance:** 530.

WHITEHAVEN 84 WEST WALES RAIDERS 6

WHITEHAVEN: 14 Dan Abram; 15 Danny Green; 3 Chris Taylor; 4 Jessie Joe Parker; 24 Phil Lister; 6 Dion Aiye; 7 Callum Phillips; 19 Lewis Brown; 26 Josh Eaves; 10 Carl Forster; 11 Connor Holliday; 5 Dave Thompson; 27 Liam Cooper. Subs (all used): 25 Jake Bradley; 8 Marc Shackley; 20 Lewis Reece; 9 James Tilley.
Tries: D Thompson (2), Green (6, 9), Taylor (17, 56), Cooper (27), Reece (29, 69), Abram (34, 47), Holliday (37, 74), Aiye (39), Parker (49), Eaves (64), Phillips (67), Shackley (80); **Goals:** Abram 7/15, Parker 1/2.
RAIDERS: 1 Matt Davies; 2 Liam Silver; 3 Kurtis Haile; 24 Aneurin Walker; 26 Louis Ford; 19 Fraser Stroud; 23 Karlin Claridge; 17 Harry Boots; 22 Macauley Harris; 10 Morgan Evans; 12 Harrison Elliott; 11 Ellis Simon; 20 Archie Snook. Subs (all used): 5 Rowland Kaye; 14 Dalton Desmond-Walker; 15 Dean Higgs; 4 Sam Fraser.
Try: Boots (15); **Goals:** Stroud 1/1.
Dismissal: Desmond-Walker (27) - high tackle.
Rugby Leaguer & League Express Men of the Match:
Whitehaven: Chris Taylor; *Raiders:* Morgan Evans.
Penalty count: 8-5; **Half-time:** 46-6;
Referee: Steve Race; **Attendance:** 401.

YORK CITY KNIGHTS 66 LONDON SKOLARS 6

CITY KNIGHTS: 30 Kieren Moss; 1 Ash Robson; - Will Oakes; 22 Jake Normington; 5 Judah Mazive; 2 Ben Cockayne; 6 Connor Robinson; 34 Jordan Walne; 9 Andy Ellis; 15 Chris Siddons; 19 Mike Kelly; 12 Sam Scott; 13 Tim Spears. Subs (all used): 26 Dan Hawksworth; 28 Aaron Smith; 16 Ronan Dixon; 17 Joe Porter.
Tries: Mazive (6, 58, 77), Ellis (10), Scott (33), Moss (38, 41), Smith (50, 62), Oakes (52), Ronan Dixon (71);
Goals: C Robinson 11/12.
SKOLARS: 1 Elliot Hall; 2 Vinny Finigan; 3 Michael Brown; 4 Jake Melling; 5 Lameck Juma; 6 Jy-mel Coleman; 7 Neil Thorman; 19 Michael Sykes; 9 Billy Driver; 8 Will Martin; 11 Quinn Ngawati; 22 Sam Nash; 13 Ryan Chester. Subs (all used): 16 Louis Robinson; 14 Eddie Mbaraga; 25 Charlie Lawrence; 24 Phil Lyon.
Try: Hall (15); **Goals:** Thorman 1/1.
Rugby Leaguer & League Express Men of the Match:
City Knights: Kieren Moss; *Skolars:* Neil Thorman.
Penalty count: 13-7; **Half-time:** 24-6;
Referee: Marcus Griffiths; **Attendance:** 916.

ROUND 2

Sunday 22nd April 2018

NEWCASTLE THUNDER 14 KEIGHLEY COUGARS 34

THUNDER: 1 Theerapol Ritson; 5 Mo Agoro; 4 Joe Brown; 12 Aaron Ollett; 24 Ben Calland; 6 Lewis Young; 16 Tom Shaw; 8 Liam McAvoy; 9 Evan Simons; 13 Jack Aldous; 15 Sam Luckley; 20 Conor Fitzsimmons; 7 Danny Nicklas. Subs (all used): 11 Harry Aldous; 14 Vincent Rennie; 21 Ben Pointer; 26 Ryan Lloyd.
Tries: Ollett (34, pen), Calland (62); **Goals:** Shaw 3/3.
Sin bin: Fitzsimmons (60) - fighting.
COUGARS: 1 Ritchie Hawkyard; 17 Cameron Leeming; 34 Perry Whiteley; 4 Adam Ryder; 2 Andy Gabriel; 23 Benn Hardcastle; 7 Matty Beharrell; 35 Darrell Griffin; 15 Ryan Wright; 19 Matthew Bailey; 37 Ben Morris; 18 Josh Tonks; 13 Mike Emmett. Subs (all used): 8 Scott Law; 9 Nathan Conroy; 11 Josh Lynam; 29 Brad Nicholson.
Tries: Griffin (9), Wright (14), Ryder (50), Gabriel (58, 73), Tonks (77); **Goals:** Hardcastle 5/6.
Sin bin: Hawkyard (60) - fighting.
Rugby Leaguer & League Express Men of the Match:
Thunder: Liam McAvoy; *Cougars:* Matty Beharrell.
Penalty count: 11-7; **Half-time:** 8-12;
Referee: Billy Pearson; **Attendance:** 623.

WORKINGTON TOWN 20
NORTH WALES CRUSADERS 12

TOWN: 3 Elliott Miller; 24 John Patrick; 5 Perry Singleton; 4 Scott Akehurst; 1 Scott Rooke; 6 Jamie Doran; 7 Carl Forber; 8 Oliver Wilkes; 9 James Newton; 10 Stevie Scholey; - Nick Gregson; 18 Karl Olstrom; 13 Larne Patrick. Subs (all used): 14 Jonah Cunningham; 12 Kurt Maudling; 20 Jack Blagbrough; 22 Caine Barnes.
Tries: Doran (9), Barnes (70); **Goals:** Forber 6/7.
Sin bin: Miller (23) - high tackle on Norman.
CRUSADERS: 1 Tommy Johnson; 24 Gavin Conroy; 12 Simon Atherton; 26 Alex Trumper; - Jake Knox; - Joe Lyons; 7 Ryan Smith; 10 Warren Thompson; 9 Lee Hudson; 17 Kenny Baker; 11 Jack Houghton; 14 James Dandy; 25 Jordan Case. Subs (all used): 19 Aaron Moore; - Dan Norman; 16 Alex Davidson; 22 Brad Brennan.
Tries: Brennan (39), Knox (73); **Goals:** Johnson 2/3.
Sin bin: Johnson (80) - professional foul.
Rugby Leaguer & League Express Men of the Match:
Town: Jamie Doran; *Crusaders:* Aaron Moore.
Penalty count: 16-10; **Half-time:** 6-8;
Referee: Tom Crashley; **Attendance:** 597.

ROUND 8

Sunday 29th April 2018

NORTH WALES CRUSADERS 40 HEMEL STAGS 16

CRUSADERS: 1 Tommy Johnson; - Owen Buckley; 12 Simon Atherton; 26 Alex Trumper; 24 Gavin Conroy; 6 Steve Roper; - Joe Lyons; 17 Kenny Baker; 14 James Dandy; 10 Warren Thompson; 11 Jack Houghton; 27 Liam Hulme; 25 Jordan Case. Subs (all used): 19 Aaron Moore; - Dan Norman; 16 Alex Davidson; 22 Brad Brennan.
Tries: Johnson (11), Buckley (13), Lyons (18), Moore (33), Atherton (40), Houghton (55), Dandy (71);
Goals: Johnson 6/7.
STAGS: 22 Louis Sheriff; 9 Mark Barlow; 12 Alex Williams; 4 Chris Heil; 5 Darren Forde; 14 Jack Mitchell; 7 Kieran Smith; 21 James Thornton; 1 Paul Stamp; 10 Jack Howieson; 3 Kadeem Williams; 11 Sonny Esslemont; 19 Marcus Stock. Subs (all used): 18 Ricky Hough; 17 Wayne Jowett; 16 Reece Williams; 8 Corey Hanson.
Tries: Reece Williams (26), Smith (43), Mitchell (57);
Goals: Mitchell 0/1, Smith 2/2.
Rugby Leaguer & League Express Men of the Match:
Crusaders: Aaron Moore; *Stags:* Kieran Smith.
Penalty count: 9-8; **Half-time:** 28-4;
Referee: Michael Mannifield; **Attendance:** 215.

COVENTRY BEARS 20 LONDON SKOLARS 28

BEARS: 1 Rhys Gant; 2 Dante Morley-Samuels; 20 Kameron Pearce-Paul; 4 Jason Bass; 5 Hayden Freeman; 6 Paul Emanuelli; 7 Ben Stead; 8 Joel Thomas; 9 Lewis Lord; 10 Chris Vitalini; 11 Ben Gray; 12 James Mason; 13 Zak Williams. Subs (all used): 14 Liam Rice-Wilson; 16 Ashley Bateman; 17 James Geurtjens; 18 Dan Gover.
Tries: Morley-Samuels (10, 43), Pearce-Paul (24), Freeman (30); **Goals:** Stead 2/5.
SKOLARS: 1 Elliot Hall; 2 Vinny Finigan; 4 Michael Brown; 3 Quinn Ngawati; 5 Jerome Yates; 6 Jy-mel Coleman; 7 Neil Thorman; 8 Michael Sykes; 9 Billy Driver; 10 Will Martin; 22 Sam Nash; 12 Lamont Bryan; 13 Ryan Chester. Subs (all used): 25 Charlie Lawrence; 14 Eddie Mbaraga; 20 Ollie Purslow; 11 Jordan Williams.
Tries: Driver (4), Bryan (19), Thorman (48), Finigan (68), Chester (72); **Goals:** Thorman 4/5.
Sin bin: Yates (64) - late challenge on Emanuelli.
Rugby Leaguer & League Express Men of the Match:
Bears: Dante Morley-Samuels; *Skolars:* Neil Thorman.
Penalty count: 11-9; **Half-time:** 14-12;
Referee: Steve Race; **Attendance:** 266.

DONCASTER 6 BRADFORD BULLS 32

DONCASTER: 7 Liam Harris; 5 Sam Doherty; 3 Liam Welham; 4 Jason Tali; 2 Aaron Jones-Bishop; 17 Jack Miller; 6 Jordan Howden; 10 Ryan Boyle; 15 Kieran Cross; 8 Russ Spiers; 18 Charlie Martin; 30 Jack Downs; 26 Brandan Wilkinson. Subs (all used): 13 Jordie Hedges; 14 Connor Scott; 28 Frankie Mariano; 21 Jez Litten.
Try: Jones-Bishop (24); **Goals:** Miller 1/1.
BULLS: 24 Brandon Pickersgill; 35 Jy Hitchcox; 3 Ashley Gibson; 1 Lee Smith; 2 Ethan Ryan; 6 Joe Keyes; 7 Dane Chisholm; 15 Callum Bustin; 9 Sam Hallas; 10 Steve Crossley; 11 Matt Garside; 36 James Laithwaite; 12 Elliot Minchella. Subs (all used): 21 George Flanagan; 8 Liam Kirk; 17 Ross Peltier; 19 Mikey Wood.
Tries: Ryan (6), Minchella (34, 45), Wood (47), Flanagan (56); **Goals:** Keyes 6/6.
Rugby Leaguer & League Express Men of the Match:
Doncaster: Liam Welham; *Bulls:* George Flanagan.
Penalty count: 7-12; **Half-time:** 6-14;
Referee: Billy Pearson; **Attendance:** 2,780.

KEIGHLEY COUGARS 24 WHITEHAVEN 30

COUGARS: 1 Ritchie Hawkyard; 28 Harry Aaronson; 34 Perry Whiteley; 4 Adam Ryder; 2 Andy Gabriel; 23 Benn Hardcastle; 7 Matty Beharrell; 35 Darrell Griffin; 15 Ryan Wright; 19 Matthew Bailey; 11 Josh Lynam; 18 Josh Tonks; 13 Mike Emmett. Subs (all used): 8 Scott Law; 9 Nathan Conroy; 17 Cameron Leeming; 29 Brad Nicholson.
Tries: Lynam (29), Beharrell (36), Aaronson (58), Leeming (64); **Goals:** Hardcastle 4/4.
WHITEHAVEN: 14 Dan Abram; 15 Danny Green; 3 Chris Taylor; 23 Jason Mossop; 5 Dave Thompson; 6 Dion Aiye; 7 Callum Phillips; 19 Lewis Brown; 9 James Tilley; 16 Kris Coward; 18 Ellis Gillam; 27 Liam Cooper; 10 Carl Forster. Subs (all used): 4 Jessie Joe Parker; 11 Connor Holliday; 20 Lewis Reece; 26 Josh Eaves.
Tries: Abram (5, 9), Aiye (11), Green (43), Eaves (49);
Goals: Abram 5/7.
Rugby Leaguer & League Express Men of the Match:
Cougars: Matty Beharrell; *Whitehaven:* Dion Aiye.
Penalty count: 11-7; **Half-time:** 12-20;
Referee: Andrew Sweet; **Attendance:** 648.

NEWCASTLE THUNDER 28 HUNSLET 10

THUNDER: 1 Theerapol Ritson; 2 Ali Blair; 3 Tyler Craig; 4 Joe Brown; 5 Mo Agoro; 6 Lewis Young; 16 Tom Shaw; 8 Liam McAvoy; 9 Evan Simons; 13 Jack Aldous; 15 Sam Luckley; 10 Rhys Clarke; 11 Harry Aldous. Subs (all used): 14 Vincent Rennie; 25 Sam Blake; 20 Conor Fitzsimmons; 24 Ben Calland.
Tries: Young (9), Brown (31), Rennie (38), Agoro (64), Craig (70); **Goals:** Shaw 4/6.
HUNSLET: 1 Jimmy Watson; 2 David Foggin-Johnston; 23 Tom Ashton; 3 Danny Grimshaw; 22 Niall Walker; 6 Joe Sanderson; 7 Cain Southernwood; 42 Joe Chandler; 9 Jack Lee; 13 Matt Nicholson; 39 Josh Jordan-Roberts; 12 Duane Straugheir; 11 Liam Mackay. Subs (all used): 31 Daniel Halmshaw; 32 Alex Bretherton; 8 Michael Haley; 17 Nyle Flynn.
Tries: Lee (13), Mackay (28); **Goals:** Sanderson 1/2.
Sin bin: Walker (43) - professional foul.
Rugby Leaguer & League Express Men of the Match:
Thunder: Lewis Young; *Hunslet:* Duane Straugheir.
Penalty count: 8-7; **Half-time:** 16-10;
Referee: Liam Staveley; **Attendance:** 837.

WORKINGTON TOWN 10 OLDHAM 32

TOWN: 1 Jordan Tansey; 24 John Patrick; 3 Elliott Miller; 4 Jamie Foster; 2 Scott Rooke; 6 Jamie Doran; 7 Carl Forber; 8 Oliver Wilkes; 9 James Newton; 10 Stevie Scholey; - Nick Gregson; 18 Karl Olstrom; 22 Caine Barnes. Subs (all used): 14 Scott Leatherbarrow; 5 Perry Singleton; 16 Jack Blagbrough; 20 Jonah Cunningham.
Tries: Gregson (9), Miller (65); **Goals:** Foster 1/2.
Sin bin: Doran (54) - shoulder charge.
OLDHAM: 15 Luke Hooley; 2 Dave Eccleston; 3 Matt Reid; 14 Kieran Gill; 28 Lee Kershaw; 6 Paul Crook; 7 Dave Hewitt; 8 Phil Joy; 21 Kenny Hughes; 13 Jack Spencer; 25 Danny Bridge; 12 Danny Langtree; 24 Liam Bent. Subs (all used): 19 Adam Jones; 9 Gareth Owen; 20 Matt Wilkinson; 23 Luke Nelmes.
Tries: Bent (1), Langtree (19), Kershaw (39), Hooley (49), Joy (54), Hewitt (79); **Goals:** Crook 4/6.
Sin bin: Bent (76) - punching.
Rugby Leaguer & League Express Men of the Match: *Town:* Jamie Doran; *Oldham:* Danny Langtree.
Penalty count: 11-8; **Half-time:** 6-14;
Referee: Nick Bennett; **Attendance:** 712.

YORK CITY KNIGHTS 144 WEST WALES RAIDERS 0

CITY KNIGHTS: 30 Kieren Moss; 1 Ash Robson; 3 Jake Butler-Fleming; 4 Brad Hey; 5 Judah Mazive; 6 Connor Robinson; 27 Liam Jackson; 8 Adam Robinson; 28 Aaron Smith; 26 Dan Hawksworth; 11 Joe Batchelor; 19 Mike Kelly; 17 Joe Porter. Subs (all used): 20 Will Jubb; 15 Chris Siddons; 16 Ronan Dixon; 10 Graeme Horne.
Tries: Jackson (1), Moss (7, 27, 46, 51, 54, 66, 74), C Robinson (10, 23), Hey (12), Porter (15), Robson (18, 79), Batchelor (30), Ronan Dixon (33, 77), Horne (35, 44, 49), Mazive (42), Smith (58, 70), Kelly (60), A Robinson (68); **Goals:** C Robinson 14/17, Robson 8/8.
RAIDERS: 2 Mike Ward; 23 Karlin Claridge; 24 Aneurin Walker; 4 Liam Smith; 25 James Smith; 6 Luke Williams; 21 Steve Parry; 12 Harrison Elliott; 22 Macauley Harris; 17 Harry Boots; 20 Archie Snook; 18 Craig Lewis; 13 Robert Bonehill. Subs (all used): 14 Danny Hunter; 26 Craig Kelly; 5 Rowland Kaye; 11 Ellis Simon.
Rugby Leaguer & League Express Men of the Match: *City Knights:* Kieren Moss; *Raiders:* Harry Boots.
Penalty count: 11-4; **Half-time:** 60-0;
Referee: Brandon Robinson; **Attendance:** 1,089.

ROUND 9

Saturday 5th May 2018

LONDON SKOLARS 18 DONCASTER 42

SKOLARS: 1 Elliot Hall; 2 Vinny Finigan; 22 Omari Caro; 3 Michael Brown; 5 Ryan Burroughs; 6 Jy-mel Coleman; 7 Neil Thorman; 20 Michael Sykes; 9 Billy Driver; 8 Will Martin; 11 Quinn Ngawati; 12 Lamont Bryan; 13 Ryan Chester. Subs (all used): 14 Eddie Mbaraga; 15 Matthew Davies; 16 Rob Butler; 17 Jordan Williams.
Tries: Bryan (21), Hall (32, 69); **Goals:** Thorman 3/3.
DONCASTER: 1 Richard Owen; 24 Jack Sanderson; 3 Liam Welham; 4 Jason Tali; 2 Aaron Jones-Bishop; 30 Hakim Miloudi; 7 Liam Harris; 14 Connor Scott; 9 Kyle Kesik; 8 Russ Spiers; 18 Charlie Martin; 33 Jack Downs; 26 Brandan Wilkinson. Subs (all used): 12 Jason Muranka; 28 Frankie Mariano; 15 Kieran Cross; 16 Zac Braham.
Tries: Wilkinson (2), Miloudi (14, 77), Cross (39, 46), Braham (49), Jones-Bishop (72), Welham (80);
Goals: Miloudi 5/8.
Rugby Leaguer & League Express Men of the Match: *Skolars:* Elliot Hall; *Doncaster:* Hakim Miloudi.
Penalty count: 9-10; **Half-time:** 12-16;
Referee: Matt Rossleigh; **Attendance:** 186.

Sunday 6th May 2018

HEMEL STAGS 12 WORKINGTON TOWN 60

STAGS: 7 Kieran Smith; 2 Marcus Elliott; 13 Alex Williams; 4 Chris Heil; 5 Darren Forde; 22 Louis Sheriff; 1 Paul Stamp; 10 Rory Dixon; 18 Ricky Hough; 15 Jack Howieson; 11 Sonny Esslemont; 21 James Thornton; 12 Kieran Moran. Subs (all used): 14 Blake Broadbent; 19 Marcus Stock; 16 Reece Williams; 17 Lewis Taylor.
Tries: Moran (25), Taylor (78); **Goals:** Smith 1/1, Hough 1/1.
TOWN: 2 Sam Forrester; 1 Ricky Bailey; 3 Elliott Miller; 18 Karl Olstrom; 5 Joe Hambley; 6 Jamie Doran; 7 Carl Forber; 8 Oliver Wilkes; 9 James Newton; 16 Jack Blagbrough; 11 Larne Patrick; 21 Jake Moore; 22 Caine Barnes. Subs (all used): 10 Stevie Scholey; 15 Tom Curwen; 19 Andrew Dawson; 12 Kurt Maudling.
Tries: Barnes (5, 65), Miller (8, 20, 54), Wilkes (17), Hambley (28), Doran (31), Forrester (46), Olstrom (50), Forber (67); **Goals:** Forber 8/11.
Rugby Leaguer & League Express Men of the Match: *Stags:* Louis Sheriff; *Town:* Jamie Doran.
Penalty count: 5-4; **Half-time:** 6-34;
Referee: Steve Race; **Attendance:** 110.

BRADFORD BULLS 124 WEST WALES RAIDERS 0

BULLS: 35 Jy Hitchcox; 2 Ethan Ryan; 3 Ashley Gibson; 1 Lee Smith; 5 Dalton Grant; 24 Brandon Pickersgill; 7 Dane Chisholm; 8 Liam Kirk; 21 George Flanagan; 15 Callum Bustin; 11 Matt Garside; 36 James Laithwaite; 9 Sam Hallas. Subs (all used): 26 Vila Halafihi; 17 Ross Peltier; 19 Mikey Wood; 12 Elliot Minchella.
Tries: Bustin (5), Grant (9, 63), Ryan (11, 68), Hallas (15), Chisholm (17, 38), Laithwaite (23), Smith (27), Garside (31, 56, 73), Pickersgill (34, 54), Minchella (44, 49, 65), Peltier (47), Halafihi (59), Flanagan (79); **Goals:** Chisholm 20/21.
RAIDERS: 2 Mike Ward; 1 Matt Davies; 24 Aneurin Walker; 3 Kurtis Haile; 5 Sam Baker; 16 Shaun Tennant; 7 Danny Hunter; 8 Connor Parker; 22 Macauley Harris; 12 Harrison Elliott; 20 Archie Snook; 18 Craig Lewis; 21 Steve Parry. Subs (all used): 11 Ross Price; 4 Rowland Kaye; 19 Ellis Simon; 14 Dalton Desmond-Walker.
Rugby Leaguer & League Express Men of the Match: *Bulls:* Dane Chisholm; *Raiders:* Harrison Elliott.
Penalty count: 12-3; **Half-time:** 60-0;
Referee: Andrew Sweet; **Attendance:** 3,398.

HUNSLET 24 YORK CITY KNIGHTS 26

HUNSLET: 1 Jimmy Watson; 2 David Foggin-Johnston; 30 Nathan Chappell; 28 Will Cooke; 23 Tom Ashton; 6 Joe Sanderson; 7 Cain Southernwood; 32 Aiden Hema; 9 Jack Lee; 13 Matt Nicholson; 39 Josh Jordan-Roberts; 12 Duane Straugheir; 15 Brad Foster. Subs (all used): 31 Daniel Halmshaw; 8 Michael Haley; 21 Jack Walton; 10 Lewis Reed.
Tries: Jordan-Roberts (30), Chappell (40, 76), Walton (60);
Goals: Sanderson 4/4.
Sin bin: Walton (42) - dangerous contact on Dagger.
CITY KNIGHTS: 28 Will Dagger; 25 Tom Saxton; 3 Jake Butler-Fleming; 4 Brad Hey; 5 Judah Mazive; 2 Ben Cockayne; 6 Connor Robinson; 8 Adam Robinson; 9 Andy Ellis; 10 Graeme Horne; 11 Joe Batchelor; 12 Sam Scott; 13 Tim Spears. Subs (all used): 20 Will Jubb; 15 Chris Siddons; 16 Ronan Dixon; 17 Joe Porter.
Tries: Mazive (10, 22), Dagger (15), Cockayne (26);
Goals: C Robinson 5/6.
Rugby Leaguer & League Express Men of the Match: *Hunslet:* Nathan Chappell; *City Knights:* Ben Cockayne.
Penalty count: 7-6; **Half-time:** 12-24;
Referee: John McMullen; **Attendance:** 729.

KEIGHLEY COUGARS 98 COVENTRY BEARS 6

COUGARS: 1 Ritchie Hawkyard; 28 Harry Aaronson; 34 Perry Whiteley; 4 Adam Ryder; 2 Andy Gabriel; 23 Benn Hardcastle; 7 Matty Beharrell; 12 Brendon Rawlins; 15 Ryan Wright; 19 Matthew Bailey; 32 Dan Parker; 18 Josh Tonks; 13 Mike Emmett. Subs (all used): 8 Scott Law; 9 Nathan Conroy; 17 Cameron Leeming; 29 Brad Nicholson.
Tries: Hardcastle (2), Bailey (15), Ryder (19, 45, 59), Aaronson (22, 28), Gabriel (36, 70), Tonks (40), Parker (41), Law (47), Nicholson (55), Hawkyard (61), Beharrell (67), Rawlins (75, 77); **Goals:** Hardcastle 14/16, Beharrell 1/1.
BEARS: 1 Rhys Gant; 2 Dante Morley-Samuels; 20 Kameron Pearce-Paul; 4 Jason Bass; 5 Jake Ogden; 6 Paul Emanuelli; 7 Ben Stead; 8 James Geurtjens; 9 Zak Williams; 10 Dan Gover; 11 Ashley Bateman; 12 James Mason; 13 Chris Vitalini. Subs (all used): 14 Lewis Lord; 16 Malikhi Lloyd-Jones; 17 Joel Thomas; 25 Richard Hughes.
Try: Gant (11); **Goals:** Stead 1/1.
Rugby Leaguer & League Express Men of the Match: *Cougars:* Brad Nicholson; *Bears:* Rhys Gant.
Penalty count: 11-6; **Half-time:** 42-6;
Referee: Michael Mannifield; **Attendance:** 446.

OLDHAM 28 NEWCASTLE THUNDER 12

OLDHAM: 15 Luke Hooley; 2 Dave Eccleston; 14 Kieran Gill; 3 Matt Reid; 28 Lee Kershaw; 6 Paul Crook; 7 Dave Hewitt; 8 Phil Joy; 9 Gareth Owen; 13 Jack Spencer; 12 Danny Langtree; 25 Danny Bridge; 24 Liam Bent. Subs (all used): 23 Luke Nelmes; 20 Matt Wilkinson; 19 Adam Jones; 11 Craig Briscoe.
Tries: Gill (15), Bridge (30), Eccleston (35), Joy (48), Briscoe (69); **Goals:** Crook 4/5.
THUNDER: 1 Theerapol Ritson; 2 Ali Blair; 3 Tyler Craig; 4 Joe Brown; 5 Mo Agoro; 6 Lewis Young; 16 Tom Shaw; 8 Liam McAvoy; 9 Evan Simons; 13 Jack Aldous; 15 Sam Luckley; 10 Rhys Clarke; 11 Harry Aldous. Subs (all used): 14 Vincent Rennie; 25 Sam Blake; 20 Conor Fitzsimmons; 12 Aaron Ollett.
Tries: Blair (55), Young (80); **Goals:** Shaw 2/2.
Sin bin: Agoro (68) - professional foul.
Rugby Leaguer & League Express Men of the Match: *Oldham:* Danny Bridge; *Thunder:* Theerapol Ritson.
Penalty count: 7-4; **Half-time:** 16-0;
Referee: Nick Bennett; **Attendance:** 455.

WHITEHAVEN 22 NORTH WALES CRUSADERS 25

WHITEHAVEN: 14 Dan Abram; 15 Danny Green; 3 Chris Taylor; 23 Jason Mossop; 5 Dave Thompson; 6 Dion Aiye; 7 Callum Phillips; 8 Marc Shackley; 22 Stuart Howarth; 19 Lewis Brown; 18 Ellis Gillam; 27 Liam Cooper; 10 Carl Forster. Subs (all used): 16 Kris Coward; 20 Lewis Reece; 11 Connor Holliday; 26 Josh Eaves.
Tries: Phillips (36), Taylor (48), D Thompson (71), Abram (79); **Goals:** Abram 3/4.
CRUSADERS: 1 Tommy Johnson; - Jake Knox; 12 Simon Atherton; 26 Alex Trumper; 24 Gavin Conroy; 6 Steve Roper; - Joe Lyons; 17 Kenny Baker; 14 James Dandy; 15 Joe Bate; 11 Jack Houghton; 25 Jordan Case; - Brad Walker. Subs (all used): - Dan Norman; 19 Aaron Moore; 22 Brad Brennan; 7 Ryan Smith.
Tries: Roper (11), Conroy (14), Smith (55), Baker (59);
Goals: Johnson 4/5; **Field goal:** B Walker (66).
Rugby Leaguer & League Express Men of the Match: *Whitehaven:* Dan Abram; *Crusaders:* Brad Walker.
Penalty count: 17-7; **Half-time:** 6-12;
Referee: Jon Roberts; **Attendance:** 603.

ROUND 2

Saturday 12th May 2018

BRADFORD BULLS 54 LONDON SKOLARS 16

BULLS: 24 Brandon Pickersgill; 5 Dalton Grant; 3 Ashley Gibson; 1 Lee Smith; 2 Ethan Ryan; 33 Rowan Milnes; 7 Dane Chisholm; 10 Steve Crossley; 21 George Flanagan; 15 Callum Bustin; 11 Matt Garside; 36 James Laithwaite; 12 Elliot Minchella. Subs (all used): 17 Ross Peltier; 19 Mikey Wood; 9 Sam Hallas; 26 Vila Halafihi.
Tries: Pickersgill (7), Ryan (16, 19, 53, 72), Grant (28, 62), Peltier (35), Smith (40), Gibson (48), Bustin (77);
Goals: Chisholm 5/11.
SKOLARS: 1 Elliot Hall; 2 Vinny Finigan; 4 Matty Fleming; 18 Omari Caro; 5 Ryan Burroughs; 7 Neil Thorman; 24 Phil Lyon; 20 Michael Sykes; 9 Billy Driver; 10 Lamont Bryan; 11 Quinn Ngawati; 12 Jordan Williams; 13 Ryan Chester. Subs (all used): 16 Rob Butler; 14 Eddie Mbaraga; 15 Matthew Davies; 22 Sam Nash.
Tries: Burroughs (32), Mbaraga (58), Lyon (75);
Goals: Thorman 2/3.
Sin bin: Butler (41) - dangerous challenge on Minchella.
Rugby Leaguer & League Express Men of the Match: *Bulls:* Ethan Ryan; *Skolars:* Neil Thorman.
Penalty count: 9-3; **Half-time:** 28-4;
Referee: Steve Race; **Attendance:** 3,041.

COVENTRY BEARS 18 YORK CITY KNIGHTS 58

BEARS: 1 Jason Bass; 2 Jamahl Hunte; 21 Kameron Pearce-Paul; 4 Jake Ogden; 5 Hayden Freeman; 6 Liam Rice-Wilson; 7 Ben Stead; 8 James Geurtjens; 9 Richard Hughes; 10 Peter Ryan; 11 Ashley Bateman; 12 Ben Gray; 13 Chris Vitalini. Subs (all used): 14 Lewis Lord; 15 Harry Kaufman; 16 Malikhi Lloyd-Jones; 17 Zak Williams.
Tries: Ogden (15), Hughes (25), Ryan (29);
Goals: Stead 3/3.
CITY KNIGHTS: 2 Ben Cockayne; 5 Judah Mazive; 11 Joe Batchelor; 4 Brad Hey; 1 Ash Robson; 27 Liam Jackson; 6 Connor Robinson; 8 Adam Robinson; 20 Will Jubb; 15 Chris Siddons; 19 Mike Kelly; 12 Sam Scott; 13 Tim Spears. Subs (all used): 26 Dan Hawksworth; 37 Danny Maskill; 16 Ronan Dixon; 17 Joe Porter.
Tries: A Robinson (3), Jubb (8), Spears (12), Hawksworth (36), Ronan Dixon (47), Robson (52), Mazive (56), Batchelor (64, 67), Hey (74);
Goals: C Robinson 9/10.
Rugby Leaguer & League Express Men of the Match: *Bears:* Peter Ryan; *City Knights:* Joe Batchelor.
Penalty count: 11-9; **Half-time:** 18-24;
Referee: Brandon Robinson; **Attendance:** 252.

Sunday 13th May 2018

OLDHAM 74 HEMEL STAGS 6

OLDHAM: 1 Kyran Johnson; 5 Steven Nield; 4 Jack Holmes; 29 Zack McComb; 30 Ben West; 6 Paul Crook; 9 Gareth Owen; 8 Phil Joy; 20 Matt Wilkinson; 28 Levy Nzoungou; 12 Danny Langtree; 25 Danny Bridge; 16 Gavin Bennion. Subs (all used): 23 Luke Nelmes; 21 Kenny Hughes; 19 Adam Jones; 22 Danny Rasool.
Tries: Owen (8), West (19), Bridge (28, 50), Nelmes (32, 40), Johnson (38, 64), McComb (43, 56, 67), Wilkinson (61), Bennion (80); **Goals:** Crook 11/13.

STAGS: 14 Jack Mitchell; 2 Darren Forde; 13 Alex Williams; 3 Chris Heil; 5 Marcus Elliott; 22 Louis Sheriff; 1 Paul Stamp; 10 Rory Dixon; 18 Ricky Hough; 16 Reece Williams; 11 Sonny Esslemont; 21 James Thornton; 19 Blake Broadbent. Subs (all used): 7 Chris Cullimore; 4 Santino Decaro; 8 Wayne Jowett; 17 Lewis Taylor.
Try: Forde (4); **Goals:** Mitchell 1/1.
Rugby Leaguer & League Express Men of the Match: *Oldham:* Luke Nelmes; *Stags:* Jack Mitchell.
Penalty count: 11-9; **Half-time:** 34-6;
Referee: Billy Pearson; **Attendance:** 411.

WEST WALES RAIDERS 18 DONCASTER 70

RAIDERS: 1 Matt Davies; 2 Liam Silver; 16 Shaun Tennant; 24 Aneurin Walker; 5 Sam Baker; 23 Karlin Claridge; 21 Steve Parry; 17 Harry Boots; 22 Macauley Harris; 11 Alan Pope; 8 Connor Parker; 20 Archie Snook; 10 Morgan Evans. Subs (all used): 14 Dalton Desmond-Walker; 9 Connor Farrer; 19 Ellis Simon; 26 Louis Ford.
Tries: Farrer (54), Silver (62), Parry (70);
Goals: Tennant 3/3.
DONCASTER: 1 Richard Owen; 24 Jack Sanderson; 3 Liam Welham; 4 Jason Tali; 2 Aaron Jones-Bishop; 6 Jordan Howden; 17 Jack Miller; 14 Connor Scott; 9 Kyle Kesik; 23 Ross Osborne; 19 Connor Bower; 28 Frankie Mariano; 25 Jack Downs. Subs (all used): 16 Zac Braham; 12 Jason Muranka; 13 Jordie Hedges; 5 Sam Doherty.
Tries: Connor Scott (6), Downs (9), Miller (15), Osborne (18, 42), Mariano (21), Kesik (26), Jones-Bishop (31), Tali (35, 44), Muranka (48, 76), Doherty (67); **Goals:** Miller 9/13.
Rugby Leaguer & League Express Men of the Match: *Raiders:* Steve Parry; *Doncaster:* Ross Osborne.
Penalty count: 6-3; **Half-time:** 0-42;
Referee: Nick Bennett; **Attendance:** 188.

ROUND 10

Friday 18th May 2018

NEWCASTLE THUNDER 16 BRADFORD BULLS 26

THUNDER: 1 Theerapol Ritson; 5 Mo Agoro; 33 Tuoyo Egodo; 3 Tyler Craig; 2 Ali Blair; 6 Lewis Young; 17 Adam Brook; 8 Liam McAvoy; 9 Evan Simons; 11 Harry Aldous; 15 Sam Luckley; 12 Aaron Ollett; 13 Jack Aldous. Subs (all used): 14 Vincent Rennie; 10 Rhys Clarke; 20 Conor Fitzsimmons; 25 Sam Blake.
Tries: Ritson (16), Craig (18), Egodo (76); **Goals:** Brook 2/3.
Dismissal: J Aldous (72) - fighting.
Sin bin: Clarke (40) - high tackle.
BULLS: 24 Brandon Pickersgill; 5 Dalton Grant; 3 Ashley Gibson; 1 Lee Smith; 2 Ethan Ryan; 12 Elliot Minchella; 7 Dane Chisholm; 10 Steve Crossley; 26 Vila Halafihi; 15 Callum Bustin; 11 Matt Garside; 36 James Laithwaite; 13 George Milton. Subs (all used): 17 Ross Peltier; 8 Liam Kirk; 33 Rowan Milnes; 21 George Flanagan.
Tries: Minchella (24), Ryan (30), Flanagan (39), Chisholm (48); **Goals:** Chisholm 5/6.
Dismissal: Grant (72) - fighting.
Rugby Leaguer & League Express Men of the Match: *Thunder:* Lewis Young; *Bulls:* Dane Chisholm.
Penalty count: 7-11; **Half-time:** 12-18;
Referee: John McMullen; **Attendance:** 4,137.

Saturday 19th May 2018

LONDON SKOLARS 26 WHITEHAVEN 44

SKOLARS: 1 Elliot Hall; 2 Vinny Finigan; 22 Omari Caro; 4 Matty Fleming; 5 Ryan Burroughs; 7 Neil Thorman; 24 Phil Lyon; 20 Michael Sykes; 9 Billy Driver; 10 Lamont Bryan; - Sam Nash; 12 Jordan Williams; 13 Ryan Chester. Subs (all used): 11 Quinn Ngawati; 15 Matthew Davies; 16 Rob Butler; 14 Eddie Mbaraga.
Tries: Caro (42), Butler (53), Hall (65), Fleming (69), Burroughs (74); **Goals:** Thorman 3/5.
Sin bin: Fleming (38) - obstruction.
WHITEHAVEN: 14 Dan Abram; 15 Danny Green; 3 Chris Taylor; 23 Jason Mossop; 4 Jessie Joe Parker; 6 Dion Aiye; 7 Callum Phillips; 27 Liam Cooper; 9 James Tilley; 10 Carl Forster; 11 Connor Holliday; 5 Dave Thompson; 22 Stuart Howarth. Subs (all used): 26 Josh Eaves; 18 Ellis Gillam; 8 Marc Shackley; 16 Kris Coward.
Tries: Forster (19), Aiye (22, 30), Green (26), Holliday (34), D Thompson (40), Taylor (58), Phillips (61);
Goals: Abram 6/9.
Rugby Leaguer & League Express Men of the Match: *Skolars:* Ryan Burroughs; *Whitehaven:* Carl Forster.
Penalty count: 10-11; **Half-time:** 0-32;
Referee: Michael Mannifield; **Attendance:** 346.

WEST WALES RAIDERS 0 OLDHAM 74

RAIDERS: 3 Kurtis Haile; 2 Liam Silver; 16 Shaun Tennant; 24 Aneurin Walker; 19 Andrew Rees-Spowart; 21 Steve Parry; 23 Karlin Claridge; 10 Morgan Evans; 9 Connor Farrer; 11 Ross Price; 12 Harrison Elliott; 20 Archie Snook; 8 Connor Parker. Subs (all used): 4 Rowland Kaye; 17 Harry Boots; 18 Craig Lewis; 22 Macauley Harris.
Sin bin: Evans (70) - dissent.
OLDHAM: 1 Kyran Johnson; 2 Dave Eccleston; 3 Matt Reid; 29 Zack McComb; 30 Ben West; 9 Gareth Owen; 7 Dave Hewitt; 8 Phil Joy; 21 Kenny Hughes; 13 Jack Spencer; 25 Danny Bridge; 12 Danny Langtree; 24 Liam Bent. Subs (all used): 20 Matt Wilkinson; 23 Luke Nelmes; 22 Danny Rasool; 11 Craig Briscoe.
Tries: Eccleston (4), McComb (7, 53, 63), Hughes (12), Bridge (22), Reid (26, 78), West (34), Wilkinson (37), Rasool (42), Hewitt (48, 58), Joy (73);
Goals: Hewitt 5/7, Johnson 4/7.
Sin bin: Bridge (30) - punching.
Rugby Leaguer & League Express Men of the Match: *Raiders:* Connor Parker; *Oldham:* Dave Hewitt.
Penalty count: 5-13; **Half-time:** 0-38;
Referee: Paul Marklove; **Attendance:** 424.

Sunday 20th May 2018

NORTH WALES CRUSADERS 28 KEIGHLEY COUGARS 46

CRUSADERS: - Joe Lyons; 5 Dale Bloomfield; 12 Simon Atherton; 26 Alex Trumper; 24 Gavin Conroy; 6 Steve Roper; 7 Ryan Smith; 17 Kenny Baker; 19 Aaron Moore; 15 Joe Bate; 11 Jack Houghton; 25 Jordan Case; - Brad Walker. Subs (all used): 27 Liam Hulme; - Ted Chapelhow; 22 Brad Brennan; - Dan Norman.
Tries: Baker (4, 63), B Walker (65), Brennan (77, 79);
Goals: B Walker 3/3, Roper 1/2.
COUGARS: 1 Ritchie Hawkyard; 5 Davey Dixon; 34 Perry Whiteley; 4 Adam Ryder; 2 Andy Gabriel; 23 Benn Hardcastle; 7 Matty Beharrell; 12 Brendon Rawlins; 15 Ryan Wright; 19 Matthew Bailey; 32 Dan Parker; 18 Josh Tonks; 13 Mike Emmett. Subs (all used): 8 Scott Law; 9 Nathan Conroy; 35 Darrell Griffin; 29 Brad Nicholson.
Tries: Parker (18, 71), Whiteley (27, 60), Ryder (32, 40), Conroy (36), Law (56); **Goals:** Hardcastle 6/7, Beharrell 1/1.
Rugby Leaguer & League Express Men of the Match: *Crusaders:* Aaron Moore; *Cougars:* Benn Hardcastle.
Penalty count: 8-9; **Half-time:** 6-28;
Referee: Nick Bennett; **Attendance:** 337.

COVENTRY BEARS 4 WORKINGTON TOWN 52

BEARS: 1 Dante Morley-Samuels; 2 Hayden Freeman; 21 Kameron Pearce-Paul; 4 Jake Ogden; 5 Reece Rance; 6 Liam Rice-Wilson; 7 Ben Stead; 8 James Geurtjens; 9 Sam Davis; 10 Peter Ryan; 11 Ashley Bateman; 12 Jacob Jones; 13 Chris Vitalini. Subs (all used): 14 Lewis Lord; 15 Harry Kaufman; 16 Malikhi Lloyd-Jones; 17 John Aldred.
Try: Pearce-Paul (72); **Goals:** Rice-Wilson 0/1.
Sin bin: Ryan (22) - shoulder charge on Moimoi; Vitalini (22) - dissent.
TOWN: 2 Sam Forrester; 3 Elliott Miller; 18 Karl Olstrom; 5 Perry Singleton; 4 Ricky Bailey; 6 Jamie Doran; 7 Carl Forber; 8 Oliver Wilkes; 20 Sean Penkywicz; 10 Stevie Scholey; 21 Jake Moore; 22 Caine Barnes; 16 Jack Blagbrough. Subs (all used): 9 James Newton; 15 Tom Curwen; 19 Andrew Dawson; 23 Fuifui Moimoi.
Tries: Miller (4), Singleton (8, 28), Blagbrough (12), Doran (17), Scholey (20), Penkywicz (25), Forrester (48), Olstrom (64), Ricky Bailey (67); **Goals:** Forber 6/10.
Rugby Leaguer & League Express Men of the Match: *Bears:* Dante Morley-Samuels; *Town:* Sean Penkywicz.
Penalty count: 7-11; **Half-time:** 0-38;
Referee: Brandon Robinson; **Attendance:** 264.

DONCASTER 16 HUNSLET 35

DONCASTER: 1 Richard Owen; 5 Sam Doherty; 19 Connor Bower; 4 Jason Tali; 24 Jack Sanderson; 6 Jordan Howden; 17 Jack Miller; 14 Connor Scott; 9 Kyle Kesik; 10 Ryan Boyle; 18 Charlie Martin; 28 Frankie Mariano; 25 Jack Downs. Subs (all used): 23 Ross Osborne; 8 Russ Spiers; 13 Jordie Hedges; 26 Brandan Wilkinson.
Tries: Doherty (4), Osborne (24), Kesik (44);
Goals: Miller 2/3.
Sin bin: Kesik (70) - fighting.
HUNSLET: 1 Jimmy Watson; 2 David Foggin-Johnston; 30 Nathan Chappell; 4 Mufaro Mvududu; 23 Tom Ashton; 6 Joe Sanderson; 7 Cain Southernwood; 32 Aiden Hema; 9 Jack Lee; 13 Matt Nicholson; 39 Josh Jordan-Roberts; 12 Duane Straugheir; 15 Brad Foster. Subs (all used): 31 Daniel Halmshaw; 8 Michael Haley; 19 Jack Coventry; 21 Jack Walton.
Tries: Southernwood (19), Walton (33), Chappell (53), Sanderson (65), Straugheir (74); **Goals:** Sanderson 7/7;
Field goal: Southernwood (70).
Sin bin: Watson (15) - holding down; Chappell (70) - fighting.
Rugby Leaguer & League Express Men of the Match: *Doncaster:* Kyle Kesik; *Hunslet:* Joe Sanderson.
Penalty count: 9-11; **Half-time:** 10-14;
Referee: Andrew Sweet; **Attendance:** 597.

YORK CITY KNIGHTS 90 HEMEL STAGS 0

CITY KNIGHTS: 28 Will Dagger; 2 Ben Cockayne; 11 Joe Batchelor; 4 Brad Hey; 1 Ash Robson; 6 Connor Robinson; 32 Matty Marsh; 8 Adam Robinson; 37 Danny Maskill; 10 Graeme Horne; 19 Mike Kelly; 12 Sam Scott; 13 Tim Spears. Subs (all used): 26 Dan Hawksworth; 15 Chris Siddons; 16 Ronan Dixon; 17 Joe Porter.
Tries: Dagger (3, 34), Robson (13, 49, 80), C Robinson (18), Marsh (25, 56, 59, 68), Siddons (28), Kelly (31, 53), Maskill (61), Spears (66), Batchelor (79);
Goals: C Robinson 13/16.
STAGS: 14 Marcus Elliott; 2 Darren Forde; 13 Alex Williams; 3 Tom Bonillo; 5 Jordan Fitzpatrick-Parry; 22 Louis Sheriff; 7 Chris Cullimore; 10 Rory Dixon; 18 Ricky Hough; 16 Reece Williams; 21 James Thornton; 4 Santino Decaro; 19 Blake Broadbent. Subs (all used): 1 Mark Barlow; 17 Lewis Taylor; 11 Stefanos Bastas; 8 Wayne Jowett.
Rugby Leaguer & League Express Men of the Match: *City Knights:* Matty Marsh; *Stags:* Reece Williams.
Penalty count: 8-7; **Half-time:** 38-0;
Referee: Joe Stearne; **Attendance:** 987.

ROUND 11

Sunday 27th May 2018

HEMEL STAGS 0 BRADFORD BULLS 68

STAGS: 5 Matt Welham; 2 Darren Forde; 13 Alex Williams; 1 Tom Bonillo; 14 Marcus Elliott; 22 Louis Sheriff; 7 Chris Cullimore; 10 Rory Dixon; 9 Paul Stamp; 21 James Thornton; 4 Santino Decaro; 12 Sonny Esslemont; 17 Kieran Moran. Subs (all used): 19 Blake Broadbent; 16 Reece Williams; 3 Stefanos Bastas; 8 Wayne Jowett.
Sin bin: Esslemont (31) - repeated team offences; Moran (34) - use of the knees; Elliott (39) - interference.
BULLS: 24 Brandon Pickersgill; 5 Dalton Grant; 3 Ashley Gibson; 1 Lee Smith; 2 Ethan Ryan; 12 Elliot Minchella; 7 Dane Chisholm; 10 Steve Crossley; 26 Vila Halafihi; 15 Callum Bustin; 11 Matt Garside; 36 James Laithwaite; 9 Sam Hallas. Subs (all used): 17 Ross Peltier; 18 Liam Johnson; 19 Mikey Wood; 21 George Flanagan.
Tries: Chisholm (3), Garside (21), Peltier (31), Flanagan (35), Ryan (45), Minchella (49, 68), Pickersgill (60), Grant (72, 74), Laithwaite (77), Halafihi (79); **Goals:** Chisholm 10/12.
Sin bin: Peltier (41) - dissent.
Rugby Leaguer & League Express Men of the Match: *Stags:* Matt Welham; *Bulls:* Dane Chisholm.
Penalty count: 6-19; **Half-time:** 0-24;
Referee: Michael Mannifield; **Attendance:** 736.

NORTH WALES CRUSADERS 42 COVENTRY BEARS 6

CRUSADERS: 1 Tommy Johnson; - Olly Ashall-Bott; 20 Alex Thompson; 26 Alex Trumper; 5 Dale Bloomfield; 7 Ryan Smith; - Joe Lyons; 15 Joe Bate; 19 Aaron Moore; 17 Kenny Baker; 11 Jack Houghton; 25 Jordan Case; - Brad Walker. Subs (all used): 6 Steve Roper; 22 Brad Brennan; 8 Jonny Walker; - Dan Norman.
Tries: Johnson (3, 28), Ashall-Bott (11, 65), Lyons (54), Bloomfield (67), Moore (73); **Goals:** Johnson 7/7.
Sin bin: Roper (35) - dangerous challenge.
BEARS: 1 Harry Chapman; 2 Reece Rance; 21 Kameron Pearce-Paul; 4 Jake Ogden; 5 Dante Morley-Samuels; 6 Liam Rice-Wilson; 7 Ben Stead; 8 James Geurtjens; 9 Richard Hughes; 10 Peter Ryan; 11 Ashley Bateman; 12 Ben Gray; 13 Harry Kaufman. Subs (all used): 14 Lewis Lord; 15 Zak Williams; 16 Malikhi Lloyd-Jones; 17 John Aldred.
Try: Rance (36); **Goals:** Stead 1/1.
Rugby Leaguer & League Express Men of the Match: *Crusaders:* Kenny Baker; *Bears:* Kameron Pearce-Paul.
Penalty count: 3-3; **Half-time:** 18-6;
Referee: Nick Bennett; **Attendance:** 301.

HUNSLET 86 WEST WALES RAIDERS 0

HUNSLET: 1 Jimmy Watson; 2 David Foggin-Johnston; 30 Nathan Chappell; 23 Tom Ashton; 4 Mufaro Mvududu; 6 Joe Sanderson; 7 Cain Southernwood; 32 Aiden Hema; 9 Jack Lee; 13 Matt Nicholson; 39 Josh Jordan-Roberts; 12 Duane Straugheir; 15 Brad Foster. Subs (all used): 8 Michael Haley; 21 Jack Walton; 10 Lewis Reed; 33 Luke Million.
Tries: Straugheir (2), Watson (4, 58), Lee (7, 75), Chappell (17), Foggin-Johnston (19), Walton (37), Mvududu (40), Southernwood (46), Ashton (52, 69), Hema (61, 65), Sanderson (72); **Goals:** Sanderson 13/15.

RAIDERS: 2 Mike Ward; 26 Louis Ford; 24 Aneurin Walker; 15 Joe McClean; 3 Kurtis Haile; 21 Steve Parry; 23 Karlin Claridge; 10 Morgan Evans; 22 Macauley Harris; 14 Dalton Desmond-Walker; 12 Harrison Elliott; 20 Archie Snook; 8 Connor Parker. Subs (all used): 7 Danny Hunter; 13 Robert Bonehill; 19 Ellis Simon; 17 Harry Boots.
Rugby Leaguer & League Express Men of the Match: *Hunslet:* Duane Straugheir; *Raiders:* Danny Hunter.
Penalty count: 6-5; **Half-time:** 38-0;
Referee: Billy Pearson; **Attendance:** 415.

KEIGHLEY COUGARS 26 LONDON SKOLARS 18

COUGARS: 1 Ritchie Hawkyard; 5 Davey Dixon; 34 Perry Whiteley; 4 Adam Ryder; 2 Andy Gabriel; 32 Dan Parker; 7 Matty Beharrell; 12 Brendon Rawlins; 15 Ryan Wright; 19 Matthew Bailey; 17 Cameron Leeming; 18 Josh Tonks; 13 Mike Emmett. Subs (all used): 8 Scott Law; 9 Nathan Conroy; 16 Harvey Hallas; 29 Brad Nicholson.
Tries: Ryder (24), Gabriel (48, 71), Nicholson (52), Whiteley (62); **Goals:** Beharrell 3/6, Parker 0/1.
SKOLARS: 1 Ryan Burroughs; 2 Vinny Finigan; 3 Jake Melling; 4 Michael Brown; 5 Jerome Yates; 7 Neil Thorman; 24 Phil Lyon; 10 Lamont Bryan; 9 Billy Driver; 14 Eddie Mbaraga; 22 Sam Nash; 12 Jordan Williams; 13 Ryan Chester. Subs (all used): 11 Quinn Ngawati; 15 Matthew Davies; 16 Callum Field; 20 Michael Sykes.
Tries: Thorman (9), Burroughs (33); **Goals:** Thorman 5/5.
Sin bin: Finigan (71) - dangerous challenge on Gabriel.
Rugby Leaguer & League Express Men of the Match: *Cougars:* Andy Gabriel; *Skolars:* Ryan Burroughs.
Penalty count: 9-11; **Half-time:** 6-14;
Referee: John McMullen; **Attendance:** 521.

WHITEHAVEN 26 YORK CITY KNIGHTS 18

WHITEHAVEN: 14 Dan Abram; 5 Dave Thompson; 3 Chris Taylor; 23 Jason Mossop; 4 Jessie Joe Parker; 6 Dion Aiye; 7 Callum Phillips; 8 Marc Shackley; 9 James Tilley; 10 Carl Forster; 27 Liam Cooper; 18 Ellis Gillam; 22 Stuart Howarth. Subs (all used): 19 Lewis Brown; 11 Connor Holliday; 16 Kris Coward; 26 Josh Eaves.
Tries: Parker (16), Gillam (41), Phillips (63), D Thompson (69); **Goals:** Abram 5/6.
CITY KNIGHTS: 2 Ben Cockayne; 1 Ash Robson; 11 Joe Batchelor; 4 Brad Hey; 3 Jake Butler-Fleming; 10 Graeme Horne; 6 Connor Robinson; 8 Adam Robinson; 9 Andy Ellis; 15 Chris Siddons; 29 Jordan Walne; 12 Sam Scott; 13 Tim Spears. Subs (all used): 20 Will Jubb; 19 Mike Kelly; - Colton Roche; 17 Joe Porter.
Tries: C Robinson (5), Horne (35), A Robinson (37);
Goals: C Robinson 3/3.
Rugby Leaguer & League Express Men of the Match: *Whitehaven:* Dion Aiye; *City Knights:* Graeme Horne.
Penalty count: 14-3; **Half-time:** 8-18;
Referee: Tom Crashley; **Attendance:** 640.

WORKINGTON TOWN 38 NEWCASTLE THUNDER 18

TOWN: 2 Sam Forrester; - Ricky Bailey; 3 Elliott Miller; 5 Perry Singleton; 24 John Patrick; 6 Jamie Doran; 7 Carl Forber; 8 Oliver Wilkes; 20 Sean Penkywicz; 10 Stevie Scholey; 13 Kyle Lovett; 22 Caine Barnes; 16 Jack Blagbrough. Subs (all used): 21 Jake Moore; 15 Tom Curwen; 19 Andrew Dawson; 17 Fuifui Moimoi.
Tries: Wilkes (16), Ricky Bailey (20), Penkywicz (26, 33, 78), Barnes (61), Blagbrough (64); **Goals:** Forber 5/8.
THUNDER: 1 Theerapol Ritson; 5 Mo Agoro; 4 Joe Brown; 2 Ali Blair; 3 Tyler Craig; 6 Lewis Young; 17 Adam Brook; 8 Liam McAvoy; 9 Evan Simons; 11 Harry Aldous; 10 Rhys Clarke; 12 Aaron Ollett; 13 Jack Aldous. Subs (all used): 35 Remy Marginet; 20 Conor Fitzsimmons; 14 Vincent Rennie; 24 Ben Calland.
Tries: Marginet (43, 70), McAvoy (75); **Goals:** Brook 3/3.
Dismissal: Ollett (52) - shoulder charge.
Rugby Leaguer & League Express Men of the Match: *Town:* Sean Penkywicz; *Thunder:* Adam Brook.
Penalty count: 9-7; **Half-time:** 18-0;
Referee: Marcus Griffiths; **Attendance:** 696.

ROUND 2

Saturday 2nd June 2018

HUNSLET 39 WHITEHAVEN 32

HUNSLET: 1 Jimmy Watson; 2 David Foggin-Johnston; 30 Nathan Chappell; 4 Mufaro Mvududu; 23 Tom Ashton; 6 Joe Sanderson; 7 Cain Southernwood; 32 Aiden Hema; 9 Jack Lee; 10 Lewis Reed; 39 Josh Jordan-Roberts; 12 Duane Straugheir; 15 Brad Foster. Subs (all used): 8 Michael Haley; 21 Jack Walton; 11 Liam Mackay; 31 Daniel Halmshaw.
Tries: Sanderson (17), Ashton (35), Foggin-Johnston (37, 69), Watson (76), Mvududu (80);
Goals: Sanderson 7/8; **Field goal:** Southernwood (78).
Sin bin: Watson (51) - retaliation.

WHITEHAVEN: 14 Dan Abram; 1 Jordan Burns; 23 Jason Mossop; 3 Chris Taylor; 4 Jessie Joe Parker; 6 Dion Aiye; 7 Callum Phillips; 8 Marc Shackley; 9 James Tilley; 10 Carl Forster; 18 Ellis Gillam; 5 Dave Thompson; 22 Stuart Howarth. Subs (all used): 27 Liam Cooper; 11 Connor Holliday; 16 Kris Coward; 26 Josh Eaves.
Tries: Aiye (28), Forster (40), Taylor (45), Parker (55), Cooper (66); **Goals:** Abram 6/6.
Sin bin: Eaves (51) - late challenge on Watson.
On report: Gillam (61) - alleged punching.
Rugby Leaguer & League Express Men of the Match: *Hunslet:* Aiden Hema; *Whitehaven:* Carl Forster.
Penalty count: 10-6; **Half-time:** 22-14;
Referee: Matt Rossleigh; **Attendance:** 576.

ROUND 1

Sunday 3rd June 2018

WEST WALES RAIDERS 20 NEWCASTLE THUNDER 82

RAIDERS: 18 Phil Cowburn; 3 Kurtis Haille; 15 Brad Kislingbury; 6 Luke Williams; 5 Sam Baker; 23 Karlin Claridge; 21 Steve Parry; 10 Morgan Evans; 22 Macauley Harris; 11 Ross Price; 12 Harrison Elliott; 8 Connor Parker; 4 Rowland Kaye. Subs (all used): 13 Alan Pope; 14 Dalton Desmond-Walker; 19 Ellis Simon; 24 Aneurin Walker.
Tries: Baker (7), Parry (11), Elliott (53), Kislingbury (69);
Goals: Williams 2/4.
THUNDER: 1 Theerapol Ritson; 4 Joe Brown; 23 Ben Dent; 6 Lewis Young; 28 Niall Sidney; 17 Adam Brook; 35 Remy Marginet; 8 Liam McAvoy; 9 Evan Simons; 10 Rhys Clarke; 11 Harry Aldous; 12 Aaron Ollett; 20 Conor Fitzsimmons. Subs (all used): 18 Dan Turland; 21 Ben Pointer; 24 Ben Calland; - Frazer Morris.
Tries: Clarke (16, 58), Sidney (22, 76), Fitzsimmons (25, 65), Young (30, 40, 43), Calland (34), Morris (37), McAvoy (46), Ritson (48), Brook (72), Marginet (80);
Goals: Marginet 5/9, Brook 6/6.
Rugby Leaguer & League Express Men of the Match: *Raiders:* Steve Parry; *Thunder:* Lewis Young.
Penalty count: 7-9; **Half-time:** 10-36;
Referee: Marcus Griffiths; **Attendance:** 272.

ROUND 11

Sunday 3rd June 2018

OLDHAM 32 DONCASTER 12

OLDHAM: 15 Luke Hooley; 30 Ben West; 4 Jack Holmes; 3 Matt Reid; 28 Lee Kershaw; 6 Paul Crook; 7 Dave Hewitt; 8 Phil Joy; 9 Gareth Owen; 16 Gavin Bennion; 12 Danny Langtree; 25 Danny Bridge; 24 Liam Bent. Subs (all used): 23 Luke Nelmes; 20 Matt Wilkinson; 19 Adam Jones; 11 Craig Briscoe.
Tries: Langtree (21), Hooley (33), Nelmes (42), Kershaw (68), Joy (75); **Goals:** Crook 6/7.
DONCASTER: 1 Richard Owen; 5 Sam Doherty; 19 Connor Bower; 4 Jason Tali; 24 Jack Sanderson; 6 Jordan Howden; 7 Liam Harris; 14 Connor Scott; 9 Kyle Kesik; 10 Ryan Boyle; 18 Charlie Martin; 25 Jack Downs; 26 Brandan Wilkinson. Subs (all used): 32 Lewis Bienek; 16 Zac Braham; 12 Jason Muranka; 21 Jez Litten.
Tries: Wilkinson (55), Tali (80);
Goals: Howden 1/1, Sanderson 1/1.
Sin bin: Owen (62) - dissent.
Rugby Leaguer & League Express Men of the Match: *Oldham:* Danny Bridge; *Doncaster:* Jez Litten.
Penalty count: 8-9; **Half-time:** 16-0;
Referee: Liam Staveley; **Attendance:** 453.

ROUND 12

Saturday 9th June 2018

BRADFORD BULLS 50 NORTH WALES CRUSADERS 12

BULLS: 24 Brandon Pickersgill; 5 Dalton Grant; 3 Ashley Gibson; 1 Lee Smith; 2 Ethan Ryan; 6 Joe Keyes; 7 Dane Chisholm; 10 Steve Crossley; 9 Sam Hallas; 8 Liam Kirk; 11 Matt Garside; 36 James Laithwaite; 12 Elliot Minchella. Subs (all used): 14 Gregg McNally; 19 Mikey Wood; 17 Ross Peltier; 26 Vila Halafihi.
Tries: Chisholm (8), Smith (14, 18), Pickersgill (25), Ryan (39, 69), Garside (43, 74), Keyes (47);
Goals: Chisholm 7/9.
CRUSADERS: 7 Ryan Smith; 24 Gavin Conroy; 20 Alex Thompson; 26 Alex Trumper; 5 Dale Bloomfield; 6 Steve Roper; - Joe Lyons; 8 Jonny Walker; 14 James Dandy; 15 Joe Bate; 11 Jack Houghton; 12 Simon Atherton; 17 Kenny Baker. Subs (all used): 19 Aaron Moore; 27 Liam Hulme; 22 Brad Brennan; - Wellington Albert.
Tries: Bloomfield (61), Atherton (64); **Goals:** Baker 2/2.
Sin bin: Trumper (42) - dangerous contact on Grant.

Rugby Leaguer & League Express Men of the Match: *Bulls:* Dane Chisholm; *Crusaders:* Aaron Moore.
Penalty count: 7-6; **Half-time:** 28-0;
Referee: Jon Roberts; **Attendance:** 3,112.

LONDON SKOLARS 30 HUNSLET 37

SKOLARS: 1 Ryan Burroughs; 5 Iliess Macani; 4 Michael Brown; 3 Jake Melling; 2 Lameck Juma; 7 Neil Thorman; 24 Phil Lyon; 8 Matt Ross; 9 Billy Driver; 10 Eddie Mbaraga; 12 Lamont Bryan; 11 Sam Nash; 13 Ryan Chester. Subs (all used): 20 Michael Sykes; - Jordan Williams; - Lewis Wray; 25 Charlie Lawrence.
Tries: Brown (14), Juma (17), Bryan (28), Burroughs (72), Thorman (75); **Goals:** Thorman 5/5.
HUNSLET: 1 Jimmy Watson; 2 David Foggin-Johnston; 30 Nathan Chappell; 4 Mufaro Mvududu; 28 Will Cooke; 6 Joe Sanderson; 7 Cain Southernwood; 32 Aiden Hema; 9 Jack Lee; 10 Lewis Reed; 39 Josh Jordan-Roberts; 11 Liam Mackay; 13 Matt Nicholson. Subs (all used): 31 Daniel Halmshaw; 21 Jack Walton; 40 Zac Braham; 8 Michael Haley.
Tries: Lee (32), Haley (35), Southernwood (43, 53), Halmshaw (49), Cooke (57); **Goals:** Sanderson 6/6;
Field goal: Southernwood (78).
Rugby Leaguer & League Express Men of the Match: *Skolars:* Ryan Burroughs; *Hunslet:* Cain Southernwood.
Penalty count: 10-11; **Half-time:** 18-12;
Referee: Nick Bennett; **Attendance:** 389.

WEST WALES RAIDERS 12 HEMEL STAGS 48

RAIDERS: 18 Phil Cowburn; 5 Sam Baker; 3 Kurtis Hale; 15 Brad Kislingbury; 2 Liam Silver; 23 Karlin Claridge; 19 Frazer Stroud; 11 Ross Price; 21 Steve Parry; 8 Connor Parker; 12 Harrison Elliott; 10 Joe McClean; 14 Dalton Desmond-Walker. Subs (all used): 22 Macauley Harris; 24 Aneurin Walker; 13 Alan Pope; 17 Harry Boots.
Tries: Elliott (25), Cowburn (63); **Goals:** Stroud 2/2.
STAGS: 22 Louis Sheriff; 2 Darren Forde; 4 Alex Williams; 3 Matt Welham; 5 Jordan Fitzpatrick-Parry; 6 Shaun Roberts; 7 Kieran Smith; 18 James Thornton; 9 Paul Stamp; 10 Rory Dixon; 11 Santino Decaro; 21 Dean Roberts; 13 Marcus Stock. Subs (all used): 14 Chris Cullimore; 17 Blake Broadbent; 16 Reece Williams; 8 Wayne Jowett.
Tries: Thornton (6, 73), Fitzpatrick-Parry (9), Sheriff (29, 68), Stamp (36, 47, 53), A Williams (78);
Goals: Smith 6/9.
Rugby Leaguer & League Express Men of the Match: *Raiders:* Phil Cowburn; *Stags:* Paul Stamp.
Penalty count: 10-6; **Half-time:** 6-24;
Referee: Matt Rossleigh; **Attendance:** 319.

Sunday 10th June 2018

COVENTRY BEARS 0 OLDHAM 60

BEARS: 1 Harry Chapman; 2 Jamahl Hunte; 3 Jason Bass; 21 Kameron Pearce-Paul; 5 Errol Carter; 6 Paul Emanuelli; 7 Ben Stead; 8 James Geurtjens; 9 Zak Williams; 10 Peter Ryan; 11 Ben Gray; 12 Chris Barratt; 13 Chris Vitalini. Subs (all used): 14 Liam Rice-Wilson; 15 James Mason; 16 Malikhi Lloyd-Jones; 17 John Aldred.
OLDHAM: 1 Kyran Johnson; 28 Lee Kershaw; 4 Jack Holmes; 3 Matt Reid; 30 Ben West; 6 Paul Crook; 7 Dave Hewitt; 8 Phil Joy; 9 Gareth Owen; 18 Ben Davies; 11 Craig Briscoe; 12 Danny Langtree; 24 Liam Bent. Subs (all used): 23 Luke Nelmes; 20 Matt Wilkinson; 22 Danny Rasool; 29 Zack McComb.
Tries: Davies (4), West (11), Wilkinson (21), Briscoe (27, 75), Langtree (33, 58), Rasool (37), Crook (46), Johnson (63), Hewitt (70); **Goals:** Crook 6/8, Hewitt 2/3.
Rugby Leaguer & League Express Men of the Match: *Bears:* James Geurtjens; *Oldham:* Danny Langtree.
Penalty count: 7-9; **Half-time:** 0-32;
Referee: Steve Race; **Attendance:** 337.

DONCASTER 29 KEIGHLEY COUGARS 20

DONCASTER: 1 Richard Owen; 5 Sam Doherty; 19 Connor Bower; 4 Jason Tali; 24 Jack Sanderson; 6 Jordan Howden; 13 Jordie Hedges; 10 Ryan Boyle; 9 Kyle Kesik; 33 Lewis Bienek; 11 Brad England; 22 Jordan Lane; 26 Brandan Wilkinson. Subs (all used): 23 Ross Osborne; 8 Russ Spiers; 18 Charlie Martin; 15 Kieran Cross.
Tries: Sanderson (28), Martin (39), Doherty (49), Cross (57); **Goals:** Hedges 5/5, Howden 1/1;
Field goal: Howden (76).
COUGARS: 1 Ritchie Hawkyard; 28 Harry Aaronson; 34 Perry Whiteley; 4 Adam Ryder; 2 Andy Gabriel; 23 Benn Hardcastle; 7 Matty Beharrell; 19 Matthew Bailey; 15 Ryan Wright; 35 Darrell Griffin; 17 Cameron Leeming; 32 Dan Parker; 13 Mike Emmett. Subs (all used): 8 Scott Law; 9 Nathan Conroy; 12 Brendon Rawlins; 29 Brad Nicholson.
Tries: Bailey (7), Nicholson (25), Ryder (65);
Goals: Hardcastle 4/5.
On report: Hawkyard (44) - alleged punch on Hedges.

Rugby Leaguer & League Express Men of the Match:
Doncaster: Jordie Hedges; *Cougars:* Matthew Bailey.
Penalty count: 9-9; **Half-time:** 12-14;
Referee: Greg Dolan; **Attendance:** 678.

NEWCASTLE THUNDER 30 WHITEHAVEN 22

THUNDER: 1 Theerapol Ritson; 5 Mo Agoro; 33 Tuoyo Egodo; 6 Lewis Young; 23 Ben Dent; 17 Adam Brook; 35 Remy Marginet; 8 Liam McAvoy; 21 Ben Pointer; 14 Vincent Rennie; 10 Rhys Clarke; 12 Aaron Ollett; 11 Harry Aldous. Subs (all used): 31 Frazer Morris; 20 Conor Fitzsimmons; 24 Ben Calland; 30 Curtis Davies.
Tries: Clarke (8), Egodo (10, 49), Dent (32), Young (35, 52);
Goals: Marginet 2/6, Brook 1/2.
WHITEHAVEN: 14 Dan Abram; 5 Dave Thompson; 3 Chris Taylor; 23 Jason Mossop; 1 Jordan Burns; 6 Dion Aiye; 7 Callum Phillips; 8 Marc Shackley; 9 James Tilley; 10 Carl Forster; 18 Ellis Gillam; 27 Liam Cooper; 22 Stuart Howarth. Subs (all used): 16 Kris Coward; 26 Josh Eaves; 11 Connor Holliday; 4 Jessie Joe Parker.
Tries: Cooper (39), Forster (45), Eaves (76), Burns (78);
Goals: Abram 3/4.
Rugby Leaguer & League Express Men of the Match:
Thunder: Lewis Young; *Whitehaven:* Liam Cooper.
Penalty count: 4-8; **Half-time:** 20-6;
Referee: Marcus Griffiths; **Attendance:** 759.

YORK CITY KNIGHTS 40 WORKINGTON TOWN 8

CITY KNIGHTS: 28 Will Dagger; 35 Will Oakes; 11 Joe Batchelor; 4 Brad Hey; 1 Ash Robson; 2 Ben Cockayne; 6 Connor Robinson; 26 Dan Hawksworth; 9 Andy Ellis; 8 Adam Robinson; 19 Mike Kelly; 12 Sam Scott; 13 Tim Spears. Subs (all used): 20 Will Jubb; 10 Graeme Horne; - Colton Roche; 17 Joe Porter.
Tries: Scott (13), Oakes (19), Kelly (31), Batchelor (45, 71), Cockayne (63), Horne (68); **Goals:** C Robinson 6/7.
TOWN: 1 Sam Forrester; 2 Joe Hambley; - Elliott Miller; 5 Perry Singleton; 24 John Patrick; 6 Jamie Doran; 7 Carl Forber; 8 Oliver Wilkes; 20 Sean Penkywicz; 10 Stevie Scholey; 21 Jake Moore; 18 Karl Olstrom; 16 Jack Blagbrough. Subs (all used): 12 Kurt Maudling; 15 Tom Curwen; 19 Andrew Dawson; 17 Fuifui Moimoi.
Try: Dawson (38); **Goals:** Forber 2/2.
Rugby Leaguer & League Express Men of the Match:
City Knights: Ben Cockayne; *Town:* John Patrick.
Penalty count: 10-8; **Half-time:** 18-8;
Referee: Liam Staveley; **Attendance:** 1,399.

ROUND 13

Sunday 17th June 2018

HEMEL STAGS 8 NEWCASTLE THUNDER 56

STAGS: 22 Louis Sheriff; 2 Darren Forde; 3 Kadeem Williams; 4 Sonny Esslemont; 5 Jordan Fitzpatrick-Parry; 6 Jack Mitchell; 7 Kieran Smith; 17 Blake Broadbent; 9 Paul Stamp; 10 Rory Dixon; 21 Paddy Burns; 11 Marcus Stock; 18 Kieran Moran. Subs (all used): 14 Jono Burns; - Max Garcia; 13 Lewis Taylor; 8 Wayne Jowett.
Tries: Forde (69, 79); **Goals:** Smith 0/2.
THUNDER: 23 Ben Dent; 30 Conor McGrath; 3 Tyler Craig; 6 Lewis Young; 4 Joe Brown; 17 Adam Brook; 16 Tom Shaw; 19 Liam Scott; 21 Ben Pointer; 15 Sam Luckley; 10 Rhys Clarke; 12 Aaron Ollett; 11 Harry Aldous. Subs (all used): - Liam Richmond; 27 David Weetman; 8 Liam McAvoy; 14 Vincent Rennie.
Tries: Scott (3, 61), Shaw (19, 46), Brown (24), McGrath (31, 74), Dent (42), Luckley (57), Pointer (74);
Goals: Shaw 8/10.
Rugby Leaguer & League Express Men of the Match:
Stags: Kadeem Williams; *Thunder:* Tom Shaw.
Penalty count: 2-6; **Half-time:** 0-22;
Referee: Steve Race; **Attendance:** 109.

NORTH WALES CRUSADERS 4
YORK CITY KNIGHTS 31

CRUSADERS: 1 Tommy Johnson; - Jake Knox; - Earl Hurst; 26 Alex Trumper; 5 Dale Bloomfield; - Joe Lyons; 7 Ryan Smith; 8 Jonny Walker; 14 James Dandy; 15 Joe Bate; 11 Jack Houghton; 12 Simon Atherton; 17 Kenny Baker. Subs (all used): 9 Lee Hudson; 22 Brad Brennan; - Samir Tahraoui; 27 Liam Hulme.
Try: Bloomfield (73); **Goals:** Johnson 0/1.
CITY KNIGHTS: - Will Dagger; 28 Will Oakes; 11 Joe Batchelor; 4 Brad Hey; 1 Ash Robson; 2 Ben Cockayne; 6 Connor Robinson; - Josh Johnson; 9 Andy Ellis; 26 Dan Hawksworth; - Jordan Walne; 12 Sam Scott; 13 Tim Spears. Subs (all used): 14 Harry Carter; 10 Graeme Horne; 8 Adam Robinson; 17 Joe Porter.
Tries: Robson (18), Oakes (35), Cockayne (57), Hawksworth (64), Ellis (68); **Goals:** C Robinson 5/6;
Field goal: C Robinson (40).

Rugby Leaguer & League Express Men of the Match:
Crusaders: Kenny Baker; *City Knights:* Ben Cockayne.
Penalty count: 6-10; **Half-time:** 0-13;
Referee: Michael Mannifield; **Attendance:** 408.

HUNSLET 40 COVENTRY BEARS 16

HUNSLET: 1 Jimmy Watson; 2 David Foggin-Johnston; 30 Nathan Chappell; 4 Mufaro Mvududu; 38 Marcus Elliott; 6 Joe Sanderson; 7 Cain Southernwood; 32 Aiden Hema; 9 Jack Lee; 13 Matt Nicholson; 39 Josh Jordan-Roberts; 28 Will Cooke; 11 Liam Mackay. Subs (all used): 8 Michael Haley; 10 Lewis Reed; 23 Tom Ashton; 31 Daniel Halmshaw.
Tries: Lee (4), Foggin-Johnston (23, 27), Chappell (42, 72, 77), Watson (68); **Goals:** Sanderson 6/7.
BEARS: 1 Jason Bass; 2 Errol Carter; 3 Jake Ogden; 4 Kameron Pearce-Paul; 5 Reece Rance; 6 Paul Emanuelli; 7 Ben Stead; 8 James Geurtjens; 9 Joe Cator; 10 Chris Vitalini; 11 Brad Clavering; 12 Chris Barratt; 13 Ashley Bateman. Subs (all used): 14 Zak Williams; 15 James Mason; 16 Malikhi Lloyd-Jones; 17 Dan Gover.
Tries: Cator (10), Barratt (35), Mason (58);
Goals: Stead 2/3.
Rugby Leaguer & League Express Men of the Match:
Hunslet: Nathan Chappell; *Bears:* Joe Cator.
Penalty count: 9-5; **Half-time:** 18-10;
Referee: Liam Staveley; **Attendance:** 511.

KEIGHLEY COUGARS 94 WEST WALES RAIDERS 0

COUGARS: 1 Ritchie Hawkyard; 28 Harry Aaronson; 34 Perry Whiteley; 4 Adam Ryder; 2 Andy Gabriel; 32 Dan Parker; 23 Benn Hardcastle; 16 Harvey Hallas; 15 Ryan Wright; 35 Darrell Griffin; 17 Cameron Leeming; 18 Josh Tonks; 13 Mike Emmett. Subs (all used): 8 Scott Law; 9 Nathan Conroy; 12 Brendon Rawlins; 29 Brad Nicholson.
Tries: Ryder (2, 49, 57), Parker (10, 72), Hawkyard (17, 43, 47, 60), Law (23), Whiteley (29, 35, 78), Gabriel (52, 68, 70), Griffin (74); **Goals:** Hardcastle 13/17.
RAIDERS: 18 Phil Cowburn; 2 Liam Silver; 3 Kurtis Haile; 11 Brad Kislingbury; 1 Matt Davies; 23 Karlin Claridge; 19 Frazer Stroud; 12 Harrison Elliott; 22 Macauley Harris; 8 Connor Parker; 20 Archie Snook; 10 Joe McClean; 4 Rowland Kaye. Subs (all used): 14 Dalton Desmond-Walker; 15 Dean Higgs; 24 Aneurin Walker; 26 Ellis Simon.
Rugby Leaguer & League Express Men of the Match:
Cougars: Adam Ryder; *Raiders:* Brad Kislingbury.
Penalty count: 7-3; **Half-time:** 32-0;
Referee: Cameron Worsley; **Attendance:** 470.

OLDHAM 44 LONDON SKOLARS 12

OLDHAM: 15 Luke Hooley; 2 Dave Eccleston; 4 Jack Holmes; 29 Zack McComb; 28 Lee Kershaw; 6 Paul Crook; 7 Dave Hewitt; 8 Phil Joy; 9 Gareth Owen; 13 Jack Spencer; 12 Danny Langtree; 25 Danny Bridge; 24 Liam Bent. Subs (all used): 18 Ben Davies; 20 Matt Wilkinson; 19 Adam Jones; 11 Craig Briscoe.
Tries: Hewitt (2), McComb (6), Wilkinson (40), Langtree (59), Bridge (67, 76, 80), Holmes (71);
Goals: Crook 6/8.
Sin bin: Jones (50) - use of the elbow.
SKOLARS: 1 Neil Thorman; 5 Iliess Macani; 4 Michael Brown; 15 Jake Melling; 2 Lameck Juma; 6 Jermaine Coleman; 7 Phil Lyon; 8 Matt Ross; 9 Billy Driver; 10 Mike Greenhalgh; 12 Eddie Mbaraga; 11 Sam Nash; 13 Ryan Chester. Subs (all used): 20 Samy Kibula; 22 Oliver Partington; 16 Lewis Wray; 17 Charlie Lawrence.
Tries: Macani (28), Mbaraga (52); **Goals:** Thorman 2/2.
Rugby Leaguer & League Express Men of the Match:
Oldham: Gareth Owen; *Skolars:* Neil Thorman.
Penalty count: 9-5; **Half-time:** 18-6;
Referee: Jon Roberts; **Attendance:** 419.

WHITEHAVEN 20 BRADFORD BULLS 27

WHITEHAVEN: 14 Dan Abram; 15 Danny Green; 23 Jason Mossop; 4 Jessie Joe Parker; 1 Jordan Burns; 22 Stuart Howarth; 7 Callum Phillips; 8 Marc Shackley; 9 James Tilley; 16 Kris Coward; 18 Ellis Gillam; 6 Dion Aiye; 10 Carl Forster. Subs (all used): 19 Lewis Brown; 27 Liam Cooper; 11 Connor Holliday; 26 Josh Eaves.
Tries: Gillam (4), Aiye (42), Eaves (74); **Goals:** Abram 4/4.
BULLS: 24 Brandon Pickersgill; 5 Dalton Grant; 3 Ashley Gibson; 1 Lee Smith; 2 Ethan Ryan; 6 Joe Keyes; 7 Dane Chisholm; 10 Steve Crossley; 26 Vila Halafihi; 8 Liam Kirk; 11 Matt Garside; 36 James Laithwaite; 12 Elliot Minchella. Subs (all used): 17 Ross Peltier; 19 Mikey Wood; 9 Sam Hallas; 18 Liam Johnson.
Tries: Crossley (16), Keyes (21, 55), Halafihi (79);
Goals: Chisholm 5/6; **Field goal:** Keyes (61).
Rugby Leaguer & League Express Men of the Match:
Whitehaven: Marc Shackley; *Bulls:* Joe Keyes.
Penalty count: 7-11; **Half-time:** 8-14;
Referee: John McMullen; **Attendance:** 1,476.

WORKINGTON TOWN 34 DONCASTER 6

TOWN: 1 Sam Forrester; 3 Elliott Miller; 5 Perry Singleton; 18 Karl Olstrom; 24 John Patrick; 6 Jamie Doran; 7 Carl Forber; 8 Oliver Wilkes; 20 Sean Penkywicz; 15 Tom Curwen; 21 Jake Moore; 22 Ben Morris; 16 Jack Blagbrough. Subs (all used): 9 James Newton; 10 Stevie Scholey; 19 Andrew Dawson; 17 Fuifui Moimoi.
Tries: Miller (5, 24), Moimoi (36, 77), Singleton (39), Doran (67); **Goals:** Forber 5/6.
Sin bin: Curwen (13) - late challenge.
DONCASTER: 24 Jack Sanderson; 5 Sam Doherty; - Cameron Scott; 4 Jason Tali; 2 Aaron Jones-Bishop; 6 Jordan Howden; 13 Jordie Hedges; - Lewis Bienek; 9 Kyle Kesik; 10 Ryan Boyle; 22 Jordan Lane; 11 Brad England; 26 Brandan Wilkinson. Subs (all used): 15 Kieran Cross; 12 Jason Muranka; 14 Connor Scott; 8 Russ Spiers.
Try: Cameron Scott (52); **Goals:** Hedges 1/1.
Rugby Leaguer & League Express Men of the Match:
Town: Jack Blagbrough; *Doncaster:* Kyle Kesik.
Penalty count: 12-8; **Half-time:** 22-0;
Referee: Billy Pearson; **Attendance:** 550.

ROUND 14

Saturday 23rd June 2018

LONDON SKOLARS 28
NORTH WALES CRUSADERS 36

SKOLARS: 1 Iliess Macani; 5 Vinny Finigan; 22 Sam Nash; 4 James Worthington; 2 Lameck Juma; 6 Jermaine Coleman; 7 Neil Thorman; 8 Matt Ross; 16 Charlie Lawrence; 10 Mike Greenhalgh; 18 Lamont Bryan; - Eddie Mbaraga; 13 Oliver Partington. Subs (all used): 9 Billy Driver; 20 Samy Kibula; 19 Michael Sykes; 17 Jordan Williams.
Tries: M Greenhalgh (4), Kibula (26, 77), Juma (28), Bryan (69); **Goals:** Thorman 4/5.
CRUSADERS: 1 Tommy Johnson; 5 Dale Bloomfield; - Earl Hurst; 12 Simon Atherton; - Jake Knox; - Joe Lyons; 7 Ryan Smith; 15 Joe Bate; 9 Lee Hudson; 8 Jonny Walker; 11 Jack Houghton; 14 James Dandy; 17 Kenny Baker. Subs (all used): 19 Aaron Moore; 20 Alex Thompson; 13 Ryan Millington; 27 Liam Hulme.
Tries: Houghton (9, 18), Atherton (47), A Thompson (54), Johnson (59), Baker (75); **Goals:** Johnson 6/7.
Rugby Leaguer & League Express Men of the Match:
Skolars: Samy Kibula; *Crusaders:* Jack Houghton.
Penalty count: 7-11; **Half-time:** 16-10;
Referee: Matt Rossleigh; **Attendance:** 275.

WEST WALES RAIDERS 6 WHITEHAVEN 66

RAIDERS: 18 Phil Cowburn; 2 Liam Silver; 15 Brad Kislingbury; 16 Shaun Tennant; 3 Kurtis Haile; 19 Frazer Stroud; 23 Karlin Claridge; 8 Connor Parker; 21 Steve Parry; 24 Aneurin Walker; 10 Joe McClean; 20 Archie Snook; 13 Alan Pope. Subs (all used): 5 Sam Baker; 6 Luke Williams; 17 Harry Boots; 22 Macauley Harris.
Try: Parry (11); **Goals:** Stroud 1/1.
WHITEHAVEN: 1 Jordan Burns; 15 Danny Green; 3 Chris Taylor; 4 Jessie Joe Parker; 5 Dave Thompson; 7 Callum Phillips; 22 Stuart Howarth; 16 Kris Coward; 26 Josh Eaves; 19 Lewis Brown; 11 Connor Holliday; 18 Ellis Gillam; 10 Carl Forster. Subs (all used): 6 Dion Aiye; 27 Scott McAvoy; 8 Marc Shackley; 9 James Tilley.
Tries: Burns (2), Gillam (7, 72), Phillips (33, 46), Shackley (36), Aiye (49), D Thompson (55, 58, 64), Coward (61), McAvoy (79); **Goals:** Burns 9/12.
Rugby Leaguer & League Express Men of the Match:
Raiders: Karlin Claridge; *Whitehaven:* Marc Shackley.
Penalty count: 5-8; **Half-time:** 6-22;
Referee: Liam Staveley; **Attendance:** 296.

Sunday 24th June 2018

BRADFORD BULLS 56 DONCASTER 14

BULLS: 24 Brandon Pickersgill; 5 Dalton Grant; 3 Ashley Gibson; 1 Lee Smith; 2 Ethan Ryan; 6 Joe Keyes; 7 Dane Chisholm; 10 Steve Crossley; 26 Vila Halafihi; 15 Callum Bustin; 11 Matt Garside; 36 James Laithwaite; 19 Mikey Wood. Subs (all used): 9 Sam Hallas; 18 Liam Johnson; 17 Ross Peltier; 8 Liam Kirk.
Tries: Ryan (2, 17, 69, 78), Crossley (20), Pickersgill (40, 65), Chisholm (49), Laithwaite (63), Bustin (73);
Goals: Chisholm 8/10.
DONCASTER: 1 Richard Owen; 5 Sam Doherty; 30 Cameron Scott; 4 Jason Tali; 24 Jack Sanderson; 13 Jordie Hedges; 17 Jack Miller; 8 Russ Spiers; 9 Kyle Kesik; 10 Ryan Boyle; 22 Jordan Lane; 11 Brad England; 18 Charlie Martin. Subs (all used): 31 Lewis Bienek; 21 Jez Litten; 12 Jason Muranka; 14 Connor Scott.
Tries: Hedges (7), Tali (23), Cameron Scott (49);
Goals: Hedges 1/3.

Rugby Leaguer & League Express Men of the Match: *Bulls:* Ethan Ryan; *Doncaster:* Lewis Bienek.
Penalty count: 5-5; **Half-time:** 22-8;
Referee: Tom Crashley; **Attendance:** 4,060.

NEWCASTLE THUNDER 46 COVENTRY BEARS 12

THUNDER: 1 Theerapol Ritson; 5 Mo Agoro; 4 Joe Brown; 3 Tyler Craig; 6 Lewis Young; 17 Adam Brook; 34 Remy Marginet; 13 Jack Aldous; 21 Ben Pointer; 8 Liam McAvoy; 10 Rhys Clarke; 24 Ben Calland; 15 Sam Luckley. Subs (all used): 33 Ollie Gowing; 14 Vincent Rennie; 20 Conor Fitzsimmons; 19 Liam Scott.
Tries: Young (7, 20, 36, 52), Agoro (24, 71), Ritson (45, 49), Craig (80); **Goals:** Marginet 5/9.
BEARS: 1 Harry Chapman; 2 Reece Rance; 20 Kameron Pearce-Paul; 4 Jake Ogden; 5 Errol Carter; 6 Paul Emanuelli; 7 Ben Stead; 8 James Geurtjens; 9 Joe Cator; 10 Dan Gover; 11 Brad Clavering; 12 Chris Barratt; 13 Chris Vitalini. Subs (all used): 14 Zak Williams; 15 James Mason; 16 Malikhi Lloyd-Jones; 17 Rob Butler.
Tries: Clavering (14), Barratt (43); **Goals:** Stead 2/2.
Rugby Leaguer & League Express Men of the Match: *Thunder:* Lewis Young; *Bears:* Chris Barratt.
Penalty count: 5-5; **Half-time:** 22-6;
Referee: Jon Roberts; **Attendance:** 903.

WORKINGTON TOWN 60 HEMEL STAGS 12

TOWN: 3 Elliott Miller; - Scott Rooke; 5 Perry Singleton; 18 Karl Olstrom; 2 Joe Hambley; 6 Jamie Doran; 7 Carl Forber; 8 Oliver Wilkes; 9 James Newton; 19 Andrew Dawson; 21 Jake Moore; 12 Kurt Maudling; 16 Jack Blagbrough. Subs (all used): 20 Sean Penkywicz; 10 Stevie Scholey; 24 John Patrick; 17 Fuifui Moimoi.
Tries: Wilkes (19), Singleton (22), Moimoi (24), Miller (30), Rooke (33), Hambley (37), Scholey (39), Penkywicz (47), Forber (53, 68), Blagbrough (78);
Goals: Forber 8/11.
STAGS: 1 Matt Welham; 2 Darren Forde; 3 Kadeem Williams; 4 Sonny Esslemont; 21 Alex Williams; 6 Shaun Roberts; 7 Kieran Smith; 14 Blake Broadbent; 9 Louis Sheriff; 10 Rory Dixon; 11 Marcus Stock; 22 Dean Roberts; 18 Kieran Moran. Subs (all used): 16 Reece Williams; 8 Wayne Jowett; 13 Lewis Taylor; 17 Stefanos Bastas.
Tries: Welham (11), Stock (71); **Goals:** Smith 2/2.
Rugby Leaguer & League Express Men of the Match: *Town:* Jack Blagbrough; *Stags:* Matt Welham.
Penalty count: 5-4; **Half time:** 40-6;
Referee: Nick Bennett; **Attendance:** 444.

HUNSLET 16 OLDHAM 12

HUNSLET: 1 Jimmy Watson; 2 David Foggin-Johnston; 30 Nathan Chappell; 4 Mufaro Mvududu; 23 Tom Ashton; 6 Joe Sanderson; 7 Cain Southernwood; 10 Lewis Reid; 9 Jack Lee; 13 Matt Nicholson; 39 Josh Jordan-Roberts; 15 Brad Foster; 11 Liam Mackay. Subs (all used): 17 Nyle Flynn; 19 Jack Coventry; 31 Daniel Halmshaw; 34 Zac Braham.
Tries: Braham (22), Mvududu (59), Southernwood (73);
Goals: Sanderson 2/3.
Sin bin: Halmshaw (45) - persistent team offences.
OLDHAM: 15 Luke Hooley; 30 Ben West; 3 Matt Reid; 29 Zack McComb; 28 Lee Kershaw; 6 Paul Crook; 7 Dave Hewitt; 8 Phil Joy; 9 Gareth Owen; 13 Jack Spencer; 25 Danny Bridge; 11 Craig Briscoe; 24 Liam Bent. Subs (all used): 23 Luke Nelmes; 20 Matt Wilkinson; 19 Adam Jones; 22 Danny Rasool.
Tries: Hooley (13), Wilkinson (37); **Goals:** Crook 2/3.
Rugby Leaguer & League Express Men of the Match: *Hunslet:* Zac Braham; *Oldham:* Paul Crook.
Penalty count: 8-12; **Half-time:** 6-12;
Referee: Marcus Griffiths; **Attendance:** 605.

KEIGHLEY COUGARS 14 YORK CITY KNIGHTS 46

COUGARS: 1 Ritchie Hawkyard; 28 Harry Aaronson; 34 Perry Whiteley; 4 Adam Ryder; 2 Andy Gabriel; 23 Benn Hardcastle; 7 Matty Beharrell; 19 Matthew Bailey; 15 Ryan Wright; 35 Darrell Griffin; 32 Dan Parker; 18 Josh Tonks; 13 Mike Emmett. Subs (all used): 8 Scott Law; 9 Nathan Conroy; 12 Brendon Rawlins; 29 Brad Nicholson.
Tries: Whiteley (26), Gabriel (31), Nicholson (68);
Goals: Hardcastle 1/3.
Sin bin:
Nicholson (21) - fighting, (54) - high tackle on C Robinson.
CITY KNIGHTS: 1 Ash Robson; 28 Will Oakes; 11 Joe Batchelor; 4 Brad Hey; 5 Judah Mazive; 2 Ben Cockayne; 6 Connor Robinson; 16 Ronan Dixon; 9 Andy Ellis; 26 Dan Hawksworth; 19 Mike Kelly; 12 Sam Scott; 13 Tim Spears. Subs (all used): 8 Adam Robinson; 10 Graeme Horne; 17 Joe Porter; 20 Will Jubb.
Tries: Spears (12), Jubb (23), C Robinson (39), Batchelor (47), Horne (61), Porter (78), Kelly (80);
Goals: C Robinson 4/4, Robson 5/5.
Sin bin: Spears (21) - fighting.
Rugby Leaguer & League Express Men of the Match: *Cougars:* Adam Ryder; *City Knights:* Ben Cockayne.
Penalty count: 10-12; **Half-time:** 10-18;
Referee: Billy Pearson; **Attendance:** 698.

ROUND 15

Saturday 30th June 2018

COVENTRY BEARS 12 BRADFORD BULLS 62

BEARS: 1 Jason Bass; 2 Harry Chapman; 3 Jake Ogden; 20 Kameron Pearce-Paul; 5 Hayden Freeman; 6 Paul Emanuelli; 7 Ben Stead; 8 Chris Vitalini; 9 Zak Williams; 10 Malikhi Lloyd-Jones; 11 Kieran Sherratt; 12 Chris Barratt; 13 Ashley Bateman. Subs (all used): 14 Liam Rice-Wilson; 15 James Mason; 16 Peter Ryan; 17 Dan Gover.
Tries: Pearce-Paul (4), Barratt (48); **Goals:** Stead 2/2.
BULLS: 24 Brandon Pickersgill; 5 Dalton Grant; 3 Ashley Gibson; 4 Ross Oakes; 2 Ethan Ryan; 6 Joe Keyes; 7 Dane Chisholm; 8 Liam Kirk; 9 Sam Hallas; 15 Callum Bustin; 18 Liam Johnson; 12 Elliot Minchella; 19 Mikey Wood. Subs (all used): 17 Ross Peltier; 26 Vila Halafihi; 13 George Milton; 36 James Laithwaite.
Tries: Ryan (16), Milton (28), Minchella (31, 45, 78), Peltier (41), Laithwaite (43), Keyes (51), Johnson (64), Hallas (74, 80); **Goals:** Chisholm 9/11.
Rugby Leaguer & League Express Men of the Match: *Bears:* Ben Stead; *Bulls:* Elliot Minchella.
Penalty count: 13-10; **Half-time:** 6-16;
Referee: Joe Stearne; **Attendance:** 1,465.

WEST WALES RAIDERS 12 LONDON SKOLARS 62

RAIDERS: 14 Phil Cowburn; 3 Kurtis Haile; 11 Brad Kislingbury; 16 Shaun Tennant; 10 Andrew Rees-Spowart; 19 Frazer Stroud; 23 Karlin Claridge; 24 Aneurin Walker; 21 Steve Parry; 13 Alan Pope; 20 Archie Snook; 4 Rowland Kaye; 8 Connor Parker. Subs (all used): 6 Luke Williams; 9 Connor Farrer; 18 Craig Lewis; 17 Harry Boots.
Tries: Walker (54), Cowburn (75); **Goals:** Stroud 2/2.
Sin bin: Farrer (64) - fighting.
SKOLARS: 1 Elliot Hall; 2 Vinny Finigan; 22 Sam Nash; 4 Lameck Juma; 5 Iliess Macani; 6 Phil Lyon; 7 Neil Thorman; 8 Will Martin; 9 Billy Driver; 10 Mike Greenhalgh; 18 Lamont Bryan; 12 Eddie Mbaraga; 13 Ryan Chester. Subs (all used): 14 Michael Sykes; 15 Mike Bishay; 16 Matt Ross; 17 Rob Butler.
Tries: Bryan (7, 40, 80), Hall (10), Macani (13, 34, 58), Finigan (15, 45), Juma (24, 71), Mbaraga (31);
Goals: Thorman 5/9, Bishay 2/3.
Sin bin: Driver (64) - fighting.
Rugby Leaguer & League Express Men of the Match: *Raiders:* Aneurin Walker; *Skolars:* Lamont Bryan.
Penalty count: 7-11; **Half-time:** 0-42;
Referee: Craig Smith; **Attendance:** 224.

Sunday 1st July 2018

HEMEL STAGS 10 DONCASTER 74

STAGS: 1 Jack Mitchell; 2 Darren Forde; 3 Kadeem Williams; 13 Sonny Esslemont; 5 Matt Welham; 6 Shaun Roberts; 7 Kieran Smith; 15 Blake Broadbent; 9 Paul Stamp; 10 Rory Dixon; 11 Marcus Stock; 18 Dean Roberts; 8 Kieran Moran. Subs (all used): 14 Jono Burns; 4 Corey Hanson; 16 Reece Williams; 17 Stefanos Bastas.
Tries: Forde (27), Welham (78); **Goals:** Smith 1/2.
DONCASTER: 24 Jack Sanderson; 1 Richard Owen; 30 Cameron Scott; 4 Jason Tali; 2 Aaron Jones-Bishop; 6 Jordan Howden; 13 Jordie Hedges; 8 Russ Spiers; 9 Kyle Kesik; 10 Ryan Boyle; 25 Jack Downs; 11 Brad England; 31 Jansin Turgut. Subs (all used): 21 Jez Litten; 12 Jason Muranka; 14 Connor Scott; 18 Charlie Martin.
Tries: Turgut (4, 31), Sanderson (7, 15, 37, 41), Downs (10), Tali (21), Kesik (24), Hedges (35, 43), Jones-Bishop (55, 80), Litten (60);
Goals: Hedges 2/5, Sanderson 3/4, Howden 4/5.
Rugby Leaguer & League Express Men of the Match: *Stags:* Darren Forde; *Doncaster:* Jack Sanderson.
Penalty count: 2-5; **Half-time:** 6-46;
Referee: Jon Roberts; **Attendance:** 108.

NORTH WALES CRUSADERS 18 HUNSLET 19

CRUSADERS: 1 Tommy Johnson; - Olly Ashall-Bott; - Earl Hurst; 12 Simon Atherton; 5 Dale Bloomfield; 7 Ryan Smith; - Joe Lyons; 15 Joe Bate; 14 James Dandy; 8 Jonny Walker; 11 Jack Houghton; 17 Kenny Baker; - Brad Walker. Subs (all used): 19 Aaron Moore; 20 Alex Thompson; 10 Warren Thompson; - Dan Norman.
Tries: W Thompson (21), B Walker (32), Bloomfield (71);
Goals: Johnson 3/4.
HUNSLET: 1 Jimmy Watson; 2 David Foggin-Johnston; 30 Nathan Chappell; 4 Mufaro Mvududu; 23 Tom Ashton; 6 Joe Sanderson; 7 Cain Southernwood; 13 Matt Nicholson; 9 Jack Lee; 10 Lewis Reed; 39 Josh Jordan-Roberts; 15 Brad Foster; 11 Liam Mackay. Subs (all used): 31 Daniel Halmshaw; 34 Zac Braham; 8 Michael Haley; 12 Duane Straugheir.
Tries: Straugheir (16), Sanderson (26), Mvududu (57);
Goals: Sanderson 3/4; **Field goal:** Southernwood (77).
Rugby Leaguer & League Express Men of the Match: *Crusaders:* Brad Walker; *Hunslet:* Duane Straugheir.
Penalty count: 6-6; **Half-time:** 12-12;
Referee: Andrew Sweet; **Attendance:** 317.

OLDHAM 14 WORKINGTON TOWN 16

OLDHAM: 1 Kyran Johnson; 2 Dave Eccleston; 29 Zack McComb; 3 Matt Reid; 30 Ben West; 6 Paul Crook; 7 Dave Hewitt; 8 Phil Joy; 9 Gareth Owen; 13 Jack Spencer; 11 Craig Briscoe; 25 Danny Bridge; 24 Liam Bent. Subs (all used): 23 Luke Nelmes; 20 Matt Wilkinson; 19 Adam Jones; 22 Danny Rasool.
Tries: Reid (13), West (59), Johnson (66); **Goals:** Crook 1/3.
Sin bin: West (33) - delaying restart.
TOWN: 3 Elliott Miller; 24 John Patrick; 4 Sam Wood; 12 Kurt Maudling; 2 Joe Hambley; 6 Jamie Doran; 7 Carl Forber; 8 Oliver Wilkes; 20 Sean Penkywicz; 15 Tom Curwen; 21 Jake Moore; 22 Ben Morris; 10 Stevie Scholey. Subs (all used): 9 James Newton; 11 Andrew Dawson; - Scott Rooke; 17 Fuifui Moimoi.
Tries: Morris (23), Miller (25), Hambley (47);
Goals: Forber 1/3, Wood 1/2, Doran 0/1.
Sin bin: Moimoi (68) - high tackle.
Rugby Leaguer & League Express Men of the Match: *Oldham:* Liam Bent; *Town:* Jamie Doran.
Penalty count: 10-8; **Half-time:** 4-10;
Referee: Tom Crashley; **Attendance:** 486.

WHITEHAVEN 28 KEIGHLEY COUGARS 14

WHITEHAVEN: 1 Jordan Burns; 15 Danny Green; 3 Chris Taylor; 4 Jessie Joe Parker; 5 Dave Thompson; 22 Stuart Howarth; 7 Callum Phillips; 8 Marc Shackley; 26 Josh Eaves; 16 Kris Coward; 6 Dion Aiye; 18 Ellis Gillam; 10 Carl Forster. Subs (all used): 14 Dan Abram; 27 Liam Cooper; 23 Jason Mossop; 9 James Tilley.
Tries: Parker (39), D Thompson (46, 69), Taylor (67);
Goals: Burns 6/6.
COUGARS: 28 Harry Aaronson; 5 Davey Dixon; 34 Perry Whiteley; 4 Adam Ryder; 17 Cameron Leeming; 32 Dan Parker; 23 Benn Hardcastle; 35 Darrell Griffin; 15 Ryan Wright; 19 Matthew Bailey; 12 Brendon Rawlins; 29 Brad Nicholson; 13 Mike Emmett. Subs (all used): 8 Scott Law; 9 Nathan Conroy; 10 Trae O'Sullivan; 16 Harvey Hallas.
Tries: Hardcastle (54, 78); **Goals:** Hardcastle 3/3.
Dismissal: Parker (64) - high tackle on Aiye.
Rugby Leaguer & League Express Men of the Match: *Whitehaven:* Dave Thompson; *Cougars:* Benn Hardcastle.
Penalty count: 9-5; **Half-time:** 8-2;
Referee: Nick Bennett; **Attendance:** 592.

YORK CITY KNIGHTS 24 NEWCASTLE THUNDER 6

CITY KNIGHTS: 1 Ash Robson; 33 Will Oakes; 11 Joe Batchelor; 4 Brad Hey; 5 Judah Mazive; 2 Ben Cockayne; 32 Matty Marsh; 26 Dan Hawksworth; 37 Danny Maskill; 16 Ronan Dixon; 19 Mike Kelly; 12 Sam Scott; 17 Joe Porter. Subs (all used): 14 Harry Carter; - Jordan Walne; - Josh Johnson; 8 Adam Robinson.
Tries: Robson (31), Scott (38), Oakes (73), Marsh (78);
Goals: Robson 4/5.
Sin bin: Carter (59) - fighting.
THUNDER: 6 Lewis Young; 5 Mo Agoro; 4 Joe Brown; 3 Tyler Craig; 23 Ben Dent; 17 Adam Brook; 16 Tom Shaw; 8 Liam McAvoy; 21 Ben Pointer; 13 Jack Aldous; 15 Sam Luckley; 12 Aaron Ollett; 11 Harry Aldous. Subs (all used): - Joe Cator; - Ollie Gowing; 14 Vincent Rennie; 20 Conor Fitzsimmons.
Try: Dent (29); **Goals:** Shaw 1/2.
Sin bin: Luckley (59) - fighting.
Rugby Leaguer & League Express Men of the Match: *City Knights:* Ash Robson; *Thunder:* Lewis Young.
Penalty count: 8-10; **Half-time:** 10-6;
Referee: Steve Race; **Attendance:** 1,212.

ROUND 16

Friday 6th July 2018

BRADFORD BULLS 24 NEWCASTLE THUNDER 4

BULLS: 24 Brandon Pickersgill; 5 Dalton Grant; 3 Ashley Gibson; 4 Ross Oakes; 2 Ethan Ryan; 6 Joe Keyes; 7 Dane Chisholm; 10 Steve Crossley; 9 Sam Hallas; 15 Callum Bustin; 12 Elliot Minchella; 36 James Laithwaite; 19 Mikey Wood. Subs (all used): 8 Liam Kirk; 11 Matt Garside; 17 Ross Peltier; 26 Vila Halafihi.
Tries: Chisholm (8), Pickersgill (22), Ryan (79);
Goals: Chisholm 6/6.

THUNDER: 23 Ben Dent; 5 Mo Agoro; 26 Kieran Gill; 3 Tyler Craig; 4 Joe Brown; 16 Tom Shaw; 17 Adam Brook; 8 Liam McAvoy; 21 Ben Pointer; 13 Jack Aldous; 10 Rhys Clarke; 12 Aaron Ollett; 15 Sam Luckley. Subs (all used): 22 Joe Cator; 9 Evan Simons; 14 Vincent Rennie; 20 Conor Fitzsimmons.
Try: Gill (31); **Goals:** Shaw 0/1.
Sin bin: Craig (55) - professional foul.
Rugby Leaguer & League Express Men of the Match: *Bulls:* Dane Chisholm; *Thunder:* Adam Brook.
Penalty count: 12-7; **Half-time:** 14-4;
Referee: John McMullen; **Attendance:** 3,029.

Saturday 7th July 2018

LONDON SKOLARS 20 COVENTRY BEARS 24

SKOLARS: 1 Elliot Hall; 2 Vinny Finigan; 3 Matty Fleming; 4 Lameck Juma; 5 Iliess Macani; 7 Mike Bishay; 6 Charlie Lawrence; 8 Will Martin; 9 Neil Thorman; 10 Mike Greenhalgh; 12 Lamont Bryan; 11 Sam Nash; 13 Ryan Chester. Subs (all used): 14 Eddie Mbaraga; 20 Michael Sykes; 24 Billy Driver; 17 Rob Butler.
Tries: C Lawrence (2), Bryan (24), Bishay (60);
Goals: Thorman 4/4.
Dismissal:
M Greenhalgh (67) - dangerous challenge on Williams.
BEARS: 1 Jason Bass; 2 Hayden Freeman; 3 Jake Ogden; 4 Kameron Pearce-Paul; 5 Harry Chapman; 6 Liam Rice-Wilson; 7 Ben Stead; 8 Chris Vitalini; 9 Zak Williams; 15 Malikhi Lloyd-Jones; 11 Kieran Sherratt; 12 Chris Barratt; 13 Ashley Bateman. Subs (all used): 14 Brad Sheridan; 10 Peter Ryan; 16 James Mason; 17 James Geurtjens.
Tries: Vitalini (31), Pearce-Paul (40), Freeman (45, 68);
Goals: Stead 4/5.
Rugby Leaguer & League Express Men of the Match: *Skolars:* Neil Thorman; *Bears:* Hayden Freeman.
Penalty count: 11-11; **Half-time:** 14-14;
Referee: Michael Mannifield; **Attendance:** 160.

Sunday 8th July 2018

HEMEL STAGS 16 KEIGHLEY COUGARS 32

STAGS: 1 Jack Mitchell; 2 Darren Forde; 3 Kadeem Williams; 12 Matt Welham; 5 Jordan Fitzpatrick-Parry; 6 Shaun Roberts; 7 Kieran Smith; 4 Reece Williams; 9 Jono Burns; 10 Blake Broadbent; 11 Marcus Stock; 18 Dean Roberts; 13 Sonny Esslemont. Subs (all used): 8 Jack Howieson; 22 Corey Hanson; 16 Austin Bell; 17 Lewis Taylor.
Tries: J Burns (29), Welham (64), Forde (69);
Goals: Smith 2/3.
Sin bin: Hanson (67) - fighting.
COUGARS: 28 Harry Aaronson; 5 Davey Dixon; 17 Cameron Leeming; 3 Hamish Barnes; 2 Andy Gabriel; 32 Dan Parker; 23 Benn Hardcastle; 19 Matthew Bailey; - Chris Cullimore; 16 Harvey Hallas; 39 Aaron Levy; 12 Brendon Rawlins; 13 Mike Emmett. Subs (all used): 8 Scott Law; 9 Nathan Conroy; 10 Trae O'Sullivan; 31 Jose Kenga.
Tries: Cullimore (5), Leeming (9), Dixon (19), Levy (41), Gabriel (43), Rawlins (57); **Goals:** Hardcastle 4/6.
Sin bin: Hardcastle (67) - fighting.
Rugby Leaguer & League Express Men of the Match: *Stags:* Darren Forde; *Cougars:* Benn Hardcastle.
Penalty count: 6-15; **Half-time:** 6-14;
Referee: Brandon Robinson; **Attendance:** 136.

NORTH WALES CRUSADERS 14 WHITEHAVEN 22

CRUSADERS: - Olly Ashall-Bott; - Ryan Ince; 12 Simon Atherton; - Earl Hurst; 5 Dale Bloomfield; 7 Ryan Smith; 6 Steve Roper; 15 Joe Bate; 9 Lee Hudson; 8 Jonny Walker; 11 Jack Houghton; 17 Kenny Baker; - Brad Walker. Subs (all used): 19 Aaron Moore; 22 Brad Brennan; 10 Warren Thompson; - Dan Norman.
Tries: Ashall-Bott (10), Baker (56); **Goals:** B Walker 3/3.
Sin bin: Bloomfield (36) - delaying restart.
WHITEHAVEN: 14 Dan Abram; 1 Jordan Burns; 3 Chris Taylor; 4 Jessie Joe Parker; 5 Dave Thompson; 22 Stuart Howarth; 7 Callum Phillips; 8 Marc Shackley; 9 James Tilley; 19 Lewis Brown; 18 Ellis Gillam; 6 Dion Aiye; 10 Carl Forster. Subs (all used): 27 Liam Cooper; 26 Josh Eaves; 11 Connor Holliday; 23 Jason Mossop.
Tries: Burns (7, 50), Aiye (36), Eaves (65);
Goals: Abram 3/4.
Sin bin: Gillam (30) - late challenge on Smith.
Rugby Leaguer & League Express Men of the Match: *Crusaders:* Olly Ashall-Bott; *Whitehaven:* Stuart Howarth.
Penalty count: 9-6; **Half-time:** 8-10;
Referee: Tom Crashley; **Attendance:** 321.

OLDHAM 102 WEST WALES RAIDERS 6

OLDHAM: 15 Luke Hooley; 28 Lee Kershaw; 4 Jack Holmes; 29 Zack McComb; 30 Ben West; 6 Paul Crook; 7 Dave Hewitt; 18 Ben Davies; 9 Gareth Owen; 13 Jack Spencer; 11 Craig Briscoe; 25 Danny Bridge; 24 Liam Bent. Subs (all used): 23 Luke Nelmes; 14 Jonah Cunningham; 16 Jordan Dezaria; 19 Adam Jones.
Tries: Hooley (2, 19, 59, 77), Holmes (7, 24, 55), Spencer (17), Cunningham (31, 37, 46), Dezaria (34), Hewitt (39, 50, 52), Kershaw (42), West (68), McComb (71);
Goals: Crook 7/9, Hewitt 8/9.
RAIDERS: 1 Phil Cowburn; 2 Matt Davies; 11 David Kearns; 4 Brad Kislingbury; 5 Sam Baker; 21 Steve Parry; 6 Luke Williams; 24 Aneurin Walker; 22 Macauley Harris; 12 Harrison Elliott; 20 Archie Snook; 7 Rowland Kaye; 13 Dewi Billingham. Subs (all used, only three named): 26 Craig Kelly; 17 Harry Boots; 16 Shaun Tennant.
Try: Kislingbury (10); **Goals:** Williams 1/1.
Rugby Leaguer & League Express Men of the Match: *Oldham:* Jonah Cunningham; *Raiders:* Phil Cowburn.
Penalty count: 4-2; **Half-time:** 50-6;
Referee: Jon Roberts; **Attendance:** 274.

WORKINGTON TOWN 28 HUNSLET 18

TOWN: 4 Sam Wood; - Scott Rooke; 12 Kurt Maudling; 18 Karl Olstrom; 2 Joe Hambley; 6 Jamie Doran; 7 Carl Forber; 8 Oliver Wilkes; 20 Sean Penkywicz; 15 Tom Curwen; 22 Ben Morris; 10 Stevie Scholey; 23 Tyler Dickinson. Subs (all used): 3 Matthew Johnson; 11 Andrew Dawson; 9 James Newton; 17 Fuifui Moimoi.
Tries: K Maudling (23), Scholey (47), Wilkes (51), Doran (57), Rooke (78); **Goals:** Forber 4/5.
HUNSLET: 41 Gavin Duffy; 28 Will Cooke; 36 Daley Williams; 4 Mufaro Mvududu; 23 Tom Ashton; 6 Joe Sanderson; 7 Cain Southernwood; 10 Lewis Reed; 9 Jack Lee; 13 Matt Nicholson; 33 Josh Tonks; 12 Duane Straugheir; 11 Liam Mackay. Subs (all used): 37 Ryan Wright; 39 Josh Jordan-Roberts; 17 Nyle Flynn; 34 Zac Braham.
Tries: Straugheir (6), Mvududu (18, 72);
Goals: Sanderson 3/4.
Sin bin: Flynn (42) - persistent team offences.
Rugby Leaguer & League Express Men of the Match: *Town:* Oliver Wilkes; *Hunslet:* Duane Straugheir.
Penalty count: 9-7; **Half-time:** 4-14;
Referee: Nick Bennett; **Attendance:** 601.

YORK CITY KNIGHTS 31 DONCASTER 16

CITY KNIGHTS: 1 Ash Robson; 2 Ben Cockayne; 11 Joe Batchelor; 4 Brad Hey; 5 Judah Mazive; 6 Connor Robinson; 32 Matty Marsh; 34 Josh Johnson; 9 Andy Ellis; - Jordan Walne; 19 Mike Kelly; 12 Sam Scott; 13 Tim Spears. Subs (all used): 14 Harry Carter; 10 Graeme Horne; - Colton Roche; 17 Joe Porter.
Tries: Mazive (9), Robson (29), Marsh (64), Horne (78), Cockayne (80); **Goals:** C Robinson 5/6;
Field goal: C Robinson (48).
Dismissal: Johnson (4) - fighting.
DONCASTER: 24 Jack Sanderson; 1 Richard Owen; 5 Sam Doherty; 4 Jason Tali; 2 Aaron Jones-Bishop; 6 Jordan Howden; 29 Matty Beharrell; 8 Russ Spiers; 9 Kyle Kesik; 10 Ryan Boyle; 22 Jordan Lane; 11 Brad England; 30 Jansin Turgut. Subs (all used): 21 Jez Litten; 28 Frankie Mariano; 23 Ross Osborne; 14 Connor Scott.
Tries: Owen (5, 58), Howden (68); **Goals:** Sanderson 2/4.
Dismissal: Spiers (4) - fighting.
Rugby Leaguer & League Express Men of the Match: *City Knights:* Ben Cockayne; *Doncaster:* Richard Owen.
Penalty count: 9-9; **Half-time:** 12-6;
Referee: Marcus Griffiths; **Attendance:** 1,311.

ROUND 17

Friday 13th July 2018

KEIGHLEY COUGARS 15 OLDHAM 8

COUGARS: 28 Harry Aaronson; 5 Davey Dixon; 17 Cameron Leeming; 3 Hamish Barnes; 2 Andy Gabriel; - Anthony Bowman; 23 Benn Hardcastle; 16 Harvey Hallas; - Chris Cullimore; 19 Matthew Bailey; 12 Brendon Rawlins; 35 Darrell Griffin; 13 Mike Emmett. Subs (all used): 8 Scott Law; 9 Nathan Conroy; 31 Jose Kenga; 42 Kieran Moran.
Try: Emmett (22); **Goals:** Hardcastle 5/5;
Field goal: Hardcastle (31).
Sin bin: Rawlins (55) - fighting.
OLDHAM: 15 Luke Hooley; 28 Lee Kershaw; 29 Zack McComb; 4 Jack Holmes; 30 Ben West; 6 Paul Crook; 7 Dave Hewitt; 13 Jack Spencer; 9 Gareth Owen; 8 Phil Joy; 25 Danny Bridge; 11 Craig Briscoe; 24 Liam Bent. Subs (all used): 14 Jonah Cunningham; 18 Ben Davies; 19 Adam Jones; 23 Luke Nelmes.
Try: Hooley (15); **Goals:** Crook 2/2.
Sin bin: Jones (55) - fighting.
Rugby Leaguer & League Express Men of the Match: *Cougars:* Darrell Griffin; *Oldham:* Jack Spencer.
Penalty count: 10-12; **Half-time:** 7-8;
Referee: Cameron Worsley; **Attendance:** 510.

Saturday 14th July 2018

LONDON SKOLARS 20 YORK CITY KNIGHTS 22

SKOLARS: 1 Elliot Hall; 2 Vinny Finigan; 22 Sam Nash; 4 Lameck Juma; 5 Jerome Yates; 6 James Meadows; 7 Mike Bishay; 8 Will Martin; 9 Neil Thorman; 10 Mike Greenhalgh; 11 Eddie Mbaraga; 12 Lamont Bryan; 13 Ryan Chester. Subs (all used): 24 Billy Driver; 16 Matt Ross; 17 Rob Butler; - Jordan Williams.
Tries: Finigan (53), Meadows (67), Bishay (74);
Goals: Bishay 4/4.
Sin bin: Juma (78) - punching.
CITY KNIGHTS: 1 Ash Robson; 27 Liam Jackson; 3 Jake Butler-Fleming; 4 Brad Hey; 5 Judah Mazive; 2 Ben Cockayne; 6 Connor Robinson; 8 Adam Robinson; 20 Will Jubb; 26 Dan Hawksworth; 11 Joe Batchelor; 19 Mike Kelly; 13 Tim Spears. Subs (all used): 14 Harry Carter; 10 Graeme Horne; 16 Ronan Dixon; 17 Joe Porter.
Tries: Mazive (35), C Robinson (40), Porter (48), Batchelor (62); **Goals:** C Robinson 3/4.
Rugby Leaguer & League Express Men of the Match: *Skolars:* James Meadows; *City Knights:* Joe Porter.
Penalty count: 5-3; **Half-time:** 2-10;
Referee: Nick Bennett; **Attendance:** 258.

Sunday 15th July 2018

DONCASTER 102 WEST WALES RAIDERS 6

DONCASTER: 7 Liam Harris; 5 Sam Doherty; 30 Cameron Scott; 4 Jason Tali; 1 Richard Owen; 6 Jordan Howden; 29 Matty Beharrell; 8 Russ Spiers; 9 Kyle Kesik; 14 Connor Scott; 11 Brad England; 28 Frankie Mariano; 13 Jordie Hedges. Subs (all used): 12 Jason Muranka; 2 Aaron Jones-Bishop; 21 Jez Litten; 10 Ryan Boyle.
Tries: Owen (8), Harris (11, 48), Howden (14), Mariano (17, 36), Kesik (25, 73), Doherty (33), Litten (38, 41, 53), England (50), Hedges (55), Cameron Scott (58), Spiers (68), Muranka (74), Jones-Bishop (78); **Goals:** Harris 15/18.
RAIDERS: 1 Phil Cowburn; 2 Matt Davies; 4 Brad Kislingbury; 6 Luke Williams; 7 Rowland Kaye; 21 Steve Parry; 19 Frazer Stroud; 12 Harrison Elliott; 22 Macauley Harris; 24 Aneurin Walker; 20 Archie Snook; 10 Joe McClean; 13 Dewi Billingham. Subs (all used): 26 Craig Kelly; 15 Dean Higgs; 8 Connor Parker; 17 Harry Boots.
Try: Parry (30); **Goals:** Stroud 1/1.
Rugby Leaguer & League Express Men of the Match: *Doncaster:* Liam Harris; *Raiders:* Steve Parry.
Penalty count: 6-3; **Half-time:** 42-6;
Referee: Brandon Robinson; **Attendance:** 306
(at LD Nutrition Stadium, Featherstone).

HUNSLET 16 BRADFORD BULLS 36

HUNSLET: 1 Jimmy Watson; 2 David Foggin-Johnston; 4 Mufaro Mvududu; 23 Tom Ashton; 41 Gavin Duffy; 6 Joe Sanderson; 7 Cain Southernwood; 32 Aidan Hema; 9 Jack Lee; 10 Lewis Reed; 33 Josh Tonks; 12 Duane Straugheir; 11 Liam Mackay. Subs (all used): 19 Jack Coventry; 31 Daniel Halmshaw; 8 Michael Haley; 36 Daley Williams.
Tries: Duffy (5), Straugheir (56); **Goals:** Sanderson 4/4.
BULLS: 14 Gregg McNally; 5 Dalton Grant; 3 Ashley Gibson; 4 Ross Oakes; 2 Ethan Ryan; 6 Joe Keyes; 7 Dane Chisholm; 10 Steve Crossley; 9 Sam Hallas; 15 Callum Bustin; 11 Matt Garside; 36 James Laithwaite; 12 Elliot Minchella. Subs (all used): 24 Brandon Pickersgill; 37 James Green; 21 George Flanagan; 17 Ross Peltier.
Tries: Gibson (16, 19), Crossley (43), Keyes (58), Flanagan (60, 77); **Goals:** Chisholm 6/8.
Rugby Leaguer & League Express Men of the Match: *Hunslet:* Lewis Reed; *Bulls:* George Flanagan.
Penalty count: 6-6; **Half-time:** 10-12;
Referee: Michael Smaill; **Attendance:** 1,536.

WORKINGTON TOWN 22 WHITEHAVEN 24

TOWN: 3 Elliott Miller; 5 Joe Hambley; 23 Ilias Bergal; 4 Perry Singleton; 2 Scott Rooke; 6 Jamie Doran; 7 Carl Forber; 8 Oliver Wilkes; 20 Sean Penkywicz; 15 Tom Curwen; 18 Karl Olstrom; 25 Ben Morris; 10 Stevie Scholey. Subs (all used): 9 James Newton; 12 Kurt Maudling; 19 Andrew Dawson; 26 Tyler Dickinson.
Tries: Rooke (55, 66), Dickinson (73); **Goals:** Forber 5/6.
Sin bin: Olstrom (38) - punching Forster.
WHITEHAVEN: 1 Jordan Burns; 4 Jessie Joe Parker; 23 Jason Mossop; 3 Chris Taylor; 5 Dave Thompson; 7 Callum Phillips; 22 Stuart Howarth; 8 Marc Shackley; 14 Dan Abram; 10 Carl Forster; 18 Ellis Gillam; 6 Dion Aiye; 19 Lewis Brown. Subs (all used): 27 Liam Cooper; 26 Josh Eaves; 11 Connor Holliday; 15 Danny Green.
Tries: Gillam (28, 78), Green (80); **Goals:** Abram 6/6.
Sin bin: Shackley (51) - dangerous contact on Curwen.
Rugby Leaguer & League Express Men of the Match: *Town:* Tyler Dickinson; *Whitehaven:* Liam Cooper.
Penalty count: 11-9; **Half-time:** 4-10;
Referee: Marcus Griffiths; **Attendance:** 1,258.

COVENTRY BEARS 20 HEMEL STAGS 18

BEARS: 1 Jason Bass; 2 Hayden Freeman; 3 Jake Ogden; 21 Kameron Pearce-Paul; 5 Harry Chapman; 6 Brad Sheridan; 7 Ben Stead; 8 Chris Vitalini; 9 Zak Williams; 16 Malikhi Lloyd-Jones; 11 Kieran Sherratt; 12 Chris Barratt; 13 Ashley Bateman. Subs (all used): 14 Sam Davis; 17 James Geurtjens; 15 James Mason; 10 Dan Gover.
Tries: Bass (4, 23), Sherratt (67), Chapman (73);
Goals: Stead 2/4.
STAGS: 1 Jack Mitchell; 2 Darren Forde; 4 Alex Williams; 3 Matt Welham; 5 Ricky Williams; 6 Shaun Roberts; 7 Kieran Smith; 8 Reece Williams; 9 Jono Burns; 10 Blake Broadbent; 11 Marcus Stock; 18 Dean Roberts; 13 Sonny Esslemont. Subs (all used): 14 Paul Stamp; 22 Corey Hanson; 16 Austin Bell; - Lewis Taylor.
Tries: Broadbent (12), A Williams (35), Smith (69);
Goals: Smith 3/4.
Rugby Leaguer & League Express Men of the Match:
Bears: Jason Bass; *Stags:* Kieran Smith.
Penalty count: 6-16; **Half-time:** 10-10;
Referee: Paul Marklove; **Attendance:** 281.

NEWCASTLE THUNDER 20 NORTH WALES CRUSADERS 24

THUNDER: 23 Ben Dent; 5 Mo Agoro; - Tuoyo Egodo; 3 Tyler Craig; 4 Joe Brown; 16 Tom Shaw; 17 Adam Brook; 8 Liam McAvoy; 21 Ben Pointer; 13 Jack Aldous; 10 Rhys Clarke; 12 Aaron Ollett; 15 Sam Luckley. Subs (all used): 9 Evan Simons; 11 Harry Aldous; 14 Vincent Rennie; 20 Conor Fitzsimmons.
Tries: Brown (3), Shaw (18, 43); **Goals:** Shaw 4/4.
CRUSADERS: 24 Gavin Conroy; - Patrick Ah Van; - Earl Hurst; 12 Simon Atherton; 5 Dale Bloomfield; - Joe Lyons; 7 Ryan Smith; 15 Joe Bate; 9 Lee Hudson; 10 Warren Thompson; 14 James Dandy; 26 Alex Trumper; 17 Kenny Baker. Subs (all used): 19 Aaron Moore; 22 Brad Brennan; 20 Alex Thompson; - Dan Norman.
Tries: Smith (37), Bloomfield (39), Norman (47), Baker (78); **Goals:** Ah Van 3/3, Baker 1/1.
Sin bin: Bate (5) - late challenge.
Rugby Leaguer & League Express Men of the Match:
Thunder: Tom Shaw; *Crusaders:* Dale Bloomfield.
Penalty count: 7-7; **Half-time:** 12-12;
Referee: Liam Staveley; **Attendance:** 637.

ROUND 18

Saturday 21st July 2018

COVENTRY BEARS 30 KEIGHLEY COUGARS 20

BEARS: 1 Mikey Russell; 2 Errol Carter; 3 Jake Ogden; 21 Kameron Pearce-Paul; 5 Hayden Freeman; 6 Paul Emanuelli; 7 Brad Delaney; 8 Chris Vitalini; 9 Zak Williams; 16 Malikhi Lloyd-Jones; 11 Kieran Sherratt; 12 Chris Barratt; 13 Sam Davis. Subs (all used): 14 Dante Morley-Samuels; 10 James Geurtjens; 15 Cameron Stewart; 17 John Aldred.
Tries: M Russell (6, 55, 80), Barratt (9), Ogden (63);
Goals: Emanuelli 5/7.
COUGARS: 28 Harry Aaronson; 5 Davey Dixon; 17 Cameron Leeming; 3 Hamish Barnes; 2 Andy Gabriel; 32 Dan Parker; 23 Benn Hardcastle; 19 Matthew Bailey; 21 Chris Cullimore; 16 Harvey Hallas; 35 Darrell Griffin; 12 Brendon Rawlins; 13 Mike Emmett. Subs (all used): 8 Scott Law; 9 Nathan Conroy; 31 Jose Kenga; 42 Kieran Moran.
Tries: Conroy (32), Aaronson (35), Hallas (62), Parker (71);
Goals: Hardcastle 2/4.
Rugby Leaguer & League Express Men of the Match:
Bears: Mikey Russell; *Cougars:* Harry Aaronson.
Penalty count: 12-11; **Half-time:** 12-10;
Referee: Joe Stearne; **Attendance:** 303.

WEST WALES RAIDERS 6 WORKINGTON TOWN 46

RAIDERS: 1 Phil Cowburn; 2 Matt Davies; 18 Brad Kislingbury; 3 Kurtis Haile; 5 Sam Baker; 6 Luke Williams; 21 Steve Parry; 24 Aneurin Walker; 15 Dean Higgs; 13 Alan Pope; 12 Harrison Elliott; 10 Joe McClean; 7 Rowland Kaye. Subs: 26 Rhys Pope; 11 Barrie Phillips (not used); 4 Liam Silver; 25 Dafydd Phillips.
Try: A Pope (62); **Goals:** Williams 1/1.
TOWN: 1 Elliott Miller; 6 Ilias Bergal; 22 Ben Morris; 3 Perry Singleton; 2 Joe Hambley; 5 Sam Forrester; 7 Carl Forber; 8 Oliver Wilkes; 20 Sean Penkywicz; 15 Tom Curwen; 18 Karl Olstrom; 21 Jake Moore; 10 Stevie Scholey. Subs (all used): 19 Andrew Dawson; 24 Jordan Dezaria; 4 Gordon Maudling; 12 Kurt Maudling.
Tries: Bergal (7, 21, 51, 73), Curwen (10), Hambley (18), Wilkes (70), Dawson (76); **Goals:** Forber 7/9.
Rugby Leaguer & League Express Men of the Match:
Raiders: Steve Parry; *Town:* Ilias Bergal.
Penalty count: 8-10; **Half-time:** 0-22;
Referee: Craig Smith; **Attendance:** 246.

Sunday 22nd July 2018

BRADFORD BULLS 28 YORK CITY KNIGHTS 30

BULLS: 14 Gregg McNally; 5 Dalton Grant; 18 Liam Johnson; 4 Ross Oakes; 2 Ethan Ryan; 6 Joe Keyes; 7 Dane Chisholm; 10 Steve Crossley; 9 Sam Hallas; 15 Callum Bustin; 12 Elliot Minchella; 11 Matt Garside; 19 Mikey Wood. Subs (all used): 21 George Flanagan; 8 Liam Kirk; 17 Ross Peltier; 37 James Green.
Tries: Grant (38, 78), McNally (51), Peltier (56), Ryan (62);
Goals: Chisholm 4/6.
CITY KNIGHTS: 31 Matty Marsh; 1 Ash Robson; 3 Jake Butler-Fleming; 4 Brad Hey; 5 Judah Mazive; 2 Ben Cockayne; 6 Connor Robinson; 32 Josh Johnson; 9 Andy Ellis; 29 Jordan Walne; 11 Joe Batchelor; 12 Sam Scott; 13 Tim Spears. Subs (all used): 10 Graeme Horne; 30 Jack Ormondroyd; 17 Joe Porter; 14 Harry Carter.
Tries: Johnson (6), Cockayne (12), Mazive (19, 69), Batchelor (25); **Goals:** C Robinson 5/6.
Rugby Leaguer & League Express Men of the Match:
Bulls: Dane Chisholm; *City Knights:* Ben Cockayne.
Penalty count: 17-6; **Half-time:** 4-24;
Referee: Matt Rossleigh; **Attendance:** 6,441.

HUNSLET 14 DONCASTER 30

HUNSLET: 1 Jimmy Watson; 2 David Foggin-Johnston; 30 Nathan Chappell; 4 Mufaro Mvududu; 23 Tom Ashton; 6 Joe Sanderson; 7 Cain Southernwood; 32 Aiden Hema; 9 Jack Lee; 10 Lewis Reed; 33 Josh Tonks; 12 Duane Straugheir; 15 Brad Foster. Subs (all used): 37 Ryan Wright; 8 Michael Haley; 13 Matt Nicholson; 28 Will Cooke.
Tries: Lee (22), Chappell (34); **Goals:** Sanderson 3/3.
Sin bin: Watson (77) - dissent.
DONCASTER: 24 Jack Sanderson; 5 Sam Doherty; 30 Cameron Scott; 4 Jason Tali; 1 Richard Owen; 6 Jordan Howden; 29 Matty Beharrell; 8 Russ Spiers; 9 Kyle Kesik; 14 Connor Scott; 28 Frankie Mariano; 11 Brad England; 22 Jordan Lane. Subs (all used): 10 Ryan Boyle; 13 Jordie Hedges; 21 Jez Litten; 18 Charlie Martin.
Tries: Connor Scott (19), Martin (42), Beharrell (60), Tali (63), Sanderson (68);
Goals: Sanderson 4/4, Beharrell 1/1.
Sin bin: Beharrell (33) - high tackle on Foggin-Johnston.
Rugby Leaguer & League Express Men of the Match:
Hunslet: Jack Lee; *Doncaster:* Matty Beharrell.
Penalty count: 7-7; **Half-time:** 14-6;
Referee: Steve Race; **Attendance:** 517.

NEWCASTLE THUNDER 42 HEMEL STAGS 14

THUNDER: 23 Ben Dent; 5 Mo Agoro; 2 Ali Blair; 30 Kieran Hudson; 28 Niall Sidney; 16 Tom Shaw; 17 Adam Brook; 8 Liam McAvoy; 9 Evan Simons; 13 Jack Aldous; 15 Sam Luckley; 12 Aaron Ollett; 11 Harry Aldous. Subs (all used): - Joe Cator; 14 Vincent Rennie; 25 Sam Blake; 27 David Weetman.
Tries: Blair (6), Agoro (14), Simons (22, 64), Weetman (31), Ollett (40), Sidney (44, 75); **Goals:** Shaw 5/8.
Sin bin: Cator (64) - professional foul.
STAGS: 1 Matt Welham; 2 Darren Forde; 18 Alex Williams; 4 Corey Hanson; 5 Ricky Williams; 6 Jack Mitchell; 7 Shaun Roberts; 17 Reece Williams; 9 Jono Burns; 10 Blake Broadbent; 11 Santino Decaro; 21 Dean Roberts; 13 Sonny Esslemont. Subs (all used): 14 Paul Stamp; 8 Austin Bell; 16 Stefanos Bastas; 22 Wayne Jowett.
Tries: D Roberts (17, 72), Jowett (55); **Goals:** S Roberts 1/3.
Rugby Leaguer & League Express Men of the Match:
Thunder: Evan Simons; *Stags:* Dean Roberts.
Penalty count: 7-7; **Half-time:** 28-4;
Referee: Andrew Sweet; **Attendance:** 676.

OLDHAM 50 NORTH WALES CRUSADERS 6

OLDHAM: 15 Luke Hooley; 28 Lee Kershaw; 29 Zack McComb; 3 Matt Reid; 2 Dave Eccleston; 6 Paul Crook; 7 Dave Hewitt; 8 Phil Joy; 9 Gareth Owen; 13 Jack Spencer; 25 Danny Bridge; 12 Danny Langtree; 24 Liam Bent. Subs (all used): 14 Jonah Cunningham; 16 Nick Gregson; 23 Luke Nelmes; 11 Craig Briscoe.
Tries: Langtree (5, 11, 15, 57), Nelmes (34), Cunningham (42, 60), Reid (64), Joy (70); **Goals:** Crook 7/9.
CRUSADERS: 1 Tommy Johnson; 24 Gavin Conroy; 26 Alex Trumper; - Earl Hurst; 5 Dale Bloomfield; - Joe Lyons; 7 Ryan Smith; 15 Joe Bate; 9 Lee Hudson; 10 Warren Thompson; 11 Jack Houghton; 14 James Dandy; 17 Kenny Baker. Subs (all used): 19 Aaron Moore; 22 Brad Brennan; 20 Alex Thompson; - Dan Norman.
Try: Houghton (25); **Goals:** Johnson 1/1.
Rugby Leaguer & League Express Men of the Match:
Oldham: Danny Langtree; *Crusaders:* Ryan Smith.
Penalty count: 4-5; **Half-time:** 24-6;
Referee: Michael Mannifield; **Attendance:** 466.

WHITEHAVEN 28 LONDON SKOLARS 18

WHITEHAVEN: 14 Dan Abram; 1 Jordan Burns; 23 Jason Mossop; 3 Chris Taylor; 15 Danny Green; 22 Stuart Howarth; 7 Callum Phillips; 8 Marc Shackley; 9 James Tilley; 19 Lewis Brown; 11 Connor Holliday; 5 Dave Thompson; 10 Carl Forster. Subs (all used): 16 Kris Coward; 27 Liam Cooper; 26 Josh Eaves; 28 Scott McAvoy.
Tries: Burns (17, 27), Eaves (35), Holliday (68), Taylor (72);
Goals: Abram 2/5, Burns 2/2.
SKOLARS: 1 Mike Bishay; 2 Vinny Finigan; 15 Matty Fleming; 4 Lameck Juma; 5 Michael Brown; 6 James Meadows; 7 Neil Thorman; 8 Will Martin; 9 Billy Driver; 10 Daymeric Pelo; 12 Eddie Mbaraga; 18 Lamont Bryan; 13 Ryan Chester. Subs (all used): 16 Jy-mel Coleman; 22 Matt Ross; 17 Rob Butler; 25 Jordan Williams.
Tries: Juma (50, 75), Jy-mel Coleman (59);
Goals: Thorman 3/3.
Sin bin: Ross (37) - persistent team offences.
Rugby Leaguer & League Express Men of the Match:
Whitehaven: Stuart Howarth; *Skolars:* Daymeric Pelo.
Penalty count: 18-7; **Half-time:** 16-0;
Referee: Brandon Robinson; **Attendance:** 661.

ROUND 4

Wednesday 25th July 2018

COVENTRY BEARS 64 WEST WALES RAIDERS 6

BEARS: 1 Jason Bass; 2 Hayden Freeman; 3 Dante Morley-Samuels; 21 Kameron Pearce-Paul; 4 Harry Chapman; 6 Paul Emanuelli; 7 Ben Stead; 8 Dan Gover; 9 Zak Williams; 16 Malikhi Lloyd-Jones; 11 Kieran Sherratt; 12 Chris Barratt; 13 Chris Vitalini. Subs (all used): 14 Liam Rice-Wilson; 10 James Geurtjens; 15 James Mason; 17 Cameron Stewart.
Tries: Barratt (3), Bass (8), Freeman (14, 33, 75), Geurtjens (29), Pearce-Paul (38, 62, 65), Stead (45), Sherratt (57), Chapman (61); **Goals:** Stead 8/12.
RAIDERS: 1 Phil Cowburn; 26 Aseri Biutanaseva; 22 Brad Kislingbury; 3 Kurtis Haile; 2 Liam Silver; 6 Luke Williams; 21 Steve Parry; 24 Aneurin Walker; 15 Dean Higgs; 8 Connor Parker; 13 Dewi Billingham; 7 Rowland Kaye; 12 Harrison Elliott. Subs (all used): 14 David Kearns; 25 Dafydd Phillips; 18 Craig Lewis; 11 Callum Mulkeen.
Try: Cowburn (59); **Goals:** Williams 1/1.
Sin bin: Lewis (51) - professional foul.
Rugby Leaguer & League Express Men of the Match:
Bears: Kameron Pearce-Paul; *Raiders:* Phil Cowburn.
Penalty count: 12-9; **Half-time:** 34-0;
Referee: Cameron Worsley; **Attendance:** 272.

ROUND 19

Saturday 28th July 2018

LONDON SKOLARS 12 BRADFORD BULLS 58

SKOLARS: 1 Mike Bishay; 2 Billy Driver; 3 Matty Fleming; 4 Lameck Juma; 5 Michael Brown; 6 Jy-mel Coleman; 7 Charlie Lawrence; 8 Will Martin; 9 Neil Thorman; 10 Daymeric Pelo; 11 Lamont Bryan; 12 Jordan Williams; 13 Ryan Chester. Subs (all used): 14 Matthew Davies; 15 Matt Ross; 16 Eddie Mbaraga; 17 Michael Sykes.
Tries: Juma (24, 71); **Goals:** Thorman 2/2.
BULLS: 24 Brandon Pickersgill; 5 Dalton Grant; 39 Tuoyo Egodo; 4 Ross Oakes; 2 Ethan Ryan; 38 Jordan Lilley; 7 Dane Chisholm; 37 James Green; 21 George Flanagan; 10 Steve Crossley; 12 Eliot Minchella; 11 Matt Garside; 19 Mikey Wood. Subs (all used): 17 Ross Peltier; 26 Vila Halafihi; 13 George Milton; 8 Liam Kirk.
Tries: Green (8), Chisholm (10, 58), Ryan (14, 41, 54), Peltier (34), Halafihi (49), Lilley (61), Pickersgill (67), Minchella (75); **Goals:** Chisholm 7/11.
Rugby Leaguer & League Express Men of the Match:
Skolars: Jordan Williams; *Bulls:* Dane Chisholm.
Penalty count: 7-8; **Half-time:** 6-20;
Referee: Craig Smith; **Attendance:** 1,178.

Sunday 29th July 2018

HEMEL STAGS 30 WEST WALES RAIDERS 22

STAGS: 1 Matt Welham; 2 Joe Barron; 22 Louis Sheriff; 4 Corey Hanson; 5 Ricky Williams; 6 Jack Mitchell; 7 Shaun Roberts; 16 Stefanos Bastas; 9 Jono Burns; 10 Blake Broadbent; 11 Santino Decaro; 21 Dean Roberts; 18 Jack Howieson. Subs (all used): 14 Paul Stamp; 13 Marcus Stock; 8 Austin Bell; 17 Wayne Jowett.
Tries: Decaro (5), Welham (30, 53), Hanson (35, 58), Sheriff (48); **Goals:** Mitchell 3/6.
RAIDERS: 1 Phil Cowburn; 5 Sam Baker; 14 Brad Kislingbury; 6 Luke Williams; 2 Matt Davies; 21 Steve Parry; 19 Frazer Stroud; 24 Aneurin Walker; 15 Dean Higgs; 13 Alan Pope; 10 Joe McClean; 20 Rowland Kaye; 12 Harrison Elliott. Subs: 22 Macauley Harris; 26 Rhys Pope; 16 Craig Lewis; 17 Harry Boots (not used).

Tries: Cowburn (11), Williams (15), A Pope (68), McClean (80); **Goals:** Stroud 1/2, Williams 2/2.
Rugby Leaguer & League Express Men of the Match: *Stags:* Louis Sheriff; *Raiders:* Rowland Kaye.
Penalty count: 10-9; **Half-time:** 16-10;
Referee: Michael Smaill; **Attendance:** 118.

NORTH WALES CRUSADERS 22 WORKINGTON TOWN 36

CRUSADERS: 1 Tommy Johnson; 5 Dale Bloomfield; - Earl Hurst; 26 Alex Trumper; 24 Gavin Conroy; 7 Ryan Smith; - Joe Lyons; 17 Kenny Baker; 14 James Dandy; 10 Warren Thompson; 11 Jack Houghton; - Stephen Wild; - Brad Walker. Subs (all used): - Karl Ashall; 8 Jonny Walker; 15 Joe Bate; - Dan Norman.
Tries: Hurst (5), Trumper (16), Bloomfield (52);
Goals: Johnson 4/4, B Walker 1/1.
TOWN: 1 Sam Forrester; - Scott Rooke; 3 Elliott Miller; 24 Perry Singleton; 5 Joe Hambley; 6 Jamie Doran; 7 Carl Forber; 8 Oliver Wilkes; 20 Sean Penkywicz; 15 Tom Curwen; 4 Gordon Maudling; 16 Ben Morris; 10 Stevie Scholey. Subs (all used): 17 Fuifui Moimoi; 19 Andrew Dawson; 21 Jake Moore; 12 Kurt Maudling.
Tries: Forrester (11), Wilkes (24), Morris (35), Penkywicz (54, 63), Curwen (66); **Goals:** Forber 6/6.
Rugby Leaguer & League Express Men of the Match: *Crusaders:* Alex Trumper; *Town:* Sean Penkywicz.
Penalty count: 7-5; **Half-time:** 14-18;
Referee: Steve Race; **Attendance:** 340.

DONCASTER 26 OLDHAM 22

DONCASTER: 20 Hakim Miloudi; 5 Sam Doherty; 30 Jack Logan; 4 Jason Tali; 2 Aaron Jones-Bishop; 6 Jordan Howden; 29 Matty Beharrell; 14 Connor Scott; 9 Kyle Kesik; 10 Ryan Boyle; 11 Brad England; 28 Frankie Mariano; 25 Jack Downs. Subs (all used): 23 Ross Osborne; 18 Charlie Martin; 13 Jordie Hedges; 21 Jez Litten.
Tries: Doherty (24), England (44), Jones-Bishop (49), Logan (64); **Goals:** Beharrell 5/7.
Sin bin: Hedges (42) - fighting.
OLDHAM: 15 Luke Hooley; 28 Lee Kershaw; 3 Matt Reid; 29 Zack McComb; 2 Dave Eccleston; 6 Paul Crook; 7 Dave Hewitt; 8 Phil Joy; 9 Gareth Owen; 13 Jack Spencer; 11 Craig Briscoe; 12 Danny Langtree; 24 Liam Bent. Subs (all used): 20 Matt Wilkinson; 23 Luke Nelmes; 18 Ben Davies; 22 Danny Rasool.
Tries: Langtree (69), Reid (74), Eccleston (77);
Goals: Crook 3/3, Hooley 1/2, Hewitt 1/1.
Sin bin: Langtree (42) - fighting.
Rugby Leaguer & League Express Men of the Match: *Doncaster:* Brad England; *Oldham:* Gareth Owen.
Penalty count: 10-11; **Half-time:** 8-6;
Referee: Andrew Sweet; **Attendance:** 647.

KEIGHLEY COUGARS 16 HUNSLET 24

COUGARS: 1 Ritchie Hawkyard; 5 Davey Dixon; 17 Cameron Leeming; 3 Hamish Barnes; 28 Harry Aaronson; 32 Dan Parker; 23 Benn Hardcastle; 19 Matthew Bailey; 9 Nathan Conroy; 16 Harvey Hallas; 35 Darrell Griffin; 11 Josh Lynam; 13 Mike Emmett. Subs (all used): 8 Scott Law; 10 Trae O'Sullivan; 31 Jose Kenga; 42 Kieran Moran.
Tries: Lynam (8), Hardcastle (31); **Goals:** Hardcastle 4/4.
Dismissal: Emmett (79) - dissent.
Sin bin: Lynam (60) - late challenge on Watson; Barnes (74) - persistent team offences; Hawkyard (75) - holding down.
HUNSLET: 1 Jimmy Watson; 2 David Foggin-Johnston; 30 Nathan Chappell; 4 Mufaro Mvududu; 36 Daley Williams; 6 Joe Sanderson; 7 Cain Southernwood; 32 Aiden Hema; 9 Jack Lee; 13 Matt Nicholson; 33 Josh Tonks; 12 Duane Straugheir; 15 Brad Foster. Subs (all used): 8 Michael Haley; 10 Lewis Reed; 11 Liam Mackay; 31 Daniel Halmshaw.
Tries: Watson (35), Mackay (67), Mvududu (77), Haley (79);
Goals: Sanderson 4/4.
Dismissal: Reed (19) - shoulder charge on Parker.
Rugby Leaguer & League Express Men of the Match: *Cougars:* Benn Hardcastle; *Hunslet:* Duane Straugheir.
Penalty count: 2-12; **Half-time:** 16-6;
Referee: Brandon Robinson; **Attendance:** 793.

WHITEHAVEN 12 NEWCASTLE THUNDER 8

WHITEHAVEN: 1 Jordan Burns; 15 Danny Green; 3 Chris Taylor; 23 Jason Mossop; 5 Dave Thompson; 7 Callum Phillips; 22 Stuart Howarth; 8 Marc Shackley; 26 Josh Eaves; 9 James Tilley; 11 Connor Holliday; 18 Ellis Gillam; 10 Carl Forster. Subs (all used): 14 Dan Abram; 16 Kris Coward; 28 Scott McAvoy; 4 Jessie Joe Parker.
Tries: D Thompson (21), Parker (70); **Goals:** Burns 2/4.
THUNDER: 1 Theerapol Ritson; 5 Mo Agoro; 23 Ben Dent; 6 Lewis Young; 2 Ali Blair; 17 Adam Brook; - Remy Marginet; 8 Liam McAvoy; 9 Evan Simons; 13 Jack Aldous; 10 Rhys Clarke; 15 Sam Luckley; 11 Harry Aldous. Subs (all used): 14 Vincent Rennie; 20 Conor Fitzsimmons; 21 Ben Pointer; 24 Ben Calland.
Try: Young (39); **Goals:** Marginet 2/3.
Rugby Leaguer & League Express Men of the Match: *Whitehaven:* Marc Shackley; *Thunder:* Vincent Rennie.
Penalty count: 7-9; **Half-time:** 8-6;
Referee: Michael Mannifield; **Attendance:** 551.

YORK CITY KNIGHTS 68 COVENTRY BEARS 6

CITY KNIGHTS: 35 Matt Chilton; 1 Ash Robson; 4 Brad Hey; 11 Joe Batchelor; 5 Judah Mazive; 6 Connor Robinson; 2 Ben Cockayne; 16 Ronan Dixon; 9 Andy Ellis; 10 Graeme Horne; 28 Josh Jordan-Roberts; 19 Mike Kelly; 34 Joel Edwards. Subs (all used): 20 Will Jubb; 26 Dan Hawksworth; 17 Joe Porter; 24 Jack Ormondroyd.
Tries: Jordan-Roberts (5, 65), Ronan Dixon (10), Horne (20), C Robinson (22), Batchelor (27, 45, 59, 67), Kelly (33), Hey (55), Robson (62), Ormondroyd (74);
Goals: C Robinson 8/13.
BEARS: 1 Jason Bass; 2 Hayden Freeman; 3 Jake Ogden; 21 Kameron Pearce Paul; 5 Dante Morley-Samuels; 6 Liam Rice-Wilson; 7 Ben Stead; 8 Chris Vitalini; 9 Zak Williams; 10 Malikhi Lloyd-Jones; 11 Kieran Sherratt; 12 Chris Barratt; 13 Ashley Bateman. Subs (all used): 14 Sam Davis; 17 James Geurtjens; 15 James Mason; 18 Dan Gover.
Try: Bass (76); **Goals:** Stead 1/1.
Rugby Leaguer & League Express Men of the Match: *City Knights:* Josh Jordan-Roberts; *Bears:* Ben Stead.
Penalty count: 10-6; **Half-time:** 34-0;
Referee: Liam Staveley; **Attendance:** 1,104.

ROUND 20

Saturday 4th August 2018

BRADFORD BULLS 46 WHITEHAVEN 0

BULLS: 24 Brandon Pickersgill; 5 Dalton Grant; 39 Tuoyo Egodo; 4 Ross Oakes; 2 Ethan Ryan; 38 Jordan Lilley; 7 Dane Chisholm; 10 Steve Crossley; 9 Sam Hallas; 37 James Green; 11 Matt Garside; 12 Elliot Minchella; 19 Mikey Wood. Subs (all used): 8 Liam Kirk; 40 Jonny Pownall; 17 Ross Peltier; 26 Vila Halafihi.
Tries: Hallas (5), Ryan (11, 50, 79), Lilley (15), Pickersgill (35), Minchella (60, 70); **Goals:** Chisholm 6/8, Lilley 1/1.
WHITEHAVEN: 1 Jordan Burns; 15 Danny Green; 3 Chris Taylor; 23 Jason Mossop; 5 Dave Thompson; 7 Callum Phillips; 22 Stuart Howarth; 8 Marc Shackley; 9 James Tilley; 10 Carl Forster; 11 Connor Holliday; 4 Jessie Joe Parker; 18 Ellis Gillam. Subs (all used): 16 Kris Coward; 26 Josh Eaves; - Jordan Herve; 27 Jordan Thompson.
Rugby Leaguer & League Express Men of the Match: *Bulls:* Brandon Pickersgill; *Whitehaven:* Jordan Burns.
Penalty count: 12-13; **Half-time:** 24-0;
Referee: Tom Grant; **Attendance:** 2,818.

WEST WALES RAIDERS 6 HUNSLET 86

RAIDERS: 1 Phil Cowburn; 3 Kurtis Haile; 14 Brad Kislingbury; 11 Rowland Kaye; 5 Liam Silver; 6 Luke Williams; 21 Steve Parry; 13 Alan Pope; 15 Dean Higgs; 12 Harrison Elliott; 10 Joe McClean; 18 Craig Lewis; 26 Rhys Pope. (No subs named).
Try: Silver (36); **Goals:** Williams 1/1.
HUNSLET: 38 Tommy Brierley; 2 David Foggin-Johnston; 36 Daley Williams; 4 Mufaro Mvududu; 41 Gavin Duffy; 30 Nathan Chappell; 6 Joe Sanderson; 13 Matt Nicholson; 9 Jack Lee; 32 Aiden Hema; 12 Duane Straugheir; 33 Josh Tonks; 15 Brad Foster. Subs (all used): 31 Daniel Halmshaw; 10 Lewis Reed; 28 Will Cooke; 17 Nyle Flynn.
Tries: Foggin-Johnston (2), Lee (6), Williams (10), Tonks (13, 33, 65, 74), Mvududu (17, 60), Duffy (20), Flynn (51), Chappell (58), Cooke (67), Hema (71), Nicholson (77); **Goals:** Sanderson 13/15.
Rugby Leaguer & League Express Men of the Match: *Raiders:* Rhys Pope; *Hunslet:* Josh Tonks.
Penalty count: 6-8; **Half-time:** 6-40;
Referee: Andrew Sweet; **Attendance:** 258.

Sunday 5th August 2018

HEMEL STAGS 28 OLDHAM 60

STAGS: 16 Louis Sheriff; 2 Kieran Smith; 4 Marcus Stock; 18 Corey Hanson; 5 Jordan Fitzpatrick-Parry; 6 Jack Mitchell; 7 Shaun Roberts; 8 Austin Bell; 9 Jono Burns; 10 Stefanos Bastas; 11 Santino Decaro; 21 Dean Roberts; 13 Sonny Esslemont. Subs (all used): 14 Paul Stamp; 22 Lewis Taylor; 15 Blake Broadbent; 17 Wayne Jowett.
Tries: D Roberts (4), Hanson (35), Smith (51), Taylor (66), Stock (74); **Goals:** Mitchell 4/5.
OLDHAM: 1 Kyran Johnson; 2 Dave Eccleston; 3 Matt Reid; 29 Zack McComb; 28 Lee Kershaw; 6 Paul Crook; 7 Dave Hewitt; 13 Jack Spencer; 9 Gareth Owen; 8 Phil Joy; 22 Danny Rasool; 12 Danny Langtree; 24 Liam Bent. Subs (all used): 23 Luke Nelmes; 18 Ben Davies; 20 Matt Wilkinson; 10 Adam Neal.
Tries: Langtree (10, 31), Reid (17), Hewitt (20), Crook (28, 70), Spencer (39), Wilkinson (42), Kershaw (47, 56); **Goals:** Crook 10/10.
Rugby Leaguer & League Express Men of the Match: *Stags:* Marcus Stock; *Oldham:* Paul Crook.
Penalty count: 4-6; **Half-time:** 12-36;
Referee: Matt Rossleigh; **Attendance:** 109.

COVENTRY BEARS 4 DONCASTER 46

BEARS: 1 Jason Bass; 2 Hayden Freeman; 3 Jake Ogden; 21 Kameron Pearce-Paul; 5 Reece Rance; 6 Paul Emanuelli; 7 Ben Stead; 8 Dan Gover; 9 Liam Rice-Wilson; 10 Chris Vitalini; 11 Kieran Sherratt; 12 Chris Barratt; 13 James Mason. Subs (all used): 25 Mikey Russell; 18 James Geurtjens; 16 Peter Ryan; 17 Cameron Stewart.
Try: M Russell (44); **Goals:** Stead 0/1.
DONCASTER: 1 Richard Owen; 5 Sam Doherty; 19 Connor Bower; 4 Jason Tali; 2 Aaron Jones-Bishop; 6 Jordan Howden; 29 Matty Beharrell; 8 Russ Spiers; 9 Kyle Kesik; 14 Connor Scott; 28 Frankie Mariano; 11 Brad England; 12 Jason Muranka. Subs (all used): 10 Ryan Boyle; 13 Jordie Hedges; - Karim Madani; 23 Ross Osborne.
Tries: Howden (9), Owen (16), Bower (19, 51), Mariano (21), Jones-Bishop (32), Boyle (38), Spiers (68), England (78);
Goals: Beharrell 5/9, Owen 0/1.
Sin bin: Doherty (74) - professional foul.
Rugby Leaguer & League Express Men of the Match: *Bears:* Mikey Russell; *Doncaster:* Connor Bower.
Penalty count: 12-9; **Half-time:** 0-30;
Referee: Steve Race; **Attendance:** 300.

NEWCASTLE THUNDER 46 LONDON SKOLARS 14

THUNDER: 1 Theerapol Ritson; 5 Mo Agoro; 4 Joe Brown; 6 Lewis Young; 2 Ali Blair; 17 Adam Brook; - Remy Marginet; 8 Liam McAvoy; 9 Evan Simons; 13 Jack Aldous; 15 Sam Luckley; 12 Aaron Ollett; 11 Harry Aldous. Subs (all used): 22 Liam Richmond; 19 Liam Scott; 14 Vincent Rennie; 21 Ben Pointer.
Tries: Marginet (20), Blair (31), Ritson (38, 44), Ollett (52), Young (55, 78), Pointer (71); **Goals:** Marginet 7/8.
SKOLARS: 1 Mike Bishay; 2 Billy Driver; 22 Sam Nash; 4 Matty Fleming; 5 Michael Brown; 18 Jy-mel Coleman; 6 Phil Lyon; 8 Will Martin; 7 Neil Thorman; 10 Matt Ross; 12 Daymeric Pelo; 11 Jordan Williams; 13 Ryan Chester. Subs (all used): 15 Matthew Davies; 17 Rob Butler; 14 Eddie Mbaraga; 20 Michael Sykes.
Tries: Brown (25), Pelo (75), Williams (80);
Goals: Thorman 1/3.
Rugby Leaguer & League Express Men of the Match: *Thunder:* Remy Marginet; *Skolars:* Jy-mel Coleman.
Penalty count: 7-6; **Half-time:** 16-6;
Referee: Liam Staveley; **Attendance:** 554.

WORKINGTON TOWN 34 KEIGHLEY COUGARS 12

TOWN: 1 Sam Forrester; 24 Tyllar Mellor; 3 Elliott Miller; 16 Ben Morris; 2 Joe Hambley; 6 Jamie Doran; 7 Carl Forber; 8 Oliver Wilkes; 20 Sean Penkywicz; 15 Tom Curwen; 21 Jake Moore; 4 Gordon Maudling; 10 Stevie Scholey. Subs (all used): 9 James Newton; 11 Andrew Dawson; 12 Kurt Maudling; 17 Fuifui Moimoi.
Tries: Forrester (11), Penkywicz (37), Mellor (46), Miller (50, 63, 72), Doran (77); **Goals:** Forber 3/7.
Sin bin: Doran (32) - dissent.
COUGARS: 1 Ritchie Hawkyard; 5 Davey Dixon; - James Haynes; 3 Hamish Barnes; 28 Harry Aaronson; 32 Dan Parker; 23 Benn Hardcastle; 19 Matthew Bailey; 25 James Feather; 16 Harvey Hallas; 11 Josh Lynam; 17 Cameron Leeming; 13 Mike Emmett. Subs (all used): 8 Scott Law; 31 Jose Kenga; - Chris Cullimore; 34 Aaron Levy.
Try: Levy (42); **Goals:** Hardcastle 4/5.
Rugby Leaguer & League Express Men of the Match: *Town:* Elliott Miller; *Cougars:* Mike Emmett.
Penalty count: 8-8; **Half-time:** 10-6;
Referee: Michael Mannifield; **Attendance:** 607.

YORK CITY KNIGHTS 30 NORTH WALES CRUSADERS 0

CITY KNIGHTS: 35 Matt Chilton; 1 Ash Robson; 4 Brad Hey; 11 Joe Batchelor; 5 Judah Mazive; 2 Ben Cockayne; 6 Connor Robinson; 16 Ronan Dixon; 20 Will Jubb; - Jack Ormondroyd; 28 Josh Jordan-Roberts; 12 Sam Scott; 34 Joel Edwards. Subs (all used): 9 Andy Ellis; 8 Adam Robinson; 19 Mike Kelly; 17 Joe Porter.
Tries: Scott (6, 15), C Robinson (47), Mazive (57), Hey (75);
Goals: C Robinson 5/5.
CRUSADERS: 1 Tommy Johnson; - Jake Knox; 17 Kenny Baker; 26 Alex Trumper; 5 Dale Bloomfield; - Joe Lyons; 7 Ryan Smith; 10 Warren Thompson; 13 Karl Ashall; - Dan Norman; - Brad Walker; 14 James Dandy; 9 Lee Hudson. Subs (all used): 19 Aaron Moore; 15 Joe Bate; 22 Brad Brennan; - Lewis Fairhurst.

Rugby Leaguer & League Express Men of the Match: *City Knights:* Connor Robinson; *Crusaders:* Joe Bate.
Penalty count: 9-9; **Half-time:** 12-0;
Referee: Greg Dolan; **Attendance:** 981.

ROUND 21

Saturday 11th August 2018

WEST WALES RAIDERS 0 YORK CITY KNIGHTS 130

RAIDERS: 23 Karlin Claridge; 2 Lewys Willacott; 3 Kurtis Haile; 11 Rowland Kaye; 5 Liam Silver; 6 Luke Williams; 21 Steve Parry; 13 Alan Pope; 19 David Kearns; 26 Rhys Pope; 18 Craig Lewis; 20 Archie Snook; 10 Callum Mulkeen. Subs (only one named): 8 Barrie Phillips (not used).
CITY KNIGHTS: - Matt Chilton; 1 Ash Robson; 11 Joe Batchelor; - Perry Whiteley; 5 Judah Mazive; 2 Ben Cockayne; 6 Connor Robinson; 8 Adam Robinson; 20 Will Jubb; 26 Dan Hawksworth; - Josh Jordan-Roberts; 12 Sam Scott; 34 Joel Edwards. Subs (all used): 14 Harry Carter; 10 Graeme Horne; 24 Jack Ormondroyd; 17 Joe Porter.
Tries: Robson (2, 5, 12, 69), Scott (9), Jubb (18), Whiteley (20, 22, 42), Chilton (25, 73, 76), Porter (32), Carter (34, 56), Jordan-Roberts (39), Cockayne (47), C Robinson (53), Edwards (60), Hawksworth (62), Batchelor (70, 78); **Goals:** C Robinson 21/23.
Rugby Leaguer & League Express Men of the Match: *Raiders:* Steve Parry; *City Knights:* Ash Robson.
Penalty count: 2-9; **Half-time:** 0-68;
Referee: Michael Mannifield; **Attendance:** 196.

Sunday 12th August 2018

NORTH WALES CRUSADERS 0 BRADFORD BULLS 48

CRUSADERS: - Lewis Fairhurst; 5 Dale Bloomfield; - Earl Hurst; 26 Alex Trumper; - Jake Knox; 7 Ryan Smith; - Joe Lyons; 10 Warren Thompson; - Karl Ashall; 17 Kenny Baker; 11 Jack Houghton; - Stephen Wild; 14 James Dandy. Subs (all used): 9 Lee Hudson; 22 Brad Brennan; 15 Joe Bate; - Dan Norman.
BULLS: 24 Brandon Pickersgill; 5 Dalton Grant; 39 Tuoyo Egodo; 4 Ross Oakes; 2 Ethan Ryan; 7 Dane Chisholm; 38 Jordan Lilley; 37 James Green; 9 Sam Hallas; 10 Steve Crossley; 11 Matt Garside; 12 Elliot Minchella; 19 Mikey Wood. Subs (all used): 6 Joe Keyes; 8 Liam Kirk; 40 Jonny Pownall; 17 Ross Peltier.
Tries: Ryan (4), Minchella (26), Egodo (31), Chisholm (47, 57), Garside (62), Pownall (65), Keyes (75); **Goals:** Chisholm 8/9.
Sin bin: Peltier (79) - late challenge.
Rugby Leaguer & League Express Men of the Match: *Crusaders:* Earl Hurst; *Bulls:* Dane Chisholm.
Penalty count: 4-8; **Half-time:** 0-20;
Referee: Michael Smaill; **Attendance:** 886.

DONCASTER 38 LONDON SKOLARS 6

DONCASTER: 20 Hakim Miloudi; 24 Jack Sanderson; 33 Jack Logan; 4 Jason Tali; 1 Richard Owen; 6 Jordan Howden; 29 Matty Beharrell; 14 Connor Scott; 9 Kyle Kesik; 8 Russ Spiers; 11 Brad England; 28 Frankie Mariano; 18 Charlie Martin. Subs (all used): 23 Ross Osborne; 12 Jason Muranka; 13 Jordie Hedges; 21 Jez Litten.
Tries: Tali (4), Owen (8), Miloudi (11), Logan (29, 73), Connor Scott (50), Kesik (69); **Goals:** Beharrell 5/7.
SKOLARS: 1 Mike Bishay; 2 Billy Driver; 22 Sam Nash; 4 Matty Fleming; 5 Lameck Juma; 18 Jy-mel Coleman; 7 Phil Lyon; 8 Will Martin; 9 Neil Thorman; 10 Eddie Mbaraga; 12 Daymeric Pelo; 11 Jordan Williams; 13 Ryan Chester. Subs (all used): 15 Matthew Davies; 20 Michael Sykes; 17 Rob Butler; 19 Judd Greenhalgh.
Try: Juma (24); **Goals:** Thorman 1/1.
Rugby Leaguer & League Express Men of the Match: *Doncaster:* Frankie Mariano; *Skolars:* Neil Thorman.
Penalty count: 9-7; **Half-time:** 20-6;
Referee: Andrew Sweet; **Attendance:** 589.

HUNSLET 54 HEMEL STAGS 6

HUNSLET: 1 Jimmy Watson; 2 David Foggin-Johnston; 11 Liam Mackay; 4 Mufaro Mvududu; 41 Gavin Duffy; 6 Joe Sanderson; 7 Cain Southernwood; 32 Aidan Hema; 9 Jack Lee; 13 Matt Nicholson; 33 Josh Tonks; 12 Duane Straugheir; 15 Brad Foster. Subs (all used): 37 Ryan Wright; 10 Lewis Reed; 21 Jack Walton; 28 Will Cooke.
Tries: Nicholson (23), Duffy (25, 30, 43), Straugheir (34), Walton (40, 61), Mackay (68), Foggin-Johnston (69), Cooke (80); **Goals:** Sanderson 7/10.
STAGS: 22 Louis Sheriff; 2 Kieran Smith; 3 Ricky Williams; 4 Corey Hanson; 5 Darren Forde; 6 Jack Mitchell; 7 Shaun Roberts; 13 Blake Broadbent; 9 Jono Burns; 10 Stefanos Bastas; 11 Marcus Stock; 21 Dean Roberts; 18 Jack Howieson. Subs (all used): 14 Paul Stamp; 12 Mark Barlow; 17 Lewis Taylor; 8 Austin Bell.
Try: Hanson (54); **Goals:** Mitchell 1/2.
Rugby Leaguer & League Express Men of the Match: *Hunslet:* Cain Southernwood; *Stags:* Louis Sheriff.
Penalty count: 9-6; **Half-time:** 26-2;
Referee: Jon Roberts; **Attendance:** 610.

KEIGHLEY COUGARS 24 NEWCASTLE THUNDER 16

COUGARS: 1 Ritchie Hawkyard; 5 Davey Dixon; 43 James Haynes; 17 Cameron Leeming; 28 Harry Aaronson; 23 Benn Hardcastle; 30 Billy Gaylor; 42 Kieran Moran; 25 James Feather; 31 Jose Kenga; 32 Dan Parker; 11 Josh Lynam; 21 Emmerson Whittel. Subs (all used): 8 Scott Law; 33 Chris Cullimore; 34 Aaron Levy; 22 Alfie Seeley.
Tries: Dixon (13), Lynam (28), Seeley (35), Hawkyard (75); **Goals:** Hardcastle 4/8.
THUNDER: 1 Theerapol Ritson; 5 Mo Agoro; 4 Joe Brown; 6 Lewis Young; 2 Ali Blair; 16 Tom Shaw; - Remy Marginet; 8 Liam McAvoy; 9 Evan Simons; 14 Vincent Rennie; 15 Sam Luckley; 12 Aaron Ollett; 13 Jack Aldous. Subs (all used): 11 Harry Aldous; 20 Conor Fitzsimmons; 21 Ben Pointer; 26 Liam Richmond.
Tries: Ollett (6), Ritson (64), Richmond (75); **Goals:** Shaw 2/3.
Sin bin: Fitzsimmons (79) - punching.
Rugby Leaguer & League Express Men of the Match: *Cougars:* Ritchie Hawkyard; *Thunder:* Theerapol Ritson.
Penalty count: 6-5; **Half-time:** 16-6;
Referee: Paul Marklove; **Attendance:** 732.

OLDHAM 20 WHITEHAVEN 0

OLDHAM: 1 Kyran Johnson; 2 Dave Eccleston; 29 Zack McComb; 3 Matt Reid; 28 Lee Kershaw; 6 Paul Crook; 7 Dave Hewitt; 8 Phil Joy; 9 Gareth Owen; 13 Jack Spencer; 11 Craig Briscoe; 12 Danny Langtree; 24 Liam Bent. Subs (all used): 23 Luke Nelmes; 18 Ben Davies; 20 Matt Wilkinson; 10 Adam Neal.
Tries: Briscoe (26), Hewitt (33), Langtree (77); **Goals:** Crook 4/4.
WHITEHAVEN: 7 Callum Phillips; 1 Jordan Burns; 23 Jason Mossop; 3 Chris Taylor; 5 Dave Thompson; 22 Stuart Howarth; 14 Dan Abram; 8 Marc Shackley; 9 James Tilley; 27 Jordan Thompson; 6 Dion Aiye; 18 Ellis Gillam; 10 Carl Forster. Subs (all used): 16 Kris Coward; 26 Josh Eaves; 11 Connor Holliday; 4 Jessie Joe Parker.
Rugby Leaguer & League Express Men of the Match: *Oldham:* Kyran Johnson; *Whitehaven:* James Tilley.
Penalty count: 7-10; **Half-time:** 12-0;
Referee: Steve Race; **Attendance:** 413.

WORKINGTON TOWN 40 COVENTRY BEARS 16

TOWN: 1 Sam Forrester; 24 Tyllar Mellor; 3 Elliott Miller; 19 Ben Morris; 2 Joe Hambley; 6 Jamie Doran; 7 Carl Forber; 8 Oliver Wilkes; 9 James Newton; 15 Tom Curwen; 4 Gordon Maudling; 12 Kurt Maudling; 18 Karl Olstrom. Subs (all used): - Scott Rooke; 11 Andrew Dawson; 21 Jake Moore; 17 Fuifui Moimoi.
Tries: Newton (10), Doran (13), Hambley (15, 24), Curwen (54), Wilkes (61), Morris (69); **Goals:** Forber 6/7.
Sin bin: G Maudling (50) - high tackle; Doran (52) - high tackle.
BEARS: 1 Dante Morley-Samuels; 2 Hayden Freeman; 3 Jason Bass; 20 Kameron Pearce-Paul; 5 Reece Rance; 6 Paul Emanuelli; 7 Ben Stead; 17 James Geurtjens; 9 Liam Rice-Wilson; 10 Peter Ryan; 11 Kieran Sherratt; 12 Chris Barratt; 13 Cameron Stewart. Subs (all used): 14 Brad Sheridan; 8 Dan Gover; 16 Chris Vitalini; 15 James Mason.
Tries: Stead (19), Freeman (75), Bass (79); **Goals:** Stead 2/3.
Rugby Leaguer & League Express Men of the Match: *Town:* Tom Curwen; *Bears:* Jason Bass.
Penalty count: 7-9; **Half-time:** 24-6;
Referee: James Jones; **Attendance:** 556.

ROUND 22

Sunday 19th August 2018

HEMEL STAGS 0 NORTH WALES CRUSADERS 50

STAGS: 1 Kieran Smith; 2 Darren Forde; 4 Alex Williams; 3 Ricky Williams; 5 Jordan Fitzpatrick-Parry; 6 Paul Stamp; 7 Shaun Roberts; 16 Marcus Stock; 9 Jono Burns; 10 Stefanos Bastas; 22 Corey Hanson; 21 Dean Roberts; 13 Sonny Esslemont. Subs (all used): 14 Mark Barlow; 18 Santino Decaro; 17 Lewis Taylor; 8 Jack Howieson.
CRUSADERS: - Lewis Fairhurst; 24 Gavin Conroy; 26 Alex Trumper; - Earl Hurst; 5 Dale Bloomfield; - Joe Lyons; 7 Ryan Smith; 8 Jonny Walker; - Karl Ashall; 10 Warren Thompson; 11 Jack Houghton; - Brad Walker; 17 Kenny Baker. Subs (all used): 19 Aaron Moore; 15 Joe Bate; 22 Brad Brennan; 9 Lee Hudson.
Tries: B Walker (3), Conroy (12, 48), Bate (33), Smith (52), Moore (60), Hurst (65), Fairhurst (70), Baker (80); **Goals:** B Walker 7/9.
Rugby Leaguer & League Express Men of the Match: *Stags:* Dean Roberts; *Crusaders:* Earl Hurst.
Penalty count: 6-7; **Half-time:** 0-14;
Referee: Cameron Worsley; **Attendance:** 110.

WHITEHAVEN 14 DONCASTER 23

WHITEHAVEN: 7 Callum Phillips; 5 Dave Thompson; 23 Jason Mossop; 3 Chris Taylor; 1 Jordan Burns; - Steve Roper; 14 Dan Abram; 8 Marc Shackley; 22 Stuart Howarth; 27 Jordan Thompson; 6 Dion Aiye; 28 Scott McAvoy; 10 Carl Forster. Subs (all used): 16 Kris Coward; 4 Jessie Joe Parker; 26 Josh Eaves; 18 Ellis Gillam.
Tries: McAvoy (28), Mossop (69); **Goals:** Abram 3/4.
Sin bin: Roper (62) - holding down.
DONCASTER: 20 Hakim Miloudi; 24 Jack Sanderson; 33 Jack Logan; 4 Jason Tali; 1 Richard Owen; 6 Jordan Howden; 29 Matty Beharrell; 8 Russ Spiers; 9 Kyle Kesik; 14 Connor Scott; 11 Brad England; 28 Frankie Mariano; 13 Jordie Hedges. Subs (all used): 23 Ross Osborne; 10 Ryan Boyle; 19 Connor Bower; 21 Jez Litten.
Tries: Miloudi (15), Bower (35), Logan (40), England (74); **Goals:** Beharrell 3/4; **Field goal:** Miloudi (54).
Sin bin: Sanderson (60) - repeated team offences.
Rugby Leaguer & League Express Men of the Match: *Whitehaven:* Jordan Thompson; *Doncaster:* Russ Spiers.
Penalty count: 12-8; **Half-time:** 10-16;
Referee: Michael Mannifield; **Attendance:** 871.

BRADFORD BULLS 18 WORKINGTON TOWN 24

BULLS: 24 Brandon Pickersgill; 5 Dalton Grant; 4 Ross Oakes; 39 Tuoyo Egodo; 2 Ethan Ryan; 38 Jordan Lilley; 7 Dane Chisholm; 10 Steve Crossley; 21 George Flanagan; 37 James Green; 11 Matt Garside; 12 Elliot Minchella; 9 Sam Hallas. Subs (all used): 8 Liam Kirk; 19 Mikey Wood; 17 Ross Peltier; 6 Joe Keyes.
Tries: Minchella (14), Chisholm (22), Garside (47); **Goals:** Chisholm 0/1, Lilley 3/4, Keyes 0/1.
Sin bin: Flanagan (70) - fighting.
TOWN: 1 Sam Forrester; 24 Tyllar Mellor; 22 Elliott Miller; 5 Perry Singleton; 2 Joe Hambley; 6 Jamie Doran; 7 Carl Forber; 8 Oliver Wilkes; 20 Sean Penkywicz; 15 Tom Curwen; 18 Karl Olstrom; 16 Ben Morris; 19 Stevie Scholey. Subs (all used): 9 James Newton; 11 Andrew Dawson; 23 Tyler Dickinson; 17 Fuifui Moimoi.
Tries: Forrester (4), Miller (36), Doran (66), Penkywicz (75); **Goals:** Forber 4/4.
Sin bin: Scholey (70) - fighting.
Rugby Leaguer & League Express Men of the Match: *Bulls:* Matt Garside; *Town:* Sean Penkywicz.
Penalty count: 14-13; **Half-time:** 10-12;
Referee: John McMullen; **Attendance:** 3,320.

NEWCASTLE THUNDER 24 OLDHAM 18

THUNDER: 1 Theerapol Ritson; 5 Mo Agoro; 3 Tyler Craig; 6 Lewis Young; 23 Ben Dent; 17 Adam Brook; - Remy Marginet; 11 Harry Aldous; 9 Evan Simons; 13 Jack Aldous; 22 Jed Charlton; 12 Aaron Ollett; 15 Sam Luckley. Subs (all used): 30 Liam Richmond; 20 Conor Fitzsimmons; 14 Vincent Rennie; 25 Sam Blake.
Tries: Agoro (23), Ritson (65, 78), Marginet (67); **Goals:** Marginet 4/4.
OLDHAM: 1 Kyran Johnson; 2 Dave Eccleston; 3 Matt Reid; 29 Zack McComb; 28 Lee Kershaw; 6 Paul Crook; 7 Dave Hewitt; 13 Jack Spencer; 9 Gareth Owen; 8 Phil Joy; 11 Craig Briscoe; 12 Danny Langtree; 24 Liam Bent. Subs (all used): 10 Adam Neal; 20 Matt Wilkinson; 18 Ben Davies; 23 Luke Nelmes.
Tries: Bent (6), Kershaw (45), Nelmes (50); **Goals:** Crook 3/3.
Rugby Leaguer & League Express Men of the Match: *Thunder:* Theerapol Ritson; *Oldham:* Lee Kershaw.
Penalty count: 6-4; **Half-time:** 6-6;
Referee: Craig Smith; **Attendance:** 749.

WEST WALES RAIDERS 18 COVENTRY BEARS 28

RAIDERS: 1 Phil Cowburn; 2 Liam Silver; 18 Brad Kislingbury; 24 Aneurin Walker; 5 Sam Baker; 6 Luke Williams; 19 Frazer Stroud; 13 Alan Pope; 21 Steve Parry; 12 Harrison Elliott; 10 Rowland Kaye; 20 Archie Snook; 11 Callum Mulkeen. Subs (all used): 14 Dalton Desmond-Walker; 15 Dean Higgs; 22 Macauley Harris; 8 James Walter.
Tries: Parry (25, 58), Baker (38); **Goals:** Williams 3/3.
BEARS: 1 Dante Morley-Samuels; 2 Hayden Freeman; 3 Jason Bass; 20 Kameron Pearce-Paul; 5 Reece Rance; 6 Paul Emanuelli; 7 Ben Stead; 8 Chris Vitalini; 9 Liam Rice-Wilson; 10 Peter Ryan; 11 Kieran Sherratt; 12 Chris Barratt; 13 Ben Gray. Subs (all used): 14 Zak Williams; 15 Ashley Bateman; 16 Malikhi Lloyd-Jones; 18 Dan Gover.
Tries: Freeman (7, 49), Rice-Wilson (21), Bateman (44), Sherratt (75); **Goals:** Stead 1/1, Emanuelli 3/4.
Rugby Leaguer & League Express Men of the Match: *Raiders:* Steve Parry; *Bears:* Ashley Bateman.
Penalty count: 8-6; **Half-time:** 12-12;
Referee: Joe Stearne; **Attendance:** 409.

YORK CITY KNIGHTS 48 HUNSLET 6

CITY KNIGHTS: 32 Matty Marsh; 1 Ash Robson; 11 Joe Batchelor; 4 Brad Hey; 33 Will Oakes; 2 Ben Cockayne; 6 Connor Robinson; 8 Adam Robinson; 20 Will Jubb; 10 Graeme Horne; - Josh Jordan-Roberts; 12 Sam Scott; 13 Tim Spears. Subs (all used): 14 Harry Carter; 34 Joel Edwards; 24 Jack Ormondroyd; 17 Joe Porter.
Tries: Horne (1), Oakes (19, 60), Cockayne (31), Ormondroyd (34), Marsh (49), Robson (65), C Robinson (75); **Goals:** C Robinson 8/9.
HUNSLET: 1 Jimmy Watson; 2 David Foggin-Johnston; 3 Danny Grimshaw; 4 Mufaro Mvududu; 38 Tommy Brierley; 6 Joe Sanderson; 7 Cain Southernwood; 10 Lewis Reed; 9 Jack Lee; 13 Matt Nicholson; 12 Duane Straugheir; 15 Brad Foster; 11 Liam Mackay. Subs (all used): 37 Ryan Wright; 32 Aiden Hema; 19 Jack Coventry; 21 Jack Walton.
Try: Brierley (52); **Goals:** Sanderson 1/1.
Sin bin: Walton (26) - persistent team offences.
Rugby Leaguer & League Express Men of the Match: *City Knights:* Connor Robinson; *Hunslet:* Ryan Wright.
Penalty count: 10-11; **Half-time:** 26-0;
Referee: Liam Staveley; **Attendance:** 1,491.

Friday 24th August 2018

LONDON SKOLARS 20 KEIGHLEY COUGARS 6

SKOLARS: 1 Matty Fleming; 2 Vinny Finigan; 22 Sam Nash; 4 Lameck Juma; 16 Omari Caro; 7 Mike Bishay; 6 Jermaine Coleman; 8 Will Martin; 9 Neil Thorman; 10 Michael Sykes; 11 Jordan Williams; 12 Daymeric Pelo; 18 Lamont Bryan. Subs (all used): 24 Billy Driver; 17 Rob Butler; 19 Judd Greenhalgh; 13 Matt Ross.
Tries: Bishay (5), Pelo (7), Nash (12), Caro (29);
Goals: Thorman 2/5.
COUGARS: 1 Ritchie Hawkyard; 5 Davey Dixon; 22 Alfie Seeley; 39 Aaron Levy; 28 Harry Aaronson; 32 Dan Parker; 30 Billy Gaylor; 19 Matthew Bailey; 25 James Feather; 42 Kieran Moran; 11 Josh Lynam; 21 Emmerson Whittel; 13 Mike Emmett. Subs (all used): 9 Nathan Conroy; 12 Brendon Rawlins; 31 Jose Kenga; 35 Darrell Griffin.
Try: Feather (70); **Goals:** Aaronson 1/1.
Rugby Leaguer & League Express Men of the Match: *Skolars:* Mike Bishay; *Cougars:* James Feather.
Penalty count: 6-11; **Half-time:** 18-0;
Referee: Matt Rossleigh; **Attendance:** 1,043.

ROUND 23

Sunday 2nd September 2018

HEMEL STAGS 13 WHITEHAVEN 50

STAGS: 4 Louis Sheriff; 2 Darren Forde; 3 Kadeem Williams; 1 Ricky Williams; 5 Jordan Fitzpatrick-Parry; 6 Paul Stamp; 7 Kieran Smith; 8 Lewis Taylor; 9 Jono Burns; 10 Stefanos Bastas; 11 Marcus Stock; 18 Alex Williams; 13 Sonny Esslemont. Subs (all used): 14 Shaun Roberts; 21 Dean Roberts; 16 Santino Decaro; 17 Wayne Jowett.
Tries: Taylor (19), Esslemont (31); **Goals:** Smith 2/2;
Field goal: Smith (40).
WHITEHAVEN: 14 Dan Abram; 15 Danny Green; 23 Jason Mossop; 4 Jessie Joe Parker; 1 Jordan Burns; 22 Stuart Howarth; 28 Steve Roper; 8 Marc Shackley; 26 Josh Eaves; 27 Jordan Thompson; 6 Dion Aiye; 5 Dave Thompson; 10 Carl Forster. Subs (all used): 16 Kris Coward; 18 Ellis Gillam; 30 Jordan Herve; 31 Scott McAvoy.
Tries: Green (13), Forster (16, 53, 63), Coward (24), Mossop (43), D Thompson (47), Eaves (68), Aiye (79);
Goals: Abram 5/7, Roper 1/1, Aiye 1/1.
Rugby Leaguer & League Express Men of the Match: *Stags:* Ricky Williams; *Whitehaven:* Carl Forster.
Penalty count: 12-10; **Half-time:** 13-16;
Referee: Billy Pearson; **Attendance:** 109.

NORTH WALES CRUSADERS 66
WEST WALES RAIDERS 0

CRUSADERS: - Lewis Fairhurst; 24 Gavin Conroy; 26 Alex Trumper; - Earl Hurst; 5 Dale Bloomfield; 7 Ryan Smith; - Joe Lyons; 10 Warren Thompson; - Karl Ashall; 17 Kenny Baker; 11 Jack Houghton; - Stephen Wild; - Brad Walker. Subs (all used): 9 Lee Hudson; 22 Brad Brennan; 15 Joe Bate; 8 Jonny Walker.
Tries: Conroy (4, 19, 72), B Walker (16), Fairhurst (24, 66), Hurst (39), J Walker (42), Brennan (50), Wild (53), Ashall (63), Bloomfield (80);
Goals: B Walker 3/4, Fairhurst 6/8.
RAIDERS: 1 Phil Cowburn; 2 Liam Silver; 3 Kurtis Haile; 18 Craig Lewis; 5 Sam Baker; 6 Luke Williams; 19 Frazer Stroud; 10 Morgan Evans; 21 Steve Parry; 12 Harrison Elliott; 26 Rowland Kaye; 11 Callum Mulkeen; 20 Archie Snook. Subs (all used): 14 Dalton Desmond-Walker; 13 Alan Pope; 24 Aneurin Walker; 22 Macauley Harris.
Rugby Leaguer & League Express Men of the Match: *Crusaders:* Lewis Fairhurst; *Raiders:* Phil Cowburn.
Penalty count: 8-7; **Half-time:** 28-0;
Referee: Michael Mannifield; **Attendance:** 368.

BRADFORD BULLS 54 KEIGHLEY COUGARS 4

BULLS: 14 Gregg McNally; 2 Ethan Ryan; 39 Tuoyo Egodo; 3 Ashley Gibson; 40 Jonny Pownall; 38 Jordan Lilley; 6 Joe Keyes; 10 Steve Crossley; 9 Sam Hallas; 8 Liam Kirk; 11 Matt Garside; 12 Elliot Minchella; 19 Mikey Wood. Subs (all used): 17 Ross Peltier; 21 George Flanagan; 24 Brandon Pickersgill; 37 James Green.
Tries: Keyes (4), Egodo (13, 61, 77), Ryan (32, 39, 74), Flanagan (47, 65), Minchella (53); **Goals:** Keyes 7/10.
COUGARS: 1 Ritchie Hawkyard; 28 Harry Aaronson; 43 James Haynes; 17 Cameron Leeming; 2 Andy Gabriel; 32 Dan Parker; 30 Billy Gaylor; 19 Matthew Bailey; 25 James Feather; 35 Darrell Griffin; 11 Josh Lynam; 12 Brendon Rawlins; 13 Mike Emmett. Subs (all used): 8 Scott Law; 9 Nathan Conroy; 29 Brad Nicholson; 31 Jose Kenga.
Try: Leeming (79); **Goals:** Aaronson 0/1.
Dismissal: Rawlins (23) - punching.
Rugby Leaguer & League Express Men of the Match: *Bulls:* Tuoyo Egodo; *Cougars:* Ritchie Hawkyard.
Penalty count: 12-9; **Half-time:** 20-0;
Referee: Steve Race; **Attendance:** 3,119.

DONCASTER 38 NEWCASTLE THUNDER 21

DONCASTER: 20 Hakim Miloudi; 24 Jack Sanderson; 33 Jack Logan; 4 Jason Tali; 5 Sam Doherty; 6 Jordan Howden; 29 Matty Beharrell; 14 Connor Scott; 9 Kyle Kesik; 8 Russ Spiers; 11 Brad England; 28 Frankie Mariano; 12 Jason Muranka. Subs (all used): 10 Ryan Boyle; 13 Jordie Hedges; 32 Karim Madani; 19 Connor Bower.
Tries: Miloudi (20), Beharrell (29), Sanderson (37), Tali (49, 76), Howden (62), Logan (72); **Goals:** Beharrell 5/7.
THUNDER: 1 Theerapol Ritson; 5 Mo Agoro; 3 Tyler Craig; 6 Lewis Young; 23 Ben Dent; 17 Adam Brook; - Remy Marginet; 11 Harry Aldous; 9 Evan Simons; 13 Jack Aldous; 22 Jed Charlton; 12 Aaron Ollett; 20 Conor Fitzsimmons. Subs (all used): 21 Ben Pointer; 4 Joe Brown; 14 Vincent Rennie; 27 David Weetman.
Tries: Weetman (33), Pointer (58), Rennie (68);
Goals: Marginet 4/4; **Field goal:** Marginet (40).
Dismissal: H Aldous (74) - punching.
Rugby Leaguer & League Express Men of the Match: *Doncaster:* Hakim Miloudi; *Thunder:* Vincent Rennie.
Penalty count: 7-11; **Half-time:** 18-9;
Referee: Liam Staveley; **Attendance:** 741.

HUNSLET 48 LONDON SKOLARS 12

HUNSLET: 1 Jimmy Watson; 41 Gavin Duffy; 3 Danny Grimshaw; 4 Mufaro Mvududu; 23 Tom Ashton; 6 Joe Sanderson; 7 Cain Southernwood; 10 Lewis Reed; 9 Jack Lee; 13 Matt Nicholson; 33 Josh Tonks; 12 Duane Straugheir; 15 Brad Foster. Subs (all used): 37 Ryan Wright; 11 Liam Mackay; 17 Nyle Flynn; 8 Michael Haley.
Tries: Watson (20), Southernwood (25, 45), Wright (34, 80), Tonks (48), Nicholson (73), Foster (79);
Goals: Sanderson 8/8.
Sin bin: Wright (58) - tripping.
SKOLARS: 1 Matty Fleming; 2 Vinny Finigan; 22 Sam Nash; 4 Lameck Juma; 5 Billy Driver; 6 Jermaine Coleman; 7 Phil Lyon; 8 Will Martin; 9 Neil Thorman; 10 Michael Sykes; 11 Jordan Williams; 12 Daymeric Pelo; 18 Lamont Bryan. Subs (all used): 15 Matthew Davies; 17 Rob Butler; 19 Judd Greenhalgh; 13 Matt Ross.
Tries: Bryan (40), Driver (61); **Goals:** Lyon 2/2.
Rugby Leaguer & League Express Men of the Match: *Hunslet:* Joe Sanderson; *Skolars:* Daymeric Pelo.
Penalty count: 3-3; **Half-time:** 18-6;
Referee: Tom Crashley; **Attendance:** 453.

OLDHAM 58 COVENTRY BEARS 6

OLDHAM: 15 Luke Hooley; 30 Ben West; 4 Jack Holmes; 22 Danny Rasool; 28 Lee Kershaw; 6 Paul Crook; 9 Gareth Owen; 8 Phil Joy; 21 Kenny Hughes; 10 Adam Neal; 11 Craig Briscoe; 12 Danny Langtree; 13 Jack Spencer. Subs (all used): 23 Luke Nelmes; 18 Ben Davies; 19 Adam Jones; 20 Matt Wilkinson.
Tries: Holmes (4, 25), Briscoe (11), Langtree (37, 40), Wilkinson (43, 46), Hooley (58), West (63), Joy (78);
Goals: Crook 7/8, Hooley 2/2.
BEARS: 1 Errol Carter; 2 Hayden Freeman; 3 Jason Bass; 4 Dante Morley-Samuels; 5 Reece Rance; 6 Liam Rice-Wilson; 7 Ben Stead; 8 Peter Ryan; 9 Zak Williams; 10 Malikhi Lloyd-Jones; 11 Kieran Sherratt; 12 Chris Barratt; 13 Ashley Bateman. Subs (all used): 14 Brad Sheridan; 15 Richard Hughes; 16 Harry Kaufman; 17 Cameron Stewart.
Try: Morley-Samuels (20); **Goals:** Stead 1/1.
Rugby Leaguer & League Express Men of the Match: *Oldham:* Matt Wilkinson; *Bears:* Ben Stead.
Penalty count: 5-5; **Half-time:** 28-6;
Referee: John McMullen; **Attendance:** 373.

WORKINGTON TOWN 14 YORK CITY KNIGHTS 18

TOWN: 1 Sam Forrester; 24 Tyllar Mellor; 3 Elliott Miller; 4 Perry Singleton; 2 Joe Hambley; 6 Jamie Doran; 7 Carl Forber; 8 Oliver Wilkes; 9 Sean Penkywicz; 15 Tom Curwen; 16 Ben Morris; 18 Karl Olstrom; 10 Stevie Scholey. Subs (all used): 11 Andrew Dawson; 23 Tyler Dickinson; - James Newton; 17 Fuifui Moimoi.
Tries: Mellor (35), Moimoi (41), Miller (66);
Goals: Forber 1/3.
CITY KNIGHTS: 35 Matty Marsh; 1 Ash Robson; 11 Joe Batchelor; 4 Brad Hey; 33 Will Oakes; 2 Ben Cockayne; 6 Connor Robinson; 16 Ronan Dixon; 9 Andy Ellis; 10 Graeme Horne; 29 Josh Jordan-Roberts; 12 Sam Scott; 13 Tim Spears. Subs (all used): 14 Harry Carter; 34 Joel Edwards; 8 Adam Robinson; 17 Joe Porter.
Tries: Robson (30), C Robinson (48), Batchelor (55);
Goals: C Robinson 3/4.
Rugby Leaguer & League Express Men of the Match: *Town:* Elliott Miller; *City Knights:* Tim Spears.
Penalty count: 11-9; **Half-time:** 4-6;
Referee: Marcus Griffiths; **Attendance:** 1,623.

ROUND 24

Saturday 8th September 2018

LONDON SKOLARS 76 HEMEL STAGS 6

SKOLARS: 1 Matty Fleming; 2 Vinny Finigan; 22 Sam Nash; 17 Omari Caro; 4 Lameck Juma; 24 Phil Lyon; 7 Mike Bishay; 10 Matt Ross; 9 Neil Thorman; 8 Rob Butler; 11 Jordan Williams; 12 Daymeric Pelo; 18 Lamont Bryan. Subs (all used): 23 Billy Driver; 19 Mike Greenhalgh; 20 Judd Greenhalgh; 13 Ryan Chester.
Tries: Pelo (18), Juma (30), Finigan (36, 53), Caro (40, 63), Lyon (41), Bishay (46), Nash (56, 58), Bryan (61), Fleming (67, 73), Thorman (71);
Goals: Thorman 8/10, Lyon 2/3, Bishay 0/1.
STAGS: 1 Matt Welham; 2 Darren Forde; 16 Kadeem Williams; 3 Ricky Williams; 5 Jordan Fitzpatrick-Parry; 6 Paul Stamp; 22 Louis Sheriff; 8 Lewis Taylor; 9 Mark Barlow; 10 Wayne Jowett; 18 Jack Howieson; 13 Marcus Stock; 4 Alex Williams. Subs: 11 Santino Decaro (not used); 14 Jack Mitchell (not used); 15 Reece Williams (not used); 17 Austin Bell (not used).
Try: Howieson (10); **Goals:** Sheriff 1/1.
Rugby Leaguer & League Express Men of the Match: *Skolars:* Sam Nash; *Stags:* Louis Sheriff.
Penalty count: 6-8; **Half-time:** 24-6;
Referee: Michael Mannifield; **Attendance:** 172.

NEWCASTLE THUNDER 50 WORKINGTON TOWN 22

THUNDER: 1 Theerapol Ritson; 5 Mo Agoro; 6 Lewis Young; 23 Ben Dent; 4 Joe Brown; 17 Adam Brook; - Remy Marginet; 11 Harry Aldous; 21 Ben Pointer; 13 Jack Aldous; 24 Ben Calland; 12 Aaron Ollett; 9 Evan Simons. Subs (all used): 20 Conor Fitzsimmons; 8 Liam McAvoy; 14 Vincent Rennie; 19 Liam Scott.
Tries: Pointer (12), Young (14), Calland (17), Ritson (32), H Aldous (38), Brook (59), Dent (62), Scott (70), Agoro (75); **Goals:** Marginet 7/10.
TOWN: 1 Sam Forrester; 24 Tyllar Mellor; 3 Elliott Miller; 4 Perry Singleton; 2 Joe Hambley; 6 Jamie Doran; 7 Carl Forber; 8 Oliver Wilkes; 20 Sean Penkywicz; 15 Tom Curwen; 18 Karl Olstrom; 16 Ben Morris; 10 Stevie Scholey. Subs (all used): 9 James Newton; 11 Andrew Dawson; 23 Tyler Dickinson; 17 Fuifui Moimoi.
Tries: Hambley (5, 79), Mellor (22), Dickinson (26);
Goals: Forber 2/3, Doran 1/1.
Rugby Leaguer & League Express Men of the Match: *Thunder:* Remy Marginet; *Town:* Jamie Doran.
Penalty count: 9-7; **Half-time:** 28-16;
Referee: Steve Race; **Attendance:** 769.

Sunday 9th September 2018

COVENTRY BEARS 12 NORTH WALES CRUSADERS 36

BEARS: 1 Jason Bass; 2 Errol Carter; 3 Hayden Freeman; 4 Dante Morley-Samuels; 5 Reece Rance; 25 Paul Emanuelli; 7 Ben Stead; 8 James Geurtjens; 9 Liam Rice-Wilson; 10 Peter Ryan; 11 Kieran Sherratt; 12 Chris Barratt; 13 Ben Gray. Subs (all used): 14 Brad Sheridan; 15 Ashley Bateman; 16 Malikhi Lloyd-Jones; 18 Dan Gover.
Tries: Rance (45), Bass (76); **Goals:** Stead 2/3.
CRUSADERS: 1 Tommy Johnson; 24 Gavin Conroy; 26 Alex Trumper; - Earl Hurst; 5 Dale Bloomfield; - Karl Ashall; 7 Ryan Smith; 8 Jonny Walker; 9 Lee Hudson; 10 Warren Thompson; 11 Jack Houghton; 12 Simon Atherton; 17 Kenny Baker. Subs (all used): 19 Aaron Moore; 15 Joe Bate; - Dan Norman; 22 Brad Brennan.

Tries: Hurst (7), Ashall (14), Baker (24, 58), Moore (52), Conroy (55), Bloomfield (64); **Goals:** Johnson 4/7.
Rugby Leaguer & League Express Men of the Match: *Bears:* Ben Stead; *Crusaders:* Aaron Moore.
Penalty count: 8-4; **Half-time:** 0-16;
Referee: Paul Marklove; **Attendance:** 288.

KEIGHLEY COUGARS 6 DONCASTER 50

COUGARS: 1 Ritchie Hawkyard; 41 Alfie Seeley; 32 Dan Parker; 17 Cameron Leeming; 2 Andy Gabriel; 23 Benn Hardcastle; 30 Billy Gaylor; 19 Matthew Bailey; 44 James Feather; 35 Darrell Griffin; 11 Josh Lynam; 21 Emmerson Whittel; 13 Mike Emmett. Subs (all used): 8 Scott Law; 9 Nathan Conroy; 29 Brad Nicholson; 42 Kieran Moran.
Try: Gabriel (65); **Goals:** Hardcastle 1/1.
Sin bin: Hawkyard (17) - punching Beharrell.
DONCASTER: 24 Jack Sanderson; 5 Sam Doherty; 33 Jack Logan; 4 Jason Tali; 1 Richard Owen; 6 Jordan Howden; 29 Matty Beharrell; 8 Russ Spiers; 9 Kyle Kesik; 10 Ryan Boyle; 28 Frankie Mariano; 11 Brad England; 12 Jason Muranka. Subs (all used): 13 Jordie Hedges; 14 Connor Scott; 15 Kieran Cross; 32 Karim Madani.
Tries: Mariano (3), Spiers (19, 42), Owen (27), Logan (50), Tali (54), Doherty (70), Muranka (73, 79);
Goals: Beharrell 7/9.
Dismissal: Hedges (31) - high tackle on Leeming.
Rugby Leaguer & League Express Men of the Match: *Cougars:* Alfie Seeley; *Doncaster:* Matty Beharrell.
Penalty count: 7-10; **Half-time:** 0-16;
Referee: Andrew Sweet; **Attendance:** 596.

WEST WALES RAIDERS 0 BRADFORD BULLS 104

RAIDERS: 3 Kurtis Haile; 19 Rowland Kaye; 18 Craig Lewis; 24 Aneurin Walker; 2 Liam Silver; 5 Sam Baker; 6 Luke Williams; 13 Alan Pope; 15 Dean Higgs; 10 Morgan Evans; 20 Archie Snook; 11 Callum Mulkeen; 12 Harrison Elliott. Subs (all used): 14 Dalton Desmond-Walker; 22 Macauley Harris; 26 James Walter; 8 Connor Parker.
BULLS: 14 Gregg McNally; 2 Ethan Ryan; 39 Tuoyo Egodo; 35 Jy Hitchcox; 5 Dalton Grant; 6 Joe Keyes; 7 Dane Chisholm; 15 Callum Bustin; 38 Jordan Lilley; 8 Liam Kirk; 32 Matthew Storton; 12 Elliot Minchella; 13 George Milton. Subs (all used): 10 Steve Crossley; 17 Ross Peltier; 18 Liam Johnson; 19 Mikey Wood.
Tries: Grant (3, 47), Minchella (9, 20, 70), Bustin (12, 73), Ryan (16, 58), Hitchcox (23, 50, 79), Crossley (30), Peltier (37), McNally (40, 63), Storton (43), Egodo (65), Chisholm (77); **Goals:** Keyes 14/19.
Rugby Leaguer & League Express Men of the Match: *Raiders:* Harrison Elliott; *Bulls:* Elliot Minchella.
Penalty count: 3-10; **Half-time:** 0-54;
Referee: James Jones; **Attendance:** 826.

WHITEHAVEN 46 HUNSLET 10

WHITEHAVEN: 14 Dan Abram; 1 Jordan Burns; 23 Jason Mossop; 4 Jessie Joe Parker; 5 Dave Thompson; 29 Steve Roper; 7 Callum Phillips; 8 Marc Shackley; 22 Stuart Howarth; 27 Jordan Thompson; 6 Dion Aiye; 31 Scott McAvoy; 10 Carl Forster. Subs (all used): 16 Kris Coward; 9 James Tilley; 26 Josh Eaves; 18 Ellis Gillam.
Tries: McAvoy (10), Parker (13, 79), Burns (39, 72, 76), Aiye (59, 63); **Goals:** Abram 7/10.
HUNSLET: 1 Jimmy Watson; 2 David Foggin-Johnston; 3 Danny Grimshaw; 4 Mufaro Mvududu; 23 Tom Ashton; 6 Joe Sanderson; 7 Cain Southernwood; 10 Lewis Reed; 9 Jack Lee; 13 Matt Nicholson; 33 Josh Tonks; 12 Duane Straugheir; 15 Brad Foster. Subs (all used): 37 Ryan Wright; 11 Liam Mackay; 17 Nyle Flynn; 8 Michael Haley.
Tries: Mvududu (43), Grimshaw (68); **Goals:** Sanderson 1/2.
Rugby Leaguer & League Express Men of the Match: *Whitehaven:* Dion Aiye; *Hunslet:* David Foggin-Johnston.
Penalty count: 9-9; **Half-time:** 18-0;
Referee: Billy Pearson; **Attendance:** 672.

YORK CITY KNIGHTS 10 OLDHAM 6

CITY KNIGHTS: 35 Matty Marsh; 1 Ash Robson; 11 Joe Batchelor; 4 Brad Hey; 33 Will Oakes; 2 Ben Cockayne; 6 Connor Robinson; 16 Ronan Dixon; 9 Andy Ellis; 10 Graeme Horne; 29 Josh Jordan-Roberts; 12 Sam Scott; 13 Tim Spears. Subs (all used): 14 Harry Carter; 34 Joel Edwards; 8 Adam Robinson; 17 Joe Porter.
Tries: Scott (16), C Robinson (33); **Goals:** C Robinson 1/3.
OLDHAM: 15 Luke Hooley; 28 Lee Kershaw; 3 Matt Reid; 4 Jack Holmes; 1 Kyran Johnson; 6 Paul Crook; 7 Dave Hewitt; 10 Adam Neal; 9 Gareth Owen; 8 Phil Joy; 11 Craig Briscoe; 12 Danny Langtree; 24 Liam Bent. Subs (all used): 13 Jack Spencer; 20 Matt Wilkinson; 18 Ben Davies; 19 Adam Jones.
Try: Holmes (71); **Goals:** Hooley 1/1.
Rugby Leaguer & League Express Men of the Match: *City Knights:* Tim Spears; *Oldham:* Dave Hewitt.
Penalty count: 9-13; **Half-time:** 10-0;
Referee: John McMullen; **Attendance:** 1,692.

ROUND 25

Saturday 15th September 2018

WEST WALES RAIDERS 6 KEIGHLEY COUGARS 112

RAIDERS: 3 Kurtis Haile; 2 Liam Silver; 13 Alan Pope; 18 Craig Lewis; 5 Sam Baker; 21 Steve Parry; 12 Harrison Elliott; 14 Dalton Desmond-Walker; 19 Rowland Kaye; 10 Morgan Evans; 20 Archie Snook; 8 Connor Parker. (Only twelve players named).
Try: A Pope (31); **Goals:** Elliott 1/1.
Dismissal: Lewis (47) - dissent.
Sin bin: Desmond-Walker (72) - fighting.
COUGARS: 1 Ritchie Hawkyard; 41 Alfie Seeley; 32 Dan Parker; 17 Cameron Leeming; 2 Andy Gabriel; 23 Benn Hardcastle; 30 Billy Gaylor; 31 Jose Kenga; 44 James Feather; 12 Brendon Rawlins; 11 Josh Lynam; 21 Emmerson Whittel; 13 Mike Emmett. Subs (all used): 8 Scott Law; 29 Brad Nicholson; 38 Chris Cullimore; 39 Aaron Levy.
Tries: Gabriel (4, 37, 73), Leeming (8, 24, 78), Parker (10, 40), Whittel (13), Hawkyard (16, 52, 80), Kenga (19), Feather (22), Seeley (42, 64, 75), Gaylor (55), Hardcastle (58), Cullimore (61);
Goals: Hardcastle 14/16, Gaylor 2/4.
Sin bin: Hardcastle (72) - fighting.
Rugby Leaguer & League Express Men of the Match: *Raiders:* Harrison Elliott; *Cougars:* Alfie Seeley.
Penalty count: 5-10; **Half-time:** 6-58;
Referee: Michael Mannifield; **Attendance:** 218.

Sunday 16th September 2018

HEMEL STAGS 6 YORK CITY KNIGHTS 56

STAGS: 1 Matt Welham; 2 Darren Forde; 16 Kadeem Williams; 4 Alex Williams; 5 Jordan Fitzpatrick-Parry; 6 Paul Stamp; 7 Kieran Smith; 8 Lewis Taylor; 22 Louis Sheriff; 17 Austin Bell; 13 Marcus Stock; 11 Sonny Esslemont; 10 Wayne Jowett. Subs (all used): 14 Jack Mitchell; 9 Mark Barlow; 21 Santino Decaro; 18 Jack Howieson.
Try: Howieson (73); **Goals:** Smith 1/1.
CITY KNIGHTS: 35 Matty Marsh; 31 Matt Chilton; 32 Perry Whiteley; 4 Brad Hey; 1 Ash Robson; 2 Ben Cockayne; 6 Connor Robinson; 16 Ronan Dixon; 20 Will Jubb; 10 Graeme Horne; 29 Josh Jordan-Roberts; 19 Mike Kelly; 13 Tim Spears. Subs (all used): 14 Harry Carter; 24 Jack Ormondroyd; 17 Joe Porter; 8 Adam Robinson.
Tries: Cockayne (5, 13, 35), Spears (10), C Robinson (18), Kelly (20), Carter (42), Marsh (58, 67), Hey (64);
Goals: C Robinson 8/10.
Rugby Leaguer & League Express Men of the Match: *Stags:* Paul Stamp; *City Knights:* Ben Cockayne.
Penalty count: 6-6; **Half-time:** 0-36;
Referee: Andrew Sweet; **Attendance:** 175.

NORTH WALES CRUSADERS 12 DONCASTER 36

CRUSADERS: 1 Tommy Johnson; - Aled Davies; - Earl Hurst; 26 Alex Trumper; - Jake Knox; 7 Ryan Smith; - Karl Ashall; 8 Jonny Walker; 19 Aaron Moore; 10 Warren Thompson; 11 Jack Houghton; 12 Simon Atherton; - Stephen Wild. Subs (all used): 9 Lee Hudson; - Dan Norman; 22 Brad Brennan; 15 Joe Bate.
Tries: Davies (21), Houghton (68); **Goals:** Johnson 2/2.
Sin bin: Houghton (75) - professional foul.
DONCASTER: 1 Richard Owen; 2 Aaron Jones-Bishop; 19 Connor Bower; 4 Jason Tali; 5 Sam Doherty; 6 Jordan Howden; 13 Jordie Hedges; 8 Russ Spiers; 9 Kyle Kesik; 10 Ryan Boyle; 28 Frankie Mariano; 18 Charlie Martin; 12 Jason Muranka. Subs (all used): 14 Connor Scott; 23 Ross Osborne; 15 Kieran Cross; 24 Jack Sanderson.
Tries: Spiers (16), Tali (29, 73), Owen (36), Jones-Bishop (45), Doherty (65), Martin (79);
Goals: Hedges 3/6, Sanderson 1/1.
Rugby Leaguer & League Express Men of the Match: *Crusaders:* Earl Hurst; *Doncaster:* Jason Tali.
Penalty count: 6-3; **Half-time:** 6-16;
Referee: Tom Crashley; **Attendance:** 296.

HUNSLET 10 NEWCASTLE THUNDER 46

HUNSLET: 38 Tommy Brierley; 2 David Foggin-Johnston; 3 Danny Grimshaw; 36 Daley Williams; 41 Gavin Duffy; 6 Joe Sanderson; 7 Cain Southernwood; 17 Nyle Flynn; 9 Jack Lee; 32 Aiden Hema; 12 Duane Straugheir; 33 Josh Tonks; 15 Brad Foster. Subs (all used): 37 Ryan Wright; 28 Will Cooke; 19 Jack Coventry; 11 Liam Mackay.
Tries: Foggin-Johnston (42), Williams (50);
Goals: Sanderson 1/2.
Sin bin: Tonks (54) - fighting.
THUNDER: 6 Lewis Young; 5 Mo Agoro; 4 Joe Brown; 2 Ali Blair; 1 Theerapol Ritson; 17 Adam Brook; - Remy Marginet; 8 Liam McAvoy; 21 Ben Pointer; 13 Jack Aldous; 20 Conor Fitzsimmons; 12 Aaron Ollett; 9 Evan Simons. Subs (all used): 28 Niall Sidney; 27 David Weetman; 14 Vincent Rennie; 35 Liam Richmond.
Tries: Marginet (3, 45), Ritson (12), Young (34), Pointer (38, 41), Blair (61), Agoro (67); **Goals:** Marginet 7/10.
Sin bin: Fitzsimmons (54) - fighting.
Rugby Leaguer & League Express Men of the Match: *Hunslet:* Danny Grimshaw; *Thunder:* Remy Marginet.
Penalty count: 7-11; **Half-time:** 0-24;
Referee: Liam Staveley; **Attendance:** 560.

OLDHAM 16 BRADFORD BULLS 24

OLDHAM: 15 Luke Hooley; 1 Kyran Johnson; 4 Jack Holmes; 3 Matt Reid; 28 Lee Kershaw; 9 Gareth Owen; 7 Dave Hewitt; 8 Phil Joy; 21 Kenny Hughes; 10 Adam Neal; 11 Craig Briscoe; 12 Danny Langtree; 24 Liam Bent. Subs (all used): 23 Luke Nelmes; 18 Ben Davies; 20 Matt Wilkinson; 13 Jack Spencer.
Tries: Hewitt (12), Reid (16), Briscoe (74); **Goals:** Hooley 2/3.
Dismissals: Davies (50) - dissent; Nelmes (76) - punching.
Sin bin: Hooley (76) - tripping.
BULLS: 24 Brandon Pickersgill; 2 Ethan Ryan; 39 Tuoyo Egodo; 3 Ashley Gibson; 35 Jy Hitchcox; 6 Joe Keyes; 7 Dane Chisholm; 8 Liam Kirk; 38 Jordan Lilley; 10 Steve Crossley; 32 Matthew Storton; 12 Elliot Minchella; 19 Mikey Wood. Subs (all used): 21 George Flanagan; 37 James Green; 17 Ross Peltier; 15 Callum Bustin.
Tries: Storton (21), Hitchcox (30), Flanagan (33), Peltier (36); **Goals:** Keyes 4/4.
Rugby Leaguer & League Express Men of the Match: *Oldham:* Danny Langtree; *Bulls:* Dane Chisholm.
Penalty count: 9-12; **Half-time:** 10-24;
Referee: Matt Rossleigh; **Attendance:** 1,038.

WHITEHAVEN 24 COVENTRY BEARS 20

WHITEHAVEN: 14 Dan Abram; 15 Danny Green; 23 Jason Mossop; 4 Jessie Joe Parker; 1 Jordan Burns; 29 Steve Roper; 7 Callum Phillips; 8 Marc Shackley; 26 Josh Eaves; 27 Jordan Thompson; 18 Ellis Gillam; 6 Dion Aiye; 10 Carl Forster. Subs (all used): 31 Carl Sice; 22 Stuart Howarth; 11 Connor Holliday; 16 Kris Coward.
Tries: Shackley (1), Forster (39, 66, 77); **Goals:** Abram 4/4.
BEARS: 1 Jason Bass; 2 Dante Morley-Samuels; 3 Hayden Freeman; 4 Kameron Pearce-Paul; 5 Reece Rance; 6 Brad Sheridan; 7 Ben Stead; 8 Peter Ryan; 9 Liam Rice-Wilson; 18 Dan Gover; 11 Kieran Sherratt; 12 Chris Barratt; 13 Harry Kaufman. Subs (all used): 14 Errol Carter; 16 James Mason; 15 Malikhi Lloyd-Jones; 10 James Geurtjens.
Tries: Pearce-Paul (9), Freeman (27), Rance (61);
Goals: Stead 4/4.
Rugby Leaguer & League Express Men of the Match: *Whitehaven:* Carl Forster; *Bears:* Brad Sheridan.
Penalty count: 12-6; **Half-time:** 12-12;
Referee: Billy Pearson; **Attendance:** 691.

WORKINGTON TOWN 38 LONDON SKOLARS 6

TOWN: 1 Sam Forrester; 24 Tyllar Mellor; 4 Perry Singleton; 12 Kurt Maudling; - Scott Rooke; 6 Jamie Doran; 7 Carl Forber; 8 Oliver Wilkes; 20 Sean Penkywicz; 23 Tyler Dickinson; 18 Gordon Maudling; 16 Ben Morris; 10 Stevie Scholey. Subs (all used): 9 James Newton; 15 Tom Curwen; 11 Andrew Dawson; 17 Fuifui Moimoi.
Tries: Mellor (12, 20), Dickinson (16), Rooke (43, 67), Wilkes (54), Moimoi (73); **Goals:** Forber 5/7.
SKOLARS: 1 Matty Fleming; 2 Vinny Finigan; 22 Sam Nash; 4 Lameck Juma; 25 Michael Brown; 6 Charlie Lawrence; 7 Mike Bishay; 10 Michael Sykes; 9 Neil Thorman; 8 Rob Butler; 11 Jordan Williams; 12 Daymeric Pelo; 13 Ryan Chester. Subs (all used): 19 Mike Greenhalgh; 14 Judd Greenhalgh; 24 Billy Driver; 16 Matt Ross.
Try: Fleming (50); **Goals:** C Lawrence 1/1.
Sin bin: Fleming (26) - professional foul;
M Greenhalgh (38) - late challenge; Driver (58) - dissent.
Rugby Leaguer & League Express Men of the Match: *Town:* Scott Rooke; *Skolars:* Mike Bishay.
Penalty count: 10-5; **Half-time:** 14-0;
Referee: Steve Race; **Attendance:** 545.

ROUND 26

Saturday 22nd September 2018

COVENTRY BEARS 14 HUNSLET 4

BEARS: 1 Jason Bass; 2 Dante Morley-Samuels; 3 Hayden Freeman; 21 Kameron Pearce-Paul; 5 Reece Rance; 6 Brad Sheridan; 7 Ben Stead; 8 Dan Gover; 11 Kieran Sherratt; 10 Peter Ryan; 14 Ben Gray; 12 Chris Barratt; 13 Harry Kaufman. Subs (all used): - Errol Carter; - James Geurtjens; 15 Malikhi Lloyd-Jones; 9 Liam Rice-Wilson.
Tries: Barratt (5), Gray (69); **Goals:** Stead 3/3.
HUNSLET: 38 Tommy Brierley; 2 David Foggin-Johnston; 36 Daley Williams; 4 Mufaro Mvududu; 41 Gavin Duffy; 3 Danny Grimshaw; 37 Ryan Wright; 13 Matt Nicholson; 9 Jack Lee; 10 Lewis Reed; 12 Duane Straugheir; 33 Josh Tonks; 15 Brad Foster. Subs (all used): 17 Nyle Flynn; 8 Michael Haley; 31 Daniel Halmshaw; 11 Liam Mackay.

York's Andy Ellis halted against Whitehaven as the City Knights clinch the League 1 title

Try: Williams (50); **Goals:** Brierley 0/1.
Sin bin: Duffy (35) - punching;
Foggin-Johnston (53) - repeated team offences.
Rugby Leaguer & League Express Men of the Match:
Bears: Ben Stead; *Hunslet:* Mufaro Mvududu.
Penalty count: 10-7; **Half-time:** 6-0;
Referee: Steve Race; **Attendance:** 380.

LONDON SKOLARS 18 OLDHAM 46

SKOLARS: 1 Matty Fleming; 2 Jerome Yates; 18 Lamont Bryan; 4 Lameck Juma; 22 Omari Caro; 24 Phil Lyon; 7 Mike Bishay; 19 Mike Greenhalgh; 9 Neil Thorman; 20 Judd Greenhalgh; 11 Jordan Williams; 12 Daymeric Pelo; 13 Ryan Chester. Subs (all used): 15 Billy Driver; 10 Michael Sykes; 8 Matt Ross; 14 Eddie Mbaraga.
Tries: Mbaraga (26, 61), Caro (54);
Goals: Thorman 1/1, Lyon 2/2.
OLDHAM: 15 Luke Hooley; 1 Kyran Johnson; 3 Matt Reid; 4 Jack Holmes; 28 Lee Kershaw; 6 Paul Crook; 7 Dave Hewitt; 10 Adam Neal; 9 Gareth Owen; 8 Phil Joy; 11 Craig Briscoe; 12 Danny Langtree; 13 Jack Spencer. Subs (all used): 20 Matt Wilkinson; 23 Luke Nelmes; 18 Ben Davies; 21 Kenny Hughes.
Tries: Crook (4), Kershaw (11, 64, 72), Langtree (22), Briscoe (31), Hughes (51), Reid (80);
Goals: Crook 6/6, Hooley 1/2.
Rugby Leaguer & League Express Men of the Match:
Skolars: Eddie Mbaraga; *Oldham:* Lee Kershaw.
Penalty count: 3-6; **Half-time:** 6-24;
Referee: Nick Bennett; **Attendance:** 402.

Sunday 23rd September 2018

BRADFORD BULLS 52 HEMEL STAGS 7

BULLS: 24 Brandon Pickersgill; 5 Dalton Grant; 3 Ashley Gibson; 35 Jy Hitchcox; 40 Jonny Pownall; 38 Jordan Lilley; 37 Dane Chisholm; 37 James Green; 9 Sam Hallas; 15 Callum Bustin; 32 Matthew Storton; 11 Matt Garside; 13 George Milton. Subs (all used): 31 Oliver Wilson; 26 Vila

Halafihi; 17 Ross Peltier; 4 Ross Oakes.
Tries: Grant (8, 23), Bustin (11), Pownall (32, 70), Hitchcox (43), Pickersgill (49), Storton (51, 68), Oakes (53);
Goals: Chisholm 6/10.
STAGS: 1 Matt Welham; 2 Darren Forde; 16 Kadeem Williams; 4 Alex Williams; 5 Jordan Fitzpatrick-Parry; 14 Jack Mitchell; 7 Kieran Smith; 8 Lewis Taylor; 12 Jono Burns; 10 Wayne Jowett; 13 Marcus Stock; 11 Sonny Esslemont; 22 Louis Sheriff. Subs (all used): 6 Paul Stamp; 9 Mark Barlow; 17 Austin Bell; 18 Jack Howieson.
Try: Barlow (80); **Goals:** Jowett 1/1; **Field goal:** Sheriff (29).
Rugby Leaguer & League Express Men of the Match:
Bulls: Matthew Storton; *Stags:* Matt Welham.
Penalty count: 4-4; **Half-time:** 20-1;
Referee: Liam Staveley; **Attendance:** 2,855.

DONCASTER 44 WORKINGTON TOWN 32

DONCASTER: 24 Jack Sanderson; 5 Sam Doherty; 33 Jack Logan; 2 Aaron Jones-Bishop; 1 Richard Owen; 7 Liam Harris; 29 Matty Beharrell; 8 Russ Spiers; 9 Kyle Kesik; 23 Ross Osborne; 11 Brad England; 28 Frankie Mariano; 12 Jason Muranka. Subs (all used): 15 Kieran Cross; 4 Jason Tali; 18 Charlie Martin; 14 Connor Scott.
Tries: Logan (2, 40), Sanderson (11, 68), Beharrell (18), Jones-Bishop (21), Muranka (48), Harris (51);
Goals: Beharrell 6/8.
Sin bin: Cross (28) - high tackle on Forber.
TOWN: 24 Tyllar Mellor; - Scott Rooke; 14 John Patrick; 12 Kurt Maudling; 2 Joe Hambley; 1 Sam Forrester; 7 Carl Forber; 11 Andrew Dawson; 9 James Newton; 23 Tyler Dickinson; 16 Ben Morris; 21 Jake Moore; 18 Karl Olstrom. Subs (all used): 6 Jamie Doran; 20 Sean Penkywicz; 17 Fuifui Moimoi; 10 Stevie Scholey.
Tries: Mellor (6), Moore (37, 45), Penkywicz (56), Hambley (75), Moimoi (80); **Goals:** Forber 4/6.
Rugby Leaguer & League Express Men of the Match:
Doncaster: Matty Beharrell; *Town:* Jake Moore.
Penalty count: 5-10; **Half-time:** 26-10;
Referee: Tom Crashley; **Attendance:** 689.

KEIGHLEY COUGARS 24
NORTH WALES CRUSADERS 22

COUGARS: 1 Ritchie Hawkyard; 41 Alfie Seeley; 32 Dan Parker; 17 Cameron Leeming; 2 Andy Gabriel; 13 Mike Emmett; 23 Benn Hardcastle; 12 Brendon Rawlins; 44 James Feather; 19 Matthew Bailey; 11 Josh Lynam; 39 Aaron Levy; 21 Emmerson Whittel. Subs (all used): 8 Scott Law; 29 Brad Nicholson; 31 Jose Kenga; 38 Chris Cullimore.
Tries: Lynam (3), Gabriel (15), Rawlins (75), Seeley (80); **Goals:** Hardcastle 4/5.
Sin bin: Gabriel (38) - retaliation.
CRUSADERS: 1 Tommy Johnson; 24 Gavin Conroy; 26 Alex Trumper; - Earl Hurst; 5 Dale Bloomfield; - Karl Ashall; 7 Ryan Smith; - Dan Norman; 9 Lee Hudson; 10 Warren Thompson; 12 Simon Atherton; 11 Jack Houghton; 17 Kenny Baker. Subs (all used): 8 Jonny Walker; 15 Joe Bate; 19 Aaron Moore; 22 Brad Brennan.
Tries: Johnson (10), Bloomfield (25), Houghton (56), W Thompson (70); **Goals:** Johnson 3/4.
Rugby Leaguer & League Express Men of the Match:
Cougars: Ritchie Hawkyard; *Crusaders:* Kenny Baker.
Penalty count: 8-5; **Half-time:** 10-10;
Referee: Jon Roberts; **Attendance:** 592.

NEWCASTLE THUNDER 98 WEST WALES RAIDERS 6

THUNDER: 6 Lewis Young; 2 Ali Blair; 3 Tyler Craig; - Alex Clegg; 28 Niall Sidney; 16 Tom Shaw; - Remy Marginet; 14 Vincent Rennie; 9 Evan Simons; 19 Liam Scott; 20 Conor Fitzsimmons; 22 Jed Charlton; 15 Sam Luckley. Subs (all used): 35 Adam Bielby; 29 Ollie Gowing; - Rory Nettleton; 27 David Weetman.
Tries: Craig (4, 22, 76), Sidney (9, 13, 17, 74), Clegg (38), Marginet (40), Young (43), Nettleton (45, 80), Blair (49, 62), Gowing (51, 78), Luckley (57), Fitzsimmons (65); **Goals:** Shaw 10/15, Marginet 3/3.
RAIDERS: 3 Kurtis Haile; 2 Liam Silver; 11 Rowland Kaye; 18 Craig Lewis; 26 Aseri Biutanaseva; 19 Frazer Stroud; 6 Luke Williams; 14 Dalton Desmond-Walker; 21 Steve Parry; 10 Morgan Evans; 20 Archie Snook; 13 David

Bradford's Steve Crossley on the charge during the Bulls' Promotion Final win against Workington

Kearns; 12 Harrison Elliott. Sub (used, only one named): 22 Macauley Harris.
Try: Elliott (24); **Goals:** Elliott 1/1.
Rugby Leaguer & League Express Men of the Match: *Thunder:* Niall Sidney; *Raiders:* Harrison Elliott.
Penalty count: 1-3; **Half-time:** 36-6;
Referee: Brandon Robinson; **Attendance:** 889.

YORK CITY KNIGHTS 32 WHITEHAVEN 14

CITY KNIGHTS: 35 Matty Marsh; 1 Ash Robson; 11 Joe Batchelor; 4 Brad Hey; 31 Matt Chilton; 2 Ben Cockayne; 6 Connor Robinson; 16 Ronan Dixon; 9 Andy Ellis; 10 Graeme Horne; 29 Josh Jordan-Roberts; 12 Sam Scott; 13 Tim Spears. Subs (all used): 14 Harry Carter; 34 Joel Edwards; 24 Jack Ormondroyd; 17 Joe Porter.
Tries: Chilton (34, 72), Scott (50), Edwards (63);
Goals: C Robinson 8/10.
WHITEHAVEN: 14 Dan Abram; 1 Jordan Burns; 23 Jason Mossop; 4 Jessie Joe Parker; 15 Danny Green; 28 Steve Roper; 27 Callum Phillips; 27 Jordan Thompson; 22 Stuart Howarth; 9 James Tilley; 6 Dion Aiye; 18 Ellis Gillam; 10 Carl Forster. Subs (all used): 16 Kris Coward; 26 Josh Eaves; 11 Connor Holliday; 5 Dave Thompson.
Tries: Eaves (37), Burns (67); **Goals:** Abram 3/3.
Rugby Leaguer & League Express Men of the Match: *City Knights:* Tim Spears; *Whitehaven:* Carl Forster.
Penalty count: 10-6; **Half-time:** 10-8;
Referee: Jack Smith; **Attendance:** 3,223.

SEMI-FINALS

Sunday 30th September 2018

BRADFORD BULLS 47 OLDHAM 0

BULLS: 14 Gregg McNally; 35 Jy Hitchcox; 39 Tuoyo Egodo; 3 Ashley Gibson; 2 Ethan Ryan; 6 Joe Keyes; 7 Dane Chisholm; 8 Liam Kirk; 38 Jordan Lilley; 10 Steve Crossley; 32 Matthew Storton; 12 Elliot Minchella; 19

Mikey Wood. Subs (all used): 37 James Green; 21 George Flanagan; 17 Ross Peltier; 11 Matt Garside.
Tries: Ryan (19, 60), Keyes (28), Peltier (40), Minchella (52, 55), Hitchcox (57), Gibson (74);
Goals: Keyes 7/10; **Field goal:** Chisholm (38).
Sin bin: Peltier (77) - punching Owen.
OLDHAM: 1 Kyran Johnson; 28 Lee Kershaw; 3 Matt Reid; 29 Zack McComb; 2 Dave Eccleston; 6 Paul Crook; 7 Dave Hewitt; 10 Adam Neal; 9 Gareth Owen; 8 Phil Joy; 11 Craig Briscoe; 12 Danny Langtree; 24 Liam Bent. Subs (all used): 13 Jack Spencer; 21 Kenny Hughes; 20 Matt Wilkinson; 19 Adam Jones.
Sin bin: Kershaw (51) - dissent;
Owen (77) - high tackle on Garside.
Rugby Leaguer & League Express Men of the Match: *Bulls:* Dane Chisholm; *Oldham:* Danny Langtree.
Penalty count: 12-7; **Half-time:** 19-0;
Referee: Jack Smith; **Attendance:** 2,788.

DONCASTER 18 WORKINGTON TOWN 30

DONCASTER: 24 Jack Sanderson; 5 Sam Doherty; 2 Aaron Jones-Bishop; 4 Jason Tali; 1 Richard Owen; 7 Liam Harris; 29 Matty Beharrell; 8 Russ Spiers; 9 Kyle Kesik; 14 Connor Scott; 11 Brad England; 28 Frankie Mariano; 12 Jason Muranka. Subs (all used): 10 Ryan Boyle; 23 Ross Osborne; 18 Charlie Martin; 15 Kieran Cross.
Tries: Harris (7), England (44), Tali (64);
Goals: Beharrell 3/4.
TOWN: 24 Tyllar Mellor; - Scott Rooke; 3 Elliott Miller; 16 Ben Morris; 2 Joe Hambley; 6 Jamie Doran; 7 Carl Forber; 8 Oliver Wilkes; 20 Sean Penkywicz; 23 Tyler Dickinson; 5 Gordon Maudling; 18 Karl Olstrom; 10 Stevie Scholey. Subs (all used): 9 James Newton; 11 Andrew Dawson; 17 Fuifui Moimoi; 21 Jake Moore.
Tries: G Maudling (20), Wilkes (24), Dickinson (52), Hambley (59); **Goals:** Forber 7/7.
Rugby Leaguer & League Express Men of the Match: *Doncaster:* Jason Tali; *Town:* Jamie Doran.
Penalty count: 6-12; **Half-time:** 8-16;
Referee: Nick Bennett; **Attendance:** 542.

PROMOTION FINAL

Sunday 7th October 2018

BRADFORD BULLS 27 WORKINGTON TOWN 8

BULLS: 14 Gregg McNally; 35 Jy Hitchcox; 3 Ashley Gibson; 4 Ross Oakes; 2 Ethan Ryan; 6 Joe Keyes; 7 Dane Chisholm; 8 Liam Kirk; 38 Jordan Lilley; 10 Steve Crossley; 12 Elliot Minchella; 11 Matt Garside; 19 Mikey Wood. Subs (all used): 37 James Green; 21 George Flanagan; 17 Ross Peltier; 32 Matthew Storton.
Tries: Hitchcox (4, 63, 74), Flanagan (35), Keyes (38), Chisholm (79); **Goals:** Keyes 0/2, Chisholm 1/4, Crossley 0/1;
Field goal: Chisholm (67).
Sin bin: Garside (14) - dissent.
TOWN: 24 Tyllar Mellor; 2 Joe Hambley; 22 Elliot Miller; 16 Ben Morris; - Scott Rooke; 6 Jamie Doran; 7 Carl Forber; 8 Oliver Wilkes; 20 Sean Penkywicz; 28 Tyler Dickinson; 21 Jake Moore; 18 Karl Olstrom; 10 Stevie Scholey. Subs (all used): 9 James Newton; 15 Tom Curwen; 11 Andrew Dawson; 17 Fuifui Moimoi.
Try: Miller (51); **Goals:** Forber 2/2.
Dismissal: Moimoi (68) - high tackle on Kirk.
Rugby Leaguer & League Express Men of the Match: *Bulls:* Jy Hitchcox; *Town:* Tyllar Mellor.
Penalty count: 11-9; **Half-time:** 12-2;
Referee: Marcus Griffiths; **Attendance:** 6,011.

CHALLENGE CUP 2018
Round by Round

ROUND 3

Saturday 24th February 2018

KELLS 30 BRITISH ARMY 4

KELLS: 1 Lewis Smith; 2 Grant Gainford; 3 Craig Benson; 4 Tyrone Dalton; 5 Jordan Herve; 6 Ross Gainford; 7 Dominic Wear; 8 David Lowery; 9 Troy Armstrong; 10 Ross Ainley; 11 Scott Lofthouse; 12 Connor Hetherington; 13 Tony Burns. Subs (all used): 14 Grant McLaughlin; 15 Barry Boyd; 19 Paul Culnean; 20 Adam Blake.
Tries: Dalton (3), Armstrong (18, 56), Smith (38), Boyd (43), Herve (63); **Goals:** R Gainford 3/6.
BRITISH ARMY: 1 Mike Harrison; 2 Loz Hamzat; 3 Jamie Laing; 4 Pete Holmes; 5 Marcus Mercer; 6 Tony Lawless; 7 Kieron Roche; 8 Dan Turner; 9 Matt Scott; 10 Ben Cartmell; 11 Jordan Kerman; 12 Micky Hoyle; 13 George Clarke. Subs (all used): 14 Dec Baines; 15 Chris Brand; 16 Joe Peters; 17 Shaun Allen.
Try: Hamzat (74); **Goals:** Kerman 0/1.
Rugby Leaguer & League Express Men of the Match:
Kells: Dominic Wear; *British Army:* Loz Hamzat.
Penalty count: 9-9; **Half-time:** 14-0;
Referee: Craig Smith; **Attendance:** 300.

NORMANTON KNIGHTS 18 BATLEY BOYS 0

KNIGHTS: 1 Connor Wilson; 2 Aaron Butterfield; 3 Connor Taylor; 4 Ash Haynes; 5 Lee Hammond; 6 Tom Alexander; 7 Tom Carrol; 8 Patrick Waterton; 9 Craig Wright; 10 David Evans; 11 James Senkiw; 12 Jordan Siddons; 13 Ben Tyers. Subs (all used): 18 Lee Starbuck; 17 Stuart Biscomb; 19 Shaun Smith; 20 Clark Thompson.
Tries: Alexander (16), Taylor (22), Starbuck (33), Hammond (50); **Goals:** Taylor 1/4.
Sin bin: Haynes (72) - kicking the ball away.
BATLEY BOYS: 1 Josh Scruton; 2 Michael Dyson; 3 Josh Whitehead; 4 Damon Fletcher; 5 Josh Ritcher; 6 Adam Bingham; 7 Luke Sheridan; 8 Mark Grayshon; 9 Ryan Crossley; 10 Gavin Davis; 11 Josh O'Sullivan; 12 Aaron James; 13 Declan Tomlinson. Subs (all used): 14 Josh Knowles; 15 Jordan Brown; 16 Lewis Hardy; 17 Sean Sheard.
Sin bin: Davis (67) - persistent team offences.
Rugby Leaguer & League Express Men of the Match:
Knights: Connor Wilson, *Batley Boys:* Gavin Davis.
Penalty count: 13-12; **Half-time:** 14-0;
Referee: Michael Smaill; **Attendance:** 350.

PILKINGTON RECS 32 MILLOM 16

PILKINGTON RECS: 1 Ryan Hilliard; 2 Kyran Knapper; 3 Johnathan Frodsham; 4 Ian Stanley; 5 Jake Hodson; 6 Tom Roughley; 7 Danny Lynch; 13 Mike Garrity; 9 Ryan Liptrot; 10 Mark Briody; 11 Terry Riley; 12 Luke Riley; 17 Jonathan Peers. Subs (all used): 16 Tommy Chisnall; 19 Chris Clayton; 15 Joe Chow; 14 Connor Mulchay.
Tries: Stanley (20), Hilliard (28), Roughley (36), Knapper (52), T Riley (65), Clayton (78); **Goals:** Lynch 4/6.
MILLOM: 1 Ross Brookes; 2 Niall Harris; 3 Tyler Lancaster; 4 Chris Warren; 5 Lee Posslethwaite; 6 Owen Myers; 7 Tom Newbigin; 8 Ethan Kelly; 9 Noah Robinson; 10 Dane Kelly; 11 Hanley Dawson; 12 Joe Wright; 13 Tom Sibley. Subs (all used): 14 Kyle Evans; 15 Charlie Elmsue; 16 Scott Fisher; 17 Luke Brady.
Tries: Dawson (24), E Kelly (56), Myers (76);
Goals: Posslethwaite 2/4.
Rugby Leaguer & League Express Men of the Match:
Pilkington Recs: Danny Lynch; *Millom:* Tom Newbigin.
Penalty count: 7-10; **Half-time:** 14-6;
Referee: Joe Stearne; **Attendance:** 251.

ASKAM 6 YORK CITY KNIGHTS 64

ASKAM: 1 Krystian Tyson; 2 Tom Askew; 3 Mark Tyson; 4 Russ Bolton; 5 Brad Jackson; 6 Joe Satterthwaite; 7 Mike Wilson; 8 Liam Saunders; 9 Sam Dowsett; 10 Tom Spedding; 11 Tom Hopkins; 12 Stuart High; 13 Tom Wilkinson. Subs (all used): 14 Adam Jackson; 15 Jake Spedding; 16 Brad Kavanagh; 17 Jamie Butler.
Try: Wilkinson (42); **Goals:** K Tyson 1/1.
CITY KNIGHTS: - Kieren Moss; 1 Ash Robson; 22 Jake Normington; 4 Brad Hey; 5 Judah Mazive; 27 Liam Jackson; 6 Connor Robinson; 8 Adam Robinson; 9 Andy Ellis; 15 Chris Siddons; 11 Joe Batchelor; 19 Mike Kelly; 13 Tim Spears. Subs (all used): 14 Harry Carter; 21 Rory Dixon; 17 Joe Porter; 26 Dan Hawksworth.
Tries: A Robinson (12), Siddons (16), Kelly (23), Batchelor (26), Moss (32), Mazive (35), Normington (55), Hey (60, 63, 75), Robson (72), Porter (80);
Goals: C Robinson 8/12.
Rugby Leaguer & League Express Men of the Match:
Askam: Sam Dowsett; *City Knights:* Liam Jackson.
Penalty count: 8-7; **Half-time:** 0-36;
Referee: Brad Milligan; **Attendance:** 750.

HUNSLET CLUB PARKSIDE 16 WORKINGTON TOWN 24

PARKSIDE: 1 Craig McShane; 2 Omar Alrawi; 3 Dalke Harris; 4 Michael Waite; 5 Dale Harrison; 6 Andrew Hullock; 7 Daniel Rowse; 8 Luke Pettman; 9 Jamie Bradley; 10 Jamie Field; 11 Ben Shulver; 12 Liam Thompson; 13 Jay Cunningham. Subs (all used): 14 Michael Hayward; 15 Ryan Gaunt; 16 Mark Stubley; 17 Adam Biscomb.
Tries: Alrawi (29), Bradley (50), Field (79); **Goals:** Field 2/3.
Dismissal: Biscomb (72) - gouging.
Sin bin: Harrison (30) - dissent.
TOWN: 1 Jordan Tansey; 5 Joe Hambley; 3 Perry Singleton; 4 Scott Akehurst; 2 Sam Forrester; 6 Jamie Doran; - Carl Forber; 8 Oliver Wilkes; 20 Sean Penkywicz; 10 Stevie Scholey; 18 Gordon Maudling; 12 Kurt Maudling; 13 Joe Ryan. Subs (all used): 9 James Newton; 24 Scott Leatherbarrow; 19 Andrew Dawson; 22 Caine Barnes.
Tries: Doran (10), Forrester (35), Singleton (48), K Maudling (62), Penkywicz (77);
Goals: Forber 1/1, Leatherbarrow 1/4.
Rugby Leaguer & League Express Men of the Match:
Parkside: Jamie Bradley; *Town:* Sean Penkywicz.
Penalty count: 9-14; **Half-time:** 4-10;
Referee: Tom Crashley; **Attendance:** 285
(at South Leeds Stadium).

WHITEHAVEN 16 LONDON SKOLARS 14

WHITEHAVEN: 14 Dan Abram; 5 Dave Thompson; 3 Chris Taylor; 4 Jessie Joe Parker; 23 Jason Mossop; 6 Dion Aiye; 7 Callum Phillips; 16 Kris Coward; 9 James Tilley; 8 Marc Shackley; 18 Ellis Gillam; 13 Karl Olstrom; 27 Matty While. Subs (all used): 10 Carl Forster; 17 Brad Billsborough; 20 Lewis Reece; 22 Stuart Howarth.
Tries: Gillam (31), Abram (59), Tilley (64);
Goals: Phillips 0/1, Billsborough 2/2.
SKOLARS: 1 Elliot Hall; 22 Sam Nash; 4 Michael Brown; 3 Jake Melling; 5 Lameck Juma; 6 Jy-mel Coleman; 7 Mike Bishay; 8 Will Martin; 9 Phil Lyon; 10 Lamont Bryan; 20 Omari Caro; 12 Eddie Mbaraga; 13 Ryan Chester. Subs (all used): 24 Billy Driver; 25 Jordan Williams; 14 Ollie Purslow; 19 Michael Sykes.
Tries: Melling (13, 43), Driver (69);
Goals: Jy-mel Coleman 0/2, Lyon 1/1, Nash 0/1.
Rugby Leaguer & League Express Men of the Match:
Whitehaven: Chris Taylor; *Skolars:* Jake Melling.
Penalty count: 10-6; **Half-time:** 4-4;
Referee: Marcus Griffiths; **Attendance:** 439.

Sunday 25th February 2018

HEMEL STAGS 0 NEWCASTLE THUNDER 74

STAGS: 22 Louis Sheriff; 2 Darren Forde; 3 Kadeem Williams; 15 Brad Adams; 5 Mitch Vincent; 6 Liam Darville; 7 Liam Coe; 10 Wayne Jowett; 9 Jono Burns; 17 Reece Williams; 11 Sonny Esslemont; 21 James Thornton; 18 Ricky Hough. Subs (all used): 14 Jack Mitchell; 19 Marcus Stock; 16 Lewis Taylor; 8 Corey Hanson.
Sin bin: Mitchell (58) - persistent team offences.
THUNDER: 1 Theerapol Ritson; 5 Mo Agoro; 4 Joe Brown; 24 Ben Calland; 2 Ali Blair; 6 Lewis Young; 16 Tom Shaw; 13 Jack Aldous; 9 Evan Simons; 14 Vincent Rennie; 12 Aaron Ollett; 15 Sam Luckley; 8 Liam McAvoy. Subs (all used): 11 Harry Aldous; 18 Dan Turland; 20 Conor Fitzsimmons; 21 Ben Pointer.
Tries: Young (4, 8), Agoro (28, 79), Ollett (32, 70), Ritson (35, 61, 64), Fitzsimmons (38), Calland (48), Blair (56), Rennie (59); **Goals:** Shaw 11/13.
Rugby Leaguer & League Express Men of the Match:
Stags: Kadeem Williams; *Thunder:* Tom Shaw.
Penalty count: 6-14; **Half-time:** 0-34;
Referee: Andrew Sweet; **Attendance:** 115.

NORTH WALES CRUSADERS 28 KEIGHLEY COUGARS 24

CRUSADERS: 1 Tommy Johnson; 2 Dan Price; 12 Simon Atherton; 3 Callan Beckett; 24 Gavin Conroy; 6 Steve Roper; 29 Billy Sheen; 16 Alex Davidson; 9 Lee Hudson; 8 Jonny Walker; 11 Jack Houghton; 25 Jordan Case; 13 Ryan Millington. Subs (all used): 19 Aaron Moore; 15 Joe Bate; 26 Alex Trumper; 22 Brad Brennan.
Tries: Roper (17), Houghton (50), Atherton (55, 67, 71);
Goals: Johnson 4/6.
COUGARS: 1 Ritchie Hawkyard; 28 Harry Aaronson; 3 Hamish Barnes; 4 Adam Ryder; 2 Andy Gabriel; 23 Benn Hardcastle; 7 Matty Beharrell; 27 Samir Tahraoui; 9 Nathan Conroy; 19 Matthew Bailey; 12 Brendon Rawlins; 18 Josh Tonks; 13 Mike Emmett. Subs (all used): 8 Scott Law; 15 Ryan Wright; 16 Harvey Hallas; 29 Brad Nicholson.
Tries: Rawlins (8, 23), Tonks (26), Hawkyard (37);
Goals: Hardcastle 4/4.
Sin bin: Law (55) - professional foul.
Rugby Leaguer & League Express Men of the Match:
Crusaders: Simon Atherton; *Cougars:* Brendon Rawlins.
Penalty count: 12-3; **Half-time:** 6-24;
Referee: James Jones; **Attendance:** 281.

BRADFORD BULLS 82 WEST WALES RAIDERS 6

BULLS: 14 Gregg McNally; 5 Dalton Grant; 3 Ashley Gibson; 1 Lee Smith; 2 Ethan Ryan; 6 Joe Keyes; 24 Brandon Pickersgill; 17 Ross Peltier; 9 Sam Hallas; 10 Steve Crossley; 12 Elliot Minchella; 18 Liam Johnson; 13 George Milton. Subs (all used): 7 Dane Chisholm; 15 Callum Bustin; 26 Vila Halafihi; 19 Mikey Wood.
Tries: Johnson (4, 52), Crossley (8), Ryan (10), McNally (23, 29), Minchella (25, 34, 57, 59, 69), Bustin (50), Gibson (62, 80), Chisholm (66); **Goals:** Keyes 11/15.
RAIDERS: 25 James Smith; 3 Kurtis Haile; 13 Ashley Bateman; 16 Shaun Tennant; 20 Archie Snook; 21 Steve Parry; 19 Frazer Stroud; 10 Morgan Evans; 15 Dean Higgs; 14 Dalton Desmond-Walker; 18 Craig Lewis; 12 Harrison Elliott; 8 Connor Parker. Subs (all used): 17 Harry Boots; 26 Barrie Phillips; 24 Ellis Simon; 23 Rowland Kaye.
Try: Parry (76); **Goals:** Stroud 1/1.
Rugby Leaguer & League Express Men of the Match:
Bulls: Elliot Minchella; *Raiders:* Frazer Stroud.
Penalty count: 11-5; **Half-time:** 38-0;
Referee: Nick Woodward; **Attendance:** 1,505.

COVENTRY BEARS 42 DISTINGTON 12

BEARS: 1 Harry Chapman; 2 Hayden Freeman; 3 Dante Morley-Samuels; 4 Jason Bass; 5 Errol Carter; 6 Paul Emanuelli; 7 Ben Stead; 8 Dan Gover; 9 Lewis Lord; 10 Callum Bradbury; 11 Kieran Sherratt; 12 Chris Barratt; 13 Chris Vitalini. Subs (all used): 15 Lewis Russell; 16 Harry Kaufman; 19 James Geurtjens; 18 John Aldred.
Tries: Chapman (13, 75), Bass (35, 38), Barratt (54), Lord (58), Freeman (64); **Goals:** Stead 7/7.
DISTINGTON: 1 Steven Conway; 2 Greg Bedford; 3 Liam Friel; 4 Gavin Martin; 5 Ryan Hodgson; 6 Clayton Sutton; 7 Sean Sutton; 8 Bryan Ritchie; 9 Jamie Friel; 10 Carl Stephenson; 11 Grant Dryden; 12 Kieran Ritchie; 13 Aiden Worthington. Subs (all used): 14 Matt Hewer; 15 Shaun Adams; 16 Liam McNicholas; 17 Stephen Clarke.
Tries: Bedford (25, 42); **Goals:** C Sutton 2/3.
Rugby Leaguer & League Express Men of the Match:
Bears: Lewis Lord; *Distington:* Bryan Ritchie.
Penalty count: 11-12; **Half-time:** 18-8;
Referee: Cameron Worsley; **Attendance:** 267.

DONCASTER 82 MYTON WARRIORS 6

DONCASTER: 1 Richard Owen; 2 Aaron Jones-Bishop; 19 Connor Bower; 4 Jason Tali; 5 Sam Doherty; 6 Jordan Howden; 7 Liam Harris; 10 Ryan Boyle; 14 Connor Scott; 9 Kyle Kesik; 11 Brad England; 18 Charlie Martin; 26 Brandan Wilkinson. Subs (all used): 8 Russ Spiers; 15 Kieran Cross; 16 Zac Braham; 13 Jordie Hedges.
Tries: Harris (2), Kesik (13), Tali (26, 37, 42, 76), Doherty (31), Cross (34), Howden (39), Jones-Bishop (49), Martin (53), Hedges (56), Boyle (60), Bower (66, 70), Connor Scott (79); **Goals:** Harris 9/16.
WARRIORS: 1 Ryan Marrazza; 2 Ellis Wray; 3 Anthony Wheeldon; 4 Adam Piggott; 5 Lee James; 6 Nathan Slater; 7 Kris Walker; 8 Aaron Pearce; 9 Ash James; 10 Lee Fewlass; 20 Nick Walstead; 12 James Jennison; 13 Dan Spencer. Subs (all used): 14 Liam Ward; 15 Ryan Walker; 16 Sam Hoggard; 19 Christopher Penrose.
Try: Piggott (19); **Goals:** A James 1/1.
Sin bin: Penrose (32) - holding down.
Rugby Leaguer & League Express Men of the Match:
Doncaster: Liam Harris; *Warriors:* Adam Piggott.
Penalty count: 8-5; **Half-time:** 36-6;
Referee: Michael Mannifield; **Attendance:** 388.

HUNSLET 72 OULTON RAIDERS 16

HUNSLET: 1 Jimmy Watson; 23 Tom Ashton; 28 Will Cooke; 30 Nathan Chappell; 5 Joel Gibson; 6 Joe Sanderson; 7 Cain Southernwood; 10 Lewis Reed; 9 Jack Lee; 13 Matt Nicholson; 12 Duane Straugheir; 15 Brad Foster; 11 Liam Mackay. Subs (all used): 29 Jake Barnett; 8 Michael Haley; 17 Nyle Flynn; 16 Ryan Mallinder.
Tries: Cooke (9), Lee (20), Foster (24), Southernwood (30), Watson (38), Flynn (40, 46), Chappell (42), Mallinder (57), Ashton (72), Gibson (75), Mackay (79);
Goals: Sanderson 10/10, Southernwood 2/2.
RAIDERS: 1 Tom Egan; 5 Kieron Walpole; 20 Dom Flanagan; 3 Adrian Holdsworth; 2 Chris Hope; 21 Andy Williamson; 7 Jordan Gale; 8 Matty Stableford; 9 Danny Mackintosh; 10 Rob Stanley; 18 Clayton Stott; 12 Josh Lancaster; 13 James Cruickshank. Subs (all used): 11 Lee Gomersall; 14 Will Ingleby; 16 Lawrence Dibb; 17 Gary Sergeant.
Tries: Williamson (11), Ingleby (52), Walpole (60);
Goals: Egan 2/3.
Rugby Leaguer & League Express Men of the Match:
Hunslet: Jimmy Watson; *Raiders:* Rob Stanley.
Penalty count: 12-4; **Half-time:** 36-4;
Referee: Billy Pearson; **Attendance:** 896.

OLDHAM 42 FEATHERSTONE LIONS 0

OLDHAM: 1 Kyran Johnson; 2 Dave Eccleston; 4 Jack Holmes; 29 Zack McComb; 30 Ben West; 6 Paul Crook; 7 Dave Hewitt; 8 Phil Joy; 21 Kenny Hughes; 10 Adam Neal; 12 Danny Langtree; 25 Danny Bridge; 24 Liam Bent. Subs (all used): 20 Matt Wilkinson; 23 Luke Nelmes; 19 Adam Jones; 22 Danny Rasool.
Tries: Langtree (3, 74), McComb (10), West (37), Joy (49), Eccleston (57), Bridge (79); **Goals:** Crook 7/7.
LIONS: 1 Ian Jackson; 2 Kieran Redfern; 3 Gareth Gale; 4 Tom Battye; 5 Davi Garahan; 6 Tom Wandless; 7 Jake Perkins; 8 Ben Mawson; 9 Dean Gamble; 10 Daniel Gilbert; 11 Joe Fox; 12 Scott Wilson; 13 Harry McAllister. Subs (all used): 15 Brendon Gibbins; 17 Jimmy Beckett; 18 Richard Frankland; 21 Danny Glassell.
Sin bin: Gilbert (24) - persistent team offences; Garahan (36) - professional foul; Glassell (65) - interference.
Rugby Leaguer & League Express Men of the Match: *Oldham:* Kyran Johnson; *Lions:* Gareth Gale.
Penalty count: 18-5; **Half-time:** 18-0;
Referee: Liam Staveley; **Attendance:** 364.

ROUND 4

Friday 16th March 2018

KELLS 6 TORONTO WOLFPACK 56

KELLS: 1 Lewis Smith; 2 Grant Gainford; 3 Craig Benson; 4 Scott Lofthouse; 5 Jordan Herve; 6 Tyrone Dalton; 7 Ross Gainford; 8 David Lowery; 9 Troy Armstrong; 10 Ross Ainley; 11 Lewis Wilson; 12 Ryan Watson; 13 Tony Burns. Subs (all used): 14 Grant McLaughlin; 15 Bradley Smith; 16 Connor Hetherington; 19 Paul Culnean.
Try: L Smith (8); **Goals:** R Gainford 1/1.
WOLFPACK: 1 Quentin Laulu-Togagae; 5 Liam Kay; 17 Blake Wallace; 23 Nick Rawsthorne; 2 Jonny Pownall; 7 Ryan Brierley; 6 Josh McCrone; 8 Jack Buchanan; 14 Andy Ackers; 15 Adam Sidlow; 22 Richard Whiting; 16 Reni Maitua; 13 Jack Bussey. Subs: 12 Joe Westerman (not used); 28 Sam Hopkins; 29 Jake Emmitt; 18 James Laithwaite.
Tries: Wallace (2), Kay (16, 26, 53), Rawsthorne (18, 58), Laulu-Togagae (43), Pownall (63), Brierley (68), Ackers (79); **Goals:** Brierley 8/9 *(last conversion attempt declined).*
Rugby Leaguer & League Express Men of the Match: *Kells:* Lewis Smith; *Wolfpack:* Ryan Brierley.
Penalty count: 4-10; **Half-time:** 6-24;
Referee: Nick Bennett; **Attendance:** 1,000 *(at Recreation Ground, Whitehaven).*

DONCASTER 34 NEWCASTLE THUNDER 0

DONCASTER: 1 Richard Owen; 5 Sam Doherty; 19 Connor Bower; 3 Liam Welham; 24 Jack Sanderson; 6 Jordan Howden; 7 Liam Harris; 8 Russ Spiers; 15 Kieran Cross; 14 Connor Scott; 11 Brad England; 18 Charlie Martin; 26 Brandan Wilkinson. Subs (all used): 12 Jason Muranka; 2 Aaron Jones-Bishop; 16 Zac Braham; 13 Jordie Hedges.
Tries: Owen (6), Harris (24), Sanderson (47), Welham (60), Jones-Bishop (63), Doherty (68); **Goals:** Harris 5/6.
THUNDER: 1 Theerapol Ritson; 5 Mo Agoro; 24 Ben Calland; 3 Tyler Craig; 23 Ben Dent; 6 Lewis Young; 7 Danny Nicklas; 13 Jack Aldous; 9 Evan Simons; 14 Vincent Rennie; 26 Ryan Lloyd; 12 Aaron Ollett; 8 Liam McAvoy. Subs (all used): 19 Liam Scott; 11 Harry Aldous; 20 Conor Fitzsimmons; 21 Ben Pointer.
Sin bin: Calland (80) - late challenge.
Rugby Leaguer & League Express Men of the Match: *Doncaster:* Liam Harris; *Thunder:* Evan Simons.
Penalty count: 10-8; **Half-time:** 12-0;
Referee: Liam Staveley; **Attendance:** 398.

Saturday 17th March 2018

NORMANTON KNIGHTS 8 ROCHDALE HORNETS 20

KNIGHTS: 1 Connor Wilson; 2 Aaron Butterfield; 3 Connor Taylor; 4 Ash Haynes; 5 Lee Hammond; 6 Tom Alexander; 7 Kieran Hinchcliffe; 8 Patrick Waterton; 9 Tom Carrol; 10 David Evans; 12 Jordan Siddons; 13 Craig Wright; 14 Chris Woolford. Subs (all used): 15 Ben Tyers; 18 Stuart Biscomb; 19 Lee Starbuck; 20 Clark Thompson.
Tries: Wilson (30, 71); **Goals:** Taylor 0/2.
HORNETS: 21 Richard Lepori; 2 Declan Kay; 3 Earl Hurst; 31 Deon Cross; 5 Rob Massam; 6 Lewis Palfrey; 7 Danny Yates; 12 Toby Adamson; 9 Ben Moores; 19 Lee Mitchell; 23 Gary Middlehurst; 11 Dave Allen; 8 Jovili Taira. Subs (all used): 24 Declan Gregory; 16 Seta Tala; 25 Callum Mulkeen; 18 Billy Brickhill.
Tries: Massam (3, 36), Yates (15), Kay (20);
Goals: Palfrey 2/4.
Rugby Leaguer & League Express Men of the Match: *Knights:* Connor Wilson; *Hornets:* Rob Massam.
Penalty count: 11-6; **Half-time:** 4-20;
Referee: Greg Dolan; **Attendance:** N/A *(at LD Nutrition Stadium, Featherstone).*

Sunday 18th March 2018

BARROW RAIDERS 28 SHEFFIELD EAGLES 16

RAIDERS: 18 Luke Cresswell; 2 Shane Toal; 29 Gene Ormsby; 4 Andy Litherland; 5 Brett Carter; 1 Ryan Fieldhouse; 22 Dean Parata; 8 Joe Bullock; 14 Karl Ashall; 10 Tom Walker; 25 Jono Smith; 12 Jarrad Stack; 17 Alec Susino. Subs (all used): 9 Nathan Mossop; 11 Dan Toal; 15 Glenn Riley; 27 Ryan Duffy.
Tries: Fieldhouse (7), Bullock (17), Stack (21), Ormsby (32), Litherland (65); **Goals:** Carter 4/5.
EAGLES: 1 Ryan Millar; 2 Iliess Macani; 17 Daniel Igbinedion; 4 Joshua Toole; 5 Ben Blackmore; 6 Oscar Thomas; 19 Simon Brown; 8 Mark Offerdahl; 9 Matty Fozard; 12 Shaun Pick; 13 Matt James; 15 Olly Davies; 16 Kieran Moran. Subs (all used): 14 Greg Burns; 11 Nabil Djalout; 29 Ben Morris; 10 Jon Magrin.
Tries: Fozard (14), Macani (59), Millar (75);
Goals: Thomas 1/1, Brown 1/2.
Rugby Leaguer & League Express Men of the Match: *Raiders:* Ryan Fieldhouse; *Eagles:* Simon Brown.
Penalty count: 6-9; **Half-time:** 24-6;
Referee: Brandon Robinson; **Attendance:** 936.

BATLEY BULLDOGS 4 LEIGH CENTURIONS 8

BULLDOGS: 1 Dave Scott; 2 Wayne Reittie; 22 Danny Cowling; 4 Jason Crookes; 29 Lewis Galbraith; 6 Pat Walker; 7 Dominic Brambani; 20 Alex Rowe; 14 James Davey; 16 Michael Ward; 15 James Harrison; 13 Brad Day; 17 Joe Chandler. Subs (all used): 18 Tom Hemingway; 21 James Brown; 28 Keenen Tomlinson; 3 Sam Smeaton.
Goals: Walker 2/2.
CENTURIONS: 4 Peter Mata'utia; 2 Matty Dawson-Jones; 3 Ben Crooks; 5 Rhys Evans; 22 Ricky Bailey; 19 Jack Owens; 7 Drew Hutchison; 8 Paterika Vaivai; 14 Liam Hood; 18 Nathan Mason; 17 Kyle Lovett; 12 Bodene Thompson; 21 Nick Gregson. Subs (all used): 30 Micky Higham; 15 Jordan Thompson; 26 Jordan Dezaria; 13 Harrison Hansen.
Try: Ricky Bailey (19); **Goals:** Owens 2/2.
Rugby Leaguer & League Express Men of the Match: *Bulldogs:* Michael Ward; *Centurions:* Ricky Bailey.
Penalty count: 9-8; **Half-time:** 4-6;
Referee: Tom Grant; **Attendance:** 606.

WHITEHAVEN 25 DEWSBURY RAMS 18

WHITEHAVEN: 14 Dan Abram; 1 Jordan Burns; 23 Jason Mossop; 4 Jessie Joe Parker; 5 Dave Thompson; 6 Dion Aiye; 7 Callum Phillips; 8 Mark Shackley; 9 James Tilley; 10 Carl Forster; 18 Ellis Gillam; 27 Liam Cooper; 22 Stuart Howarth. Subs (all used): 11 Connor Holliday; 16 Kris Coward; 17 Brad Billsborough; 19 Lewis Brown.
Tries: Parker (7, 50), Forster (20), Mossop (33);
Goals: Burns 4/5; **Field goal:** Howarth (77).
RAMS: 25 Jared Simpson; 18 Gareth Potts; 21 Harry Woollard; 3 James Glover; 2 Rob Worrincy; 29 Danny Ansell; 7 Gareth Moore; 17 Toby Everett; 14 Dom Speakman; 22 Martyn Reilly; 15 Lucas Walshaw; 12 Michael Knowles; 24 Kyle Trout. Subs (all used): 19 Sam Day; 9 Robbie Ward; 8 Jode Sheriffe; 10 Jack Teanby.
Tries: Reilly (17), Teanby (38), Glover (55); **Goals:** Glover 3/3.
Rugby Leaguer & League Express Men of the Match: *Whitehaven:* Jessie Joe Parker; *Rams:* James Glover.
Penalty count: 10-12; **Half-time:** 20-12;
Referee: Andrew Sweet; **Attendance:** 414.

WORKINGTON TOWN 20 LONDON BRONCOS 22

TOWN: 1 Jordan Tansey; 2 Sam Forrester; 7 Jamie Foster; 18 Elliott Miller; 4 Scott Akehurst; 6 Jamie Doran; - Carl Forber; 8 Oliver Wilkes; 9 James Newton; 10 Stevie Scholey; 3 Perry Singleton; 12 Kurt Maudling; 13 Joe Ryan. Subs (all used): 5 Joe Hambley; 19 Andrew Dawson; 21 Jake Moore; 22 Caine Barnes.
Tries: Singleton (24), Doran (69, 79); **Goals:** Foster 4/4.
BRONCOS: 1 Elliot Kear; 5 Kieran Dixon; 24 Jake Ogden; 4 Matty Fleming; 2 Rhys Williams; 6 Api Pewhairangi; 27 James Meadows; 8 Tom Spencer; 9 James Cunningham; 20 Lewis Bienek; 12 Jay Pitts; 21 Will Lovell; 16 Matty Gee. Subs (all used): 26 Daniel Hindmarsh; 15 Eddie Battye; 23 Rob Butler; 29 Sam Davis.
Tries: Pewhairangi (12), Williams (14, 61), Spencer (44);
Goals: Dixon 3/4.
Rugby Leaguer & League Express Men of the Match: *Town:* Jamie Doran; *Broncos:* James Meadows.
Penalty count: 11-6; **Half-time:** 8-10;
Referee: Marcus Griffiths; **Attendance:** 548.

YORK CITY KNIGHTS 26 SWINTON LIONS 12

CITY KNIGHTS: - Kieren Moss; 1 Ash Robson; 22 Jake Normington; 4 Brad Hey; 5 Judah Mazive; 2 Ben Cockayne; 6 Connor Robinson; 26 Dan Hawksworth; 9 Andy Ellis; 10 Graeme Horne; 11 Joe Batchelor; 12 Sam Scott; 13 Tim Spears. Subs (all used): 20 Will Jubb; 15 Chris Siddons; 21 Rory Dixon; 17 Joe Porter.
Tries: Mazive (4, 75), Cockayne (9), Spears (23);
Goals: C Robinson 5/6.
LIONS: 1 Gabriel Fell; 5 Mike Butt; 3 Chris Hankinson; 4 George Tyson; 2 Marcus Webb; 35 Rob Fairclough; 7 Jack Hansen; 8 Andy Bracek; 14 Hayden Hansen; 15 Ben Austin; 11 Rhodri Lloyd; 12 Matt Sarsfield; 13 Josh Barlow. Subs (all used): 17 Kyle Shelford; 22 Conor Taylor; 24 Aaron Hall; 9 Luke Waterworth.
Tries: Tyson (32), Lloyd (56); **Goals:** Hankinson 2/3.
Sin bin: Bracek (79) - kicking.
Rugby Leaguer & League Express Men of the Match: *City Knights:* Tim Spears; *Lions:* Jack Hansen.
Penalty count: 10-12; **Half-time:** 20-8;
Referee: Michael Mannifield; **Attendance:** 525 *(at LD Nutrition Stadium, Featherstone).*

Tuesday 20th March 2018

HALIFAX 6 OLDHAM 27

HALIFAX: 16 James Woodburn-Hall; 5 James Saltonstall; 2 Ben Heaton; 3 Steve Tyrer; 21 Conor McGrath; 25 Adam Brook; 7 Ben Johnston; 8 Elliot Morris; 9 Ben Kaye; 29 Dan Fleming; 19 Will Calcott; 18 Chester Butler; 4 Ed Barber. Subs (all used): 30 Brandon Douglas; 26 Sion Jones; 14 Brandon Moore; 27 Connor Davies.
Try: Heaton (54); **Goals:** Tyrer 1/1.
OLDHAM: 27 Joe Martin; 2 Dave Eccleston; 3 Matt Reid; 29 Zack McComb; 30 Ben West; 6 Paul Crook; 7 Dave Hewitt; 13 Jack Spencer; 20 Matt Wilkinson; 10 Adam Neal; 25 Danny Bridge; 12 Danny Langtree; 24 Liam Bent. Subs (all used): 11 Craig Briscoe; 21 Kenny Hughes; 22 Danny Rasool; 23 Luke Nelmes.
Tries: Langtree (10), West (28), Reid (60), Crook (78);
Goals: Crook 5/6; **Field goal:** Hewitt (65).
Sin bin: Martin (55) - persistent team offences.
Rugby Leaguer & League Express Men of the Match: *Halifax:* Brandon Douglas; *Oldham:* Danny Langtree.
Penalty count: 13-10; **Half-time:** 0-12;
Referee: Billy Pearson; **Attendance:** 688.

NORTH WALES CRUSADERS 6 FEATHERSTONE ROVERS 66

CRUSADERS: 1 Tommy Johnson; - Kash Watkins; 20 Alex Thompson; 17 Kenny Baker; 24 Gavin Conroy; 6 Steve Roper; 7 Ryan Smith; 8 Jonny Walker; 9 Lee Hudson; 13 Ryan Millington; 11 Jack Houghton; 12 Simon Atherton; 25 Jordan Case. Subs (all used): 14 James Dandy; 22 Brad Brennan; - Luke Warburton; 26 Alex Trumper.
Try: Johnson (15); **Goals:** Johnson 1/1.
ROVERS: 1 Ian Hardman; 5 Luke Briscoe; 20 Josh Hardcastle; 4 Misi Taulapapa; 2 Shaun Robinson; 14 Matty Wildie; 19 Tom Holmes; 17 Luke Cooper; 9 Keal Carlile; 22 Sam Brooks; 11 Connor Farrell; 12 John Davies; 13 James Lockwood. Subs (all used): 15 Gareth Hock; 16 Frankie Mariano; 21 Bradley Knowles; 24 Danny Maskill.
Tries: Carlile (9, 24), Wildie (30, 76), Knowles (40), Briscoe (44, 47, 55, 73), Hardman (57), Hardcastle (60), Davies (71), Holmes (79); **Goals:** Hardman 7/13.
Rugby Leaguer & League Express Men of the Match: *Crusaders:* Ryan Smith; *Rovers:* Tom Holmes.
Penalty count: 5-8; **Half-time:** 6-22;
Referee: Jon Roberts; **Attendance:** 1,098 *(at LD Nutrition Stadium, Featherstone).*

Sunday 25th March 2018

COVENTRY BEARS 31 PILKINGTON RECS 20

BEARS: 1 Jason Bass; 2 Errol Carter; 3 Kameron Pearce Paul; 4 Dante Morley-Samuels; 5 Hayden Freeman; 6 Paul Emanuelli; 7 Ben Stead; 8 James Geurtjens; 9 Zak Williams; 10 John Aldred; 11 Kieran Sherratt; 12 James Mason; 13 Chris Vitalini. Subs (all used): 14 Liam Rice-Wilson; 18 Dan Gover; 16 Ben Gray; 19 Joel Thomas.
Tries: Mason (30, 75), Emanuelli (37), Freeman (55), Bass (62); **Goals:** Stead 5/5; **Field goal:** Emanuelli (79).
Sin bin: Mason (49) - holding down.
PILKINGTON RECS: 1 Ryan Hilliard; 2 Tommy Chisnall; 3 Ian Stanley; 4 Johnathan Frodsham; 5 Jake Hodson; 6 Tom Roughley; 7 Danny Lynch; 8 Chris Clayton; 9 Ryan Liptrot; 10 Mark Briody; 11 Terry Riley; 12 Mike Garrity; 17 Jonathan Peers. Subs (all used): 14 Luke Riley; 20 Phil Riley; 15 Joe Chow; 16 Connor Mulchay.
Tries: Clayton (5, 49), T Riley (17), Chisnall (70);
Goals: Lynch 2/5.
Rugby Leaguer & League Express Men of the Match: *Bears:* James Mason; *Pilkington Recs:* Jonathan Peers.
Penalty count: 8-10; **Half-time:** 12-10;
Referee: Steve Race; **Attendance:** 395.

Monday 2nd April 2018

HUNSLET 10 BRADFORD BULLS 34

HUNSLET: 1 Jimmy Watson; 24 Jordan Gill; 5 Joel Gibson; 28 Will Cooke; 22 Niall Walker; 6 Joe Sanderson; 7 Cain Southernwood; 8 Michael Haley; 9 Jack Lee; 10 Lewis Reed; 21 Jack Walton; 39 Josh Jordan-Roberts; 38 Jack Blagbrough. Subs (all used): 31 Daniel Halmshaw; 13 Matt Nicholson; 19 Jack Coventry; 29 Jake Barnett.
Try: Halmshaw (36); **Goals:** Sanderson 3/3.
Sin bin: Cooke (39) - delaying restart.
BULLS: 14 Gregg McNally; 25 Josh Rickett; 3 Ashley Gibson; 4 Ross Oakes; 2 Ethan Ryan; 24 Brandon Pickersgill; 7 Dane Chisholm; 8 Liam Kirk; 26 Vila Halafihi; 17 Ross Peltier; 11 Matt Garside; 18 Liam Johnson; 19 Mikey Wood. Subs (all used): 10 Steve Crossley; 12 Elliot Minchella; 21 George Flanagan; 34 Jordan Andrade.
Tries: Garside (2), Ryan (14), Johnson (52), Minchella (57), Rickett (64); **Goals:** Chisholm 7/8.
Rugby Leaguer & League Express Men of the Match: *Hunslet:* Matt Nicholson; *Bulls:* Dane Chisholm.
Penalty count: 5-9; **Half-time:** 6-14;
Referee: Nick Bennett; **Attendance:** 1,081.

ROUND 5

Saturday 21st April 2018

WIDNES VIKINGS 90 COVENTRY BEARS 0

VIKINGS: 1 Rhys Hanbury; 22 Ryan Ince; 24 Ed Chamberlain; 4 Charly Runciman; 5 Patrick Ah Van; 15 Danny Craven; 7 Tom Gilmore (C); 10 Alex Gerrard; 9 Lloyd White; 25 Jay Chapelhow; 12 Matt Whitley; 17 Sam Wilde; 28 Brad Walker. Subs (all used): 20 Macgraff Leuluai; 23 Danny Walker; 37 Stanton Albert (D); 21 Jordan Johnstone.
Tries: Hanbury (1, 15, 38), Ah Van (4, 9, 63), White (13), Craven (23, 40, 56, 59), B Walker (25), Whitley (33), Chamberlain (49), D Walker (54), J Chapelhow (67), Ince (76); **Goals:** Gilmore 11/17.
BEARS: 1 Rhys Gant; 2 Errol Carter; 29 Kameron Pearce-Paul; 4 Jason Bass; 5 Dante Morley-Samuels; 6 Paul Emanuelli; 7 Ben Stead; 8 Joel Thomas; 9 Zak Williams; 10 Chris Vitalini; 11 Ben Gray; 12 James Mason; 25 Richard Hughes. Subs (all used): 14 Liam Rice-Wilson; 16 Harry Kaufman; 17 Alex Beddows; 18 James Geurtjens.
Rugby Leaguer & League Express Men of the Match: *Vikings:* Alex Gerrard; *Bears:* Dante Morley-Samuels.
Penalty count: 5-3; **Half-time:** 54-0;
Referee: John McMullen; **Attendance:** 1,438.

WARRINGTON WOLVES 54 BRADFORD BULLS 6

WOLVES: 1 Stefan Ratchford; 27 Josh Charnley; 3 Bryson Goodwin; 4 Ryan Atkins; 21 Mitch Brown; 15 Declan Patton; 7 Tyrone Roberts; 8 Chris Hill (C); 22 Morgan Smith; 16 Sitaleki Akauola; 11 Ben Currie; 12 Jack Hughes; 19 George King. Subs (all used): 17 Joe Philbin; 20 Harvey Livett; 34 Ben Westwood; 25 Pat Moran (D).
Tries: Hill (4), Currie (13, 21), Goodwin (16, 57, 61), Charnley (23, 38, 43, 47);
Goals: Ratchford 3/6, Goodwin 4/4.
BULLS: 24 Brandon Pickersgill; 5 Dalton Grant; 3 Ashley Gibson; 4 Ross Oakes; 2 Ethan Ryan; 6 Joe Keyes; 12 Elliot Minchella; 8 Liam Kirk; 26 Vila Halafihi; 10 Steve Crossley; 11 Matt Garside; 18 Liam Johnson; 13 George Milton. Subs (all used): 21 George Flanagan; 17 Ross Peltier; 15 Callum Bustin; 19 Mikey Wood.
Try: Keyes (76); **Goals:** Keyes 1/1.
Rugby Leaguer & League Express Men of the Match: *Wolves:* Bryson Goodwin; *Bulls:* Joe Keyes.
Penalty count: 9-8; **Half-time:** 30-0;
Referee: Tom Grant; **Attendance:** 4,710.

Sunday 22nd April 2018

DONCASTER 16 FEATHERSTONE ROVERS 26

DONCASTER: 24 Jack Sanderson; 2 Aaron Jones-Bishop; 3 Liam Welham; 4 Jason Tali; 5 Sam Doherty; 17 Jack Miller; 6 Jordan Howden; 10 Ryan Boyle; 9 Kyle Kesik; 14 Connor Scott; 11 Brad England; 18 Charlie Martin; 26 Brandan Wilkinson. Subs (all used): 8 Russ Spiers; 16 Zac Braham; 15 Kieran Cross; 12 Jason Muranka.
Tries: Jones-Bishop (15), England (23), Tali (27);
Goals: Miller 2/4.
Sin bin: Howden (47) - dissent.
ROVERS: 7 Anthony Thackeray; 5 Luke Briscoe; 20 Josh Hardcastle; 4 Misi Taulapapa; 2 Shaun Robinson; 6 Martyn Ridyard; 19 Tom Holmes; 17 Luke Cooper; 14 Matty Wildie; 10 Richard Moore; 11 Connor Farrell; 12 John Davies; 13 James Lockwood. Subs (all used): 8 Scott Wheeldon; 22 Sam Brooks; 21 Bradley Knowles; 9 Keal Carlile.
Tries: Briscoe (3, 9), Holmes (55), Robinson (57, 70);
Goals: Ridyard 3/5.
Rugby Leaguer & League Express Men of the Match: *Doncaster:* Jason Tali; *Rovers:* Luke Briscoe.
Penalty count: 5-9; **Half-time:** 14-10;
Referee: Matt Rossleigh; **Attendance:** 1,076.

LEIGH CENTURIONS 40 LONDON BRONCOS 0

CENTURIONS: 4 Peter Mata'utia; 2 Matty Dawson-Jones; 3 Ben Crooks; 1 Craig Hall; 19 Jack Owens; 6 Ben Reynolds; 7 Drew Hutchison; 18 Nathan Mason; 14 Liam Hood; 10 Jamie Acton; 13 Harrison Hansen; 12 Bodene Thompson; 15 Jordan Thompson. Subs (all used): 30 Micky Higham; 29 Ryan Bailey; 20 Greg Richards; 11 Kevin Larroyer.
Tries: Dawson-Jones (18), Hood (20), Hall (22), Owens (35), Crooks (49, 52), Hansen (69); **Goals:** Reynolds 6/7.
BRONCOS: 5 Kieran Dixon; 1 Elliot Kear; 17 Michael Channing; 4 Matty Fleming; 2 Rhys Williams; 6 Api Pewhairangi; 27 James Meadows; 8 Tom Spencer; 7 Jarrod Sammut; 15 Eddie Battye; 12 Jay Pitts; 16 Matty Gee; 13 Matt Davis. Subs (all used): 29 Sam Davis; 20 Lewis Bienek; 19 Sadiq Adebiyi; 23 Rob Butler.
Rugby Leaguer & League Express Men of the Match: *Centurions:* Ben Reynolds; *Broncos:* Sam Davis.
Penalty count: 10-8; **Half-time:** 22-0;
Referee: Liam Moore; **Attendance:** 2,507.

OLDHAM 0 HULL KINGSTON ROVERS 32

OLDHAM: 14 Luke Hooley; 2 Dave Eccleston; 3 Matt Reid; 4 Jack Holmes; 15 Lee Kershaw; 6 Paul Crook; 7 Dave Hewitt; 8 Phil Joy; 9 Gareth Owen; 13 Jack Spencer; 25 Danny Bridge; 12 Danny Langtree; 24 Liam Bent. Subs (all used): 11 Craig Briscoe; 19 Adam Jones; 21 Kenny Hughes; 23 Luke Nelmes.
ROVERS: 1 Adam Quinlan; 5 Ryan Shaw; 22 Liam Salter; 2 Junior Vaivai; 27 Will Oakes; 24 Chris Atkin; 20 Matty Marsh; 23 Josh Johnson; 30 Joe Cator; 8 Nick Scruton; 29 Jordan Walne; 34 Danny Tickle; 15 James Donaldson. Subs (all used): 10 Mose Masoe; 11 Maurice Blair (C); 12 James Greenwood; 28 Will Dagger.
Tries: Atkin (6), Quinlan (25, 38, 48), Oakes (35), Dagger (57); **Goals:** Shaw 4/6.
Rugby Leaguer & League Express Men of the Match: *Oldham:* Danny Langtree; *Rovers:* Junior Vaivai.
Penalty count: 10-5; **Half-time:** 0-20;
Referee: Gareth Hewer; **Attendance:** 1,064.

TORONTO WOLFPACK 16 BARROW RAIDERS 12

WOLFPACK: 31 Gareth O'Brien; 19 Adam Higson; 33 Chase Stanley; 23 Nick Rawsthorne; 5 Liam Kay; 7 Ryan Brierley; 6 Josh McCrone; 29 Jake Emmitt; 14 Andy Ackers; 10 Ashton Sims; 13 Jack Bussey; 22 Richard Whiting; 28 Sam Hopkins. Subs (all used): 32 Darcy Lussick; 15 Adam Sidlow; 8 Jack Buchanan; 9 Bob Beswick.
Tries: O'Brien (5), Beswick (24), Rawsthorne (48);
Goals: Brierley 2/3.
RAIDERS: 1 Ryan Fieldhouse; 2 Shane Toal; 12 Jarrad Stack; 3 Declan Hulme; 29 Gene Ormsby; 6 Jamie Dallimore; 21 Ryan Johnston; 8 Joe Bullock; 9 Nathan Mossop; 17 Alec Susino; 24 Danny Morrow; 25 Jono Smith; 13 Martin Aspinwall. Subs (all used): 27 Ryan Duffy; 22 Dean Parata; 19 Bradd Crellin; 10 Tom Walker.
Tries: Mossop (18), Aspinwall (24); **Goals** Dallimore 2/2.
Rugby Leaguer & League Express Men of the Match: *Wolfpack:* Gareth O'Brien; *Raiders:* Jono Smith.
Penalty count: 7-6; **Half-time:** 10-12;
Referee: Greg Dolan; **Attendance:** 1,140
(at Craven Park, Barrow).

WHITEHAVEN 38 ROCHDALE HORNETS 0

WHITEHAVEN: 14 Dan Abram; 5 Dave Thompson; 3 Chris Taylor; 23 Jason Mossop; 15 Danny Green; 6 Dion Aiye; 7 Callum Phillips; 8 Marc Shackley; 9 James Tilley; 16 Kris Coward; 27 Liam Cooper; 18 Ellis Gillam; 10 Carl Forster. Subs (all used): 19 Lewis Brown; 11 Connor Holliday; 20 Lewis Reece; 4 Jessie Joe Parker.
Tries: Phillips (22, 35), Abram (42), Holliday (58), Parker (64); **Goals:** Abram 9/9.
Sin bin: Forster (18) - persistent team offences; Reece (48) - interference.
HORNETS: 2 Declan Kay; 21 Richard Lepori; 18 Billy Brickhill; 3 Earl Hurst; 4 Taylor Welch; 31 Deon Cross; 7 Danny Yates; 13 Luke Adamson; 9 Ben Moores; 19 Lee Mitchell; 12 Toby Adamson; 11 Dave Allen; 23 Gary Middlehurst. Subs (all used): 15 Lewis Hatton; 24 Declan Gregory; 8 Jovili Taira; 10 Matty Hadden.
Sin bin: Allen (35) - holding down.
On report: Allen (2) - alleged late challenge on Aiye; Taira (67) - alleged late challenge on Phillips.
Rugby Leaguer & League Express Men of the Match: *Whitehaven:* Callum Phillips; *Hornets:* Lee Mitchell.
Penalty count: 7-13; **Half-time:** 18-0;
Referee: Liam Staveley; **Attendance:** 604.

YORK CITY KNIGHTS 22 CATALANS DRAGONS 34

CITY KNIGHTS: 30 Kieren Moss; 1 Ash Robson; 3 Jake Butler-Fleming; 4 Brad Hey; 5 Judah Mazive; 2 Ben Cockayne; 6 Connor Robinson; 8 Adam Robinson; 9 Andy Ellis; 15 Chris Siddons; 11 Joe Batchelor; 12 Sam Scott; 13 Tim Spears. Subs (all used): 26 Dan Hawksworth; 22 Jake Normington; 16 Ronan Dixon; 17 Joe Porter.
Tries: Porter (34, 37), Moss (52), Batchelor (78);
Goals: C Robinson 3/4.
DRAGONS: 1 David Mead; 2 Jodie Broughton; 31 Tony Gigot; 16 Vincent Duport; 5 Fouad Yaha; 6 Samisoni Langi; 22 Lucas Albert; 23 Antoni Maria; 19 Michael Mcllorum; 10 Sam Moa; 13 Greg Bird; 12 Benjamin Garcia (C); 17 Jason Baitieri. Subs (all used): 9 Paul Aiton; 14 Julian Bousquet; 18 Thibaut Margalet; 15 Mickael Simon.
Tries: Yaha (5), Baitieri (18), Simon (40), Albert (49), Broughton (69), Bird (73); **Goals:** Albert 5/6.
Rugby Leaguer & League Express Men of the Match: *City Knights:* Joe Batchelor; *Dragons:* Lucas Albert.
Penalty count: 9-13; **Half-time:** 10-16;
Referee: Chris Kendall; **Attendance:** 3,081.

ROUND 6

Thursday 10th May 2018

FEATHERSTONE ROVERS 20 HULL FC 38

ROVERS: 7 Anthony Thackeray; 5 Luke Briscoe; 20 Josh Hardcastle; 4 Misi Taulapapa; 2 Shaun Robinson; 6 Martyn Ridyard; 19 Tom Holmes; 8 Scott Wheeldon; 9 Keal Carlile; 21 Bradley Knowles; 11 Connor Farrell; 12 John Davies; 13 James Lockwood. Subs (all used): 14 Matty Wildie; 15 Gareth Hock; 17 Luke Cooper; 22 Sam Brooks.
Tries: Thackeray (22), Briscoe (36, 46), Hock (75);
Goals: Ridyard 2/4.
Sin bin: Briscoe (56) - professional foul; Davies (66) - high tackle on Litten; Knowles (77) - dangerous challenge on Connor.
HULL FC: 1 Jamie Shaul; 2 Bureta Faraimo; 4 Josh Griffin; 11 Dean Hadley; 5 Fetuli Talanoa; 14 Jake Connor; 3 Carlos Tuimavave; 15 Chris Green; 9 Danny Houghton (C); 13 Josh Bowden; 21 Sika Manu; 12 Mark Minichiello; 33 Joe Westerman. Subs (all used): 29 Masi Matongo; 17 Danny Washbrook; 22 Jez Litten; 26 Jordan Lane.
Tries: Connor (4, 13), Manu (9), Shaul (25), Griffin (32), Faraimo (50, 63); **Goals:** Connor 5/7.
Dismissal: Faraimo (80) - late challenge on Thackeray.
Sin bin: Washbrook (74) - use of the knees; Connor (77) - retaliation; Shaul (78) - delaying restart.
Rugby Leaguer & League Express Men of the Match: *Rovers:* Gareth Hock; *Hull FC:* Jake Connor.
Penalty count: 10-10; **Half-time:** 10-30;
Referee: Scott Mikalauskas; **Attendance:** 3,222.

Friday 11th May 2018

LEIGH CENTURIONS 22 SALFORD RED DEVILS 10

CENTURIONS: 4 Peter Mata'utia; 2 Matty Dawson-Jones; 3 Ben Crooks; 1 Craig Hall; 19 Jack Owens; 6 Ben Reynolds; 7 Drew Hutchison; 29 Ryan Bailey; 30 Micky Higham; 10 Jamie Acton; 13 Harrison Hansen; 12 Bodene Thompson; 15 Jordan Thompson. Subs (all used): 9 Daniel Mortimer; 11 Kevin Larroyer; 20 Greg Richards; 26 Jordan Dezaria.
Tries: Reynolds (16), Hansen (20), Mortimer (49), Hutchison (77); **Goals:** Reynolds 3/4.
RED DEVILS: 5 Niall Evalds; 22 Derrell Olpherts; 3 Kris Welham; 4 Junior Sa'u; 2 Greg Johnson; 28 Jake Shorrocks; 7 Jack Littlejohn; 18 Ben Nakubuwai; 9 Logan Tomkins; 23 Lee Mossop; 12 Weller Hauraki; 10 George Griffin; 13 Mark Flanagan (C). Subs (all used): 19 Josh Wood; 14 Lama Tasi; 17 Tyrone McCarthy; 8 Craig Kopczak.
Tries: Evalds (2), Griffin (12); **Goals:** Shorrocks 1/2.
Rugby Leaguer & League Express Men of the Match: *Centurions:* Harrison Hansen; *Red Devils:* Tyrone McCarthy.
Penalty count: 8-7; **Half-time:** 12-10;
Referee: Liam Moore; **Attendance:** 4,024.

HUDDERSFIELD GIANTS 24 WAKEFIELD TRINITY 14

GIANTS: 15 Jordan Rankin; 2 Jermaine McGillvary; 6 Lee Gaskell; 1 Jake Mamo; 23 Darnell McIntosh; 4 Jordan Turner; 7 Danny Brough; 8 Sebastine Ikahihifo; 21 Adam O'Brien; 18 Paul Clough; 22 Alex Mellor; 17 Ukuma Ta'ai; 13 Ryan Hinchcliffe (C). Subs (all used): 9 Kruise Leeming; 12 Michael Lawrence; 19 Daniel Smith; 27 Matty English.
Tries: O'Brien (16), English (45), Ta'ai (55), Gaskell (65);
Goals: Brough 4/4.
Sin bin: Leeming (27) - persistent team offences.
TRINITY: 21 Max Jowitt; 24 Mason Caton-Brown; 3 Bill Tupou; 18 Joe Arundel; 2 Tom Johnstone; 6 Jacob Miller (C); 7 Liam Finn; 10 Anthony England; 9 Kyle Wood; 8 David Fifita; 11 Matty Ashurst; 15 Pauli Pauli; 14 Justin Horo. Subs (all used): 16 Tinirau Arona; 19 James Batchelor; 20 Keegan Hirst; 25 Ryan Hampshire.
Tries: Caton-Brown (6), Hampshire (68); **Goals:** Finn 3/4.

Rugby Leaguer & League Express Men of the Match:
Giants: Matty English; *Trinity:* Pauli Pauli.
Penalty count: 11-12; **Half-time:** 6-8;
Referee: Gareth Hewer; **Attendance:** 2,631.

WIDNES VIKINGS 20 LEEDS RHINOS 23

VIKINGS: 1 Rhys Hanbury; 22 Ryan Ince; 4 Charly Runciman; 24 Ed Chamberlain; 2 Stefan Marsh; 7 Tom Gilmore (C); 33 Aaron Heremaia; 10 Alex Gerrard; 9 Lloyd White; 19 Greg Burke; 12 Matt Whitley; 17 Sam Wilde; 13 Hep Cahill. Subs (all used): 20 Macgraff Leuluai; 16 Tom Olbison; 36 Wellington Albert; 21 Jordan Johnstone.
Tries: Whitley (26, 48), Gerrard (57), Runciman (60);
Goals: Gilmore 2/4.
RHINOS: 24 Jack Walker; 2 Tom Briscoe; 3 Kallum Watkins (C); 22 Ash Handley; 1 Ashton Golding; 6 Joel Moon; 7 Richie Myler; 28 Mikolaj Oledzki; 9 Matt Parcell; 8 Adam Cuthbertson; 12 Carl Ablett; 13 Stevie Ward; 11 Jamie Jones-Buchanan. Subs (all used): 21 Nathaniel Peteru; 16 Anthony Mullally; 14 Brad Dwyer; 19 Brett Ferres.
Tries: Grace (14), Barba (31, 43, 70), Morgan (52), Richardson (63); **Goals:** Richardson 6/7.
Tries: T Briscoe (15), Myler (23), Golding (44), Ward (46);
Goals: Watkins 3/4; **Field goal:** Myler (37).
Sin bin: Golding (11) - holding down.
Rugby Leaguer & League Express Men of the Match:
Vikings: Matt Whitley; *Rhinos:* Stevie Ward.
Penalty count: 8-6; **Half-time:** 4-11;
Referee: Greg Dolan; **Attendance:** 1,865.

Saturday 12th May 2018

CASTLEFORD TIGERS 18 ST HELENS 36

TIGERS: 4 Michael Shenton (C); 2 Greg Minikin; 3 Jake Webster; 16 Joe Wardle; 24 Jy Hitchcox; 6 Jamie Ellis; 9 Paul McShane; 32 Liam Watts; 13 Adam Milner; 15 Jesse Sene-Lefao; 11 Oliver Holmes; 12 Mike McMeeken; 17 Alex Foster. Subs (all used): 8 Junior Moors; 10 Grant Millington; 18 Matt Cook; 21 Jake Trueman.
Tries: Trueman (48), Minikin (59), McMeeken (80);
Goals: Ellis 3/3.
SAINTS: 23 Ben Barba; 2 Tommy Makinson; 3 Ryan Morgan; 4 Mark Percival; 19 Regan Grace; 1 Jonny Lomax; 18 Danny Richardson; 10 Kyle Amor; 9 James Roby (C); 16 Luke Thompson; 17 Dominique Peyroux; 11 Zeb Taia; 12 Jon Wilkin. Subs (all used): 6 Theo Fages; 13 Louie McCarthy-Scarsbrook; 14 Luke Douglas; 15 Morgan Knowles.
Tries: Grace (14), Barba (31, 43, 70), Morgan (52), Richardson (63); **Goals:** Richardson 6/7.
Rugby Leaguer & League Express Men of the Match:
Tigers: Adam Milner; *Saints:* Ben Barba.
Penalty count: 5-6; **Half-time:** 0-12;
Referee: James Child; **Attendance:** 5,342.

CATALANS DRAGONS 56 WHITEHAVEN 10

DRAGONS: 31 Tony Gigot; 2 Jodie Broughton; 3 Iain Thornley; 16 Vincent Duport; 20 Lewis Tierney; 6 Samisoni Langi; 33 Josh Drinkwater; 15 Mickael Simon; 19 Michael McIlorum; 10 Sam Moa; 21 Benjamin Jullien; 12 Benjamin Garcia (C); 17 Jason Baitieri. Subs (all used): 14 Julian Bousquet; 23 Antoni Maria; 24 Alrix Da Costa; 32 Mickael Goudemand (D).
Tries: Broughton (3, 4, 67), McIlorum (10), Drinkwater (27), Goudemand (35, 65), Maria (48), Bousquet (56), Duport (73), Gigot (78); **Goals:** Drinkwater 6/11.
WHITEHAVEN: 14 Dan Abram; 15 Danny Green; 23 Jason Mossop; 4 Jessie Joe Parker; 5 Dave Thompson; 22 Stuart Howarth; 7 Callum Phillips; 8 Marc Shackley; 9 James Tilley; 27 Liam Cooper; 6 Dion Aiye; 18 Ellis Gillam; 10 Carl Forster. Subs (all used): 3 Chris Taylor; 16 Kris Coward; 19 Lewis Brown; 26 Josh Eaves.
Tries: Parker (16), D Thompson (19); **Goals:** Abram 1/2.
Rugby Leaguer & League Express Men of the Match:
Dragons: Jason Baitieri; *Whitehaven:* Callum Phillips.
Penalty count: 10-5; **Half-time:** 24-10;
Referee: Matt Rossleigh; **Attendance:** 2,533.

Sunday 13th May 2018

HULL KINGSTON ROVERS 10 WIGAN WARRIORS 28

ROVERS: 1 Adam Quinlan; 5 Ryan Shaw; 22 Liam Salter; 2 Junior Vaivai; 37 Elliot Wallis (D); 19 Tommy Lee; 11 Maurice Blair (C); 21 Robbie Mulhern; 24 Chris Atkin; 23 Josh Johnson; 34 Danny Tickle; 12 James Greenwood; 30 Joe Cator. Subs (all used): 10 Mose Masoe; 15 James Donaldson; 29 Jordan Walne; 20 Matty Marsh.
Tries: Atkin (21), Vaivai (51); **Goals:** Shaw 1/3.
Dismissal: Tickle (40) - punching Bateman.
Sin bin: Quinlan (29) - delaying restart.
WARRIORS: 1 Sam Tomkins; 2 Tom Davies; 3 Dan Sarginson; 4 Oliver Gildart; 22 Liam Marshall; 34 Josh Woods; 7 Sam Powell; 8 Tony Clubb; 9 Thomas Leuluai; 10 Ben Flower; 14 John Bateman; 12 Liam Farrell; 13 Sean O'Loughlin (C). Subs (all used): 19 Willie Isa; 15 Ryan Sutton; 11 Joel Tomkins; 17 Taulima Tautai.

St Helens' Theo Fages looks for a way through the Castleford defence

Tries: Woods (11), Marshall (24), S Tomkins (62), Clubb (74), Davies (78); **Goals:** S Tomkins 4/6.
Sin bin: Bateman (40) - retaliation.
Rugby Leaguer & League Express Men of the Match:
Rovers: Robbie Mulhern; *Warriors:* Sam Tomkins.
Penalty count: 11-10; **Half-time:** 4-10;
Referee: Chris Kendall; **Attendance:** 3,524.

TORONTO WOLFPACK 10 WARRINGTON WOLVES 66

WOLFPACK: 31 Gareth O'Brien; 19 Adam Higson; 33 Chase Stanley; 3 Greg Worthington; 5 Liam Kay; 6 Josh McCrone; 7 Ryan Brierley; 32 Darcy Lussick; 9 Bob Beswick; 10 Ashton Sims; 11 Andrew Dixon; 24 Cory Paterson; 29 Jake Emmitt. Subs (all used): 15 Adam Sidlow; 13 Jack Bussey; 14 Andy Ackers; 28 Sam Hopkins.
Tries: Higson (7), Kay (16); **Goals:** Brierley 1/3.
Dismissal: Dixon (38) - punching Livett.
Sin bin: Kay (29) - dangerous challenge on Charnley; McCrone (47) - dissent; Lussick (53) - dissent.
WOLVES: 1 Stefan Ratchford; 2 Tom Lineham; 3 Bryson Goodwin; 4 Ryan Atkins; 27 Josh Charnley; 6 Kevin Brown; 7 Tyrone Roberts; 8 Chris Hill (C); 9 Daryl Clark; 10 Mike Cooper; 20 Harvey Livett; 12 Jack Hughes; 34 Ben Westwood. Subs (all used): 17 Joe Philbin; 13 Ben Murdoch-Masila; 15 Declan Patton; 16 Sitaleki Akauola.
Tries: Cooper (23), Charnley (40, 72), Livett (41), Murdoch-Masila (45, 70), Hughes (51), Westwood (55), Lineham (57, 67, 80), Roberts (59); **Goals:** Goodwin 9/12.
Rugby Leaguer & League Express Men of the Match:
Wolfpack: Gareth O'Brien; *Wolves:* Stefan Ratchford.
Penalty count: 8-16; **Half-time:** 10-12;
Referee: Ben Thaler; **Attendance:** 6,507
(at Halliwell Jones Stadium, Warrington).

QUARTER FINALS

Thursday 31st May 2018

HUDDERSFIELD GIANTS 6 CATALANS DRAGONS 20

GIANTS: 15 Jordan Rankin; 2 Jermaine McGillvary; 3 Leroy Cudjoe (C); 1 Jake Mamo; 23 Darnell McIntosh; 4 Jordan Turner; 7 Danny Brough; 8 Sebastine Ikahihifo; 21 Adam O'Brien; 18 Paul Clough; 5 Aaron Murphy; 22 Alex Mellor; 13 Ryan Hinchcliffe. Subs (all used): 9 Kruise Leeming; 19 Daniel Smith; 27 Matty English; 16 Oliver Roberts.
Try: Cudjoe (42); **Goals:** Brough 1/1.
Sin bin: Brough (22) - dangerous contact on Edwards.
DRAGONS: 31 Tony Gigot; 2 Jodie Broughton; 1 David Mead; 4 Brayden Wiliame; 20 Lewis Tierney; 13 Greg Bird; 33 Josh Drinkwater; 15 Mickael Simon; 19 Michael McIlorum; 10 Sam Moa; 21 Benjamin Jullien; 12 Benjamin Garcia; 8 Remi Casty (C). Subs (all used): 14 Julian Bousquet; 23 Antoni Maria; 11 Louis Andersen; 34 Kenny Edwards (D).
Tries: Mead (45), Bird (67); **Goals:** Drinkwater 6/6.
Sin bin: Garcia (72) - dangerous challenge.
Rugby Leaguer & League Express Men of the Match:
Giants: Leroy Cudjoe; *Dragons:* Josh Drinkwater.
Penalty count: 10-11; **Half-time:** 0-4;
Referee: Gareth Hewer; **Attendance:** 2,151.

Friday 1st June 2018

LEEDS RHINOS 52 LEIGH CENTURIONS 22

RHINOS: 24 Jack Walker; 2 Tom Briscoe; 18 Jimmy Keinhorst; 22 Ash Handley; 5 Ryan Hall; 25 Jordan Lilley; 7 Richie Myler; 8 Adam Cuthbertson; 9 Matt Parcell; 28 Mikolaj Oledzki; 12 Carl Ablett. Subs (all used): 16 Anthony Mullally; 30 Josh Walters; 1 Ashton Golding; 27 Cameron Smith.
Tries: T Briscoe (10, 15), Walker (20), Handley (22), Keinhorst (25), Golding (27), Myler (36), Smith (48), Cuthbertson (79); **Goals:** Lilley 8/10.
CENTURIONS: 4 Peter Mata'utia; 2 Matty Dawson-Jones; 3 Ben Crooks; 1 Craig Hall; 5 Rhys Evans; 6 Ben Reynolds; 7 Drew Hutchison; 10 Jamie Acton; 14 Liam Hood; 18 Nathan Mason; 12 Bodene Thompson; 13 Harrison Hansen; 15 Jordan Thompson. Subs (all used): 31 Jordan Baldwinson; 20 Greg Richards; 30 Micky Higham; 11 Kevin Larroyer.
Tries: Mason (5), Hutchison (29), Crooks (63), Hood (72);
Goals: Reynolds 3/4.
Dismissals: Mata'utia (9) - dangerous challenge on Parcell; Dawson-Jones (79) - dissent.
Sin bin: Acton (77) - persistent offences.
On report: Crooks (35) - alleged use of the forearm on Myler.
Rugby Leaguer & League Express Men of the Match:
Rhinos: Jack Walker; *Centurions:* Greg Richards.
Penalty count: 8-7; **Half-time:** 40-12;
Referee: Chris Kendall; **Attendance:** 3,277
(at LD Nutrition Stadium, Featherstone).

Saturday 2nd June 2018

WARRINGTON WOLVES 23 WIGAN WARRIORS 0

WOLVES: 1 Stefan Ratchford; 2 Tom Lineham; 3 Bryson Goodwin; 4 Ryan Atkins; 27 Josh Charnley; 6 Kevin Brown; 7 Tyrone Roberts; 8 Chris Hill (C); 9 Daryl Clark; 10 Mike Cooper; 20 Harvey Livett; 12 Jack Hughes; 34 Ben Westwood. Subs (all used): 13 Ben Murdoch-Masila; 17 Joe Philbin; 15 Declan Patton; 16 Sitaleki Akauola.
Tries: K Brown (12), Murdoch-Masila (40), Charnley (40), Patton (80); **Goals:** Livett 2/3, Goodwin 1/2;
Field goal: Roberts (76).
WARRIORS: 1 Sam Tomkins; 2 Tom Davies; 14 John Bateman; 4 Oliver Gildart; 22 Liam Marshall; 6 George Williams; 7 Sam Powell; 8 Tony Clubb; 9 Thomas Leuluai; 10 Ben Flower; 19 Willie Isa; 12 Liam Farrell; 13 Sean O'Loughlin (C). Subs (all used): 20 Morgan Escare; 15 Ryan Sutton; 11 Joel Tomkins; 17 Taulima Tautai.
Sin bin: Leuluai (60) - dangerous challenge on Westwood.
Rugby Leaguer & League Express Men of the Match:
Wolves: Tyrone Roberts; *Warriors:* John Bateman.
Penalty count: 6-5; **Half-time:** 16-0;
Referee: Robert Hicks; **Attendance:** 10,213.

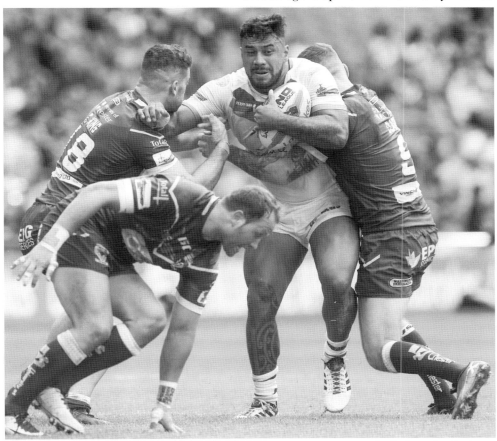

Catalans' Kenny Edwards takes on Warrington's Daryl Clark and Toby King during the Challenge Cup Final

Sunday 3rd June 2018

ST HELENS 25 HULL FC 22

SAINTS: 23 Ben Barba; 2 Tommy Makinson; 3 Ryan Morgan; 4 Mark Percival; 19 Regan Grace; 1 Jonny Lomax; 18 Danny Richardson; 10 Kyle Amor; 9 James Roby (C); 16 Luke Thompson; 17 Dominique Peyroux; 11 Zeb Taia; 12 Jon Wilkin. Subs (all used): 6 Theo Fages; 13 Louie McCarthy-Scarsbrook; 14 Luke Douglas; 15 Morgan Knowles.
Tries: Percival (13, 36), Grace (16, 33);
Goals: Richardson 4/5; **Field goal:** Richardson (40).
HULL FC: 1 Jamie Shaul; 2 Bureta Faraimo; 24 Jack Logan; 3 Carlos Tuimavave; 28 Hakim Miloudi; 6 Albert Kelly; 14 Jake Connor; 15 Chris Green; 9 Danny Houghton (C); 8 Scott Taylor; 12 Mark Minichiello; 21 Sika Manu; 11 Dean Hadley. Subs (all used): 17 Danny Washbrook; 20 Brad Fash; 23 Mickey Paea; 29 Masi Matongo.
Tries: Kelly (19), Green (22), Taylor (53), Miloudi (70);
Goals: Connor 3/4.
Sin bin: Houghton (27) - dangerous contact; Washbrook (30) - use of the knees; Matongo (56) - late challenge on Lomax.
Rugby Leaguer & League Express Men of the Match: *Saints:* Mark Percival; *Hull FC:* Chris Green.
Penalty count: 9-5; **Half-time:** 23-12;
Referee: Ben Thaler; **Attendance:** 8,928.

SEMI-FINALS

Sunday 5th August 2018

CATALANS DRAGONS 35 ST HELENS 16

DRAGONS: 31 Tony Gigot; 20 Lewis Tierney; 1 David Mead; 4 Brayden Wiliame; 5 Fouad Yaha; 6 Samisoni Langi; 33 Josh Drinkwater; 15 Mickael Simon; 19 Michael McIlorum;
10 Sam Moa; 21 Benjamin Jullien; 12 Benjamin Garcia; 8 Remi Casty (C). Subs (all used): 14 Julian Bousquet; 11 Louis Anderson; 34 Kenny Edwards; 17 Jason Baitieri.
Tries: Tierney (20), Garcia (29, 39), Gigot (36), Moa (62);
Goals: Drinkwater 7/8; **Field goal:** Gigot (32).
SAINTS: 23 Ben Barba; 5 Adam Swift; 2 Tommy Makinson; 4 Mark Percival; 19 Regan Grace; 1 Jonny Lomax; 18 Danny Richardson; 10 Kyle Amor; 9 James Roby (C); 16 Luke Thompson; 15 Morgan Knowles; 11 Zeb Taia; 12 Jon Wilkin. Subs (all used): 6 Theo Fages; 13 Louie McCarthy-Scarsbrook; 14 Luke Douglas; 20 Matty Lees.
Tries: Percival (14), McCarthy-Scarsbrook (55);
Goals: Richardson 2/3.
Sin bin: Knowles (34) - high tackle on Edwards.
Rugby Leaguer & League Express Men of the Match: *Dragons:* Tony Gigot; *Saints:* Mark Percival.
Penalty count: 10-9; **Half-time:** 27-0;
Referee: Robert Hicks.

LEEDS RHINOS 12 WARRINGTON WOLVES 48

RHINOS: 24 Jack Walker; 2 Tom Briscoe; 22 Ash Handley; 4 Liam Sutcliffe; 5 Ryan Hall; 6 Joel Moon; 7 Richie Myler; 8 Adam Cuthbertson; 9 Matt Parcell; 10 Brad Singleton (C); 19 Brett Ferres; 12 Carl Ablett; 11 Jamie Jones-Buchanan. Subs (all used): 14 Brad Dwyer; 28 Mikolaj Oledzki; 21 Nathaniel Peteru; 30 Josh Walters.
Tries: Hall (13), Cuthbertson (45); **Goals:** Sutcliffe 2/2.
WOLVES: 1 Stefan Ratchford; 2 Tom Lineham; 3 Bryson Goodwin; 18 Toby King; 27 Josh Charnley; 6 Kevin Brown; 7 Tyrone Roberts; 8 Chris Hill (C); 9 Daryl Clark; 10 Mike Cooper; 20 Harvey Livett; 12 Jack Hughes; 34 Ben Westwood. Subs (all used): 13 Ben Murdoch-Masila; 19 George King; 15 Declan Patton; 17 Joe Philbin.
Tries: Lineham (22, 77), Charnley (24, 58), K Brown (30), Murdoch-Masila (39), T King (69), Goodwin (74);
Goals: Roberts 8/9, Westwood 0/1.

Rugby Leaguer & League Express Men of the Match: *Rhinos:* Brad Dwyer; *Wolves:* Daryl Clark.
Penalty count: 3-6; **Half-time:** 6-26;
Referee: Chris Kendall.

Attendance: 26,086
(both at University of Bolton Stadium).

FINAL

Saturday 25th August 2018

CATALANS DRAGONS 20 WARRINGTON WOLVES 14

DRAGONS: 31 Tony Gigot; 20 Lewis Tierney; 1 David Mead; 4 Brayden Wiliame; 5 Fouad Yaha; 6 Samisoni Langi; 33 Josh Drinkwater; 15 Mickael Simon; 19 Michael McIlorum; 10 Sam Moa; 21 Benjamin Jullien; 12 Benjamin Garcia; 8 Remi Casty (C). Subs (all used): 14 Julian Bousquet; 17 Jason Baitieri; 34 Kenny Edwards; 32 Mickael Goudemand.
Tries: Tierney (2), Garcia (34), Wiliame (46);
Goals: Drinkwater 4/4.
WOLVES: 1 Stefan Ratchford; 2 Tom Lineham; 3 Bryson Goodwin; 18 Toby King; 27 Josh Charnley; 6 Kevin Brown; 7 Tyrone Roberts; 8 Chris Hill (C); 9 Daryl Clark; 10 Mike Cooper; 20 Harvey Livett; 12 Jack Hughes; 34 Ben Westwood. Subs (all used): 13 Ben Murdoch-Masila; 19 George King; 15 Declan Patton; 17 Joe Philbin.
Tries: Murdoch-Masila (28), G King (56);
Goals: Roberts 3/3.
Rugby Leaguer & League Express Men of the Match: *Dragons:* Tony Gigot; *Wolves:* Toby King.
Penalty count: 6-10; **Half-time:** 14-6;
Referee: Robert Hicks; **Attendance:** 50,672
(at Wembley Stadium).

GRAND FINALS
1998-2017

Grand Finals 1998-2017

1998

DIVISION ONE GRAND FINAL

Saturday 26th September 1998

FEATHERSTONE ROVERS 22 WAKEFIELD TRINITY 24

ROVERS: 1 Steve Collins; 2 Carl Hall; 3 Shaun Irwin; 4 Danny Baker; 5 Karl Pratt; 6 Jamie Coventry; 7 Ty Fallins; 8 Chico Jackson; 9 Richard Chapman; 10 Stuart Dickens; 11 Gary Price; 12 Neil Lowe; 13 Richard Slater. Subs: 14 Paddy Handley for Coventry (70); 15 Asa Amone for Lowe (50); 16 Micky Clarkson for Jackson (50); 17 Steve Dooler (not used).
Tries: Baker (15), Jackson (45), Collins (49), Hall (69);
Goals: Chapman 3.
TRINITY: 1 Martyn Holland; 2 Josh Bostock; 3 Adam Hughes; 4 Martin Law; 5 Kevin Gray; 6 Garen Casey; 7 Roger Kenworthy; 8 Francis Stephenson; 9 Roy Southernwood; 10 Gary Lord; 11 Ian Hughes; 12 Sonny Whakarau; 13 Matt Fuller. Subs: 14 Sean Richardson for I Hughes (32); 15 Andy Fisher for Lord (26); 16 David Mycoe (not used); 17 Wayne McDonald for Whakarau (70); Lord for Stephenson (40); Stephenson for Lord (70).
Tries: Southernwood (2), Bostock (7, 25), Casey (58), Stephenson (76); **Goals:** Casey 2.
League Express Men of the Match:
Rovers: Richard Chapman; *Trinity:* Garen Casey.
Penalty count: 8-3; **Half time:** 6-12;
Referee: Nick Oddy (Halifax); **Attendance:** 8,224
(at McAlpine Stadium, Huddersfield).

SUPER LEAGUE GRAND FINAL

Saturday 24th October 1998

LEEDS RHINOS 4 WIGAN WARRIORS 10

RHINOS: 1 Iestyn Harris (C); 22 Leroy Rivett; 3 Richie Blackmore; 4 Brad Godden; 5 Francis Cummins; 13 Daryl Powell; 7 Ryan Sheridan; 8 Martin Masella; 21 Terry Newton; 25 Darren Fleary; 11 Adrian Morley; 17 Anthony Farrell; 12 Marc Glanville. Subs: 20 Jamie Mathiou for Masella (25); 24 Marcus St Hilaire for Powell (40); 14 Graham Holroyd for Newton (49); 27 Andy Hay for Fleary (54); Powell for Godden (58); Masella for Mathiou (71).
Try: Blackmore (20).
WARRIORS: 1 Kris Radlinski; 2 Jason Robinson; 3 Danny Moore; 4 Gary Connolly; 5 Mark Bell; 6 Henry Paul; 7 Tony Smith; 16 Terry O'Connor; 9 Robbie McCormack; 10 Tony Mestrov; 20 Lee Gilmour; 17 Stephen Holgate; 13 Andy Farrell (C). Subs: 8 Neil Cowie for O'Connor (18BB, rev 48); 14 Mick Cassidy for McCormack (19BB, rev 27); 25 Paul Johnson for Moore (37); 12 Simon Haughton for Gilmour (27BB, rev 33); Haughton for Holgate (33); Cowie for Mestrov (54); Cassidy for Haughton (64); Holgate for Cowie (68); Haughton for Gilmour (71BB, rev 75); Mestrov for O'Connor (75BB).
Try: Robinson (37); **Goals:** Farrell 3.
League Express Men of the Match:
Rhinos: Iestyn Harris; *Warriors:* Jason Robinson.
Penalty count: 7-13; **Half-time:** 4-6;
Referee: Russell Smith (Castleford); **Attendance:** 43,553
(at Old Trafford, Manchester).

1999

NORTHERN FORD PREMIERSHIP GRAND FINAL

Saturday 25th September 1999

DEWSBURY RAMS 11 HUNSLET HAWKS 12

RAMS: 1 Nathan Graham; 2 Alex Godfrey; 3 Paul Evans; 4 Brendan O'Meara; 5 Adrian Flynn; 6 Richard Agar; 7 Barry Eaton; 8 Alan Boothroyd; 9 Paul Delaney; 10 Matthew Long; 11 Andy Spink; 12 Mark Haigh; 13 Damian Ball. Subs: 14 Brendan Williams for Eaton (5BB, rev 15); 15 Sean Richardson for Haigh (50); 16 Simon Hicks for Long (25); 17 Paul Medley for Spink (50); Williams for Evans (61); Long for Boothroyd (71); Spink for Long (78).
Tries: Flynn (27), Ball (54); **Goal:** Eaton; **Field goal:** Agar.
HAWKS: 1 Abraham Fatnowna; 2 Chris Ross; 3 Shaun Irwin; 4 Paul Cook; 5 Iain Higgins; 6 Marcus Vassilakopoulos; 7 Latham Tawhai; 8 Richard Hayes; 9 Richard Pachniuk; 10 Steve Pryce; 11 Rob Wilson; 12 Jamie Leighton; 13 Lee St Hilaire. Subs: 14 Mick Coyle for Wilson (57); 15 Phil Kennedy for Pryce (35); 16 Jamie Thackray for St Hilaire (25); 17 Richard Baker for Higgins (55); Higgins for Fatnowna (62); Pryce for Kennedy (65).
Tries: Cook (31), Higgins (46); **Goal:** Ross;
Field goals: Tawhai, Leighton.
League Express Men of the Match:
Rams: Barry Eaton; *Hawks:* Latham Tawhai.
Penalty count: 8-5; **Half-time:** 7-7;
Referee: Steve Ganson (St Helens); **Attendance:** 5,783
(at Headingley Stadium, Leeds).

SUPER LEAGUE GRAND FINAL

Saturday 9th October 1999

BRADFORD BULLS 6 ST HELENS 8

BULLS: 28 Stuart Spruce; 2 Tevita Vaikona; 20 Scott Naylor; 5 Michael Withers; 17 Leon Pryce; 6 Henry Paul; 1 Robbie Paul (C); 10 Paul Anderson; 9 James Lowes; 29 Stuart Fielden; 15 David Boyle; 23 Bernard Dwyer; 13 Steve McNamara. Subs: 14 Paul Deacon for R Paul (53); 4 Nathan McAvoy (not used); 12 Mike Forshaw for McNamara (18); 22 Brian McDermott for Anderson (18); Anderson for Fielden (61); Fielden for Dwyer (65); R Paul for Deacon (72).
Try: H Paul (18); **Goal:** H Paul.
SAINTS: 1 Paul Atcheson; 14 Chris Smith; 3 Kevin Iro; 4 Paul Newlove; 5 Anthony Sullivan; 13 Paul Sculthorpe; 20 Tommy Martyn; 8 Apollo Perelini; 9 Keiron Cunningham; 10 Julian O'Neill; 2 Fereti Tuilagi; 21 Sonny Nickle; 11 Chris Joynt (C). Subs: 26 Paul Wellens for Martyn (52); 6 Sean Hoppe for Newlove (43); 16 Vila Matautia for O'Neill (20); 7 Sean Long for Perelini (24); Perelini for Matautia (46); O'Neill for Perelini (69).
Tries: Iro (65); **Goals:** Long 2.
League Express Men of the Match:
Bulls: Henry Paul; *Saints:* Kevin Iro.
Penalty count: 4-7; **Half-time:** 6-2;
Referee: Stuart Cummings (Widnes);
Attendance: 50,717 *(at Old Trafford, Manchester).*

2000

NORTHERN FORD PREMIERSHIP GRAND FINAL

Saturday 29th July 2000

DEWSBURY RAMS 13 LEIGH CENTURIONS 12

RAMS: 1 Nathan Graham; 2 Richard Baker; 4 Dan Potter; 3 Brendan O'Meara; 5 Adrian Flynn; 6 Richard Agar; 7 Barry Eaton; 8 Shayne Williams; 9 David Mycoe; 10 Mark Haigh; 11 Sean Richardson; 12 Daniel Frame; 13 Damian Ball. Subs: 14 Gavin Wood (not used); 15 Paul Delaney for Mycoe (53); 16 Ryan McDonald for Haigh (30); 17 Matthew Long for Williams (23); Haigh for McDonald (64).
Tries: Eaton (2), Long (23); **Goals:** Eaton 2;
Field goal: Agar.
Sin bin: Williams (66) - use of the elbow.
On report: Richardson (20) - high tackle on Donlan.
CENTURIONS: 1 Stuart Donlan; 5 David Ingram; 3 Paul Anderson; 4 Andy Fairclough; 2 Alan Cross; 6 Liam Bretherton; 7 Kieron Purtill; 8 Tim Street; 9 Mick Higham; 10 Andy Leathem; 11 Simon Baldwin; 12 Heath Cruckshank; 13 Adam Bristow. Subs: 14 James Arkwright for Cross (68); 15 Paul Norman for Street (36); 16 Radney Bowker (not used); 17 David Whittle for Leathem (24); Street for Norman (62).
Tries: Higham (29, 69); **Goals:** Bretherton 2.
Sin bin: Whittle (66) - retaliation.
League Express Men of the Match:
Rams: Richard Agar; *Centurions:* Mick Higham.
Penalty count: 4-4; **Half-time:** 10-6;
Referee: Robert Connolly (Wigan); **Attendance:** 8,487
(at Gigg Lane, Bury).

SUPER LEAGUE GRAND FINAL

Saturday 14th October 2000

ST HELENS 29 WIGAN WARRIORS 16

SAINTS: 17 Paul Wellens; 24 Steve Hall; 3 Kevin Iro; 15 Sean Hoppe; 5 Anthony Sullivan; 20 Tommy Martyn; 7 Sean Long; 8 Apollo Perelini; 9 Keiron Cunningham; 10 Julian O'Neill; 11 Chris Joynt (C); 22 Tim Jonkers; 13 Paul Sculthorpe. Subs: 14 Fereti Tuilagi for O'Neill (20); 12 Sonny Nickle for Perelini (28); 26 John Stankevitch for Jonkers (50); 23 Scott Barrow (not used); Perelini for Nickle (52); Jonkers for Stankevitch (66); Stankevitch for Perelini (67BB); O'Neill for Hall (74).
Tries: Hoppe (7), Joynt (28, 50), Tuilagi (69), Jonkers (80); **Goals:** Long 4; **Field goal:** Sculthorpe.
WARRIORS: 5 Jason Robinson; 2 Brett Dallas; 1 Kris Radlinski; 3 Steve Renouf; 26 David Hodgson; 6 Tony Smith; 7 Willie Peters; 8 Terry O'Connor; 9 Terry Newton; 10 Neil Cowie; 11 Mick Cassidy; 12 Denis Betts; 13 Andy Farrell (C). Subs: 23 Brady Malam for Cowie (30); 17 Tony Mestrov for O'Connor (43); 19 Chris Chester for Cassidy (47BB, rev 69); 14 Lee Gilmour for Betts (51); O'Connor for Mestrov (61); Cowie for Malam (67); Chester for Newton (75).
Tries: Farrell (13), Hodgson (58), Smith (61);
Goals: Farrell 2.
League Express Men of the Match:
Saints: Chris Joynt; *Warriors:* Andy Farrell.
Penalty count: 10-6; **Half-time:** 11-4;
Referee: Russell Smith (Castleford); **Attendance:** 58,132
(at Old Trafford, Manchester).

2001

NORTHERN FORD PREMIERSHIP GRAND FINAL

Saturday 28th July 2001

OLDHAM 14 WIDNES VIKINGS 24

OLDHAM: 1 Mark Sibson; 2 Joey Hayes; 3 Anthony Gibbons; 4 Pat Rich; 5 Joe McNicholas; 6 David Gibbons; 7 Neil Roden; 8 Leo Casey; 9 Keith Brennan; 10 Paul Norton; 11 Phil Farrell; 12 Bryan Henare; 13 Kevin Mannion. Subs: 14 Mike Ford for Mannion (27); 15 Jason Clegg for Casey (18); 16 John Hough for Brennan (44); 17 Danny Guest for Norton (40BB, rev 54); Mannion for Henare (66); Guest for Clegg (73).
Tries: Brennan (9), Ford (74), Mannion (80); **Goal:** Rich.
VIKINGS: 1 Paul Atcheson; 2 Damian Munro; 3 Craig Weston; 4 Jason Demetriou; 5 Chris Percival; 6 Richard Agar; 7 Martin Crompton; 8 Simon Knox; 9 Phil Cantillon; 10 Stephen Holgate; 11 Steve Gee; 12 Sean Richardson; 13 Tommy Hodgkinson. Subs: 14 Andy Craig for Percival (65); 15 Chris McKinney for Gee (41); 16 Joe Faimalo for Knox (32); 17 Matthew Long for Holgate (23); Knox for Long (49BB, rev 61); Holgate for Long (74).
Tries: Gee (17), Demetriou (38, 60), Cantillon (50), Munro (69); **Goals:** Weston 2.
League Express Men of the Match:
Oldham: Jason Clegg; *Vikings:* Phil Cantillon.
Penalty count: 8-5; **Half-time:** 4-10;
Referee: Steve Ganson (St Helens); **Attendance:** 8,974
(at Spotland, Rochdale).

SUPER LEAGUE GRAND FINAL

Saturday 13th October 2001

BRADFORD BULLS 37 WIGAN WARRIORS 6

BULLS: 5 Michael Withers; 2 Tevita Vaikona; 20 Scott Naylor; 23 Graham Mackay; 3 Leon Pryce; 6 Henry Paul; 1 Robbie Paul (C); 8 Joe Vagana; 9 James Lowes; 22 Brian McDermott; 11 Daniel Gartner; 19 Jamie Peacock; 12 Mike Forshaw. Subs: 29 Stuart Fielden for McDermott (21BB, rev 65); 10 Paul Anderson for Vagana (22); 15 Shane Rigon for Pryce (40); 7 Paul Deacon for R Paul (69); Vagana for Anderson (53); Fielden for Gartner (72); Anderson for Vagana (74).
Tries: Lowes (9), Withers (11, 27, 31), Fielden (65), Mackay (72); **Goals:** H Paul 5, Mackay; **Field goal:** H Paul.
WARRIORS: 1 Kris Radlinski; 2 Brett Dallas; 4 Gary Connolly; 3 Steve Renouf; 5 Brian Carney; 6 Matthew Johns; 7 Adrian Lam; 8 Terry O'Connor; 9 Terry Newton; 20 Harvey Howard; 11 Mick Cassidy; 14 David Furner; 13 Andy Farrell (C). Subs: 15 Paul Johnson for Carney (12BB); 10 Neil Cowie for Howard (17); 12 Denis Betts for O'Connor (32); 19 Chris Chester for Farrell (59); O'Connor for Cowie (55); Howard for Newton (64); Cowie for Cassidy (72).
Try: Lam (63); **Goal:** Furner.
League Express Men of the Match:
Bulls: Michael Withers; *Warriors:* Adrian Lam.
Penalty count: 6-7; **Half-time:** 26-0;
Referee: Stuart Cummings (Widnes);
Attendance: 60,164 *(at Old Trafford, Manchester).*

2002

NORTHERN FORD PREMIERSHIP GRAND FINAL

Saturday 12th October 2002

HUDDERSFIELD GIANTS 38 LEIGH CENTURIONS 16

GIANTS: 1 Ben Cooper; 2 Hefin O'Hare; 3 Eorl Crabtree; 4 Graeme Hallas; 5 Marcus St Hilaire; 6 Stanley Gene; 7 Chris Thorman; 8 Michael Slicker; 9 Paul March; 10 Jeff Wittenberg; 11 David Atkins; 12 Robert Roberts; 13 Steve McNamara. Subs: 14 Heath Cruckshank for Roberts (24BB); 15 Chris Molyneux for Slicker (53); 16 Darren Turner for March (21); 17 Andy Rice for Cruckshank (57); Roberts for Wittenberg (34); Wittenberg for Roberts (74).
Tries: O'Hare (12, 78), St Hilaire (34, 53), Thorman (46), Gene (57); **Goals:** McNamara 7.
Sin bin: Roberts (47) - fighting.
CENTURIONS: 1 Neil Turley; 2 Leon Felton; 4 Jon Roper; 3 Dale Cardoza; 5 Oliver Marns; 6 Willie Swann; 7 Bobbie Goulding; 8 Vila Matautia; 9 Paul Rowley; 10 David Bradbury; 11 Simon Baldwin; 12 Andrew Isherwood; 13 Adam Bristow. Subs: 14 Gareth Price for Bradbury (24BB, rev 35); 15 John Duffy for Swann (32); 16 John Hamilton for Bristow (46BB, rev 57); 17 David Whittle for Matautia (22); Matautia for Bradbury (53BB); Swann for Goulding (58); Hamilton for Whittle (67); Bradbury for Turley (72); Goulding for Swann (75).
Tries: Cardoza (9), Marns (18), Hamilton (70);
Goals: Turley 2.

Sin bin: Whittle (47) - fighting; Bristow (74) - interference.
On report: Isherwood (66) - high tackle on Roberts.
Rugby Leaguer & League Express Men of the Match:
Giants: Chris Thorman; *Centurions:* Adam Bristow.
Penalty count: 11-11; **Half-time:** 14-10;
Referee: Karl Kirkpatrick (Warrington);
Attendance: 9,051 *(at Halton Stadium, Widnes).*

SUPER LEAGUE GRAND FINAL

Saturday 19th October 2002

BRADFORD BULLS 18 ST HELENS 19

BULLS: 6 Michael Withers; 2 Tevita Vaikona; 20 Scott Naylor; 15 Brandon Costin; 5 Lesley Vainikolo; 1 Robbie Paul (C); 7 Paul Deacon; 8 Joe Vagana; 9 James Lowes; 29 Stuart Fielden; 11 Daniel Gartner; 12 Jamie Peacock; 13 Mike Forshaw. Subs: 14 Lee Gilmour for Gartner (21); 10 Paul Anderson for Vagana (25); 22 Brian McDermott for Fielden (34); 3 Leon Pryce for Vainikolo (53); Fielden for Anderson (55); Vainikolo for Paul (77).
Tries: Naylor (3), Paul (44), Withers (47); **Goals:** Deacon 3.
SAINTS: 1 Paul Wellens; 5 Darren Albert; 3 Martin Gleeson; 4 Paul Newlove; 19 Anthony Stewart; 13 Paul Sculthorpe; 7 Sean Long; 8 Darren Britt; 9 Keiron Cunningham; 10 Barry Ward; 23 Mike Bennett; 15 Tim Jonkers; 11 Chris Joynt (C). Subs: 2 Sean Hoppe for Wellens (3); 12 Peter Shiels for Ward (27); 14 John Stankevitch for Britt (31BB, rev 58); 17 Mick Higham for Joynt (54); Stankevitch for Shiels (58); Joynt for Britt (75); Shiels for Jonkers (77).
Tries: Bennett (24), Long (32), Gleeson (56);
Goals: Long 3; **Field goal:** Long.
Rugby Leaguer & League Express Men of the Match:
Bulls: Paul Deacon; *Saints:* Mike Bennett.
Penalty count: 5-4; **Half-time:** 12-8;
Referee: Russell Smith (Castleford); **Attendance:** 61,138 *(at Old Trafford, Manchester).*

2003

NATIONAL LEAGUE TWO GRAND FINAL

Sunday 5th October 2003

KEIGHLEY COUGARS 13 SHEFFIELD EAGLES 11

COUGARS: 1 Matt Foster; 2 Max Tomlinson; 3 David Foster; 4 James Rushforth; 5 Andy Robinson; 6 Paul Ashton; 7 Matt Firth; 8 Phil Stephenson; 9 Simeon Hoyle; 10 Danny Ekis; 11 Oliver Wilkes; 12 Ian Sinfield; 13 Lee Patterson. Subs (all used): 14 Chris Wainwright; 15 Richard Mervill; 16 Mick Durham; 17 Jason Ramshaw.
Tries: M Foster (7), Robinson (74); **Goals:** Ashton 2;
Field goal: Firth.
EAGLES: 1 Andy Poynter; 2 Tony Weller; 3 Richard Goddard; 4 Tom O'Reilly; 5 Greg Hurst; 6 Gavin Brown; 7 Mark Aston; 8 Jack Howieson; 9 Gareth Stanley; 10 Dale Laughton; 11 Andy Raleigh; 12 Craig Brown; 13 Wayne Flynn. Subs (all used): 14 Peter Reilly; 15 Simon Tillyer; 16 Nick Turnbull; 17 Mitchell Stringer.
Try: O'Reilly (51); **Goals:** G Brown 3; **Field goal:** Reilly.
Rugby Leaguer & League Express Men of the Match:
Cougars: Simeon Hoyle; *Eagles:* Andy Raleigh.
Penalty count: 6-8; **Half-time:** 9-4;
Referee: Peter Taberner (Wigan).
(at Halton Stadium, Widnes).

NATIONAL LEAGUE ONE GRAND FINAL

Sunday 5th October 2003

LEIGH CENTURIONS 14 SALFORD CITY REDS 31

CENTURIONS: 1 Neil Turley; 2 Damian Munro; 3 Alan Hadcroft; 4 Danny Halliwell; 5 Leroy Rivett; 6 John Duffy; 7 Tommy Martyn; 8 Sonny Nickle; 9 Patrick Weisner; 10 Paul Norman; 11 Sean Richardson; 12 Willie Swann; 13 Adam Bristow. Subs (all used): 14 David Bradbury; 15 Lee Sanderson; 16 Bryan Henare; 17 Ricky Bibey.
Tries: Richardson (33), Halliwell (38), Swann (65);
Goal: Turley.
On report: Nickle (60) - late tackle on Clinch.
CITY REDS: 1 Jason Flowers; 2 Danny Arnold; 3 Stuart Littler; 4 Alan Hunte; 5 Andy Kirk; 6 Cliff Beverley; 7 Gavin Clinch; 8 Neil Baynes; 9 Malcolm Alker; 10 Andy Coley; 11 Simon Baldwin; 12 Paul Highton; 13 Chris Charles. Subs (all used): 14 Steve Blakeley; 15 David Highton; 16 Martin Moana; 17 Gareth Haggerty.
Tries: Hunte (3, 52), Beverley (23), Littler (73);
Goals: Charles 6, Blakeley; **Field goal:** Blakeley.
Rugby Leaguer & League Express Men of the Match:
Centurions: Willie Swann; *City Reds:* Gavin Clinch.
Penalty count: 10-10; **Half-time:** 10-16;
Referee: Richard Silverwood (Dewsbury);
Attendance: 9,186 *(at Halton Stadium, Widnes).*

SUPER LEAGUE GRAND FINAL

Saturday 18th October 2003

BRADFORD BULLS 25 WIGAN WARRIORS 12

BULLS: 17 Stuart Reardon; 2 Tevita Vaikona; 6 Michael Withers; 4 Shontayne Hape; 5 Lesley Vainikolo; 15 Karl Pratt; 7 Paul Deacon; 8 Joe Vagana; 9 James Lowes; 29 Stuart Fielden; 11 Daniel Gartner; 12 Jamie Peacock; 13 Mike Forshaw. Subs (all used): 10 Paul Anderson; 18 Lee Radford; 3 Leon Pryce; 1 Robbie Paul (C).
Tries: Reardon (51), Hape (59), Lowes (75);
Goals: Deacon 6/6; **Field goal:** Deacon.
WARRIORS: 1 Kris Radlinski; 5 Brian Carney; 18 Martin Aspinwall; 14 David Hodgson; 2 Brett Dallas; 15 Sean O'Loughlin; 20 Luke Robinson; 30 Quentin Pongia; 9 Terry Newton; 10 Craig Smith; 11 Mick Cassidy; 12 Danny Tickle; 13 Andy Farrell (C). Subs (all used): 4 Paul Johnson; 8 Terry O'Connor; 23 Gareth Hock; 17 Mark Smith.
Tries: Tickle (17), Radlinski (72); **Goals:** Farrell 2/3.
Rugby Leaguer & League Express Men of the Match:
Bulls: Stuart Reardon; *Warriors:* Kris Radlinski.
Penalty count: 7-6; **Half-time:** 4-6;
Referee: Karl Kirkpatrick (Warrington);
Attendance: 65,537 *(at Old Trafford, Manchester).*

2004

NATIONAL LEAGUE ONE GRAND FINAL

Sunday 10th October 2004

LEIGH CENTURIONS 32 WHITEHAVEN 16
(after extra-time)

CENTURIONS: 1 Neil Turley; 2 Rob Smyth; 3 Danny Halliwell; 4 Ben Cooper; 5 David Alstead; 6 John Duffy; 7 Tommy Martyn; 8 Simon Knox; 9 Paul Rowley; 10 Matt Sturm; 11 David Larder; 12 Oliver Wilkes; 13 Ian Knott. Subs (all used): 14 Dave McConnell; 15 Heath Cruckshank; 16 Richard Marshall; 17 Willie Swann.
Tries: Cooper (27, 83), Martyn (61), Turley (87);
Goals: Turley 6/8; **Field goals:** Turley 2, Rowley, Martyn.
WHITEHAVEN: 1 Gary Broadbent; 2 Craig Calvert; 3 David Seeds; 4 Mick Nanyn; 5 Wesley Wilson; 6 Leroy Joe; 7 Sam Obst; 8 Marc Jackson; 9 Aaron Lester; 10 David Fatialofa; 11 Paul Davidson; 12 Howard Hill; 13 Craig Walsh. Subs (all used): 14 Spencer Miller; 15 Carl Sice; 16 Chris McKinney; 17 Ryan Tandy.
Tries: Wilson (2, 71), Calvert (45); **Goals:** Nanyn 2/6.
Rugby Leaguer & League Express Men of the Match:
Centurions: Neil Turley; *Whitehaven:* Aaron Lester.
Penalty count: 5-9; **Half-time:** 7-6; **Full-time:** 16-16;
Referee: Ronnie Laughton (Barnsley);
Attendance: 11,005 *(at Halton Stadium, Widnes).*

SUPER LEAGUE GRAND FINAL

Saturday 16th October 2004

BRADFORD BULLS 8 LEEDS RHINOS 16

BULLS: 6 Michael Withers; 17 Stuart Reardon; 16 Paul Johnson; 4 Shontayne Hape; 5 Lesley Vainikolo; 18 Iestyn Harris; 7 Paul Deacon; 8 Joe Vagana; 1 Robbie Paul (C); 29 Stuart Fielden; 12 Jamie Peacock; 13 Logan Swann; 11 Lee Radford. Subs: 10 Paul Anderson for Vagana (14); 15 Karl Pratt for Paul (23); 27 Rob Parker for Anderson (24); 19 Jamie Langley for Peacock (32); Paul for Withers (ht); Peacock for Radford (48); Radford for Swann (54); Vagana for Parker (56); Parker for Fielden (63); Fielden for Vagana (67); Swann for Langley (68).
Tries: Vainikolo (7), Hape (43); **Goals:** Deacon 0/2.
RHINOS: 21 Richard Mathers; 18 Mark Calderwood; 5 Chev Walker; 4 Keith Senior; 22 Marcus Bai; 13 Kevin Sinfield (C); 6 Danny McGuire; 19 Danny Ward; 9 Matt Diskin; 8 Ryan Bailey; 3 Chris McKenna; 29 Ali Lauitiiti; 11 David Furner. Subs: 16 Willie Poching for Furner (19); 10 Barrie McDermott for Ward (22); Ward for Bailey (29); 7 Rob Burrow for Lauitiiti (30); Bailey for McDermott (41); 20 Jamie Jones-Buchanan for McKenna (48); Lauitiiti for Ward (50); Furner for Sinfield (60); McKenna for Poching (63); Sinfield for Diskin (67); Poching for McKenna (72); Ward for Bailey (73).
Tries: Diskin (15), McGuire (75); **Goals:** Sinfield 4/4.
Rugby Leaguer & League Express Men of the Match:
Bulls: Lesley Vainikolo; *Rhinos:* Richard Mathers.
Penalty count: 5-5; **Half-time:** 4-10;
Referee: Steve Ganson (St Helens);
Attendance: 65,547 *(at Old Trafford, Manchester).*

2005

NATIONAL LEAGUE ONE GRAND FINAL

Sunday 9th October 2005

CASTLEFORD TIGERS 36 WHITEHAVEN 8

TIGERS: 1 Michael Platt; 2 Waine Pryce; 3 Michael Shenton; 4 Jon Hepworth; 5 Damien Blanch; 6 Brad Davis; 7 Andrew Henderson; 8 Adam Watene; 9 Aaron Smith; 10 Richard Fletcher; 11 Tom Haughey; 12 Steve Crouch; 13 Deon Bird. Subs (all used): 14 Paul Handforth; 15 Craig Huby; 16 Adrian Vowles; 17 Frank Watene.
Tries: Huby (22), Crouch (24), Blanch (26), Davis (33, 45), Haughey (52); **Goals:** Fletcher 2/3, Huby 3/4, Hepworth 1/1.
WHITEHAVEN: 1 Gary Broadbent; 2 Craig Calvert; 3 David Seeds; 4 Mick Nanyn; 5 Wesley Wilson; 6 Leroy Joe; 7 Joel Penny; 8 Ryan Tandy; 9 Carl Sice; 10 David Fatialofa; 11 Spencer Miller; 12 Howard Hill; 13 Aaron Lester. Subs (all used): 14 Carl Rudd; 15 Aaron Summers; 16 Craig Chambers; 17 Marc Jackson.
Tries: Seeds (56), Calvert (78); **Goals:** Nanyn 0/2.
Sin bin: Joe (16) - late tackle on Davis.
On report: Joe (16) - late tackle on Davis;
Sice (40) - alleged biting.
Rugby Leaguer & League Express Men of the Match:
Tigers: Brad Davis; *Whitehaven:* Wesley Wilson.
Penalty count: 4-9; **Half-time:** 26-0;
Referee: Steve Ganson (St Helens);
Attendance: 13,300 *(at Halton Stadium, Widnes).*

SUPER LEAGUE GRAND FINAL

Saturday 15th October 2005

BRADFORD BULLS 15 LEEDS RHINOS 6

BULLS: 6 Michael Withers; 3 Leon Pryce; 13 Ben Harris; 4 Shontayne Hape; 5 Lesley Vainikolo; 18 Iestyn Harris; 7 Paul Deacon; 12 Jamie Peacock (C); 9 Ian Henderson; 29 Stuart Fielden; 16 Paul Johnson; 10 Brad Meyers; 11 Lee Radford. Subs (all used): 24 Adrian Morley for Johnson (5); 19 Jamie Langley for Peacock (24); 8 Joe Vagana for Fielden (24); Johnson for Radford (24); 1 Robbie Paul for Henderson (31); Peacock for Vagana (45); Fielden for Morley (49); Henderson for Paul (54); Radford for Meyers (60); Morley for Peacock (62); Meyers for Langley (73); Peacock for Johnson (74).
Tries: L Pryce (29), Vainikolo (53); **Goals:** Deacon 3/5;
Field goal: I Harris.
RHINOS: 1 Richard Mathers; 2 Mark Calderwood; 3 Chev Walker; 12 Chris McKenna; 5 Marcus Bai; 6 Danny McGuire; 7 Rob Burrow; 8 Ryan Bailey; 14 Andrew Dunemann; 15 Danny Ward; 20 Gareth Ellis; 16 Willie Poching; 13 Kevin Sinfield (C). Subs (all used): 10 Barrie McDermott for Ward (17); 11 Ali Lauitiiti for Poching (21); 18 Jamie Jones-Buchanan for Bailey (31); Ward for McDermott (34); 9 Matt Diskin for Ellis (48); Poching for Lauitiiti (48); McDermott for Ward (54); Ellis for Poching (54); Lauitiiti for McDermott (61); Poching for Dunemann (65); Ward for Jones-Buchanan (68); Dunemann for Ellis (71).
Try: McGuire (22); **Goals:** Sinfield 1/2.
Rugby Leaguer & League Express Men of the Match:
Bulls: Leon Pryce; *Rhinos:* Danny McGuire.
Penalty count: 6-8; **Half-time:** 8-6;
Referee: Ashley Klein (Keighley); **Attendance:** 65,537 *(at Old Trafford, Manchester).*

2006

NATIONAL LEAGUE TWO GRAND FINAL

Sunday 8th October 2006

SHEFFIELD EAGLES 35 SWINTON LIONS 10

EAGLES: 1 Johnny Woodcock; 5 Greg Hurst; 4 Jimmy Walker; 3 James Ford; 2 Rob Worrincy; 6 Brendon Lindsay; 7 Gavin Brown; 8 Jack Howieson; 9 Paul Pickering; 10 Mitchell Stringer; 11 Andy Hay; 12 Dale Holdstock; 13 Andy Smith. Subs (all used): 14 Craig Poucher; 15 Martin Ostler; 16 Sean Dickinson; 17 Waisale Sovatabua.
Tries: Worrincy (21, 43), Lindsay (38), Woodcock (39), Walker (51), Hay (60); **Goals:** Woodcock 5/6;
Field goal: G Brown.
LIONS: 1 Wayne English; 2 Andy Saywell; 3 Darren Woods; 4 David Alstead; 5 Marlon Billy; 6 Martin Moana; 7 Chris Hough; 8 Bruce Johnson; 9 Phil Wood; 10 Dave Newton; 11 Kris Smith; 12 Ian Sinfield; 13 Lee Marsh. Subs (all used): 14 Liam McGovern; 15 Chris Morley; 16 Danny Aboushakra; 17 Ian Parry.
Tries: Saywell (35), Alstead (74); **Goals:** McGovern 1/2.
Rugby Leaguer & League Express Men of the Match:
Eagles: Johnny Woodcock; *Lions:* Wayne English.
Penalty count: 3-4; **Half-time:** 16-4;
Referee: Peter Taberner (Wigan).
(at Halliwell Jones Stadium, Warrington).

Dewsbury Rams were National League Two Champions in 2006. This game was to determine who took the second promotion place.

Grand Finals 1998-2017

NATIONAL LEAGUE ONE GRAND FINAL

Sunday 8th October 2006

HULL KINGSTON ROVERS 29 WIDNES VIKINGS 16

ROVERS: 1 Ben Cockayne; 2 Leroy Rivett; 3 Gareth Morton; 4 Jon Goddard; 5 Byron Ford; 6 Scott Murrell; 7 James Webster; 8 Makali Aizue; 9 Ben Fisher; 10 David Tangata-Toa; 11 Iain Morrison; 12 Michael Smith; 13 Tommy Gallagher. Subs (all used): 14 Pat Weisner; 15 Dwayne Barker; 16 Jason Netherton; 17 Dave Wilson.
Tries: Ford (6), Goddard (18, 36), Murrell (24), Weisner (43); **Goals:** Morton 4/6; **Field goal:** Murrell.
VIKINGS: 1 Gavin Dodd; 2 Damien Blanch; 3 Sean Gleeson; 4 Daryl Cardiss; 5 John Kirkpatrick; 6 Dennis Moran; 7 Ian Watson; 8 Terry O'Connor; 9 Mark Smith; 10 Barrie McDermott; 11 Mick Cassidy; 12 David Allen; 13 Bob Beswick. Subs (all used): 14 Aaron Summers; 15 Oliver Wilkes; 16 Jordan James; 17 Ryan Tandy.
Tries: Dodd (32), Tandy (57), Blanch (70);.**Goals:** Dodd 2/3.
Rugby Leaguer & League Express Men of the Match: *Rovers:* James Webster; *Vikings:* Mark Smith.
Penalty count: 8-5; **Half-time:** 22-4;
Referee: Phil Bentham (Warrington); **Attendance:** 13,024 *(at Halliwell Jones Stadium, Warrington).*

SUPER LEAGUE GRAND FINAL

Saturday 14th October 2006

HULL FC 4 ST HELENS 26

HULL: 1 Shaun Briscoe; 14 Motu Tony; 4 Sid Domic; 3 Kirk Yeaman; 5 Gareth Raynor; 13 Paul Cooke; 7 Richard Horne; 8 Ewan Dowes; 9 Richard Swain (C); 10 Garreth Carvell; 11 Lee Radford; 12 Shayne McMenemy; 24 Danny Washbrook. Subs: 15 Paul King for Carvell (17); 19 Graeme Horne for Radford (23); 26 Scott Wheeldon for Dowes (27); 6 Richard Whiting for McMenemy (29); Dowes for Wheeldon (49); Carvell for King (49); Radford for G Horne (51); McMenemy for Whiting (54); King for Carvell (68); Wheeldon for Dowes (73); Whiting for Tony (76); G Horne for Radford (77).
Try: Domic (24); **Goals:** Cooke 0/1.
SAINTS: 1 Paul Wellens; 2 Ade Gardner; 3 Jamie Lyon; 4 Willie Talau; 5 Francis Meli; 6 Leon Pryce; 7 Sean Long (C); 17 Paul Anderson; 9 Keiron Cunningham; 10 Jason Cayless; 11 Lee Gilmour; 12 Jon Wilkin; 16 Jason Hooper. Subs: 23 Maurie Fa'asavalu for P Anderson (12); 19 James Graham for Cayless (25); 15 Mike Bennett for Fa'asavalu (28); 14 James Roby for Cunningham (31); P Anderson for Wilkin (33); Cunningham for Gilmour (49); Cayless for P Anderson (52); Wilkin for Hooper (56); Fa'asavalu for Cayless (58); Gilmour for Graham (66); Cayless for Fa'asavalu (72); P Anderson for Wilkin (75).
Tries: Meli (17), Pryce (29), Talau (49), Gardner (52), Cunningham (62); **Goals:** Lyon 3/5.
Rugby Leaguer & League Express Men of the Match: *Hull:* Shaun Briscoe; *Saints:* Paul Wellens.
Penalty count: 4-2; **Half-time:** 4-10;
Referee: Karl Kirkpatrick (Warrington);
Attendance: 72,582 *(at Old Trafford, Manchester).*

2007

NATIONAL LEAGUE TWO GRAND FINAL

Sunday 7th October 2007

FEATHERSTONE ROVERS 24 OLDHAM 6

ROVERS: 1 Loz Wildbore; 2 Danny Kirmond; 3 Jon Whittle; 4 Wayne McHugh; 5 Ade Adebisi; 6 Andy Kain; 7 Paul Handforth; 8 Gareth Handford; 9 Joe McLocklan; 10 Stuart Dickens; 11 Jamie Field; 12 Richard Blakeway; 13 Tom Haughey. Subs (all used): 14 Jamie Benn; 15 Ian Tonks; 16 James Houston; 17 Gavin Swinson.
Tries: McHugh (39, 49), Handforth (46);
Goals: Dickens 5/6; **Field goals:** Wildbore (66, 70).
Dismissal: Blakeway (64) – head butt on Roberts.
OLDHAM: 1 Gareth Langley; 2 Byron Ford; 3 Craig Littler; 4 Adam Hughes; 5 Lucas Onyango; 6 Neil Roden; 7 James Coyle; 8 Anthony Stewart; 9 Simeon Hoyle; 10 Richard Mervill; 11 Ian Sinfield; 12 Robert Roberts; 13 Geno Costin. Subs (all used): 14 Ian Hodson; 15 Alex Wilkinson; 16 Said Tamghart; 17 Matty Brooks.
Try: Hughes (31); **Goals:** Langley 1/2.
Rugby Leaguer & League Express Men of the Match: *Rovers:* Paul Handforth; *Oldham:* Robert Roberts.
Penalty count: 9-5; **Half-time:** 10-6;
Referee: Gareth Hewer. *(at Headingley Carnegie, Leeds).*

Celtic Crusaders were National League Two Champions in 2007. This game was to determine who took the second promotion place.

NATIONAL LEAGUE ONE GRAND FINAL

Sunday 7th October 2007

CASTLEFORD TIGERS 42 WIDNES VIKINGS 10

TIGERS: 1 Stuart Donlan; 2 Danny Williams; 3 Michael Shenton; 4 Ryan McGoldrick; 5 Kirk Dixon; 6 Anthony Thackeray; 7 Danny Brough; 8 Liam Higgins; 9 Andrew Henderson; 10 Awen Guttenbeil; 11 Joe Westerman; 12 Ryan Clayton; 13 Peter Lupton. Subs (all used): 14 Mark Leafa; 15 Chris Charles; 16 Michael Wainwright; 17 Ryan Boyle.
Tries: Wainwright (20), McGoldrick (29), Guttenbeil (44, 76), M Shenton (52), Westerman (62), Clayton (66);
Goals: Brough 6/9; **Field goals:** Brough (25, 55).
VIKINGS: 1 Scott Grix; 2 Damien Blanch; 3 Toa Kohe-Love; 4 Mick Nanyn; 5 Gavin Dodd; 6 Dennis Moran; 7 Joel Penny; 8 Mick Cassidy; 9 Mark Smith; 10 Oliver Wilkes; 11 Joel Tomkins; 12 Paul Noone; 13 Bob Beswick. Subs (all used): 14 Aaron Summers; 15 Jordan James; 16 Ian Webster; 17 Lee Doran.
Tries: Nanyn (35), Wilkes (69); **Goals:** Nanyn 1/2.
Rugby Leaguer & League Express Men of the Match: *Tigers:* Danny Brough; *Vikings:* Scott Grix.
Penalty count: 7-2; **Half-time:** 13-4;
Referee: Phil Bentham; **Attendance:** 20,814 *(at Headingley Carnegie, Leeds).*

SUPER LEAGUE GRAND FINAL

Saturday 13th October 2007

LEEDS RHINOS 33 ST HELENS 6

RHINOS: 1 Brent Webb; 5 Lee Smith; 3 Clinton Toopi; 4 Keith Senior; 2 Scott Donald; 6 Danny McGuire; 7 Rob Burrow; 8 Kylie Leuluai; 9 Matt Diskin; 10 Jamie Peacock; 11 Jamie Jones-Buchanan; 12 Gareth Ellis; 13 Kevin Sinfield (C). Subs (all used): 14 Ali Lauitiiti for Diskin (23); 16 Ryan Bailey for Leuluai (18); 18 Ian Kirke for Jones-Buchanan (33); 22 Carl Ablett for Kirke (57); Leuluai for Bailey (55); Jones-Buchanan for Lauitiiti (60); Diskin for Ablett (63); Kirke for Leuluai (65); Bailey for Kirke (76).
Tries: Webb (19), Lauitiiti (50), Donald (52), Smith (69), Jones-Buchanan (80); **Goals:** Sinfield 6/7;
Field goal: Burrow (80).
SAINTS: 1 Paul Wellens; 2 Ade Gardner; 3 Matt Gidley; 4 Willie Talau; 5 Francis Meli; 6 Leon Pryce; 7 Sean Long; 8 Nick Fozzard; 9 Keiron Cunningham (C); 10 Jason Cayless; 11 Lee Gilmour; 30 Chris Flannery; 12 Jon Wilkin. Subs (all used): 17 James Graham for Cayless (15); 14 James Roby for Cunningham (23); 23 Maurie Fa'asavalu for Fozzard (23); 15 Mike Bennett for Wilkin (31); Cayless for Fa'asavalu (34); Cunningham for Flannery (51); Wilkin for Bennett (55); Fa'asavalu for Cayless (55); Fozzard for Graham (57); Cayless for Fozzard (68); Graham for Fa'asavalu (68); Bennett for Gilmour (72).
Try: Roby (27); **Goals:** Long 1/2.
Rugby Leaguer & League Express Men of the Match: *Rhinos:* Rob Burrow; *Saints:* Sean Long.
Penalty count: 4-5; **Half-time:** 8-6; **Referee:** Ashley Klein; **Attendance:** 71,352 *(at Old Trafford, Manchester).*

2008

NATIONAL LEAGUE TWO GRAND FINAL

Sunday 28th September 2008

DONCASTER 18 OLDHAM 10

DONCASTER: 1 Zebastian Luisi; 2 Dean Colton; 3 Andreas Bauer; 4 Shaun Leaf; 5 Wayne Reittie; 6 Kyle Wood; 7 Luke Gale; 8 Nathan Freer; 9 Corey Lawrie; 10 Alex Benson; 11 Peter Green; 12 Craig Lawton; 13 Josh Weeden. Subs (all used): 14 Kyle Briggs; 15 Chris Buttery; 16 Michael Haley; 17 Mark Castle.
Tries: Buttery (44), Gale (49), Briggs (73); **Goals:** Gale 3/4.
OLDHAM: 1 Paul O'Connor; 2 Gareth Langley; 3 Marcus St Hilaire; 4 Mick Nanyn; 5 Daryl Cardiss; 6 Phil Joseph; 7 James Coyle; 8 Adam Robinson; 9 Marcus Brooks; 10 Richard Mervill; 11 Tommy Goulden; 12 Danny Halliwell; 13 Robert Roberts. Subs (all used): 14 Ian Hodson; 15 Luke Menzies; 16 Chris Baines; 17 Said Tamghart.
Tries: Hodson (34), Nanyn (62); **Goals:** Nanyn 1/4.
Rugby Leaguer & League Express Men of the Match: *Doncaster:* Luke Gale; *Oldham:* Adam Robinson.
Penalty count: 7-8; **Half-time:** 2-6;
Referee: Ronnie Laughton.
(at Halliwell Jones Stadium, Warrington).

Gateshead Thunder were National League Two Champions in 2008. This game was to determine who took the second promotion place.

NATIONAL LEAGUE ONE GRAND FINAL

Sunday 28th September 2008

CELTIC CRUSADERS 18 SALFORD CITY REDS 36
(after extra-time)

CRUSADERS: 1 Tony Duggan; 2 Luke Dyer; 3 Josh Hannay; 4 Mark Dalle Cort; 5 Anthony Blackwood; 6 Damien Quinn; 7 Jace Van Dijk; 8 Jordan James; 9 Neil Budworth; 10 David Tangata-Toa; 11 Chris Beasley; 12 Darren Mapp; 13 Terry Martin. Subs (all used): 14 Aaron Summers; 15 Ian Webster; 16 Mark Lennon; 17 Neale Wyatt.
Tries: Blackwood (38), Dyer (50), J James (54), Tangata-Toa (66); **Goals:** Hannay 0/1, Lennon 1/3.
CITY REDS: 1 Karl Fitzpatrick; 2 Matt Gardner; 3 Stuart Littler; 4 John Wilshere; 5 Paul White; 6 Robbie Paul; 7 Richard Myler; 8 Paul Highton; 9 Malcolm Alker; 10 Craig Stapleton; 11 Ian Sibbit; 12 Jason Turner. Subs (all used): 14 Stefan Ratchford; 15 Steve Bannister; 16 Lee Jewitt; 17 Phil Leuluai.
Tries: White (5, 86), Gardner (26), Fitzpatrick (63), Sibbit (83), Myler (99); **Goals:** Wilshere 6/7.
Rugby Leaguer & League Express Men of the Match: *Crusaders:* Tony Duggan; *City Reds:* John Wilshere.
Penalty count: 5-5; **Half-time:** 4-10; **Full-time:** 18-18;
Referee: Ben Thaler; **Attendance:** 7,104 *(at Halliwell Jones Stadium, Warrington).*

SUPER LEAGUE GRAND FINAL

Saturday 4th October 2008

LEEDS RHINOS 24 ST HELENS 16

RHINOS: 5 Lee Smith; 22 Ryan Hall; 19 Carl Ablett; 4 Keith Senior; 2 Scott Donald; 6 Danny McGuire; 7 Rob Burrow; 8 Kylie Leuluai; 9 Matt Diskin; 10 Jamie Peacock; 11 Jamie Jones-Buchanan; 12 Gareth Ellis; 13 Kevin Sinfield (C). Subs (all used): 17 Nick Scruton; 14 Ali Lauitiiti; 18 Ian Kirke; 16 Ryan Bailey.
Tries: Smith (23), Hall (37), McGuire (49, 63);
Goals: Sinfield 4/4.
SAINTS: 1 Paul Wellens; 2 Ade Gardner; 3 Matt Gidley; 4 Willie Talau; 5 Francis Meli; 6 Leon Pryce; 7 Sean Long; 18 Bryn Hargreaves; 9 Keiron Cunningham (C); 17 James Graham; 11 Lee Gilmour; 12 Jon Wilkin; 16 Chris Flannery. Subs (all used): 8 Nick Fozzard; 21 Paul Clough; 14 James Roby; 23 Maurie Fa'asavalu.
Tries: Graham (6), Gidley (43), Gardner (59);
Goals: Long 2/3.
Rugby Leaguer & League Express Men of the Match: *Rhinos:* Jamie Peacock; *Saints:* Sean Long.
Penalty count: 6-8; **Half-time:** 12-6;
Referee: Ashley Klein; **Attendance:** 68,810 *(at Old Trafford, Manchester).*

2009

CHAMPIONSHIP ONE GRAND FINAL

Sunday 4th October 2009

KEIGHLEY COUGARS 28 OLDHAM 26

COUGARS: 1 George Rayner; 2 Sam Gardner; 3 Dan Potter; 4 Oliver Pursglove; 5 Gavin Duffy; 6 Jon Presley; 7 Danny Jones; 17 Scott Law; 14 Jamaine Wray; 8 Andy Shickell; 11 Will Cartledge; 18 Greg Nicholson; 13 Carl Hughes. Subs (all used): 21 Ryan Smith; 28 Ryan Benjafield; 9 James Feather; 16 Brendan Rawlins.
Tries: Gardner (24), Jones (42, 50), Presley (63), Pursglove (67); **Goals:** Jones 4/5.
OLDHAM: 4 Paul Reilly; 21 Lucas Onyango; 24 Marcus St Hilaire; 22 Phil Joseph; 1 Paul O'Connor; 18 Neil Roden; 7 Thomas Coyle; 15 Jason Boults; 30 Martin Roden; 16 Wayne Kerr; 23 Chris Baines; 12 Tommy Goulden; 28 Craig Lawton. Subs (all used): 10 Jamie I'Anson; 25 Luke Menzies; 27 Matt Ashe; 29 Ben Heaton.
Tries: Menzies (35, 76), N Roden (54), St Hilaire (70), Kerr (78); **Goals:** Baines 3/4, Ashe 0/1.
Rugby Leaguer & League Express Men of the Match: *Cougars:* Danny Jones; *Oldham:* Luke Menzies.
Penalty count: 9-2; **Half-time:** 4-6;
Referee: Ronnie Laughton.
(at Halliwell Jones Stadium, Warrington).

Dewsbury Rams were Championship One Champions in 2009. This game was to determine who took the second promotion place.

CHAMPIONSHIP GRAND FINAL

Sunday 4th October 2009

BARROW RAIDERS 26 HALIFAX 18

RAIDERS: 1 Gary Broadbent; 36 Andy Ballard; 32 Andreas Bauer; 4 Liam Harrison; 5 James Nixon; 24 Jamie Rooney; 31 James Coyle; 34 Rob Roberts; 9 Andy Ellis; 8 Brett McDermott; 33 Dave Allen; 22 Ned Catic; 26 Zebastian Luisi. Subs (all used): 15 Chris Young; 13 Andy Bracek; 35 Danny Halliwell; 14 Paul Noone.
Tries: Harrison (33), Ballard (37), Allen (61), Bauer (66, 78); **Goals:** Rooney 3/5.
HALIFAX: 4 Shad Royston; 5 James Haley; 15 Mark Roberts; 2 Lee Paterson; 23 Rob Worrincy; 19 Mick Govin; 7 Ben Black; 21 Neil Cherryholme; 9 Sean Penkywicz; 22 David Wrench; 11 David Larder; 27 Steve Bannister; 12 Paul Smith. Subs (all used): 13 Bob Beswick; 14 Mark Gleeson; 16 Said Tamghart; 26 Dominic Maloney.
Tries: Haley (12), Royston (31), Black (45), Govin (70); **Goals:** Paterson 1/5.
Rugby Leaguer & League Express Men of the Match: *Raiders:* Gary Broadbent; *Halifax:* Mick Govin.
Penalty count: 8-5; **Half-time:** 10-10;
Referee: Phil Bentham; **Attendance:** 11,398
(at Halliwell Jones Stadium, Warrington).

SUPER LEAGUE GRAND FINAL

Saturday 10th October 2009

LEEDS RHINOS 18 ST HELENS 10

RHINOS: 1 Brent Webb; 2 Scott Donald; 3 Lee Smith; 4 Keith Senior; 5 Ryan Hall; 6 Danny McGuire; 7 Rob Burrow; 8 Kylie Leuluai; 14 Matt Diskin; 10 Jamie Peacock; 11 Jamie Jones-Buchanan; 18 Carl Ablett; 13 Kevin Sinfield (C). Subs (all used): 16 Ryan Bailey for Leuluai (19); 19 Luke Burgess for Peacock (29); 17 Ian Kirke for Jones-Buchanan (29); 12 Ali Lauitiiti for Ablett (29); Jones-Buchanan for Lauitiiti (36); Peacock for Burgess (46); Leuluai for Bailey (53); Ablett for Kirke (57); Burgess for Diskin (62); Bailey for Leuluai (67); Diskin for Burgess (69); Kirke for Jones-Buchanan (76).
Tries: Diskin (30), Smith (37, 72); **Goals:** Sinfield 2/4; **Field goals:** Sinfield (42), Burrow (78).
SAINTS: 1 Paul Wellens; 2 Ade Gardner; 3 Matt Gidley; 18 Kyle Eastmond; 5 Francis Meli; 6 Leon Pryce; 7 Sean Long; 10 James Graham; 9 Keiron Cunningham (C); 16 Tony Puletua; 12 Jon Wilkin; 11 Lee Gilmour; 13 Chris Flannery. Subs (all used): 14 James Roby for Cunningham (25); 15 Bryn Hargreaves for Puletua (24); 17 Paul Clough for Gilmour (31); 23 Maurie Fa'asavalu for Graham (31); Graham for Fa'asavalu (48); Puletua for Hargreaves (50); Gilmour for Wilkin (55); Cunningham for Clough (61); Wilkin for Roby (65); Roby for Flannery (73).
Try: Eastmond (13); **Goals:** Eastmond 3/3.
Rugby Leaguer & League Express Men of the Match: *Rhinos:* Kevin Sinfield; *Saints:* James Graham.
Penalty count: 8-7; **Half-time:** 8-8;
Referee: Steve Ganson; **Attendance:** 63,259
(at Old Trafford, Manchester).

2010

CHAMPIONSHIP ONE GRAND FINAL

Sunday 26th September 2010

OLDHAM 4 YORK CITY KNIGHTS 25

OLDHAM: 1 Paul O'Connor; 2 Lucas Onyango; 24 Marcus St Hilaire; 4 Mick Fogerty; 5 John Gillam; 6 Neil Roden; 28 Gregg McNally; 8 Jason Boults; 9 Martin Roden; 16 Wayne Kerr; 18 Chris Clarke; 13 Joe Chandler; 21 Valu Bentley. Subs (all used): 10 Dave Ellison; 19 Ben Heaton; 17 Danny Whitmore; 7 Matt Ashe.
Try: Fogerty (20); **Goals:** McNally 0/1.
CITY KNIGHTS: 31 James Haynes; 2 Wayne Reittie; 3 Mike Mitchell; 4 Lee Waterman; 28 Danny Wilson; 6 Chris Thorman; 1 Danny Ratcliffe; 17 Nathan Freer; 33 Jack Lee; 10 Alex Benson; 11 Jordan Ross; 29 Ryan Esders; 15 Luke Hardbottle. Subs (all used): 32 Paul Stamp; 36 Callum Dinsdale; 26 Steve Lewis; 30 Jack Stearman.
Tries: Reittie (7), Haynes (26), Thorman (64), Lewis (74); **Goals:** Waterman 2/3, Thorman 2/2;
Field goal: Thorman (69).
Rugby Leaguer & League Express Men of the Match: *Oldham:* Neil Roden; *City Knights:* Chris Thorman.
Penalty count: 2-7; **Half-time:** 4-10;
Referee: Gareth Hewer.
(at Halliwell Jones Stadium, Warrington).

Hunslet Hawks were Championship One Champions in 2010. This game was to determine who took the second promotion place.

CHAMPIONSHIP GRAND FINAL

Sunday 26th September 2010

FEATHERSTONE ROVERS 22 HALIFAX 23
(after golden point extra-time)

ROVERS: 1 Ian Hardman; 26 Zak Hardaker; 3 Sam Smeaton; 4 Liam Welham; 2 Tom Saxton; 6 Kyle Briggs; 9 Liam Finn; 17 Tony Tonks; 31 Ben Kaye; 10 Stuart Dickens; 18 Tim Spears; 13 Jamie Field; 11 Matty Dale. Subs (all used): 19 Ross Divorty; 16 Dane Manning; 12 Jon Grayshon; 7 Andy Kain.
Tries: Briggs (28), Hardaker (30, 52), Dale (45); **Goals:** Briggs 3/4.
HALIFAX: 4 Shad Royston; 2 Lee Paterson; 6 Luke Branighan; 18 Dylan Nash; 23 Rob Worrincy; 26 Graham Holroyd; 7 Ben Black; 10 Neil Cherryholme; 13 Bob Beswick; 8 Makali Aizue; 11 David Larder; 22 David Wrench; 27 Sam Barlow. Subs (all used): 9 Sean Penkywicz; 17 Frank Watene; 19 Dominic Maloney; 24 Steve Bannister.
Tries: Worrincy (20), Black (58), Branighan (60), Bannister (75); **Goals:** Paterson 3/4; **Field goal:** Black (82).
On report: Barlow (35) - alleged high tackle on Divorty.
Rugby Leaguer & League Express Men of the Match: *Rovers:* Tom Saxton; *Halifax:* Ben Black.
Penalty count: 6-3; **Half-time:** 12-4; **Full-time:** 22-22;
Referee: Robert Hicks; **Attendance:** 9,443
(at Halliwell Jones Stadium, Warrington).

SUPER LEAGUE GRAND FINAL

Saturday 2nd October 2010

ST HELENS 10 WIGAN WARRIORS 22

SAINTS: 1 Paul Wellens; 30 Jamie Foster; 3 Matt Gidley; 5 Francis Meli; 24 Jonny Lomax; 12 Jon Wilkin; 34 Matty Smith; 10 James Graham; 9 Keiron Cunningham (C); 15 Bryn Hargreaves; 4 Iosia Soliola; 13 Chris Flannery; 11 Tony Puletua. Subs (all used): 17 Paul Clough; 14 James Roby; 22 Andrew Dixon; 25 Jacob Emmitt.
Tries: Dixon (28), Meli (74); **Goals:** Foster 1/2.
WARRIORS: 6 Sam Tomkins; 24 Darrell Goulding; 3 Martin Gleeson; 4 George Carmont; 5 Pat Richards; 19 Paul Deacon; 7 Thomas Leuluai; 8 Stuart Fielden; 15 Michael McIlorum; 10 Andy Coley; 11 Harrison Hansen; 12 Joel Tomkins; 13 Sean O'Loughlin (C). Subs (all used): 9 Mark Riddell; 17 Iafeta Palea'aesina; 25 Liam Farrell; 14 Paul Prescott.
Tries: Gleeson (4, 16), Goulding (20), S Tomkins (53); **Goals:** Richards 2/3, Riddell 1/3, S Tomkins 0/1.
Rugby Leaguer & League Express Men of the Match: *Saints:* Tony Puletua; *Warriors:* Thomas Leuluai.
Penalty count: 6-11; **Half time:** 6-16;
Referee: Richard Silverwood; **Attendance:** 71,526
(at Old Trafford, Manchester).

2011

CHAMPIONSHIP ONE GRAND FINAL

Sunday 2nd October 2011

KEIGHLEY COUGARS 32 WORKINGTON TOWN 12

COUGARS: 18 James Haythornthwaite; 4 Danny Lawton; 22 Ben Sagar; 33 Jake Normington; 5 Gavin Duffy; 6 Jason Demetriou; 36 Jy-Mel Coleman; 17 Ryan Benjafield; 9 James Feather; 10 Scott Law; 11 Will Cartledge; 12 Oliver Pursglove; 21 Richard Jones. Subs (all used): 14 Jamaine Wray; 8 Andy Shickell; 16 Brendan Rawlins; 7 Ryan Smith.
Tries: Lawton (5), Feather (20), Rawlins (25), Pursglove (32), Normington (69, 77); **Goals:** Lawton 4/6.
TOWN: 1 Brett Carter; 2 Elliott Miller; 3 Jason Mossop; 4 Aaron Low; 5 Neil Frazer; 24 Darren Holt; 7 Scott Kaighan; 10 Kris Coward; 13 Karl Olstrum; 29 Dave Armitstead; 11 Mike Whitehead; 18 Joe McKenna; 12 Jarrad Stack. Subs (all used): 23 Marc Bainbridge; 15 Ruairi McGoff; 32 Chris Clough; 17 James Robinson.
Tries: Kaighan (65), Frazer (74); **Goals:** Holt 2/2.
Rugby Leaguer & League Express Men of the Match: *Cougars:* Jason Demetriou; *Town:* Jarrad Stack.
Penalty count: 7-5; **Half-time:** 22-0; **Referee:** Tim Roby.
(at Halliwell Jones Stadium, Warrington).

Swinton Lions were Championship One Champions in 2011. This game was to determine who took the second promotion place.

CHAMPIONSHIP GRAND FINAL

Sunday 2nd October 2011

FEATHERSTONE ROVERS 40 SHEFFIELD EAGLES 4

ROVERS: 1 Ian Hardman; 33 Ben Cockayne; 3 Sam Smeaton; 17 Greg Worthington; 5 Tom Saxton; 6 Andy Kain; 7 Liam Finn; 8 Tony Tonks; 9 Ben Kaye; 10 Stuart Dickens; 11 Jon Grayshon; 12 Tim Spears; 28 Jon Hepworth. Subs (all used): 18 Ross Divorty; 13 Matty Dale; 4 Andrew Bostock; 30 Kirk Netherton.
Tries: Spears (4), Finn (7, 39), Hardman (42), Cockayne (56), Hepworth (59), Saxton (79); **Goals:** Finn 6/7.
Sin bin: Netherton (54) - fighting.
EAGLES: 6 Quentin Laulu-Togagae; 5 Tim Bergin; 26 Corey Hanson; 1 Misi Taulapapa; 16 Vinny Finigan; 13 Dane McDonald; 7 Simon Brown; 8 Jack Howieson; 9 Andrew Henderson; 10 Mitchell Stringer; 11 Alex Szostak; 12 Peter Green; 19 Joe Hirst. Subs (all used): 22 Ryan Hepworth; 30 Sam Scott; 20 Pat Smith; 14 Jonny Woodcock.
Try: McDonald (12); **Goals:** Brown 0/1.
Sin bin: Hirst (54) - fighting.
Rugby Leaguer & League Express Men of the Match: *Rovers:* Liam Finn; *Eagles:* Joe Hirst.
Penalty count: 7-11; **Half-time:** 18-4;
Referee: Matthew Thomason; **Attendance:** 7,263
(at Halliwell Jones Stadium, Warrington).

SUPER LEAGUE GRAND FINAL

Saturday 8th October 2011

LEEDS RHINOS 32 ST HELENS 16

RHINOS: 1 Brent Webb; 23 Ben Jones-Bishop; 27 Zak Hardaker; 12 Carl Ablett; 5 Ryan Hall; 13 Kevin Sinfield (C); 6 Danny McGuire; 8 Kylie Leuluai; 9 Danny Buderus; 10 Jamie Peacock; 11 Jamie Jones-Buchanan; 3 Brett Delaney; 21 Chris Clarkson. Subs (all used): 7 Rob Burrow; 16 Ryan Bailey; 17 Ian Kirke; 14 Ali Lauitiiti.
Tries: Burrow (34), Webb (65), Hall (70), Ablett (74), Hardaker (80); **Goals:** Sinfield 6/7.
SAINTS: 1 Paul Wellens (C); 28 Tom Makinson; 3 Michael Shenton; 5 Francis Meli; 22 Jamie Foster; 25 Lee Gaskell; 20 Jonny Lomax; 10 James Graham (C); 9 James Roby; 11 Tony Puletua; 12 Jon Wilkin; 4 Iosia Soliola; 16 Paul Clough. Subs (all used): 19 Andrew Dixon; 14 Scott Moore; 15 Louie McCarthy-Scarsbrook; 17 Gary Wheeler.
Tries: Makinson (50), Shenton (55); **Goals:** Foster 4/5.
Rugby Leaguer & League Express Men of the Match: *Rhinos:* Rob Burrow; *Saints:* Lee Gaskell.
Penalty count: 5-7; **Half-time:** 8-2;
Referee: Phil Bentham; **Attendance:** 69,107
(at Old Trafford, Manchester).

2012

CHAMPIONSHIP ONE GRAND FINAL

Sunday 30th September 2012

BARROW RAIDERS 13 DONCASTER 16

RAIDERS: 1 Andy Ballard; 2 Lee Haney; 3 Chris Larkin; 4 Aaron Low; 5 James Nixon; 6 Scott Kaighan; 7 Liam Campbell; 8 Jamie Butler; 9 James Dandy; 10 Ryan Duffy; 11 Liam Harrison; 12 James Gordon; 13 Daniel Toal. Subs (all used): 14 Liam Finch; 15 Martin Ostler; 16 Ruairi McGoff; 17 Andrew Dawson.
Tries: Larkin (4), Low (77); **Goals:** Ballard 2/3;
Field goal: Kaighan (39).
DONCASTER: 1 Lee Waterman; 2 Tom Hodson; 3 Chris Spurr; 4 Danny Cowling; 5 Stewart Sanderson; 6 Kyle Kesik; 7 Craig Fawcett; 8 Mark Castle; 9 Mike Emmett; 10 Russ Spiers; 11 Lucas Walshaw; 12 Michael Kelly; 13 Carl Hughes. Subs (all used): 14 Nathan Powley; 15 Craig Robinson; 16 Grant Edwards; 17 Liam Cunningham.
Tries: Sanderson (11), Waterman (46), Fawcett (57); **Goals:** Hodson 2/3.
Rugby Leaguer & League Express Men of the Match: *Raiders:* Liam Harrison; *Doncaster:* Craig Fawcett.
Penalty count: 4-5; **Half-time:** 7-4; **Referee:** Jamie Leahy.
(at Halliwell Jones Stadium, Warrington).

CHAMPIONSHIP GRAND FINAL

Sunday 30th September 2012

FEATHERSTONE ROVERS 16 SHEFFIELD EAGLES 20

ROVERS: 1 Ian Hardman; 2 Tangi Ropati; 3 Nathan Chappell; 4 Greg Worthington; 5 Tom Saxton; 6 Andy Kain; 7 Liam Finn; 8 Anthony England; 9 Ben Kaye; 10 James Lockwood; 11 Matty Dale; 12 Tim Spears; 13 Kyle Briggs. Subs (all used): 14 Dominic Maloney; 15 Stuart Dickens; 16 Andrew Bostock; 17 Jon Hepworth.
Tries: Hardman (17), Hepworth (51); **Goals:** Finn 4/4.
On report:
Maloney (57) - alleged use of the elbow on Turner.
EAGLES: 1 Quentin Laulu-Togagae; 2 Misi Taulapapa; 3 Duane Straugheir; 4 Menzie Yere; 5 Scott Turner; 6 Simon Brown; 7 Dominic Brambani; 8 Jack Howieson; 9 Andrew Henderson; 10 Mitchell Stringer; 11 Michael Knowles; 12 Sam Scott; 13 Alex Szostak. Subs (all used): 14 James Davey; 15 Peter Green; 16 Dane McDonald; 17 Liam Higgins.
Tries: Turner (9), Laulu-Togagae (32), McDonald (46), Taulapapa (57); **Goals:** Brown 2/5.
Rugby Leaguer & League Express Men of the Match: *Rovers:* Ian Hardman; *Eagles:* Michael Knowles.
Penalty count: 4-6; **Half-time:** 8-10; **Referee:** Tim Roby; **Attendance:** 6,409
(at Halliwell Jones Stadium, Warrington).

Grand Finals 1998-2017

SUPER LEAGUE GRAND FINAL

Saturday 6th October 2012

LEEDS RHINOS 26 WARRINGTON WOLVES 18

RHINOS: 4 Zak Hardaker; 2 Ben Jones-Bishop; 3 Kallum Watkins; 12 Carl Ablett; 5 Ryan Hall; 13 Kevin Sinfield (C); 6 Danny McGuire; 8 Kylie Leuluai; 7 Rob Burrow; 10 Jamie Peacock; 11 Jamie Jones-Buchanan; 15 Brett Delaney; 16 Ryan Bailey. Subs (all used): 17 Ian Kirke; 20 Darrell Griffin; 25 Stevie Ward; 31 Shaun Lunt.
Tries: Sinfield (19), Jones-Bishop (28), Ablett (59), Hall (72); **Goals:** Sinfield 5/5.
WOLVES: 1 Brett Hodgson; 5 Joel Monaghan; 19 Stefan Ratchford; 4 Ryan Atkins; 2 Chris Riley; 6 Lee Briers; 7 Richard Myler; 20 Chris Hill; 14 Mick Higham; 13 Ben Harrison; 12 Ben Westwood; 11 Trent Waterhouse; 15 Simon Grix. Subs (all used): 8 Adrian Morley (C); 9 Michael Monaghan; 16 Paul Wood; 17 Michael Cooper.
Tries: Myler (4), J Monaghan (38), Atkins (45); **Goals:** Hodgson 3/4.
Rugby Leaguer & League Express Men of the Match: *Rhinos:* Kevin Sinfield; *Wolves:* Richard Myler.
Penalty count: 6-5; **Half-time:** 14-14;
Referee: Richard Silverwood; **Attendance:** 70,676 *(at Old Trafford, Manchester).*

2013

CHAMPIONSHIP ONE GRAND FINAL

Sunday 29th September 2013

OLDHAM 18 ROCHDALE HORNETS 32

OLDHAM: 1 Richard Lepori; 2 Mo Agoro; 21 David Cookson; 25 Jonathan Ford; 5 Dale Bloomfield; 23 Lewis Palfrey; 26 Kenny Hughes; 18 Phil Joy; 9 Sam Gee; 10 Jason Boults; 11 Josh Crowley; 12 Danny Langtree; 13 Mark Hobson. Subs (all used): 14 Adam Files; 19 Michael Ward; 22 Liam Thompson; 28 Matthew Haggarty.
Tries: Ford (12), Hughes (38), Cookson (44); **Goals:** Palfrey 3/3.
HORNETS: 1 Wayne English; 2 Gareth Langley; 20 Daniel Davies; 23 Dave Hull; 17 Martin Waring; 6 Paul Crook; 7 Steve Roper; 29 Carl Forster; 31 Chris Hough; 10 Warren Thompson; 26 Dave Llewellyn; 14 Alex Trumper; 18 Joe Greenwood. Subs (all used): 8 John Cookson; 9 Alex McClurg; 11 Chris Baines; 13 Jordan Case.
Tries: Llewellyn (5), Davies (20), Hull (58), Cookson (71), English (78); **Goals:** Crook 6/6.
Rugby Leaguer & League Express Men of the Match: *Oldham:* Lewis Palfrey; *Hornets:* Paul Crook.
Penalty count: 1-2; **Half-time:** 12-12;
Referee: Chris Leatherbarrow. *(at Leigh Sports Village).*

North Wales Crusaders were Championship One Champions in 2013. This game was to determine who took the second promotion place.

CHAMPIONSHIP GRAND FINAL

Sunday 29th September 2013

BATLEY BULLDOGS 12 SHEFFIELD EAGLES 19

BULLDOGS: 1 Miles Greenwood; 5 Johnny Campbell; 3 Jason Walton; 4 Danny Maun; 21 Greg Johnson; 6 Ben Black; 7 Gareth Moore; 8 Byron Smith; 9 Paul Mennell; 28 Anthony Mullally; 11 Alex Bretherton; 16 John Davies; 13 Ashley Lindsay. Subs (all used): 14 George Flanagan; 15 Keegan Hirst; 19 Alex Rowe; 17 Liam Walmsley.
Try: Campbell (13); **Goals:** Moore 4/5.
EAGLES: 1 Quentin Laulu-Togagae; 5 Misi Taulapapa; 4 Tom Armstrong; 3 Menzie Yere; 2 Scott Turner; 6 Pat Walker; 7 Dominic Brambani; 25 Eddie Battye; 9 Andrew Henderson; 10 Mitchell Stringer; 11 Michael Knowles; 15 Alex Szostak; 13 Joe Hirst. Subs (all used): 14 James Davey; 12 Peter Green; 16 Duane Straugheir; 21 Matt Garside.
Tries: Turner (56, 67), Yere (61), Laulu-Togagae (70); **Goals:** Brambani 1/5; **Field goal:** Walker (74).
Rugby Leaguer & League Express Men of the Match: *Bulldogs:* Keegan Hirst; *Eagles:* Dominic Brambani.
Penalty count: 6-7; **Half-time:** 12-0;
Referee: Matthew Thomason; **Attendance:** 6,374 *(at Leigh Sports Village).*

SUPER LEAGUE GRAND FINAL

Saturday 5th October 2013

WARRINGTON WOLVES 16 WIGAN WARRIORS 30

WOLVES: 19 Stefan Ratchford; 5 Joel Monaghan; 3 Chris Bridge; 4 Ryan Atkins; 2 Chris Riley; 6 Lee Briers; 7 Richard Myler; 16 Paul Wood; 14 Mick Higham; 18 Chris Hill; 13 Ben Harrison; 12 Ben Westwood; 15 Simon Grix. Subs (all used): 9 Michael Monaghan; 8 Adrian Morley (C); 17 Michael Cooper; 10 Garreth Carvell.

Tries: J Monaghan (20), Grix (24), Westwood (27); **Goals:** Ratchford 2/3.
On report: Westwood (2) - alleged punch on Green.
WARRIORS: 1 Sam Tomkins; 2 Josh Charnley; 3 Darrell Goulding; 17 Iain Thornley; 5 Pat Richards; 6 Blake Green; 7 Matty Smith; 10 Lee Mossop; 9 Michael McIlorum; 20 Gil Dudson; 11 Harrison Hansen; 12 Liam Farrell; 13 Sean O'Loughlin (C). Subs (all used): 15 Ben Flower; 4 Jack Hughes; 26 Dominic Crosby; 21 Scott Taylor.
Tries: Goulding (37), McIlorum (47), Charnley (53), Green (65), Richards (74); **Goals:** Richards 5/6.
Rugby Leaguer & League Express Men of the Match: *Wolves:* Chris Hill; *Warriors:* Michael McIlorum.
Penalty count: 7-10; **Half-time:** 16-6;
Referee: Richard Silverwood; **Attendance:** 66,281 *(at Old Trafford, Manchester).*

2014

CHAMPIONSHIP ONE GRAND FINAL

Sunday 5th October 2014

HUNSLET HAWKS 17 OLDHAM 16
(after golden point extra-time)

HAWKS: 2 Jimmy Watson; 36 Gavin Duffy; 4 Danny Maun; 3 Lee Brickwood; 37 James Duckworth; 6 Thomas Coyle; 29 Danny Ansell; 38 Richard Moore; 9 David March; 10 James Houston; 11 John Oakes; 12 Aaron Lyons; 31 Luke Briscoe. Subs (all used): 27 Liam Hood; 8 Michael Haley; 1 Stuart Kain; 40 Luke Hardbottle.
Tries: Watson (22), Duckworth (45), T Coyle (53); **Goals:** March 2/3; **Field goal:** T Coyle (85).
OLDHAM: 4 Steven Nield; 29 Adam Clay; 21 David Cookson; 25 Jonathan Ford; 5 Dale Bloomfield; 6 Lewis Palfrey; 26 Steve Roper; 8 Phil Joy; 30 Gareth Owen; 10 Jason Boults; 11 Josh Crowley; 12 Danny Langtree; 22 Liam Thompson. Subs (all used): 19 Michael Ward; 28 Nathan Mason; 16 Kenny Hughes; 20 George Tyson.
Tries: Roper (5), Bloomfield (31), Langtree (74); **Goals:** Roper 2/3.
Rugby Leaguer & League Express Men of the Match: *Hawks:* Liam Hood; *Oldham:* Jonathan Ford.
Penalty count: 4-3; **Half-time:** 6-10; **Referee:** Joe Cobb. *(at Headingley Carnegie, Leeds).*

CHAMPIONSHIP GRAND FINAL

Sunday 5th October 2014

FEATHERSTONE ROVERS 12 LEIGH CENTURIONS 36

ROVERS: 2 Will Sharp; 35 Jason Crookes; 1 Ian Hardman; 18 Jamie Cording; 36 Ben Blackmore; 23 Andy Kain; 7 Gareth Moore; 8 Steve Crossley; 9 Andy Ellis; 13 Matt James; 31 Shaun Pick; 11 James Lockwood; 12 Tim Spears. Subs (all used): 10 Luke Teasdale; 6 Jack Bussey; 42 Chris Annakin; 10 Keegan Hirst.
Tries: Sharp (27, 51); **Goals:** Moore 2/2.
Sin bin: Crookes (68) - high tackle on Armstrong.
CENTURIONS: 1 Gregg McNally; 22 Adam Higson; 34 Michael Platt; 4 Tom Armstrong; 15 Liam Kay; 6 Martyn Ridyard; 7 Ryan Brierley; 29 Jake Emmitt; 14 Sean Penkywicz; 10 Oliver Wilkes; 11 Matt Sarsfield; 30 Kurt Haggerty; 13 Sam Barlow. Subs (all used): 9 Bob Beswick; 18 Jamie Acton; 16 Martin Aspinwall; 33 Jonathan Walker.
Tries: Sarsfield (5), McNally (17), Armstrong (22), Higson (65), Barlow (70), Brierley (80); **Goals:** Ridyard 6/8.
Sin bin: Penkywicz (68) - retaliation.
Rugby Leaguer & League Express Men of the Match: *Rovers:* Jack Bussey; *Centurions:* Tom Armstrong.
Penalty count: 6-8; **Half-time:** 6-20;
Referee: Matthew Thomason; **Attendance:** 9,164 *(at Headingley Carnegie, Leeds).*

SUPER LEAGUE GRAND FINAL

Saturday 11th October 2014

ST HELENS 14 WIGAN WARRIORS 6

SAINTS: 17 Paul Wellens (C); 2 Tom Makinson; 22 Mark Percival; 4 Josh Jones; 5 Adam Swift; 15 Mark Flanagan; 6 Lance Hohaia; 16 Kyle Amor; 9 James Roby; 8 Mose Masoe; 10 Louie McCarthy-Scarsbrook; 11 Iosia Soliola; 3 Jordan Turner. Subs (all used): 28 Luke Thompson; 13 Willie Manu; 18 Alex Walmsley; 27 Greg Richards.
Tries: Soliola (54), Makinson (69); **Goals:** Percival 3/3.
WARRIORS: 1 Matt Bowen; 2 Josh Charnley; 5 Anthony Gelling; 23 Dan Sarginson; 32 Joe Burgess; 6 Blake Green; 7 Matty Smith; 10 Ben Flower; 19 Sam Powell; 17 Dominic Crosby; 11 Joel Tomkins; 12 Liam Farrell; 13 Sean O'Loughlin (C). Subs (all used): 22 Eddy Pettybourne; 24 Tony Clubb; 25 John Bateman; 27 George Williams.
Try: Burgess (40); **Goals:** Smith 1/3.
Dismissal: Flower (2) - punching Hohaia.

Rugby Leaguer & League Express Men of the Match: *Saints:* James Roby; *Warriors:* Liam Farrell.
Penalty count: 9-7; **Half-time:** 2-6;
Referee: Phil Bentham; **Attendance:** 70,102 *(at Old Trafford, Manchester).*

2015

SUPER LEAGUE GRAND FINAL

Saturday 10th October 2015

LEEDS RHINOS 22 WIGAN WARRIORS 20

RHINOS: 1 Zak Hardaker; 2 Tom Briscoe; 3 Kallum Watkins; 4 Joel Moon; 5 Ryan Hall; 13 Kevin Sinfield (C); 6 Danny McGuire; 30 Mitch Garbutt; 7 Rob Burrow; 10 Jamie Peacock; 12 Carl Ablett; 15 Brett Delaney; 19 Brad Singleton. Subs (all used): 8 Kylie Leuluai; 17 Adam Cuthbertson; 20 Jimmy Keinhorst; 21 Josh Walters.
Tries: McGuire (7, 35), Moon (27), Walters (64); **Goals:** Sinfield 3/4.
WARRIORS: 1 Matt Bowen; 22 Dominic Manfredi; 14 John Bateman; 34 Oliver Gildart; 5 Joe Burgess; 6 George Williams; 7 Matty Smith; 8 Dominic Crosby; 9 Michael McIlorum; 10 Ben Flower; 11 Joel Tomkins; 12 Liam Farrell; 13 Sean O'Loughlin (C). Subs (all used): 16 Sam Powell; 17 Tony Clubb; 23 Lee Mossop; 25 Larne Patrick.
Tries: Burgess (4), Manfredi (46), Bowen (49); **Goals:** Bowen 4/4.
Rugby Leaguer & League Express Men of the Match: *Rhinos:* Danny McGuire; *Warriors:* Matt Bowen.
Penalty count: 5-4; **Half-time:** 16-6;
Referee: Ben Thaler; **Attendance:** 73,512 *(at Old Trafford, Manchester).*

2016

SUPER LEAGUE GRAND FINAL

Saturday 8th October 2016

WARRINGTON WOLVES 6 WIGAN WARRIORS 12

WOLVES: 6 Stefan Ratchford; 2 Tom Lineham; 3 Rhys Evans; 4 Ryan Atkins; 5 Matthew Russell; 1 Kurt Gidley; 26 Declan Patton; 8 Chris Hill (C); 9 Daryl Clark; 10 Ashton Sims; 27 Sam Wilde; 12 Jack Hughes; 16 Joe Westerman. Subs (all used): 24 Toby King; 18 George King; 7 Chris Sandow; 33 Ryan Bailey.
Try: Patton (21); **Goals:** Patton 1/1.
WARRIORS: 4 Dan Sarginson; 2 Josh Charnley; 3 Anthony Gelling; 20 Oliver Gildart; 22 Lewis Tierney; 6 George Williams; 7 Matty Smith; 24 Frank-Paul Nuuausala; 16 Sam Powell; 10 Ben Flower; 14 John Bateman; 12 Liam Farrell; 25 Willie Isa. Subs (all used): 8 Dominic Crosby; 19 Taulima Tautai; 21 Ryan Sutton; 13 Sean O'Loughlin (C).
Tries: Gildart (55), Charnley (63); **Goals:** Smith 2/4.
Rugby Leaguer & League Express Men of the Match: *Wolves:* Kurt Gidley; *Warriors:* Liam Farrell.
Penalty count: 4-6; **Half-time:** 6-2;
Referee: Robert Hicks; **Attendance:** 70,202 *(at Old Trafford, Manchester).*

2017

SUPER LEAGUE GRAND FINAL

Saturday 7th October 2017

CASTLEFORD TIGERS 6 LEEDS RHINOS 24

TIGERS: 5 Greg Eden; 2 Greg Minikin; 3 Jake Webster; 4 Michael Shenton (C); 25 Jy Hitchcox; 16 Ben Roberts; 7 Luke Gale; 14 Nathan Massey; 9 Paul McShane; 15 Jesse Sene-Lefao; 11 Oliver Holmes; 12 Mike McMeeken; 13 Adam Milner. Subs (all used): 10 Grant Millington; 17 Junior Moors; 18 Matt Cook; 34 Alex Foster.
Try: Foster (79); **Goals:** Gale 1/1.
RHINOS: 31 Jack Walker; 2 Tom Briscoe; 3 Kallum Watkins; 14 Liam Sutcliffe; 5 Ryan Hall; 4 Joel Moon; 6 Danny McGuire (C); 16 Brad Singleton; 9 Matt Parcell; 17 Mitch Garbutt; 13 Stevie Ward; 11 Jamie Jones-Buchanan; 10 Adam Cuthbertson. Subs (all used): 20 Anthony Mullally; 12 Carl Ablett; 7 Rob Burrow; 19 Brett Ferres.
Tries: Briscoe (11, 59), McGuire (51, 70); **Goals:** Watkins 3/4; **Field goal:** McGuire (40, 77).
Rugby Leaguer & League Express Men of the Match: *Tigers:* Matt Cook; *Rhinos:* Danny McGuire.
Penalty count: 5-1; **Half-time:** 0-7;
Referee: James Child; **Attendance:** 72,827 *(at Old Trafford, Manchester).*

2018 SEASON
Stats round-up

ATTENDANCES

SUPER LEAGUE CLUBS - AVERAGES

	2018 Avg	2017 Avg	Diff
Leeds Rhinos	12,352	14,573	-2,221
Hull FC	11,854	11,459	+395
Wigan Warriors	11,648	13,669	-2,021
St Helens	11,169	10,946	+223
Warrington Wolves	9,782	10,164	-382
Catalans Dragons	8,145	8,612	-467
Hull Kingston Rovers	7,873	7,429	+444
(Championship)			
Castleford Tigers	7,604	8,945	-1,341
Huddersfield Giants	5,471	5,873	-402
Wakefield Trinity	5,056	5,283	-227
Widnes Vikings	4,624	5,587	-963
Salford Red Devils	2,823	3,941	-1,118
2018 Average	8,200		
2017 Average	8,779		
Difference	-579		

CHAMPIONSHIP CLUBS - AVERAGES

	2018 Avg	2017 Avg	Diff
Toronto Wolfpack	6,565	6,960	-395
(League 1)			
Leigh Centurions	3,247	6,301	-3,054
(Super League)			
Toulouse Olympique	2,538	1,814	+724
Featherstone Rovers	2,084	2,624	-540
Halifax	2,008	1,796	+212
Barrow Raiders	1,223	1,042	+181
(League 1)			
Batley Bulldogs	1,029	998	+31
Dewsbury Rams	969	1,028	-59
London Broncos	896	891	+5
Swinton Lions	768	775	-7
Sheffield Eagles	684	637	+47
Rochdale Hornets	573	832	-259
2018 Average	1,882		
2017 Average	1,957		
Difference	-75		

LEAGUE 1 CLUBS - AVERAGES

	2018 Avg	2017 Avg	Diff
Bradford Bulls	3,684	3,877	-193
(Championship)			
York City Knights	1,624	1,055	+569
Newcastle Thunder	1,023	863	+160
Doncaster	807	572	+235
Workington Town	782	631	+151
Keighley Cougars	781	784	-3
Whitehaven	752	703	+49
Hunslet	616	423	+193
Oldham	505	777	-272
(Championship)			
London Skolars	401	451	-50
Coventry Bears	387	366	+21
North Wales Crusaders	374	342	+32
West Wales Raiders	322	N/A	N/A
Hemel Stags	177	116	+61
2018 Average	874		
2017 Average	930		
Difference	-56		

BEST ATTENDANCES

		Round	Date
64,892	Warrington v Wigan	SLGF	13/10/18
	(at Old Trafford, Manchester)		
50,672	Catalans Dragons v Warrington	CCF	25/8/18
	(at Wembley Stadium)		
23,246	Leeds v Castleford	SLR7	23/3/18
	(at Elland Road)		
19,062	Melbourne v Leeds	WCC	16/2/18
17,980	St Helens v Wigan	SLR8	30/3/18
17,564	Hull FC v Hull KR	SLR23	27/7/18
16,149	Leeds v Hull KR	SLR2	8/2/18
	(at Elland Road)		
16,047	Wigan v St Helens	SLR22	19/7/18
14,623	Hull FC v Castleford	SLR14	5/5/18
14,061	St Helens v Wigan	SLS8R3	31/8/18
13,704	Hull FC v Huddersfield	SLR1	1/2/18
13,461	Wigan v Castleford	SLSF	5/10/18
13,256	Hull FC v Wigan	SLR18	16/6/18
13,249	Wigan v Warrington	SLR20	6/7/18
13,108	St Helens v Castleford	SLR1	2/2/18
12,454	St Helens v Warrington	SLR23	26/7/18
12,416	Wigan v Hull FC	SLR2	10/2/18
	(at WIN Stadium, Wollongong)		
12,372	Wigan v Warrington	SLS8R5	14/9/18
12,309	St Helens v Warrington	SLSF	4/10/18
12,268	Warrington v St Helens	SLR5	9/3/18

LEADING SCORERS

CHAMPIONSHIP *(Regular season only)*

TRIES

1	Luke Briscoe	Featherstone Rovers	24
2	Kieran Dixon	London Broncos	22
	Liam Kay	Toronto Wolfpack	22
4	Craig Hall	Leigh Centurions	20
	Rhys Williams	London Broncos	20
	Mark Kheirallah	Toulouse Olympique	20
7	Jarrod Sammut	London Broncos	19
8	Alex Walker	London Broncos	17
9	Steve Tyrer	Halifax	15
10	Josh Hardcastle	Featherstone Rovers	14
	Liam Hood	Leigh Centurions	14
	Blake Wallace	Toronto Wolfpack	14
	Bastien Ader	Toulouse Olympique	14

GOALS

1	Mark Kheirallah	Toulouse Olympique	127
2	Ben Reynolds	Leigh Centurions	98
3	Steve Tyrer	Halifax	90
4	Jarrod Sammut	London Broncos	87
5	Ryan Brierley	Toronto Wolfpack	71
6	Ian Hardman	Featherstone Rovers	68
7	Jamie Dallimore	Barrow Raiders	56
8	Kieran Dixon	London Broncos	50
	Chris Hankinson	Swinton Lions	50
10	Martyn Ridyard	Featherstone Rovers	49
	Paul Sykes	Dewsbury Rams	49

POINTS

			T	G	FG	Pts
1	Mark Kheirallah	Toulouse Olympique	20	127	0	334
2	Jarrod Sammut	London Broncos	19	87	1	251
3	Steve Tyrer	Halifax	15	90	0	240
4	Ben Reynolds	Leigh Centurions	5	98	1	217
5	Ryan Brierley	Toronto Wolfpack	11	71	2	188
	Kieran Dixon	London Broncos	22	50	0	188
7	Ian Hardman	Featherstone Rovers	7	68	1	165
8	Gareth O'Brien	Toronto Wolfpack	10	45	0	130
9	Jamie Dallimore	Barrow Raiders	4	56	0	128
10	Martyn Ridyard	Featherstone Rovers	7	49	0	126

Mark Kheirallah

CHAMPIONSHIP SHIELD

TRIES

1	Johnny Campbell	Batley Bulldogs	9
2	John Davies	Featherstone Rovers	7
	Harry Newman	Featherstone Rovers	7
4	Deon Cross	Rochdale Hornets	6
5	Brad Delaney	Dewsbury Rams	5
	Adam Ryder	Dewsbury Rams	5
	Connor Farrell	Featherstone Rovers	5
	Anthony Thackeray	Featherstone Rovers	5
	Ilias Bergal	Leigh Centurions	5

GOALS

1	Ian Hardman	Featherstone Rovers	33
2	Paul Sykes	Dewsbury Rams	32
3	Jamie Dallimore	Barrow Raiders	18
	Tyler Whittaker	Rochdale Hornets	18
5	Ben Reynolds	Leigh Centurions	17
	Dave Scott	Batley Bulldogs	17

POINTS

			T	G	FG	Pts
1	Paul Sykes	Dewsbury Rams	2	32	0	72
2	Ian Hardman	Featherstone Rovers	1	33	0	70
3	Ben Reynolds	Leigh Centurions	3	17	0	46
	Dave Scott	Batley Bulldogs	3	17	0	46
5	Jamie Dallimore	Barrow Raiders	2	18	0	44

CHALLENGE CUP

TRIES

1	Josh Charnley	Warrington Wolves	9
2	Luke Briscoe	Featherstone Rovers	8
3	Elliot Minchella	Bradford Bulls	6
4	Tom Lineham	Warrington Wolves	5
	Ben Murdoch-Masila	Warrington Wolves	5
	Jason Tali	Doncaster	5

GOALS

1	Josh Drinkwater	Catalans Dragons	23
2	Connor Robinson	York City Knights	16
3	Bryson Goodwin	Warrington Wolves	14
	Liam Harris	Doncaster	14
5	Tom Gilmore	Widnes Vikings	13
	Joe Sanderson	Hunslet	13

Josh Charnley

POINTS

			T	G	FG	Pts
1	Josh Drinkwater	Catalans Dragons	1	23	0	50
2	Bryson Goodwin	Warrington Wolves	4	14	0	44
3	Josh Charnley	Warrington Wolves	9	0	0	36
	Liam Harris	Doncaster	2	14	0	36
5	Luke Briscoe	Featherstone Rovers	8	0	0	32
	Connor Robinson	York City Knights	0	16	0	32

LEADING SCORERS

SUPER LEAGUE

(Regular season, Super 8s, Semi-finals & Grand Final.
Super 8s (Qualifiers) not included)

TRIES

1	Ben Barba	St Helens	28
2	Tom Johnstone	Wakefield Trinity	24
3	Mark Percival	St Helens	20
4	Greg Eden	Castleford Tigers	18
	Ben Jones-Bishop	Wakefield Trinity	18
	Tom Lineham	Warrington Wolves	18
7	Bureta Faraimo	Hull FC	17
	Jonny Lomax	St Helens	17
9	Josh Charnley	Warrington Wolves	16
	Liam Marshall	Wigan Warriors	16

GOALS

1	Danny Richardson	St Helens	135
2	Sam Tomkins	Wigan Warriors	96
3	Danny Brough	Huddersfield Giants	62
4	Ryan Hampshire	Wakefield Trinity	61
5	Ryan Shaw	Hull Kingston Rovers	56
6	Jamie Ellis	Castleford Tigers	54
7	Josh Drinkwater	Catalans Dragons	53
8	Marc Sneyd	Hull FC	51
9	Luke Gale	Castleford Tigers	48
10	Jake Connor	Hull FC	40

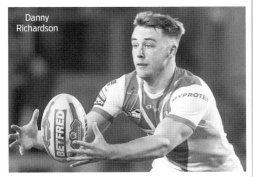

Danny Richardson

GOALS PERCENTAGE

			G	Att	%
1	Paul McShane	Castleford Tigers	10	11	90.90
2	Declan Patton	Warrington Wolves	17	19	89.47
3	Luke Gale	Castleford Tigers	48	55	87.27
4	Jake Connor	Hull FC	40	46	86.95
5	Ryan Shaw	Hull Kingston Rovers	56	65	86.15
6	Tom Gilmore	Widnes Vikings	33	39	84.61
7	Krisnan Inu	Widnes Vikings	21	25	84.00
8	Ryan Hampshire	Wakefield Trinity	61	74	82.43
9	James Batchelor	Wakefield Trinity	13	16	81.25
10	Tyrone Roberts	Warrington Wolves	32	40	80.00

(10 minimum attempts to qualify)

POINTS

			T	G	FG	Pts
1	Danny Richardson	St Helens	5	135	6	296
2	Sam Tomkins	Wigan Warriors	11	96	6	242
3	Ryan Shaw	Hull Kingston Rovers	11	56	0	156
4	Ryan Hampshire	Wakefield Trinity	5	61	1	143
5	Josh Drinkwater	Catalans Dragons	7	53	0	134
6	Danny Brough	Huddersfield Giants	1	62	2	130
7	Jamie Ellis	Castleford Tigers	2	54	1	117
8	Stefan Ratchford	Warrington Wolves	15	27	0	114
9	Ben Barba	St Helens	28	0	0	112
10	Marc Sneyd	Hull FC	1	51	5	111

CONSECUTIVE APPEARANCES *(all club games included)*

1	Bill Tupou	Wakefield Trinity	43
2	Danny Richardson	St Helens	34
3	Chris Atkin	Hull Kingston Rovers	31
4	Tom Briscoe	Leeds Rhinos	30
5	Morgan Knowles	St Helens	28
6	Tony Clubb	Wigan Warriors	26
	Sam Powell	Wigan Warriors	26
8	Harrison Hansen	Widnes Vikings/Leigh Centurions	25
9	Danny Tickle	Hull Kingston Rovers	23
10	Tom Davies	Wigan Warriors	22
	Ryan Hinchcliffe	Huddersfield Giants	22

SUPER 8s - THE QUALIFIERS

TRIES

1	Craig Hall	Hull Kingston Rovers	12
2	Chris Centrone	Toulouse Olympique	8
3	Chris Atkin	Hull Kingston Rovers	6
	Joel Moon	Leeds Rhinos	6
	Stan Robin	Toulouse Olympique	6

GOALS

1	Liam Sutcliffe	Leeds Rhinos	32
2	Jarrod Sammut	London Broncos	27
3	Gareth O'Brien	Toronto Wolfpack	24
4	Ed Chamberlain	Salford Red Devils	23
5	Mark Kheirallah	Toulouse Olympique	22

POINTS

			T	G	FG	Pts
1	Craig Hall	Hull Kingston Rovers	12	16	0	80
2	Liam Sutcliffe	Leeds Rhinos	2	32	0	72
3	Jarrod Sammut	London Broncos	2	27	3	65
4	Ed Chamberlain	Salford Red Devils	2	23	0	54
	Gareth O'Brien	Toronto Wolfpack	1	24	2	54

Craig Hall

LEADING SCORERS

Connor
Robinson

Luke
Briscoe

LEAGUE 1 *(Regular season & play-offs)*

TRIES

1	Ethan Ryan	Bradford Bulls	34
2	Elliot Minchella	Bradford Bulls	27
3	Joe Batchelor	York City Knights	21
4	Lewis Young	Newcastle Thunder	20
5	Andy Gabriel	Keighley Cougars	19
6	Dalton Grant	Bradford Bulls	18
	Jason Tali	Doncaster	18
	Danny Langtree	Oldham	18
9	Dane Chisholm	Bradford Bulls	16
	Elliott Miller	Workington Town	16
	Ash Robson	York City Knights	16

GOALS

1	Connor Robinson	York City Knights	166
2	Benn Hardcastle	Keighley Cougars	125
3	Dane Chisholm	Bradford Bulls	114
4	Joe Sanderson	Hunslet	111
5	Paul Crook	Oldham	110
6	Carl Forber	Workington Town	97
7	Dan Abram	Whitehaven	85
8	Neil Thorman	London Skolars	78
9	Joe Keyes	Bradford Bulls	70
10	Tom Shaw	Newcastle Thunder	66

POINTS

			T	G	FG	Pts
1	Connor Robinson	York City Knights	13	166	4	388
2	Dane Chisholm	Bradford Bulls	16	114	2	294
3	Benn Hardcastle	Keighley Cougars	6	125	1	275
4	Joe Sanderson	Hunslet	6	111	0	246
5	Paul Crook	Oldham	4	110	0	236
6	Carl Forber	Workington Town	5	97	0	214
7	Dan Abram	Whitehaven	7	85	0	198
8	Joe Keyes	Bradford Bulls	11	70	1	185
9	Neil Thorman	London Skolars	4	78	0	172
10	Tom Shaw	Newcastle Thunder	5	66	0	152

ALL COMPETITIONS

TRIES

1	Luke Briscoe	Leeds Rhinos/Featherstone Rovers	38
2	Ethan Ryan	Bradford Bulls	36
3	Craig Hall	Hull Kingston Rovers/	
		Leigh Centurions	35
4	Elliot Minchella	Bradford Bulls	33
5	Ben Barba	St Helens	31
6	Kieran Dixon	London Broncos	27
7	Liam Kay	Toronto Wolfpack	26
8	Josh Charnley	Warrington Wolves	25
	Kieren Moss	Halifax/Hull Kingston Rovers/	
		York City Knights	25
	Rhys Williams	London Broncos	25

GOALS

1	Connor Robinson	York City Knights	182
2	Mark Kheirallah	Toulouse Olympique	149
3	Danny Richardson	St Helens	147
4	Benn Hardcastle	Keighley Cougars	129
5	Ben Reynolds	Leigh Centurions	127
6	Joe Sanderson	Hunslet	124
7	Paul Crook	Oldham	122
8	Dane Chisholm	Bradford Bulls	121
9	Jarrod Sammut	London Broncos	114
10	Ian Hardman	Featherstone Rovers	108

POINTS

			T	G	FG	Pts
1	Connor Robinson	York City Knights	13	182	4	420
2	Mark Kheirallah	Toulouse Olympique	22	149	0	386
3	Danny Richardson	St Helens	6	147	7	325
4	Jarrod Sammut	London Broncos	21	114	4	316
5	Dane Chisholm	Bradford Bulls	17	121	2	312
6	Ben Reynolds	Leigh Centurions	9	127	1	291
7	Benn Hardcastle	Keighley Cougars	6	129	1	283
8	Joe Sanderson	Hunslet	6	124	0	272
9	Paul Crook	Oldham	5	122	0	264
10	Steve Tyrer	Halifax	17	94	0	256

FIELD GOALS

1	Tony Gigot	Catalans Dragons	7
	Danny Richardson	St Helens	7
3	Sam Tomkins	Wigan Warriors	6
4	Marc Sneyd	Hull FC	5
	Cain Southernwood	Hunslet	5
	Josh Woods	Swinton Lions/Wigan Warriors	5

FINAL TABLES

SUPER LEAGUE - SUPER 8s

	P	W	D	L	F	A	D	Pts
St Helens	30	26	0	4	895	408	487	52
Wigan Warriors	30	23	0	7	740	417	323	46
Castleford Tigers	30	20	1	9	767	582	185	41
Warrington Wolves	30	18	1	11	767	561	206	37
Wakefield Trinity	30	13	1	16	747	696	51	27
Huddersfield Giants	30	13	1	16	539	794	-255	27
Catalans Dragons	30	12	1	17	596	750	-154	25
Hull FC	30	11	0	19	615	787	-172	22

SUPER 8s - THE QUALIFIERS

	P	W	D	L	F	A	D	Pts
Salford Red Devils	7	5	0	2	218	75	143	10
Leeds Rhinos	7	5	0	2	216	137	79	10
Hull Kingston Rovers	7	5	0	2	197	162	35	10
Toronto Wolfpack	7	5	0	2	136	118	18	10
London Broncos	7	4	0	3	161	164	-3	8
Toulouse Olympique	7	3	0	4	156	190	-34	6
Widnes Vikings	7	1	0	6	92	173	-81	2
Halifax	7	0	0	7	68	225	-157	0

CHAMPIONSHIP SHIELD

	P	W	D	L	F	A	D	Pts
Featherstone Rovers	30	23	0	7	1040	524	516	46
Leigh Centurions	30	20	0	10	1059	644	415	40
Batley Bulldogs	30	14	0	16	753	805	-52	28
Dewsbury Rams	30	10	1	19	650	899	-249	21
Barrow Raiders	30	8	3	19	491	1006	-515	19
Sheffield Eagles	30	8	0	22	549	1091	-542	16
Rochdale Hornets	30	6	0	24	465	1093	-628	12
Swinton Lions	30	4	2	24	502	1112	-610	10

LEAGUE 1

	P	W	D	L	F	A	D	Pts
York City Knights	26	24	0	2	1130	308	822	48
Bradford Bulls	26	23	0	3	1197	282	915	46
Doncaster	26	19	0	7	956	495	461	38
Workington Town	26	17	0	9	833	517	316	34
Oldham	26	16	0	10	902	345	557	32
Whitehaven	26	16	0	10	702	529	173	32
Hunslet	26	15	0	11	735	596	139	30
Newcastle Thunder	26	14	0	12	841	520	321	28
Keighley Cougars	26	13	0	13	839	657	182	26
North Wales Crusaders	26	9	1	16	589	660	-71	19
Coventry Bears	26	7	0	19	406	1058	-652	14
London Skolars	26	6	1	19	626	887	-261	13
Hemel Stags	26	2	0	24	314	1286	-972	4
West Wales Raiders	26	0	0	26	176	2106	-1930	0

SUPER LEAGUE - REGULAR SEASON

	P	W	D	L	F	A	D	Pts
St Helens	23	21	0	2	713	298	415	42
Wigan Warriors	23	16	0	7	573	345	228	32
Castleford Tigers	23	15	1	7	567	480	87	31
Warrington Wolves	23	14	1	8	531	410	121	29
Huddersfield Giants	23	11	1	11	427	629	-202	23
Hull FC	23	11	0	12	534	544	-10	22
Wakefield Trinity	23	10	1	12	581	506	75	21
Catalans Dragons	23	10	1	12	488	531	-43	21
Leeds Rhinos	23	8	2	13	441	527	-86	18
Hull Kingston Rovers	23	8	1	14	476	582	-106	17
Salford Red Devils	23	7	0	16	384	597	-213	14
Widnes Vikings	23	3	0	20	387	653	-266	6

CHAMPIONSHIP - REGULAR SEASON

	P	W	D	L	F	A	D	Pts
Toronto Wolfpack	23	20	1	2	866	374	492	41
London Broncos	23	16	1	6	907	423	484	33
Toulouse Olympique	23	16	1	6	900	438	462	33
Halifax	23	16	1	6	643	416	227	33
Featherstone Rovers	23	16	0	7	819	420	399	32
Leigh Centurions	23	16	0	7	849	508	341	32
Batley Bulldogs	23	8	0	15	523	703	-180	16
Sheffield Eagles	23	7	0	16	437	843	-406	14
Dewsbury Rams	23	6	1	16	424	746	-322	13
Barrow Raiders	23	5	3	15	382	816	-434	13
Swinton Lions	23	3	2	18	402	866	-464	8
Rochdale Hornets	23	4	0	19	327	926	-599	8